New Perspectives on

Microsoft® Office Word 2007

Comprehensive

What is the Microsoft Business Certification Program?

The Microsoft Business Certification Program enables candidates to show that they have something exceptional to offer – proven expertise in Microsoft Office programs. The two certification tracks allow candidates to choose how they want to exhibit their skills, either through validating skills within a specific Microsoft product or taking their knowledge to the next level and combining Microsoft programs to show that they can apply multiple skill sets to complete more complex office tasks. Recognized by businesses and schools around the world, over 3 million certifications have been obtained in over 100 different countries. The Microsoft Business Certification Program is the only Microsoft-approved certification program of its kind.

What is the Microsoft Certified Application Specialist Certification?

The Microsoft Certified Application Specialist Certification exams focus on validating specific skill sets within each of the Microsoft® Office system programs. The candidate can choose which exam(s) they want to take according to which skills they want to validate. The available Application Specialist exams include:

- Using Windows Vista™
- Using Microsoft® Office Word 2007
- Using Microsoft® Office Excel® 2007
- Using Microsoft® Office PowerPoint® 2007
- Using Microsoft® Office Access 2007
- Using Microsoft® Office Outlook® 2007

What is the Microsoft Certified Application Professional Certification?

The Microsoft Certified Application Professional Certification exams focus on a candidate's ability to use the 2007 Microsoft® Office system to accomplish industry-agnostic functions, for example Budget Analysis and Forecasting, or Content Management and Collaboration. The available Application Professional exams currently include:

- Organizational Support
- Creating and Managing Presentations
- Content Management and Collaboration
- Budget Analysis and Forecasting

What do the Microsoft Business Certification Vendor of Approved Courseware logos represent?

The logos validate that the courseware has been approved by the Microsoft® Business Certification Vendor program and that these courses cover objectives that will be included in the relevant exam. It also means that after utilizing this courseware, you may be prepared to pass the exams required to become a Microsoft Certified Application Specialist or Microsoft Certified Application Professional.

For more information:

To learn more about Microsoft Certified Application Specialist or Professional exams, visit
www.microsoft.com/learning/msbc.
To learn about other Microsoft Certified Application Specialist approved courseware from Course Technology, visit
www.course.com.
*The availability of Microsoft Certified Application exams varies by Microsoft Office program, program version and language.
Visit www.microsoft.com/learning for exam availability.
Microsoft, the Office Logo, Outlook, and PowerPoint are either registered trademarks or trademarks of Microsoft
Corporation in the United States and/or other countries. The Microsoft Certified Application Specialist and Microsoft
Certified Application Professional Logos are used under license from Microsoft Corporation.

New Perspectives on

Microsoft® Office Word 2007

Comprehensive

S. Scott Zimmerman
Brigham Young University

Beverly B. Zimmerman
Brigham Young University

Ann Shaffer

Katherine T. Pinard

COURSE TECHNOLOGY
CENGAGE Learning™

Australia • Brazil • Japan • Korea • Mexico • Singapore • Spain • United Kingdom • United States

COURSE TECHNOLOGY
CENGAGE Learning™

**New Perspectives on Microsoft Office
Word 2007—Comprehensive**

Acquisitions Editor: Kristina Matthews

Senior Product Manager: Kathy Finnegan

Product Manager: Erik Herman

Associate Product Manager: Brandi Henson

Editorial Assistant: Leigh Robbins

Senior Marketing Manager: Joy Stark

Marketing Coordinator: Jennifer Hankin

Developmental Editor: Mary Kemper

Senior Content Project Manager:
    Catherine G. DiMassa

Composition: GEX Publishing Services

Text Designer: Steve Deschene

Cover Designer: Elizabeth Paquin

Cover Art: Bill Brown

For product information and technology assistance, contact us at
Cengage Learning Academic Resource Center, 1-800-423-0563
For permission to use material from this text or product, submit all requests online at
www.cengage.com/permissions
Further permissions questions can be emailed to **permissionrequest@cengage.com**

ISBN-13: 978-1-4239-0582-0
ISBN-10: 1-4239-0582-2

Course Technology Cengage Learning
25 Thomson Place
Boston, MA 02210
USA

Cengage Learning products are represented in Canada by Nelson Education, Ltd.

For your lifelong learning solutions, visit **course.cengage.com**

Visit our corporate website at **www.cengage.com**

Some of the product names and company names used in this book have been used for identification purposes only and may be trademarks or registered trademarks of their respective manufacturers and sellers.

Microsoft and the Office logo are either registered trademarks or trademarks of Microsoft Corporation in the United States and/or other countries. Course Technology Cengage Learning is an independent entity from the Microsoft Corporation, and not affiliated with Microsoft in any manner.

Disclaimer: Any fictional data related to persons or companies or URLs used throughout this book is intended for instructional purposes only. At the time this book was printed, any such data was fictional and not belonging to any real persons or companies.

Printed in the United States of America
2 3 4 5 6 7 8 9 RRD-WI 11 10 09 08 07

Preface

The New Perspectives Series' critical-thinking, problem-solving approach is the ideal way to prepare students to transcend point-and-click skills and take advantage of all that Microsoft Office 2007 has to offer.

In developing the New Perspectives Series for Microsoft Office 2007, our goal was to create books that give students the software concepts and practical skills they need to succeed beyond the classroom. We've updated our proven case-based pedagogy with more practical content to make learning skills more meaningful to students.

With the New Perspectives Series, students understand *why* they are learning *what* they are learning, and are fully prepared to apply their skills to real-life situations.

"I really love the Margin Tips, which add 'tricks of the trade' to students' skills package. In addition, the Reality Check exercises provide for practical application of students' knowledge. I can't wait to use them in the classroom when we adopt Office 2007."

—Terry Morse Colucci
Institute of Technology, Inc.

About This Book

This book provides thorough, hands-on coverage of the new Microsoft Office Word 2007 software, and includes the following:

- A new "Getting Started with Microsoft Office 2007" tutorial that familiarizes students with the new Office 2007 features and user interface
- Complete coverage of Word 2007 basics, including creating, editing, and formatting documents; working with multi-page documents; and desktop publishing
- Expanded and in-depth coverage of higher level skills, including working with templates, styles, and tables of contents; customizing document themes; performing a mail merge; revising and merging documents with tracked changes; creating Web pages; customizing Word and automating your work; creating on-screen forms using advanced tables; and managing long documents
- Instruction in using the exciting new features of Word 2007, including sampling document elements with Live Preview; creating diagrams with SmartArt; using Quick Styles to format a document; storing and managing document elements as Building Blocks; using content controls to create interactive documents; inserting citations and creating bibliographies; and protecting private information with the Document Inspector
- New business case scenarios throughout, which provide a rich and realistic context for students to apply the concepts and skills presented
- Certification requirements for the Microsoft Certified Application Specialist exam, "Using Microsoft® Office Word 2007"

System Requirements

This book assumes a typical installation of Microsoft Office Word 2007 and Microsoft Windows Vista Ultimate with the Aero feature turned off (or Windows Vista Home Premium or Business edition). Note that you can also complete the tutorials in this book using Windows XP; you will notice only minor differences if you are using Windows XP. Refer to the tutorial "Getting Started with Microsoft Office 2007" for Tips noting these differences. The browser used in this book for any steps that require a browser is Internet Explorer 7.

www.course.com/NewPerspectives

"I appreciate the real-world approach that the New Perspective Series takes. It enables the transference of knowledge from step-by-step instructions to a far broader application of the software tools."

—Monique Sluymers
Kaplan University

The New Perspectives Approach

Context

Each tutorial begins with a problem presented in a "real-world" case that is meaningful to students. The case sets the scene to help students understand what they will do in the tutorial.

Hands-on Approach

Each tutorial is divided into manageable sessions that combine reading and hands-on, step-by-step work. Colorful screenshots help guide students through the steps. **Trouble?** tips anticipate common mistakes or problems to help students stay on track and continue with the tutorial.

InSight

InSight Boxes

New for Office 2007! InSight boxes offer expert advice and best practices to help students better understand how to work with the software. With the information provided in the InSight boxes, students achieve a deeper understanding of the concepts behind the software features and skills.

Tip

Margin Tips

New for Office 2007! Margin Tips provide helpful hints and shortcuts for more efficient use of the software. The Tips appear in the margin at key points throughout each tutorial, giving students extra information when and where they need it.

Reality Check

Reality Checks

New for Office 2007! Comprehensive, open-ended Reality Check exercises give students the opportunity to practice skills by creating practical, real-world documents, such as resumes and budgets, which they are likely to use in their everyday lives at school, home, or work.

Review

In New Perspectives, retention is a key component to learning. At the end of each session, a series of Quick Check questions helps students test their understanding of the concepts before moving on. Each tutorial also contains an end-of-tutorial summary and a list of key terms for further reinforcement.

Apply

Assessment

Engaging and challenging Review Assignments and Case Problems have always been a hallmark feature of the New Perspectives Series. Colorful icons and brief descriptions accompany the exercises, making it easy to understand, at a glance, both the goal and level of challenge a particular assignment holds.

Reference Window
Task Reference

Reference

While contextual learning is excellent for retention, there are times when students will want a high-level understanding of how to accomplish a task. Within each tutorial, Reference Windows appear before a set of steps to provide a succinct summary and preview of how to perform a task. In addition, a complete Task Reference at the back of the book provides quick access to information on how to carry out common tasks. Finally, each book includes a combination Glossary/Index to promote easy reference of material.

www.course.com/NewPerspectives

Our Complete System of Instruction

Brief
Introductory
Comprehensive

Coverage To Meet Your Needs

Whether you're looking for just a small amount of coverage or enough to fill a semester-long class, we can provide you with a textbook that meets your needs.

- Brief books typically cover the essential skills in just 2 to 4 tutorials.
- Introductory books build and expand on those skills and contain an average of 5 to 8 tutorials.
- Comprehensive books are great for a full-semester class, and contain 9 to 12+ tutorials.

So if the book you're holding does not provide the right amount of coverage for you, there's probably another offering available. Go to our Web site or contact your Course Technology sales representative to find out what else we offer.

Student Online Companion

This book has an accompanying online companion Web site designed to enhance learning. This Web site includes:

- Internet Assignments for selected tutorials
- Student Data Files
- PowerPoint presentations

COURSECASTS

CourseCasts – Learning on the Go. Always available…always relevant.

Want to keep up with the latest technology trends relevant to you? Visit our site to find a library of podcasts, CourseCasts, featuring a "CourseCast of the Week," and download them to your mp3 player at http://coursecasts.course.com.

Our fast-paced world is driven by technology. You know because you're an active participant—always on the go, always keeping up with technological trends, and always learning new ways to embrace technology to power your life.

Ken Baldauf, host of CourseCasts, is a faculty member of the Florida State University Computer Science Department where he is responsible for teaching technology classes to thousands of FSU students each year. Ken is an expert in the latest technology trends; he gathers and sorts through the most pertinent news and information for CourseCasts so your students can spend their time enjoying technology, rather than trying to figure it out. Open or close your lecture with a discussion based on the latest CourseCast.

Visit us at http://coursecasts.course.com to learn on the go!

Instructor Resources

We offer more than just a book. We have all the tools you need to enhance your lectures, check students' work, and generate exams in a new, easier-to-use and completely revised package. This book's Instructor's Manual, ExamView testbank, PowerPoint presentations, data files, solution files, figure files, and a sample syllabus are all available on a single CD-ROM or for downloading at www.course.com.

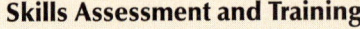

Skills Assessment and Training

SAM 2007 helps bridge the gap between the classroom and the real world by allowing students to train and test on important computer skills in an active, hands-on environment.

SAM 2007's easy-to-use system includes powerful interactive exams, training or projects on critical applications such as Word, Excel, Access, PowerPoint, Outlook, Windows, the Internet, and much more. SAM simulates the application environment, allowing students to demonstrate their knowledge and think through the skills by performing real-world tasks.

Designed to be used with the New Perspectives Series, SAM 2007 includes built-in page references so students can print helpful study guides that match the New Perspectives textbooks used in class. Powerful administrative options allow instructors to schedule exams and assignments, secure tests, and run reports with almost limitless flexibility.

Blackboard

Online Content

Blackboard is the leading distance learning solution provider and class-management platform today. Course Technology has partnered with Blackboard to bring you premium online content. Content for use with *New Perspectives on Microsoft Office Word 2007, Comprehensive* is available in a Blackboard Course Cartridge and may include topic reviews, case projects, review questions, test banks, practice tests, custom syllabi, and more.

Course Technology also has solutions for several other learning management systems. Please visit http://www.course.com today to see what's available for this title.

Acknowledgments

Thanks to Kristina Matthews, the fearless leader of the New Perspective Series. To Kathy Finnegan, amazing and resourceful project manager, thank you for the great ideas and much-needed encouragement. Thanks, also, to Brandi Henson, Associate Product Manager, and Leigh Robbins, Editorial Assistant, for their support during the development of this text. My thanks to Mary Kemper, Developmental Editor extraordinaire, who made this a far better book than it would have been without her careful edits. A special thanks to Kitty Pinard and Lisa Ruffolo for their patient advice and explanations at all hours of the day and night. Thank you to Cathie DiMassa, our hard-working Production Editor, who managed the million details involved in transforming the manuscript into a printed book. As always, I relied on the ace Manuscript Quality Assurance testers at Course Technology, who provided detailed comments on every tutorial, at several stages in the process. Many thanks to Christian Kunciw, MQA Project Leader, and to the following QA testers for their help and suggestions: John Freitas, Serge Palladino, Danielle Shaw, Marianne Snow, and Susan Whalen.

Finally, I'm extremely grateful to our reviewers, who provided valuable insights into the needs of their students: Carla Jones, Middle Tennessee State University; Pamela Silvers, Asheville-Buncombe Technical Community College; and Monique Sluymers, Kaplan University.

–Ann Shaffer

We likewise want to thank all those who made this book possible. We especially want to thank Ann Shaffer, our co-author, for her expertise, hard work, and creative talents. Special thanks also go to Mary Kemper for her dedication and expertise as Developmental Editor in bringing this new edition to fruition.

–Beverly and Scott Zimmerman
–Katherine T. Pinard

Brief Contents

Table of Contents

Tutorial 4 Desktop Publishing and Mail Merge

Word Level II Tutorials

Tutorial 5 Working with Templates and Outlines

Word Level III Tutorials

Tutorial 8 Customizing Word and Automating Your Work

Automating Documents for a Function Hall . . . .*WD 377*

Tutorial 9 Creating On-Screen Forms Using Advanced Table Techniques

Developing an Order Form . . . .*WD 455*

Objectives

- Develop file management strategies
- Explore files and folders
- Create, name, copy, move, and delete folders
- Name, copy, move, and delete files
- Work with compressed files

Managing Your Files

Creating and Working with Files and Folders in Windows Vista

Case | Distance Learning Company

The Distance Learning Company specializes in distance-learning courses for people who want to participate in college-level classes to work toward a degree or for personal enrichment. Distance learning is formalized education that typically takes place using a computer and the Internet, replacing normal classroom interaction with modern communications technology. The company's goal is to help students gain new skills and stay competitive in the job market. The head of the Customer Service Department, Shannon Connell, interacts with the Distance Learning Company's clients on the phone and from her computer. Shannon, like all other employees, is required to learn the basics of managing files on her computer.

In this tutorial, you'll work with Shannon to devise a strategy for managing files. You'll learn how Windows Vista organizes files and folders, and you'll examine Windows Vista file management tools. You'll create folders and organize files within them. You'll also explore options for working with compressed files.

Starting Data Files

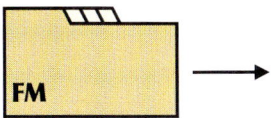

FM

Tutorial
Agenda.docx
Holiday.bmp
Members.htm
New Logo.bmp
Proposal.docx
Resume.docx
Stationery.bmp
Vinca.jpg

Review
Billing.xlsx
Car Plan.xlsx
Commissions.xlsx
Contracts.xlsx
Customers.xlsx
Loan.docx
Photos.pptx
Speech.wav
Water lilies.jpg

Case1
Inv Feb.xlsx
Inv Jan.xlsx
Inv March.xlsx
Painting-Agenda.docx
Painting-Eval.docx
Painting-Manual.docx
Paris.jpg
Still Life.jpg

Organizing Files and Folders

Knowing how to save, locate, and organize computer files makes you more productive when you are working with a computer. A **file**, often referred to as a **document**, is a collection of data that has a name and is stored on a computer. After you create a file, you can open it, edit its contents, print it, and save it again—usually using the same program you used to create it. You organize files by storing them in **folders**, which are containers for your files. You need to organize files so that you can find them easily and work efficiently.

A file cabinet is a common metaphor for computer file organization. A computer is like a file cabinet that has two or more drawers—each drawer is a storage device, or **disk**. Each disk contains folders that hold documents, or files. To make it easy to retrieve files, you arrange them logically into folders. For example, one folder might contain financial data, another might contain your creative work, and another could contain information you're collecting for an upcoming vacation.

A computer can store folders and files on different types of disks, ranging from removable media—such as **USB drives** (also called USB flash drives), **compact discs (CDs)**, and **digital video discs (DVDs)**—to **hard disks**, or fixed disks, which are permanently stored on a computer. Hard disks are the most popular type of computer storage because they can contain many gigabytes of data and are economical.

To have your computer access a removable disk, you must insert the disk into a **drive**, which is a computer device that can retrieve and sometimes record data on a disk. See Figure 1. A hard disk is already contained in a drive, so you don't need to insert it each time you use the computer.

| **Figure 1** | **Comparing drives and disks** |

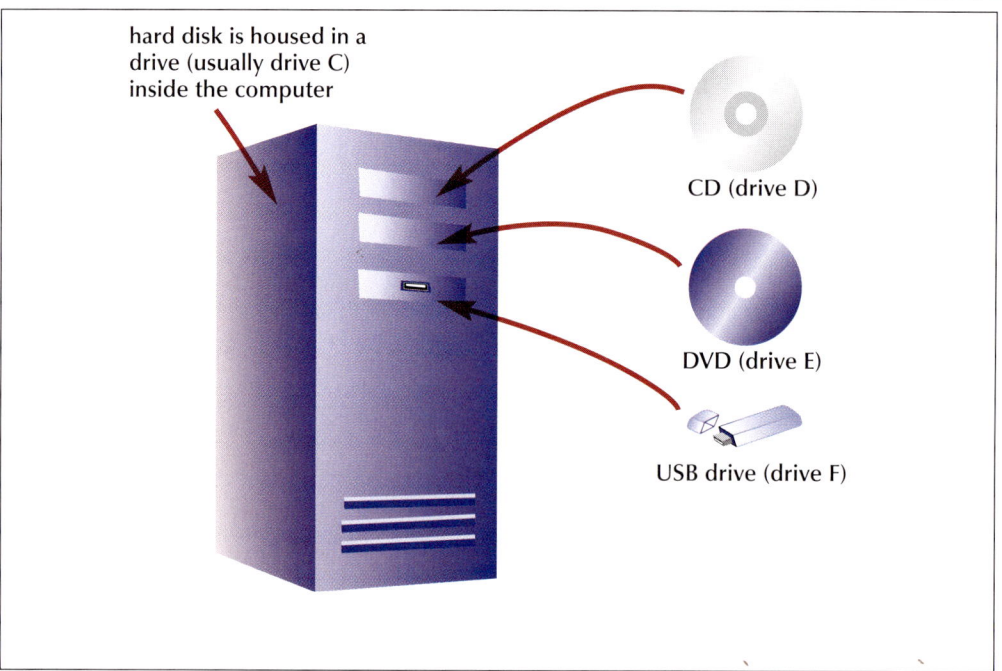

hard disk is housed in a
drive (usually drive C)
inside the computer

CD (drive D)

DVD (drive E)

USB drive (drive F)

A computer distinguishes one drive from another by assigning each a drive letter. The hard disk is usually assigned to drive C. The remaining drives can have any other letters, but are usually assigned in the order that the drives were installed on the computer—so your USB drive might be drive D or drive F. Most contemporary computers have ports for more than one USB drive.

Understanding the Need for Organizing Files and Folders

Windows Vista stores thousands of files in many folders on the hard disk of your computer. These are system files that Windows Vista needs to display the desktop, use drives, and perform other operating system tasks. To ensure system stability and find files quickly, Windows Vista organizes the folders and files in a hierarchy, or **file system**. At the top of the hierarchy, Windows Vista stores folders and important files that it needs when you turn on the computer. This location is called the **root directory**, and is usually drive C (the hard disk). The term "root" refers to another popular metaphor for visualizing a file system—an upside-down tree, which reflects the file hierarchy that Windows Vista uses. In Figure 2, the tree trunk corresponds to the root directory, the branches to the folders, and the leaves to the files.

Windows file hierarchy | Figure 2

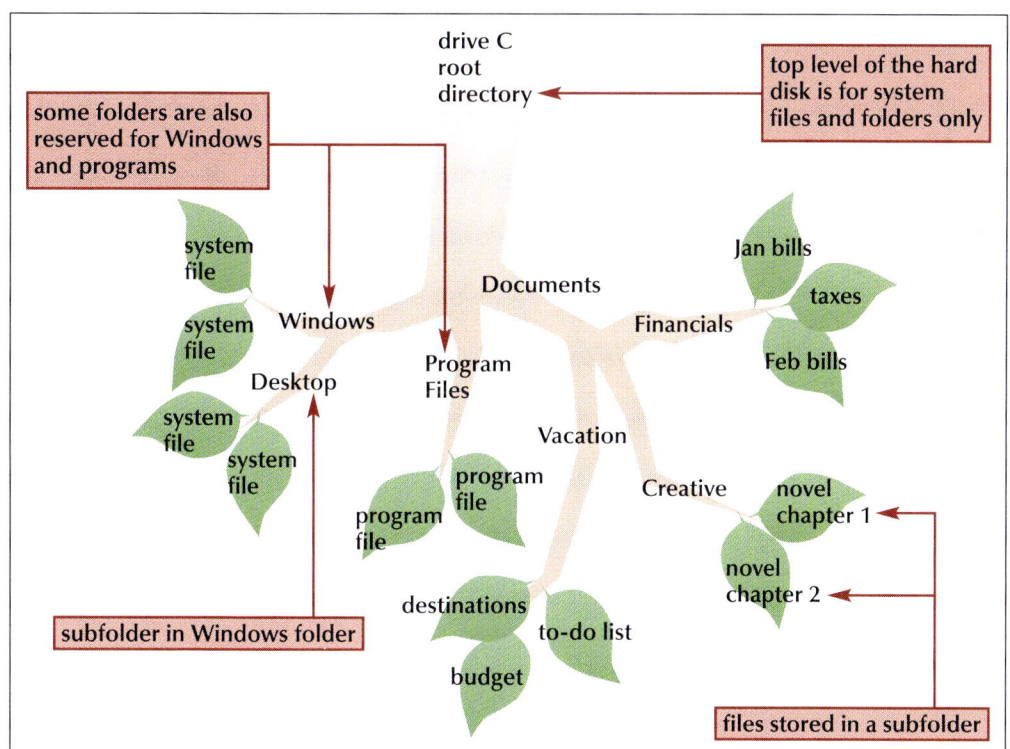

Note that some folders contain other folders. An effectively organized computer contains a few folders in the root directory, and those folders contain other folders, also called **subfolders**.

The root directory, or top level, of the hard disk is for system files and folders only—you should not store your own work here because it could interfere with Windows or a program. (If you are working in a computer lab, you might not be allowed to access the root directory.)

Do not delete or move any files or folders from the root directory of the hard disk—doing so could mean that you cannot run or start the computer. In fact, you should not reorganize or change any folder that contains installed software because Windows Vista expects to find the files for specific programs within certain folders. If you reorganize or change these folders, Windows Vista cannot locate and start the programs stored in that folder. Likewise, you should not make changes to the folder that contains the Windows Vista operating system (usually named Windows or Winnt).

Because the top level of the hard disk is off-limits for your files—the ones that you create, open, and save on the hard disk—you must store your files in subfolders. If you are working on your own computer, you should store your files within the Documents folder. If you are working in a computer lab, you will probably use a different location that your instructor specifies. If you simply store all your files in one folder, however, you will soon have trouble finding the files you want. Instead, you should create folders within a main folder to separate files in a way that makes sense for you.

Likewise, if you store most of your files on removable media, such as USB drives, you need to organize those files into folders and subfolders. Before you start creating folders, whether on a hard disk or removable disk, you should plan the organization you will use.

Developing Strategies for Organizing Files and Folders

The type of disk you use to store files determines how you organize those files. Figure 3 shows how you could organize your files on a hard disk if you were taking a full semester of distance-learning classes. To duplicate this organization, you would open the main folder for your documents, create four folders—one each for the Basic Accounting, Computer Concepts, Management Skills II, and Professional Writing courses—and then store the writing assignments you complete in the Professional Writing folder.

Figure 3	Organizing folders and files on a hard disk

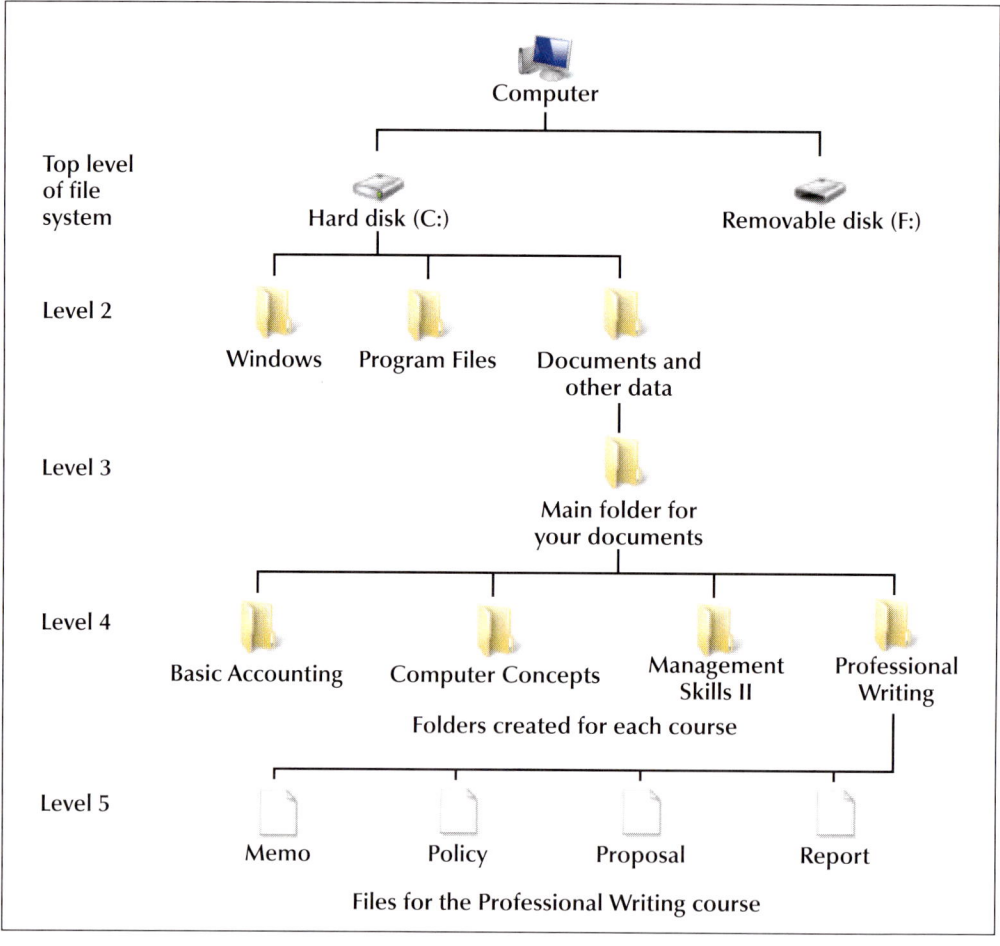

If you store your files on removable media, such as a USB drive or rewritable CD, you can use a simpler organization because you do not have to account for system files. In general, the larger the medium, the more levels of folders you should use because large media can store more files, and, therefore, need better organization. For example, you could organize your files on a 128-MB USB drive. In the top level of the USB drive, you could create folders for each general category of documents you store—one each for Courses, Creative, Financials, and Vacation. The Courses folder could then include one folder for each course, and each of those folders could contain the appropriate files.

If you work on two computers, such as one computer at an office or school and another computer at home, you can duplicate the folders you use on both computers to simplify transferring files from one computer to another. For example, if you have four folders in your Documents folder on your work computer, you would create these same four folders on your removable media as well as in the Documents folder of your home computer. If you change a file on the hard disk of your home computer, you can copy the most recent version of the file to the corresponding folder on your removable media so that it is available when you are at work. You also then have a **backup**, or duplicate copy, of important files that you need.

Planning Your Organization

Now that you've explored the basics of organizing files on a computer, you can plan the organization of your files for this book by writing in your answers to the following questions:

1. How do you obtain the files for this book (on a USB drive from your instructor, for example)?_____

2. On what drive do you store your files for this book (drive A, C, D, for example)? _____

3. Do you use a particular folder on this drive? If so, which folder do you use?_____
_____

4. Is this folder contained within another folder? If so, what is the name of that main folder?_____

5. On what type of disk or drive do you save your files for this book (hard disk, USB drive, CD, or network drive, for example)?_____

If you cannot answer any of these questions, ask your instructor for help.

Exploring Files and Folders

Windows Vista provides two tools for exploring the files and folders on your computer—Windows Explorer and the Computer window. Both display the contents of your computer, using icons to represent drives, folders, and files. However, by default, each presents a slightly different view of your computer. **Windows Explorer** shows the files, folders, and drives on your computer, making it easy to navigate, or move from one location to another within the file hierarchy. The **Computer** window shows the drives on your computer and makes it easy to perform system tasks, such as viewing system information. Most of the time, you use one of these tools to open a **folder window** that displays the files and subfolders in a folder.

The Windows Explorer and Computer windows are divided into two sections, called **panes**. The left pane is the **Navigation pane**. It contains a **Favorite Links list**, which can provide quick access to the folders you use often, and a **Folders list**, which shows the hierarchy of the folders and other locations on your computer. The right pane lists the contents of these folders and other locations. If you select a folder in the left pane, for example, the files stored in that folder appear in the right pane.

Tip

The term "folder window" refers to any window that displays the contents of a folder, including the Computer, Windows Explorer, and Recycle Bin windows. In all of these windows, you can use the same techniques to display folders and their contents, navigate your computer, and work with files.

If the Folders list showed all the folders on your computer at once, it could be a very long list. Instead, you open drives and folders only when you want to see what they contain. If a folder contains subfolders, an expand icon ▷ appears to the left of the folder icon. (The same is true for drives.) To view the folders contained in an object, you click the expand icon. A collapse icon ◢ then appears next to the folder icon; click the collapse icon to hide the folder's subfolders. To view the files contained in a folder, you click the folder icon, and the files appear in the right pane. See Figure 4.

Figure 4 **Viewing folder contents in Windows Explorer**

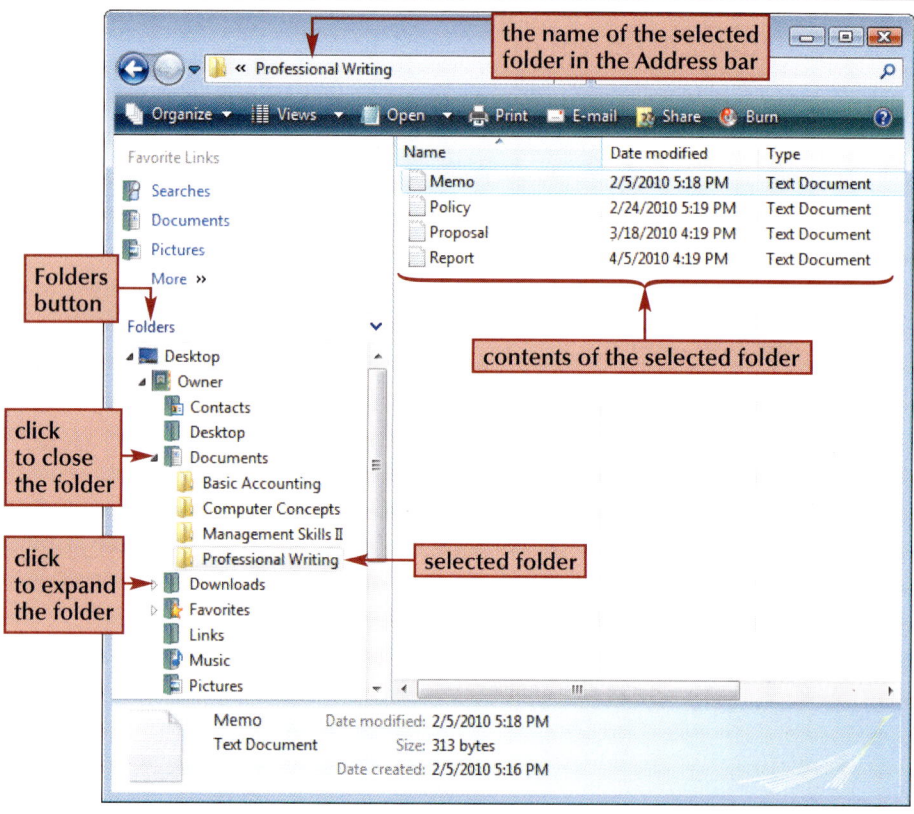

Using the Folders list helps you navigate your computer and orients you to your current location. As you move, copy, delete, and perform other tasks with the files in the right pane of a folder window, you can refer to the Folders list to see how your changes affect the overall organization.

Both Windows Explorer and the Computer window let you view, organize, and access the drives, folders, and files on your computer. In addition to using the Folders list, you can navigate your computer in other ways:

- **Opening drives and folders in the right pane**: To view the contents of a drive or folder, double-click the drive or folder icon in the right pane of a folder window.
- **Using the Address bar**: Use the Address bar to navigate to a different folder. The Address bar displays your current folder as a series of locations separated by arrows. Click a folder name or an arrow button to navigate to a different location.

Tip

To display or hide the Folders list in a folder window, click the Folders button in the Navigation pane.

- **Clicking the Back, Forward, and Recent Pages buttons**: Use the Back, Forward, and Recent Pages buttons to navigate to other folders you have already opened. After you change folders, use the Back button to return to the original folder or click the Recent Pages button to navigate to a location you've visited recently.
- **Using the Search box**: To find a file or folder stored in the current folder or its subfolders, type a word or phrase in the Search box. The search begins as soon as you start typing. Windows finds files based on text in the filename, text within the file, and other characteristics of the file, such as tags (descriptive words or phrases you add to your files) or the author.

These navigation controls are available in Windows Explorer, Computer, and other folder windows, including many dialog boxes. In fact, all of these folder windows share common tools. By default, when you first open Computer, it shows all the drives available on your computer, whereas Windows Explorer shows the folders on your computer. However, by changing a single setting, you can make the two windows interchangeable. If you open the Folders list in Computer, you have the same setup as Windows Explorer. Likewise, if you close the Folders list in the Windows Explorer window, you have the same setup as in the Computer window.

Shannon prefers to use Windows Explorer to manage her files. You'll use Windows Explorer to manage files in the rest of this tutorial.

Using Windows Explorer

Windows Vista also provides a folder for your documents—your **personal folder**, which is designed to store the files and folders you work with regularly and is labeled with the name you use to log on to Windows Vista, such as Shannon. On your own computer, this is where you can keep your data files—the memos, videos, graphics, music, and other files that you create, edit, and manipulate in a program. Windows Vista provides a few built-in folders in your personal folder, including Music (for songs and other music files), Pictures (for photos and other image files), and Documents (for text, spreadsheets, presentations, and other files you create). If you are working in a computer lab, you might not have a personal folder or be able to access the Documents folder, or you might have a personal folder or be able to store files there only temporarily because that folder is emptied every night. Instead, you might permanently store your Data Files on removable media or in a different folder on your computer or network.

When you start Windows Explorer from the All Programs menu, it opens to the Documents folder by default. If you cannot access the Documents folder, the screens you see as you perform the following steps will differ. However, you can still perform the steps accurately.

To examine the organization of your computer using Windows Explorer:

▶ 1. Click the **Start** button 🏁 on the taskbar, click **All Programs**, click **Accessories**, and then click **Windows Explorer**. The Windows Explorer window opens.

▶ 2. Scroll the Folders list, point to the **Folders list**, and then click the **expand** icon ▷ next to the Computer icon. The drives and other useful locations on your computer appear under the Computer icon, as shown in Figure 5. The contents of your computer will differ.

Figure 5 | **Viewing the contents of your computer**

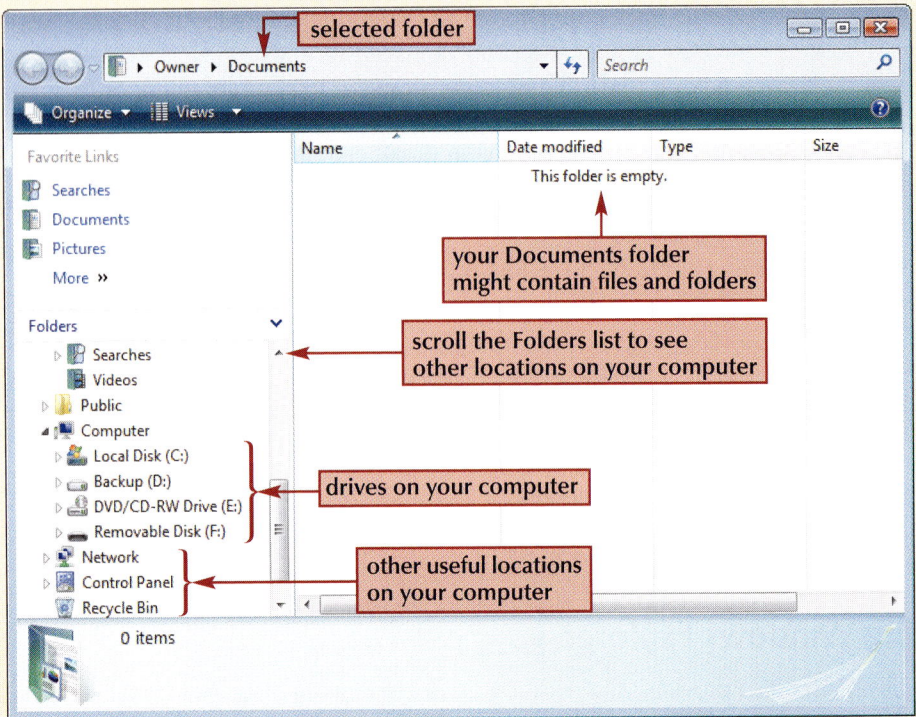

3. Click the **expand** icon ▷ next to the Local Disk (C:) icon. The contents of your hard disk appear under the Local Disk (C:) icon.

   Trouble? If you do not have permission to access drive C, skip Step 3 and read but do not perform the remaining steps.

   Documents is still the selected folder. To view the contents of an object in the right pane, you can click the object's icon in the Folders list.

4. If necessary, scroll up the list, and then click the **Public** folder in the Folders list. Its contents appear in the right pane. Public is a built-in Windows Vista folder that contains folders any user can access on this computer.

Navigating to Your Data Files

The **file path** is a notation that indicates a file's location on your computer. The file path leads you through the Windows file system to your file. For example, the Holiday file is stored in the Tutorial subfolder of the FM folder. If you are working on a USB drive, for example, the path to this file might be as follows:

F:\FM\Tutorial\Holiday.bmp

This path has four parts, and each part is separated by a backslash (\ ):

- **F**: The drive name; for example, drive F might be the name for the USB drive. If this file were stored on the hard disk, the drive name would be C.
- **FM**: The top-level folder on drive F.
- **Tutorial**: A subfolder in the FM folder.
- **Holiday.bmp**: The full filename with the file extension.

If someone tells you to find the file F:\FM\Tutorial\Holiday.bmp, you know you must navigate to your USB drive, open the FM folder, and then open the Tutorial folder to find the Holiday file. By default, the Address bar includes arrow buttons instead of backslashes when displaying a path. To navigate to a different folder in the FM folder, for example, you can click the arrow button to right of FM in the Address bar, and then click the folder name.

You can use Windows Explorer to navigate to the Data Files you need for the rest of this tutorial. Refer to the information you provided in the "Planning Your Organization" section and note the drive on your system that contains your Data Files. In the following steps, this is drive F, a USB drive. If necessary, substitute the appropriate drive on your system when you perform the steps.

To navigate to your Data Files:

▶ **1.** Make sure your computer can access your Data Files for this tutorial. For example, if you are using a USB drive, insert the drive into the USB port.

   Trouble? If you don't have the Data Files, you need to get them before you can proceed. Your instructor will either give you the Data Files or ask you to obtain them from a specified location (such as a network drive). In either case, be sure that you make a backup copy of your Data Files before you start using them, so that the original files will be available on your copied disk in case you need to start over because of an error or problem. If you have any questions about the Data Files, see your instructor or technical support person for assistance.

▶ **2.** In the Windows Explorer window, click the **expand** icon ▷ next to the drive containing your Data Files, such as Removable Disk (F:). A list of the folders on that drive appears.

▶ **3.** If the list of folders does not include the FM folder, continue clicking the **expand** icon ▷ to navigate to the folder that contains the FM folder.

▶ **4.** Click the **expand** icon ▷ next to the FM folder, and then click the **FM** folder. Its contents appear in the Folders list and in the right pane of the Windows Explorer window. The FM folder contains the Case1, Review, and Tutorial folders, as shown in Figure 6. The other folders on your system might vary.

Figure 6 ▸ Navigating to the FM folder

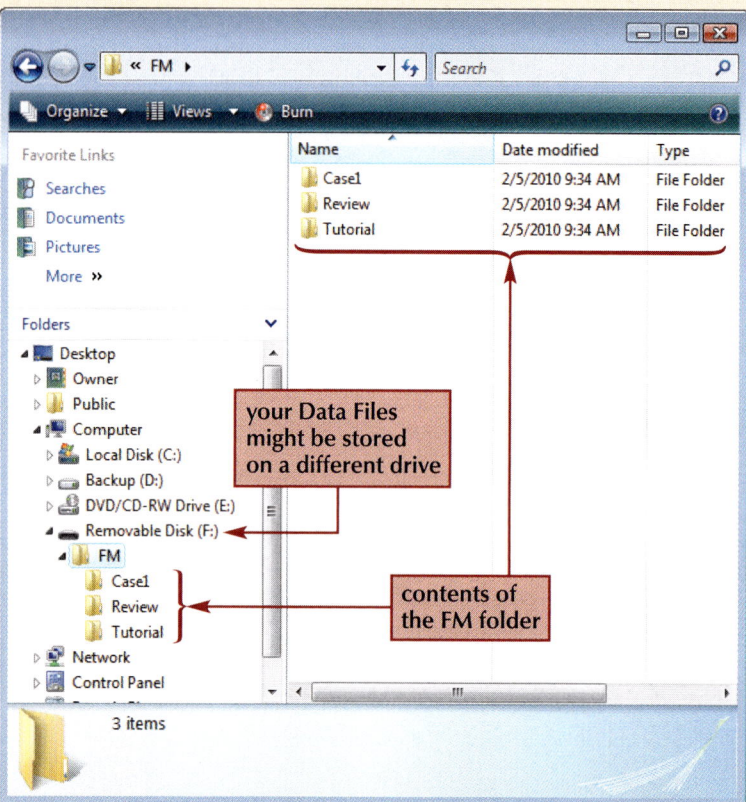

5. In the left pane, click the **Tutorial** folder. The files it contains appear in the right pane. You want to view them as a list.

6. Click the **Views button arrow** on the toolbar, and then click **List**. The files appear in List view in the Windows Explorer window. See Figure 7.

Figure 7 ▸ Files in the Tutorial folder in List view

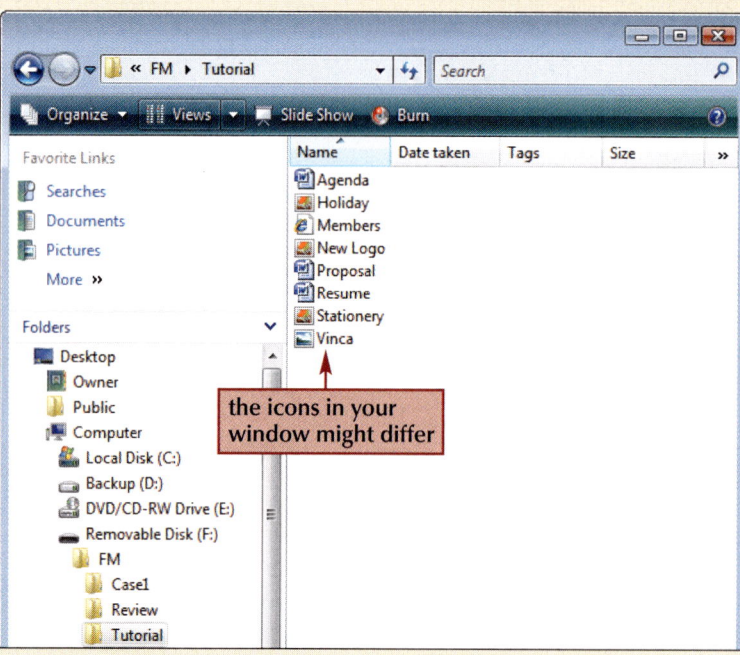

The file icons in your window depend on the programs installed on your computer, so they might be different from the ones shown in Figure 7.

Working with Folders and Files

After you devise a plan for storing your files, you are ready to get organized by creating folders that will hold your files. For this tutorial, you create folders in the Tutorial folder. When you are working on your own computer, you usually create folders within the Documents folder in your personal folder.

Examine the files shown in Figure 7 again and determine which files seem to belong together. Holiday, New Logo, and Vinca are all graphics files containing pictures or photos. The Resume and Stationery files were created for a summer job hunt. The other files were created for a neighborhood association to update a playground.

One way to organize these files is to create three folders—one for graphics, one for the job hunt files, and another for the playground files. When you create a folder, you give it a name, preferably one that describes its contents. A folder name can have up to 255 characters, except / \ : * ? " < > or |. Considering these conventions, you could create three folders as follows:

- **Graphics folder**: Holiday, New Logo, and Vinca files
- **Job Hunt folder**: Resume and Stationery files
- **Playground folder**: Agenda, Proposal, and Members files

Guidelines for Creating Folders | InSight

- **Keep folder names short and familiar**: Long filenames can be cut off in a folder window, so use names that are short but clear. Choose names that will be meaningful later, such as project names or course numbers.
- **Develop standards for naming folders**: Use a consistent naming scheme that is clear to you, such as one that uses a project name as the name of the main folder, and includes step numbers in each subfolder name, such as 01Plan, 02Approvals, 03Prelim, and so on.
- **Create subfolders to organize files**: If a file listing in a folder window is so long that you must scroll the window, consider organizing those files into subfolders.

Creating Folders

You've already seen folder icons in the windows you've examined. Now, you'll create folders in the Tutorial folder using the Windows Explorer toolbar.

Creating a Folder | Reference Window

- In the left pane, click the drive or folder where you want to create a folder.
- Click the Organize button on the toolbar, and then click New Folder (or right-click a blank area in the folder window, point to New, and then click Folder).
- Type a name for the folder, and then press the Enter key.

Next you will create three folders in your Tutorial folder. The Windows Explorer window should show the contents of the Tutorial folder in List view.

To create folders in a folder window:

▶ **1.** Click the **Organize** button on the toolbar, and then click **New Folder**. A folder icon with the label "New Folder" appears in the right pane. See Figure 8.

Figure 8 Creating a folder in the Tutorial folder

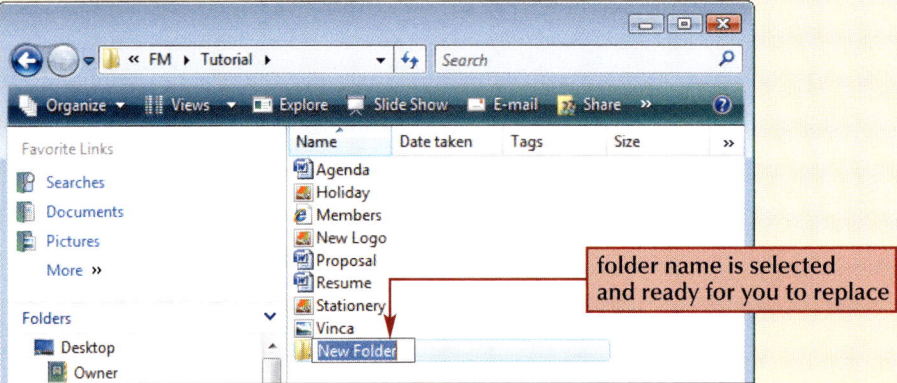

Trouble? If the "New Folder" name is not selected, right-click the new folder, click Rename, and then continue with Step 2.

Windows Vista uses "New Folder" as a placeholder, and selects the text so that you can replace it with the name you want.

▶ **2.** Type **Graphics** as the folder name, and then press the **Enter** key. The new folder is named "Graphics" and is the selected item in the right pane.

You are ready to create a second folder. This time, you'll use a shortcut menu to create a folder.

▶ **3.** Right-click a blank area near the Graphics folder, point to **New** on the shortcut menu, and then click **Folder**. A folder icon with the label "New Folder" appears in the right pane with the "New Folder" text selected.

▶ **4.** Type **Job Hunt** as the name of the new folder, and then press the **Enter** key.

▶ **5.** Using the toolbar or the shortcut menu, create a folder named **Playground**. The Tutorial folder contains three new subfolders.

Moving and Copying Files and Folders

If you want to place a file into a folder from another location, you can either move the file or copy it. **Moving** a file removes it from its current location and places it in a new location you specify. **Copying** places the file in both locations. Windows Vista provides several techniques for moving and copying files. The same principles apply to folders—you can move and copy folders using a variety of methods.

Reference Window | **Moving a File or Folder**

- Right-click and drag the file or folder you want to move to the destination folder.
- Click Move Here on the shortcut menu.
or
- Right-click the file or folder you want to move, and then click Cut on the shortcut menu.
- Navigate to and right-click the destination folder, and then click Paste on the shortcut menu.

Next, you'll move the Agenda, Proposal, and Members files to the Playground folder.

To move a file using the right mouse button:

▶ **1.** Point to the **Agenda** file in the right pane, and then press and hold the *right* mouse button.

▶ **2.** With the right mouse button still pressed down, drag the **Agenda** file to the **Playground** folder. When a "Move to Playground" ScreenTip appears, release the button. A shortcut menu opens.

▶ **3.** With the left mouse button, click **Move Here** on the shortcut menu. The Agenda file is removed from the main Tutorial folder and stored in the Playground subfolder.

   Trouble? If you release the mouse button before dragging the Agenda file to the Playground folder, the shortcut menu opens, letting you move the file to a different folder. Press the Esc key to close the shortcut menu without moving the file, and then repeat Steps 1 through 3.

▶ **4.** In the right pane, double-click the **Playground** folder. The Agenda file is in the Playground folder.

▶ **5.** In the left pane, click the **Tutorial** folder to see its contents. The Tutorial folder no longer contains the Agenda file.

The advantage of moving a file or folder by dragging with the right mouse button is that you can efficiently complete your work with one action. However, this technique requires polished mouse skills so that you can drag the file comfortably. Another way to move files and folders is to use the **Clipboard**, a temporary storage area for files and information that you have copied or moved from one place and plan to use somewhere else. You can select a file and use the Cut or Copy commands to temporarily store the file on the Clipboard, and then use the Paste command to insert the file elsewhere. Although using the Clipboard takes more steps, some users find it easier than dragging with the right mouse button.

You'll move the Resume file to the Job Hunt folder next.

To move files using the Clipboard:

▶ **1.** Right-click the **Resume** file, and then click **Cut** on the shortcut menu. Although the file icon is still displayed in the folder window, Windows Vista removes the Resume file from the Tutorial folder and stores it on the Clipboard.

▶ **2.** In the Folders list, right-click the **Job Hunt** folder, and then click **Paste** on the shortcut menu. Windows Vista pastes the Resume file from the Clipboard to the Job Hunt folder. The Resume file icon no longer appears in the folder window.

▶ **3.** In the Folders list, click the **Job Hunt** folder to view its contents in the right pane. The Job Hunt folder now contains the Resume file.

   You'll move the Stationery file from the Tutorial folder to the Job Hunt folder.

▶ **4.** Click the **Back** button ⬅ on the Address bar to return to the Tutorial folder, right-click the **Stationery** file in the folder window, and then click **Cut** on the shortcut menu.

▶ **5.** Right-click the **Job Hunt** folder, and then click **Paste** on the shortcut menu.

▶ **6.** Click the **Back** button ⬅ on the Address bar to return to view the contents of the Job Hunt folder. It now contains the Resume and Stationery files. See Figure 9.

Figure 9 ▶ **Moving files**

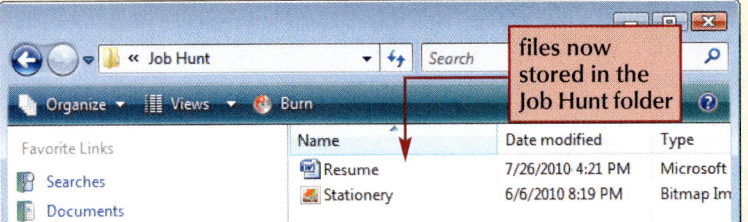

▶ **7.** Click the **Forward** button ➡ to return to the Tutorial folder.

Tip

To use keyboard shortcuts to move files, click the file you want to move, press Ctrl+X to cut the file, navigate to a new location, and then press Ctrl+V to paste the file.

You can also copy a file using the same techniques as when you move a file—by dragging with the right mouse button or by using the Clipboard. You can copy more than one file at the same time by selecting all the files you want to copy, and then clicking them as a group. To select files that are listed together in a window, click the first file in the list, hold down the Shift key, click the last file in the list, and then release the Shift key. To select files that are not listed together, click one file, hold down the Ctrl key, click the other files, and then release the Ctrl key.

Reference Window | **Copying a File or Folder**

- Right-click and drag the file or folder you want to copy to the destination folder.
- Click Copy Here on the shortcut menu.

or

- Right-click the file or folder you want to copy, and then click Copy on the shortcut menu.
- Navigate to the destination folder.
- Right-click a blank area of the destination folder window, and then click Paste on the shortcut menu.

You'll copy the three graphics files from the Tutorial folder to the Graphics folder now.

To copy files using the shortcut menu:

▶ **1.** In the Tutorial window, click the **Holiday** file.

▶ **2.** Hold down the **Ctrl** key, click the **New Logo** file, click the **Vinca** file, and then release the **Ctrl** key. Three files are selected in the Tutorial window.

Tip

It's easiest to select multiple files in List view or Details view.

▶ **3.** Right-click a selected file, and then click **Copy** on the shortcut menu.

▶ **4.** In the right pane, double-click the **Graphics** folder to open it.

▶ **5.** Right-click a blank area in the right pane, and then click **Paste** on the shortcut menu. Windows Vista copies the three files to the Graphics folder.

▶ **6.** Switch to List view, if necessary.

Now that you are familiar with two ways to copy files, you can use the technique you prefer to copy the Proposal and Members files to the Playground folder.

To copy the two files:

▶ **1.** In the Graphics folder window, click the **Back** button ⬅ on the toolbar to return to the Tutorial folder.

▶ **2.** Use any technique you've learned to copy the **Proposal** and **Members** files from the Tutorial folder to the Playground folder.

You can move and copy folders in the same way that you move and copy files. When you do, you move or copy all the files contained in the folder.

Naming and Renaming Files

As you work with files, pay attention to **filenames**—they provide important information about the file, including its contents and purpose. A filename such as Car Sales.docx has three parts:

- **Main part of the filename**: The name you provide when you create a file, and the name you associate with a file
- **Dot**: The period (.) that separates the main part of the filename from the file extension
- **File extension**: Usually three or four characters that follow the dot in the filename

The main part of a filename can have up to 260 characters—this gives you plenty of room to name your file accurately enough so that you'll know the contents of the file just by looking at the filename. You can use spaces and certain punctuation symbols in your filenames. Like folder names, however, filenames cannot contain the symbols \ / ? : * " < > | because these characters have special meaning in Windows Vista.

A filename might display an **extension**—three or more characters following a dot—that identifies the file's type and indicates the program in which the file was created. For example, in the filename Car Sales.docx, the extension "docx" identifies the file as one created by Microsoft Office Word 2007, a word-processing program. You might also have a file called Car Sales.xlsx—the "xlsx" extension identifies the file as one created in Microsoft Office Excel 2007, a spreadsheet program. Though the main parts of these filenames are identical, their extensions distinguish them as different files. You usually do not need to add extensions to your filenames because the program that you use to create the file adds the file extension automatically. Also, although Windows Vista keeps track of extensions, not all computers are set to display them.

Be sure to give your files and folders meaningful names that help you remember their purpose and contents. You can easily rename a file or folder by using the Rename command on the file's shortcut menu.

Guidelines for Naming Files | InSight

The following are a few suggestions for naming your files:

- **Use common names**: Avoid cryptic names that might make sense now, but could cause confusion later, such as nonstandard abbreviations or imprecise names like Stuff08.
- **Don't change the file extension**: When renaming a file, don't change the file extension. If you do, Windows might not be able to find a program that can open it.
- **Find a comfortable balance between too short and too long**: Use filenames that are long enough to be meaningful, but short enough to read easily on the screen.

Next, you'll rename the Agenda file to give it a more descriptive name.

To rename the Agenda file:

▶ **1.** In the Tutorial folder window, double-click the **Playground** folder to open it.

▶ **2.** Right-click the **Agenda** file, and then click **Rename** on the shortcut menu. The file-name is highlighted and a box appears around it.

▶ **3.** Type **Meeting Agenda**, and then press the **Enter** key. The file now appears with the new name.

> **Trouble?** If you make a mistake while typing and you haven't pressed the Enter key yet, press the Backspace key until you delete the mistake, and then complete Step 3. If you've already pressed the Enter key, repeat Steps 1 through 3 to rename the file again.

> **Trouble?** If your computer is set to display file extensions, a message might appear asking if you are sure you want to change the file extension. Click the No button, right-click the Agenda file, click Rename on the shortcut menu, type "Meeting Agenda.docx", and then press the Enter key.

All the files in the Tutorial folder are now stored in appropriate subfolders. You can streamline the organization of the Tutorial folder by deleting the files you no longer need.

Deleting Files and Folders

Tip

To retrieve a deleted file from the hard disk, double-click the Recycle Bin, right-click the file you want to retrieve, and then click Restore.

You should periodically delete files and folders you no longer need so that your main folders and disks don't get cluttered. In the Computer window or Windows Explorer, you delete a file or folder by deleting its icon. Be careful when you delete a folder, because you also delete all the files it contains. When you delete a file from a hard disk, Windows Vista removes the filename from the folder, but stores the file contents in the Recycle Bin. The **Recycle Bin** is an area on your hard disk that holds deleted files until you remove them permanently; an icon on the desktop allows you easy access to the Recycle Bin. If you change your mind and want to retrieve a file deleted from your hard disk, you can use the Recycle Bin to recover it or return it to its original location. However, after you empty the Recycle Bin, you can no longer recover the files that were in it.

When you delete a file from removable media, it does not go into the Recycle Bin. Instead, it is deleted as soon as its icon disappears—and you cannot recover it.

Shannon reminds you that because you copied the Holiday, New Logo, Proposal, Members, and Vinca files to the Graphics and Playground folders, you can safely delete the original files in the Tutorial folder. As with moving, copying, and renaming files and folders, you can delete a file or folder in many ways, including using a shortcut menu.

To delete files in the Tutorial folder:

▶ **1.** Use any technique you've learned to navigate to and open the **Tutorial** folder.

▶ **2.** Click **Holiday** (the first file in the file list), hold down the **Shift** key, click **Vinca** (the last file in the file list), and then release the **Shift** key. All the files in the Tutorial folder are now selected. None of the subfolders should be selected.

▶ **3.** Right-click the selected files, and then click **Delete** on the shortcut menu. Windows Vista asks if you're sure you want to delete these files.

▶ **4.** Click the **Yes** button.

So far, you've moved, copied, renamed, and deleted files, but you haven't viewed any of their contents. To view file contents, you can preview or open the file. When you double-click a file in a folder window, Windows Vista starts the appropriate program and opens the file. To preview the file contents, you can select the file in a folder window, and then open the Preview pane by clicking the Organize button, pointing to Layout, and then clicking Preview Pane.

Working with Compressed Files

If you transfer files from one location to another, such as from your hard disk to a removable disk or vice versa, or from one computer to another via e-mail, you can store the files in a **compressed (zipped) folder** so that they take up less disk space. You can then transfer the files more quickly. When you create a compressed folder, Windows Vista displays a zipper on the folder icon.

You compress a folder so that the files it contains use less space on the disk. Compare two folders—a folder named Pictures that contains about 8.6 MB of files and a compressed folder containing the same files, but requiring only 6.5 MB of disk space. In this case, the compressed files use about 25 percent less disk space than the uncompressed files.

You can create a compressed folder using the Compressed (zipped) Folder command on the New submenu of the shortcut menu in a folder window. Then, you can compress files or other folders by dragging them into the compressed folder. You can open files directly from a compressed folder, although you cannot modify the file. To edit and save a compressed file, you must extract it first. When you **extract** a file, you create an uncompressed copy of the file and folder in a folder you specify. The original file remains in the compressed folder.

If a different compression program has been installed on your computer, such as WinZip or PKZIP, the Compressed (zipped) Folder command might not appear on the New submenu. Instead, it might be replaced by the name of your compression program. In this case, refer to your compression program's Help system for instructions on working with compressed files.

Shannon suggests you compress the files and folders in the Tutorial folder so that you can more quickly transfer them to another location.

To compress the folders and files in the Tutorial folder:

▶ **1.** If necessary, navigate to the Tutorial folder.

▶ **2.** Right-click a blank area of the right pane, point to **New** on the shortcut menu, and then click **Compressed (zipped) Folder**. A new compressed folder with a zipper icon appears in the Tutorial window. See Figure 10. Your window might appear in a different view.

Creating a compressed folder ◀ **Figure 10**

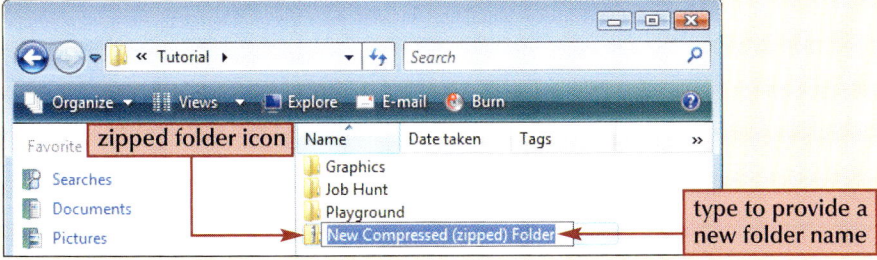

Trouble? If the Compressed (zipped) Folder command does not appear on the New submenu, a different compression program is probably installed on your computer. Click a blank area of the Tutorial window to close the shortcut menu, and then read but do not perform the remaining steps.

▶ **3.** Type **Final Files**, and then press the **Enter** key. Windows Vista names the compressed folder in the Tutorial folder.

4. Click the **Graphics** folder, hold down the **Shift** key, click the **Playground** folder in the right pane, and then release the **Shift** key. Three folders are selected in the Tutorial window.

5. Drag the three folders to the **Final Files** compressed folder. Windows Vista copies the files to the folder, compressing them to save space.

You open a compressed folder by double-clicking it. You can then move and copy files and folders in a compressed folder, although you cannot rename them. When you extract files, Windows Vista uncompresses and copies them to a location that you specify, preserving the files in their folders as appropriate.

To extract the compressed files:

1. Right-click the **Final Files** compressed folder, and then click **Extract All** on the shortcut menu. The Extract Compressed (Zipped) Folders dialog box opens.

2. Press the **End** key to deselect the path in the text box, press the **Backspace** key as many times as necessary to delete "Final Files," and then type **Extracted**. The final three parts of the path in the text box should be "\FM\Tutorial\Extracted." See Figure 11.

Figure 11 ▶ **Extracting compressed files**

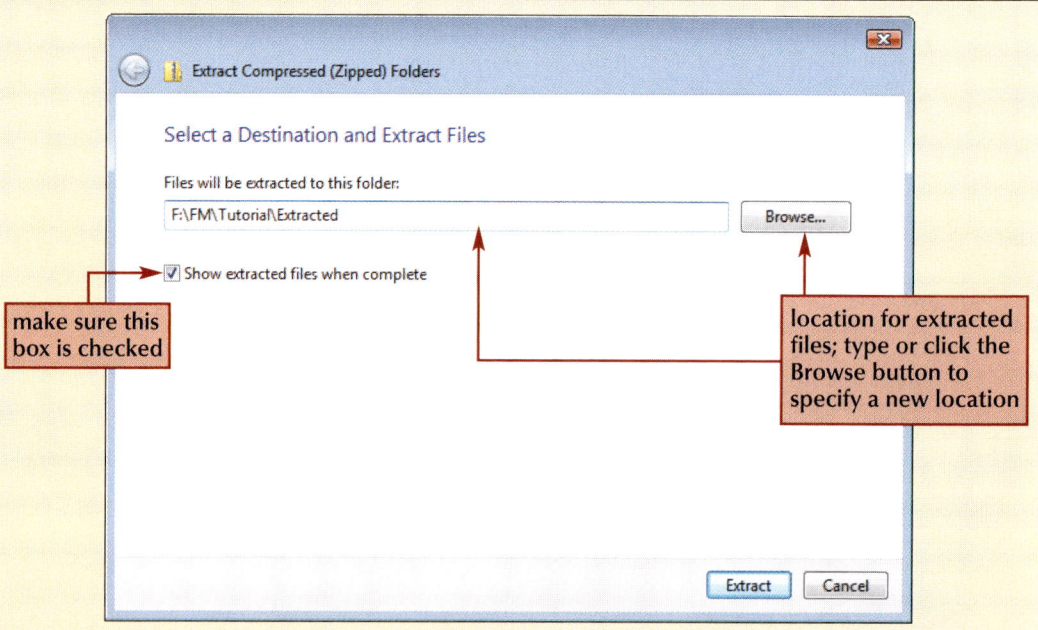

make sure this box is checked

location for extracted files; type or click the Browse button to specify a new location

3. Make sure the **Show extracted files when complete** check box is checked, and then click the **Extract** button. The Extracted folder opens, showing the Graphics, Job Hunt, and Playground folders.

4. Open each folder to make sure it contains the files you worked with in this tutorial.

5. Close all open windows.

Quick Check | Review

1. What do you call a named collection of data stored on a disk?
2. Name two types of removable media for storing files.
3. The letter C is typically used for the _____ drive of a computer.
4. What are the two tools that Windows Vista provides for exploring the files and folders on your computer?
5. What is the notation you can use to indicate a file's location on your computer?
6. True or False: The advantage of moving a file or folder by dragging with the right mouse button is that you can efficiently complete your work with one action.
7. What part of a filename indicates the file type and program that created it?
8. Is a file deleted from a compressed folder when you extract it?

Tutorial Summary | Review

In this tutorial, you examined Windows Vista file organization, noting that you need to organize files and folders to work efficiently. You learned about typical file management strategies, including how to organize files and folders by creating folders, moving and copying files, and renaming and deleting files. You also learned how to copy files to a compressed (zipped) folder, and then extract files from a compressed folder.

Key Terms

backup	extract	move
Clipboard	Favorite Links list	Navigation pane
compact disc (CD)	file	pane
compressed (zipped) folder	file path	personal folder
Computer	file system	Recycle Bin
copy	filename	root directory
disk	folder	subfolder
document	folder window	USB drive
drive	Folders list	Windows Explorer
extension	hard disk	

Practice	**Review Assignments**

Practice the skills you learned in the tutorial.

Data Files needed for the Review Assignments: Billing.xlsx, Car Plan.xlsx, Commissions.xlsx, Contracts.xlsx, Customers.xlsx, Loan.docx, Photos.pptx, Speech.wav, Water lilies.jpg

Complete the following steps, recording your answers to any questions:

1. Use the Computer window or Windows Explorer as necessary to record the following information:
   - Where are you supposed to store the files you use in the Review Assignments for this tutorial?
   - Describe the method you will use to navigate to the location where you save your files for this book.
   - Do you need to follow any special guidelines or conventions when naming the files you save for this book? For example, should all the filenames start with your course number or tutorial number? If so, describe the conventions.
   - When you are instructed to open a file for this book, what location are you supposed to use?
   - Describe the method you will use to navigate to this location.
2. Use the Computer window or Windows Explorer to navigate to and open the FM\Review folder provided with your Data Files.
3. Examine the nine files in the Review folder included with your Data Files, and then answer the following questions:
   - How will you organize these files?
   - What folders will you create?
   - Which files will you store in these folders?
   - Will you use any built-in Windows folders? If so, which ones? For which files?
4. In the Review folder, create three folders: Business, Finances, and Project.
5. Move the **Billing**, **Commissions**, **Contracts**, and **Customers** files from the Review folder to the Business folder.
6. Move the **Car Plan** and **Loan** files to the Finances folder.
7. Copy the remaining files to the Project folder.
8. Delete the files in the Review folder (do *not* delete any folders).
9. Rename the **Speech** file in the Project folder to **Ask Not**.
10. Create a compressed (zipped) folder in the Review folder named **Final Review** that contains all the files and folders in the Review folder.
11. Extract the contents of the Final Review files folder to a new folder named **Extracted**. (*Hint:* The file path will end with "\FM\Review\Extracted.")
12. Locate all copies of the **Loan** file in the subfolders of the Review folder. In which locations did you find this file?
13. Close all open windows.
14. Submit the results of the preceding steps to your instructor, either in printed or electronic form, as requested.

Apply	**Case Problem 1**

Use the skills you learned in the tutorial to manage files and folders for an arts organization.

Data Files needed for this Case Problem: Inv Feb.xlsx, Inv Jan.xlsx, Inv March.xlsx, Painting–Agenda.docx, Painting–Eval.docx, Painting–Manual.docx, Paris.jpg, Still Life.jpg

Jefferson Street Fine Arts Center   Rae Wysnewski owns the Jefferson Street Fine Arts Center (JSFAC) in Pittsburgh, and offers classes and gallery, studio, and practice space for aspiring and fledgling artists, musicians, and dancers. Rae opened JSFAC two years ago, and this year the center has a record enrollment in its classes. She hires you to teach a painting class and to show her how to manage her files on her new Windows Vista computer. Complete the following steps:

1. In the FM\Case1 folder in your Data Files, create two folders: Invoices and Painting Class.
2. Move the **Inv Jan**, **Inv Feb**, and **Inv March** files from the Case1 folder to the Invoices folder.
3. Rename the three files in the Invoices folder to remove "Inv" from each name.
4. Move the three text documents from the Case1 folder to the Painting Class folder. Rename the three documents, using shorter but still descriptive names.
5. Copy the remaining files to the Painting Class folder.
6. Switch to Details view, if necessary, and then answer the following questions:
    a.   What is the largest file in the Painting Class folder?
    b.   How many files in the Painting Class folder are JPEG images?
7. Delete the **Paris** and **Still Life** files from the Case1 folder.
8. Open the Recycle Bin folder by double-clicking the Recycle Bin icon on the desktop. Do the Paris and Still Life files appear in the Recycle Bin folder? Explain why or why not. Close the Recycle Bin window.
9. Copy the Painting Class folder to the Case1 folder. The duplicate folder appears as "Painting Class – Copy." Rename the Painting Class – Copy folder as **Graphics**.
10. Delete the text files from the Graphics folder.
11. Delete the **Paris** and **Still Life** files from the Painting Class folder.
12. Close all open windows, and then submit the results of the preceding steps to your instructor, either in printed or electronic form, as requested.

Challenge	**Case Problem 2**

Extend what you've learned to discover other methods of managing files for a social service organization.

There are no Data Files needed for this Case Problem.

First Call Outreach   Victor Crillo is the director of a social service organization named First Call Outreach in Toledo, Ohio. Its mission is to connect people who need help from local and state agencies to the appropriate service. Victor has a dedicated staff, but they are all relatively new to Windows Vista. In particular, they have trouble finding files that they have saved on their hard disks. He asks you to demonstrate how to find files in Windows Vista. Complete the following:

⊕ **EXPLORE**

1. Windows Vista Help and Support includes topics that explain how to search for files on a disk without looking through all the folders. Click the Start button, click Help and Support, and then use one of the following methods to locate topics on searching for files.
    • In the Windows Help and Support window, click the Windows Basics icon. Click the Working with files and folders link. In the "In this article" list, clicking Finding your files.

- In the Windows Help and Support window, click the Table of Contents icon. (If necessary, click the Home icon first, and then click the Table of Contents icon.) the Files and folders link, and then click Working with files and folders. In the "In this article" list, click Finding your files.
- In the Search Help box, type **searching for files**, and then press the Enter key. Click the Find a file or folder link. In the article, click the Show all link.

⊕ **EXPLORE**
2. Read the topic and click any See also or For more information links in the topic, if necessary, to provide the following information:
   a. Where is the Search box located?
   b. Do you need to type the entire filename to find the file?
   c. Name three file characteristics you can use as search options.

⊕ **EXPLORE**
3. Use the Windows Vista Help and Support window to locate topics related to managing files and folders. Write out two procedures for working with files and folders that were not covered in the tutorial.

4. Submit the results of the preceding steps to your instructor, either in printed or electronic form, as requested.

| Assess | **SAM Assessment and Training** |

If you have a SAM user profile, you may have access to hands-on instruction, practice, and assessment of the skills covered in this tutorial. Log in to your SAM account (**http://sam2007.course.com**) to launch any assigned training activities or exams that relate to the skills covered in this tutorial.

| Review | **Quick Check Answers** |

1. file
2. USB drives, CDs, and DVDs
3. hard disk
4. Windows Explorer and the Computer window
5. file path
6. True
7. extension
8. No

Ending Data Files

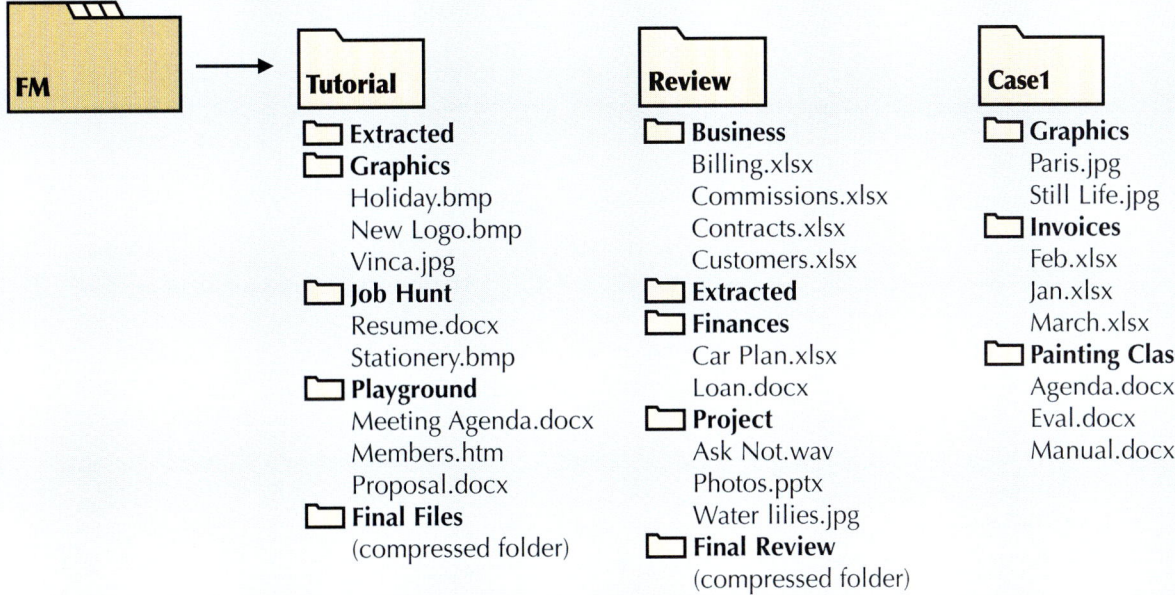

FM → **Tutorial**
- 📁 **Extracted**
- 📁 **Graphics**
  - Holiday.bmp
  - New Logo.bmp
  - Vinca.jpg
- 📁 **Job Hunt**
  - Resume.docx
  - Stationery.bmp
- 📁 **Playground**
  - Meeting Agenda.docx
  - Members.htm
  - Proposal.docx
- 📁 **Final Files**
  - (compressed folder)

Review
- 📁 **Business**
  - Billing.xlsx
  - Commissions.xlsx
  - Contracts.xlsx
  - Customers.xlsx
- 📁 **Extracted**
- 📁 **Finances**
  - Car Plan.xlsx
  - Loan.docx
- 📁 **Project**
  - Ask Not.wav
  - Photos.pptx
  - Water lilies.jpg
- 📁 **Final Review**
  - (compressed folder)

Case1
- 📁 **Graphics**
  - Paris.jpg
  - Still Life.jpg
- 📁 **Invoices**
  - Feb.xlsx
  - Jan.xlsx
  - March.xlsx
- 📁 **Painting Class**
  - Agenda.docx
  - Eval.docx
  - Manual.docx

Reality Check

Now that you have reviewed the fundamentals of managing files, organize the files and folders you use for course work or for other projects on your own computer. Be sure to follow the guidelines presented in this tutorial for developing an organization strategy, creating folders, naming files, and moving, copying, deleting, and compressing files. To manage your own files, complete the following tasks:

1. Use a program such as Word or Notepad to create a plan for organizing your files. List the types of files you work with, and then determine whether you want to store them on your hard disk or on removable media. Then sketch the folders and subfolders you will use to manage these files. If you choose a hard disk as your storage medium, make sure you plan to store your work files and folders in a subfolder of the Documents folder.

2. Use Windows Explorer or the Computer window to navigate to your files. Determine which tool you prefer for managing files, if you have a preference.

3. Create or rename the main folders you want to use for your files. Then create or rename the subfolders you will use.

4. Move and copy files to the appropriate folders according to your plan, and rename and delete files as necessary.

5. Create a backup copy of your work files by creating a compressed file and then copying the compressed file to a removable disk, such as a USB flash drive.

6. Submit your finished plan to your instructor, either in printed or electronic form, as requested.

Objectives

- Explore the programs that comprise Microsoft Office
- Start programs and switch between them
- Explore common window elements
- Minimize, maximize, and restore windows
- Use the Ribbon, tabs, and buttons
- Use the contextual tabs, Mini toolbar, and shortcut menus
- Save, close, and open a file
- Use the Help system
- Print a file
- Exit programs

Getting Started with Microsoft Office 2007

Preparing a Meeting Agenda

Case | Recycled Palette

Recycled Palette, a company in Oregon founded by Ean Nogella in 2006, sells 100 percent recycled latex paint to both individuals and businesses in the area. The high-quality recycled paint is filtered to industry standards and tested for performance and environmental safety. The paint is available in both 1 gallon cans and 5 gallon pails, and comes in colors ranging from white to shades of brown, blue, green, and red. The demand for affordable recycled paint has been growing each year. Ean and all his employees use Microsoft Office 2007, which provides everyone in the company with the power and flexibility to store a variety of information, create consistent files, and share data. In this tutorial, you'll review how the company's employees use Microsoft Office 2007.

Starting Data Files

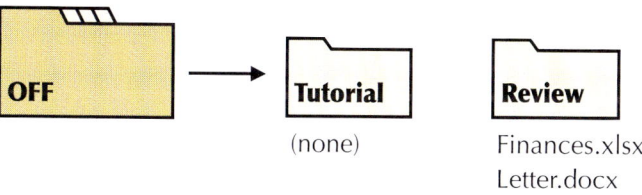

OFF → Tutorial

(none)

Review

Finances.xlsx
Letter.docx

Exploring Microsoft Office 2007

Microsoft Office 2007, or **Office**, is a collection of Microsoft programs. Office is available in many suites, each of which contains a different combination of these programs. For example, the Professional suite includes Word, Excel, PowerPoint, Access, Outlook, and Publisher. Other suites are available and can include more or fewer programs (for additional information about the available suites, go to the Microsoft Web site). Each Office program contains valuable tools to help you accomplish many tasks, such as composing reports, analyzing data, preparing presentations, compiling information, sending e-mail, and planning schedules.

Microsoft Office Word 2007, or **Word**, is a computer program you use to enter, edit, and format text. The files you create in Word are called **documents**, although many people use the term *document* to refer to any file created on a computer. Word, often called a word processing program, offers many special features that help you compose and update all types of documents, ranging from letters and newsletters to reports, brochures, faxes, and even books—all in attractive and readable formats. You can also use Word to create, insert, and position figures, tables, and other graphics to enhance the look of your documents. For example, the Recycled Palette employees create business letters using Word.

Microsoft Office Excel 2007, or **Excel**, is a computer program you use to enter, calculate, analyze, and present numerical data. You can do some of this in Word with tables, but Excel provides many more tools for recording and formatting numbers as well as performing calculations. The graphics capabilities in Excel also enable you to display data visually. You might, for example, generate a pie chart or a bar chart to help people quickly see the significance of and the connections between information. The files you create in Excel are called **workbooks** (commonly referred to as spreadsheets), and Excel is often called a spreadsheet program. The Recycled Palette accounting department uses a line chart in an Excel workbook to visually track the company's financial performance.

Microsoft Office Access 2007, or **Access**, is a computer program used to enter, maintain, and retrieve related information (or data) in a format known as a database. The files you create in Access are called **databases**, and Access is often referred to as a database or relational database program. With Access, you can create forms to make data entry easier, and you can create professional reports to improve the readability of your data. The Recycled Palette operations department tracks the company's inventory in a table in an Access database.

Microsoft Office PowerPoint 2007, or **PowerPoint**, is a computer program you use to create a collection of slides that can contain text, charts, pictures, sound, movies, multimedia, and so on. The files you create in PowerPoint are called **presentations**, and PowerPoint is often called a presentation graphics program. You can show these presentations on your computer monitor, project them onto a screen as a slide show, print them, share them over the Internet, or display them on the World Wide Web. You can also use PowerPoint to generate presentation-related documents such as audience handouts, outlines, and speakers' notes. The Recycled Palette marketing department has created an effective slide presentation with PowerPoint to promote its paints to a wider audience.

Microsoft Office Outlook 2007, or **Outlook**, is a computer program you use to send, receive, and organize e-mail; plan your schedule; arrange meetings; organize contacts; create a to-do list; and jot down notes. You can also use Outlook to print schedules, task lists, phone directories, and other documents. Outlook is often referred to as an information management program. The Recycled Palette staff use Outlook to send and receive e-mail, plan their schedules, and create to-do lists.

Although each Office program individually is a strong tool, their potential is even greater when used together.

Integrating Office Programs

One of the main advantages of Office is **integration**, the ability to share information between programs. Integration ensures consistency and accuracy, and it saves time because you don't have to reenter the same information in several Office programs. The staff at Recycled Palette uses the integration features of Office daily, including the following examples:

- The accounting department created an Excel bar chart on the previous two years' fourth-quarter results, which they inserted into the quarterly financial report created in Word. They included a hyperlink in the Word report that employees can click to open the Excel workbook and view the original data.
- The operations department included an Excel pie chart of sales percentages by paint colors on a PowerPoint slide, which is part of a presentation to stockholders.
- The marketing department produced a mailing to promote its recycled paints to local contractors and designers by combining a form letter created in Word with an Access database that stores the names and addresses of these potential customers.
- A sales representative wrote a letter in Word about an upcoming promotion for new customers and merged the letter with an Outlook contact list containing the names and addresses of prospective customers.

These are just a few examples of how you can take information from one Office program and integrate it with another.

Starting Office Programs

You can start any Office program by clicking the Start button on the Windows taskbar, and then selecting the program you want from the All Programs menu. As soon as the program starts, you can immediately begin to create new files or work with existing ones. If an Office program appears in the most frequently used programs list on the left side of the Start menu, you can click the program name to start the program.

Starting Office Programs | Reference Window

- Click the Start button on the taskbar.
- Click All Programs.
- Click Microsoft Office.
- Click the name of the program you want to start.

or

- Click the name of the program you want to start in the most frequently used programs list on the left side of the Start menu.

You'll start Excel using the Start button.

To start Excel and open a new, blank workbook:

▶ **1.** Make sure your computer is on and the Windows desktop appears on your screen.

Trouble? If your screen varies slightly from those shown in the figures, your computer might be set up differently. The figures in this book were created while running Windows Vista with the Aero feature turned off, but how your screen looks depends on the version of Windows you are using, the background settings, and so forth.

Windows XP Tip

The Start button is the green button with the word "start" on it, located at the bottom left of the taskbar.

2. Click the **Start** button on the taskbar, and then click **All Programs** to display the All Programs menu.

3. Click **Microsoft Office** on the All Programs list, and then point to **Microsoft Office Excel 2007**. Depending on how your computer is set up, your desktop and menu might contain different icons and commands.

   Trouble? If you don't see Microsoft Office on the All Programs list, click Microsoft Office Excel 2007 on the All Programs list. If you still don't see Microsoft Office Excel 2007, ask your instructor or technical support person for help.

4. Click **Microsoft Office Excel 2007**. Excel starts, and a new, blank workbook opens. See Figure 1.

Figure 1 New, blank Excel workbook

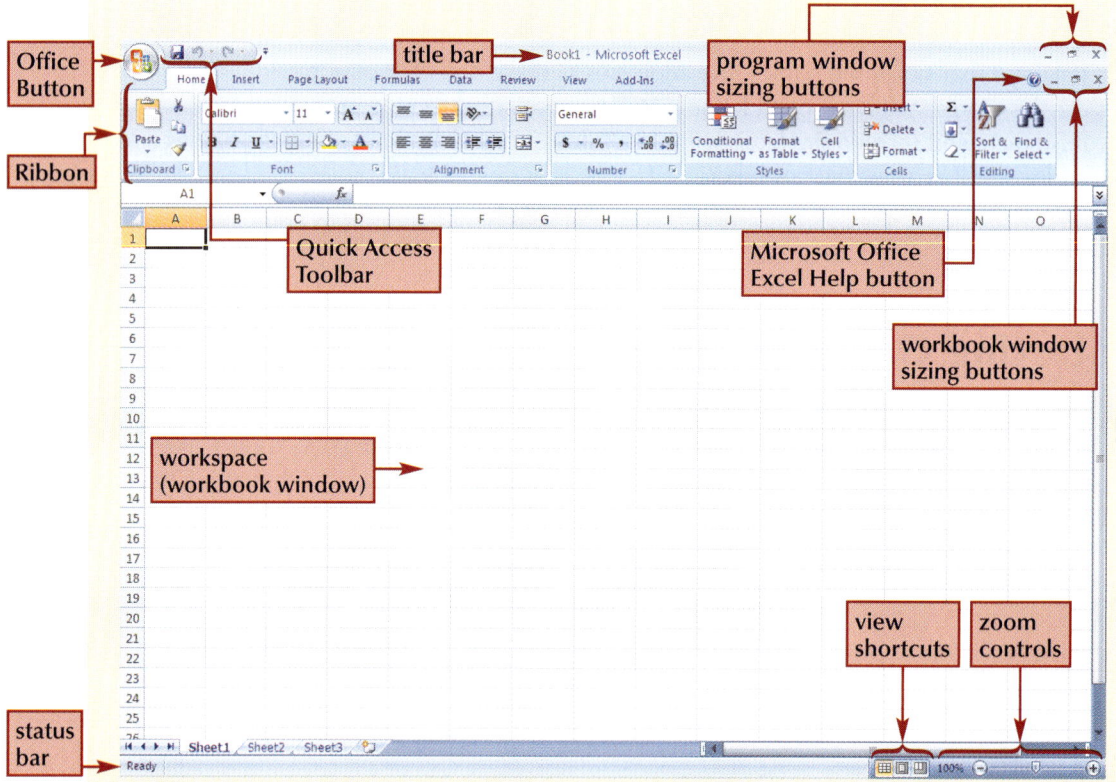

Trouble? If the Excel window doesn't fill your entire screen, the window is not maximized, or expanded to its full size. You'll maximize the window shortly.

You can have more than one Office program open at once. You'll use this same method to start Word and open a new, blank document.

To start Word and open a new, blank document:

1. Click the **Start** button on the taskbar, click **All Programs** to display the All Programs list, and then click **Microsoft Office**.

   Trouble? If you don't see Microsoft Office on the All Programs list, click Microsoft Office Word 2007 on the All Programs list. If you still don't see Microsoft Office Word 2007, ask your instructor or technical support person for help.

2. Click **Microsoft Office Word 2007**. Word starts, and a new, blank document opens. See Figure 2.

New, blank document in Word ◀ **Figure 2**

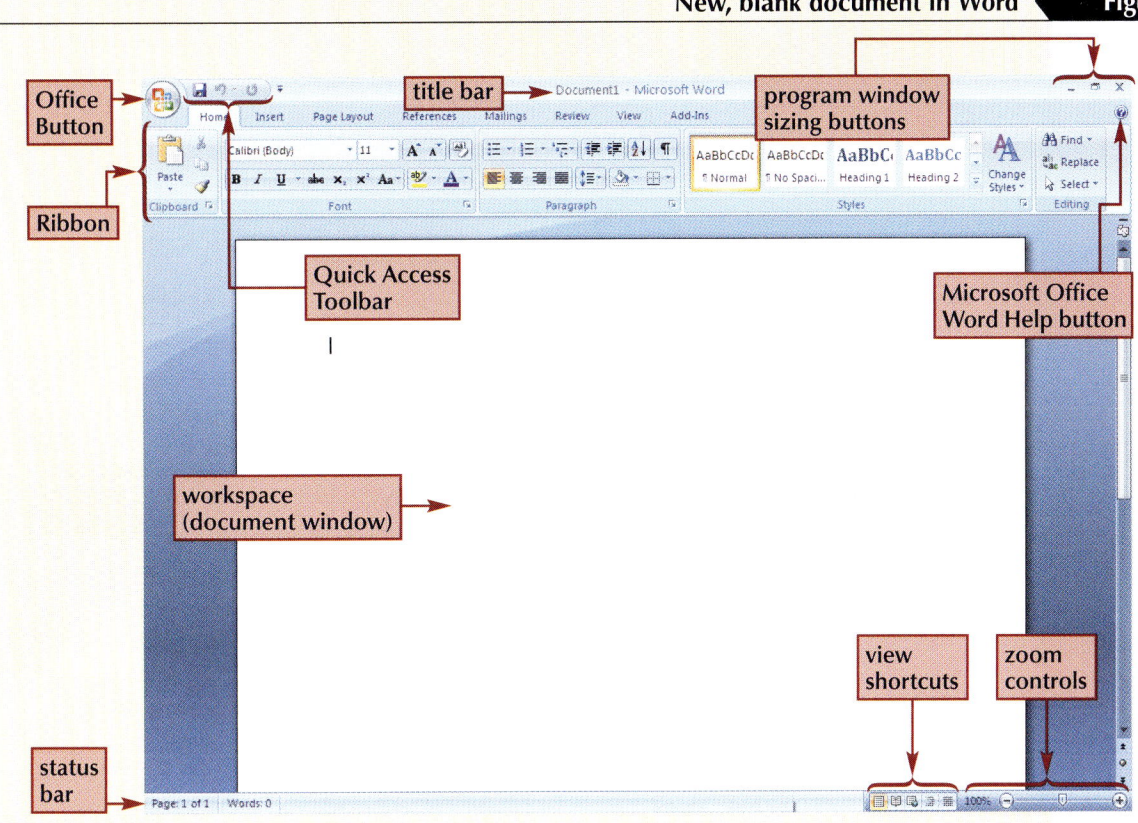

Trouble? If the Word window doesn't fill your entire screen, the window is not maximized. You'll maximize the window shortly.

Switching Between Open Programs and Files

Two programs are running at the same time—Excel and Word. The taskbar contains buttons for both programs. When you have two or more programs running or two files within the same program open, you can use the taskbar buttons to switch from one program or file to another. The button for the active program or file is darker. The employees at Recycled Palette often work in several programs at once.

To switch between Word and Excel files:

▶ 1. Click the **Microsoft Excel – Book1** button on the taskbar. The active program switches from Word to Excel. See Figure 3.

Excel and Word programs opened simultaneously ◀ **Figure 3**

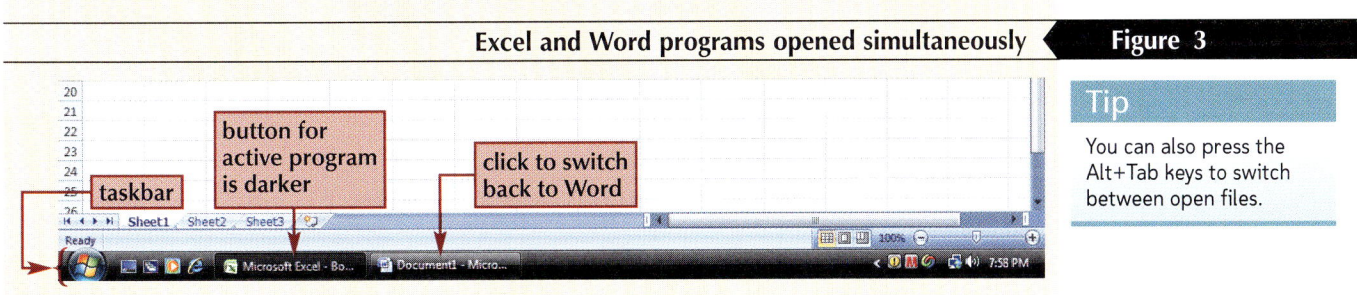

Tip

You can also press the Alt+Tab keys to switch between open files.

▶ 2. Click the **Document1 – Microsoft Word** button on the taskbar to return to Word.

Exploring Common Window Elements

The Office programs consist of windows that have many similar features. As you can see in Figures 1 and 2, many of the elements in both the Excel program window and the Word program window are the same. In fact, all the Office programs have these same elements. Figure 4 describes some of the most common window elements.

| Figure 4 | Common window elements |

Element	Description
Office Button	Provides access to document-level features and program settings
Quick Access Toolbar	Provides one-click access to commonly used commands, such as Save, Undo, and Repeat
Title bar	Contains the name of the open file, the program name, and the sizing buttons
Sizing buttons	Resize and close the program window or the workspace
Ribbon	Provides access to the main set of commands organized by task into tabs and groups
Microsoft Office Help button	Opens the Help window for that program
Workspace	Displays the file you are working on (Word document, Excel workbook, Access database, or PowerPoint slide)
Status bar	Provides information about the program, open file, or current task as well as the view shortcuts and zoom controls
View shortcuts	Change how a file is displayed in the workspace
Zoom controls	Magnify or shrink the content displayed in the workspace

Because these elements are the same in each program, after you've learned one program, it's easy to learn the others. The next sections explore these common features.

Resizing the Program Window and Workspace

There are three different sizing buttons. The Minimize button ▬ , which is the left button, hides a window so that only its program button is visible on the taskbar. The middle button changes name and function depending on the status of the window—the Maximize button ☐ expands the window to the full screen size or to the program window size, and the Restore Down button ❐ returns the window to a predefined size. The Close button ✕ , on the right, exits the program or closes the file. Excel has two sets of sizing buttons. The top set controls the program window and the lower set controls the workspace. The workspace sizing buttons look and function in exactly the same way as the program window sizing buttons, except the button names change to Minimize Window and Restore Window when the workspace is maximized.

Most often, you'll want to maximize the program window and workspace to take advantage of the full screen size you have available. If you have several files open, you might want to restore down their windows so that you can see more than one window at a time, or you might want to minimize programs or files you are not working on at the moment. You'll try minimizing, maximizing, and restoring down windows and workspaces now.

To resize windows and workspaces:

▶ **1.** Click the **Minimize** button [—] on the Word title bar. The Word program window reduces to a taskbar button. The Excel program window is visible again.

▶ **2.** If necessary, click the **Maximize** button [□] on the Excel title bar. The Excel program window expands to fill the screen.

▶ **3.** Click the **Restore Window** button [□] in the lower set of Excel sizing buttons. The workspace is resized and is now smaller than the full program window. See Figure 5.

Resized Excel window and workspace ◀ **Figure 5**

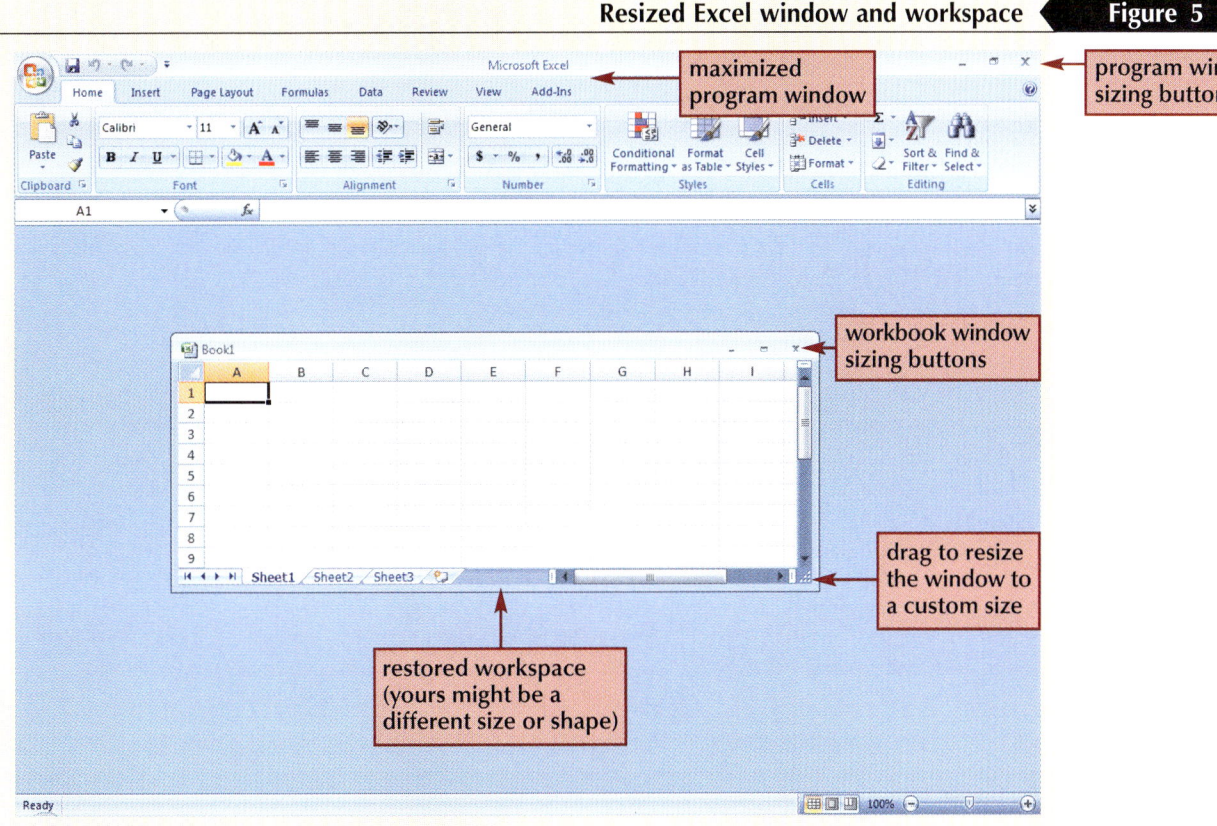

maximized program window

program window sizing buttons

workbook window sizing buttons

drag to resize the window to a custom size

restored workspace (yours might be a different size or shape)

▶ **4.** Click the **Maximize** button [□] on the Excel workbook window title bar. The Excel workspace expands to fill the program window.

▶ **5.** Click the **Document1 - Microsoft Word** button on the taskbar. The Word program window returns to its previous size.

▶ **6.** If necessary, click the **Maximize** button [□] on the Word title bar. The Word program window expands to fill the screen.

The sizing buttons give you the flexibility to arrange the program and file windows on your screen to best fit your needs.

Getting Information from the Status Bar

The **status bar** at the bottom of the program window provides information about the open file and current task or selection. It also has buttons and other controls for working with the file and its content. The status bar buttons and information displays are specific to the individual programs. For example, the Excel status bar displays summary information about a selected range of numbers (such as their sum or average), whereas the Word status bar shows the current page number and total number of words in a document. The right side of the status bar includes buttons that enable you to switch the workspace view in Word, Excel, PowerPoint, and Access as well as zoom the workspace in Word, Excel, and PowerPoint. You can customize the status bar to display other information or hide the **default** (original or preset) information.

Switching Views

Each program has a variety of views, or ways to display the file in the workspace. For example, Word has five views: Print Layout, Full Screen Reading, Web Layout, Outline, and Draft. The content of the file doesn't change from view to view, although the presentation of the content will. In Word, for example, Page Layout view shows how a document would appear as the printed page, whereas Web Layout view shows how the document would appear as a Web page. You can quickly switch between views using the shortcuts at the right side of the status bar. You can also change the view from the View tab on the Ribbon. You'll change views in later tutorials.

Zooming the Workspace

Zooming is a way to magnify or shrink the file content displayed in the workspace. You can zoom in to get a closer look at the content of an open document, worksheet, or slide, or you can zoom out to see more of the content at a smaller size. There are several ways to change the zoom percentage. You can use the Zoom slider at the right of the status bar to quickly change the zoom percentage. You can click the Zoom level button to the left of the Zoom slider in the status bar to open the Zoom dialog box and select a specific zoom percentage or size based on your file. You can also change the zoom settings using the Zoom group in the View tab on the Ribbon.

Reference Window | **Zooming the Workspace**

- Click the Zoom Out or Zoom In button on the status bar (or drag the Zoom slider button left or right) to the desired zoom percentage.

or

- Click the Zoom level button on the status bar.
- Select the appropriate zoom setting, and then click the OK button.

or

- Click the View tab on the Ribbon, and then in the Zoom group, click the zoom setting you want.

The figures shown in these tutorials are zoomed to enhance readability. You'll zoom the Word and Excel workspaces.

To zoom the Word and Excel workspaces:

▶ **1.** On the Zoom slider on the Word status bar, drag the **slider button** to the left until the Zoom percentage is **10%**. The document reduces to its smallest size, which makes the entire page visible but unreadable. See Figure 6.

Word document zoomed to 10% **Figure 6**

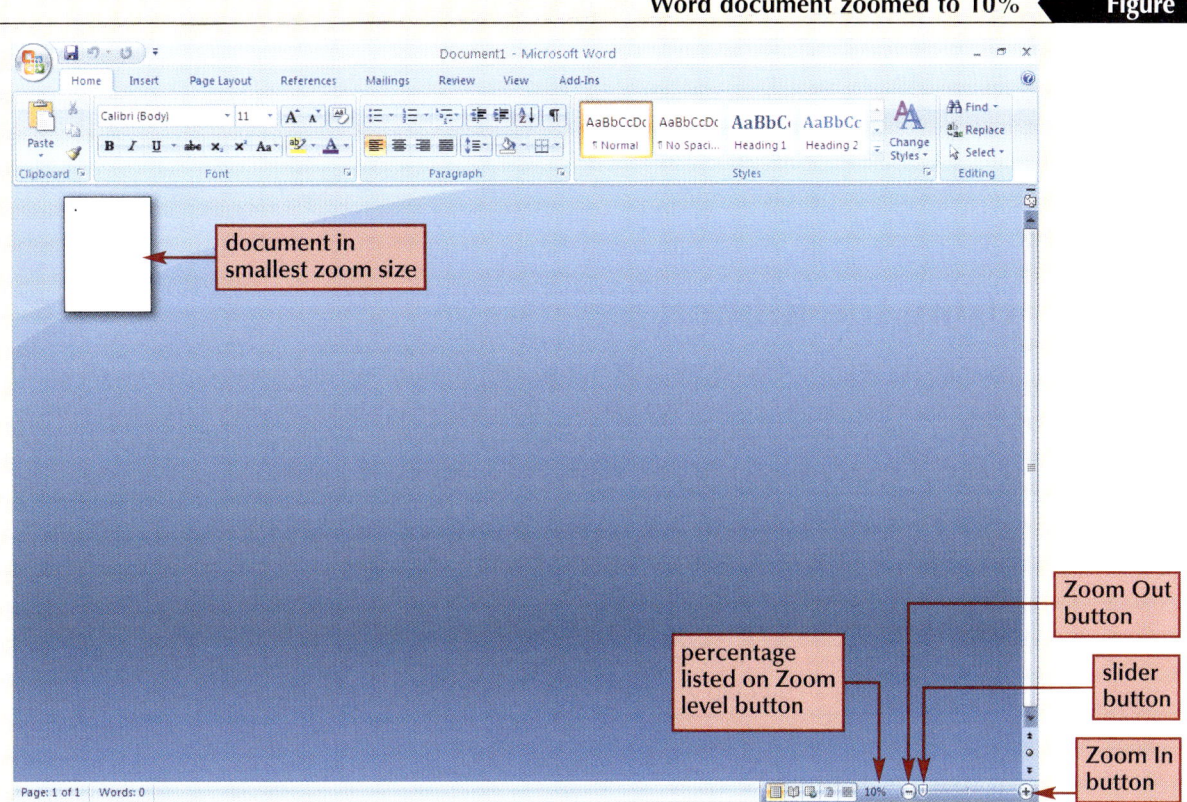

document in smallest zoom size

Zoom Out button

percentage listed on Zoom level button

slider button

Zoom In button

You'll zoom the document so its page width fills the workspace.

▶ **2.** Click the **Zoom level** button `10%` on the Word status bar. The Zoom dialog box opens. See Figure 7.

Zoom dialog box **Figure 7**

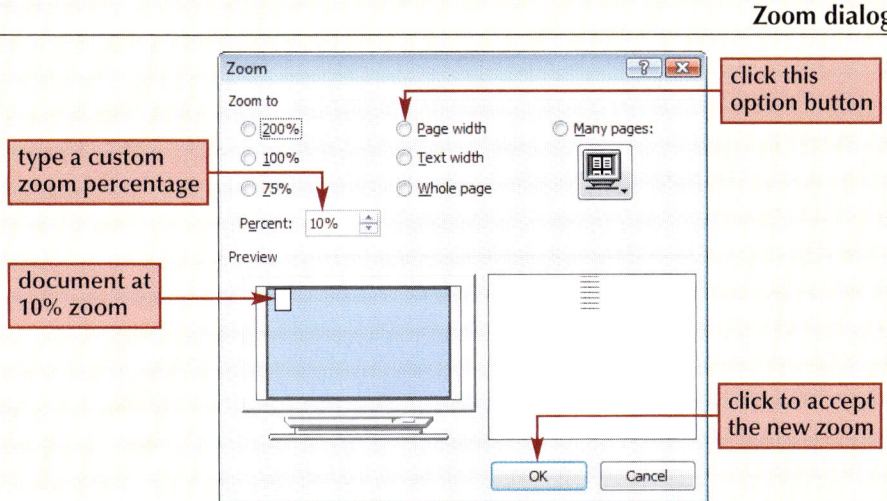

type a custom zoom percentage

click this option button

document at 10% zoom

click to accept the new zoom

▶ **3.** Click the **Page width** option button, and then click the **OK** button. The Word document magnifies to its page width to match the rest of the Word figures shown in these tutorials.

Now, you'll zoom the workbook to 120%.

4. Click the **Microsoft Excel – Book1** button on the taskbar. The Excel program window is displayed.

5. Click the **Zoom In** button ⊕ on the status bar two times. The workspace magnifies to 120%. This is the zoom percentage that matches the rest of the Excel figures shown in these tutorials.

6. Click the **Document1 – Microsoft Word** button on the taskbar. The Word program window is displayed.

Using the Ribbon

The **Ribbon** at the top of the program window just below the title bar is the main set of commands that you click to execute tasks. The Ribbon is organized into tabs. Each **tab** has commands related to particular activities. For example, in Word, the Insert tab on the Ribbon provides access to all the commands for adding objects such as shapes, pages, tables, illustrations, text, and symbols to a document. Although the tabs differ from program to program, the first tab in each program, called the Home tab, contains the commands for the most frequently performed activities, including cutting and pasting, changing fonts, and using editing tools. In addition, the Insert, Review, View, and Add-Ins tabs appear on the Ribbon in all the Office programs except Access, although the commands they include might differ from program to program. Other tabs are program specific, such as the Design tab in PowerPoint and the Datasheet tab in Access.

To use the Ribbon tabs:

1. In Word, point to the **Insert** tab on the Ribbon. The Insert tab is highlighted, though the Home tab with the options for using the Clipboard and formatting text remains visible.

2. Click the **Insert** tab. The Ribbon displays the Insert tab, which provides access to all the options for adding objects such as shapes, pages, tables, illustrations, text, and symbols to a document. See Figure 8.

Figure 8	Insert tab on the Ribbon

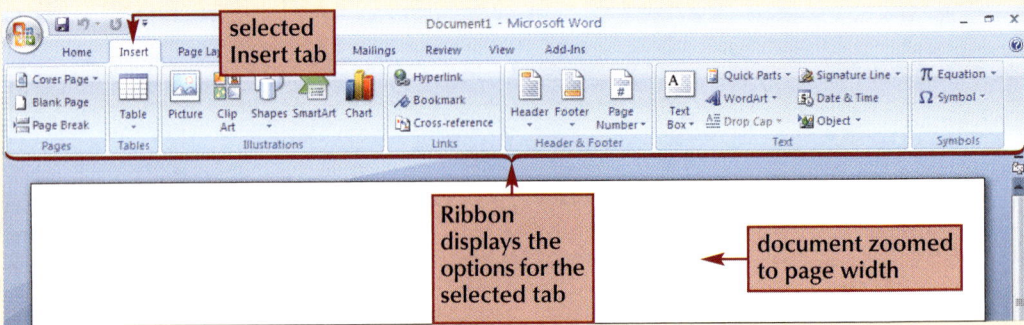

3. Click the **Home** tab on the Ribbon. The Ribbon displays the Home options.

Clicking Button Icons

Each **button**, or icon, on the tabs provides one-click access to a command. Most buttons are labeled so that you can easily find the command you need. For the most part, when you click a button, something happens in your file. If you want to repeat that action, you click the button again. Buttons for related commands are organized on a tab in **groups**. For example, the Clipboard group on the Home tab includes the Cut, Copy, Paste, and Format Painter buttons—the commands for moving or copying text, objects, and formatting.

Buttons can be toggle switches: one click turns on the feature and the next click turns off the feature. While the feature is on, the button remains colored or highlighted to remind you that it is active. For example, in Word, the Show/Hide button on the Home tab in the Paragraph group displays the nonprinting screen characters when toggled on and hides them when toggled off.

Some buttons have two parts: a button that accesses a command and an arrow that opens a menu of all the commands available for that task. For example, the Paste button on the Home tab includes the default Paste command and an arrow that opens the menu of all the Paste commands—Paste, Paste Special, and Paste as Hyperlink. To select a command on the menu, you click the button arrow and then click the command on the menu.

The buttons and groups change based on your monitor size, your screen resolution, and the size of the program window. With smaller monitors, lower screen resolutions, and reduced program windows, buttons can appear as icons without labels and a group can be condensed into a button that you click to display the group options. The figures in these tutorials were created using a screen resolution of 1024 × 768 and, unless otherwise specified, the program and workspace windows are maximized. If you are using a different screen resolution or window size, the button icons on the Ribbon might show more or fewer button names, and some groups might be condensed into buttons.

You'll type text in the Word document, and then use the buttons on the Ribbon.

To use buttons on the Ribbon:

▶ **1.** Type **Recycled Palette**, and then press the **Enter** key. The text appears in the first line of the document and the insertion point moves to the second line.

   Trouble? If you make a typing error, press the Backspace key to delete the incorrect letters, and then retype the text.

▶ **2.** In the Paragraph group on the Home tab, click the **Show/Hide** button ¶. The nonprinting screen characters appear in the document, and the Show/Hide button remains toggled on. See Figure 9.

   Trouble? If the nonprinting characters are removed from your screen, the Show/Hide button ¶ was already selected. Repeat Step 2 to show the nonprinting screen characters.

Button toggled on   Figure 9

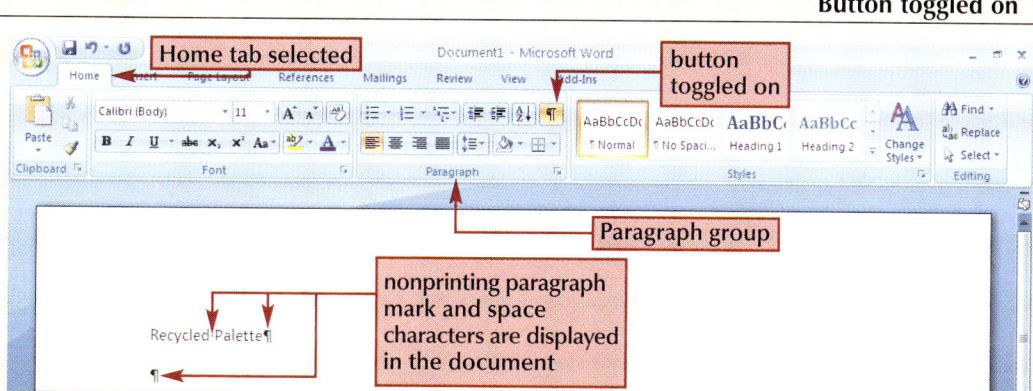

▶ **3.** Drag to select all the text in the first line of the document (but not the paragraph mark).

▶ **4.** In the Clipboard group on the Home tab, click the **Copy** button. The selected text is copied to the Clipboard.

▶ **5.** Press the ↓ key. The text is deselected and the insertion point moves to the second line in the document.

▶ **6.** In the Clipboard group on the Home tab, point to the top part of the **Paste** button. Both parts of the Paste button are highlighted, but the icon at top is darker to indicate it will be clicked if you press the mouse button.

▶ **7.** Point to the **Paste button arrow**. The button arrow is now darker.

▶ **8.** Click the **Paste button arrow**. A menu of paste commands opens. See Figure 10. To select one of the commands on the list, you click it.

Figure 10	Two-part Paste button

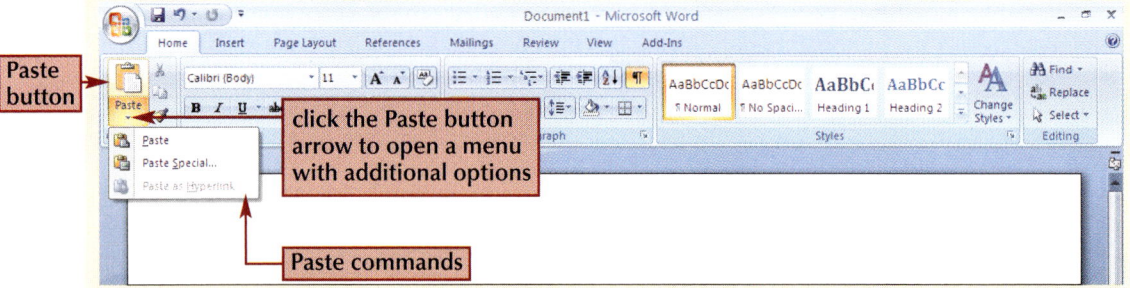

▶ **9.** Click **Paste**. The menu closes, and the text is duplicated in the second line of the document.

As you can see, you can quickly access commands and turn features on and off with the buttons on the Ribbon.

InSight	**Using Keyboard Shortcuts and Key Tips**

Keyboard shortcuts can help you work faster and more efficiently. A **keyboard shortcut** is a key or combination of keys you press to access a tool or perform a command. To quickly access options on the Ribbon, the Quick Access Toolbar, and the Office Button without removing your hands from the keyboard:

1. Press the Alt key. Key Tips appear that list the keyboard shortcut for each Ribbon tab, each Quick Access Toolbar button, and the Office Button.
2. Press the key for the tab or button you want to use. An action is performed or Key Tips appear for the buttons on the selected tab or the commands for the selected button.
3. Continue to press the appropriate key listed in the Key Tip until the action you want is performed.

You can also use keyboard shortcuts to perform specific commands. For example, Ctrl+S is the keyboard shortcut for the Save command (you hold down the Ctrl key while you press the S key). This type of keyboard shortcut appears in ScreenTips next to the command's name. Not all commands have this type of keyboard shortcut. Identical commands in each Office program use the same keyboard shortcut.

Using Galleries and Live Preview

A button can also open a **gallery**, which is a grid or menu that shows a visual representation of the options available for that command. For example, the Bullet Library gallery in Word shows an icon of each bullet style you can select. Some galleries include a More button that you click to expand the gallery to see all the options in it. When you hover the pointer over an option in a gallery, **Live Preview** shows the results you would achieve in your file if you clicked that option. To continue the bullets example, when you hover over a bullet style in the Bullet Library gallery, the current paragraph or selected text previews that bullet style. By moving the pointer from option to option, you can quickly see the text set with different bullet styles; you can then select the style that works best for your needs.

To use a gallery and Live Preview:

1. In the Paragraph group on the Home tab, click the **Bullets button arrow** 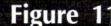. The Bullet Library gallery opens.

2. Point to the **check mark bullet** style. Live Preview shows the selected bullet style in your document, so you can determine if you like that bullet style. See Figure 11.

Live Preview of bullet style   Figure 11

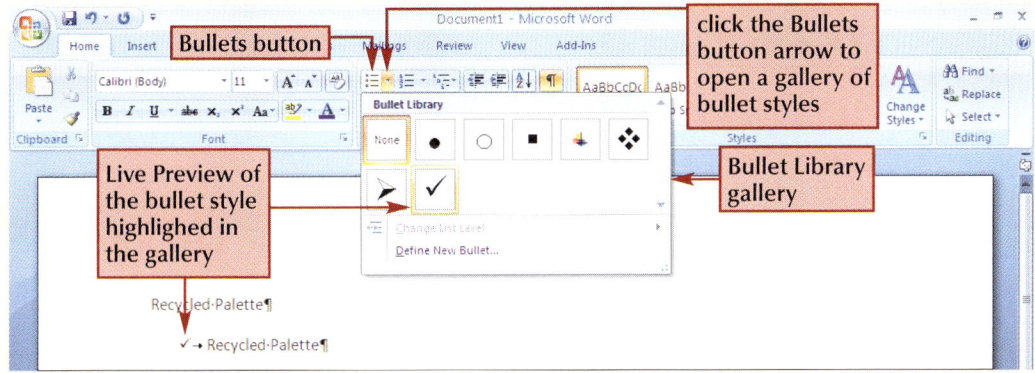

3. Place the pointer over each of the remaining bullet styles and preview them in your document.

    You don't want to add bullets to your document right now, so you'll close the Bullet Library gallery and deselect the Bullets button.

4. Press the **Esc** key on the keyboard. The Bullet Library gallery closes and the Bullets button is deselected.

5. Press the **Backspace** key on the keyboard to delete the text "Recycled Palette" on the second line.

Galleries and Live Preview let you quickly see how your file will be affected by a selection.

Opening Dialog Boxes and Task Panes

The button to the right of the group names is the **Dialog Box Launcher**, which you click to open a task pane or dialog box that provides more advanced functionality for that group of tasks. A **task pane** is a window that helps you navigate through a complex task or feature. For example, the Clipboard task pane allows you to paste some or all of the items that have been cut or copied from any Office program during the current work session and the Research task pane allows you to search a variety of reference resources from within a file. A **dialog box** is a window from which you enter or choose settings for how you want to perform a task. For example, the Page Setup dialog box in Word contains options for how you want a document to look. Some dialog boxes organize related information into tabs, and related options and settings are organized into groups, just as they are on the Ribbon. You select settings in a dialog box using option buttons, check boxes, text boxes, lists, and other controls to collect information about how you want to perform a task.

In Excel, you'll use the Dialog Box Launcher for the Page Setup group to open the Page Setup dialog box.

To open the Page Setup dialog box using the Dialog Box Launcher:

▶ **1.** Click the **Microsoft Excel – Book1** button on the taskbar to switch from Word to Excel.

▶ **2.** Click the **Page Layout** tab on the Ribbon.

▶ **3.** In the Page Setup group, click the **Dialog Box Launcher**, which is the small button to the right of the Page Setup group name. The Page Setup dialog box opens with the Page tab displayed. See Figure 12.

| Figure 12 | Page tab in the Page Setup dialog box |

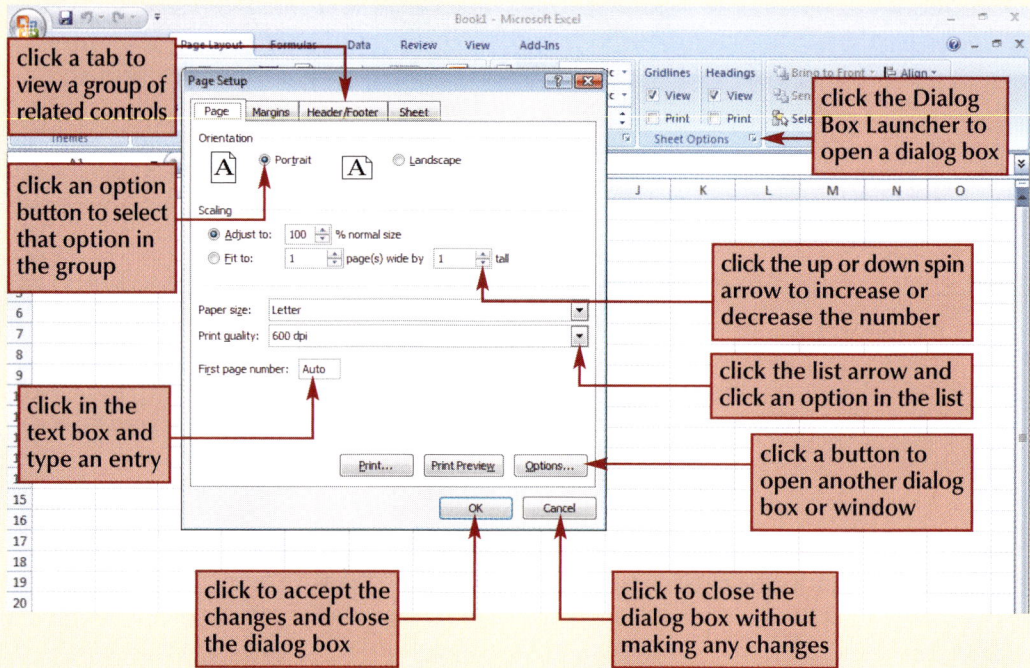

- click a tab to view a group of related controls
- click the Dialog Box Launcher to open a dialog box
- click an option button to select that option in the group
- click the up or down spin arrow to increase or decrease the number
- click the list arrow and click an option in the list
- click in the text box and type an entry
- click a button to open another dialog box or window
- click to accept the changes and close the dialog box
- click to close the dialog box without making any changes

▶ **4.** Click the **Landscape** option button. The workbook's page orientation changes to a page wider than it is long.

▶ **5.** Click the **Sheet** tab. The dialog box displays options related to the worksheet. You can click a check box to turn an option on (checked) or off (unchecked). You can check more than one check box in a group, whereas you can select only one option button in a group.

▶ **6.** In the Print group, click the **Gridlines** check box and the **Row and column headings** check box. Check marks appear in both check boxes, indicating that these options are selected.

You don't want to change the page setup right now, so you'll close the dialog box.

▶ **7.** Click the **Cancel** button. The dialog box closes without making any changes to the page setup.

Using Contextual Tools

Some tabs, toolbars, and menus come into view as you work. Because these tools become available only as you might need them, the workspace on your screen remains more open and less cluttered. However, tools that appear and disappear as you work can be distracting and take some getting used to.

Displaying Contextual Tabs

Any object that you can select in a file has a related contextual tab. An **object** is anything that appears on your screen that can be selected and manipulated as a whole, such as a table, a picture, a text box, a shape, a chart, WordArt, an equation, a diagram, a header, or a footer. A **contextual tab** is a Ribbon tab that contains commands related to the selected object so you can manipulate, edit, and format that object. Contextual tabs appear to the right of the standard Ribbon tabs just below a title label. For example, Figure 13 shows the Table Tools contextual tabs that appear when you select a table in a Word document. Although the contextual tabs appear only when you select an object, they function in the same way as standard tabs on the Ribbon. Contextual tabs disappear when you click elsewhere on the screen and deselect the object. Contextual tabs can also appear as you switch views. You'll use contextual tabs in later tutorials.

Table Tools contextual tabs ◀ **Figure 13**

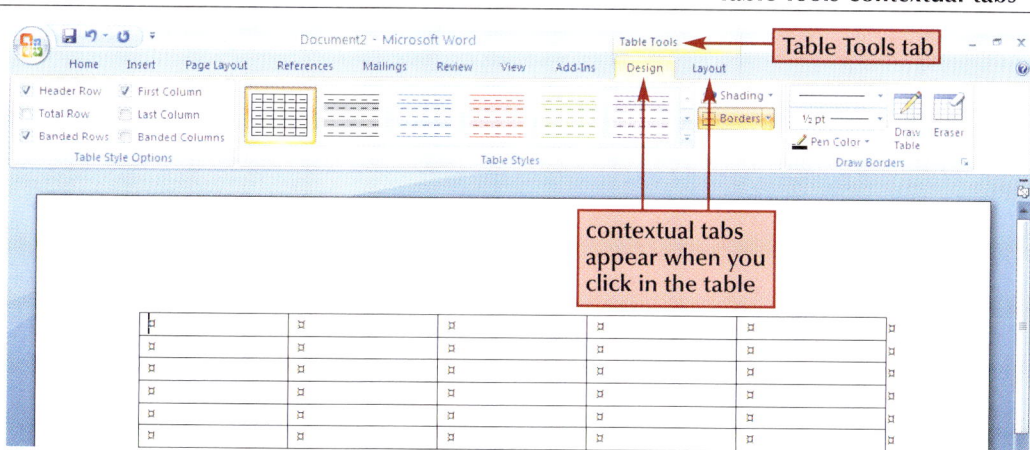

Table Tools tab

contextual tabs appear when you click in the table

Accessing the Mini Toolbar

The **Mini toolbar** is a toolbar that appears next to the pointer whenever you select text, and it contains buttons for the most commonly used formatting commands, such as font, font size, styles, color, alignment, and indents that may appear in different groups or tabs on the Ribbon. The Mini toolbar buttons differ in each program. A transparent version of the Mini toolbar appears immediately after you select text. When you move the pointer over the Mini toolbar, it comes into full view so you can click the appropriate formatting button or buttons. The Mini toolbar disappears if you move the pointer away from the toolbar, press a key, or press a mouse button. The Mini toolbar can help you format your text faster, but initially you might find that the toolbar disappears unexpectedly. All the commands on the Mini toolbar are also available on the Ribbon. Be aware that Live Preview of selected styles does not work in the Mini toolbar.

You'll use the Mini toolbar to format text you enter in the workbook.

Tip

You can turn off the Mini toolbar and Live Preview in Word, Excel, and PowerPoint. Click the Office Button, click the Options button at the bottom of the Office menu, uncheck the first two check boxes in the Popular category, and then click the OK button.

To use the Mini toolbar to format text:

▶ **1.** If necessary, click cell **A1** (the rectangle in the upper-left corner of the worksheet).

▶ **2.** Type **Budget**. The text appears in the cell.

▶ **3.** Press the **Enter** key. The text is entered in cell A1 and cell A2 is selected.

▶ **4.** Type **2008**, and then press the **Enter** key. The year is entered in cell A2 and cell A3 is selected.

You'll use the Mini toolbar to make the word in cell A1 boldface.

▶ **5.** Double-click cell **A1** to place the insertion point in the cell. Now you can select the text you typed.

▶ **6.** Double-click **Budget** in cell A1. The selected text appears white in a black background, and the transparent Mini toolbar appears directly above the selected text. See Figure 14.

Figure 14 | Transparent Mini toolbar

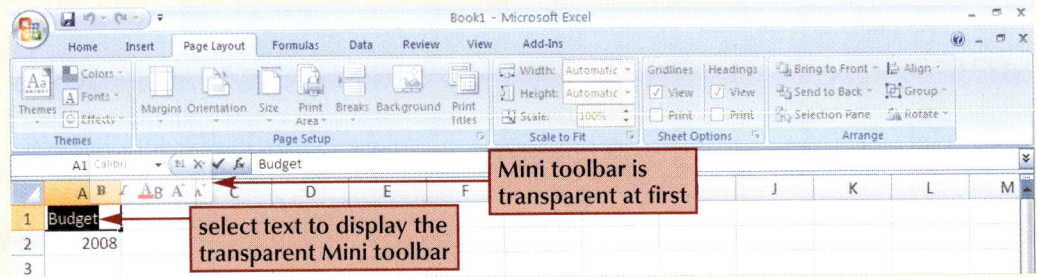

▶ **7.** Move the pointer over the Mini toolbar. The Mini toolbar is now completely visible, and you can click buttons.

Trouble? If the Mini toolbar disappears, you probably moved the pointer to another area of the worksheet. To redisplay the Mini toolbar, repeat Steps 5 through 7, being careful to move the pointer directly over the Mini toolbar in Step 7.

▶ **8.** Click the **Bold** button **B** on the Mini toolbar. The text in cell A1 is bold and the Mini toolbar remains visible so you can continue formatting the selected text. See Figure 15.

Tip

You can redisplay the Mini toolbar if it disappears by right-clicking the selected text.

Figure 15 | Mini toolbar with the Bold button selected

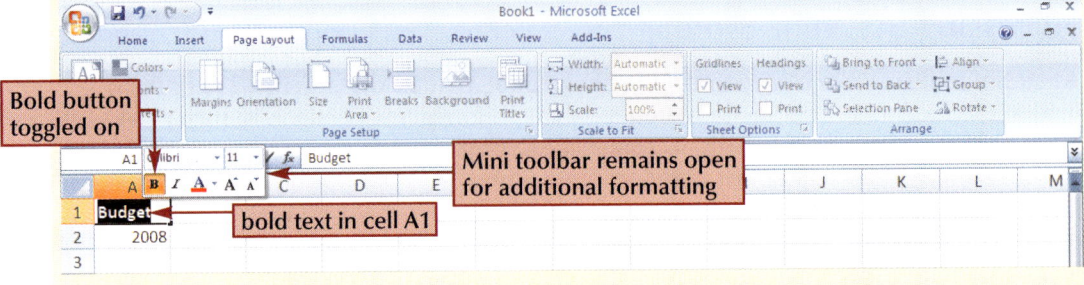

You don't want to make any other changes, so you'll close the Mini toolbar.

▶ **9.** Press the **Enter** key. The Mini toolbar disappears and cell A2 is selected.

Opening Shortcut Menus

A **shortcut menu** is a list of commands related to a selection that opens when you click the right mouse button. Each shortcut menu provides access to the commands you'll most likely want to use with the object or selection you right-click. The shortcut menu includes commands that perform actions, commands that open dialog boxes, and galleries of options that provide Live Preview. The Mini toolbar also opens when you right-click. If you click a button on the Mini toolbar, the rest of the shortcut menu closes while the Mini toolbar remains open so you can continue formatting the selection. Using a shortcut menu provides quick access to the commands you need without having to access the tabs on the Ribbon. For example, you can right-click selected text to open a shortcut menu with a Mini toolbar, text-related commands, such as Cut, Copy, and Paste, as well as other program-specific commands.

You'll use a shortcut menu in Excel to delete the content you entered in cell A1.

To use a shortcut menu to delete content:

▶ 1. Right-click cell **A1**. A shortcut menu opens, listing commands related to common tasks you'd perform in a cell, along with a Mini toolbar. See Figure 16.

Shortcut menu with Mini toolbar ◀ **Figure 16**

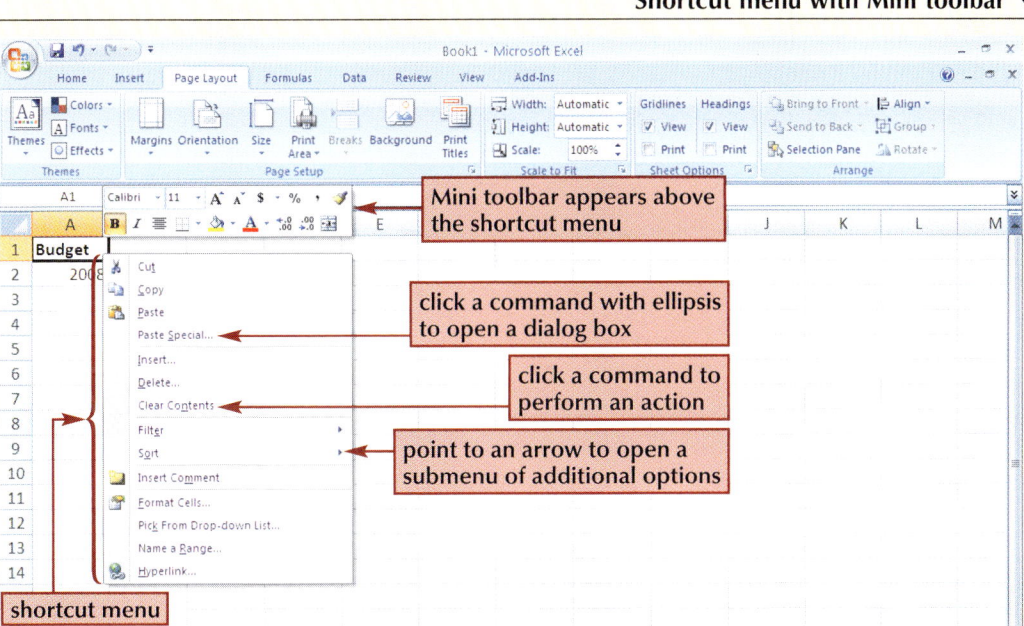

You'll use the Clear Contents command to delete the bold text from cell A1.

▶ 2. Click **Clear Contents** on the shortcut menu. The shortcut menu closes, the Mini toolbar disappears, and the formatted text is removed from cell A1.

You'll use the Clear Contents command again to delete the year from cell A2.

▶ 3. Right-click cell **A2**, and then click **Clear Contents** on the shortcut menu. The year is removed from cell A2.

Shortcut menus enable you to quickly access commands that you're most likely to need in the context of the task you're performing.

Tip

Press the Esc key to close an open menu, shortcut menu, list, gallery, and so forth without selecting an option.

Working with Files

The most common tasks you perform in any Office program are to create, open, save, and close files. The processes for these tasks are basically the same in all the Office programs. In addition, there are several methods for performing most tasks in Office. This flexibility enables you to use Office in a way that best fits how you like to work.

The **Office Button** provides access to document-level features, such as creating new files, opening existing files, saving files, printing files, and closing files, as well as the most common program options, called **application settings**. The **Quick Access Toolbar** is a collection of buttons that provide one-click access to commonly used commands, such as Save, Undo, and Repeat.

To begin working in a program, you need to create a new file or open an existing file. When you start Word, Excel, or PowerPoint, the program opens along with a blank file—ready for you to begin working on a new document, workbook, or presentation. When you start Access, the Getting Started with Microsoft Access window opens, displaying options for creating a new database or opening an existing one.

Ean has asked you to continue working on the agenda for the stockholder meeting. You already started typing in the document that opened when you started Word. Next, you will enter more text in the Word document.

To enter text in the Word document:

▶ 1. Click the **Document1 – Microsoft Word** button on the taskbar to activate the Word program window.

▶ 2. Type **Meeting Agenda** on the second line of the document, and then press the **Enter** key. The text you typed appears in the document.

   Trouble? If you make a typing error, press the Backspace key to delete the incorrect letters, and then retype the text.

Saving a File

As you create and modify Office files, your work is stored only in the computer's temporary memory, not on a hard disk. If you were to exit the programs without saving, turn off your computer, or experience a power failure, your work would be lost. To prevent losing work, save your file to a disk frequently—at least every 10 minutes. You can save files to the hard disk located inside your computer, a floppy disk, an external hard drive, a network storage drive, or a portable storage disk, such as a USB flash drive.

Reference Window | **Saving a File**

To save a file the first time or with a new name or location:
- Click the Office Button, and then click Save As (or for an unnamed file, click the Save button on the Quick Access Toolbar or click the Office Button, and then click Save).
- In the Save As dialog box, navigate to the location where you want to save the file.
- Type a descriptive title in the File name box, and then click the Save button.

To resave a named file to the same location:
- Click the Save button on the Quick Access Toolbar (or click the Office Button, and then click Save).

The first time you save a file, you need to name it. This **filename** includes a descriptive title you select and a file extension assigned by Office. You should choose a descriptive title that accurately reflects the content of the document, workbook, presentation, or database, such as "Shipping Options Letter" or "Fourth Quarter Financial Analysis." Your descriptive title can include uppercase and lowercase letters, numbers, hyphens, and spaces in any combination, but not the following special characters: ? " / \ < > * | and :. Each filename ends with a **file extension**, a period followed by several characters that Office adds to your descriptive title to identify the program in which that file was created. The default file extensions for Office 2007 are .docx for Word, .xlsx for Excel, .pptx for PowerPoint, and .accdb for Access. Filenames (the descriptive title and the file extension) can include a maximum of 255 characters. You might see file extensions depending on how Windows is set up on your computer. The figures in these tutorials do not show file extensions.

You also need to decide where to save the file—on which disk and in what folder. A **folder** is a container for your files. Just as you organize paper documents within folders stored in a filing cabinet, you can organize your files within folders stored on your computer's hard disk or a removable disk, such as a USB flash drive. Store each file in a logical location that you will remember whenever you want to use the file again. The default storage location for Office files is the Documents folder; you can create additional storage folders within that folder or navigate to a new storage location.

You can navigate the Save As dialog box by clicking a folder or location on your computer in the Navigation pane along the left side of the dialog box, and then double-clicking folders in the file list until you display the storage location you want. You can also navigate to a storage location with the Address bar, which displays the current file path. Each location in the file path has a corresponding arrow that you can click to quickly select a folder within that location. For example, you can click the Documents arrow in the Address bar to open a list of all the folders in the Documents folder, and then click the folder you want to open. If you want to return to a specific spot in the file hierarchy, you click that folder name in the Address bar. The Back and Forward buttons let you quickly move between folders.

Saving and Using Files with Earlier Versions of Office | InSight

The default file types in Office 2007 are different from those used in earlier versions. This means that someone using Office 2003 or earlier cannot open files created in Office 2007. Files you want to share with earlier Office users must be saved in the earlier formats, which use the following extensions: .doc for Word, .xls for Excel, .mdb for Access, and .ppt for PowerPoint. To save a file in an earlier format, open the Save As dialog box, click the Save as type list arrow, and then click the appropriate 97-2003 format. A compatibility checker reports which Office 2007 features or elements are not supported by the earlier version of Office, and you can choose to remove them before saving. You can use Office 2007 to open and work with files created in earlier versions of Office. You can then save the file in its current format or update it to the Office 2007 format.

The lines of text you typed are not yet saved on disk. You'll do that now.

To save a file for the first time:

Windows XP Tip

To navigate to a location in the Save As dialog box, you use the Save in arrow.

1. Click the **Save** button 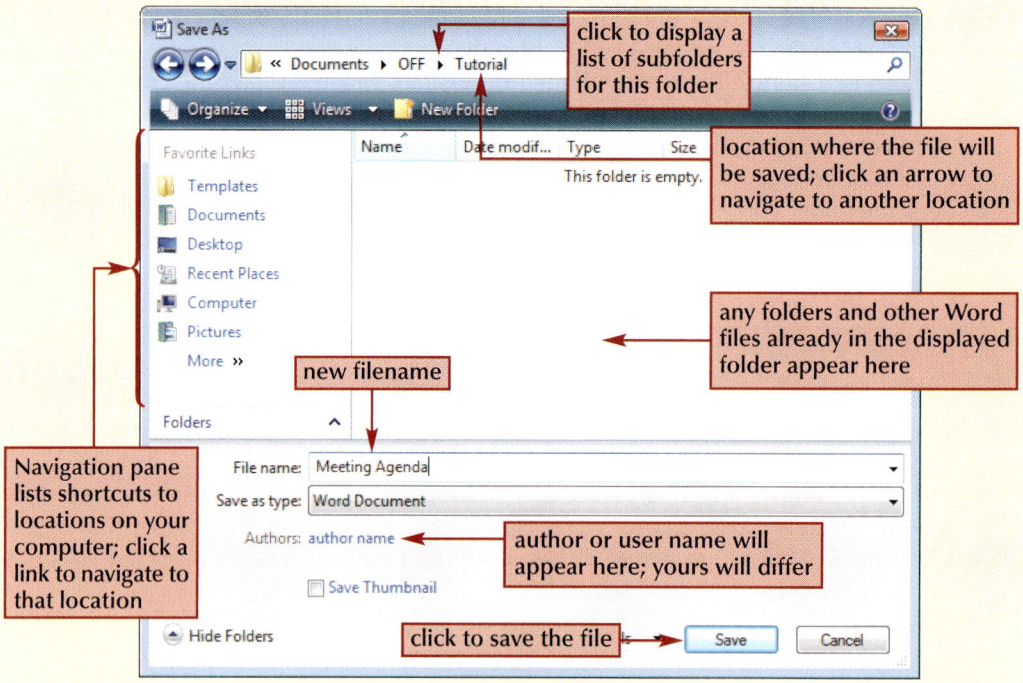 on the Quick Access Toolbar. The Save As dialog box opens because you have not yet saved the file and need to specify a storage location and filename. The default location is set to the Documents folder, and the first few words of the first line appear in the File name box as a suggested title.

2. In the Navigation pane, click the link for the location that contains your Data Files, if necessary.

   Trouble? If you don't have the starting Data Files, you need to get them before you can proceed. Your instructor will either give you the Data Files or ask you to obtain them from a specified location (such as a network drive). In either case, make a backup copy of the Data Files before you start so that you will have the original files available in case you need to start over. If you have any questions about the Data Files, see your instructor or technical support person for assistance.

3. Double-click the **OFF** folder in the file list, and then double-click the **Tutorial** folder. This is the location where you want to save the document.

   Next, you'll enter a more descriptive title for the filename.

4. Type **Meeting Agenda** in the File name box. See Figure 17.

Figure 17	Completed Save As dialog box

click to display a list of subfolders for this folder

location where the file will be saved; click an arrow to navigate to another location

any folders and other Word files already in the displayed folder appear here

new filename

Navigation pane lists shortcuts to locations on your computer; click a link to navigate to that location

author or user name will appear here; yours will differ

click to save the file

Trouble? If the .docx file extension appears after the filename, your computer is configured to show file extensions. Continue with Step 5.

5. Click the **Save** button. The Save As dialog box closes, and the name of your file appears in the title bar.

The saved file includes everything in the document at the time you last saved it. Any new edits or additions you make to the document exist only in the computer's memory and are not saved in the file on the disk. As you work, remember to save frequently so that the file is updated to reflect the latest content of the document.

Because you already named the document and selected a storage location, the Save As dialog box doesn't open whenever you save the document again. If you want to save a copy of the file with a different filename or to a different location, you reopen the Save As dialog box by clicking the Office Button, and then clicking Save As. The previous version of the file remains on your disk as well.

You need to add your name to the agenda. Then, you'll save your changes.

To modify and save the Word document:

▶ 1. Type your name, and then press the **Enter** key. The text you typed appears on the next line.

▶ 2. Click the **Save** button 🖫 on the Quick Access Toolbar to save your changes.

Closing a File

Although you can keep multiple files open at one time, you should close any file you are no longer working on to conserve system resources as well as to ensure that you don't inadvertently make changes to the file. You can close a file by clicking the Office Button and then clicking the Close command. If that's the only file open for the program, the program window remains open and no file appears in the window. You can also close a file by clicking the Close button in the upper-right corner of the title bar or double-clicking the Office Button. If that's the only file open for the program, the program also closes.

As a standard practice, you should save your file before closing it. However, Office has an added safeguard: If you attempt to close a file without saving your changes, a dialog box opens, asking whether you want to save the file. Click the Yes button to save the changes to the file before closing the file and program. Click the No button to close the file and program without saving changes. Click the Cancel button to return to the program window without saving changes or closing the file and program. This feature helps to ensure that you always save the most current version of any file.

You'll add the date to the agenda. Then, you'll attempt to close it without saving.

To modify and close the Word document:

▶ 1. Type today's date, and then press the **Enter** key. The text you typed appears below your name in the document.

▶ 2. In the upper-left corner of the program window, click the **Office Button** 🔵. A menu opens with commands for creating new files, opening existing files, saving files, printing files, and closing files.

▶ 3. Click **Close**. A dialog box opens, asking whether you want to save the changes you made to the document.

▶ 4. Click the **Yes** button. The current version of the document is saved to the file, and then the document closes. Word is still running.

After you have a program open, you can create additional new files for the open program or you can open previously created and saved files.

Opening a File

When you want to open a blank document, workbook, presentation, or database, you create a new file. When you want to work on a previously created file, you must first open it. Opening a file transfers a copy of the file from the storage disk (either a hard disk or a portable disk) to the computer's memory and displays it on your screen. The file is then in your computer's memory and on the disk.

Reference Window | **Opening an Existing File or Creating a New File**

- Click the Office Button, and then click Open.
- In the Open dialog box, navigate to the storage location of the file you want to open.
- Click the filename of the file you want to open.
- Click the Open button.

or

- Click the Office Button, and then click a filename in the Recent Documents list.

or

- Click the Office Button, and then click New.
- In the New dialog box, click Blank Document, Blank Workbook, Blank Presentation, or Blank Database (depending on the program).
- Click the Create button.

Ean asks you to print the agenda. To do that, you'll reopen the file.

To open the existing Word document:

1. Click the **Office Button** 🗔, and then click **Open**. The Open dialog box, which works similarly to the Save As dialog box, opens.

2. Use the Navigation pane or the Address bar to navigate to the **OFF\Tutorial** folder included with your Data Files. This is the location where you saved the agenda document.

3. Click **Meeting Agenda** in the file list. See Figure 18.

Figure 18 ▶ Open dialog box

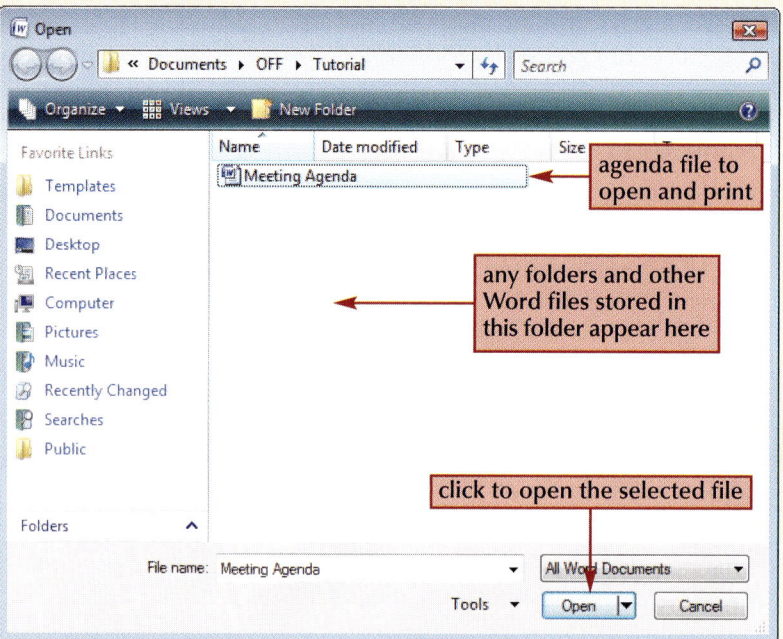

4. Click the **Open** button. The agenda file opens in the Word program window.

Next, you'll use Help to get information about printing files in Word.

Getting Help

If you don't know how to perform a task or want more information about a feature, you can turn to Office itself for information on how to use it. This information, referred to simply as **Help**, is like a huge encyclopedia available from your desktop. You can get Help in ScreenTips, from the Help window, and in Microsoft Office Online.

Viewing ScreenTips

ScreenTips are a fast and simple method you can use to get help about objects you see on the screen. A **ScreenTip** is a box with the button's name, its keyboard shortcut if it has one, a description of the command's function, and, in some cases, a link to more information. Just position the mouse pointer over a button or object to view its ScreenTip. If a link to more information appears in the ScreenTip, press the F1 key while the Screen-Tip is displayed to open the Help window with the appropriate topic displayed.

To view ScreenTips:

▶ **1.** Point to the **Microsoft Office Word Help** button ⓦ. The ScreenTip shows the button's name, its keyboard shortcut, and a brief explanation of the button. See Figure 19.

ScreenTip for the Help button ◀ **Figure 19**

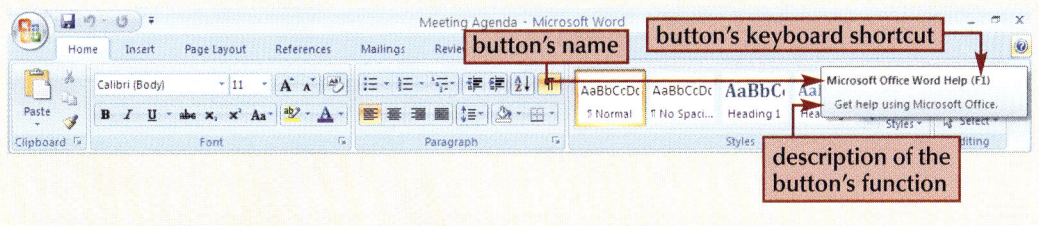

▶ **2.** Point to other buttons on the Ribbon to display their ScreenTips.

Using the Help Window

For more detailed information, you can use the **Help window** to access all the Help topics, templates, and training installed on your computer with Office and available on Microsoft Office Online. **Microsoft Office Online** is a Web site maintained by Microsoft that provides access to the latest information and additional Help resources. For example, you can access current Help topics, templates of predesigned files, and training for Office. To connect to Microsoft Office Online, you need Internet access on your computer. Otherwise, you see only those topics stored locally.

| Reference Window | **Getting Help** |

- Click the Microsoft Office Help button (the button name depends on the Office program).
- Type a keyword or phrase in the "Type words to search for" box, and then click the Search button.
- Click a Help topic in the search results list.
- Read the information in the Help window. For more information, click other topics or links.
- Click the Close button on the Help window title bar.

You open the Help window by clicking the Microsoft Office Help button 🔘 located below the sizing buttons in every Office program. Each program has its own Help window from which you can find information about all the Office commands and features as well as step-by-step instructions for using them. You can search for information in the Help window using the "Type words to search for" box and the Table of Contents pane.

The "Type words to search for" box enables you to search the Help system using key-words or phrases. You type a specific word or phrase about a task you want to perform or a topic you need help with, and then click the Search button to search the Help system. A list of Help topics related to the keyword or phrase you entered appears in the Help window. If your computer is connected to the Internet, your search results come from Microsoft Office Online rather than only the Help topics stored locally on your computer. You can click a link to open a Help topic with step-by-step instructions that will guide you through a specific procedure and/or provide explanations of difficult concepts in clear, easy-to-understand language. For example, if you type "format cell" in the Excel Help window, a list of Help topics related to the words you typed appears in the Help window. You can navigate through the topics you've viewed using the buttons on the Help window toolbar. These buttons—including Back, Forward, Stop, Refresh, Home, and Print—are the same as those in the Microsoft Internet Explorer Web browser.

You'll use the "Type words to search for" box in the Help window to obtain more information about printing a document in Word.

To use the "Type words to search for" box:

▶ **1.** Click the **Microsoft Office Word Help** button 🔘 . The Word Help window opens.

▶ **2.** Click the **Type words to search for** box, if necessary, and then type **print document**. You can set where you want to search.

▶ **3.** Click the **Search button arrow**. The Search menu shows the online and local con-tent available.

▶ **4.** If your computer is connected to the Internet, click **All Word** in the Content from Office Online list. If your computer is not connected to the Internet, click **Word Help** in the Content from this computer list.

▶ **5.** Click the **Search** button. The Help window displays a list of topics related to your keywords. See Figure 20.

Search results displaying Help topics   Figure 20

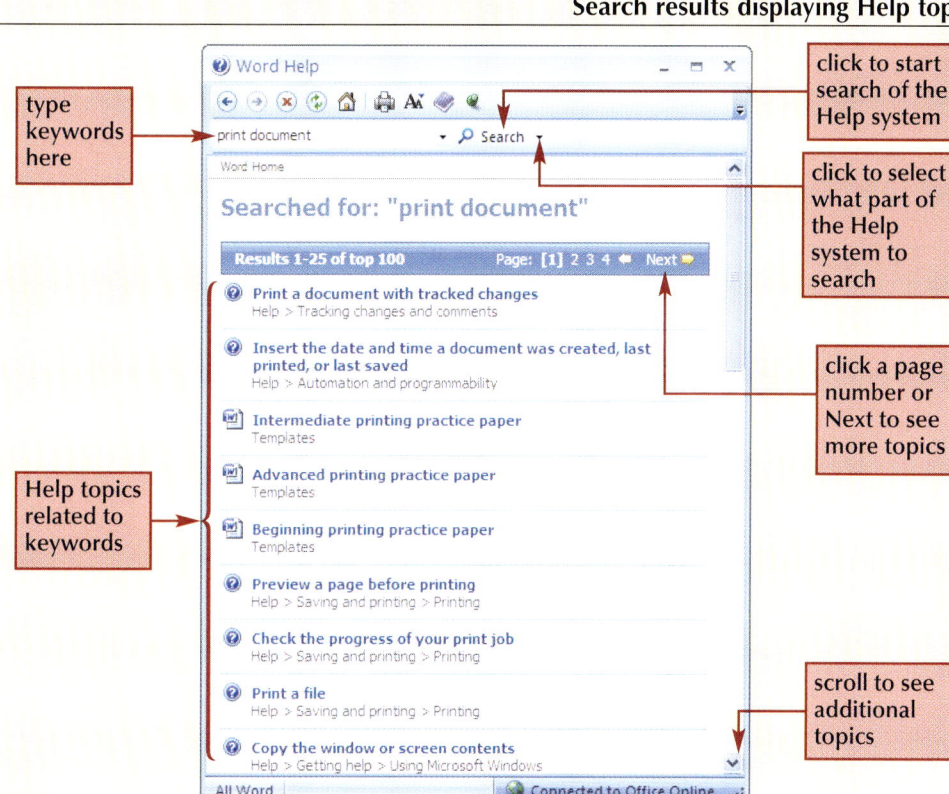

Trouble? If your search results list differs from the one shown in Figure 20, your computer is not connected to the Internet or Microsoft has updated the list of available Help topics since this book was published. Continue with Step 6.

▶ **6.** Scroll through the list to review the Help topics.

▶ **7.** Click **Print a file**. The Help topic is displayed in the Help window so you can learn more about how to print a document. See Figure 21.

Figure 21 Print a file Help topic

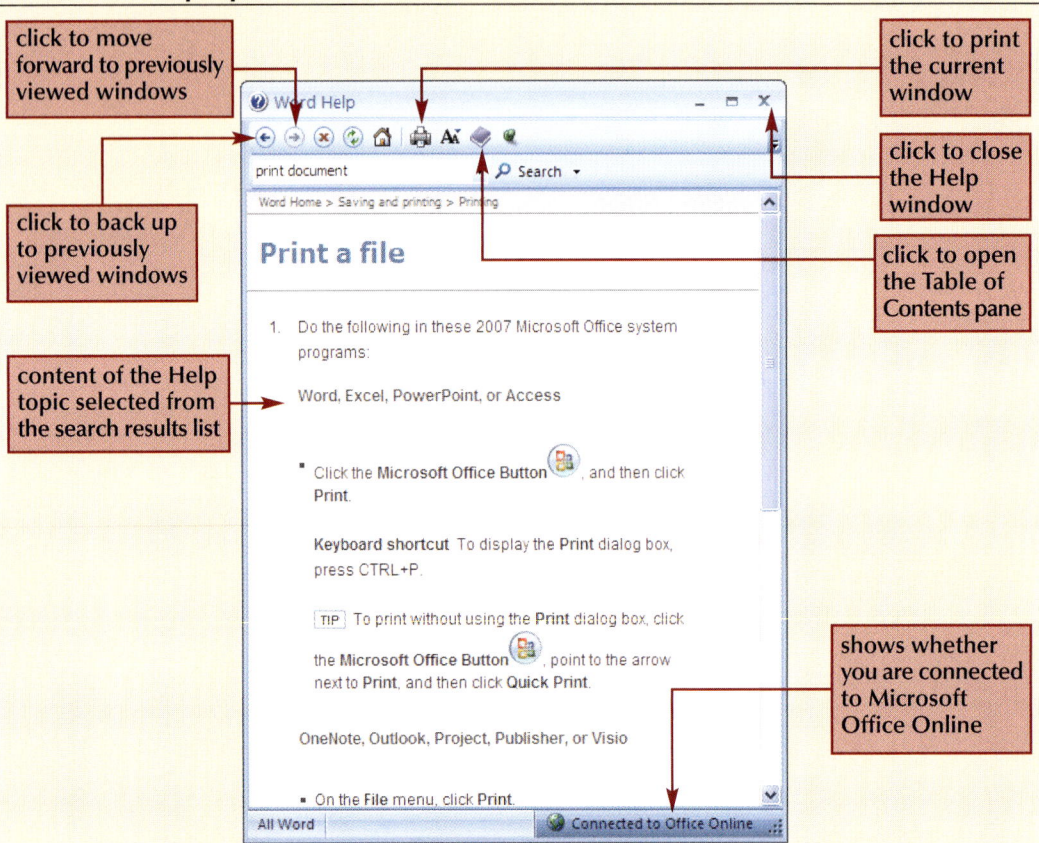

click to move forward to previously viewed windows

click to print the current window

click to back up to previously viewed windows

click to close the Help window

click to open the Table of Contents pane

content of the Help topic selected from the search results list

shows whether you are connected to Microsoft Office Online

Trouble? If you don't see the Print a file Help topic on page 1, its current location might be on another page. Click the Next link to move to the next page, and then scroll down to find the Print a file topic, repeating to search additional pages until you locate the topic.

▶ **8.** Read the information.

Another way to find information in the Help system is to use the Table of Contents pane. The Show Table of Contents button on the Help window toolbar opens a pane that displays a list of the Help system content organized by subjects and topics, similar to a book's table of contents. You click main subject links to display related topic links. You click a topic link to display that Help topic in the Help window. You'll use the Table of Contents to find information about getting help in Office.

To use the Help window table of contents:

▶ **1.** Click the **Show Table of Contents** button on the Help window toolbar. The Table of Contents pane opens on the left side of the Help window.

▶ **2.** Click **Getting help** in the Table of Contents pane, scrolling up if necessary. The Getting help "book" opens, listing the topics related to that subject.

▶ **3.** Click the **Work with the Help window** topic, and then click the **Maximize** button on the title bar. The Help topic is displayed in the maximized Help window, and you can read the text to learn more about the various ways to obtain help in Word. See Figure 22.

Table of Contents pane in the Help window | Figure 22

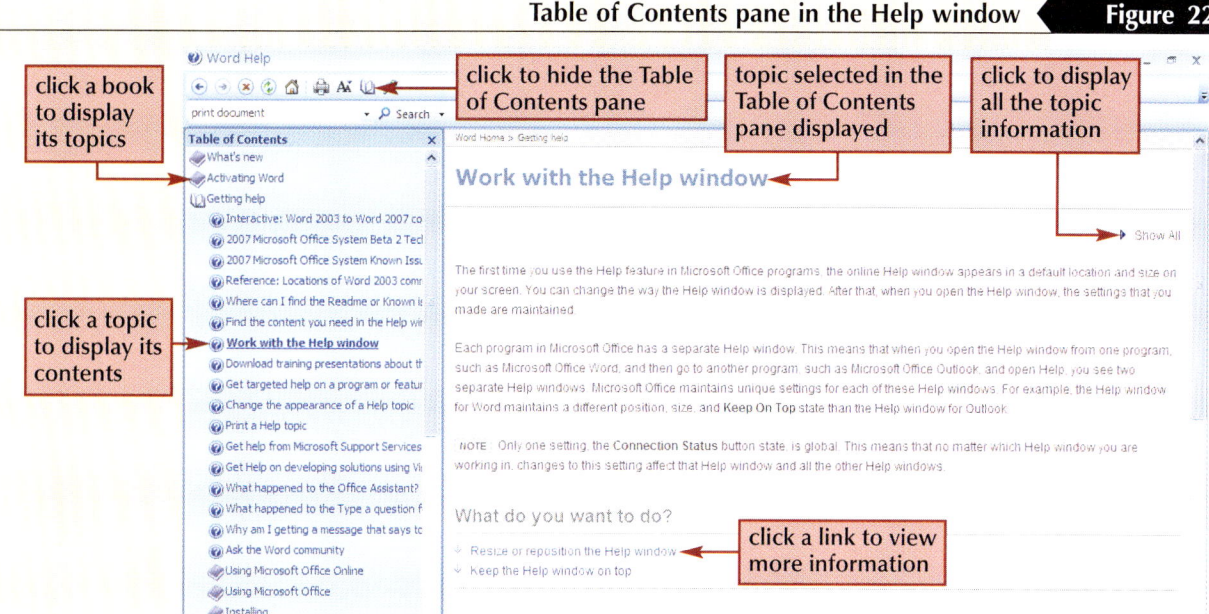

Trouble? If your search results list differs from the one shown in Figure 22, your computer is not connected to the Internet or Microsoft has updated the list of available Help topics since this book was published. Continue with Step 4.

4. Click **Using Microsoft Office Online** in the Table of Contents pane, click the **Get online Help, templates, training, and additional content** topic to display information about that topic, and then read the information.

5. Click the links within this topic and read the information.

6. Click the **Close** button on the Help window title bar to close the window.

Printing a File

At times, you'll want a paper copy of your Office file. The first time you print during each session at the computer, you should use the Print command to open the Print dialog box so you can verify or adjust the printing settings. You can select a printer, the number of copies to print, the portion of the file to print, and so forth; the printing settings vary slightly from program to program. If you want to use the same default settings for subsequent print jobs, you can use the Quick Print button to print without opening the dialog box.

Printing a File	Reference Window

- Click the Office Button, and then click Print.
- Verify the print settings in the Print dialog box.
- Click the OK button.

or

- Click the Office Button, point to Print, and then click Quick Print.

Now that you know how to print, you'll print the agenda for Ean.

To print the Word document:

▶ **1.** Make sure your printer is turned on and contains paper.

▶ **2.** Click the **Office Button** (⊕), and then click **Print**. The Print dialog box opens. See Figure 23.

| Figure 23 | Print dialog box |

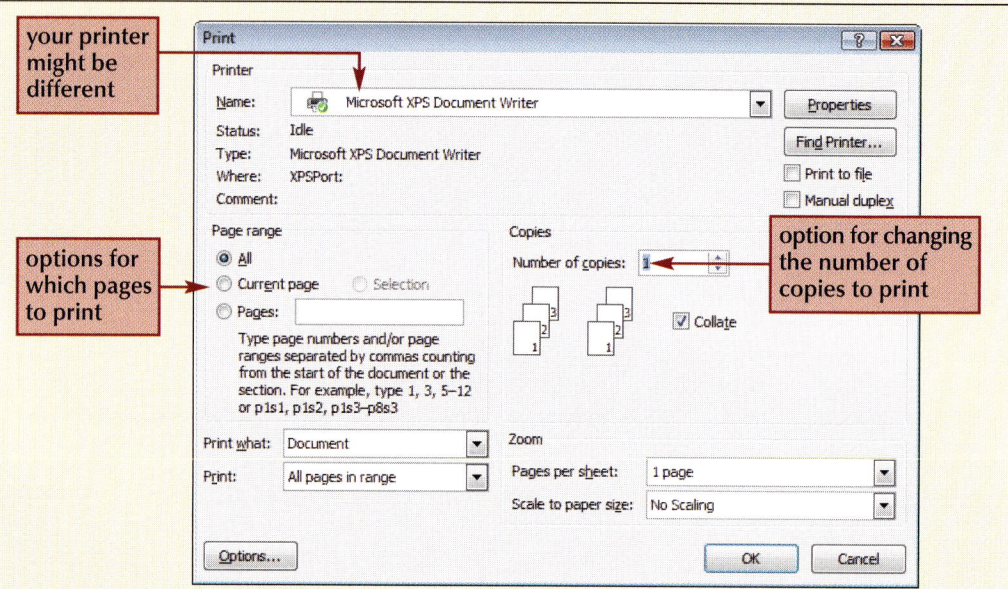

your printer might be different

options for which pages to print

option for changing the number of copies to print

Trouble? If a menu of Print commands opens, you clicked the Print button arrow on the two-part Print button. Click Print on the menu to open the Print dialog box.

▶ **3.** Verify that the correct printer appears in the Name box in the Printer group. If necessary, click the **Name** arrow, and then click the correct printer from the list of available printers.

▶ **4.** Verify that **1** appears in the Number of copies box.

▶ **5.** Click the **OK** button to print the document.

Trouble? If the document does not print, see your instructor or technical support person for help.

Exiting Programs

When you finish working with a program, you should exit it. As with many other aspects of Office, you can exit programs with a button or a command. You'll use both methods to exit Word and Excel. You can use the Exit command to exit a program and close an open file in one step. If you haven't saved the final version of the open file, a dialog box opens, asking whether you want to save your changes. Clicking the Yes button saves the open file, closes the file, and then exits the program.

To exit the Word and Excel programs:

▶ **1.** Click the **Close** button ⊠ on the Word title bar to exit Word. The Word document closes and the Word program exits. The Excel window is visible again.

> **Trouble?** If a dialog box opens, asking if you want to save the document, you might have inadvertently made a change to the document. Click the No button.

▶ **2.** Click the **Office Button** 🔘, and then click **Exit Excel**. A dialog box opens, asking whether you want to save the changes you made to the workbook. If you click the Yes button, the Save As dialog box opens and Excel exits after you finish saving the workbook. This time, you don't want to save the workbook.

▶ **3.** Click the **No** button. The workbook closes without saving a copy, and the Excel program exits.

Exiting programs after you are done using them keeps your Windows desktop uncluttered for the next person using the computer, frees up your system's resources, and prevents data from being lost accidentally.

Quick Check | Review

1. What Office program would be best to use to create a budget?
2. How do you start an Office program?
3. Explain the difference between Save and Save As.
4. How do you open an existing Office file?
5. What happens if you open a file, make edits, and then attempt to close the file or exit the program without saving the current version of the file?
6. What are two ways to get Help in Office?

Tutorial Summary | Review

You have learned how to use features common to all the programs included in Microsoft Office 2007, including starting and exiting programs; resizing windows; using the Ribbon, dialog boxes, shortcut menus, and the Mini toolbar; opening, closing, and printing files; and getting Help.

Key Terms

Access	Help window	Office Button
application settings	integration	Outlook
button	keyboard shortcut	PowerPoint
contextual tab	Live Preview	presentation
database	Microsoft Office 2007	Quick Access Toolbar
default	Microsoft Office Access 2007	Ribbon
dialog box	Microsoft Office Excel 2007	ScreenTip
Dialog Box Launcher	Microsoft Office Online	shortcut menu
document	Microsoft Office	status bar
Excel	Outlook 2007	tab
file extension	Microsoft Office	task pane
filename	PowerPoint 2007	Word
folder	Microsoft Office Word 2007	workbook
gallery	Mini toolbar	zoom
group	object	
Help	Office	

Practice	**Review Assignments**

Practice the skills you learned in the tutorial.

Data Files needed for the Review Assignments: Finances.xlsx, Letter.docx

You need to prepare for an upcoming meeting at Recycled Palette. You'll open and print documents for the presentation. Complete the following:

1. Start PowerPoint.
2. Use the Help window to search Office Online for the PowerPoint demo "Demo: Up to Speed with PowerPoint 2007." (*Hint*: Use "demo" as the keyword to search for, and make sure you search All PowerPoint in the Content from Office Online list. If you are not connected to the Internet, continue with Step 3.) Open the Demo topic, and then click the Play Demo link to view it. Close Internet Explorer and the Help window when you're done.
3. Start Excel.
4. Switch to the PowerPoint window using the taskbar, and then close the presentation but leave open the PowerPoint program. (*Hint:* Click the Office Button and then click Close.)
5. Open a new, blank PowerPoint presentation from the New Presentation dialog box.
6. Close the PowerPoint presentation and program using the Close button on the PowerPoint title bar; do not save changes if asked.
7. Open the **Finances** workbook located in the OFF\Review folder included with your Data Files.
8. Use the Save As command to save the workbook as **Recycled Palette Finances** in the OFF\Review folder.
9. Type your name, press the Enter key to insert your name at the top of the worksheet, and then save the workbook.
10. Print one copy of the worksheet using the Print button on the Office Button menu.
11. Exit Excel using the Office Button.
12. Start Word, and then open the **Letter** document located in the OFF\Review folder included with your Data Files.
13. Use the Save As command to save the document with the filename **Recycled Palette Letter** in the OFF\Review folder.
14. Press and hold the Ctrl key, press the End key, and then release both keys to move the insertion point to the end of the letter, and then type your name.
15. Use the Save button on the Quick Access Toolbar to save the change to the Recycled Palette Letter document.
16. Print one copy of the document, and then close the document.
17. Exit the Word program using the Close button on the title bar.

Assess	**SAM Assessment and Training**

If you have a SAM user profile, you may have access to hands-on instruction, practice, and assessment of the skills covered in this tutorial. Log in to your SAM account (**http://sam2007.course.com**) to launch any assigned training activities or exams that relate to the skills covered in this tutorial.

Review	**Quick Check Answers**

1. Excel
2. Click the Start button on the taskbar, click All Programs, click Microsoft Office, and then click the name of the program you want to open.
3. Save updates a file to reflect its latest contents using its current filename and location. Save As enables you to change the filename and storage location of a file.
4. Click the Office Button, and then click Open.
5. A dialog box opens asking whether you want to save the changes to the file.
6. Two of the following: ScreenTips, Help window, Microsoft Office Online

Ending Data Files

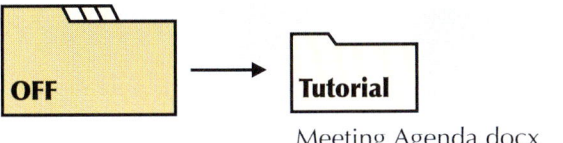

OFF → **Tutorial**
Meeting Agenda.docx

Review
Recycled Palette Finances.xlsx
Recycled Palette Letter.docx

Reality Check

At home, school, or work, you probably complete many types of tasks, such as writing letters and balancing a checkbook, on a regular basis. You can use Microsoft Office to streamline many of these tasks.

Note: Please be sure *not* to include any personal information of a sensitive nature in the documents you create to be submitted to your instructor for this exercise. Later on, you can update the documents with such information for your own personal use.

1. Start Word, and open a new document, if necessary.
2. In the document, type a list of all the personal, work, and/or school tasks you do on a regular basis.
3. For each task, identify the type of Office file (document, workbook, presentation, or database) you would create to complete that task. For example, you would create a Word document to write a letter.
4. For each file, identify the Office program you would use to create that file, and explain why you would use that program. For example, Word is the best program to use to create a document for a letter.
5. Save the document with an appropriate filename in an appropriate folder location.
6. Use a Web browser to visit the Microsoft Web site at *www.microsoft.com* and research the different Office 2007 suites available. Determine which suite includes all the programs you need to complete the tasks on your list.
7. At the end of the task list you created in your Word document, type which Office suite you decided on and a brief explanation of why you chose that suite. Then save the document.
8. Double-click the Home tab on the Ribbon to minimize the Ribbon to show only the tab names and extend the workspace area. At the end of the Word document, type your opinion of whether minimizing the Ribbon is a helpful feature. When you're done, double-click the Home tab to display the full Ribbon.
9. Print the finished document, and then submit it to your instructor.

Creating a Document

Writing a Business Letter

Case | Carlyle University Press

Carlyle University Press is a nonprofit book publisher associated with Carlyle State University in Albany, New York. The Press, as it is referred to by both editors and authors, publishes scholarly books, with an emphasis on history and literature. When a new author signs a contract for a book, he or she receives the *Author's Guide*, a handbook describing the process of creating a manuscript. In this tutorial, you will help one of the editors, Andrew Suri, create a cover letter to accompany a copy of the *Author's Guide*.

You will create the letter using **Microsoft Office Word 2007** (or simply **Word**), a popular word-processing program. Before you begin typing the letter, you will learn how to start the Word program, identify and use the elements of the Word window, and adjust some Word settings. Next, you will create a new Word document, type the text of the cover letter, save the letter, and then print the letter. In the process of entering the text, you'll learn several ways to correct typing errors. Finally, you will create an envelope for the letter.

Starting Data Files

There are no starting Data Files needed for this tutorial.

Session 1.1

Four Steps to a Professional Document

With Word, you can create polished, professional documents in a minimal amount of time. You can type a document in Word, adjust margins and spacing, create columns and tables, add graphics, and then quickly make revisions and corrections. The most efficient way to produce a document is to follow these four steps: (1) planning, (2) creating and editing, (3) formatting, and (4) printing or distributing online.

In the long run, planning saves time and effort. First, you should determine what you want to say. State your purpose clearly and include enough information to achieve that purpose without overwhelming or boring your reader. Be sure to organize your ideas logically. Decide how you want your document to look as well. In this case, your letter will take the form of a standard business letter, in the block style.

Figure 1-1 shows what the completed, block style letter will look like when it is printed on Carlyle University Press letterhead. You will create the letter in this tutorial by following detailed steps. Throughout the tutorial, you might want to refer back to Figure 1-1 for help locating the various parts of a block style letter.

Figure 1-1   **Completed block style letter**

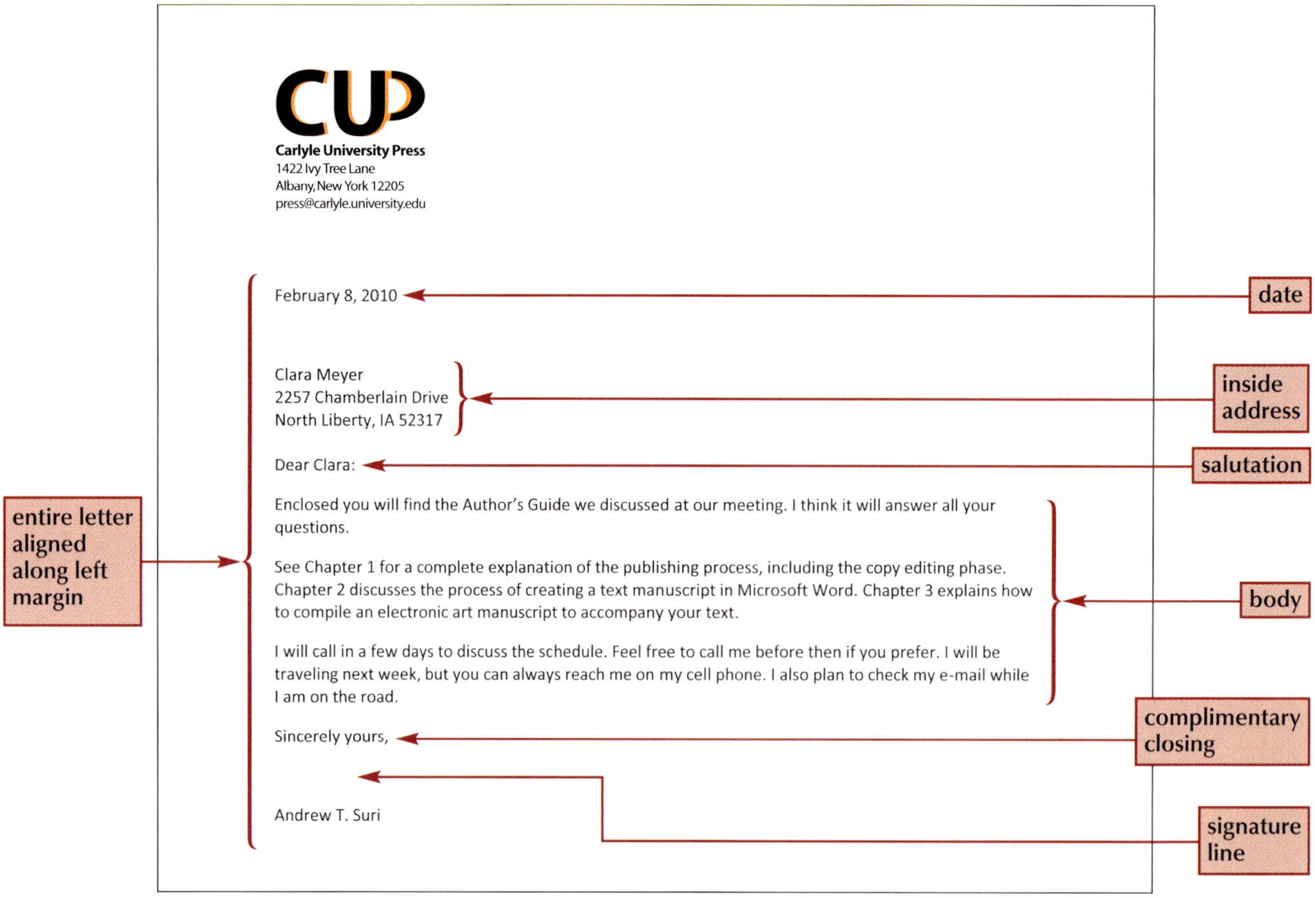

CUP
Carlyle University Press
1422 Ivy Tree Lane
Albany, New York 12205
press@carlyle.university.edu

February 8, 2010 — **date**

Clara Meyer
2257 Chamberlain Drive
North Liberty, IA 52317 — **inside address**

Dear Clara: — **salutation**

entire letter aligned along left margin

Enclosed you will find the Author's Guide we discussed at our meeting. I think it will answer all your questions.

See Chapter 1 for a complete explanation of the publishing process, including the copy editing phase. Chapter 2 discusses the process of creating a text manuscript in Microsoft Word. Chapter 3 explains how to compile an electronic art manuscript to accompany your text. — **body**

I will call in a few days to discuss the schedule. Feel free to call me before then if you prefer. I will be traveling next week, but you can always reach me on my cell phone. I also plan to check my e-mail while I am on the road.

Sincerely yours, — **complimentary closing**

Andrew T. Suri — **signature line**

There are several accepted styles for business letters. The main differences among them have to do with how parts of the letter are indented from the left margin. In the block style, which you will use to create the letter in this tutorial, each line of text starts at the left margin. In other words, nothing is indented. Another style is to indent the first line of each paragraph. The choice of style is largely a matter of personal preference, or it can be determined by the standards used in a particular business or organization.

After you plan your document, you can create and edit it using Word. Creating the document generally means typing the text of your document. Editing consists of reading the document you've created; correcting, adding, deleting, or moving text to make the document easy to read; and finally, correcting your errors.

To make your document visually appealing, you need to format it. Formatting—for example, adjusting margins, setting line spacing, and using bold and italic—can help make your document easier to read.

Finally, you will usually want to print your document so that you can give it to other people, or you might want to distribute it via e-mail. Whether you print the document yourself or e-mail it to others, it is important to preview it first to make sure it is suitable for printing.

Exploring the Word Window

Before you can apply these four steps to produce a letter in Word, you need to start Word and learn about the general organization of the Word window. You'll do that now.

To start Microsoft Word:

▶ 1. Click the **Start** button 🟦 on the taskbar, click **All Programs**, click **Microsoft Office**, and then click **Microsoft Office Word 2007**. The Word window opens. See Figure 1-2.

Figure 1-2 Maximized Word window

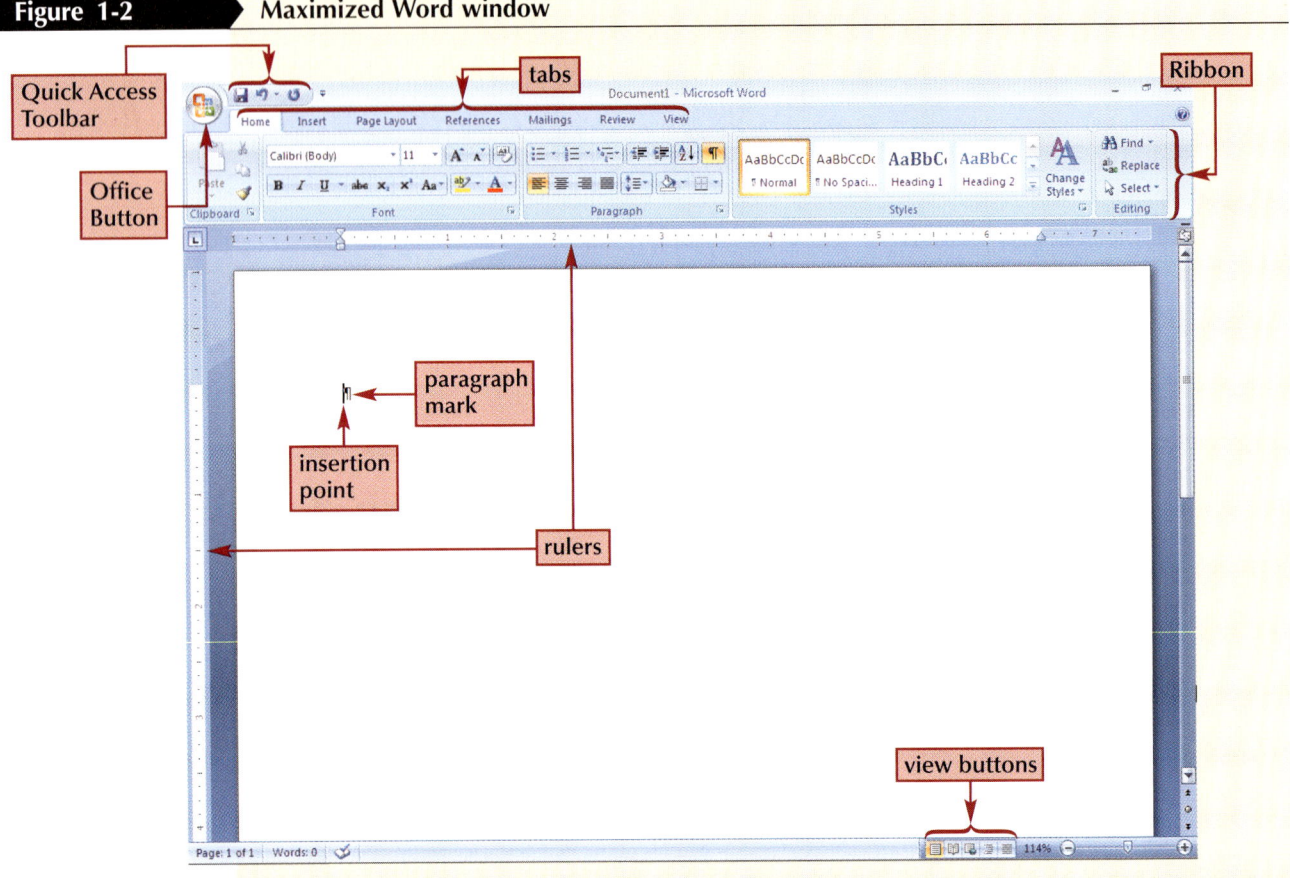

Trouble? If you don't see the Microsoft Office Word 2007 option on the Microsoft Office submenu, look for it in a different submenu or as an option on the All Programs menu. If you still can't find the Microsoft Office Word 2007 option, ask your instructor or technical support person for help.

2. If the Word window does not fill the entire screen, click the **Maximize** button in the upper-right corner of the Word window. Your screen should now resemble Figure 1-2.

Trouble? If your screen looks slightly different from Figure 1-2, just continue with the steps. You will learn how to change the appearance of the Word window shortly.

Word is now running and ready to use. Don't be concerned if you don't see everything shown in Figure 1-2. You'll learn how to adjust the appearance of the Word window soon.

The Word window is made up of a number of elements, which are described in Figure 1-3. You might be familiar with some of these elements, such as the Office Button and the Ribbon, because they are common to all Microsoft Office 2007 programs.

Parts of the Word window ◄ **Figure 1-3**

Window Element	Description
Office Button	Provides access to the Word Options dialog box and to commands that control what you can do with a document that you have created, such as saving, printing, and so on
Ribbon	Provides access to commands that are grouped according to the tasks you perform in Word
Tabs	Provide one-click access to the groups of commands on the Ribbon; the tabs you see change depending on the task you are currently performing
Quick Access Toolbar	Provides access to common commands you use frequently, such as Save
Rulers	Show page margins, tab stops, row heights, and column widths
Insertion point	Shows where characters will appear when you start typing
Paragraph mark	Marks the end of a paragraph
View buttons	Allow you to change the way the document is displayed

If at any time you would like to learn more about an item on the Ribbon, position your mouse pointer over the item without clicking anything. A **ScreenTip**, a small box with information about the item, will appear.

Opening a New Document

You'll begin by opening a new blank document (in case you accidentally typed something in the current page while you were examining the Word window).

To open a new document:

▶ **1.** Click the **Office Button** in the upper-left corner of the Word window and view the menu of commands that opens. These commands are all related to working with Word documents. See Figure 1-4.

Microsoft Office menu ◄ **Figure 1-4**

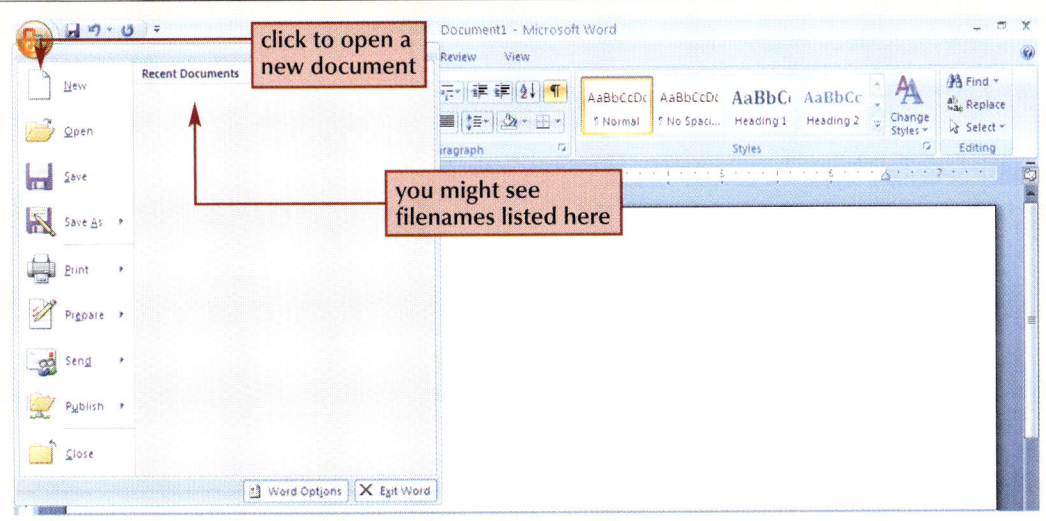

> **2.** Click **New**. The New Document dialog box opens. See Figure 1-5. In this dialog box, you can choose from several different types of documents. In this case, you simply want a new, blank document, which is already selected for you, as in Figure 1-5.

Figure 1-5 **New Document dialog box**

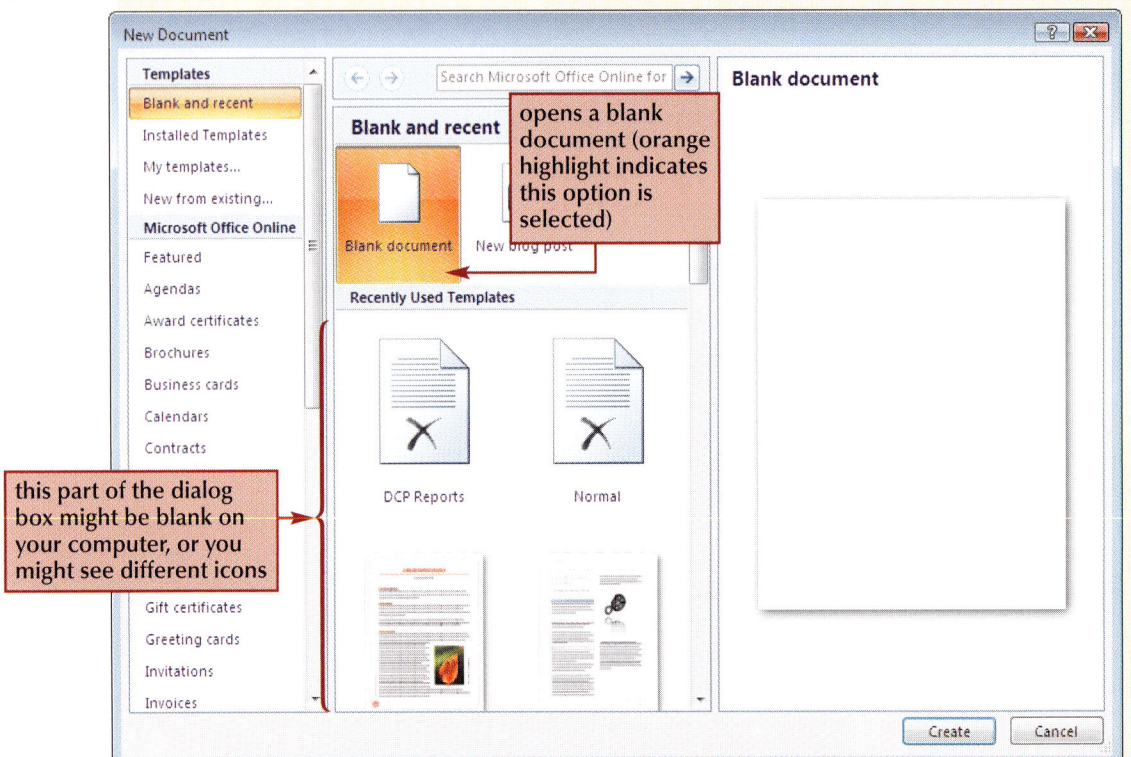

> **3.** Verify that the **Blank document** option is selected (that is, highlighted in orange), and then click the **Create** button at the bottom of the dialog box. The New Document dialog box closes and a new document (named Document2) opens. Later in this tutorial, you'll choose a more descriptive name for this document.

Setting Up the Word Window

To make it easier to follow the steps in these tutorials, you should take care to arrange your window to match the tutorial figures. The rest of this section explains what your window should look like and how to make it match those in the tutorials. After you've set up your window to match the figures, you'll begin writing the letter for Andrew.

Selecting Print Layout View

You can use the View buttons in the lower-right corner of the Word window to change the way your document is displayed. You will learn how to select the appropriate view for a document as you gain more experience with Word. For now, you want your letter displayed in Print Layout view because this view most closely resembles how your letter will look when you print it.

To make sure Print Layout view is selected:

▶ **1.** Click the **Print Layout** button ▤ , as shown in Figure 1-6. If your window was not in Print Layout view, it changes to Print Layout view now. The Print Layout button is now highlighted in orange, indicating that it is selected. See Figure 1-6.

Selecting Print Layout view ◀ **Figure 1-6**

Print Layout button is orange to show it is selected

other view buttons

Page: 1 of 1 | Words: 0 | 114%

Displaying the Rulers and Selecting the Home Tab

Depending on the choices made by the last person to use your computer, you might not see the rulers. The options controlling the rulers are located on the Ribbon's View tab. When Word opens, the Home tab is typically displayed, so to display the rulers, you need to switch to the View tab. Even if the rulers are currently displayed on your computer, perform the following steps to get some practice moving among the tabs on the Ribbon.

Displaying the Rulers | Reference Window

- Click the View tab.
- In the Show/Hide group, click the Ruler check box to display a check mark.

To display the rulers:

▶ **1.** At the top of the Word window, click the **View** tab. This tab contains buttons and commands related to displaying the document.

▶ **2.** In the Show/Hide group on the View tab, locate the Ruler check box. If it already contains a check mark, the rulers are already displayed on your screen. If the Ruler check box is empty, click it to insert a check mark. You should now see a vertical ruler on the left side of the document and a horizontal ruler below the Ribbon. See Figure 1-7.

Figure 1-7 **Displaying the rulers**

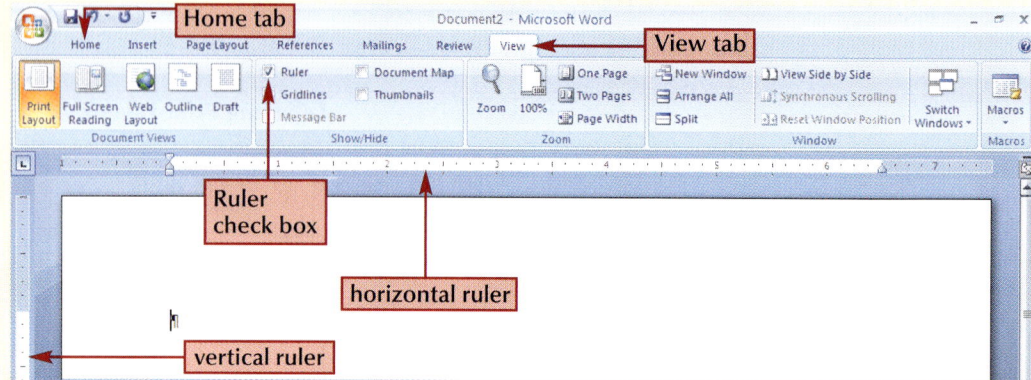

3. Click the **Home** tab. The Ribbon changes to show Word's basic text-editing options, as shown earlier in Figure 1-2.

Displaying Nonprinting Characters

Nonprinting characters are symbols that appear on the screen but are not visible on the printed page; they help you see details that you might otherwise miss. For example, one nonprinting character (¶) marks the end of a paragraph, and another (•) marks the space between words. It is helpful to display nonprinting characters so you can see whether you've typed an extra space, ended a paragraph, and so on.

Depending on how your computer is set up, nonprinting characters might be displayed automatically when you start Word. In Figure 1-8, you can see the paragraph symbol (¶) in the blank document window. Also, the Show/Hide ¶ button is highlighted on the Ribbon. Both of these indicate that nonprinting characters are displayed. If they are not displayed on your screen, you need to perform the following step.

To display nonprinting characters:

1. In the Paragraph group on the Home tab, click the **Show/Hide ¶** button ¶ if it is not already selected. A paragraph mark (¶) appears at the top of the document window. Your screen should match Figure 1-8.

Figure 1-8 **Nonprinting characters displayed**

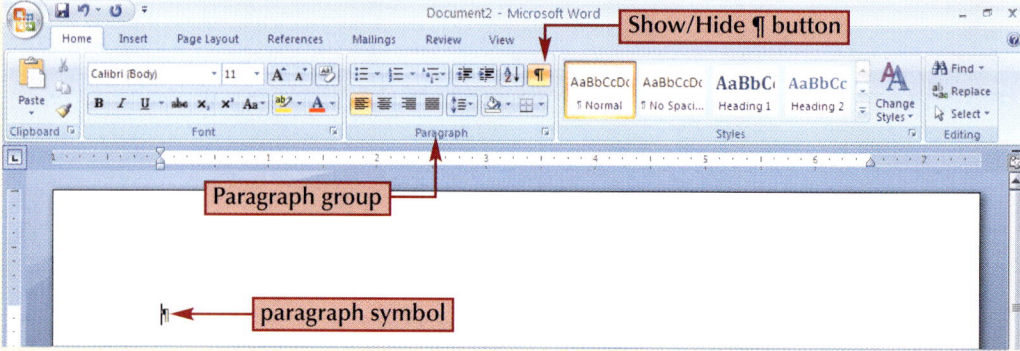

Trouble? If the Show/Hide ¶ button was already highlighted before you clicked it, you turned off nonprinting characters instead of turning them on. Click the Show/Hide ¶ button a second time to select it.

Checking the Font and Font Size

Next, you need to make sure the correct font and font size are selected. The term **font** refers to the shape of the characters in a document. **Font size** refers to the size of the characters. You'll learn more about fonts in Tutorial 2. For now, you just need to make sure that the font and font size selected on your computer match those selected in the figures in this book. The figures in this book were created using the default font and font size. (The term **default** refers to settings that are automatically selected.)

To verify that the correct font is selected:

▶ **1.** In the Font group on the Home tab, locate the **Font** and **Font Size** boxes. See Figure 1-9.

Font settings ◣ **Figure 1-9**

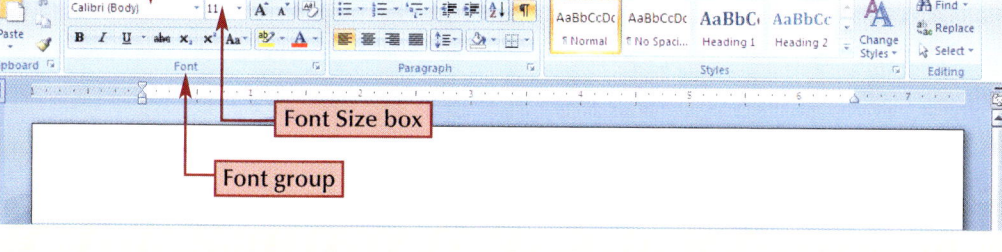

The setting in the Font box should read "Calibri (Body)" as in Figure 1-9. If you see something else in your Font box, click the **Font** list arrow, and then click **Calibri (Body)**.

Trouble? If you see just "Calibri" in your font box instead of "Calibri (Body)" you should still perform Step 1.

▶ **2.** The setting in your Font Size box should read "11." If you see something else in your Font size box, click the **Font Size** list arrow, and then click **11**.

Checking the Zoom Setting

Next, you'll take care of the document **Zoom level**, which controls the document's on-screen magnification. A Zoom level of 100% shows the document as if it were printed on paper. It is often helpful to increase the Zoom level to more than 100% (zoom in) to make the text easier to read. Other times, you may want to decrease the Zoom level to less than 100% (zoom out) so that you can see more of the document at a glance. To make your screen match the figures in this tutorial, you need to set the Zoom level to **Page width**, a setting that shows the entire width of the document on your screen. You can change the Zoom level by using the Zoom buttons in the lower-right corner of the Word window.

Tip

Changing the zoom affects only the way the document is displayed on the screen; it does not affect the document itself.

To check your Zoom setting:

▶ **1.** In the lower-right corner of the Word window, locate the current Zoom level, the Zoom Out button, the Zoom In button, and the Zoom slider. In Figure 1-10, the current Zoom setting is 114%, but yours might be higher or lower. In the next two steps you'll practice zooming in and zooming out. Then you will select the Page width setting.

Figure 1-10	Options for changing the Zoom setting

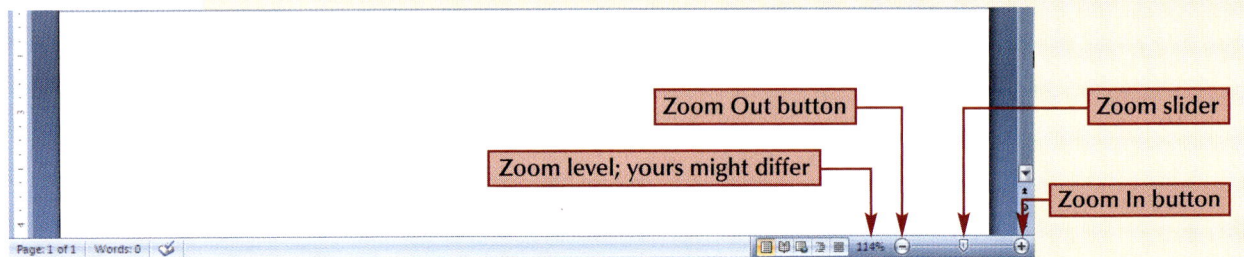

Tip

You can also drag the Zoom slider button left or right to change the Zoom level.

▶ **2.** Click the **Zoom In** button ⊕ several times to increase the document magnification. The Zoom level increases and the Zoom slider moves to the right.

▶ **3.** Click the **Zoom Out** button ⊖ several times to decrease the document magnification. The Zoom level decreases and the Zoom slider button moves to the left.

▶ **4.** Click the **Zoom level**. The Zoom dialog box opens. The Zoom level in the Zoom dialog box matches the Zoom level shown in the lower-right corner of the Word window. In Figure 1-11, the current Zoom setting is 110%, but yours might be different.

Figure 1-11	Zoom dialog box

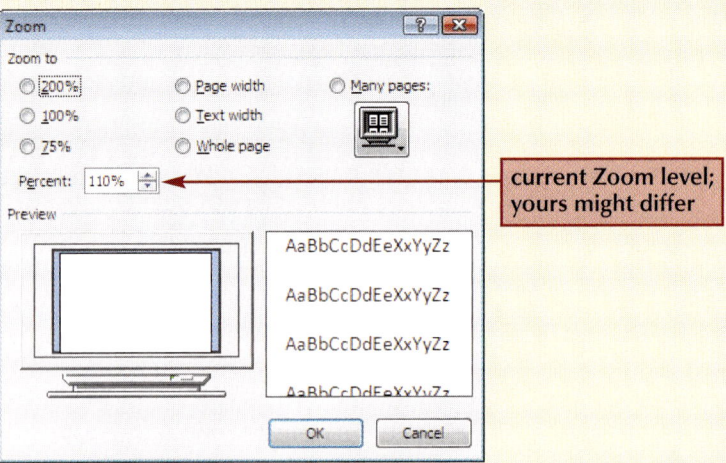

▶ **5.** Click the **Page width** option button to select it, and then click the **OK** button. The Zoom dialog box closes and the Zoom level adjusts to display the full width of the document page. The exact Zoom level on your computer will depend on the size of your monitor. On a 15-inch monitor, the Zoom level is probably 114%.

To make sure your window always matches the figures in these tutorials, remember to complete the checklist in Figure 1-12 each time you are working in this book.

Window Element	Setting
Document view	Print Layout
Nonprinting characters	Displayed
Rulers	Displayed
Word window	Maximized
Zoom	Page width
Font	Identical to setting shown in figures
Font size	Identical to setting shown in figures

Now that you have planned your letter, opened Word, identified screen elements, and adjusted settings, you are ready to begin your letter to Clara Meyer, Carlyle Press's new author.

Beginning a Letter

Before you begin writing, you should insert some blank lines to ensure that you leave enough room for the Carlyle University Press letterhead. The amount of space you leave at the top of a letter depends on the size of the letterhead. In this case, pressing Enter four times should add enough space.

Adjusting Margins vs. Inserting Blank Lines | InSight

As you gain experience with Word, you'll learn how to adjust a document's margin to add blank space at the beginning of a document. (The term **margin** refers to the blank space around the top, bottom, and sides of document.) Adjusting margins is a better method than inserting blank lines, because it ensures that you won't accidentally delete a blank line as you edit the document. However, until you learn more about margins, inserting blank lines is a useful shortcut that enables you to jump right into the task of typing your letter.

To insert blank lines in the document:

▶ 1. Press the **Enter** key four times. Each time you press the Enter key, a nonprinting paragraph mark appears, and the insertion point moves down to the next line. By default, Word inserts some space between each paragraph mark. You'll learn how to change this setting later in this tutorial. For now, you can ignore this space. On the vertical ruler, you can see that the insertion point is about 1.5 inches from the top margin. Although you might find it hard to see on the ruler, the top margin itself is 1 inch. This means the insertion point is now located a total of 2.5 inches from the top of the page. See Figure 1-13.

Figure 1-13 **Document window after inserting blank lines**

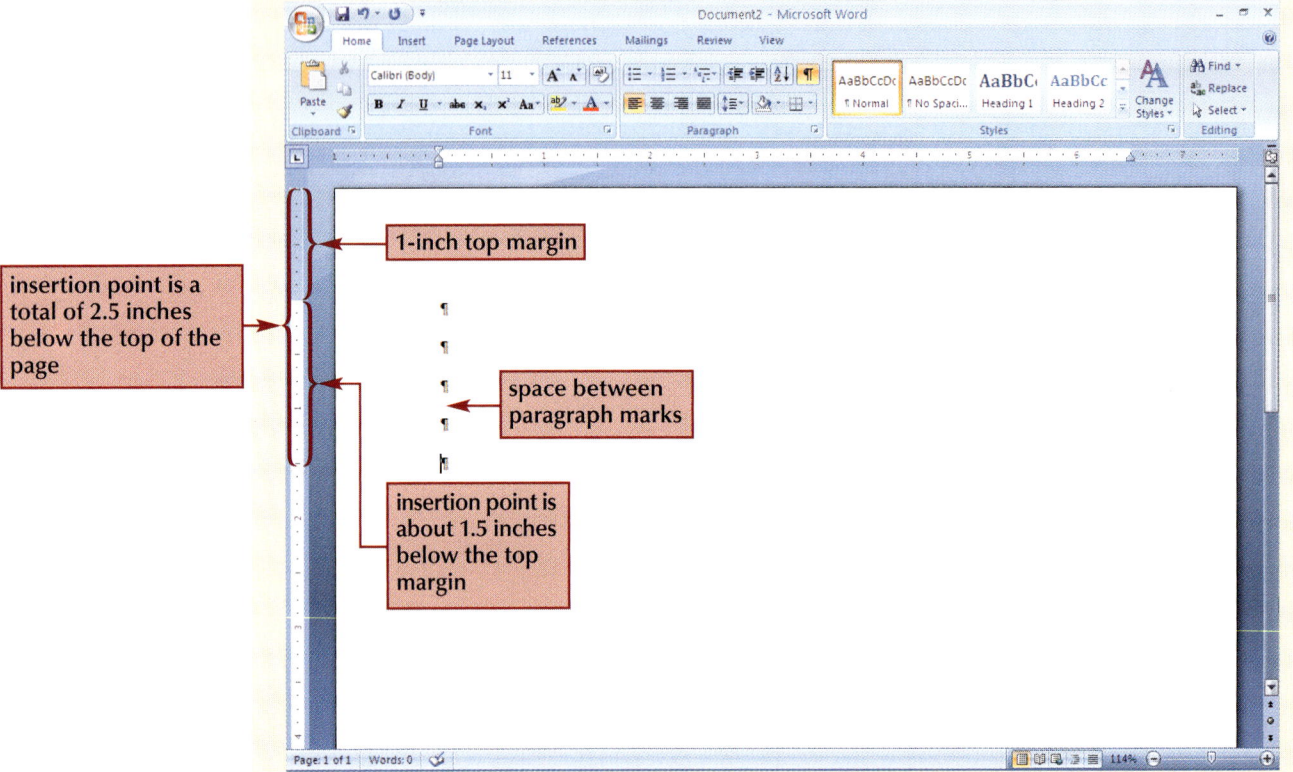

Trouble? If your insertion point is higher or lower on the vertical ruler than in Figure 1-13, don't worry. Different monitors produce slightly different measurements when you press the Enter key.

The insertion point is now low enough in your document to allow room for the letterhead when you print the document. You are ready to start typing.

Entering Text

Normally, you begin a letter by typing the date followed by the inside address. However, typing these two items involves using some specialized Word features. To give you some experience with simply typing text, you'll start with the salutation and the body of the letter. Then you'll go back later to add the date and the inside address.

You'll start by typing the salutation (the "Dear Clara:" text, shown earlier in Figure 1-1). If you make a mistake while typing, press the Backspace key to delete the incorrect character and then type the correct character.

To type the salutation:

1. Type **Dear Clara:** and then pause to notice the nonprinting character (•) that appears to indicate a space between the two words.

2. Press the **Enter** key to start a new paragraph for the body of the letter. If you have typed a block style business letter before, you might be accustomed to pressing Enter twice between paragraphs. However, because Word is set up to insert extra space between paragraphs by default, you need to press the Enter key only once to start a new paragraph. See Figure 1-14.

Letter with salutation ◄ **Figure 1-14**

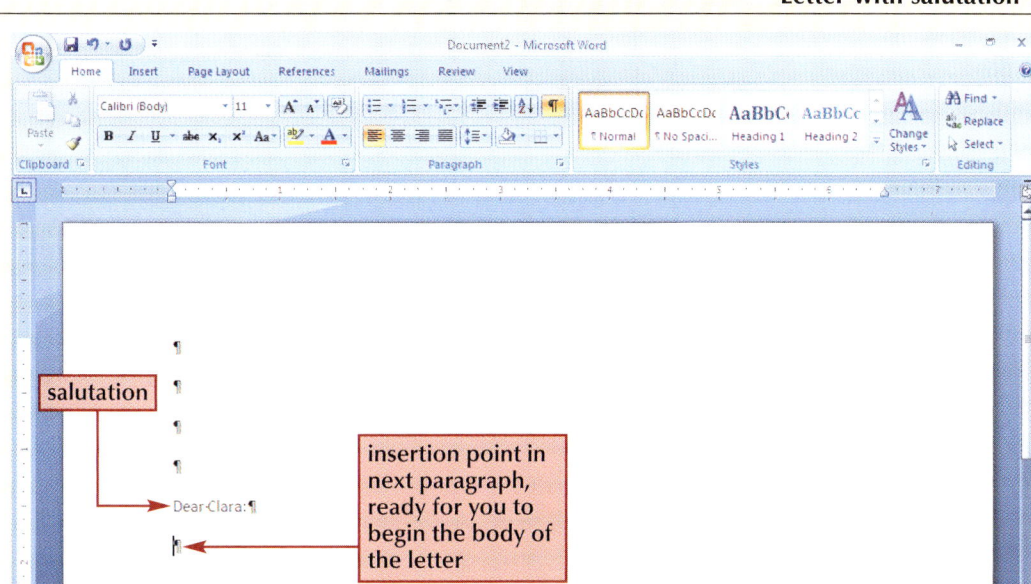

Now you are ready to begin typing the body of the letter (shown earlier in Figure 1-1). As you do, notice that when you reach the end of a line, you can keep typing; the insertion point just moves down to the next line. Depending on the length of the word you are typing when you reach the end of the line, the word will either stay on that line, or if it is long, it will move to the next line. This automatic line breaking is called **word wrap**. You'll see how word wrap works as you begin typing the body of the letter.

To begin typing the body of the letter:

1. Type the following sentence, including the period: **Enclosed you will find the Author's Guide we discussed at our meeting.**

2. Press the **spacebar**.

3. Type the following sentence: **I think it will answer all your questions.**

   Notice how Word moves the insertion point to a new line when the preceding line is full.

4. Press the **Enter** key to end the first paragraph. When you are finished, your screen should look similar to Figure 1-15. Notice that, in addition to inserting space between paragraphs, Word also inserts a smaller amount of space between lines within a paragraph.

Figure 1-15 | Completed first main paragraph

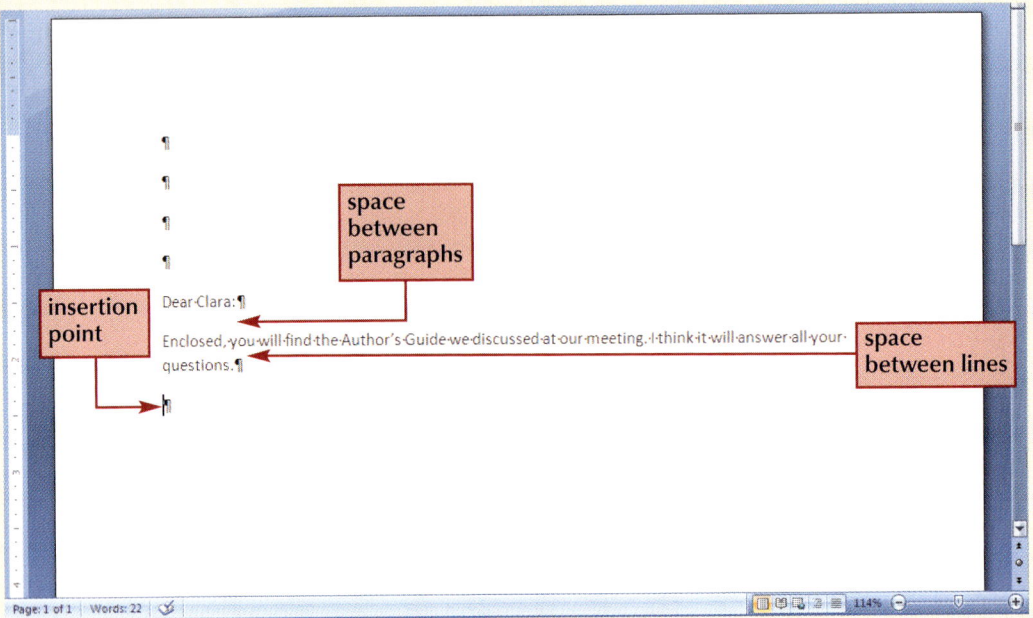

Before you continue with the rest of the letter, you should save what you have typed so far.

Reference Window | **Saving a Document for the First Time**

- Click the Save button on the Quick Access Toolbar.
- Type a name in the File name text box.
- Select the location where you want to save the file.
- Click the Save button at the bottom of the Save As dialog box.

To save the document:

▶ **1.** On the Quick Access Toolbar, click the **Save** button 🔲 . The Save As dialog box opens. Note that Word suggests using the first line you typed ("Dear Clara") as the filename. You will replace the suggested filename with something more descriptive.

▶ **2.** Type **Meyer Letter** in the File name text box, replacing the suggested filename.

Next, you need to tell Word where you want to save the document. In this case, you want to use the Tutorial subfolder in the Tutorial.01 folder provided with your Data Files.

Trouble? The Tutorial.01 folder is included with the Data Files for this text. If you don't have the Word Data Files, you need to get them before you can proceed. Your instructor will either give you the Data Files or ask you to obtain them from a specified location (such as a network drive). In either case, be sure that you make a backup copy of your Data Files before you start using them, so that the original files will be available on your copied disk in case you need to start over because of an error or problem. If you have any questions about the Data Files, see your instructor or technical support person for assistance.

> **3.** Use the options in the Save As dialog box to select the Tutorial subfolder within the Tutorial.01 folder. See Figure 1-16.

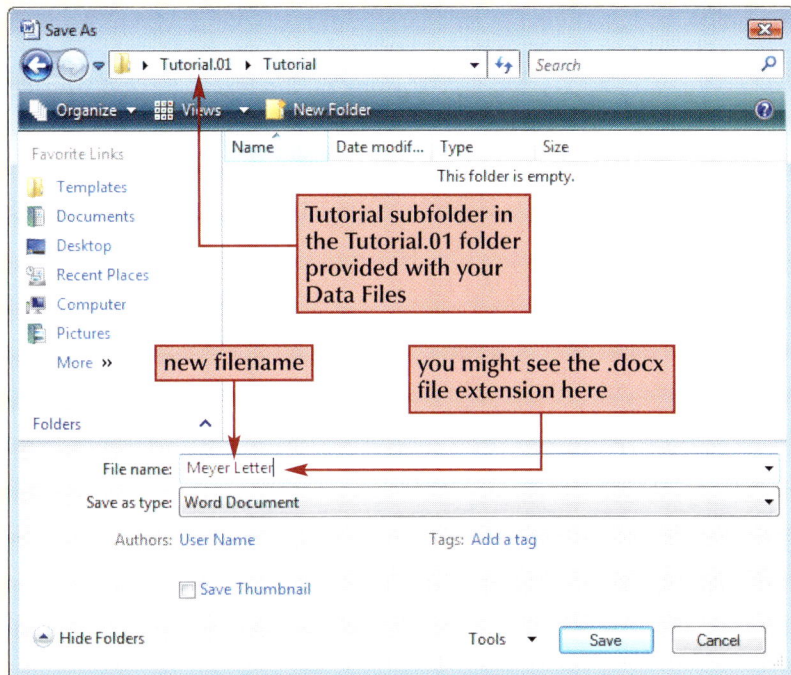

Trouble? If Word adds the .docx extension to your filename, your computer is configured to show file extensions. Just continue with the tutorial.

> **4.** Click the **Save** button in the Save As dialog box. The dialog box closes, and you return to the document window. The new document name (Meyer Letter) appears in the title bar.

Note that Word adds the .docx extension to document filenames to identify them as Microsoft Word 2007 documents, whether your computer is set up to display them or not. These tutorials assume that file extensions are hidden, but it is okay if they are displayed.

You've made a good start on the letter, and you've saved your work so far. In the next session, you'll finish typing the letter, and then you'll print it.

Session 1.1 Quick Check | Review

1. In your own words, explain the importance of planning a document.
2. On what tab is the Ruler check box located?
3. Explain how to change the document view to Print Layout.
4. True or False: Nonprinting characters are symbols that can appear on the screen but are not visible on the printed page.
5. True or False: Pressing the Enter key is the only way to insert blank space at the top of a document.
6. What is the file extension for Microsoft Word 2007 documents?

Session 1.2

Scrolling a Document

At this point, unless you are working on a large monitor, your screen probably looks as if it doesn't have enough room to type the rest of Andrew's letter—but of course there is room. As you continue to add text to your document, the text at the top will **scroll** (or shift up) and disappear from the top of the document window. You'll see how scrolling works as you type the second paragraph in the body of the letter.

To observe scrolling while you're typing text:

▶ 1. If you took a break after the previous session, make sure that Word is running and that the Meyer Letter document is open. Also, review the checklist in Figure 1-12 and verify that your screen is set up to match the figures in this tutorial.

▶ 2. Make sure the insertion point is positioned to the left of the paragraph symbol below the first paragraph in the body of the letter (as shown earlier in Figure 1-15). If it is not, move the insertion point by clicking in that location now.

▶ 3. Type the following two paragraphs:

   See Chapter 1 for a complete explanation of the publishing process, including the copy editing phase. Chapter 2 discusses the process of creating a text manuscript in Microsoft Word. Chapter 3 explains how to compile an electronic art manuscript to accompany your text.

   I will call in a few days to discuss the schedule. Feel free to call me before then if you prefer. I will be traveling next week, but you can always reach me on my cell phone. I also plan to check my e-mail while I am on the road.

   Trouble? If you make a mistake while typing, press the Backspace key or the Delete key to delete any incorrect characters, and then type the correct characters.

▶ 4. Press the **Enter** key.

▶ 5. Type **Sincerely yours,** (including the comma) to enter the complimentary closing.

▶ 6. Press the **Enter** key 10 times so you can see the document scroll up to accommodate the blank paragraphs. You're doing this only to demonstrate how a document scrolls up. You'll delete the extra blank paragraphs shortly.

   As you pressed the Enter key repeatedly, the upper part of the document probably scrolled off the top of the document window. Exactly when this happens depends on the size of your monitor. See Figure 1-17.

Part of the document scrolled off the window ◀ **Figure 1-17**

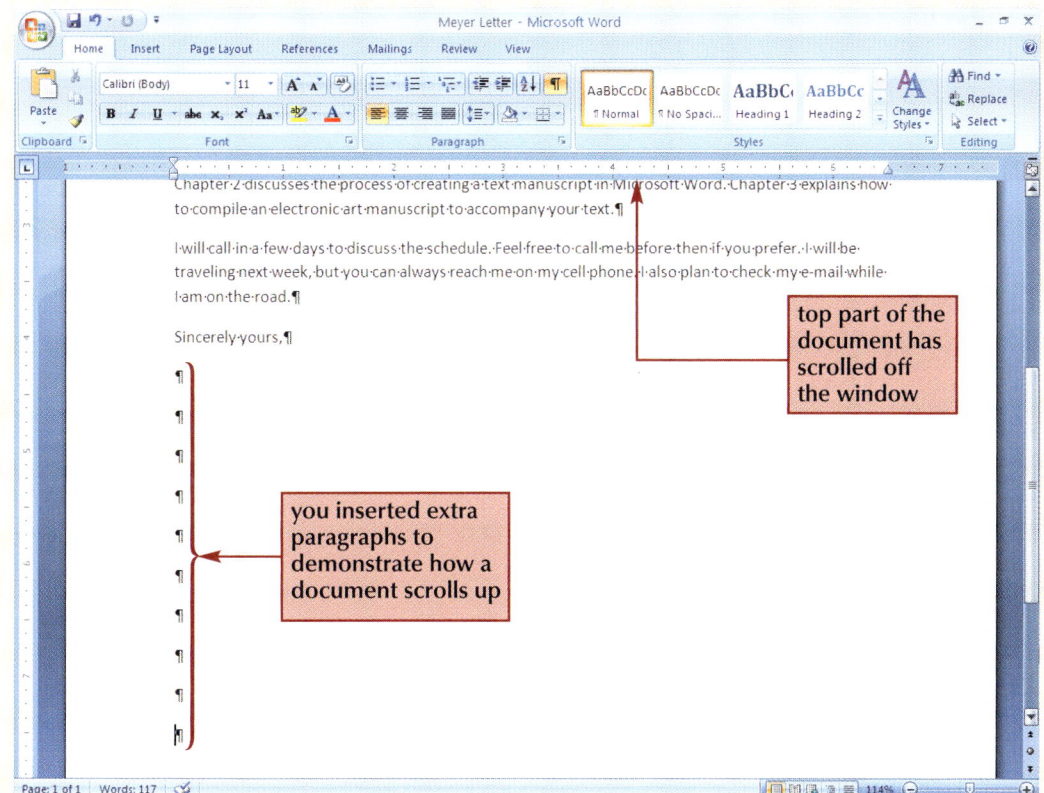

You don't really want all those blank paragraph marks after the complimentary closing, so you need to delete them.

▶ **7.** Press the **Backspace** key eight times. When you finish, you should see two paragraph marks below the complimentary closing, with the insertion point blinking to the left of the bottom one. This allows enough space for a signature.

▶ **8.** Type **Andrew Suri**, and then press the **Enter** key. A wavy red line appears below "Suri." In Word, such lines indicate possible spelling errors. Because Andrew's last name is not in the Word dictionary, Word suggests that it might be spelled incorrectly. You'll learn more about Word's error-checking features in a moment. For now, you can ignore the wavy red line.

You've completed most of the letter, so you should save your work.

▶ **9.** On the Quick Access Toolbar, click the **Save** button ⊟ . Word saves your letter with the same name and in the same location you specified earlier. Don't be concerned about any typing errors. You'll learn how to correct them later in this tutorial.

In the previous set of steps, you watched paragraph marks and text at the top of your document move off the window. Anytime you need to see the beginning of the letter, you can scroll this hidden text back into view. When you do, the text at the bottom of the window will scroll out of view. There are three ways to scroll the document window: click the up or down arrows in the vertical scroll bar, click anywhere in the vertical scroll bar, or drag the scroll box. See Figure 1-18.

Figure 1-18 ▶ Scrolling the document window

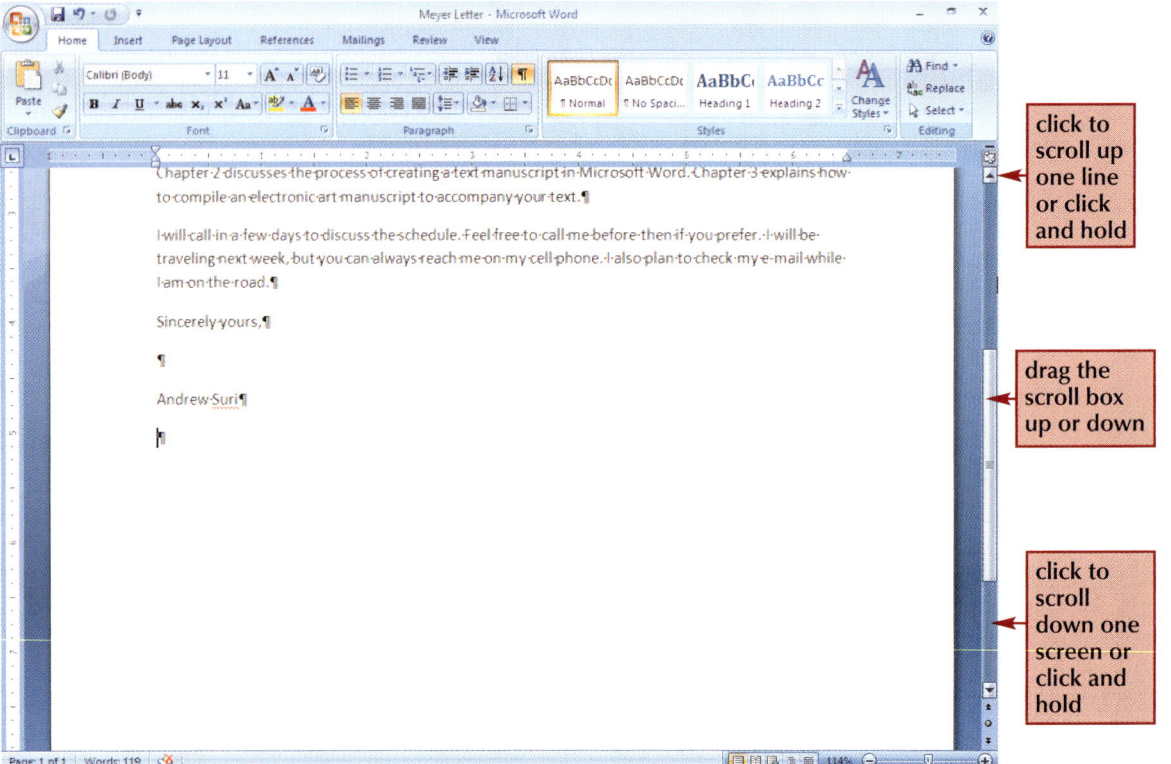

To practice scrolling the document using the vertical scroll bar:

▶ **1.** Position the mouse pointer over the arrow at the top of the vertical scroll bar. Press and hold the mouse button to scroll the text. When the text stops scrolling, you have reached the top of the document and can see the beginning of the letter. Note that scrolling does not change the location of the insertion point in the document.

▶ **2.** Click the down arrow on the vertical scroll bar several times. The document scrolls down one line at a time.

▶ **3.** Click anywhere in the vertical scroll bar below the scroll box. The document scrolls down one full screen.

▶ **4.** Drag the scroll box up to the top of the scroll bar, so you can see the beginning of the letter.

▶ **5.** Continue practicing these steps until you feel comfortable scrolling up and down. When you are finished, scroll the document so you can see the complimentary closing at the end of the letter.

Andrew asks you to include his middle initial in the signature line. Performing this task will give you a chance to practice moving the insertion point around the document.

Moving the Insertion Point Around a Document

When you scroll a document, you change the part of the document that is displayed on the screen. But to change the location in the document where new text will appear when you type, you need to move the insertion point. One way to move the insertion point is to scroll up or down and then click where you want to insert new text. However, it is often more efficient to use the keyboard so you don't have to move your hand to the mouse, move the insertion point, and then move your hand back to the keyboard to type. You can use the arrow keys, ←, ↑, →, and ↓, to move the insertion point one character at a time to the left or right or one line at a time up or down. In addition, you can press a variety of key combinations to move the insertion point from one paragraph to another, to the beginning or end of the document, and so on. As you become more experienced with Word, you'll learn which methods you prefer.

Before you add Andrew's middle initial to the signature line, you'll take some time to practice moving the insertion point around the document.

To move the insertion point with keystrokes:

▶ **1.** Press the **Ctrl+Home** keys (that is, press the Ctrl key and hold it down while you press the Home key). The insertion point moves to the beginning of the document.

▶ **2.** Press the **Page Down** key to move the insertion point down to the next screen.

▶ **3.** Press the ↑ key several times to move the insertion point up one line at a time, and then press the → key several times to move the insertion point to the right one character at a time.

▶ **4.** Press the **Ctrl+End** keys. The insertion point moves to the end of the document.

▶ **5.** Use the arrow keys to position the insertion point to the right of the "w" in "Andrew." Now you can add Andrew's middle initial.

▶ **6.** Press the **spacebar**, and then type the letter **T** followed by a period so that the signature line reads "Andrew T. Suri."

Figure 1-19 summarizes the keystrokes you can use to move the insertion point around a document.

Keystrokes for moving the insertion point ◀ **Figure 1-19**

To move the insertion point	Press
Left or right one character at a time	← or →
Up or down one line at a time	↑ or ↓
Left or right one word at a time	Ctrl+ ← or Ctrl+ →
Up or down one paragraph at a time	Ctrl+ ↑ or Ctrl+ ↓
To the beginning or to the end of the current line	Home or End
To the beginning or to the end of the document	Ctrl+Home or Ctrl+End
To the previous screen or to the next screen	Page Up or Page Down
To the top or to the bottom of the document window	Alt+Ctrl+Page Up or Alt+Ctrl+Page Down

Using the Undo and Redo Commands

To undo (or reverse) the last thing you did in a document, you can click the **Undo button** on the Quick Access Toolbar. If you want to restore your original change, the **Redo button** reverses the action of the Undo button (or redoes the undo). To undo more than your last action, you can click the Undo button arrow on the Quick Access Toolbar. A list will open that shows your most recent actions.

Andrew asks you to undo the addition of his middle initial, to see how the signature line looks without it.

To undo the addition of the "T.":

▶ **1.** On the Quick Access Toolbar, place the mouse pointer over the **Undo** button 🔄, but don't click it. The ScreenTip "Undo Typing (Ctrl + Z)" appears, indicating that your most recent action involved typing. The item in parentheses is the keyboard shortcut for the Undo command. See Figure 1-20.

Figure 1-20 ▶ **Using the Undo button**

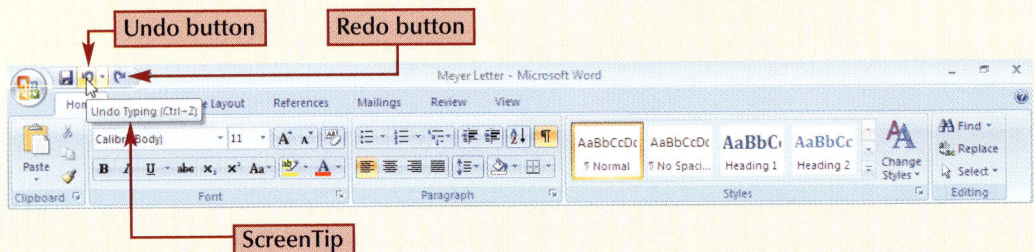

▶ **2.** Click the **Undo** button 🔄 on the Quick Access Toolbar. The letter "T," the period, and the space you typed earlier are deleted.

Trouble? If something else changes, you probably made another edit or change to the document between the addition of Andrew's middle initial and the undo action. Click the Undo button on the Quick Access Toolbar until the letter "T," the period, and the space following it are deleted. If a list of possible changes appears under the Undo button, you clicked the arrow next to the Undo button rather than the Undo button itself. Press the Esc key to close the list.

Andrew decides that he does want to include his middle initial after all. Instead of retyping it, you'll redo the undo.

▶ **3.** On the Quick Access Toolbar, place the mouse pointer over the **Redo** button and observe the "Redo Typing (Ctrl + Y)" ScreenTip.

▶ **4.** Click the **Redo** button 🔄 on the Quick Access Toolbar. Andrew's middle initial (along with the period and an additional space) are reinserted into the signature line.

▶ **5.** Click the **Save** button 💾 on the Quick Access Toolbar to save your changes to the document.

Correcting Errors

If you notice a typing error as soon as you make it, you can press the Backspace key, which deletes the characters and spaces to the left of the insertion point one at a time. Backspacing erases both printing and nonprinting characters. After you erase the error, you can type the correct character(s). You can also press the Delete key, which deletes characters to the right of the insertion point one at a time.

In many cases, however, Word's **AutoCorrect** feature will do the work for you. Among other things, AutoCorrect automatically corrects common typing errors, such as typing "adn" for "and." For example, you might have noticed AutoCorrect at work if you forgot to capitalize the first letter in a sentence as you typed the letter. AutoCorrect can automatically correct this error as you type the rest of the sentence. You'll learn more about using AutoCorrect as you become a more experienced Word user. For now, just keep in mind that AutoCorrect corrects certain typing errors automatically. Depending on how your computer is set up, some or all AutoCorrect features might be turned off. You'll learn how to turn AutoCorrect on in the following steps.

Whether or not AutoCorrect is turned on, you can always rely on Word's **spelling checker**. By default, this feature continually checks your document against Word's built-in dictionary. If you type a word that doesn't match the correct spelling in Word's dictionary, or if a word is not in the dictionary at all (as is the case with Andrew's last name, Suri), a wavy red line appears beneath the word. A wavy red line also appears if you type duplicate words (such as "the the"). Word also includes a grammar checker, which is turned off by default. You will learn how to use the grammar checker in Tutorial 2.

Before you can practice using AutoCorrect and the spelling checker, you need to verify that you have the correct settings in the Word Options dialog box.

To verify the spelling checker and AutoCorrect settings:

▶ **1.** Click the **Office Button** 🔘 , and then (at the bottom of the Office menu) click the **Word Options** button. The Word Options dialog box opens.

▶ **2.** In the left pane, click **Proofing**. Options related to proofing a document are displayed in the right pane.

▶ **3.** Verify that the **Check spelling as you type** check box contains a check mark.

▶ **4.** Verify that the **Mark grammar errors as you type** check box does *not* contain a check mark. (This option is typically turned off by default.)

▶ **5.** Near the top of the right pane, click the **AutoCorrect Options** button. The AutoCorrect: English (United States) dialog box opens.

▶ **6.** Locate the **Capitalize first letter of sentences** check box and the **Replace text as you type** check box. If they are not already checked, click them to insert check marks now. (It is okay if other check boxes have check marks.) See Figure 1-21.

Figure 1-21 **Selecting AutoCorrect options**

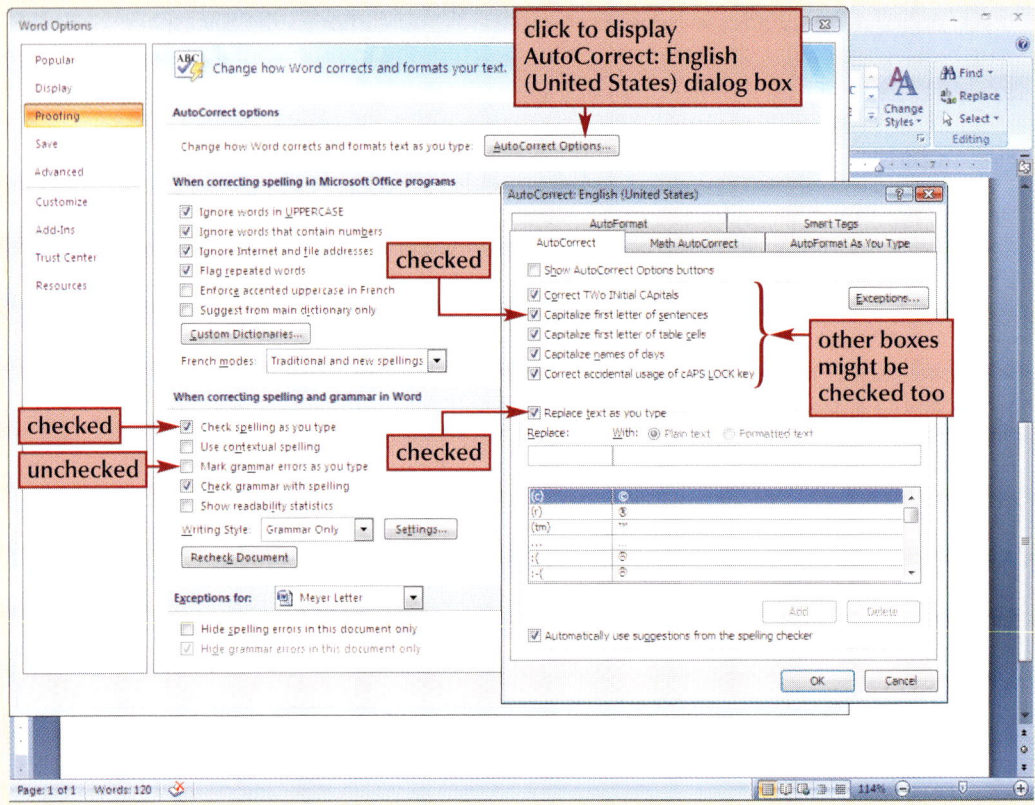

7. Click the **OK** button to close the AutoCorrect English (United States) dialog box, and then click the **OK** button again to close the Word Options dialog box.

The easiest way to see how these features work is to make some intentional typing errors.

To correct intentional typing errors:

▶ **1.** Use the arrow keys to move the insertion point to the left of the last paragraph mark in the document.

▶ **2.** Carefully and slowly type the following sentence exactly as it is shown, including the spelling errors: **notice how microsoft Word corects teh commen typing misTakes you make**. See Figure 1-22.

Intentional typing errors ◀ **Figure 1-22**

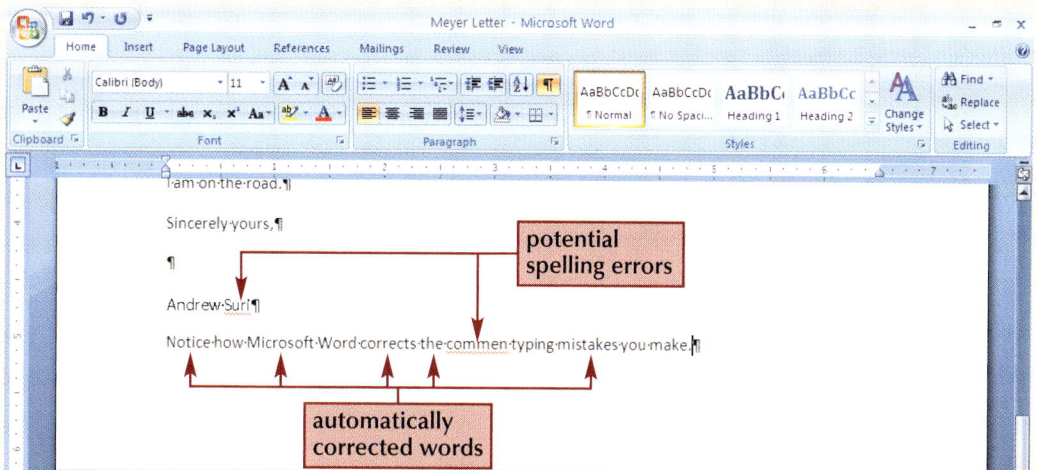

Trouble? If you see wavy green underlines, the grammar checker is turned on and you made a mistake not included in Step 2. Delete the text you just typed, repeat Steps 1–4 in the preceding set of steps to turn the grammar checker off, click the OK button to close the Word Options dialog box, and then begin these steps again with Step 1.

When you pressed the spacebar after the word "commen," a wavy red line appeared beneath it, indicating that the word might be misspelled. Also, Word automatically capitalized the word "Notice" (because it is the first word in the sentence) and "Microsoft" (because it is a proper noun). And, when you pressed the spacebar after the words "corects," "teh," and "misTakes," Word automatically corrected the typing errors.

Correcting Spelling Errors

After you verify that AutoCorrect made the changes you want, you should review your document for red wavy underlines, which indicate potential spelling errors. In the following steps, you will learn a quick way to correct such errors.

To correct spelling and grammar errors:

▶ **1.** Position the I-beam pointer over the word "commen," and then click the right mouse button. A shortcut menu appears with suggested spellings. You also see the Mini toolbar, which provides easy access to some of the most commonly used options in the Home tab for the object you've right-clicked. You'll learn more about the Mini toolbar as you gain more experience with Word. See Figure 1-23.

Figure 1-23 | **Shortcut menu with suggested spellings**

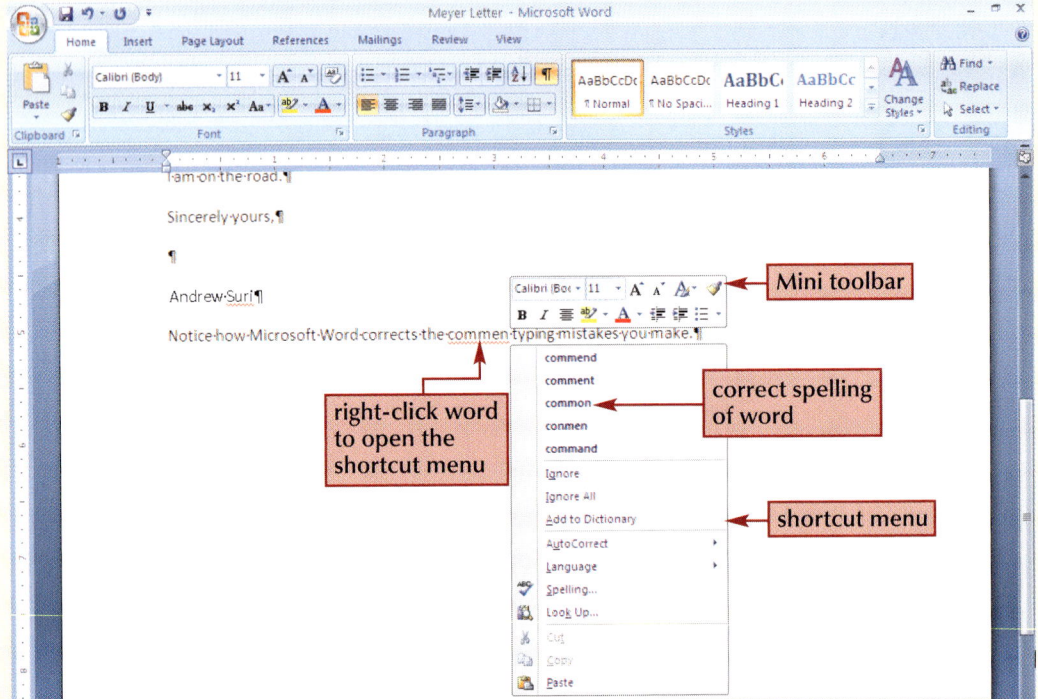

Trouble? If the shortcut menu doesn't appear, repeat Step 1, making sure you click the right mouse button, not the left one. If you see a different menu from the one shown in Figure 1-23, you didn't right-click exactly on the word "commen." Press the Esc key to close the menu, and then repeat Step 1.

▸ **2.** Click **common** in the shortcut menu. The menu closes (along with the Mini toolbar), and the correct spelling appears in your document. Notice that the wavy red line disappears after you correct the error.

Proofreading the Letter

You can see how quick and easy it is to correct common typing errors with AutoCorrect and the spelling checker. Remember, however, to proofread each document you create thoroughly. AutoCorrect will not catch words that are spelled correctly but used improperly (such as "your" for "you're"). Before you can proofread your letter, you need to delete the practice sentence.

To delete the practice sentence:

▸ **1.** Make sure the insertion point is to the right of "common" in the sentence you just typed, and then press the **Delete** key repeatedly to delete any spaces and characters to the right of the insertion point.

▸ **2.** Press the **Backspace** key repeatedly until the insertion point is located just left of the paragraph mark below Andrew's name. There should only be one paragraph mark below his name. If you accidentally delete part of the letter, retype it, using Figure 1-1 as a guide.

Now you can proofread the letter for any typos. You can also get rid of the wavy red underline below Andrew's last name.

To proofread the document:

▶ **1.** Be sure the signature line is visible. Because Word doesn't recognize "Suri" as a word, it is marked as a potential error. You need to tell Word to ignore this name wherever it occurs in the letter.

▶ **2.** Right-click **Suri**. A shortcut menu and the Mini toolbar open.

▶ **3.** Click **Ignore All** on the shortcut menu. This tells Word to ignore the word "Suri" each time it occurs in this document. The wavy red underline disappears from below Andrew's last name.

▶ **4.** Scroll up to the beginning of the letter and proofread it for typing errors. If a word has a wavy red underline, right-click it and choose an option on the shortcut menu. To correct other errors, click to the right or left of the error, use the Backspace or Delete key to remove it, and then type a correction.

▶ **5.** On the Quick Access Toolbar, click the **Save** button 🖫 . Word saves your letter with the same name and to the same location you specified earlier.

Next, you need to return to the beginning of the document and insert the date. In the process, you'll learn how to use Word's AutoComplete feature.

Inserting a Date with AutoComplete

The advantage of using a word-processing program such as Microsoft Word is that you can easily make changes to text you have already typed. In this case, you need to insert the current date at the beginning of the letter. Andrew tells you that he wants to send the *Author's Guide* to Clara Meyer on February 8, so you need to insert that date into the letter now.

Before you can enter the date, you need to move the insertion point to the correct location.

To move the insertion point and add some blank lines:

▶ **1.** Scroll up to display the top of the document.

▶ **2.** Click to the left of the "D" in "Dear Clara" in the salutation, press the **Enter** key twice, then press the ↑ key twice to move the insertion point up to two paragraphs above the salutation. There are now six blank paragraphs before the salutation. The insertion point is located in the second blank paragraph above the salutation. The vertical ruler tells you that the insertion point is located about 1.5 inches from the top margin (that is, the insertion point is now located where the salutation used to be). As you'll recall, the top margin is one inch deep, so the insertion point is now approximately 2.5 inches from the top of the page. This is where you will insert the date. See Figure 1-24.

Figure 1-24	Insertion point positioned for adding date

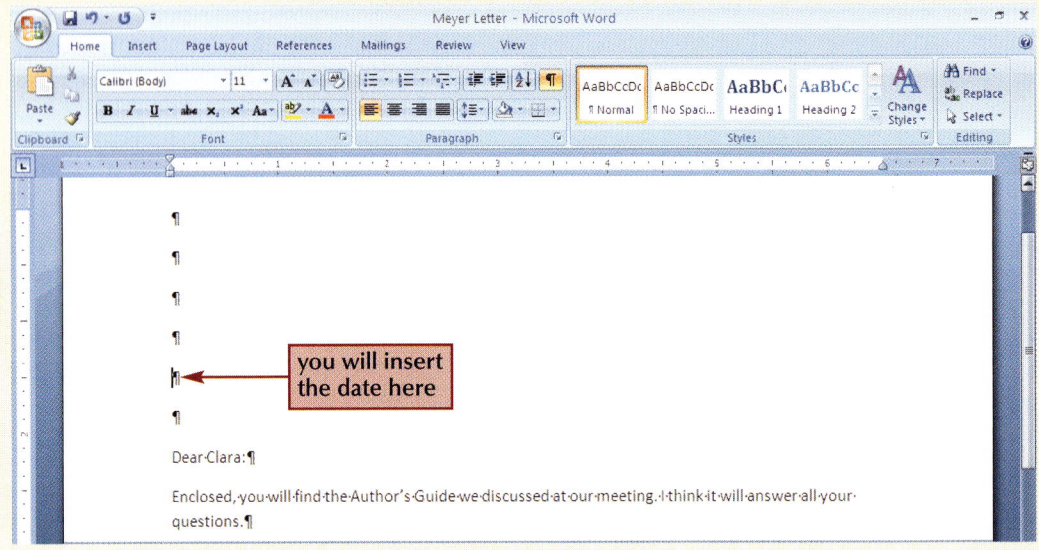

To insert the date, you can take advantage of Word's **AutoComplete** feature, which automatically inserts dates and other regularly used items for you. In this case, you can type the first few characters of the month, and let Word insert the rest.

To insert the date:

▸ 1. Type **Febr** (the first four letters of February). A rectangular box appears above the line, as shown in Figure 1-25. If you wanted to type something other than February, you could continue typing to complete the word. In this case, though, you want to accept the AutoComplete suggestion.

Figure 1-25	AutoComplete suggestion

Tip

AutoComplete works for long month names like February, but not shorter ones like May, because "Ma" could be the beginning of many words, not just "May."

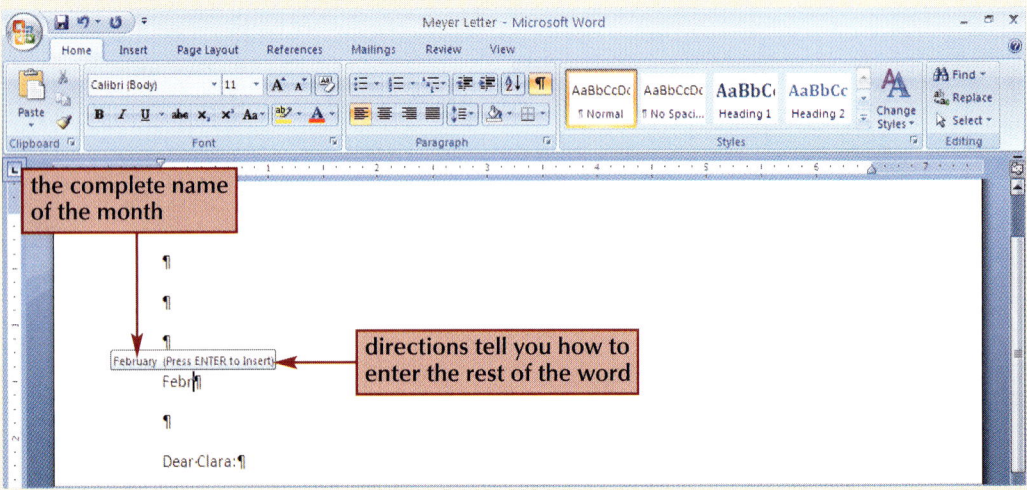

▸ 2. Press the **Enter** key. The rest of the word "February" is inserted in the document.

▶ **3.** Press the **spacebar**, type **8, 2010**, and then press the **Enter** key twice. The date is finished, and the insertion point is now located where you want to begin typing the inside address.

   Trouble? If February happens to be the current month, you will see a second AutoComplete suggestion displaying the current date after you press the spacebar. To ignore that AutoComplete suggestion, continue typing the rest of the date as instructed in Step 3.

You're ready to type the inside address. But first, you need to learn a little more about paragraph and line spacing in Microsoft Word.

Understanding Line and Paragraph Spacing

In Word, any text that ends with a paragraph mark symbol (¶) is a paragraph. A **paragraph** can be a group of words that is many lines long, a single word, or even a blank line, in which case you see a paragraph mark alone on a single line. (Recall that the letter to Clara Meyer includes several blank paragraphs at the beginning of the document.) As you work with paragraphs in a document, you need to be concerned with two types of spacing—line spacing and paragraph spacing.

Line spacing determines the amount of space between lines of text within a paragraph. Lines that are closely positioned one on top of another are said to be single spaced. Technically speaking, single spacing allows for the tallest character in a line of text. All other line spacing options are measured as multiples of single spacing. For example, 1.5 line spacing allows for one and one-half times the space of single spacing. Likewise, double spacing allows for twice the space of single spacing. By default, the line spacing in Word 2007 documents is set to 1.15 times the space allowed in single spacing. This allows for the largest character in a particular line as well as a small amount of extra space.

The other type of spacing you need to be concerned with, **paragraph spacing**, determines the amount of space before and after a paragraph. Paragraph spacing is measured in points; a **point** is approximately $1/72$ of an inch. The default setting for paragraph spacing in Word is 0 points before each paragraph and 10 points after each paragraph.

Although line spacing and paragraph spacing are two different things, it is common to refer to paragraph spacing with the same terms used to refer to line spacing. So, paragraphs that appear very close together, with no space for text in between, are often referred to as single spaced. Paragraphs that have space enough for a single line of text between them are said to be double spaced. The default paragraph spacing in Word (10 points after each paragraph) is designed to look like double spacing (although it is slightly tighter than true double spacing). Figure 1-26 shows the Meyer Letter document zoomed to 90%, so you can see its spacing at a glance.

Figure 1-26   **Line and paragraph spacing in the letter to Clara Meyer**

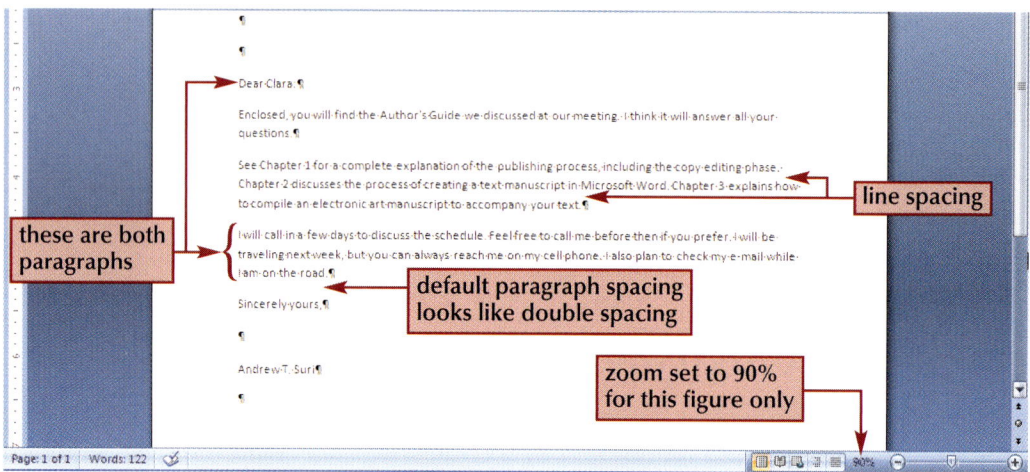

In a block style letter, the inside address (shown earlier in Figure 1-1) should be single spaced. However, with Word's default paragraph spacing, when you press the Enter key to move from the name line in the inside address, to the street address line, and then to the city and state line, Word inserts extra space after each paragraph. This results in an inside address that is double spaced. You'll see how this works in the following steps. Then you'll learn how to correct the problem.

To type the inside address:

1. Type the following: **Clara Meyer**, press the **Enter** key, type **2257 Chamberlain Drive**, press the **Enter** key, and then type **North Liberty, IA 52317**. Do not press the Enter key after typing the zip code; you should already see one blank paragraph before and after the inside address. See Figure 1-27.

Letter with inside address ◀ **Figure 1-27**

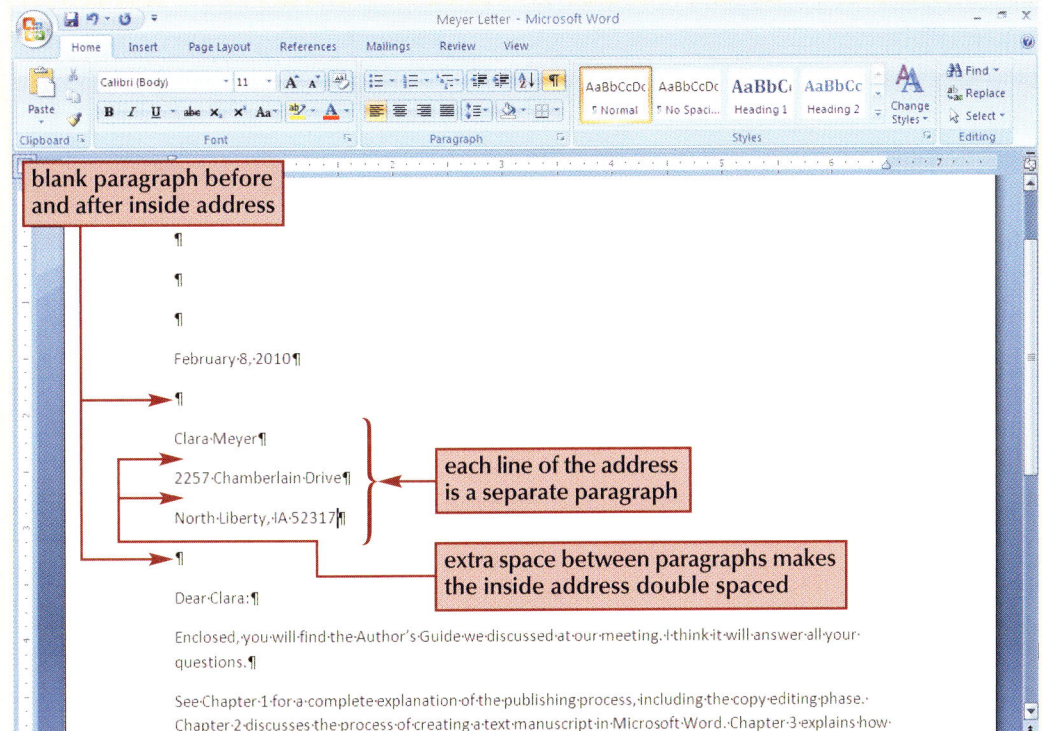

Remember that each line of the inside address is actually a separate paragraph. As you can see in Figure 1-27, the extra space Word inserted between these separate paragraphs results in an inside address that appears to be double spaced.

To correct this problem, you need to **select**, or highlight, the inside address and then change the paragraph spacing. Andrew is also concerned about the document's line spacing. He doesn't really like the extra space between lines, so he asks you to remove it. To change this, you need to select the entire document and then change the line spacing.

Selecting Parts of a Document

You can select one or more paragraphs, one or more words, any other part of a document, or even the entire document, by using the mouse or the keyboard. However, most people find that the mouse is easier and more efficient to use. With the mouse you can quickly select a line or paragraph by clicking the **selection bar** (the blank space in the left margin area of the document window). You can also select text using various combinations of keys. Figure 1-28 summarizes methods for selecting text with the mouse and the keyboard. A notation such as "Ctrl+Shift" means you press and hold the two keys at the same time.

Figure 1-28 | Methods for selecting text

To Select	Mouse	Keyboard	Mouse and Keyboard
A word	Double-click the word	Move the insertion point to the beginning of the word, hold down Ctrl+Shift, and then press →	
A line	Click in the selection bar next to the line	Move the insertion point to the beginning of the line, hold down Shift, and then press ↓	
A sentence	Click at the beginning of the sentence, then drag the pointer until the sentence is selected		Press and hold down Ctrl, and then click within the sentence
Multiple lines	Click and drag in the selection bar next to the lines	Move the insertion point to the beginning of the first line, hold down Shift, and then press ↓ until all the lines are selected	
A paragraph	Double-click in the selection bar next to the paragraph, or triple-click within the paragraph	Move the insertion point to the beginning of the paragraph, hold down Ctrl+Shift, and then press ↓	
Multiple paragraphs	Click in the selection bar next to the first paragraph in the group, and then drag in the selection bar to select the paragraphs	Move the insertion point to the beginning of the first paragraph, hold down Ctrl+Shift, and then press ↓ until all the paragraphs are selected	
An entire document	Triple-click in the selection bar	Press Ctrl+A	Press and hold down Ctrl, and then click in the selection bar
A block of text	Click at the beginning of the block, and then drag the pointer until the entire block is selected		Click at the beginning of the block, press and hold down Shift, and then click at the end of the block
Nonadjacent blocks of text	Press and hold down Ctrl, and then drag the mouse pointer to select multiple blocks of nonadjacent text		

You'll practice many of these selection methods in Tutorial 2. For now, you will focus on selecting the multiple paragraphs of the inside address and the entire document. You'll start by selecting the inside address.

To select the inside address:

▶ 1. Click to the left of the "C" in "Clara Meyer" in the inside address, and then drag the mouse right and down until the entire inside address is selected. Make sure the paragraph mark to the right of the zip code is also selected. See Figure 1-29.

Selected inside address ◀ Figure 1-29

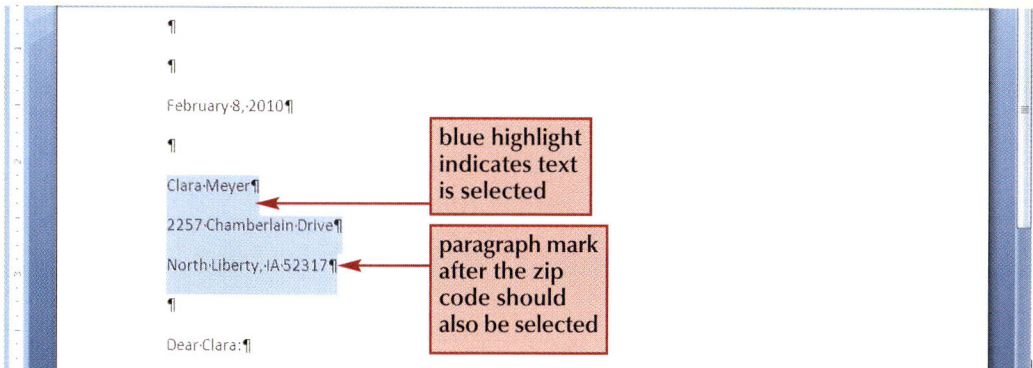

Trouble? If you selected only part of the inside address, or selected a different part of the document, click anywhere in the document to remove the blue highlight, and then begin again with Step 1.

Trouble? Don't be concerned if you see the Mini toolbar hovering over the selected text.

Now that the inside address is selected, you are ready to remove the extra space after each paragraph. You'll also adjust the line spacing, as Andrew requested.

Adjusting Paragraph and Line Spacing

There are several ways to adjust paragraph and line spacing in Word. The quickest method, which you'll use in this tutorial, is to click the Line spacing button in the Paragraph group on the Home tab. (In Tutorial 2, you'll learn another technique that offers more options.)

Clicking the Line spacing button opens a menu with some commonly used line spacing options: single spacing (listed on the Line spacing menu as 1.0), double spacing (listed as 2.0), and so on. The paragraph spacing options offered by the Line spacing button are more streamlined: you can choose to add or remove a default amount of extra space before or after each paragraph. You cannot specify a particular amount of space.

Understanding Spacing Between Paragraphs	InSight

To many people, "to single space between paragraphs" means pressing the Enter key once after each paragraph. Likewise, "to double space between paragraphs" means pressing the Enter key twice after each paragraph. With the default paragraph spacing in Word 2007, however, you only need to press the Enter key once to insert a double space after a paragraph. Keep this in mind if you're used to pressing the Enter key twice; otherwise, you could end up with more space than you want between paragraphs.

Andrew asks you to remove the extra space between the lines within paragraphs. This means you need to change the line spacing from 1.15 to 1.0 (that is, to single spacing). You'll start by adjusting the paragraph spacing in the inside address, and then turn your attention to the line spacing for the entire document.

To adjust the paragraph spacing in the inside address:

1. Verify that the inside address is still selected.

2. In the Paragraph group on the Home tab, click the **Line spacing** button ![line spacing icon]. A menu of line spacing options appears, with two paragraph spacing options at the bottom. The current line spacing setting for the selected text (1.15) is indicated by a check mark. Because the line spacing is the same throughout the document, this is also the current line spacing setting for the entire document. At the moment, you are more interested in the paragraph spacing options. Your goal is to remove the extra space after each paragraph in the inside address, so you need to use the last option on the menu, Remove Space After Paragraph. See Figure 1-30.

Figure 1-30 Line and paragraph spacing options

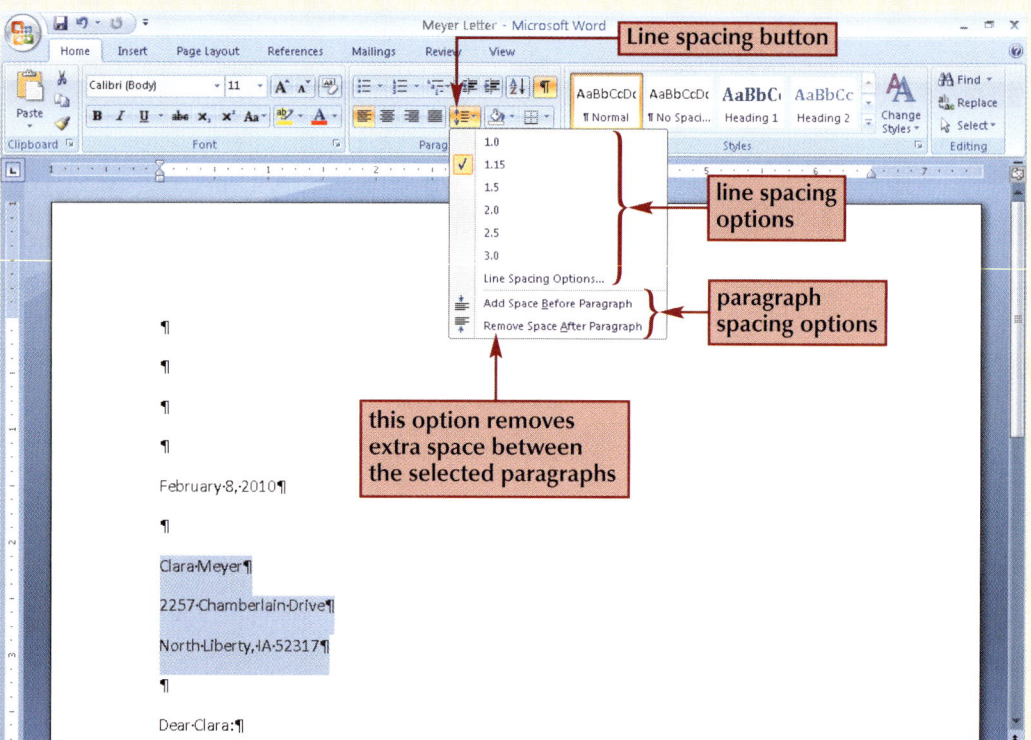

3. Click **Remove Space After Paragraph**. The menu closes, and the extra space after each of the three paragraphs of the inside address is removed. The paragraphs are now closer together.

4. Click anywhere in the document to deselect the inside address. Notice that the change in paragraph spacing in the inside address did not affect the rest of the document because you had selected only the inside address. The paragraphs in the body of the letter are still separated by extra space, so that they appear to be double spaced.

The three paragraphs of the inside address are closer together, but they don't exactly look single spaced. That's because the default line spacing setting (which you'll recall adds a small amount of space below each line) remains in effect, adding a small amount of extra space below the single line of text in each of the three inside address paragraphs. When you change the line spacing for the entire document to single spaced in the next set of steps, the inside address will finally look single spaced.

To adjust the line spacing for the entire document:

▶ **1.** Press the **Ctrl + A** keys. The entire document is selected, as indicated by the blue highlight.

▶ **2.** In the Paragraph group on the Home tab, click the **Line spacing** button. The Line spacing menu opens. As you saw earlier, the default line spacing setting of 1.15 is currently selected, as indicated by the check mark. You want to change the setting to single spacing, or 1.0.

▶ **3.** Click **1.0**. The Line spacing menu closes.

▶ **4.** Click anywhere in the document to deselect it. The lines of the entire document move closer together, and the inside address is now single spaced. The lines within the paragraphs in the rest of the document are also single spaced. The double spacing between paragraphs everywhere in the letter except the inside address remains unchanged. See Figure 1-31.

New line spacing in the document ◀ **Figure 1-31**

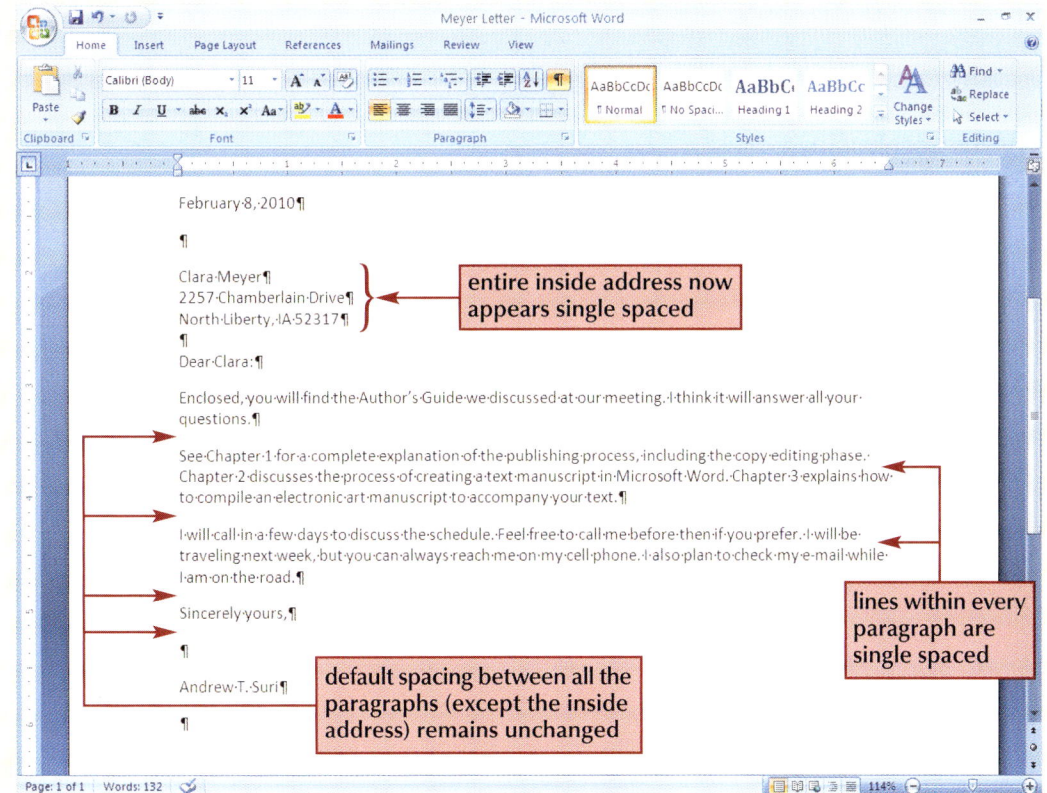

Previewing and Printing a Document

Do you think the letter is ready to print? If you print too soon, you risk wasting paper and printer time. For example, if you failed to insert enough space for the company letterhead, you would have to add more space, and then print the letter again. To avoid wasting paper and time, you should first display the document in the **Print Preview window**. By default, the Print Preview window shows you the full page; there's no need to scroll through the document.

To preview the document:

▶ **1.** Proof the document one last time and correct any new errors. Always remember to proof your document immediately before printing it.

▶ **2.** Click to the left of the last paragraph mark in the document (just below Andrew's name), press the **Enter** key and type your first, middle, and last initials in lowercase. In a block style letter, it is customary for the typist to include his or her initials below the signature line. In this case, adding your initials also ensures that you will be able to identify your copy of the letter when you retrieve it from the printer.

▶ **3.** Click the **Office Button** 🔵, point to **Print**, and then click **Print Preview**. The Print Preview window opens and displays a full-page version of your letter, as shown in Figure 1-32. This shows how the letter will fit on the printed page. The Ribbon in Print Preview includes a number of useful options for changing the way the printed page will look.

| Figure 1-32 | Full page displayed in the Print Preview window |

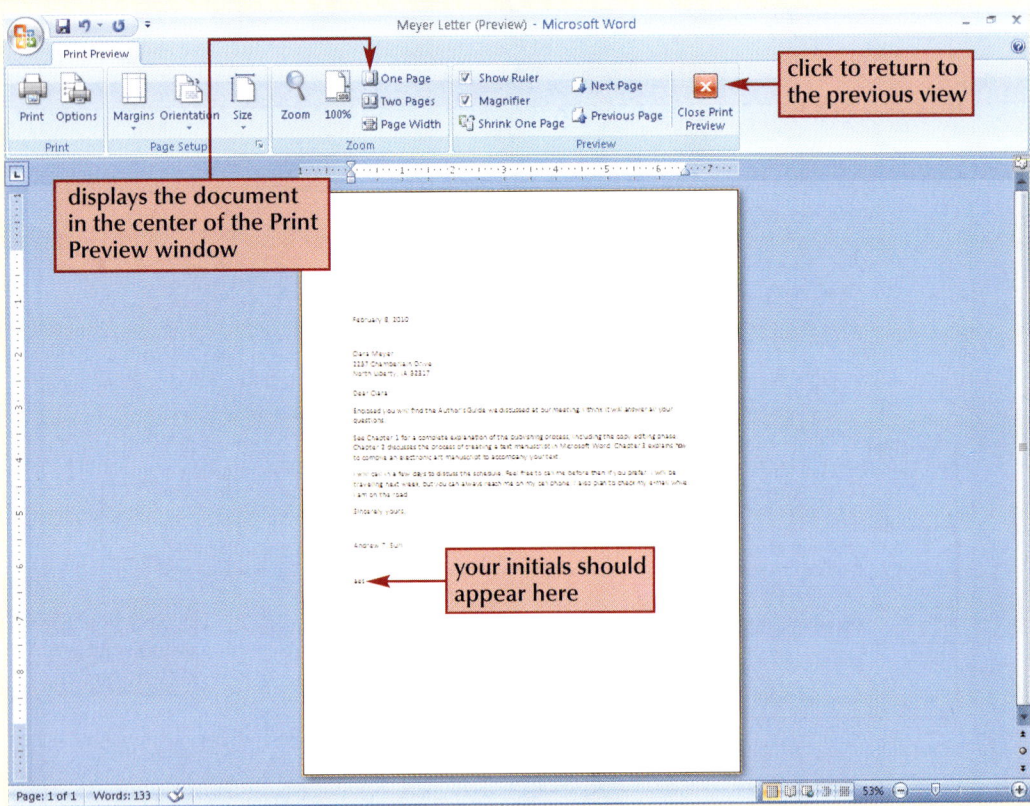

Trouble? If your letter is not centered in the Print Preview window, click the One Page button in the Zoom group on the Print Preview tab.

Trouble? If you don't see a ruler above the document, click the Show Ruler check box in the Preview group on the Print Preview tab to insert a check mark and display the ruler.

4. Review your document and make sure its overall layout matches the document in Figure 1-32. If you notice a problem with paragraph breaks or spacing, click the Close Print Preview button in the Preview group on the Print Preview tab, edit the document, and then open the Print Preview window again and check your work.

5. In the Preview group on the Print Preview tab, click the **Close Print Preview** button to return to Print Layout view.

6. Click the **Save** button 🔲 on the Quick Access Toolbar to save the letter with your newly added initials.

In Andrew's letter, the text looks well spaced, and the letterhead will fit at the top of the page. You are ready to print the letter.

To print a document, click the Office Button, and then click Print. This opens the Print dialog box, where you can adjust various printer settings. Or, if you prefer, you can click the Office Button, point to Print, and then click Quick Print. This prints the document using default settings, without opening a dialog box. In these tutorials, the first time you print, you should check the settings in the Print dialog box and make sure the number of copies is set to 1. After that, you can use the Quick Print command.

To print the letter document:

1. Make sure your printer is turned on and contains paper.

2. Click the **Office Button** 🔘 , and then click **Print**. The Print dialog box opens.

3. Make sure the Printer section of the dialog box shows the correct printer. Also, make sure the number of copies is set to 1.

   Trouble? If the Name list box in the Print dialog box shows the wrong printer, click the Name list arrow, and then select the correct printer from the list of available printers. If you're not sure what the correct printer is, check with your instructor or technical support person.

4. Click the **OK** button. Assuming your computer is attached to a printer, the letter prints.

Your printed letter should look similar to Figure 1-1, but without the Carlyle University letterhead. Also, your initials should appear below Andrew's name, on the last line of the letter.

Printing Documents on a Shared Printer	InSight

If your computer is connected to a network, be sure to print only those documents that you need in hard copy format. You should avoid tying up a shared printer with unnecessary printing.

Creating an Envelope

After you print the letter, Andrew asks you to create an envelope in which to mail the *Author's Guide*. Creating an envelope is a simple process because Word automatically uses the inside address from the letter as the address on the envelope. By default, Word does not add extra space between the paragraphs on an envelope, and the line spacing is set to 1.0. As a result, addresses on an envelope are single spaced.

Creating an Envelope

- Click the Mailings tab on the Ribbon.
- In the Create group, click the Envelopes button to open the Envelopes and Labels dialog box.
- Verify that the Delivery address box contains the correct address. If necessary, type a new address or edit the existing one.
- If necessary, type a return address. If you are using preprinted stationery that already includes a return address, click the Omit check box to insert a check mark.
- To print the envelope immediately, insert an envelope in your printer, and then click the Print button.
- To store the envelope along with the rest of the document, click the Add to Document button.
- To print the envelope after you have added it to the document, insert an envelope in your printer, open the Print dialog box, and print the page containing the envelope.

Andrew tells you that your printer is not currently stocked with envelopes. He asks you to create the envelope and add it to the document. Then he will print the envelope later, when he is ready to mail the *Author's Guide* to Clara.

To create an envelope:

▶ 1. Click the **Mailings** tab on the Ribbon.

▶ 2. In the Create group on the Mailings tab, click the **Envelopes** button. The Envelopes and Labels dialog box opens, as shown in Figure 1-33. By default, Word uses the inside address from the letter as the delivery address. Depending on how your computer is set up, you might see an address in the Return address box. Because Andrew will be using his company's printed envelopes, you don't need to print a return address on this envelope.

Figure 1-33 | **Envelopes and Labels dialog box**

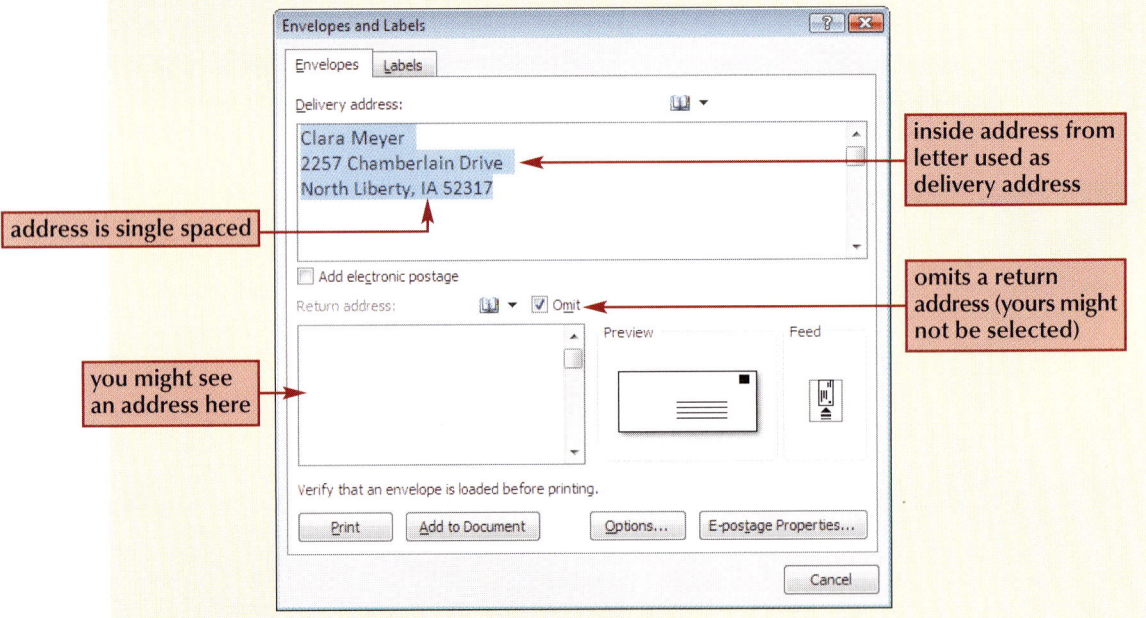

▶ 3. If necessary, click the **Omit** check box to insert a check mark.

▶ **4.** Click the **Add to Document** button. The dialog box closes, and you return to the document window. The envelope is inserted at the top of the document, with the address single spaced. The double line with the words "Section Break (Next Page)" indicate how the envelope is formatted, and will not be visible when you print the envelope. The envelope will print in the standard business envelope format. (You'll have a chance to print an envelope in the exercises at the end of this tutorial.)

▶ **5.** Save your changes to the document. You are finished with the letter and the envelope, so you can close the document.

▶ **6.** Click the **Close** button ☒ on the Word program title bar. The Meyer Letter document closes. If you have no other documents open, Word closes also.

Trouble? If you see a dialog box with the message "Do you want to save the changes to 'Meyer Letter?'" click the Yes button.

Congratulations on creating your first letter in Microsoft Word 2007. You'll be able to use the skills you learned in this tutorial to create a variety of professional documents.

Session 1.2 Quick Check | Review

1. True or False: The spelling checker is turned off by default.
2. True or False: To accept an AutoComplete suggestion, such as the name of a month, you need to click a button on the Ribbon.
3. Explain how to correct a misspelled word using a shortcut menu.
4. What's the difference between paragraph spacing and line spacing?
5. Explain how to preview a document before you print it.
6. What tab on the Ribbon do you use to create an envelope?

Tutorial Summary | Review

In this tutorial, you learned how to set up your Word window to match the figures in this book, create a new document from scratch, and type a professional-looking letter. You practiced correcting errors and moving the insertion point around a document. You learned how to undo and redo changes and how to insert a date with AutoComplete. You adjusted paragraph and line spacing, and then you previewed and printed a document. Finally, you created an envelope.

Key Terms

AutoComplete	nonprinting characters	scroll
AutoCorrect	Page width	select
default	paragraph	selection bar
font	paragraph spacing	spelling checker
font size	point	Undo button
line spacing	Print Preview window	Word
margin	Redo button	word wrap
Microsoft Office Word	ScreenTip	Zoom level

| Practice | | **Review Assignments** |

Practice the skills you learned in the tutorial using the same case scenario.

There are no Data Files needed for the Review Assignments.

Andrew asks you to write a letter to a local author, Philippa Gallatin, inviting her to an upcoming convention. He also asks you to create an envelope for the letter. You'll create the letter and envelope by completing the following steps. (Note: Text you need to type is shown in bold for ease of reference only; do not bold the text unless otherwise instructed.)

1. Open a new blank document.
2. Compare your screen to the checklist in Figure 1-12, and change any settings if necessary. In particular, make sure that nonprinting characters are displayed.
3. Press the Enter key four times to insert enough space for the company letterhead.
4. Type the date **November 25, 2010** using AutoComplete for "November."
5. Press the Enter key twice, then type the following inside address, using the default paragraph spacing for now:
   Philippa Gallatin
   787 First Street
   Albany, NY 12205
6. Press the Enter key twice, then type the letter's salutation, body, complimentary closing, and signature line, as shown in Figure 1-34. Accept any relevant AutoCorrect suggestions. Use the default line and paragraph spacing; do not insert any extra blank paragraphs.

Figure 1-34

Dear Philippa:

The Albany Visitors Bureau will be hosting the 2011 convention for the National Editorial Association. The convention is scheduled for the first week in March. As a major publishing force in the Albany area, we'd like to make a strong showing at the convention. In particular, we'd like to invite you to attend the opening banquet as our guest. Our own editor-in-chief, Sally Ann Hamilton, will be the keynote speaker.

The complete convention schedule will be posted on the National Editorial Association's Web site after the New Year. I'll e-mail you shortly afterward to confirm your reservation for the opening banquet. At that time, you can tell me if you'll be available to attend any of the afternoon seminars.

Sincerely,

Andrew T. Suri

7. Save your work as **Gallatin Letter** in the Tutorial.01\Review folder provided with your Data Files.
8. Practice using the keyboard to move the insertion point around the document. Use the arrow keys so the insertion point is positioned immediately to the right of the "a" in "Philippa" in the inside address.

9. Press the spacebar and then type **M.**, so the first line of the inside address reads "Philippa M. Gallatin." (Don't forget the period after the middle initial.)

10. Undo the change and then redo it.

11. Scroll to the beginning of the document and proofread your work.

12. Correct any misspelled words marked by wavy red lines. If the correct spelling of a word does not appear in the shortcut menu, close the list, and then make the correction yourself. Remove any red wavy lines below words that are spelled correctly.

13. Click at the end of Andrew's name in the signature line, press the Enter key twice, and type your initials in lowercase.

14. Select the inside address and remove the extra paragraph spacing from the selected paragraphs.

15. Select the entire document and change the line spacing to single spacing.

16. Save your changes to the letter, and then preview and print it.

17. Add an envelope to the document. Use your own address as the delivery address. Do not include a return address.

18. Save your changes and close the document.

| Apply | | **Case Problem 1** |

Apply the skills you learned to create a letter about a health-care lecture.

There are no Data Files needed for this Case Problem.

Wingra Family Practice Clinic You are a nurse at Wingra Family Practice Clinic. You have organized a lunchtime lecture series for the clinic staff in which regional medical professionals will discuss topics related to pediatric health care. You have hired your first speaker and need to write a letter confirming your agreement and asking a few questions. Create the letter by completing the following steps. As you type the document, accept the default paragraph and line spacing until you are asked to change them. Because the clinic is currently out of letterhead, you will start the letter by typing a return address. (Note: Text you need to type is shown in bold for ease of reference only; do not bold the text unless otherwise instructed.)

1. Open a new blank document. Compare your screen to the checklist in Figure 1-12, and change any settings if necessary. In particular, make sure that nonprinting characters are displayed.

2. Type your name, press the Enter key, and then type the following return address:
   Wingra Family Practice Clinic
   2278 Norwood Place
   Middleton, WI 52247

3. Press the Enter key twice, and then type **May 8, 2010** as the date.

4. Press the Enter key twice, and then type this inside address:
   Dr. Susanna Trevay
   James Madison Medical Center
   56 Ingersoll Drive
   Madison, WI 53788

5. Press the Enter key twice, type the salutation **Dear Dr. Trevay:** (don't forget the colon), and then press the Enter key once.

6. Type the following paragraph: **Thank you so much for agreeing to lecture about early childhood vaccinations on Friday, May 21. Before I can publicize your talk, I need some information. Please call by Tuesday with your answers to these questions:**

7. Press the Enter key, and then type the following questions as separate paragraphs, using the default paragraph spacing:

   Which vaccines will you cover in detail?

   Will you discuss common immune responses to vaccine antigens?

   Will you provide hand-outs with suggested vaccination schedules?

8. Save the document as **Lecture Series Letter** in the Tutorial.01\Case1 folder provided with your Data Files.

9. Move the insertion point to the beginning of the third question (which begins "Will you provide..."). Insert a new paragraph, and add the following as the new third question in the list: **Would you be willing to take questions from the audience?**

10. Correct any spelling errors indicated by red wavy lines. Because "Wingra" is spelled correctly, use the shortcut menu to remove the wavy red line under the word "Wingra" and prevent Word from marking the word as a misspelling. Repeat this to ignore "Trevay," "Ingersoll," and any other words that are spelled correctly but are marked as misspellings.

11. Insert a new paragraph after the last question, and then type the complimentary closing **Sincerely,** (including the comma).

12. Press the Enter key twice to leave room for your signature, and then type your full name. Press the Enter key and type **Wingra Family Practice Clinic**. Notice that "Wingra" is not marked as a spelling error this time.

13. Select the return address and remove the extra paragraph spacing. Do the same for the inside address. Do not attempt to change them both at the same time by selecting the return address, the date, and the inside address all at once, or you will end up with too little space before and after the date.

14. Select the entire document and change the line spacing to single spacing.

15. Save the document, preview and print it, and then close it.

| Apply | | Case Problem 2 |

Apply the skills you learned to create a letter informing a client about a new investment program.

There are no Data Files needed for this Case Problem.

Pear Tree Investment Services As a financial planner at Pear Tree Investment Services, you are responsible for keeping your clients informed about new investment options. You have just learned about a program called HigherEdVest, which encourages parents to save for their children's college educations. You'll write a letter to Joseph Robbins, a client of yours, in which you introduce the program and ask him to call for more information. Create the letter by completing the following steps. (Note: Text you need to type is shown in bold for ease of reference only; do not bold the text unless otherwise instructed.)

1. Open a new blank document. Compare your screen to the checklist in Figure 1-12, and change any settings if necessary. In particular, make sure that nonprinting characters are displayed.

2. To leave room for the company letterhead, press the Enter key until the insertion point is positioned about three inches from the top of the page. (Remember that you can see the exact position of the insertion point, in inches, on the vertical ruler.)

 **EXPLORE**

3. Type the current date, accepting any AutoComplete suggestions that appear.

4. Press the Enter key twice and type the inside address: **Joseph Robbins, 5788 Rugby Road, Hillsborough, CO 80732**.

5. Press the Enter key twice, type the salutation **Dear Joseph:**, and then press the Enter key once.

6. Write one paragraph introducing the HigherEdVest program, explaining that you think the client might be interested, and asking him to call your office at (555) 555-5555 for more details.

7. In the next paragraph, type the complimentary closing **Sincerely,**.

8. Press the Enter key twice to leave room for your signature, and then type your name and title.

9. Save the letter as **EdVest Letter** in the Tutorial.01\Case2 folder provided with your Data Files.

10. Reread your letter carefully and correct any errors. Use the keyboard to move the insertion point as necessary.

11. Remove the extra paragraph spacing in the inside address, and then change the entire document to single spacing.

12. Save your changes, and then preview and print the letter.

EXPLORE

13. Create an envelope for the letter. Click the Omit check box to deselect it (if necessary), and then, for the return address, type your own address. Add the envelope to the document. If you are asked if you want to save the return address as the new default return address, answer No. If your computer is connected to a printer that is stocked with envelopes, click the Office Button, click Print, click the Pages option button, type **1** in the Pages text box, and then click the OK button.

14. Save and close the document.

Create	Case Problem 3

Use your skills to create the letter of recommendation shown in Figure 1-35.

There are no Data Files needed for this Case Problem.

Monterrey Mountain Bike Tours You are the owner of Monterrey Mountain Bike Tours, located in Eugene, Oregon. One of your tour guides, Melissa Coia, has decided to move to the Midwest to be closer to her family. She has applied for a job as a tour guide at Horicon Marsh in Wisconsin, and has asked you to write a letter of recommendation. To create the letter, complete the following steps:

1. Open a new blank document. Compare your screen to the checklist in Figure 1-12, and change any settings if necessary. In particular, make sure that nonprinting characters are displayed.

2. Type the letter shown in Figure 1-35. Assume that you will print the letter on the company's letterhead, with the date positioned about 2.5 inches from the top of the page. Replace "Your Name" with your first and last name.

Figure 1-35

June 27, 2010

Peter Roundtree
Horicon Marsh Ranger Station
9875 Scales Bend Road
Horicon, Wisconsin 57338

Dear Mr. Roundtree:

I am writing on behalf of Melissa Coia, who has applied for a job as a tour guide at Horicon Marsh. I highly recommend that you hire Melissa. She is enthusiastic, energetic, and extremely well organized.

I would be glad to tell you more about Melissa over the phone. You can reach me during business hours at (555) 555-5555.

Sincerely,

Your Name

3. Save the document as **Melissa** in the Tutorial.01\Case3 folder provided with your Data Files.
4. Correct any typing errors.
5. Change the paragraph and line spacing so that the entire letter is single spaced, including the inside address.
6. Preview and print the letter.
7. Create an envelope for the letter. Click the Omit check box to deselect it (if necessary), and then, for the return address, type your own address. Add the envelope to the document. If you are asked if you want to save the return address as the new default return address, answer No. If your computer is connected to a printer that is stocked with envelopes, click the Office Button, click Print, click the Pages option button, type **1** in the Pages text box, and then click the OK button.
8. Save the document and close it.

| Challenge | **Case Problem 4** |

Go beyond what you've learned to write a fax coversheet for a small engineering company.

There are no Data Files needed for this Case Problem.

Gladstone Engineering As the office manager for Gladstone Engineering, you are responsible for faxing technical drawings to clients. Along with each set of drawings, you need to include a coversheet that explains what you are faxing, lists the total number of pages, and provides the name and cell phone number of the engineer who created the drawings. The fastest way to create a professional-looking coversheet is to use a template—a special Word document that comes with predefined headings, line and paragraph spacing, and other types of formatting. To create the fax coversheet, perform the following steps. (Note: Text you need to type is shown in bold for ease of reference only; do not bold the text unless otherwise instructed.)

⊕ **EXPLORE**

1. Click the Microsoft Office Button, and then click New. The New Document dialog box opens. In the Template list (on the left), click Installed Templates.

EXPLORE

2. In the Installed Templates pane (on the right), click Equity Fax, and then click Create. A fax template opens, containing generic text called placeholders that you replace with your own information. (You should always take care to remove any placeholders you don't replace with other text.)

3. Compare your screen to the checklist in Figure 1-12 and change any settings if necessary. In particular, make sure that nonprinting characters are displayed.

EXPLORE

4. Click the text "[Type the recipient name]." The placeholder text appears in a blue box with blue highlighting. The box containing the highlighted text (with the small rectangle attached) is called a document control, or a content control. You can enter text in this document control just as you enter text in a dialog box. You'll learn more about document controls in Tutorial 3.

5. Type **Robert Mason**, and then press the Tab key twice. A document control is now visible to the right of the word "From." If you see a name here, click in the document control (if necessary) and delete the name.

6. Type your first and last name in the document control, and then press the Tab key to highlight the placeholder text "[Type the recipient fax number]."

7. Type **(555) 555-5555**, and then continue using the Tab key as necessary to enter **4** as the number of pages and **(333) 333-3333** as the phone number. If you press the Tab key too many times and skip past a document control, you can click the document control to highlight it. If you make a typing mistake, use the Undo button to reverse the error.

EXPLORE

8. Use the Tab key to select the placeholder text "[Pick the date]," click the list arrow on the document control, click the right facing arrow above the calendar as necessary until you see the calendar for December 2010, and then click 10 in the calendar. The date 12.10.2010 appears in the Date document control.

9. Use the Tab key to select the placeholder text in the "Re:" section, and then press the Delete key to delete the placeholder text. Delete the "CC:" placeholder text as well.

10. Click the box to the left of "Please Reply," and then type an uppercase **X**.

11. Click the placeholder text "[Type comments]," and then type the following message: **Here are the latest drawings, created for you by Matt Xio. After you review them, please call Matt on his cell phone to discuss the next phase of this project. Thank you very much**.

12. Save the coversheet as **Mason Fax** in the Tutorial.01\Case4 folder provided with your Data Files.

EXPLORE

13. Zoom the document out until you can see the entire page on the screen. When you are finished reviewing the document, zoom the document until it returns to its original zoom setting.

14. Review the coversheet and correct any typos. Save the coversheet again, preview it, and then print it.

15. Close the document.

Research | Internet Assignments

Go to the Web to find information you can use to create documents.

The purpose of the Internet Assignments is to challenge you to find information on the Internet that you can use to work effectively with this software. The actual assignments are updated and maintained on the Course Technology Web site. Log on to the Internet and use your Web browser to go to the Student Online Companion for New Perspectives Office 2007 at **www.course.com/np/office2007**. Then navigate to the Internet Assignments for this tutorial.

| Review | **Quick Check Answers** |

Session 1.1

1. Planning a document saves time and effort. It ensures that you include enough information to achieve the document's purpose without overwhelming or boring the reader. It also ensures that the document is organized logically and has the appearance you want.
2. View tab
3. Click the Print Layout button on the bottom-right area of the window.
4. True
5. False
6. .docx

Session 1.2

1. False
2. False
3. Right-click the word, and then click the correct spelling in the shortcut menu.
4. Paragraph spacing controls the amount of space inserted between paragraphs. Line spacing controls the amount of space inserted between lines within a paragraph.
5. Click the Office Button, point to Print, and then click Print Preview. In the Preview group on the Print Preview tab, click the Close Print Preview button to return to the previous view.
6. Mailings tab

Ending Data Files

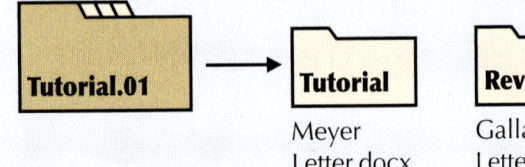

Tutorial.01 →	Tutorial	Review	Case1	Case2	Case3	Case4
	Meyer Letter.docx	Gallatin Letter.docx	Lecture Series Letter.docx	EdVest Letter.docx	Melissa.docx	Mason Fax.docx

Editing and Formatting a Document

Preparing a Handout on Choosing a Design Style

Case | Pemberly Furniture and Interiors

Natalie Lanci is the lead designer at Pemberly Furniture and Interiors, a design and furniture firm. Over the years, she has found that new customers are often intimidated by the prospect of decorating their homes. To make things easier, she has decided to create a series of handouts about interior styles and furniture. She's just finished a draft of her first handout, "Getting the Look You Want." She has marked up a printed copy of the document with notes about what she wants changed. As her assistant, it's your job to make the necessary changes and reprint the document.

In this tutorial, you will edit the handout according to Natalie's comments. You will open a draft of the document, save it with a different name, and then make the changes Natalie requested. First, you will check the document's grammar and spelling, and then you'll move text using two different methods. You will also use Word's Find and Replace feature to replace one version of the company name with another.

Next, you will change the overall look of the document by changing margins, indenting and justifying paragraphs, and copying the formatting from one paragraph to another. You'll create two bulleted lists and one numbered list. Then you'll make the title and subtitle more prominent by centering them, changing their font, and enlarging them. You'll also change the font of the company name in the body of the document, and you'll add bold to the headings to set them off from the rest of the text. You will experiment with changing the document's theme, and finally, you will preview and print the formatted document.

Starting Data Files

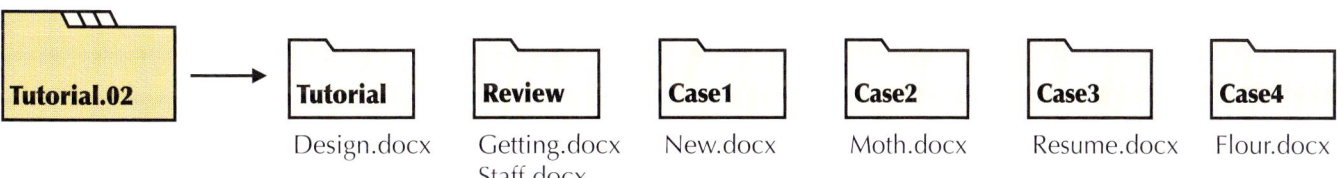

Tutorial.02 → Tutorial — Design.docx

Review — Getting.docx, Staff.docx

Case1 — New.docx

Case2 — Moth.docx

Case3 — Resume.docx

Case4 — Flour.docx

Session 2.1

Reviewing the Document

You'll begin by opening Natalie's first draft of the document, which has the filename Design.

To open the document:

▶ **1.** Start Word.

▶ **2.** On the Quick Access Toolbar, click the **Office Button** , and then click **Open**. The Open dialog box opens.

▶ **3.** Use the options in the Open dialog box to open the **Tutorial** subfolder within the **Tutorial.02** folder included with your Data Files.

▶ **4.** Click **Design** to select the file, if necessary. The name of the selected file appears in the File name text box. See Figure 2-1.

Figure 2-1 | Open dialog box

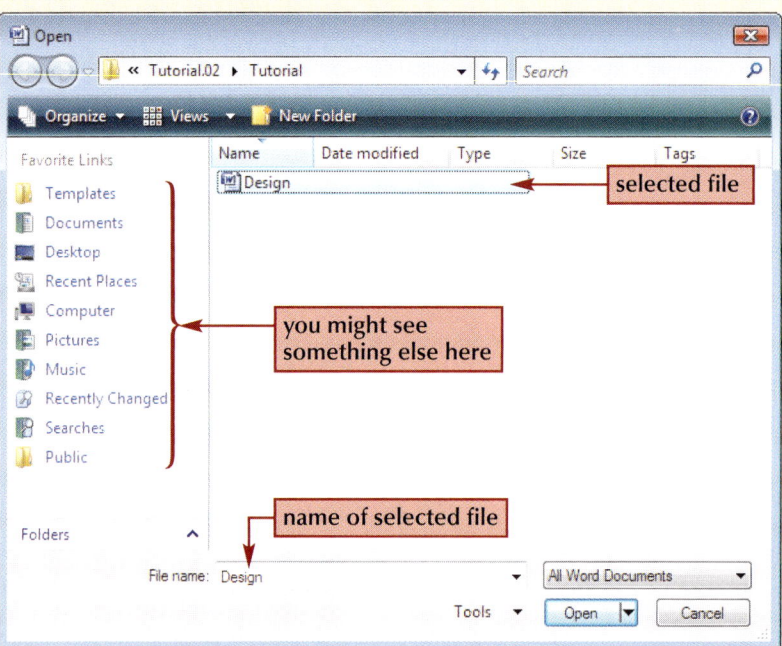

Trouble? If you see "Design.docx" in the folder, it's okay; click Design.docx and continue with Step 5. This just means that Windows is configured to display file extensions. If you can't find the file with or without the file extension, make sure you're looking in the Tutorial subfolder within the Tutorial.02 folder included with your Data Files, and check to make sure the list box next to the File name text box displays All Word Documents or All Files. If you still can't locate the file, ask your instructor or technical support person for help.

▶ **5.** Click the **Open** button. The document opens with the insertion point at the beginning.

Before revising a document for someone else, it's a good idea to familiarize yourself with its overall structure. You'll do that now, and in the process make sure the document is displayed in a way that makes editing it as easy as possible.

To review the document:

▶ **1.** Verify that the document is displayed in Print Layout view, and if necessary, in the Paragraph group, click the **Show/Hide ¶** button ¶ to display nonprinting characters. If the rulers are not visible, switch to the **View** tab, and then click the **Ruler** check box to display the rulers.

▶ **2.** Take a moment to read the document. It consists of a series of headings, with explanatory text below each heading. Right now, the headings (such as "Ask Yourself Some Questions" and "Pick a Style") are hard to spot because they don't look any different from the surrounding text. You'll change that when you format the document. The document also includes some lists; you will format these later in this tutorial to make them easier to read. Natalie used the default font size, 11-point, and the default font, Calibri (Body), for the entire document. She relied on Word's default paragraph spacing to provide a visual separation between paragraphs.

▶ **3.** Scroll down until you can see the line "Stay True to Your Style." The white space after this line is the page's bottom margin. The blue space below the margin indicates a page break. This tells you that the line "Stay True to Your Style" appears on the last line of the first page. Word starts a new page whenever your text fills up a page. The Page box in the lower-left corner of the document window tells you the total number of pages in the document and which page currently contains the insertion point.

Figure 2-2 shows the page break, along with other important elements of the document. Note that in Figure 2-2 the Word window has been zoomed to 80%; this is to make it easy to see several parts of the document at once. At this point, your Zoom setting is probably 100%. To make sure you can see the entire width of the page, you'll select Page width in the Zoom dialog box in the next step.

Document with two pages ◀ **Figure 2-2**

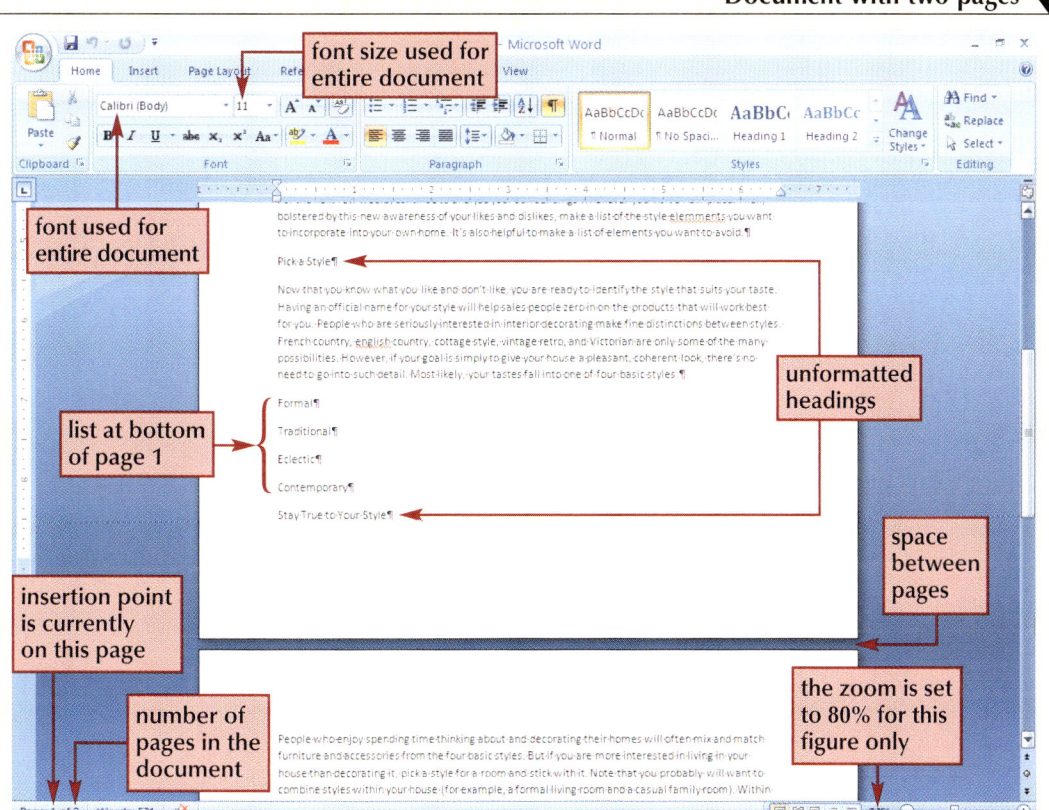

Tip

To hide the blue space between pages, double-click the blue space. To redisplay the blue space, double-click the black line.

> **4.** In the bottom-right corner of the Word window, click the current Zoom setting to open the Zoom dialog box, click **Page width**, and then click the **OK** button to close the Zoom dialog box. Word displays the full width of the document.

Now that you are familiar with Natalie's document, you can turn your attention to the edits she has requested. Natalie's editing marks and notes on the first draft are shown in Figure 2-3.

Figure 2-3 ▶ **Draft of handout with Natalie's edits (page 1)**

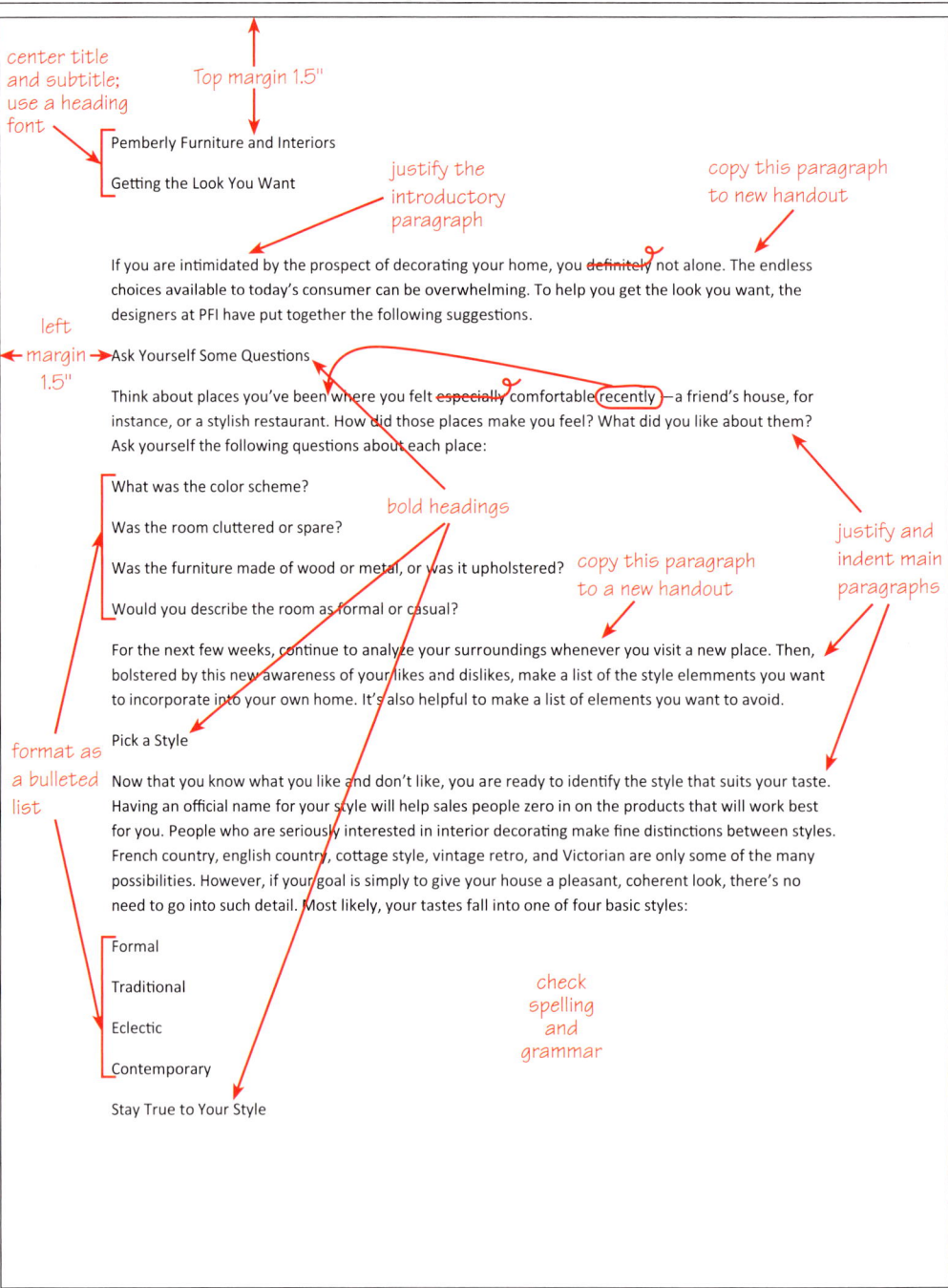

Draft of handout with Natalie's edits (page 2) **Figure 2-3 (cont.)**

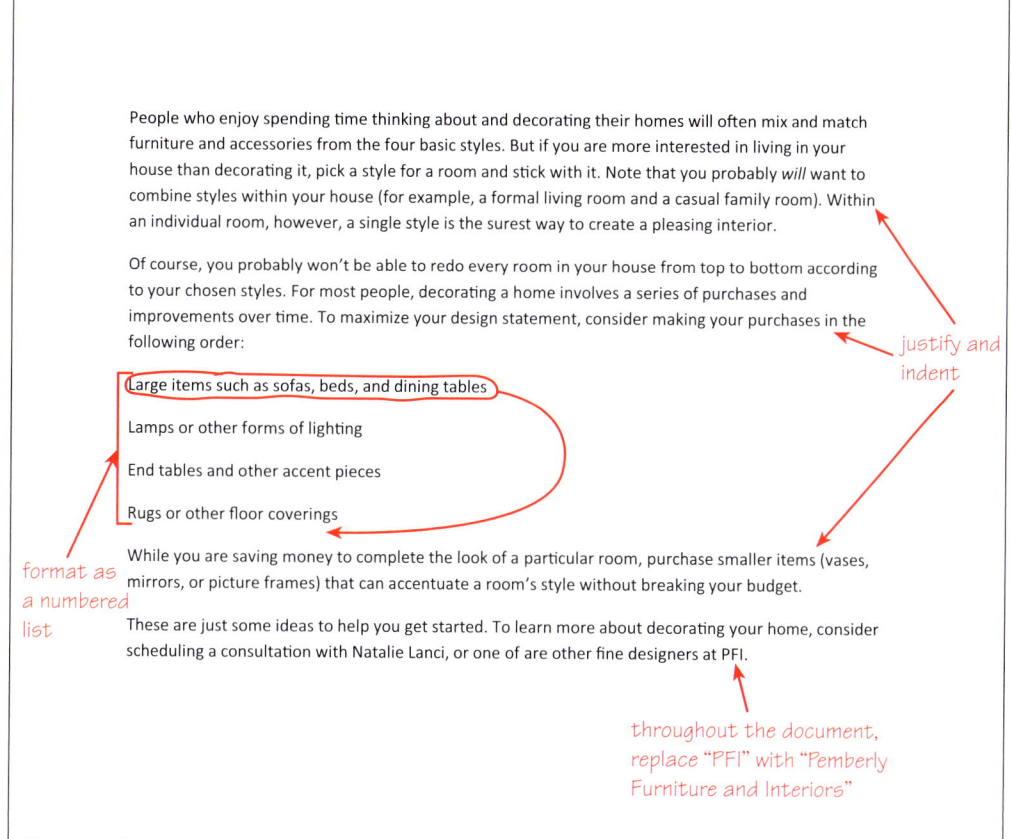

People who enjoy spending time thinking about and decorating their homes will often mix and match furniture and accessories from the four basic styles. But if you are more interested in living in your house than decorating it, pick a style for a room and stick with it. Note that you probably *will* want to combine styles within your house (for example, a formal living room and a casual family room). Within an individual room, however, a single style is the surest way to create a pleasing interior.

Of course, you probably won't be able to redo every room in your house from top to bottom according to your chosen styles. For most people, decorating a home involves a series of purchases and improvements over time. To maximize your design statement, consider making your purchases in the following order:

justify and indent

Large items such as sofas, beds, and dining tables

Lamps or other forms of lighting

End tables and other accent pieces

Rugs or other floor coverings

format as a numbered list

While you are saving money to complete the look of a particular room, purchase smaller items (vases, mirrors, or picture frames) that can accentuate a room's style without breaking your budget.

These are just some ideas to help you get started. To learn more about decorating your home, consider scheduling a consultation with Natalie Lanci, or one of are other fine designers at PFI.

throughout the document, replace "PFI" with "Pemberly Furniture and Interiors"

Before you begin editing the document, you should save it with a new name. Saving the document with a different filename creates a copy of the file and leaves the original file unchanged in case you want to work through the tutorial again.

To save the document with a new name:

1. Click the **Office Button** , and then click **Save As**. The Save As dialog box opens with the current filename highlighted in the File name text box. You could type an entirely new filename, or you could edit the current one.

2. Click to the right of the current filename to place the insertion point after the "n" in "Design."

3. Press the **spacebar**, and then type **Handout** so that the filename is "Design Handout."

4. Verify that the **Tutorial** folder is selected as the location for saving the file.

5. Click the **Save** button. The document is saved with the new filename "Design Handout" in the Tutorial folder, and the original Design file closes, remaining unchanged.

Now you're ready to begin working with the document. First, you will check it for spelling and grammatical errors.

Using the Spelling and Grammar Checker

As you type a document, Word marks possible spelling errors with a red wavy underline. When you're working on a document that someone else typed, it's a good idea to start by using the **Spelling and Grammar Checker**, a feature that checks a document word by word for a variety of errors.

Reference Window | **Checking a Document for Spelling and Grammar Errors**

- Move the insertion point to the beginning of the document, click the Review tab on the Ribbon, and then, in the Proofing group, click the Spelling & Grammar button.
- In the Spelling and Grammar dialog box, review any items highlighted in color. Possible grammatical errors appear in green; possible spelling errors appear in red. Review the suggested corrections in the Suggestions list box.
- To accept a suggested correction, click on it in the Suggestions list box, click the Change button to make the correction, and then continue searching the document for errors.
- To skip the current instance of the highlighted text and continue searching the document for errors, click the Ignore Once button.
- Click the Ignore All button to skip all instances of the highlighted text and continue searching the document for errors. Click the Ignore Rule button to skip all instances of a highlighted grammatical error.
- To type your correction directly in the document, click outside the Spelling and Grammar dialog box, make the correction, and then click the Resume button in the Spelling and Grammar dialog box.
- To add an unrecognized word to the dictionary, click the Add to Dictionary button.
- When you see a dialog box informing you that the spelling and grammar check is complete, click the OK button.

You'll see how the Spelling and Grammar Checker works as you check the Design Handout document for mistakes.

To check the Design Handout document for spelling and grammatical errors:

▶ **1.** Press the **Ctrl+Home** keys to verify that the insertion point is located at the beginning of the document, to the left of the "P" in "Pemberly Furniture and Interiors."

▶ **2.** Click the **Review** tab on the Ribbon, and then, in the Proofing group, click the **Spelling & Grammar** button. The Spelling and Grammar: English (United States) dialog box opens with the word "Pemberly" displayed in red, indicating a possible spelling error. In the document, "Pemberly" is highlighted in blue. Typically, the Suggestions box would contain one or more possible corrections for you to choose from, but in this case, Word doesn't recognize the name of Natalie's company because it is not included in the main dictionary. This isn't really an error. See Figure 2-4.

Spelling and Grammar dialog box ◀ **Figure 2-4**

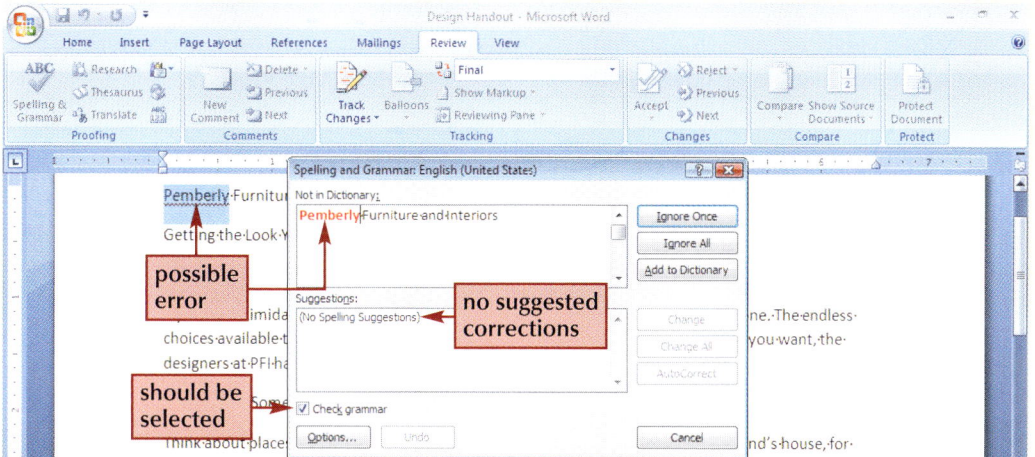

▶ **3.** Click the **Ignore All** button. This tells Word to ignore all instances of "Pemberly" throughout the document. Now the first sentence of the document appears in green in the dialog box and in a blue highlight in the document. The Suggestions box tells you that the highlighted text is a sentence fragment. The last part of the sentence should read "you definitely are not alone," but the word "are" is missing. You can fix this problem by clicking outside the Spelling and Grammar dialog box and typing the change directly in the document.

▶ **4.** Click the blue highlighted sentence outside the Spelling and Grammar dialog box. The blue highlight disappears, and the insertion point appears at the end of the sentence.

 Trouble? If you can't see the entire highlighted sentence, move the mouse pointer over the title bar of the Spelling and Grammar dialog box, press and hold the left mouse button, drag the mouse pointer until the dialog box is out of the way, and then release the mouse button.

▶ **5.** Click to the left of the "n" in "not," type **are**, and then press the **spacebar**. Verify that the last part of the sentence now reads "you definitely are not alone." (You might notice that the word "definitely" makes the sentence awkward; you will delete this word in the next section.)

 You've edited the document to correct the error. Now you need to return to the Spelling and Grammar dialog box to continue checking the document.

To continue checking the document:

▶ **1.** Click the **Resume** button in the Spelling and Grammar dialog box to continue checking the rest of the document. The misspelled word "elemments" is highlighted in the Spelling and Grammar dialog box and in the document. The correct spelling, "elements," appears in the Suggestions box.

▶ **2.** Verify that "elements" is highlighted in the Suggestions box, and then click the **Change** button. "Elements" is inserted into the document, and the word "english" is highlighted in the document. This should be "English," with an uppercase "E," instead.

▶ **3.** Verify that "English" is selected in the Suggestions box, and then click the **Change** button. The word "English" is inserted in the document. A message box opens indicating that the spelling and grammar check is complete.

▶ **4.** Click the **OK** button. The Spelling and Grammar dialog box closes. You return to the Design Handout document.

▶ **5.** Click the **Home** tab to display the options related to editing a document again. You'll need to use these options as you continue the tutorial.

Although the Spelling and Grammar Checker is a useful tool, there is no substitute for careful proofreading. Always take the time to read through your document to check for errors the Spelling and Grammar Checker might have missed. Keep in mind that the Spelling and Grammar checker cannot pinpoint phrases that are inaccurate. You'll have to find those yourself. To produce a professional document, you must read it carefully several times. It's a good idea to ask a coworker to read your documents, too.

To proofread the Design Handout document:

▶ **1.** Scroll to the beginning of the document and proofread the document. In the last sentence of the document, notice that the word "are" is used instead of the word "our." You will correct this error in the next section.

▶ **2.** Finish proofreading the Design Handout document, and then click the **Save** button 🖫 on the Quick Access Toolbar to save the changes you've made so far.

Your next job is to delete some text (as shown earlier in Figure 2-3).

Deleting Text

You already have experience using the Backspace and Delete keys to delete a few characters. To delete an entire word or multiple words, it's faster to select the text first. Then you can either replace it with something else by typing over it, or you can delete it by pressing the Delete key. Right now, you need to change the word "are" to "our."

To replace "are" with "our":

▶ **1.** Press the **Ctrl+End** keys. The insertion point moves to the end of the document.

▶ **2.** In the last line of the document, double-click the word **are** (in the phrase "are other fine designers...").

▶ **3.** Type **our**. The selected word is replaced with the correction. The phrase now correctly reads: "...our other fine designers...."

Next, Natalie wants you to delete the word "definitely" in the introductory paragraph at the beginning of the document and the word "especially" in the paragraph below the heading "Ask Yourself Some Questions." You can do this quickly by selecting multiple items and then pressing the Delete key.

To select and delete multiple items:

▶ **1.** Press the **Ctrl+Home** keys. The insertion point is now located at the beginning of the document.

▶ **2.** In the introductory paragraph, which begins "If you are intimidated by...," double-click the word **definitely**. The word and the space following it are selected.

▶ **3.** Press and hold the **Ctrl** key, double-click the word **especially** in the paragraph below the heading "Ask Yourself Some Questions," and then release the **Ctrl** key. At this point the words "definitely" and "especially" should be selected. See Figure 2-5.

Text to be deleted ◀ Figure 2-5

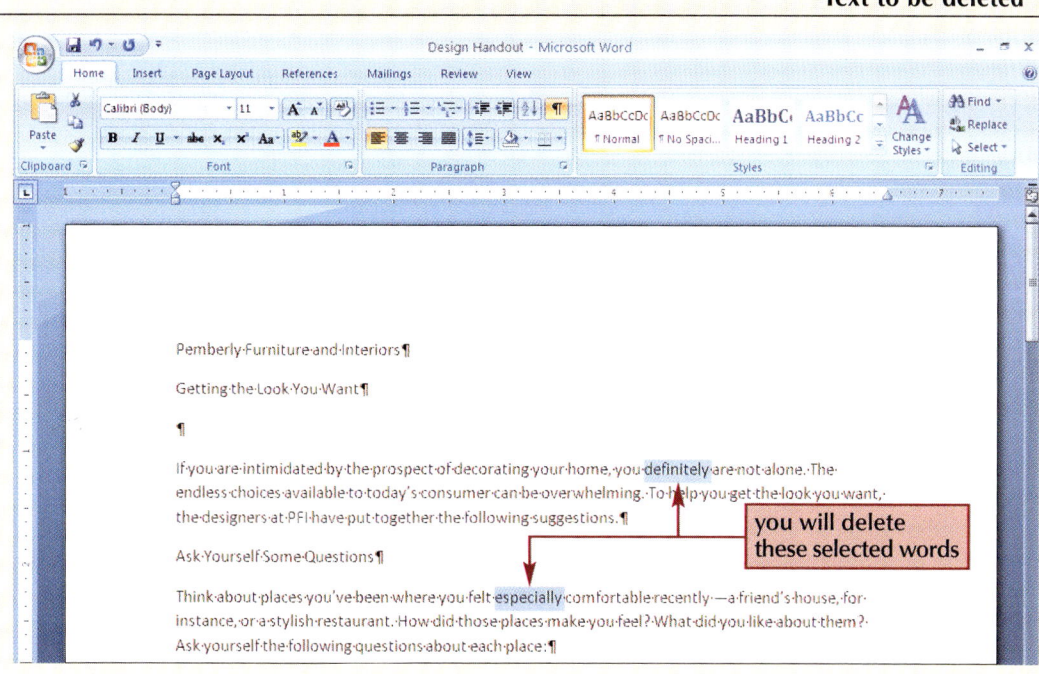

Trouble? If you don't get Step 3 right the first time, click anywhere in the document, and then repeat Steps 2 and 3.

▶ **4.** Press the **Delete** key. The selected items are deleted, and the words around them move in to fill the space. See Figure 2-6.

Paragraphs after deleting text ◀ Figure 2-6

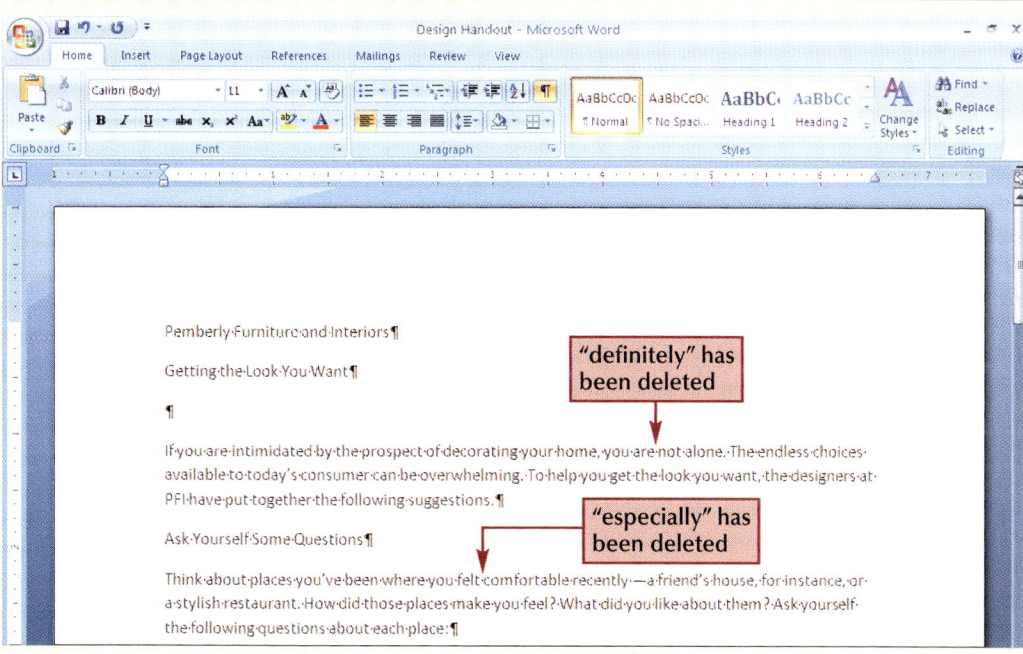

> **Trouble?** If you deleted the wrong text, click the Undo button on the Quick Access Toolbar to reverse your mistake, and then begin again with Step 2.

▶ **5.** Scroll down to display the last line of the document, drag the mouse pointer to select "Natalie Lanci," press the **Delete** key, press the **spacebar** if necessary, and then type your first and last name. This change will make it easier for you to find your document if you print it on a network printer used by other students.

▶ **6.** Save the document.

You have edited the document by replacing "are" with "our" and by removing the text that Natalie marked for deletion. Now you are ready to make the rest of the edits she suggested.

Moving Text in a Document

One of the most useful features of a word-processing program is the ability to move text. For example, Natalie wants to reorder the four points in the section "Stay True to Your Style" on page 2. You could reorder the list by deleting an item and then retyping it at a new location, but it's easier to select and then move the text. Word provides several ways to move text: drag and drop, cut and paste, and copy and paste.

Dragging and Dropping Text

To move text with **drag and drop**, you select the text you want to move, press and hold down the mouse button while you drag the selected text to a new location, and then release the mouse button.

Reference Window | **Dragging and Dropping Text**

- Select the text you want to move.
- Press and hold down the mouse button until the drag-and-drop pointer appears, and then drag the selected text to its new location.
- Use the dotted insertion point as a guide to determine exactly where the text should be inserted.
- Release the mouse button to "drop" the text at the insertion point.

Natalie wants you to change the order of the items in the list on page 2 of the document. You'll use the drag-and-drop method to reorder these items. Because you need to select text before you can move it, you'll get practice using the selection bar (the white space in the left margin) to highlight a line of text as you do these steps.

To move text using drag and drop:

▶ **1.** Scroll up slightly until you see the list of suggested purchases, which begins "Large items such as sofas, beds, and dining tables." Natalie wants you to move the first item to the bottom of the list.

2. Move the pointer to the selection bar to the left of the line "Large items such as sofas, beds, and dining tables." The pointer changes to a right-facing arrow ⌐.

3. Click in the selection bar to the left of the line "Large items such as sofas, beds, and dining tables." The line is selected. Notice that the paragraph mark at the end of the line is also selected. See Figure 2-7.

Selected text to drag and drop ◄ **Figure 2-7**

to·your·chosen·styles.·For·most·people,·decorating·a·home·involves·a·series·of·purchases·and·improvements·over·time.·To·maximize·your·design·statement,·consider·making·your·purchases·in·the·following·order:¶

pointer in selection bar

Large·items·such·as·sofas,·beds,·and·dining·tables¶ — **selected text to be moved**

Lamps·or·other·forms·of·lighting¶

End·tables·and·other·accent·pieces¶ — **new location for selected text**

Rugs·or·other·floor·coverings¶

While·you·are·saving·money·to·complete·the·look·of·a·particular·room,·purchase·smaller·items·(vases,·mirrors,·or·picture·frames)·that·can·accentuate·a·room's·style·without·breaking·your·budget.·¶

These·are·just·some·ideas·to·help·you·get·started.·To·learn·more·about·decorating·your·home,·consider·scheduling·a·consultation·with·Natalie·Lanci,·or·one·of·our·other·fine·designers·at·PFI.¶

you should have replaced Natalie's name with yours

4. Position the pointer over the selected text. The pointer changes from a right-facing arrow ⌐ to a left-facing arrow ⌐.

5. Press and hold down the mouse button until the drag-and-drop pointer ⌐ appears. Note that a dotted insertion point appears within the selected text. (You may have to move the mouse pointer slightly left or right to see the drag-and-drop pointer or the dotted insertion point.)

6. Without releasing the mouse button, drag the selected text down until the dotted insertion point is positioned to the left of the first paragraph below the list (to the left of the "W" in "While you are saving..."). Make sure you use the dotted insertion point, rather than the mouse pointer, to guide the text to its new location. The dotted insertion point indicates exactly where the text will appear when you release the mouse button. See Figure 2-8.

Figure 2-8 ▸ **Moving text with drag-and-drop pointer**

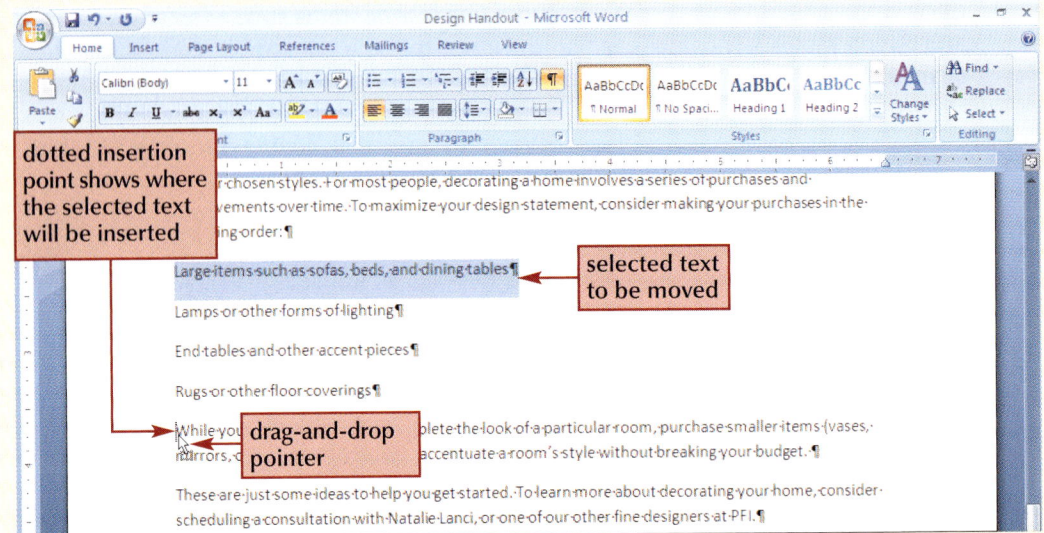

▸ **7.** Release the mouse button. The selected text moves to its new location at the end of the list, as shown in Figure 2-9. Near the newly inserted text you might see the Paste Options button, which gives you access to more advanced options related to pasting text. You don't need to use the Paste Options button right now, so you can ignore it. It will disappear when you start performing another task.

Figure 2-9 ▸ **Text in new location**

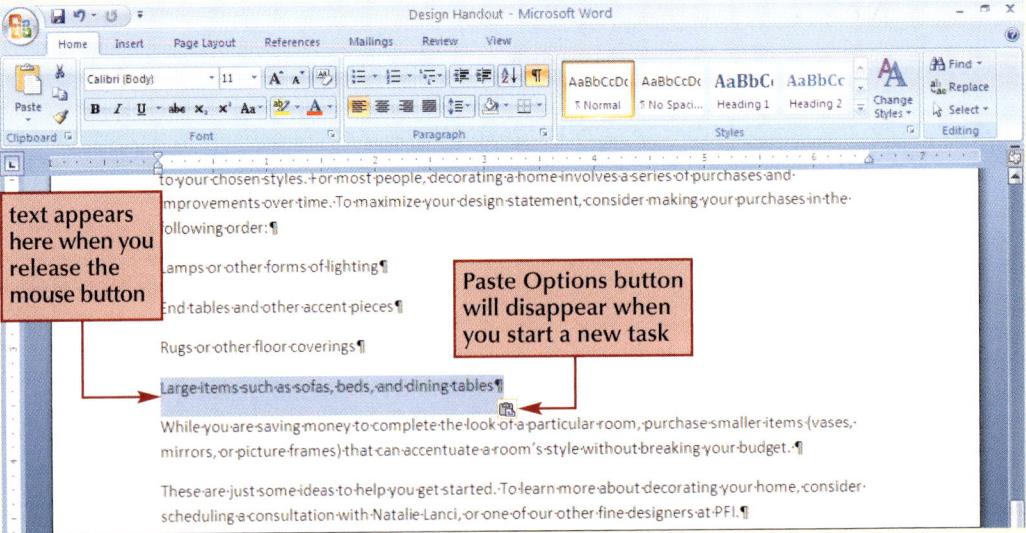

Trouble? If the selected text moves to the wrong location, click the Undo button on the Quick Access Toolbar, and then repeat Steps 2 through 7. Remember to hold down the mouse button until the dotted insertion point appears to the left of the paragraph just below the list.

▸ **8.** Deselect the highlighted text by clicking anywhere in the document, and then save the document.

Dragging and dropping works well if you're moving text a short distance in a document. For moving text longer distances, another method, called cut and paste, works better. You can also use cut and paste to move text short distances, if you find that you prefer it over drag and drop.

Cutting or Copying and Pasting Text

The key to cutting and pasting is the **Clipboard**, a temporary storage area on your computer that holds text or graphics until you need them. To **cut** means to remove something from a document and place it on the Clipboard. Once you've cut something, you can paste it somewhere else. To **paste** means to place a copy of whatever is on the Clipboard into the document; it gets pasted at the insertion point.

To **cut and paste**, you select the text you want to cut (or remove) from the document, click the Cut button, and then use the Paste button to paste (or insert) it into the document in a new location. If you don't want to remove the text from its original location, you can copy it (rather than cutting it), and then paste the copy in a new location. To **copy** means to copy text (or other material, such as pictures) to the Clipboard, leaving the material in its original location.

Note that when you paste an item from the Clipboard into a document, the item also remains on the Clipboard so you can paste it again somewhere else if you want.

Cutting (or Copying) and Pasting Text	Reference Window

- Select the text or graphics you want to cut or copy.
- To remove the text or graphics, click the Cut button in the Clipboard group on the Home tab, or to copy, click the Copy button in the Clipboard group on the Home tab.
- Move the insertion point to the target location in the document.
- Click the Paste button in the Clipboard group on the Home tab.

If you need to keep track of multiple pieces of cut or copied text, it's helpful to open the **Clipboard task pane**, a special part of the Word window that displays the contents of the Clipboard. You open the Clipboard task pane by clicking the Clipboard button on the Home tab. When the Clipboard task pane is not displayed, the Clipboard can hold only one item at a time. (Each newly copied item replaces the current contents of the Clipboard.) However, when the Clipboard task pane is displayed, the Clipboard can store up to 24 items. The last item cut or copied to the Clipboard is the first item listed in the Clipboard task pane.

As indicated in Figure 2-3, Natalie suggested moving the word "recently" (in the paragraph under the heading "Ask Yourself Some Questions") to a new location. You'll use cut and paste to move this word.

To move text using cut and paste:

▶ **1.** Scroll up until you can see the paragraph below the heading "Ask Yourself Some Questions" on page 1.

▶ **2.** Double-click the word **recently**. As you can see in Figure 2-10, you need to move this word to after the phrase "places you've been."

Figure 2-10 **Text to move using cut and paste**

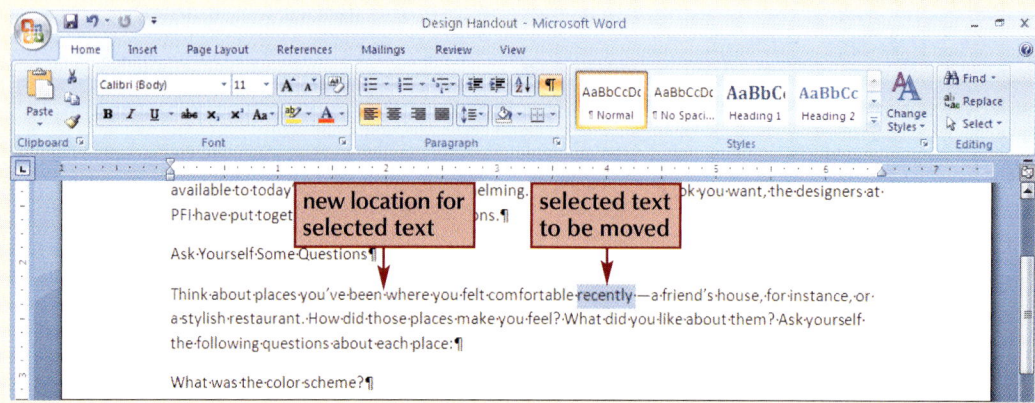

▶ **3.** In the Clipboard group on the Home tab, click the **Cut** button 📎 . The selected text is removed from the document.

Trouble? If the Clipboard task pane opens, your computer is set up to have it open by default when you click the Cut or Copy buttons. Click its Close button for now. You'll have a chance to use the Clipboard task pane shortly.

Trouble? If you don't see the Cut button in the Clipboard group, you may have forgotten to switch back to the Home tab earlier. Click the Home tab on the Ribbon and repeat Step 3.

▶ **4.** In the same line, click to the left of the "w" in "where." The insertion point is now located between the "w" and the blank space after the word "been."

▶ **5.** In the Clipboard group, click the **Paste** button. The word "recently" appears in its new location. Note that Word also included a space after the word "recently," so that the sentence reads "...places you've been recently where you felt...." See Figure 2-11.

Trouble? If a menu opens below the Paste button, you clicked the Paste button arrow instead of the Paste button. Press the Esc key to close the menu, and then begin again with Step 5, taking care not to click the arrow below the Paste button.

Figure 2-11 **The word "recently" pasted in new location**

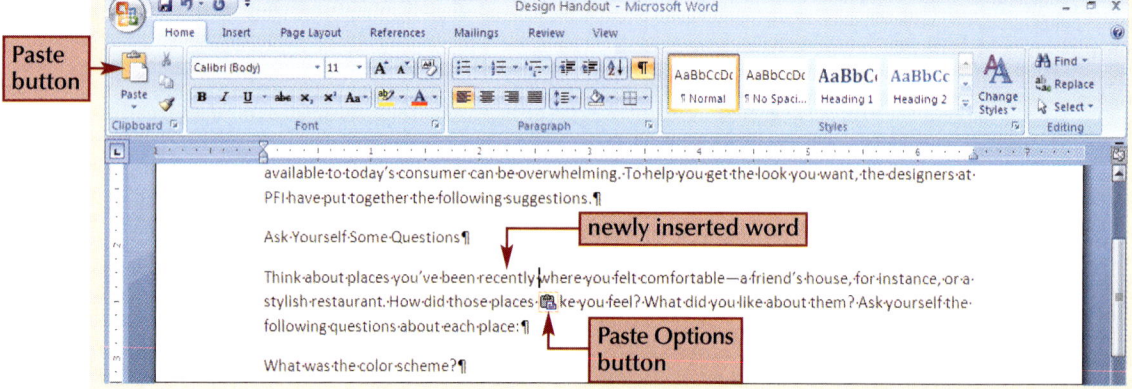

Natalie mentions that she'll be using two paragraphs from the Design Handout document as the basis for a new handout entitled "Formal Designs." She asks you to copy that information and paste it in a new document. You can do this using copy and paste. In the process, you'll have a chance to use the Clipboard task pane.

To copy and paste text into a new document:

▶ **1.** In the Clipboard group, click the **Dialog Box Launcher**. The Clipboard task pane opens on the left side of the document window. It contains the word "recently," which you copied to the Clipboard in the last set of steps. The document zooms out so that you can still see the full width of the page, even though the Clipboard task pane is open. See Figure 2-12. To minimize the clutter on the Clipboard, you will delete its current contents in the next step.

Clipboard task pane ◀ **Figure 2-12**

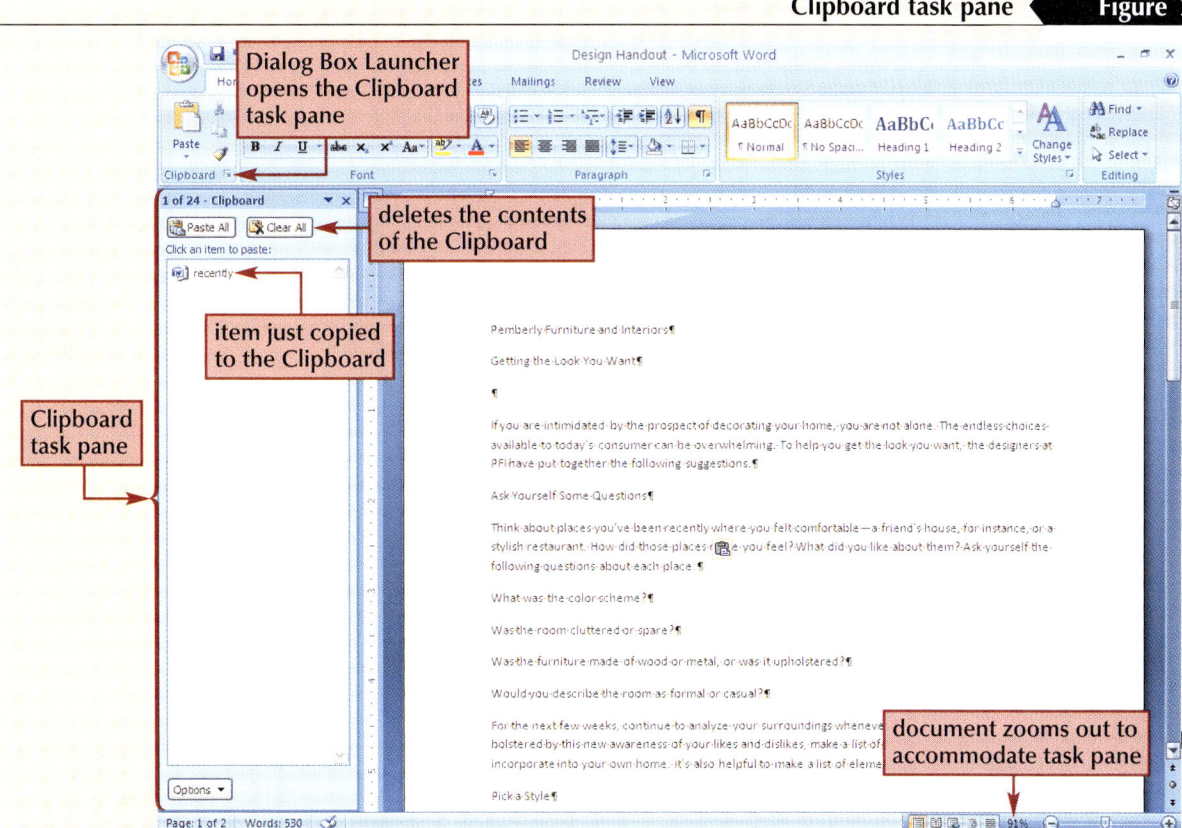

▶ **2.** Click the **Clear All** button near the top of the task pane. The current contents of the Clipboard are deleted, and you see the following message on the Clipboard task pane: "Clipboard empty. Copy or cut to collect items."

▶ **3.** Move the mouse pointer to the selection bar and double-click in the margin next to the paragraph that begins "If you are intimidated by the prospect...." The entire paragraph is selected.

▶ **4.** In the Clipboard group, click the **Copy** button 🔲. The first part of the paragraph appears in the Clipboard task pane, but a copy of all the text you selected—the whole paragraph—is now stored on the Clipboard.

▶ **5.** If necessary, scroll down until you can see the paragraph below the list of questions, which begins "For the next few weeks, continue...."

▶ **6.** Select the paragraph that begins "For the next few weeks, continue...."

▶ **7.** Click the **Copy** button. The first part of the paragraph appears in the Clipboard task pane, as shown in Figure 2-13.

Tip

To have the Clipboard task pane open each time you cut or copy an item, click Options at the bottom of the Clipboard task pane, and then select Show Office Clipboard Automatically.

Figure 2-13 | **Items in the Clipboard task pane**

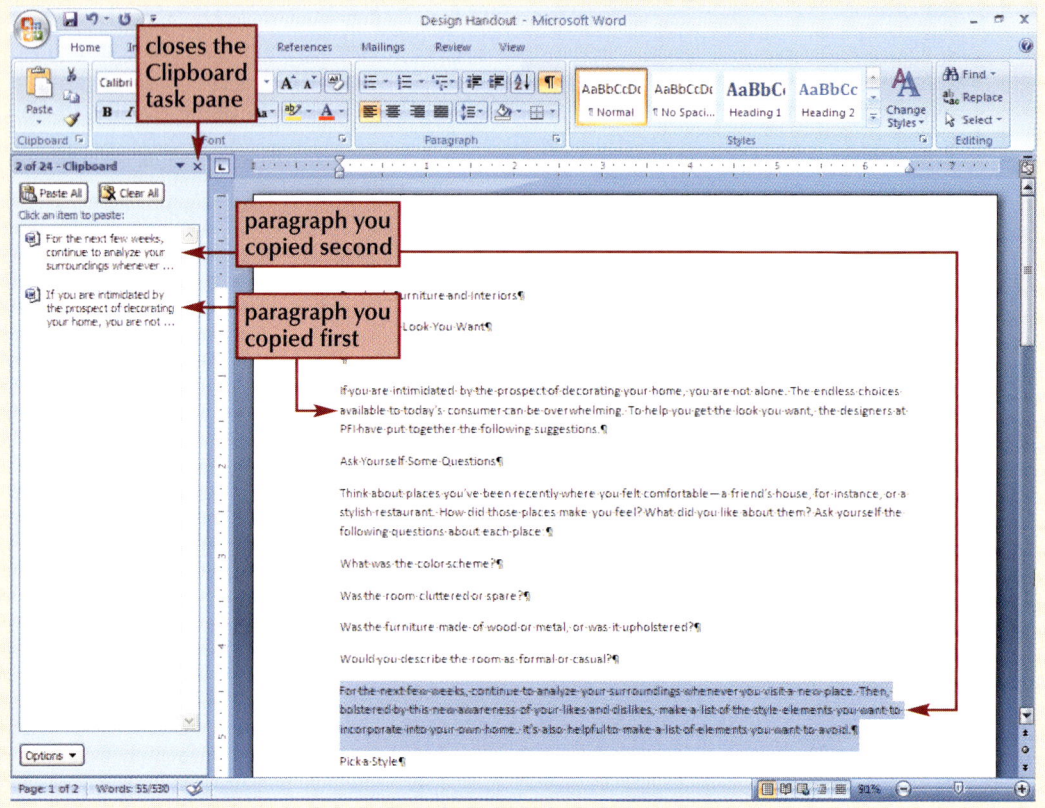

Now you can use the Clipboard task pane to insert the copied text into a new document. You'll start by opening a new, blank document.

To insert the copied text into the new document:

▶ 1. Click the **Office Button** 🖫, click **New**, verify that **Blank document** is selected, and then click the **Create** button. A new, blank document opens.

▶ 2. If the Clipboard task pane is not open, click the **Dialog Box Launcher** in the Clipboard group to open it.

▶ 3. In the Clipboard task pane, click the item that begins "**For the next few weeks**...." The text is inserted in the document.

▶ 4. Click the item that begins "**If you are intimidated by**...." The text is inserted as the second paragraph in the document.

▶ 5. Save the document as **Formal Designs** in the Tutorial.02\Tutorial folder.

▶ 6. Close the Formal Designs document. Natalie will be using this document later. You return to the Design Handout document, where the Clipboard task pane is still open. You are finished using the Clipboard task pane. In the next step you will clear the Clipboard so that you can start with an empty Clipboard when you begin work on the Review Assignments and Case Problems at the end of this tutorial.

7. Click the **Clear All** button on the Clipboard task pane. The copied items are removed from the Clipboard.

8. Click the **Close** button ☒ on the Clipboard task pane. The Clipboard task pane closes.

9. Click anywhere in the document to deselect the highlighted paragraph, and then save the document.

Finding and Replacing Text

When you're working with a longer document, the quickest and easiest way to locate a particular character, word, or phrase is to use the **Find and Replace dialog box**. This dialog box contains three tabs:

- Find, for finding a word or phrase in a document (for example, you need to know where you referred to "textiles" in a document on interior design)
- Replace, for finding a word or phrase in a document and replacing it with something else (for example, you want to replace "formal design" with "formal style" throughout a document)
- Go To, for moving the cursor directly to a specific part of a document (for example, you want to go directly to page 29)

To open the Find and Replace dialog box, click the Find button or the Replace button (in the Editing group on the Home tab), depending on what you want to do. For example, to find a word or phrase, click the Find button, type the text you want to find in the Find what text box, and then click the Find Next button. The text you type in the Find what text box is known as the **search text**. After you click the Find Next button, Word finds and highlights the first instance of the search text. You continue clicking Find Next to find more occurrences of the search text in your document.

To replace text with something else, click the Replace button, and then type your search text in the Find what text box and the text you want to substitute in the Replace with text box. As with the Find feature, you click the Find Next button to find the next occurrence of the search text; Word stops and highlights each occurrence, allowing you to determine whether or not to substitute the replacement text. If you want to substitute the highlighted occurrence, click the Replace button. If you want to substitute every occurrence of the search text with the replacement text, without locating and reviewing each occurrence, you can click the Replace All button.

Finding and Replacing the Right Words | InSight

When using the Replace All button with single words, keep in mind that the search text might be found within other words. To prevent Word from making incorrect substitutions in such cases, it's a good idea to select the Find whole words only check box. (If you don't see this check box, click the More button to display additional options.) For example, suppose you want to replace the word "figure" with "illustration." Unless you select the Find whole words only check box, Word replaces "figure" in "configure" with "illustration" so the word becomes "conillustration."

Reference Window | **Finding and Replacing Text**

- Click either the Find button or the Replace button on the Home tab.
- Click the More button to expand the dialog box to display additional options, including the Find whole words only option. If you see the Less button, the additional options are already displayed.
- In the Search list box, select Down if you want to search from the insertion point to the end of the document, select Up if you want to search from the insertion point to the beginning of the document, or select All to search the entire document.
- Type the characters you want to find in the Find what text box.
- If you are replacing text, type the replacement text in the Replace with text box.
- Click the Find whole words only check box to search for complete words.
- Click the Match case check box to insert the replacement text with the same case (upper or lower) as in the Replace with text box. For example, if the Replace with text box contained the words "Pemberly Interiors," this would ensure that Word inserted the text with a capital (uppercase) "P" and a capital (uppercase) "I."
- Click the Find Next button.
- Click the Replace button to substitute the found text with the replacement text and find the next occurrence.
- Click the Replace All button to substitute all occurrences of the found text with the replacement text, without reviewing each occurence.

Throughout the document, Natalie wants to replace the initials "PFI" with the full company name, "Pemberly Furniture and Interiors." You'll use the Replace feature to make this change quickly and easily.

To replace "PFI" with "Pemberly Furniture and Interiors":

▶ 1. Press the **Ctrl+Home** keys to move the insertion point to the beginning of the document.

▶ 2. In the Editing group on the Home tab, click the **Replace** button. The Find and Replace dialog box opens, with the Replace tab displayed.

▶ 3. If you see a **More** button in the lower-left corner of the dialog box, click it to display the additional search options. (If you see a Less button, the additional options are already displayed.) Verify that **All** is selected in the Search list box, so Word will search the entire document.

▶ 4. Click the **Find what** text box if necessary, type **PFI**, press the **Tab** key, and then, in the Replace with text box, type **Pemberly Furniture and Interiors**.

   Trouble? If you already see the text "PFI" and "Pemberly Furniture and Interiors" in your Find and Replace dialog box, someone has recently performed these steps on your computer without closing Word afterward. Skip Step 4 and continue with Step 5.

▶ 5. Click the **Match case** check box to insert a check. This ensures that Word will search only for "PFI" and not "pfi" in the document.

▶ 6. Click the **Find whole words only** check box to insert a check. Your Find and Replace dialog box should look like Figure 2-14.

Find and Replace dialog box ◄ **Figure 2-14**

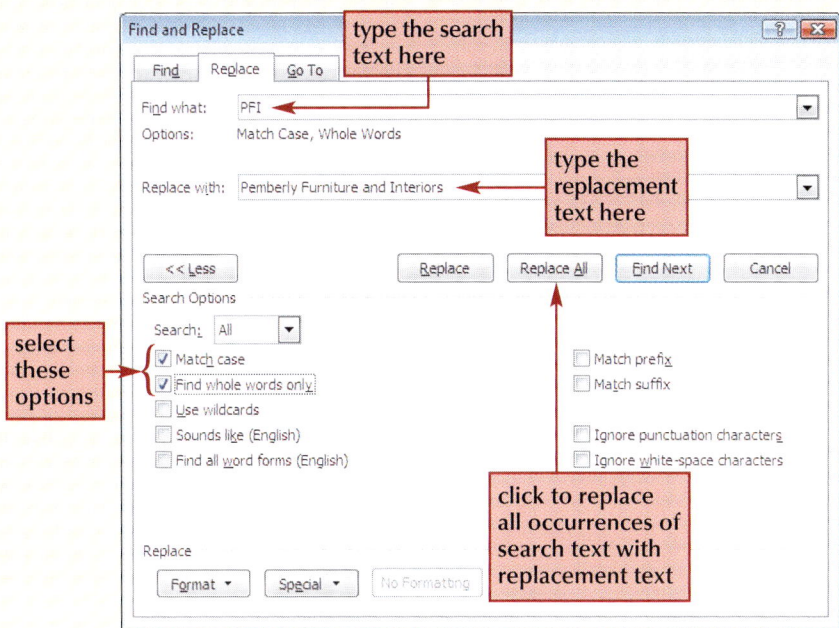

▶ **7.** Click the **Replace All** button to replace all occurrences of the search text with the replacement text. When Word finishes making the replacements, you see a message box telling you that two replacements were made.

▶ **8.** Click the **OK** button to close the message box, and then click the **Close** button in the Find and Replace dialog box to return to the document. The full company name has been inserted near the beginning of the document, as shown in Figure 2-15. If you scroll down to the end of the document, you'll see that it was also inserted in the last sentence.

Document with "Pemberly Furniture and Interiors" inserted ◄ **Figure 2-15**

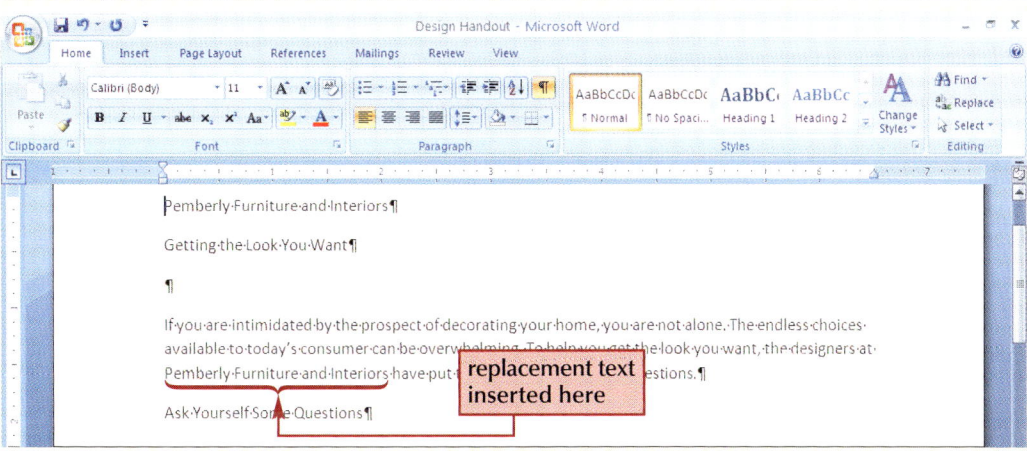

▶ **9.** Save the document.

InSight | **Searching for Formatting**

You can search for formatting, such as bold or italics, using the Find and Replace dialog box in the same way that you can find text. For example, you might want to check a document to see where you used bold. Or you might need to find where you used a certain font, font size, or style. This is especially useful in long documents where scrolling to look for something would take a long time. To search for formatting, click the Format button at the bottom of the Find and Replace dialog box, click the category of formatting that you want to look for (such as Font, Paragraph, Style, and so on), and then select the formatting you want to find. You can also use the Replace tab to replace formatting in the same way you use it to replace text. To replace formatting, click the Replace tab, and then repeat the previous steps to specify the formatting that should replace the other formatting. Whether you are replacing formatting or not, note that you can look for formatting that occurs only on specific text, or you can look for formatting that occurs anywhere in a document. If you're looking for formatting on certain text (such as all instances of "Contemporary Furniture" that are bold), enter the text in the Find what text box and then specify the formatting you're looking for. To find formatting on any text in a document, leave the Find what text box empty and then specify the formatting.

You have completed the content changes Natalie requested. In the next session, you will make changes that affect the document's appearance.

Review | **Session 2.1 Quick Check**

1. True or False: You should move the insertion point to the beginning of the document before starting the Spelling and Grammar checker.
2. True or False: You need to select text before you can move it.
3. Explain how to drag and drop text.
4. Explain how to cut and paste text.
5. Suppose you want to find a word in a document. How do you open the Find and Replace dialog box?
6. How can you ensure that Word will insert "ZIP code" instead of "zip code" when you use the Find and Replace dialog box?

Session 2.2

Changing Margins

When you **format** a document, you make changes that affect the way the document looks. You'll start formatting Natalie's handout by adjusting the document's margins. By default, the margins for a Word document are one inch on the top, bottom, and sides.

When adjusting a document's margins, you'll find that the rulers are essential. They show you the current margin settings, as well as the amount that individual paragraphs are indented from the margin. On the horizontal ruler, the right edge of the left margin serves as the zero point, with the numbers to the right measuring the distance to the right edge of the page, and the numbers on the left measuring the distance to the left edge of the page. This allows you to see the exact width of the left margin at a glance. See Figure 2-16. The measurements on the vertical ruler work similarly, with the bottom edge of the top margin serving as the zero point from which all other vertical distances are measured.

Using the horizontal ruler to view margins | **Figure 2-16**

Tip

The Zoom setting affects how much of the margin you can see on the screen. If you zoom in to make the text larger and easier to read, you see less of the margin. If you zoom out, you see more of the margin.

As you'll see in the upcoming steps, you can change the page margins in the Page Setup dialog box. You can also quickly adjust a document's margins in Print Layout view by clicking an option in the Margins menu. You'll have a chance to practice these techniques in the Case Problems at the end of this tutorial.

Changing Margins for a Document | Reference Window

- Make sure no text is selected, and then, in the Page Setup group on the Page Layout tab, click the Dialog Box Launcher. If necessary, click the Margins tab to display the margin settings.
- Use the arrows to change the settings in the Top, Bottom, Left, or Right text boxes, or type a new margin value in each text box.
- Make sure the Apply to list box displays Whole document.
- Click the OK button.
- To choose from groups of predefined margin settings, click the Margins button in the Page Setup group on the Page Layout tab. In the Margins menu, click the group of margin settings that is appropriate for your document.

You need to change the top and left margins of the Design Handout document to 1.5 inches, per Natalie's note in Figure 2-3. The left margin needs to be wider than the right to allow space for holes so that the document can be inserted in a three-ring binder. Also, the top margin needs to be wider than the bottom margin so the document can be printed on the company letterhead. In the next set of steps, you'll change the margins using the Page Setup dialog box.

To change the margins in the Design Handout document:

▶ 1. Click anywhere in the document to make sure no text is selected.

▶ 2. Click the **Page Layout** tab on the Ribbon, and then, in the Page Setup group, click the **Margins** button. The Margins menu appears, displaying some common margin settings. The Normal option contains the default margin settings. You can always click Normal to return a document to the default margin settings. The item at the top of the menu, Last Custom Setting, reflects the last margin settings selected in the Page Setup dialog box. See Figure 2-17.

Figure 2-17	Margins menu

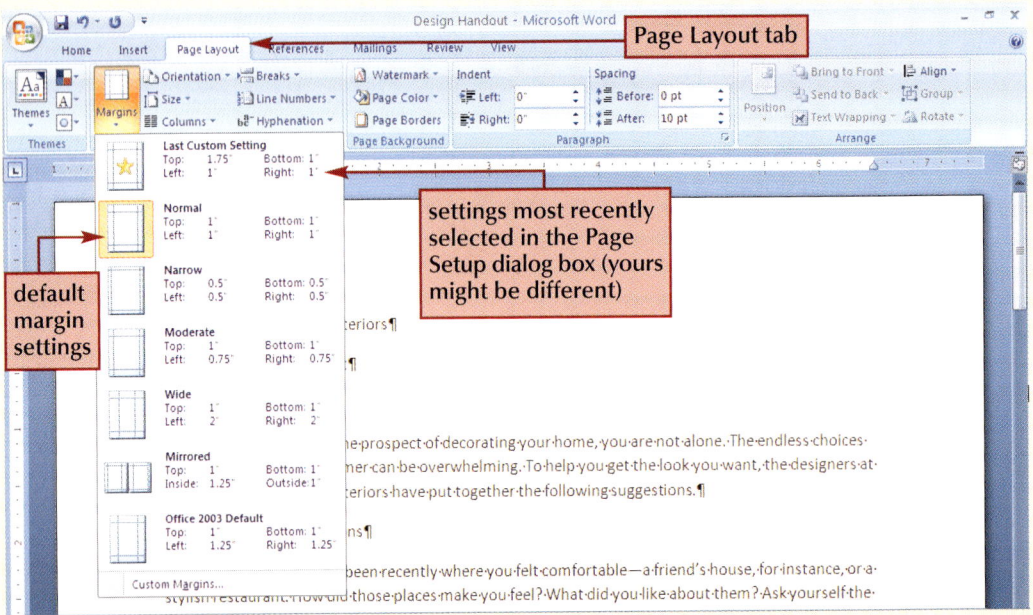

It's possible that the Last Custom Setting option matches the margin settings you want to use in the Design Handout document, but if so, ignore it. Instead, you'll open the Page Setup dialog box in the next step, so you can practice using it. You can open the Page Setup dialog box via the Custom Margins option at the bottom of the Margins menu, or you can use the Dialog Box Launcher in the Page Setup group on the Page Layout tab. You'll try the Custom Margins option now.

3. At the bottom of the Margins menu, click **Custom Margins**. The Page Setup dialog box opens.

4. Click the **Margins** tab, if it is not already selected, to display the margin settings. The Top margin setting is selected. See Figure 2-18. As you complete the following steps, keep an eye on the Preview in the bottom-left part of the dialog box, which changes to reflect changes you make to the margins.

Page Setup dialog box ◀ **Figure 2-18**

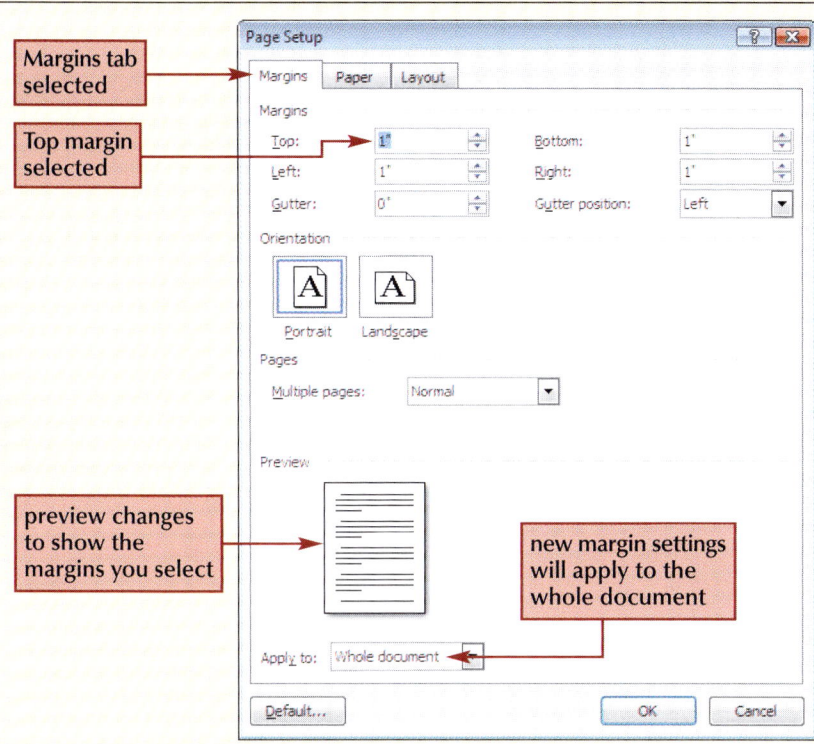

Margins tab selected

Top margin selected

preview changes to show the margins you select

new margin settings will apply to the whole document

▶ **5.** Type **1.5** to change the Top margin setting. (You do not have to type the inches symbol.)

▶ **6.** Press the **Tab** key twice to select the Left text box and highlight the current margin setting. The text area in the Preview box moves down to reflect the larger top margin.

▶ **7.** Verify that the insertion point is in the Left text box, type **1.5**, and then press the **Tab** key. The left margin in the Preview box increases.

▶ **8.** In the Apply to list box, make sure **Whole document** is selected, and then click the **OK** button to return to your document. Notice that the ruler has changed to reflect the new margin settings and the resulting reduced page area. The document text is now 6 inches wide. See Figure 2-19.

Figure 2-19 ▶ **Rulers after setting top and left margins to 1.5 inches**

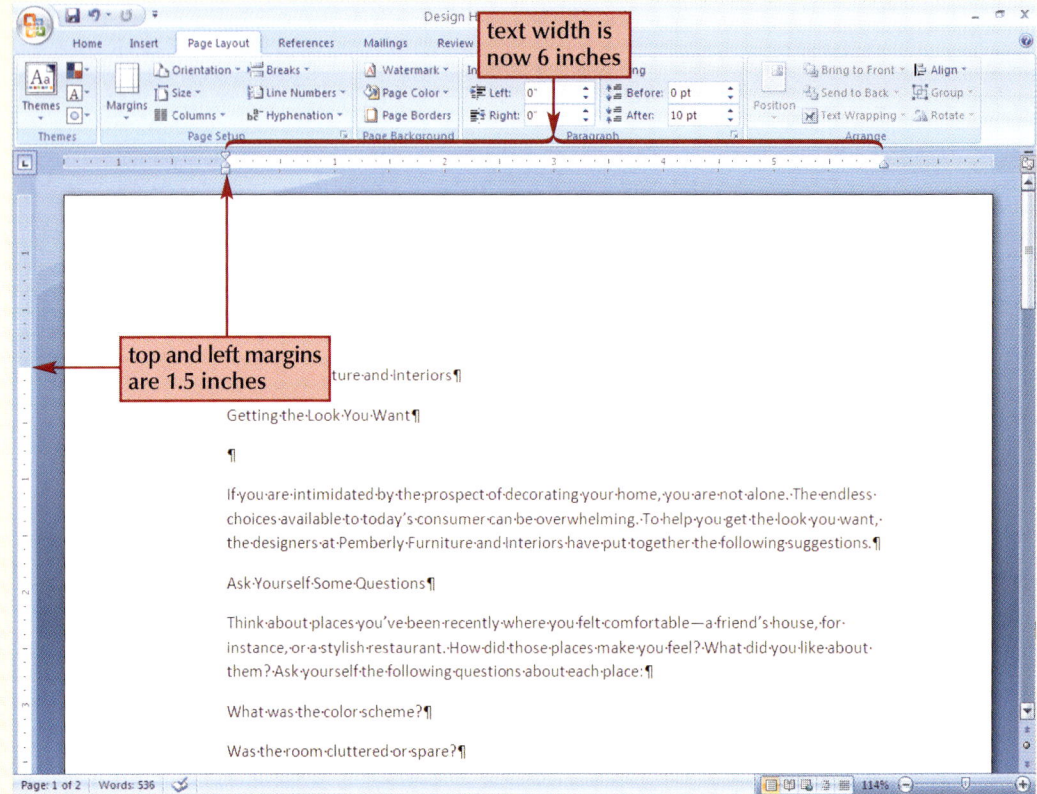

Trouble? If a double-dotted line and the words "Section Break" appear in your document, Whole document wasn't selected in the Apply to list box. If this occurs, click the Undo button ⟲ on the Quick Access Toolbar and repeat Steps 1 through 8, making sure you select the Whole document option in the Apply to list box.

▶ 9. Save the document and then click the **Home** tab.

Recall that in Tutorial 1 you inserted a series of blank paragraphs at the beginning of a document in order to allow room for the company letterhead. Now that you know how to change margins, you should use this method to insert extra space in a document rather than inserting blank paragraphs. Adjusting margins allows you to be more precise, because you can specify an exact amount. Also, if you know you will usually need to use a particular margin setting for your documents, you can click the Default button on the Margins tab of the Page Setup dialog box to make your settings the default for all new documents.

In the next section, you will make some changes that will affect the way certain paragraphs are positioned between the left and right margins.

Aligning Text

The term **alignment** refers to the way a paragraph lines up horizontally between the margins. By default, text is aligned along the left margin and is **ragged**, or uneven, along the right margin. This is called **left alignment**. With **right alignment**, the text is aligned along the right margin and is ragged along the left margin. With **center alignment**, text is centered between the left and right margins and is ragged along both the left and right margins. With **justified alignment**, full lines of text are spaced between both the left and the right margins, and the text is not ragged. Text in newspaper columns is often justified. See Figure 2-20.

Varieties of text alignment   **Figure 2-20**

left alignment
If you are intimidated by the prospect of decorating your home, you are not alone. The endless choices available to today's consumer can be overwhelming. To help you get the look you want, the designers at Pemberly Furniture and Interiors have put together the following suggestions.

right alignment
If you are intimidated by the prospect of decorating your home, you are not alone. The endless choices available to today's consumer can be overwhelming. To help you get the look you want, the designers at Pemberly Furniture and Interiors have put together the following suggestions.

center alignment
If you are intimidated by the prospect of decorating your home, you are not alone. The endless choices available to today's consumer can be overwhelming.

justified alignment
If you are intimidated by the prospect of decorating your home, you are not alone. The endless choices available to today's consumer can be overwhelming. To help you get the look you want, the designers at Pemberly Furniture and Interiors have put together the following suggestions.

The Paragraph group on the Home tab includes a button for each of the four major types of alignment. The Mini toolbar, which appears when you select text in a document, includes just the Center button, which is commonly used to center titles in a document.

To align a single paragraph, click anywhere in that paragraph and then click the appropriate alignment button. To align multiple paragraphs, select the paragraphs first, and then click an alignment button.

Figure 2-3 indicates that the title and subtitle of the Design Handout should be centered and that the main paragraphs should be justified. First, you'll center the title and subtitle using the Center button on the Mini toolbar.

To center-align the title:

▶ **1.** Click and drag in the selection bar to select the title ("Pemberly Furniture and Interiors") and the subtitle ("Getting the Look You Want"). A faint image of the Mini toolbar appears near the selected text. To fully display the Mini toolbar, you need to move the mouse pointer over it.

▶ **2.** Move the mouse pointer near the Mini toolbar. The Mini toolbar is now fully visible and remains visible until you move the mouse pointer away from it. It contains one alignment button, the Center button. The Align Text Left button on the Home tab is highlighted in orange, indicating that the selected text is currently left-aligned. See Figure 2-21.

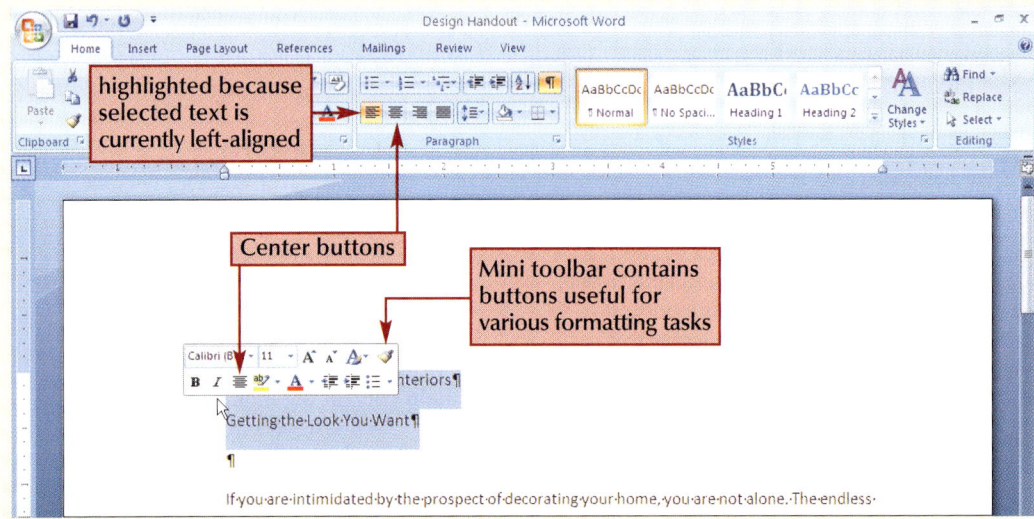

▶ **3.** On the Mini toolbar, click the **Center** button ▤. The text is centered between the left and right margins. Both Center buttons are now highlighted in orange, indicating that the selected text is centered. The Mini toolbar remains visible until you move the mouse pointer away from it.

Trouble? If the Mini toolbar disappears before you click the Center button, click anywhere in the document to deselect the text, and then repeat Steps 1 through 3.

Next, you'll justify the text in the first two main paragraphs.

To justify the first two main paragraphs:

▶ **1.** Click anywhere in the paragraph that begins "If you are intimidated by...." If the Mini toolbar was still visible, it disappears and the insertion point is now located in the paragraph you want to align. The Align Text Left button in the Paragraph group is highlighted in orange, indicating that the paragraph containing the insertion point is left-aligned.

▶ **2.** In the Paragraph group, click the **Justify** button ▤. The paragraph text spreads out so that it lines up evenly along the left and right margins.

▶ **3.** Scroll down if necessary and click in the paragraph that begins "Think about places you've been recently.... "

▶ **4.** Click the **Justify** button ▤ in the Paragraph group again. The text is evenly spaced between the left and right margins. See Figure 2-22.

Justified paragraphs | **Figure 2-22**

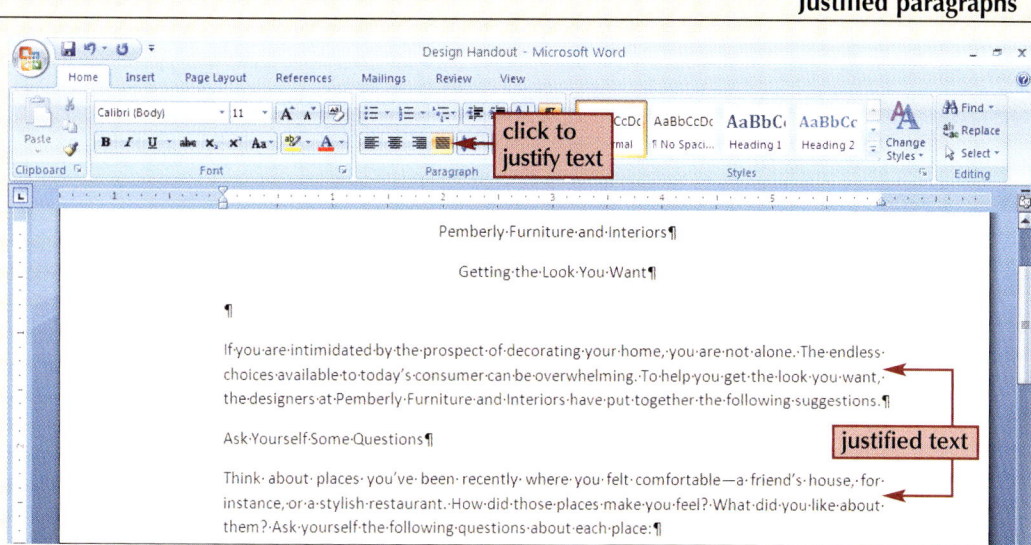

You'll justify the other paragraphs later. But first, you turn your attention to indenting a paragraph.

Indenting a Paragraph

When you **indent** a paragraph, you move the entire paragraph to the right. You can use the indent buttons on the Home tab to increase or decrease paragraph indenting in increments of 0.5 inches. The **indent markers** on the horizontal ruler allow you to see at a glance a paragraph's current indent settings. See Figure 2-23.

Indent markers on horizontal ruler | **Figure 2-23**

By dragging the indent markers individually, you can create specialized indents, such as a **hanging indent** (where all lines except the first line of the paragraph are indented from the left margin) or a **right indent** (where all lines of the paragraph are indented from the right margin). You'll have a chance to try some of these specialized indents in the Case Problems at the end of this tutorial. In this document, though, you only need to indent the main paragraphs 0.5 inches. When you do a simple indent like this, the three indent markers, shown stacked on top of one another in Figure 2-23, move as a unit along with the paragraphs you are indenting.

To indent a paragraph using the Increase Indent button:

▶ **1.** Verify that the insertion point is still located within the paragraph that begins "Think about places you've been...."

▶ **2.** In the Paragraph group, click the **Increase Indent** button [icon] twice. (Be careful not to click the Decrease Indent button by mistake.) The entire paragraph and the stacked indent markers in the horizontal ruler move right 0.5 inches each time you click the Increase Indent button. The paragraph is indented 1 inch, which is 0.5 inches more than Natalie wants.

▶ **3.** Click the **Decrease Indent** button [icon] in the Paragraph group to move the paragraph left 0.5 inches. The paragraph is now indented 0.5 inches from the left margin. Don't be concerned about the list of questions. You will indent this list later, when you format it as a bulleted list. See Figure 2-24.

Figure 2-24 ▶ **Indented paragraph**

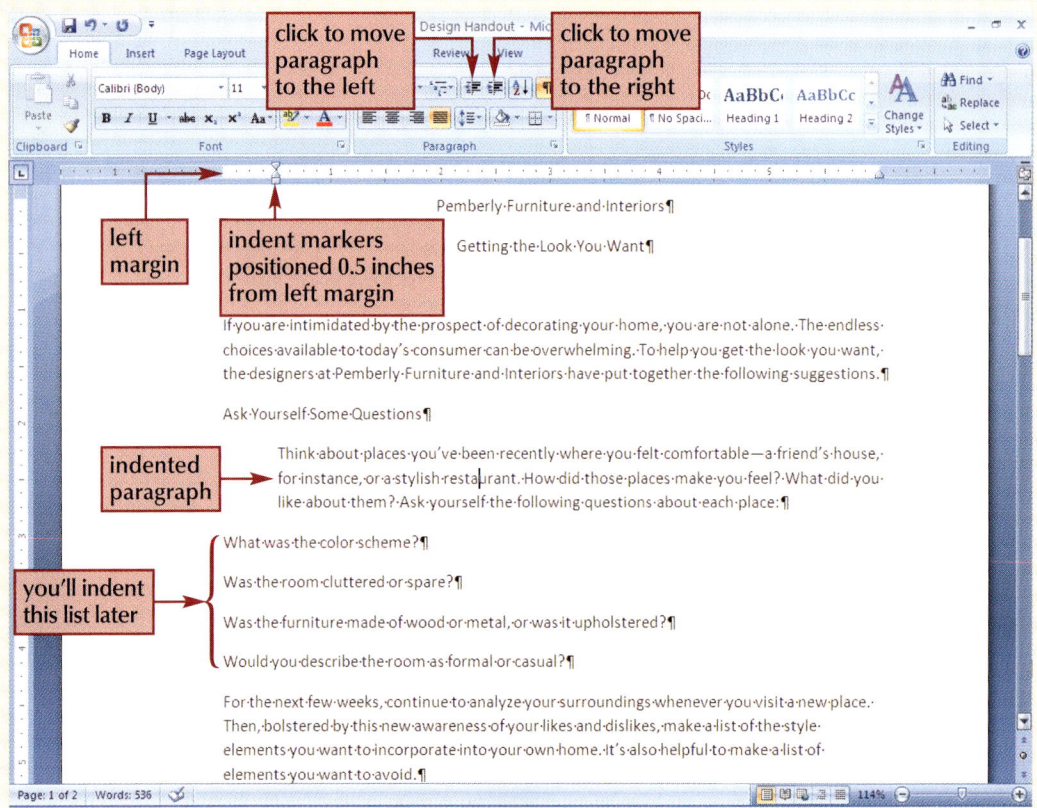

You could continue to indent and then justify each paragraph. However, it's faster to use the Format Painter button. With the Format Painter, you can easily copy both the indentation and alignment changes to the remaining paragraphs in the document.

Using the Format Painter

The **Format Painter** makes it easy to copy all the formatting features of one paragraph to other paragraphs (or from one heading to other headings, or from one word to other words). You can use this button to copy formatting to just one item or to multiple items.

Using the Format Painter

- Select the text whose formatting you want to copy. If you are trying to copy the formatting of an entire paragraph, you can just click anywhere in the paragraph.
- To copy formatting to one item, click the Format Painter button in the Clipboard group on the Home tab, and then select the text you want to format, or click anywhere in the paragraph you want to format.
- To copy formatting to multiple items, double-click the Format Painter button in the Clipboard group on the Home tab, and then select, one by one, each text item you want to format, or click anywhere in each paragraph you want to format. When you are finished, click the Format Painter button again to deselect it.

You'll use the Format Painter now to copy the formatting of the second paragraph to the other main paragraphs. The first step is to move the insertion point to the paragraph whose formatting you want to copy.

To copy paragraph formatting with the Format Painter:

▶ **1.** Verify that the insertion point is located in the paragraph that begins "Think about places you've been...."

▶ **2.** In the Clipboard group, double-click the **Format Painter** button 🗸. When you double-click the Format Painter button, it stays selected until you click it again; you can paste the copied formatting as many times as you wish. Also, notice that when you move the pointer over text, the pointer changes to 🗸⌶ to indicate that the format of the paragraph containing the insertion point can be "painted" (or copied) onto another paragraph.

▶ **3.** Scroll down, and then click anywhere in the paragraph that begins "For the next few weeks...." The format of this paragraph changes to match the format of the indented and justified paragraph above it. See Figure 2-25. Two paragraphs are now indented and justified. The Format Painter pointer is still visible, indicating that you can continue formatting paragraphs with it.

Formatting copied with Format Painter ◀ **Figure 2-25**

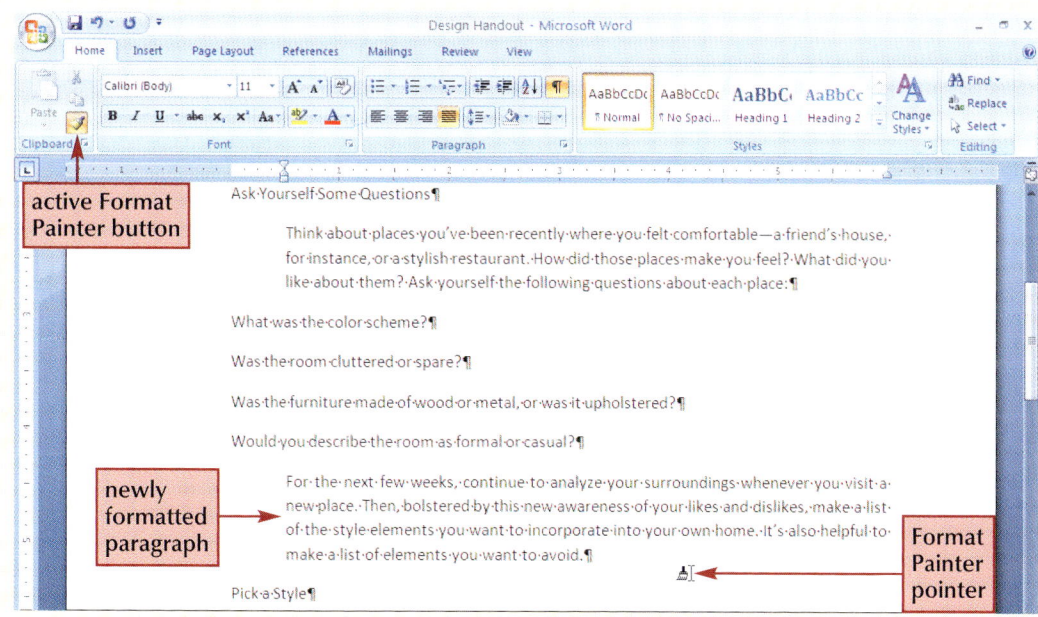

Now you need to continue copying the indented and justified formatting to the main paragraphs of text. You do not want to copy this formatting to the document headings or to the several lists. (You'll format these elements later in this tutorial.)

4. Scroll down and click in the paragraph below the "Pick a Style" subheading, which begins "Now that you know what you like...." Also, click the paragraphs that begin "People who enjoy spending time..." and "Of course you probably won't be able...." Finally, click the paragraph that begins "While you are saving money...." Do not click the document title or subtitle, the lists, or the last paragraph of text.

   Trouble? If you click a paragraph and the formatting doesn't change to match the indented and justified paragraphs, you single-clicked the Format Painter button rather than double-clicked it. Move the insertion point to a paragraph that has the desired format, double-click the Format Painter button, and then repeat Step 4.

   Trouble? If you accidentally click a heading or one line of a list, click the Undo button on the Quick Access Toolbar to return the line to its original formatting. Then select a paragraph that has the desired format, double-click the Format Painter button, and repeat Step 4 to finish copying the format to the desired paragraphs.

5. After you are finished formatting paragraphs with the Format Painter pointer, click the **Format Painter** button to turn off the feature.

6. Save the document.

You've saved considerable time using the Format Painter to format all the main paragraphs in your document with the correct indentation and alignment. Your next job is to make the lists easier to read by adding bullets and numbers.

Adding Bullets and Numbers

You can emphasize a list of items by adding a heavy dot, or **bullet**, before each item in the list. Bulleted lists are usually much easier to read and follow than lists that do not have bullets. For a list of items that have a particular order (such as steps in a procedure), you can use numbers instead of bullets. Natalie's printout requests that you add bullets to the list of questions on page 1 to make them stand out. She also wants you to add bullets to the list of four basic styles on page 1.

To apply bullets to a list of questions:

1. Scroll up until you see the list of questions on page 1, which begins "What was the color scheme?"

2. Select the four questions in the list.

3. In the Paragraph group, click the **Bullets** button. Black circles called bullets appear before each item in the list. Also, the list is indented and the paragraph spacing between the items is reduced. After reviewing the default, circular bullet style in the document, Natalie decides she would prefer square bullets.

   Trouble? If no bullets are applied and a menu opens instead, you clicked the Bullets button arrow instead of the Bullets button. Press the Esc key to close the menu, and then repeat Step 3, taking care to click the Bullets button.

4. In the Paragraph group, click the **Bullets button arrow** (make sure to click the arrow, not just the button). A gallery of bullet styles opens.

At the top of the gallery of bullet styles is the Recently Used Bullets section; these are the bullet styles that have been used since you started Word. You'll probably see just the round black bullets, which were applied by default when you clicked the Bullets button. However, if you had used several different bullet styles, you would see them here. Below the Recently Used Bullets section is the **Bullet Library**, which offers a variety of bullet styles. For the Design Handout, you want to use a black square, which is an option in the Bullet Library. See Figure 2-26.

Bullets gallery | Figure 2-26

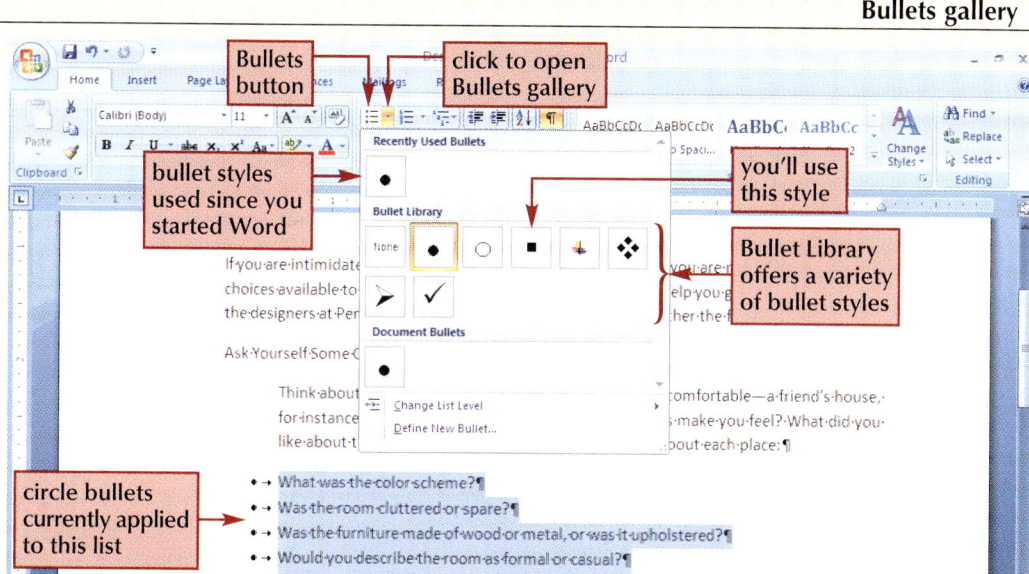

5. Move the mouse pointer over the options in the Bullet Library and observe a live preview of the bullet styles in the document. The blue highlight disappears from the selected list in the document so you can clearly see the live preview.

6. Click the **black square** in the Bullet Library. The round bullets are replaced with square bullets.

7. To align the bullets with the first paragraph, make sure the list is still selected, and then, in the Paragraph group, click the **Increase Indent** button. The bulleted list moves to the right. Figure 2-27 shows the indented bulleted list.

Indented bulleted list | Figure 2-27

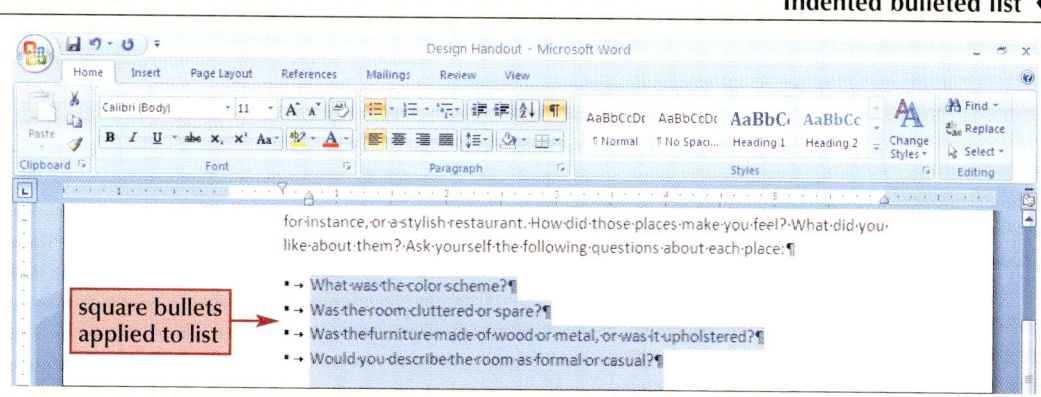

Next, you need to format the list of decorating styles on page 1 with square bullets. When you first start Word, the Bullets button applies the round bullets you saw earlier. But after you select a new bullet style, the Bullets button applies that last bullet style you used. So, to add square bullets to the decorating styles list, you just have to select the list and click the Bullets button.

To add bullets to the list of decorating styles:

1. Scroll down and select the list of four basic decorating styles (**Formal, Traditional, Eclectic, Contemporary**) at the bottom of page 1.

2. In the Paragraph group, click the **Bullets** button ≣, and then click the **Increase Indent** button. The list is now formatted with square black bullets. The list is also indented, similar to the list of questions shown earlier in Figure 2-27.

Your next step is to format the list of suggested purchases on page 2. Natalie wants you to format this information as a numbered list because it specifies purchases in a sequential order. Adding numbers to a list of items is a quick task thanks to the Numbering button, which numbers selected paragraphs with consecutive numbers. If you insert a new paragraph, delete a paragraph, or reorder the paragraphs, Word adjusts the numbers to make sure they remain consecutive.

To apply numbers to the list of suggested purchases:

1. Scroll down and select the list that begins with **Lamps or other forms of lighting** and ends with **Large items such as sofas, beds, and dining tables**.

2. In the Paragraph group, click the **Numbering** button ≣. Consecutive numbers appear in front of each item in the list, with a period after each number. As you'll see in the next step, you can choose from more options by clicking the Numbering button arrow instead.

   Trouble? If you see a gallery of numbering options, you clicked the Numbering button arrow instead of the Numbering button. Press the Esc key to close the gallery, and then click the Numbering button.

3. Make sure the list is still selected in the document, and then click the **Numbering button arrow** ≣ ▾. A gallery of numbering formats opens. Recently used numbering formats appear at the top of the list. Below the recently used formats you see the **Numbering Library**, which contains a variety of numbering formats. The style currently applied to the numbered list is highlighted in orange. You can move the mouse pointer over the options in the Numbering Library to see a live preview of the other formats in the document. See Figure 2-28.

Numbering Gallery **Figure 2-28**

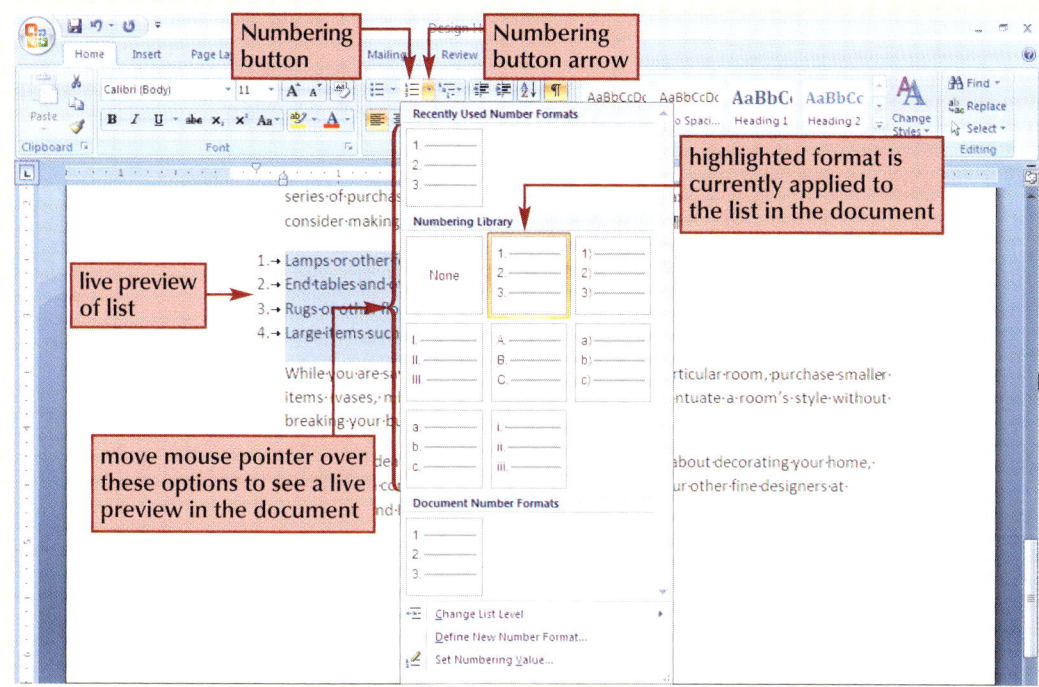

4. Move the mouse pointer over the options in the Numbering Library to display the live preview in the document. The blue highlight disappears from the selected list in the document so you can clearly see the live preview.

5. In the first row of the Numbering Library, click the far-right option, which shows numbers with a parenthesis after each number. The Numbering Gallery closes and each number is now followed by a parenthesis.

6. Make sure the list is still selected, and then in the Paragraph group, click the **Increase Indent** button. The list moves to the right so that the numbers align with the paragraph of text above it.

7. Click anywhere in the document to deselect the text. Figure 2-29 shows the indented and numbered list.

Indented numbered list **Figure 2-29**

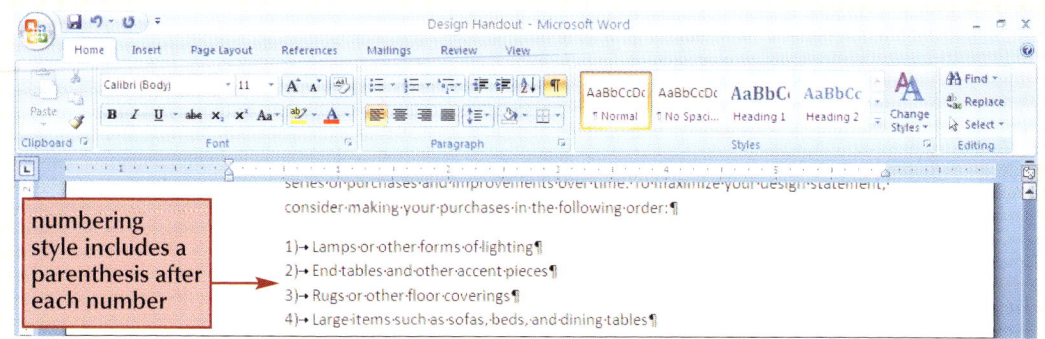

The text of the document is now properly aligned and indented. The bullets and numbers make the lists easy to read and give readers visual clues about the type of information they contain. Next, you need to adjust the formatting of individual words.

Emphasizing Text Using Bold and Italic

You can emphasize text by formatting it with bold, underline, or italic. These styles help make specific words or phrases stand out. You add bold, underline, or italics by using the corresponding buttons in the Font group on the Home tab. These buttons are **toggle buttons**, which means you can click them once to format the selected text, and click again to remove the formatting from the selected text.

Natalie wants to draw attention to the headings by formatting them in bold.

To format the headings in bold:

1. On page 1, click in the selection bar to select the heading **Ask Yourself Some Questions**.

2. In the Font group, click the **Bold** button **B**. The heading is formatted in bold. In the next step, you'll learn a useful method for repeating the task you just performed.

3. Scroll down and click in the selection bar to select the next heading in the document ("Pick a Style"). Press the **F4** key. The selected heading is formatted in bold. The F4 key repeats your most recent action. It is especially helpful when formatting parts of a document.

4. Select the last heading, **Stay True to Your Style** (at the bottom of page 1), and then press the **F4** key.

5. Click anywhere in the document to deselect the text, and then scroll up to return to the beginning of the document. The three headings appear in bold. Two of them are shown in Figure 2-30.

Figure 2-30 ▶ **Formatting headings with bold**

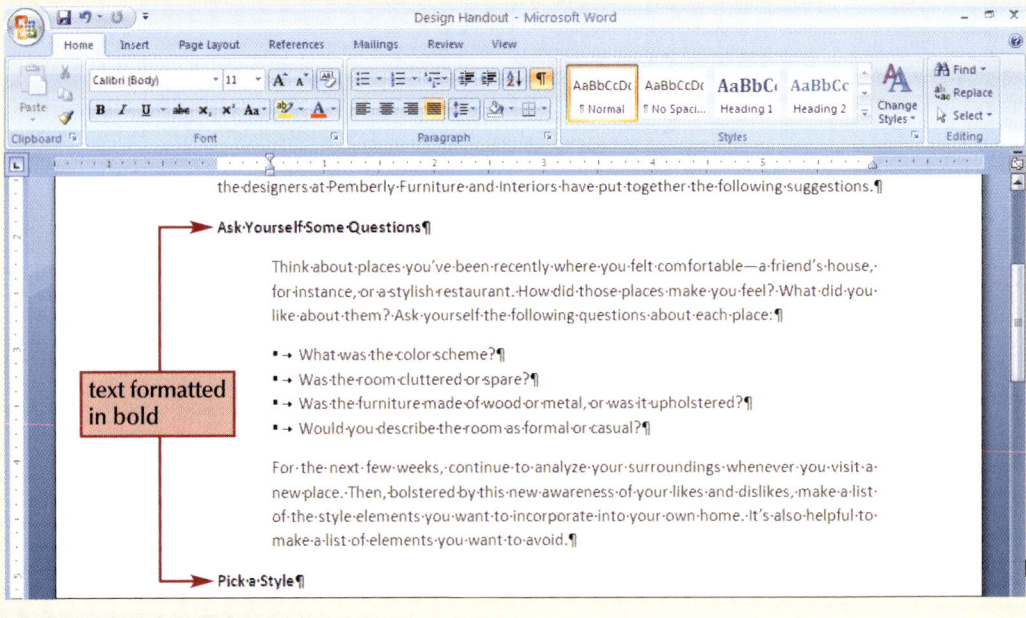

Now that it is formatted in bold, it's easy to see that the last heading, "Stay True to Your Style," is stranded at the bottom of page 1. The handout would look better if the heading was at the top of page 2, just above the first paragraph of the "Stay True to Your Style" section. To fix this problem, you need to tell Word to keep one paragraph (the heading paragraph) on the same page as the next paragraph.

To keep one paragraph with another:

1. Scroll down and click anywhere in the heading **Stay True to Your Style**.

2. In the Paragraph group, click the **Dialog Box Launcher**, and then, in the Paragraph dialog box, click the **Line and Page Breaks** tab.

3. Click the **Keep with next** check box to insert a check mark, and then click the **OK** button. The Paragraph dialog box closes, and the "Stay True to Your Style" heading moves to the top of page 2.

The Underline and Italic buttons on the Home tab work in the same way as the Bold button. You'll try formatting the title and subtitle in italics now, to see how they look.

To format the title and subtitle in italics:

1. On page 1, select the title **Pemberly Furniture and Interiors** and the subtitle **Getting the Look You Want**.

2. In the Font group, click the **Italic** button I. The title and subtitle are italicized, meaning they lean slightly to the right. The Italic button is selected, indicating that the selected text is italicized. See Figure 2-31.

Formatting headings with italics | **Figure 2-31**

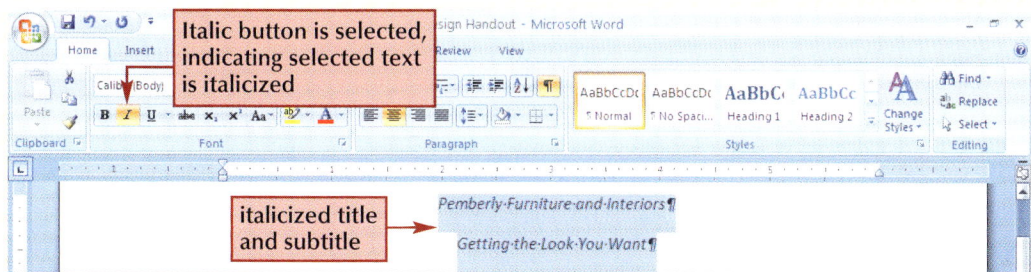

3. After reviewing the change, Natalie decides she doesn't care for the italics and asks you to remove them.

4. Click the **Italic** button I. The italic formatting toggles off. The selected text looks the way it did before you italicized it.

5. Save the document, leaving the title and subtitle selected.

Helpful Keyboard Shortcuts

For common tasks, such as applying bold and italics, it's often faster to use a **keyboard shortcut** (a combination of keys pressed at the same time) instead of clicking buttons with the mouse. For each of the keyboard shortcuts listed below, press and hold the Ctrl key, press the indicated number or letter key, and then release both keys.

• Bold selected text: Ctrl+B
• Italicize selected text: Ctrl+I

- Underline selected text: Ctrl+U
- Single-space lines within paragraph that currently contains the insertion point: Ctrl+1
- Double-space lines within paragraph that currently contains the insertion point: Ctrl+2
- Select entire document: Ctrl+A
- Cut selected text: Ctrl+X
- Copy selected text to Clipboard: Ctrl+C
- Paste most recently copied item at location of insertion point: Ctrl+V
- Undo your most recent action: Ctrl+Z

You can also save time by using **KeyTips**, sometimes called access keys, to select buttons and commands. To use KeyTips, press the Alt key and notice the letters that are displayed over each tab. Press the letter for the tab that contains the feature you want. For example, "P" is the KeyTip for the Page Layout tab; pressing it displays the Page Layout tab, with KeyTips showing for each feature on that tab. Press the KeyTip for the feature you want (for example, "B" for the Breaks button), and then notice the KeyTips that appear in the menu or gallery that opens. Press the KeyTip for the option you want. The change you select is applied to your document, and the KeyTips are hidden. You can press the Alt key to display them again for your next task. To hide KeyTips without using them, press the Esc key.

Working with Themes and Fonts

In addition to drawing attention to text with bold, italics, or underlining, you can change the shape and size of the individual letters by changing the font and font size. (As you learned in Tutorial 1, the term "font" refers to the shape of the characters in a document, and "font size" refers to the size of the characters.) You'll learn how to change the font in the Design Handout document soon, but first you need to take a few moments to learn about a related topic, document themes.

The document **theme** controls the variety of fonts, colors, and other visual effects available to you as you format a document. Twenty different themes are included in Word, with each offering a coordinated assortment of fonts, colors, and visual effects. By default, the Office theme is selected in each new Word document, including the Design Handout document you are working on now. You'll learn more about themes as you gain experience with Word. For now, you need to focus only on the relationship between themes and fonts.

One secret to creating a harmonious-looking document is to use no more than two fonts. For this reason, each theme includes only two fonts: one for headings and one for body text (that is, anything that is not a heading). In the Office theme, the heading font is Cambria, and the body font is Calibri. These two fonts were designed specifically for easy reading onscreen as well as on the printed page. A long list of other fonts is available. You can experiment with them and use them in your documents, but take care not to use too many fonts. This will create a document with a cluttered, disjointed appearance.

Applying a New Font and Font Size

To apply a font, select the text you want to format, then in the Font group on the Home tab, click the Font arrow, and click the font you want. The heading and body font for a document's theme are listed first, at the top of the font list.

To select a font size, make sure the text you want to format is selected, then in the Font group, click the Font Size arrow, and click the font size you want. Both the Font and Font Size lists allow you to see a live preview of selections by moving the mouse pointer over a font name or font size.

Natalie typed the entire Design Handout document in the Calibri font, which is intended primarily for body text, and the font size for the entire document is 11-point. She wants you to format the title and the subtitle in Cambria, which is the heading font for the Office theme. She also wants you to increase the size of the title and subtitle to 14-point.

To apply the Cambria heading font to the Design Handout document:

▶ **1.** On page 1, verify that the title **Pemberly Furniture and Interiors** and the subtitle **Getting the Look You Want** are selected.

▶ **2.** In the Font group, click the **Font** arrow. A list of available fonts appears. The heading and body font for the Office theme (Cambria and Calibri) appear at the top of the list. The intended use of these two fonts (Headings or Body) is specified after each font name. Calibri (Body) is highlighted in orange, indicating that this font is currently applied to the selected text. (Calibri also appears in the Font box, above the list, for the same reason.) Below the heading and body fonts is a list of fonts that have been used recently on your computer, followed by a complete alphabetical list of all available fonts. (You need to scroll the list to see all the fonts.) Each name in the list is formatted with the relevant font. For example, "Cambria" appears in the Cambria font, and "Calibri" appears in the Calibri font. See Figure 2-32.

Font list **Figure 2-32**

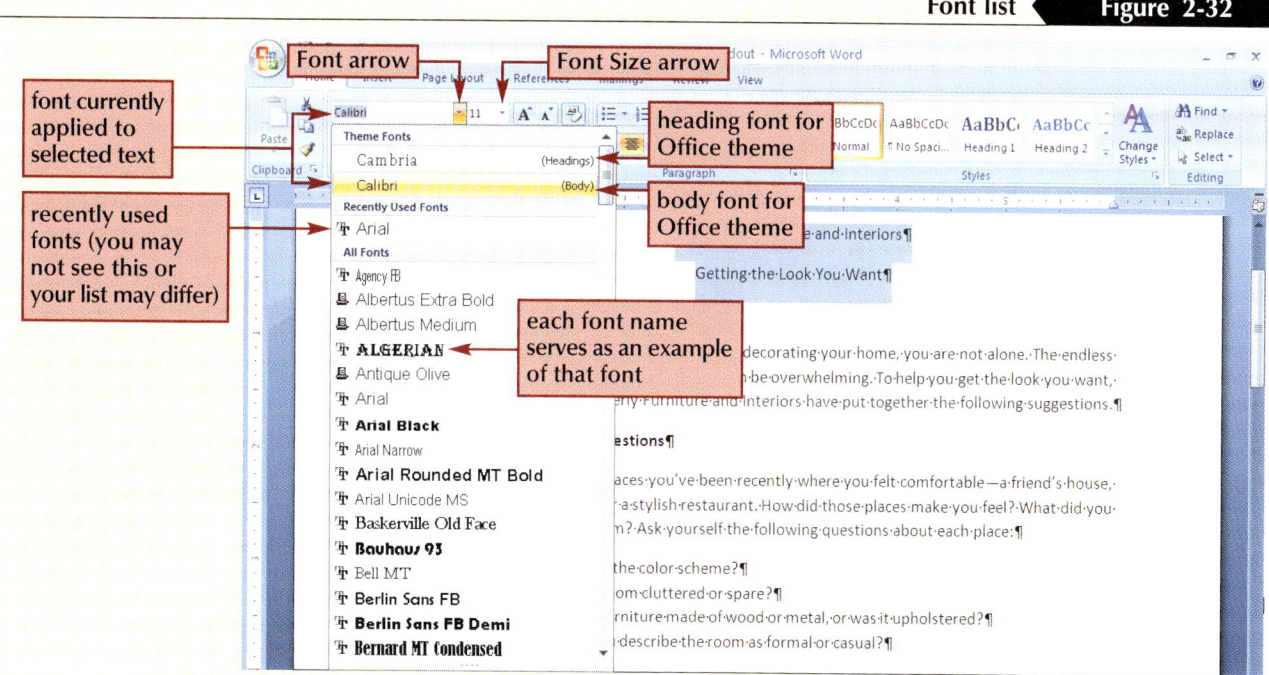

▶ **3.** Without clicking, move the mouse pointer over a dramatic-looking font in the font list, such as Algerian or Arial Black, and then drag the pointer over another font. The selected text in the document shows a live preview of the font, changing again to a new font when you drag the mouse pointer to a different font name.

▶ **4.** At the top of the list, click **Cambria (Headings)**. Take care to select Cambria (Headings) at the top of the list. Do not click Cambria where it appears farther down, in the alphabetical list of fonts. (The reason for this will become clear in the next section, when you learn more about document themes.) The selected title and subtitle are now formatted in Cambria, and the font list closes. "Cambria (Headings)" appears in the Font box, indicating the font currently applied to the selected text. Next, you need to increase the font size of the selected text from 11 point to 14 point.

Trouble? If you see "Cambria" in the font box rather than "Cambria (Headings)," you selected Cambria where it appears in the alphabetical list of fonts rather than at the top of the list. Begin again with Step 2, taking care to select Cambria (Headings) at the top of the list.

▶ 5. Verify that the title and subtitle are still selected, and then in the Font group click the **Font Size** arrow (shown earlier in Figure 2-32). A list of font sizes appears, with the currently selected font size (11) displayed in the Font Size box. Like the Font box, the Font Size box allows you to preview options before selecting one.

▶ 6. Drag the mouse pointer over a few font sizes, and notice how the size of the selected text changes accordingly.

▶ 7. Click **14**. The Font Size list closes and the selected text increases from 11-point to 14-point Cambria. Click within the title to deselect the text.

Tip

The font and font size settings in the Font group reflect the settings of the text that is currently selected, or, if no text is selected, of the text currently containing the insertion point.

You've finished formatting the document's title and subtitle in the Cambria font, the preferred heading font for the Office theme. You could also apply the Cambria font to the headings within the document (such as the heading "Ask Yourself Some Questions"). However, Natalie thinks the bold you applied earlier emphasizes them enough, so you'll leave the headings as they are.

The only remaining font change has to do with the company name. Wherever it appears in the body of the document, Natalie wants to format it in the Arial font, so that it matches the sign outside the company's storefront. Arial is not one of the suggested fonts for the Office theme, and using it breaks the general rule of two fonts per document, but this is a small change that won't affect the overall look of the document.

To format the company name in the Arial font:

▶ 1. At the end of the introductory paragraph, select **Pemberly Furniture and Interiors**.

▶ 2. In the Font group click the **Font** arrow, and then click **Arial** in either in the Recently used Fonts section of the list or in the All Fonts section. The font for the company name changes from Calibri to Arial. Arial appears in the Font box, indicating that the selected text is formatted in this font.

Trouble? If you don't see Arial in your font list, choose another font in the All Fonts section that is easy to distinguish from Calibri or Cambria but still looks suitable for a business document.

▶ 3. Scroll down to the last paragraph of the document, select **Pemberly Furniture and Interiors**, and format it in the Arial font. See Figure 2-33.

Figure 2-33 | Company name formatted in Arial

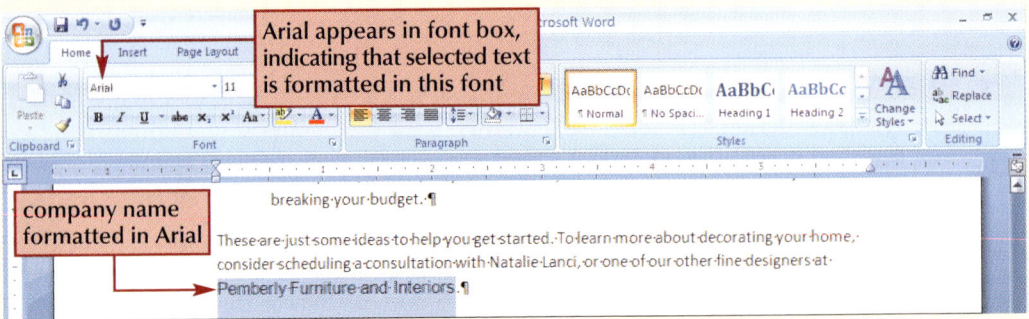

▶ 4. Deselect the company name, and then save the document.

You are finished changing the document fonts. In the next section, you'll select a new theme for the document and observe how this affects your font choices.

Changing the Document's Theme

Each document theme is designed to convey a specific look and feel. For example, the Office theme is designed to be appropriate for standard business documents. By contrast, some of the other themes are designed to give documents a more informal look, such as sleek for a new product announcement or earthy for a flyer on environmental news.

The advantage of sticking with a theme's suggested heading and body fonts (the two fonts at the top of the font list) is that if you switch to a different theme, the fonts in the document automatically change to the body and heading fonts for that theme. If you select any fonts on the font list other than the two heading and body fonts at the top of the list, they will remain unchanged in the document as you switch from one theme to another.

Natalie is considering using a different theme for future handouts. She asks you to apply the Metro theme to the Design Handout document to see how it looks.

To change the document's theme:

▶ **1.** Make sure that you saved the document using the current name (Design Handout) at the end of the last section. If you aren't sure, save the document again.

▶ **2.** Save the document as **Design Handout Metro** in the Tutorial folder.

▶ **3.** Press the **Ctrl+Home** keys to move the insertion point up to the headings at the beginning of the document. With the title and subtitle visible, you will more easily be able to see what happens when you change the document's theme.

▶ **4.** Click the **Page Layout** tab, and then click the **Themes** button. The Themes gallery opens. You might have to wait a moment until the various themes appear in the gallery. See Figure 2-34.

Themes gallery **Figure 2-34**

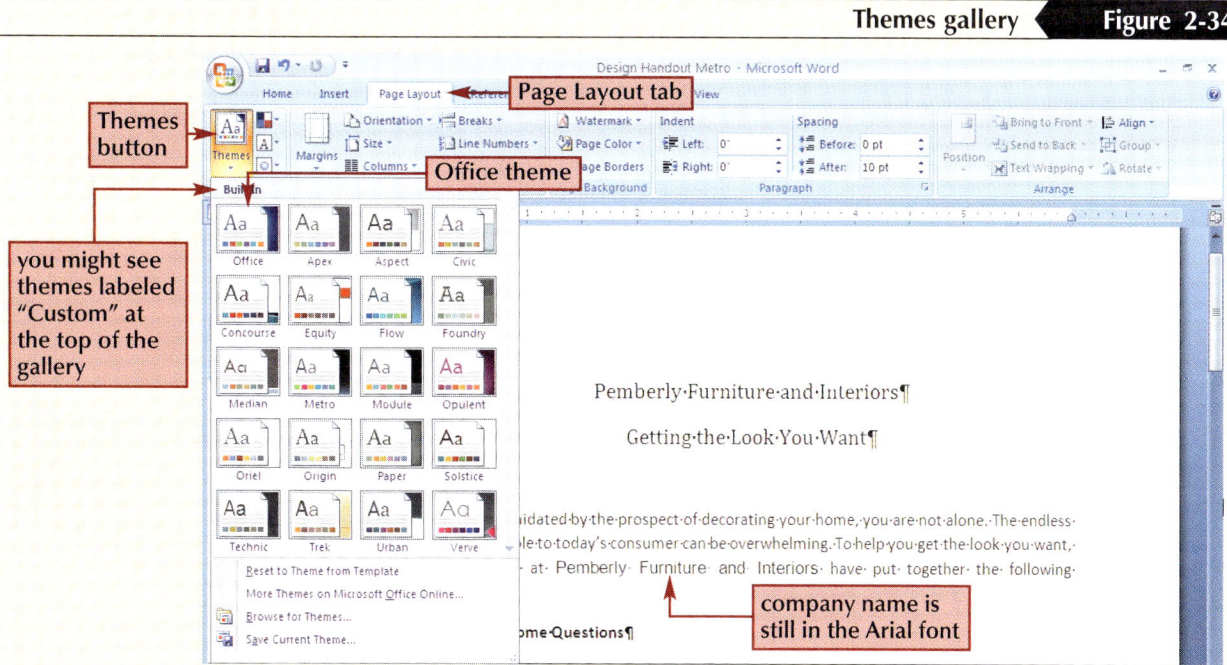

5. Without clicking, hold the mouse over the various themes in the gallery, and observe the live preview of each theme in the document. The heading and body fonts change to reflect the fonts associated with the various themes.

6. Click **Metro**. Except for the two instances of the company name (which you formatted earlier in Arial), the text in the Design Handout Metro document changes to the body and heading fonts of the Metro theme. To see exactly what the Metro theme fonts are, you can point to the Theme Fonts button in the Themes group.

7. Point to the **Theme Fonts** button [A⁻] in the Themes group. A ScreenTip appears, listing the currently selected theme (Metro), the heading font (Consolas), and the body font (Corbel).

   Trouble? If a menu appears, you clicked the Theme Fonts button instead of pointing to it. Press the Esc key, and then repeat Step 7.

8. Save the document and then close it. You can give the Design Handout Metro file to Natalie later, so she can decide whether or not to use the Metro theme for future handouts. Because you saved the Design Handout document before changing the theme, you can reopen it now and continue with the tutorial.

9. Reopen the Design Handout document, which is formatted with the Office theme.

InSight | **Changing Fonts by Changing Themes**

The two fonts at the top of the font list are not actually specific fonts; they are instructions that tell Word to use the heading and body fonts for the currently selected theme. By contrast, the other fonts in the Font list (such as Arial or Calibri where they appear in the alphabetical list of fonts) are more straightforward. When you apply one of these fonts to text in a document, it doesn't change when you change the document theme. The same is true for other kinds of formatting, such as bold, italics, or font size changes. These types of formatting remain unchanged no matter what theme you choose.

Previewing and Printing the Document

You have made all the editing and formatting changes that Natalie requested for the Design Handout document. It's helpful to preview a document after formatting it. The Print Preview window makes it easy to spot things you need to change before printing, such as text that is not aligned correctly.

To preview and print the document:

1. Click the **Office Button** 🗐, point to **Print**, and then click **Print Preview**. The document is displayed in Print Preview.

2. In the Zoom section, click the **Two Pages** button. You see both pages of the document side by side. Review the document's formatting.

   Trouble? If you notice any alignment or indentation errors, click the Close Print Preview button, correct the errors in Print Layout view, save your changes, and then return to the Print Preview window.

3. On the Print Preview tab in the Print group, click the **Print** button, check the print settings, and then click the **OK** button. After a pause, the document prints.

▶ **4.** Click the **Close Print Preview** button. You return to Print Layout view.

▶ **5.** Save the document if necessary and then close it.

You now have a printed copy of the final Design Handout document, as shown in Figure 2-35.

Final version of Design Handout document ◀ **Figure 2-35**

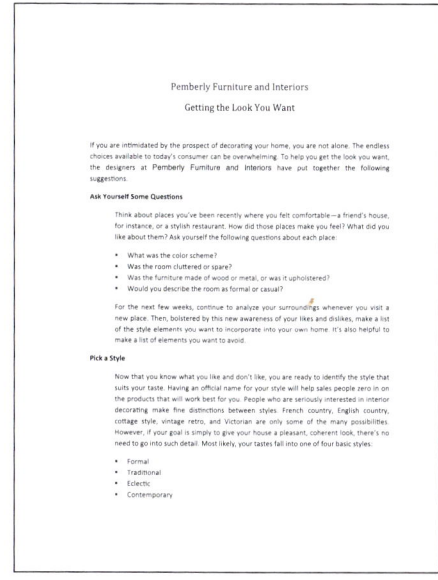
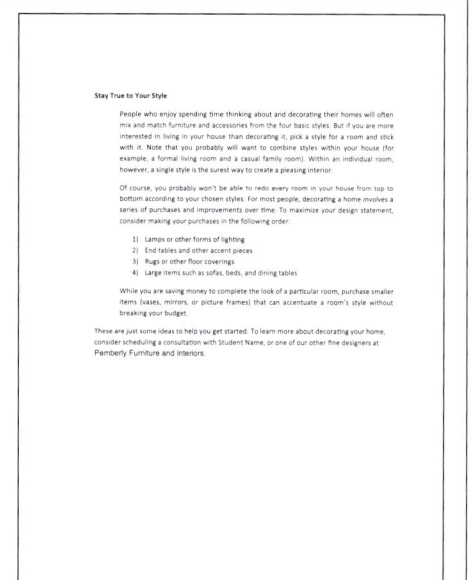

Session 2.2 Quick Check | Review

1. The term _____ refers to the way a paragraph lines up horizontally between the margins.
2. Explain how to indent a paragraph 1 inch or more from the left margin.
3. Explain how to copy formatting to multiple paragraphs.
4. What is the Numbering Library?
5. Explain the effect a theme has on the overall look of a document.
6. Explain how to change a paragraph's font.
7. Explain the relationship between the two items at the top of the Font list and the document's theme.

Tutorial Summary | Review

In this tutorial, you learned how to use the Spelling and Grammar checker, select parts of a document, delete text, and move text within a document. You also learned how to find and replace text. Next, you focused on formatting a document, including changing margins, aligning text, indenting paragraphs, using the Format Painter, and emphasizing text with bold and italics. Finally, you learned how to change the font and font size for selected text and you explored the relationship between fonts and themes.

Key Terms

alignment
bullet
Bullet Library
center alignment
Clipboard
Clipboard task pane
copy
cut
cut and paste
drag and drop
Find and Replace
   dialog box

format
Format Painter
hanging indent
indent
indent markers
justified alignment
keyboard shortcut
Key Tips
left alignment
Numbering Library
paste

ragged
right alignment
right indent
search text
Spelling and Grammar
   checker
theme
toggle buttons

| Practice | | **Review Assignments** |

Apply the skills you learned in the tutorial using the same case scenario.

Data Files needed for the Review Assignments: Getting.docx, Staff.docx

Natalie asks you to work on a document that explains how to get started working with the designers at Pemberly Furniture and Interiors. The document starts by introducing the entire Pemberly design staff and then lists the steps involved in a major home renovation. Natalie also asks you to create a document listing the names of the firm's interior designers and interior decorators.

1. Open the file **Getting** located in the Tutorial.02\Review folder included with your Data Files, and then check your screen to make sure your settings match those in the tutorial.
2. Save the document as **Getting Started** in the same folder.
3. Use the Spelling and Grammar checker to correct any errors in the document. Assume that all names in the document and the term "Feng Shui" are spelled correctly.
4. Proofread the document carefully to check for any additional errors. Look for and correct errors in the last two paragraphs of the document that were not reported when you used the Spelling and Grammar checker.
5. Change the left and top margins to 1.5 inches using the Page Setup dialog box. Make sure to apply the change to the whole document.
6. In the list on the second page of the document, select the paragraph that begins "Interview potential construction..." and move it so that it follows the paragraph that reads "Review the final design plan."
7. Format the heading and subheading in the suggested heading font for the Office theme. Change the font size to 16 point.
8. Make all edits and formatting changes shown in Figure 2-36, and then save your work.

Figure 2-36

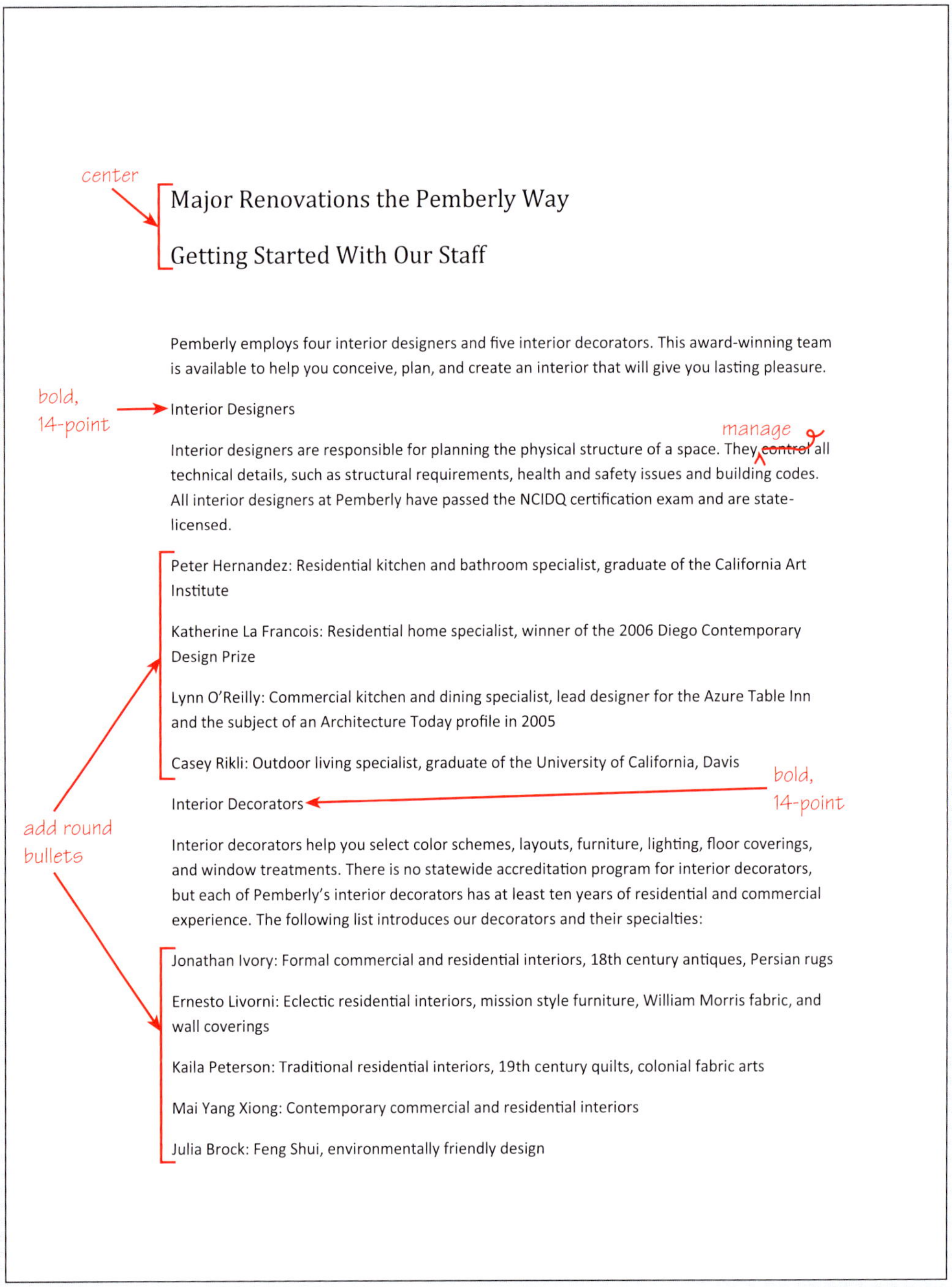

center

Major Renovations the Pemberly Way

Getting Started With Our Staff

Pemberly employs four interior designers and five interior decorators. This award-winning team is available to help you conceive, plan, and create an interior that will give you lasting pleasure.

bold, 14-point → Interior Designers

manage

Interior designers are responsible for planning the physical structure of a space. They ~~control~~ all technical details, such as structural requirements, health and safety issues and building codes. All interior designers at Pemberly have passed the NCIDQ certification exam and are state-licensed.

Peter Hernandez: Residential kitchen and bathroom specialist, graduate of the California Art Institute

Katherine La Francois: Residential home specialist, winner of the 2006 Diego Contemporary Design Prize

Lynn O'Reilly: Commercial kitchen and dining specialist, lead designer for the Azure Table Inn and the subject of an Architecture Today profile in 2005

Casey Rikli: Outdoor living specialist, graduate of the University of California, Davis

Interior Decorators ← *bold, 14-point*

add round bullets

Interior decorators help you select color schemes, layouts, furniture, lighting, floor coverings, and window treatments. There is no statewide accreditation program for interior decorators, but each of Pemberly's interior decorators has at least ten years of residential and commercial experience. The following list introduces our decorators and their specialties:

Jonathan Ivory: Formal commercial and residential interiors, 18th century antiques, Persian rugs

Ernesto Livorni: Eclectic residential interiors, mission style furniture, William Morris fabric, and wall coverings

Kaila Peterson: Traditional residential interiors, 19th century quilts, colonial fabric arts

Mai Yang Xiong: Contemporary commercial and residential interiors

Julia Brock: Feng Shui, environmentally friendly design

Figure 2-36 (cont.)

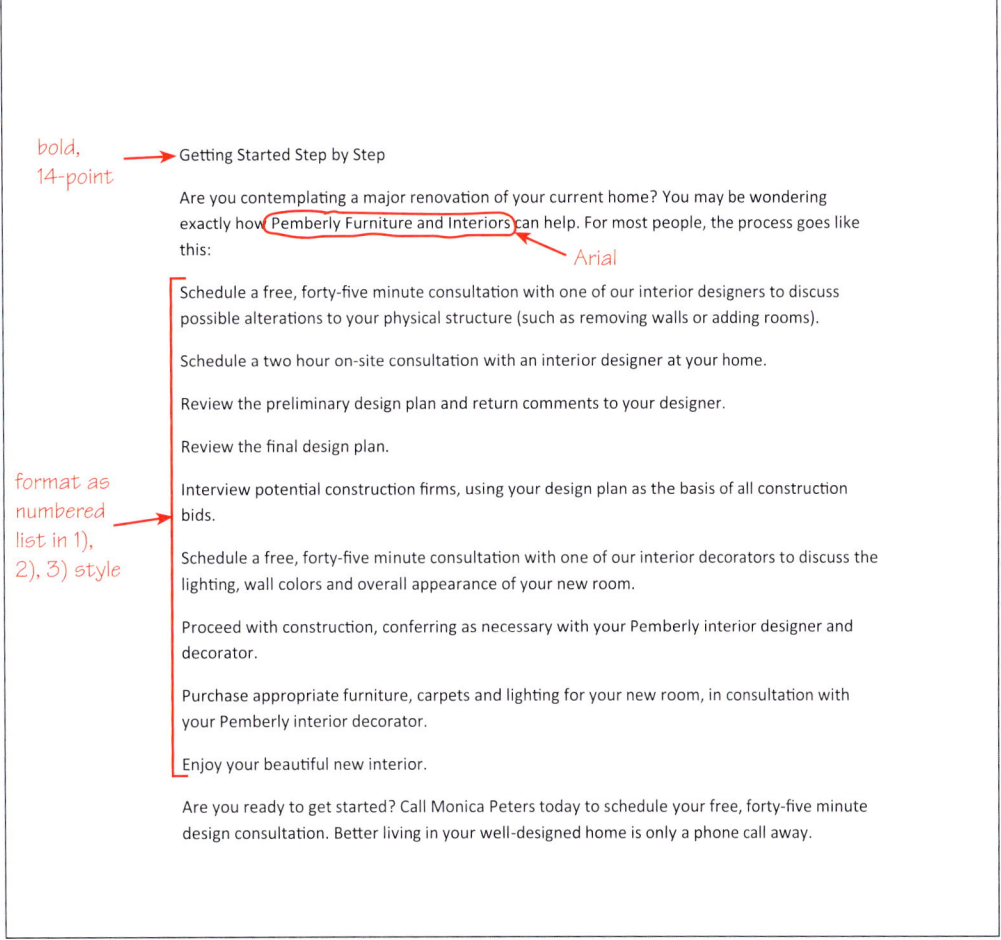

9. In the last paragraph of the document, replace "Monica Peters" with your first and last name.

10. Below the heading "Interior Designers," justify the paragraph that begins "Interior designers are responsible for...." Click the Increase Indent button once. Note that Word indents the justified paragraph slightly to match the bulleted list below it. Click the Increase Indent button again to indent the paragraph a full 0.5 inch. Similarly, justify and indent the paragraph below the heading "Interior Decorators" and the paragraph below the heading "Getting Started Step by Step." Finally, justify and indent the last paragraph in the document, and then indent the two bulleted lists and the numbered list to match the other indented paragraphs. When you are finished, the text and lists below the three boldface headings should all be indented by 0.5 inch. Save the document.

11. If necessary, move the heading "Getting Started Step by Step" to the top of page 2.

12. Display the Clipboard task pane. Copy the list of interior designers and their specialties (starting with Peter Hernandez and ending with Casey Rikli) to the Clipboard. Also copy the list of interior decorators and their specialties (beginning with Jonathan Ivory and ending with Julia Brock) to the Clipboard.

13. Open the file **Staff** located in the Tutorial.02\Review folder included with your Data Files, and save the document as **Pemberly Staff** in the same folder. In the subtitle, insert your first and last name after the word "by."

14. Display the Clipboard task pane. Below the heading "Interior Designers," paste the list of interior designers, which begins "Peter Hernandez." Below the heading "Interior Decorators," paste the list of interior decorators, which begins "Jonathan Ivory." In each case, start by moving the insertion point to the blank paragraph below the heading. Notice that text inserted from the Clipboard retains its original formatting.

15. Clear the contents of the Clipboard task pane, and then print the document.

16. Save the Pemberly Staff document and close it. Close the Clipboard task pane.

17. Save the Getting Started document, deselect any selected text, preview the document, and print it.

18. Save the Getting Started document as **Verve Sample** in the same folder.

19. Select the Verve theme, and then review the newly formatted document and its list of fonts. Check the company name in the paragraph below the heading "Getting Started Step by Step" and make sure it is still formatted in Arial.

20. Save the Verve Sample document, preview it, print it, and close it. Close any other open documents. Submit the finished documents to your instructor, either in printed or electronic form, as requested.

Apply | **Case Problem 1**

Apply the skills you learned to create a one-page flyer.

Data File needed for this Case Problem: New.docx

Peach Tree School of the Arts Students at Peach Tree School of the Arts, in Savannah, Georgia, can choose from a wide range of after-school classes in fine arts, music, and theater. Amanda Reinhard, the school director, has created a flyer informing parents of some additional offerings. It's your job to format the flyer to make it professional looking and easy to read.

1. Open the file **New** located in the Tutorial.02\Case1 folder included with your Data Files, and save the file as **New Classes** in the same folder.

2. Correct any spelling or grammar errors. Ignore the sentence fragments highlighted by the grammar checker. These fragments will make sense once they are formatted as part of a bulleted list.

3. Proofread for other errors, such as words that are spelled correctly but used incorrectly. Use the Replace command to replace "P.M." with "p.m." throughout the document.

4. Replace "Marcus Cody" with your name.

5. Change the top, left, right, and bottom margins to 1.5 inches, and then save your work.

6. Format everything in the document except the title and subtitle in 12-point Times New Roman font. Format the title and subtitle in Arial, 16 point, bold.

7. Format the list of new classes (which begins "Advanced Drawing") as a bulleted list, using the square bullet style.

8. Move the third bulleted item (which begins "Jazz Dance...") up to make it the first bulleted item in the list.

9. Format the four-step check list near the end of the document as a numbered list, using the default numbering style.

10. Save your work, preview the document, switch back to Print Layout view to make any changes you think necessary, print the document, and then close it. Submit the finished document to your instructor, either in printed or electronic form, as requested.

Apply | Case Problem 2

Use your skills to format the summary document shown in Figure 2-37.

Data File needed for this Case Problem: Moth.docx

Hamilton Polytechnic Institute Finn Hansen is an associate researcher in the Department of Entomology at Hamilton Polytechnic Institute. He is working on a nationwide program that aims to slow the spread of a devastating forest pest, the gypsy moth. He has created a one-page document that will be used as part of a campaign to inform the public about current efforts to manage gypsy moths in North America. Format the document by completing the following steps.

1. Open the file **Moth** located in the Tutorial.02\Case2 folder included with your Data Files, and then check your screen to make sure your settings match those in the tutorial.
2. Save the file as **Gypsy Moth** in the same folder.
3. Format the document as shown in Figure 2-37.

Figure 2-37

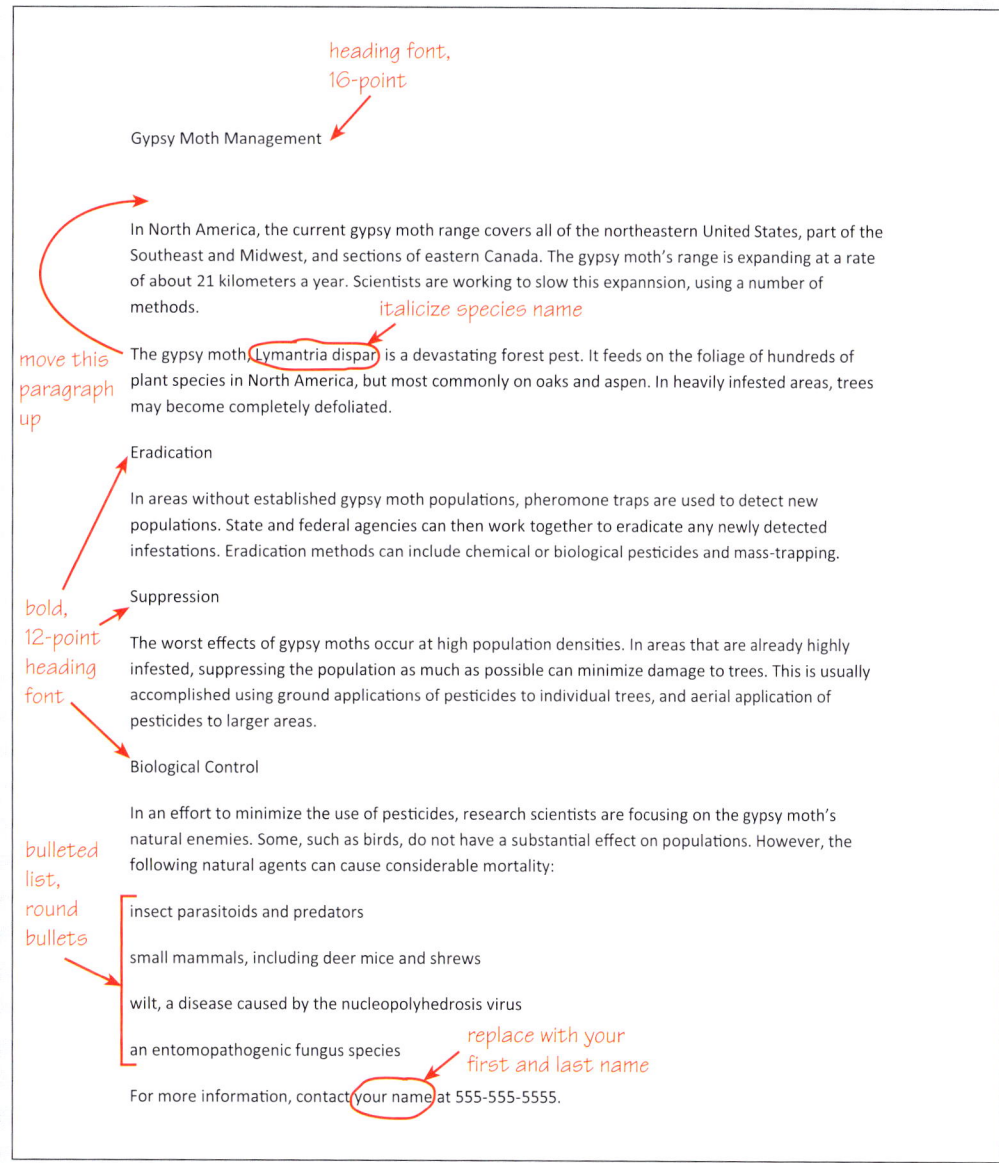

⟐ EXPLORE
4. Use the ruler to indent a paragraph, as follows:

a. Make sure the horizontal ruler is displayed and the document is in Print Layout view.

b. Click anywhere in the paragraph below the heading "Eradication."

c. Position the pointer on the small gray rectangle on the ruler at the left margin (the rectangle is below the two triangles). A ScreenTip with the words "Left Indent" appears.

d. Press and hold down the mouse button. A vertical dotted line appears in the document window, indicating the current left margin. Drag the Left Indent marker right to the 0.5-inch mark on the ruler, and then release the mouse button.

5. Use the Format Painter to copy the indent to the paragraph below the heading "Suppression" and the heading "Biological Control."

6. Indent the bulleted list so it aligns below the preceding paragraph.

7. Use the Spelling and Grammar checker to make corrections as needed, proofread for additional errors, save, and preview the document.

8. Print the document, and then close it. Submit the finished document to your instructor, either in printed or electronic form, as requested.

Challenge | Case Problem 3

Expand your formatting skills to create a resume for an aspiring sales representative.

Data File needed for this Case Problem: Resume.docx

Educational Publishing   Elena Pelliterri has over a decade of experience in education. She worked as a writing teacher and then as a college supervisor of student teachers. Now she would like to pursue a career as a sales representative for a company that publishes textbooks and other educational materials. She has asked you to edit and format her resume. Complete the resume by completing the following steps.

1. Open the file **Resume** located in the Tutorial.02\Case3 folder included with your Data Files, and then check your screen to make sure your settings match those in the tutorial.

2. Save the file as **Elena Resume** in the same folder.

3. Search for the text "your name", and replace it with your first and last name.

4. Replace all occurrences of "Aroyo" with "Arroyo."

5. Use the Spelling and Grammar checker to correct any errors in the document. Note that this document contains lines that the Spelling and Grammar checker might consider sentence fragments but that are acceptable in a resume.

6. Delete the word "traveling" from the sentence below the "OBJECTIVE" heading.

7. Change the document theme to Metro.

8. Format the resume as described in Figure 2-38. Use the Format Painter to copy formatting as necessary.

Figure 2-38

Resume Element	Format
Name "Elena Pelliterri"	16-point, heading font, bold, with underline
Address, phone number, and e-mail address	14-point, heading font, bold
Uppercase headings (OBJECTIVE, EXPERIENCE, etc.)	11-point, heading font, bold
Two subheadings below EXPERIENCE, which begin "Rio Mesa College..." and "Middleton Public Schools..."	11-point, heading font, bold, italic
Lists of teaching experience, educational history, and so on, below the resume headings and subheadings	Bulleted list with square bullets

9. Reorder the two items under the "COMPUTER SKILLS" heading so that the second item becomes the first.

EXPLORE 10. Open a new, blank document, type some text, and experiment with the Change Case button in the Font group on the Home tab. Close the document without saving it, and then change the name "Elena Pelliterri" at the top of the resume to all uppercase.

11. Save, preview, and print the document.

EXPLORE 12. Experiment with two special paragraph alignment options: first line and hanging.

   a. Save the document as **Alignment Samples**. Make sure the horizontal ruler is displayed and the document is in Print Layout view.

   b. Select the two bulleted items under the subheading "Middleton Public Schools." Click the Bullets button to remove the bulleted list format.

   c. With the paragraphs still selected, locate the alignment markers on the left side of the horizontal ruler. Position the pointer over the bottom, triangle-shaped alignment marker. A ScreenTip with the words "Hanging Indent" appears. (If you see a different ScreenTip, such as "Left Indent," you don't have the pointer positioned properly.)

   d. Press and hold down the mouse button. A vertical dotted line appears in the document window, indicating the current left margin. Drag the Hanging Indent marker right to the 1-inch mark on the ruler, and then release the mouse button.

   e. Select the two bulleted items under the heading "Educational History" and remove the bulleted list formatting. Position the mouse pointer over the top, triangle-shaped alignment marker until you see the ScreenTip "First Line Indent." Drag the First Line Indent marker right to the 1-inch mark on the ruler, and then release the mouse button.

13. Save, preview, and print the document.

14. Close the document. Close any other open documents. Submit the finished documents to your instructor, either in printed or electronic form, as requested.

Challenge		**Case Problem 4**

Explore new ways to format an order form for a baking supply company.

Data File needed for this Case Problem: Flour.docx

McElmeel Baking Supply Melissa Martinez is the sales manager for McElmeel Baking Supply, a wholesale distributor of gourmet baking ingredients based in Ames, Iowa. The company is currently offering a special on flour. Melissa has started work on an order form that explains the special offer. She plans to include the form with each invoice sent out next month. It's your job to format the order form to make it easy to use.

1. Open the file **Flour** located in Tutorial.02\Case4 folder included with your Data Files, and save the file as **Flour Form** in the same folder.

EXPLORE
2. When you type Web addresses or e-mail addresses in a document, Word formats them as links. When you click a Web address formatted as a link, Windows opens a Web browser (such as Microsoft Internet Explorer) and, if your computer is connected to the Internet, displays that Web page. Likewise, Word recognizes text that looks like an e-mail address, and formats such text as links as well. If you click an e-mail address formatted as a link, Windows opens a program in which you can type an e-mail message. The address you clicked is included, by default, as the recipient of the e-mail. You'll see how this works as you add a Web address and e-mail address to the order form. At the top of the document, click at the end of the company name, add a new line, and then type the address for the company's Web site: **www.McElmeelBaking.course.com**. (The company is fictitious and does not really have a Web site.) When you are finished, press the Enter key. Word formats the address in blue with an underline, marking it as a link. Move the mouse pointer over the link and read the ScreenTip.

EXPLORE
3. In the line below the Web address, type **McElmeel_Baking@course.com** and then press the Enter key. Word formats the e-mail address as a link. Press and hold the Ctrl key and then click the e-mail link. Your default e-mail program opens, displaying a window where you could type an e-mail message to McElmeel Baking Supply. (If your computer is not set up for email, close any error messages or wizard dialog boxes that open.) Close the e-mail window without saving any changes. The e-mail link is now formatted in a color other than blue, indicating that the link has been clicked.

EXPLORE
4. Right-click the Web site address, and then click Remove Hyperlink in the shortcut menu. Do the same for the e-mail address. The links are now formatted as ordinary text.

5. Delete the phrase "regular clients," and replace it with "loyal customers."

6. Use the Margins menu to change the top and bottom margins to 1 inch and the left and right margins to 2 inches.

7. Format the entire document in the Arial font.

8. At the top of the document, center and single space the company name, Web address, and e-mail address. Remove extra paragraph spacing from all three paragraphs.

9. Change the font size for the company name at the top of the document to 16 points.

10. Near the middle of the document, bold and single space the company address. Remove extra paragraph spacing from all three paragraphs.

11. Format the blank ruled lines at the bottom of the order form as a numbered list.

12. Insert your name in the form to the right of "Name:".

EXPLORE
13. Save your work and preview the document. Click the One Page button on the Print Preview tab to view the entire document on the screen at one time. Print the document and then close the Print Preview window.

EXPLORE 14. The Words box in the bottom, left-hand corner of the document window shows you the number of words in a document. To see more useful statistics, you can use the Word Count dialog box. Click the Words box in the lower-left corner of the document window to open the Word Count dialog box. Note the number of characters (not including spaces), paragraphs, and lines in the document, and then write these statistics in the upper-right corner of the printout. Close the Word Count dialog box.

15. Save and close the document. Submit the finished document to your instructor, either in printed or electronic form, as requested.

| Research | **Internet Assignments** |

Go to the Web to find information you can use to create documents.

The purpose of the Internet Assignments is to challenge you to find information on the Internet that you can use to work effectively with this software. The actual assignments are updated and maintained on the Course Technology Web site. Log on to the Internet and use your Web browser to go to the Student Online Companion for New Perspectives Office 2007 at **www.course.com/np/office2007**. Then navigate to the Internet Assignments for this tutorial.

| Assess | **SAM Assessment and Training** |

If you have a SAM user profile, you may have access to hands-on instruction, practice, and assessment of the skills covered in this tutorial. Log in to your SAM account (**http://sam2007.course.com**) to launch any assigned training activities or exams that relate to the skills covered in this tutorial.

| Review | **Quick Check Answers** |

Session 2.1

1. True
2. True
3. Select the text you want to move. Press and hold down the mouse button until the drag-and-drop pointer appears, and then drag the selected text to its new location. Use the dotted insertion point as a guide to determine exactly where the text will be inserted. Release the mouse button to drop the text at the insertion point.
4. Select the text you want to cut, and then click the Cut button in the Clipboard group on the Home tab. Move the insertion point to the target location in the document, and then click the Paste button in the Clipboard group on the Home tab.
5. Click the Find button in the Editing group on the Home tab.
6. Select the Match case check box.

Session 2.2

1. alignment

2. Click the Increase Indent button in the Paragraph group on the Home tab.

3. Move the insertion point to the paragraph whose formatting you want to copy, double-click the Format Painter button, and then click each paragraph you want to format. When you are finished, click the Format Painter button again to deselect it.

4. A gallery of numbered list styles. To display it (along with other numbered list options), click the Numbering button arrow in the Paragraph group on the Home tab.

5. A theme controls the variety of fonts, colors, and other visual effects available to you as you format a document. Each theme is designed to provide a coordinated, harmonious-looking document.

6. Select the text you want to change. Click the Font arrow in the Font group to display the list of fonts. Move the mouse pointer over the list of font names and observe a preview of the fonts in the selected text. Click the font you want to use.

7. They are the heading and body fonts for the document's theme. They are really instructions that tell Word to use the heading and body fonts for the currently selected theme.

Ending Data Files

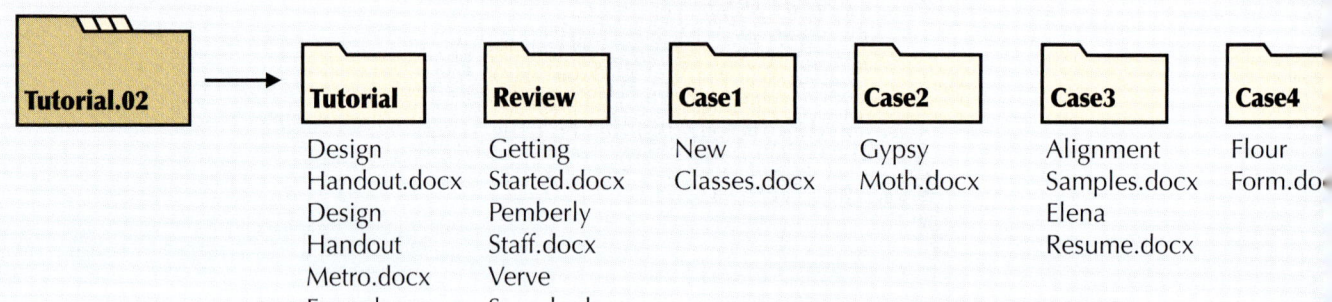

Tutorial.02

Tutorial
Design
Handout.docx
Design
Handout
Metro.docx
Formal
Designs.docx

Review
Getting
Started.docx
Pemberly
Staff.docx
Verve
Sample.docx

Case1
New
Classes.docx

Case2
Gypsy
Moth.docx

Case3
Alignment
Samples.docx
Elena
Resume.docx

Case4
Flour
Form.do

Objectives

Session 3.1
- Format headings with Quick Styles
- Insert a manual page break
- Create and edit a table
- Sort rows in a table
- Modify a table's structure
- Format a table

Session 3.2
- Set tab stops
- Create footnotes and endnotes
- Divide a document into sections
- Create a SmartArt graphic
- Create headers and footers
- Insert a cover page

Creating a Multiple-Page Report

Writing a Recommendation

Case | Parkside Housing Coalition

Robin Kinsella is the director of Parkside Housing Coalition, a nonprofit organization that provides low-cost rental housing in Evanston, Illinois, at more than 50 properties it owns and manages in the Evanston area. Robin has been investigating a plan to reduce utility bills for Parkside residents through a process known as an energy audit. Robin has written a multiple-page report for the board of directors at Parkside Housing Coalition summarizing basic information about energy audits. It's your job to finish formatting the report. She also needs some help adding a table to the end of the report.

In this tutorial, you will format headings with Quick Styles and insert a manual page break. Then you will insert a table, select all or part of a table, sort a table's rows, insert and delete rows or columns, change column widths, and format a table to improve its appearance. You will also set tab stops, create footnotes and endnotes, and insert a section break. Finally, you will create a SmartArt graphic, add headers and footers, and insert a cover page.

Starting Data Files

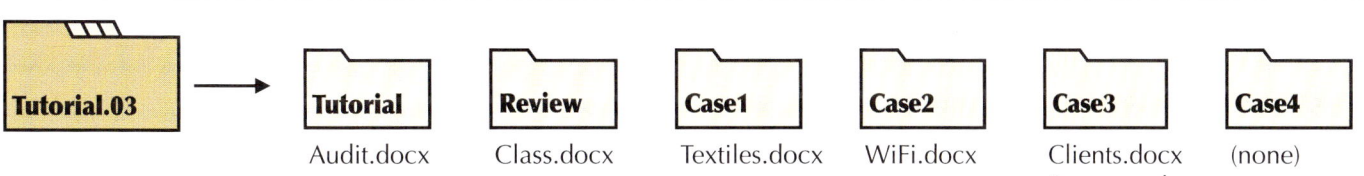

Tutorial.03 →	Tutorial	Review	Case1	Case2	Case3	Case4
	Audit.docx	Class.docx	Textiles.docx	WiFi.docx	Clients.docx Expenses.docx	(none)

Session 3.1

Planning the Document

Robin saved her draft of the report as a Word document named Audit. In its current form, the report is two pages long. By the time you are finished, it will be five pages long, containing a title page, a table, and an illustration, each on a separate page. Figure 3-1 illustrates the revisions you'll be making to the report.

Figure 3-1   **Revisions planned for Audit document**

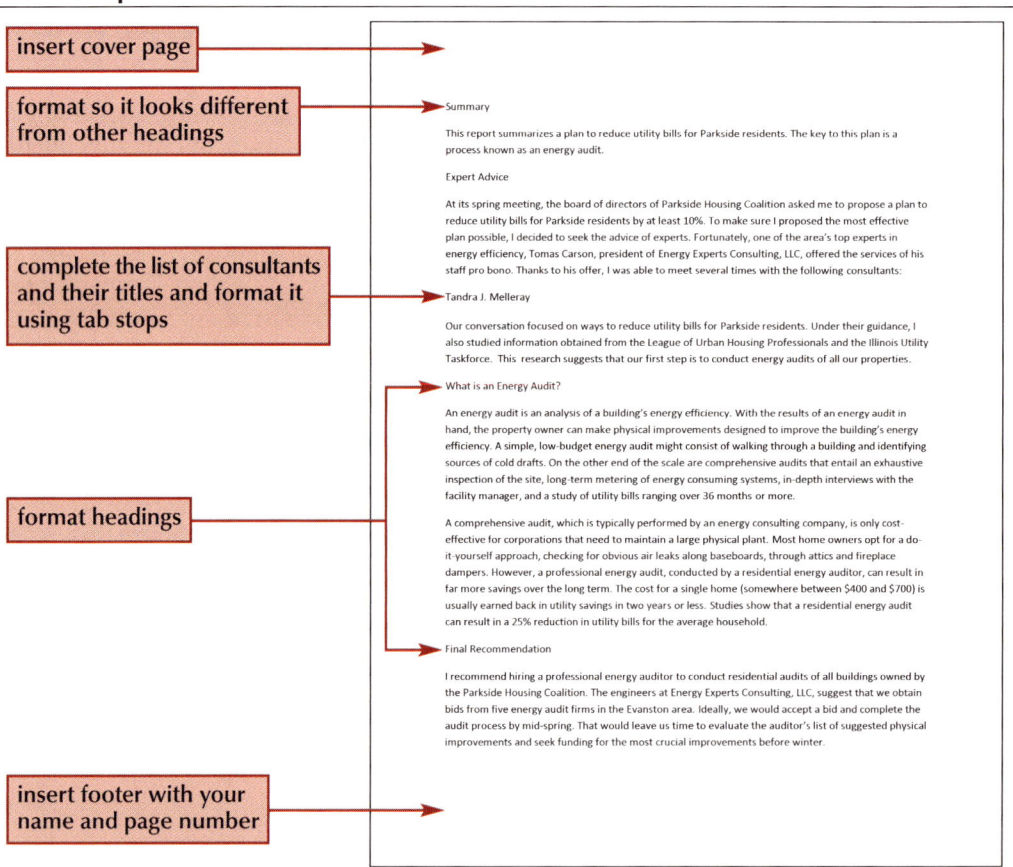

- insert cover page
- format so it looks different from other headings
- complete the list of consultants and their titles and format it using tab stops
- format headings
- insert footer with your name and page number

Summary

This report summarizes a plan to reduce utility bills for Parkside residents. The key to this plan is a process known as an energy audit.

Expert Advice

At its spring meeting, the board of directors of Parkside Housing Coalition asked me to propose a plan to reduce utility bills for Parkside residents by at least 10%. To make sure I proposed the most effective plan possible, I decided to seek the advice of experts. Fortunately, one of the area's top experts in energy efficiency, Tomas Carson, president of Energy Experts Consulting, LLC, offered the services of his staff pro bono. Thanks to his offer, I was able to meet several times with the following consultants:

Tandra J. Melleray

Our conversation focused on ways to reduce utility bills for Parkside residents. Under their guidance, I also studied information obtained from the League of Urban Housing Professionals and the Illinois Utility Taskforce. This research suggests that our first step is to conduct energy audits of all our properties.

What is an Energy Audit?

An energy audit is an analysis of a building's energy efficiency. With the results of an energy audit in hand, the property owner can make physical improvements designed to improve the building's energy efficiency. A simple, low-budget energy audit might consist of walking through a building and identifying sources of cold drafts. On the other end of the scale are comprehensive audits that entail an exhaustive inspection of the site, long-term metering of energy consuming systems, in-depth interviews with the facility manager, and a study of utility bills ranging over 36 months or more.

A comprehensive audit, which is typically performed by an energy consulting company, is only cost-effective for corporations that need to maintain a large physical plant. Most home owners opt for a do-it-yourself approach, checking for obvious air leaks along baseboards, through attics and fireplace dampers. However, a professional energy audit, conducted by a residential energy auditor, can result in far more savings over the long term. The cost for a single home (somewhere between $400 and $700) is usually earned back in utility savings in two years or less. Studies show that a residential energy audit can result in a 25% reduction in utility bills for the average household.

Final Recommendation

I recommend hiring a professional energy auditor to conduct residential audits of all buildings owned by the Parkside Housing Coalition. The engineers at Energy Experts Consulting, LLC, suggest that we obtain bids from five energy audit firms in the Evanston area. Ideally, we would accept a bid and complete the audit process by mid-spring. That would leave us time to evaluate the auditor's list of suggested physical improvements and seek funding for the most crucial improvements before winter.

Revisions planned for Audit document (page 2) | **Figure 3-1 (cont.)**

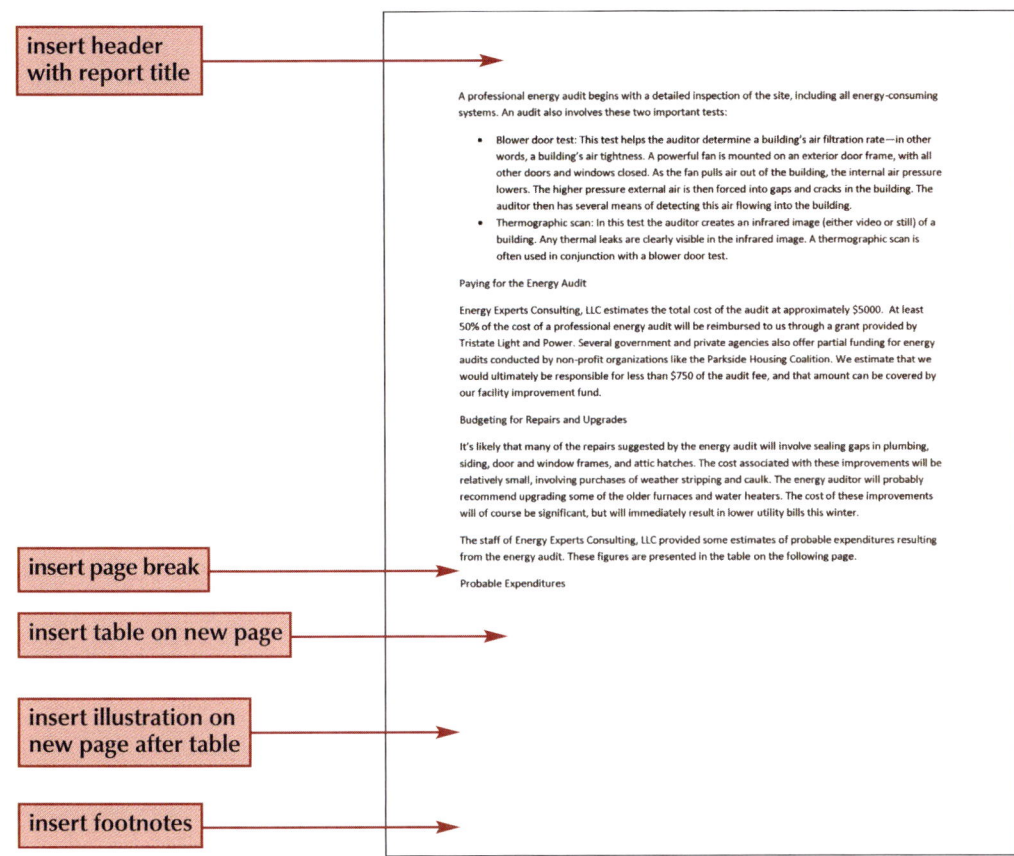

insert header with report title

insert page break

insert table on new page

insert illustration on new page after table

insert footnotes

Now that you have a sense of the revisions you'll be making, you are ready to get started.

To open the document:

1. Start Word, and then open the file **Audit** located in the Tutorial.03\Tutorial folder included with your Data Files.

2. To avoid altering the original file, save the document as **Audit Report** in the same folder.

3. Check your settings to make sure your screen matches the figures in this tutorial. In particular, be sure to display the nonprinting characters, switch to Print Layout view if necessary, display the rulers, and set the zoom so you can see the entire width of the page.

Formatting Headings with Quick Styles

Your first job is to format the headings to make them easier to distinguish from the body text. You already know how to draw attention to text by adding bold, italic, or underline formatting. You also know how to use a heading font. To give a document a really polished look, you can use **Quick Styles**, which allow you to apply an entire set of formatting choices with one click. A Quick Style typically applies many formatting options at once, such as, bold, a specific font, a specific indent setting, and a new color for the text (that is, a new **font color**).

Some Quick Styles apply **paragraph-level formatting**—that is, they are set up to format an entire paragraph (for example, adding space before and after a heading paragraph). Other Quick Styles apply **character-level formatting**—that is, they are set up to format only a few characters or words (for example, formatting a book title in italics).

The Quick Styles gallery on the Home tab gives you access to the document's Quick Styles (or just "styles," as they are sometimes called). One row of the gallery is always visible on the Home tab. When you first open a document, the visible row contains the four most commonly used Quick Styles (Normal, No Spacing, Heading 1, and Heading 2). These are all paragraph-level Quick Styles, so to use one, you place the insertion point anywhere in the paragraph you want to format, and then click one of the four visible styles. To use any other Quick Style, click the More button in the Styles group to display the entire Quick Styles gallery, and then click the Quick Style you want.

The Quick Styles that are available in a given document are controlled by the document's theme. Each theme uses the same names for its Quick Styles (starting with Normal, No Spacing, Heading 1, and Heading 2), but the formatting applied by a given Quick Style depends on the document's theme. For example, in the Office theme (the default theme for new documents), the Heading 1 style applies the Cambria font in blue. But in the Equity theme, the Heading 1 style applies the Franklin Gothic Book font in dark red.

Robin decided that the Office theme (the default) works fine for the Energy Audit document, so you'll be working with the Quick Styles that come with that theme. She would like you to apply the Intense Quote style to the Summary heading and the Heading 1 style to the other headings. As its name suggests, the Intense Quote style is useful for drawing attention to quotations from a document; however, because it indents text, it's also useful for certain types of headings. It applies paragraph-level formatting, so you need to start by moving the insertion point to the paragraph you want to format.

To format the "Summary" heading with the Intense Quote style:

▶ 1. Click in the paragraph containing the heading **Summary** at the beginning of the document (if necessary), and then on the Home tab, locate the More button in the Styles group, as shown in Figure 3-2.

| Figure 3-2 | Locating the More button |

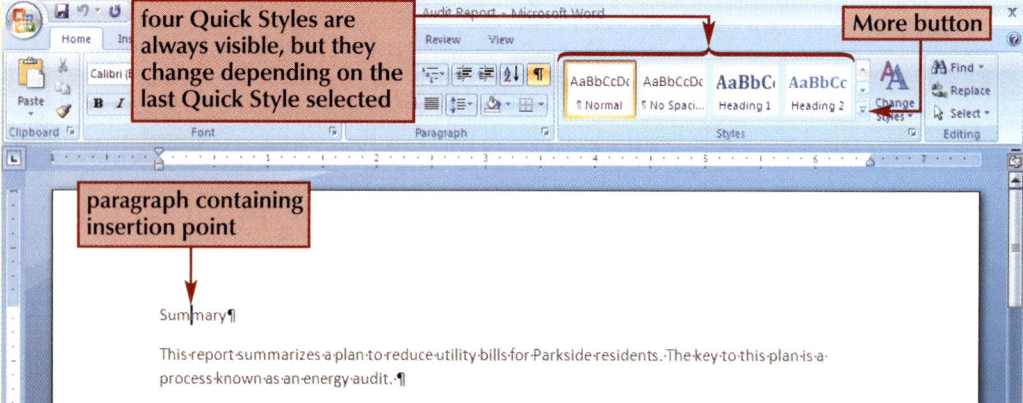

▶ 2. In the Styles group, click the **More** button. The Quick Styles gallery opens, displaying a total of 16 possible Quick Styles.

▶ 3. Move the mouse pointer over the styles in the Quick Styles Gallery. When you point to a style, a ScreenTip displays the style's full name, and the text in your document that contains the insertion point is formatted with a preview of that style.

▶ **4.** Point to (but don't click) the **Intense Quote** style. A preview of the style appears in the document, as shown in Figure 3-3. The Intense Quote style indents text 0.5 inch, inserts a blue line below the text, changes the font color to blue, and adds bold and italic to the text. It does not change the font, which remains 11-point Calibri.

Quick Styles Gallery ◀ **Figure 3-3**

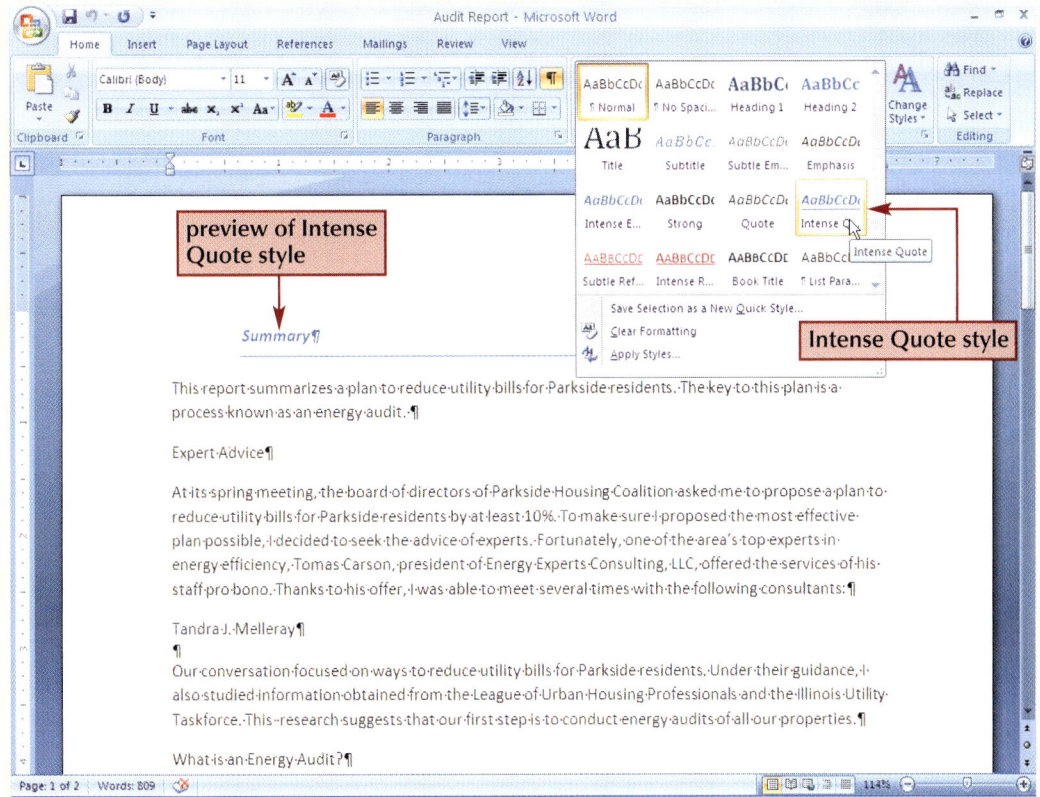

▶ **5.** Click the **Intense Quote** style. The Quick Style is applied to the paragraph containing the heading "Summary." The row of buttons visible on the Ribbon is now the row containing the Intense Quote style. Next, you need to indent the summary itself so it matches the heading.

▶ **6.** Click anywhere in the paragraph that begins "This report summarizes…" and then in the Paragraph group, click the **Increase Indent** button 🔲 twice. (Make sure to click it twice.) The summary paragraph indents to match the "Summary" heading.

Trouble? If the summary paragraph is not indented as far as the "Summary" heading, you probably clicked the Increase Indent button just once. Try clicking it again.

Next, Robin would like you to format the remaining headings in the document with the Heading 1 style. She would also like the table heading at the end of the document to be formatted with the Heading 2 style.

To format the remaining headings with the Heading 1 style:

▶ **1.** Click the heading **Expert Advice**. The Heading 1 style is no longer visible in the Styles group because when you used the Intense Quote style in the last set of steps, the default row was replaced with the row containing the button you just used. This means that you need to open the Quick Styles gallery again.

  2. In the Styles group, click the **More** button, and then click the **Heading 1** style in the Quick Styles gallery. The heading is formatted in blue, 14-point Cambria, with bold. The Heading 1 style also inserts some extra space above the heading. The gallery row containing the Heading 1 style is now visible in the Styles group.

  3. If necessary, scroll down, click the heading **What is an Energy Audit?**, and then press the **F4** key to apply the Heading 1 Quick Style. (Recall that the F4 key repeats your most recent action.) Continue to format these headings with the Heading 1 style: **Final Recommendation**, **Paying for the Energy Audit**, and **Budgeting for Repairs and Upgrades**.

  4. At the end of the document, click the heading **Probable Expenditures** (the caption for the table that you will create later in this tutorial), and format it with the **Heading 2** Quick Style.

  5. Save your work. Figure 3-4 shows two headings formatted with the Heading 1 Quick Style and one with the Heading 2 Quick Style.

Figure 3-4 ▶ **Formatted headings**

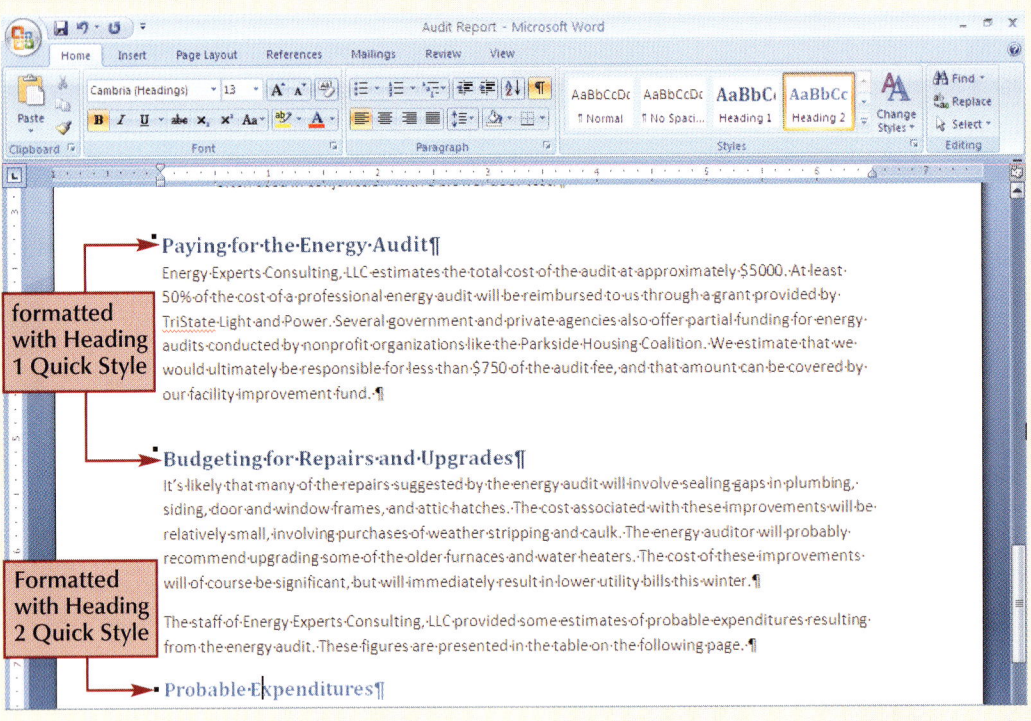

Next, you need to start working on the table of expenditures. Robin wants the table to appear on its own page (to allow plenty of room for the board of directors to make notes on it), so first you need to insert a page break.

Inserting a Manual Page Break

There are two kinds of page breaks in Word—automatic page breaks and manual page breaks. You've already seen how Word inserts automatic page breaks, by starting a new page every time the current page fills up. A **manual page break** is one you insert at a specific location; it doesn't matter if the previous page is full or not. You insert a manual page break by clicking the Page Break button on the Insert tab or by holding down the Ctrl key and pressing the Enter key. Note that the Page Break button and the Ctrl+Enter keys insert a new page *after* the insertion point. To insert a new page *before* the insertion point, use the Blank Page button (also on the Insert tab).

You need to insert a manual page break just before the table caption. This will ensure that the caption and the table are on their own page.

To insert a manual page break:

▶ 1. If necessary, scroll down to the bottom of page 2 until you can see the table caption "Probable Expenditures," and then click to the left of the "P" in "Probable."

▶ 2. Click the **Insert** tab, and then, in the Pages group, click the **Page Break** button. The caption "Probable Expenditures" moves to the top of the new page 3. A dotted line with the words "Page Break" is inserted on page 2, where you positioned the insertion point in Step 1.

   Trouble? If you don't see the dotted line with the words "Page Break," check to make sure your document is displayed in Print Layout view and that nonprinting characters are displayed.

You are now ready to insert the table on the new page 3, just below the table caption.

Organizing Information in Tables

A **table** is information arranged in horizontal rows and vertical columns. It's common to organize text or numerical data in a table, but you can also insert graphics, charts, and other kinds of art into tables. You can format text in various ways in different parts of a table, turning some text so it stretches vertically from top to bottom, while centering other text between the left and right margins. You can even insert one table inside another. All of these options make tables extremely useful for setting up complicated documents. You'll have a chance to explore some of the more advanced table features in the Case Problems at the end of this tutorial. Right now, you'll focus on creating the simple table Robin needs for her report. In the process, you'll gain a good understanding of how to work with tables in Word.

When you first insert a table into a document, it appears as a simple grid structure, with black **gridlines** defining the rows and columns. The area where a row and column intersect is called a **cell**. Depending on your needs, you can create a blank table and then insert information into it (as you'll do next), or you can convert existing text into a table (as you'll do in the Case Problems at the end of this tutorial).

Inserting a Blank Table

Figure 3-5 shows a sketch of what Robin wants the table to look like. The top row of the table, called the **header row**, identifies the type of information in each column. Some tables also include a **header column**, which is a column on the left that identifies the type of information in each row.

Table sketch ◀ **Figure 3-5**

Item	Materials Cost
Weather stripping	$350
High-efficiency water heaters	$8,500
High-efficiency furnaces	$10,000
Insulation	$700

In the following steps, you will insert a blank table by using the Table button on the Insert tab. The Table button allows you to drag the mouse pointer across a blank grid to select the numbers of rows and columns you want to include in your table. A live preview of the table structure appears in the document as you drag the mouse pointer. The table is inserted in the document when you click the mouse button. Keep in mind that the table you insert has the same paragraph and line spacing settings as the paragraph that currently contains the insertion point.

To insert a blank table:

1. Press the **Ctrl+End** keys to move the insertion point to the end of the document (to the blank paragraph below the heading "Probable Expenditures").

2. Make sure the Insert tab is displayed and then, in the Tables group, click the **Table** button. A table grid opens, with a menu at the bottom.

3. Position the pointer in the upper-left cell of the grid, and then drag the pointer down and across the grid until you highlight **two columns** and **five rows**. (The outline of a cell turns orange when it is highlighted.) As you drag the pointer across the grid, Word indicates the size of the table (columns by rows) at the top of the grid. A live preview of the table structure appears in the document. See Figure 3-6.

   Trouble? If the rows of the live preview table are spaced more widely than shown in Figure 3-6, the insertion point is located in a heading, rather than at the end of the document. Press the Esc key to close the Table grid, and begin again with Step 1, taking care to press the Ctrl+End keys as instructed.

Figure 3-6 Inserting a blank table

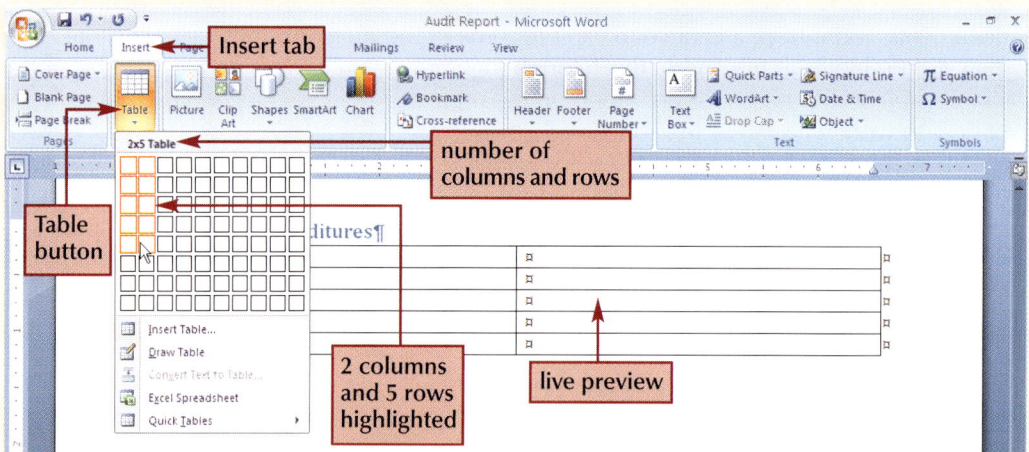

4. When the table size is 2 × 5 (as in Figure 3-6), click the mouse button. An empty table, two columns by five rows, appears below the table caption, with the insertion point in the upper-left cell. The two columns are of equal width. Each cell contains an end-of-cell mark, and each row contains an end-of-row mark, which are important for selecting parts of a table. Two new tabs appear on the Ribbon; the label "Table Tools" identifies them as Table contextual tabs. They are visible only when the table is selected or the insertion point is located inside the table.

   Trouble? If you inserted a table with the wrong number of rows or columns, click the Undo button to remove the table, and then repeat Steps 1 through 4.

▶ **5.** Move the mouse pointer over the empty table. The Table Move handle appears in the table's upper-left corner, and the Table Resize handle appears in the lower-right corner. See Figure 3-7. You don't need to use either of these handles now, but you should understand their function. To select the entire table quickly, you can click the Table Move handle. Then you can move the entire table by dragging the Table Move handle. To change the size of the entire table, you can drag the Table Resize handle.

Trouble? If you don't see the end-of-cell and end-of-row marks, you need to display nonprinting characters. Click the Show/Hide ¶ button on the Home tab.

Tip

To delete a table, select it, right-click it, and then click Cut. If you press the Delete key instead, you'll delete the contents of the table, but not the table itself.

Blank table inserted in document — **Figure 3-7**

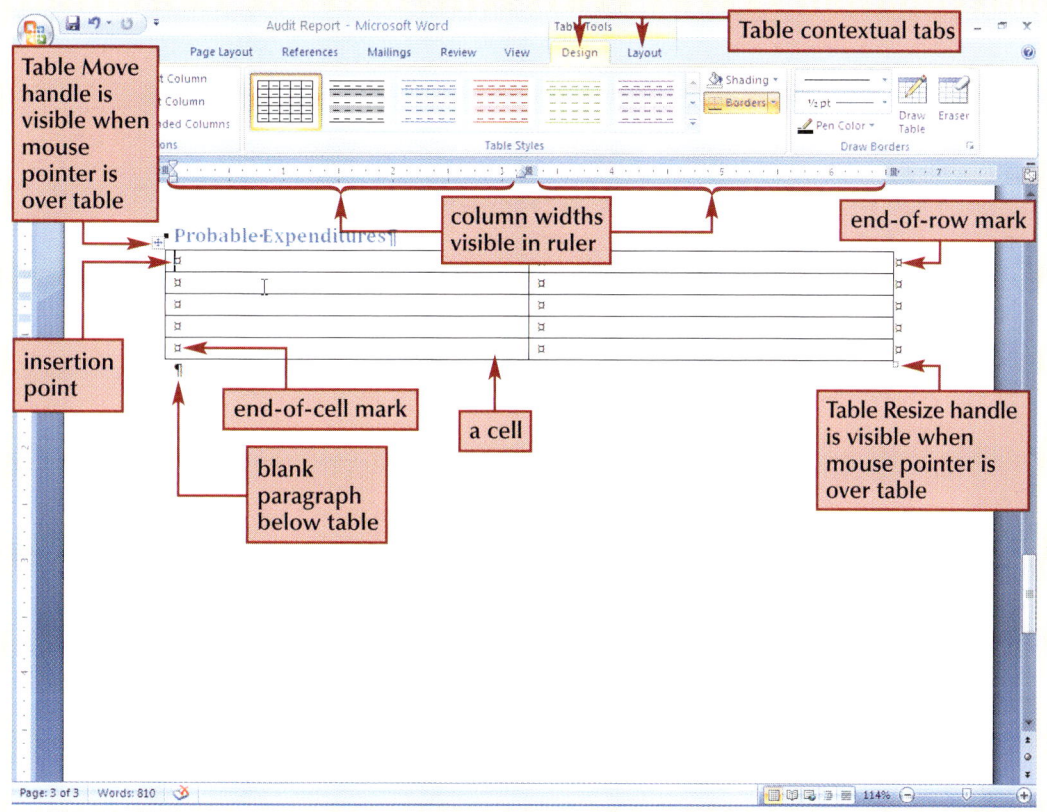

The blank table is ready for you to begin entering information. You'll do that next.

Entering Data in a Table

You can enter data in a table by moving the insertion point to a cell and typing. If the data takes up more than one line in the cell, Word automatically wraps the text to the next line and increases the height of that cell (and all the cells in that row). To move the insertion point to another cell in the table, you can click in that cell, use the arrow keys, or use the Tab key.

To enter data into the table:

▶ **1.** Verify that the insertion point is located in the upper-left cell.

▶ **2.** Type **Item**. As you type, the end-of-cell mark moves right to accommodate the text.

3. Press the **Tab** key to move to the next cell to the right.

Trouble? If Word created a new paragraph in the first cell rather than moving the insertion point to the second cell, you pressed the Enter key instead of the Tab key. Press the Backspace key to remove the paragraph mark, and then press the Tab key to move to the second cell in the first row.

4. Type **Materials Cost**, and then press the **Tab** key to move to the first cell in the second row. Notice that when you press the Tab key in the right column, the insertion point moves to the first column in the next row.

You have finished entering the header row—the row that identifies the information in each column. Now you can enter the information about the various expenditures.

To continue entering information in the table:

1. Type **weather stripping**, and then press the **Tab** key to move to the second cell in the second row. Notice that the "w" in "weather stripping" is capitalized, even though you typed it in lowercase. By default, AutoCorrect capitalizes the first letter in a cell entry.

2. Type **$350**, and then press the **Tab** key to move the insertion point to the first cell in the third row.

3. Type the following information to complete the table, pressing the Tab key to move from cell to cell. When you are finished, your table should look like the one in Figure 3-8.

High-efficiency water heaters	**$8,500**
High-efficiency furnaces	**$10,000**
Insulation	**$700**

Figure 3-8 Table with all data entered

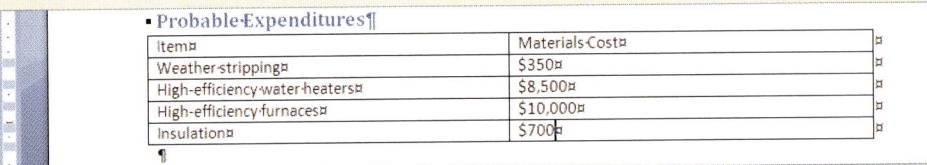

• Probable·Expenditures¶	
Item¤	Materials·Cost¤
Weather·stripping¤	$350¤
High-efficiency·water·heaters¤	$8,500¤
High-efficiency·furnaces¤	$10,000¤
Insulation¤	$700¤

Trouble? If a new row (row 6) appears at the bottom of your table, you pressed the Tab key when the insertion point was in the last cell in the table. Click the Undo button on the Quick Access Toolbar to remove row 6 from the table.

The table you've just created presents information about expenditures in an easy-to-read structure. Your next job is to format the header row in bold so it stands out from the rest of the table. To do that, you need to know how to select a table row.

Selecting Part of a Table

As you have learned, you can select the entire table by clicking the Table Move handle (just above the upper-left corner of the table). You can also click the Select button on the Table Tools Layout tab and then click Select Table.

To select part of a table, you can drag the mouse pointer, just as you would to select regular text in a document—but that's not a good idea, because you can easily miss the end-of-cell mark in a cell or the end-of-row mark at the end of a row. This can produce unpredictable results when you are performing certain formatting or editing tasks. The most foolproof way to select part of a table is to use the Select button on the Table Tools Layout tab. A third method, which is often the most convenient, is to select a row by clicking in the left margin next to the row. Similarly, to select a column, you can click just above the column. After you've selected an entire row or column, you can drag the mouse to select more rows or columns.

You'll get some practice selecting a row in the following steps, as you format the header row in bold. Formatting the header row in bold is helpful for two reasons: (1) it makes it easier to distinguish between the header row and the rest of the data in the table; and (2) when you are using certain table commands, it allows Word to recognize the header row as a special part of the table. Later in this tutorial, you'll apply more elaborate formatting to the table.

To select and format the header row:

▶ 1. Move the mouse pointer to the left of the table next to the first row (which contains the word "Item"). The pointer changes to a right-facing arrow 𝒜.

▶ 2. Click the left mouse button. The entire header row, including the end-of-cell mark in each cell and the end-of-row mark, is selected. See Figure 3-9. To format this row in bold, you could switch to the Home tab and click the Bold button or use the Mini toolbar, but it's faster to use a keyboard shortcut.

Header row selected ◀ **Figure 3-9**

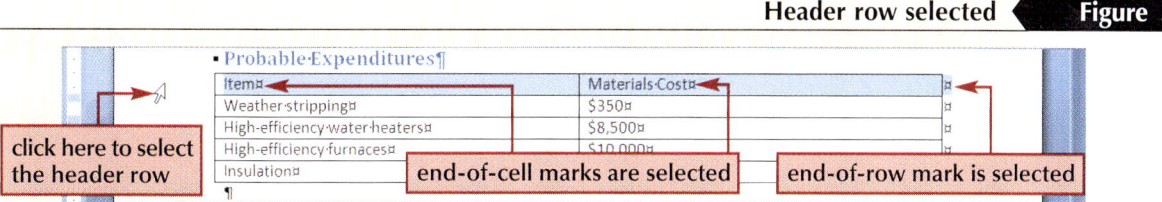

▶ 3. Press the **Ctrl+B** keys. The headers are formatted in bold.

▶ 4. Click anywhere in the table to deselect the header row, and then save your work.

You've created a very basic table. Now you can sort the information in the table and improve its appearance.

Sorting Rows in a Table

The term **sort** refers to the process of rearranging information in alphabetical, numerical, or chronological order. You can sort a series of paragraphs, such as a list or the rows of a table.

When you sort a table, you arrange the rows based on the contents of one of the columns. For example, you could sort the table you just created based on the contents of the Item column—either in ascending alphabetical order (from *A* to *Z*) or in descending alphabetical order (from *Z* to *A*). Alternately, you could sort the table based on the contents of the Materials Cost column—either in ascending numerical order (lowest to highest) or in descending numerical order (highest to lowest).

To sort a table, select the table, then, on the Table Tools Layout tab, click the Sort button. This opens the Sort dialog box, which provides a number of options that allow you to fine-tune the sorting process. You'll have to change fewer settings in the Sort dialog box if you first take the time to format the headers in bold, as you just did. That way Word recognizes the bold text as headers and excludes them from the sorting process, leaving them unsorted at the top of the table.

| Reference Window | **Sorting the Rows of a Table** |

- Format the column headers in bold, and then select the entire table.
- In the Data group on the Table Tools Layout tab, click the Sort button.
- In the Sort dialog box, click the Sort by arrow, and then select the header for the column you want to sort by. For example, if you want to organize the rows in the table according to the contents of the Last Name column, click "Last Name."
- In the Type list box located to the right of the Sort by list box, select the type of information stored in the column you want to sort by. You can choose to sort text, dates, or numbers.
- To sort in alphabetical, chronological, or numeric order, click the Ascending option button. To sort in reverse order, click the Descending option button.
- If you also want to sort by a second column, click the Then by arrow and click a column header. This is useful if, for example, you want to organize the table rows by last name, and then, within each last name, by first name. You can also specify the type of information in the Then by column, and whether you want to sort in ascending or descending order.
- Make sure the Header row option button is selected. This tells Word that the table you want to sort includes a header row that should not be sorted along with the other rows.
- Click the OK button.

Robin would like you to sort the table in ascending alphabetical order, based on the contents of the Item column.

To sort the information in the table:

1. Make sure the insertion point is somewhere in the table, and then click the **Table Tools Layout** tab.

2. In the Table group, click the **Select** button, and then click **Select Table**. The entire table is selected.

3. In the Data group, click the **Sort** button. The Sort dialog box opens, as shown in Figure 3-10. By default, the far-left column heading ("Item") is already selected in the Sort by list box. This tells Word to sort the rows of the table according to the contents of the Item column, which is what you want. Word recognizes the information in the Item column as text, so "Text" is selected by default in the Type list box. (If the column contained dates or numbers, you would see Date or Number in the Type list box instead.) The Ascending option button next to the Sort by list box is selected by default, indicating that Word will sort the contents of the Item column from *A* to *Z*. The Header row option button is selected in the lower-left corner of the dialog box. This indicates that the table contains a header row that should not be sorted along with the rest of the rows. The default settings in the Sort dialog box are all correct, so you can go ahead and complete the sort process.

Sort dialog box Figure 3-10

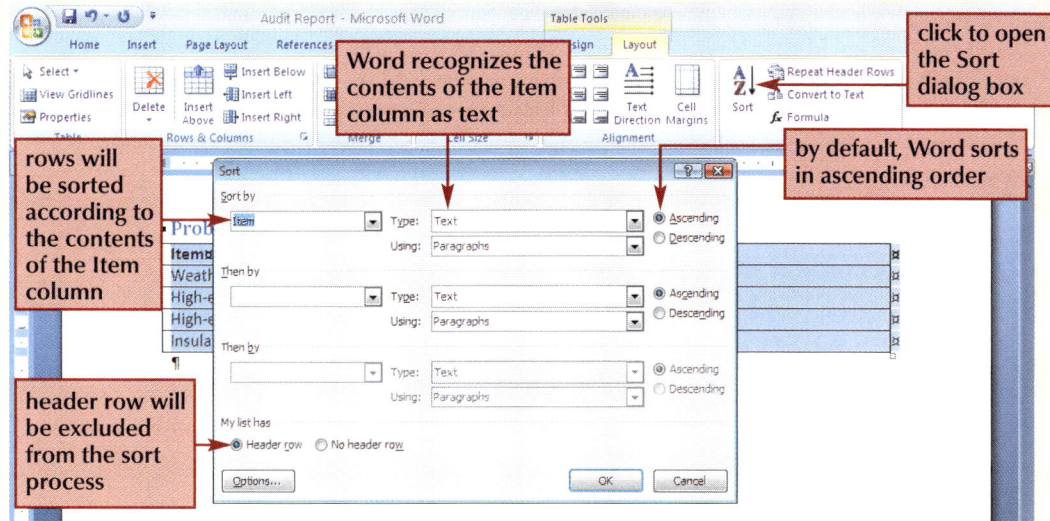

4. Click the **OK** button. The Sort dialog box closes.

5. Click anywhere in the table to deselect it. Rows 2 through 5 are now arranged alphabetically according to the text in the Item column, with the "Weather strip-ping" row now at the bottom. When you sort a table, all the items in a row move together as one entity. In this table, that means the materials cost doesn't become separated from its item during the sort process. Also note that the header row remains in its original position at the top of the table. See Figure 3-11.

Trouble? If the sort was unsuccessful, click the Undo button on the Quick Access Toolbar, and then repeat Steps 1 through 5.

Table after being sorted Figure 3-11

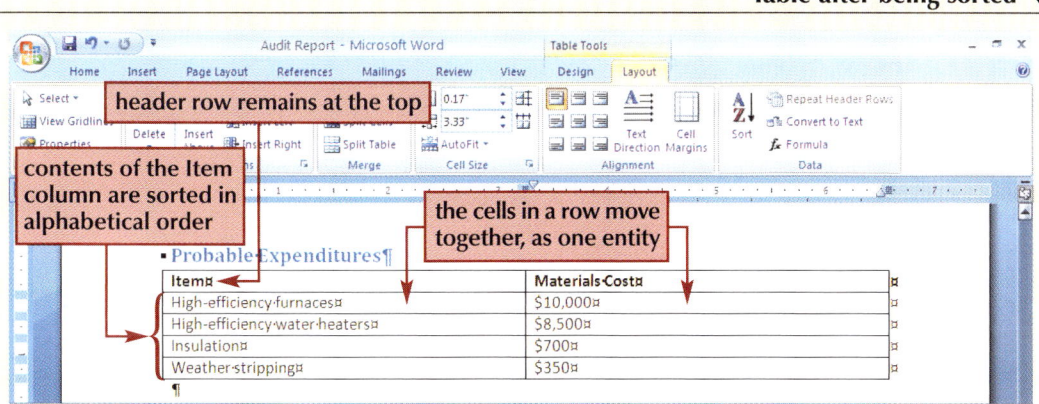

The table looks good, but after reviewing it, Robin decides that she should include an estimate of the labor cost for each item. She asks you to insert a "Labor Cost" column.

Inserting Rows and Columns in a Table

You will often need to modify a table structure by adding or deleting rows and columns. With the buttons in the Rows & Columns group on the Table Tools Layout tab, this is a straightforward task. You'll see how these buttons work in the following steps, as you insert a new column between the Item column and the Materials Cost column. To insert a column, you begin by selecting a column to the left or right of the location where you want to insert a column.

To insert a column in the table:

1. Click any cell in the Item column, click the **Select** button in the Table group, and then click **Select Column**. The Item column is selected.

2. In the Rows & Columns group, click the **Insert Right** button. A new, blank column is inserted to the right of the Item column. The three columns in the table are narrower than the original two columns; the overall width of the table does not change.

3. Click in the top cell of the new column, and enter the following header and data. Use the ↓ key to move the insertion point down through the column.

Labor Cost

$3,000 to $4,500

$2,000 to $3,000

$1,000

$1,500

When you are finished, your table should look like the one in Figure 3-12. Because you selected the entire header row when you formatted the original headers in bold, the newly inserted header, "Labor Cost," is also formatted in bold.

Tip

Word inserts the same number of new columns as are selected. For example, if you had selected two columns in Step 1, Word would have inserted two new columns in the table.

Figure 3-12 | New Labor Cost column

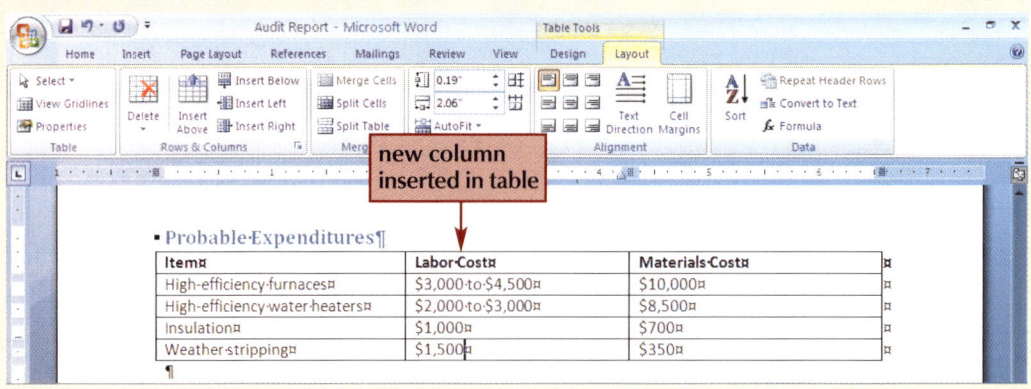

Inserting a row is similar to inserting a column. First, you select a row below the location where you want to insert a row, and then, in the Rows & Columns group, click the Insert Above button. Alternatively, you could select a row above where you want to insert a row, and then click the Insert Below button.

You're almost finished adjusting the structure of the table. But first Robin would like to delete the Insulation row because she's just learned that the costs listed for weather stripping actually cover both weather stripping and insulation.

Deleting Rows and Columns

When you consider deleting a row, you need to be clear about whether you want to delete the *contents* of the row, or the contents and the *structure* of the row. You can delete the *contents* of a row by selecting the row and pressing the Delete key. The same is true for deleting the contents of an individual cell, a column, or the entire table. To delete the *structure* of a row, column, or the entire table—including its contents—you select the row (or column or the entire table) and then use the Delete button in the Rows & Columns group. To delete multiple rows or columns, start by selecting all the rows or columns you want to delete.

Before you delete the Insulation row, you need to edit the bottom row.

To delete the Insulation row:

▶ 1. In the cell containing the text "Weather stripping," click to the right of the "g," press the **spacebar**, and then type **and insulation**. The cell now reads "Weather stripping and insulation." Next, you can delete the Insulation row, which is no longer necessary.

▶ 2. Select the Insulation row by clicking to the left of the row in the left margin.

▶ 3. In the Rows & Columns group, click the **Delete** button. The Delete menu opens, displaying options for deleting cells, columns, rows, or the entire table. See Figure 3-13.

Deleting a row   Figure 3-13

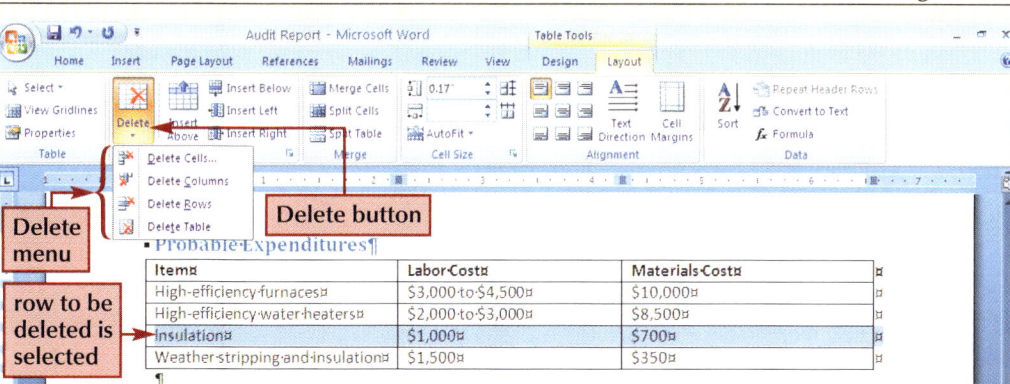

▶ 4. Click **Delete Rows**. The Insulation row is removed from the table.

▶ 5. Save your work.

The table now contains all the information Robin wants to include. Your next job is to adjust the widths of the three columns to make the table attractive and easy to read.

Changing Column Widths

Columns that are too wide for the material they contain can make a table hard to read. You can quickly change a column's width by dragging the column's right border to a new position. Or, if you prefer, you can double-click a column border to make the column width adjust automatically to accommodate the widest entry in the column.

You'll adjust the columns in Robin's table by double-clicking the right column borders. You need to start by making sure that no part of the table is selected. Otherwise, when you double-click the border, only the width of the selected part of the table will change.

To change the width of the columns in the table:

▶ **1.** Verify that no part of the table is selected, and then position the mouse pointer over the right border of the Labor Cost column until the pointer changes to ◄||► . See Figure 3-14.

Figure 3-14 ▶ **Changing the column width**

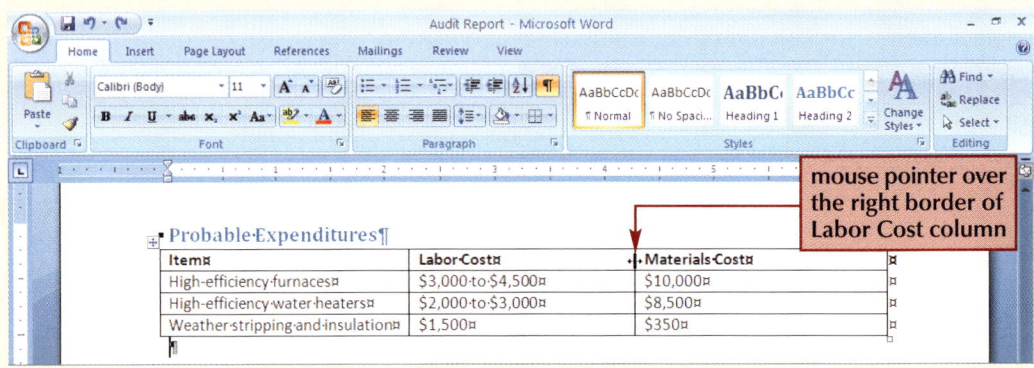

> mouse pointer over the right border of Labor Cost column

Tip

To change the height of a row, position the mouse pointer over the bottom row border and drag the border up or down.

▶ **2.** Double-click the left mouse button. The right column border moves left so that the column is just wide enough to accommodate the widest entry in the column.

▶ **3.** Double-click the right border of the Materials Cost column. The Materials Cost column becomes narrower, leaving just enough room for the widest entry in the column (the column header "Materials Cost").

▶ **4.** Repeat this procedure to adjust the width of the Item column. All three columns in the table are now just wide enough to accommodate their widest entries.

The table is almost finished. Your final job is to add some color and modify the cell borders. As you'll see in the next section, Word's predefined table styles make quick work of these tasks.

Formatting Tables with Styles

Word includes a variety of built-in table styles that you can use to add shading, color, borders, and other design elements with a single click. You can choose a style that includes different formatting for the header row than for the rest of the table. Or you can choose a style that instead applies different formatting to the **first column**, or header column (that is, the far-left column, which sometimes contains headers that identify the type of information in each row). Some styles format the rows in alternating colors, called banded rows, while others format the columns in alternating colors, called banded columns.

At first, the variety of styles available for formatting your tables may seem overwhelming, but once you become familiar with the basic variations (header row formatting, first row formatting, banded rows, banded columns, etc.), you'll grow comfortable with choosing a style that suits your needs. Six table styles are always visible in the Table Styles group on the Table Tools Design tab. To see the complete collection, click the More button in the Table Styles group. After you apply a table style, you can modify it by selecting or deselecting the check boxes in the Table Style Options group on the Table Tools Design tab.

- Click in the table you want to format, and then click the Table Tools Design tab.
- In the Table Styles group, click the More button to display the Table Styles gallery.
- Position the mouse pointer over a style in the Table Styles gallery to see a live preview of the style in the document.
- In the Table Styles gallery, click the style you want.
- To apply or remove style elements (such as special formatting for the header row, banded rows, or banded columns), select or deselect check boxes as necessary in the Table Style Options group.

Robin wants to use a table style that emphasizes the header row with special formatting, that does not include column borders, and that uses color to separate the rows.

To apply a table style to the Probable Expenditures table:

▶ 1. Click anywhere in the table, and then click the **Table Tools Design** tab. Within the six visible styles, the plain black and white grid style is highlighted, indicating that it is the current style of the table in the document. See Figure 3-15.

Table styles visible on the Table Tools Design tab ◀ Figure 3-15

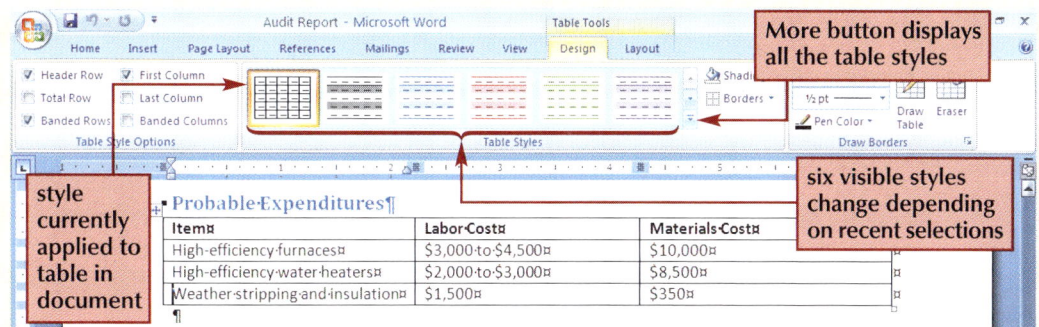

▶ 2. In the Table Styles group, click the **More** button. The Table Styles gallery opens. Now the plain black and white grid style appears at the top of the gallery, under the heading "Plain Tables." The more elaborate Table Styles appear below, in the "Built-In" section of the gallery.

▶ 3. Use the gallery's vertical scroll bar to view the complete collection of table styles. When you are finished looking, scroll up until you can see the Built-In heading again.

▶ 4. Move the mouse pointer over the style located in the fourth row down, second column from the left. See Figure 3-16. A ScreenTip displays the style's official name, "Medium Shading 1 – Accent 1." The style consists of a dark blue heading row, with alternating rows of light blue and white below and no borders between the columns. A live preview of the style is visible in the document, although the size of the Table Styles gallery makes this hard to see.

Figure 3-16 | **Table Styles gallery**

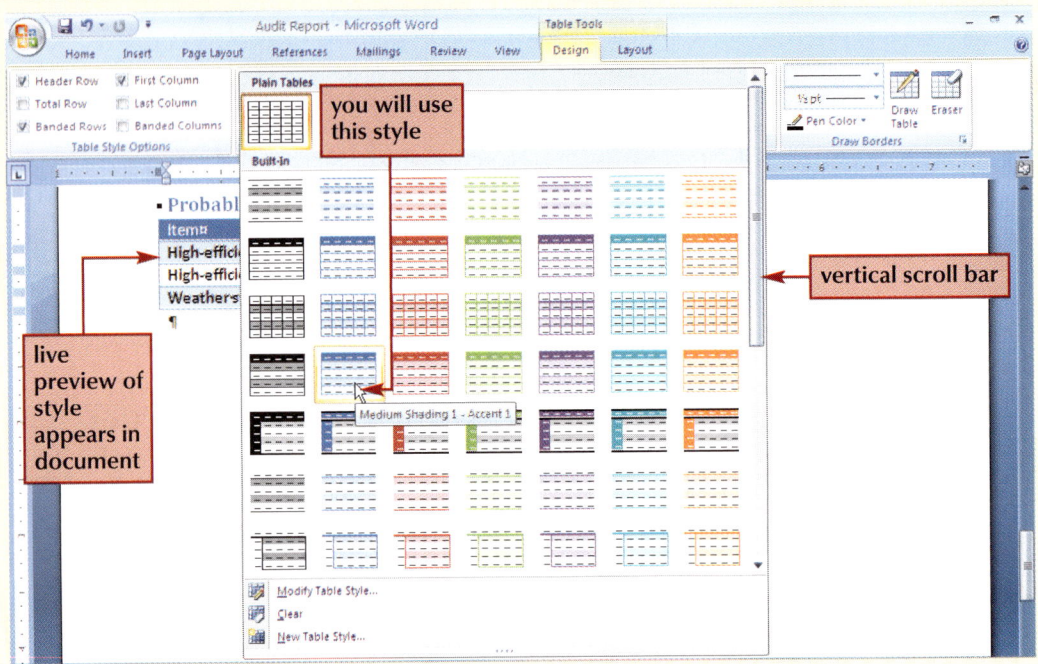

▶ **5.** Click the **Medium Shading 1 – Accent 1** style. The Table Styles gallery closes. The table's header row is formatted with dark blue shading and white text. The rows below are shaded light blue and white.

The only problem with the newly formatted table is that the text in the first column is formatted in bold. In tables where the first column contains headers, bold would be appropriate, but this isn't the case with Robin's table. You'll fix this by deselecting the First Column check box in the Table Style Options group.

To remove the bold formatting from the first column:

▶ **1.** In the Table Style Options group, click the **First Column** check box to remove the check. The bold formatting is removed from the entries in the Item column. Note that the Header Row check box is selected. This indicates that the table's header row is emphasized with special formatting (dark blue shading with white text). The Banded Rows check box is also selected because the table is formatted with banded rows of blue and white. See Figure 3-17.

Figure 3-17 | **Deselecting the First Column check box**

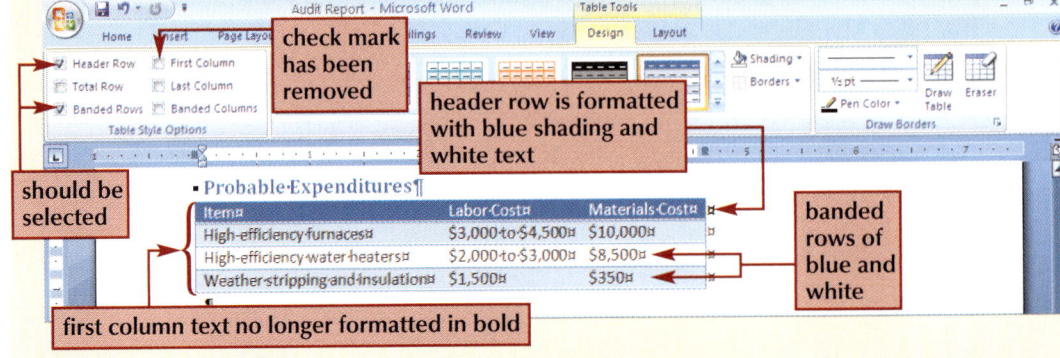

Using Table Styles vs. Manually Formatting a Table | InSight

You can create a table by formatting it "manually" with the buttons on the Table Tools Design tab. For example, you can change the thickness and color of the table borders using the options in the Draw Borders group, and you can add shading using the Shading button in the Table Styles group. However, applying formatting by clicking individual buttons is time consuming. Also, it's easy to make mistakes. For example, you might omit a necessary column border or apply color inconsistently. Instead of formatting a table manually, it's better to start with the built-in table style that most closely resembles the formatting you want. Then you can fine tune the formatting. And remember, if you don't like the selection of table styles available in your document, change the document's theme and look again at the available table styles. Each theme includes a complete set of table styles.

The completed table looks crisp and professional. In the next session, you'll turn your attention to completing the rest of the report.

Session 3.1 Quick Check | Review

1. Explain how to format a heading with a Quick Style.
2. True or False: To insert a manual page break, you can press the Ctrl+End key combination.
3. Explain how to insert a table in a document.
4. What key can you press to move the insertion point from one cell to another in a table?
5. What's the most foolproof way to select part of a table?
6. Explain how to sort a table.
7. True or False: To insert a column, you begin by selecting a column to the left or right of the location where you want to insert a column.

Session 3.2

Setting Tab Stops

A **tab stop** (often called just a **tab**) is a location on the horizontal ruler where the insertion point moves when you press the Tab key. Tab stops are useful for aligning small amounts of data in columns. There are default tab stops every one-half inch on the horizontal ruler, indicated by the small gray tick marks along the bottom edge of the ruler. When you press the Tab key, the insertion point moves to the next tab stop to the right. It's helpful to have the Show/Hide ¶ button selected when you work with tab stops, because then you can see the nonprinting tab character (➜) that is inserted when you press the Tab key. A tab is just like any other character you type; you can delete it by pressing the Backspace key or the Delete key.

Text next to tab stops can be aligned in a variety of ways. The five major styles are Left, Center, Right, Decimal, and Bar, as shown in Figure 3-18. The Left style is selected by default and is probably the tab style you'll use most often.

| Figure 3-18 | Tab stop alignment styles |

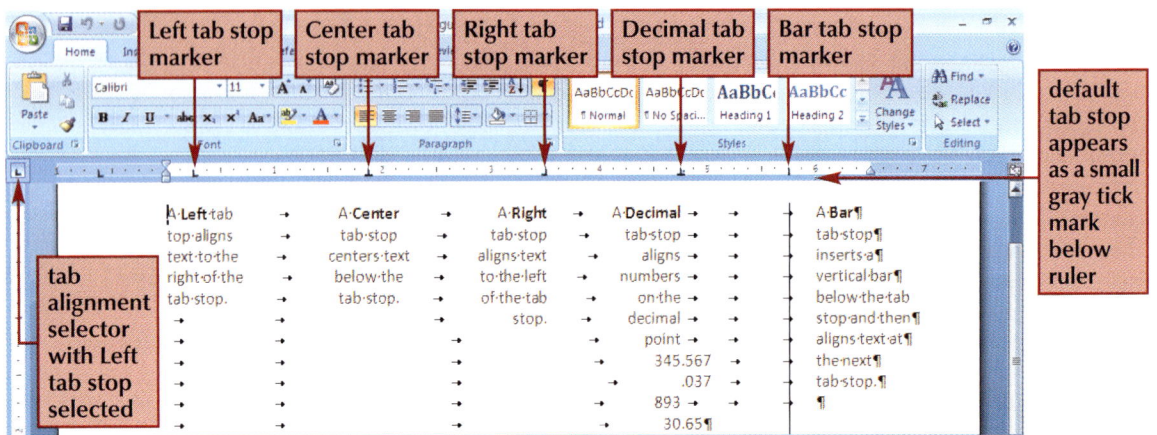

You can set tab stops a few different ways. The simplest is to first select an alignment style from the tab alignment selector, located at the left end of the horizontal ruler, and then click the horizontal ruler where you want the tab stop. When you insert a tab stop in this way, all of the default tab stops to its left are removed. This means you have to press the Tab key only once to move the insertion point to your new tab stop.

<table>
<tr><td>Reference Window |</td><td>**Setting and Clearing Tab Stops**</td></tr>
</table>

- To set a tab stop, click the tab alignment selector on the far left of the horizontal ruler until the appropriate tab stop alignment style appears, and then click the horizontal ruler where you want to position the tab stop. Press the Tab key to move the insertion point to the new tab stop.
- To align text that already contains a nonprinting tab character, select the text and then insert a tab stop on the horizontal ruler.
- To remove a tab stop, locate it on the ruler, click it, and drag it off the ruler (into the document window).
- To clear all tab stops in the document or in a selected paragraph, click the Dialog Box Launcher in the Paragraph group, click the Indents and Spacing tab, click the Tabs button, and then click the Clear All button. Click the OK button to close the Tabs dialog box.

In the report, you need to type the list of consultants and their titles. As you type, you'll discover whether Word's default tab stops are appropriate for this document or whether you need to add a new tab stop.

To enter the list of consultants using tabs:

▶ **1.** If you took a break after the previous session, make sure Word is running and that the Audit Report document is open. Check that the ruler and nonprinting characters are displayed and that the document is displayed in Print Layout view.

▶ **2.** Scroll as necessary to display the Expert Advice section, and then click to the right of the "y" in "Tandra J. Melleray."

▶ **3.** Press the **Tab** key. A tab character appears, and the insertion point moves to the first tab stop after the "y" in "Melleray." This tab stop is one of the default tabs and is located at the 1.5-inch mark on the horizontal ruler. See Figure 3-19.

Tab character ◄ Figure 3-19

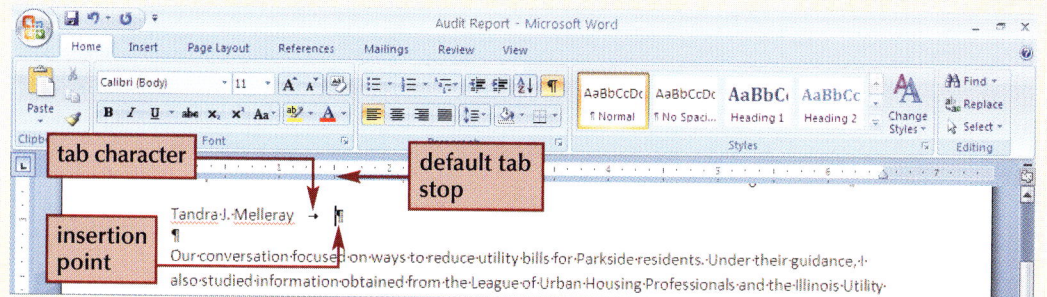

▶ **4.** Type **Associate Engineer**. You've finished typing the first row in the list of consultants. You could press the Enter key now to end the paragraph and start a new paragraph for the next row in the list. However, remember that Word inserts extra space after every paragraph; this will result in a list in which the items are spaced too far apart. Instead, you can use the **Shift+Enter key combination** to insert a manual line break. A **manual line break** moves the insertion point to the next line without actually starting a new paragraph, so no extra space is inserted.

▶ **5.** Press the **Shift+Enter** keys. The insertion point moves to the next line and Word inserts a manual line break nonprinting character. See Figure 3-20.

Starting a new line without starting a new paragraph ◄ Figure 3-20

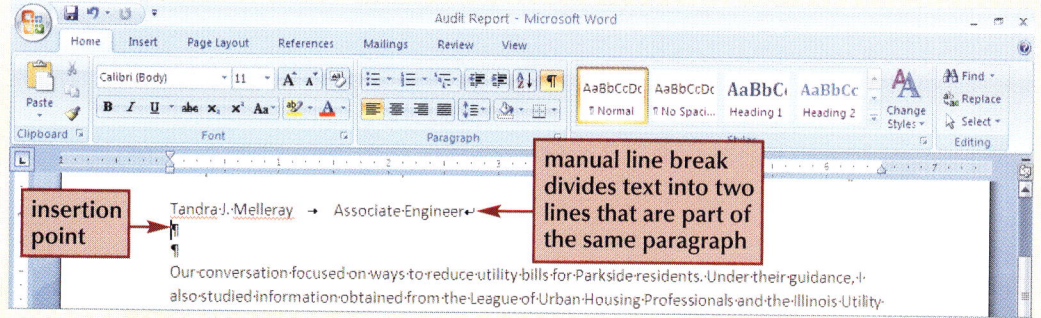

▶ **6.** Type **Susan Tiu** and then press the **Tab** key. The insertion point moves to the first available tab stop, which is another default tab stop, this time located at the 1-inch mark on the horizontal ruler.

▶ **7.** Type **Senior Engineer** and then press the **Shift+Enter** keys to move to the next line.

As you can see, Susan Tiu's title does not align with Tandra J. Melleray's title on the line above it. You'll fix this in a moment by inserting a new tab stop that overrides the default tab stops. But first continue typing the list of names.

▶ **8.** Type **Peter Zaravaggio**, press the **Tab** key, and then type **Community Liaison**. When you are finished, your document should look like the one in Figure 3-21.

Trouble? If you see extra space between the names in your list, you probably forgot to press the Shift+Enter keys at the end of one or more of the lines in the list. Delete the paragraph mark at the end of such a line, and then press the Shift+Enter keys. Repeat for the other lines, if necessary.

Figure 3-21 List of consultants

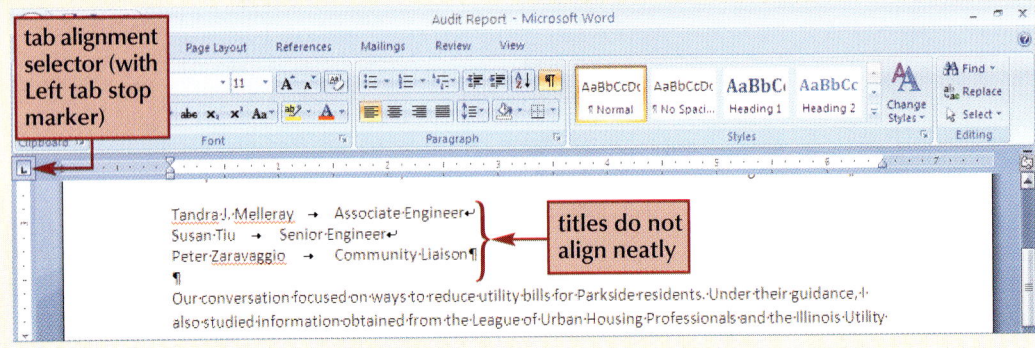

The list of names and titles is not aligned properly. You'll fix this by inserting a new tab stop.

To add a new tab stop to the horizontal ruler:

1. Click and drag the mouse pointer to select the list of consultants and their titles.

2. Make sure the current tab stop alignment style is Left tab ⌊L⌋, as shown in Figure 3-21. If the Left tab marker is not displayed as in Figure 3-21, click the tab alignment selector one or more times until ⌊L⌋ appears.

3. Click the tick mark on the ruler that is at 2.5 inches. Word inserts a Left tab stop at that location and removes the default tab stops to its left. The column of titles shifts to the new tab stop.

4. Click anywhere in the list of names and titles. See Figure 3-22.

Figure 3-22 Titles aligned at the new tab stop

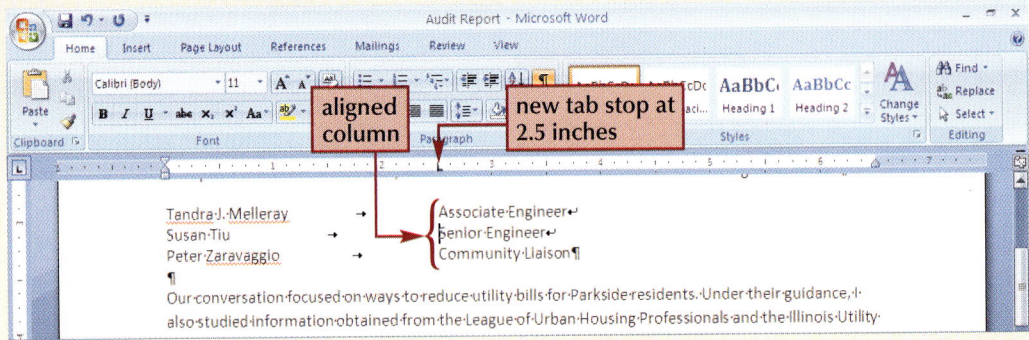

5. Save your work.

The two columns of information are now aligned, as Robin requested. In the Case Problems at the end of this tutorial, you'll have a chance to work with tab stops using the Tabs dialog box, which you can open via the Tabs button in the Paragraph dialog box. Among other things, the Tabs dialog box allows you to insert a **dot leader**, which is a row of dots (or other characters) between tabbed text. A dot leader makes it easier to read a long list of tabbed material because the eye can follow the dots from one item to the next.

Choosing Between Tabs and Tables | InSight

What's the best way to align text in columns? It depends. Tabs work well for small amounts of information, such as two columns with three rows, but they become cumbersome when you need to organize a lot of data. For larger amounts of information, tables are better. Unlike with tabbed columns of data, it's easy to add data to tables by inserting columns. Also, you can format tables more elaborately than you can format tabbed columns.

Whatever you do, don't try to align columns of data by adding extra spaces with the spacebar. Although the text might seem precisely aligned on the screen, it might not be aligned when you print the document. Furthermore, if you edit the text, the spaces you inserted to align your columns will be affected by your edits; they get moved just like regular text, ruining your alignment. One of the main advantages of tab stops and tables is that when you edit data, the alignment remains intact.

Your next job is to add two footnotes to the document that provide further information about topics discussed in Robin's report.

Creating Footnotes and Endnotes

A **footnote** is an explanatory comment or reference that appears at the bottom of a page. When you create a footnote, Word inserts a small, superscript number (called a **reference marker**) in the text. The term "superscript" means that the number is raised slightly above the line of text. Word then inserts the same number in the page's bottom margin and positions the insertion point next to it so you can type the text of the footnote. **Endnotes** are similar, except that the text of an endnote appears at the end of a document. Also, by default, the reference marker for an endnote is a lowercase Roman numeral.

Word automatically manages the reference markers for you, keeping them sequential from the beginning of the document to the end, no matter how many times you add, delete, or move footnotes or endnotes. For example, if you move a paragraph containing footnote 4 so that it falls before the paragraph containing footnote 1, Word renumbers all the footnotes in the document to keep them sequential.

Working with Footnotes and Endnotes | Reference Window

- To create a footnote, click where you want to insert a footnote, click the References tab, in the Footnotes group click the Insert Footnote button, and then type the text of the footnote in the bottom margin.
- To create an endnote, click where you want to insert an endnote, click the References tab, in the Footnotes group click the Insert Endnote button, and then type the text of the endnote at the end of the document.
- When you are finished typing the text of a footnote or endnote, click in the body of the document to continue working on it.
- To delete a footnote or endnote, delete its reference marker (the small, superscript number) in the text.
- To edit the text of a footnote or endnote, click in the bottom margin or at the end of the document and edit the note.

Robin asks you to insert a footnote at the end of the paragraph just above the heading "Final Recommendation." The last sentence of this paragraph refers to studies on the effectiveness of residential energy audits. Robin wants a footnote that explains where more information about those studies can be found.

To add a footnote to the report:

▶ **1.** Near the bottom of page 1, locate the paragraph just above the heading "Final Recommendation."

▶ **2.** Click to the right of the period after "household" at the end of the paragraph. The insertion point is now located at the end of the paragraph, where you want the footnote.

▶ **3.** Click the **References** tab, and then in the Footnotes group, click the **Insert Footnote** button. A superscript "1" is inserted to the right of the period after "household." Word also inserts the number "1" in the bottom margin below a separator line. The insertion point is now located next to the number in the bottom margin, ready for you to type the text of the footnote. See Figure 3-23.

Figure 3-23	Inserting a footnote

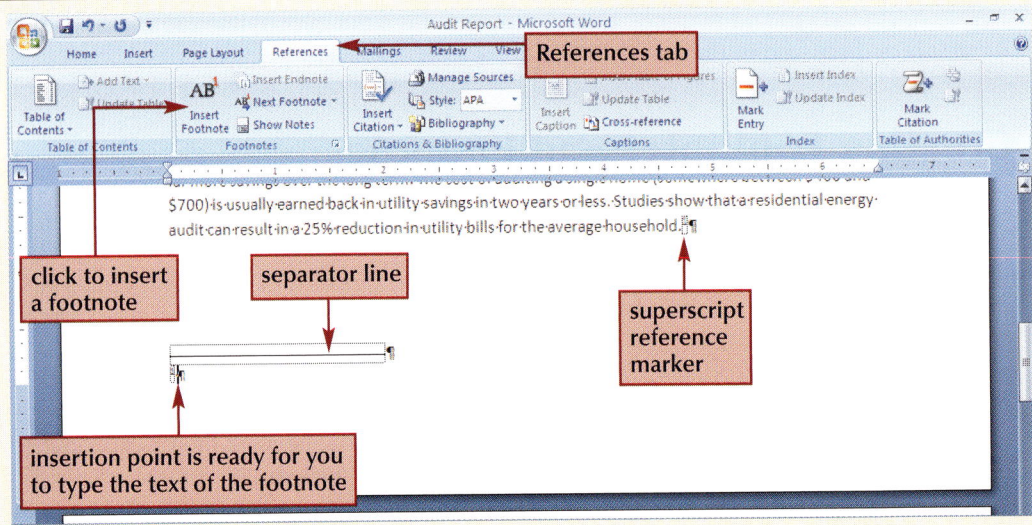

▶ **4.** Type the following footnote text:

For more information, see "A Consumer's Guide to Energy," available at www.course.com/consumer/energy. This helpful Web site is maintained by Course Energy Consultants.

When you press the spacebar after the Web address in the footnote, Word underlines the address and formats it in blue, indicating that it is a live hyperlink, as shown in Figure 3-24. This means people reading the document in Word can open the Web site by pressing the Ctrl key and clicking the link. Because Robin plans to distribute only a hard copy of the report, she asks you to disable the hyperlink.

Figure 3-24	Footnote containing live hyperlink

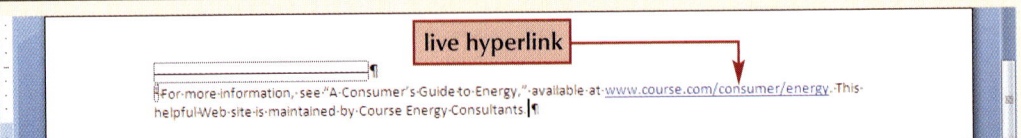

▶ **5.** Right-click the **hyperlink** and then click **Remove Hyperlink** in the shortcut menu. The disabled hyperlink is formatted to match the surrounding text.

The first footnote is complete. Robin would like you to insert a second footnote explaining more about the cost of a typical residential home energy audit. You start by clicking the location in the main document where you want to insert the footnote's reference marker.

To insert a second footnote:

▶ **1.** In the same paragraph (the paragraph above the heading "Final Recommendation"), locate the second to last sentence, which begins "The cost of auditing a single home..." and then click at the end of the sentence. The insertion point should be positioned to the right of the period after "less."

▶ **2.** In the Footnotes group, click the **Insert Footnote** button. Because this footnote is placed earlier in the document than the one you just created, Word inserts a super-script "1" for this footnote, and the other footnote is now numbered "2." See Figure 3-25.

Inserting a second footnote | **Figure 3-25**

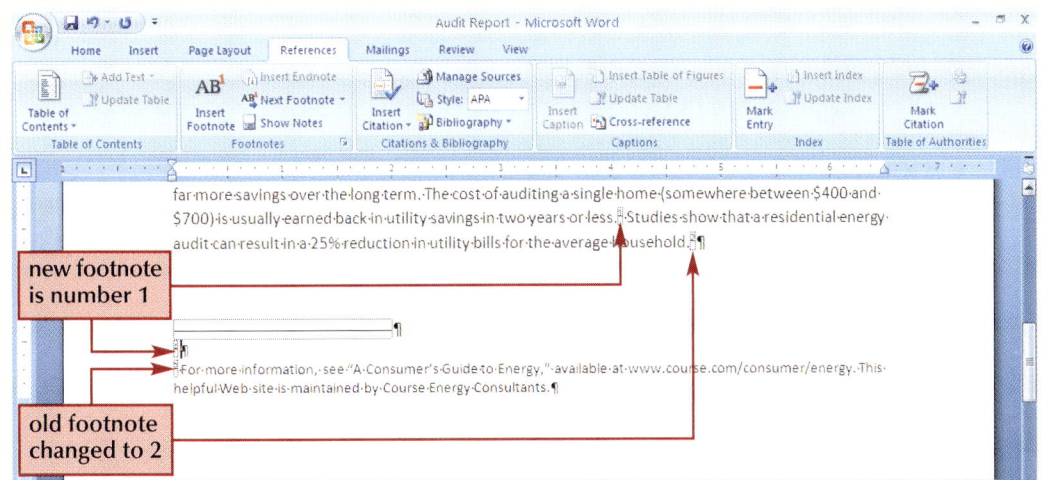

▶ **3.** Type the following footnote text:

While cost varies by auditor, the price of an audit is usually based on a home's square footage.

▶ **4.** Zoom out so you can see the entire page, with the footnotes at the bottom. Note that to make room for the two footnotes, the "Final Recommendation" heading and the paragraph that follows it were moved to the next page. One of the advantages of using Word's heading styles (such as the Heading 1 Quick Style you applied earlier) is that they tell Word to keep the heading and the paragraph that follows it together.

▶ **5.** Zoom back in so you can read the document, and then save your work.

The footnotes will provide helpful information for the board of directors. Next, Robin wants to include a sample of the type of handout she plans to post on community bulletin boards at Parkside, encouraging residents to take part in the energy audit process. Before you can create the handout, you need to divide the document into sections.

Formatting a Document in Sections

Robin wants to format the handout in **landscape orientation**—that is, with the page turned so it is wider than it is tall. The rest of the report is currently formatted in **portrait orientation** (with the page taller than it is wide), which is the default orientation for all Word documents and is appropriate for a report. To format part of a document in an orientation different from the rest of the document, you need to divide the document into sections.

A **section** is a part of a document that can have its own page orientation, margins, headers, footers, and so on. Each section, in other words, is like a document within a document. To divide a document into sections, you insert a **section break**, which appears as a dotted line with the words "Section Break." When you insert a section break, you can choose to have the section start a new page (a Next Page section break) or have the section start at the location of the insertion point, without changing the page flow (a Continuous section break). You insert section breaks with the Breaks button on the Page Layout tab.

To insert a section break below the table:

▶ 1. Press the **Ctrl+End** keys to move the insertion point to the end of the document (to the blank paragraph below the table).

▶ 2. Click the **Page Layout** tab, and then, in the Page Setup group, click the **Breaks** button. The Breaks menu opens, as shown in Figure 3-26. The Page Breaks part of the menu includes options for controlling how the text flows from page to page. The first option, Page, inserts a page break (just like the Page Break button on the Insert tab that you used earlier). The Section Breaks part of the menu includes four types of section breaks. The two you'll use most often are Next Page, which starts a section on a new page, and Continuous, which starts a new section at the location of the insertion point, without starting a new page.

Figure 3-26 ▶ **Breaks menu**

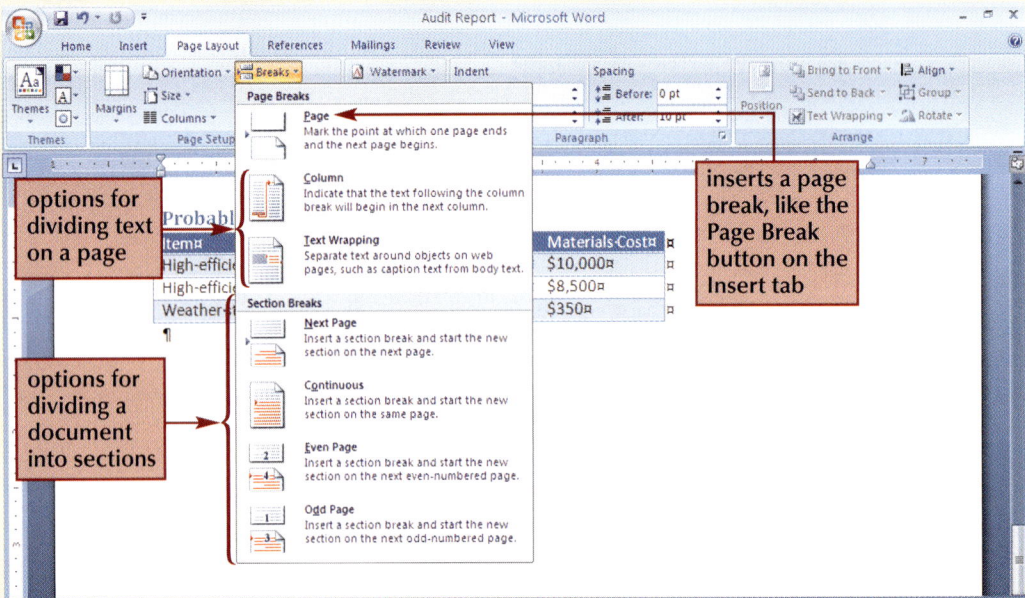

3. Under "Section Breaks," click **Next Page**. A section break is inserted, and the insertion point moves to the top of the newly inserted page.

4. Scroll up until you can see the double-dotted line and the words "Section Break (Next Page)" below the table. This line indicates that a new section begins on the next page.

Trouble? If you see a single dotted line and the words "Page Break," you inserted a page break rather than a Next Page section break. Click the Undo button on the Quick Access Toolbar, and then repeat Steps 1 through 4.

5. Save your work.

Tip

To delete a section break, click the line representing the break, and then press the Delete key.

You've created a new page that is a separate section from the rest of the report. The sections are numbered consecutively, so that the first part of the document is section 1 and the new page is section 2. Now you can format section 2 in landscape orientation without affecting the rest of the document.

To format section 2 in landscape orientation:

1. Scroll down if necessary and verify that the insertion point is positioned at the top of the new page 4.

2. Change the zoom setting to 50% (this will allow you to see clearly the page orientation change in the next steps), and then scroll down, if necessary, so you can see the page containing the table and the new page 4, which is blank.

3. In the Page Setup group, click the **Orientation** button. The Orientation menu opens.

4. Click **Landscape**. Section 2, which consists solely of page 4, changes to landscape orientation, as shown in Figure 3-27. Section 1, which consists of pages 1–3, remains in portrait orientation.

Page 4 formatted in landscape orientation ◄ **Figure 3-27**

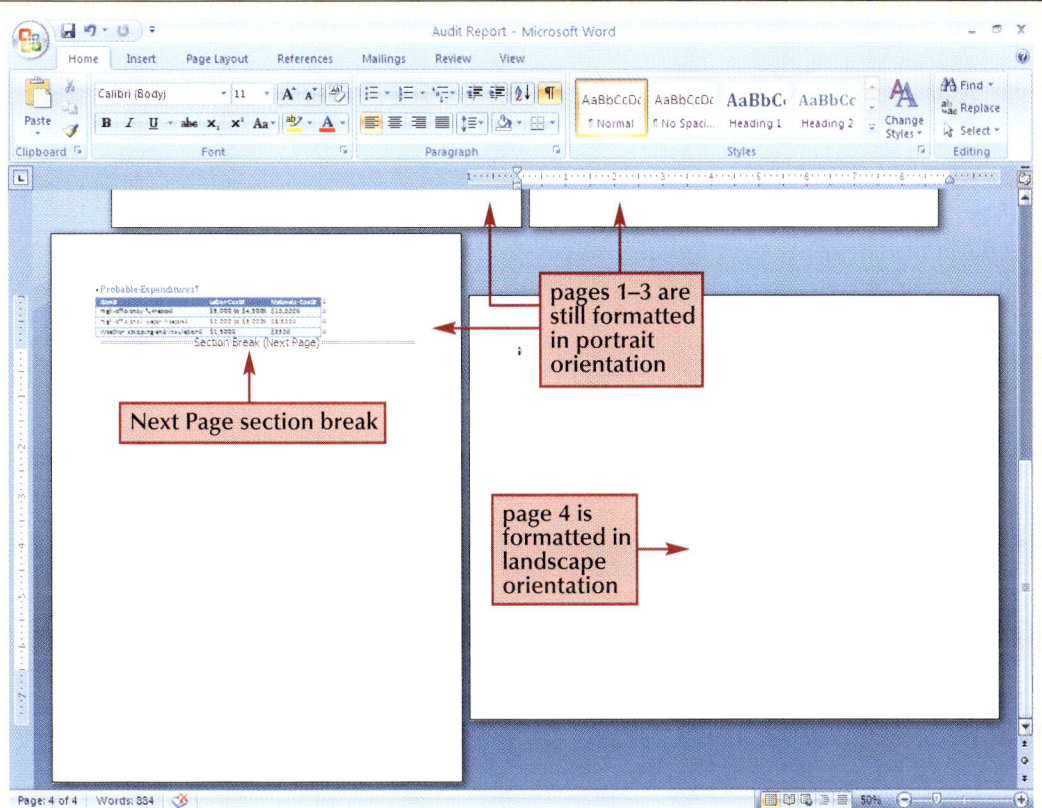

pages 1–3 are still formatted in portrait orientation

Next Page section break

page 4 is formatted in landscape orientation

▶ **5.** Zoom back in so you can read the document text, and then save your work.

Page 4 is now formatted in landscape orientation, ready for you to create Robin's handout, which will consist of an illustration, or **graphic**, that explains the stages and ultimate goal of the energy audit process. With Word's SmartArt feature, you can quickly create great looking illustrations for a wide variety of purposes.

Creating SmartArt

The **SmartArt** feature allows you to create diagrams and charts to illustrate concepts that would otherwise require several paragraphs of explanation. To begin creating a SmartArt graphic, you switch to the Insert tab and then, in the Illustrations group, click the SmartArt button. This opens the Choose a SmartArt Graphic dialog box, where you can select from seven categories of graphics, including graphics designed to illustrate relationships, processes, and hierarchies. Within each category, you can then choose from numerous designs. Once inserted into your document, a SmartArt graphic contains placeholder text that you replace with something appropriate for your needs. When a SmartArt graphic is selected, the SmartArt tools appear on the Ribbon, with two tabs of editing options. In the following steps, you will begin creating a SmartArt graphic that summarizes the energy audit process.

To create a SmartArt graphic:

▶ **1.** Verify that the insertion point is located at the top of page 4, which is blank.

▶ **2.** Click the **Insert** tab, and then, in the Illustrations group, click the **SmartArt** button. The Choose a SmartArt Graphic dialog box opens. This dialog box consists of three panels. The left panel lists the categories of SmartArt Graphics; the middle panel displays the graphics associated with the category selected in the left panel; and the right panel displays a larger image of the graphic that is currently selected in the middle panel, along with an explanation of the graphic's purpose. Currently, All is selected in the left panel. This means you could use the scroll bar in the middle panel to see all of the possible SmartArt graphics.

▶ **3.** Explore the Choose a SmartArt Graphic dialog box by selecting categories in the left panel and viewing the graphics displayed in the middle panel.

▶ **4.** In the left panel, click **Relationship**, and then, in the middle panel, click the **Equation** graphic (in the far-left column, fifth row from the top), which shows three circles in an equation. In the right panel, you see an explanation of the Equation graphic, as shown in Figure 3-28.

Tip

To see a detailed view of a graphic, click that graphic in the middle panel and view the details that appear in the right panel.

Selecting a SmartArt graphic | Figure 3-28

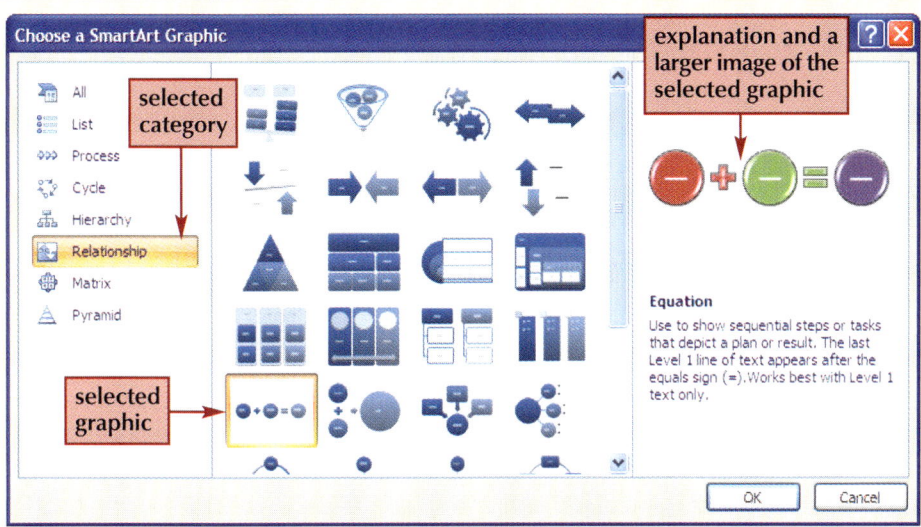

5. Click the **OK** button. The Choose a SmartArt Graphic dialog box closes, and the Equation graphic, with placeholder text, is inserted at the top of page 4. The graphic is surrounded by a rectangular border, indicating that it is selected. The SmartArt tools are visible on the Ribbon. To the left or right of the graphic, you might also see the Text Pane, a small window with a title bar that reads "Type your text here."

6. If you do *not* see the Text Pane, click the **left-facing arrow** on the left side of the SmartArt Border, as shown in Figure 3-29.

SmartArt graphic with Text Pane displayed | Figure 3-29

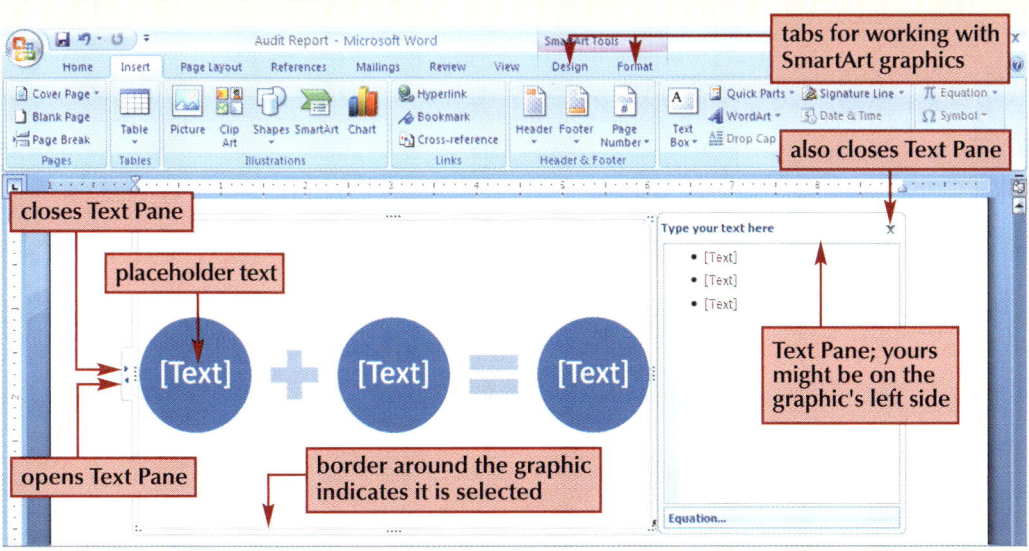

The Text Pane is useful for complicated graphics containing many parts. However, the Equation graphic is simple enough that you can type the text directly in the circles, so you will close the Text Pane in the next step.

Trouble? If you inserted a graphic other than the equation graphic, click the Undo button on the Quick Access Toolbar and start again with Step 1.

Trouble? If you see other elements in your SmartArt graphic, such as a square border around one of the blue circles, or if you see the insertion point blinking inside the Text Pane, don't be concerned. Just continue with the steps.

▶ **7.** Click the **Close** button ✕ in the upper-right corner of the Text Pane (shown in Figure 3-29). You will type the text directly into the circles.

Now you are ready to begin typing text in the graphic.

To add text to the SmartArt graphic:

▶ **1.** In the blue circle on the left, click the placeholder text (which reads "[Text]"). The placeholder text disappears and the insertion point blinks inside the left circle. (The insertion point might be hard to see on the dark blue background.) The left circle is surrounded by a box consisting of a dotted line, with small white circles on the corners and a small white square in the middle of each side. This box indicates that the blue circle is selected, ready for you to replace the placeholder text with your text. The circles and squares along the border of the box are called **handles**; you can drag them to change the shape of the item inside the box. You'll learn more about dragging handles to change the shape of a graphic in Tutorial 4. For now, you can ignore them. See Figure 3-30.

Trouble? If the circle is selected, but the placeholder text is still visible, you clicked the circle, but not the placeholder text within the circle. Repeat Step 1, but take care to click the placeholder text.

Figure 3-30 ▶ **Entering text in the SmartArt graphic**

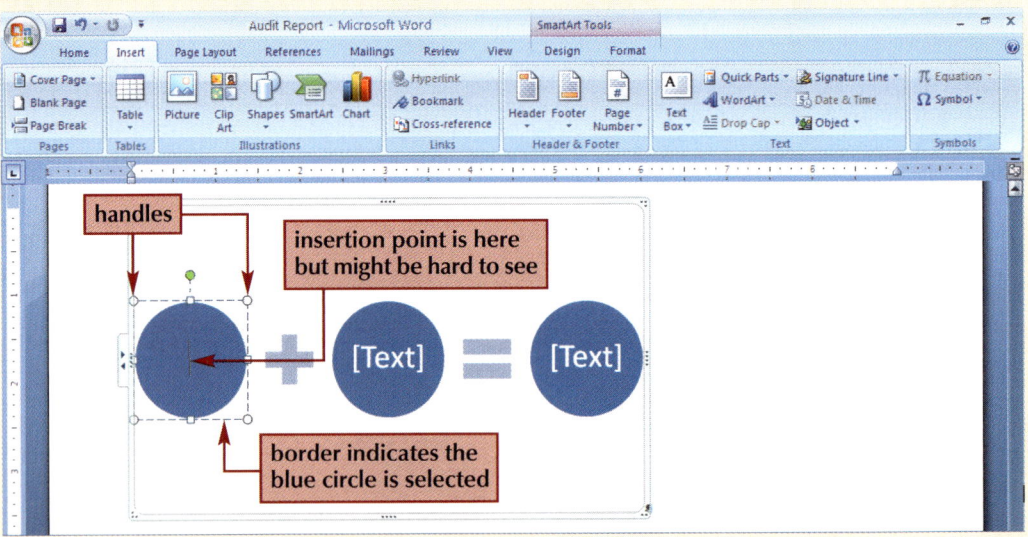

▶ **2.** Type **Energy Audit**. The font size gets smaller as you type, shrinking to accommodate each new letter without increasing the size of the circle.

▶ **3.** Click the placeholder text in the middle circle, type **Repairs and Upgrades**, click the **right circle** to select it, and type **Lower Utility Bills**. The right circle remains selected.

Trouble? If you make a typing mistake, click the circle containing the error and edit the text as you would ordinary text, using the Backspace or Delete keys as necessary.

▶ **4.** Click in the white area inside the SmartArt border to deselect the right circle. The equation now reads "Energy Audit + Repairs and Upgrades = Lower Utility Bills."

The graphic is almost finished. Your last task is to increase its size so it fills the page. To resize the entire SmartArt graphic, you drag the outer border.

To adjust the size of the SmartArt graphic:

▶ **1.** Zoom out so you can see the entire page.

▶ **2.** Position the mouse pointer over the lower-right corner of the SmartArt border. The pointer changes to a diagonal, double-sided arrow ⤢. As you can see on the ruler, the SmartArt border is currently about six inches wide. See Figure 3-31.

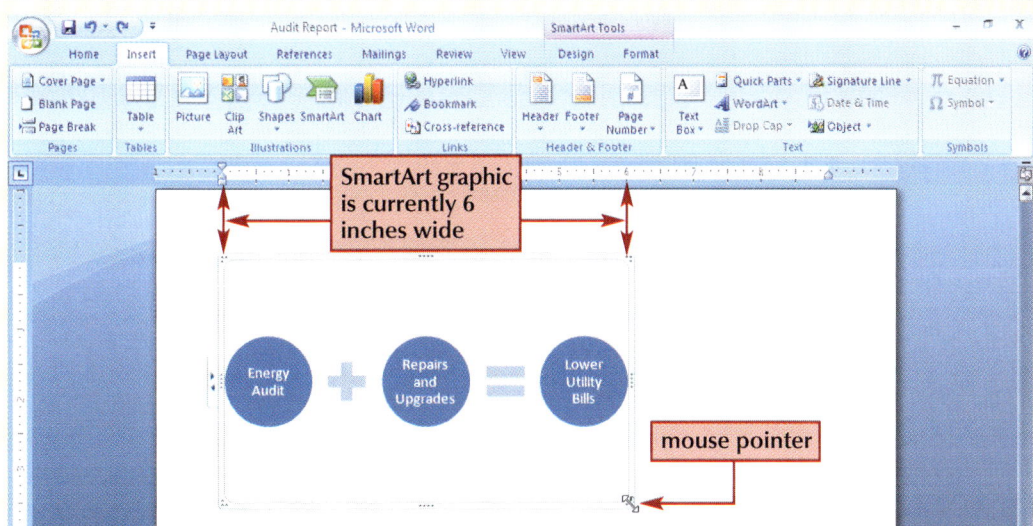

Trouble? If the pointer changes to a four-sided arrow ✛, you haven't positioned the pointer correctly over the lower-right corner. Reposition the pointer until it changes to a diagonal, double-sided arrow, as shown in Figure 3-31.

▶ **3.** Drag the pointer down and to the right. As you drag, the pointer changes to a crosshair ╋. A rectangular outline moves with the pointer, showing how the dimensions of the SmartArt border will appear when you release the mouse button. The size of the graphic won't actually change until you release the mouse button.

Trouble? If the graphic changes size, you released the mouse button too early. Undo the change, and begin again with Step 2.

▶ **4.** Position the pointer in the lower-right corner of the page, so the outline is approximately 9 inches wide and 6.5 inches high, but do *not* release the mouse button yet. Compare your screen to Figure 3-32 to make sure you have the pointer in the correct location.

Figure 3-32 **Dragging the SmartArt border**

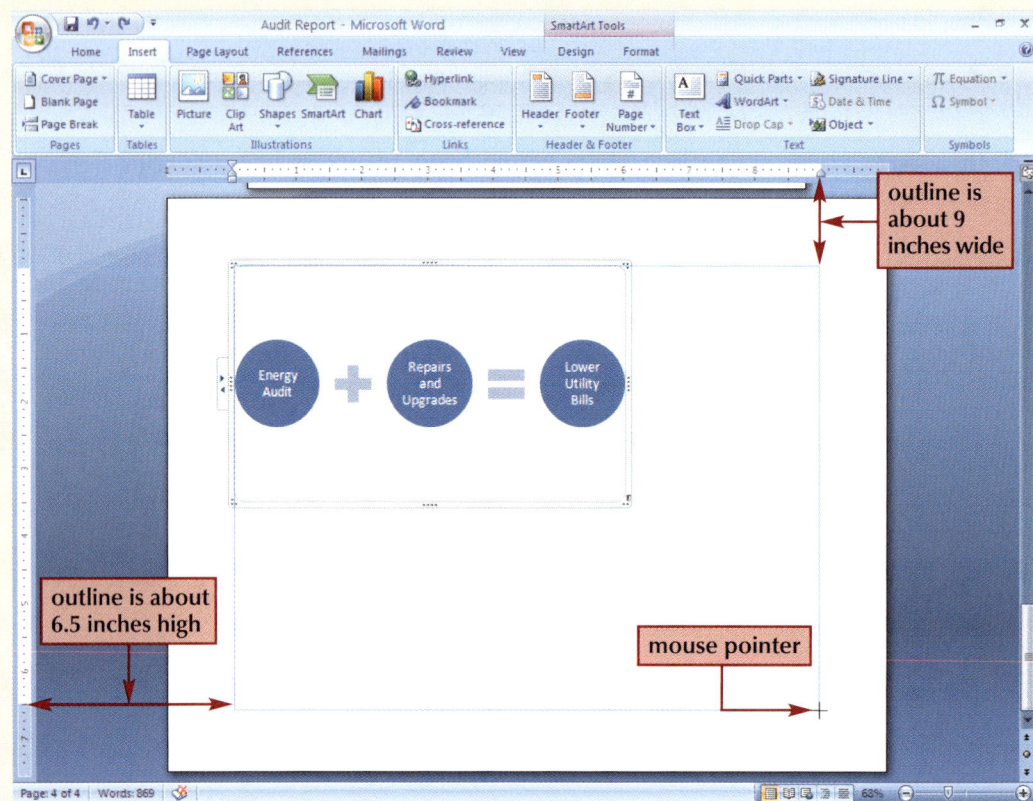

▶ **5.** Release the mouse button. The SmartArt graphic resizes, so that it is now 9 inches wide and 6.5 inches high, taking up most of the page.

▶ **6.** Click outside the SmartArt border to view the graphic centered on the page.

The SmartArt graphic is eye-catching and succinctly explains the goal of the energy audit. Robin will add a heading and some text introducing the graphic later. Your next job is to insert headers and footers in the report. This will involve working with the two sections separately.

Adding Headers and Footers

Text that is printed at the top of every page is called a **header**. For example, the information printed at the top of this textbook page is a header. A **footer** is text that is printed at the bottom of every page.

There are two ways to begin inserting a header or footer: (1) you can double-click in the header area (in a page's top margin) or in the footer area (in a page's bottom margin); or (2) you can click the Header button or the Footer button on the Insert tab. Either way, the document switches to **Header and Footer view**, with special tools related to working with headers and footers displayed on the Ribbon. In Header and Footer view, the document text is dimmed, indicating that it cannot be edited while you are in this view.

Some headers and footers also include **document controls**, which are similar to the kinds of controls (text boxes, list boxes, etc.) that you might encounter in a dialog box. Most of the document controls you'll see in headers and footers are text boxes, where you can enter important information such as the document title or the name of the document's author. Any information that you enter in a document control is displayed in the header or footer as ordinary text, but it is also stored in the Word file so that Word can easily reuse it in other parts of the document. For example, later in this tutorial you will create a cover page for the report. Word's predefined cover pages include document controls similar to those found in headers and footers. So if you use a document control to enter the document title in the header, that same document title will show up in the cover page; there's no need to retype it. You'll see how this works shortly.

Two Ways to Insert a Header or Footer		InSight

Double-clicking in the top or bottom margin is the simplest way to begin inserting a header or footer. After Word switches to Header and Footer view, you type the text of the header or footer. Three default tab stops allow you to left-align, center, or right-align the text in the header or footer. Many documents require page numbers; you can use the Page Number button on the Insert tab to insert the page number, which Word updates as you add and delete pages from your document.

For a more elaborate header or footer, use the Header and Footer buttons on the Insert tab. These buttons open menus that you can use to select from a number of predefined headers and footers, some of which include page numbers and graphic elements such as horizontal lines or shaded boxes.

You'll create a footer for the whole document (pages 1 through 4) that includes the page number and your name. You'll also create a header for section 1 (pages 1 through 3) that includes the document title and the date. When creating a header or footer for an entire document, you can work in the header or footer area for any page in the document. In the following steps, you'll start on page 1, so you can see how the footer fits below the footnotes at the bottom of the page.

To create a footer for the entire document:

▶ **1.** Zoom back in so you can read the text, and then scroll up until you can see the bottom of page 1.

▶ **2.** Double-click in the bottom margin of page 1, below the footnotes. The document switches to Header and Footer view. On the Ribbon, the Design tab appears below the label "Header & Footer Tools." The insertion point is positioned on the left side of the footer area, ready for you to begin typing. The label "Footer - Section 1" tells you that the insertion point is located in the footer for section 1. The document text (including the footnotes) is gray, indicating that you cannot edit it in Header and Footer view. The header area for section 1 is also visible on top of page 2. The default footer tab stops are visible on the ruler. See Figure 3-33.

Figure 3-33 ▶ Creating a footer

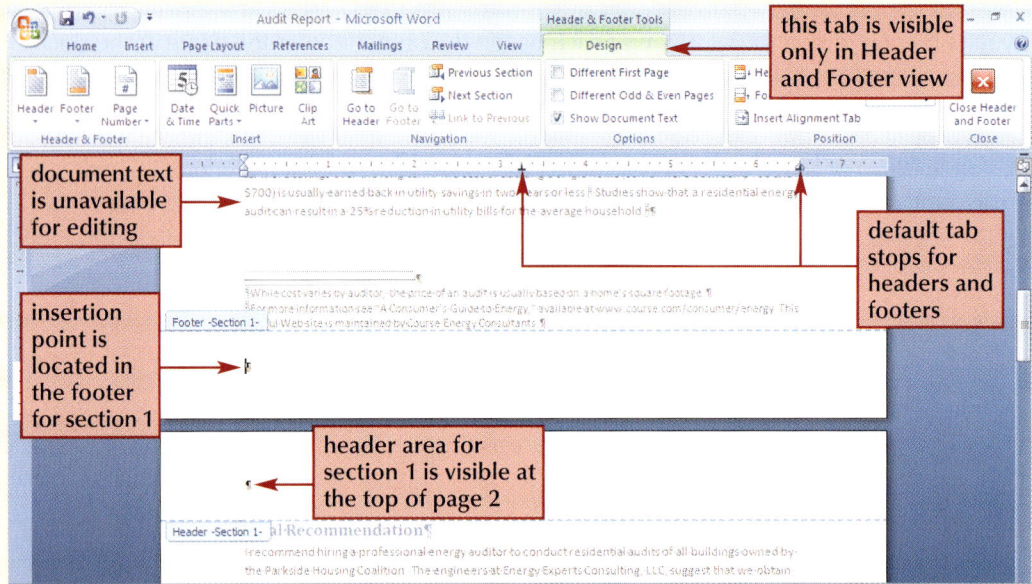

Trouble? If the document does not switch to Header and Footer view, you probably did not double-click in the right place in Step 2. Try again.

▶ **3.** Type your first and last name, and then press the **Enter** key. The insertion point moves to the second line in the footer, on the left margin. This is where you will insert the page number.

▶ **4.** In the Header & Footer group, click the **Page Number** button. The Page Number menu opens. This menu allows you to insert a page number at the top, bottom, or side of the page. Because the insertion point is already located where you want to insert the page number, you need to use the Current Position option.

▶ **5.** Point to **Current Position**. A gallery of page number styles opens. The Plain Number style at the top simply inserts a page number, whereas other styles include the word "Page" or design elements such as special shapes or colors. Robin wants to use the Accent Bar 2 style. See Figure 3-34.

Inserting the page number in the footer ◀ **Figure 3-34**

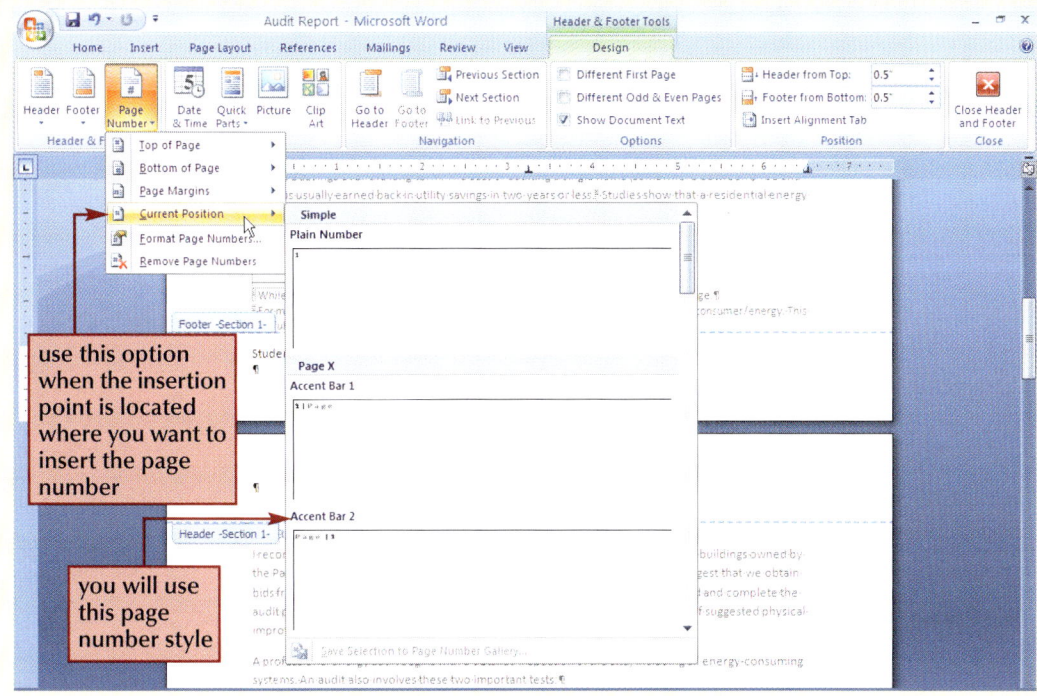

use this option when the insertion point is located where you want to insert the page number

you will use this page number style

▶ **6.** Scroll down the page number gallery to get a sense of the types of page number styles available, then scroll back up and click the **Accent Bar 2** style (the third from the top). The word "Page," a vertical bar, and the page number are inserted in the document. Next, you'll check to make sure that the footer you just created for section 1 also appears in section 2.

▶ **7.** Scroll down to the end of the document until you can see the footer at the bottom of page 4. Scroll left or right, if necessary, so you can see the entire footer. The label at the top of the footer area on page 4, "Footer – Section 2," tells you that you are looking at the footer for section 2. You see the same text (your name, plus the page number) in this footer as in section 1.

You have successfully created a footer for the entire document. Now you can turn your attention to creating a header for section 1. Robin does not want to include a header in section 2 because it would distract attention from the SmartArt graphic. So your first task is to separate the header for section 1 from the header for section 2.

To separate the headers for section 1 and section 2:

▶ **1.** Click anywhere in the section 2 footer area, at the bottom of page 4. The insertion point moves to the section 2 footer.

▶ **2.** In the Navigation group, click the **Go to Header** button. The insertion point moves to the section 2 header at the top of page 4. Notice that in the Navigation group, the Link to Previous button is selected. This tells you that the section 2 header is linked to the header in the previous section (that is, the section 1 header). In other words, anything you add to the section 1 header will also be added to the section 2 header—but Robin wants the header to appear only in section 1. To make the section 2 header a separate entity, you need to break that link.

3. In the Navigation group, click the **Link to Previous** button to deselect it. Deselecting this button ensures that the header you create in section 1 will not appear in section 2. See Figure 3-35.

Figure 3-35 **Breaking the link between the section 1 and section 2 headers**

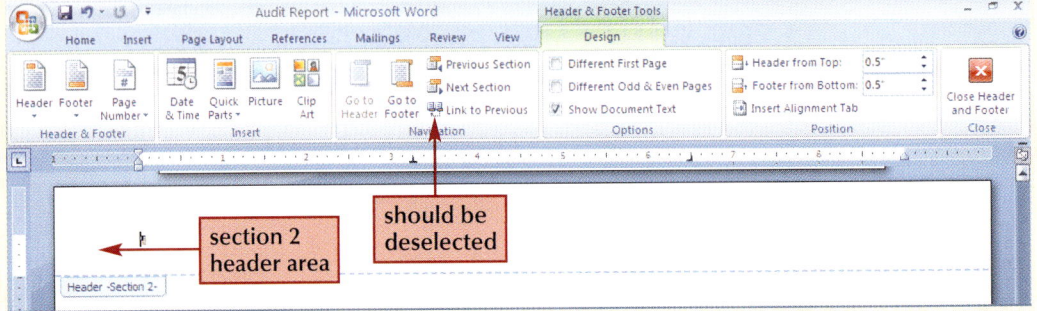

Next, you need to move the insertion point to the section 1 header.

Tip

When you create a header for a section, it doesn't matter what page you're working on, as long as the insertion point is located in a header in that section.

4. In the Navigation group, click the **Previous Section** button. The insertion point moves up to the nearest section 1 header, which is at the top of page 3. The label "Header – Section 1" identifies this as a section 1 header.

5. In the Header & Footer group, click the **Header** button. A gallery of header styles opens. See Figure 3-36.

Figure 3-36 **Header gallery**

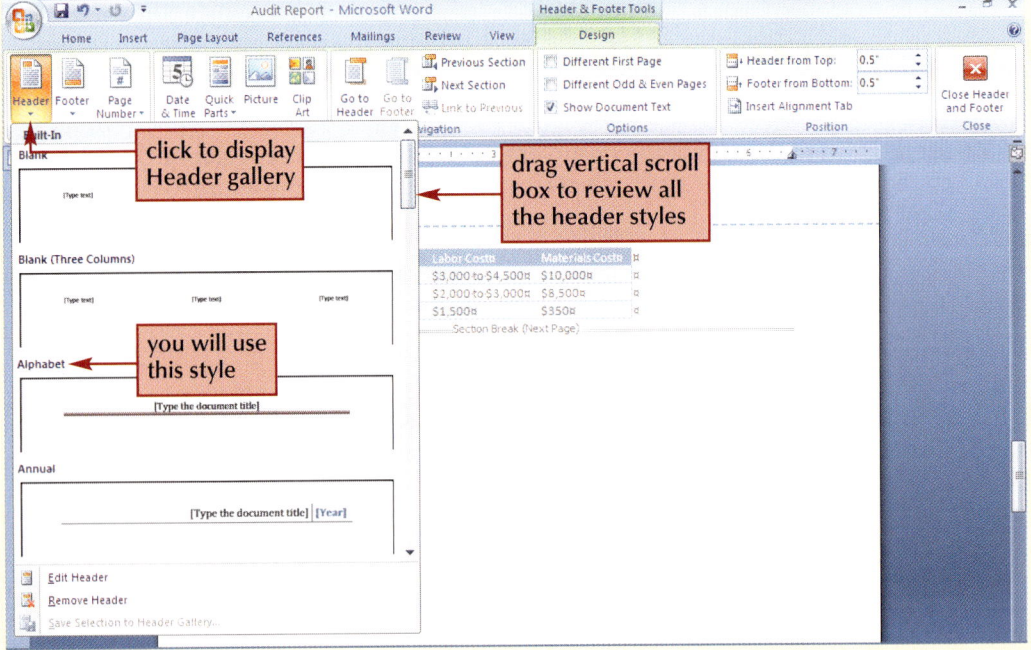

▶ **6.** Scroll down and review the various header styles, and then click the **Alphabet style** (third from the top). A horizontal line is inserted in the document, along with the placeholder text "[Type the document title]." The placeholder text is actually contained within a document control, although right now you can't see anything that would indicate this is anything other than ordinary text.

▶ **7.** Click the placeholder text **[Type the document title]**. The text is highlighted in blue, and a blue label with the word "Title" appears above the highlighted text. The blue highlighting and the blue label indicate that this is a document control. This particular document control is a text box; currently it contains the placeholder text "[Type the document title]." Now that the placeholder text is selected (as indicated by the blue highlight), you can replace it with something appropriate for Robin's report. See Figure 3-37.

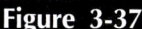

Adding a header to section 1   ◀   **Figure 3-37**

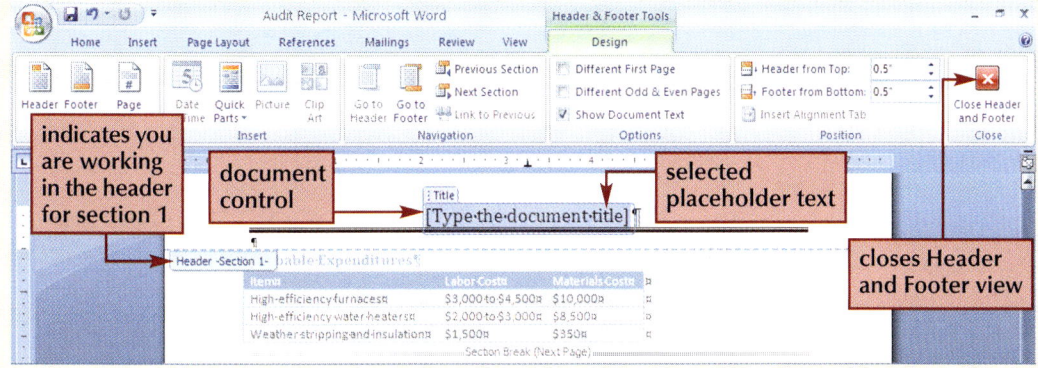

▶ **8.** Type **Parkside Energy Audit**. As soon as you begin typing, the placeholder text and the blue highlight disappear. The new title, "Parkside Energy Audit," is displayed in the document control. You are finished creating the header and footer for Robin's report, so you can close Header and Footer view and return to Print Layout view.

▶ **9.** In the Close group, click the **Close Header and Footer** button, save your work, and then zoom out until you can see all four pages of the document, including the header at the top of pages 1-3 and the footer at the bottom of pages 1–4. See Figure 3-38.

Figure 3-38   **Document with new header and footer**

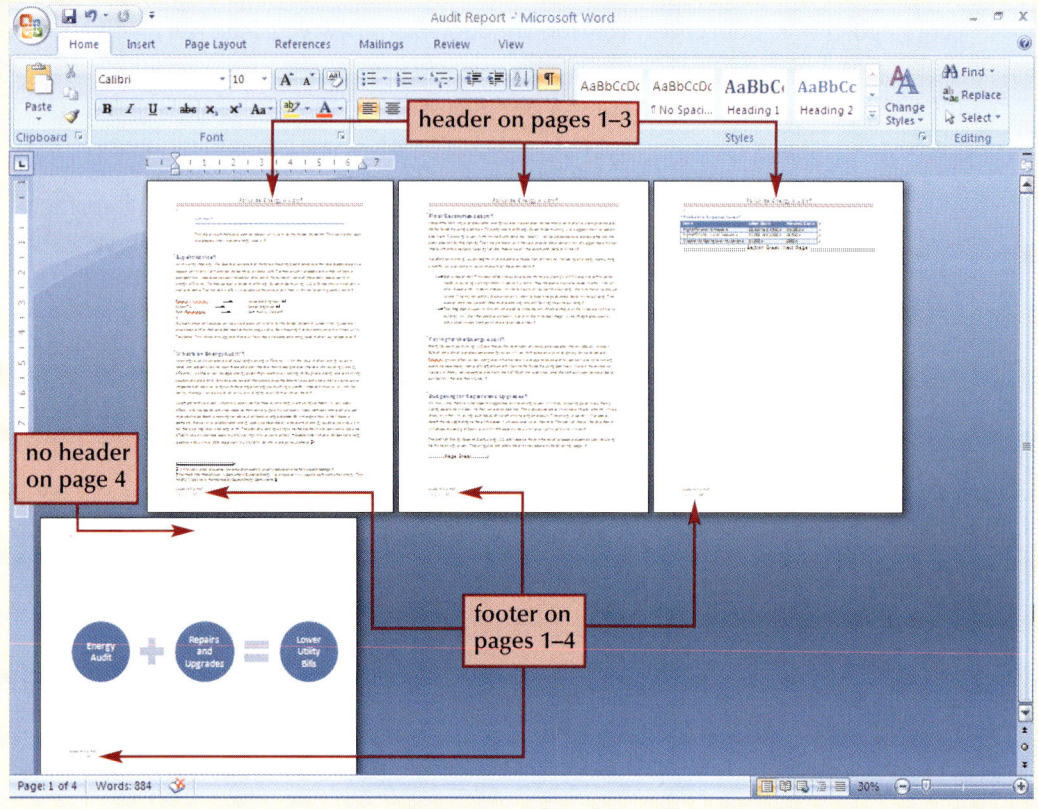

The header and footer will make it easier for Parkside board members to keep track of the pages of the printed report. This will be especially helpful as Robin adds more pages to the report. Your last job is to create an attractive cover page.

Inserting a Cover Page

A document's cover page typically includes the title and the author of the report. Some writers also prefer to include a summary on the cover page rather than on the first page of the report itself, as Robin chose to do. In addition, you might include the date, the name and possibly the logo of your company or organization, and a subtitle. A cover page should not include the document header or footer.

To create a simple cover page for a report, you can do the following: insert a Next Page section break at the beginning of the document, adjust the header and footer settings for the new section 1 so the header and footer do not appear on the cover page, type the title and other information, and, finally, format the text to add emphasis. To center cover page text between the top and bottom margins, click the Page Layout tab. In the Page Setup group, click the Dialog Box Launcher, click the Layout tab, click the Vertical alignment arrow, and then click Center.

To create a more elaborate cover page—one that includes design elements such as color, lines, and graphics—you can use the Cover Page button on the Insert tab. The Cover Page button inserts a predefined cover page at the beginning of the document.

As with Word's predefined headers and footers, a predefined cover page includes document controls in which you can enter the document title, the document's author, the date, and so on. These document controls are linked to any other document controls in the document. You already entered the document title into a control in the header of Robin's report. You'll see the advantages of that choice in the following steps, as you insert a cover page into Robin's report.

To insert a cover page at the beginning of the report:

▶ **1.** Verify that the document is still zoomed so that you can see all four pages, and then press the **Ctrl+Home** keys. The insertion point moves to the beginning of the document. (You don't have to move the insertion point to the beginning of the document before you insert a cover page, but as a general rule it's a good idea to know where the insertion point is before you start a new task.)

▶ **2.** Click the **Insert** tab, and then, in the Pages group, click the **Cover Page** button. A gallery of cover pages opens. Notice that the names of the cover page styles match the names of the preformatted header styles you saw earlier. For example, the list includes an Alphabet cover page, which is similar in design to the Alphabet header you inserted earlier. To give a document a coherent look, it's helpful to use elements (such as cover pages and headers) with the same name throughout. However, in this case, the Alphabet cover page is more complicated than Robin wants, so you will use the Stacks style instead.

▶ **3.** Scroll down through the gallery to see the choice of cover pages and locate the Stacks cover page, in the left column, bottom row. See Figure 3-39.

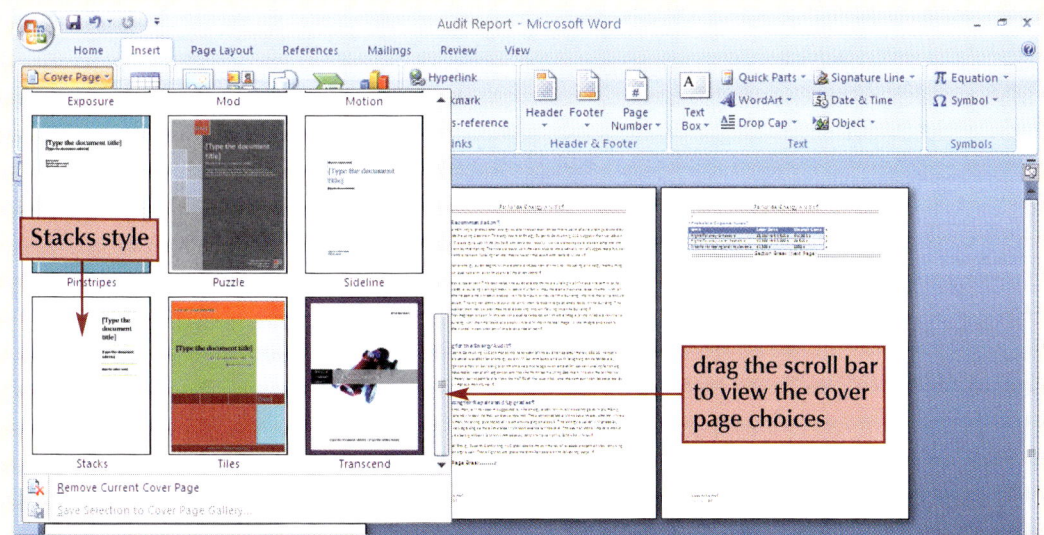

▶ **4.** Click the **Stacks** cover page. The new cover page is inserted at the beginning of the document.

▶ **5.** Zoom back in so you can read the document, and then scroll to view the new cover page. The insertion point is positioned in the upper-left corner of the document, just above a page break line. (In pages with complicated formatting, such as this one, a page break line sometimes appears in places you might not expect; you can ignore it.) On the right side of the document, you see controls for the title and the subtitle. Because you already entered "Parkside Energy Audit" in the Title document control in the header, the same text appears in the Title document control in the cover page. The Author document control (for entering the author's name) is located directly below the Subtitle document control. You might not be able to see the Author control. If you can see it, it probably contains a name inserted automatically by Word. See Figure 3-40.

Tip

To delete a cover page that you inserted from the Cover Page gallery, click the Cover Page button in the Pages group, and then click Remove Current Cover Page.

Trouble? If the header is on the new cover page, click the Cover Page button in the Pages group, click Remove Current Cover Page, and then repeat Steps 1 through 5.

Figure 3-40 ▶ **Newly inserted cover page**

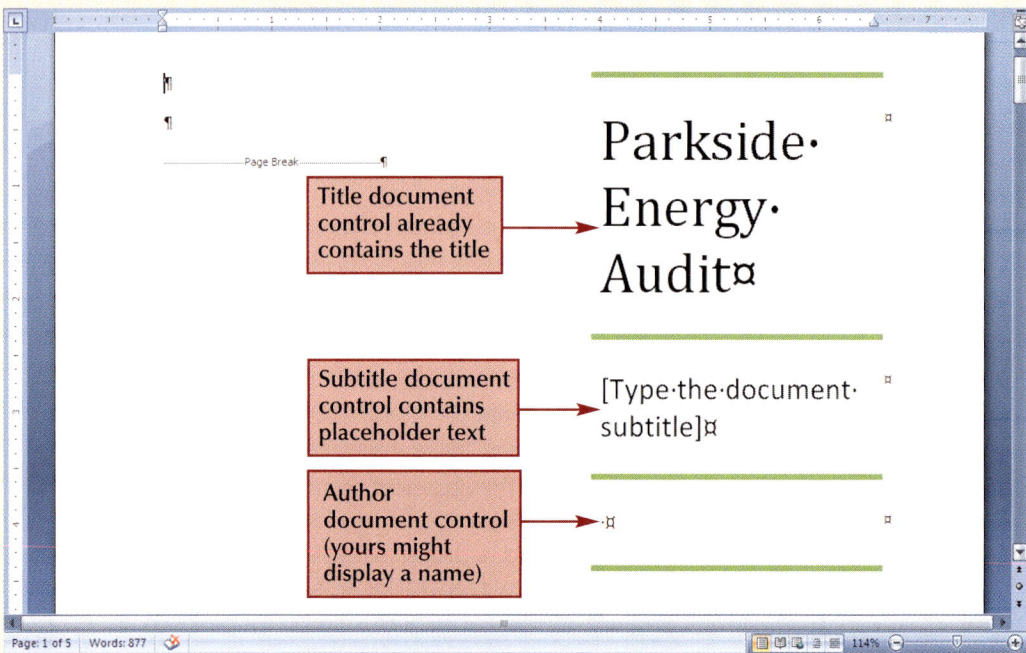

▶ **6.** Click the text **[Type the document subtitle]**. The text is selected, and the document control label "Subtitle" is visible. The Table Tools contextual tabs appear on the Ribbon because, although you can't tell by looking at them, the document controls are actually organized on the page in a table structure. When you clicked the Subtitle document control, you clicked within the table.

▶ **7.** Type **A Recommendation Report for the Parkside Housing Coalition Board of Directors**. Word formats the subtitle in a table cell below the title.

▶ **8.** Press the **Tab** key to display and select the Author control, and then type **Robin Kinsella**. The cover page now includes a title, a subtitle, and Robin's name.

▶ **9.** Save your work.

Your work on the report is finished. All that remains is to preview it and print it.

To preview and print the report:

▶ **1.** Click the **Office Button** (📄), point to **Print**, and then click **Print Preview**. The document is displayed in the Print Preview window.

▶ **2.** On the Print Preview tab, in the Zoom group, click the **Two Pages** button to display the first two pages of the report side by side, and then use the **Next Page** and **Previous Page** buttons in the Preview group to move back and forth among the pages of the report. Make sure that the header is only visible on pages 2–4, and that the footer is visible on pages 2–5. Also, notice that Word renumbered the pages to account for the addition of the cover page, which is the new page 1.

▶ **3.** If you need to make any changes to the report, return to Print Layout view, edit the document, and then return to Print Preview.

▶ **4.** When you are satisfied with the document, click the **Print** button in the Print group, verify that the printer settings are correct, and then click the **OK** button.

▶ **5.** Close the document.

You now have a draft of the Parkside Housing Coalition report, including a cover page, the report text, a nicely formatted table, and the SmartArt graphic (printed in landscape orientation). Eventually, Robin will add more information to the report, including an introduction to the table.

Session 3.2 Quick Check | Review

1. True or False: There are default tab stops every one-half inch on the horizontal ruler.
2. Explain how to create a footnote.
3. What button do you use to insert a section break, and where is it located?
4. How do you know if a SmartArt graphic is selected?
5. Explain two ways to switch to Header and Footer view.
6. True or False: For page numbering purposes, a cover page inserted from the Cover Page gallery is considered page 1.

Review | Tutorial Summary

In this tutorial, you learned how to format headings with Quick Styles and insert a manual page break. Then you learned how to insert a table, select all or part of a table, sort the rows of a table, insert and delete rows or columns, change column widths, and format a table to improve its appearance. You also learned how to set tab stops, create footnotes and endnotes, and insert a section break. Finally, you learned how to create a SmartArt graphic, add headers and footers, and insert a cover page.

Key Terms

cell
character-level formatting
document controls
dot leader
endnote
first column
font color
footer
footnote
graphic
gridlines
handles
header
Header and Footer view
header column
header row
landscape orientation
manual line break
manual page break
paragraph-level formatting
portrait orientation
Quick Styles
reference marker
Shift+Enter key combination
SmartArt
section
section break
sort
tab
tab stop
table

Practice	**Review Assignments**

Apply the skills you learned in the tutorial using the same case scenario.

Data File needed for the Review Assignments: Class.docx

In conjunction with a local community college, Robin Kinsella has organized a series of computer training classes for Parkside residents to be held in the Parkside community center. She has begun work on a report for the board that outlines basic information about the classes and introduces the instructors. It's your job to format the report, add a table at the end containing a preliminary schedule, and create a sample graphic that Robin could use in a handout advertising the classes. When you are finished, Robin will expand each section of the report, adding more text to each. (*Note*: Text you need to type is shown in bold for ease of reference only; do not bold the text unless otherwise instructed.) Complete the following:

1. Open the file **Class** located in the Tutorial.03\Review folder included with your Data Files, and then save it as **Class Report** in the same folder.
2. Display the rulers and nonprinting characters and make sure the document is displayed in Print Layout view.
3. Format the document headings with the Heading 2 Quick Style. Use the Intense Quote style for the "Summary" heading and then indent the summary paragraph to match.
4. Click to the left of the heading "Schedule," insert a page break, move the insertion point to the end of the document, and then create the table shown in Figure 3-41.

Figure 3-41

Start Date	Topic
March 17	The Internet
April 21	Spreadsheets
January 13	Computer literacy
May 12	Simple database
June 9	HTML

5. Sort the table by the contents of the Start Date column in ascending order.
6. In the appropriate location, insert a new row for a word-processing class that starts on February 10.
7. Delete the HTML row at the bottom of the table.
8. Modify the widths of both columns to accommodate the widest entry in each.
9. Format the table with banded rows of pink and white and dark red shading for the header row, and then save your work.
10. On page 1, replace the text "[instructor names]" with the following list of instructors and their specialties. Insert a tab after each name, remembering that the list of specialties won't align properly until you complete Step 11. Remember to use the Shift+Enter key combination (instead of just the Enter key) to insert a new line for each name without adding extra space:
    Felicity J. Connelly-Porter   **Word processing**
    Antonio Morales   **Multimedia software**
    Jon Davis   **Web design**
    Amelia Guntz   **Database design and SQL programming**
11. Select the list of instructors and their specialties, and then insert a left tab stop 2.5 inches from the left margin.
12. Below the heading "Equipment Needs," locate the first sentence of the second paragraph, which begins "There are currently five...." At the end of that sentence, insert a footnote that reads **The computers should run either Windows Vista or Windows XP.**

13. Insert a Next Page section break after the table, format the new page 3 in landscape orientation, and then insert a SmartArt graphic that illustrates the advantages of computer classes. Use the Continuous Block Process graphic from the Process category, and, from left to right, include the following text: **Computer Education, Technological Advantage**, and **New Career Prospects**. Size the SmartArt graphic to fill the page.

14. Create a footer for sections 1 and 2 that aligns your name at the left margin. Insert the page number, without any design elements and without the word "Page," below your name.

15. Create a header for just section 1 using the Alphabet header style, enter **Parkside Computer Classes** as the document title, close Header and Footer view, and then save your work.

16. Insert a cover page using the Stacks style, verify that the document title is automatically inserted in the cover page, enter **An Informational Report** for the subtitle, and then enter your name for the author.

17. Save and preview the report, and then submit the finished document to your instructor, either in printed or electronic form, as requested.

Apply	**Case Problem 1**

Apply the skills you learned to create an annual report for a textile store.

Data File needed for this Case Problem: Textiles.docx

Noblewood Textiles, Inc. As an assistant manager of Noblewood Textiles in San Diego, California, you must help prepare an annual report for the board of directors. (*Note*: Text you need to type is shown in bold for ease of reference only; do not bold the text unless otherwise instructed.) Complete the following:

1. Open the file **Textiles** located in the Tutorial.03\Case1 folder included with your Data Files, and then save it as **Textiles Report** in the same folder.

2. Check your screen to make sure your settings match those in the tutorials, with the document displayed in Print Layout view.

3. Format the headings using the Heading 1 Quick Style. (There are 11 headings, beginning with "Introduction" and ending with "Sales Forecast.")

◈ **EXPLORE**

4. Select the list of members under the heading "Board of Directors," and then click the Page Layout tab. In the Paragraph group, click the Dialog Box Launcher, click the Indents and Spacing tab if necessary, and then click the Tabs button at the bottom of the dialog box. To insert a tab stop with a dot leader at the 4-inch mark, type 4 in the Tab stop position text box, verify that the Left option button is selected in the Alignment section, and then click the 2..... option button in the Leader section. Click the Set button. (Notice the Clear button, which you can use to clear the tab stop you just set, and the Clear All button, which you can use to clear all the custom tab stops from a document.) Click the OK button to close the Tabs dialog box. Notice the tab setting and the dot leaders.

5. On page 2, at the end of the paragraph below the heading "Summer Fiber Art Festival," insert the following endnote: **The Noblewood Web site is currently hosted by NetMind Solutions, but that may change in the coming year.**

6. At the end of the paragraph below the heading "Company Philosophy," insert the following endnote: **Our major, statewide competitor continues to be Boardman Fabrics, which has five retail outlets.**

7. Move the insertion point to the blank paragraph at the end of the Sales Forecast section (above the endnote), and then insert a table consisting of three columns and four rows.

8. Enter the following column headers and data. Format the header row in bold.

Department	January–June	Projected July–December
Yarn	$150,000	$180,000
Quilting	$120,000	$140,000
Garment	$75,000	$100,000

9. Sort the table in ascending order by department.
10. Insert a row above the Garment row and enter the following information:

Embroidery	$100,000	$120,000

11. Adjust the column widths so each column accommodates the widest entry.
12. Format the table using the Light List - Accent 1 table style, which applies blue shading to the header row, no shading in the other rows, and no column borders. Save the document.
13. Create a footer for the document that aligns your name at the left margin and the page number (in the Accent Bar 3 style) at the right margin. (*Hint:* Press the Tab key twice to move the insertion point to the right margin before inserting the page number.)

⊕ EXPLORE 14. Insert a cover page using the Sideline style. Enter the company name, **Noblewood Textiles**, and the title, **Annual Report**. In the subtitle document control, enter **Prepared by Student Name** (but replace "Student Name" with your first and last name). Click the date document control, click the arrow, and then click the current date in the calendar.
15. Save and preview the document, and then submit the finished document to your instructor, either in printed or electronic form, as requested.

Apply	**Case Problem 2**

Apply the skills you learned to create a report summarizing information on a municipal wireless network.

Data File needed for this Case Problem: WiFi.docx

Report on a Municipal Wireless Network   Like many communities, the town of Grand Island, Nebraska, is considering a citywide wireless (or WiFi) network to provide low-cost Internet access for all residents. A task force appointed by the mayor has investigated the issue and summarized its findings in a report. As you format the report in the following steps, you will focus on creating a cover page and a header from scratch, without relying on predefined elements provided by Word. You will also create and edit a SmartArt graphic to illustrate the process of creating the network. (*Note:* Text you need to type is shown in bold for ease of reference only; do not bold the text unless otherwise instructed.) Complete the following:

1. Open the file named **WiFi** located in the Tutorial.03\Case2 folder included with your Data Files, and then save it as **WiFi Report** in the same folder. Check your screen to make sure your settings match those in the tutorials.
2. Replace "Student Name" in the first page with your first and last name.
3. Divide the document into two sections. Begin the second section just before the heading "Summary" and have the second section begin a new page.
4. Position the insertion point somewhere in the page 1 text.

⊕ EXPLORE 5. Click the Page Layout tab. In the Page Setup group, click the Dialog Box Launcher, and then click the Layout tab. Click the Vertical alignment arrow, click Center, and then click the OK button. Zoom out so you can see the entire page and review the newly formatted cover page, with the text centered in the middle of the page.

6. Zoom in again so you can read the document text, and format the text of the title and the subtitle using the Title and Subtitle Quick Styles. Leave the line containing your name in Normal style.

7. Format the document headings using the Heading 1 Quick Style.

8. Insert a tab stop at the 2-inch mark in the list of task force members.

9. Change the section 2 header so it is no longer linked to section 1, move the insertion point to the center tab stop in the section 2 header, and then type the header **WiFi Network Report**. Format the header text in italic, 14-point Calibri.

10. Create a footer for just section 2 using the Alphabet style. Replace the placeholder text with your first and last name. Close Header and Footer view. Zoom out and verify that the header and footer appear only in section 2.

11. Move the insertion point to the end of the document, insert a page break, and insert a SmartArt graphic in the new page. In the Process category, select the Upward Arrow graphic. Enter the text **Hire Networking Firm**, **Construct Network**, and **Sell Broadband Rights**.

⊕ **EXPLORE** 12. In the Create Graphic group, click the Add Shape button (not the Add Shape button arrow), and then type **Sell Network Subscriptions**. Click anywhere in the white area of the SmartArt Graphic, inside the border, to deselect the text.

13. Save the document, preview it, and then submit the finished document to your instructor, either in printed or electronic form, as requested.

| Challenge | **Case Problem 3** |

Go beyond what you've learned to convert text into a table and then use other advanced table options to enhance the table.

Data Files needed for this Case Problem: Clients.docx and Expenses.docx

Contact List for Parson's Graphic Design   Amanda Parson recently launched a new graphic design firm that specializes in creating Web ads for small businesses in the Seattle area. A colleague has just e-mailed her a list of potential clients. The list consists of names, e-mail addresses, and phone numbers. Because it was exported from another program, the information is formatted as simple text, with the pieces of information separated by commas. Amanda asks you to convert this text into a table and then format the table to make it easy to read. When you're finished, she needs you to sum a column of numbers in her Office Expense table. (*Note*: Text you need to type is shown in bold for ease of reference only; do not bold the text unless otherwise instructed.) Complete the following:

1. Open the file named **Clients** located in the Tutorial.03\Case3 folder included with your Data Files, and then save it as **Potential Clients** in the same folder. Check your screen to make sure your settings match those in the tutorials.

⊕ **EXPLORE** 2. Use Word Help to learn how to convert text to a table. Use what you learned to convert the document to a table. Adjust the column widths to accommodate the widest entry in each column.

3. Insert a header row using the bold headers **Company**, **Contact**, **Phone**, and **E-Mail**.

4. Sort the list alphabetically by Company, and then replace the name "Katherine Shropshire" with your first and last name.

⊕ **EXPLORE** 5. Change the page orientation to landscape, and then drag the Table Resize handle (located just outside the lower-right corner of the table) until the table is 7 inches wide and 3 inches high. Notice that all the parts of the table increase proportionally.

6. Format the table using a Quick Style that includes row borders but not column borders.

7. Save and preview the document, and then submit the finished document to your instructor, either in printed or electronic form, as requested. Close the document.

8. Open the file named **Expenses** located in the Tutorial.03\Case3 folder included with your Data Files, and then save it as **Office Expenses** in the same folder.

⊕ EXPLORE
9. Use Word Help to learn how to merge cells. Use what you learned to merge the cell containing the word "TOTAL" with the blank cell to its right.

⊕ EXPLORE
10. In the Alignment group, click the Align Top Right button to align the word "TOTAL" on the right side of the new, larger cell. Select the four cells below the Expense header (including the blank cell at the bottom of the Expense column), and then click the Align Top Right button.

⊕ EXPLORE
11. Click the blank cell at the bottom of the Expenses column and then, in the Data group, click the Formula button. The Formula dialog box opens. Make sure the formula "=SUM(ABOVE)" appears in the Formula text box, make sure the other two text boxes are blank, and then click the OK button. Word sums the costs in the Expense column and displays the total ($9587.00) in the selected cell.

12. Save and preview the document, and then submit the finished document to your instructor, either in printed or electronic form, as requested.

| Create | **Case Problem 4**

Use your table skills to create the instruction sheet shown in Figure 3-42.

There are no Data Files needed for this Case Problem.

Hammond Astronomical Society Sarah Vernon coordinates star-gazing tours for the Hammond Astronomical Society. To ensure that participants can see as well as possible in the night sky, they are asked to follow a set of rules that astronomers refer to as a dark sky protocol. You can use Word table features to create an instruction sheet describing the club's dark sky protocol. Figure 3-42 shows Sarah's sketch. (*Note*: Text you need to type is shown in bold for ease of reference only; do not bold the text unless otherwise instructed.)

Figure 3-42

Dark Sky Protocol

Hammond Astronomical Society

Personal Items

Turn off flashlights.

Shield computers with red foil.

Shield all lights for charts and confine them to the target area.

Rationale

Most people need 30 minutes to achieve optimum night vision. Accidental exposure to light from cars, computers or flashlights means the period of dark adaption must begin again. Some individuals can tolerate small amounts of red light without significant vision degradation, as long as the light source is dim and does not shine into the eyes. For more information, see Sarah Vernon.

Vehicle

Turn off all interior lights before arrival.

Turn off headlights.

Park so backup lights are not required upon exit.

Complete the following steps:

1. Open a new, blank document, and save it as **Dark Sky Protocol** in the Tutorial.03\Case4 folder included with your Data Files.

2. If necessary, zoom out so you can see the entire page, switch to Print Layout view, and display the rulers.

3. Change the document's orientation to landscape.

EXPLORE

4. On the Insert tab, click the Table button, and then click Draw Table at the bottom of the Insert Table menu. The Draw Table pointer (which looks like a pencil) appears. You drag this pointer horizontally or vertically to create a straight line, and diagonally to create a rectangle.

EXPLORE

5. Click in the upper-left corner of the document (near the paragraph mark), and then drag down and to the right to draw a rectangle that stretches to the right and bottom margins. The rectangle should be a little less than nine inches wide and a little more than six inches high. If you make the rectangle too big, Word will insert a second page in the document. In that case, undo the change and redraw the rectangle.

EXPLORE

6. Use the Draw Table pointer to draw the columns and rows shown in Figure 3-42. For example, to draw the column border for the "Dark Sky Protocol" column, click the top of the rectangle where you want the column to begin, and drag down to the bottom of the rectangle. Use the same technique to draw rows. (If you make a mistake, use the Undo button. To delete a border, click the Eraser button on the Table Tools Design tab, click the border you want to erase, and then click the Eraser button again to turn it off. Click the Draw Table button to turn on the Draw Table pointer again.) Don't expect to draw the table perfectly the first time. You may have to practice until you become comfortable with the Draw Table pointer, but once you can use it well, you will find it a helpful tool for creating complex tables.

7. Press the Escape key to turn off the Draw Table pointer.

EXPLORE

8. In the left column, type the text **Dark Sky Protocol**. With the pointer still in that cell, click the Table Tools Layout tab, then in the Alignment group, click the Text Direction button twice to position the text vertically so that it reads from bottom to top. Using the formatting options on the Home tab, format the text in 36-point Cambria. Click the Table Tools Layout tab, and then, in the Alignment group, click the Align Center button. (*Hint*: You will probably have to adjust and readjust the row and column borders throughout these steps, until all the elements of the table are positioned properly.)

9. Type the remaining text, as shown in Figure 3-42. Replace "Sarah Vernon" with your own name. Use bold as shown in Figure 3-42 to draw attention to key elements. Change the font and font sizes as necessary to make your table look like the one in Figure 3-42. Likewise, use the Center Align button on the Table Tools Layout tab as necessary. (*Hint:* For the bottom three cells, use 16-point or 18-point Cambria for the bold items and 14-point or 16-point Calibri for the other text.)

EXPLORE

10. Switch to the Insert tab. In the Illustrations group, click the Shapes button and then, under "Stars and Banners," click the 5-Point Star shape. In the blank cell in the top row, position the mouse pointer over the upper-left corner, and then click and drag the mouse pointer down and to the right to draw a five-pointed star. If the star isn't centered neatly in the cell, click the Undo button, and try again until you draw a star that looks similar to the one in Figure 3-42. The star is selected, as indicated by the small squares (called selection handles) that surround it. A new tab, named Format, appears on the Ribbon with a label identifying it as a Drawing Tools contextual tab. On the Drawing Tools Format tab, in the Shape Styles group, click the Shape Fill button arrow and, under "Standard Colors," click the orange square. Click anywhere outside the star to deselect it.

⊕ **EXPLORE**

11. Now that you have organized the information using the Word table tools, you can remove the borders. Select the entire table, click the Table Tools Design tab, click the Borders button arrow (in the Table Styles group) and then click No Border. (You may still see dotted blue gridlines, which will not be visible in the printed document. If you would like to turn off the dotted blue gridlines, click the Table Tools Layout tab, and then click View Gridlines in the Tables group.)

12. Save your work, preview the document, make any necessary adjustments, and then submit the finished document to your instructor, either in printed or electronic form, as requested.

Research | **Internet Assignments**

Go to the Web to find information you can use to create documents.

The purpose of the Internet Assignments is to challenge you to find information on the Internet that you can use to work effectively with this software. The actual assignments are updated and maintained on the Course Technology Web site. Log on to the Internet and use your Web browser to go to the Student Online Companion for New Perspectives Office 2007 at **www.course.com/np/office2007**. Then navigate to the Internet Assignments for this tutorial.

Assess | **SAM Assessment and Training**

If you have a SAM user profile, you may have access to hands-on instruction, practice, and assessment of the skills covered in this tutorial. Log in to your SAM account (**http://sam2007.course.com**) to launch any assigned training activities or exams that relate to the skills covered in this tutorial.

Review | **Quick Check Answers**

Session 3.1

1. Click the paragraph containing the heading; on the Home tab in the Styles group, click the More button; and then click the Quick Style you want. (If the Quick Style you want is already visible in the Styles group, you don't have to click the More button.)
2. False
3. Click where you want to insert the table, click the Insert Tab, in the Tables group click the Tables button, drag the mouse pointer to select the desired number of rows and columns, and then release the mouse button.
4. Tab key
5. Select button on the Table Tools Layout tab
6. In the Data group on the Table Tools Layout tab, click the Sort button. Click the Sort by arrow, and select the header for the column you want to sort by. In the Type list box located to the right of the Sort by list box, select the type of information stored in the column you want to sort by. To sort in alphabetical, chronological, or numeric order, click the Ascending option button. To sort in reverse order, click the Descending option button. If you also want to sort by a second column, click the Then by arrow and click a column header. If the table includes headers, make sure the Header row option button is selected, and then click the OK button.
7. True

Session 3.2

1. True
2. Click where you want to insert a footnote, click the References tab, in the Footnotes group click the Insert Footnote button, and then type the text of the footnote in the bottom margin.
3. The Breaks button on the Page Layout tab
4. The SmartArt graphic appears with a blue border around it.
5. Click in the header area (in a page's top margin) or in the footer area (in a page's bottom margin); or click the Header button or the Footer button on the Insert tab.
6. False

Ending Data Files

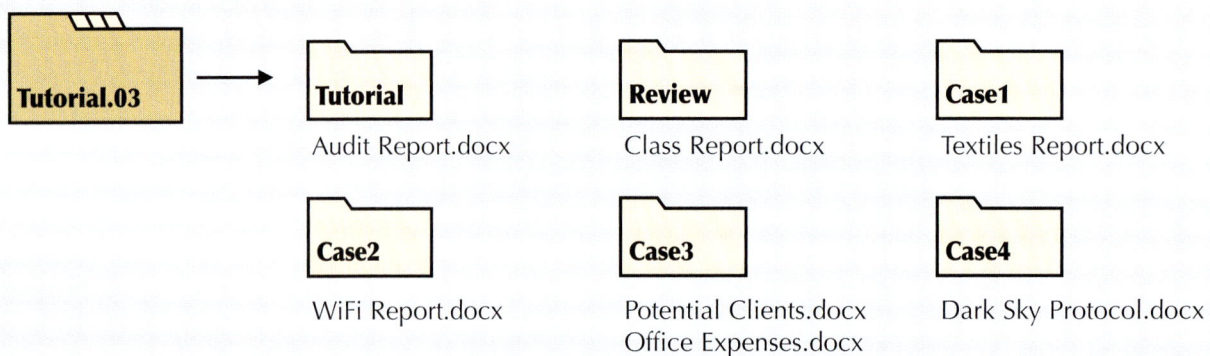

Tutorial.03 → Tutorial
Audit Report.docx

Review
Class Report.docx

Case1
Textiles Report.docx

Case2
WiFi Report.docx

Case3
Potential Clients.docx
Office Expenses.docx

Case4
Dark Sky Protocol.docx

Desktop Publishing and Mail Merge

Creating a Newsletter, Cover Letter, and Blog Post

Case | Shepherd Bay Medical Center

Joel Conchola, a public outreach specialist at Shepherd Bay Medical Center, needs to create a one-page newsletter that explains the importance of exercise and diet in preventing type II diabetes. He has asked you to help him create the newsletter and a cover letter that will accompany the newsletter. He is also interested in creating a blog for Shepherd Bay Medical and needs your help to create a blog post.

Joel has already written the text of the newsletter. He wants you to transform this text into a publication that is neat, organized, and professional looking. He would like the newsletter to contain headings and an eye-catching headline. He also wants to include a picture that reinforces the newsletter content.

In this tutorial, you'll get acquainted with some desktop publishing features available in Word that you'll use to create the newsletter. You'll format the title as a prominent-looking headline and divide the document into newspaper-style columns to make it easier to read. To add interest and focus to the text, you'll include a graphic. You'll then fine-tune the newsletter layout, give it a more professional appearance with typographic characters, and you'll put a border around the page to give the newsletter a finished look. Next, you will use Word's mail merge feature to insert personalized information into the cover letter that will accompany the newsletter. Finally, you'll experiment with creating a blog post.

Starting Data Files

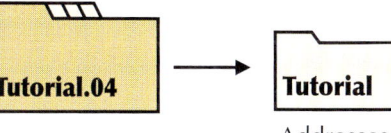

Tutorial.04 →	Tutorial	Review	Case1	Case2	Case3	Case4
	Addresses.docx	Addresses.docx	Audio.docx	Island.jpg	Hill.docx	(none)
	Letter.docx	Eating.docx		News.docx		
	Prevention.docx	Nutrition.docx				

Session 4.1

Elements of Desktop Publishing

Desktop publishing is the process of preparing commercial-quality printed material using a desktop computer system. In addition to newsletters, you can desktop-publish brochures, posters, and other documents that include text and graphics.

The following elements are commonly associated with desktop publishing:

- Columns and other page layout features—Columns of text, pull quotes (small portions of text pulled out of the main text and enlarged), drop caps (large initial letters at the beginning of paragraphs), page borders, and other special formatting features that you don't frequently see in letters and other documents distinguish desktop-published documents.
- Graphics—Clip art, horizontal or vertical lines (called **rules**), text boxes, and photographs help illustrate a concept or product, draw a reader's attention to the document, and make the text visually appealing.
- Multiple fonts—Two or three fonts, font sizes, and font colors provide visual interest, guide the reader through the text, and convey the tone of the document.
- High-quality printing—A laser printer or high-resolution inkjet printer produces the final output.

Although professional desktop publishers use software specially designed for desktop publishing, you can use Word to create basic desktop-published documents. You already know how to format text in multiple fonts and font sizes, and you know how to create a graphic using SmartArt. In this tutorial, you'll incorporate more of the desktop publishing elements listed to produce the newsletter shown in Figure 4-1.

Figure 4-1 **Shepherd Bay Medical Center newsletter**

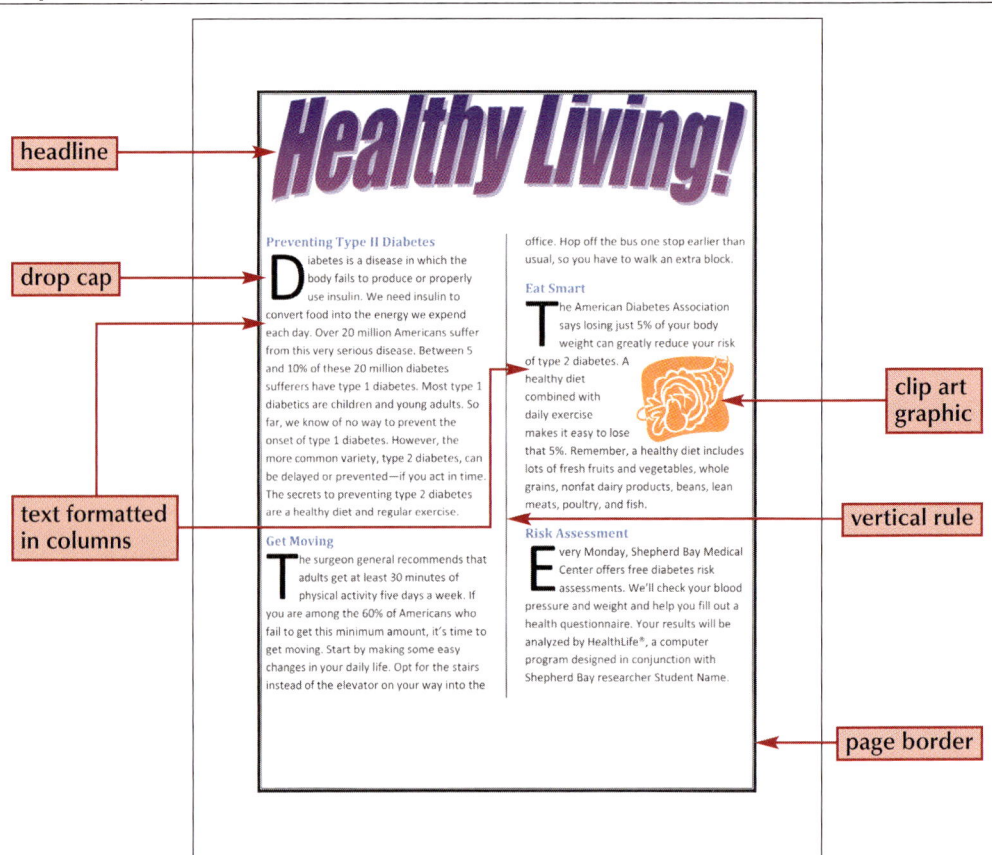

Before you can start creating the newsletter shown in Figure 4-1, you need to open Joel's document and review the text of the newsletter.

To open the newsletter document:

▶ **1.** Start Word and open the file **Prevention** from the Tutorial.04\Tutorial folder included with your Data Files.

▶ **2.** To avoid altering the original file, save the document as **Prevention Newsletter** in the same folder.

▶ **3.** Display nonprinting characters, switch to Print Layout view, display the rulers, and set the zoom so you can see the entire width of the newsletter. Throughout this tutorial, feel free to zoom in or zoom out if you prefer to see more or less of the newsletter.

▶ **4.** Read the document to familiarize yourself with its content.

▶ **5.** At the end of the document, replace "Shawn Kampa" with your first and last name. This will make it easier for you to find your copy of the newsletter when you print it.

Now that the newsletter contains all the necessary details, you can turn your attention to your first desktop publishing task—adding a headline.

Using WordArt to Create a Headline

Joel wants the title of the newsletter, "Healthy Living," to be eye-catching and dramatic. You can create such a headline using **WordArt**, a feature that allows you to create specially formatted text. You type the text for a piece of WordArt in the Edit WordArt Text dialog box and then insert it into the document. Unlike regular text, a WordArt headline is considered an **object**—that is, something that you can manipulate independently of the text. You can think of the WordArt object as a thing that lies on top of, or next to, the text in a document. This means that, for example, to alter its size you drag its handles, just as you would for a SmartArt graphic. A set of WordArt tools appears on the Ribbon when the WordArt is selected. You can use these tools to change its shape, size, and color and to add special effects such as 3-D and shadowing.

Creating WordArt | Reference Window

- Click the Insert tab, and then, in the Text group, click the WordArt button.
- In the WordArt gallery, click the style of text you want to insert.
- Type the text you want in the Edit WordArt Text dialog box.
- Click the Font and Size arrows to select the font and font size you want. If you want, click the Bold or Italic button, or both.
- Click the OK button.
- Use the tools on the WordArt Tools Format tab to format the WordArt.
- Drag any handle to resize and reshape the WordArt. To avoid altering the WordArt's proportions, press and hold down the Ctrl key while you drag a handle.

You're ready to use WordArt to create the newsletter title.

To create the title of the newsletter using WordArt:

▶ **1.** Press the **Ctrl+Home** keys to move the insertion point to the beginning of the document, and then click the **Insert** tab.

▶ **2.** In the Text group, click the **WordArt** button. The WordArt gallery opens. Joel wants to use the WordArt style in the middle row, second column from the left. See Figure 4-2.

Figure 4-2 ▶ **WordArt gallery**

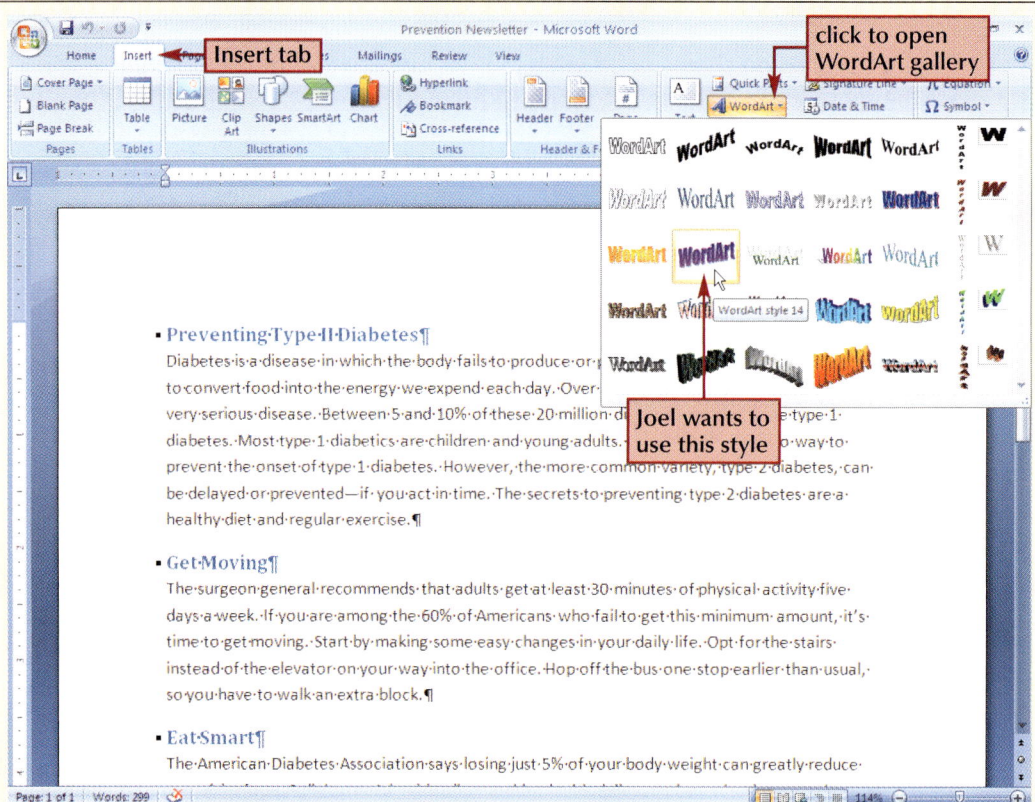

▶ **3.** Position the mouse pointer over the style Joel wants to use, as shown in Figure 4-2. A ScreenTip displays the name of this style: "WordArt style 14."

▶ **4.** Click **WordArt style 14**. The Edit WordArt Text dialog box opens, displaying the placeholder text "Your Text Here," which you will replace with the newsletter title. See Figure 4-3.

Edit WordArt Text dialog box ◀ **Figure 4-3**

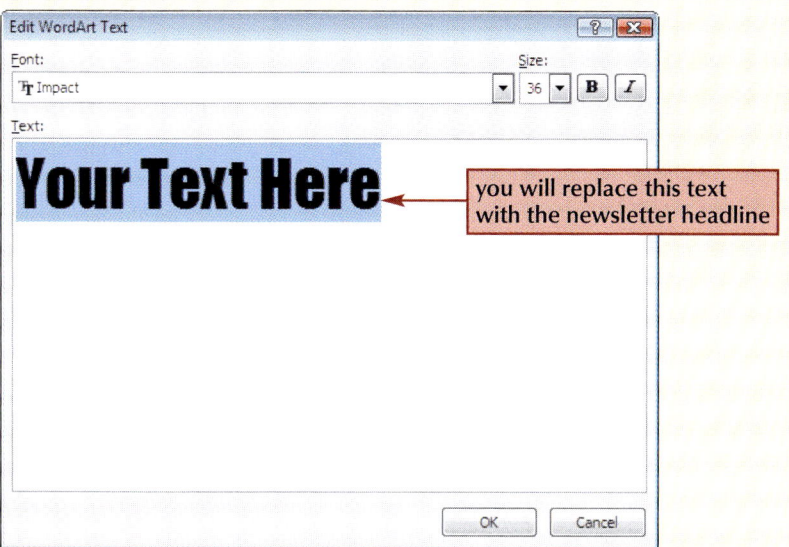

> you will replace this text with the newsletter headline

▶ **5.** Type **Healthy Living** to replace the placeholder text with the newsletter title, and then click the **OK** button. The Edit WordArt Text dialog box closes, and the Word-Art is inserted as a graphic at the beginning of the newsletter. The "Preventing Type II Diabetes" heading moves to the right to accommodate the new headline. The WordArt Tools Format tab appears on the Ribbon. The border around the Wor-dArt tells you that it is currently selected. The squares on the border are **sizing handles**, which you can drag to change the size of the WordArt. See Figure 4-4.

WordArt inserted into document ◀ **Figure 4-4**

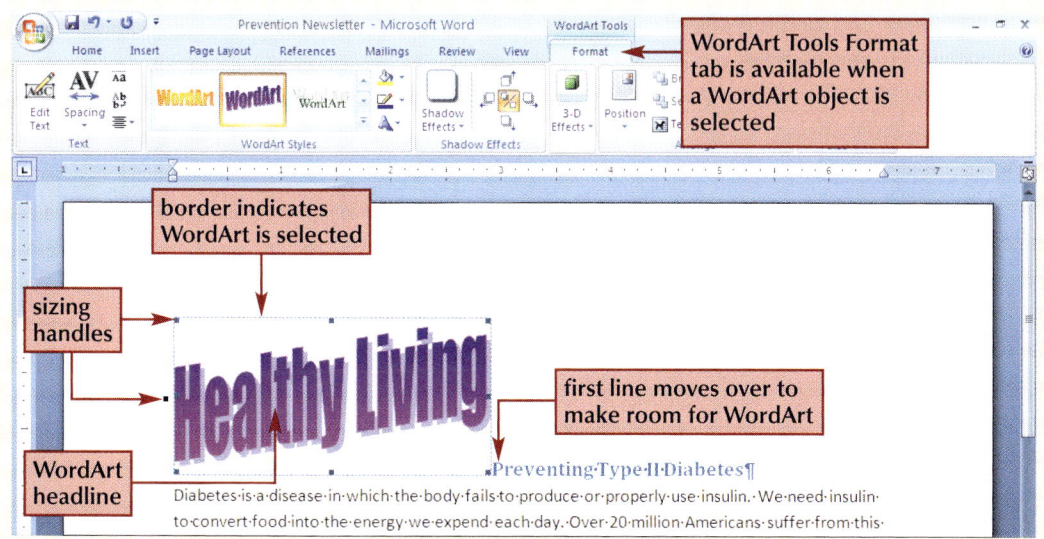

> WordArt Tools Format tab is available when a WordArt object is selected

> border indicates WordArt is selected

> sizing handles

> first line moves over to make room for WordArt

> WordArt headline

Eventually, you will position and resize the headline, so that it stretches from margin to margin. But for now, you can leave it in its current position.

Editing a WordArt Object

The WordArt object you have created is not regular text. You cannot edit it as you would other text. You can think of WordArt as an object that lies on top of or next to the text in a document. To edit WordArt, it must be selected. Then you can make changes using the tools on the WordArt Tools Format tab or by dragging its sizing handles.

The WordArt object you just created is already selected, so you can get to work modifying its appearance. First, Joel would like you to add an exclamation point at the end of the headline and format the headline in italic.

To edit the text and formatting of the WordArt object:

▶ **1.** Verify that the WordArt object is selected, as indicated by the border and the sizing handles. The WordArt Tools Format tab, which is visible only when a WordArt object is selected, contains tools for editing WordArt.

▶ **2.** In the Text group on the WordArt Tools Format tab, click the **Edit Text** button. The Edit WordArt Text dialog box opens. You used this dialog box earlier when you first created the WordArt object.

▶ **3.** Click at the end of the headline (to the right of the "g" in "Living"), and then type **!** (an exclamation point).

▶ **4.** Click the **Italic** button I in the Edit WordArt Text dialog box. The headline in the text box is now formatted in italic.

▶ **5.** Click the **OK** button. The Edit WordArt Text dialog box closes, and you can see the edited headline in the document. See Figure 4-5.

Figure 4-5 ▶ **Edited WordArt headline**

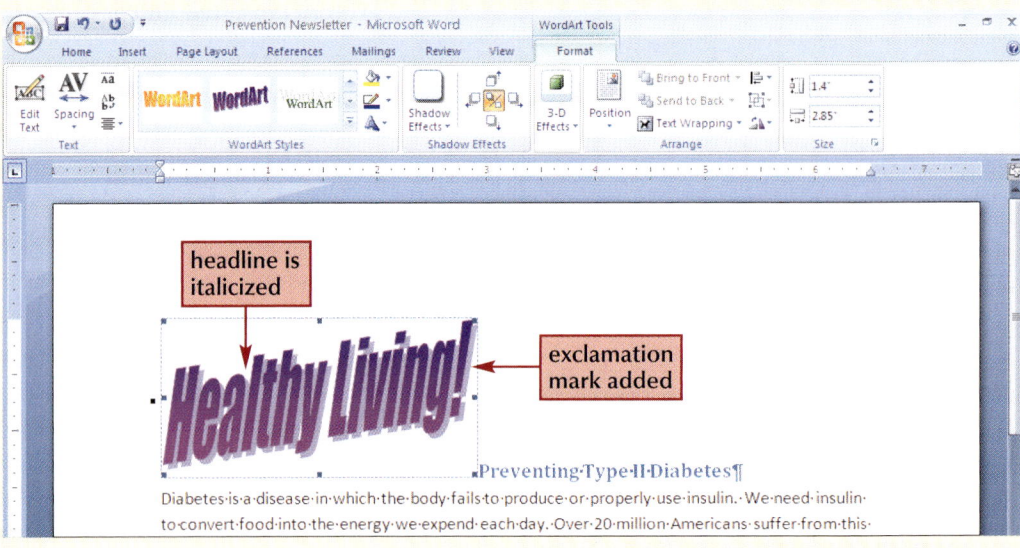

Changing the Shape of a WordArt Object

You can quickly change the shape of a WordArt graphic using the Change WordArt Shape button in the WordArt Styles group on the WordArt Tools Format tab. Right now, the WordArt headline has a straight shape, without any curve to it. Joel wants to use an arched shape.

To change the shape of the WordArt object:

▶ **1.** Verify that the WordArt object is selected, and then, in the WordArt Styles group, click the **Change WordArt Shape** button ![A]. A palette of shape options opens.

▶ **2.** Move the mouse pointer over each option in the palette to display a ScreenTip with the name of each shape and to see the live preview of each shape in the document.

▶ **3.** Point to (but don't click) the **Can Up** shape (top row in the Warp section, third column from the left), as shown in Figure 4-6.

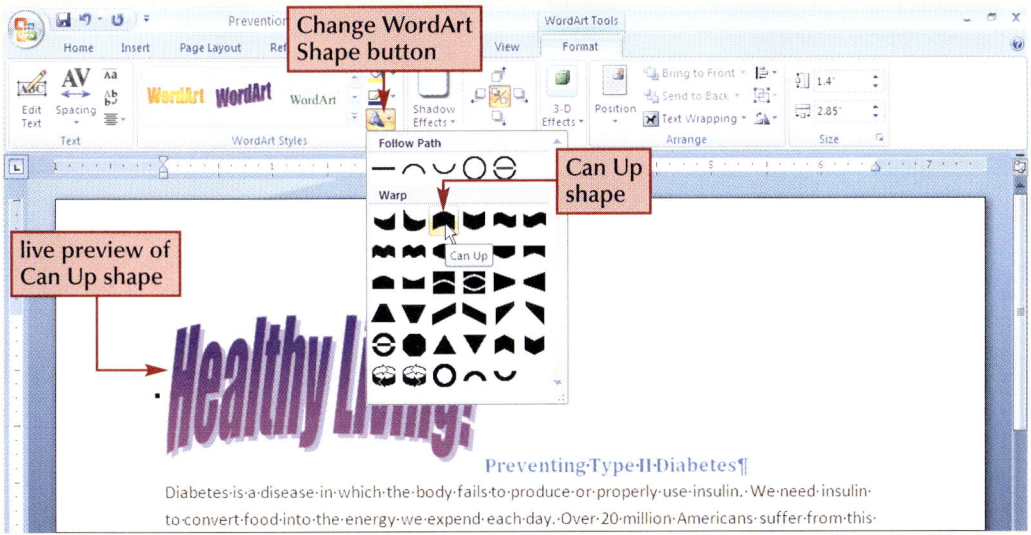

Selecting a new WordArt shape   **Figure 4-6**

▶ **4.** Click the **Can Up** shape. The newsletter title is formatted in the new WordArt shape, which arches upward in the middle.

▶ **5.** Save your work.

The headline has the shape you want. Now you can position the WordArt object in relation to the text of the newsletter.

Wrapping Text Below a WordArt Object

At this point, the WordArt object is an **inline graphic**, which means it is located in a specific position in a specific line of the document (in this case, at the beginning of the first line). If you type text before an inline graphic, the graphic moves to accommodate the new text. You have more control over the position of a graphic, such as a WordArt object, if you change it to a floating graphic. A **floating graphic** is attached, or **anchored**, to a specific paragraph; however, you can drag a floating graphic to any location in the document. The text then flows, or **wraps**, around it. Adding or deleting text does not affect the position of a floating graphic.

To change an inline WordArt object to a floating graphic, you need to select a text wrapping style. You can wrap text around graphics many different ways. For example, you can have the text wrap above and below the graphic, or so the text follows the shape of the graphic, even if it has an irregular shape. The Arrange group on the WordArt Tools Format tab contains two useful tools for controlling the way text wraps around all graphics, including WordArt, pictures, and charts. First, there's the Position button, which allows you to position the WordArt or graphic in one of several locations on the page (top left, top middle, top right, and so on) and to wrap the document text around it. Second, there's the Text Wrapping button, which assumes the WordArt is already positioned where you want it and allows you to choose from a number of more refined wrapping options. Because the WordArt object is already located at the beginning of the document, where you want it, you'll use the Text Wrapping button in the Arrange group.

To wrap the newsletter text below the WordArt object:

▶ **1.** With the WordArt object selected, click the **Text Wrapping** button in the Arrange group. A menu of text wrapping options opens. See Figure 4-7.

Figure 4-7 ▶ **Text Wrapping menu**

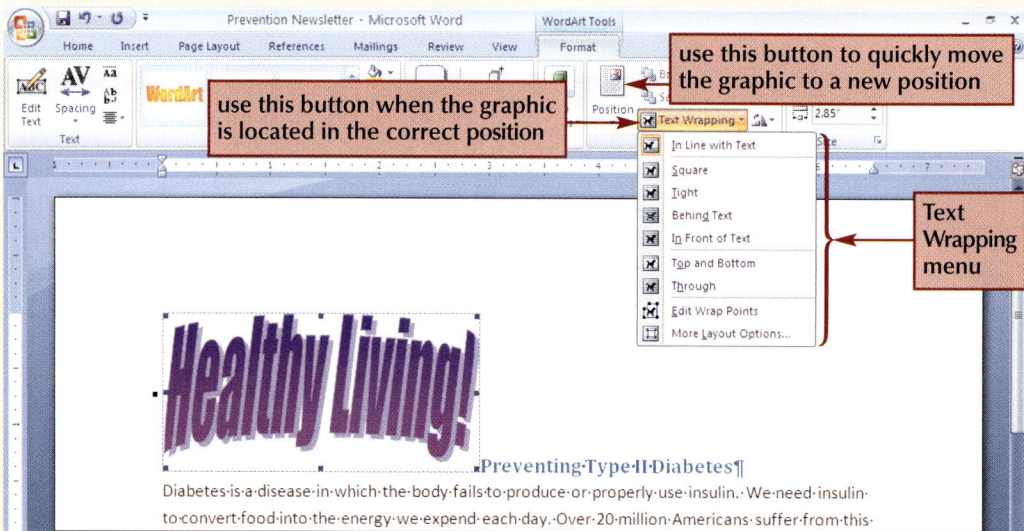

▶ **2.** Click **Top and Bottom**. The heading text is moved below the WordArt object. The WordArt is still selected, although now you see only the sizing handles, without the box. Also, there are more handles, and not all the handles are squares. Like the blue squares, the blue circles are sizing handles. However, the circle-shaped handles indicate that the graphic is a floating graphic. A number of other items appear around the WordArt object, as shown in Figure 4-8. The anchor symbol to the left of the heading "Preventing Type II Diabetes" tells you that the WordArt is attached, or anchored, to that paragraph.

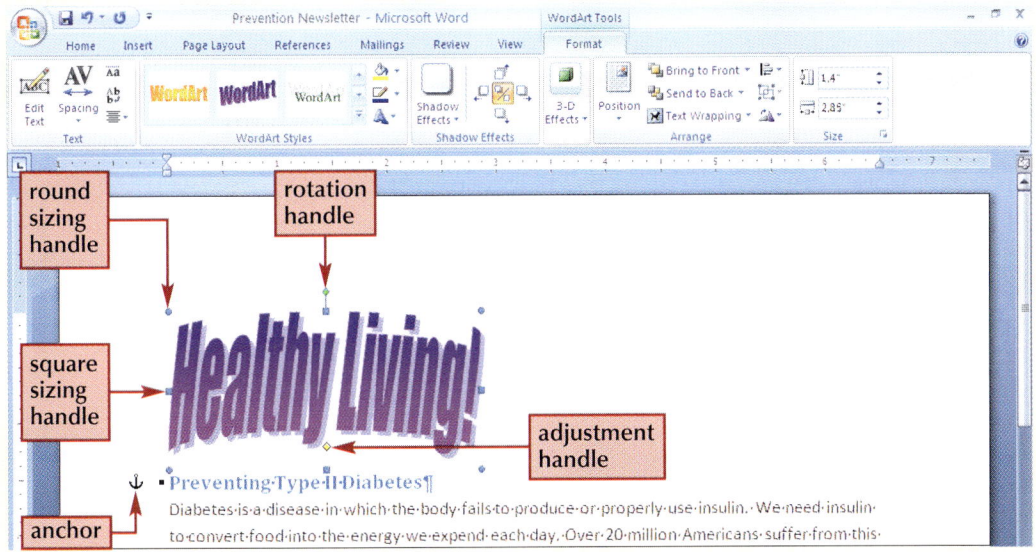

Trouble? If you can't see the anchor symbol, your Zoom setting is probably too high. Zoom out until you can see the full width of the page.

Positioning and Sizing the WordArt Object

After you choose a text wrapping style for a WordArt object, you can adjust its position in the document by dragging it with the mouse pointer. To change the size of a WordArt object, drag one of its sizing handles. To keep the headline the same proportion as the original, hold down the Ctrl key as you drag the sizing handle. This prevents "stretching" the headline more in one direction than the other.

Joel asks you to widen the headline so it stretches neatly across the margins. Before you enlarge the headline, you will drag it to a new position.

To position and enlarge the WordArt object:

▶ **1.** Move the mouse pointer over the headline.

▶ **2.** Use the 🔀 pointer to drag the WordArt object to the right until it is centered below the 3-inch mark on the horizontal ruler. Release the mouse button.

▶ **3.** With the WordArt object still selected, position the pointer over the lower-right sizing handle. The pointer changes to ⤡ .

▶ **4.** Press and hold the **Ctrl** key while you drag the sizing handle almost to the right margin. Use the horizontal ruler as a guide. As you drag the handle, the pointer changes to ╋ and a dotted outline appears to show you how big the WordArt will be when you release the mouse button. Take care not to drag the handle down too far, or the WordArt object will be too tall. See Figure 4-9.

Figure 4-9 Resizing the WordArt

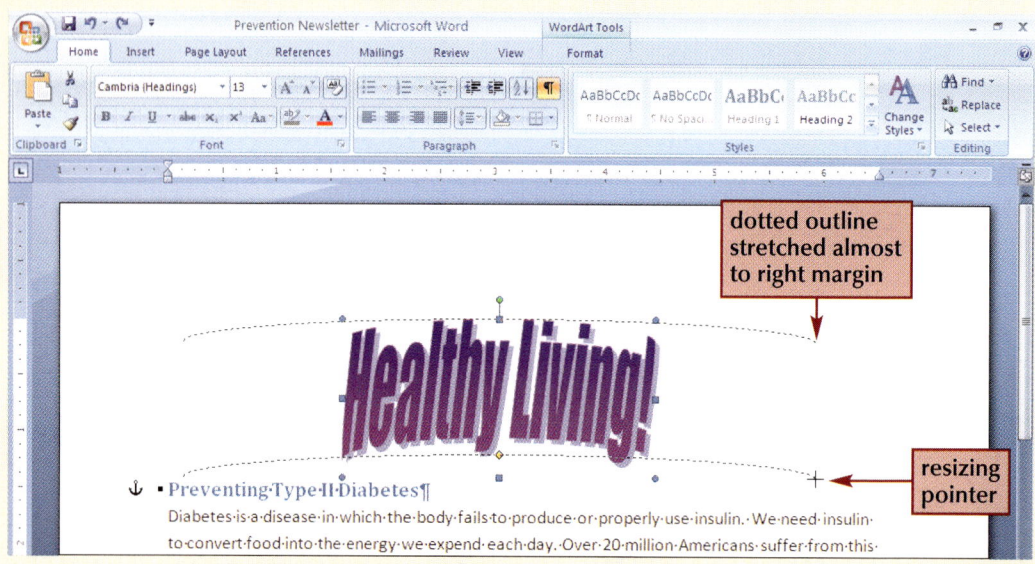

5. Release the mouse button when the dotted horizontal line stretches almost from the left to the right margin. The WordArt heading should be about 5.5 inches wide and a little less than 1.5 inches high at its tallest.

Trouble? If the WordArt heading spans the margins, but is not tall enough to read easily, you probably didn't hold down the Ctrl key when you dragged the mouse pointer. Undo the change and repeat Steps 4 and 5.

6. If necessary, drag the headline down slightly, so that the top of the headline does not extend into the top margin.

Trouble? If the headline jumps to the middle of the first paragraph of text, you dragged it too far. Undo the change, and then repeat Step 6.

Tip

You can drag the rotation handle (the green circle) to rotate a WordArt object. You can use the adjustment handle (the yellow diamond) to increase or decrease the arch of a WordArt object.

Next, you need to turn your attention to the anchor symbol located by the lower-left corner of the WordArt headline.

Anchoring the WordArt Object to a Blank Paragraph

The text wrapping that you applied earlier changed the WordArt object into a floating graphic that is anchored to the paragraph containing the heading "Preventing Type II Diabetes." Later in this tutorial, you will format the newsletter text in narrow, newspaper-style columns. To prevent the column format from affecting the WordArt object, you need to anchor it to its own, blank paragraph. Then you can format that paragraph as a separate section.

At this point, the anchor symbol is probably located to the left of, and just above, the first paragraph (the heading "Preventing Type II Diabetes"). However, yours may be in a different position—for instance, it might be positioned above and to the left of the WordArt. In the next set of steps, you will move the anchor to a new, blank paragraph at the beginning of the document.

To anchor the WordArt object to a blank paragraph:

▶ **1.** Press the **Ctrl+Home** keys. The insertion point moves to the left of the "P" in the heading "Preventing Type II Diabetes," where you need to insert a blank paragraph. The WordArt object is no longer selected, so you cannot see the anchor at this point.

▶ **2.** Press the **Enter** key. A new paragraph symbol is inserted just above the Preventing Type II Diabetes heading.

▶ **3.** If the new paragraph symbol is inserted above the WordArt heading, drag the WordArt heading up slightly until the paragraph mark moves below the WordArt heading.

▶ **4.** Click the **WordArt** object. The selection handles and the anchor symbol appear. The anchor symbol is probably positioned to the left of, and just above, the new paragraph, although it might be positioned to the left of the "Preventing Type II Diabetes" paragraph instead.

▶ **5.** If necessary, click the anchor and drag it up to position it to the left of the new, blank paragraph, as shown in Figure 4-10, if it is not already positioned there.

Properly anchored WordArt | **Figure 4-10**

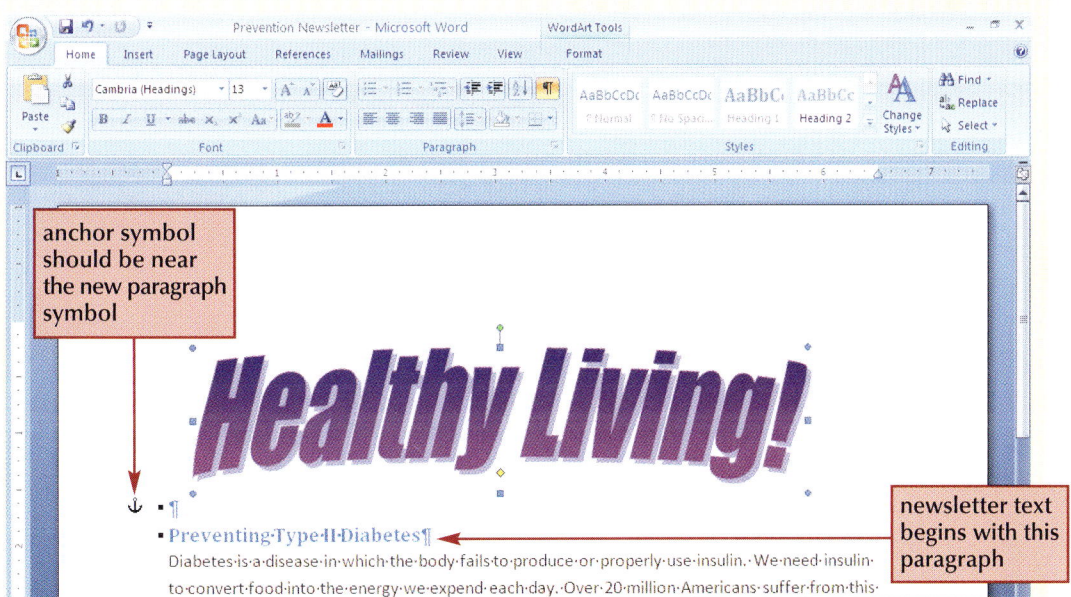

Trouble? If you notice any other differences between your headline and the one shown in Figure 4-10, edit the headline to make it match the figure. For example, you may need to drag the WordArt left or right slightly, or you may need to adjust its size by dragging one of its sizing handles.

▶ **6.** Click anywhere in the newsletter to deselect the WordArt, and then save your work.

Your WordArt is finished. The headline draws attention to the newsletter and makes it visually appealing.

Formatting Text in Newspaper-Style Columns

Because newsletters are meant for quick reading, they are usually laid out in newspaper-style columns. In **newspaper-style columns**, a page is divided into two or more vertical blocks, or columns. Text flows down one column, continues at the top of the next column, flows down that column, and so forth. The columns allow the eye to take in a lot of text and to scan a newspaper quickly for interesting information.

To quickly format a document in columns, click the Columns button on the Page Layout tab, and then select the number of columns you want on the Columns menu. If your document is already divided into sections, the column format is applied only to the section that currently contains the insertion point. For more detailed options, use the More Columns command (at the bottom of the Columns menu), which opens the Columns dialog box. In the Columns dialog box, you can insert a vertical line between columns, select a specific column width, and insert a section break at the same time you apply the column formatting, so that only part of a document is formatted in columns.

Joel wants you to format the text below the WordArt object into two columns and add a vertical line between them. To accomplish this, you need to use the Columns dialog box.

To apply newspaper-style columns to the body of the newsletter:

▶ 1. Click to the left of the "P" in "Preventing Type II Diabetes."

▶ 2. Click the **Page Layout** tab, and then, in the Page Setup group, click the **Columns** button. The Columns menu opens. You could click an option on the menu to format the entire document, including the paragraph containing the WordArt, in columns. However, you don't want the WordArt to be part of a column, so you need to start the columns below the paragraph to which the WordArt object is anchored. To do this, you need to use the More Columns command at the bottom of the menu.

▶ 3. Click **More Columns**. The Columns dialog box opens.

▶ 4. In the Presets section, click the **Two** icon, and then verify that the Equal column width check box (in the lower-left corner of the dialog box) is selected.

▶ 5. Click the **Line between** check box to select it. The text in the Preview box changes to a two-column format with a vertical rule between the columns.

   You don't want the WordArt object to be included in the columns; you want the columns to start at the current location of the insertion point and to continue through the rest of the document.

▶ 6. Click the **Apply to** arrow, and then click **This point forward**. This tells Word to insert a section break at the insertion point and format the columns starting there. See Figure 4-11.

Correct settings in Columns dialog box ◀ Figure 4-11

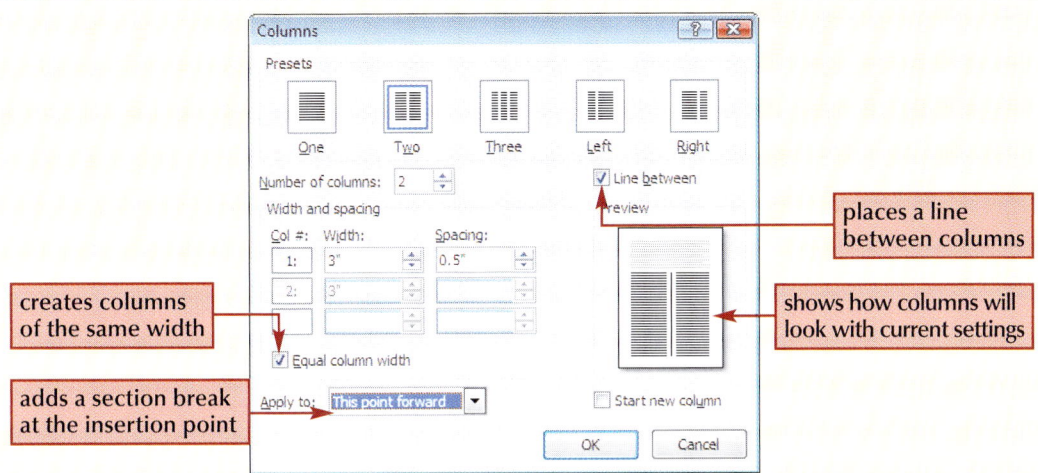

creates columns of the same width

adds a section break at the insertion point

places a line between columns

shows how columns will look with current settings

7. Click the **OK** button to return to the document window. A continuous section break appears below the WordArt object; the first section contains the WordArt and the second section contains the rest of the document, which is now formatted in columns. The word "Continuous" indicates that the new section continues on the same page as the preceding text—i–n other words, the section break does not start a new page.

8. Zoom out so you can see the entire page. The newsletter headline is centered over the two columns of text. The text fills the left column but not the right column. You'll fix this later, after you add a graphic and formatting to some of the text. See Figure 4-12.

Document formatted in two columns ◀ Figure 4-12

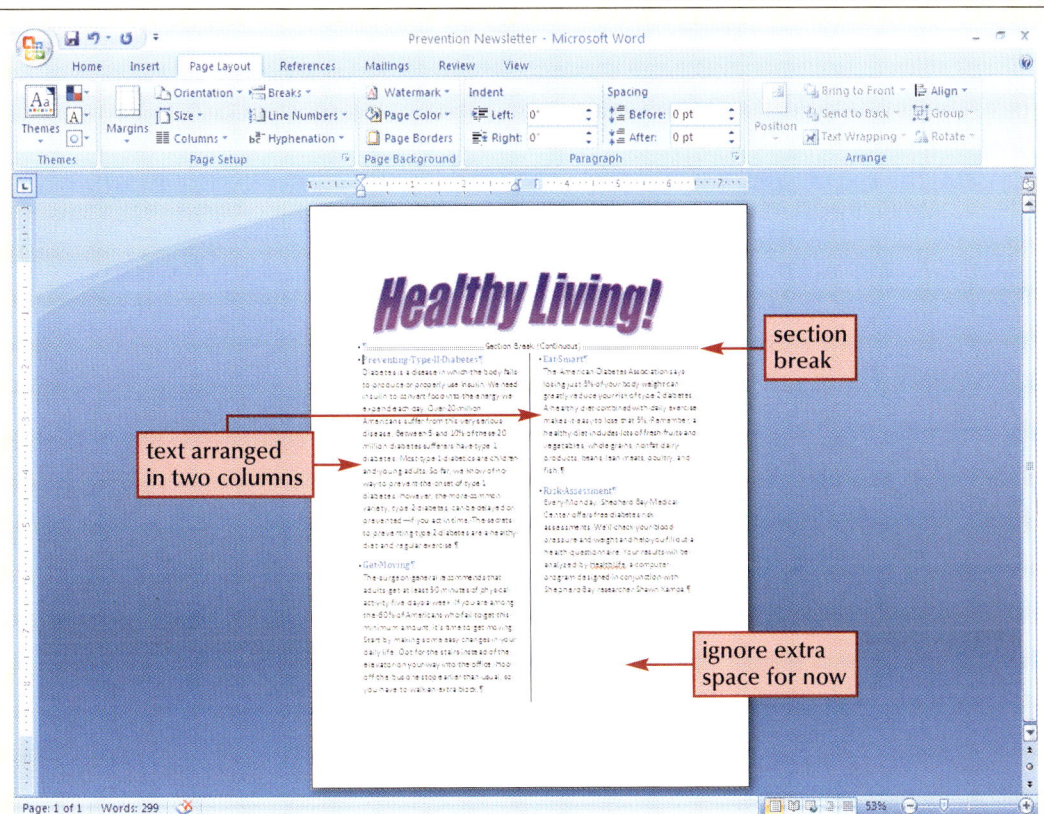

section break

text arranged in two columns

ignore extra space for now

▶ **9.** Save your work.

Trouble? Your columns may break at a slightly different line of text from those shown in the figure. This is not a problem.

Keep in mind that you can modify columns as you work on a document; you can change the number of columns or return the document to its original format by formatting it as one column. You can also insert column breaks to control where text moves from one column to the next.

Inserting Graphics

Word makes it easy to insert graphics, or illustrations, in your documents. The term **graphic** can refer to a drawing, a photograph, clip art, a chart, and so on. The Illustrations group on the Insert tab contains five buttons, for five types of graphics, as described below:

- The Picture button opens a dialog box where you can locate and insert an image that already exists, such as a picture taken with a digital camera or a scan of a paper drawing.
- The Clip Art button opens the Clip Art task pane on the right side of the Word window, where you can select from premade images known as **clip art**. A collection of clip art images is installed with Word, and you are free to use them in your documents. You can also search the Web for free clip art, available from the Microsoft Web site and from other Web sites devoted to clip art.
- The Shapes button opens a gallery where you can select from over a hundred basic shapes, such as arrows, stars, and banners. You click the shape you want in the gallery, and then drag the mouse pointer in the document to draw the shape. When the shape is selected in the document, you can change its color, shape, text wrapping settings, and so on using the options on the Drawing Tools Format tab.
- The SmartArt button, as you already know, opens a dialog box where you can create diagrams.
- The Chart button opens the Insert Chart dialog box, where you can create a variety of charts similar to the charts you can create in a spreadsheet program such as Microsoft Excel. You can choose from bar charts, pie charts, and line charts, to name a few. After you select a chart type, a spreadsheet window opens where you can enter the chart data. When the chart is selected in the document, you can edit it using the three tabs that appear under the label "Chart Tools."

Working with Graphics Files | InSight

There are several types of graphics files, many of which were developed for use in Web pages. In desktop publishing, you will often work with **bitmaps**. The most common types of bitmaps are:

- BMP—Used by Microsoft Paint and other graphics programs to store graphics you create. These files, which have the .bmp file extension, tend to be very large.
- TIFF—Commonly used for photographs or scanned images. TIFF files are usually much larger than GIF or JPEG files, but smaller than BMP files. A TIFF file has the file extension .tif.
- GIF—Suitable for most types of simple art. A GIF file is compressed, so it doesn't take up much room on your computer. A GIF file has the file extension .gif.
- JPEG—Suitable for photographs and drawings. Files stored using the JPEG format are even more compressed than GIF files. A JPEG file has the file extension .jpg.

A document containing graphics can take up a lot of memory, making it difficult to work with. To save file space, use JPEG graphics as much as possible.

You'll have a chance to work with graphics files in the Case Problems at the end of this tutorial. You'll also have a chance to work with text boxes, which are similar to graphics. A **text box**, as its name implies, is a box in which you can type text. The box sets off the text and draws special attention to it. You can use a text box to create a **pull quote**—a brief quotation from the main document.

Joel wants you to insert a clip art image in the newsletter. He asks you to use one of the food-related images that are installed with Word.

To insert the clip art image into the newsletter:

▶ **1.** With the document still zoomed out so you can see the whole page, and the insertion point located anywhere in the document, click the **Insert** tab, and then in the Illustrations group, click the **Clip Art** button. The Clip Art task pane opens, as shown in Figure 4-13. You use the top part of the Clip Art task pane to search for graphics related to a specific topic. The Search for text box on your computer may contain text left from a previous search. You can click the Organize clips option (near the bottom) to open the Microsoft Clip Organizer window, where you can browse among the various clip art images stored on your computer. You'll use the Microsoft Clip Organizer to insert an image into the newsletter.

Figure 4-13 Clip Art task pane

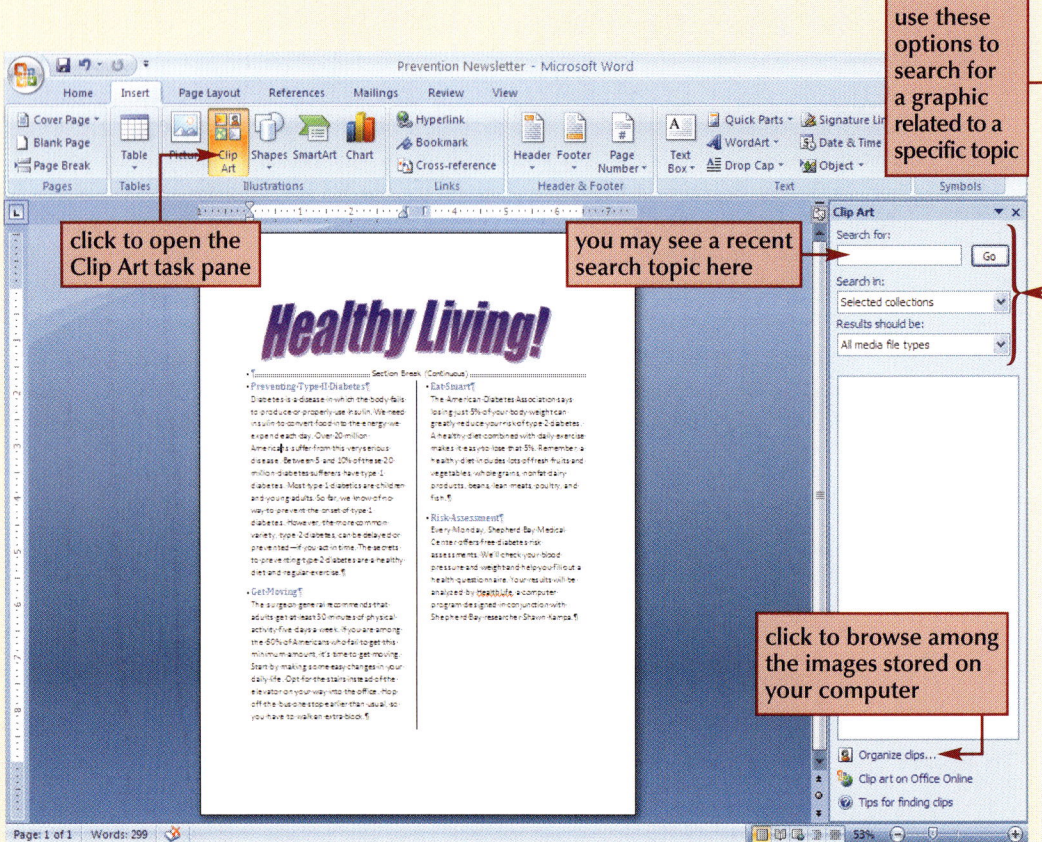

2. Click **Organize clips** near the bottom of the Clip Art task pane. The Favorites - Microsoft Clip Organizer window opens. This window is similar to Windows Explorer. For example, you click the plus sign next to a folder to display its subfolders. You select a subfolder to display its contents in the right pane. The default Microsoft Office clip art is stored in subfolders within the Office Collections folder. See Figure 4-14. You might see different folders from those shown in Figure 4-14, but you should see the Office Collections folder.

Microsoft Clip Organizer | **Figure 4-14**

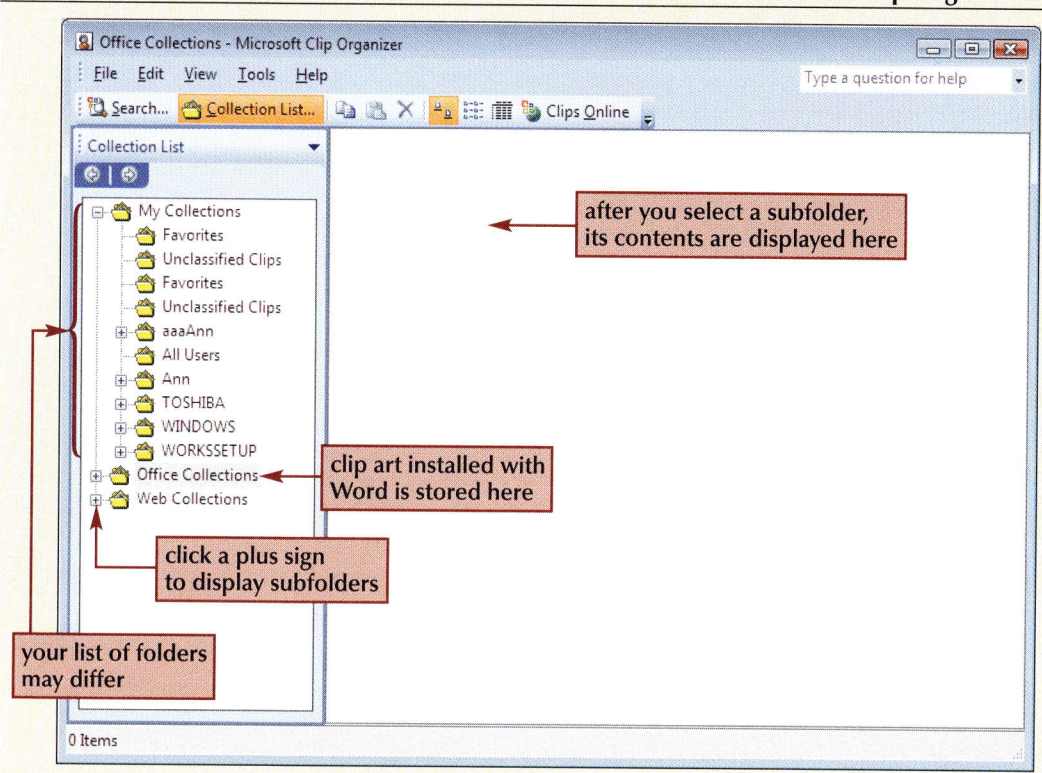

3. If necessary, scroll down to display the Office Collections folder in the left pane, and then click the **plus sign** next to the Office Collections folder. A list of subfolders within the Office Collections folder appears. This list of folders, which is created when you install Word, organizes clip art images into related categories. The folders with plus signs next to them contain subfolders and clip art images.

4. Scroll down and examine the list of folders. Click any plus signs to open subfolders, and then click folders to display clip art images in the right pane.

5. Click the **Food** folder to select it. Four images stored in the Food folder are displayed in the right pane.

6. Move the pointer over the image of the cornucopia (the second image from the left). An arrow button appears on the right side of the image. You might also see a ScreenTip with information about the file.

7. Click the **arrow button** that appears when your pointer is over the image. A menu of options opens, as shown in Figure 4-15.

Figure 4-15 ▷ **Selected image in Food folder**

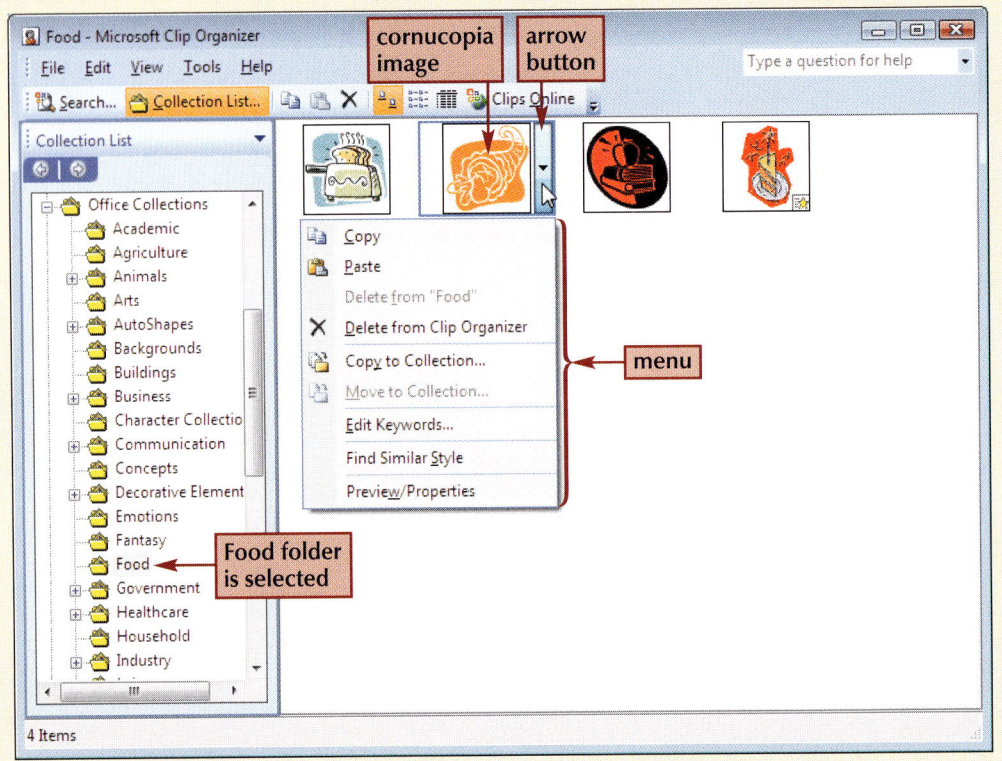

> **8.** Click **Copy** in the menu. The image is copied to the Clipboard.

Now that you have copied the image to the Clipboard, you can paste it into the document at the insertion point. Joel asks you to insert the graphic in the paragraph below the heading "Eat Smart." Before you insert the image, you will close the Clip Art task pane.

To paste the clip art into the document:

> **1.** Click the **Close** button ❌ in the Microsoft Clip Organizer title bar, and then click **Yes** when you see a dialog box asking if you want the item to remain on the Clipboard. You return to the document window.

> **2.** Click the **Close** button ❌ on the Clip Art task pane.

> **3.** Zoom back in so you can read the document, and then position the insertion point to the left of the word "The" below the heading "Eat Smart." At this point, you could switch to the Home tab and click the Paste button, but it's faster to use a keyboard shortcut.

> **4.** Press the **Ctrl+V** keys. The cornucopia clip art is inserted into the document at the insertion point. The text moves right to accommodate the image, which nearly fills the right column. Don't be concerned if one of the headings moves. You'll have a chance to fix that later.

> **5.** Save the document.

> **6.** Click the **cornucopia** image. A border with sizing handles appears, indicating that the image is selected. The Picture Tools Format tab also appears, containing tools related to working with graphics. The Insert tab is still selected, however, so at this point you can't actually see the tools on the Picture Tools Format tab. See Figure 4-16.

Newsletter with the clip art graphic selected

Figure 4-16

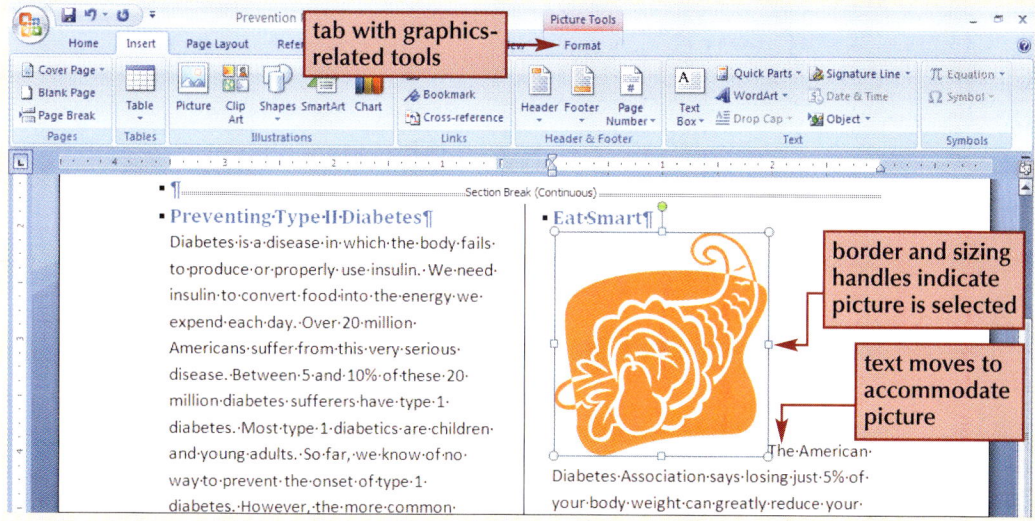

Joel would like the image to be smaller so it is better balanced with the text. You'll make that change in the next section.

Resizing a Graphic

It's often necessary to change the size of a graphic to make it fit into a document. This is sometimes called **scaling** the image. You can resize a graphic either by dragging its sizing handles or, for more precise control, by specifying an exact height and width in the Size group on the Picture Tools Format tab. For Joel's newsletter, the dragging technique will work well. You can then use the height and width controls on the Picture Tools Format tab to check the exact size of the graphic.

To resize the clip art graphic:

1. Make sure the clip art graphic is selected, click the **Picture Tools Format** tab, and then locate the Shape Height and Shape Width boxes in the Size group on the right edge of the Picture Tools Format tab. These boxes tell you that the cornucopia graphic is currently 1.98 inches high and 1.95 inches wide.

2. Move the mouse pointer over the lower-right sizing handle of the clip art. The pointer changes to ⬉. When you drag the pointer in the next step, a faint copy of the cornucopia image will resize accordingly, allowing you to see how the image will alter when you release the mouse button.

3. Drag the handle up and to the left until the faint copy of the cornucopia image is approximately 1.5 inches wide. Use the horizontal ruler as a guide. The measurements in the Shape Height and Shape Width boxes will not change until you release the mouse button, in the next step. See Figure 4-17.

Figure 4-17 | **Resizing the graphic**

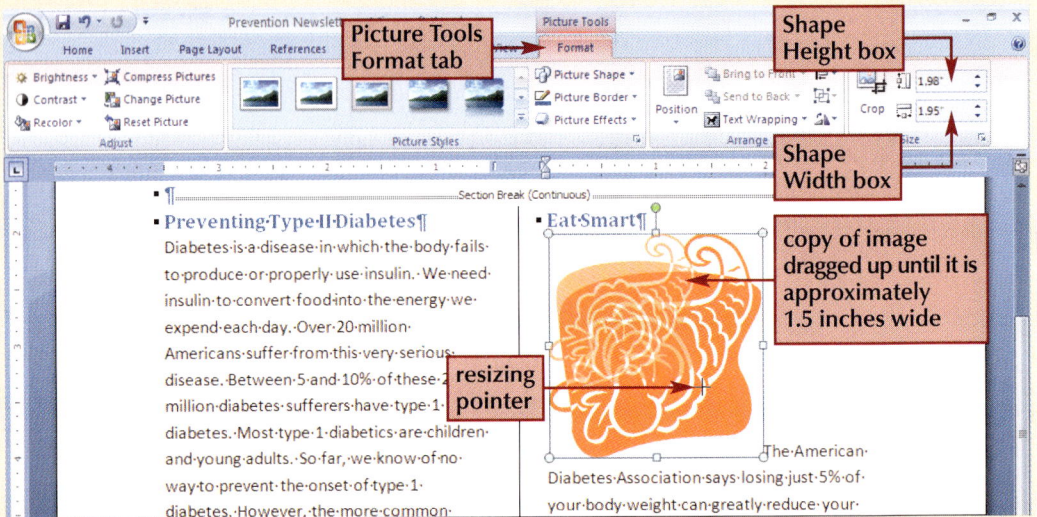

4. Release the mouse button. The cornucopia image is now about half as wide as the left column. According to the Shape Height and Shape Width boxes in the Size group, the graphic is approximately 1.5 inches wide.

   Trouble? If the measurement in your Shape Width box is greater than 1.53 inches, or less than 1.45 inches, resize the graphic until its width is closer to 1.5 inches.

Joel wonders if the graphic would take up less space if you deleted the tip of the cornucopia at the top of the image. You'll make that change in the next section.

Cropping a Graphic

You can **crop** a graphic—that is, cut off one or more of its edges—using the Crop button on the Picture Tools Format tab. Once you crop a graphic, the part you cropped is hidden from view. It remains a part of the graphic, which means you can change your mind and restore a cropped graphic to its original form.

To crop the graphic:

1. If necessary, click the clip art to select it. The sizing handles appear.

2. Click the **Crop** button in the Size group on the Picture Tools Format tab. The Crop button turns orange, indicating that it is currently selected; it stays selected until you click it again. The graphic is surrounded by a broken black box, and the pointer changes to ⛏ when you move it over the text.

3. Position the pointer directly over the middle sizing handle on the top of the picture. The pointer changes to ⊥.

4. Press and hold down the mouse button. The pointer changes to ┼.

5. Drag the handle down. As you drag, a solid outline appears to indicate the new shape of the graphic.

6. Position the top edge of the solid outline along the top of the cornucopia's orange background. See Figure 4-18.

Cropping the graphic — **Figure 4-18**

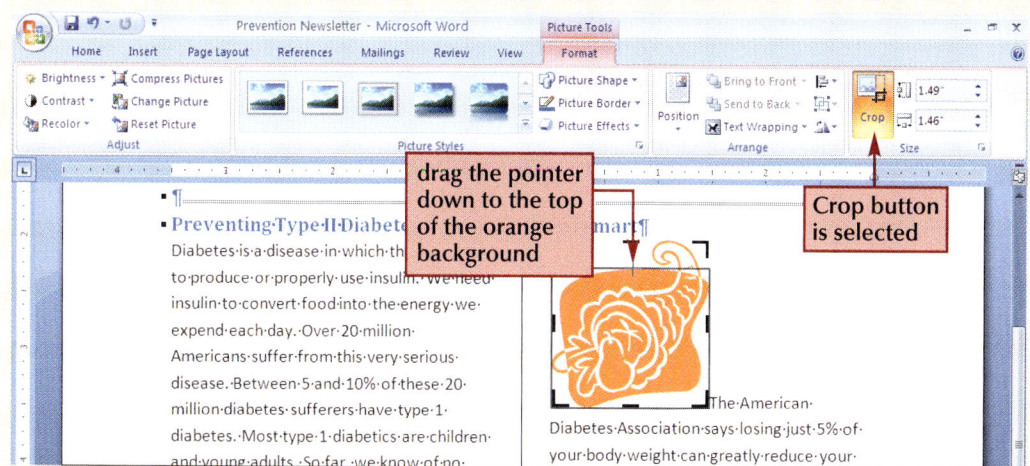

7. Release the mouse button. The tip of the cornucopia is cropped from the image. The Crop button is still selected. The cropping pointer and the broken black box around the graphic remain visible, in case you want to crop the graphic some more. You are finished cropping the graphic, so you can turn off the cropping feature.

8. Click the **Crop** button in the Size group to deselect it. The broken black box around the graphic is replaced with the solid box with the round and square selection handles (shown earlier in Figure 4-16).

In the next session you will wrap the newsletter text around the graphic and move the graphic to a new location. Then you'll finalize the newsletter and turn your attention to creating the cover letter with mail merge.

Session 4.1 Quick Check | Review

1. List four elements you might see in a desktop-published document.
2. Explain how to change the text of a WordArt object after you've already inserted it into the document.
3. True or False: To avoid altering the proportions of a WordArt object, you press and hold down the Alt key while you drag a handle.
4. What button should you use to change the way text flows around a WordArt object? Where is this button located?
5. Suppose you want to format only part of a document in columns, and you haven't inserted any section breaks. Should you use the Columns menu or the Columns dialog box?
6. Name four types of bitmap files.
7. On what tab are the buttons for inserting graphics located?

Session 4.2

Wrapping Text Around a Graphic

Earlier in this tutorial, you used Top and Bottom text wrapping with the WordArt object so the WordArt would appear above the columns of text. Now you'll apply Tight text wrapping to make the text follow the shape of the cornucopia.

To wrap text around the graphic:

▶ 1. If you took a break after the previous session, make sure Word is still running and that the Prevention Newsletter file is open with the document in Print Layout view and with the nonprinting characters and rulers displayed.

▶ 2. If necessary, click the cornucopia graphic to select it, and, if necessary, click the Picture Tools Format tab to display it.

▶ 3. In the Arrange group on the Picture Tools Format tab, click the **Text Wrapping** button. A menu of text wrapping options appears.

▶ 4. Click **Tight**. The text wraps to the right of the cornucopia, roughly following its shape. See Figure 4-19.

Figure 4-19 ▶ **Text wrapped around the graphic**

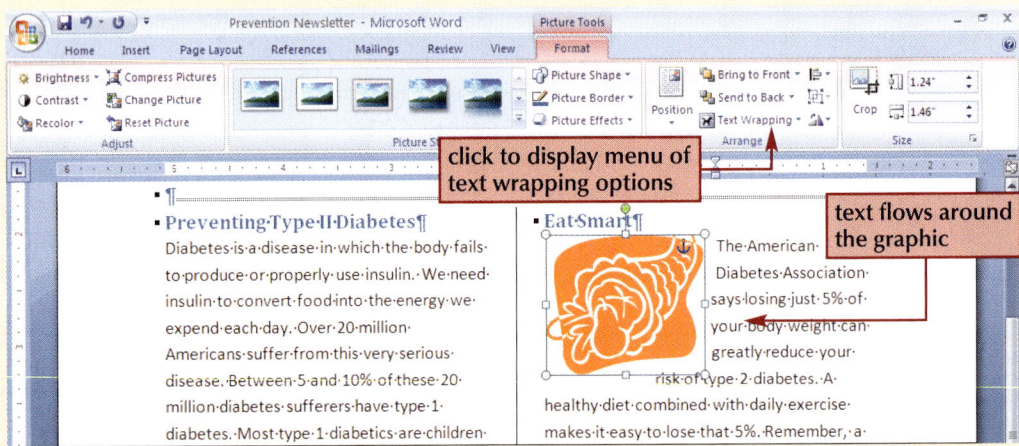

▶ 5. Click anywhere in the newsletter text to deselect the graphic, and then save the newsletter. Don't be concerned if the heading "Eat Smart" wraps to the right of the graphic. You will move the graphic away from the heading in the next section. If the heading does not wrap around the graphic, that's fine too.

Trouble? If the heading "Eat Smart" moves back down to the bottom of the left column, you probably didn't make the WordArt object tall enough. Undo the insertion of the graphic, increase the height of the WordArt object so that it is about 1.5 inches tall at its highest point, drag it down if necessary so it doesn't overlap the top margin, click at the beginning of the paragraph under the heading "Eat Smart," and begin again with Step 2.

You are almost finished with the graphic. You just need to move it to the middle of the paragraph, so that it is not so close to the heading.

Moving and Aligning a Graphic

You can move a graphic by dragging it, just as you dragged the WordArt object. Like WordArt, a clip art graphic is anchored to a specific paragraph in a document. When you drag a graphic to a new paragraph, the anchor symbol moves to the beginning of that paragraph. When you drag a graphic to a new position within the same paragraph, the anchor symbol remains in its original position and only the graphic moves. You'll see how this works when you move the cornucopia clip art to the middle of its current paragraph, next to the right margin.

When you move a graphic, it's a good idea to specify exactly where you want to align it. For example, you can choose to align a graphic along any one of the page margins, or you can choose to align it along the edge of the page. Specifying an alignment option prevents the graphic from moving if you make changes to the document later. The Align button in the Arrange group on the Picture Tools Format tab provides some preset alignment options that are appropriate for most documents. You'll see how this works in the following steps.

To move the graphic:

1. Click the graphic to select it if necessary. You should see an anchor symbol either within the graphic or to the left of the heading "Eat Smart."

2. Move the mouse pointer over the graphic.

3. Click and slowly drag the pointer down. As you move the mouse, a faint copy of the image moves too, so that you can see where you're moving the image.

4. Position the image near the middle of the paragraph, next to the right margin, and then release the mouse button. The graphic moves to its new position, with the text wrapped to its left. The anchor is probably located to the left of the first line under the heading "Eat Smart," although it may have moved to somewhere else near the top of the newsletter. In the next few steps, you'll make some adjustments to make sure the position of your graphic and anchor matches Figure 4-20. First, you'll align the graphic along the right margin.

   Trouble? If paragraph text wraps to the right of the graphic, you need to drag the graphic farther to the right.

Tip

To move a graphic to one of several preset positions on the page, click the Position button in the Arrange group on the Picture Tools Format tab.

Graphic in new position | **Figure 4-20**

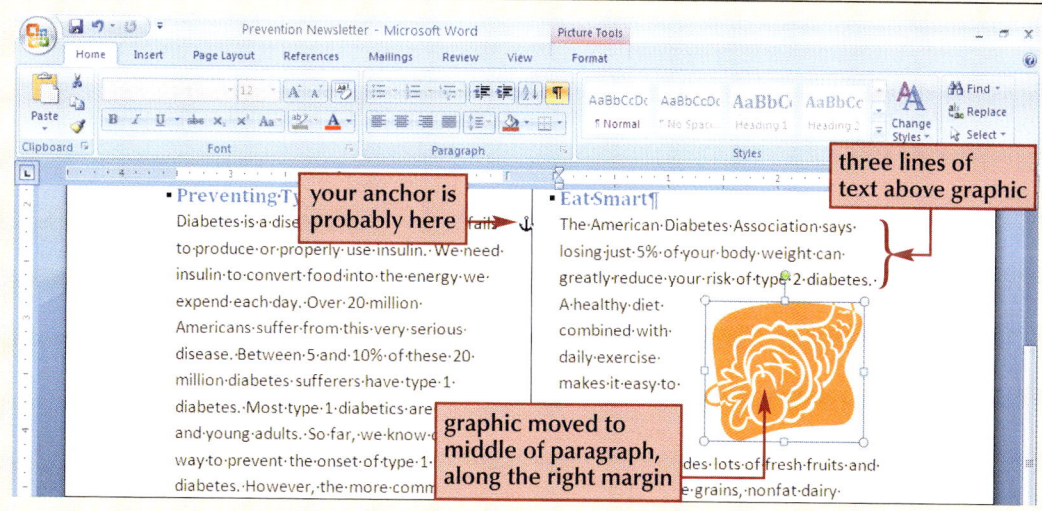

5. On the Picture Tools Format tab in the Arrange group, click the **Align** button. A menu of alignment options opens. You want to align the graphic along the right margin. It's possible to align the graphic along the edge of the page, so first you have to make sure the Align to Margin option is selected.

6. Verify that you see a check mark before "Align to Margin." Now you can specify what margin you want to align the graphic to.

7. Near the top of the Align menu, click **Align Right**.

8. If necessary, drag the anchor up or down slightly until it is positioned as in Figure 4-20, with three lines of text wrapped above it. If the anchor is not located next to the first line under the heading "Eat Smart," click it and drag it there now. When you are finished, your newsletter should match Figure 4-20.

   Trouble? If you can't get the text to wrap properly around the graphic (for example, if individual words wrap to the right of the graphic), try reducing the size of the graphic slightly by dragging the lower-right sizing handle.

9. Click anywhere outside the graphic to deselect it and save your work.

The graphic helps draw the reader's attention to the newsletter, but the rest of the text looks plain. Joel suggests adding a drop cap at the beginning of each section.

Inserting Drop Caps

A **drop cap** is a large, capital letter that begins the text of a paragraph, chapter, or some other document section. You can place a drop cap in the margin, next to the paragraph, or you can have the text of the paragraph wrap around the drop cap. In the following steps, you will create a drop cap for each of the four paragraphs that follow each heading in the newsletter. The drop cap will extend three lines into the paragraph, with the text wrapping around it.

To insert drop caps in the newsletter:

1. Click in the paragraph below the heading "Preventing Type II Diabetes."

2. Click the **Insert** tab, and then, in the Text group, click the **Drop Cap** button. The Drop Cap menu opens.

3. Move the mouse pointer over the In margin option and then the Dropped option, and observe the live preview of the two types of drop caps in the document. The default settings applied by these two options are fine for most documents. Clicking Drop Cap Options, at the bottom of the menu, opens the Drop Cap dialog box, where you can select more detailed settings. See Figure 4-21.

| Figure 4-21 | Drop Cap menu |

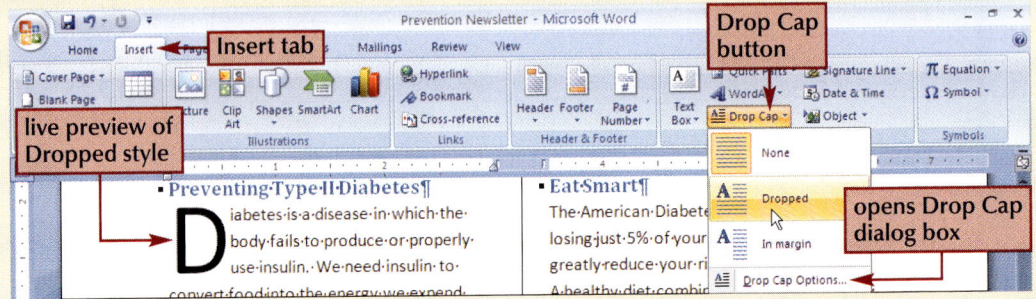

▶ **4.** Click **Dropped** in the Drop Cap menu. The Drop Cap menu closes, and Word formats the first character of the paragraph as a drop cap, just as in the live preview in Figure 4-21. The blue box with square selection handles around the drop cap tells you the drop cap is selected.

▶ **5.** Click in the paragraph following the heading "Get Moving," and then repeat Steps 3 and 4 to insert a drop cap in that paragraph.

▶ **6.** Insert a drop cap in the paragraph following the heading "Eat Smart." Word adjusts the text wrapping around the graphic.

Trouble? If a drop cap does not appear after you perform Step 6, there might be a blank space at the beginning of the paragraph that is left over from when you inserted the graphic. Delete the space and repeat Step 6.

▶ **7.** Insert a drop cap in the paragraph following the last heading, click anywhere in the text to deselect the drop cap, and scroll so you can see the drop caps.

Tip

To change the size of the drop cap, you can drag one of the sizing handles.

The drop caps are a nice, eye-catching detail. Next, you turn your attention to inserting a registered trademark symbol (®) next to a registered trademark name.

Inserting Symbols and Special Characters

In printed publications, it is customary to change some of the characters available on the standard keyboard into more polished-looking characters called **typographic characters**. Word's AutoCorrect feature automatically converts some standard characters into typographic characters as you type. For instance, as Joel typed the paragraph under the heading "Preventing Type II Diabetes," he typed two hyphens after the phrase "be delayed or prevented." As he began to type the rest of the sentence, "if you act in time," Word automatically converted the two hyphens into a single, longer character called an em dash.

Figure 4-22 lists some of the other character combinations that AutoCorrect automatically converts to typographic characters. In most cases you need to press the spacebar and type more characters before Word inserts the appropriate typographic character. If you don't like the typographic character inserted by Word, click the Undo button to revert to the characters you originally typed.

Common typographic characters ◀ **Figure 4-22**

To insert this symbol or character	Type	After you press the spacebar, Word converts to
Em dash	word--word	word—word
Smiley	:)	☺
Copyright symbol	(c)	©
Trademark symbol	(tm)	™
Ordinal numbers	1st, 2nd, 3rd, etc.	1st, 2nd, 3rd, etc.
Fractions	1/2, 1/4	½, ¼
Arrows	--> or <--	← or →

In addition to characters inserted by AutoCorrect, Word also has many typographic characters that you can insert into a document. You can access these with the Symbol button on the Insert tab.

Reference Window | **Inserting Symbols and Special Characters**

- Move the insertion point to the location where you want to insert a particular symbol or special character.
- Click the Insert tab, and then, in the Symbols group, click the Symbol button.
- If you see the symbol or character you want in the Symbol gallery, click it. For a more extensive set of choices, click More Symbols to open the Symbol dialog box.
- In the Symbol dialog box, locate the symbol or character you want on either the Symbols tab or the Special Characters tab.
- Click the symbol or special character you want, click the Insert button, and then click the Close button.

Joel needs to include a registered trademark symbol (®) after "HealthLife" in the last paragraph of the newsletter.

To insert the registered trademark symbol:

▶ **1.** Scroll down to display the paragraph below the heading "Risk Assessment" at the bottom of the right column, and then click to the right of the word "HealthLife." (Take care to click between the final "e" and the comma.)

▶ **2.** Click the **Insert** tab, if necessary, click the **Symbol** button in the Symbols group, and then click **More Symbols**. The Symbol dialog box opens.

▶ **3.** If necessary, click the **Special Characters** tab. See Figure 4-23.

Figure 4-23 ▶ **Symbol dialog box**

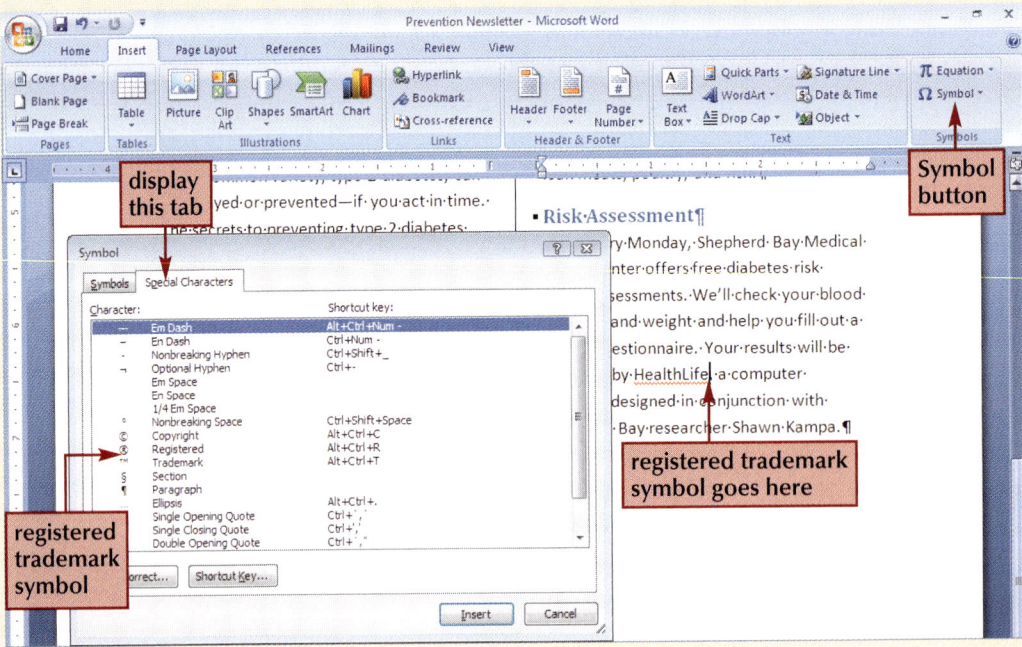

▶ **4.** Click **Registered** to select it, and then click the **Insert** button.

▶ **5.** Close the Symbol dialog box. Word inserts an ® immediately after and slightly above the word "HealthLife."

Next, you need to adjust the columns of text, so they are approximately the same length.

Balancing the Columns

You can shift text from one column to another by adding blank paragraphs to move the text into the next column or by deleting blank paragraphs to shorten the text, so it will fit into one column. The problem with this approach is that any edits you make later could throw off the balance. Instead, you can insert a continuous section break at the end of the document. This tells Word to automatically **balance** the columns, or make them of equal length. You'll balance the columns in the newsletter next.

To balance the columns:

1. Press the **Ctrl+End** keys to move the insertion point to the end of the text in the right column, just after the period following your name.

2. Zoom out, so you can see the entire newsletter at once.

3. Click the **Page Layout** tab, and then, in the Page Setup group, click the **Breaks** button. The Breaks menu opens.

4. Below "Section Breaks," click **Continuous**. Word inserts a continuous section break at the end of the text. As shown in Figure 4-24, Word balances the text between the two columns, so they are approximately the same length.

Newsletter with balanced columns | **Figure 4-24**

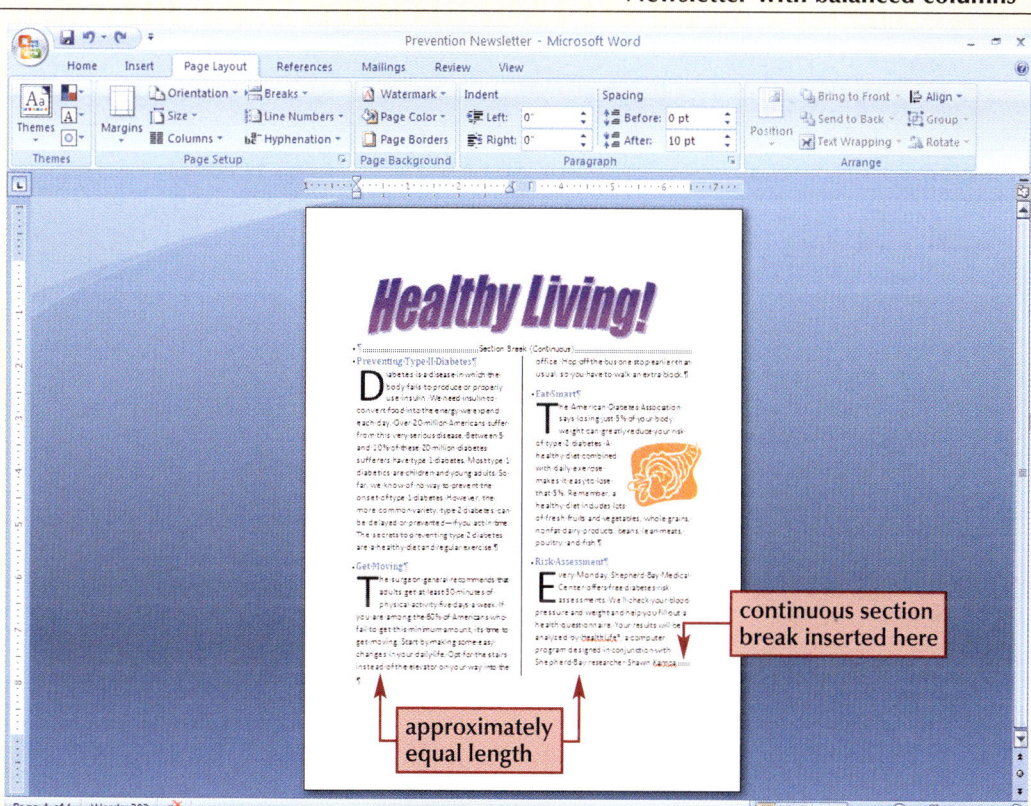

Inserting a Border Around a Page

You can add definition to a paragraph or an entire page by adding a border. Borders can be simple lines or they can be elaborate artwork. You can also emphasize pages and paragraphs by adding shading (a colored background). In both cases, you use the Page Borders button on the Page Layout tab, which opens the Borders and Shading dialog box. Right now, Joel wants to add a border around the entire newsletter page.

To insert a border around the newsletter:

1. Make sure the document is still zoomed out, so you can see the whole page and that the Page Layout tab is selected.

2. In the Page Background group, click the **Page Borders** button. The Borders and Shading dialog box opens.

3. If necessary, click the **Page Border** tab. (Take care not to click the Borders tab by mistake.) You use the Setting options on the left side of this tab to specify the type of border you want. In this case, you want a simple box.

4. In the Setting section, click the **Box** option. Now that you have selected the type of border you want, you can choose the style of line that will be used to create the border.

5. In the Style list box, scroll down and select the ninth style down from the top (the thick line with the thin line underneath), and then verify that the Apply to option is set to **Whole document**. See Figure 4-25. While the Borders and Shading dialog box is open, notice the Art arrow, which you can use to select a border consisting of graphical elements such as lightening bolts, boxes, or specially designed borders.

Tip

Use the Borders tab in the Borders and Shading dialog box to add a border around a selected paragraph. Use the Shading tab to add a colored background to a page or a selected paragraph.

Figure 4-25 | Adding a border to the newsletter

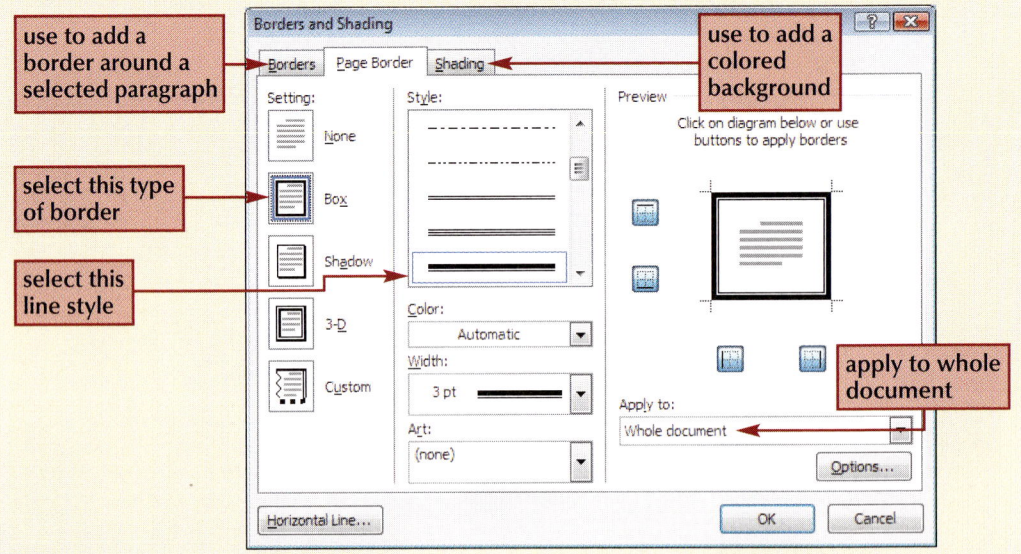

▶ **6.** Click the **Options** button in the lower-right corner of the Borders and Shading dialog box. The Border and Shading Options dialog box opens. Here you can change settings that control where the border is positioned on the page. By default, the border is positioned 24 points from the edges of the page. To ensure that your printer will print the entire border, you need to change the Measure from setting so that it is positioned relative to the outside edge of the text rather than the edge of the page.

▶ **7.** Click the **Measure from** arrow, and then click **Text**. The settings in the Top and Bottom boxes change to 1 pt, and the settings in the Left and Right boxes change to 4 pt, indicating the border's position relative to the edge of the text. You can leave the other settings as they are. See Figure 4-26.

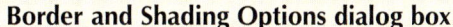 Border and Shading Options dialog box 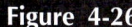 Figure 4-26

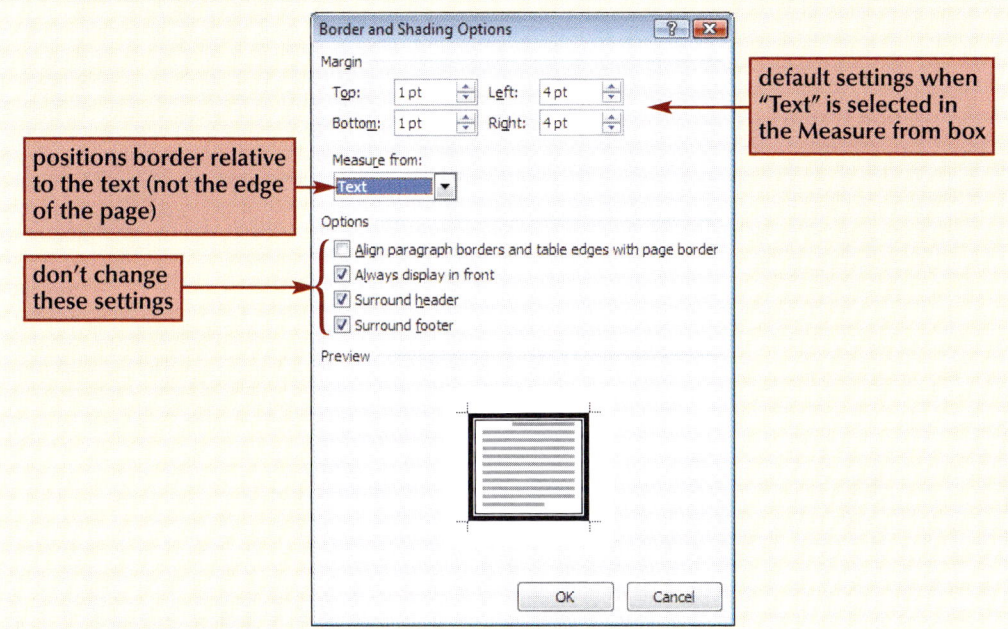

default settings when "Text" is selected in the Measure from box

positions border relative to the text (not the edge of the page)

don't change these settings

▶ **8.** Click the **OK** button in the Border and Shading Options dialog box, click the **OK** button in the Borders and Shading dialog box, and then save your work. The newsletter now has an attractive border, although the cornucopia graphic may not be positioned neatly inside the border.

▶ **9.** If necessary, drag the cornucopia graphic to position it inside the border, as shown in Figure 4-27. You may also need to drag the graphic up or down, so that the text wraps neatly around it. When you are finished, save the document.

Figure 4-27 ▶ **Newsletter with border**

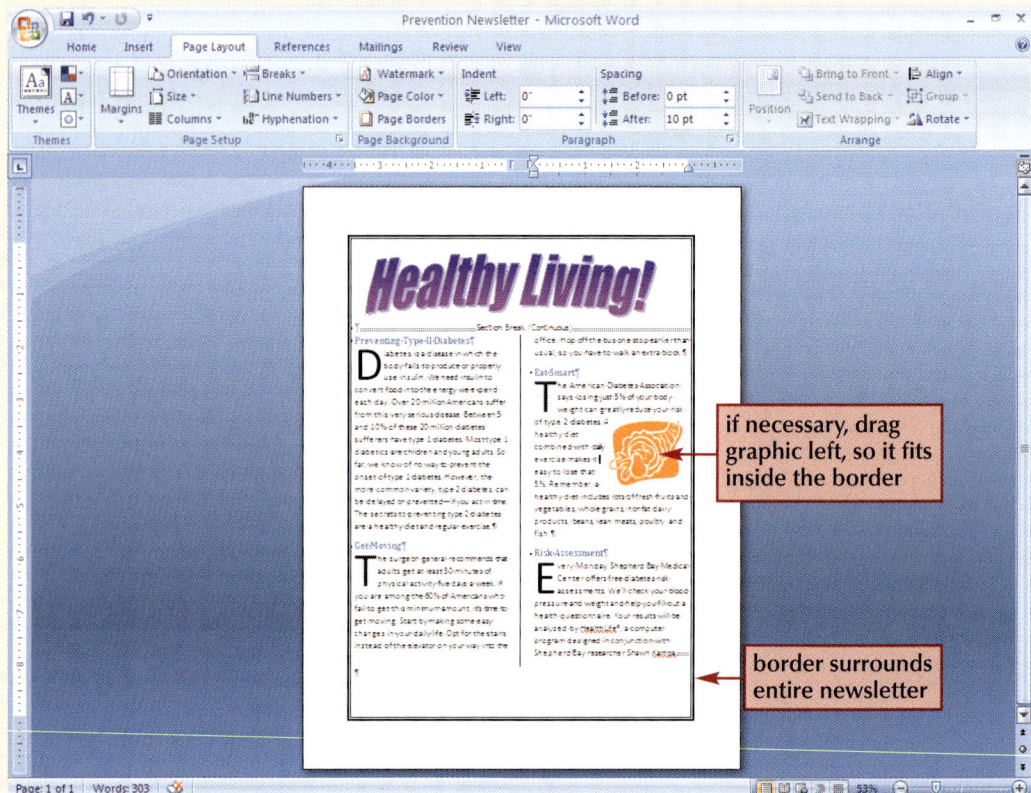

▶ **10.** Print the newsletter, and then close the document, saving it if prompted to do so.

Joel will print the newsletter later on a high-quality color printer. But first, he asks you to use Word's mail merge feature to insert customer names and addresses into a cover letter he's written. He plans to send the cover letter with the newsletter.

Performing a Simple Mail Merge

The term **mail merge** refers to the process of combining information from two separate documents to create many final documents, each containing customized information. The two separate documents are called a main document and a data source. A **main document** is a document that contains text, such as a business letter, as well as place-holders called **merge fields**. The merge fields tell Word where to insert customized information such as a name or an address. You can distinguish merge fields from the text of the main document because each merge field name is enclosed by pairs of angled brackets like this: << >>.

Joel's main document is a letter that contains the text shown in Figure 4-28. You will replace the text in brackets with merge fields.

Joel's main document | **Figure 4-28**

> June 26, 2010
>
> [INSERT ADDRESS FIELDS]
>
> Dear [INSERT FIRST NAME FIELD]:
>
> Enclosed you will find an informational newsletter published by Shepherd Bay Medical Center. We would like to make this a regular publication that focuses on health-related topics. To ensure that it is as helpful as possible, we are soliciting feedback from potential readers. Would you have a moment to give me your opinion regarding the newsletter's content and layout? My office is located at the South Clinic. You can reach me everyday from noon to 5 P.M. at 555-5555.
>
> Sincerely,
>
> Joel Conchola
>
> Public Outreach Specialist

A **data source** is a document that contains the data, such as clients' names and addresses, that you can insert into the main document. Joel plans to send the newsletter to a small test group of clients. His data source is a table in a Word document that contains the names and addresses of five Shepherd Bay Medical Center clients. This table is shown in Figure 4-29. The header row in the table contains the names of the merge fields. Each row in the table contains information about an individual client. In mail merge terminology, all of the information about one person or one object is called a **record**.

Joel's data source | **Figure 4-29**

a merge field name

header row includes all merge field names for this data source

record for individual client

First Name	Last Name	Street Address	City	State	ZIP
Rhoda	Carey	3545 Route 14	Brandon	MS	39875
Marley	Delisle	1234 E. Pascagoula	Jackson	MS	39204
Catherine	Larke	36 Capers Avenue	Jackson	MS	39211
Luca	Peters	3453 River Lane	Richland	MS	39345
Daniel	Shorba	4533 Terry Road	Jackson	MS	39298

During a mail merge, the merge fields in the main document instruct Word to retrieve information from the data source. For example, one merge field in the main document might retrieve a first name from the data source; another merge field might retrieve a street address. For each record in the data source, Word will create a separate letter in the final document, which is called the **merged document**. Thus, if the data source contains five sets of client names and addresses, the merged document will contain five separate letters, each one containing a different client name and address in the appropriate places.

The Mailings tab contains all the options you need for performing a mail merge. However, when you're just getting started with mail merge, it's helpful to use the Mail Merge task pane, which walks you through the process.

In the following steps, you'll open the Word document that you'll use as the data source, so you can see how it's set up. Then you'll open the Mail Merge task pane and start the mail merge.

To begin the mail merge process:

▶ 1. Open the document named **Addresses** from the Tutorial.04\Tutorial folder included with your Data Files. Review the table, which contains addresses for five clients of Shepherd Bay Medical Center.

▶ 2. Close the Addresses document without making any changes, and then open the document named **Letter** from the Tutorial.04\Tutorial folder included with your Data Files. When he typed this letter, Joel included text in brackets as placeholders to indicate where he wants to insert the merge fields.

▶ 3. Near the end of the letter, replace "Joel Conchola" with your first and last name, and then save the document as **Cover Letter** in the Tutorial.04\Tutorial folder included with your Data Files.

▶ 4. Click the **Mailings** tab, and then, in the Start Mail Merge group, click the **Start Mail Merge** button. The Start Mail Merge menu opens.

▶ 5. In the Start Mail Merge menu, click **Step by Step Mail Merge Wizard**. The Mail Merge task pane opens, displaying the first of six steps related to completing a mail merge. See Figure 4-30. Your first task is to specify the type of main document you want to use for the merge.

| Figure 4-30 | Mail Merge task pane |

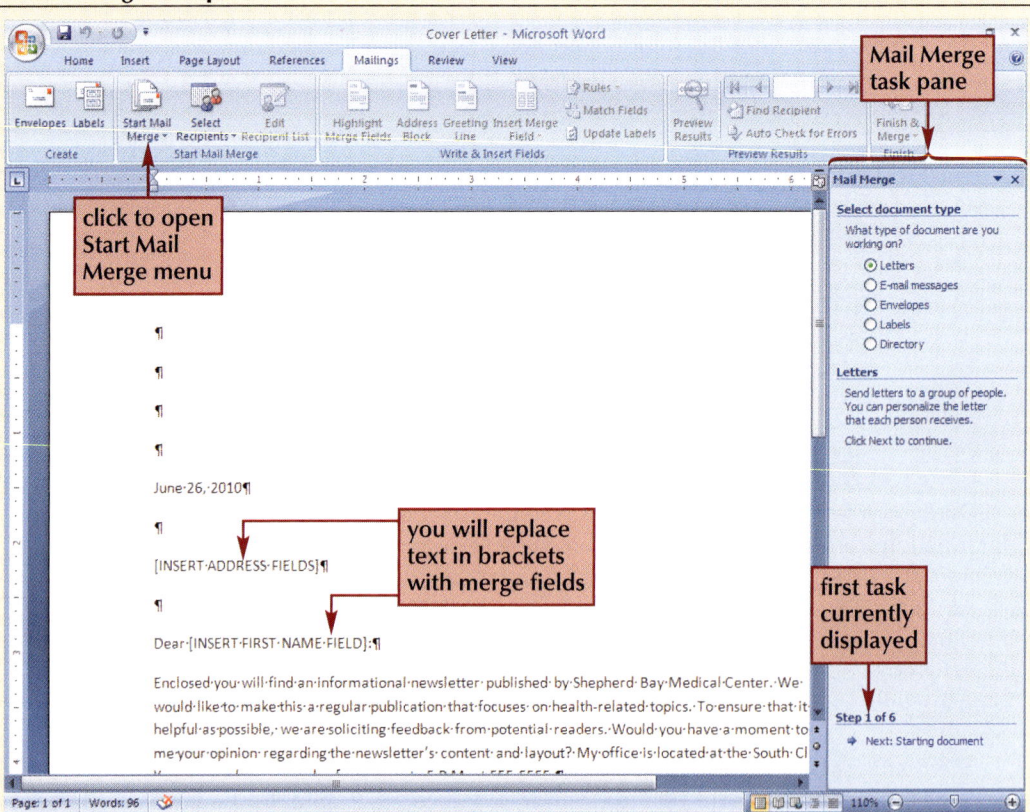

▶ 6. Verify that the **Letters** option button is selected in the Mail Merge task pane.

▶ 7. At the bottom of the Mail Merge task pane, click **Next: Starting document**. The Mail Merge task pane now displays information and options that you can use to select a starting document—that is, to select a main document. In this case, you want to use the current document, Cover Letter.

▶ **8.** Verify that the **Use the current document** option button is selected.

▶ **9.** At the bottom of the Mail Merge task pane, click **Next: Select recipients**. You'll continue working with the Mail Merge task pane in the next set of steps.

You've finished the first two tasks, which relate to selecting the main document. Now you are ready to tell Word where to find the list of recipients for Joel's letter.

Selecting a Data Source

You can use many kinds of files as data sources for a mail merge, including Word tables, Excel worksheets, Access databases, or Contacts lists from Microsoft Outlook. You can select a preexisting file or you can create a new data source. In this case, you will use the table in the Addresses document, which you examined earlier.

To select the data source:

▶ **1.** In the Mail Merge task pane, verify that the **Use an existing list** option button is selected.

▶ **2.** Click **Browse** in the Mail Merge task pane. The Select Data Source dialog box opens. This dialog box works similarly to Word's Open dialog box.

▶ **3.** Navigate to the Tutorial.04\Tutorial folder, select the **Addresses** document, and then click the **Open** button. The table from the Addresses document is displayed in the Mail Merge Recipients dialog box. See Figure 4-31.

Mail Merge Recipients dialog box ◀ **Figure 4-31**

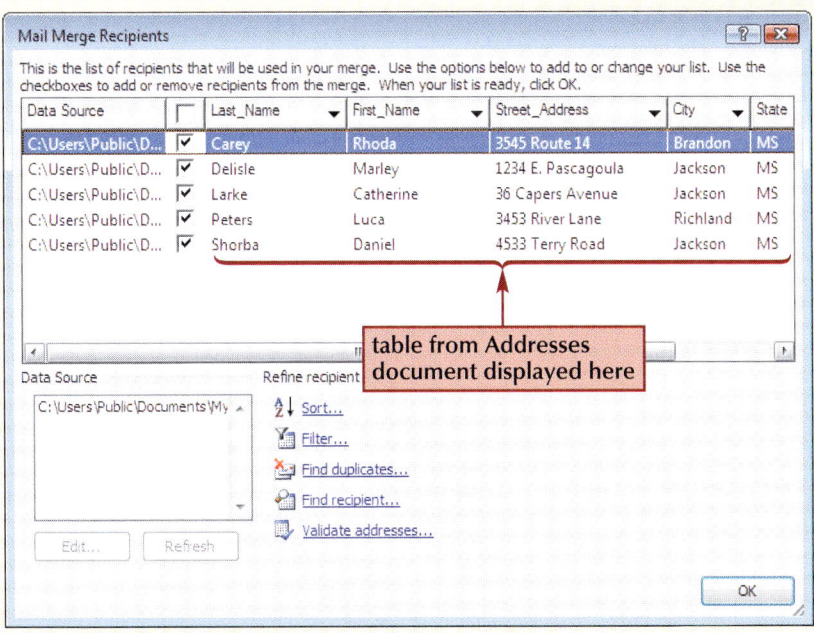

▶ **4.** Click the **OK** button. The Mail Merge Recipients dialog box closes, and you return to the Cover Letter document with the Mail Merge task pane open. Under "Use an existing list," you see the name of the file selected as the data source—or, depending on where you store your Data Files, you may see only the beginning of a directory path, which identifies the location where the data source file is stored.

▶ **5.** Click **Next: Write your letter** at the bottom of the Mail Merge task pane. The task pane displays options related to inserting merge fields in the main document, which you'll learn about next.

Inserting Merge Fields

Joel's letter is a standard business letter, so you'll place the recipient's name and address below the date. You could insert individual merge fields for the client's first name, last name, address, city, and ZIP code. But it's easier to use the **Address block** link in the Mail Merge task pane, which inserts a merge field for the entire address with one click.

To insert an Address Block merge field:

▶ **1.** Select the text **[INSERT ADDRESS FIELDS]**, and then delete it. Remember to delete the opening and closing brackets. Do not delete the paragraph mark following the text.

▶ **2.** Verify that there are three blank paragraphs between the date and the salutation and that the insertion point is positioned in the second blank paragraph below the date.

▶ **3.** Click **Address block** in the Mail Merge task pane. The Insert Address Block dialog box opens. See Figure 4-32. The options in this dialog box allow you to fine-tune the way the address will be inserted in the letter. The Preview box shows you how the address will look in the document after the merge is complete.

Figure 4-32 ▶ **Insert Address Block dialog box**

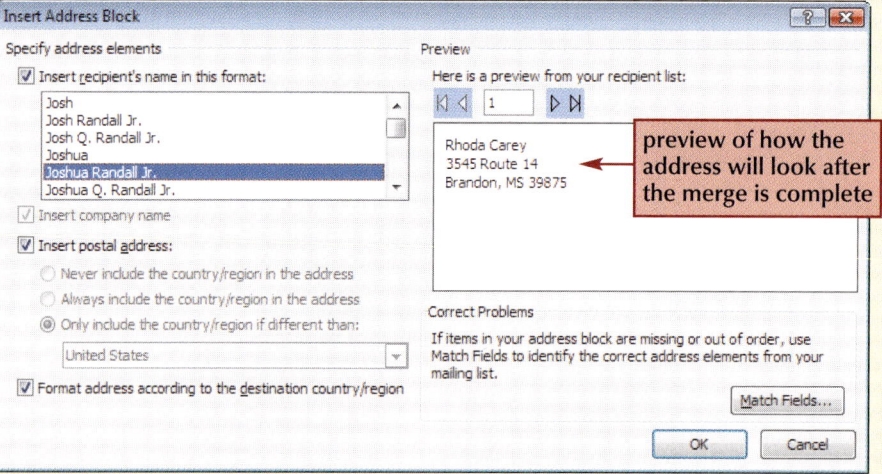

▶ **4.** Verify that the **Insert recipient's name in this format** check box is selected, and also verify that **Joshua Randall Jr.** is selected in the list box. This ensures that Word will insert each recipient's first and last name. (The other options in this list are useful with more complicated data sources.)

▶ **5.** Verify that the **Insert postal address** check box is selected. It doesn't matter whether the other check box and option buttons are selected; you only need to be concerned with them when working with more complicated data sources.

> **6.** Click the **OK** button. An Address Block merge field is inserted in the letter. See Figure 4-33. Depending on how your computer is set up, you might see a gray background behind the merge field. Notice the angled brackets that surround the merge field. The angled brackets are automatically inserted when you insert a merge field. It is important to note that you cannot type the angled brackets and merge field information—you must enter it via a dialog box selection.

Tip

A selected merge field is highlighted with a gray background to distinguish it from regular text.

Address Block merge field in letter | **Figure 4-33**

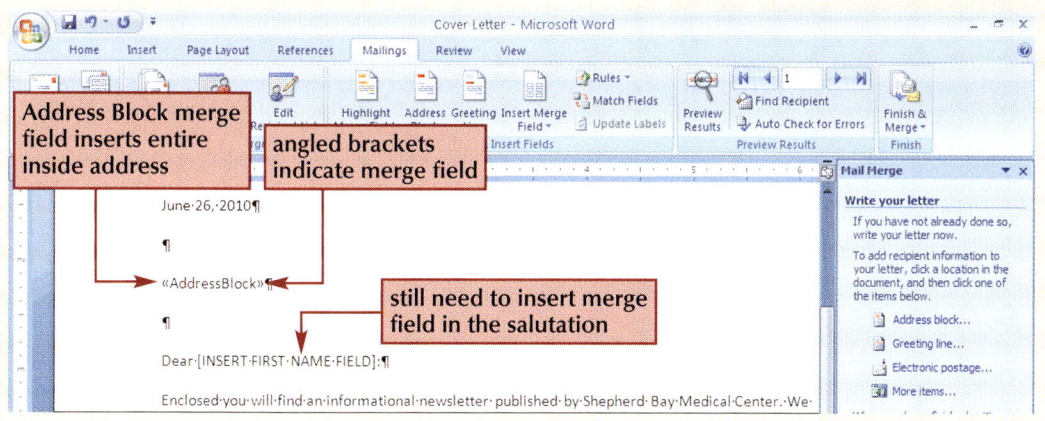

Later, when you merge the main document with the data source, Word will replace the Address Block merge field with the address information for each record in the data source. Your next job is to insert a merge field that will include each client's first name in the salutation. To insert an individual merge field (rather than a field for the entire address), you need to use the More items option in the Mail Merge task pane.

To insert the merge field for the salutation:

> **1.** Select and delete **[INSERT FIRST NAME FIELD]** in the salutation. Remember to delete the opening and closing brackets. Do not delete the colon.

> **2.** If necessary, insert a space to the left of the colon. When you finish, the insertion point should be positioned between the space and the colon.

> **3.** In the Mail Merge task pane, click **More items**. The Insert Merge Field dialog box opens. The Fields list shows all the merge fields in the data source. See Figure 4-34. Note that merge fields cannot contain spaces, so Word replaces any spaces in the merge field names with underlines. You want to insert the client's first name into the main document, so you need to make sure the First_Name merge field is selected.

Figure 4-34 ▶ **Insert Merge Field dialog box**

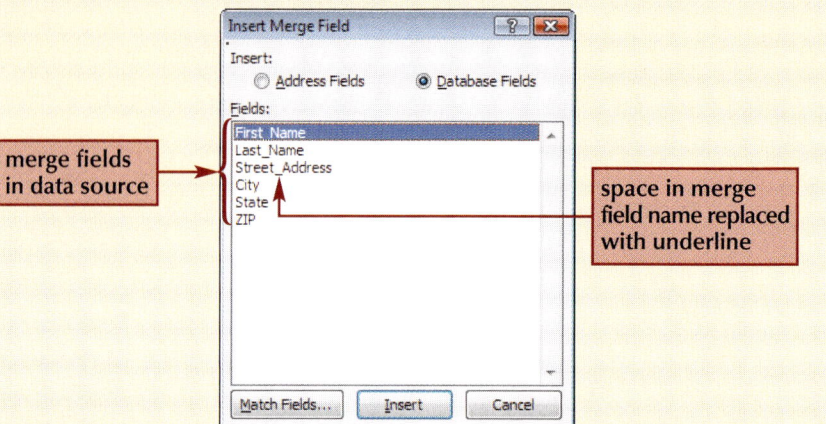

merge fields
in data source

space in merge
field name replaced
with underline

▶ **4.** Verify that **First_Name** is selected, click the **Insert** button, and then close the Insert Merge Field dialog box. The First_Name merge field is inserted in the document at the location of the insertion point. See Figure 4-35.

Figure 4-35 ▶ **First_Name merge field inserted in document**

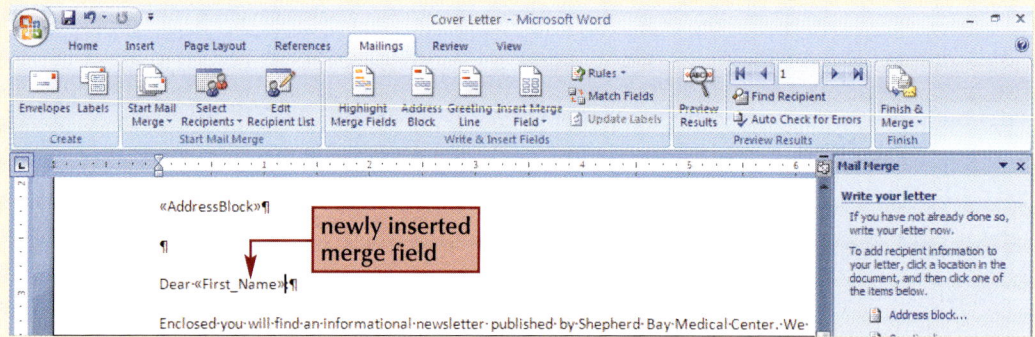

newly inserted
merge field

Trouble? If you make a mistake and insert the wrong merge field or insert the correct field in the wrong location, undo the insertion and then repeat Steps 1 through 4.

▶ **5.** Save your changes to the main document.

The main document now contains all the necessary merge fields, so you're ready to merge the main document with the data source. First, however, you should preview the merged document.

Previewing the Merged Document

When you preview the merged document, you see the main document with the customized information inserted in place of the merge fields. Previewing a merged document allows you to check for errors or formatting problems before you perform the merge.

To preview the merged document:

▶ 1. In the Mail Merge task pane, click **Next: Preview your letters**. The data for the first client in the data source (Rhoda Carey) replaces the merge fields in the cover letter. The top of the task pane indicates which record is currently displayed in the document. As shown in Figure 4-36, Word's default paragraph and line spacing results in too much space between the lines of the address. You can fix this by adjusting the spacing for the paragraph containing the Address Block merge field.

Trouble? If the address is highlighted with a gray background, the merge field is selected. Click anywhere in the document outside the address to deselect the merge field.

Previewing the merge document ◀ **Figure 4-36**

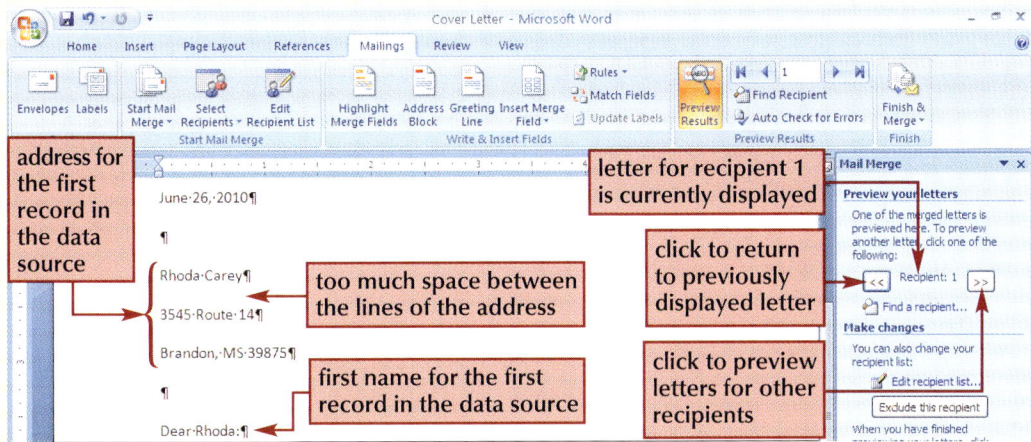

▶ 2. At the bottom of the Mail Merge task pane, click **Previous: Write your letter**. This moves you back one step in the Mail Merge task pane, to where the letter is displayed with the merge fields, rather than the recipient data, as shown earlier in Figure 4-35.

▶ 3. Click in the margin to the left of the **<<AddressBlock>>** merge field to select the merge field, as well as the paragraph mark to its right.

▶ 4. Click the **Home** tab, and in the Styles group, click the **No Spacing** Quick Style, and then, at the bottom of the Mail Merge task pane, click **Next: Preview your letters**. Now the address for Rhoda Carey is single spaced.

▶ 5. Carefully check the rest of the letter to make sure the text and formatting are correct. In particular, check to make sure that the spacing before and after the first name in the salutation is correct; it is easy to omit spaces or add extra spaces around merge fields.

Adjusting the Spacing in an Inside Address | InSight

In Tutorial 1, you used the Line spacing button to reduce the paragraph and line spacing in an inside address. Here, you used the No Spacing Quick Style. Which is better? The No Spacing Quick Style is faster, because it involves just one click. But keep in mind that it adjusts the line spacing and paragraph spacing at the same time. If you want more control over your spacing selections, use the Line spacing button instead.

You are ready for the final step—completing the merge.

Merging the Main Document and Data Source

Because your data source consists of five records, merging the main document with the data source will result in five copies of the letter to five different clients of Shepherd Bay Medical Center. Each letter will appear on its own page. Keep in mind that mail merges often involve hundreds or even thousands of records. As a result, the resulting document can be extremely long, with one page for every record in the data source.

To complete the mail merge:

1. In the Mail Merge task pane, click **Next: Complete the merge**. The task pane displays options related to merging the main document and the data source. You can use the Print option to have Word print the customized letters immediately, without displaying them on the screen. Instead, you'll use the Edit individual letters option to merge to a new document.

2. Click **Edit individual letters** in the Mail Merge task pane. The Merge to New Document dialog box opens. Here, you need to specify which records you want to include in the merge. You want to include all the records in the data source.

3. Verify that the **All** option button is selected, click the **OK** button, and then scroll as needed to display the entire first letter. Word creates a new document (the merged document) called Letters1, which contains five pages, one for each record in the data source. Each letter is separated from the one that follows it by a Next Page section break. See Figure 4-37. The main document with the merge fields (Cover Letter) remains open, as indicated by its button on the taskbar.

Figure 4-37	Newly merged document with customized letters

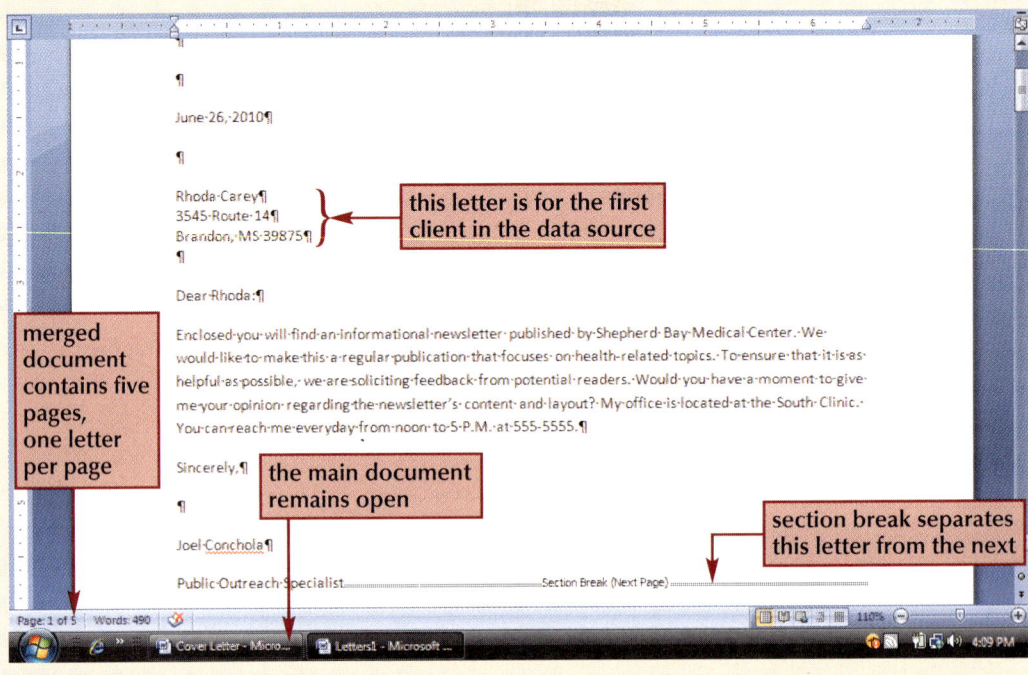

▶ **4.** Save the merged document in the Tutorial.04\Tutorial folder, using the filename **Merged Cover Letters**.

▶ **5.** Scroll down and review the five letters. Note the different address and salutation in each.

▶ **6.** Close the Merged Cover Letters document. The document named Cover Letter reappears, along with the Mail Merge task pane.

▶ **7.** Save the document and then close it.

Tip

There's usually no need to waste disk space by saving large merged documents. Typically, you would just print the merged document and close it without saving it.

You have completed a mail merge and generated a merged document. Joel will send the cover letters out with sample copies of his newsletter. Next, he wants to explore another means of communicating with the public—a blog.

Creating a Blog Post

A **blog** is an online journal that other people can read via the World Wide Web. The word "blog" is short for "Web log." Blogs typically include headings, paragraphs of text, pictures, and links to other blogs or Web sites. Although individuals often use blogs for personal reasons, in the business world a blog can serve the same function as a printed newsletter—providing news, product updates, and schedules of events. Because it can be updated instantly, and because the business doesn't incur printing costs, a blog is an effective way for a business or organization to communicate with the public.

A **blog post** is an addition to a blog, similar to an entry in a journal. When you create a blog post in Word, the file is a regular .docx file like an ordinary Word document, except that it doesn't have any of the formatting that controls the way a document looks on a printed page. It doesn't need that kind of formatting, because a blog is meant to be read on a computer screen. For example, the margins of a blog post are not fixed; instead, the margins change to accommodate the current zoom setting, with the text rewrapping as necessary. When it's finished, you can **post** it, or publish it—that is, add it to your online blog. At that point, the file is changed to an HTML file, so that it can easily be transferred over the Web.

Before you can post material to a blog, you need to create an account with a service that manages blogs and makes them available on the Web. Joel hasn't yet set up an account, but he wants to experiment with creating a blog post in Word. You can take an existing document and save it as a blog post, or you can start with a new, blank blog post. Joel wants to create a blog post from scratch. In the Case Problems at the end of this tutorial you'll save an existing document as a blog post.

To create a new blog post:

▶ **1.** If necessary, start Word.

▶ **2.** Click the **Office Button** (icon), and then click **New**. The New Document dialog box opens. The middle pane contains an option for creating a new blog post. (Note that your New Document dialog box may not include the Recently Used Templates section.) See Figure 4-38.

Figure 4-38 ▶ **Selecting a blog post in the New Document dialog box**

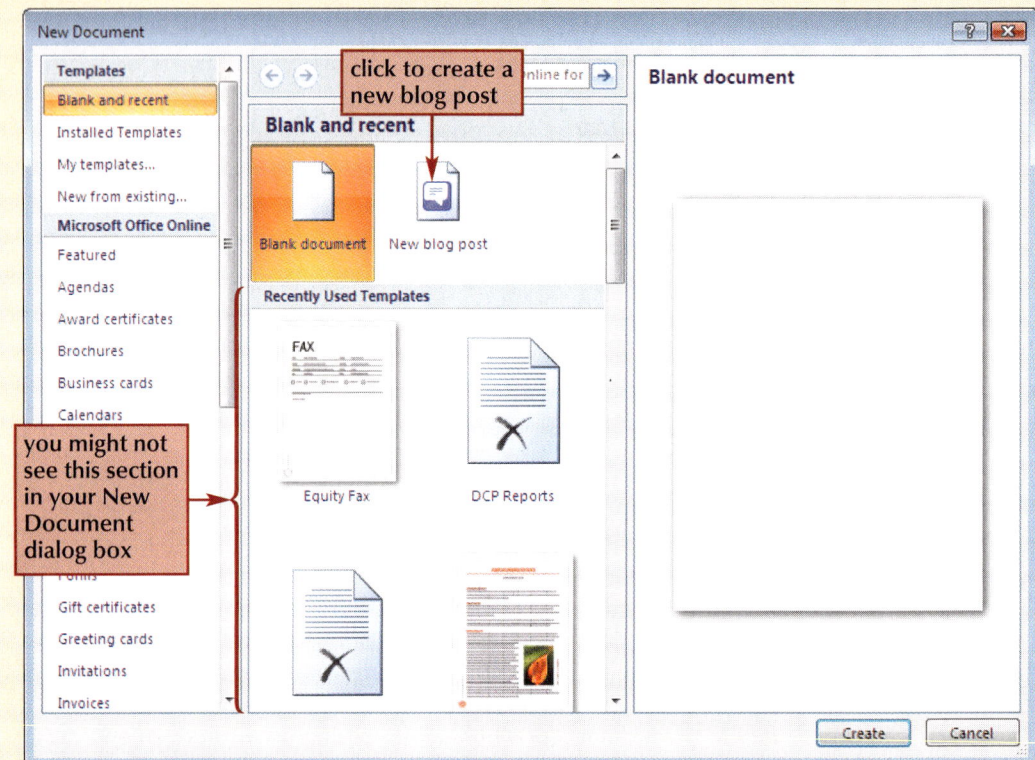

▶ **3.** Click **New blog post**, and then click the **Create** button. The New Document dialog box closes and the Register a Blog Account dialog box opens. You don't need to create a blog account in order to create a blog post, so you'll skip this step. Later, if you decide to start an online blog, you could use this dialog box to register with a blog provider.

▶ **4.** Click **Register Later**. The Register a Blog Account dialog box closes. A blank blog post opens. It includes some placeholder text, which you can replace with a title for the new post. Notice that the Ribbon has only two tabs, both containing tools related to working with blog posts. See Figure 4-39.

Figure 4-39 ▶ **Blank blog post**

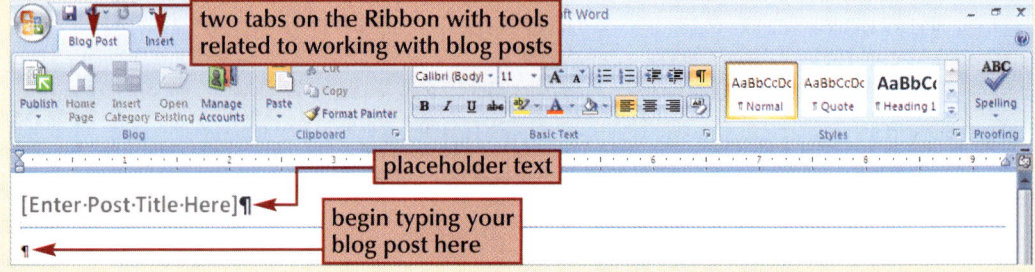

▶ **5.** Click the placeholder text **[Enter Post Title Here]** and type **Shepherd Bay Medical Center's New Blog**. The placeholder text is replaced with the new post title.

▶ **6.** Click in the blank paragraph below the horizontal line and type **This is a sample blog post for Shepherd Bay Medical Center.** See Figure 4-40. A typical blog post is at least several lines long, and may contain graphics, tables, and links to other information on the Web. The Insert tab simplifies the process of adding this type of material. If you had registered with a blog provider, you could click the Publish button in the Blog group to post this to your online blog. Because you have not registered with a blog provider, you will simply save the blog post instead. Even if you publish a blog post, you should always save a copy on your computer, so you have a complete record of all your posts.

Sample blog post ◀ **Figure 4-40**

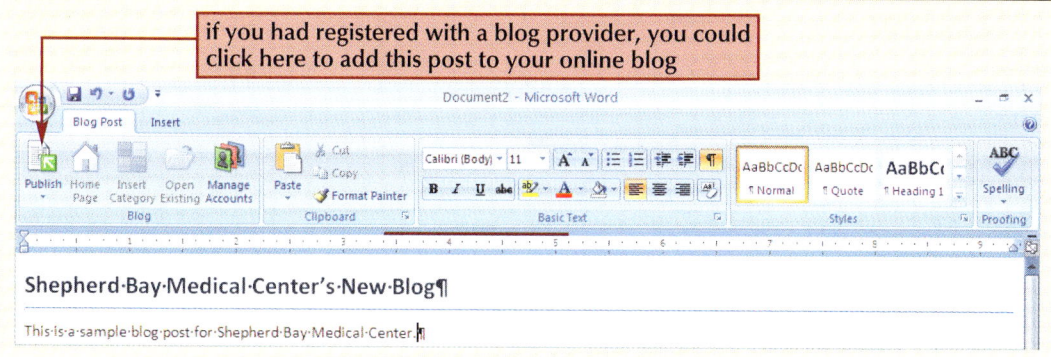

▶ **7.** Click the **Save** button 🖫 on the Quick Access Toolbar, and then save the blog post as **Sample Blog Post** in the Tutorial.04\Tutorial folder included with your Data Files.

▶ **8.** Print the blog post just as you would print an ordinary Word document, and then close the blog post.

Now that Joel understands how easy it is to create a blog post in Word, he will look into registering with a blog provider. A blog, along with the newsletter and the mass mailings he can create in Word, will help him communicate important information to the clients of Shepherd Bay Medical Center.

Session 4.2 Quick Check | Review

1. What type of text wrapping makes text follow the shape of the graphic?
2. True or False: When inserting a drop cap, you can specify the number of lines you want the drop cap to extend into the paragraph.
3. Explain how to open the Borders and Shading dialog box.
4. Name the two types of documents you need in a mail merge.
5. Define "record" as a mail merge term.
6. List the steps in performing a mail merge.
7. Explain how to open a new, blank blog post.

In this tutorial, you planned a newsletter and learned about the elements of desktop publishing. You created a headline using WordArt, anchored the WordArt object, and formatted text in newspaper-style columns. You also inserted a graphic into a document, edited the graphic, inserted drop caps, and inserted symbols and special characters. Next, you balanced the newsletter columns, drew a border around the page, and used mail merge to create customized cover letters to accompany the newsletter. Finally, you created a blog post.

Key Terms

anchoring	floating graphic	pull quote
balance	graphic	record
bitmap	inline graphic	rules
blog	mail merge	scaling
blog post	main document	sizing handles
clip art	merge fields	template
crop	merged document	text box
data source	newspaper-style column	typographic symbols
desktop publishing	object	WordArt
drop cap	post	wrap

Practice	**Review Assignments**

Apply the skills you learned in the tutorial using the same case scenario.

Data Files needed for the Review Assignments: Addresses.docx, Eating.docx, and Nutrition.docx

Joel's Healthy Living newsletter was well received. Now the Nutrition Department of the Shepherd Bay Medical Center has asked him to create a newsletter providing information and encouragement for Shepherd Bay clients to eat well. Joel has already written the text of the newsletter and asks you to transform it into a professional-looking newsletter. He asks you to create an accompanying cover letter using Word's mail merge feature, and then to create the first blog post for a new nutrition blog. (Note: Text you need to type is shown in bold for ease of reference only; do not bold the text unless otherwise instructed.) Complete the following:

1. Open the file **Eating** from the Tutorial.04\Review folder included with your Data Files, and then make sure your Word document is displayed in Print Layout view and that the nonprinting characters and rulers are displayed.

2. Save the document as **Eating Well** in the same folder.

3. In the last paragraph, replace "STUDENT NAME" with your first and last name.

4. At the top of the document, create the headline **Healthy Servings** using WordArt. In the WordArt Gallery, choose the fourth style from the left in the third row down from the top (the rainbow style with the shadow—WordArt style 16).

5. Change the shape of the WordArt object to Double Wave 2, and then italicize the WordArt text.

6. Apply the Top and Bottom text wrapping style to the WordArt object.

7. Drag the WordArt object to center it at the top of the page, then enlarge the Word-Art object to span the width of the page. When you are finished, the WordArt object should be slightly less than one inch high and a little more than six inches wide.

8. Insert a blank paragraph at the beginning of the document, anchor the WordArt object to the new blank paragraph, and then save your work. If the WordArt moves below the new paragraph symbol, drag it up above the new paragraph. When you are finished, the anchor symbol should be positioned to the left of, and just above, the new paragraph symbol, with the WordArt object positioned above the new paragraph symbol.

9. Position the insertion point at the beginning of the newsletter text (to the left of the heading "Eat Light, Eat Right"), and then format the newsletter text in two columns. Insert a section break so that the two-column formatting is applied below the insertion point and insert a line between the two columns.

10. Click at the beginning of the paragraph below the heading "Eating Well in a Busy World."

11. At the insertion point, insert the clip art graphic of the running person with the cell phone from the Business folder in the Office Collections folder. (The image is black and blue.)

12. Close the Clip Art task pane, and then resize the graphic, so it is approximately 1.5 inches square.

13. Crop the image slightly on the top to remove most of the dotted blue line. Make sure not to crop any part of the satellite dish or the black and blue background behind the running figure.

14. Wrap text around the graphic using Tight text wrapping, and then drag the graphic down to position it near the middle of the paragraph, next to the left margin. Three lines of the paragraph text should wrap below the graphic. Use the Align button to align the graphic at the left margin. You may have to move the graphic around a bit until you find a location that allows the text to wrap neatly around it.

15. Create a drop cap in the first paragraph under each heading. When you are finished, adjust the position of the graphic if necessary, so the text wraps neatly around it, without excessive space between words.

16. In the paragraph below the heading "Eating Well in a Busy World," insert the trademark symbol after "20 Fast Food Friends."

17. Check to make sure the document is still only one page long. If the text has flowed to the second page, then you probably made the WordArt headline too tall. Resize the WordArt object (and the graphic, if necessary) until the document is only one page long.

18. If you think it's necessary, balance the columns by inserting a Continuous section break at the bottom of the document. If you do insert a Continuous section break, and a new page is added at the end of the document, delete the section break. You probably sized the WordArt object and the graphic in a way that makes the section break unnecessary.

19. Add a border around the page using the Box setting and the border style with three thin lines (eighth from the top). Remember to position the border relative to the text, and not the edge of the page. Adjust the position of the clip art graphic if necessary.

20. Preview, save, and print the newsletter. When you are finished, close the document.

21. Open the file **Nutrition** located in the Tutorial.04\Review folder, replace "Joel Conchola" at the end of the letter with your name, and then save the document as **Nutrition Letter** in the same folder.

22. Merge the Nutrition Cover Letter document with the Addresses file found in the Tutorial.04\Review folder. Use the Address Block merge field for the inside address. Next, include a merge field that will insert the customer's first name in the salutation. Preview the merged letters and make any necessary changes before completing the merge. Remember to adjust the spacing for the Address Block field, so the inside address is single spaced.

23. Save the merged document as **Merged Nutrition Letters** and close it. Save your changes to the main document and close it. Close the task pane if necessary.

24. Create a new blog post. Use "Eating Right for Life" as the post title. For the blog post, type two sentences introducing a health and nutrition blog sponsored by the Nutrition Department at Shepherd Bay Medical Center. Save the blog post as **Nutrition Blog** in the Tutorial.04\Review folder included with your Data Files, and then close it.

25. Submit the finished documents to your instructor, either in printed or electronic form, as requested.

Apply	**Case Problem 1**

Apply the skills you learned to create a newsletter and a blog post for a public library.

Data File needed for this Case Problem: Audio.docx

Florentina, Arizona, Public Library   Michaela Novoa is the director of the Florentina, Arizona, Public Library. She and her staff have developed a new program that makes it possible for library patrons to download audio books over the Web as MP3 files. Michaela has written the text of a newsletter explaining the download system. She asks you to finalize the newsletter and then create a blog post from the formatted newsletter. (Note: Text you need to type is shown in bold for ease of reference only; do not bold the text unless otherwise instructed.) Complete the following:

1. Open the file **Audio** located in the Tutorial.04\Case1 folder included with your Data Files. Make sure your document is displayed in Print Layout view at Page width zoom and that the ruler and the nonprinting characters are displayed.

2. At the end of the document, replace "STUDENT NAME" with your first and last name. Save the document as **Audio Books** in the same folder.

3. At the top of the document, create the headline **Downloading Audio Books** using WordArt. In the WordArt Gallery, choose WordArt style 11, in the second column from the right, second row from the top (blue block letters).

4. Set the text wrapping style to Top and Bottom.

5. Drag the WordArt object to center it at the top of the page, and then enlarge the WordArt object to span the entire width of the page. When you are finished, the WordArt object should be a little less than 1 inch high and about 6.5 inches wide.

6. Edit the WordArt object to set the font to Arial and to apply bold to it. Then apply the Inflate Top shape to the headline and save your work.

7. Make sure the WordArt is anchored to the paragraph containing the subtitle of the newsletter, "Florentina, Arizona, Public Library." (The anchor should be located in the margin, on the same line as the subtitle.) In this newsletter, you don't need to insert a blank paragraph and anchor the WordArt to it, because the columns will begin below the subtitle, not directly below the WordArt.

⊕ **EXPLORE**

8. Select the paragraph containing the subtitle and center and italicize it. Open the Borders and Shading dialog box, click the Borders tab, and apply a Box border with the default line style. Make sure the Apply to box shows Paragraph. Click the Shading tab, click the Fill arrow, and click the pink box in the second row from the top. Be sure Paragraph is still selected in the Apply to list box, and then click the OK button.

9. Format all the text below the subtitle in two newspaper style columns, without a line between them. The subtitle should be centered over the two columns.

10. Open the Clip Art task pane and use the Clip Organizer to locate the image of a man in a brown suit typing on a keyboard. The image is stored in the Business folder within the Office Collections folder. Paste the image at the beginning of the first paragraph under the heading "How do I Listen to a Downloaded Book?" Close the Clip Art task pane.

11. Resize the picture, so that it is 1.5 inches wide.

12. Apply the Square text wrapping option. Drag the graphic down to the middle of the paragraph, next to the right column border. Align the graphic using the Align Right option in the Align menu.

13. Balance the columns if necessary, then zoom out, so you can see the whole page and review your work. If the newsletter text flows to a second page, reduce the height of the WordArt object until the newsletter is again only one page long.

14. Save and print the newsletter.

⊕ **EXPLORE**

15. Click anywhere in the document text to make sure the graphic and the WordArt object are not selected. Click the Office Button, point to Publish, and then click Blog. If you are asked to register a blog account, click Register Later. Save the new blog post as **Audio Books Blog** in the Tutorial.04\Case1 folder included with your Data Files. When saved as a blog post, the document loses the two-column formatting. You can format a blog in columns, but you need to do it through the blog provider, not when you create individual blog posts in Word.

16. Increase the zoom setting to at least 130%, so you can easily read the text. Notice how, in a blog post, the text wraps to fit the zoom size.

17. Click the WordArt title and delete it. Enter **Downloading Audio Books** as the post title. Select the subtitle in the pink box, and align it on the left margin. Delete the section break, as it is no longer necessary. If necessary, drag the clip art down to the paragraph below the heading "How do I download a book from ListenBooks?" Note that the final position of graphics in an online blog is often determined by the blog service provider.

18. Save your work, submit the finished documents to your instructor, either in printed or electronic form, as requested, and then close the files.

Apply | **Case Problem 2**

Apply the skills you learned to create an employee newsletter.

Data Files needed for this Case Problem: Island.jpg and News.docx

Flannery Investments   You work in the Personnel Department for Flannery Investments, a national investment company with headquarters in Minneapolis, Minnesota. You've been assigned the task of preparing the monthly newsletter *Flannery News*, which provides news about employees of Flannery Investments. You will use text written by other employees for the body of the newsletter. The newsletter will ultimately be three pages long, but at this point you have enough text to fill only one page and part of another. Complete the following:

1. Open the file **News** located in the Tutorial.04\Case2 folder included with your Data Files, and then save it as **Flannery Newsletter** in the same folder.

2. Use the Find and Replace command to replace all instances of the name "Daniela" with your first name. Then replace all instances of "Alford" with your last name.

3. At the top of the newsletter, create a **Flannery News** WordArt headline. Use the WordArt style in the second row down, third column from the left (WordArt style 9), select Arial as the font, and apply bold formatting. Set the wrapping style to Top and Bottom, and then anchor the WordArt to the blank paragraph at the top of the document, if it isn't already.

4. Center the WordArt if necessary, and resize the WordArt proportionally, so that it spans the width of the page and is about 1 inch high and 6 inches wide.

5. Make sure the WordArt object is positioned above the blank paragraph and anchored to the blank paragraph. Format the body of the newsletter into three newspaper-style columns. Place a vertical rule between the columns.

◆ EXPLORE 6. Position the insertion point at the beginning of the paragraph below the heading "Win a Vacation Get-Away." Click the Insert tab, and then, in the Illustrations group, click the Picture button. In the Picture dialog box, navigate to the Tutorial.04\Case2 folder, select the **Island** file, and then click the Insert button.

7. Crop about a third of the photo from the left and right sides, so that you only see the pier stretching out into the water. When you are finished, the image should be about .5 inches wide.

◆ EXPLORE 8. Make sure the photo is still selected and that the Picture Tools Format tab is displayed. In the Arrange group, click the Position button, and then, under With Text Wrapping, click the option in the left column, middle row. This aligns the photo on the left margin, halfway down the page, with the text wrapped around it. You don't need to select an alignment option on the Align menu when you use the Position button.

9. Click in the first paragraph under the heading "Win a Vacation Get-Away," and insert a drop cap that drops two lines into the paragraph. Insert a similar drop cap in the first paragraph after each of the other two headings in the newsletter.

10. Zoom out so you can see the whole page and review your work. Don't be concerned that the newsletter spans more than one page.

11. Add a page border to the newsletter. Select yellow stars as the art for the border. Apply the border to both pages of the newsletter (the entire document).

12. Save your work, submit the finished documents to your instructor, either in printed or electronic form, as requested, and then close any open files.

Challenge | **Case Problem 3**

Explore new techniques as you create the two-sided brochure shown in Figure 4-41.

Data File needed for this Case Problem: Hill.docx

Hill Star Dairy Cooperative Haley Meskin is the publicity director for Hill Star Dairy Cooperative in Lawrence, Kansas. Local residents pay a membership fee to join the co-op and then receive a 10% discount on purchases of organic dairy products. Many members don't realize that they can take advantage of other benefits, such as free cooking classes and monthly mailings with recipe cards and coupons. To spread the word, Haley would like to create a brochure describing the benefits of joining the co-op. She has already written the text of the brochure. She would like the brochure to consist of one piece of paper folded in three parts, with text on both sides of the paper, as shown in Figure 4-41. (Note: Text you need to type is shown in bold for ease of reference only; do not bold the text unless otherwise instructed.)

Figure 4-41

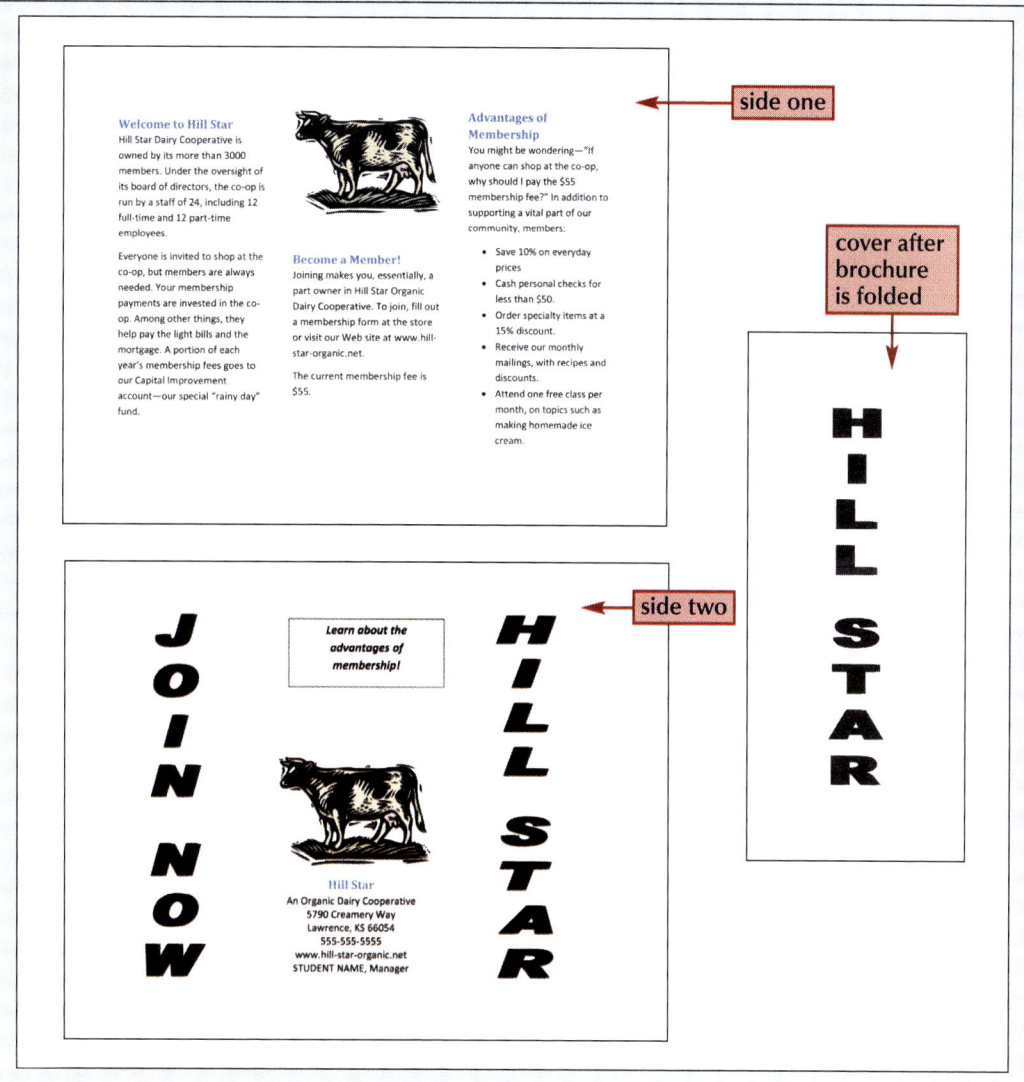

Complete the following:

1. Open the file **Hill** located in the Tutorial.04\Case3 folder included with your Data Files, and then save it as **Hill Star Brochure** in the same folder. This document contains a graphic of a cow. Because no text wrapping has been applied to it, it is an inline graphic. In this case, you want the graphic to remain an inline graphic, because you want it to move with the text as you edit the document.

2. On the second page, below the cow graphic, replace "STUDENT NAME" with your first and last name.

3. Format the entire document in three columns of equal width. Do not include a vertical line between columns. Ignore the page break at the bottom of page 1.

⊕ EXPLORE 4. You are already familiar with adding section breaks and page breaks to a document. You can also add a column break, which forces the text after the insertion point to move to the next column. Click at the beginning of the heading "Become a Member!" (just to the left of the "B"), click the Page Layout tab, and then, in the Page Setup group, click the Breaks button. In the Breaks menu, click Column. Insert another column break before the heading "Advantages of Membership." On the second page, click the second blank paragraph on the page, and then insert another column break. This column break moves the cow graphic and the text below it to the middle column. Press the Ctrl+End keys to move the insertion point to the blank paragraph at the end of the document, and insert another column break; this moves the blank paragraph to the third column on the second page.

5. Zoom out so you can see the whole page and review your work. The document should consist of two pages, with three columns each. The cow graphic and the co-op address should appear in the middle column on the second page.

⊕ EXPLORE 6. Click the cow graphic in the second page, copy the graphic to the Clipboard, click to the left of the heading "Become a Member!", and then insert two blank paragraphs. Click in the first new paragraph (at the top of the column), and then paste the graphic from the Clipboard. The middle column of the first page now contains the cow graphic, with the heading "Become a Member!" below, followed by two paragraphs of text.

7. On page 2, click in the blank paragraph at the top of the left column. Insert a WordArt object. In the WordArt Gallery, select the style in the left column, fourth row down. Use **JOIN NOW** (use uppercase letters) as the text. *Save your work.*

⊕ EXPLORE 8. Select the WordArt object if it is not already selected, and make sure the WordArt Tools Format tab is visible. In the Text group, click the WordArt Vertical Text button. This arranges the letters vertically down the column.

9. Adjust the size of the WordArt object (by dragging a sizing handle), so that it spans the height of the column—do *not* press the Shift key as you drag the handle. When you are finished, the WordArt object should be approximately 6 inches high and 1 inch wide. If you make it too wide, the WordArt will be hard to read. If you increase the height too much, the WordArt will disturb the column breaks, possibly resulting in a third page being added to the document. If that happens, click the Undo button and try again.

⊕ EXPLORE 10. In the WordArt Styles group on the WordArt Tools Format tab, click the Shape Fill button arrow. Click the black square in the top row of the palette. The WordArt changes from a marbleized brown to all black. Save your work.

11. Copy the WordArt object to the Clipboard. Paste a copy of the WordArt in the right column of page 2, select the newly pasted copy, click the Edit Text button in the Text group on the Format tab, and then change the text to **HILL STAR**. When you are finished, page 2 should consist of the JOIN NOW WordArt in the left column, the graphic and address information in the middle column, and the HILL STAR WordArt in the right column. Zoom out so you can see the whole page and examine your work.

12. Use the Center button on the Home tab to center both WordArt objects in their respective columns.

EXPLORE 13. Click the Page Layout tab, and then, in the Page Setup group, click the Dialog Box Launcher. In the Page Setup dialog box, click the Layout tab, click the Vertical align-ment arrow, click Center, and then click the OK button. This centers the text verti-cally on the page (between the top and bottom margins) and ensures that the brochure will look right when folded. Save your work.

EXPLORE 14. Change the Zoom setting to 100% and scroll to display the top of the middle column on the second page. Click the top of the middle column, insert five blank paragraphs, click the Insert tab, and then, in the Text group, click the Text Box button. In the Text Box gallery, click Simple Text Box, and then, in the text box inserted in the document, type **Learn about the advantages of membership!**. Select the text in the text box and, using the appropriate tools on the Home tab, format the text in 16-point Calibri, italic, and bold. Center the text in the text box. Place the mouse pointer on the border of the text box, and drag the text box up to position it at the top of the middle column, above the cow. Drag the border of the text box to make the text box narrower than the col-umn, and only as tall as necessary to display all of the text. Zoom out, so you can see the whole page, and adjust the text box size and the position of the graphic as needed, so that the content of the middle column fits nicely on the page. Save your work.

15. To print the brochure, you need to print the first page and then print the second page on the reverse side. Ask your instructor if you should print the brochure before doing so. To print the brochure, click the Office button, click Print, click the Pages option button, type **1**, and then click the OK button. Retrieve the printed page, and then insert it into your printer's paper tray, so that "JOIN NOW" prints on the reverse side of the list of member benefits; likewise, "HILL STAR" should print on the reverse side of the "Welcome to Hill Star" text. Whether you should place the printed page upside down or right-side up depends on your printer. You may have to print a few test pages until you get it right. When you finish, you should be able to turn page 1 (the page with the heading "Welcome to Hill Star") face up, and then fold it inward in thirds, along the two column borders. Fold the brochure, so that the "HILL STAR" column lies on top.

16. Save your work, submit the finished documents to your instructor, either in printed or electronic form, as requested, and then close any open files.

Create | **Case Problem 4**

Create the table shown in Figure 4-42, and then use it as the data source for a mail merge resulting in cover letters and envelopes for your own internship search.

There are no Data Files needed for this Case Problem.

Internship Search Cover Letters You're ready to start looking for an internship, and you plan to use Word to create customized cover letters to accompany your resume. You've decided to use mail merge to customize the letters. You'll start by creating the table shown in Figure 4-42 and filling it with address information for potential internship sponsors. Then you'll create a cover letter to use as a main document, and customize it by inserting the appropriate mail merge fields. (Note: Text you need to type is shown in bold for ease of reference only; do not bold the text unless otherwise instructed.) Complete the following:

1. Open a new, blank document, and then save it as **Intern Data** in the Tutorial.04\ Case4 folder included with your Data Files.
2. Create the table shown in Figure 4-42, and then enter information for three potential internship sponsors. The information can be real or fictitious. For the First Name and Last Name columns, use a fictitious name for an appropriate contact at each company. Use Ms. or Mr. for the Title field. Note that the Title field has to be the column on the far right, or the Address Block merge field won't work correctly. (The Address Block merge field assumes the first seven columns on the left are the fields you want to include in the address.) Save your work and close the document.

Figure 4-42

First Name	Last Name	Company Name	Street Address	City	State	ZIP	Title

3. Open a new, blank document and save it as **Intern Letter** in the Tutorial.04\Case4 folder.
4. Create a cover letter that introduces yourself and describes your experience and education. Instead of an inside address, include the placeholder text **[INSIDE ADDRESS]**. For the salutation, use **Dear [TITLE] [LAST NAME]**. Refer the reader to your resume (even if you don't have one) for more information. Use a proper business letter style for your cover letter. Include a sentence in the cover letter that mentions the company name. Use the placeholder **[COMPANY NAME]** to remind you to insert the appropriate merge field later. Save your work.
5. Save the letter, and open the Mail Merge task pane and follow the steps outlined in it. Use the Intern Letter document as the main document, and select the Intern Data file as the data source.
6. Use the Address block merge field for the inside address (in the "Joshua Randall Jr." format), and verify that the Insert company name check box is selected in the Insert Address Block dialog box. Adjust the paragraph and line spacing for the paragraph containing the Address Block merge field, so the inside address is single spaced.
7. Add a merge field for the title and the last name in the salutation of the letter, and add a merge field to replace the company name placeholder text in the body of the letter. Save your changes to the main document before completing the merge.
8. Preview your letters, and then complete the merge (choosing the Edit individual letters option). Save the merged document as **Merged Intern Letters** in the Tutorial.04\ Case4 folder, close it, and close the Mail Merge task pane.
9. Print your main document, and then close it.

10. Open a new, blank document, and then save it as **Intern Envelopes** in the Tutorial.04\ Case4 folder.

◈ EXPLORE 11. Open the Mail Merge task pane, click the Envelopes option button under Select document type, and then click Next: Starting document. Click Envelope options, and then click the OK button in the Envelope Options dialog box to select the default settings. The document layout changes to resemble a business size envelope.

12. Continue with the steps in the Mail Merge task pane, selecting the Intern Data file as the data source.

13. Click Next: Arrange your envelope, and notice that the insertion point is positioned in the return address, ready for you to begin typing. Type your name and address as the return address. (Change the Zoom setting if necessary to make the text easier to read.) Click the paragraph mark in the center of the document and insert an Address block merge field in the "Joshua Randall Jr." format. You do not have to adjust the paragraph or line spacing for the Address block field for an envelope. Save your work.

14. Preview the envelopes, and complete the merge (choosing the Edit individual envelopes option). Don't worry about the section break that appears after the return address; the envelopes will print correctly. Save the merged document as **Merged Intern Envelopes** in the Tutorial.04\Case4 folder. If your computer is connected to a printer that is stocked with envelopes, print the main document. Close the Mail Merge task pane and save your changes to the main document.

15. Submit the finished documents to your instructor, either in printed or electronic form, as requested, and then close any open files.

Research | Internet Assignments

Go to the Web to find information you can use to create documents.

The purpose of the Internet Assignments is to challenge you to find information on the Internet that you can use to work effectively with this software. The actual assignments are updated and maintained on the Course Technology Web site. Log on to the Internet and use your Web browser to go to the Student Online Companion for New Perspectives Office 2007 at **www.course.com/np/office2007**. Then navigate to the Internet Assignments for this tutorial.

Assess | SAM Assessment and Training

If you have a SAM user profile, you may have access to hands-on instruction, practice, and assessment of the skills covered in this tutorial. Log in to your SAM account (**http://sam2007.course.com**) to launch any assigned training activities or exams that relate to the skills covered in this tutorial.

Session 4.1

1. The document uses multiple fonts; the document incorporates graphics; the document uses typographic symbols; the document uses columns and other special formatting features; the printing is of high quality.
2. Click the WordArt object to select it, click the Edit Text button in the Text group on the WordArt Tools Format tab, edit the text in the Edit WordArt Text dialog box, and then click the OK button.
3. False
4. Text Wrapping button; located in the Arrange group on the WordArt Tools Format tab
5. Columns dialog box
6. BMP, GIF, JPEG, and TIFF
7. Insert tab

Session 4.2

1. Tight
2. True
3. Click the Page Layout tab, and then, in the Page Background group, click the Page Borders button
4. Main document and data source
5. A single row in a data source
6. Select or create a main document. Select or create a data source. Use the Mail Merge task pane to insert merge fields into the main document. Preview the merged document. Merge the data source and the main document.
7. Click the Office button, click New, click New blog post, click the Create button.

Ending Data Files

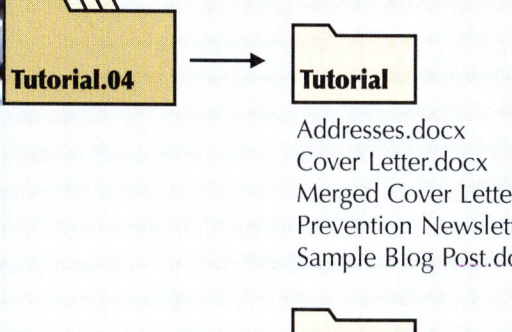

Tutorial.04 →

Tutorial
Addresses.docx
Cover Letter.docx
Merged Cover Letters.docx
Prevention Newsletter.docx
Sample Blog Post.docx

Review
Addresses.docx
Eating Well.docx
Merged Nutrition Letters.docx
Nutrition Blog.docx
Nutrition Letter.docx

Case1
Audio Books.docx
Audio Books Blog.docx

Case2
Flannery Newsletter.docx

Case3
Hill Star Brochure.docx

Case4
Intern Data.docx
Intern Envelopes.docx
Intern Letter.docx
Merged Intern Envelopes.docx
Merged Intern Letters.docx

Reality Check

You've seen how Microsoft Word 2007 allows you to create polished, professional-looking documents in a variety of business settings. The word-processing skills you've learned will be useful to you in many areas of your life. For example, you could create a Word table to keep track of a guest list for a wedding, or you could use Word's desktop publishing features to create a flyer promoting a garage sale or a concert for a friend's band. In the following exercise, you'll create a number of useful documents of your choosing using the Word skills and features presented in Tutorials 1 through 4.

Using Templates

You can create the documents in this exercise from scratch, or you can use the templates that are available in the New documents dialog box. A **template** is a special Word document that comes with predefined headings, formatting, document controls, and graphical elements. In the New Document dialog box, click Installed Templates, and then click the template you want. To use a template after you've opened it, save it like an ordinary document, and then replace the placeholder text with your own information. If a template includes a sample picture, you can replace the picture with your own JPEG photo file or a clip art image.

Note: Please be sure *not* to include any personal information of a sensitive nature in the documents you create to be submitted to your instructor for this exercise. Later on, you can update the documents with such information for your own personal use.

1. Create a resume that you could use to apply for your ideal job.
2. Create a cover letter to accompany your resume and portfolio. Where appropriate, insert placeholders for merge fields.
3. Create a data source that includes one record for each company or organization you plan to send your resume to.
4. Perform a mail merge, using your cover letter and your data source. Save the merged document.
5. Perform a second mail merge to create the envelopes for your cover letter and resume. In the first step of the Mail Merge task pane, click the Envelopes option button. In the second step, click Envelope options, and then click the OK button to accept the default envelope settings. Continue following the steps in the Mail Merge task pane. Save the merged document.
6. Create a multiple-page report. For the text of the report, you can use a report you have already written for another class or any text of your choosing. Choose an appropriate theme. Include a cover page, header, and footer. Include at least two footnotes or endnotes, and format the headings with appropriate Quick Styles.
7. Use a Word table to design a one-page flyer for an upcoming event. Remember that you can insert graphics into a table cell and that you can format the text in each cell differently. Also, keep in mind that the buttons in the Merge group on the Table Tools Layout tab allow you to combine and divide table cells.
8. Create a newsletter containing information you want to share with friends, family, or colleagues. Include graphics, newspaper-style columns, and other desktop publishing elements, as appropriate, to enhance your newsletter.
9. Save the newsletter as a blog post. Make any changes necessary to make the blog post attractive and easy to read.
10. Review all your documents carefully in Print Preview, and then submit the finished documents to your instructor, either in printed or electronic form, as requested.

Working with Templates and Outlines

Creating a Site Selection Report

Case | Department of City Planning

Clarenbach, Tennessee is a rapidly growing suburb of Nashville. Clarenbach's Department of City Planning prepares reports on many public projects that contribute to this growing community. Sam Hooper, a senior member of the department, has asked you to help prepare a report on possible sites for a new public swimming pool. He'd like you to use one of Word's templates as the basis for the new report. He'd also like you to create a template that can be used for all the reports the department creates.

Starting Data Files

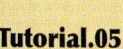

Tutorial.05 →

Tutorial
Placeholder.docx
Report.docx
Research.docx
Vilas Grove.docx

Review
Body.docx
Future.docx
Placeholder.docx
Research.docx

Case1
Characteristics.docx
Crabapple.jpg
Height.docx
Plant Headings.docx
Requirements.docx

Case2
Star.docx
Video.docx

Case3
Text.docx

Case4
(none)

Session 5.1

Creating a New Document from an Installed Template

A **template** is a file that you use as a starting point to create other files so that you don't have to re-create formatting and text for each new file. You can think of a template as a pattern for a series of similar documents. A template can contain customized Quick Styles (often referred to simply as styles), text, graphics, or any other element that you want to repeat from one document to another. Word provides numerous types of templates that you can use to create reports, fax cover sheets, letters, and other types of documents. For an even wider selection of templates, you can look online, where you'll find templates for certificates, contracts, brochures, and greeting cards, just to name a few. As you'll learn in this tutorial, you can also create your own templates to suit your specific needs.

Although you might not realize it, you already have experience working with templates. Every new, blank document that you open in Word is a copy of the Normal template. Unlike all other templates, the **Normal template** does not have any text, formatting, or graphics, but it does include all the default settings that you are accustomed to in Word. For example, the default theme in the Normal template is the Office theme. The Office theme, in turn, supplies the default body font (Calibri) and the default heading font (Cambria). The default 1.5 line spacing and the extra space after paragraphs are also specified in the Normal template.

InSight	**Changing the Normal Template**

If the settings in the Normal template don't suit your needs or tastes, you can change them. For example, you could change the default theme for the Normal template from Office to Oriel; or, instead of changing the entire theme, you could change just the default body font from Calibri to Verdana or another font. You could also change the default line spacing or the space that is supplied after each paragraph by default. It's important to remember, though, that when you change the default settings for the Normal template, the new settings will be apparent in all the new documents that you open in Word.

Tip

Templates have the file extension .dotx to differentiate them from regular Word documents, which have the extension .docx.

Sam would like to base his report on the Equity Report template, which is one of the templates installed along with Word. You open a template from the New Document dialog box. By default, when you open a new template, Word actually opens a document that is an exact copy of the template. The template itself remains untouched, so that you can continue to use it as the basis of future documents.

To open a new document based on the Equity Report template:

▶ 1. Start Word, click the **Office Button** 🏢, and then click **New**. The New Document dialog box opens. You've used the Blank document option in this dialog box before to open a new, blank document. The Templates panel on the left side of this dialog box gives you access to templates that are stored on your computer and to templates available online. In this case, you want to open a template that was installed with Word.

2. Click **Installed Templates**. The middle pane of the New Documents dialog box displays thumbnail images of the templates that were installed with Word. Scroll down, if necessary, and then click **Equity Report**. See Figure 5-1. In the lower-right corner of the New Document dialog box, the Document option button is selected by default. This indicates that Word will open a new document that is a copy of the template, not the template itself.

Selecting the Equity Report template | Figure 5-1

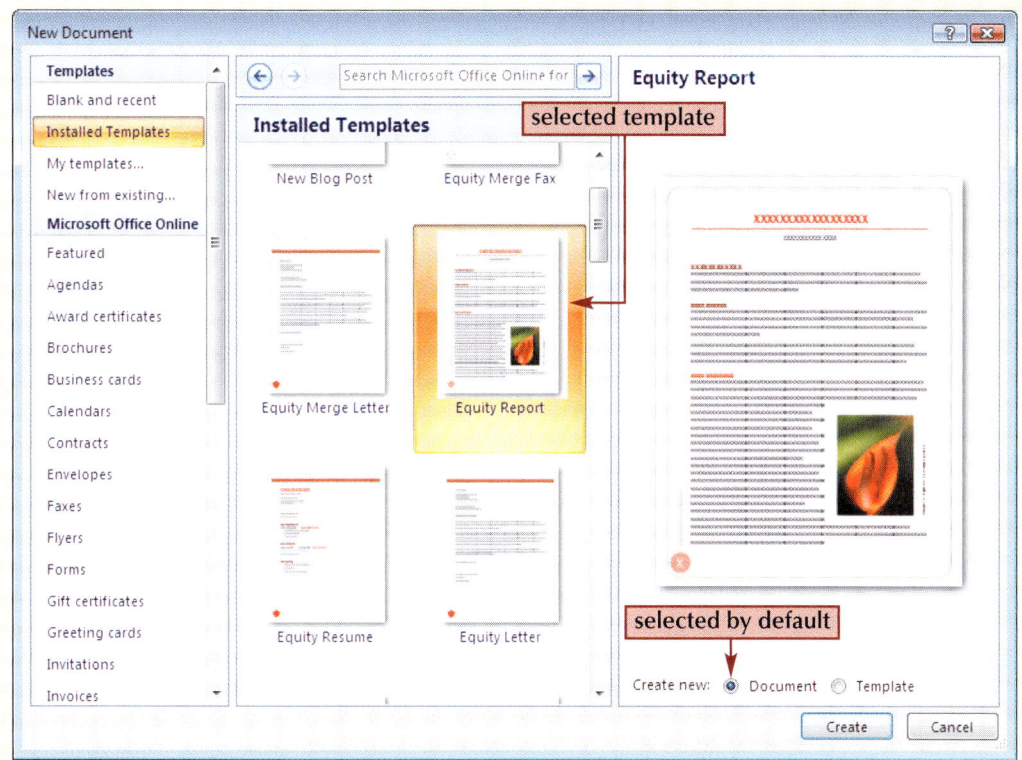

3. Click **Create**. The New Document dialog box closes, and a new document, named Document2, opens.

4. Switch to Print Layout if necessary, change the Zoom setting to Page width, display nonprinting characters if necessary, and then scroll down and review the parts of the document. The first page is a cover page with five controls: the document title, the subtitle, the company name, the date, and the author. The second page contains controls for the title and subtitle. It also contains heading and body text and a sample photograph. To the right of the photograph is a vertically formatted figure caption, which also contains a control. The lower-left corner of the second page contains a page number in an orange circle and a footer that is formatted vertically so that it runs up the left side of the page. The footer consists of two controls—one for the document title and one for the date. Each page is surrounded by a border with rounded corners. Figure 5-2 shows all the elements of the Equity Report template. The colors, the fonts, and the other elements you see in the document are specified by the Equity theme, which is the default theme for the Equity Report template.

Figure 5-2 Equity Report template

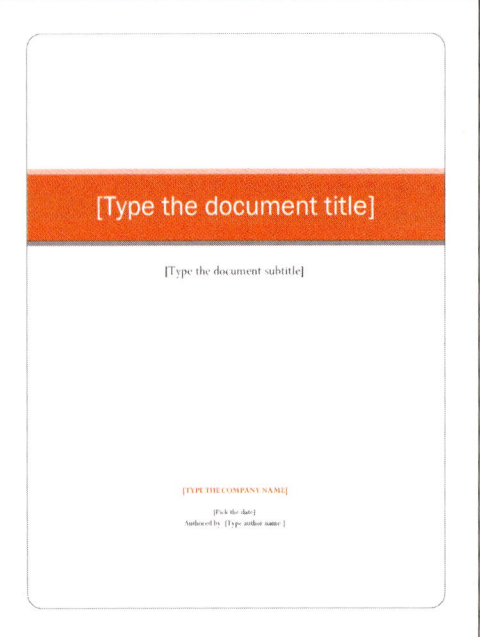
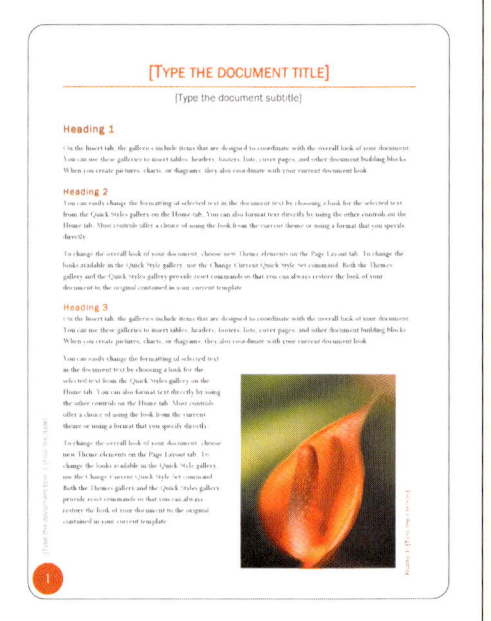

5. Save the document as **Pool Sites** in the Tutorial.05\Tutorial folder included with your Data Files.

InSight | **Using Template Elements**

When you create a document from a template, you don't have to use all the elements the template provides. For example, you could replace the default cover page with a different one by using the Cover Page button on the Insert tab, or you could delete the cover page entirely. Likewise, the sample photograph in the Equity Report template is just a suggestion; it shows how to format a photograph so that it blends harmoniously with the other elements of the Equity Report template. The same is true of the page number inside the orange circle. If you don't like it, you can switch to Header and Footer view, click the orange circle, and delete it. The secret to getting the most out of templates is to use only the elements that suit your needs.

After you open a new document based on a template, you can type the appropriate text in the controls and then replace the sample body text with text that is specific to your document. As you learned in Tutorial 3, a document control (also known as a **content control**, or just a control) serves as a repository of information; Word reuses the information from a document control in various places within the same document. For example, if you enter the title in a title document control, it will appear in all the title document controls in that document. You'll gain more practice with document controls in the following steps as you begin work on the pools report.

To enter text into the document controls:

▶ **1.** In the orange bar on the cover page, click the **[Type the document title]** place-holder text. The text is selected within the document control, ready for you to replace it. Sam wants to use the department name as the document title.

▶ **2.** Type **Department of City Planning**. The new title replaces the placeholder text. The document control is still visible around the new title, because it contains the insertion point. Next, you need to enter the subtitle.

▶ **3.** Click the **[Type the document subtitle]** placeholder text and type **Sites for New Swimming Pool**. The new subtitle appears in the control.

▶ **4.** Scroll down, if necessary, and click the **[TYPE THE COMPANY NAME]** placeholder text. The placeholder text is selected inside the company name control. A blue dot-ted rectangle with selection handles appears, enclosing the bottom of the cover page, including the company name, date, and author controls. This rectangle is part of the formatting that governs the placement of the controls on the page. You can ignore it. Sam does not want to include anything in the company name control, so you will delete it.

▶ **5.** Right-click the selected text. A shortcut menu appears. The Mini toolbar also appears, but you can ignore it. See Figure 5-3. Note that the Zoom in Figure 5-3 is set to 80% so you can see all the parts of the cover page in one figure. On your computer, the Zoom should be set to Page width.

Shortcut menu for the company name control | **Figure 5-3**

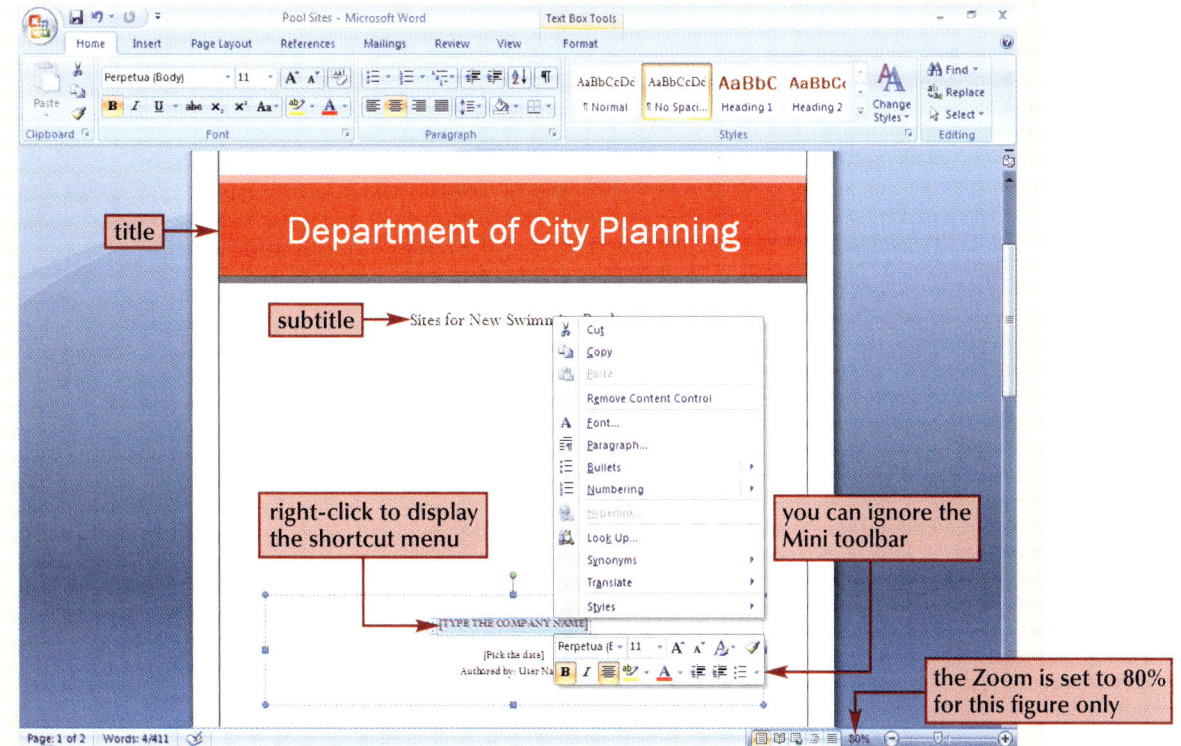

▶ **6.** Click **Remove Content Control**. The company name control is deleted.

Next, you turn your attention to inserting the date and your name as the author.

To insert the date and your name:

▶ **1.** Click the **[Pick the date]** placeholder text. A document control with an arrow button appears, surrounding the placeholder text.

▶ **2.** Click the arrow button next to the date control. A calendar appears, with a rectangle around the current date. See Figure 5-4.

Figure 5-4 ▶ **Cover page with calendar displayed**

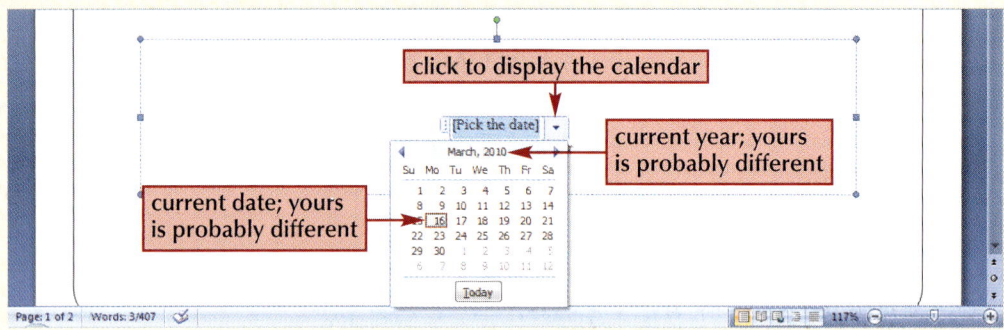

▶ **3.** Click the current date. The calendar closes and the current date is displayed in the Date control.

▶ **4.** Click to the right of the text "Authored by" to display a control where you can insert the name of the author of the report. Depending on how your computer is set up, you might see a name displayed in this control, you might see the placeholder text "[Type the author name]," or the control might be empty. See Figure 5-5.

Figure 5-5 ▶ **Author control**

▶ **5.** If the Author control is empty, click it and type your first and last name. If the control contains a name, delete it, and then type your first and last name. Press the **Escape** key to deselect the control. Your name is now displayed in the control.

The cover page for Sam's report is finished. Now you can work on the second page. Sam wants the report to begin with the heading "Contents" followed by a table of contents. You'll insert the heading now; you'll work on inserting a table of contents in Session 3 of this tutorial.

To enter the "Contents" heading on page 2:

▶ **1.** Scroll down to display page 2. Notice that the title and subtitle controls at the top of page 2 now display the title and subtitles you typed on the cover page. Likewise, the controls in the vertical footer (in the lower-left corner of the page) display the document title and the current date.

▶ **2.** Move the mouse pointer over the text in the body of the report, which begins "Heading 1." The text area is highlighted in blue.

▶ **3.** Click anywhere in the body of the report. The blue highlight darkens and now covers only the text itself. A blue tag above the highlighted text indicates that the body of the report is actually a content control. See Figure 5-6. This control is included in the document only so you can see a sample of the heading and body fonts and a suggestion for how to format a photograph, should you decide to include one in the report. Before you can create the body of the report, you need to delete this control.

Document with sample text highlighted ◀ **Figure 5-6**

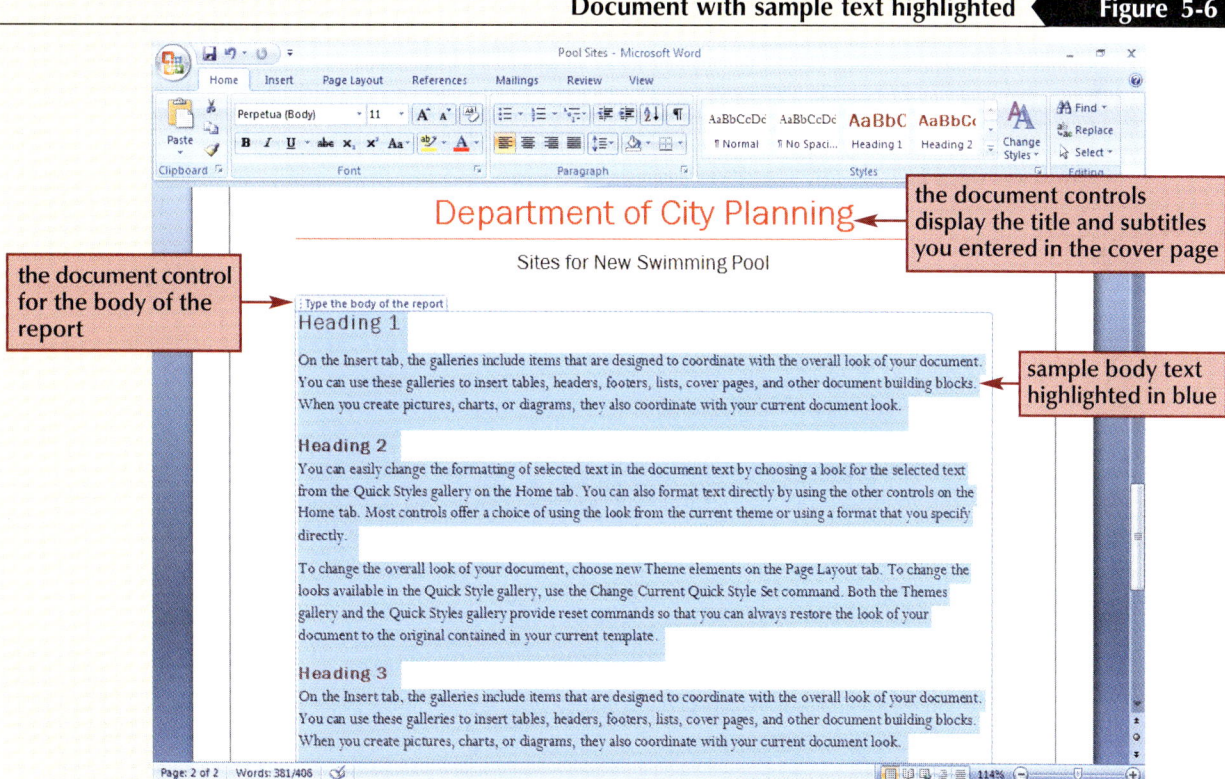

the document controls display the title and subtitles you entered in the cover page

the document control for the body of the report

sample body text highlighted in blue

▶ **4.** Right-click the **body control** to display a shortcut menu, and then click **Remove Content Control**. The control is deleted. You are ready to start typing the body of the report.

▶ **5.** Verify that the insertion point is located in the blank paragraph on the left margin below the subtitle, and then type **Contents**. The text is formatted in the Perpetua font, which is the default body font for the Equity Report template. In the next step, you'll format the text using a heading style.

▶ **6.** In the Styles group, click the **Heading 1** Quick Style. The Contents heading is formatted in 14-point Franklin Gothic Book font with a dark orange color.

▶ **7.** Press the **Enter** key to start a new paragraph, type **[Insert a table of contents.]**, and then press the **Enter** key. This placeholder text will remind Sam to insert a table of contents later. Notice that the new text is formatted in the Normal style, not in the Heading 1 style. A new paragraph after a heading is formatted in the Normal style by default. See Figure 5-7.

Figure 5-7 ▸ Page 2 of Sam's report

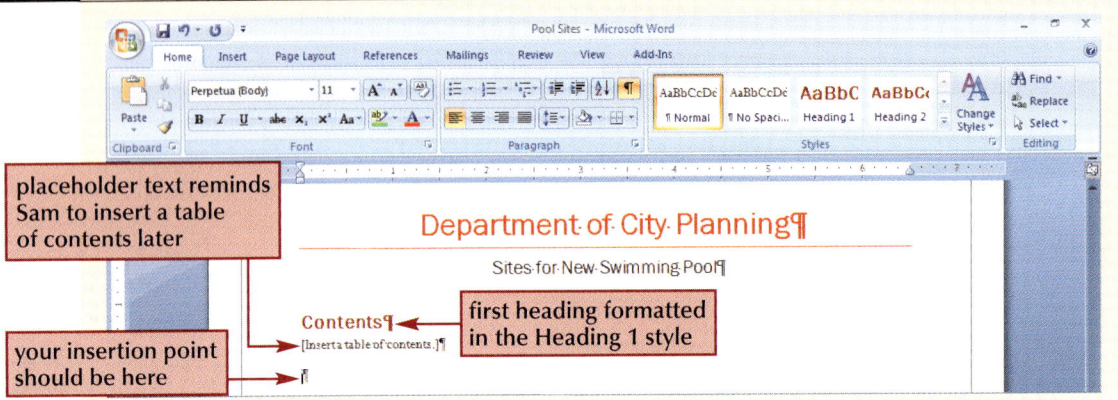

Sam has already typed the remainder of his report and saved it in a separate Word document. In the next section, you'll learn how to insert this Word file into the Pool Sites document.

Inserting a File into a Word Document

To insert a file into a document, you start by clicking the Object button in the Text group on the Insert tab. When you insert a Word file into an open Word document, the text of the inserted file is inserted at the location of the insertion point, so you need to make sure the insertion point is at the correct location. Word always inserts a blank paragraph at the end of text inserted from another file. If you don't want to include this extra paragraph, you can delete it.

To insert a file into the Pool Sites document:

▸ 1. Verify that the insertion point is located in the blank paragraph below the placeholder text, as shown earlier in Figure 5-7.

▸ 2. Click the **Insert** tab, and then, in the Text group, click the **Object** button arrow. (Take care to click the Object button arrow, and not the Object button itself.) A menu appears with two options.

   Trouble? If the Object dialog box opens, you clicked the Object button instead of the Object button arrow. Close the dialog box, and then click the Object button arrow instead.

▸ 3. In the Object menu, click **Text from File**. The Insert File dialog box opens. This looks like the Open dialog box, which you've used many times before.

▸ 4. If necessary, navigate to the Tutorial.05\Tutorial folder included with your Data Files, click the **Report** document, and then click the **Insert** button. The text of the Report document is inserted in the Pool Sites document. Sam formatted the headings of the Report document with Quick Styles when he first typed the document, so you don't need to format the headings now. Note that Word inserted a blank paragraph after the report text. You can leave that extra paragraph there for now. See Figure 5-8.

Trouble? If a menu appears below the Insert button in the Insert File dialog box, you clicked the Insert button arrow, rather than the Insert button itself. Press the Escape key to close the menu, and then click the Insert button.

Report document inserted into the Pool Sites document | Figure 5-8

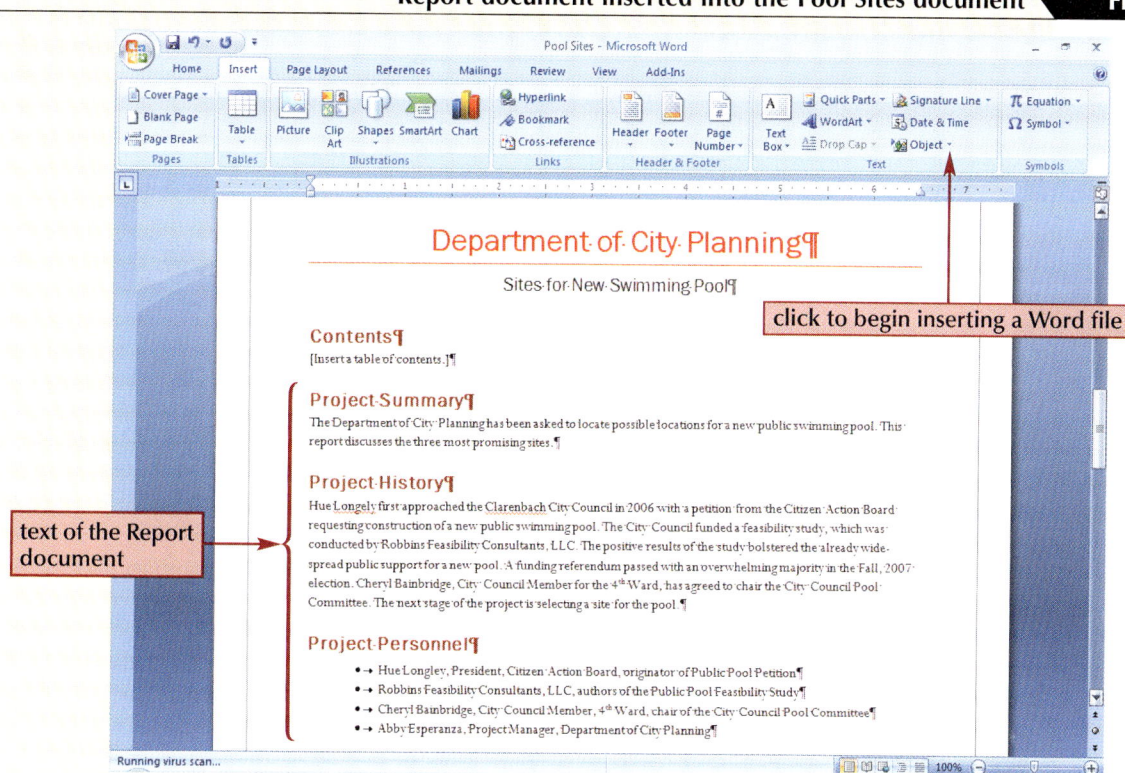

Review the document and notice that it now includes five main headings formatted with the Heading 1 style: Contents (which you typed earlier), Project Summary, Project History, Project Personnel, and Project Description. Below the Project Description heading are three subheadings: Breese Terrace Park, Langbrook Farm, and Flora Park. The subheadings Breese Terrace Park and Flora Park are formatted with the Heading 2 style. Sam mistakenly formatted the Langbrook Farm heading in the Heading 3 style. Later in this tutorial, when you learn about outlines, you will fix this problem.

▶ 5. Save your work.

Now that the document contains the report text, you can turn your attention to customizing its formatting. You'll start with the document theme.

Customizing the Document Theme

A document theme consists of three main components: colors, fonts, and effects. The **theme colors** control the colors used for every element in a document, including text, shading, hyperlinks, and so on. The **theme fonts** control the document's heading and body fonts. Remember that each theme specifies one font to be used for headings and one font to be used for body text. These two fonts appear at the top of the Font list on the Home tab. The **theme effects** control the look of a document's graphics. A specific set of colors, fonts, and effects is associated with each theme, but you can mix and match them to create a customized theme for your document. You change the theme colors, fonts, and effects for a document using the options in the Themes group on the Page Layout tab. When you change the theme colors, fonts, and effects for a document, the new elements affect only that document.

Customizing the Document Theme

- To select a different set of theme colors, click the Theme Colors button in the Themes group on the Page Layout tab, and then click the color palette you want.
- To select a different combination of heading and body fonts, click the Theme Fonts button in the Themes group on the Page Layout tab, and then click the font combination you want.
- To select a different set of theme effects, click the Theme Effects button in the Themes group on the Page Layout tab, and then click the icon for the effects you want.

The Pool Sites document, which was based on the Equity Report template, is formatted with the Equity theme. That means it draws its colors, fonts, and effects from the default settings of the Equity theme. Although Sam likes the overall layout of the document, which was provided by the Equity Report template, he doesn't like the colors or the fonts supplied by the Equity theme. He decides to select different theme colors and theme fonts for the Pool Sites document. He doesn't plan to include any graphics, so he will not take the time to customize the theme effects. He'll start with the theme colors.

Changing the Theme Colors

To get a better understanding of what happens when you change a document's theme colors, suppose you are working on a new document with the Office theme selected. The colors associated with the Office theme format headings in blue. If you prefer headings formatted in pink instead, you could select the colors of the Verve theme, which formats headings in pink.

Sam doesn't like the orange and red colors used in the Equity theme and asks you to change it to something more neutral. Before you begin customizing the theme, you will take a moment to verify that the Equity theme is in fact the current theme.

To change the theme colors in the Pool Sites document:

1. Verify that the second page of the document is displayed, so that you can see the document headings.

2. Click the **Page Layout** tab, and then position the mouse pointer over the **Themes** button. A ScreenTip appears indicating that the current theme is Equity. Next, you begin customizing the Equity theme's colors.

3. In the Themes group, click the **Theme Colors** button. A gallery of color sets appears, with one color set for each theme. A pale orange outline indicates that the Equity color set is the current color set. You see eight colors in each color set. The third color from the left in each set is the color used for headings. For example, the third color from the left in the Equity color set is dark orange, which is the color currently applied to the headings in the document. The remaining colors are used for other types of elements, such as hyperlinks, shading on cover pages, and so on. See Figure 5-9.

Tip

To see a ScreenTip that tells you the current theme colors, move the mouse pointer over the Theme Colors button in the Themes group on the Page Layout tab.

Theme Colors gallery | Figure 5-9

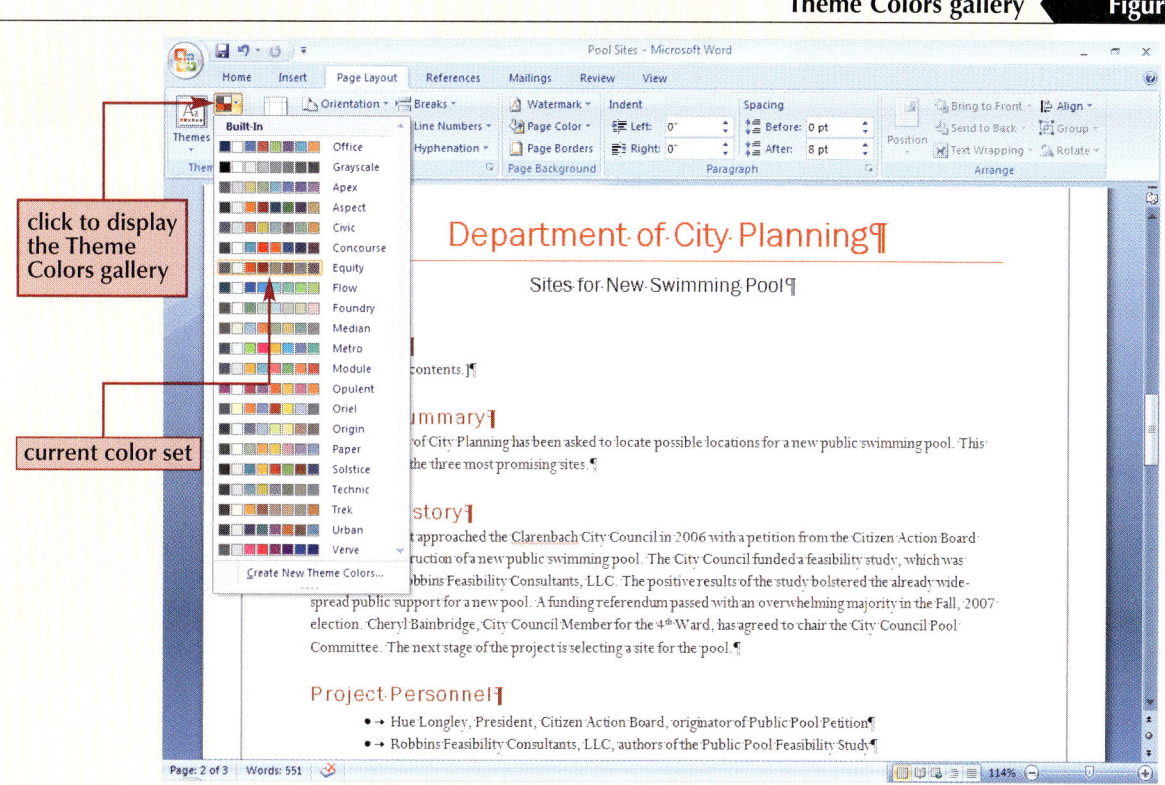

Trouble? If you see additional color sets at the top of the menu under the heading Custom, someone else created custom color sets on your computer. You can ignore them.

4. Move the mouse pointer over the options in the gallery and observe the live preview of the colors in the document.

5. Scroll down if necessary, and then click the **Urban** color set, which is the second from the bottom. The document headings are now formatted in dark blue. The page number circle in the document footing changes from orange to blue.

6. Scroll up and review the new colors applied to the cover page. The colored bar is dark blue with a brown bottom border, instead of dark orange with a light orange bottom border.

7. Save your work.

Keep in mind that the new colors you just selected affect only the Pool Sites document. Your changes do not affect the Equity theme that was installed with Word and that is available to all new documents. In the next section, you will finish customizing the document's theme by changing the theme fonts.

Customizing the Theme Fonts

Before you get to work changing the theme fonts for the Pool Sites document, you need to take a moment to learn some general principles that are useful when deciding which fonts to use in your documents:

- Fonts are divided into two types: serif and sans serif fonts. A **serif** is a small embellishment at the tips of the lines of a character, as shown in Figure 5-10. "Sans" is French for "without," thus, a **sans serif font** is a font without embellishments.

Figure 5-10 ▷ **Elements of fonts**

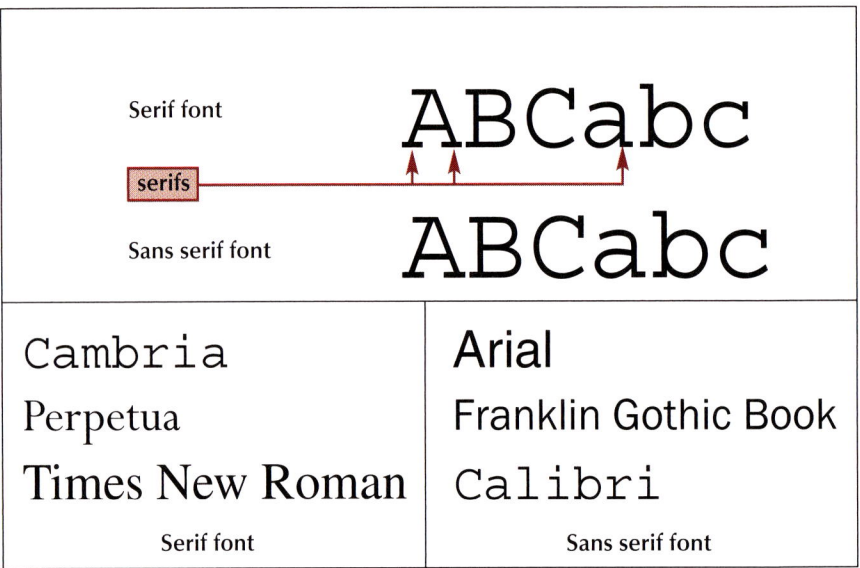

- One of the most popular serif fonts is Times New Roman. Cambria, the default Headings font in the Office theme, is a new serif font created specifically by Microsoft for Office 2007. Perpetua, the default Body font for the Equity theme, is also a serif font.
- Arial is a popular sans serif font. Calibri, the default body font in the Office theme, is a new sans serif font created specifically by Microsoft for Office 2007. Franklin Gothic Book, the default Headings font for the Equity theme, is also a sans serif font.
- As a rule, you should avoid unusual fonts, or fonts that look like handwriting, except in certificates, invitations, advertisements, and other specialty documents.
- You can add special effects to most fonts by adjusting the settings in the Font dialog box, which you open by clicking the Dialog Box Launcher in the Font group on the Home tab. For example, you can format a font as small caps (a reduced version of regular capital letters), superscript (slightly above the main line), subscript (slightly below the main line), outline (only the outline of the letters), or with shadows (light shading in the shape of the letter).

With these guidelines in mind, you are ready to select a new set of fonts for the Pool Sites document. As with theme colors, when changing the theme fonts, you can select from all the font combinations available in any of the themes installed with Word.

To select a different set of theme fonts for the Pool Sites document:

▶ **1.** Scroll down so you can see page 2 of the document.

▶ **2.** In the Themes group, move the mouse pointer over the **Theme Fonts** button Ⓐ▾. A ScreenTip appears, indicating that the current fonts are Franklin Gothic book for headings and Perpetua for body text.

▶ **3.** Click Ⓐ▾. The Theme Fonts gallery opens, displaying the heading and body font combinations for each theme.

▶ **4.** Scroll down until you see the heading and body fonts for the Equity theme. The orange highlighting indicates that these are the current fonts for the Pool Sites document. Sam prefers the Lucida Sans Unicode font, which has a bolder, more modern look than the default fonts for the Equity theme. The Concourse theme uses the Lucida Sans Unicode font for both headings and body text, so you will select the Concourse font set in the next step. (Although the Concourse font set consists of the same font for headings and body text, it's still called a "set.") See Figure 5-11.

Theme Fonts gallery ◀ **Figure 5-11**

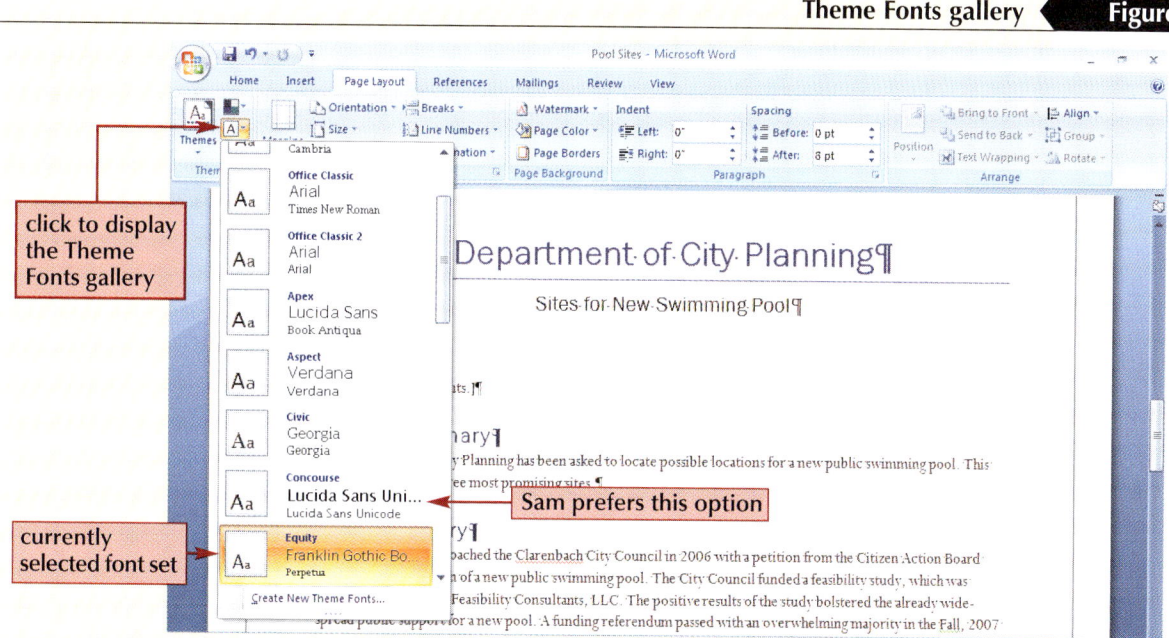

▶ **5.** Click the **Concourse** font set. The Theme Fonts gallery closes, and the Lucida Sans Unicode Font is applied to the headings and body text in the Pool Sites document. See Figure 5-12.

Figure 5-12 | **Pool Sites document with new theme fonts and colors**

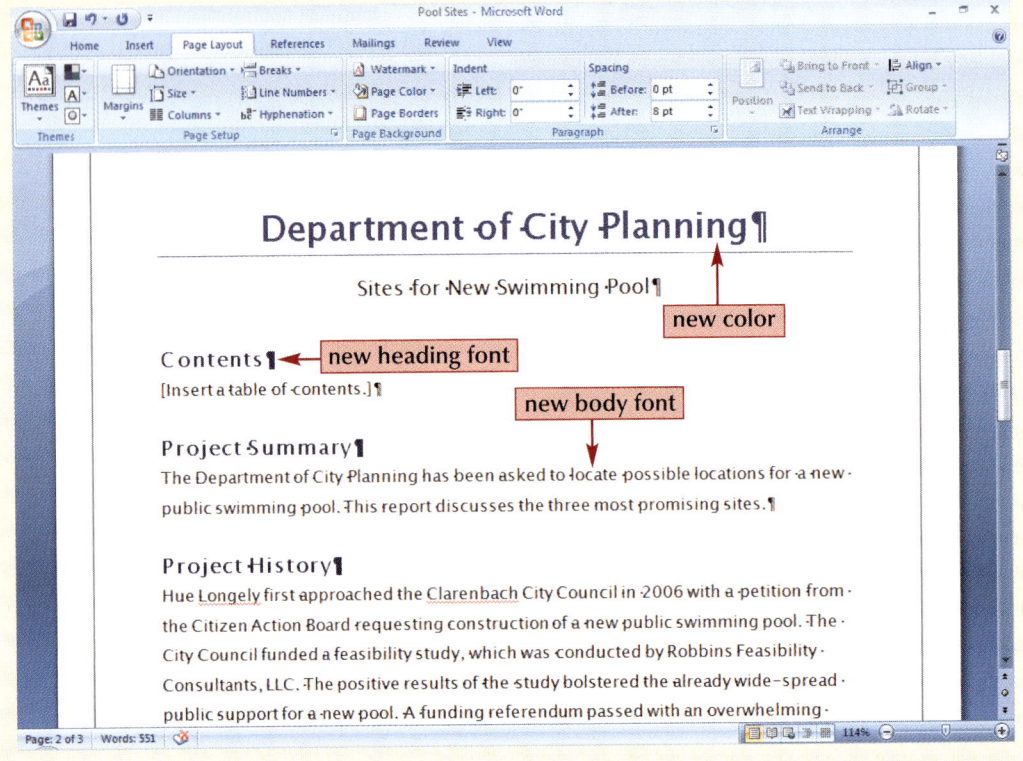

6. Save your work.

Remember that the new font set you just selected affects only the Pool Sites document. The new fonts do not affect the original Equity theme that was installed with Word and that is available to all new documents.

Creating Custom Theme Colors and Theme Fonts

It is possible to create customized sets of theme fonts and theme colors. Customized sets of theme colors and theme fonts include combinations that are not included in any of the themes installed with Word. (It is not possible to create customized theme effects in Word.) When you create a customized set of theme fonts or theme colors, they are saved as part of Word, so that you can use them in other documents.

- To create a custom set of theme colors, click the Theme Colors button in the Themes group on the Page Layout tab, click Create New Theme Colors to open the Create New Theme Colors dialog box, click the arrow for the color you want to change, click a color, repeat for additional colors as necessary, type a descriptive name for the new color scheme in the Name text box, and then click the Save button. The custom set of theme colors appears as an option in the Themes Color menu.
- To delete a custom set of theme colors, click the Theme Colors button in the Themes group on the Page Layout tab, right-click the custom set of colors you want to delete, click Delete, and then click Yes.
- To create a custom set of heading and body fonts, click the Theme Fonts button in the Themes group on the Page Layout tab, click Create New Theme Fonts to open the Create New Theme Fonts dialog box, use the list boxes to select the Heading and Body fonts you want, type a descriptive name for the new set of fonts in the Name text box, and then click the Save button. The custom set of theme fonts appears as an option in the Theme Fonts menu.
- To delete a new set of theme colors or fonts, click the Theme Colors or Theme Fonts button in the Themes group on the Page Layout tab, right-click the custom set of colors or fonts you want to delete, click Delete, and then click Yes.

The sets of theme colors and theme fonts installed with Word were created by Microsoft designers who are experts in creating harmonious-looking documents. As a rule, it's best to stick with these predesigned options, rather than trying to create your own.

Creating a Custom Theme

Keep in mind that the new theme colors and theme fonts you selected for the Pool Sites document affect only that document. To make your new choices available to other documents, you would need to create a custom theme. When you create a custom theme, it is saved as part of Word and appears as an option in the Themes gallery so that you can apply it to any document.

- Modify the document theme as much as you want by selecting new theme colors, theme fonts, and theme effects.
- In the Themes group on the Page Layout tab, click the Themes button.
- Click Save Current Theme to open the Save Current Theme dialog box, type a name for the theme in the File name text box, and then click the Save button. The new theme appears at the top of the Themes menu, under the "Custom" heading.
- To delete a custom theme, click the Themes button in the Themes group on the Page Layout tab, right-click the theme you want to delete, click Delete, and then click Yes.

Sam is happy with the new look of the Pool Sites document. He doesn't need to save his changes to the fonts and colors as a custom theme, though. In the next session, you will focus on modifying the Quick Styles used in Sam's report.

1. Which template includes all the default settings that you are accustomed to in Word?
2. How do you delete a content control?
3. What tab should you click if you want to insert a Word file into a document?
4. What are the three main components of a document theme?
5. List the two types of fonts.
6. True or False. It is not possible to create a new theme.

Session 5.2

Understanding Themes, Styles, and Style Sets

Before you begin working more extensively with styles, you need to make sure you understand the relationship between styles and themes. The elements of a theme (colors, fonts, and effects) are like the building materials for a house. Styles, on the other hand, are like blueprints for the many types of houses that you can create with those building materials.

For example, by default, the Heading 1 style applies the heading font specified in the document theme. However, it doesn't just apply to the heading font. That would be like a blueprint that said only that a house should be made out of brick, but failed to specify the number of rooms, the style of windows, and so on. The Heading 1 style, for example, includes numerous additional details that, taken together, format text with a particular look—its style. Among other things, the Heading 1 style applies a particular font size and adds boldface. It also adds color—whatever color specified by the current Accent 1 color for the current theme.

As you know, you select a style from the Quick Styles gallery on the Home tab. By default, the Quick Styles gallery displays 20 different styles. Additional sets of styles are also available via the Change Styles button in the Styles group on the Home tab.

You can modify an existing style, or you can create a new style by modifying an existing one and saving it with a new name. By default, a new or modified style is saved only in the current document. If you prefer, you can save a new or modified style as part of the current template, so that it is available in all new documents based on that template.

InSight | **Saving Styles to the Current Document**

Keep in mind that all new, blank documents are based on the Normal template. So if you open a blank document, modify or create a style, and then save the style to the current template (rather than to the current document), the style will be available in all new blank documents that you open in Word in the future. Continually modifying or creating styles in the Normal template can result in a Quick Styles gallery that is disorganized, making it hard to find the styles you want. To avoid this problem, consider saving specialized styles to the current document (rather than to the current template), and then saving the current document as a template. All future documents based on that new template will contain your new styles. Meanwhile, the Normal template will remain unaffected by the new styles.

Sam wants to select a different style set for the Pool Sites document. Then he would like to modify the Heading 1 style, and finally, create a new style for the Project Summary heading.

Selecting a Style Set

Every built-in theme comes with 11 sets of styles, with names such as Elegant, Modern, and Manuscript. Each style set is, in turn, made up of 31 styles. So far, you've worked with only the sixteen styles, such as Heading 1 and Heading 2, that are available from the Quick Styles gallery on the Home tab. You can access additional styles via the Styles window, by clicking the More button in the Styles group on the Home tab.

The **style sets** have the same names in each theme, but they look different from one theme to the next. Likewise, the styles that make up the style sets have the same name in each style set, but they look different from one style set to the next. The default style set for built-in themes is the Office 2007 style set. This is the style set you are used to seeing in the Quick Styles gallery whenever you open a new, blank document.

Each set of styles includes a Normal style for formatting body text, several heading styles, and styles for titles, captions, and other special types of text. To select a different style set, you use the Change Styles button in the Styles group on the Home tab. The Style Sets menu allows you to preview the various style sets in your document before actually selecting one.

In the following steps, you select a new style set for the Pool Sites document.

To select a new style set for the Pool Sites document:

▶ 1. Verify that the Pool Sites document is open, in Print Layout view, the Zoom set at Page width, and nonprinting characters displayed. If necessary, scroll down so the second page of the document is visible. This will allow you to see how changing the style set affects the document headings. Recall that some headings are formatted with various heading styles. The body text below each of the headings is formatted in the Normal style.

▶ 2. Click the **Home** tab if necessary, and then in the Styles group, click the **Change Styles** button. The Change Styles menu opens. To select a new style set, you use the Style Set option.

▶ 3. Point to **Style Set**. The Style Set menu opens, displaying a list of style sets.

▶ 4. Drag the mouse pointer down and point to **Modern**. In the document, you see a preview of some of the styles that make up the Modern style set. In the Modern style set, the Heading 1 style applies a blue box that spans the left and right margins, with the heading text in white. The font for the document is still Lucida Sans Unicode for both headings and the body text, as you specified in Session 1 when you changed the theme fonts. The colors are still the colors you picked when you changed the theme colors in Session 1. See Figure 5-13.

Tip

To restore the default style set specified by the document's template, click Reset to Quick Styles from *Name* Template (where *Name* stands for the template's name) at the bottom of the Style Set menu.

Figure 5-13 ▶ Live Preview of the Modern style set

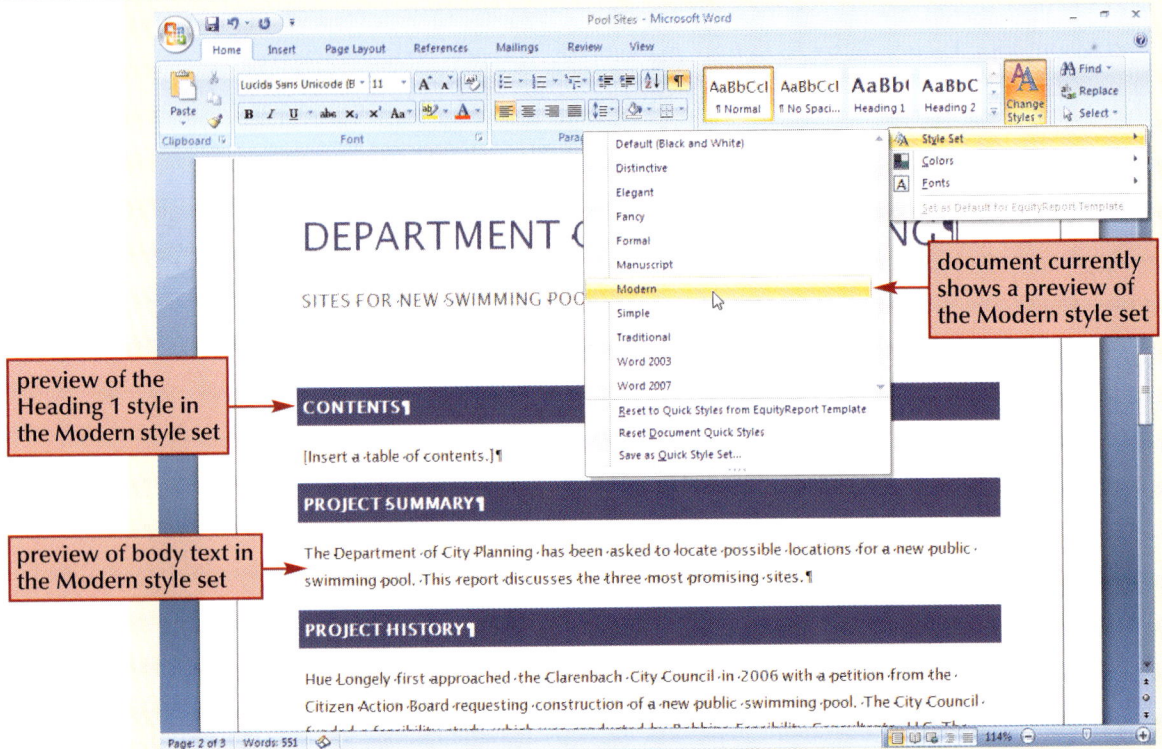

preview of the Heading 1 style in the Modern style set

preview of body text in the Modern style set

document currently shows a preview of the Modern style set

▶ 5. Move the mouse pointer over other options in the Style Set menu and observe the live preview in the document.

▶ 6. Click **Modern** in the Style Set menu. The styles in the document change to reflect the styles in the Modern style set, and the Quick Styles gallery in the Styles group displays the first four styles in the Modern Style set.

▶ 7. In the Styles group, click the **More** button ⬇ to review the set of styles available in the Quick Styles gallery, and then click anywhere in the document to close the Quick Styles gallery.

Now that you've selected the Modern style set for Sam's document, you can customize the styles in the Modern style set. You'll start by modifying the Heading 1 style.

Modifying Styles

To modify a style, you select text formatted with the style you want to modify, apply new formatting, and then save your changes to the style. You'll start modifying the Heading 1 style by selecting some text formatted in that style and then applying the new formatting. Specifically, you will expand its character spacing, paragraph spacing, and apply italics. After you finish applying this new formatting, you will modify the Heading 1 style to match the newly formatted heading. To apply this formatting, you need to turn your attention briefly away from styles to focus on character spacing and paragraph spacing.

Changing Character Spacing

Word offers a number of ways to adjust the spacing between characters—that is, to adjust **character spacing**. In some situations, you might want to use **kerning**, the process of adjusting the spacing between characters to make them look like they are spaced evenly. Kerning is helpful because in text formatted in large font sizes, characters sometimes look unevenly spaced, even though they are in fact spaced evenly. Turning on Word's automatic kerning feature ensures that the spacing is adjusted automatically so that letters appear evenly spaced. In most documents, however, it's easiest to select a group of characters and then uniformly expand or condense the spacing between them. Notice that space between characters is measured in points, with one point equal to 1/72 of an inch.

You are ready to modify the character spacing of the Contents heading. While you have the Font dialog box open, you will also add italics.

To modify the character spacing of the Contents heading:

▶ 1. Click in the left margin to select the heading **Contents**. Note that the blue selection highlighting might be hard to see in the blue box surrounding the "Contents" heading.

▶ 2. In the Font group on the Home tab, click the Dialog Box Launcher. The Font dialog box opens.

▶ 3. Click the **Character Spacing** tab. This tab includes several options for changing the space between characters. Currently, the setting in the Spacing list box is Expanded. The setting you see here depends on the style applied to the text that is selected in the document. If you wanted to move the selected character closer together, you could click the Spacing arrow and then click Condensed. In this case, you will keep the Expanded setting but increase the space between the characters by changing the setting in the By box next to the Spacing list box.

▶ 4. Next to the Spacing list box, delete the contents of the By text box, type **2** (you don't have to type "pt"), and then press the **Tab** key. The Preview section shows a sample of the expanded character spacing. See Figure 5-14.

Figure 5-14 | **Changing character spacing in the Font dialog box**

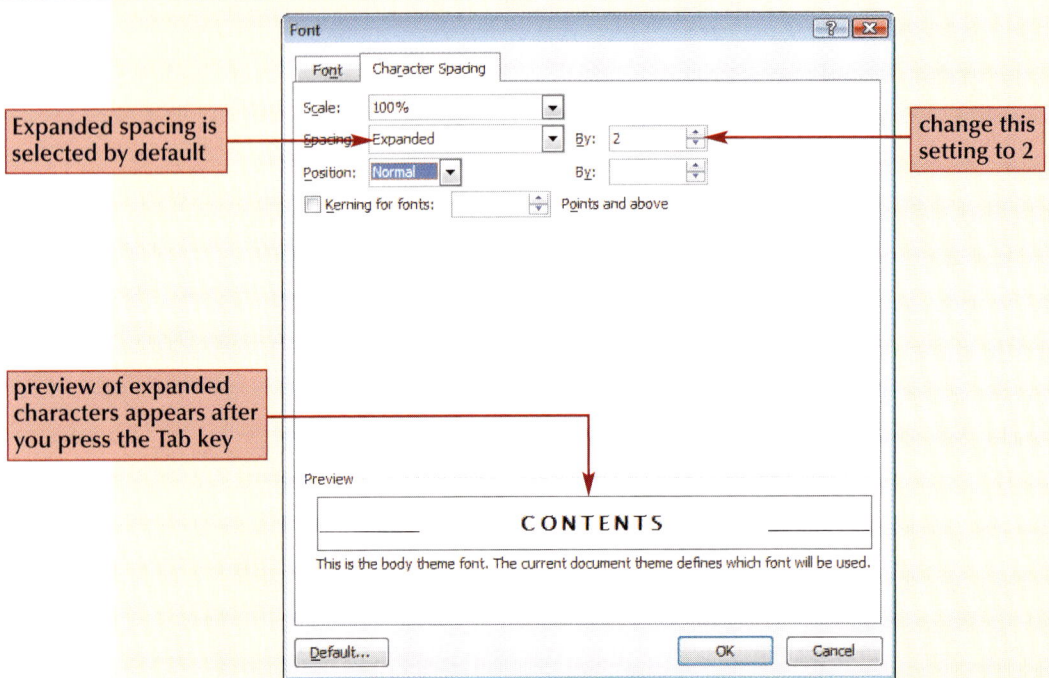

Expanded spacing is selected by default

preview of expanded characters appears after you press the Tab key

change this setting to 2

Next, you need to apply italics. It's normally easiest to use the buttons on the Home tab to perform this task. However, since the Font dialog box is open, it makes sense to make these changes there.

▶ **5.** In the Font dialog box, click the **Font** tab. Here you can make numerous changes affecting the appearance of the selected text, including adding special effects such as shadows or outlines. The "Contents" heading is already formatted in all capital letters, so the All caps check box is selected. This setting was specified by the Heading 1 style. In the Font style list box, Bold is also selected, indicating that the Heading 1 style also applied bold formatting to the "Contents" heading. (In the case of the white font color applied to the "Contents" heading, bold makes the white characters thicker rather than darker.) You want to keep the bold formatting and also add italics.

▶ **6.** In the Font style list box, click **Bold Italic**. The Preview section of the Font tab shows a preview of the new formatting. See Figure 5-15.

Applying italics in the Font dialog box ◄ **Figure 5-15**

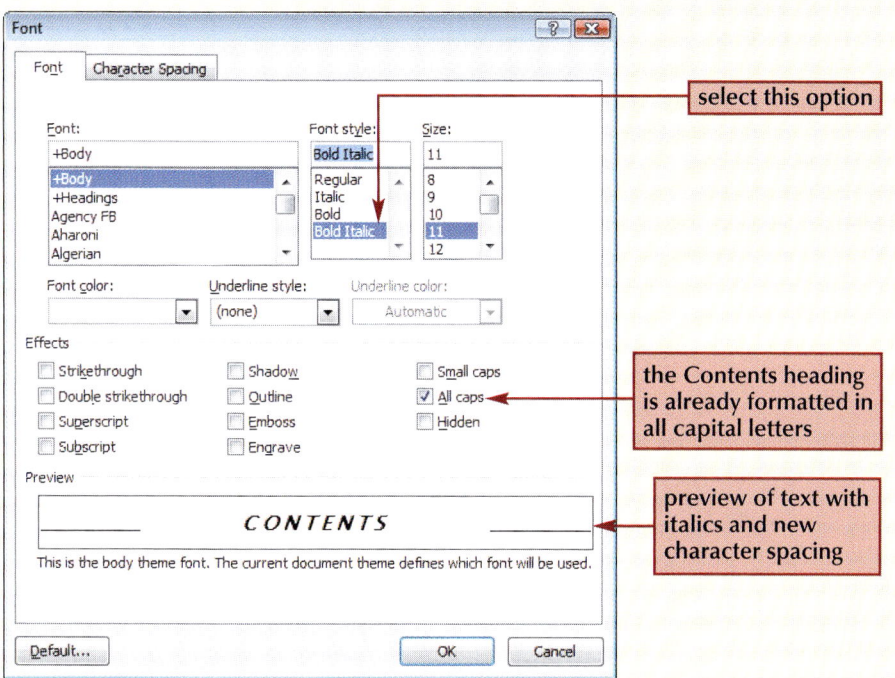

> select this option

> the Contents heading is already formatted in all capital letters

> preview of text with italics and new character spacing

▶ **7.** Click the **OK** button to close the Font dialog box. The selected heading is now italicized, with the individual characters spread slightly farther apart.

▶ **8.** Save your work.

Next, you need to change the Heading 1 style so there is some extra spacing below each heading formatted with this style. Increasing the paragraph spacing is the last change Sam wants for the headings. After you're done formatting the Contents heading, you will tell Word that you want to modify the Heading 1 style to match the formatting of the Contents heading. This will affect all the headings that are currently formatted with the Heading 1 style.

Changing Paragraph Spacing

You already know how to add or delete a default amount of space before or after a paragraph using the Line spacing button in the Paragraph group on the Home tab. To specify an exact amount of space, you use the Paragraph dialog box.

Adjusting Spacing Between Paragraphs | Reference Window

- Select the paragraph whose spacing you want to adjust.
- To add or delete Word's default amount of space, click the Line spacing button in the Paragraph group on the Home tab, and then click Add Space Before Paragraph or Remove Space After Paragraph.
- To add or delete a specific amount of space, in the Paragraph group on the Home tab, click the Dialog Box Launcher to open the Paragraph dialog box, click the Indents and Spacing tab, and then use the Before box to specify the amount of space you want to insert above the selected paragraph. Use the After box to specify the amount of space you want to insert below the selected paragraph.

Sam wants 6 points of space after the Contents heading. The extra space will help draw attention to the heading.

To increase the space after the Contents heading:

▶ **1.** Verify that the Contents heading is still selected.

▶ **2.** In the Paragraph group on the Home tab, click the Dialog Box Launcher. The Paragraph dialog box opens.

▶ **3.** If necessary, click the **Indents and Spacing** tab. You use the Before and After boxes in the Spacing section of this tab to add space before or after the selected paragraph. Currently, there are 10 points of space before the selected paragraph and no points after it. Sam wants to change the After setting to 15.

▶ **4.** In the Spacing section, select the contents of the After box, and then type **15**. (You don't have to type "pt.")

▶ **5.** Press the **Tab** key to enter the new setting. The Preview section of the dialog box shows a sample of the increased paragraph spacing. See Figure 5-16.

Figure 5-16	Changing paragraph spacing

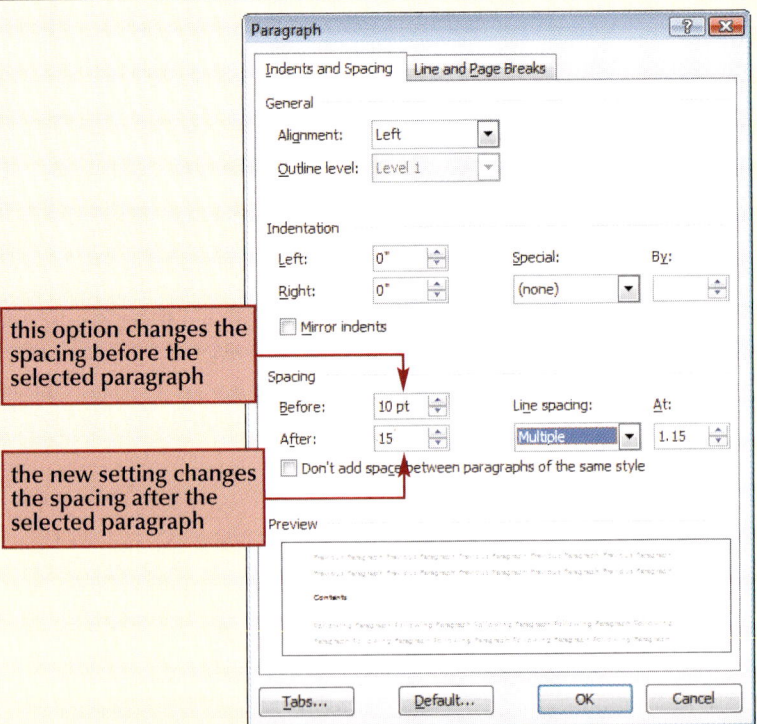

▶ **6.** Click the **OK** button. The Paragraph dialog box closes. Notice that there is now a little extra space below the Contents heading and above the paragraph of body text that says "[Insert a table of contents.]."

Adding Space Before or After a Paragraph | InSight

You might be tempted to increase the space before or after a paragraph by pressing the Enter key to insert a blank paragraph. However, inserting blank paragraphs in a document is rarely a good idea. For one thing, inserting a blank paragraph after a heading prevents Word from keeping a heading and its body text together when they span page or column breaks. Also, if you insert a blank paragraph, and then later increase the paragraph spacing in the entire document, you may end up with more blank space in the document than you really want. As a rule, using the Line spacing button in the Paragraph group on the Home tab or using the Paragraph dialog box gives you much more control over spacing before and after paragraphs. Make it a habit to use these options rather than inserting blank paragraphs.

Updating a Style to Match Selected Text

Now that the selected text is formatted the way you want, you can modify the Heading 1 style to match the selected text. As mentioned earlier, to modify a style, you select text formatted with the style you want to modify, apply new formatting, and then save your changes to the style. When saving the style, you need to decide whether you want to save the style to the current document or to the current template. If Sam modified the Heading 1 style and saved it to the current template, the modified version of the Heading 1 style would appear in all new documents based on the Equity Report template (the template his document is based on). However, Sam doesn't want to alter the Equity Report template. So in this case, it makes sense to save the modified version of the Heading 1 style just to the current document. You'll start by opening the Styles window.

Modifying Styles | Reference Window

- In the Styles group on the Home tab, click the Dialog Box Launcher to open the Styles window.
- In the document, select text formatted with the style you want to modify.
- Format the selected text with the font, paragraph, and other formatting you want.
- With the text still selected in the document, move the mouse pointer over the style you want to modify in the Styles window. A down arrow appears next to the style's name in the Styles window.
- Click the down arrow next to the style's name.
- To save the modified style to the current document, click Update *Style Name* to Match Selection (where *Style Name* is the name of the style you want to modify).
- To save the modified style to the current template, click Modify to open the Modify Style dialog box, click the New documents based on this template option button, and then click the OK button.

The **Styles window** displays a complete list of all the document's styles and provides easy access to the relevant commands. If you're doing a lot of work with styles in a document, it's often easier to use the Styles window rather than the Quick Styles gallery. You open the Styles window with the Dialog Box Launcher in the Styles group on the Home tab. You can click a style in the Styles window to apply it to selected text, just as you would click a style in the Quick Styles gallery.

To open the Styles window and modify the Heading 1 style:

1. In the Styles group on the Home tab, click the Dialog Box Launcher. The Styles window opens. It might be located on the right or left side of the document window, floating over the document text, or it might be locked on the right side, in which case the document window has been resized to accommodate it. In the following step, you will lock the Styles window on the right side of the document window, if it isn't there already.

2. Click the title bar of the Styles window, and then drag the Styles window to the right as far as you can, almost as if you are going to drag it off the screen. The Styles window snaps in place on the right side of the screen, and the document window resizes accordingly. The blue outline around the Heading 1 style in the Styles window tells you that the text currently selected in your document, the Contents heading, is formatted with the Heading 1 style—even though you've made several changes to that heading. See Figure 5-17.

| **Figure 5-17** | **Styles window** |

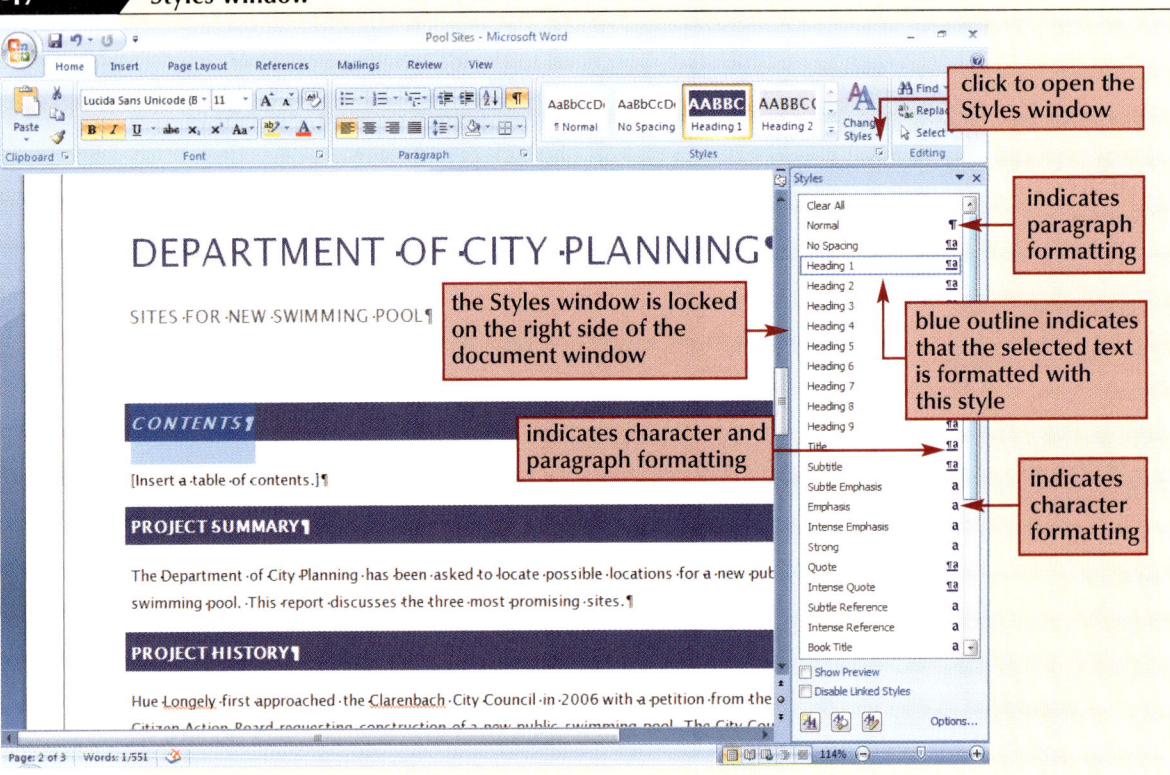

The Styles window contains a complete list of all the styles available in the document, along with some helpful commands and buttons. You can apply styles from the Styles window, just as you would from the Quick Styles gallery; just select the text you want to format and click a style in the Styles window.

Using the Styles Window

There are a lot of advantages to using the Styles window instead of the Quick Styles gallery. First, the Styles window includes styles that are not displayed in the Quick Styles gallery. Also, in the Styles window, styles are listed alphabetically, making it easier to locate a specific style in a document that contains lots of styles. So if you are looking for a style and can't find it in the Quick Styles gallery, check the Styles window. Another advantage of the Styles window is that it remains open until you close it. This makes the Styles window easier to use than the Quick Styles gallery when you need to apply a lot of styles. Finally, the symbols next to each style in the Styles window allow you to see quickly if a style is considered a paragraph style, a character style, or both.

Note that a paragraph symbol to the right of a style name in the Styles window indicates that the style applies paragraph formatting—such as line spacing, indentation, a border, and so on. A lowercase letter "a" to the right of a style name indicates the style applies character formatting—such as bold, italics, or a particular font size. Styles with both symbols next to their names apply both character and paragraph formatting. As you'll see in the following steps, you can display even more information about a style by moving the mouse pointer over the style's name in the Styles window.

To use the Styles Window to modify the Heading 1 style:

▶ **1.** In the Styles window, move the mouse pointer over **Heading 1**. A blue box with detailed information about the Heading 1 style appears, and a down arrow appears next to the style. Note that this information makes no mention of italics because, although you added italics to the "Contents" heading, you haven't yet altered the Heading 1 style itself. The information in this box relates only to the Heading 1 style.

▶ **2.** Click the **Heading 1** down arrow. A menu opens with options related to working with the Heading 1 style. The first option on the menu modifies the Heading 1 style to match the selected text and saves the newly modified style to the current document. To open a dialog box where you can save the modified style to the current template instead, you click the Modify option. Sam wants to save the newly modified Heading 1 style to the current document, so you'll use the first option. See Figure 5-18.

Figure 5-18 | **Modifying the Heading 1 style**

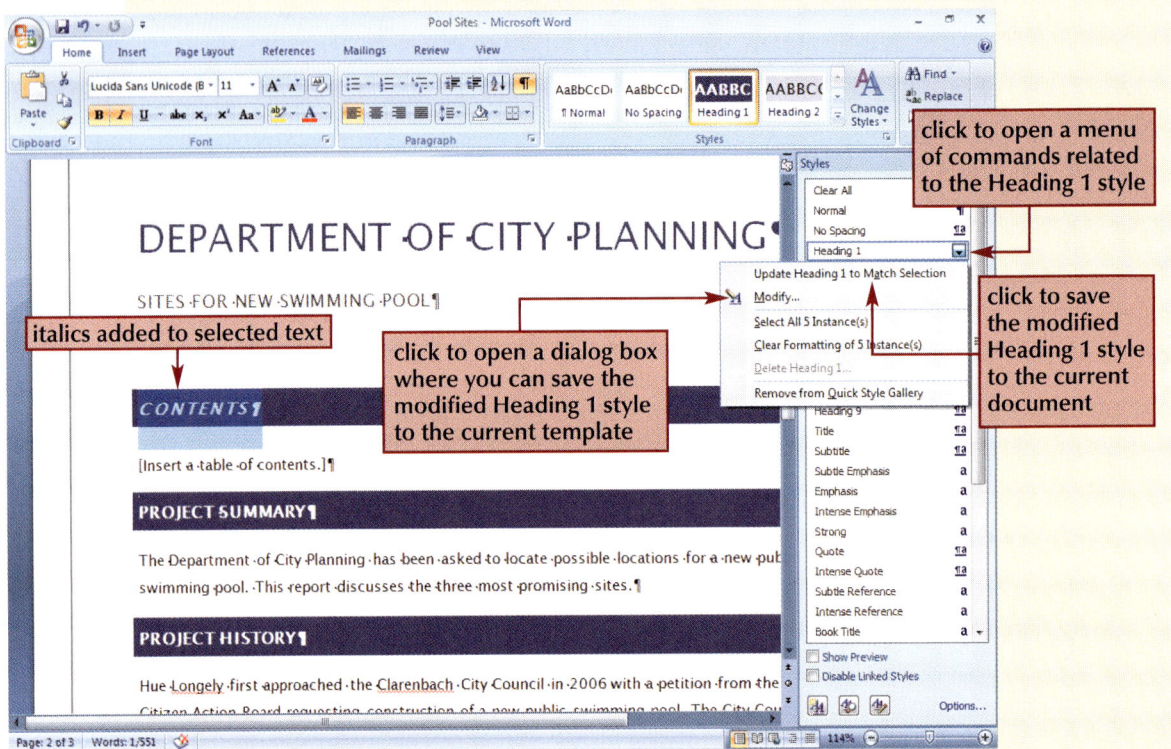

> **3.** Click **Update Heading 1 to Match Selection**. The Heading 1 style changes to include expanded character spacing, italics, and additional paragraph spacing— all the changes Sam asked you to make to the Contents heading. All the headings in the document formatted in the Heading 1 style are now formatted this way as well, and any other text you format with the Heading 1 style in this document will also have the italics, expanded character spacing, and additional paragraph spacing.

> **4.** Save your work. The modified version of the Heading 1 style is saved along with the document. No other documents are affected by this change to the Heading 1 style.

You've successfully modified the Heading 1 style by adding italics and by expanding its character and paragraph spacing. Next, you will create a new style to be used for the Project Summary heading, because it's helpful to set off a summary and its heading from the rest of a report.

Creating a New Style

When creating a new style, you have two important choices. First, as when modifying styles, you need to decide whether to save the style to the current document or to the current template. Second, you need to decide whether you want to base your new style on an existing style or create a new style from scratch.

When you base a new style on an existing style, you modify a style, as explained in the preceding section, and then, instead of updating the style to match your changes, you save the style with a new name. For example, suppose you modify the Heading 1 style by removing the bold formatting, and then save the modified style with the name "Budget," so that you can use it exclusively for formatting a "Budget" heading. A new style created in this way is called a **linked style**, because it remains linked to the style on which it is based; changes to the original style also affect the new style. This means that if you change the font for the Heading 1 style to Algerian, the font for the new Budget style would also change to Algerian. Note that the opposite is not true: changes to the new style do *not* affect the style on which it is based.

If you instead choose to create a new style from scratch—that is, if you create a style that is not based on any existing styles—the new style has no connection to any other styles. This usually isn't a good idea, because it prevents Word from enforcing the kind of formatting consistency that is possible with linked styles. As you'll see later in this tutorial, creating a style from scratch is especially troublesome in long documents, where you might want to work in Outline view.

Creating a New Style | Reference Window

- In the Styles group on the Home tab, click the Dialog Box Launcher to open the Styles window.
- Select text formatted with the style that most closely resembles the new style you want to create.
- Format the selected text with the font and paragraph formatting you want.
- In the lower-left corner of the Styles window, click the New Style button to open the Create New Style from Formatting dialog box.
- Type a name for the new style in the Name text box.
- The Style based on list box tells you which existing style the new style will be based on. If you don't want to base the new style on an existing style, click the Style based on arrow, and then click (no style).
- To save the new style to the current document, verify that the Only in this document option button is selected, and then click the OK button.
- To save the style to the current template, click the New documents based on this template option button, and then click the OK button.
- To delete a style you have created, point to the style's name in the Styles window, click the down arrow next to the style's name, click Revert to *Style Name*, (where *Style Name* is the style it was based on), and then click Yes.

Sam is ready to create a new style for the Project Summary heading. The new style will be based on the Heading 1 style. It will look just like the Heading 1 style, except that it will be not be in all uppercase (capital) letters, and it will include an underline. You'll start by selecting the text you want to format.

To format the Project Summary heading in uppercase and lowercase, with an underline:

1. Select the **Project Summary** heading. A quick way to change uppercase letters to lowercase, or vice versa, is to use the Change Case button in the Font group on the Home tab. However, in the next step you'll use the Font dialog box instead, because there you can apply a shadow effect at the same time.

2. In the Font group on the Home tab, click the Dialog Box Launcher, and then, in the Font dialog box, click the **Font** tab if necessary.

3. In the Effects section, click the **All caps** check box to remove the checkmark, click the **Underline style** arrow, scroll to the bottom of the list, and select the double-wavy underline style. The Preview section of the Font dialog box displays a preview of the new formatting. See Figure 5-19.

Figure 5-19

Formatting the Project Summary heading

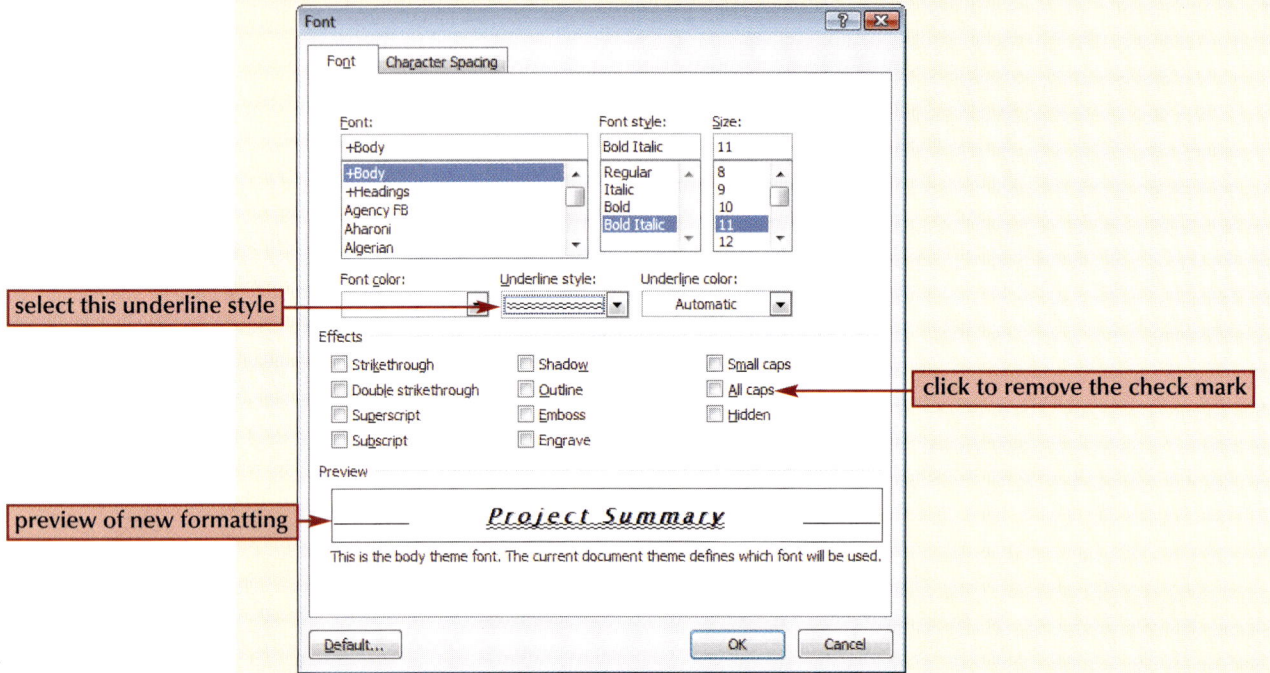

> **4.** Click the **OK** button. The Font dialog box closes.

> **5.** Click anywhere in the document to deselect the "Project Summary" heading so you can clearly see its new formatting.

Now that the text is formatted the way you want, you can create the new style.

To create a new style for the Project Summary heading:

> **1.** Select the **Project Summary** heading, and then verify that the Styles window is still open.

> **2.** In the lower-left corner of the Styles window, click the **New Style** button ⊞. The Create New Style from Formatting dialog box opens. A default name for the new style, "Style1," appears in the Name text box. In the next step, you will change the default name to something more meaningful.

> **3.** In the **Name** text box, select the default name, if necessary, and then type **Summary**. The default style name is replaced with the new one. The Style based on list box tells you that the new Summary style is based on the Heading 1 style, which is what you want. See Figure 5-20.

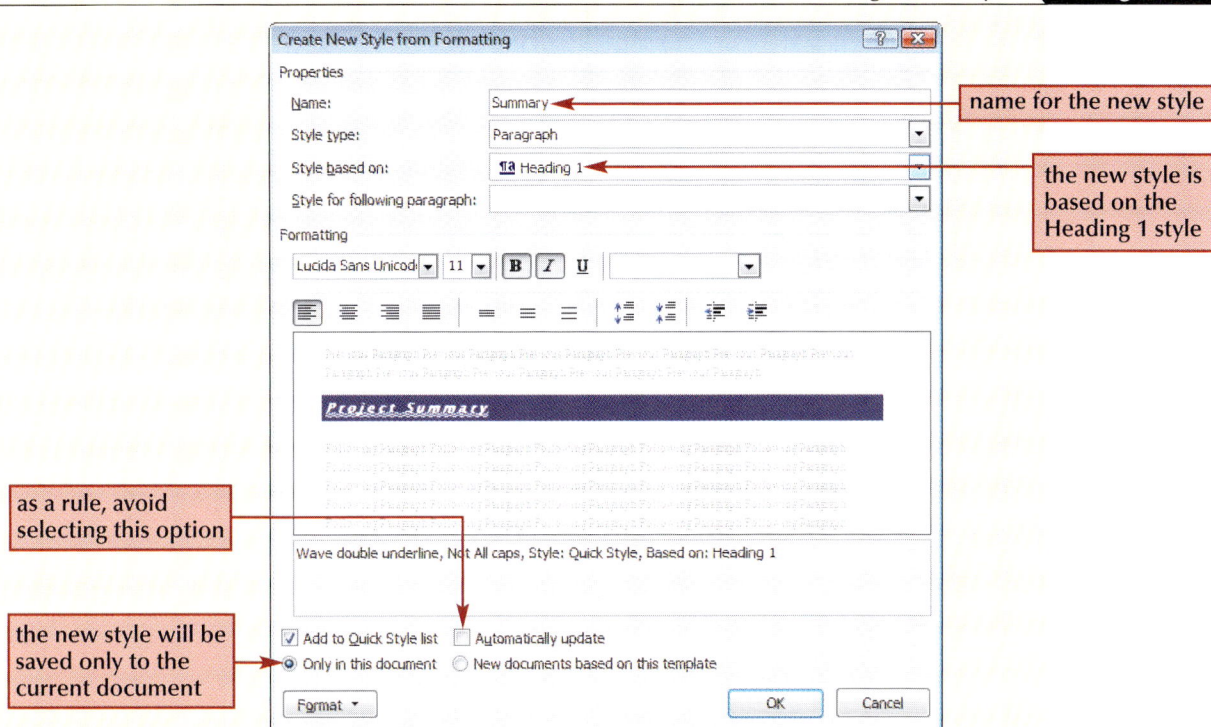

name for the new style

the new style is based on the Heading 1 style

as a rule, avoid selecting this option

the new style will be saved only to the current document

If you wanted to make the new style available to all future documents based on the current template, you would click the New documents based on this template option button. However, you want to save the new Summary style only to the current document, so you will accept the default setting, with the Only in this document option button selected. Note that, by default, the Automatically update check box is *not* selected. As a general rule, you should never select this check box. If you do select it, subsequent changes to the Summary style in future documents will be automatically updated in all documents based on the same template. This can produce unpredictable results and introduce problems that you might have difficulty resolving.

▶ **4.** Click the **OK** button. The Create New Style from Formatting dialog box closes. The new Summary style is added to the Quick Styles gallery and to the Styles window. If Sam needs to format additional headings with this new style, he can access it in either location. See Figure 5-21.

Summary style added to Quick Styles gallery and Styles window   Figure 5-21

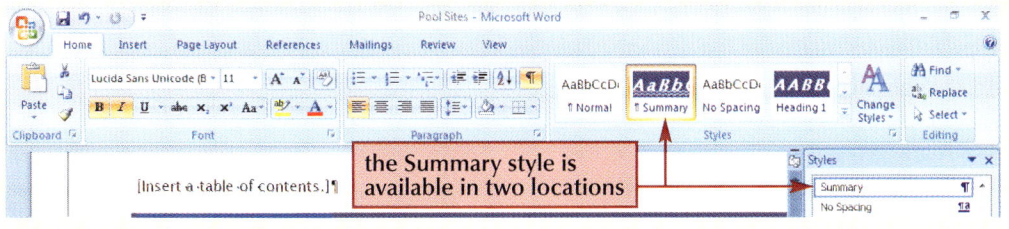

the Summary style is available in two locations

▶ **5.** Save the document.

Although it's possible create a new style that is not based on any other style, it's rarely a good idea. The link between a new style and the style it is based on ensures that changes affecting the overall look of a document are made consistently throughout the document. For example, suppose that, after creating his new Summary style, Sam decides to add extra paragraph spacing above and below the headings in the Pool Sites document. He can do that by modifying the Heading 1 style. Because his new Summary style is based on the Heading 1 style, the new paragraph spacing will automatically apply to the Summary style, thus enforcing a consistent appearance among all headings in the document. Another advantage to basing a new style on an existing style has to do with using Outline view. As you will see later in this tutorial, basing a new style on an existing style ensures that all the headings appear in the proper level in the document's outline.

Comparing Styles with the Reveal Formatting Window

If you create a document with many new or modified styles, it's easy to lose track of the formatting associated with each style. To see a quick comparison of two styles, you can use the **Reveal Formatting window**. In the following steps, you'll use the Reveal Formatting window to compare the Normal style to the Subtitle style in the document.

To compare the Heading 1 style to the Subtitle style using the Reveal Formatting window:

1. Click in the left margin to select the **[Insert a table of contents.]** paragraph.

2. At the bottom of the Styles window, click the **Style Inspector** button ⌨. The Style Inspector window opens, displaying options that allow you to quickly inspect the formatting associated with a particular style. In most situations, you'll find the Reveal Formatting window more useful, so you'll open that next.

3. At the bottom of the Style Inspector window, click the **Reveal Formatting** button ⌨. The Reveal Formatting window opens, displaying information about the style applied to the text that is currently selected in the document. Your Reveal Formatting window and Style Inspector windows might be positioned as in Figure 5-22, or they might be located elsewhere in the document window. Their position is unimportant.

Reveal Formatting window ◀ **Figure 5-22**

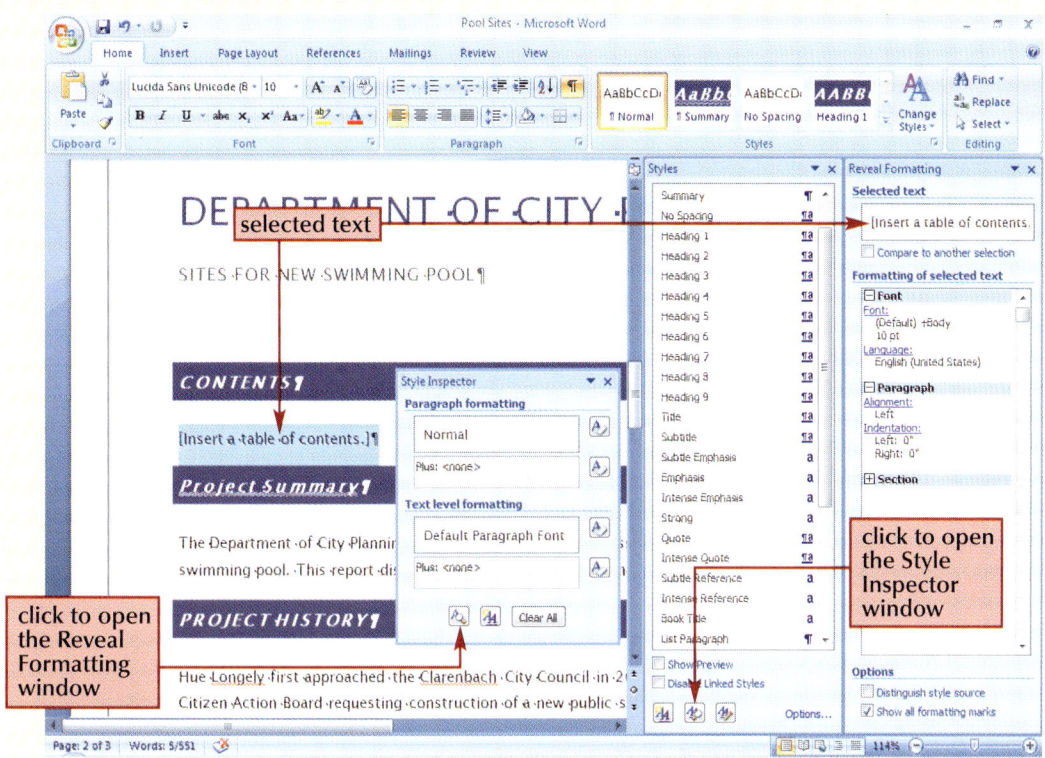

▶ **4.** In the Reveal Formatting window, click the **Compare to another selection** check box to select it. The options in the Reveal Formatting window change to allow you to compare one style to another. Under Selected text, both text boxes display copies of the text that is currently selected in the document, "[Insert a table of contents.]" This tells you that, currently the Normal style, the style applied to the text "[Insert a table of contents.]," is being compared to itself. In the next step, you'll compare the Normal style to the Subtitle style.

▶ **5.** In the document, click in the left margin to select the text **SITES FOR NEW SWIMMING POOL**, which is formatted with the Subtitle style. The text "SITES FOR NEW SWIMMING POOL" appears in the Reveal Formatting window, in the text box below "[Insert a table of contents.]" The Formatting differences section displays information about the styles to the two different text samples. This information is divided into two sections, Font and Paragraph. The information in the Reveal Formatting can sometimes be hard to interpret. But generally, if you see two settings separated by a hyphen and a greater than sign (->),the setting on the left relates to the top text box, and the item on the right relates to the bottom text box. For example, in the Font section, you see "10pt -> 12 pt." This tells you that the item in the top text box, "[Insert a table of contents.]," is formatted in a 10-point font, whereas the item in the bottom text box, "SAMPLE TEXT," is formatted in a 12-point font. See Figure 5-23.

Tip

Text formatted in a white font, such as the Contents heading, is not visible in the text boxes at the top of the Reveal Formatting window. To use the Reveal Formatting window with white text, temporarily format it in black.

Figure 5-23 | Comparing two styles

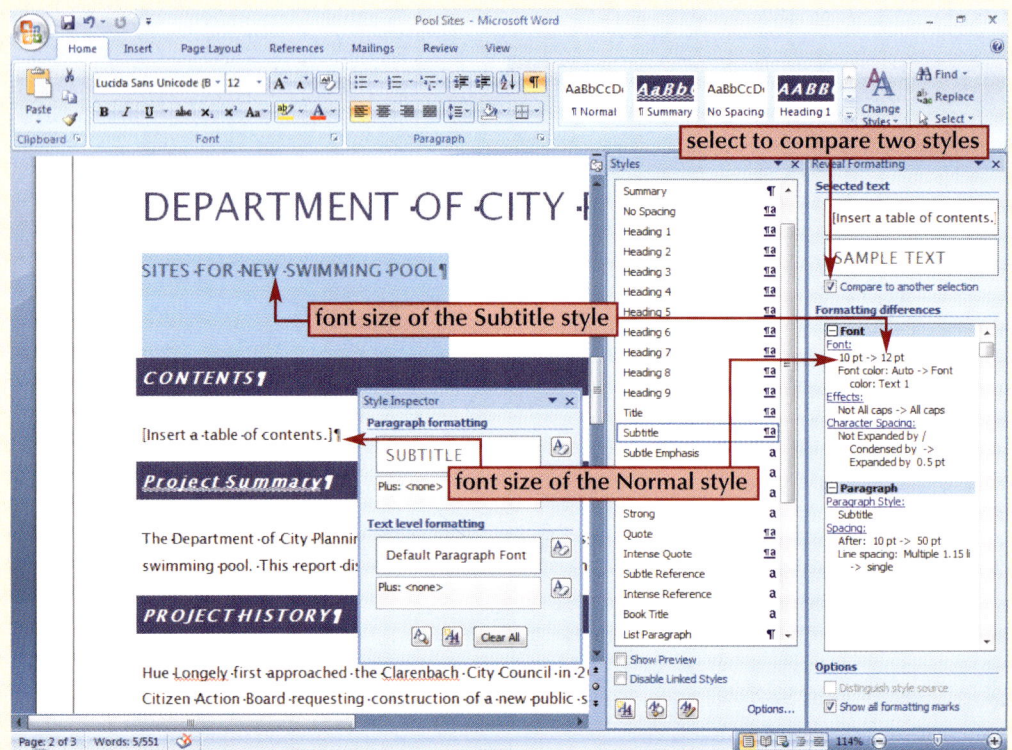

6. Click the **Close** button ☒ in the title bars of the Style Inspector window, the Reveal Formatting window, and the Styles window to close them. The document window readjusts, displaying the document at Page width zoom.

You are finished formatting the Pool Sites document. Sam likes its appearance so much that he would like to be able to reuse its formatting in the future reports issued by his department. To do that, you need to save the Pool Sites document as a template.

Saving a Document as a Template

If you know you'll often need to create a particular type of document, it's a good idea to create your own template for that type of document. In this case, Sam wants to create a template that will be used for all reports issued by the Department of City Planning. When creating a template, you can save it to any folder on the computer. However, if you save it to the Templates folder that is installed with Word, you can easily open the template later by clicking My templates in the New Document dialog box.

Saving a Document as a Template

- Click the Office Button, point to Save As, and then click Word Template.
- Navigate to the folder in which you want to save the template. To save the template to the Templates folder that is installed as part of Word, click the Templates folder under "Favorite Links."
- In the File name text box, type a name for the template.
- Click the Save button.

In the following steps, you will save the new template in the Tutorial folder for Tutorial 5, so that you can easily submit the completed tutorial files to your instructor. You'll start by saving the Pool Sites document again, just in case you didn't earlier.

To save the Pool Sites document as a new template:

1. Save the Pool Sites document.

2. Click the **Office Button** 🔘 , point to **Save As**, and then click **Word Template**. The Save As dialog box opens, with Word Template selected in the Save as type list box.

3. If necessary, navigate to the Tutorial.05\Tutorial included with your Data Files. You'll type the new filename next using "DCP," the acronym for "Department of City Planning," in the filename.

4. Delete the default filename in the File name text box, and then type **DCP Report**. See Figure 5-24.

Saving a document as a template ◀ **Figure 5-24**

5. Click the **Save** button. The Save As dialog box closes, and the document, which is now a template with the .dotx file extension, remains open.

To make the new DCP Report template really useful, you need to delete the specific information related to the Pool Sites report and replace it with placeholder text explaining what type of information is required in each section. You'll start by editing the document controls on page 1. Then you will delete the body of the report and replace it with some placeholder text that Sam has already typed and saved as a separate Word document.

To replace the Pool Sites report information with placeholder text:

▶ **1.** Scroll up to page 1. Sam wants to use the current title, "Department of City Planning," as the title in all department reports, so there's no need to change it. However, the subtitle will vary from one report to the next, so you need to replace it with a suitable placeholder.

▶ **2.** Delete the subtitle "Sites for New Swimming Pool," and then type **[Insert subtitle here.]** as a replacement. Be sure to include the brackets, so Sam's co-workers will quickly see that this is placeholder text.

▶ **3.** Scroll down, if necessary, so you can see the date, select the date in the date control, delete it, and then type **[Select current date.]** as a replacement. You'll leave your name in the Author control, so you can find the template later when you print it.

▶ **4.** Scroll down to page 2 and notice that the new subtitle placeholder has been inserted in the subtitle control at the top of page 2. Also, the placeholder for the date has been inserted in the vertical footer on the lower-left side of the page.

▶ **5.** Click in the left margin to select the **Project Summary** heading, drag down to select the remainder of the document, and press the **Delete** key. Deleting the text deleted some of the formatting codes that are included as hidden text in a Word document. (You can't see these codes, but they control the way the document is formatted.) As a result, the text "[Insert a table of contents.]" is now formatted in the Heading 1 style. You need to change it back to the Normal style.

▶ **6.** Verify that the insertion point is located within the paragraph containing the text "[Insert a table of contents.]," and then in the Quick Styles gallery in the Styles group, click the **Normal** style. The text returns to its original formatting.

▶ **7.** Press the **Enter** key to start a new paragraph. Now you are ready to insert a file containing placeholder text for the body of the report template.

▶ **8.** Click the **Insert** tab, in the Text group click the **Object** arrow, click **Text from File**, use the options in the Insert File dialog box to select the file **Placeholder** from the Tutorial.05\Tutorial folder included with your Data Files, and then click the **Insert** button. The placeholder text is inserted in the document. Scroll down to review the document and notice that the headings are all correctly formatted with the Heading 1 style. When Sam created the Placeholder document, he formatted the text in the default Heading 1 style provided by the Office theme. But when you inserted the file into the Pool Sites document, Word automatically reformatted the headings with your modified Heading 1 style. The only remaining issue is the "Project Summary" heading, which you need to format with the Summary style you created earlier.

▶ **9.** Click in the left margin to select the **Project Summary** heading, click the **Home** tab, and then in the Quick Styles gallery, click the **Summary** style. The heading is formatted with the wavy underline.

▶ **10.** Save your work and close the template.

The template you just created will simplify the process of creating new reports in Sam's department. In the next section, you'll have a chance to use the template as the basis of a new document.

| **Working Around Hidden Formatting Codes** | | InSight |

When you are working with a highly formatted document, you may sometimes encounter unexpected issues, such as in Step 5 in the preceding set of steps, when the Heading 1 style was applied to the text "[Insert a table of contents.]." Such problems are related to formatting codes that are included in a Word document, but which you can't normally see. Sometimes when you delete or insert a large amount of text, these hidden formatting codes are disrupted, causing unexpected results. Keep in mind that many hidden formatting codes are attached to the last paragraph symbol in a Word document. You can avoid formatting problems in a document by inserting a blank paragraph at the end of the document, and then taking care never to delete that last paragraph. Alternatively, if you encounter a formatting problem that you can't resolve, insert a blank paragraph at the end of the document, copy everything in the document except the last paragraph to a new document, and work with that new document instead.

Opening a New Document Based on Your Template

At this point, the new template is ready to be used by the Department of City Planning for all new reports. In fact, Sam would like to use it now to begin a report on possible sites for a new public library.

To begin a new document based on the DCP Report template:

▶ 1. Start Word, if necessary, click the **Office Button** 🔘, and then click **New**. The New Document dialog box opens.

▶ 2. In the Templates section on the left, click **My templates**. The New dialog box opens. If you had saved the DCP Report template to Word's Template folder, you would see an icon for it here. To open a new document based on the template, you could click the template's icon and then click the OK button. However, because you saved the DCP Reports template with your Data Files, you need to open it using a different method. See Figure 5-25.

Figure 5-25   New dialog box

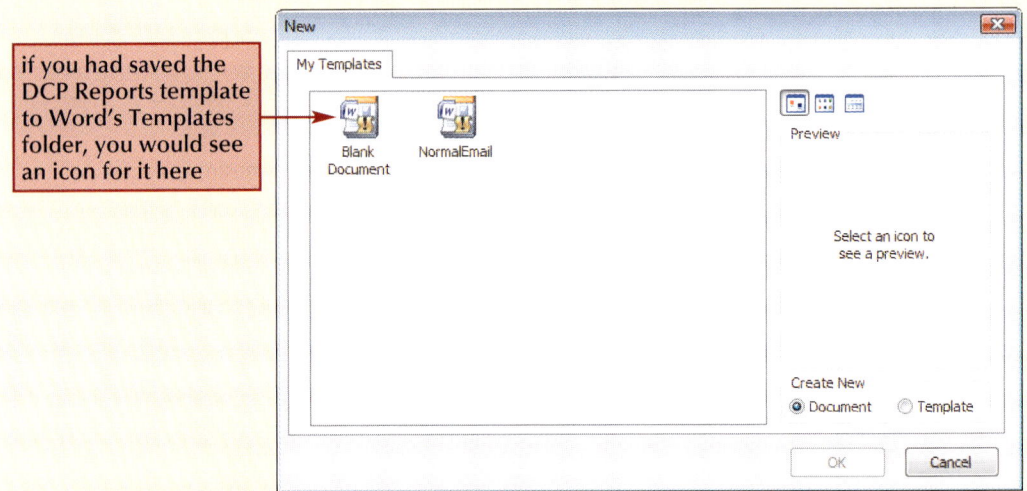

if you had saved the DCP Reports template to Word's Templates folder, you would see an icon for it here

▶ **3.** Click the **Cancel** button. The New dialog box closes, and you return to the New Document dialog box.

▶ **4.** On the left side of the New Document dialog box, under Templates, click **New from existing**. The New from Existing Document dialog box opens. This dialog box looks like the Open dialog box, which you have used many times before.

▶ **5.** If necessary, select the Tutorial.05\Tutorial folder included with your Data Files, click **DCP Report**, and then click the **Create New** button. A new document opens containing the text and formatting from the DCP Report template. The document is named "Document2" (or possibly "Document3" or "Document4," depending on whether Word was closed earlier in this tutorial). Changes you make to this new document will not affect the DCP Report template file, which remains untouched in the Tutorial.05\Tutorial folder.

▶ **6.** Delete the placeholder **[Insert subtitle here.]** on the cover page and type **Possible Sites for New Public Library**, and then click anywhere outside the Sub-title control to deselect it. That's all the work you need to do on the library report for now. Sam will finish it later. You can save the document with a new name and close it.

▶ **7.** Save the document as **Library Sites** in the Tutorial.05\Tutorial folder included with your Data Files.

   Trouble? If the Subtitle control displays the placeholder text "[Insert subtitle here.]" after you save the document, you didn't deselect the control before saving the document. Retype the subtitle, deselect the control, and save your changes to the document.

▶ **8.** Preview the document, print it, and then close it.

1. True or False. By default, a new or modified style is saved only in the current document.
2. Explain the relationship between the themes installed with Word, style sets, and styles.
3. If you can't see the style you want in the Quick Styles gallery, where should you look?
4. Explain how to open a dialog box tab where you can adjust the character spacing for selected text.
5. Explain how to open a dialog box tab where you can add a specific amount of space below a selected paragraph.
6. Where can you see a quick comparison of two styles?
7. True or False. If you save a template to the Templates folder that is installed with Word, you can easily open the template later by clicking My templates in the New Document dialog box.

Session 5.3

Using Outline View

An **outline** is a list of the basic points of a document, usually organized into main topics and subtopics. Once you have formatted a document with heading styles, you can use these headings and Word's **Outline view** to display the various levels of headings as an outline. For instance, you can display only the Heading 1 headings, or the Heading 1 and Heading 2 headings, or all the text in the document, including text formatted with the Normal style. In fact, you can display and work with as many as nine levels of headings in Outline view. The top level heading (the Heading 1 style) is Level 1, with subheadings (Heading 2, Heading 3, etc.) labeled as Level 2, Level 3, and so on.

If your document contains a heading style that you created, that heading style is assigned to the same outline level as the style on which your heading style is based. For example, the "Project Summary" heading in the Pool Sites document is formatted in the Summary style you created, which is based on the Heading 1 style. That means the "Project Summary" heading appears as Level 1 in the outline, just like the other main headings in the document. A new heading style that is not based on any other heading style is assigned an outline level that is one level lower than the lowest heading style in the document. This is why it's much wiser to base a new heading style on an existing style, rather than creating new styles from scratch.

The purpose of Outline view is to simplify the process of reorganizing a document. Imagine a long document with many Level 1 headings, several Level 2 headings for each Level 1 heading, and body text below each heading. With Outline view, you can click a heading and move it below or above other headings; the subheadings and body text associated with the heading you are moving get moved along with the heading. This is a powerful tool when you are reorganizing a large document.

Outline view has several symbols and buttons that you use in viewing and reorganizing your document. An **outline symbol** is displayed to the left of each paragraph. An outline symbol in the shape of a plus sign indicates a heading with subordinate text below it, a minus sign indicates a heading without subordinate text, and an empty gray circle indicates body text (that is, text that is not formatted with a heading style). To select an entire section, you click the outline symbol next to that section's heading. To move a section after you select it, you click the Move Up or Move Down button on the Outlining tab, which is visible only in Outline view. You can also use buttons on the Outlining tab to change the precedence of headings. For instance, you might want to change a Level 1 heading to a Level 2 heading, or to change a Level 3 heading to a Level 1 heading.

Reference Window | **Creating and Editing Outlines**

- Format a document with heading styles, such as Heading 1, Heading 2, and so on.
- Click the Outline view button in the lower-right corner of the Word window.
- If necessary, select the Show Text Formatting check box in the Outline Tools group on the Outlining tab. This ensures that you can see the document formatting.
- Use the Show Level arrow in the Outline Tools group to display the desired number of headings. For example, to see only text formatted with heading styles 1 through 3, click Level 3. To see all the document text, including the body text, click All Levels.
- To select a section, click the Outline symbol next to the section's heading.
- To move a section, select the section, and then in the Outline Tools group, click the Move Up button or the Move Down button until the section is at the desired location.
- Use the Promote button or the Demote button in the Outline Tools group to increase or decrease the levels of headings.
- Click the Page Layout button to return to Page Layout view.

Sam wants to do some more work on the Pool Sites document. Specifically, he wants to reorganize some of the sections. Outline view is the perfect tool for this task. You'll start by reopening the Pool Sites document and reviewing its organization.

To open the Pool Sites document and review its organization:

▶ 1. Open the **Pool Sites** document from the Tutorial.05\Tutorial folder included with your Data Files.

▶ 2. If necessary, switch to Print Layout view, set the Zoom to Page width, and display nonprinting characters.

▶ 3. Review pages 2 and 3 so you are familiar with the report's structure. Notice that the headings "Breese Terrace Park," "Langbrook Farm," and "Flora Park," are formatted as subheadings below the "Project Description" heading.

Sam decides that the Flora Park section should appear before the Breese Terrace Park section. First you need to switch to Outline view and display the appropriate heading levels.

To switch to Outline view and view the outline levels:

▶ 1. Scroll up, if necessary, to display the first page of the document.

▶ 2. Click the **Outline** button ⊞ in the lower-right corner of the Word window. The document is displayed in Outline view, and the Outlining tab appears on the Ribbon. At this point, you may see all of the document, just some of the headings, or all of the document except for some of the headings. In the next two steps, you will check to make sure you can see the entire document.

3. If necessary, in the Outline Tools group on the Outlining tab, click the **Show Text Formatting** check box to remove the checkmark. When this check box is selected, Word displays the document headings in the same font, font color, and font size that you see in Page Layout view. Because the major headings in the Pool Sites document are formatted in a white font, you don't want to show the document formatting in Outline view, because you wouldn't be able to see the white text on the white background. With the Show Text Formatting check box deselected, all the text in Outline view is displayed in the body text font.

4. If necessary, in the Outlining tools group on the Outlining tab, click the **Show Level** arrow, and then click **All Levels**. This tells Word to display the entire document, including the headings and the body text. At this point, your document should look like the one in Figure 5-26.

Pool Sites document in Outline view | Figure 5-26

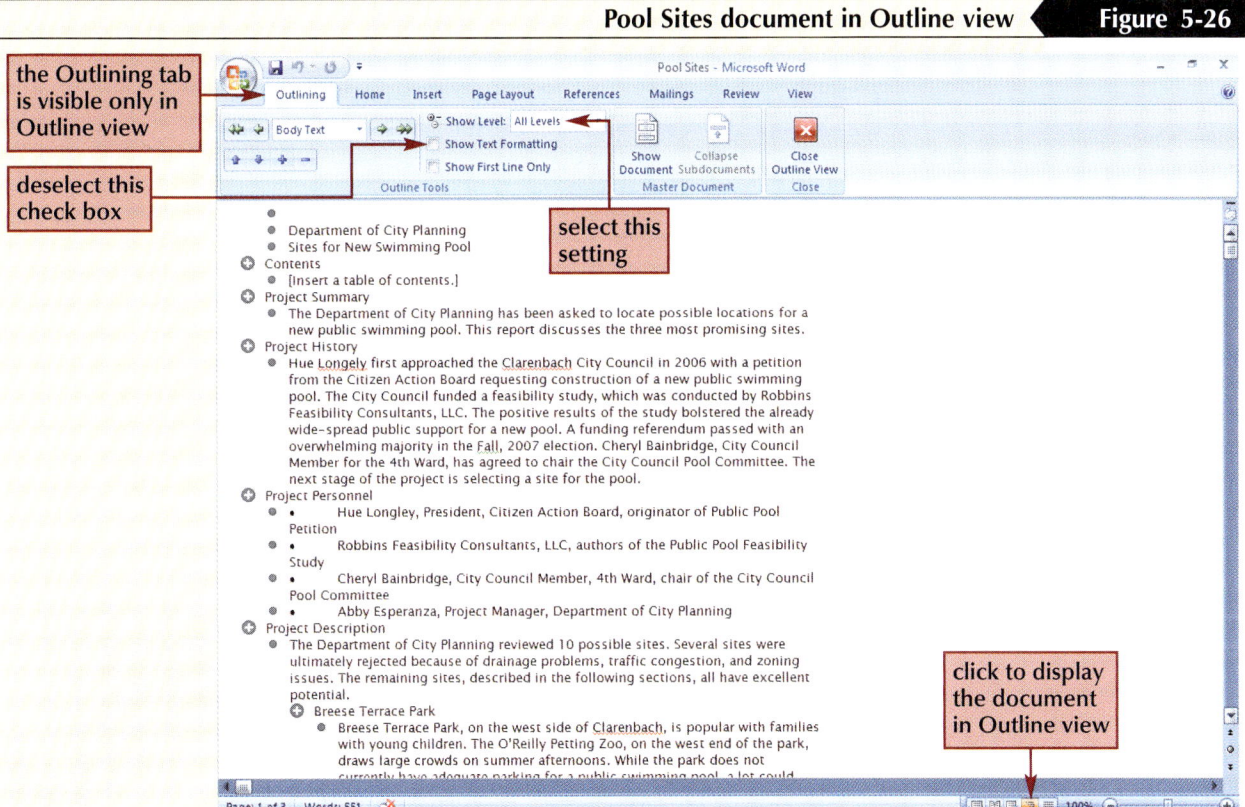

You can use the Show Level list box to display only the document headings. This is especially useful in long documents, because it allows you to see all the document headings at a glance, without having to scroll through several pages of body text. In the next step, you will display only the document headings.

5. In the Outline Tools group, click the **Show Level** arrow, and then click **Level 3**. You see only Level 1, Level 2, and Level 3 headings. In other words, you see only the text formatted with the Heading 1, Heading 2, and Heading 3 styles. Sam was concerned that he might have mistakenly applied the Heading 3 style to a heading that actually required the Heading 2 style. As you can see in Figure 5-27, he did make this mistake. You'll fix this problem later. Notice the plus sign next to each heading, indicating that the text is a heading with subordinate text. The gray lines represent text that is not currently visible.

Figure 5-27 Levels 1 through 3 displayed in Outline view

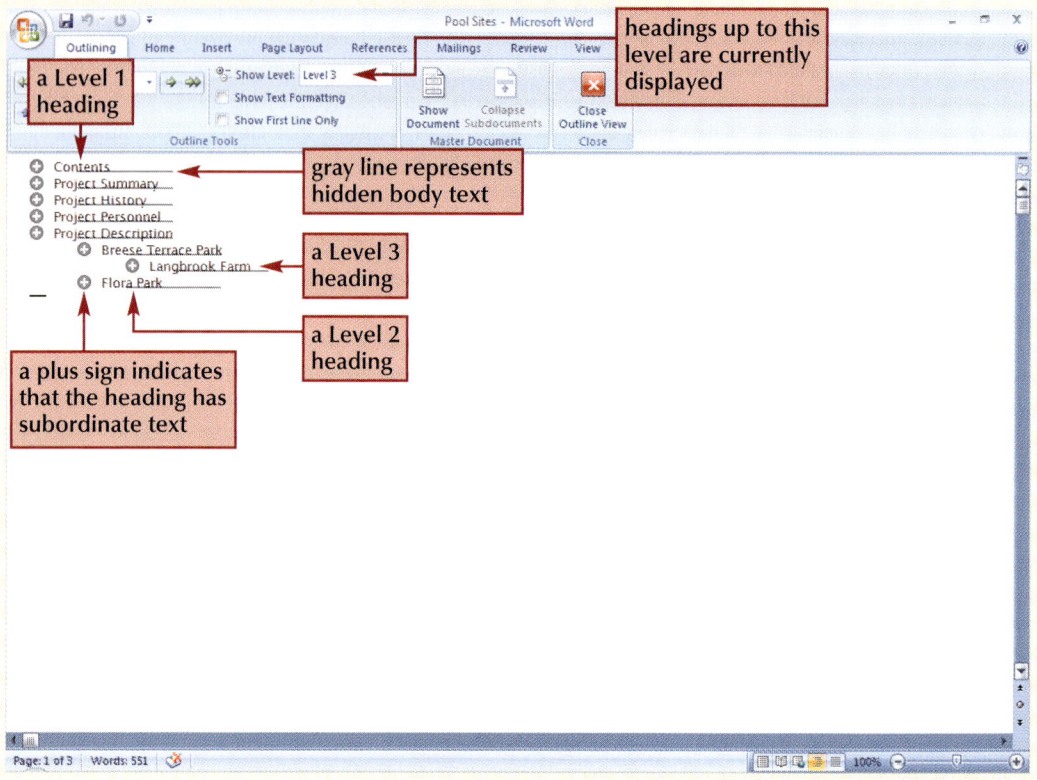

Now that you see only the document headings, you can reorder some headings and change the level of another.

Working with Headings in Outline View

When you move a heading in Outline view, any subordinate headings and all the text associated with those headings moves with the heading. In the following steps, you'll move the heading "Flora Park" so that it appears before the heading "Breese Terrace Park." As you work in Outline view, keep in mind that the Undo button reverses any mistakes, just as in Print Layout view.

To move the "Flora Park" heading and its subordinate text:

1. Double-click the **plus sign** ⊕ next to the heading "Flora Park." The subordinate text below the heading is now visible.

2. Double-click the **plus sign** ⊕ next to the heading "Flora Park" again. The subordinate text is again hidden.

3. Verify that the "Flora Park" heading and the paragraph mark following it are selected, and then click the **Move Up** button ⬆ in the Outline Tools group. The heading moves up above the heading "Langbrook Farm." Its subordinate text moved along with the heading, even though you can't see it.

4. Click the **Move Up** button ⬆ again. The "Flora Park" heading (and its subordinate text) move up above the heading "Breese Terrace Park." See Figure 5-28.

Heading moved to a new location in Outline view ◄ **Figure 5-28**

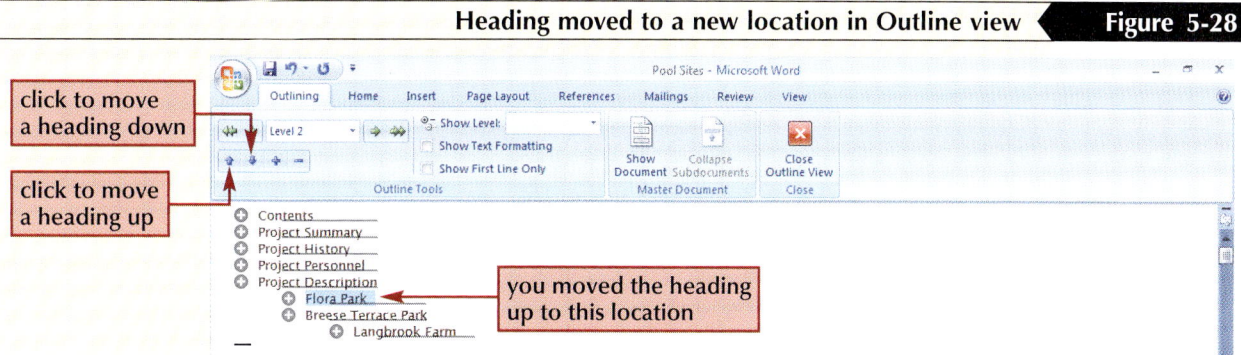

> **5.** Double-click the **plus symbol** ⊕ next to the heading "Flora Park," verify that the subordinate text did indeed move along with the heading, and then double-click ⊕ next to the heading "Flora Park" again to hide the subordinate text. Note that each time you click the Move Up button, the selected section moves up above the preceding section. To move a section down, you would use the Move Down button. Note that to select a section before moving it, you need to click the Outline symbol only once. You double-clicked it in these steps to display and then hide the subtext.

Tip

You can also use the mouse to drag selected headings up or down.

Now that the topics of the outline are in the desired order, you need to change the level of the Langbrook Farm heading, so it matches the level of the other two headings under "Project Description."

Promoting and Demoting Headings in an Outline

To **promote** a heading means to increase the level of a heading—for example, to change a Level 3 heading to a Level 2 heading. To **demote** a heading means to decrease the level—for example, to change a Level 1 heading to a Level 2 heading. When you promote or demote a heading in Outline view, the heading style applied to the heading changes accordingly. For example, if you promote a Level 3 heading to a Level 2 heading, the style applied to the heading changes from Heading 3 to Heading 2.

Sam wants to correct the error he made earlier by promoting the "Langbrook Farm" heading to a Level 2 heading.

To promote the Langbrook Farm heading:

> **1.** Click anywhere in the heading **Langbrook Farm**, and then in the Outline Tools group on the Outlining tab, click the **Promote** button ➡. (Take care not to click the Promote to Heading 1 button by mistake.) The heading moves left and becomes a Level 2 heading, formatted with the Heading 2 style. Note that demoting a heading in Outline view is similar to promoting a heading. You place the insertion point in the heading and click the Demote button. See Figure 5-29.

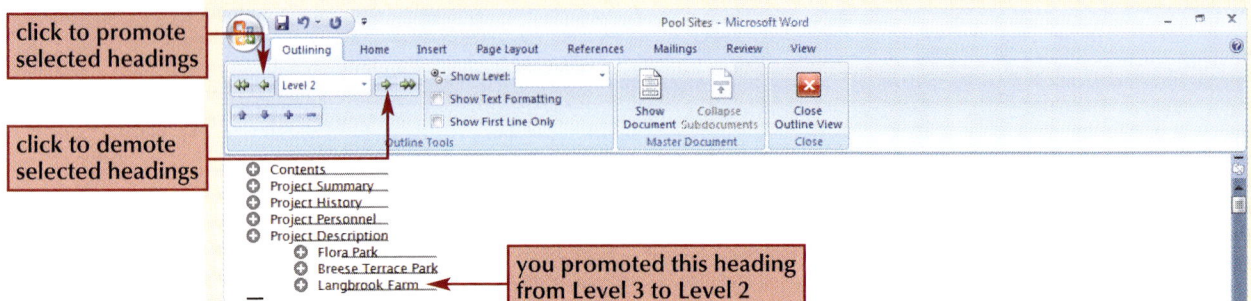

Figure 5-29 ▶ **Heading promoted in Outline view**

Trouble? If the "Langbrook Farm" heading moved all the way to the left margin, you clicked the Promote to Heading 1 button by mistake. Undo the change, and then repeat Step 1.

▶ **2.** Print the outline as you would print any other Word document.

▶ **3.** Return to Print Layout view, and then review the Project Description section and its subheadings. Note that the "Langbrook Farm" heading is formatted in the Heading 2 style, and that the Flora Park section now appears before the Breese Terrace Park section. However, the blank paragraph that was originally at the end of the document, after the Flora Park section, moved up along with the Flora Park section. You need to delete it.

▶ **4.** Click at the end of the Flora Park Section, press the **Delete** key to delete the blank paragraph, and then save your work.

Next, Sam would like to create a table of contents for his report.

> **Tip**
>
> It's important to review a document in Page Layout view after you make changes in Outline view, to make sure the document looks the way you expect.

Creating a Table of Contents

You can use Word to create a **table of contents** with page numbers for any paragraphs to which you have applied heading styles. The page numbers and headings in a table of contents in Word are actually hyperlinks that you can click to jump to a particular part of the document. If you add or delete text in the document later, and one or more headings move to a new page, you can quickly update the table of contents by clicking the Update Table button in the Table of Contents group on the References tab. After you create a table of contents, you can select additional text in the document and add it to the table of contents.

When inserting a table of contents, you can insert one of the predesigned formats available via the Table of Contents button in the Table of Contents group on the References tab. If you prefer to select from more options, you can open the Table of Contents dialog box.

Working with a Table of Contents

- Make sure you have applied heading styles such as Heading 1, Heading 2, and Heading 3 to the appropriate headings in your document.
- Move the insertion point to the location in the document where you want to insert the table of contents.
- Click the References tab, and then in the Table of Contents group, click the Table of Contents button. This opens the Table of contents menu.
- To insert a predesigned table of contents, click one of the Automatic table of contents styles in the Table of Contents menu.
- To open a dialog box where you can choose from an array of table of contents settings, click Insert Table of Contents in the Table of Contents menu, and then in the Table of Contents dialog box, click the Table of Contents tab if necessary. Click the Formats arrow and select a style, change the Show levels setting to the number of heading levels you want to include in the table of contents, verify that the Show page numbers check box is selected, and then click the OK button.
- To update a table of contents, click the Update Table button in the Table of Contents group on the References tab.
- To add text to a table of contents, select the text in the document, then in the Table of Contents group on the References tab, click the Add Text button. In the Add Text menu, click the level at which you want to insert the selected text, and then update the table of contents.
- To delete a table of contents, click the Table of Contents button, and then click Remove Table of Contents.

The current draft of Sam's report is fairly short, but the final document will be much longer. He asks you to create a table of contents for the report now, just after the "Contents" heading. Then, as Sam adds sections to the report, he can update the table of contents.

To insert the table of contents into the Pool Sites document:

1. Below the heading "Contents," select and delete the placeholder text **[Insert a table of contents.]**. Do not delete the paragraph mark after the placeholder text. When you are finished, your insertion point should be in the blank paragraph between the "Contents" heading and the "Project Summary" heading.

2. Click the **References** tab, and then in the Table of Contents group, click the **Table of Contents** button. The Table of Contents menu opens, displaying two Automatic table of contents formats, one Manual Table option, and two commands to insert and delete a table of contents. The Automatic options insert a table of contents made up of the first three levels of document headings, in a predefined format. Each of the Automatic options also includes a heading for the Table of Contents. Because Sam's document already contains the heading "Contents," you do not want to use either of the Automatic options. The Manual option is useful only if you need to type the table of contents yourself. In this case, you want to take advantage of the document headings and allow Word to build the table of contents for you, so you will use the Insert Table of Contents command at the bottom of the menu. See Figure 5-30.

Figure 5-30 **Table of Contents menu**

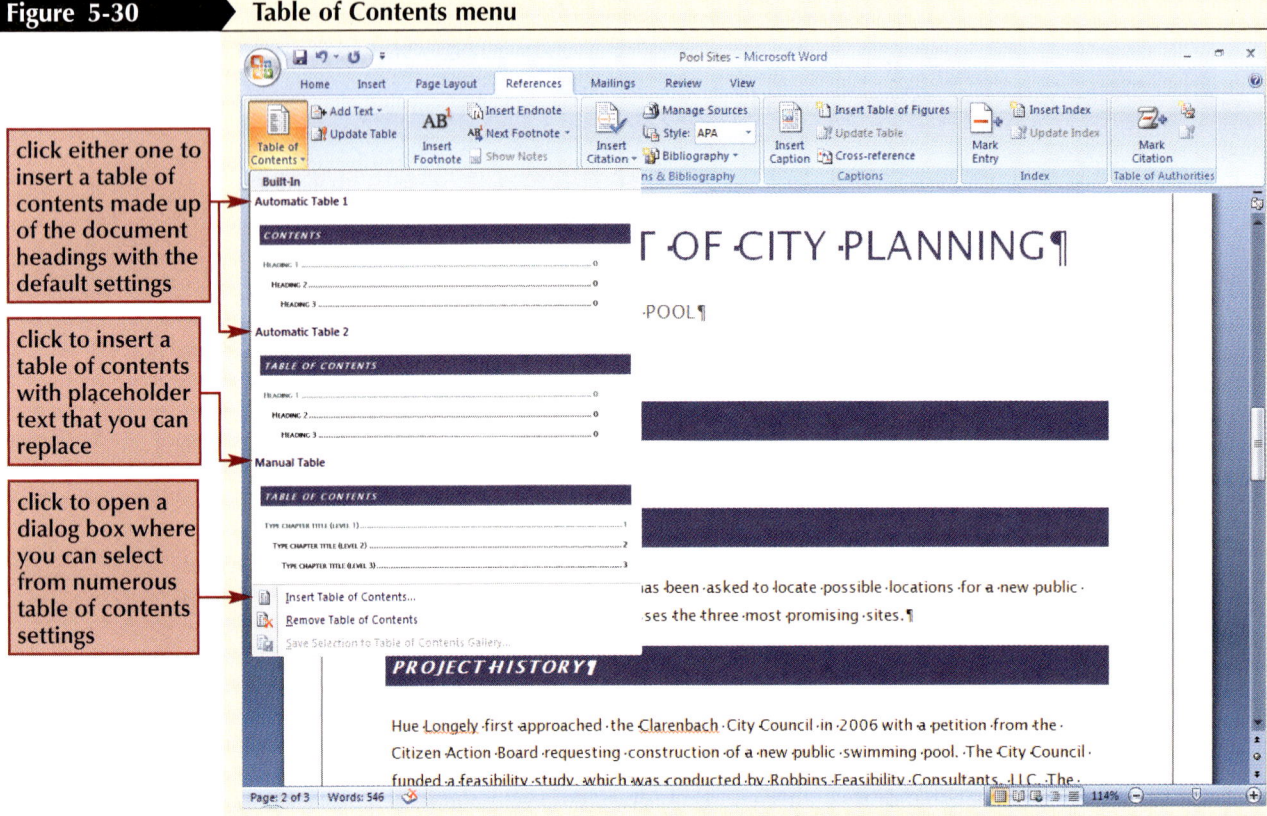

click either one to insert a table of contents made up of the document headings with the default settings

click to insert a table of contents with placeholder text that you can replace

click to open a dialog box where you can select from numerous table of contents settings

3. At the bottom of the Table of Contents menu, click **Insert Table of Contents**. The Table of Contents dialog box opens, with the Table of Contents tab displayed. The Formats list box allows you to select a format for your table of contents. The default option, From template, uses the styles provided by the document's template. In this case, you'll accept that default setting. Note that the Show page numbers check box is selected by default, so the table of contents will include a page number for each heading. Also by default, the "Use hyperlinks instead of page numbers" check box is selected. This setting means that Word will make each entry in the table of contents a hyperlink that links to the relevant section in the document. You can accept this default setting. Finally, you need to consider the Show levels headings. The document contains two levels of headings (Heading 1 and Heading 2). However, Sam might add some headings formatted in the Heading 3 style later, so you will leave the Show levels setting at 3. See Figure 5-31.

Table of Contents dialog box ◄ **Figure 5-31**

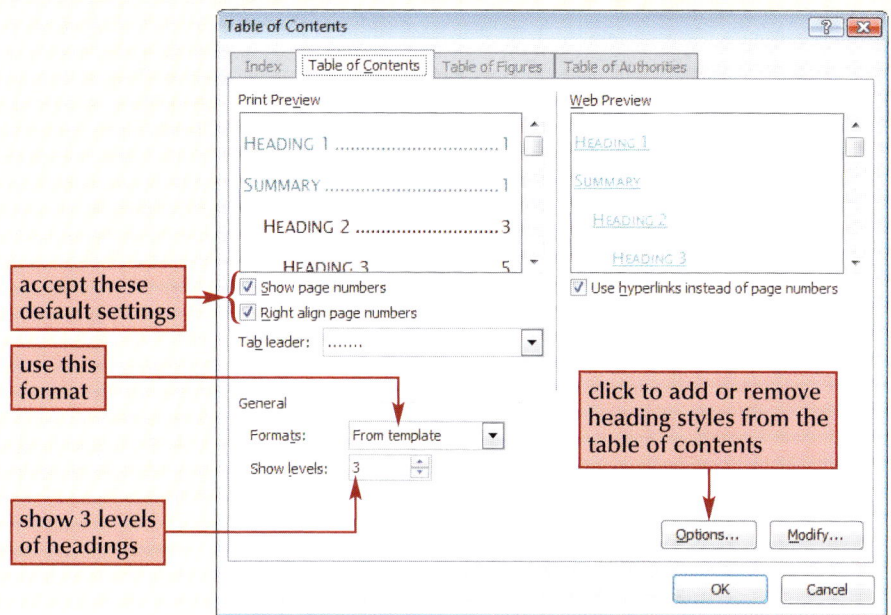

Sam knows that Word will compile the table of contents based on the heading styles in the document. But what about the Summary style, which you created earlier? Remember that the Summary style is based on the Heading 1 style, so Word will treat it as a heading of the same level as the Heading 1 style, just like in Outline view. To verify that this is true, you can check the heading levels by clicking the Options button.

▶ **4.** Click the **Options** button in the lower-right corner of the Table of Contents dialog box. The Table of Contents Options dialog box opens. The Styles check box is selected, indicating that Word will compile the table of contents based on the styles applied to the document headings.

▶ **5.** Use the vertical scroll in the TOC level list to see how the various styles in the document are assigned levels in the table of contents. (Note that "TOC" is short for "Table of Contents.") You can see that Heading 1 is assigned to Level 1, and Heading 2 is assigned to Level 2. Like Heading 1, the Summary style is also assigned to Level 1. If you wanted to change the level of a heading style, you could type a different number for it in the style's TOC level text box. To add a style to the table of contents, you could type a level number in the style's TOC level text box. See Figure 5-32.

Figure 5-32 ▶ **Checking the styles used in the table of contents**

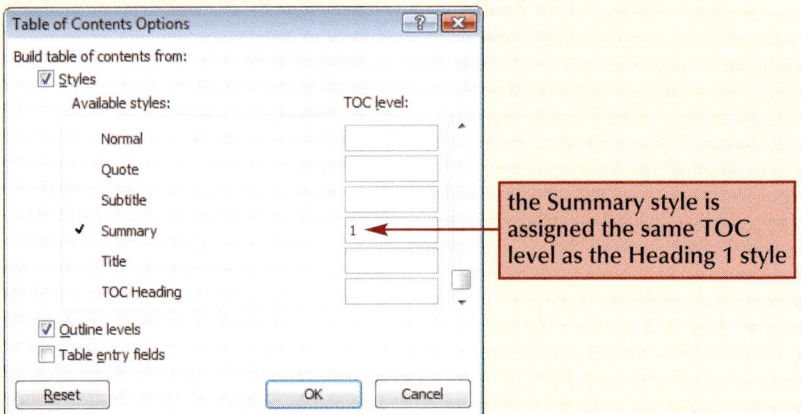

the Summary style is assigned the same TOC level as the Heading 1 style

The settings in the Table of Contents Options dialog box are all correct, so you can close it.

▶ **6.** Click the **Cancel** button to close the Table of Contents Options dialog box without making any changes.

▶ **7.** Click the **OK** button to accept the default settings in the Table of Contents dialog box. Word searches for text formatted with styles Heading 1, Heading 2, and Heading 3, and then places those headings and their corresponding page numbers in a table of contents. The table of contents is inserted below the "Contents" heading, where you placed the insertion point in Step 1. Depending on how your computer is set up, the table of contents might appear on a light gray background. See Figure 5-33.

Figure 5-33 ▶ **Table of contents inserted into document**

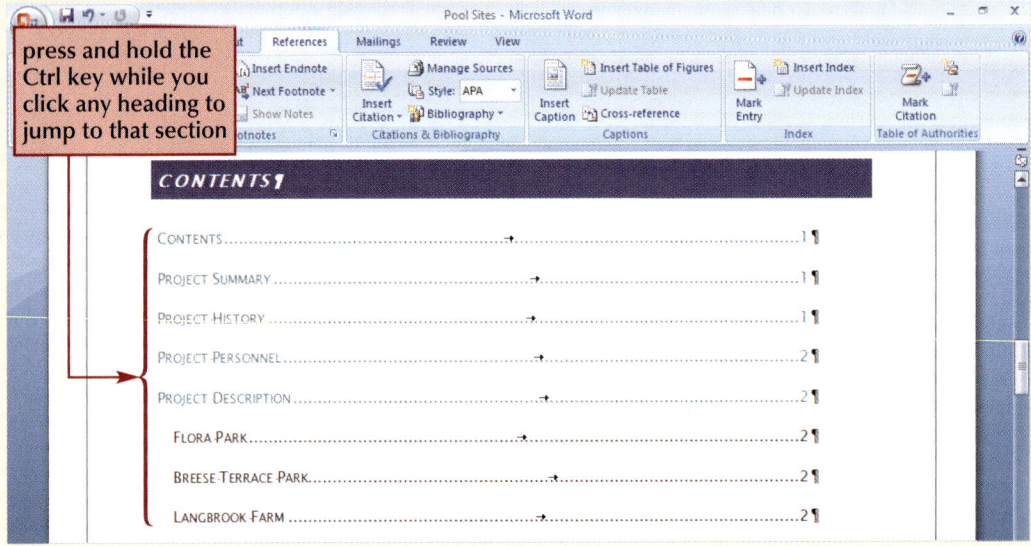

press and hold the Ctrl key while you click any heading to jump to that section

In the following step, you'll check the hyperlink formatting to make sure the headings really do function as links.

▶ **8.** Press and hold down the **Ctrl** key while you click **LANGBROOK FARM** in the table of contents. The Langbrook Farm section is displayed.

▶ **9.** Save the report.

Sam remembers that he needs to add a new section to the document describing another potential pool site. He's already typed the new section and saved it as a Word file. He asks you to insert it at the end of the Pool Sites document and then add the new heading to the table of contents. You can do this using the Add Text button in the Table of Contents group in the References tab. You start by selecting the text you want to add to the table of contents. Then you use the Add Text button in the Table of Contents group on the References tab to format the text in the appropriate heading level. Finally, you update the table of contents.

To add a section to the Pool Sites document, add the heading text to the table of contents, and update the table of contents:

▶ **1.** Press the **Ctrl+End** keys to move the insertion point to the end of the document, insert a new blank paragraph, and then insert the file **Vilas Grove** from the Tutorial.05\Tutorial folder included with your Data Files.

▶ **2.** Select the heading **Vilas Grove**.

▶ **3.** Click the **References** tab, and then, in the Table of Contents group on the References tab, click the **Add Text** button. The Add Text menu opens. See Figure 5-34.

Add Text menu | **Figure 5-34**

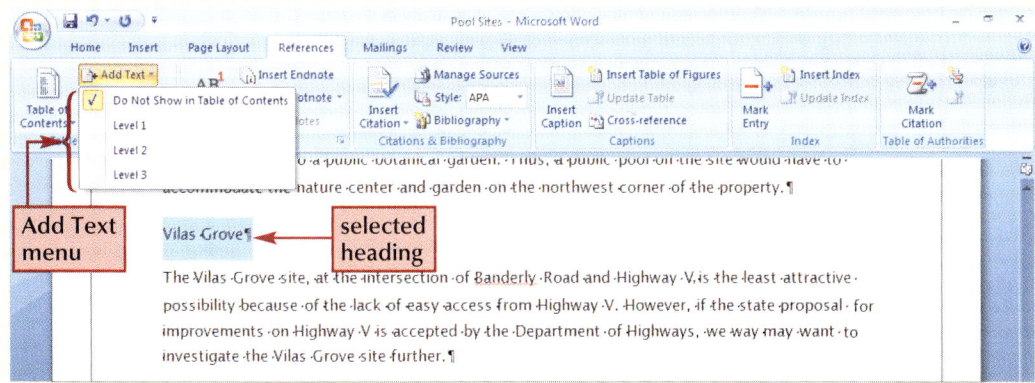

In the Add Text menu, you need to indicate at what level you want to insert the selected text in the table of contents.

▶ **4.** Click **Level 2**. The text is formatted with the Heading 2 style, to match the headings for the sections about the other possible pool sites. Now that the text is formatted with a heading style, you can update the table of contents.

▶ **5.** Scroll up so you can see the table of contents, and then in the Table of Contents group in the References tab, click the **Update Table** button. The Update Table of Contents dialog box opens. You can use the Update page numbers only option button if you don't want to update the headings in the table of contents. However, it's usually best to use the Update entire table option because it ensures that the table of contents is completely up to date.

▶ **6.** Click the **Update entire table** option button to select it, and then click the **OK** button. The table of contents is updated to include the Vilas Grove heading. See Figure 5-35.

Tip

You can also format new text with a heading style in the Quick Styles gallery, and then update the table of contents.

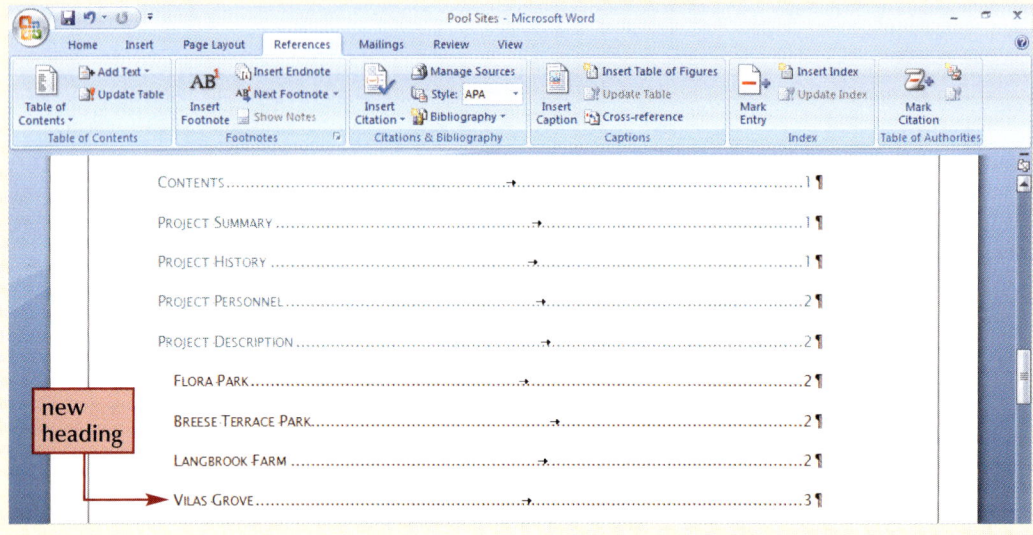
new heading

7. Save your work.

Sam is finished with the Pool Sites report for now, so you can print it and close it.

To print the document:

1. Preview the document, and then print it. If you see a dialog box asking about updating the table of contents, update the entire table.

2. Close the document.

Sam will continue work on the Pool Sites report later. Right now, he needs to do some research for another city project: an open-air theater.

Using the Research Task Pane

You can use the **Research task pane** to look up dictionary definitions and to search for synonyms in Word's thesaurus. In addition, you can search for information in online general interest encyclopedias and in sources devoted to particular topics, such as business and finance. If you prefer, you can use the MSN search engine to search the entire Web from the Research task pane. You can even use the Research task pane to translate a word or phrase into the language of your choice.

The Department of City Planning has been asked to evaluate a proposed open-air theater, which will be funded by a grant from a state arts organization. The proposal includes a number of theater-related terms. Sam wants to make sure he understands the term *proscenium* and decides to use Word's Research task pane to look it up in Encarta, the dictionary installed with Word. He also wants to experiment with looking up synonyms in Word's thesaurus.

To look up a definition in the Research task pane:

▶ **1.** Open the document named **Research** from the Tutorial.05\Tutorial folder and save it as **Theater Research** in the same folder. This document contains the terms you will look up, along with space to insert the results of your research.

▶ **2.** If necessary, set the Zoom to Page width and display nonprinting characters. To open the Research task pane, you need to switch to the Review tab.

▶ **3.** Click the **Review** tab, and then locate the Proofing group on the left side of the Review tab. The Research, Thesaurus, and Translate buttons in the Proofing group all open the Research task pane, although each with different options displayed. Once the Research task pane is open, you can easily switch among the various options, depending on whether you want to research a topic, look up a word in the thesaurus, or translate some text.

▶ **4.** In the Proofing group, click the **Research** button. The Research task pane opens on the right side of the document window. For starters, Sam wants to look up the word *proscenium*, one of the terms in the theater proposal.

▶ **5.** Delete any text in the Search for text box, and then type **proscenium**. Next, you need to specify where you want to search for information.

▶ **6.** In the list box that currently contains the text "All Reference Books," click the arrow to open a drop-down menu, and then click **Encarta Dictionary: English (North America)**. Two definitions of the term *proscenium* are displayed in the Research task pane. See Figure 5-36.

Tip

If you select a new reference source and don't see the information you expect in the Research task pane, click the green Start searching arrow at the top of the task pane to start the search.

Definitions displayed in the Research task pane   **Figure 5-36**

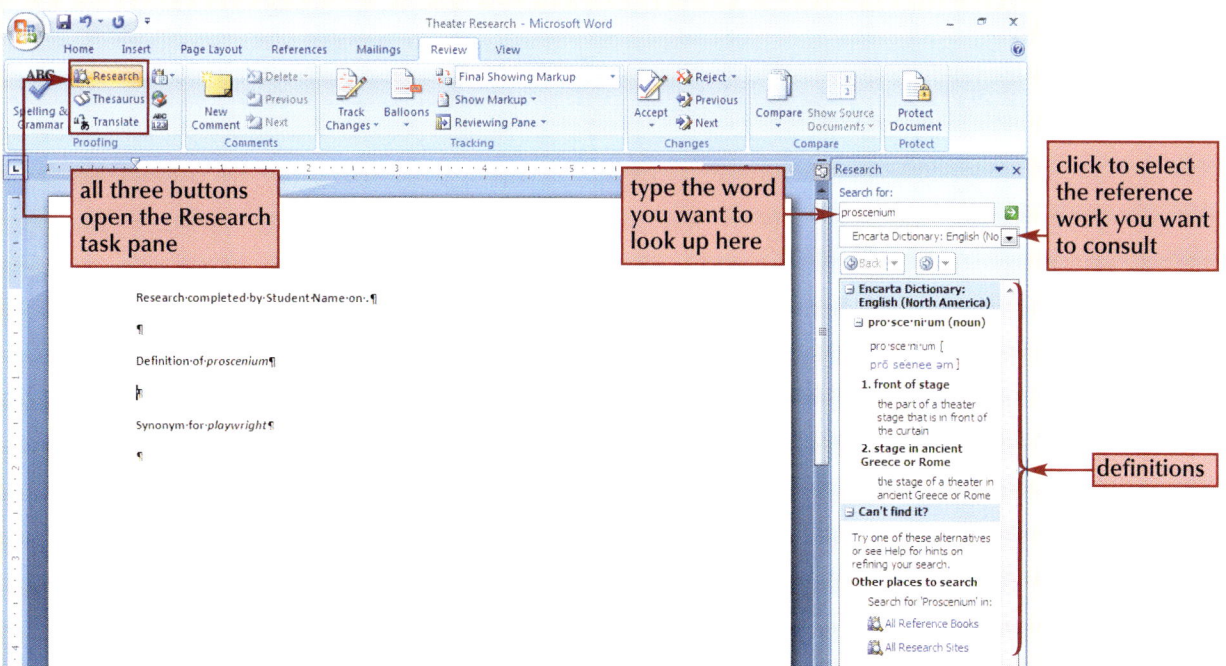

▶ **7.** Drag the mouse pointer to select the first definition, which reads **the part of a theater stage that is in front of the curtain**, right-click the selected text, click **Copy**, click in the blank paragraph below the text "Definition of *proscenium*" in the document, and press the **Ctrl+V** keys to paste the definition into the document.

Next, Sam wants to look up a synonym for *playwright*. If he didn't have the Research task pane open already, he would begin his search by clicking the Thesaurus button in the Proofing group. But because the Research task pane is already open, he can simply select a new reference work.

To look up a synonym in the thesaurus:

1. In the document, click in the blank paragraph below the text "Synonym for *playwright.*"

2. In the Research task pane, delete the word **proscenium** from the Search for text box, and then type **playwright**.

3. Click the arrow button below the Search for text box, and then click **Thesaurus: English (United States)**. Synonyms for *playwright* are displayed in the Research task pane, where the definitions for *proscenium* appeared earlier.

4. Move the mouse pointer over **writer**, the second synonym in the list. A list box appears around the word.

5. Click the down arrow next to the word "writer." A menu of options appears. See Figure 5-37.

Figure 5-37 Synonyms displayed in the Research task pane

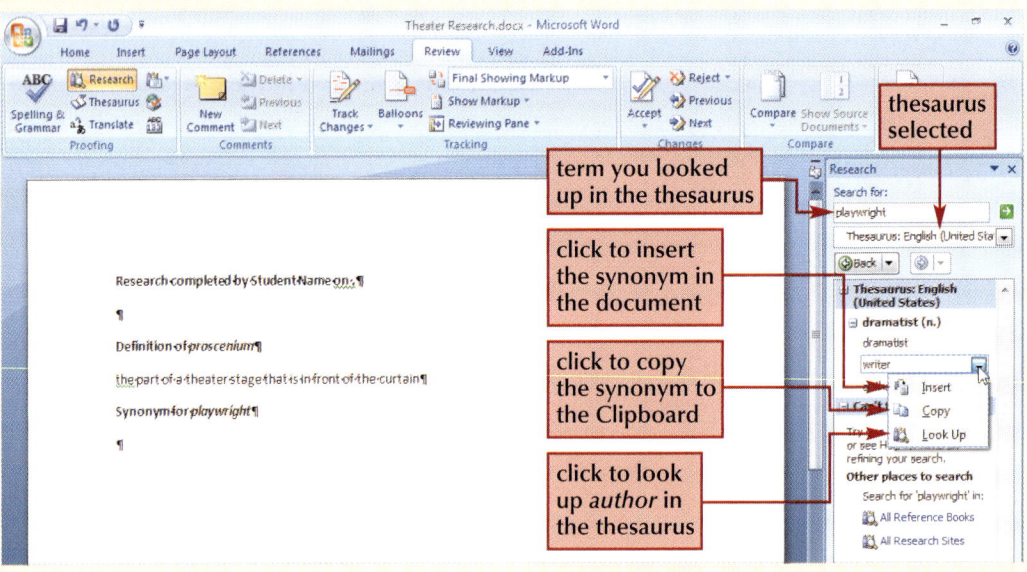

You can click Insert to insert the synonym in the document at the insertion point, or you can click Copy to copy the synonym to the Clipboard, so that you can paste it into other locations in the document or in other documents. To look up synonyms of *writer*, you could click Look Up. Right now, Sam simply wants to insert the word *writer* into the document.

6. Click **Insert**. The term *writer* is inserted into the document, below "Synonym for *playwright.*"

7. Save the document, and then click the **Close** button in the title bar of the Research task pane to close it.

If your computer is connected to the Internet, you can type a word or phrase in the Search for box, click the down arrow and select Translation, and then use the options that appear in the Research task pane to retrieve a translation of your word or phrase over the Internet. The translations provided by the Research task pane are performed by computers, and therefore are useful only when you need a quick idea of what a term or phrase refers to.

You are finished with your research. All that remains is to insert your name and the current date at the top of the document.

Inserting the Current Date

You could begin typing the current date and have Word finish it for you using AutoComplete. But by using the Date and Time button in the Text group on the Insert tab, you can take advantage of several formatting options. These formats allow you to include the time or the day of the week. You can also choose to have Word update the date every time you open the document. Sam wants to use one of the date formats available via the Date and Time dialog box.

To insert your name and the current date into the Theater Research document:

▶ **1.** In the first line of the document, replace **Student Name** with your first and last name.

▶ **2.** Click at the end of the first line, just to the left of the period. This is where you want to insert the current date.

▶ **3.** Click the **Insert** tab, and then, in the Text group, click the **Date & Time** button. The Date and Time dialog box opens. The Available formats list shows the different ways you can insert the current date.

▶ **4.** In the Available formats list box, click the format that provides the day of the week and the date—for example, Friday, March 05, 2010. This is probably the second item in the Available formats list. See Figure 5-38.

Date and Time dialog box ◀ **Figure 5-38**

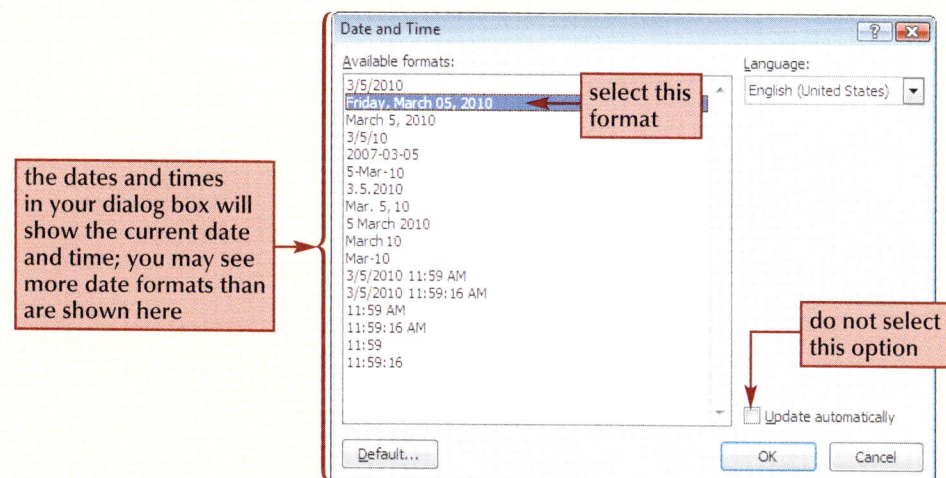

Note that your Date & Time dialog box will show the current date, and not the date shown in Figure 5-38. Notice the Update automatically check box, which you could click if you wanted Word to update the date and time each time you open the document. In this case, you want to insert today's date without Word updating it when you reopen the document.

▶ **5.** Verify that the Update automatically check box is *not* selected.

▶ **6.** Click the **OK** button. Word inserts the date into the document.

▶ **7.** Save the document, print it, and then close it.

Review | **Session 5.3 Quick Check**

1. What type of outline symbol indicates a heading with subordinate text under it?
2. Define *promote* as it relates to Outline view.
3. What do you have to do before you can create a table of contents?
4. What button can you click to revise a table of contents, and where is the button located?
5. True or False. You can use the Research task pane to look up definitions, but not synonyms.
6. What's the advantage of using the Date & Time button in the Text group on the Insert tab to insert a date?

Review | **Tutorial Summary**

In this tutorial, you learned how to create a new document from a template, insert a Word file into a document, and customize the document theme. You also learned how to select a style set, modify a style, create a new style, and compare styles with the Reveal Formatting window. Finally, you learned how to create a new template, use Outline view, create a table of contents, use the Research task pane, and insert the current date into the document.

Key Terms

character spacing	outline symbol	style sets
content control	Outline view	Styles window
demote	promote	table of contents
kerning	Research task pane	template
linked style	Reveal Formatting window	theme colors
Normal template	sans serif font	theme fonts
outline	serif	theme effects

Practice | **Review Assignments**

Apply the skills you learned in the tutorial using the same case scenario.

Data Files needed for the Review Assignments: Body.docx, Placeholder.docx, Future.docx, Research.docx

Sam's DCP Report template is now used for all reports created by employees of Clarenbach Department of City Planning. Inspired by Sam's success with the template, the director of the Department of Water Safety (DWS), Heather Sheehan, wants you to help with a report on improving the city's water testing system. After you format the report, she'd like you to save the document as a new template. Finally, she'd like you to look up some terms using the Research task pane. (*Note:* Text you need to type is shown in bold for ease of reference only; do not bold the text unless otherwise instructed.)

Complete the following:

1. Start Word if necessary, open a new document based on the **Oriel Report** template, and then save the document as **Water Testing** in the Tutorial.05\Review folder included with your Data Files.
2. Make sure that nonprinting characters are displayed, and if necessary, switch to Print Layout view.
3. Replace the placeholder text in the Title control with **Department of Water Safety**. Replace the subtitle placeholder text with **Plans for Improving City Water Testing**.
4. Replace the placeholder text in the Abstract control with **This report analyzes possibilities for improving the city's water testing system.** Type your name in the Author control and select the current date in the Date control.
5. Delete the placeholder text in the Body control on page 2, and then insert the file named **Body** from the Tutorial.05\Review folder included with your Data Files. This is just a skeletal draft of the report, but it includes the necessary headings.
6. Format the five headings (Table of Contents, Project History, Improved Bacterial Testing, Protecting the Municipal Reservoir, and Installing New Pumping Stations) with the Heading 1 style.
7. Change the theme colors to Concourse, and then change the theme's fonts to the Apex fonts.
8. Select the Formal style set, and then open the Styles window.
9. Select the Project History heading and modify it by changing its character spacing to condensed, changing the paragraph spacing after the heading to 20 points, and adding italics.
10. Update the Heading 1 style to match the newly formatted Project History heading.
11. Create a new style for the Table of Contents heading that is based on the Heading 1 style. The style should be identical to the Heading 1 style, except that it should format text in 18-point font, in bold. Name the new style **Contents** and save it to the current document.
12. Open the Reveal Formatting window and compare the Contents style with the Heading 1 style.
13. Save your changes to the Water Testing document.
14. Save the Water Testing document as a template named **DWS Template** in the Tutorial.05\Review folder included with your Data Files.
15. On page 1, replace the subtitle with the placeholder **[Insert subtitle here.]**. Replace the abstract with the placeholder **[Insert report abstract here.]**.
16. Delete the body of the report, beginning with the Table of Contents heading to the end of the report (Tip: To maintain the formatting of the subtitle at the top of page 2, do not delete the last paragraph of the document.)

17. In the blank paragraph below the subtitle on page 2, insert the Word file **Placeholder** from the Tutorial.05\Review folder included with your Data Files.

18. Format the Table of Contents heading with the Contents style.

19. Save the template, preview it, print it, and close it.

20. Open a new document based on the DWS Template, enter **Estimate for New Wells** as the document subtitle, save the new document as **New Wells** in the Tutorial.05\Review folder included with your Data Files, preview it, print it, and close it.

21. Open the **Water Testing** document from the Tutorial.05\Review folder included with your Data Files.

22. In Outline view, demote the last three headings in the document to Level 2, and then move the heading Protecting the Municipal Reservoir up so it comes before the heading Improved Bacterial Testing.

23. Save your work and print the outline.

24. Insert a table of contents below the Table of Contents heading. Use the default settings in the Table of Contents dialog box.

25. At the end of the document, insert the Word file **Future** from the Tutorial.05\Review folder included with your Data Files, and then add the heading Future Plans to the table contents as a Level 1 heading.

26. Save, preview, print, and close the Water Testing document.

27. Open the document named **Research** from the Tutorial.05\Review folder included with your Data Files, and then save it as **Water Research** in the same folder.

28. Open the Research task pane, look up the definition of *aquifer*, and then insert the definition into the document in the appropriate place. Look up synonyms for *reservoir*, and insert the third synonym in the list into the appropriate place in the document.

29. At the top of the document, replace STUDENT NAME with your first and last name, replace DATE with the current date and time in the format 3/04/10 10:25 AM, and then save, preview, print, and close the document.

30. Submit the finished documents to your instructor, either in printed or electronic form, as requested.

Apply | **Case Problem 1**

Apply the skills you learned to create a template for a plant information handout.

Data Files needed for this Case Problem: Characteristics.docx, Crabapple.jpg, Height.docx, Plant Headings.docx, Requirements.docx.

Bluestem Landscape Design Carla Niedenthal is the manager of the retail store owned by Bluestem Landscape Design. Customers often ask her for information about particular plants. Over the years, she has created fact sheets for some of the most popular plants, but now Carla would like to create a set of one-page plant descriptions. Her first step is to create a template that will serve as the basis of the handouts. As you'll see in the following steps, you can use templates intended for one purpose, such as a letter, for another purpose, such as a handout. (*Note:* Text you need to type is shown in bold for ease of reference only; do not bold the text unless otherwise instructed.)

Complete the following:

1. Open a new document based on the **Median Letter** template, and then save the document as **Plant** in the Tutorial.05\Case1 folder included with your Data Files.

2. Make sure that nonprinting characters are displayed and that Print Layout view is selected.

3. Replace the placeholder text in the Company Name control with **Bluestem Landscape Design**. Replace the company address placeholder text with **Plant-at-a-Glance**.

4. Delete the date control, and then type **[Insert common plant name]** in the brown box that used to contain the date control. Click the blue bar next to the brown box and type **[Insert Latin plant name.]**.

5. Below the blue bar, delete the sender company address control, the recipient title control, the recipient address control, and the salutation control. Delete the body text control, the closing control, and the name control. If a name remains visible in the document after you delete the name control, delete the name as well.

6. Delete all the blank paragraphs in the document below the brown and blue boxes except one. Make sure the remaining blank paragraph below the brown box is formatted with the Normal style, and that it is positioned at the left margin.

7. With the insertion point located in the blank paragraph below the brown box, insert the file Plant Headings from the Tutorial.05\Case1 folder included with your Data Files.

8. Format the three headings with the Heading 1 style. Remember that if you can't find a style in the Quick Styles gallery, you can look in the Styles window.

9. Change the theme colors to Foundry.

10. Change the theme's fonts to Verve.

11. Modify the Heading 1 style for the current document by changing its character spacing to Expanded, changing the paragraph spacing after the heading to 12 points, and adding italics.

12. At the bottom of the document, replace "STUDENT NAME" with your first and last name. Save and print the Plant document.

13. Save the Plant document as a template named **Plant Template** in the Tutorial.05\Case1 folder included with your Data Files, and then close the template.

14. Open a document based on your template. Save the new document as **Crabapple** in the Tutorial.05\Case1 folder included with your Data Files.

15. For the common plant name, enter **Crabapple**. For the Latin plant name, enter **Malus**.

16. Under the Characteristics heading, delete the placeholder text but not the paragraph mark at the end of the paragraph, verify that the blank paragraph is formatted in the Normal style, and insert the Word file **Characteristics** from the Tutorial.05\Case1 folder included with your Data Files. Delete the extra paragraph mark at the end of the new text. Replace the placeholder text below the Mature Height heading and the Requirements heading with the files **Height** and **Requirements** from the Tutorial.05\Case1 folder included with your Data Files. Delete any extra new paragraphs.

17. At the bottom of the document, read the placeholder text about inserting a photograph. Select the placeholder text (but not the paragraph mark at the end of it), and delete it so you can insert a photo in its place.

⊕ EXPLORE

18. Verify that the insertion point is positioned in the blank paragraph just above the line that begins "Created by..." and then insert the photo named **Crabapple.jpg** from the Tutorial.05\Case1 folder included with your Data Files. (*Hint*: Use the Picture button in the Illustrations group on the Insert tab.) With the photograph selected, click the Drop Shadow Rectangle style in the Picture Styles group on the Picture Tools Format tab.

19. At the bottom of the document, replace DATE with the current date, including the day of the week.

20. Save, print, and close the Crabapple document.

21. Submit the finished documents to your instructor, either in printed or electronic form, as requested.

Case Problem 2

Data Files needed for this Case Problem: Star.docx, Video.docx

Star Avenue Consulting Steven Yang is a consultant for Star Avenue Consulting, a firm that helps retail chains evaluate and improve the organization of their retail floor space. Steven and his colleagues often have to produce reports that summarize their recommendations. Your job is to create a template they can use to generate these reports. (*Note:* Text you need to type is shown in bold for ease of reference only; do not bold the text unless otherwise instructed.)

Complete the following:

1. Open the document **Star** from the Tutorial.05\Case2 folder included with your Data Files, and then save it as **Star Report** in the same folder.

2. Make sure that nonprinting characters are displayed. If necessary, switch to Print Layout view. This document is based on the Normal template, and was created using all the default settings.

3. Format the five headings (starting with Recommendation and ending with Advantages of Current Layout) with the Heading 1 style.

4. Select the Opulent theme, and change the theme colors to Flow. Change the style set to Traditional.

5. Format the "Recommendation" heading by changing its character spacing to Expanded, changing the font size to 16 points, and changing the paragraph spacing after the paragraph to 12 points. Update the Heading 1 style for the current document to match the "Recommendation" heading.

6. Create a new style for the company name at the top of the document that is based on the Title style. The style should be identical to the Title style, except that it should format text in 20-point font, with bold and italic formatting, and should include 6 points of space after the paragraph. Name the new style **Company**, and save it to the current document.

7. Open the Reveal Formatting window and compare the Company style to the Title style.

8. In Outline view, move the Recommendation section down so it is the last section in the document. Demote the headings "Variations by Location," "Disadvantages of Current Layout," and "Advantages of Current Layout" to Level 2 headings.

9. In the blank paragraph above the heading "Assessment of Current Store Layout," insert a table of contents using the Automatic Table 2 format. Delete any extra blank paragraphs after the table of contents. The table of contents might seem unnecessary in such a short document, but as consultants create their multipage reports, they will need a table of contents.

10. Save your changes to the Star Report document, and then save the Star Report document as a template named **Star Report Template** in the Tutorial.05\Case2 folder included with your Data Files. Close the template.

11. Open a document based on your new template. You will use this document as the basis of a new report for HomeFlix Video Outlets. You will not complete the entire report; instead you'll leave the placeholder text in the body of the report for another consultant to replace.

12. Save the new document as **HomeFlix** in the Tutorial.05\Case2 folder included with your Data Files.

13. For the client name, insert **HomeFlix Video Outlets**. Replace CONSULTANT NAME with your first and last name.

EXPLORE   14. Replace DATE with the current date and time in the format 3/4/2010 3:25:25 PM. Select the Update automatically check box. Note the exact time inserted into the document, save the document, close it, pause briefly, and reopen the document. Note the updated time. Click the date, and then click Update. Note the updated time.

15. Save, print, and close the HomeFlix document.

16. Open the document named **Video** from the Tutorial.05\Case2 folder included with your Data Files, and then save it as **Video Research**. Open the Research task pane, look up the definition of *video*, and insert the third definition into the document in the appropriate place. Look up synonyms for *video* and insert the last synonym under "videotape" into the appropriate place in the document.

17. Save, print, and close the document.

18. Submit the finished documents to your instructor, either in printed or electronic form, as requested.

Challenge	**Case Problem 3**

Go beyond what you've learned to edit a business plan for a new Internet company named AllSecure, Incorporated.

Data File needed for this Case Problem: Text.docx

AllSecure, Inc.   Camden Lui has written a business plan for his new Internet business, AllSecure, Incorporated. On its Web site, the company will publish security information on data storage and transmission services. Camden has written part of the report and needs help formatting it. (*Note:* Text you need to type is shown in bold for ease of reference only; do not bold the text unless otherwise instructed.)

Complete the following:

1. Open a new document based on the Origin Report template and save it as **AllSecure Plan** in the Tutorial.05\Case3 folder included with your Data Files.

2. Remove the cover page at the beginning of the document. (*Hint*: Use the Cover Page button on the Insert tab.)

3. Use **AllSecure, Inc.** for the document title and **Business Plan** for the subtitle.

4. Delete the body control, and insert the file named **Text** from the Tutorial.05\Case3 folder included with your Data Files.

5. Format the four headings in the left column with the Heading 1 style. In the right column, format the first three headings in the Heading 1 style. Format the last three headings in the right column in the Heading 2 style.

EXPLORE   6. Create a new character style for the company name where it is used in the body of the report. Base the style on the Intense Reference style. It should be identical to the Intense Reference style, but without underline formatting. In the Create New Style from Formatting dialog box, select Character in the Style type list box. If necessary, select Intense Reference in the Style based on list box and deselect the Underline button. Name the style **Company Name** and save it to the current document.

EXPLORE   7. Open the Find and Replace dialog box, find all instances of "AllSecure" in the body of the document, and format them with the new Company Name style. After you find the first instance using the Find and Replace dialog box, close the dialog box, and click the button with the double blue down arrows at the bottom of the vertical scroll bar to find additional instances without using the Find and Replace dialog box. Use the button with the double blue up arrows at the bottom of the vertical scroll bar to move back to preceding instances.

⊕ EXPLORE

8. Use Word Help to look up information on Find and Replace. Click the "Find and replace text or other items" topic, and then read about how to find and highlight text on the screen. Use this feature to highlight all instances of "AllSecure" in the document. Turn off the highlighting and close the Find and Replace dialog box.

9. Insert a new paragraph before the Executive Summary heading, format the new paragraph with the Normal style, type **Contents**, and insert a new paragraph. Format the paragraph containing the heading Contents in the Heading 1 style.

10. Use the Table of Contents dialog box to insert a table of contents in the blank paragraph below the Contents heading. Use the Distinctive format. Deselect the Right align page numbers check box so the entire table of contents is aligned in the left column.

11. At the end of the document, change the heading Audience Needs to **Audience Requirements**, and then update the table of contents.

⊕ EXPLORE

12. Click the Select Browse Object button (the circle near the bottom of the vertical scroll bar). Move the pointer over the buttons in the palette and review the name of each option. Click the Go To button in the palette, and then use the Go To tab of the Find and Replace dialog box to move the insertion point to the top of page 2. Close the Find and Replace dialog box. Click the Select Browse Object button again, click the Browse by Heading button, and then click the button with the double blue down arrows (at the bottom of the vertical scroll bar) to move from one heading to the next. Use the double blue up arrow button to browse up through the document by heading.

13. Save, print, and close the document.

14. Submit the finished documents to your instructor, either in printed or electronic form, as requested.

Create | **Case Problem 4**

Create the outline shown in Figure 5-39 by using the Numbering button in the Paragraph group on the Home tab.

There are no Data Files needed for this Case Problem.

Public Health Report Outline Shakira Ankor is a communications specialist at the Municipal Association for Public Health (MAPH). Each year she begins her work on the association's annual report by creating an outline using Word's multilevel list feature. She has asked you to help. (*Note*: Text you need to type is shown in bold for ease of reference only; do not bold the text unless otherwise instructed.)

1. Open a new Word document, and save it as **MAPH Report** in the Tutorial.05\Case4 folder included with your Data Files.

2. Switch to Print Layout view, if necessary, and make sure nonprinting characters are displayed.

3. To begin creating the report outline, insert a new paragraph, click the Numbering button in the Paragraph group on the Home tab, and type **A Message from the Director**. Press the Enter key, and then type **Report Highlights**. Press the Enter key, and then type **Summaries from Regional Committees**.

⊕ EXPLORE

4. To demote a heading to a lower level, you can press the Tab key or click the Increase Indent button in the Paragraph group on the Home tab. Press the Enter key, press the Tab key, and then type **Northeast Region**. Continue typing the names of the following regions on separate lines: **Southeast Region**, **Midwest Region**, **West Region**. Insert another paragraph, click the Decrease Indent button, and then type **National Health Information Campaigns**.

5. Continue using the techniques described in Step 4 to complete the outline shown in Figure 5-39.

Figure 5-39

1. A Message from the Director
2. Report Highlights
3. Summaries from Regional Committees
    a. Northeast Region
    b. Southeast Region
    c. Midwest Region
    d. West Region
4. National Health Information Campaigns
    a. Vaccinations for Adolescents and Young Adults
        i. Special Needs of High School Students
        ii. Considerations for the College-Bound
    b. Lupus Signs and Symptoms
    c. Childhood Obesity
    d. Geriatric Nutrition Needs
        i. Calcium Intake
        ii. Protein Requirements

 **EXPLORE**

6. Select the outline, click the Multilevel List button in the Paragraph group on the Home tab, and then select the style that uses Roman numerals and capital letters (in the lower-left corner of the Multilevel List gallery).

7. In Outline view, move the Southeast Region heading up before the Northeast Region heading.

8. Switch to Print Layout view, click at the beginning of the document, and then add **Municipal Association for Public Health** and the subtitle **Annual Report Outline**. Below the subtitle, insert **Created by Student Name**. (Replace "Student Name" with your first and last name.) On a line below your name, insert the current date in the March 7, 2010, format.

9. Format the title in the Title style, and then reduce the title's font size to 18 point. (Do not modify the Title style.) Format the subtitle in the Subtitle style.

10. Save your work, preview the document, and print it.

11. Submit the finished documents to your instructor, either in printed or electronic form, as requested.

| Research | **Internet Assignments** |

Go to the Web to find information you can use to create documents.

The purpose of the Internet Assignments is to challenge you to find information on the Internet that you can use to work effectively with this software. The actual assignments are updated and maintained on the Course Technology Web site. Log on to the Internet and use your Web browser to go to the Student Online Companion for New Perspectives Office 2007 at **www.course.com/np/office2007**. Then navigate to the Internet Assignments for this tutorial.

| Assess | **SAM Assessment and Training** |

If you have a SAM user profile, you may have access to hands-on instruction, practice, and assessment of the skills covered in this tutorial. Log in to your SAM account (**http://sam2007.course.com**) to launch any assigned training activities or exams that relate to the skills covered in this tutorial.

Session 5.1

1. Normal template
2. Right-click the content control, and then click Remove Content Control.
3. Insert tab
4. Colors, fonts, effects
5. Serif and sans serif
6. False

Session 5.2

1. True
2. Every built-in theme comes with 11 sets of styles. Each style set is, in turn, made up of 31 styles.
3. Styles window
4. In the Font group on the Home tab, click the Dialog Box Launcher to open the Font dialog box, and then click the Character Spacing tab.
5. Click the Dialog Box Launcher in the Paragraph group on the Home tab to open the Paragraph dialog box, and then click the Indents and Spacing tab.
6. Reveal Formatting window
7. True

Session 5.3

1. Plus sign
2. To increase the level of a heading
3. Format the document headings with heading styles.
4. Update Table button in the Table of Contents group in the References tab
5. False
6. It allows you to choose from a variety of date and time formats.

Ending Data Files

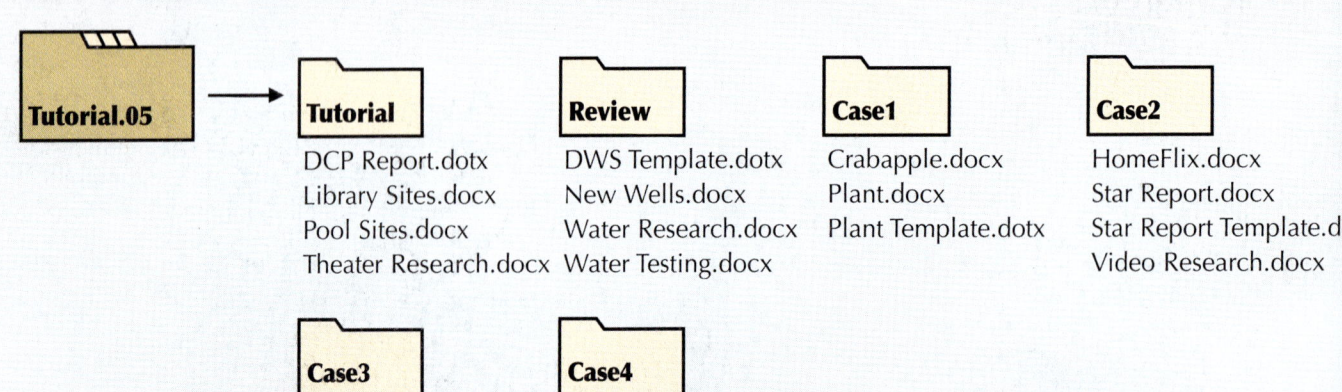

Tutorial.05 → Tutorial
DCP Report.dotx
Library Sites.docx
Pool Sites.docx
Theater Research.docx

Review
DWS Template.dotx
New Wells.docx
Water Research.docx
Water Testing.docx

Case1
Crabapple.docx
Plant.docx
Plant Template.dotx

Case2
HomeFlix.docx
Star Report.docx
Star Report Template.d
Video Research.docx

Case3
AllSecure Plan.docx

Case4
MAPH Report.docx

Using Mail Merge

Creating a Form Letter, Mailing Labels, and a List

Case | Lily Road Yoga Studio

Nina Ranabhat is the owner and chief instructor at Lily Road Yoga Studio in Boise, Idaho. The studio has just moved to a new, expanded location. Nina wants to invite clients to try out the new facility during free, open-studio days in the month of June. She plans to send a letter to each client announcing the new location and the open-studio days.

Nina doesn't have time to type a personal letter to each of the studio's many clients. Instead, she plans to create a **form letter** that contains the information she wants to send to all clients. The form letter will also contain specific details for individual clients, such as name, address, and each client's favorite class and instructor. Nina has already written the text of the form letter. She plans to use the mail merge process to add the personal information for each client. She asks you to create the form letter using Word's Mail Merge feature. She also needs a set of letters that will go just to the clients who take power yoga classes. After you create the merged letters, she'd like you to create the mailing labels for the envelopes and a telephone directory that lists a phone number for each teacher. Next, you will create an additional document with name and address information by converting text to a table. Finally, you will create and format a list of names by converting a table to text.

Starting Data Files

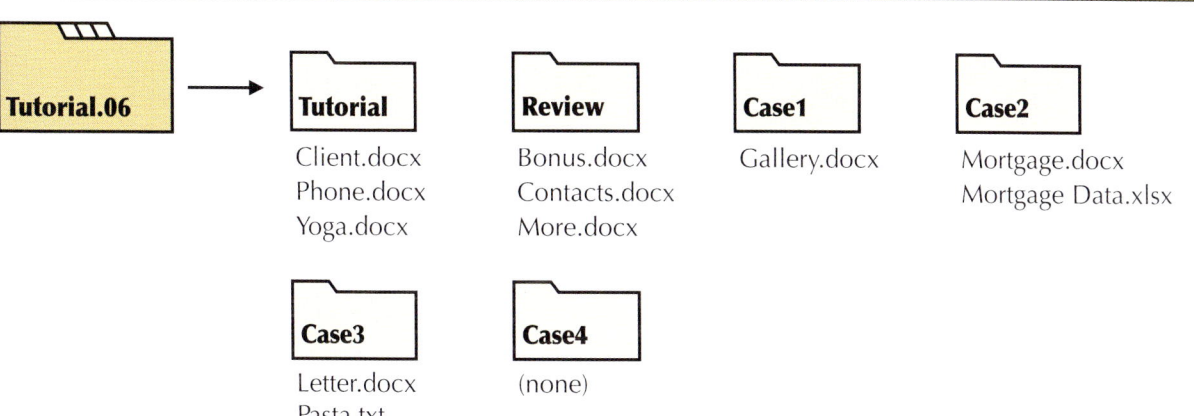

Tutorial.06 →	Tutorial	Review	Case1	Case2
	Client.docx	Bonus.docx	Gallery.docx	Mortgage.docx
	Phone.docx	Contacts.docx		Mortgage Data.xlsx
	Yoga.docx	More.docx		

Case3	Case4
Letter.docx	(none)
Pasta.txt	

Session 6.1

Understanding the Mail Merge Process

To insert individualized information into a form letter, you combine, or **merge**, a form letter with a separate file containing specific information, whether that information is names and addresses, product information, or another type of data. The form letter is called a **main document**, and the file containing the specific information is called the **data source**.

A main document can be a letter or any other kind of document. It contains codes called **fields** that tell Word where to insert names, addresses, and other variable information. A field can be a data field, such as date and time fields, or **merge fields**, such as First Name and Last Name fields. As you will see in this tutorial, one of the steps you must complete before merging the main document with the data source is inserting the merge fields into the main document. Nina's main document is the letter shown in Figure 6-1. As you complete the steps in this tutorial, you will replace the red text with merge fields.

Figure 6-1	Nina's main document

[Date]

[First Name] [Last Name]
[Street Address]
[City], ID [ZIP Code]

Dear [First Name]:

I am happy to announce that Lily Road Yoga Studio has moved to an expanded location at 4722 Lily Road. This is just two blocks south of our original location, but it feels like a whole new world. Our sunny new studio offers off-street parking, private changing rooms, and a much larger studio space. We also have a separate, smaller space for individual instruction.

To welcome you to our new home, we are hosting open studio hours every Thursday through the month of June. Classes on open studio days are free. Of course, we will continue to offer a full range of yoga instruction, including group classes and private practice.

Please check out our schedule online at *www.lilyroad.course.com*. You'll be glad to know that we now offer two additional [Favorite Type] classes. Also, keep in mind that [Favorite Teacher] is available for individual instruction.

We hope to see you soon at one of our open-studio Thursdays. Come soon, and bring a friend!

Sincerely yours,

Nina Ranabhat

Owner and Certified Ashtanga Instructor

Nina's data source will include the name and address of each client, as well as information about each client's preferred type of class and favorite teacher.

Inserting information from a data source into a main document produces a final document called a **merged document**. Figure 6-2 illustrates how the data source and main document combine to form a merged document.

Merging a main document with a data source to create a merged document   **Figure 6-2**

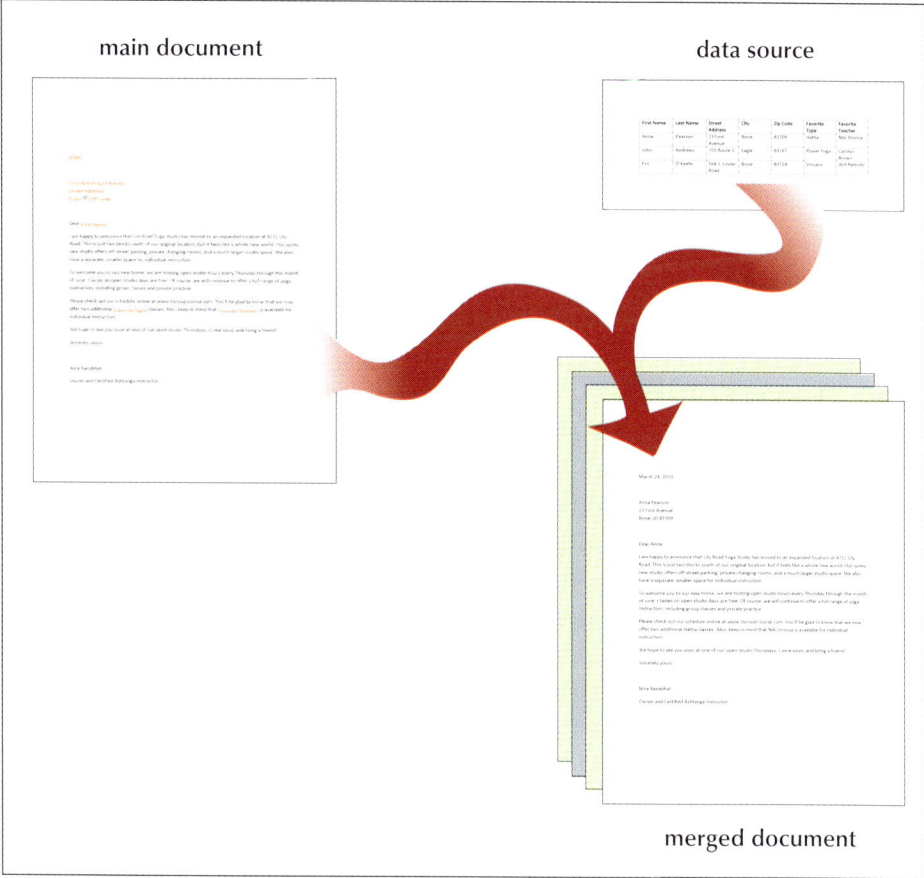

main document

data source

merged document

Merge Fields and Records

Merge fields appear in the main document and tell Word which pieces of information to retrieve from the data source. One merge field might retrieve an address from the data source; another merge field might retrieve a telephone number. Merge fields are easy to spot in the main document because each merge field name is enclosed by pairs of angled brackets, which look like this: << >>. You can insert merge fields into a main document only by using the Mail Merge task pane or the tools in the Mailings tab. You cannot simply type merge fields into the main document—even if you type the brackets.

A data source is a table of information similar to the one shown in Figure 6-3. The header row, the first row of the table, contains the name of each merge field. The cells below the header row contain the specific information that replaces the merge fields in the main document. This information is called **data**. Each row of data in the table makes up a complete **record**. You can also think of a record as the information about one individual or object.

Figure 6-3 Sample data source

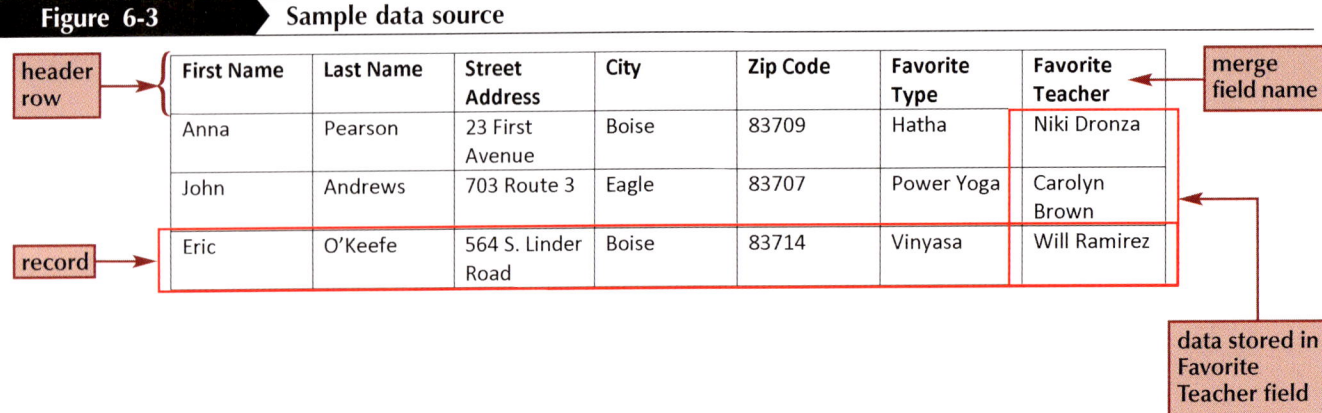

Data sources are commonly used to store names and addresses. However, you can also create data sources with inventory records, records of suppliers, or records of equipment. After you understand how to manage and manipulate the records in a data source, you'll be able to use them for many different types of information.

Using the Mail Merge Task Pane

The **Mail Merge task pane** walks you through the following six steps for merging documents:

1. Select the type of document you want to use as the main document. Possible types of main documents include letters, envelopes, e-mails, labels, and directories.
2. Select the document you want to use as the main document. You can create a new document or edit an existing one.
3. Select the list of recipients (that is, the data source) you want to use for the merge or create a new list of recipients.
4. Complete the main document by adding merge fields.
5. Preview the merged document.
6. Complete the mail merge.

To ensure that you see the same thing in the Mail Merge task pane each time you open it, start with a new, blank document before you open the Mail Merge task pane. Once you are familiar with merging documents, you can also use the options on the Mailings tab to perform the same tasks described in the Mail Merge task pane.

Nina is ready for you to start the mail merge process for her form letter.

To start Word and open the Mail Merge task pane:

▶ **1.** Start Word and make sure a new, blank document is displayed. Note that this new document is named "Document1."

▶ **2.** Switch to Print Layout view, and then display nonprinting characters, if necessary. Use any Zoom setting you want for now. You won't need the rulers in this tutorial, so close them if they are displayed.

▶ **3.** Click the **Mailings** tab, then in the Start Mail Merge group, click the **Start Mail Merge** button, and then click **Step by Step Mail Merge Wizard**. The Mail Merge task pane opens, displaying information and options related to the first step in merging documents. See Figure 6-4.

Starting the mail merge process   Figure 6-4

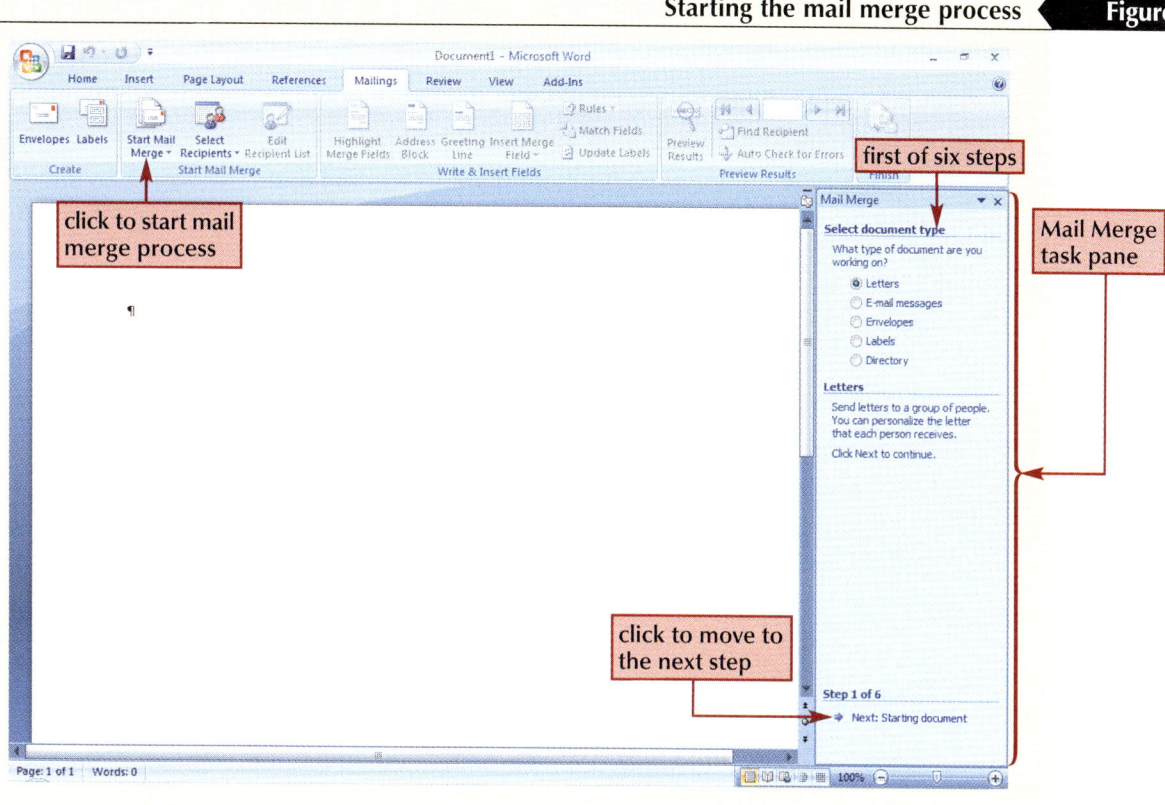

With the Mail Merge task pane open, you are ready to perform the first two steps in merging a document.

Selecting a Main Document

According to the Mail Merge task pane, your first task is to specify the type of main document you want to use for the merge. The Mail Merge task pane provides a number of options, including e-mail messages and labels. In this case, you want to create a letter.

To specify the type of merged document to create:

▶ **1.** Verify that the **Letters** option button is selected in the Mail Merge task pane.

▶ **2.** At the bottom of the task pane, click **Next: Starting document**. The Mail Merge task pane displays information and options that you can use to select a starting document—that is, to select a main document.

Now that you've selected letters as the type of document you'll use for your main document, you need to specify which document you'll use for Nina's form letter. When selecting a main document, you have three choices: use the document currently displayed in the document window; start a new document from a pre-installed mail merge template; or open an existing document. Nina has already written the letter she wants to send to all of her yoga clients, so you don't need to create a new document. Instead, you'll use her existing document, which she saved in a file named Yoga.

When you open an existing document from the Mail Merge task pane, Word actually opens a *copy* of the document you select so that any changes you make to the file will not affect the original file. You'll see how this works in the following steps.

To select a main document for the form letter:

▶ **1.** In the Mail Merge task pane, click the **Start from existing document** option button (just below the "Select starting document" heading). A list box appears, with an Open button below it. The list box contains names of files that have been used for a mail merge on your computer in the past. (If this is the first time anyone has performed a mail merge on your computer, the list box will be blank except for a More Files link.) If you perform mail merges regularly with the same group of files, you can click the name of the file you want in this list box. For now, however, you will use the Open button below the list box.

▶ **2.** In the Start from existing section of the Mail Merge task pane, click the **Open** button. The Open dialog box is displayed. You'll use this dialog box to select Nina's document.

▶ **3.** Navigate to the **Tutorial.06\Tutorial** folder included with your Data Files.

▶ **4.** Click **Yoga**, and then click the **Open** button. A copy of the file named Yoga is opened and is named Document1. The Use the current document option button is now selected in the task pane because you are now ready to use the current document as the main document. Because Nina had set the top margin of the Yoga document at 2 inches, the top margin of the Document1 document changes to 2 inches as well. This will leave enough room for Nina's letterhead.

▶ **5.** Make sure nonprinting characters are displayed.

▶ **6.** Change the zoom so you can see the entire width of the text, but not the left or right margins. On most monitors, **120%** is a good zoom setting. At the bottom of the task pane, you see the next step in the mail merge process. See Figure 6-5.

Main document Normal view ◄ **Figure 6-5**

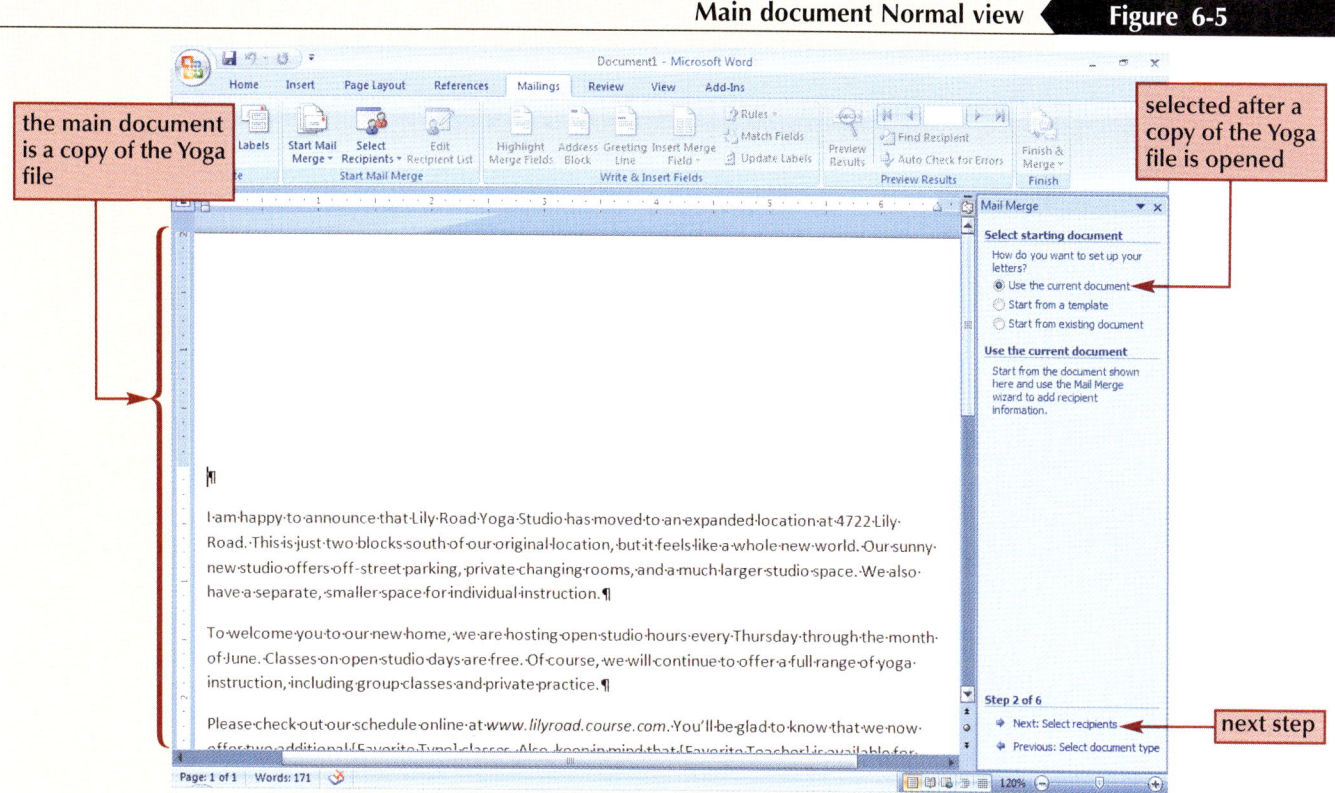

the main document is a copy of the Yoga file

selected after a copy of the Yoga file is opened

next step

7. Scroll down to display the letter's closing, change "Nina Ranabhat" to your name, and then scroll back up to the beginning of the letter.

8. Save the file as **Yoga Letter with Merge Fields** in the Tutorial.06\Tutorial folder.

Next, you need to specify your data source—the list of recipients for Nina's letter.

Creating a Data Source

As you learned earlier, a data source is a file with information organized into fields and records. Typically, the data source for a mail merge contains a list of names and addresses, but it can also contain e-mail addresses, telephone numbers, and other data. Various kinds of files can be used as the data source, including a simple text file, a Word table, an Excel worksheet, an Access database, or a Microsoft Office Address Lists file, which stores addresses for Microsoft Outlook and other Microsoft Office applications. (In Word Help, this type of file is sometimes called a Microsoft Office Contacts Lists file.) In this tutorial, you will create a Microsoft Office Address Lists file to use as your data source. Word's Mail Merge task pane walks you through the steps required to create the data source.

When performing a mail merge, you can select a data source file that already contains names and addresses, or you can create a new data source and enter names and addresses into it. When you create a new data source, the file is saved by default as a Microsoft Office Address Lists file. In this section, you will create a data source using the tools provided by the Mail Merge task pane. This involves two steps: deciding which fields to include in the data source and entering address information.

You need to create a data source that contains information on Nina's clients, including the name, address, preferred type of class, and favorite teacher. Nina collected all the necessary information by asking clients to fill out a form when they registered for their first yoga class. Figure 6-6 shows one of these forms.

Figure 6-6 **Client information form**

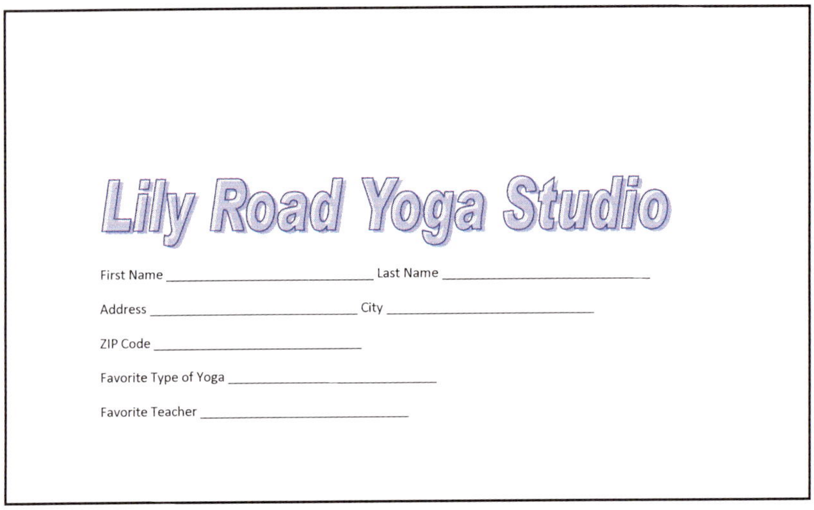
Lily Road Yoga Studio

First Name ______________ Last Name ______________

Address ______________ City ______________

ZIP Code ______________

Favorite Type of Yoga ______________

Favorite Teacher ______________

The information on each form will make up one record in the data source. Your job is to create a data source for three of Nina's clients, which means you'll have just three records. A real yoga studio would of course have tens or hundreds of records, one for each client. When you create your data source, you must include the field names shown in Figure 6-7.

Figure 6-7 **Field names to include in data source**

Field Names	Description
First Name	Client's first name
Last Name	Client's last name
Address	Client's street address
City	City in Idaho
ZIP Code	ZIP code in Idaho
Favorite Type of Yoga	Client's preferred type of yoga
Favorite Teacher	Client's preferred yoga teacher

When you create a new data source from within the Mail Merge task pane, Word provides a number of default fields, such as First Name, Last Name, and Company. You can customize the data source by adding new fields and removing the default fields that you don't plan to use. As you create a data source, keep in mind that each field name must be unique; you can't have two fields with the same name.

Creating a Data Source for a Mail Merge | Reference Window

- In Step 3 of the Mail Merge task pane, select the Type a new list option button, and then click Create; or, in the Start Mail Merge group on the Mailings tab, click the Select Recipients button, and then click Type New List.
- In the New Address List dialog box, click the Customize Columns button.
- To delete unnecessary fields, in the Customize Address List dialog box, click a field you want to delete, click the Delete button, and then click the Yes button. Continue to delete any other unnecessary fields.
- To add a new field, click the Add button, type the name of the field in the Add Field dialog box, and then click the OK button.
- To rearrange the order of the field names, click a field name, and then click the Move Up or Move Down button.
- Click the OK button to close the Customize Address List dialog box.
- In the New Address List dialog box, enter information for the first record, click the New Entry button, and type another record. Continue until you are finished entering information into the data source, and then click the OK button to open the Save Address List dialog box.
- Type a name for the data source in the File name text box, and then click the Save button. The file is saved with the .mdb file extension.

You're ready to begin creating the data source for Nina's form letter.

To begin creating the data source:

▶ 1. In the bottom of the Mail Merge task pane, click **Next: Select recipients**, and then click the **Type a new list** option button.

▶ 2. Below the heading "Type a new list," click **Create**. The New Address List dialog box opens, as shown in Figure 6-8.

Creating a data source

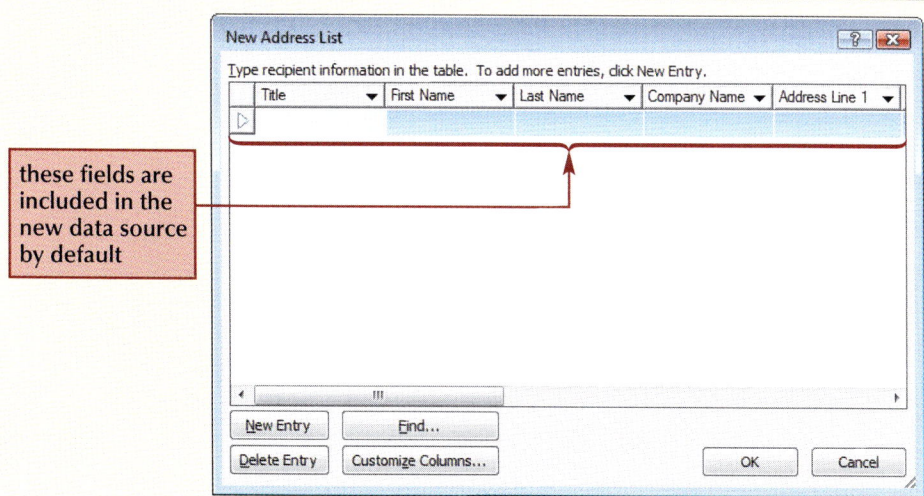

these fields are included in the new data source by default

You will use the New Address List dialog box to enter a complete set of information for one person—that is, you will enter one record into the data source. However, before you begin entering information, you need to customize the list of fields to match the fields shown earlier in Figure 6-7.

To customize the list of fields:

▶ 1. Click the **Customize Columns** button. The Customize Address List dialog box opens. Here you can delete the fields you don't need, add new ones, and arrange the fields in the order you want. You'll start by deleting fields.

▶ 2. In the Field Names list box, verify that **Title** is selected, and then click the **Delete** button. A message appears asking you to confirm the deletion.

▶ 3. Click the **Yes** button. The Title field is deleted from the list of field names.

▶ 4. Continue using the Delete button to delete the following fields: **Company Name**, **Address Line 2**, **State**, **Country or Region**, **Home Phone**, **Work Phone**, and **E-mail Address**. Next, you need to add some new fields. When you add a new field, it is inserted below the selected field, so you will start by selecting the last field in the list if it is not already selected.

▶ 5. In the Field Names list box, verify that **ZIP Code** is selected, and then click the **Add** button. The Add Field dialog box opens, instructing you to type a name for your field.

▶ 6. Type **Favorite Type**, and then click the **OK** button. The field "Favorite Type" is added.

▶ 7. Use the Add button to add a **Favorite Teacher** field below the Favorite Type field. When you are finished, your Customize Address List dialog box should look like the one shown in Figure 6-9. You could use the Move Up and Move Down buttons to rearrange the field names (for instance, to move the Favorite Teacher field above the Favorite Type field), but in this case the order is fine. You are finished customizing the list of field names.

Figure 6-9 ▷ **Customized list of field names**

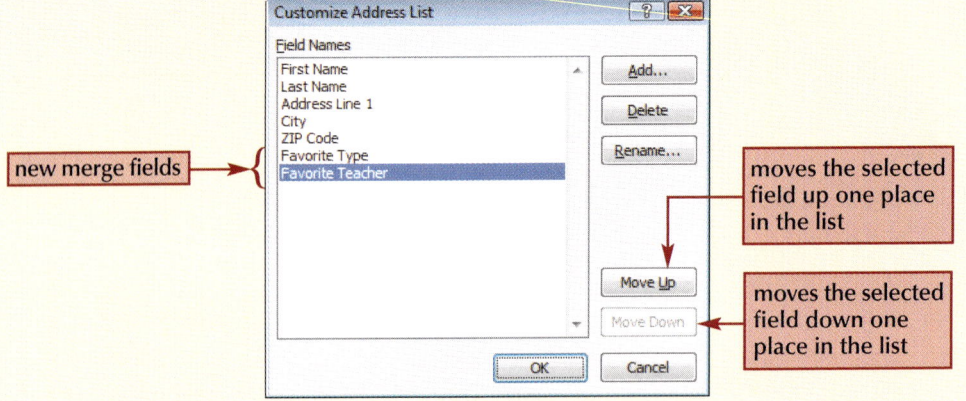

8. Click the **OK** button in the Customize Address List dialog box. The Customize Address List dialog box closes, and you return to the New Address List dialog box. This dialog box reflects the changes you just made. For instance, it no longer includes the Title field. The fields are listed in the same order they appeared in the Customize Address List dialog box. In the next step, you'll scroll right so you can see the fields you just added.

9. Use the horizontal scroll bar near the bottom of the New Address List dialog box to display the Favorite Type and Favorite Teacher fields. Although part of "Favorite Teacher" is cut off in the dialog box, the entire field name is stored as part of the data source. See Figure 6-10.

Changes made to New Address List dialog box

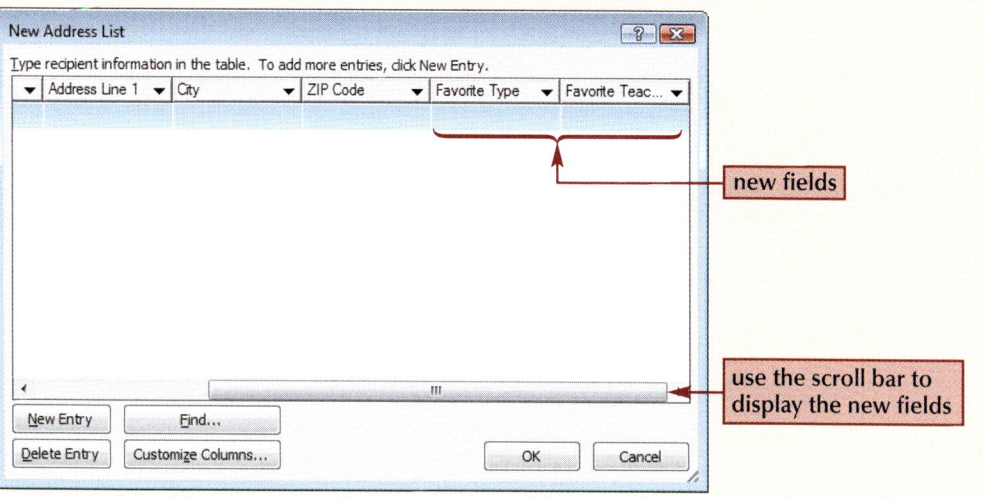

new fields

use the scroll bar to
display the new fields

Organizing Field Names | InSight

Although the order of field names in the data source doesn't affect their placement in the main document, it's a good idea to arrange field names logically in the data source so you can enter information quickly and efficiently. For example, you'll probably want the First Name field next to the Last Name field. Also, note that if you include spaces in your field names, Word will replace the spaces with underscores when you insert the fields into the main document. For example, Word transforms the field name First Name into First_Name.

Now that you have specified the fields you want to use, you are ready to enter the client information into the data source.

Entering Data into a Data Source

You are now ready to begin entering information about each client into the data source. Nina gives you three copies of the form shown earlier in Figure 6-6, with information entered in each form. She asks you to transfer the information from the paper forms into the data source. Each paper form will be used to create one new record in the data source. You'll use the New Address List dialog box to enter the information.

To enter data into a record using the New Address List dialog box:

▶ **1.** Scroll left to display the First Name field, click in the **First Name** text box, if nec-essary, and then type **Anna** to enter the first name of the first client. Make sure you do not press the spacebar after you finish typing an entry in the New Address List dialog box. You should add spaces only in the text of the main document, not in the data source, to prevent too many or too few spaces between words.

▶ **2.** Press the **Tab** key to move the insertion point to the Last Name field.

Tip

You can press the Shift+Tab keys to move the insertion point to the previous text box.

▶ **3.** Type **Pearson**, and then press the **Tab** key to move the insertion point to the Address Line 1 field.

▶ **4.** Type **23 First Avenue**, and then press the **Tab** key to move the insertion point to the City field.

▶ **5.** Type **Boise**, and then press the **Tab** key to move the insertion point to the ZIP Code field.

▶ **6.** Type **83709**, and then press the **Tab** key to move to the Favorite Type field. The Favorite Type field scrolls into view on the right side of the dialog box.

▶ **7.** Type **Hatha**, and then press the **Tab** key. The insertion point is now in the Favorite Teacher field, which has scrolled into view on the right side of the dialog box.

▶ **8.** Type **Niki Dronza**, but do *not* press the Tab key. See Figure 6-11.

Figure 6-11	Completed record 1

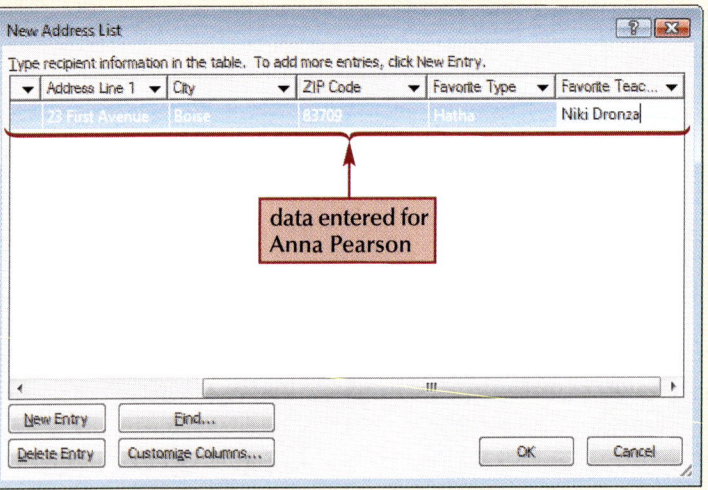

You have completed the information for the first record of the data source document. Now you're ready to enter the information for the next two records. You can create a new record by clicking the New Entry button. When the insertion point is in the far-right text box in the New Address List dialog box, you can also create a new record by pressing the Tab key. In the steps that follow, you use both methods.

To add additional records to the data source:

▶ **1.** In the New Address List dialog box, click the **New Entry** button. This creates a new, blank record.

▶ **2.** Enter the information shown in Figure 6-12 into the new record.

Information for record 2

First Name	Last Name	Street Address	City	Zip Code	Favorite Type	Favorite Teacher
John	Andrews	703 Route 3	Eagle	83707	Power Yoga	Carolyn Brown

▶ **3.** After entering data into the last field, press the **Tab** key.

▶ **4.** Enter the information for the third record, as shown in Figure 6-13. After entering the information for the third record, do not create a fourth record.

Information for record 3   Figure 6-13

First Name	Last Name	Street Address	City	Zip Code	Favorite Type	Favorite Teacher
Eric	O'Keefe	564 S. Linder Road	Boise	83714	Vinyasa	Will Ramirez

Trouble? If you create a fourth record by mistake, click the Delete Entry button to remove the blank fourth record.

You have entered the records for three clients. Next, you need to proofread each record to make sure you typed the information correctly.

To proof the records in the data source:

▶ **1.** Review the information about Anna Pearson in the first record. Compare the record to Figure 6-11, which shows all the data for Anna Pearson except for her name. Make any necessary corrections by selecting the text and retyping it.

▶ **2.** Proofread record 2 by comparing your information with Figure 6-12. Make any necessary corrections.

▶ **3.** Proofread record 3 by comparing your information with Figure 6-13. Make any necessary corrections.

Nina's data source eventually will contain hundreds of records for Lily Road Yoga Studio clients. The current data source, however, contains only the records Nina wants to work with now. Next, you need to save the data source.

Saving a Data Source

You have finished entering data, so you are ready to close the New Address List dialog box. When you close this dialog box, a new dialog box opens, where you can save the data source as a Microsoft Office Address Lists file.

To save the data source:

▶ 1. In the New Address List dialog box, click the **OK** button. The New Address List dialog box closes, and the Save Address List dialog box opens, as shown in Figure 6-14. By default, Word offers to save the file to the My Data Sources folder, which is a subfolder of the Documents folder. In this case, however, you will save the data source in the Tutorial.06\Tutorial folder. Notice that the Save as type box indicates that the data source will be saved as a Microsoft Office Address Lists file.

Figure 6-14 **Saving the data source**

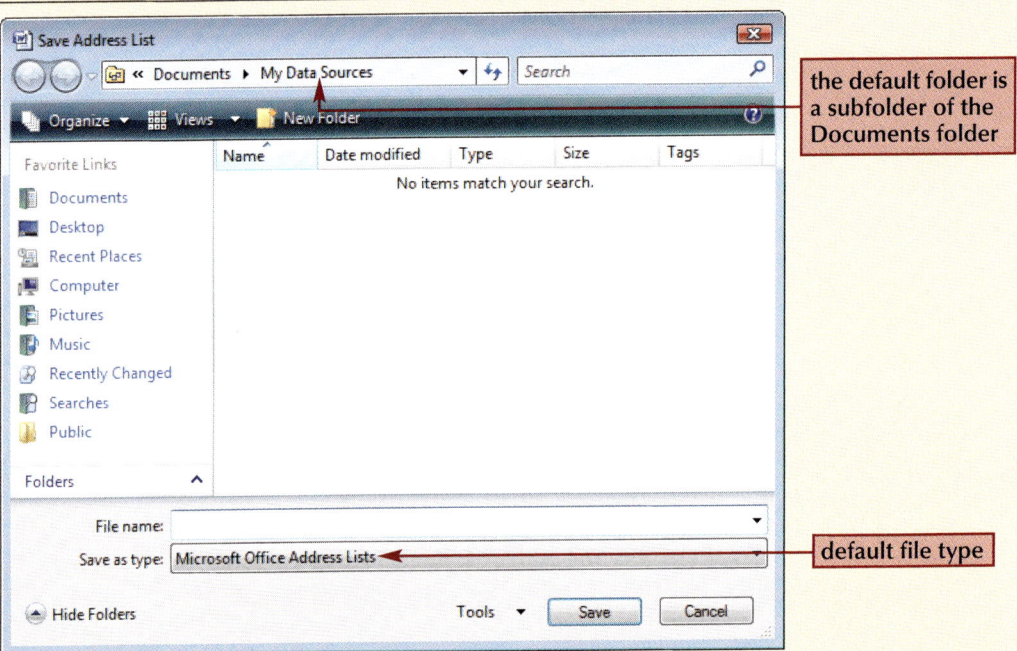

▶ 2. Navigate to the **Tutorial.06\Tutorial** folder.

▶ 3. Click the **File name** text box, type **Yoga Data**, and then click the **Save** button. The Mail Merge Recipients dialog box opens, as shown in Figure 6-15. As in the New Address List dialog box, the header row in this dialog box contains the names of the fields. You need to scroll right to see all the fields. You can use the Mail Merge Recipients dialog box to rearrange the records in the list and to choose which clients you want to include in the mail merge. You'll use this dialog box later in this tutorial.

Mail Merge Recipients dialog box | **Figure 6-15**

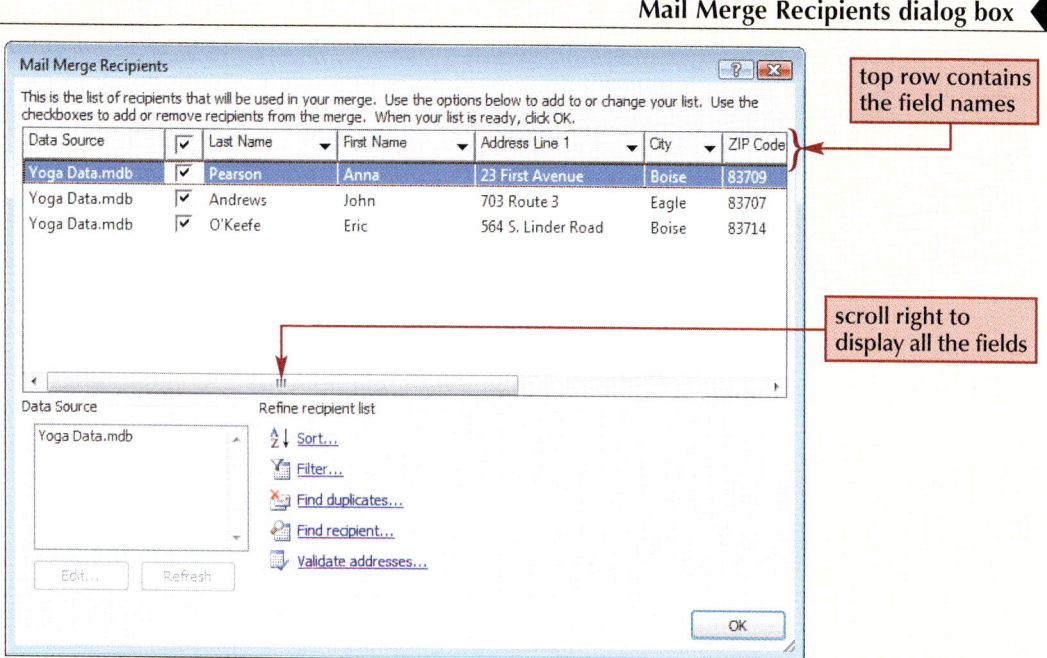

4. Click the **OK** button. The Mail Merge Recipients dialog box closes and you return to the document window. The Mail Merge task pane indicates that you have selected an Office Address List file named "Yoga Data.mdb" as your data source. The task pane also indicates that the next step in the mail merge process is writing (in this case, editing) the main document. See Figure 6-16.

Tip

You can also open the Mail Recipients dialog box by clicking the Edit Recipient List button in the Start Mail Merge group on the Mailings tab.

Selected data source | **Figure 6-16**

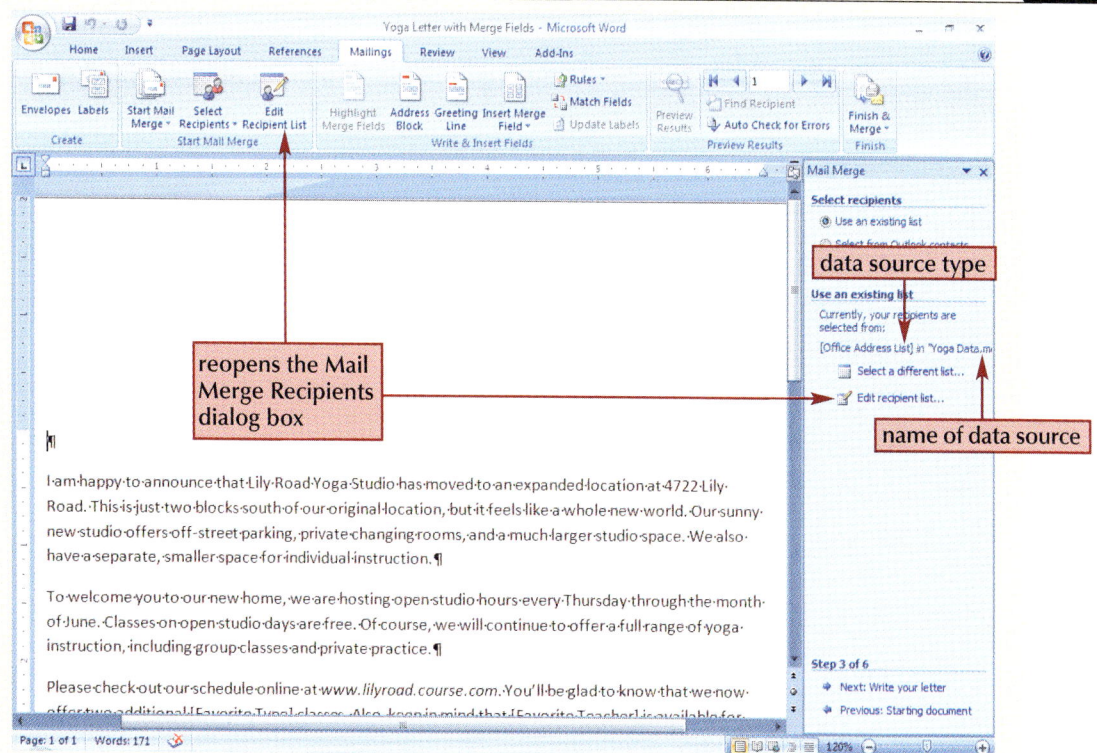

Editing a Main Document

In the first two steps of the mail merge process, you selected Nina's letter as your main document. A copy of this letter is open on your screen, next to the Mail Merge task pane. In the third step, you created and saved the data source. Now you will turn your attention back to the main document. You'll edit Nina's letter to add the current date and the merge fields.

Adding a Date Field

As you've learned, merge fields tell Word where to insert information from the data source. You can also insert other kinds of fields in a document, including a **date field**, which inserts the current date. You can set up a date field up so Word updates the field each time the document is opened.

You insert a date field via the Insert Date and Time dialog box. You already know how to use this dialog box to add the current date as text. To insert a date field that Word updates automatically, you select the Update automatically check box.

Nina wants the date to appear at the top of the document, just below where the yoga studio logo appears on the printed stationery.

To insert the date field:

▶ 1. In the Mail Merge task pane, click **Next: Write your letter**. The Mail Merge task pane displays information and options related to working with the main document. If you had originally selected a new, blank document as your main document, you would need to write the text of the form letter now. In this case, you will edit the existing letter.

▶ 2. Make sure the insertion point is at the beginning of the form letter on the first blank line. You will insert the date on the first line of the document.

▶ 3. Click the **Insert** tab, and then, in the Text group, click the **Date & Time** button. The Date and Time dialog box opens.

▶ 4. Click the third format in the Available formats list, which includes the month, the day, and the year, as in March 5, 2010.

▶ 5. If it's not selected, click the **Update automatically** check box to select it. See Figure 6-17.

| Figure 6-17 | Inserting a date field |

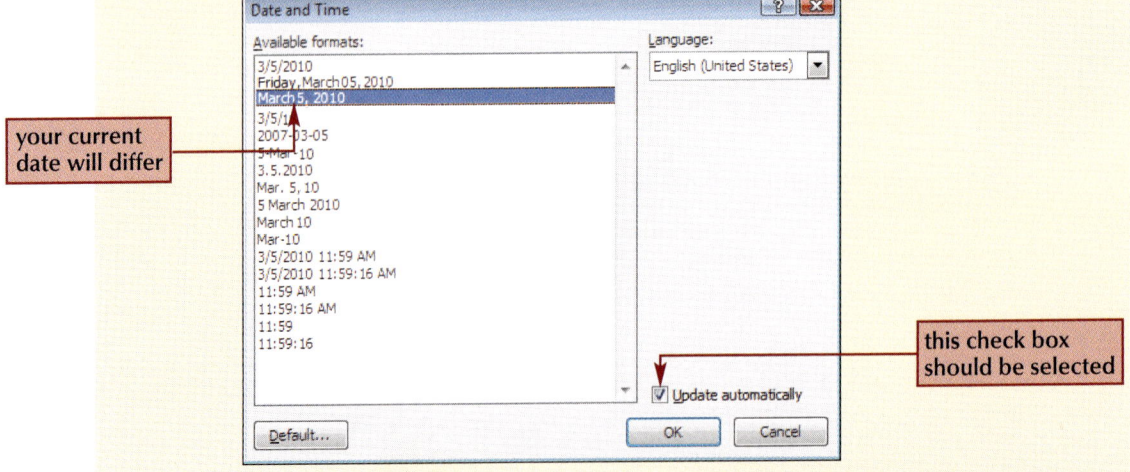

▶ **6.** Click the **OK** button. The current date appears in the document.

> **Trouble?** If you see {DATE \@ "MMMM d, yyyy"} instead of the current date, your system is set to display field codes. To view the date instead of the field code, click the Office Button, click Word Options, click Advanced, scroll down to display the Show document content section, deselect the "Show field codes instead of their values" check box, and then click the OK button.

Now, whenever you print the merged document, the current date will appear in the document. Next, you will insert the merge fields for the letter's inside address.

Inserting Merge Fields

Nina's letter is a standard business letter, so you'll place the client's name and address below the date. You'll use merge fields for the client's first name, last name, address, city, and zip code. You must enter proper spacing and punctuation around the fields so that the information in the merged document will be formatted correctly.

The Mail Merge task pane includes links, such as the Address block link, which you can use to insert a standard set of fields. The More items link offers more flexibility because it allows you to insert fields one at a time, rather than in predefined groups. In the following steps you will use the More link in the Mail Merge task pane to begin inserting merge fields in the main document. But first, you will re-display the Mailings tab, so that you can see the options on the Mailings tab that correspond to the options in the Mail merge task pane.

To insert a merge field:

▶ **1.** Click the **Mailings** tab.

▶ **2.** Verify that the insertion point is positioned in the first line immediately to the right of the date field, and then press the **Enter** key two times to leave space between the date and the first line of the inside address.

▶ **3.** In the Mail Merge task pane, click **More items**. The Insert Merge Field dialog box opens. As shown in Figure 6-18, the Database Fields option button is selected, indicating that the dialog box displays all the fields in the data source.

Inserting merge fields into the main document   **Figure 6-18**

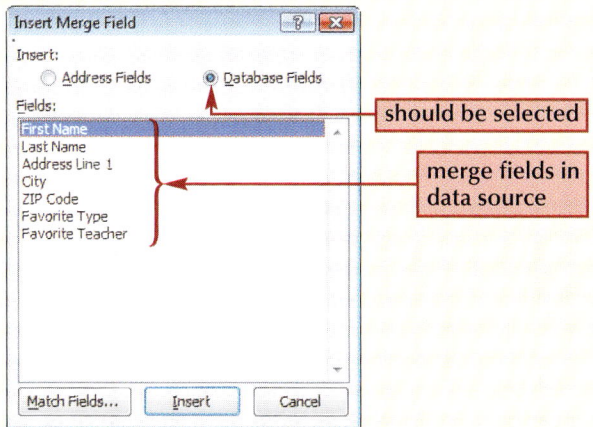

> **Trouble?** If you see a different list than the one shown in Figure 6-18, the Address Fields option button might be selected rather than the Database Fields option button. Click the Database Fields option button to select it, and then continue with Step 4.

▶ **4.** In the Fields list, click **First Name** if necessary to select it, click the **Insert** button, and then click the **Close** button. The Insert Merge Field dialog box closes, and the merge field is inserted into the document. The merge field consists of the field name surrounded by double angled brackets << >>, also called **chevrons**. Note that Word replaces spaces in field names with underscores, so the field name "First Name" is displayed as "First_Name." Also note that the Highlight Merge Fields button is now available, which means you can use it to display the merge field on a gray background.

Trouble? If you make a mistake and insert the wrong merge field, click to the left of the merge field, press the Delete key to select the field, and then press the Delete key again to delete it.

▶ **5.** In the Write & Insert Fields group, click the **Highlight Merge Fields** button. The First Name merge field is displayed on a gray background, making it easier to see in the document.

Later, when you merge the main document with the data source, Word will replace this merge field with information from the First Name field in the data source. Now, you're ready to insert the merge fields for the rest of the inside address. You'll add the necessary spacing and punctuation to the main document as well.

To insert the remaining merge fields for the inside address:

▶ **1.** Press the **spacebar** to insert a space after the First Name field, and then on the Mailings tab, click the **Insert Merge Field** button arrow. A menu appears displaying a list of the fields in the data source.

Trouble? If the Insert Merge Field dialog box opens, you clicked the Insert Merge Field button instead of the Insert Merge Field button arrow. Close the dialog box, and then click the Insert Merge Field button arrow.

▶ **2.** Click **Last_Name**. The Last_Name merge field is inserted in the document. As you continue entering the remaining merge fields in the inside address, you will use manual line breaks to avoid inserting paragraph spacing after each line. Remember that a manual line break moves the insertion point to the next line without actually starting a new paragraph, so no extra space is inserted.

▶ **3.** Press the **Shift+Enter** keys to create a manual line break, click the **Insert Merge Field** button arrow, and then click **Address Line 1**. Word inserts the Address Line 1 merge field into the form letter.

▶ **4.** Press the **Shift+Enter** keys to create another manual line break, and then, using either the Insert Merge Field button arrow on the Mailings tab or the More items link in the task pane, insert the **City** merge field. Word inserts the City merge field into the form letter.

▶ **5.** Type **,** (a comma), press the **spacebar** to insert a space after the comma, and then type **ID** to insert the abbreviation for the state of Idaho.

▶ **6.** Press the **spacebar** to insert a space after ID, and then insert the **ZIP Code** merge field. See Figure 6-19.

Form letter with merge fields | Figure 6-19

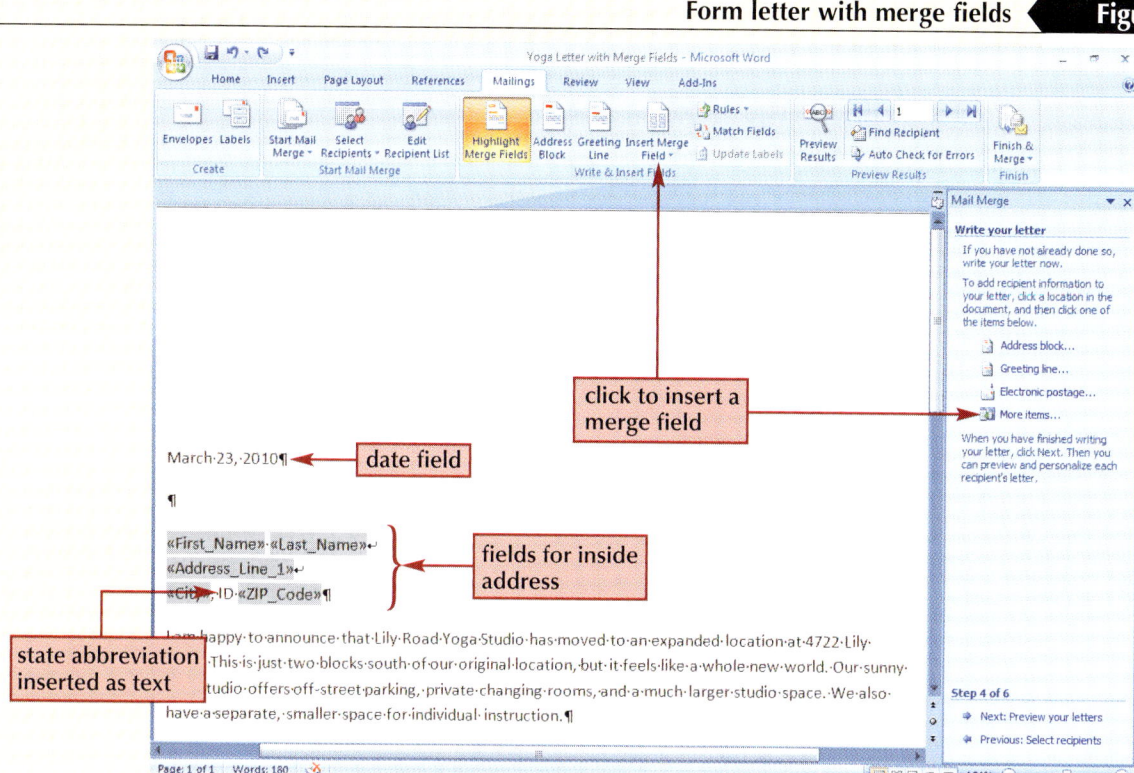

Planning Your Data Source | InSight

It's important to take some time to think about the structure of your data source before you create it. As you plan a data source, try to break information down into as many fields as seems reasonable. For example, it's always better to include a First Name field and a Last Name field, rather than simply a Name field, because including two separate fields makes it possible, later, to alphabetize the information in the data source by last name. If you entered first and last names in a single Name field, you could only alphabetize by first name, because the first name would appear first in the Name field.

If you're working with a very small data source, breaking information down into as many fields as possible is less important. However, it's very common to start with a small data source, and then, as time goes on, find that you need to keep adding information to the data source, until you have a large file. If you failed to plan the data source adequately at the beginning, the expanded data source could be hard to work with.

In this tutorial, you are working with a data source that does not include a State field because all of the yoga studio's clients live in the state of Idaho. This allows you to get some practice building an inside address out of merge fields and text. As a general rule, however, it's smart to include a State field in every address data source you create. That way, if your pool of addresses should expand in the future to include residents of other states, you won't have to make major changes to your data source to accommodate the new records. Also, if your data source includes a State field, you can use the Address Block merge field to insert an entire address at once, as you did in Tutorial 4. Finally, as you'll see later in this tutorial, including a State field in your data source simplifies the process of creating mailing labels.

The inside address is set up to match the form for a standard business letter. You can now add the salutation of the letter, which will contain each client's first name.

To insert the merge field for the salutation:

▶ **1.** Press the **Enter** key twice to insert a line between the inside address and the salutation, type **Dear**, and then press the **spacebar**.

▶ **2.** Insert the **First Name** field into the document.

▶ **3.** Type **:** (a colon), and then save your work. This completes the salutation.

You'll personalize the letter even more by including references to each client's favorite type of class and teacher.

To add each client's favorite type of class and teacher to the letter:

▶ **1.** Scroll down to display the third main paragraph of the letter, which begins "Please check out our schedule...."

▶ **2.** In the third main paragraph of the letter, select the placeholder **[Favorite Type]** (including the brackets). You'll replace this phrase with a merge field. (Don't be concerned if you also select the space following the closing bracket.)

▶ **3.** Insert the **Favorite Type** merge field. Word replaces the selected text with the Favorite Type merge field.

▶ **4.** Verify that the field has a single space before it and after it. Add a space on either side if necessary.

▶ **5.** Replace **[Favorite Teacher]** in the third main paragraph of the form letter with the **Favorite Teacher** field, and adjust the spacing as necessary.

▶ **6.** Carefully check your document to make sure the field names and spacing are correct. Your document should look like Figure 6-20.

Form letter after inserting merge fields | Figure 6-20

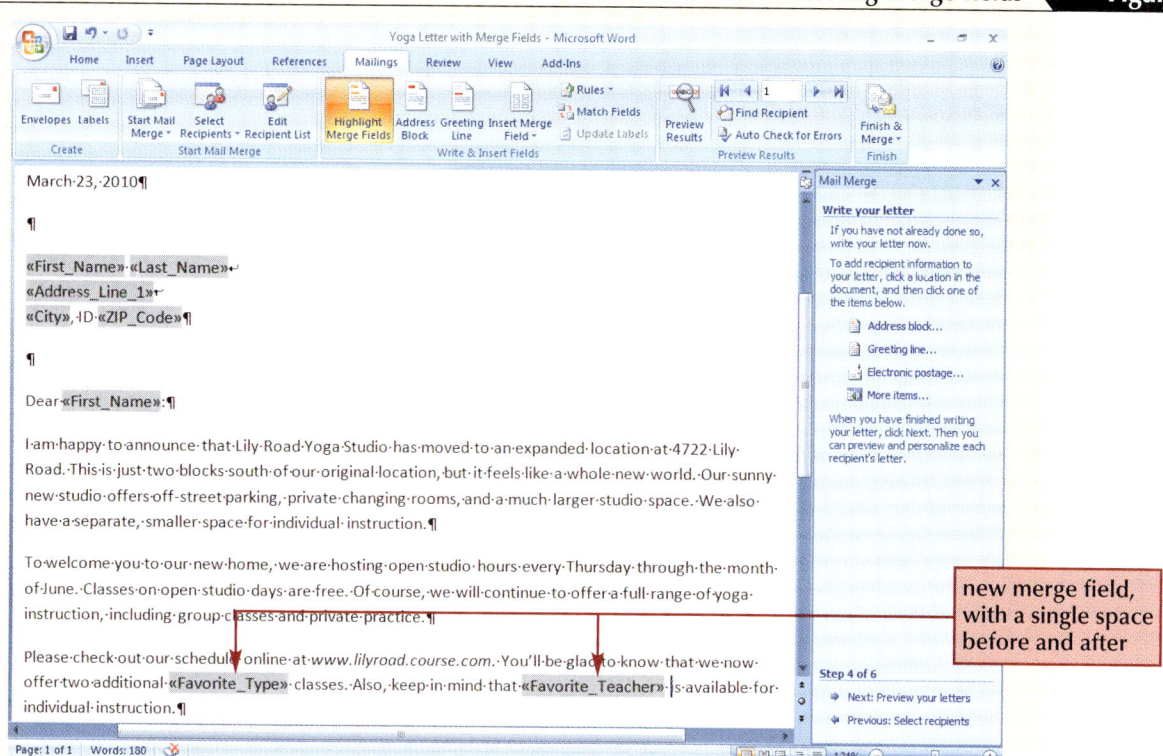

Trouble? If you see an error, edit the document as you would any other Word document. If you inserted an incorrect merge field, drag the mouse pointer to select the entire merge field, press the Delete key, and then insert the correct merge field.

▶ **7.** Save the document.

The main document now contains all the necessary merge fields. The next step is to merge the main document and the data source. Word allows you to preview the merged document before you complete the merge.

Previewing the Merged Document

Referring again to the Mail Merge task pane, your next step is to preview the merged document to see how the letter will look after Word inserts the information for each client. When you preview the merged document, you can check one last time for any missing spaces between the merge fields and the surrounding text. You can also look for any other formatting problems, and, if necessary, make final changes to the data source.

To preview the merged document:

▶ **1.** In the Mail Merge task pane, click **Next: Preview your letters**. The Mail Merge task pane displays information and options related to previewing the merged document. The data for the first record (Anna Pearson) replaces the merge fields in the form letter. See Figure 6-21. Carefully check the letter to make sure the text and formatting are correct. In particular, check to make sure that the spaces before and after the merged data are correct; it is easy to accidentally omit spaces or add extra spaces around merge fields. Finally, notice that both the task pane and the Go to Record box in the Preview Results group show which record is currently displayed in the document.

| Figure 6-21 | First letter with merged data |

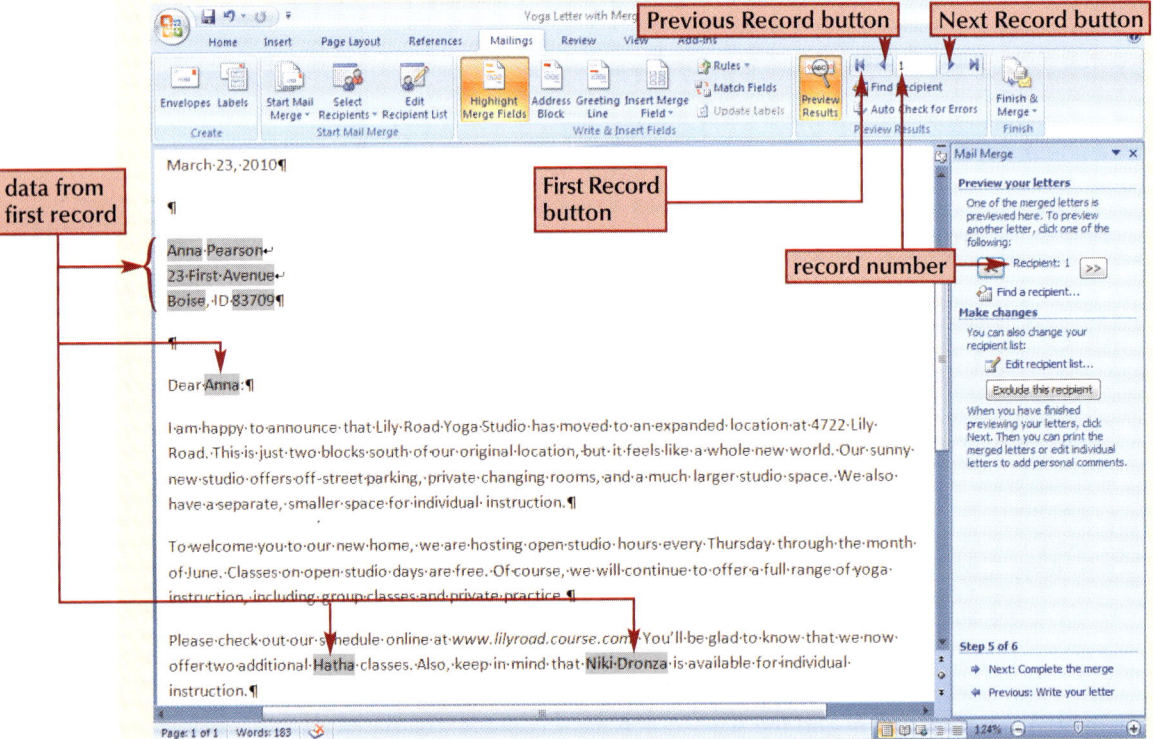

▶ **2.** If you need to make any changes to the form letter, click **Previous: Write your letter** in the Mail Merge task pane, edit the document, save your changes, and then click **Next: Preview your letters** in the task pane. When you are finished, your screen should look like Figure 6-21. Before you complete the merge, you should review the data for the other two records.

▶ **3.** In the Preview Results group on the Mailings tab, click the **Next Record** button ▶. The data for John Andrews is displayed in the letter.

▶ **4.** Click the **Next Record** button ▶ to display the data for Eric O'Keefe in the letter.

▶ **5.** Click the **First Record** button ◀ in the Preview Results group to redisplay the first record in the letter (with data for Anna Pearson).

The main document of the mail merge is completed. At this stage, you could also use the Mail Merge task pane to make changes to the data source, but Nina says the data source is fine for now. You are ready for the final step, completing the merge.

Merging the Main Document and Data Source

Now that you've created the form letter (main document) and the list of client information (data source), you're ready to merge the two files and create personalized letters to send to Nina's clients. Because the data source consists of three records, your merged document will contain three letters; each will be one page long.

When you complete a merge, you can choose to merge directly to the printer. In other words, you can choose to have Word print the merged document immediately without saving it as a separate file. However, Nina wants to keep a copy of the merged document on disk for her records. So you'll merge the data source and main document to a new document first, and then print it.

To complete the mail merge:

▶ 1. In the Mail Merge task pane, click **Next: Complete the merge**. As shown in Figure 6-22, the task pane displays options related to merging the main document and the data source. You can use the Print option to merge directly to the printer. Alternatively, you can use the Edit individual letters option to merge to a new document.

Last step in Mail Merge task pane ◀ **Figure 6-22**

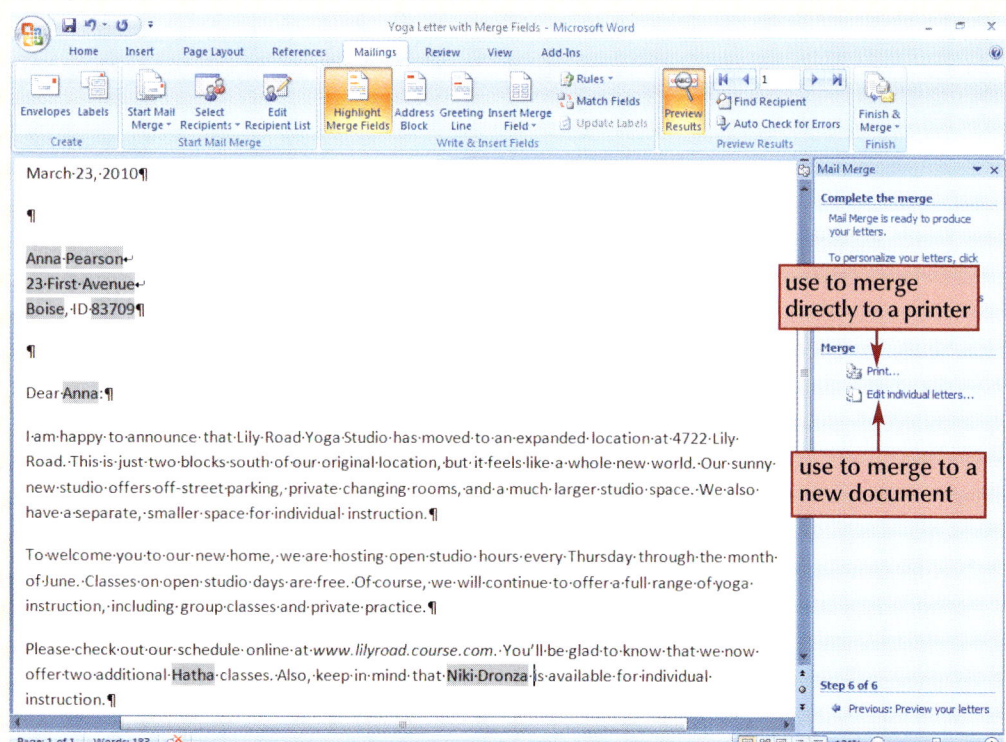

use to merge directly to a printer

use to merge to a new document

▶ 2. In the Mail Merge task pane, click **Edit individual letters**. The Merge to New Document dialog box opens. Here, you need to specify which records to include in the merge. You want to include all three records from the data source.

▶ 3. Verify that the **All** option button is selected, and then click the **OK** button. Word creates a new document called Letters1, which contains three pages, one for each record in the data source. In this new document, the merge fields have been replaced by the specific names, addresses, and so on, from the data source. See Figure 6-23. The date field, however, has not been replaced. Instead, a date field appears at the top of every page, highlighted in gray. The gray highlighting will not print.

Figure 6-23 Merged document

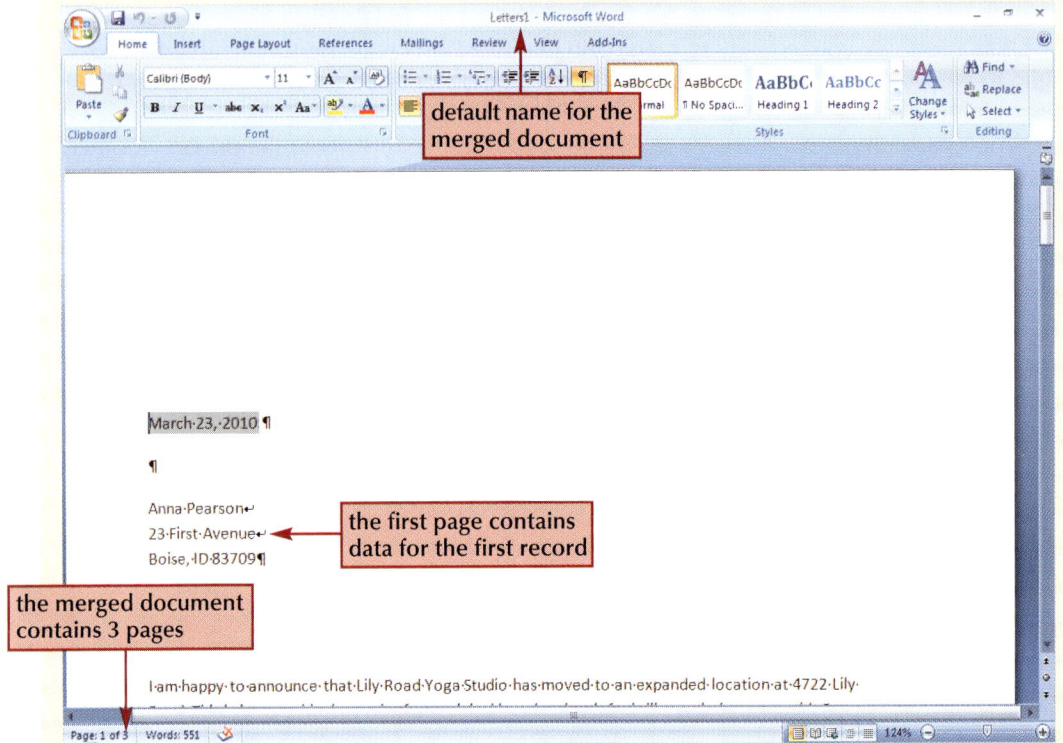

▶ **4.** Save the merged document in the Tutorial.06\Tutorial folder, using the filename **Yoga Merged Letters 1**.

▶ **5.** Zoom out so the text is large enough to read. Next, you will use the Select Browse Object button at the bottom of the vertical scroll bar to move from one page to the next.

▶ **6.** Click the **Select Browse Object** button ⊙ near the bottom of the vertical scroll bar, click the **Browse by Page** button ⬚ on the palette, and then click the **Previous Page** button ⬆ or **Next Page** button ⬇ to move among the letters. Note that each letter is addressed to a different client and that the favorite type and teacher vary from one letter to the next. A page break separates each letter from the one that follows. Nina will print the letters later. For now, you will close the file.

▶ **7.** Close the **Yoga Merged Letters 1** document. The document named "Yoga Letter with Merge Fields" is now the active document. You see the Mail Merge task pane again, displaying the last step of the mail merge process. Note that if you need to take a break while working on a mail merge, you can save the main document and close it. The data source and field information are saved along with the document. When you're ready to work on the merge again, you can open the main document again and update the connection to the data source. You'll see how this works at the beginning of the next session. For now, you will close the main document.

▶ **8.** Save and close the **Yoga Letter with Merge Fields** document.

You have completed the six steps of the Mail Merge task pane and generated a merged document. In the next session, you will learn how to use additional Mail Merge features.

Session 6.1 Quick Check | Review

1. Define the following in your own words:
   a. date field
   b. main document
   c. merge field
   d. record
2. A _____ is a file with information organized into fields and records.
3. True or False. In the Mail Merge task pane, you can select a data source file that already contains names and addresses, or you can create a new data source and enter names and addresses into it.
4. True or False. You cannot use an Excel worksheet as a data source.
5. Explain how to insert a merge field into a main document.
6. Explain how to add a date field to a document.

Session 6.2

Editing a Data Source

After you complete a mail merge, you might find that you need to make some changes to the data source and redo the merge. You can edit a data source in two ways—from within the program used to create the data source in the first place, or via the Mail Merge Recipients dialog box in Word. If you are familiar with the program used to create the data source, it's often simplest to edit the file from within that program. For example, if you were using an Excel worksheet as your data source, you could open the file in Excel, edit it (perhaps by adding new records), save it, and then reselect the file as your data source. To edit a Microsoft Office Address Lists file from within Word, you can use the Mail Merge Recipients dialog box.

Editing a Data Source in Word | Reference Window

- Open the main document for the data source you want to edit.
- In the Start Mail Merge group on the Mailings tab, click the Edit Recipient List button.
- In the Data Source list box in the Mail Merge Recipients dialog box, select the data source you want to edit, and then click the Edit button.
- To add a record, click the New Entry button, and then type a new record.
- To delete a record, click any field in the record, and then click the Delete Entry button.
- To add or remove fields from the data source, click the Customize Columns button, make any changes, and then click the OK button. Remember that if you remove a field, you will delete any data entered into that field.

In the following steps, you will reopen the main document, which you closed at the end of the last session.

After you complete a mail merge, a connection exists between the main document file and the data source file, even after you close the main document and exit Word. You can be certain the connection is maintained as long as you keep both files in their original locations. The two files don't have to be in the same folder; each file just has to remain in the folder it was in when you first created the connection between the two files.

What happens if you move one of the files to a different folder? That depends on how your computer is set up and where you move the files. On most Windows Vista computers, you can't move the *data source* file on its own, but if you move the *main document* file to another location on the same computer, the connection is usually maintained. However, if you move the document to another computer on a network, or to a different storage media (say from the hard drive to a memory stick), the connection might be broken. In that case, when you open the main document, you'll see a series of message boxes informing you that the connection to the data source has been broken. Eventually, you will see a Microsoft Word dialog box with a button labeled Find Data Source, which you can click, and then use the Select Data Source dialog box to select your data source.

To avoid difficulties with locating a data source, it's a good idea to either store the data source in the default My Data Sources folder and keep it there, or store the data source and the main document in the same folder (a folder other than the My Data Sources folder) and keep them there. The latter option is best if you think you might need to move the files to a different computer. That way, if you do need to move them, you can move the entire folder.

To add records to Nina's data source:

1. Open the document named **Yoga Letter with Merge Fields** from the Tutorial.06\Tutorial folder. You see a warning message indicating that opening the document will run an SQL command. SQL is the database programming language that controls the connection between the main document and the data source.

2. Click **Yes** to continue, and then click the **Mailings** tab. The main document still displays the data for the last record you displayed in the document when you previewed the merged document (probably Anna Pearson). As you'll see in the next step, you can alternate between displaying the merge fields and the client data by toggling the Preview Results button on the Mailings tab.

   Trouble? If you see data for a client other than Anna Pearson, don't be concerned. Simply proceed to Step 3.

   Trouble? If you see the merge fields instead of the data for one of the yoga clients, read but do not perform Step 3, and then proceed to Step 4.

3. In the Preview Results group, click the **Preview Results** button to deselect it. The merge fields are displayed in the main document.

   Trouble? If you see the data for one of the clients instead of the merge fields, click the Preview Results button again to deselect it.

4. If necessary, highlight the merge fields by clicking the **Highlight Merge Fields** button in the Write & Insert Fields group.

5. In the Start Mail Merge group, click the **Edit Recipient List** button. The Mail Merge Recipients dialog box opens. You saw this dialog box earlier, when you first selected the data source to use for the mail merge. The Data Source list box in the lower-left corner allows you to select a data source to edit. If you had multiple data sources stored in the Tutorial.06\Tutorial folder, you would see them all in this list box.

▶ **6.** In the Data Source list box, in the lower-left corner of the Mail Merge Recipients dialog box, click **Yoga Data.mdb**. The filename is selected.

▶ **7.** Click the **Edit** button. The Edit Data Source dialog box opens. Note that this dialog box looks similar to the New Address List dialog box, which you used earlier when you first entered information into the data source.

▶ **8.** Use the New Entry button to enter the information shown in Figure 6-24 into the data source. When you are finished, you should have added three new records, for a total of six.

New data ◀ **Figure 6-24**

First Name	Last Name	Street Address	City	Zip Code	Favorite Type	Favorite Teacher
Hannah	Blackmore	2054 First Avenue	Boise	83709	Hatha	Niki Dronza
Antonio	Morelos	55 Moraine Road	Eagle	83707	Hatha	Niki Dronza
Clara	Beck	34 Vilas Street	Boise	83710	Power Yoga	Carolyn Brown

After you finish entering the data for Clara Beck, review your work and make any necessary corrections.

▶ **9.** Click the **OK** button. When you are asked if you want to update the Yoga Data.mdb file, click the **Yes** button. You return to the Mail Merge Recipients dialog box, as shown in Figure 6-25. If your records look different from those in Figure 6-25, select the data source, click the Edit button, edit the data source, and then click the OK button.

New records added to data source ◀ **Figure 6-25**

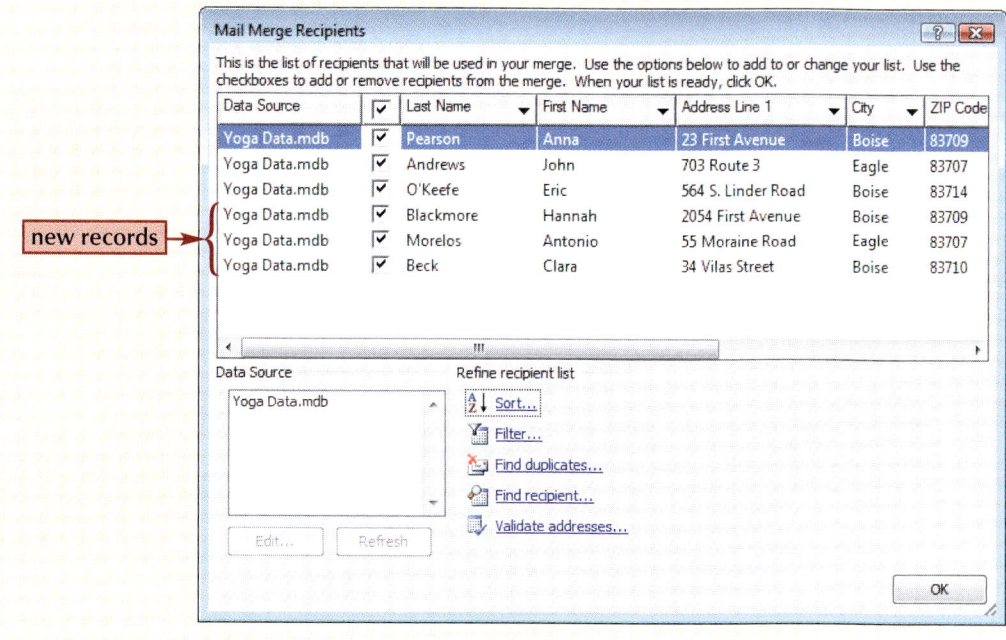

You'll leave the Mail Merge Recipients dialog box open so you can use it to make other changes to the data source.

Sorting Records

As Nina looks through the letters to her clients in the merged document, she notices one problem—the letters are not grouped by zip codes. Currently, the letters are in the order in which clients were added to the data source file. She plans to use bulk mailing rates to send her letters, and the U.S. Postal Service requires bulk mailings to be separated into groups according to zip code. She asks you to sort the data file by zip code and perform another merge, this time merging the main document with the sorted data source.

You can sort information in a data source table just as you sort information in any other table. Recall that to **sort** means to rearrange a list or a document in alphabetical, numerical, or chronological order. You can sort information in ascending order (*A* to *Z*, lowest to highest, or earliest to latest) or in descending order (*Z* to *A*, highest to lowest, or latest to earliest) by clicking a column heading in the Mail Merge Recipients dialog box. The first time you click the heading, the records are sorted in ascending order. If you click it twice, the records are sorted in descending order.

Reference Window | **Sorting a Data Source**

- In the Start Mail Merge group on the Mailings tab, click the Edit Recipient List button to display the Mail Merge Recipients dialog box.
- To sort data in ascending order, click the heading for the column you want to sort. For example, if you want to arrange the records alphabetically according to the contents of the First Name column, click the First Name column heading.
- To sort data in descending order, click the column heading a second time.

Currently, the records in the data source are listed in the order you entered them, with the information for Anna Pearson at the top. You'll sort the records in ascending order, based on the contents of the ZIP Code column.

To sort the data source by zip code:

▶ 1. Verify that the Mail Merge Recipients dialog box is still open.

▶ 2. Scroll right, if necessary, to display the entire ZIP code column.

▶ 3. Click the **ZIP Code** column heading. Word sorts the rows of the data table from lowest zip code number to highest. The information for Antonio Morelos is now at the top of the list. See Figure 6-26. When you merge the data source with the form letter, the letters will appear in the merged document in this order.

Records sorted in ascending order by ZIP code | **Figure 6-26**

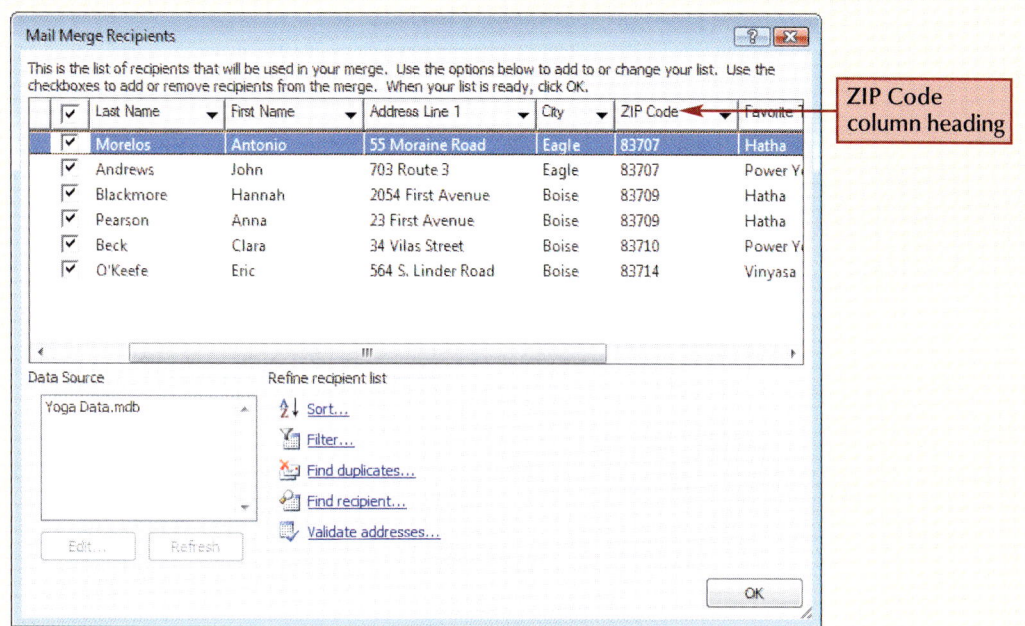

ZIP Code column heading

▶ **4.** Click the **OK** button. The Mail Merge Recipients dialog box closes.

▶ **5.** In the Finish group, click the **Finish & Merge** button, click **Edit Individual Documents**, verify that the **All** option button is selected in the Merge to New Document dialog box, and then click the **OK** button. Word generates the new merged document with six letters, one letter per page as before—but this time the first letter is to Antonio Morelos, who has the lowest zip code (83707).

▶ **6.** Use the Select Browse Object button ⊙ to browse by page and verify that the letters in the newly merged document are arranged in ascending order by zip code. Nina will print the letters later. For now, you will close the document.

▶ **7.** Save the new merged document in the Tutorial.06\Tutorial folder, using the filename **Yoga Merged Letters 2**, and then close it. You return to the main document.

As Nina requested, you've created a merged document with the letters to her clients sorted by zip code. Now she would like you to create a set of letters to just those clients who attend power yoga classes.

Selecting Records to Merge

Nina wants to inform students of Carolyn Brown that she is available for individual instruction only on Tuesdays and Thursdays. She asks you to modify the form letter slightly and then merge it with only those records of clients who have indicated that Carolyn is their favorite teacher. To select specific records in a data source, you use the Mail Merge Recipients dialog box.

To select specific records for a merge:

▶ **1.** Make sure the document named Yoga Letter with Merge Fields is displayed in the document window.

▶ **2.** Click at the end of the third main paragraph, which begins "Please check out our schedule online...."

▶ **3.** Press the ← key to move the insertion point to the left of the period, insert a space, and type **on Tuesdays and Thursdays** and then verify that the sentence reads "...is available for individual instruction on Tuesdays and Thursdays."

▶ **4.** Save the document as **Carolyn Letter with Merge Fields** in the Tutorial.06\Tutorial folder.

▶ **5.** Click the **Edit Recipient List** button in the Start Mail Merge group. The Mail Merge Recipients dialog box opens. To remove an individual record from a merge, you can deselect its check box. You want to include only the records for John Andrews and Clara Beck in this merge, because they are the only clients who listed Carolyn Brown as their favorite teacher.

▶ **6.** Click the **check box** next to the first record (for Antonio Morelos). The check mark is removed.

▶ **7.** Remove the check marks for all the records *except* for the John Andrews and Clara Beck records. See Figure 6-27. Now that you have selected only the records you want, you can complete the merge.

Figure 6-27 ▶ **Specific records selected in data source**

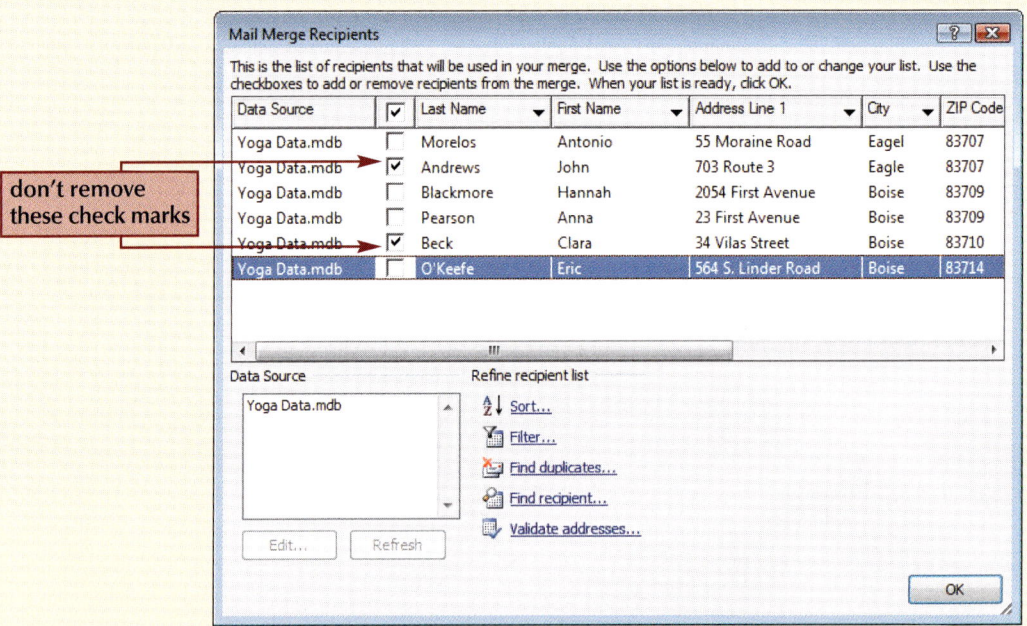

▶ **8.** Click the **OK** button. The Mail Merge Recipients dialog box closes.

▶ **9.** In the Finish group, click the **Finish & Merge** button, click **Edit Individual Documents**, in the Merge to New Document dialog box verify that the **All** option button is selected, and then click the **OK** button. Word generates the new merged document with two letters, one letter per page. This time the first letter is to John Andrews.

▶ **10.** Scroll through the letters in the new merged document to see that they are both addressed to clients who listed Carolyn Brown as their favorite teacher.

▶ **11.** Save the new merged document in the Tutorial.06\Tutorial folder using the file-name **Yoga Merged Letters 3**, close it, save your changes to the document named **Carolyn Letter with Merge Fields**, and then close it.

Next, you'll create and print mailing labels for the form letter so Nina doesn't have to address the letters by hand.

Creating Mailing Labels

Now that you've created and printed the personalized letters, Nina is ready to prepare envelopes in which to mail the letters. She could print the names and addresses directly on envelopes, or she could create mailing labels to stick on the envelopes. The latter method is easier because she can print 14 labels at once, rather than printing one envelope at a time.

Nina has purchased Avery® Laser Printer labels, which are available in most office-supply stores. Word supports most of the Avery label formats, allowing you to choose the layout that works best for you. The labels Nina has come in 8½ × 11-inch sheets designed to feed through a laser printer. Each label measures 4 × 1.33 inches. There are seven rows of labels per sheet, with two labels in each row, for a total of 14 labels. See Figure 6-28.

Layout of a sheet of Avery® labels ◀ **Figure 6-28**

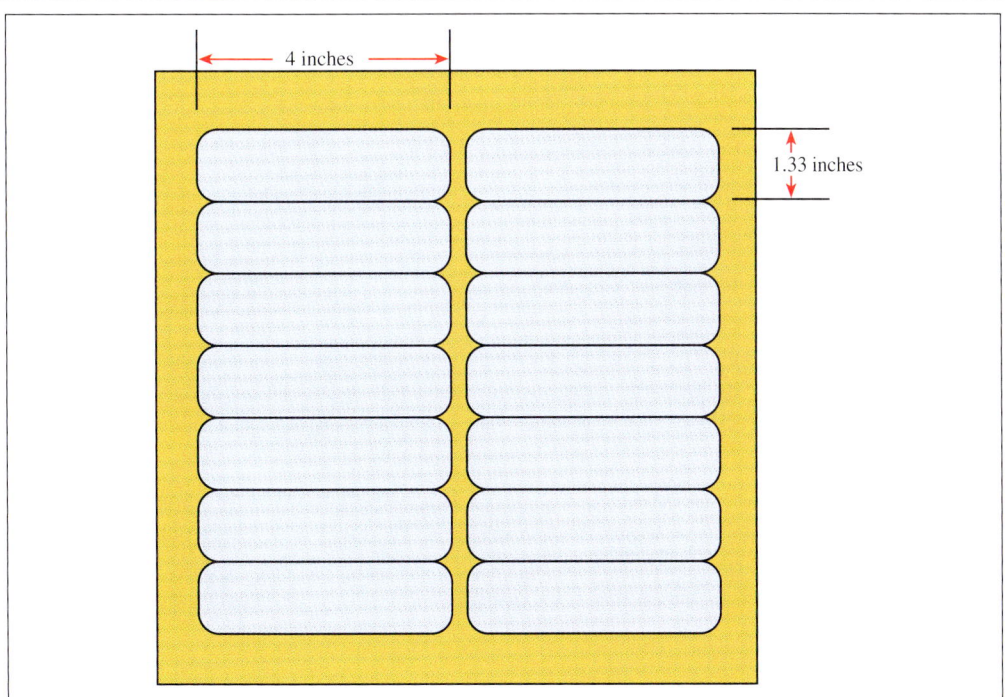

Creating mailing labels is similar to creating form letters, and the Mail Merge task pane walks you through all six steps. You'll begin creating the mailing labels by opening a blank document and the Mail Merge task pane. You can use the same data source file (Yoga Data.mdb) that you used earlier.

To specify the main document for creating mailing labels:

▶ **1.** Open a new, blank document, make sure nonprinting characters are displayed, and zoom out so you can see the whole page.

▶ **2.** Click the **Mailings** tab, and then open the Mail Merge task pane.

▶ **3.** In the Mail Merge task pane, click the **Labels** option button, and then click **Next: Starting document**. The Mail Merge task pane displays information and options for setting up the document layout for labels. (*Note:* If Nina wanted you to print envelopes instead of mailing labels, you would have selected Envelopes as the type of main document.)

▶ **4.** Under "Select starting document," verify that the **Change document layout** option button is selected, and then, under "Change document layout," click **Label options**. The Label Options dialog box opens.

▶ **5.** Click the **Label vendors** arrow, and then click **Avery US Letter**.

▶ **6.** Scroll down the Product number list box, and then click **5162**. This number is found on the packages of most labels that you buy at office supply stores. Your Label Options dialog box should look like Figure 6-29.

Figure 6-29 ▶ Label Options dialog box

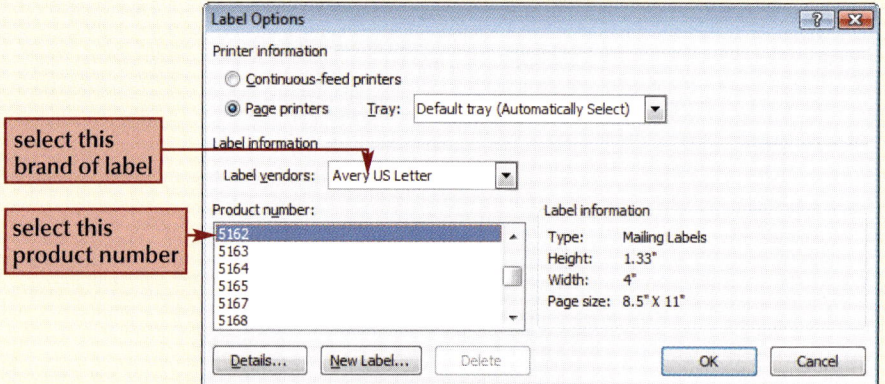

▶ **7.** Click the **OK** button. The Label Options dialog box closes. Word inserts a table structure into the document, with one cell for each of the 14 labels on the page. You might not be able to see the table structure if the table gridlines are not displayed.

▶ **8.** If you don't see the table structure, click the **Table Tools Layout** tab, and then, in the Table group, click the **View Gridlines** button to select it. You can now see that the document is divided into label-sized rectangles, as shown in Figure 6-30. The gridlines are visible only on the screen; they will not be visible on the printed labels.

Document ready for labels ◀ **Figure 6-30**

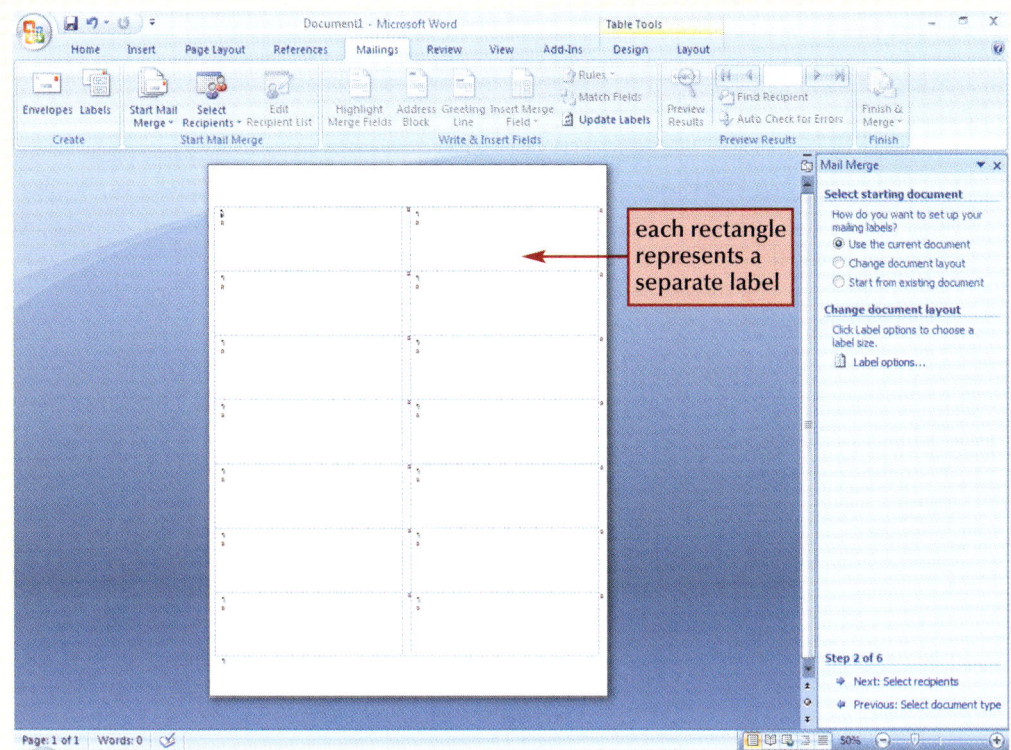

You are finished setting up the document. Next, you need to save the main document and select the data source you created earlier.

To continue the mail merge for the labels:

▶ **1.** Save the main document to the Tutorial.06\Tutorial folder using the filename **Yoga Labels with Merge Fields**.

▶ **2.** Click **Next: Select recipients**. Under "Select recipients," verify that the **Use an existing list** option button is selected, and then, under "Use an existing list," click **Browse**. The Select Data Source dialog box opens.

▶ **3.** Navigate to and select the file named **Yoga Data** in the Tutorial.06\Tutorial folder, and then click the **Open** button. The Mail Merge Recipients dialog box opens.

▶ **4.** Verify that all the records are displayed with all check boxes selected, and then click the **OK** button. The Mail Merge Recipients dialog box closes. A special code (<<Next Record>>) is inserted into all the labels except the one in the upper-left corner. To see the <<Next Record>> code, you need to adjust the Zoom setting.

▶ **5.** Zoom in so you can read the document. The <<Next Record>> code is a special code that tells Word how to insert data into the document. You can ignore it.

▶ **6.** Click **Next: Arrange your labels**. The Mail Merge task pane displays options for inserting merge fields into the document. Note that if the data source included a State field, you could use the Address block option to insert a complete set of fields for a single address. However, because the data source does not include a State field, you need to insert the fields individually, as you did when creating the form letter.

▶ **7.** Verify that the insertion point is located in the upper-left label, and then, in the Write & Insert Fields group on the Mailings tab, click the **Insert Merge Field** button arrow.

▶ **8.** Click **First_Name**, and then in the Write & Insert Fields group, click the **Highlight Merge Fields** button. The First_Name merge field is inserted in the document and displayed on a gray background.

▶ **9.** Press the **spacebar** to add a space after the First Name field, insert the **Last_ Name** field, press the **Enter** key, insert the **Address_Line_1** field, press the **Enter** key, insert the **City** field, type **,** (a comma), press the **spacebar** to insert a space, type **ID**, press the **spacebar**, and then insert the **ZIP_Code** field. You are finished inserting the fields for the first label. Now you will update your labels so the merge fields appear on all the labels.

▶ **10.** Near the bottom of the Mail Merge task pane, click the **Update all labels** button. (You might have to scroll down to see it; use the scroll button at the bottom of the task pane.) The address fields are inserted into all the labels in the document, as shown in Figure 6-31. In all except the upper-left label, the Next Record code appears to the left of the First Name merge field.

Figure 6-31   **Field codes inserted into document**

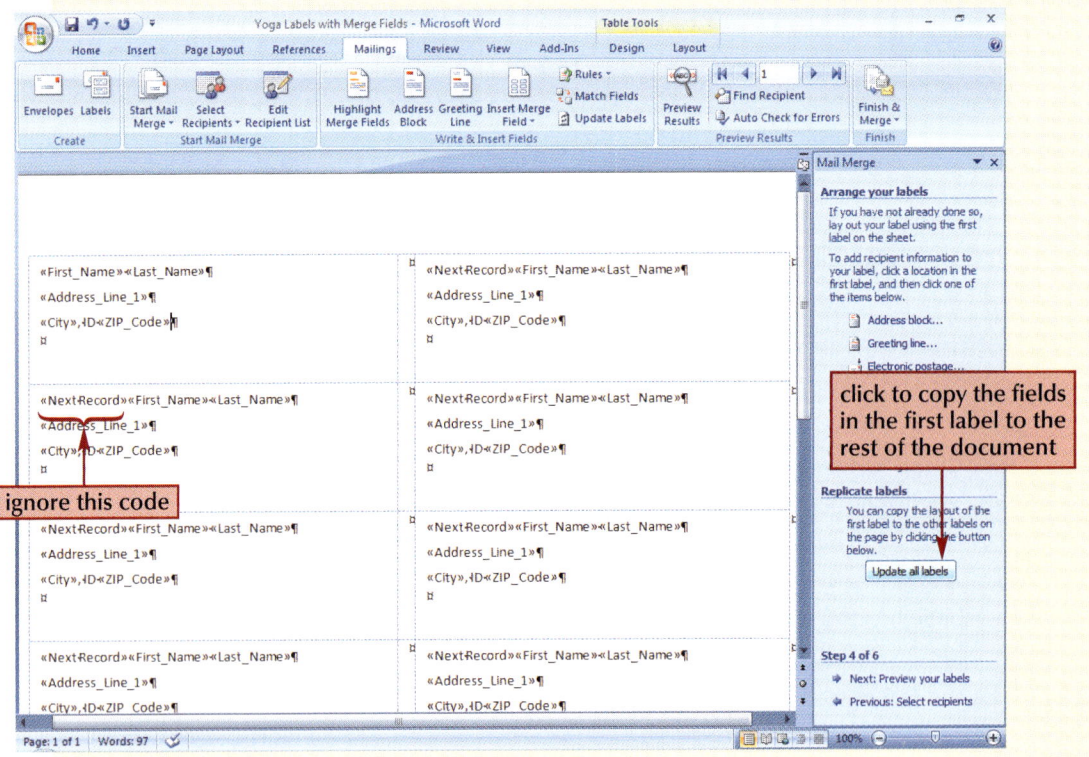

You are ready to preview the labels and complete the merge.

To preview the labels and complete the merge:

▶ **1.** Click **Next: Preview your labels** in the Mail Merge task pane. (You might have to scroll down to display this option, again using the scroll button at the bottom of the task pane.) The data for the clients is displayed in the labels. For now, ignore the extra ", ID" in labels that would otherwise be blank. You are ready to merge to a new document.

2. Click **Next: Complete the merge** in the task pane, click **Edit individual labels** in the task pane, verify that the **All** option button is selected in the Merge to New Document dialog box, and then click the **OK** button. The finished labels are displayed in a new document.

The labels are almost finished. All you need to do is edit the document to remove the "ID" text from the unused labels, save the document, and print the labels. For now, you'll just print the labels on an 8½ × 11-inch sheet of paper so you can see what they look like. Later, Nina will print them on the sheet of labels.

To edit, save, and print the labels:

1. Scroll through the document. The document contains space for 14 labels, but the data source contained only six records. However, when you clicked the Update Labels button in the task pane earlier, the comma and the state abbreviation (ID) were copied to all the labels, including those that don't contain any address information. See Figure 6-32, where the document is zoomed to show the whole page, so you can see all the labels. You can solve this problem with the extra text by deleting the extra text in the bottom four rows of labels.

Extra text in labels document   **Figure 6-32**

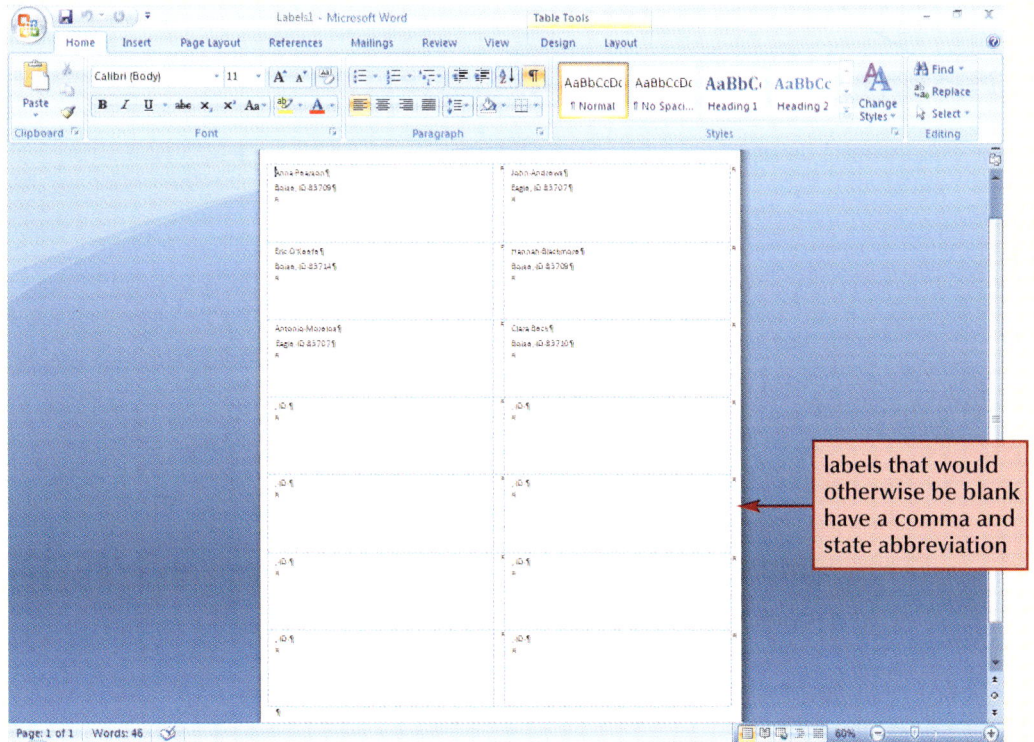

labels that would otherwise be blank have a comma and state abbreviation

2. Change the Zoom setting to **Whole Page**, drag the mouse pointer to select the bottom four rows of labels, and then press the **Delete** key. The extra text is deleted.

3. In the upper-left label, change "Anna Pearson" to your name, and then save the merged document in the Tutorial.06\Tutorial folder using the filename **Yoga Merged Labels**.

▶ **4.** Print the labels on a sheet of paper, just as you would print any other document.

   Trouble? If you want to print on a sheet of labels, ask your instructor or technical support person how to feed the label sheet into the printer. If you're using a shared printer, you might need to make special arrangements so other users' documents aren't accidentally printed on your label sheet.

▶ **5.** Close the merged document, and then close the task pane if necessary.

▶ **6.** Save changes to the main document, and then close it.

InSight	**Printing Labels**

Labels are expensive, so it's extra important to take care in completing the merge to avoid wasting label sheets. When you create labels, keep these tips in mind:

- It's a good idea to print one page of a label document on regular paper so you can check your work before printing on the more expensive sheets of adhesive labels.
- Always check the few rows of a labels document for extra text, just as you did with the Yoga studio labels.
- If you include a State field in your data source, you can avoid the problem with extra text in unused labels by inserting an Address Block merge field instead of individual merge fields mixed with regular text.

Creating a Telephone Directory

Next, Nina wants you to create a list of telephone numbers for all the teachers at Lily Road Yoga Studio. Nina has already created a Word document containing the phone numbers; you will use that document as the data source for the merge. You'll set up a mail merge as before, except this time you'll select Directory as the main document type. You'll start by examining the Word document that Nina wants you to use as the data source.

To begin creating the telephone list:

▶ **1.** Open the document named **Phone** from the Tutorial.06\Tutorial folder, and then save it as **Phone Data** in the same folder.

▶ **2.** Review the document. Note that the information is arranged in a table with three column headings: "First Name," "Last Name," and "Phone." The information in the table has already been sorted in alphabetical order by last name.

▶ **3.** In the bottom row, replace "Nina Ranabhat" with your name.

▶ **4.** Save and close the Phone Data document, open a new, blank document, display nonprinting characters, if necessary, and display the rulers.

▶ **5.** Open the Mail Merge task pane, and then zoom out if necessary so you can see the 6-inch mark on the ruler.

▶ **6.** In the Mail Merge task pane under "Select document type," click the **Directory** option button, click **Next: Starting document**, verify that the **Use the current document** option button is selected, click **Next: Select recipients**, verify that the **Use an existing list** option button is selected, and then click **Browse**. The Select Data Source dialog box opens.

7. Navigate to and select the file named **Phone Data** in the Tutorial.06\Tutorial folder as the data source, click the **Open** button, review the records in the Mail Merge Recipients dialog box, and then click the **OK** button.

8. In the task pane, click **Next: Arrange your directory**. The document is still blank; you'll insert the merge fields next.

You're ready to insert the fields in the main document. Nina wants the telephone list to include the names at the left margin of the page and the phone number at the right margin. You'll set up the main document so that the phone number is preceded by a dot leader. A **dot leader** is a dotted line that extends from the last letter of text on the left margin to the beginning of the nearest text aligned at a tab stop.

To create the main document with dot leaders:

1. With the insertion point at the top of the blank document, insert the **First_Name** merge field, insert a space, insert the **Last_Name** merge field, and then in the Write & Insert Fields group, click the **Highlight Merge Fields** button. The First Name and Last Name merge fields are displayed on a gray background. Now you'll set a tab stop at the right margin (at the 6-inch mark on the ruler) with a dot leader.

2. Click the **Page Layout** tab, then in the Paragraph group, click the **Dialog Box Launcher** to open the Paragraph dialog box, and then in the lower-left corner of the Paragraph dialog box, click the **Tabs** button. The Tabs dialog box opens.

3. Type **6** in the Tab stop position text box, then in the Alignment section, click the **Right** option button, and then in the Leader section, click the **2 ....** option button. See Figure 6-33. While the Tabs dialog box is open, notice the Clear All button, which you could click to delete all the current tab stops.

Creating a tab with a dot leader | **Figure 6-33**

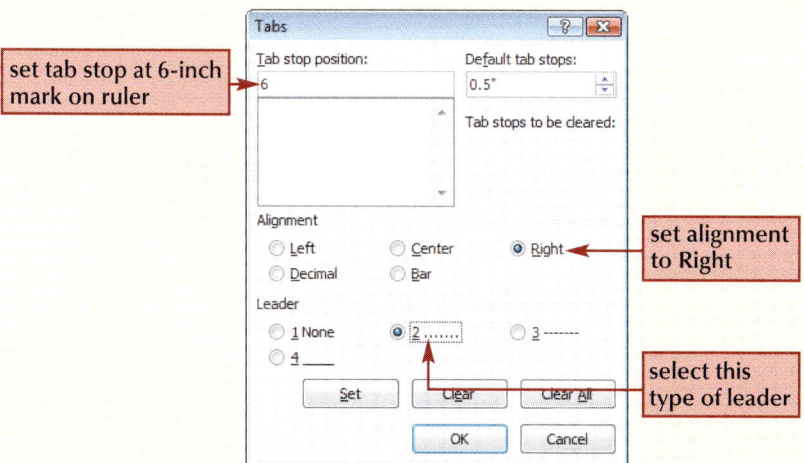

set tab stop at 6-inch mark on ruler

set alignment to Right

select this type of leader

4. Click the **OK** button. Word clears the current tab stops and inserts a right-aligned tab stop at the 6-inch mark on the horizontal ruler.

5. Press the **Tab** key to move the insertion point to the new tab stop. A dotted line stretches across the page, from the Last Name field to the right margin.

6. Switch back to the Mailings tab, and then insert the **Phone** merge field at the location of the insertion point.

7. Press the **Enter** key. You must insert a hard return here so that each name and telephone number will appear on a separate line. Notice that the dot leader shortened to accommodate the inserted field. The completed main document should look like Figure 6-34.

Completed main document for telephone directory

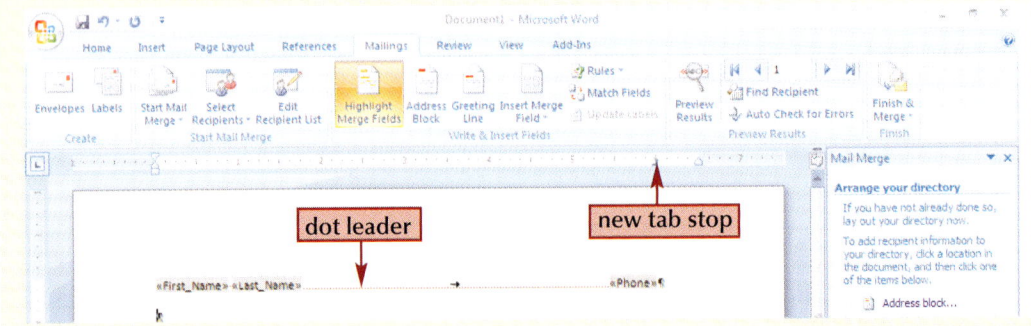

8. Save the main document in the Tutorial.06\Tutorial folder using the filename **Phone Directory with Merge Fields**.

You are now ready to merge this file with Nina's data source.

To merge the files for the phone list:

1. In the Mail Merge task pane, click **Next: Preview your directory**, and then review the data for the first record in the document.

2. Click **Next: Complete the merge** in the task pane, click **To New Document** in the task pane, verify that the **All** option button is selected in the Merge to New Document dialog box, and then click the **OK** button. Word creates a new document that contains the completed telephone list. See Figure 6-35.

Completed telephone directory

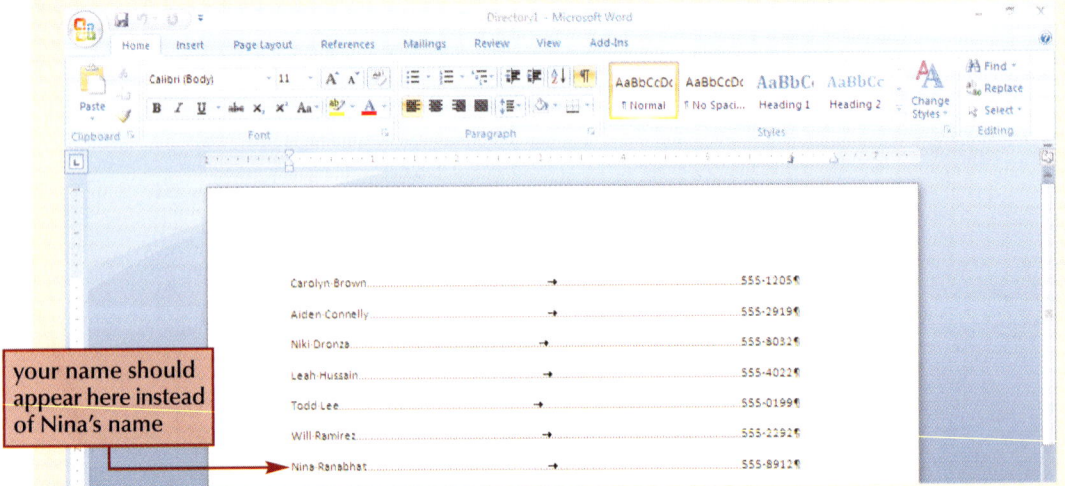

3. Save the document as **Phone Directory** in the Tutorial.06\Tutorial folder, and then close it.

4. Save and close the **Phone Directory with Merge Fields** document.

You have created the telephone list. Nina will print it and distribute it to each of the teachers. Now that you are familiar with the many types of documents you can create using Word's Mail Merge feature, you can use mail merge whenever you need to distribute customized information to a group of people.

Converting Text to Tables and Tables to Text

Nina needs your help with a few other tasks related to managing information about the teachers and clients at Lily Road Yoga Studio. First, she needs to convert names and addresses of new clients, which her assistant typed for her, into a table. She will then use the table later as the data source in a mail merge.

Before you can convert text into a table, you need to verify that the information in the document is set up properly. That is, you need to make sure that **separator characters**—typically commas or tabs—are used consistently to divide the text into individual pieces of data. Upon conversion, each data item is formatted as a separate cell in a column, and each paragraph mark starts a new row.

To convert text into a table:

▶ **1.** Open the document named **Client** from the Tutorial.06\Tutorial folder, and then save it as **Client Table** in the same folder. Display nonprinting characters, if necessary.

▶ **2.** Review the document. Notice that it consists of three paragraphs. Each paragraph contains seven separate pieces of information (first name, last name, address, city, zip code, favorite type of yoga, and favorite teacher) separated by commas.

▶ **3.** Drag the mouse to select the three paragraphs, click the **Insert** tab, click the **Table** button, and then, at the bottom of the Table menu, click **Convert Text to Table**. The Convert Text to Table dialog box opens. See Figure 6-36. Because the information in each paragraph is separated by commas, the Commas option button at the bottom of the dialog box is selected. Note that the Number of columns setting is 7. This corresponds to the seven pieces of information in each paragraph.

Converting text to a table | Figure 6-36

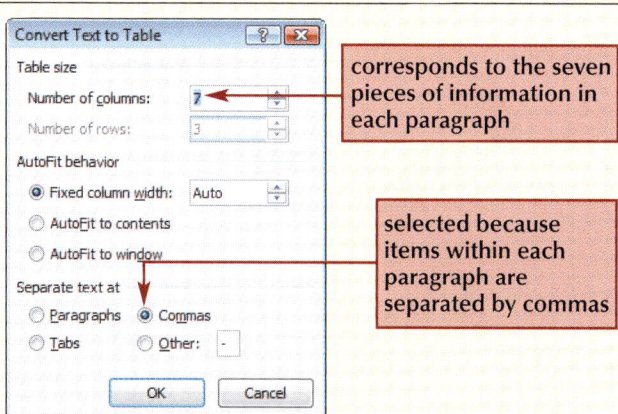

corresponds to the seven pieces of information in each paragraph

selected because items within each paragraph are separated by commas

Tip

When converting text to a table, if the result is not what you expect, undo the conversion and then review the text to make sure it is set up consistently, with each paragraph containing the same number of data items, and with the data items broken up by the same separator character.

▶ **4.** Click the **OK** button. The Convert Text to Table dialog box closes, and the text in the document is converted into a table consisting of seven columns and three rows. Next, you need to add the column headings.

▶ **5.** Click in the left margin to select the top row of the table, click the **Table Tools Layout** tab, and then in the Rows & Columns group, click the **Insert Above** button. A blank row is added at the top of the table.

▶ **6.** Enter the following column headings: **First Name**, **Last Name**, **Street Address**, **City**, **ZIP Code**, **Favorite Type**, and **Favorite Teacher**. Format the column headings in bold. When you are finished, your table should look like the one in Figure 6-37.

Figure 6-37 ▶ **Text changed to table**

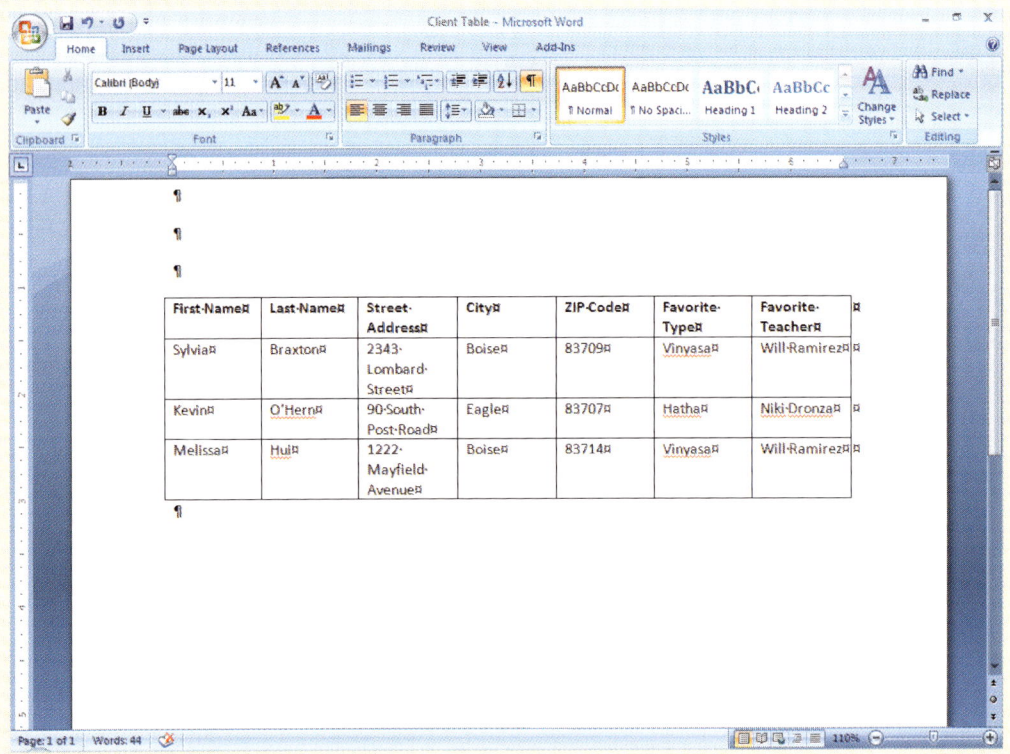

▶ **7.** Save the document, and then close it. Nina will use the Client Table in another mail merge she has planned for next month, and eventually she'll combine it with her current list of clients.

You have finished converting text into a table. Now, Nina needs your help doing the opposite—that is, converting a table into text. After the conversion, she will use the text to create a list of yoga teachers for the studio.

To convert a table into text:

▶ **1.** Open the document named **Phone Data** from the Tutorial.06\Tutorial folder, and then save it as **Teacher List** in the same folder. Display nonprinting characters, if necessary. You want to include only the names of Nina's teachers, so you will start by deleting the header row and the Phone column.

2. Click in the left margin to select the header row, click the **Table Tools Layout** tab, then in the Rows & Columns group, click the **Delete** button, and then click **Delete Rows**.

3. Select the column containing the phone numbers, and then use the Delete button in the Rows & Columns group to delete the column. The table now contains only the first and last name of each yoga teacher. You are ready to convert this table into text.

4. Select the entire table, verify that the Table Tools Layout tab is displayed, and then in the Data group, click **Convert to Text**. The Convert to Text dialog box opens.

5. Click the **Other** option button. In the text box next to this option button, you can specify how you want to divide the information in each row. In this case, you want to separate the first and last names by a space.

6. In the text box next to the Other option button, delete the hyphen, verify that the insertion point is at the far-left edge of the text box, and then press the **spacebar** to insert a space. See Figure 6-38.

Converting a table to text   **Figure 6-38**

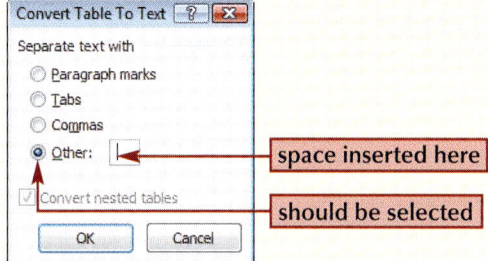

7. Click the **OK** button. The Convert Table to Text dialog box closes. The contents of the table are now formatted as seven separate paragraphs, one for each row in the table. Each first name is separated from its corresponding last name by a space.

You now have seven paragraphs, each containing the name of a teacher at Lily Road Yoga studio. In the next section, you will use Word's list features to manipulate these paragraphs, creating a useful list for Nina.

Working with Lists

Nina often has to respond to calls from potential clients asking about teachers at the yoga studio. To make her job easier, Nina wants to create a quick reference list with information about each teacher, such as what they teach and how strenuous their classes are. She wants you to format the names of the yoga teachers as a list, alphabetize it, and then add more information.

To convert the text to a list and sort it:

1. If necessary, select the seven paragraphs containing the names of the yoga teachers, and then format the selected text as a bulleted list using the default bullet style.

2. Select the bulleted list, and then, in the Paragraph group, click the **Sort** button ⬆⬇. The Sort Text dialog box opens. This is similar to the dialog box you've already used several times before to sort tables. You want to sort the paragraphs in the list in ascending alphabetical order.

► **3.** Verify that **Paragraphs** appears in the Sort by text box and that the **Ascending** option button is selected, and then click the **OK** button. The Sort Text dialog box closes, and the bulleted paragraphs are arranged alphabetically. The list begins with Aiden Connelly, unless your name comes alphabetically before "Aiden," in which case your name appears at the top of the list.

► **4.** Save the document.

Now that the list is sorted, you need to add some more information about each teacher. When working with a bulleted or numbered list, you can indent items in the list. When you do, Word automatically applies a different bullet or numbering style to the indented item, to help create a visual distinction between the various levels of the list. Indenting an item in a numbered or bulleted list is known as **demoting** the item. Moving an item in a list back to the left is known as **promoting** the item. You'll see how this works in the following steps.

To add information to the list:

► **1.** Click to the right of Aiden Connelly's name, and then press the **Enter** key to insert a new bulleted paragraph. The round, black bullet looks just like the other bullets in the list.

► **2.** In the Paragraph group on the Home tab, click the **Increase Indent** button ![icon]. The bulleted paragraph is indented, and the bullet changes to a white bullet with a black outline.

► **3.** Type **Specialties include Flow Yoga and Pilates**, and then press the **Enter** key to insert another bulleted paragraph. The new paragraph is indented at the same level as the previous paragraph, with the same style of bullet.

► **4.** Click ![icon]. The bulleted paragraph is indented even more. The bullet changes to a black square.

► **5.** Type **Flow Yoga is not recommended for beginners**, press the **Enter** key, and then type **Pilates requires four hours of individual instruction**.

► **6.** Press the **Enter** key to insert a new bulleted paragraph, click the **Decrease Indent** button ![icon] in the Paragraph group to promote the new bulleted paragraph, and then type **His classes are generally considered very challenging**. When you are finished, your bulleted list should look like the list in Figure 6-39. Nina's assistant will finish adding information to the bulleted list later. For now, you can save and close it.

Figure 6-39 | **Bulleted list with multiple levels**

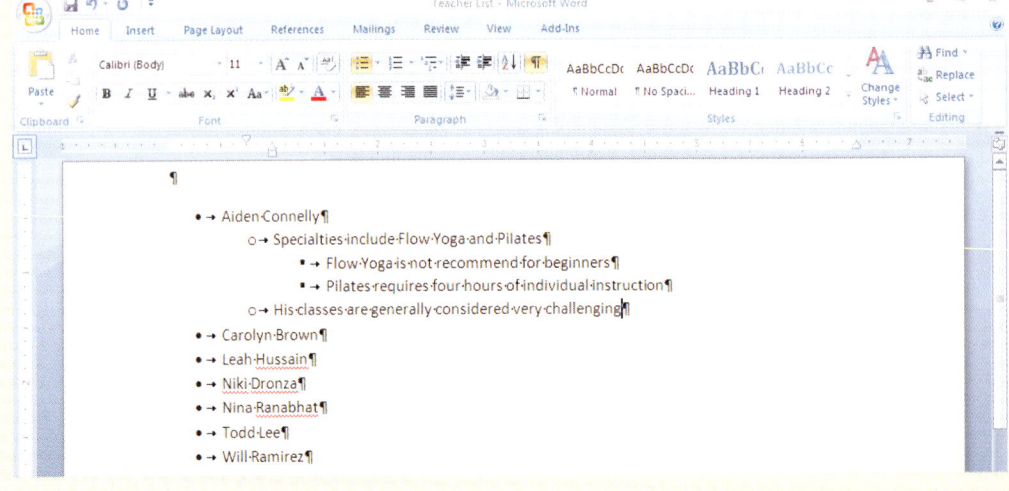

▶ **7.** Save the document and close it.

Session 6.2 Quick Check | Review

1. True or False: After you complete a mail merge and close the main document, the connection between the main document file and the data source file is broken.
2. Explain how to edit a data source for a main document that is already open.
3. Explain how to select records to merge.
4. When you create a directory with a dot leader, what do you have to do after you insert the merge field on the right side of the page?
5. True or False. You can convert data in a document to a table only if the individual pieces of data are separated by tabs.

Tutorial Summary | Review

In this tutorial, you opened the Mail Merge task pane and then completed a mail merge by selecting a main document, creating a data source, inserting merge fields into the main document, and merging the form letter with the data source. You then used the Mail Merge feature to create mailing labels and a telephone directory. In the process, you edited a data source and sorted records in a data source. Finally, you converted text to a table to create a new data source, and you converted a table to text, which you then formatted as a bulleted list with multiple levels.

Key Terms

chevrons	fields	merged document
data	form letter	promote
data source	Mail Merge task pane	record
date field	main document	sort
demote	merge	separator character
dot leader	merge fields	

Practice | **Review Assignments**

Apply the skills you learned in the tutorial using the same case scenario.

Data Files needed for the Review Assignments: Bonus.docx, Contacts.docx, More.docx

Nina's clients are happy with the new facility, and the open-studio days she offered in June were a big success. Nina was pleased with how convenient it was to send out form letters with the Word Mail Merge feature. Now she wants to send a letter inviting clients who have purchased an annual membership to sign up for their membership bonus—either a massage or a meditation session, depending on which option they selected when they purchased their membership. (*Note:* As you complete the following steps, print only those documents your instructor asks you to print.)

1. Start Word if necessary with a new, blank document, and then open the Mail Merge task pane.

2. Verify that Letters is selected as the type of main document, then in Step 2 of the Mail Merge Task pane, select the file **Bonus** in the Tutorial.06\Review folder included with your Data Files as the main document, and then save the current document as **Bonus Letter with Merge Fields** in the Tutorial.06\Review folder. In the letter's closing, replace Nina's name with yours.

3. In Step 3 of the Mail Merge task pane, create a new data source with the following fields: First Name, Last Name, Address Line 1, City, State, ZIP Code, and Bonus. Remove any extra fields so that the data source contains only seven fields.

4. Create four records using the following information (don't include the commas in the records; they are inserted here to help you see which text belongs in which fields):
   - Jane Cussler, 299 Hollister Street, Boise, ID, 83710, massage
   - May Simon, 922 Flambeau Road, Cloverdale, ID, 83712, meditation session
   - Carl Hesse, 933 Wildway Avenue, Beatty, ID, 83722, massage
   - William Greely, 52 Eton Way # 3, Boise, ID, 83714, meditation session

5. Save the data source as **Bonus Data** in the Tutorial.06\Review folder.

6. Edit the data source to replace "William Greely" with your first and last name.

7. Sort the data source by zip code from the lowest to the highest.

8. In Step 4 of the Mail Merge task pane, insert a date field in the format "March 7, 2010" at the top of the letter. Create an inside address consisting of the necessary merge fields; don't forget to use the Shift+Enter keys to prevent extra paragraph spacing. Add a salutation that includes the First Name merge field. Insert the Bonus field into the body of the letter where indicated. Add the appropriate number of blank paragraphs so the letter is formatted like a standard business letter. Insert blank paragraphs as necessary to center the letter vertically on the page.

9. Save your changes to the main document, and then preview the merged document. Correct any formatting or spacing problems.

10. In Step 6 of the Mail Merge task pane, merge to a new document and view all the letters. Save the merged document as **Merged Bonus Letters**, scroll to view the letters, and then close the file.

11. Return to Step 5 in the Mail Merge task pane, edit the data source to select only records for clients interested in a meditation session, and then complete a second merge. Save the new merged document as **Merged Meditation Letters**. Close all documents, saving all changes.

12. Open a new, blank document, open the Mail Merge task pane, and create a set of mailing labels using the vendor Avery US Letters and product number 5162. Save the main document as **Labels with Merge Fields** in the Tutorial.06\Review folder.

13. In Step 3 of the Mail Merge task pane, select the Bonus Data file you created earlier as the data source.

14. In Step 4 of the Mail Merge task pane, insert the necessary merge fields.

15. Update all the labels, preview the merged labels, merge all the records to a new document, and then save the new document as **Merged Labels** in the Tutorial.06\Review folder and close it. Save and close all open documents.

16. Create a telephone directory using the same format as the telephone directory you created in the tutorial. Use the file named **Contacts** from the Tutorial.06\Review folder as the data source. Set a right tab at six inches and use a dot leader. Save the main document as **Directory with Merge Fields** in the Tutorial.06\Review folder and the merged document as **Merged Directory** in the same folder. Close the files.

17. Open the document named **More** from the Tutorial.06\Review folder and save it as **More Bonus Data**. Convert the data in the document to a table. Insert a header row with the following column headers: First Name, Last Name, Street Address, City, State, ZIP Code, and Bonus. Replace "Sandy Martinez" with your name. Save and close the document.

18. Open the document named **Contacts** from the Tutorial.06\Review folder and save it as **Contacts Info** in the same folder. Delete the header row and the phone number column, and then convert the table to four paragraphs of text.

19. Format the company names as a bulleted list, and then add the extra information shown in Figure 6-40. Be sure to demote the subordinate bullets, as shown in Figure 6-40.

Figure 6-40

- Bright Day Window Cleaning
    - Scheduled for the first Monday of every month
        - In summer, may have to switch to the first Tuesday of every month
        - Move the table away from the front window before cleaners arrive
    - Paid by direct deposit
- Franklin Security
    - Tom Smith manages our security
    - Notify Tom if orange light blinks on alarm box
- Boise Federal Savings
    - Deposits must be in by 5 P.M.
    - Include a yellow deposit slip with every deposit
- Regent Property Management
    - Sally Thomson manages our account
    - Rent paid by direct deposit
        - Verify deposit on the 15th of every month
        - Call Sally to confirm if necessary

20. In the bullet under "Regent Property Management," change "Sally Thomson" to your name. Save and close the document.
21. Submit the documents to your instructor, either in printed or electronic form, as requested.

| Apply | **Case Problem 1** |

Apply the skills you learned to create a letter to customers of an art gallery.

Data File needed for this Case Problem: Gallery.docx

Nightingale Gallery Nell Williams owns Nightingale Gallery, a purveyor of fine art photography in Saginaw, Michigan. She wants to send out a letter to past customers informing them of an upcoming show by a local photographer. (*Note:* As you complete the following, print only those documents your instructor asks you to print.)

1. Open a new, blank document, and then begin a mail merge using Letters as the document type. For the starting document, select the document named **Gallery** from the Tutorial.06\Case1 folder, and then save it in the same folder as **Gallery Letter**. In the closing, replace "Student Name" with your name.
2. Create a data source with the following field names: Title, First Name, Last Name, Address Line1, ZIP Code, and E-mail Address.

3. Enter the following four records into the data source (don't include the commas in the records; they are inserted here to help you see what text belongs in what fields):
   - Mr., David, Joliet, 1577 Cooperville Drive, 48601, joliet@world.net
   - Mr., Paul, Robertson, 633 Wentworth, 48603, d_roberts@pmc.org
   - Ms., Maya, Suyemoto, 4424 Bedford, 48602, m_suyemoto@TaylorCulkins.com
   - Ms., Kira, Gascoyne, 844 Winter Way, 48601, gascoyne@saginaw.school.edu

4. Save the data source as **Gallery Data** in the Tutorial.06\Case1 folder, and then sort the records alphabetically by last name.

5. Edit the data source to replace "Kira Gascoyne" with your name. Change the title to "Mr." if necessary. Replace the e-mail address for that record with your e-mail address.

6. Add an inside address (use the Shift+Enter keys after each line) and a salutation to the document, using merge fields where necessary. Use "Saginaw, MI" as the city and state. Use the Title merge field and the Last Name merge field in the salutation.

7. Save your changes to the main document. Preview the merged document, and then merge to a new document. If you don't see the row of photographs at the top of the first letter, don't be concerned. You may not have a fast enough video card or enough memory to display them properly. After you close the document in the next step, and then re-open it, you will see the photographs on the first page.

8. Save the merged letters document as **Merged Gallery Letters** in the Tutorial.06\Case1 folder and then close it. If you did not see the photographs on the first page of the document in Step 7, re-open the document, verify that the photographs are properly displayed, and then close the document again.

9. Close the **Gallery Letter** document, saving any changes.

10. Open a new blank document, save it as **Gallery Envelopes** in the Tutorial.06\Case1 folder, and then open the Mail Merge task pane.

⊕ EXPLORE
11. Use the Mail Merge task pane to create envelopes, as follows:
   - In Step 1 of the Mail Merge task pane, select Envelopes as the type of main document.
   - In Step 2 of the Mail Merge task pane, verify that the Change document layout option button is selected, and then click Envelope options. In the Envelope Options dialog box, verify that Envelope size 10 ($4^1/_8 \times 9^1/_2$ in) is selected in the Envelope size box, and then click the OK button.
   - In Step 3 of the Mail Merge task pane, select the **Gallery Data** file you created earlier as the data source.
   - In Step 4 of the Mail Merge task pane, click the recipient address area of the envelope, and then insert the necessary merge fields to print a title, first name, last name, and street address and zip code on each envelope. For the city and state, use "Saginaw, MI."
   - In Step 5, preview the merged envelopes.
   - In Step 6, merge to a new document, and then save the document as **Merged Gallery Envelopes**.

12. Close all open documents, saving changes as necessary.

13. Create a customer e-mail directory that includes first and last names but not titles. Use the file named **Gallery Data** (which you created earlier) as the data source. Do not include the record for David Joliet in the merge. Use a dot leader, with the right tab stop set at the 6-inch mark, to separate the name on the left from the e-mail address on the right.

14. Save the main document for the e-mail directory as **E-mail Directory** in the Tutorial.06\Case1 folder.

15. Save the merged document as **Merged E-mail Directory** in the Tutorial.06\Case1 folder.

16. Save and close all open documents. Submit the documents to your instructor, in either printed or electronic form, as requested.

Apply | **Case Problem 2**

Apply the skills you learned to create a form letter for a mortgage company using an Excel file as a data source.

Data File needed for this Case Problem: Mortgage.docx, Mortgage Data.xlsx

Lensville Mortgage Corporation   As an account manager at Lensville Mortgage Corporation, you need to send out letters to past customers asking them to consider refinancing with a new loan. Your data source for this case problem is in an Excel file. (*Note:* As you work on this Case Problem, print only those documents your instructor asks you to print.)

1. Open a new, blank document, and begin a mail merge using Letters as the document type. For the starting document, select the document named **Mortgage** from the Tutorial.06\Case2 folder, and then save it in the same folder as **Mortgage Letter**. In the closing, replace "Student Name" with your name.

⊕ EXPLORE
2. For the data source, select the Excel file **Mortgage Data** from the Tutorial.06\Case2 folder.

3. Edit the data source to replace "Barb Russ" with your name.

4. At the beginning of the main document, insert a date field.

5. Insert an Address Block merge field for the inside address in the form "Joshua Randall Jr.," and format the Address block merge field using the No Spacing Quick Style. Insert a salutation using the First Name merge field. Use a proper business-letter format throughout.

6. In the body of the letter, replace the placeholders [NUMBER OF YEARS], [CURRENT LOAN TERM], and [NEW LOAN TERM] with the appropriate merge fields.

7. Open the Mail Merge Recipients dialog box, and then sort the records in ascending order by Current Loan Term.

8. Preview the merged document, and then merge to a new document. Save the merged document as **Merged Mortgage Letters** in the Tutorial.06\Case2 folder.

9. Close all open documents, saving all changes.

10. Create a main document for generating mailing labels on sheets of Avery US Letter Address labels, product number 5162, using the **Mortgage Data** file as your data source. Use the same Address Block merge field code that you used for the inside address of the Mortgage Letter file. Save the main document as **Mortgage Labels** in the Tutorial.06\Case2 folder.

11. Preview the merged document, merge to a new document, and then save the merged document as **Merged Mortgage Labels** in the Tutorial.06\Case2 folder. Close all open documents, saving any changes.

⊕ EXPLORE
12. Use Word Help to look up the topic "Use mail merge to create and print letters and other documents" and learn how to filter records in a data source. Open your **Mortgage Letter** file from the Tutorial.06\Case2 folder (click Yes if you are asked to run an SQL command), and save it as **Mortgage Letter Filtered**. Start a mail merge, and then select the **Mortgage Data** file as the data source. Use what you learned from Help to filter out all records except records for customers in Fort Myers. You should end up with two records displayed in the Mail Merge Recipients dialog box.

13. Preview the merged document, and then complete the merge to a new document. Save the merged document as **Merged Fort Myers** in the Tutorial.06\Case2 folder.

14. Close all open documents, saving any changes. Submit the documents to your instructor, in either printed or electronic form, as requested.

| Challenge | **Case Problem 3** |

Perform a mail merge using the Mailings tab instead of the Mail Merge task pane.

Data Files needed for this Case Problem: Letter.docx, Pasta.txt

Fierenze Pasta Kayla Souza is manager of Fierenze, a manufacturer of fresh pasta in Racine, Wisconsin. Fierenze has just bought out a competitor, JD Pasta. Now Kayla wants to send a letter to JD Pasta's longtime customers, who she hopes will become Fierenze customers. She wants to use Word's mail merge feature to create a letter that informs each customer of the price of his or her favorite type of pasta. Kayla retrieved the customer data from the JD Pasta's computer system in the form of a text file, with the data fields separated by commas. Kayla needs your help to convert the text file to a Word table, which she can then use as the data source for a mail merge. (*Note:* As you complete the following steps, print only those documents your instructor asks you to print.)

EXPLORE

1. In Word, open the text file named **Pasta.txt** from the Tutorial.06\Case3 folder. To find the text file in the Open dialog box, click the arrow next to the Files of type list box, and then click All Files. Once the file is open, save it as a Word document (in the Save As dialog box, click Word document in the Files of type list box) in the same folder using the filename **Pasta Data**.

2. Format the data in the Normal style, and then convert it to a table. Insert your first and last name where indicated. Insert a header row with the following column headers: First Name, Last Name, Street Address, City, State, ZIP Code, Type, and Price. Save the document and close it.

3. Open the file **Letter** from the Tutorial.06\Case3 folder, and then save it as **Pasta Letter** in the same folder. In the closing, replace "Student Name" with your first and last name.

EXPLORE

4. Begin a mail merge using the buttons on the Mailings tab instead of the Mail Merge task pane. Start by using the Start Mail Merge button to create a letter main document using the current document. As you perform the remaining steps in this case problem, continue to use the options on the Mailings tab rather than the Mail Merge task pane.

5. Use the Select Recipients button to select the **Pasta Data** document as the data source, and then use the Edit Recipient List button to sort the records in ascending alphabetical order by type of pasta.

6. Insert a date field where indicated by the brackets at the top of the document, and then use the Insert Merge Field button to replace the placeholder text that appears in brackets with an inside address.

EXPLORE

7. For the salutation, experiment with the Greeting Line button on the Mailings tab. Use the Greeting Line dialog box to insert a salutation that includes "Dear" and the customer's first name, followed by a colon.

8. Edit the body of the form letter to replace the placeholder text with the corresponding merge field names.

9. Save the document. Use the Preview Results button to view the merged document, and then use the Finish & Merge button to merge all the records to a new document. Save the merged document as **Merged Pasta Letters** in the Tutorial.06\Case3 folder.

10. Close all open documents, saving changes as necessary. Submit the documents to your instructor, in either printed or electronic form, as requested.

| Create | Case Problem 4 |

Use the skills you learned in the tutorial to create the list shown in Figure 6-41.

There are no Data Files needed for this Case Problem.

Chronos Steel Corporation   As a public relations specialist at Chronos Steel Corporation, you are often asked to explain the process of making steel to a general audience. To save time, you have decided to create a handout that summarizes the process. (*Note:* As you complete the following steps, print only those documents your instructor asks you to print.)

Figure 6-41

Steel Production

➢ Raw materials
     ○ Usually three components
         ▪ Iron ore
         ▪ Limestone
         ▪ Coke
             ● Coke is a byproduct of coal
             ● Created when coal is baked at a high temperature to purify it
     ○ Raw materials can vary by manufacturer
➢ Raw materials are heated in a blast furnace
➢ Slag floats to top and is drained, leaving molten iron suitable for steel
➢ Molten iron is transformed into steel
     ○ Molten iron is mixed with scrap metals
     ○ The iron and scrap metals are heated in an oxygen furnace
     ○ The resulting liquid steel is formed into slabs
➢ Slabs are milled to desired thickness and treated with acid

1. Open a new, blank document, save it as **Steel Handout** in the Tutorial.06\Case4 folder, and then change the document theme to Verve.
2. Type the multilevel bulleted list shown in Figure 6-41; don't specify the bullet type yet. Format the title, "Steel Production," in the Heading 1 style and center it.

 **EXPLORE**

3. Click in the "Raw Materials" bulleted paragraph, and then select the arrow bullet style to change all the top-level bullets to the arrow style.

⊕ **EXPLORE**

4. In Word Help, look up *bullets* and then read the topic that explains how to add picture bullets or symbols to a list. Use what you learned to change the second-level bullets (the first of which is "Usually three components") from a white circle to an orange square. Then change the third-level bullets (the first of which is "Iron ore") to green squares and the lowest level bullets to brown squares.

5. Save your changes to the document, and then save it as **Numbered Handout** in the same folder so that you can change the bullets to numbering in the next step.

6. Select the bulleted list and use the Numbering button to format it as a numbered list instead. The multiple levels of the new numbered list are numbered in outline form.

7. Delete items 1.a and 1.b, but not the items under 1.a.

⊕ **EXPLORE**

8. Using the same technique you used to promote items in a bulleted list, promote the three paragraphs containing the three raw materials so they are lettered a, b, and c. Promote the two items about coke so they are numbered i and ii.

9. Save the document and close it. Submit the documents to your instructor, in either printed or electronic form, as requested.

Research | **Internet Assignments**

Go to the Web to find information you can use to create documents.

The purpose of the Internet Assignments is to challenge you to find information on the Internet that you can use to work effectively with this software. The actual assignments are updated and maintained on the Course Technology Web site. Log on to the Internet and use your Web browser to go to the Student Online Companion for New Perspectives Office 2007 at **www.course.com/np/office2007**. Then navigate to the Internet Assignments for this tutorial.

Assess | **SAM Assessment and Training**

If you have a SAM user profile, you may have access to hands-on instruction, practice, and assessment of the skills covered in this tutorial. Log in to your SAM account (**http://sam2007.course.com**) to launch any assigned training activities or exams that relate to the skills covered in this tutorial.

Session 6.1

1. a. A date field is an instruction that tells Word to insert the current date.
   b. A main document is a document (such as a letter) that, in addition to text, contains merge fields to mark where variable information (such as a name or an address) from the data source will be inserted.
   c. A merge field is a code in a main document that tells Word where to insert specific information from the data source.
   d. A record is a collection of information about one individual or object in a data source. For example, a record might include the first name, last name, address, and phone number for a client.

2. data source

3. True

4. False

5. Position the insertion point in the main document where you want to insert the merge field. Click More Items in the Mail Merge task pane, click the field you want to insert in the Insert Merge Field dialog box, click Insert, and then click Close. Alternately, in the Write & Insert Fields group on the Mailings tab, click the Insert Merge Field button, and then click the field you want to insert. Adjust the spacing or formatting around the merge field as necessary.

6. Click the Insert tab, and then, in the Text group, click the Date and Time button. In the Date and Time dialog box, click the date format you want, select the Update automatically check box, and then click the OK button.

Session 6.2

1. False

2. In the Start Mail Merge group on the Mailings tab, click the Edit Recipient List button. In the Data Source list box in the Mail Merge Recipients dialog box, select the data source you want to edit, and then click the Edit button. To add a record, click the New Entry button, and then type a new record. To delete a record, click any field in the record, and then click the Delete Entry button. To add or remove fields from the data source, click the Customize Columns button, and make any changes.

3. Click the Edit Recipients button in the Start Mail Merge group on the Mailings tab and then deselect the check boxes for the records you do not want to include in the merge.

4. Press the Enter key to insert a blank paragraph below the directory merge fields.

5. False

Ending Data Files

Tutorial.06 →

Tutorial

Carolyn Letter with
   Merge Fields.docx
Client Table.docx
Phone Data.docx
Phone Directory.docx
Phone Directory with
   Merge Fields.docx
Teacher List.docx
Yoga Data.mdb
Yoga Labels with
   Merge Fields.docx
Yoga Letter with
   Merge Fields.docx
Yoga Merged Labels.docx
Yoga Merged Letters 1.docx
Yoga Merged Letters 2.docx
Yoga Merged Letters 3.docx

Review

Bonus Data.mdb
Bonus Letter with
   Merge Fields.docx
Contacts.docx
Contacts Info.docx
Directory with
   Merge Fields.docx
Labels with
   Merge Fields.docx
Merged Bonus Letters.docx
Merged Directory.docx
Merged Labels.docx
Merged Meditation
   Letters.docx
More Bonus Data.docx

Case1

E-mail Directory.docx
Gallery Data.mdb
Gallery Envelopes.docx
Gallery Letter.docx
Merged E-mail Directory.docx
Merged Gallery Envelopes.docx
Merged Gallery Letters.docx

Case2

Merged Fort Myers.docx
Merged Mortgage Labels.docx
Merged Mortgage Letters.docx
Mortgage Data.xlsx
Mortgage Labels.docx
Mortgage Letter.docx
Mortgage Letter Filtered.docx

Case3

Merged Pasta Letters.docx
Pasta Data.docx
Pasta Letter.docx

Case4

Numbered Handout.docx
Steel Handout.docx

Collaborating with Others and Creating Web Pages

Writing a Program Description

Case | Green Fields Fresh Lunch Program

Zoe Rios is the owner and president of Rios Communications in Dubuque, Iowa, a public relations company that specializes in developing publicity documents and Web sites. She is currently working on a program description for Green Fields, an organization that is devoted to improving the quality of meals served in area schools.

As a professional writer, Zoe knows the importance of writing and revising several drafts of a document, and she knows it's vital to ask her clients and colleagues to review her documents and make suggestions. As a first step, she asked Henry Davis, a writer at Rios Communications, to review a draft of the program description. He will read the document in Word, make some corrections, and insert some comments. While Henry is revising the program description, Zoe has asked you to work on it, making additional changes. When you are finished, Zoe wants you to merge Henry's edited version of the document with your most recent draft.

After you create a new version of the document for Zoe, she wants you to add some budget figures compiled by Alison Jorgenson, the Program Director for the Green Fields organization. She also needs you to add a pie chart created by Henry. When you are finished, she wants you to e-mail the program description to Alison. Finally, to make the program description available to the organization's members, she asks for your help to distribute it in printed form and publish it on her company's Web site.

starting Data Files

Tutorial.07 →	Tutorial	Review	Case1	Case2	Case3	Case4
	Budget.xlsx	Expenses.xlsx	Cook.docx	Kreelie.docx	Survey.xlsx	FAQ.docx
	Chart.xlsx	Menu.docx	Statement.xlsx	Sun.docx		
	Green.docx	Progress.docx				
	Green Fields HD.docx	Progress HD.docx				
	Resume.docx	Rates.xlsx				

Session 7.1

Tracking Changes and Making Comments in a Document

When you edit a printed copy of a document, it's common to use a brightly colored pen to draw lines through words or phrases you want to delete. You might write new text in the margin and then draw a line to the place in the document where you want to insert the text. You might also write notes to yourself or the writer in the margin, reminding you about facts you need to check or suggesting new sections for the writer to add. The problem with this revision method is that after you finish marking up the printed copy, you or the writer must go back to the computer and enter your changes into the document. In a long document, this can be very time-consuming. Instead of writing marks on a printed copy, it's more efficient to use Microsoft Word's Track Changes feature and the Comments feature.

Tracking Changes

When you turn on **Track Changes**, Word uses a variety of ways to mark the changes you make to the document. Any text that you insert appears in a contrasting color, with an underline. Text that you delete appears with a strikeout line, just as if you'd drawn a line through it on the printed page. If you make formatting changes, they are listed in the margin in oblong boxes known as **balloons**. In addition, a vertical line appears in the left margin next to text that has been changed in any way. Collectively, the colored text, the strikeout lines, the margin balloons, and the vertical margin lines are known as **revision marks**.

You can use the mouse to point to any marked revision in a document; this displays a ScreenTip that indicates who made the change and the date and time the change was made. By default, the name assigned to each change is taken from the User name text box on the Popular tab of the Word Options dialog box. This indication of who made a particular edit is especially useful when you are sharing revisions among a group of reviewers.

When you feel confident about the changes you or someone else has made to your document, you can accept the changes, at which point Word removes the revision marks from your document. You can accept all the changes at once, or you can go through them one by one, accepting or rejecting each one individually. When you reject a change, depending on what change you are rejecting, Word removes the text you inserted, or undoes the formatting you applied, or restores the text you deleted.

The Review tab contains all the options you need for working with track changes. Among other things, you can use the options on the Review tab to move from one change to another, to accept or reject changes, and to hide revision marks. When you hide revision marks, Word continues to track changes, but doesn't display them on the screen.

Reference Window | **Tracking Changes in a Document**

- Verify that the document is displayed in Print Layout view, click the Review tab, and then in the Tracking group, click the Track Changes button.
- Verify that Final Showing Markup is displayed in the Display for Review list box in the Tracking group.
- Edit the document as you ordinarily would. Adjust the document zoom as necessary, so you can easily see tracked changes in the document and in the margin.

Working with Comments

In addition to making changes to a document, you can also insert margin notes known as **comments**. You can attach a comment to a selected word, phrase, or paragraph. Text to which a comment has been attached is highlighted in a contrasting color so that you can easily see what the comment refers to. You type the text of your comment in a balloon that appears in the right margin. In addition to the text of your comment, the comment balloon displays the name of the person who made the comment, as well as the date and time it was made. As with tracked changes, the name assigned to each comment is taken from the User name text box on the Popular tab of the Word Options dialog box.

Although comments are often used in conjunction with the tracked changes, you don't have to turn on Track Changes in order to insert comments in a document. They are separate features. The Review tab contains all the options you need for working with Comments.

Inserting Comments | Reference Window

- Select the text to which you want to attach a comment.
- Click the Review tab, and then in the Comments group, click the New Comment button.
- Type the text of your comment in the balloon that appears in the margin.
- Adjust the document zoom as necessary so you can read the document text as well as the comment balloons in the margin.

Revising a Document with Tracked Changes and Comments

Zoe has already e-mailed a copy of her document to Henry. He will review it for her while she makes some additional changes. She decides to turn on Track Changes before she begins making these additional changes so she will have a record of the changes she makes after sending the file to Henry.

To edit Zoe's document with Track Changes turned on:

▶ 1. Open the document named **Green** from the Tutorial.07\Tutorial folder included with your Data Files, and then save it as **Green Fields** in the same folder.

▶ 2. Switch to Print Layout view if necessary, display nonprinting characters, and change the document zoom to Page width. There's no need to display the ruler.

▶ 3. Review the document, and notice that it includes three headings formatted with the Heading 1 style for the Office theme. The first heading in the document is not formatted in a heading style; instead it is simply formatted in the heading font (Cambria) and in blue. Page 1 includes two placeholders in brackets, which you will eventually replace with an Excel chart and an Excel worksheet. Also notice the photograph on page 2.

▶ 4. Click the **Review** tab, and then in the Tracking group, click the **Track Changes** button. (Do not click the Track Changes button arrow.) The Track Changes button is highlighted in orange, indicating that the Track Changes feature is turned on. You won't see any revision marks until you begin editing the document.

Trouble? If a menu appears below the Track Changes button, you clicked the Track Changes button arrow by mistake. Press the Escape key to close the menu, and then click the Track Changes button.

▶ **5.** In the Tracking group, verify that Final Showing Markup appears in the Display for Review list box. This is a default setting which tells Word to display the revision marks on the screen. See Figure 7-1.

Figure 7-1 **Track Changes turned on**

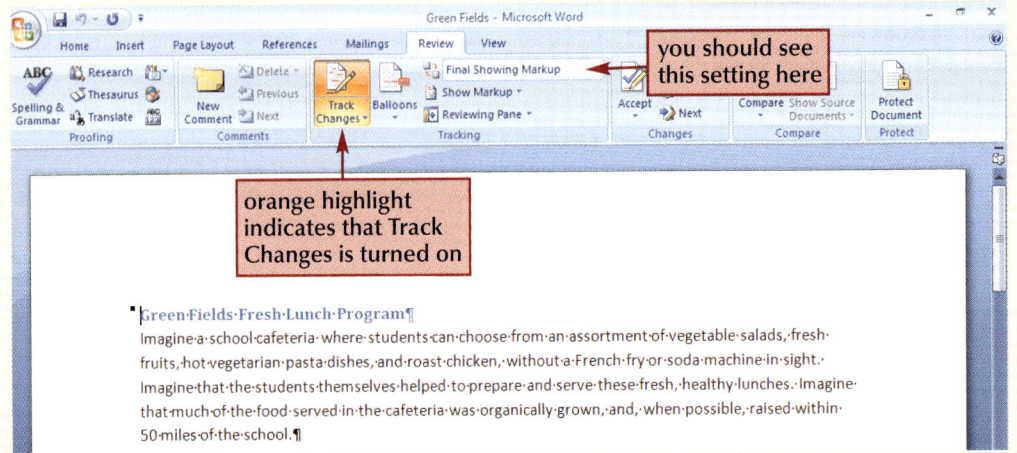

You'll start by making a change in the first main paragraph.

▶ **6.** In the paragraph below the first heading, select the number **50** in the last sentence, and then type **100**. A strikeout line appears through the number 50, and the new number, 100, appears in color. In Figure 7-2, the number 100 is red, but depending on how your computer is set up, it might be a different color. The new number is also underlined, and a vertical line appears in the left margin, drawing attention to the change.

Figure 7-2 **Edit with revision marks turned on**

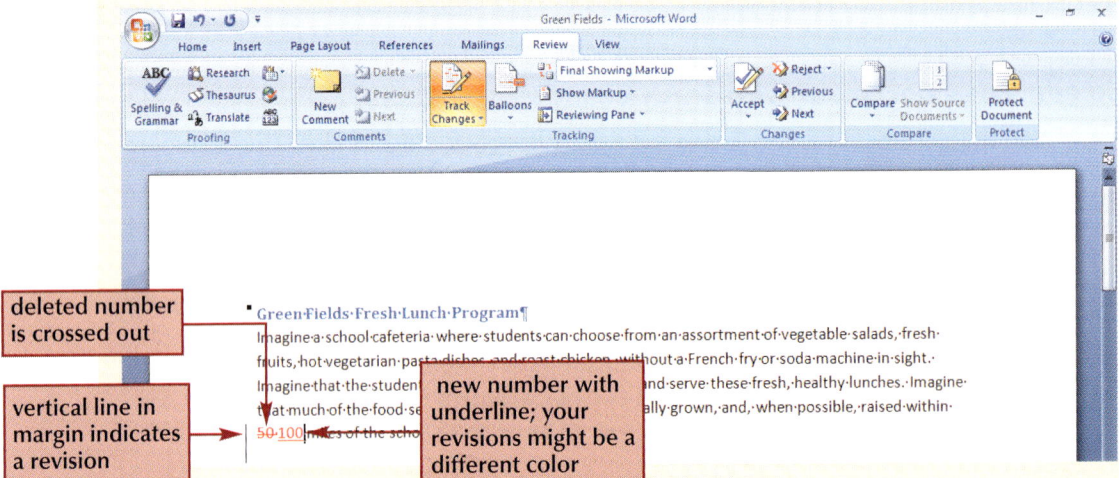

Next, you need to move a sentence. Zoe wants the second to last sentence in this paragraph to be the last sentence in the paragraph.

▶ **7.** Select the sentence **Imagine that the students themselves helped to prepare and serve these fresh, healthy lunches.** Take care to select the space after the sentence as well.

8. Drag the sentence down to insert it at the end of the paragraph, and then click any-where in the document to deselect it. The sentence is inserted with a double under-line, in color. This time the color is different from the one used for the number "100" earlier, because Word uses a separate color to denote moved text. In Figure 7-3, the sentence appears in green, but it might be a different color on your computer. The sentence is still visible in its original location, but now it is also displayed in color, with a double strikeout line through it. A vertical line appears in the left margin, next to the sentence in its original location, and also next to the sentence in its new location. When you inserted the sentence, Word automatically deleted the space after it and added a space before it, to the left of the "I" in "Imagine."

Tracked changes showing text moved to a new location | **Figure 7-3**

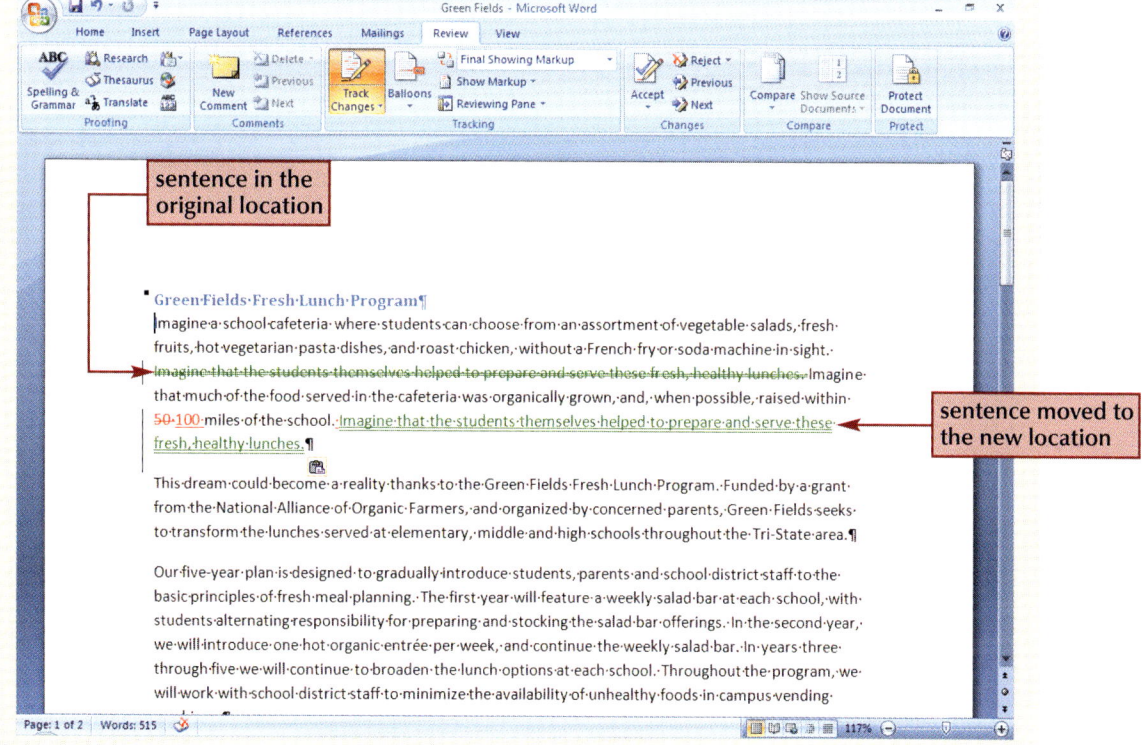

After reviewing the sentence in its new location at the end of the paragraph, Zoe decides she wants to shorten it slightly by deleting the word "healthy."

9. Click to the left of the comma after "fresh," and then press the **Delete** key repeat-edly to delete the comma, the space after it, and the word **healthy**. The deleted text ", healthy" appears with a strikeout line through it, so that the sentence reads "...serve these fresh lunches."

Finally, you need to format the first heading in the document with the Heading 1 style.

10. Click in the left margin to select the heading **Green Fields Fresh Lunch Program**, click the **Home** tab, and then click the **Heading 1** style in the Quick Styles gallery. The heading is formatted with the larger font size of the Heading 1 style, a vertical line appears in the left margin next to the heading, and a balloon appears in the right margin containing the text "Formatted: Heading 1," indicating that you for-matted the paragraph with the Heading 1 style. Because you selected Page width zoom earlier, the document zoom automatically adjusts to allow you to see the document text as well as the balloon in the right margin. See Figure 7-4.

Figure 7-4   **Tracked changes showing formatted text**

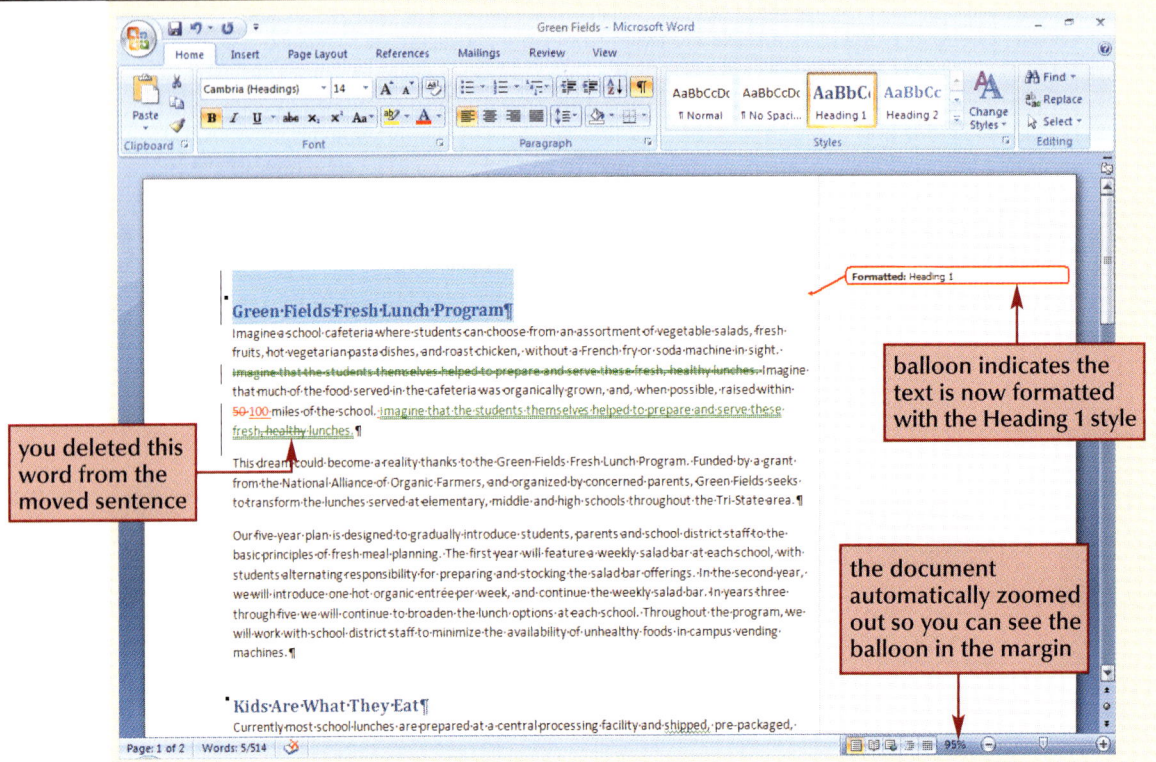

You are finished editing the document for now. For each edit, Word noted the current user name for the copy of Word on your computer, as well as the current date and time. You can display this information by moving the mouse pointer over one of your edits.

To display a ScreenTip that indicates the user name, date, and time for an edit:

1. Move the mouse pointer over the newly inserted number **100**. A ScreenTip appears displaying the type of edit (an insertion), the user name for the copy of Word in which the edit was made, and the date and time the edit was made. In Figure 7-5, the user name is Zoe Rios, but you should see either your name or another name. See Figure 7-5. Later in this tutorial you will learn how to change the user name.

ScreenTip with user name and date ◄ **Figure 7-5**

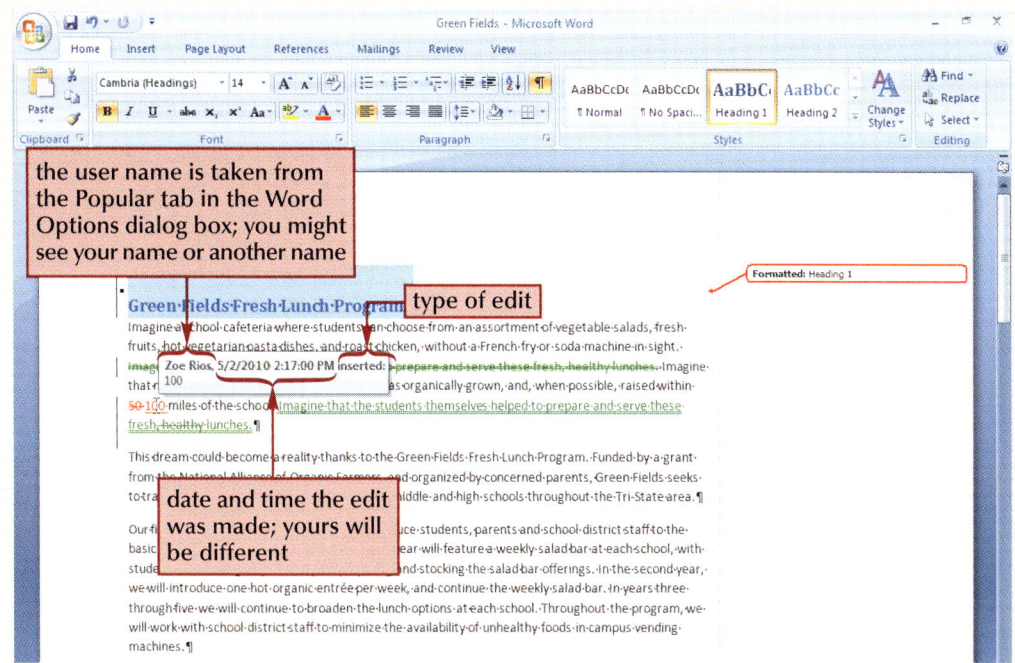

2. Move the mouse pointer over the moved sentence, the deleted sentence, and the newly formatted heading, and review the ScreenTip that appears over each edit.

Zoe would like you to add a comment in the Budget section on page 2.

To add a comment to page 2:

1. Scroll down until you can see the Budget section on the top of page 2. The second sentence says that a complete budget will be available soon. Zoe wants to include a reminder to be more precise, if possible, about exactly when the full budget will be ready. She wants to attach the comment to the word "soon," so you start by selecting that word.

2. At the end of the Budget section, select the word **soon**.

3. Click the **Review** tab, and then in the Comments group click the **New Comment** button. The word "soon" is highlighted in color, a balloon is inserted in the right margin, and the insertion point moves to the balloon, ready for you to begin typing the comment. In Figure 7-6, the highlighting and the balloon are red, but they might be a different color on your computer. Also, in Figure 7-6, you see "Comment [ZR1]." The letters "ZR" are Zoe's initials; the number 1 after the initials tells you that this is the first comment inserted by Zoe Rios. On your computer, you see your initials or some other set of initials, depending on the settings on the Popular tab of the Word Options dialog box.

Figure 7-6 | Inserting a comment

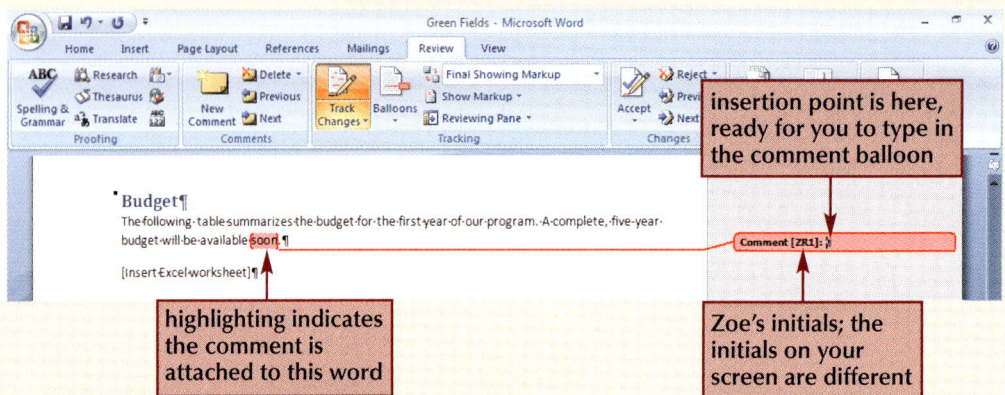

> **4.** With the insertion point in the comment balloon, as shown in Figure 7-6, type **Can we give a precise date for the new budget?** The comment is displayed in the balloon in the right margin. The insertion point remains in the comment balloon until you click in the document.

> **5.** Click anywhere in the document text, and then save your work.

Adjusting Track Changes Options

The default settings for Track Changes worked well as you edited Zoe's document. Note, however, that you can change these settings if you prefer. For instance, you could select a larger balloon for comments or a different color for inserted text. You could also change the user name that appears in the ScreenTip for each edit. You don't need to change any options now, but you will take a moment to learn how to change them, in case you want to later.

To learn how to change the Track Changes options:

> **1.** Click the **Track Changes** button arrow. A menu appears below the Track Changes button.
>
> **Trouble?** If you don't see a menu and if the Track Changes button is now deselected, you clicked the Track Changes button rather than the arrow below it. Click the Track Changes button again to select it, and then click the Track Changes button arrow to open the menu.

> **2.** Click **Change User Name**. The Popular tab of the Word Options dialog box opens. You've seen this tab before, when you used the Word Options dialog box to adjust Word settings. The User name text box on the Popular tab contains the current user name for the copy of Word installed on your computer. This is the name that appears in the ScreenTip associated with each edit when Track Changes is turned on. The letters in the Initials text box are the initials that appear in comment balloons. Do not change the user name or initials now. Simply note their location, and keep in mind that when you are working on your own computer, you should make sure the User name text box contains your full name, and that the Initials text box contains your initials.

> **3.** Click the **Cancel** button to close the Word Options dialog box. You return to the Green Fields document.

▶ **4.** Click the **Track Changes** arrow to display the menu again, and then click **Change Tracking Options**. The Track Changes Options dialog box opens. As shown in Figure 7-7, you can use the options in the Balloons section to control the size and location of the balloons in the margins. Other options in this dialog box allow you to select the colors you want to use for various types of edits. For example, you can use the Color list box next to the Insertions list box to select a color to use for inserted text. Note that the default setting for Insertions, Deletions, Comments, and Formatting is By author. This means that Word assigns one color to each person who edits the document. You'll see the significance of that later in this tutorial, when you merge your copy of the document with Henry's. Finally, note that you can deselect the Track moves check box or the Track formatting check box if you don't want to track those types of changes. Right now there's no need to change any of the settings in the Track Changes Options dialog box, so you can close it.

Examining the Track Changes Options dialog box ◀ **Figure 7-7**

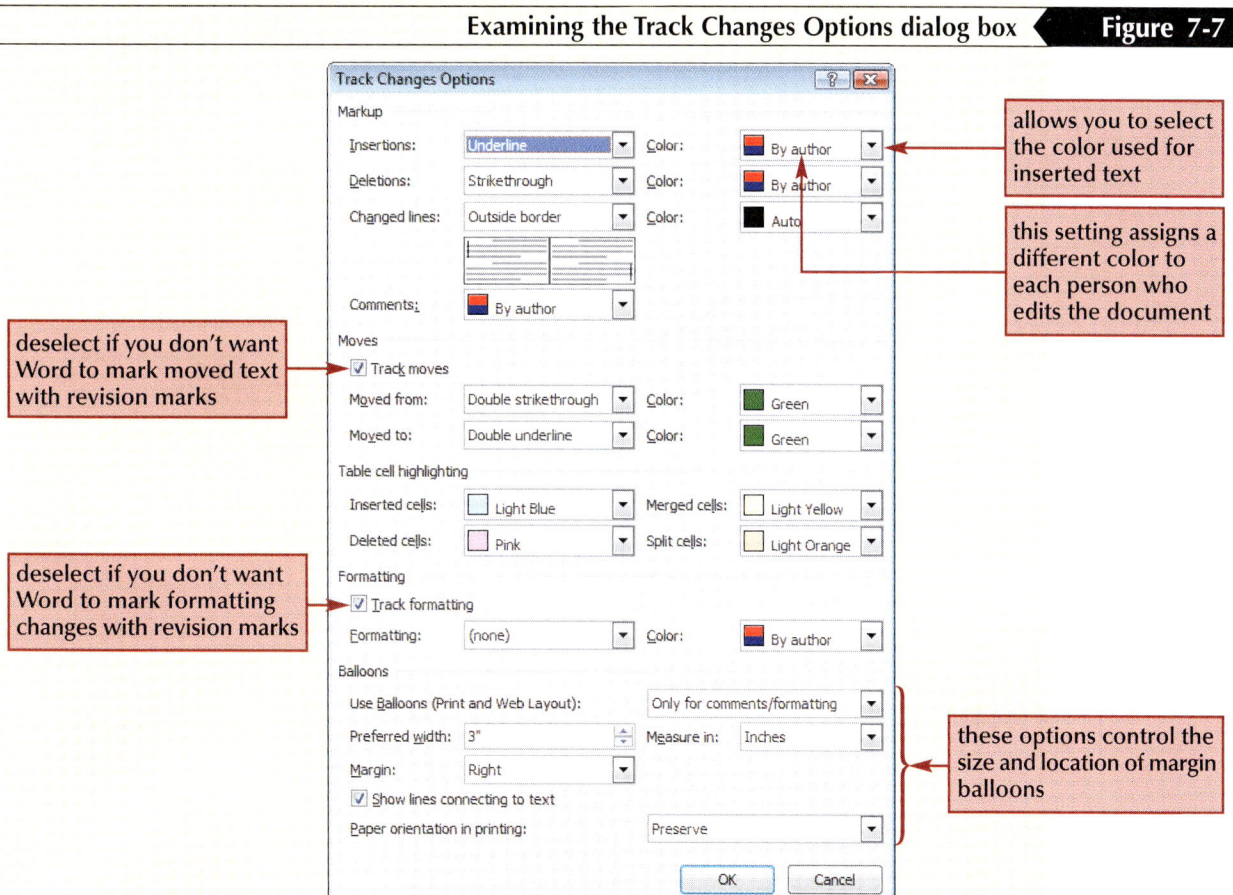

▶ **5.** Click the **Cancel** button to close the Track Changes Options dialog box, and then click the **Balloons** button in the Tracking group. A menu opens, displaying options related to the way tracked changes are displayed in margin balloons. Currently, "Show Only Comments and Formatting in Balloons" is selected. To hide the margin balloons, you could click Show All Revisions Inline. To display a margin balloon for every edit (including insertions, moves, and deletions), you could click Show Revisions in Balloons. Right now, there's no need to change the default setting.

▶ **6.** Press the **Escape** key to close the Balloons menu.

You are finished making Zoe's additional changes in the document. She has received Henry's edited copy via e-mail, and now she'd like your help in combining her copy of the Green Fields document with Henry's.

Comparing and Combining Documents

When you work in a collaborative environment, where multiple people work on the same document, Word's Compare and Combine features are essential tools. They allow you to compare documents, with revision marks highlighting the differences. The Compare and Combine features are similar, but they have different purposes.

Use the **Compare** feature when you have two different versions of a document that do not contain revision marks and you want to see the differences between the two. Use the **Combine** feature when you have two or more versions of a document that contain revision marks, which you want to combine into a single document. Note that it's also common to use the term **merge** rather than "combine" when talking about combining documents. However, keep in mind that merging, when used in this context, is different from the mail merge operation you learned about earlier.

When you compare two documents, you select one document as the original document and one as the revised document. Word then creates a new, third document, which consists of the original document with revision marks added to show how the revised document differs from the original document. The original document and the revised document are left unchanged.

For example, suppose the original document contains the sentence "The sky is blue." Also, suppose that in the revised document, the sentence reads "The sky is dark blue." When you compare these two documents, you create a third document where the sentence looks like you took the original document, turned on revision marks, and inserted the word "dark." See Figure 7-8.

Figure 7-8	Comparing two documents

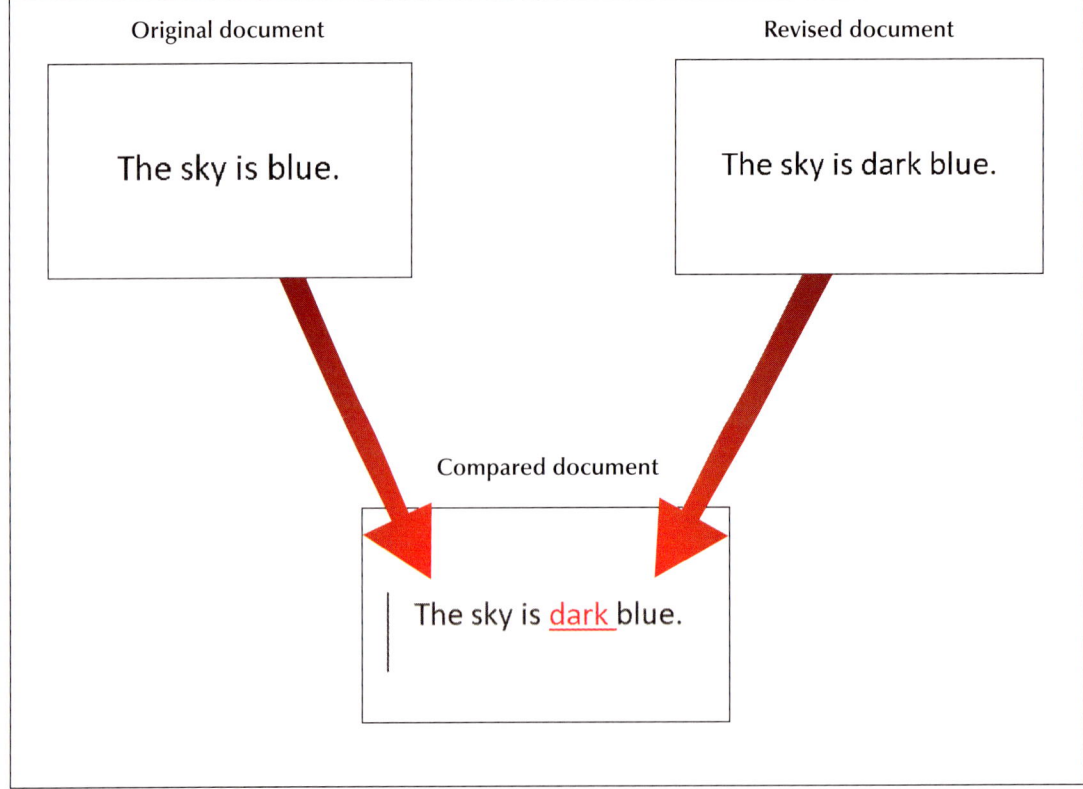

As when comparing documents, when you combine documents, you start by selecting one document as the original document and the other document as the revised document. Word then creates a new document that contains the revision marks from both the original document and the revised document. If you want, you can then take this new document and combine it with a third. In this way, you can continue, incorporating changes from as many authors as you want.

Comparing and Combining Documents | Reference Window

- With any document open in Word, click the Compare button in the Compare group on the Review tab.
- Click either Compare (to open the Compare Documents dialog box) or Combine (to open the Combine Documents dialog box). Except for their names, the two dialog boxes are identical.
- Next to the Original document list box, click the Browse for Original button, navigate to the location of the document, select the document, and then click the Open button.
- Next to the Revised document list box, click the Browse for Revised button, navigate to the location of the document, select the document, and then click the Open button.
- Click the More button, if necessary, to display options that allow you to select which items you want marked with revision marks. If the Less button is visible, these options are already displayed.
- Select or deselect any options as necessary. Verify that the New document option button is selected in the Show changes in list.
- Click the OK button, and then review the revision marks in the new document. Most likely you will want to save the combined or compared document.

You are ready to combine your document with Henry's. When you start combining or comparing documents, it doesn't matter what document is currently open in Word. It's not even necessary to have either the original document or the revised document open. In this case, the Green Fields document, which you will use as the original document, is currently open.

To combine your document with Henry's document:

▶ 1. Verify that you have saved your changes to the **Green Fields** document.

▶ 2. In the Compare group, click the **Compare** button. A menu opens. Here, you could click Compare if you wanted to compare two documents. However, you want to combine two documents, not compare them.

▶ 3. Click **Combine**. The Combine Documents dialog box opens. If you see a Less button, you also see a number of check boxes in the lower part of the document, which you can use to specify which items you want marked with revision marks. If you see a More button, you need to display these options.

▶ 4. If it is visible, click the **More** button. If the Less button is showing, skip this step. If you didn't see the check boxes earlier, you see them now. See Figure 7-9.

Figure 7-9   Combine Documents dialog box

Browse for Original button

options in bottom half of dialog box control which items will be marked by revision marks

this default option tells Word to create a new, combined document

Browse for Revised button

Note especially the New document option button, in the lower-right corner of the dialog box, which is selected by default. This tells Word to create a new, combined document, rather than importing the revision marks from the original document into the revised document, or vice versa. There's no reason to change any of the default options, so you can proceed with selecting the document you want to use as the original document. In this case, you want to use the Green Fields document as the original document. Even though this document is currently displayed on the screen, you need to select it.

▶ **5.** Next to the Original document list box, click the **Browse for Original** button 🗁. This opens an Open dialog box that is identical to the Open dialog box you have used many times before.

▶ **6.** Use the options in the Open dialog box to select the **Green Fields** document from the Tutorial.07\Tutorial folder included with your Data Files, and then click the **Open** button. You return to the Combine Documents dialog box, where the filename "Green Fields" now appears in the Original document list box. In the "Label unmarked changes with" text box, you see the user name from the Popular tab of the Word options dialog box. When you combine the documents, the edits you made earlier will be marked with this user name. Next, you need to select the document you want to use as the revised document. Henry took the file named "Green Fields" that Zoe sent to him earlier, and added his initials to the file name, to create the filename "Green Fields HD." This file is included with your Data Files.

Tip

You can also use the Original document list arrow or the Revised document list arrow to select files that you have previously opened on your computer, but using the Browse for Original and Browse for Revised buttons ensures that you select the correct file from the correct folder.

▶ **7.** Next to the Revised document list box, click the **Browse for Revised** button 🗁, use the options in the Open dialog box to navigate to and select the file named **Green Fields HD** in the Tutorial.07\Tutorial folder included with your Data Files, and then click the **Open** button. The filename "Green Fields HD" appears in the Revised document list box, and Henry's first and last name appear in the "Label unmarked changes with" text box. See Figure 7-10.

Selecting the original and revised documents ◀ **Figure 7-10**

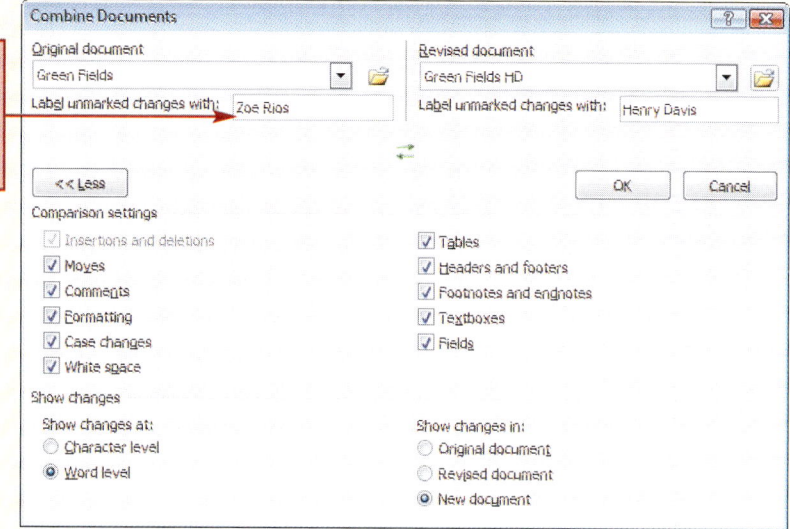

the user name from
the Popular tab in the
Word Options dialog
box is displayed here;
yours will be different

▶ **8.** Click the **OK** button. A new document opens and is named "Document1," "Document2," "Combine Result 1," or something similar. It contains the revision marks from both the original document and revised document. At this point, you might see only the new, combined document, or you might also see the original and revised documents open in separate windows. You might also see the Reviewing Pane, which lists each change in the new, combined document. In the next two steps, you will make sure your screen is set up to show the original and revised documents and the Reviewing Pane.

▶ **9.** In the Compare group, click the **Show Source Documents** button, and, if you do not see a check mark next to Show Both, click **Show Both**. If you do see a check mark next to Show Both, press the **Escape** key to close the menu.

▶ **10.** In the Tracking group, locate the Reviewing Pane button. If it is orange, then the Reviewing Pane is currently displayed. If it is not orange, click the **Reviewing Pane** button to display the Reviewing Pane. At this point, the Reviewing Pane might be displayed in a horizontal window at the bottom of the screen or vertically on the left side of the screen. In Figure 7-11, it is displayed vertically.

Figure 7-11 **Combining two documents**

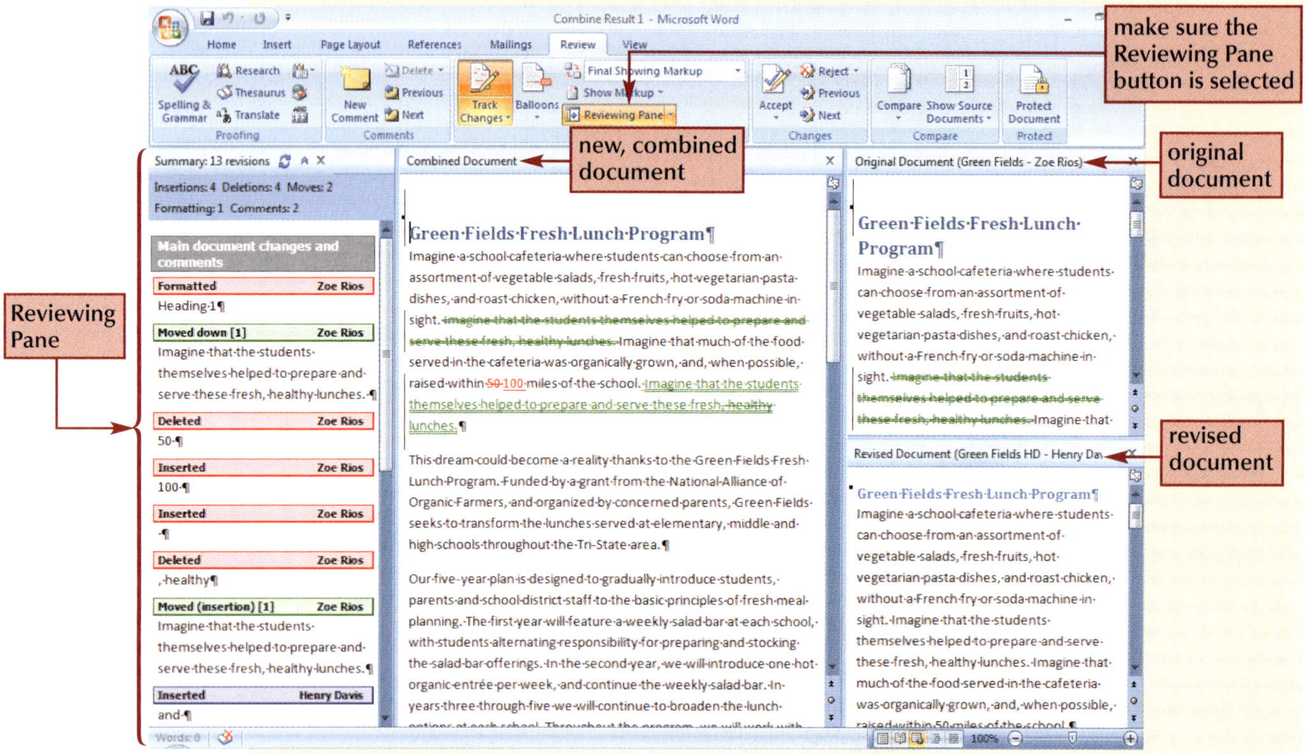

11. If your Reviewing Pane is displayed horizontally, in the Tracking group click the **Reviewing Pane** button arrow, and then click **Reviewing Pane Vertical**.

It's helpful to know how to display the original and revised documents, but if you have a small screen, having them displayed makes it harder to read the new document. You will close them in the next set of steps, and then you will take a moment to explore some options for displaying the edits made by multiple reviewers. Finally, you will save the new document with a new name.

To hide the source documents and change the reviewer options:

1. In the Compare group, click the **Show Source Documents** button, and then click **Hide Source Documents**. The panes displaying the original and revised documents close.

2. Use the vertical scroll bar in the Reviewing Pane to scroll down and review the list of edits. Notice that the document contains the edits you made earlier, as well as edits made by Henry Davis. By default, Word displays all the edits by all reviewers, but you can choose to display only the edits made by a specific reviewer or reviewers. You'll see how this works in the following step.

3. In the Tracking group, click the **Show Markup** button, and then point to **Reviewers**. A menu opens with check marks next to Henry's name and the user name for your computer. Also, you see a check mark next to "All Reviewers." This tells you that currently the document displays all the edits of all the reviewers. To hide Henry's edits, you need to deselect his name.

▶ **4.** Click **Henry Davis**. The menu closes, and the Reviewing Pane and document show only the edits you made earlier.

▶ **5.** Scroll down, if necessary, so you can see that the edits for Henry Davis are no longer displayed.

▶ **6.** Click the **Show Markup** button again, point to **Reviewers**, and then click **Henry Davis**. Henry's edits are again displayed in the Reviewing Pane and in the document. At this point, you are finished with the Reviewing Pane, so you can close it.

▶ **7.** In the Tracking group, click the **Reviewing Pane** button. (Do not click the arrow next to the Reviewing Pane button.) The Reviewing Pane closes, and the document window adjusts to show the new document in Page width zoom.

▶ **8.** Save the document as **Green Fields Rev** in the Tutorial.07\Tutorial folder included with your Data Files.

▶ **9.** Scroll down to review the document. Notice that Henry's changes, at the bottom of page 1, appear in a different color than the changes you made earlier at the top of page 1. On some computers, the word "soon" at the end of the Budget section (where you inserted a comment) might be marked as a deletion, with another instance of the word "soon" also marked as an insertion. Combining documents that contain revision marks can sometimes produce unexpected results like this. You will fix this problem later, when you accept and reject the changes in the document.

As you have seen, the document you just created contains Zoe's edits, your edits, and Henry's edits. In the following section, you will review the edits, accepting most of the changes and rejecting one.

Accepting and Rejecting Changes

When you go through revision marks in a document, it's important to be systematic, so you don't accidentally miss a change. The best approach is to move the insertion point to the beginning of the document, and then go through the document one change at a time using the Next and Previous buttons. When you click the Next button, Word moves to and selects the first change after the insertion point. Likewise, when you click the Previous button, Word moves to and selects the first change before the insertion point.

Accepting and Rejecting Changes and Deleting Comments | Reference Window

- Move the insertion point to the beginning of the document.
- To move the insertion point from one edit or comment to another, in the Changes group on the Review tab click the Next button. To move the insertion point from one comment to another, in the Comments group on the Review tab click the Next button.
- To accept a change that currently contains the insertion point, in the Changes group on the Review tab click the Accept button. To accept all the changes in the document, click the Accept button arrow, and then click Accept All Changes in Document.
- To reject the change that currently contains the insertion point, click the Reject button in the Changes group on the Review tab. To reject all the changes in the document, click the Reject button arrow, and then click Reject All Changes in Document.
- To delete a comment, click in the comment balloon, and then click the Delete button in the Comment group. To delete all the comments in a document, click the Delete button arrow, and then click Delete All Comments in Document.

You are ready to review the changes in the Green Fields Rev document, so Zoe can decide which to accept and which to reject.

To accept and reject changes in the Green Fields Rev document:

▶ 1. Press the **Ctrl+Home** keys to move the insertion point to the beginning of the document.

▶ 2. In the Changes group on the Review tab, click the **Next** button.

▶ 3. The heading "Green Fields Fresh Lunch Program" is highlighted. As you saw earlier, the margin bubble tells you that you formatted this paragraph with the Heading 1 style. This is one of your changes, and you need to accept it.

▶ 4. In the Changes group, click the **Accept** button. The heading remains formatted with the Heading 1 style, and the margin bubble disappears, indicating that the change has been accepted. The highlighting moves to the next change, which is the deleted sentence, currently displayed in green (or another color) and with a strikeout line through it. You also need to accept this change.

Trouble? If you see a menu below the Accept button, you clicked the Accept button arrow by mistake. Press the Escape key to close the menu, and then click the Accept button.

▶ 5. Click the **Accept** button. The sentence with the strikeout line through it is removed from the document, and the highlighting moves to the deleted number 50.

▶ 6. Accept the deletion of the number 50, the insertion of the number 100, the insertion of the space before the word "Imagine," and the deletion of word "healthy." After you accept the deletion of "healthy," the word "and," near the bottom of page 1, is highlighted. This is one of Henry's changes to the document. In this same paragraph, he also added a comment and deleted the word "coronary." See Figure 7-12.

| Figure 7-12 | Reviewing Henry's changes |

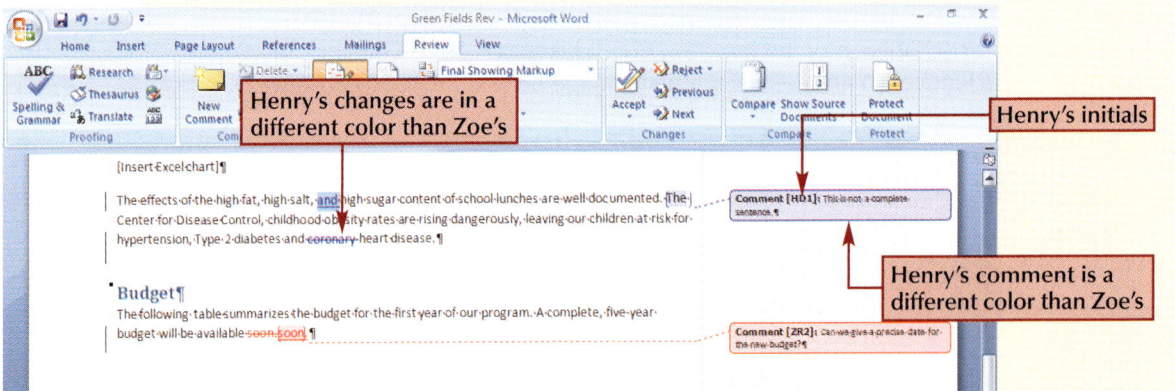

▶ 7. Click the **Accept** button to accept the insertion of the word "and." The insertion point moves to Henry's comment, which reads "This is not a complete sentence."

Henry is correct; something is missing from the sentence to which the comment is attached. You need to edit the sentence to correct it. Before you edit the sentence that Henry was concerned about, you need to turn off Track Changes if it was turned on by default when you created the combined document.

To continue accepting and rejecting changes:

▶ **1.** In the Tracking group, if the Track Changes button is highlighted, click the **Track Changes** button to deselect it.

▶ **2.** Click to the left of the word "The," press the **Delete** key to delete the "T" in "The" and then type **According to t** so that the sentence reads "According to the Center for Disease Control...". Because you turned off tracked changes, the new text looks like ordinary text. It is not displayed in revision marks. The last two letters in "The" are highlighted, indicating that the comment is still attached to them. You will delete the comment later in this set of steps.

▶ **3.** In the Changes group, click the **Next** button. The insertion point moves to the first change or comment after the insertion point, which is Henry's comment.

   Trouble? If the insertion point moves to the deleted word "coronary" instead of to Henry's comment, then the insertion point was located somewhere after the comment. In that case, skip the following step.

▶ **4.** In the Changes group, click the **Next** button again. The deleted word "coronary," which appears with a strikeout line through it, is highlighted. Both "coronary" and "heart" are unnecessary; Zoe prefers to keep "coronary" and delete "heart." That means you need to reject Henry's deletion of "coronary." You don't want to move on to the next change in the document, because you need to remain at this location and edit this sentence. So instead of using the Reject button (which would reject the change and move the insertion point to the next change in the document), you will use the Reject arrow button.

▶ **5.** In the Changes group, click the **Reject** button arrow, and then click **Reject Change**. The word "coronary" appears as ordinary text and is selected. It is no longer marked as a deletion. See Figure 7-13. Next, you will delete the word "heart," which is next to the word "coronary" and is unnecessary.

Rejected change ◀ **Figure 7-13**

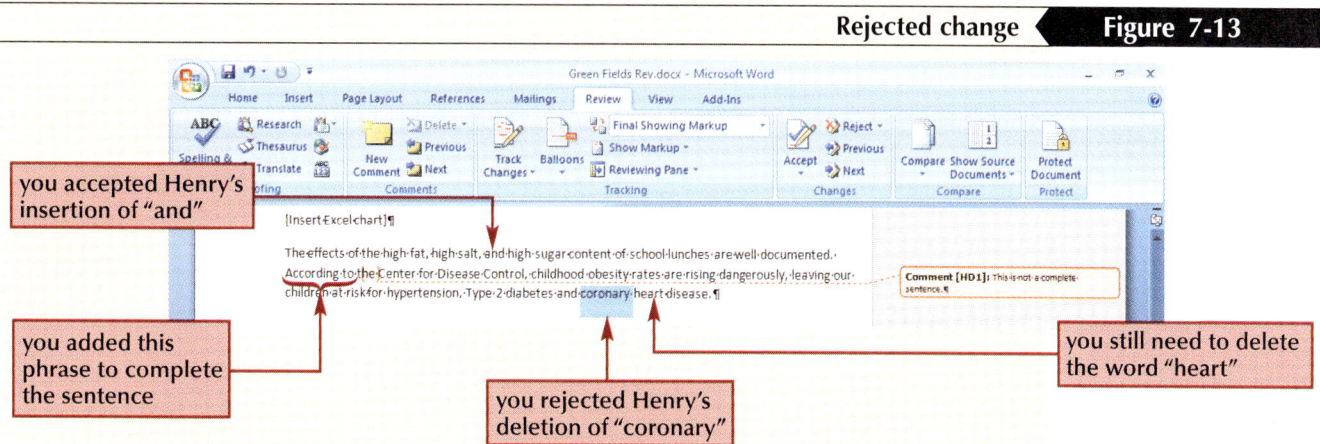

you accepted Henry's insertion of "and"

you added this phrase to complete the sentence

you rejected Henry's deletion of "coronary"

you still need to delete the word "heart"

▶ **6.** Double-click the word **heart** to select it, and then delete it, so the sentence reads "...and coronary disease." Next, as she reviews the edited sentence, Zoe notices that a comma is missing after the word "diabetes." You'll add the comma in the next step.

▶ **7.** Click to the right of the "s" in "diabetes," and then insert a comma. Finally, Zoe asks you to remove her comment, which she decides is no longer necessary. At the same time, you will delete Henry's comment. First, you need to move the insertion point to one of the comments.

▶ **8.** Click anywhere in the margin bubble for Henry's comment.

▶ **9.** In the Comments group, click the **Delete** button arrow, and then click **Delete All Comments in Document**. The comments are removed from the document.

Trouble? If only Henry's comment is deleted, and you do not see a menu with the command Delete All Comments in Document, you clicked the Delete button rather than the Delete button arrow. Undo the change, and then repeat Step 9.

If the word "soon" is marked as a deletion in your document and also marked as an insertion, then you need to complete Step 10. If the word "soon" appears in ordinary text, skip to Step 11.

▶ **10.** In the Changes group, click the **Next** button to select the deleted word "soon," accept the deletion of the word "soon," accept the insertion of the word "soon," and then click the **OK** button in the dialog box informing you that the document now contains no comments or tracked changes.

▶ **11.** Save your work on the Green Fields Rev document, click the button for the **Green Fields** document in the taskbar to display the document, and then close the **Green Fields** document. If you are asked if you want to save changes, click **Yes**. You return to the Green Fields Rev document.

| InSight | | **Understanding Tracked Changes** |

Tracked changes allow you to see the evolution of a document from draft form to the finished product. They can be extremely useful during the revision process. However, you do not want the final readers of your document to encounter any tracked changes. Inadvertently including tracked changes in a final document can be embarrassing; in other situations, it could result in serious consequences. For example, suppose you sent out a letter offering a job and specifying a salary, but you accidentally left in tracked changes that showed that you originally contemplated offering a higher salary. Such a mistake would greatly complicate the salary negotiations with a potential employee.

The problem is, you can't always tell if a document contains comments or tracked changes, because the comments or changes for some or all of the reviewers might be hidden. Also, the Display for Review list box in the Tracking group on the Review tab might be set to something other than Final Showing Markup. To determine whether or not a document contains any tracked changes or comments:

• In the Tracking group on the Review tab, verify that the Display for Review list box is set to Final Showing Markup.
• In the Tracking group on the Review tab, click the Show Markup button, point to Reviewers, and make sure you see a check mark next to All Reviewers.
• Press the Ctrl+Home keys to move the insertion point to the beginning of the document, and then in the Changes group on the Review tab, click the Next button. This will either display a dialog box informing you that the document contains no comments or tracked changes, or the insertion point will move to the next comment or tracked changes.

Now that you have incorporated Henry's suggestions, you are ready to add Alison's budget and Henry's pie chart to the document.

Embedding and Linking Objects from Other Programs

Every software program is designed to accomplish a set of specific tasks. As you've seen with Word, you can use a word-processing program to create, edit, and format documents such as letters, reports, newsletters, and proposals. A **spreadsheet program**, on the other hand, allows you to organize, calculate, and analyze numerical data. A spreadsheet created in Microsoft Excel is known as a **worksheet**. Alison created the budget for the Green Fields Fresh Lunch Program in an Excel worksheet. Henry also used Excel to create his chart.

Both the worksheet and the chart are objects. An **object** is an item such as a graphic, WordArt, chart, or paragraph of text that you can modify and move from one document to another. Zoe asks you to place the worksheet and chart objects into her document, but she also wants to be able to modify the Excel objects after they are inserted into the document. A technology called **object linking and embedding**, or **OLE**, allows you to integrate information created in one program (such as Excel) into a document created in another program (such as Word), and then modify that information using the tools originally used to create it.

The program used to create the original version of the object is called the **source program** (in this case, Excel). The program into which the object is integrated is called the **destination program** (in this case, Word). Similarly, the original file that contains the object you are inserting is called the **source file**, and the file into which you insert the object is called the **destination file**.

The next two sections describe two options for transferring data between source files and destination files: embedding and linking.

Embedding is a technique that allows you to insert a copy of an existing object into a destination document. In the destination document, you can double-click an embedded object to access the tools of the source program. This allows you to edit the object within the destination document using the tools of the source program. Because the embedded object is a copy, any changes you make to it are not reflected in the original source file, and vice versa. For instance, you could embed a worksheet named Itemized Expenses into a Word document named Travel Report. Later, if you change the Itemized Expenses file, those revisions would not appear in the Travel Report document. The opposite is also true. If you edit the embedded object from within the Travel Report file, those changes will not be reflected in the source file Itemized Expenses. The embedded object retains a connection to the source program, Excel, but not to the source file.

Figure 7-14 illustrates the relationship between an embedded Excel object in Zoe's Word document and the source file.

Figure 7-14 Embedding an Excel worksheet in a Word document

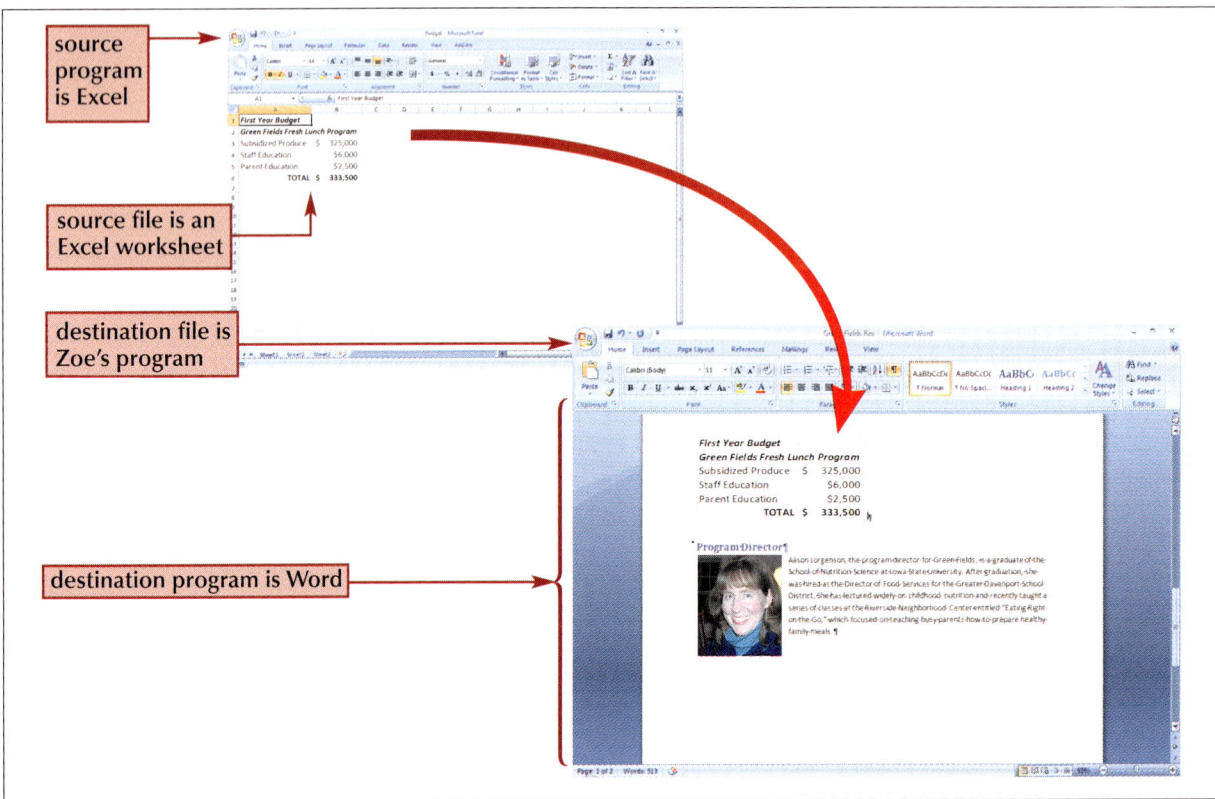

Linking is similar to embedding, except that the object inserted into the destination file maintains a connection to the source file—not just the source program. Just as with an embedded object, you can double-click a linked object to access the tools of the source program. However, unlike with an embedded object, if you edit the source file in the source program, those changes appear in the linked object; likewise, if you change the object from the destination program, the changes will also appear in the file in the source program. The linked object in the destination document is not a copy; it is a shortcut to the original object in the source file. As a result, a document that contains a linked object usually takes up less space on a disk than does a document containing an embedded version of the same object.

Figure 7-15 illustrates the relationship between the data in Henry's Excel chart and the linked object in Zoe's Word document.

Linking an Excel chart to a Word document ◄ **Figure 7-15**

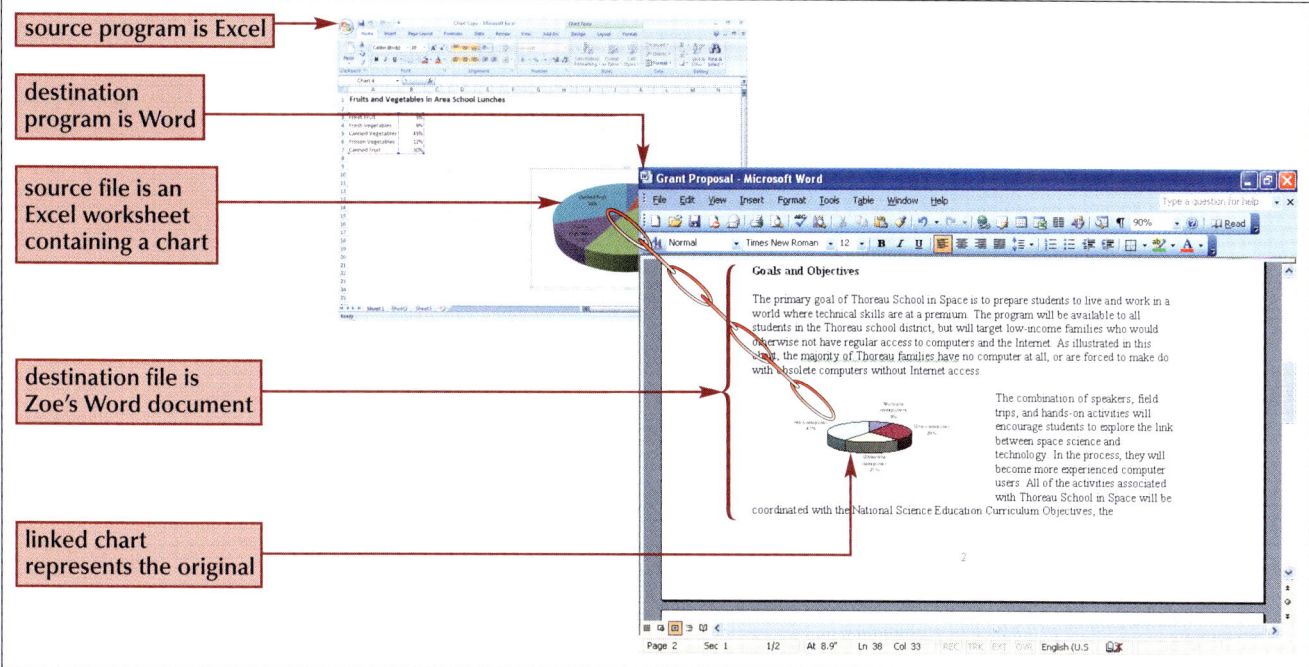

source program is Excel

destination program is Word

source file is an Excel worksheet containing a chart

destination file is Zoe's Word document

linked chart represents the original

One drawback to linking is that by moving files or folders, you can accidentally disrupt the connection between the source file and the document containing the linked object. For example, suppose you insert a linked Excel file into a Word document, close the Word document and the Excel file, and then go home. Suppose then that later a colleague moves the source file (the Excel file) to a different folder or even deletes it. The next time you open the Word document containing the linked object, you will get an error message, or you won't be able to update the linked object.

Embedding and linking are both useful when you know you'll want to edit an object after inserting it into Word. Before you can use either embedding or linking, you must verify that you have the source program installed on your computer. Then you can decide if you want to embed or link the object.

How do you decide whether to embed or link? Create an embedded object if you won't have access to the original source file in the future, or if you don't need to maintain the connection between the source file and the document containing the linked object. The source file is unaffected by any editing in the destination document. You could even delete the source file from your disk without affecting the copy embedded in your Word document.

Create a linked object whenever you have data that is likely to change over time and when you want your document to be updated with those changes. For example, suppose you created a Word document called Refinancing Options into which you want to insert an Excel file containing the latest interest rates for home mortgages. Suppose also that your assistant updates the Excel file daily to make sure it reflects current rates. By linking the Excel file to the Refinancing Options Word document, you can be certain that the mortgage rates are updated every time your assistant updates the Excel file. The advantage to linking is that the data in both the source file (the Excel file) and destination file (the Word document) can reflect recent revisions. A disadvantage to linking is that you have to keep track of two files (the Excel file and the Word file) rather than just one.

If you won't need to edit the object, you can also simply paste a copy of the object into a Word document, using the regular Paste button, similar to the way you paste a selection of copied text.

Keep in mind that you must have Excel installed on your computer to perform the steps in the rest of this session. If Excel is not installed on your computer, read the remainder of this session, but you won't be able to perform the steps.

Embedding an Excel Worksheet

Embedding all or part of an Excel worksheet in a Word document is really a special form of pasting. You start by opening the Excel file and selecting the worksheet or part of a worksheet that you want to embed in the Word document. Then you copy the selection to the Office Clipboard. When you return to Word, you click the Paste button arrow in the Clipboard group on the Home tab and select the Paste Special command to open the Paste Special dialog box. In this dialog box, you can choose to paste the copied worksheet data in a number of different forms. To embed the worksheet data, you select Microsoft Office Excel Worksheet Object.

Zoe asks you to embed the budget from Alison's Excel file into the Green Fields Rev document. In OLE terminology, the budget is the object, the Excel file is the source file, and the Green Fields Rev document is the destination file. In the following steps, you will embed the Excel object in the Word document, replacing the "[Insert Excel worksheet]" placeholder at the top of page 2. (It was originally on page 1, but it moved to page 2 after you formatted the first heading with the Heading 1 style.) Then you can use Excel commands to modify the embedded object from within Word.

To embed the Excel worksheet:

▶ **1.** Press the **Ctrl+Home** keys to move the insertion point to the beginning of the document, click the **Home** tab, in the Editing group click the **Find** button, find the placeholder **[Insert Excel worksheet]**, click **Cancel** to close the Find and Replace dialog box, and then press the **Delete** key. Take care to delete only the placeholder text and not the paragraph mark after it. When you are finished, the insertion point should be located in a blank paragraph above the heading Program Director. This is where you will embed the Excel worksheet. Now you are ready to open Alison's Excel file and copy the budget.

▶ **2.** Click the **Start** button, point to **All Programs**, click **Microsoft Office**, and then click **Microsoft Office Excel 2007**. The Excel window opens, displaying a blank worksheet named Book1.

Trouble? If you don't see Microsoft Office Excel 2007 as an option in the Start menu, or if a message indicates that Word can't find the source program, Excel might not be installed on your computer. Ask your instructor or technical support person for assistance.

▶ **3.** In Excel, click the **Office Button** 📂 , click **Open**, navigate to the Tutorial. 07\Tutorial folder included with your Data Files, click the file named **Budget,** and then click the **Open** button. The Budget worksheet opens, as shown in Figure 7-16.

Budget file open in Excel ◀ **Figure 7-16**

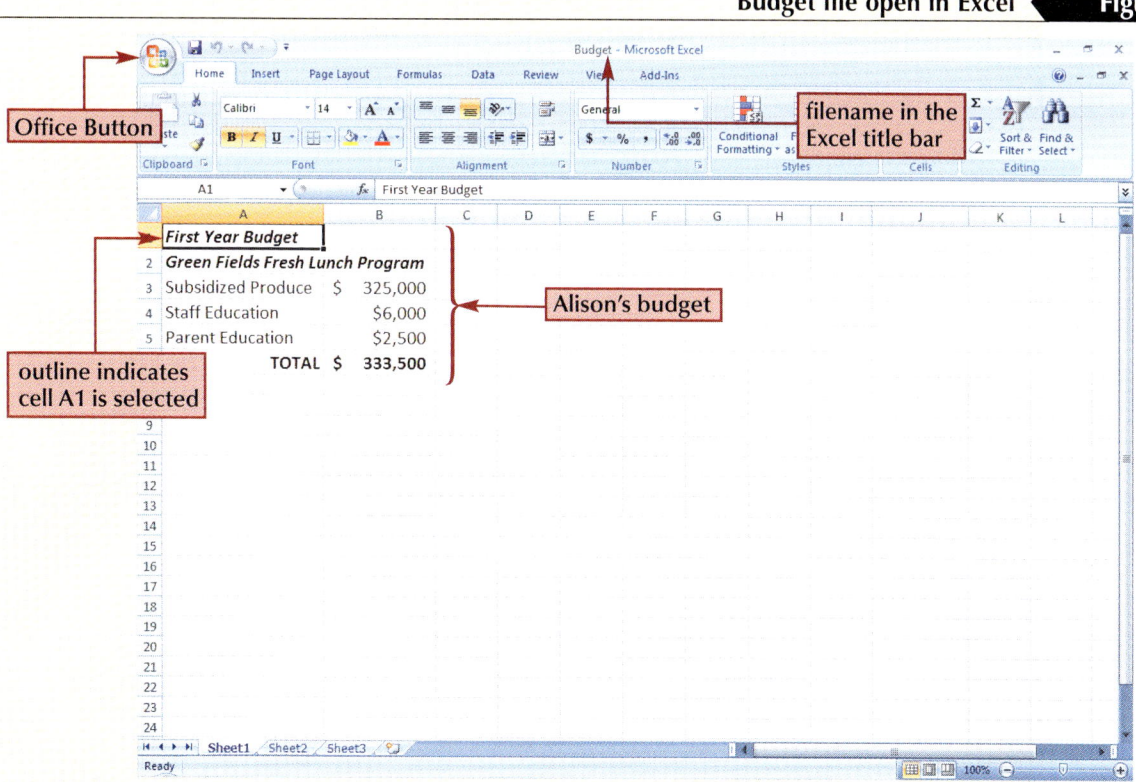

Notice that an Excel worksheet is arranged in rows and columns, just like a Word table. The intersection between a row and column is called a **cell**; an individual cell takes its name from its column letter and row number. For example, the intersection of column B and row 2 is "cell B2." Currently cell A1, in the upper-left corner of the worksheet, is selected, as indicated by its dark outline. To copy the budget data to the Office Clipboard, you need to select the entire block of cells containing the budget.

4. Click cell **A1** (the cell containing the text "First Year Budget"), drag the mouse down to select cells A1 through A6 (that is, down to the cell containing "TOTAL"), and then drag the mouse right to select the data in column B. See Figure 7-17.

Figure 7-17 **Budget data selected in the worksheet**

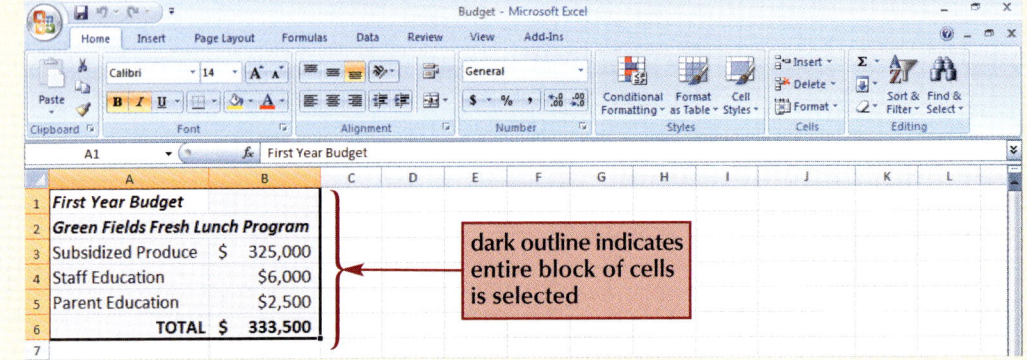

Now that the data is selected, you can copy it to the Office Clipboard and return to Word.

5. Press the **Ctrl+C** keys. The border around the selected cells is animated, indicating that you have copied the data in these cells to the Office Clipboard.

6. Click the **Green Fields Rev** button in the taskbar. You return to the Word window.

7. Verify that the insertion point is located at the top of page 2, in the blank paragraph above the heading "Program Director." You are ready to embed the copied budget into the Word document. As mentioned earlier, you need to use the Paste button arrow to do this, and not the Paste button. If you click the Paste button instead, the budget won't be embedded. Instead, Word will insert the Excel data as a Word table, which would prevent you from editing it using the Excel tabs and tools.

8. Click the **Home** tab if necessary, in the Clipboard group click the **Paste** button arrow, and then click **Paste Special**. The Paste Special dialog box opens.

   Trouble? If the budget is inserted in the document, you clicked the Paste button rather than the Paste button arrow. Undo the change, and then repeat Step 8.

   Here you can choose to embed the Excel object or link it, depending on whether you select the Paste option button or the Paste link option button. The Paste option button, which tells Word you want to embed the object, is selected by default. In the As list box, you can select the format in which you want to paste the Excel data. For example, you could click Picture (Enhanced Metafile) to insert a picture of the data, which you could not edit. In this case, you want to paste the data as a Microsoft Office Excel Worksheet Object, so you can edit it later.

9. In the As list, click **Microsoft Office Excel Worksheet Object**. See Figure 7-18.

Embedding an Excel object ◀ **Figure 7-18**

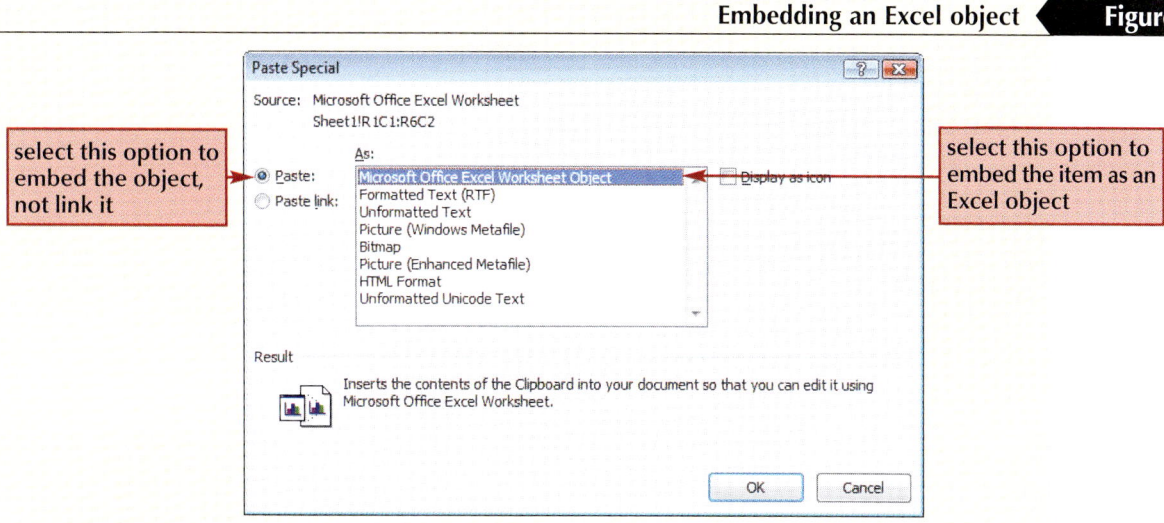

select this option to embed the object, not link it

select this option to embed the item as an Excel object

▶ **10.** Click the **OK** button. The Excel object is inserted in the Word document, as shown in Figure 7-19.

Excel object embedded in Word document ◀ **Figure 7-19**

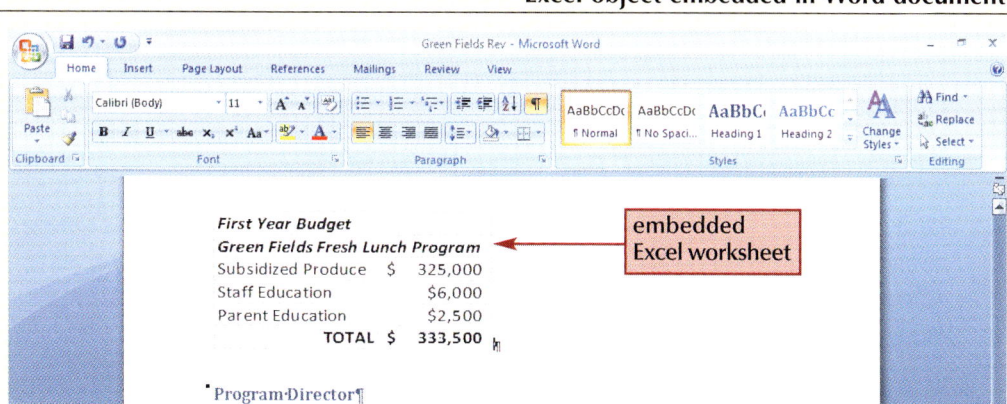

embedded Excel worksheet

Because the object is embedded, you can make changes to the object from within Word, which you'll do in the next section.

Modifying the Embedded Worksheet

After you embed an object in Word, you can modify it two different ways. First, you can click it to select it, and then move it or resize it, just as you would a picture or a piece of clip art. You can think of this as modifying the object's container—the box in which it is displayed. Second, you can double-click the object to display the tools of the source program, and then edit the contents of the object. After you modify the embedded object using the tools of the source program, you can click anywhere else in the Word document to deselect the embedded object and redisplay the usual Word tools.

Zoe would like to center the Excel object on the page. Also, Alison just e-mailed Zoe to tell her that she used an incorrect value for Staff Education, so Zoe needs to revise the worksheet data.

To modify the Excel object:

▶ **1.** Click anywhere inside the borders of the budget data. A dotted blue outline and selection handles appear around the Excel object, indicating that it is selected. With the object selected, you can center it as you would center any other selected item in a Word document. Notice that merely selecting the Excel object does not display the Excel tabs and buttons. That will happen later when you double-click the object.

▶ **2.** In the Paragraph group, click the **Center** button ▤. The Excel object moves to the center of the page. See Figure 7-20.

Figure 7-20 ▶ **Excel object centered on the page**

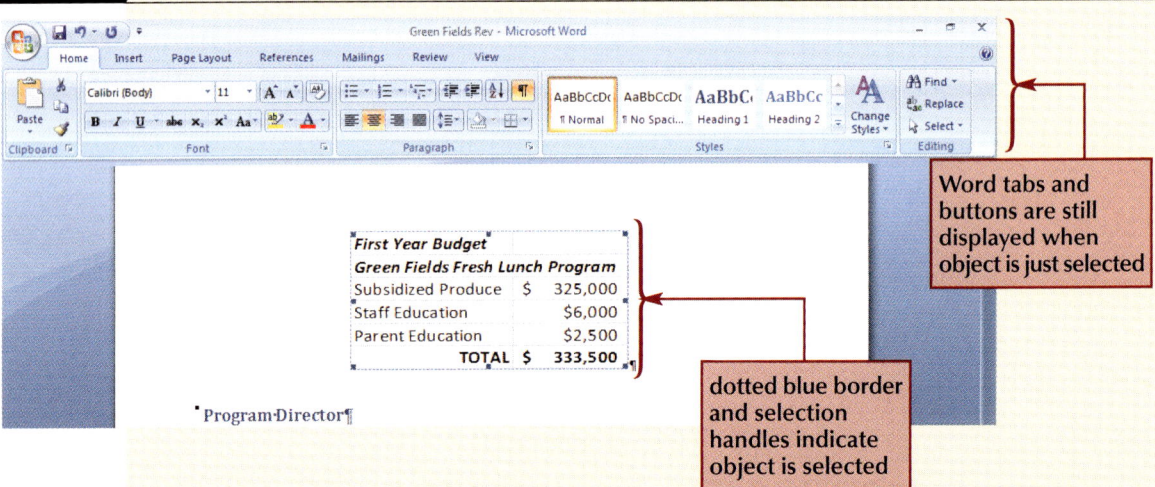

Word tabs and buttons are still displayed when object is just selected

dotted blue border and selection handles indicate object is selected

▶ **3.** Double-click the Excel object. The object's border changes to resemble the borders of an Excel worksheet, with horizontal and vertical scroll bars, row numbers, and column letters. The Word tabs at the top of the screen are replaced with Excel tabs. You need to change the value for Staff Education from $6,000 to $5,000. Decreasing the Staff Education value by $1,000 should also decrease the budget total by $1,000 because of the formula Alison entered in the worksheet.

▶ **4.** Click cell **B4**, which contains the number $6,000, type **5000** (you don't have to type a dollar sign or a comma), and then press the **Enter** key. The new value of "$5,000" replaces the old value of "$6,000." The budget total, in cell B6, decreases from $333,500 to $332,500. See Figure 7-21.

Revised data in Excel object | **Figure 7-21**

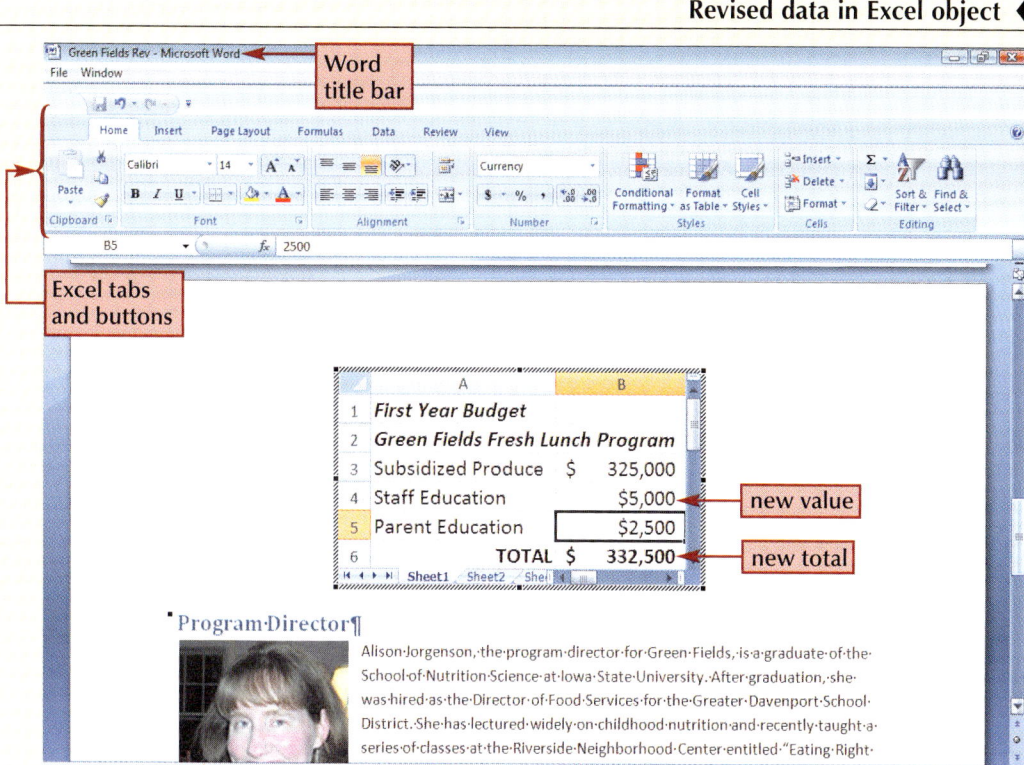

5. Click in the blank area to the left or right of the Excel object (outside its borders) to deselect it.

The source file, Budget.xlsx, remains in its original form in your Data Files, with the $6,000 as the Staff Education value. You have modified only the object in Zoe's document because it is embedded, not linked. You'll see how linking works in the next section.

Linking an Excel Chart

Next, Zoe wants you to incorporate the chart that illustrates the percentage of fresh fruits and vegetables served in school lunches in her area. Because Henry plans to revise the data soon, Zoe decides to link the chart in the Excel file rather than embed it. That way, once Henry updates the chart in the source file, the update will appear in Zoe's program description as well.

You'll use the Chart file Henry created in Excel to create the linked object in the program description document. This file is located in the Tutorial.07\Tutorial folder included with your Data Files. Because you'll make changes to the chart after you link it, you should make a copy of the Chart file before you link it. This leaves the original file in the Tutorial folder unchanged in case you want to repeat the tutorial steps later. Normally you don't need to copy a file before you link it to a Word document.

To link an Excel chart to the program description document:

▶ **1.** Use the Find dialog box to find and select the placeholder **[Insert Excel chart]**, click **Cancel** to close the Find and Replace dialog box, and then delete the place-holder **[Insert Excel chart]**. Make sure the insertion point is positioned on a blank line between the two paragraphs of text.

▶ **2.** Click the **Microsoft Excel** button in the taskbar to display the Excel window. Next, you will close the Budget file before you open the Chart file.

▶ **3.** Click the **Office Button** 🔘, and then click **Close**. The Budget worksheet closes.

▶ **4.** Click the **Office Button** 🔘, click **Open**, and then open the file named **Chart** from the Tutorial.07\Tutorial folder included with your Data Files. The worksheet includes some data in the upper-left corner and the pie chart created from the data in the lower-right corner.

▶ **5.** Click the **Office Button** 🔘, click **Save As**, and then save the Excel file with the name **Chart Copy** in the Tutorial.07\Tutorial folder included with your Data Files.

As with embedding, to link an Excel object, you start by selecting the object and copying it to the Office Clipboard. You want to copy the chart, not the data.

▶ **6.** Click the chart border. Do not click any part of the chart itself. A selection border appears around the chart. The worksheet data is also outlined in color, indicating that this is the data used to create the chart. Note that the colored outlines do not indicate that the data itself is selected. See Figure 7-22.

Figure 7-22 ▶ **Pie chart selected in worksheet**

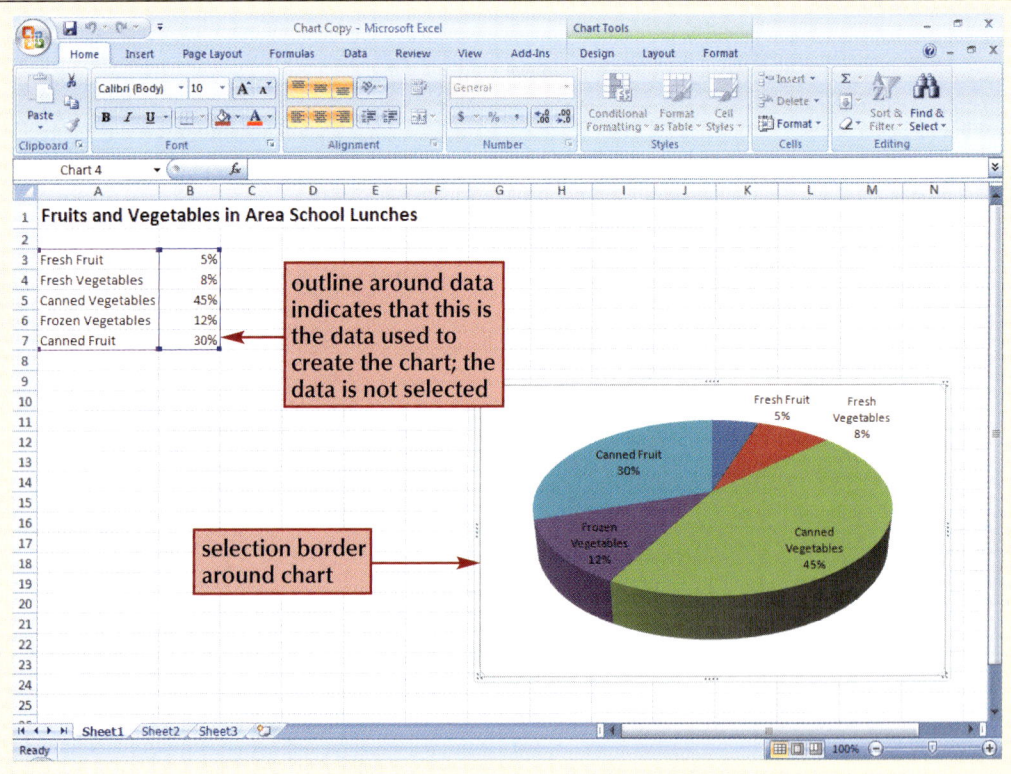

Trouble? If you see borders or handles around parts of the pie chart, click in the worksheet outside the chart border, and then repeat Step 6.

▶ **7.** Press the **Ctrl+C** keys to copy the pie chart to the Office Clipboard, and then click the **Green Fields Rev** button in the taskbar. The Green Fields Rev document is displayed in the Word window. You'll leave the Excel window open, so you can return to it in a moment.

▶ **8.** Verify that the insertion point is located in the blank paragraph between the two paragraphs of text, click the **Paste** button arrow, and then click **Paste Special**. The Paste Special dialog box opens. To link the worksheet chart to Zoe's Word document, you need to click the Paste link option button. You also need to specify that the chart is an object.

▶ **9.** Click the **Paste link** option button to select it, and then click **Microsoft Office Excel Chart Object** in the As list box. See Figure 7-23.

Inserting a linked object ◀ **Figure 7-23**

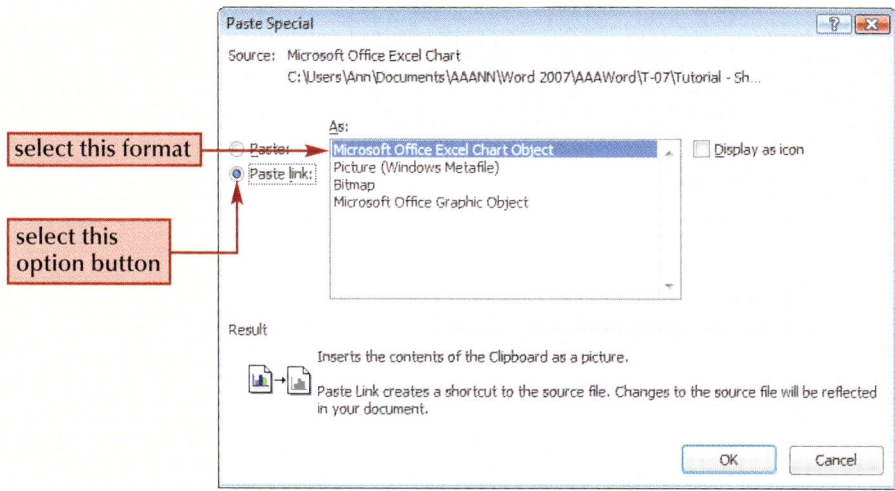

▶ **10.** Click the **OK** button. The Paste Special dialog box closes, and the Excel chart is inserted in the Word document. See Figure 7-24. It is too large to fit on page 1, so Word moved it to the top of page 2.

Figure 7-24 | Linked chart inserted in Word document

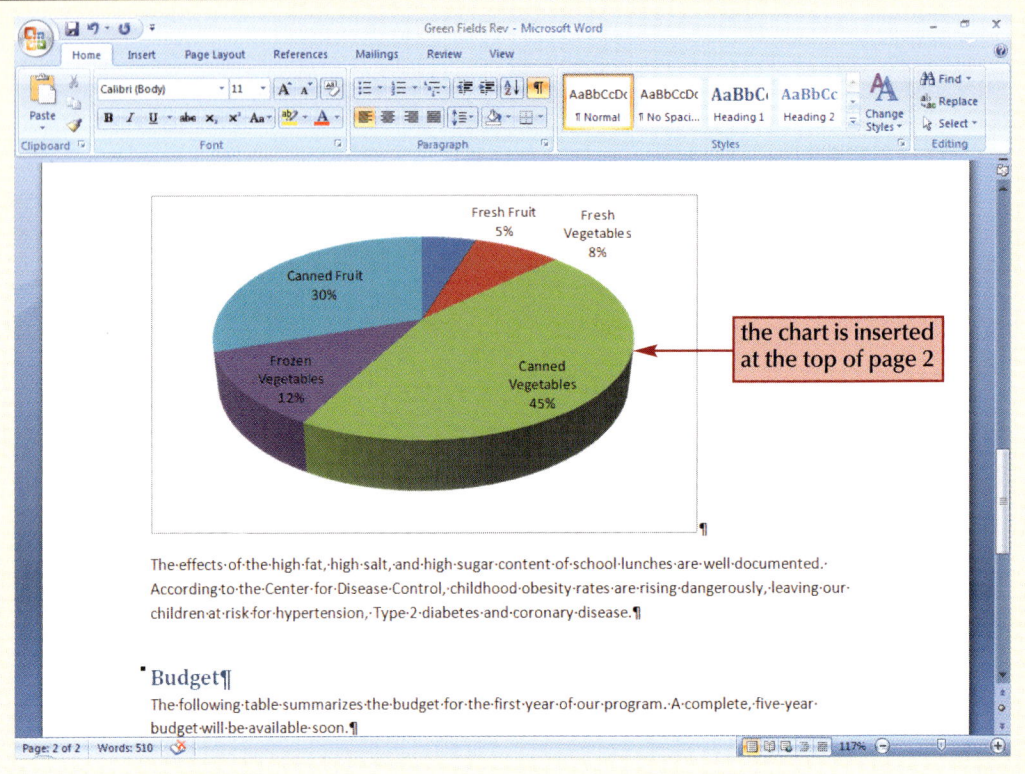

You can resize and move a linked object just as you would an embedded object. Later on, after Zoe incorporates suggestions and comments from other readers, she will resize the chart and wrap text around it. For now, she'll leave it as it is.

Modifying the Linked Chart

The advantage of linking a file over embedding it is that you can update the destination file to reflect modifications to the source file. If the destination file is closed while the source file is being modified, the linked object in the destination file will be updated automatically the next time you open the destination file. If the destination file is open while the source file is being modified, you need to right-click the linked object and then click Update Link.

In the following steps, you'll return to the Chart Copy file in Excel, change some values, and then view the updated information in the Word document.

To modify the chart in the source program:

1. Click the **Microsoft Excel** button in the taskbar. The Chart Copy workbook is displayed in the Excel window, with the chart still selected.

2. Click anywhere outside the chart to deselect it. To modify the chart, you need to edit the data in the upper-left corner of the worksheet. Currently the percentage for Fresh Fruit is 5%, and the percentage for Fresh Vegetables is 8%. In the next step, you will edit these values.

▶ **3.** Click cell **B3**, which contains the percentage for Fresh Fruit, type **9** (you don't have to type the percentage sign), and then press the **Enter** key. The new percentage is entered in cell B3, and the label in the Fresh Fruit section of the pie chart changes from 5% to 9%. Cell B4, which contains the percentage for Fresh Vegetables, is now selected, ready for you to enter a new value.

▶ **4.** Type **4**, and then press the **Enter** key. The new percentage is entered in cell B4, and the label in the Fresh Vegetables section of the pie chart changes from 8% to 4%. See Figure 7-25.

Modifying the chart in Excel ◀ **Figure 7-25**

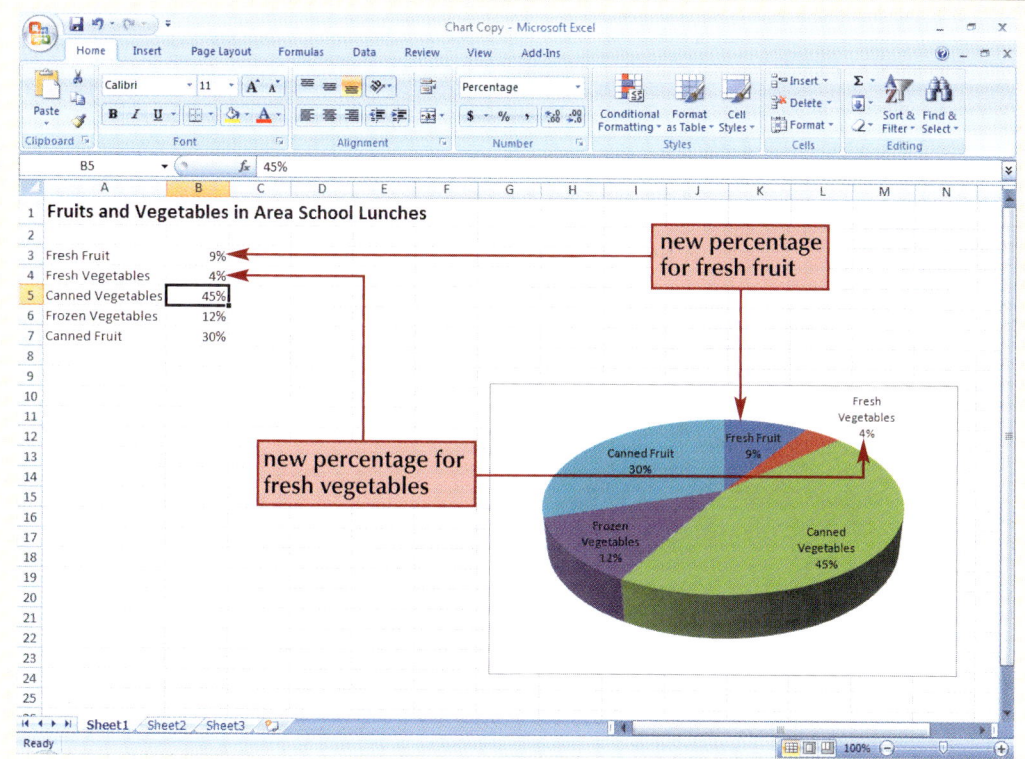

▶ **5.** On the Quick Access Toolbar, click the **Save** button 🖫 , and then close the Chart Copy file and Excel. You return to the Word window, with the pie chart displayed. Because the destination file, Green Fields Rev, was open when you edited the source file, you need to update the chart before it will show the new percentages. If the Word file had been closed, the chart would be updated when you reopened the file in Word.

▶ **6.** Right-click the chart in the Word window, and then in the shortcut menu click **Update Link**. After a pause, the chart is updated and shows a percentage of 9% for Fresh Fruit and 4% for Fresh Vegetables, just like the chart shown in Figure 7-25.

▶ **7.** Click anywhere outside the chart to deselect it, and then save your work.

Zoe's program description is finished for now. Later, after she receives everyone's comments, she will further revise it. At that time, she will add additional text, adjust the size of the pie chart, and wrap text around it.

You are ready to print the program description for distribution to the parent volunteers at Green Fields who ask for printed copies.

To print and then close the document:

▶ 1. Preview the document. Don't be concerned if the page breaks seem awkward. Zoe will add additional text to the document after her colleagues review it, so at this point she isn't concerned about adjusting page breaks in the document.

▶ 2. Print the document, click the **Office Button** 🪟, and then click **Close**. You closed the document so you can see what happens later when you open a document that contains a linked object.

Next, Zoe wants to focus on the task of distributing the document electronically, which you'll do in the next session.

Review	**Session 7.1 Quick Check**

1. Explain how to use Track Changes to edit a document.
2. What button do you use to insert a comment and on what tab is it located?
3. Suppose you want to merge two documents, each containing revision marks. Should you combine them or compare them?
4. Explain the difference between a linked object and an embedded object.
5. What term refers to an item such as a graphic, WordArt, or chart that you can modify and move from one document to another?
6. What button do you use to begin embedding or linking an object that you've copied to the Clipboard? On what tab is the button located?
7. True or False. When you modify a linked object in the destination file, your changes are also made to the source file.

Session 7.2

Distributing Word Documents Online

Tip

You can save a document as a PDF file, which can be opened on any computer running Adobe Acrobat Reader. To learn how, search for "Enable support for other file formats, such as PDF and XPS" in Word Help.

In addition to printing the document for Green Fields members, Zoe wants to make the program description available to the organization's members **online**, which means they can read it on a computer screen rather than on a printed page. You can make a document available online in one of two ways—you can either e-mail the document to specific people, or you can make it available as a Web page.

Whichever online option you choose, keep in mind that reading a document online is different from reading it in printed form. If you are certain a document will be read only online, and therefore don't have to worry about how the document will look when printed on a black and white printer, you can sometimes use more interesting formatting options, such as a fancy background. Because it is difficult to "flip through pages" online, you might also need to organize online information for easy access, or provide hyperlinks for opening related files. (You'll learn more about hyperlinks later in this tutorial.) Finally, remember that when distributing documents online, large document files can be problematic.

To e-mail a Word document, you need to use an e-mail program such as Microsoft Outlook or a Web mail service such as Yahoo. First, you create an e-mail message, type the recipient's e-mail address, and then type the text of the e-mail. Finally, you need to attach the Word document to the e-mail message. The exact steps for attaching a document to an e-mail message vary from one e-mail program to another, but in all of them, you need to find and then select the file you want to attach.

When you e-mail documents, you should keep in mind a few basic rules:

- Many e-mail programs have difficulty handling large attachments. Consider storing large files in a compressed (or zipped) folder to reduce their size before e-mailing. Alternately, you could convert the Word document to a Web page as described later in this tutorial. A Web page is usually much smaller than a Word document containing the same amount of text.

- Other word-processing programs and early versions of Word are unable to open files created in Word 2007. Before e-mailing a file, ask the recipient what word processor he or she is using. To avoid problems with conflicting versions, save the Word document as a rich text file (using the Rich Text File document, type in the Save As dialog box) before e-mailing it. All versions of Word can open rich text files.

- If you plan to e-mail a document that contains links to other files, remember to e-mail all the linked files.

- Attachments, including Word documents, are sometimes used maliciously to spread computer viruses. Remember to include an explanatory note with any e-mail attachment so that the recipient can be certain the attachment is legitimate. Also, while every computer should have a reliable virus checker program installed, this is even more important if you plan to send and receive e-mail attachments.

E-mailing Word documents is especially useful when you are collaborating with a group. You can exchange documents with colleagues in the office or around the world with just a click of the mouse. To make a document available to a larger audience, however, it's easier to publish it as a Web page, because then you don't have to take time to read and manage numerous e-mail messages. You'll learn more about working with Web pages in the next section.

Publishing Word Documents as Web Pages

Web pages are special documents designed to be viewed in a program called a **browser**. The two most popular browsers are **Microsoft Internet Explorer** and **Mozilla Firefox**. You can create a Web page on just about any kind of computer, but if you want other people to be able to view your Web page, you must store it on a computer called a **Web server**. The Web server communicates with a computer user's browser in order to display the Web page in the browser window. The process of making a Web page available to others via a Web server is called **publishing** the Web page.

Web servers are found on two different types of networks—intranets and the Internet. An **intranet** is a self-contained network belonging to a single organization. For example, the computers at Zoe's company, Rios Communications, are connected via an intranet. Zoe could publish a document as a Web page on her company's intranet Web site, so that her coworkers could view it—but it would not be available to the general public.

At the same time, Zoe's computer is also connected to the largest, most widely used computer network in the world, the **Internet**. The part of the Internet that transfers and displays Web pages is called the **World Wide Web**, or simply, the **Web**. Each Web page has its own **Web address** (or **URL**), such as *www.course.com* or *www.microsoft.com*. A group of related Web pages is called a **Web site**. The main Web page within a Web site (the one that is usually displayed first) is called a **home page**.

You probably have experience using a browser to view Web pages. If so, you know that Web pages usually contain both text and graphics, and also can contain audio and video. Web pages also include **hyperlinks**, which you can click to open or "jump to" other Web pages. A hyperlink can be a word, a phrase, or a graphic. Text hyperlinks are usually underlined and appear in a different color from the rest of the document. Hyperlinks are usually referred to as **links**, but take care not to confuse them with the OLE links you worked with earlier in this tutorial.

While hyperlinks are widely used in Web pages, you can also use them in ordinary Word documents that are intended for online reading. In the next section, you will learn more about using hyperlinks in online Word documents and Web pages.

Using Hyperlinks in Word

Hyperlinks in Word documents can link to a Web page, to a separate Word document, or to another part of the same document as the one containing the link. You can also include e-mail links, which you can click to create an e-mail message from a document. Finally, if you have many Office 2007 documents that are related to each other, you can create a useful hyperlink system that allows users to retrieve and view related material. For example, a business proposal might include links to a budget stored in an Excel file and to product photographs stored in a PowerPoint presentation. In fact, instead of inserting Henry's chart as a linked object, you could have inserted a hyperlink that users could click to open the chart in Excel. You used a linked object instead, because you wanted the chart to appear in the printed version of the program description.

Zoe wants you to add two hyperlinks to the program description—one hyperlink that jumps to a location within the program description and one that will open a different document.

Inserting a Hyperlink to a Bookmark in the Same Document

Creating a hyperlink within a document is actually a two-part process. First, you need to mark the text you want the link to jump to—either by formatting the text with a heading style or by inserting a bookmark. A **bookmark** is an electronic marker that refers to a specific point in a document. Second, you need to select the text that you want users to click, format it as a hyperlink, and specify the bookmark or heading as the target of the hyperlink. The **target** is the place in the document to which the link connects.

In this case, Zoe wants to create a hyperlink that targets Alison's name, near the end of the document. Figure 7-26 illustrates this process.

Hyperlink that targets a bookmark **Figure 7-26**

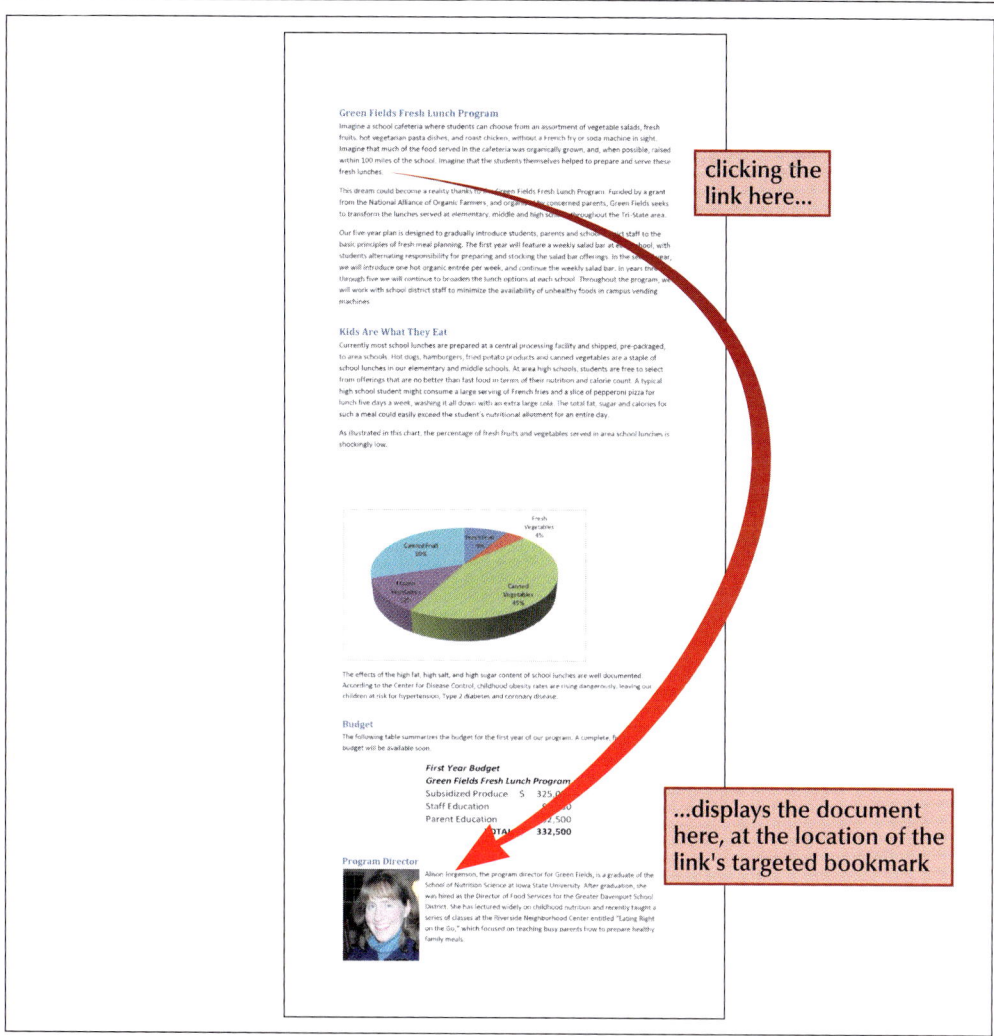

clicking the link here...

...displays the document here, at the location of the link's targeted bookmark

---

Linking to a Location in the Same Document | Reference Window

- Insert a bookmark at the target location or format text at the target location with a heading style. To insert a bookmark, select the text you want to mark as a bookmark, click the Insert tab, in the Links group click Bookmark, type a name for the bookmark, and then click the Add button.
- Select the text or graphic you want to use as the hyperlink.
- On the Insert tab in the Links group, click Hyperlink.
- Under Link to, click the Place in This Document option.
- Click the bookmark you want to link to, and then click the OK button.

To create a hyperlink in the Green Fields Rev document, you'll need to insert a bookmark in the Program Director section. But first, you need to reopen the Green Fields Rev document and update the linked object.

To reopen the document and insert a bookmark:

▶ **1.** Open the **Green Fields Rev** document from the Tutorial.07\Tutorial folder included with your Data Files. A dialog box opens, explaining that the document contains links (in this case, just one link) and asking if you want to update the data from the linked file. It's usually a good idea to click Yes in this dialog box, so you can be sure your document contains the latest version of all linked objects.

▶ **2.** Click **Yes** to update the links and close the dialog box, and then switch to Print Layout view and display nonprinting characters, if necessary.

▶ **3.** Use the Find dialog box to find and select the name **Alison Jorgenson** at the beginning of the Program Director section.

▶ **4.** Click the **Insert** tab, and then click the **Bookmark** button in the Links group. The Bookmark dialog box opens. You can now type the bookmark name, which must be one word, without spaces.

▶ **5.** Type **Director**. See Figure 7-27.

Figure 7-27 ▶ Creating a bookmark

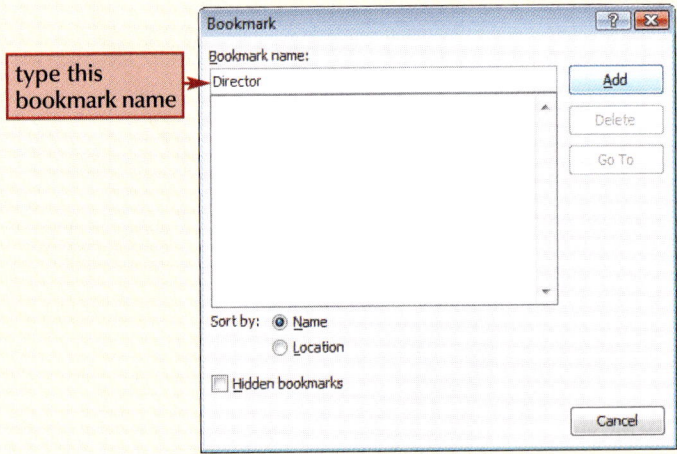

type this bookmark name

▶ **6.** Click the **Add** button. The Bookmark dialog box closes. Although you can't see it, a bookmark has been inserted before Alison's name.

This bookmark you just created will be the target of the hyperlink. When you click the hyperlink, which you will create in the next set of steps, the insertion point will jump to this bookmark.

To create a hyperlink to the bookmark:

▶ **1.** Press the **Ctrl+Home** keys to move the insertion point to the beginning of the document, and then click at the end of the second paragraph under the heading Green Fields Fresh Lunch Program. The insertion point should be positioned immediately following the phrase "...throughout the Tri-State area."

▶ **2.** Insert a space, and then type **The program director is Alison Jorgenson, an expert in childhood nutrition.** (Include the period.) Next, you'll format part of this sentence as a hyperlink.

▶ **3.** Select the name **Alison Jorgenson** in the sentence you just typed, and then in the Links group on the Insert tab, click the **Hyperlink** button. The Insert Hyperlink dialog box opens.

▶ **4.** Under Link to (on the left side of the dialog box), click **Place in This Document**. See Figure 7-28. The right side of the dialog box now lists the headings and book-marks in the document. Here you can click the bookmark or heading you want the hyperlink to jump to.

Inserting a hyperlink ◀ **Figure 7-28**

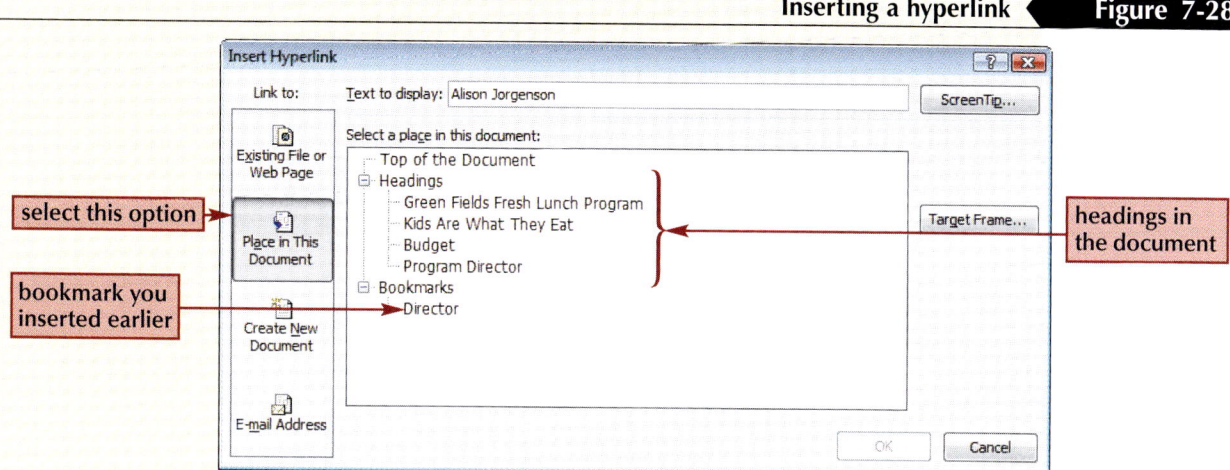

select this option →

bookmark you inserted earlier →

headings in the document

Trouble? If you don't see the document headings or the bookmark in the dialog box, click the plus signs next to Headings and Bookmarks.

▶ **5.** Under Bookmarks, click **Director**, and then click the **OK** button. The name "Alison Jorgenson" appears in underlined blue text. The hyperlink now targets the Director bookmark that you created in the last set of steps.

Trouble? If you formatted the wrong text as a hyperlink, click the Undo button and begin again with Step 3.

After inserting a hyperlink into a document, you should test it.

To test the hyperlink in your document:

▶ **1.** Without clicking, move the mouse pointer over the blue underlined hyperlink, **Alison Jorgenson**. After a moment, a ScreenTip appears with the name of the bookmark (Director) and instructions for following the link. See Figure 7-29.

Tip

To edit the text that appears in a ScreenTip when you place the mouse pointer over the hyperlink in the document, in the Insert Hyperlink dialog box click the ScreenTip button, type the text you want for a ScreenTip, and then click the OK button.

Figure 7-29 > **Displaying the hyperlink ScreenTip**

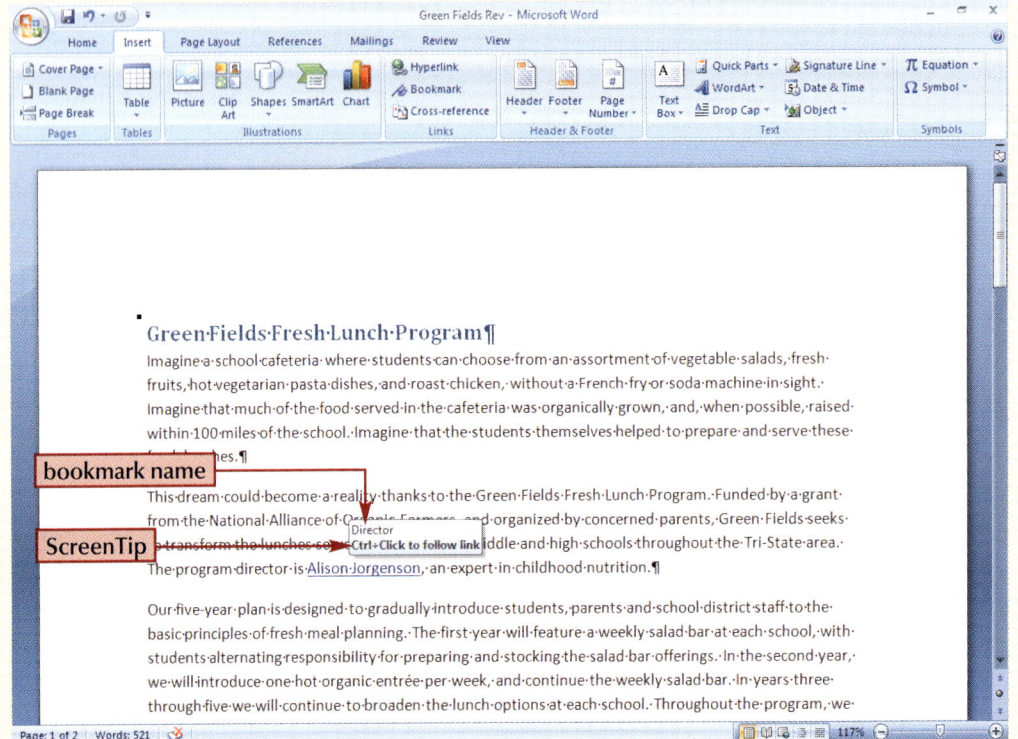

2. Press and hold the **Ctrl** key, and then click the **Alison Jorgenson** hyperlink. The insertion point jumps to the beginning of Alison's name in the Program Director section, where you inserted the bookmark.

3. Press the **Ctrl+Home** keys to move the insertion point back to the beginning of the document. The hyperlink has changed color, indicating that it has been used. If you were to close and then reopen the document, the hyperlink would again be blue until you clicked it.

4. Save your work.

You have finished creating a hyperlink that jumps to a location in the same document. Next, you will create a hyperlink that jumps to a location in a different document.

Creating Hyperlinks to Other Documents

The greatest power of hyperlinks lies not in jumping to another location within the same document, but in jumping to other documents. These documents can be located on the World Wide Web, on your computer's hard drive, or on your company's network server. When you create a hyperlink to another document, you can target the URL of a document stored on the Web or the path and filename of a file on your computer or network. When you click a hyperlink to another document, the document opens on your computer, with the beginning of the document displayed. If you want, you can also specify a particular bookmark within the other document. In that case, when you click the link, the document opens, with the bookmarked location in the document displayed.

Creating a Hyperlink to Another Document

- Select the text you want to format as a hyperlink.
- In the Links group on the Insert tab, click the Hyperlink button.
- Under Link to, click Existing File or Web Page.
- To target a specific file on your computer or network, use the Look in list arrow to open the folder containing the file, and then click the file in the file list.
- To target a Web page, type the URL in the Address text box.

Zoe wants to insert a hyperlink that will open a Word document containing Alison's resume. Because she wants the hyperlink to take users to the beginning of the resume, you don't need to insert a bookmark. Instead, you can use just the name of the target document.

To create a hyperlink to another document:

▶ **1.** Use the hyperlink again to jump to the bookmark in the Program Director section.

▶ **2.** Click at the end of the Program Director section. The insertion point should be located immediately to the right of the period that concludes the phrase "healthy family meals." This is where you'll insert text, some of which will become the hyperlink.

▶ **3.** Press the **spacebar**, and type **(See her resume.)**, making sure to include the parentheses.

▶ **4.** Select the word **resume** in the text you just typed.

▶ **5.** In the Links group on the Insert tab, click the **Hyperlink** button. The Insert Hyperlink dialog box opens.

▶ **6.** Under Link to, click **Existing File or Web Page**. The right side of the dialog box displays options related to selecting a file or a Web page.

▶ **7.** If necessary, use the **Look in** list arrow to open the Tutorial.07\Tutorial folder.

▶ **8.** Click **Resume** in the file list. See Figure 7-30.

Inserting a hyperlink to a different document ◀ **Figure 7-30**

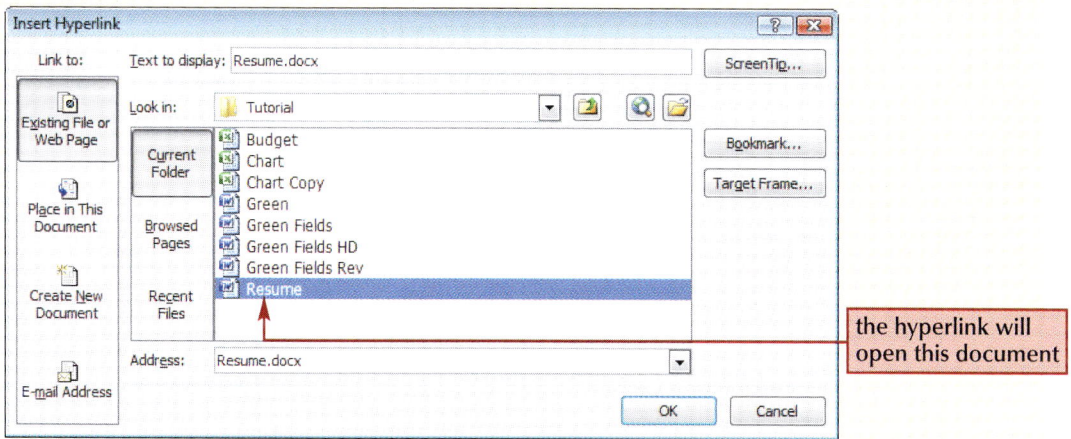

▶ **9.** Click the **OK** button. The word "resume" is now formatted as a hyperlink, in blue with an underline.

When your documents include hyperlinks to other documents, you must keep track of where you store the target documents. If you move a target document to a different location, hyperlinks to it might not function properly. In this case, you created a hyperlink in the Green Fields Rev document that links to the Resume document. Both documents are stored in the Tutorial.07\Tutorial folder, which is most likely located on your computer's hard disk. To ensure that the hyperlink in the program description document will continue to function, you must keep the two documents in the same folder as when you created the link. If you have to move a target document, then be sure to edit the hyperlink to select the target document in its new location. You'll learn how to edit hyperlinks later in this tutorial.

Now you're ready to test the hyperlink you just created.

To test the resume hyperlink:

▶ **1.** Press and hold the **Ctrl** key and click the **resume** hyperlink. The Resume document opens. See Figure 7-31.

Figure 7-31 | Resume document

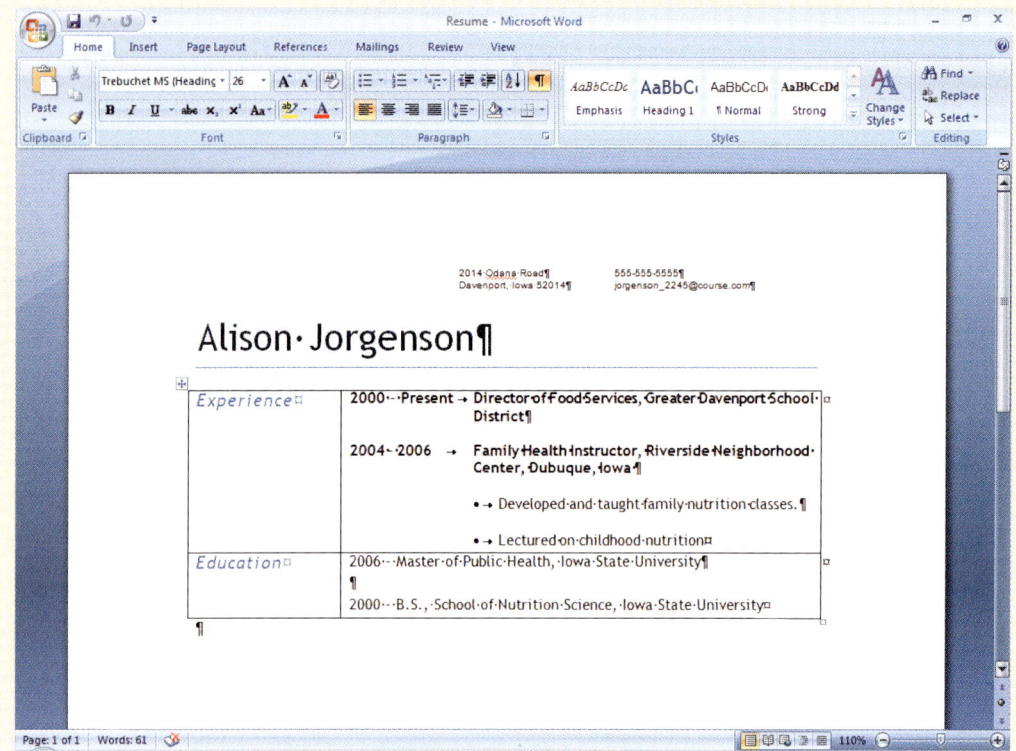

▶ **2.** Read through the Resume document, and then close it. You return to the Green Fields Rev document. Notice that the hyperlink color has changed, indicating that you have used the hyperlink.

▶ **3.** Save your work.

As you can see, hyperlinks allow you to display information instantaneously. When used thoughtfully, hyperlinks make it possible to navigate a complicated document or a set of files quickly and easily.

Viewing a Document in Web Layout View

Because the version of the program description you are now working on is intended for an online audience, Zoe suggests that you switch to Web Layout view. **Web Layout view** offers several advantages for online viewers:

- Text automatically wraps to suit the size of your screen, not the printed page.
- Documents can be displayed with a variety of background effects.
- Page setup elements, such as footers, headers, and breaks, are not displayed. Because users don't view the document as printed pages, these elements aren't necessary.

Web Layout view is useful when you need to format a document for online viewing. Text wrapping doesn't always survive the conversion from a Word document to a Web page, and graphics often shift position when you save a document as a Web page. Web Layout view prepares you for this by showing you what the graphics look like in their new positions.

Keep in mind that, despite its name, Web Layout view does not show you exactly how a document will look when saved as a Web page. Some features you see in Web Layout view, such as the embedded chart, might look different when you save the document as a Web page. (You will learn more about saving a document as a Web page later in this tutorial.)

If you switch to Web Layout view and then save the document in that view, the next time you open it, it will by default open in Web Layout view. Zoe asks you to display the program description document in Web Layout view, and then save it. Then when she e-mails the file to Alison, it will open for her in Web Layout view.

To display a document in Web Layout view:

▶ **1.** Scroll to the beginning of the document, and then click the **Web Layout** button 🗐. This button is located in the status bar in the lower-right corner of the document window. Notice that paragraphs now span the width of the document window. The line widths are no longer constrained by the margin settings for the printed page. See Figure 7-32.

Figure 7-32 ▸ **Document displayed in Web Layout view**

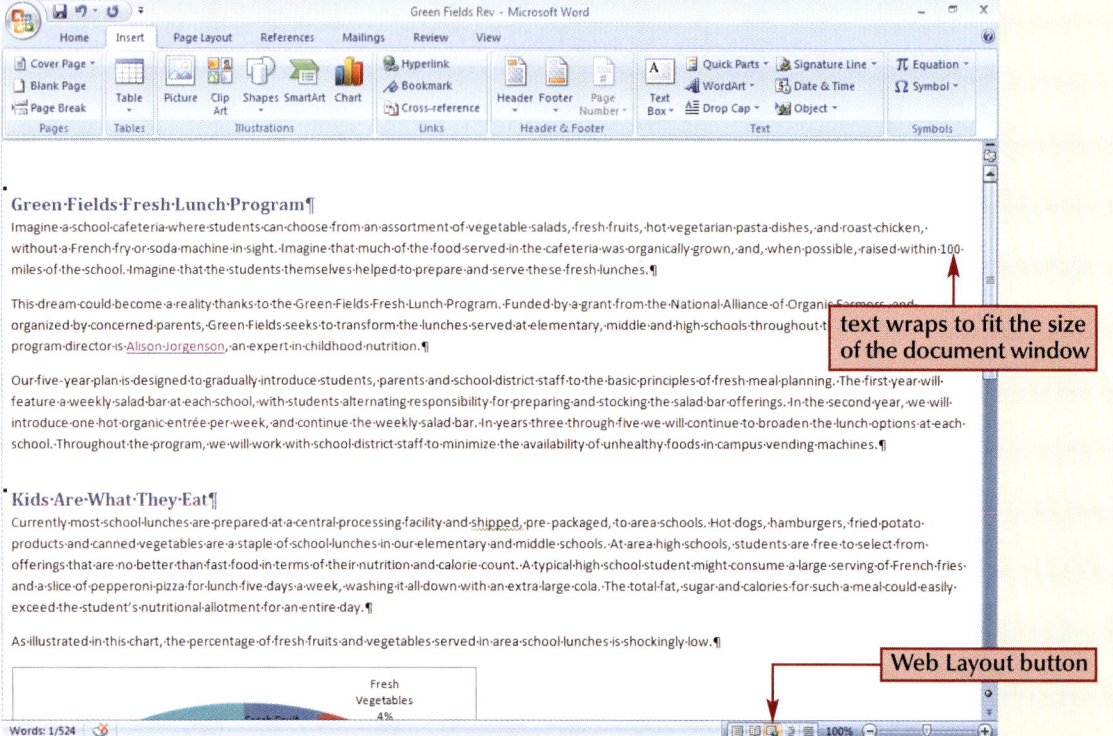

> **Trouble?** Depending on the size of your monitor, the line breaks in your document may differ from those in Figure 7-32. This has to do with the fact that Web Layout view wraps text to fit the size of the screen, and is not a problem.

▸ **2.** Scroll through the document to review its appearance in Web Layout view.

▸ **3.** Save the document.

Next, you'll make some changes to the Green Fields Rev document that will improve its online appearance.

Applying a Background Effect

To make the document more visually interesting for online viewers, Zoe would like to add a background effect. You can apply one of the following background effects:

• Solid color
• Gradient—a single color or combination of colors that varies in intensity
• Texture—a design that mimics the look of various textured materials, including linen and marble
• Pattern—a repetitive design such as checks, polka dots, and stripes, in colors you specify
• Picture—a graphic image

Note that backgrounds do not appear in printed documents; they are visible only on the screen in Web Layout view and in documents saved as Web pages. After you apply a background color or texture, you should make sure your text is still readable. In poorly designed online documents, the background might be so dark or the pattern so obtrusive that the text is illegible. Zoe suggests you use an unobtrusive textured background.

To apply a background effect to a document:

▶ **1.** Click the **Page Layout** tab, and then in the Page Background group, click the **Page Color** button. The Page Color palette opens, with a menu at the bottom. You could click a color in the palette to select it as a background color for the page. To select any other type of background effect, you need to click Fill Effects.

▶ **2.** Click **Fill Effects**, and then click the **Texture** tab if necessary. The Texture list box displays a variety of textured backgrounds.

▶ **3.** Click the gray box in the left column, fourth row down. An outline appears around the gray box, indicating that it is selected, and the name of the texture, "Newsprint," appears below the palette of tiles. See Figure 7-33.

Selecting a texture background  **Figure 7-33**

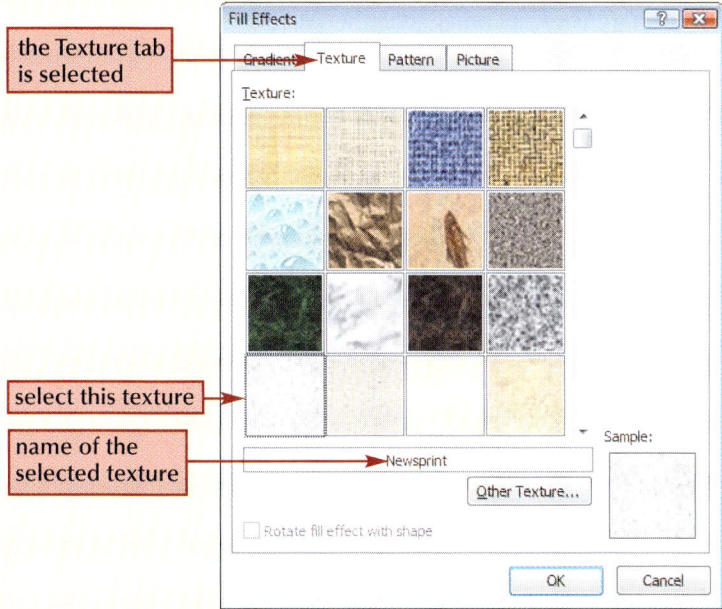

the Texture tab is selected

select this texture

name of the selected texture

▶ **4.** Click the **OK** button. The gray texture fills the background of the Green Fields Rev document.

▶ **5.** Save the document in Web Layout view.

The texture background is attractive and light enough to make the document text easy to read. Note that it's a good idea to make sure linked documents have a similar appearance. Later, Zoe plans to add a similar background to the Resume document. That way both of the linked documents will have a consistent look. She'll take care of that task, though. Instead, you can focus on saving the current document as a Web page.

Saving a Word Document as a Web Page

To create sophisticated Web pages (or a complete Web site), you'll probably want to use a dedicated HTML editor, such as Adobe Dreamweaver. But to create a simple Web page from an existing document, you can convert a document to a Web page from within Word.

So far, Zoe has created printed copies of her program description and an online version to e-mail to Alison. Next, she wants to convert her document to a Web page so she can make it available on the World Wide Web.

Another term for a Web page is **HTML document**. The acronym "HTML" is short for **Hypertext Markup Language**, a language that tells a Web browser how a Web page should look on the screen. When you save a Word document as a Web page, Word inserts HTML codes that tell the browser how to format the text and graphics. Fortunately, you don't have to learn the Hypertext Markup Language to create Web pages with Word. When you save the document as a Web page, Word creates all the necessary HTML codes (called markings, or tags). This process is transparent to you, so you won't actually see the HTML codes in your Web pages.

When you save a document as a Web page, Word saves the document as an HTML file and places the graphics that appear in the document in a separate folder. A group of smaller files travels across the Web faster than one large file, so this division of files makes it easier to share your documents on the Web.

You can choose from three different Web page file types in Word. The main differences among these file types are file size and the way special elements, such as WordArt, or embedded or linked objects, are treated when they are displayed in a browser:

- Single File Web Page—Saves the document as an MHTML file, which is slightly different from an HTML file. All graphics are stored in the file. When the Web page is open in Word, the linked and embedded objects continue to function as usual. When displayed in a browser, the file, including its linked or embedded objects, looks exactly as it did in Word. However, the linked and embedded objects do not function as embedded or linked objects when displayed in a browser. A Single File Web Page can be more than twice the size of the original Word document.
- Web Page—Saves the document as an HTML file, with all graphics stored in a separate folder. When the Web page is open in Word, the linked and embedded objects continue to function as usual. When displayed in a browser, the file, including its linked or embedded objects, looks exactly as it did in Word, but the linked and embedded objects no longer function as embedded or linked objects. A file saved using the Web Page file type might be 30 kilobytes, with 100 KB of accompanying files.
- Web Page, Filtered—Saves the document as an HTML file that contains only HTML codes, without any of the codes that ensure that special elements are displayed as they are in the Word document. Instead, these special elements are formatted by HTML codes. For example, the labels on an embedded Excel chart might look different than they did in the original Word document. Such formatting differences are apparent when you open the filtered Web page in a browser, or the next time you open the file in Word. A filtered Web page is very small, allowing it to travel quickly across the Web. A typical filtered Web page of a few hundred words might be about 4 KB, with 25 KB of accompanying files.

The Single File Web Page file type is a good choice when you plan to share your Web page only over a small network and not over the Internet. Having to manage only one file is more convenient than having to keep track of a group of files. But when you want to share your files over the Internet, it's better to use the Web Page, Filtered option. This will keep your overall file size as small as possible. Note that the folder Word creates to store the accompanying graphics files has the same name as your Web page, plus an underscore and the word "files." For instance, a Web page saved as "Finance Summary" would be accompanied by a folder named "Finance Summary_files."

Although saving a Word document as a Web page is easy, it's not foolproof, particularly when it comes to formatting. When you save your document as a Web page, some document formatting might be lost, or the formatting might look different. This is especially true if you use the Web Page, Filtered file type. Sometimes you might need to reapply formatting after a document has been saved as a Web page. As a general rule, once you save a document as a Web page, you'll want to modify it to make it more attractive for users of the Web. At the very least, you will probably need to reposition graphics.

Saving a Word Document as a Web Page | Reference Window

- Click the Office Button, and then click Save As.
- To save the Web page as a single file, click the Save as type list arrow, and then click Single File Web Page. To ensure that your Web page file is as small as possible, click the Save as type list arrow, and then click Web Page, Filtered.
- If desired, give the file a new filename. For files saved using the Single File Web Page type, Word automatically adds the .mht file extension. For files saved using the Web Page file type, Word automatically adds the .htm file extension. These extensions probably won't be visible in the Save As dialog box.
- Click the Change Title button, type a title for the Web page in the Set Page Title dialog box, and then click the OK button. This title will appear in the browser title bar.
- Click the Save button in the Save As dialog box.
- If you saved the document using the Web Page, Filtered option, click Yes in the warning dialog box.

To save the Green Fields Rev document as a Web page:

▶ **1.** Close any Internet-related programs, such as e-mail editors and browsers.

▶ **2.** Click the **Office Button** 🔘 , and then click **Save As**. The Save As dialog box opens.

▶ **3.** Click the **Save as type** list arrow, and then click **Web Page, Filtered**.

▶ **4.** Change the filename to **Green Fields Web Page**.

▶ **5.** Click the **Change Title** button to open the Set Page Title dialog box, and then type **Green Fields Fresh Lunch Program** in the Page title text box. This title will appear in the browser title bar.

▶ **6.** Click the **OK** button in the Set Page Title dialog box.

▶ **7.** Click the **Save** button in the Save As dialog box. A dialog box appears warning you that using the Web Page, Filtered file type will remove special codes, called tags, that control how the document is displayed in Word. That's fine, because you are concerned only with creating a file that is small enough to transmit quickly across the Web and that will be displayed properly in a Web browser.

▶ **8.** Click the **Yes** button. The document is converted into a Web page, although it looks the same as it did before you saved it as a Web page. The revised filename, "Green Fields Web Page," appears in the Word title bar, as usual. The title you specified in Step 5 won't be visible until you open the Web page in a browser, at which point it will be displayed in the browser's title bar.

At this point, the new Green Fields Web page looks identical to the Green Fields Rev Word document when you displayed it in Web Layout view. Because you used the Web Page, Filtered file type, you might have expected the new Web page to look different. In particular, you might have expected the linked chart or the embedded worksheet to have changed appearance. Their appearance hasn't changed yet, because your computer's memory still retains the image of these elements with the proper Word formatting. Later, when you close the Web page file and open it in a browser, you will see some differences.

Although you can't see any visible change in the file, the file size has decreased from about 61 KB to only about 9 KB, plus about 29 KB of related files. Even though you are currently looking at the Web page in Word, the new HTML file is optimized for viewing in a Web browser such as Internet Explorer.

Formatting a Web Page

You can edit and format text and graphics in a Web page the same way you edit and format a normal Word document. After you have saved a Word document as a Web page, you need to format the Web page so that it is attractive when it is displayed in a browser—you need to format it for online viewing.

Inserting Horizontal Lines

Web pages sometimes include horizontal lines that separate sections of a document. These lines make it easy to see at a glance where one section ends and another begins. You can also add horizontal lines to Word documents that you plan to read in Web Layout view. If you don't like a horizontal line after you insert one into a document, you can delete it by clicking the line and then pressing the Delete key.

Zoe wants you to add a horizontal line below the title and at the end of each section except the last one.

To insert horizontal lines into the Web page:

▶ **1.** Click at the beginning of the heading "Kids Are What They Eat."

▶ **2.** Click the **Home** tab, if necessary, click the **Borders** button arrow 🔲 ▾, and then, at the bottom of the menu, click **Borders and Shading**. The Borders and Shading dialog box opens.

▶ **3.** Click the **Borders** tab in the Borders and Shading dialog box if it is not already selected, and then click the **Horizontal Line** button. The Horizontal Line dialog box opens, displaying many styles of horizontal lines.

▶ **4.** Click the line in the left column, second box from the top. The line is selected, as shown in Figure 7-34.

Figure 7-34 ▶ Selecting a horizontal line style

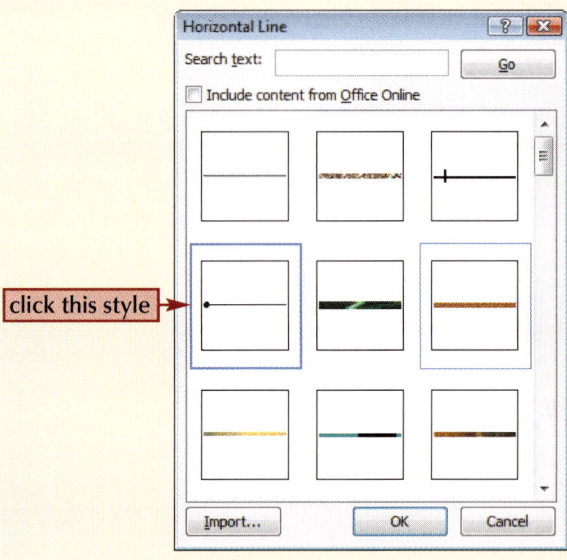

click this style

5. Click the **OK** button. A black line with a small, black circle on each end is inserted into the Web page above the "Kids Are What They Eat" heading. Your Web page should look similar to Figure 7-35.

Newly inserted horizontal line ◀ **Figure 7-35**

6. Scroll down, click to the left of the "B" in the Budget heading, and then insert the same style of horizontal line.

7. Insert the same style of horizontal line above the Program Director heading.

8. Scroll back to the top of the document and save your work. If you see the warning dialog box you saw earlier, click the **Yes** button.

Tip

You can use the F4 key to open the Horizontal Line dialog box after you complete Step 5.

Now that you've used horizontal lines to give shape to the document, you decide to improve the appearance of the document's text.

Modifying Text Size and Color

It's often helpful to format headings in a Web page in a larger size than you might use in a document that would be printed. Zoe wants you to increase the font size of the first heading in the document. She also wants you to center it.

To increase the font size for the first heading and center it:

1. Select the heading **Green Fields Fresh Lunch Program** at the beginning of the Web page.

2. In the Font group on the Home tab, click the **Grow Font** button A˄ to increase the font size from 14-point to 16-point.

3. Continue clicking the A˄ until the font size of the selected heading is **28-point**. Use the Font Size list box to see the current size of the selected text. If you increase the font size too much, use the Shrink Font button A˅ to reduce the font size.

4. In the Paragraph group, click the **Center** button ≣ to center the heading at the top of the document, and then click anywhere in the document to deselect the heading.

5. Save your work. If you see the warning dialog box, click the **Yes** button.

You've formatted Zoe's document so that it will be visually appealing when displayed in a browser. Next, you'll create additional hypertext links and edit the existing link.

Creating and Editing Hyperlinks in a Web Page

As you looked through the HTML version of the program description, you probably noticed that it still contains two hyperlinks. The Alison Jorgenson link still jumps to the Program Director section at the end of the Web page, and the resume link still jumps to a Word document containing Alison's resume. Zoe wants to save the Resume document as a Web page and then format it to match the Green Fields Rev document. She also wants you to add a hyperlink in the resume that will jump back to the Green Fields Web page. Finally, because you'll save the Resume document with a new name, you have to edit the resume hyperlink (in the Green Fields Web page) to make sure it opens the right file.

In the following steps, you will convert the resume to a Web page, create a new link from the resume back to the Green Fields Web page, and then modify the hyperlink in the Green Fields Web page so that browsers can easily jump between the two documents.

To convert the resume to a Web page:

▶ 1. Open the file named **Resume** from the Tutorial.07\Tutorial folder included with your Data Files.

▶ 2. Click the **Office Button** 🏢 , click **Save As**, navigate to the Tutorial.07\Tutorial folder, select the **Web Page, Filtered** file type, use **Resume Web Page** as the filename, and use **Alison Jorgenson's Resume** as the Web page title.

▶ 3. While the Save As dialog box is open, notice that Word has created a new folder, named "Green Fields Web Page_files," in which to store the files related to the Green Fields Web page. You should never save any other documents in this folder.

▶ 4. Click the **Save** button to save the file and close the Save As dialog box, and then click **Yes** in the warning dialog box. Word automatically switches to Web Layout view.

Next, you'll make some formatting changes to give the Resume Web page the same look as the Green Fields Web page. You'll use the procedures you learned earlier in this tutorial.

To format the resume Web page:

▶ 1. Click the **Page Layout** tab, click the **Page Color** button, click **Fill Effects**, click the **Texture** tab, and then apply the **Newsprint** style textured background.

▶ 2. Save your work. Click the **Yes** button in the warning dialog box.

The resume and the program description Web pages now have a similar appearance.

Inserting a Hyperlink to a Web Page

After users read Alison's resume, they most likely will want to return to the program description, so Zoe asks you to insert a hyperlink that jumps to the program description. You insert hyperlinks into Web pages just as you do in Word documents.

To insert a hyperlink in the Resume Web page:

▶ **1.** Press the **Ctrl+End** keys to move the insertion point to the end of the Web page, press the **Enter** key to insert a blank paragraph, and then type **Return to Green Fields Web page.** (Include the period.)

▶ **2.** Select the text **Return to Green Fields Web Page.**, click the **Insert** tab, click the **Hyperlink** button, and then, under Link to, click **Existing File or Web Page** if it is not already selected.

▶ **3.** If necessary, navigate to the Tutorial.07\Tutorial folder included with your Data Files, click **Green Fields Web Page**, and then click the **OK** button. Word inserts the hyperlink to the program description.

▶ **4.** Save the Resume Web page (clicking Yes in the warning dialog box), and then close the Web page. You return to the Green Fields Web Page.

The resume now contains a hyperlink that takes users back to the Green Fields Web page. You will test this hyperlink later in this tutorial, when you view both Web pages in a browser.

Editing a Hyperlink

The Green Fields Web page contains a hyperlink that targets the Resume document. You need to edit the hyperlink so that it targets the Web page version of the resume. Rather than deleting the hyperlink and reinserting a new one, you can edit the existing hyperlink to target the Resume Web Page document.

To edit a hyperlink:

▶ **1.** Scroll to the end of the program description, and then position the pointer over the hyperlink. A ScreenTip appears indicating that the link will jump to a document named Resume.docx.

▶ **2.** Right-click the **resume** hyperlink. A shortcut menu opens.

▶ **3.** Click **Edit Hyperlink** in the shortcut menu. The Edit Hyperlink dialog box opens. This looks just like the Insert Hyperlink dialog box, which you have already used. To edit the hyperlink, you simply select a different target file.

▶ **4.** Under Link to, verify that the **Existing File or Web Page** option is selected.

▶ **5.** If necessary, navigate to the Tutorial.07\Tutorial folder.

▶ **6.** Click **Resume Web Page** in the file list (you might have to scroll to see it), and then click the **OK** button. You return to the Green Fields Web page.

▶ **7.** Place the mouse pointer over the resume hyperlink. A ScreenTip appears, indicating that the link will now jump to a Web page named Resume Web Page.htm.

▶ **8.** Save your work, click the **Yes** button if you see a warning dialog box about the removal of Word tags, and then close Word.

The edited hyperlink in the program description Web page now correctly targets the Resume Web page. Note that if you move your Web page files to another folder or e-mail them to someone, the hyperlinks you created won't work because they refer to a specific location on your computer. Such links that refer to a specific location on a specific computer are known as absolute links. To avoid problems with absolute links, after moving a document, be sure to review all hyperlinks in the document, editing the hyperlinks as necessary to make sure they work correctly.

Breaking a Link Between Objects

When you convert a Word document to a Web page using the Single File Web Page file type or the Web Page file type, any embedded objects or linked objects continue to function as usual as long as the Web page is displayed in Word. That is, you can double-click them to display the tools of the source program. If you use the Web Page, Filtered file type, embedded and linked objects continue to function only as long as you don't close the Web page in Word. If you reopen the filtered Web page in Word, embedded and linked objects will no longer function. No matter what file type you use, when you display a Web page in a browser, the embedded or linked objects do not function. They are displayed in the Web page, but double-clicking them does not display the tools of the source program.

Even though the links to a source program continue to function in some types of Web pages when they are displayed in Word, they can be problematic. After all, the main reason to save a document as a Web page is to make transmitting it over the Web as easy as possible. You probably won't want to increase the total file size by transmitting the source file along with the Web page. Also, your readers will naturally open your Web page in a browser, not in Word, so even if the links were functional, the readers wouldn't notice them.

For these reasons, it's good idea to break any links between a Web page and a source file. When you **break a link**, the linked object becomes an embedded object, and any connection between the source file and the Web page is severed. Note that you can also break a link between a Word document and a source file. The steps are the same, whether you are working with a Word document or a Web page.

Reference Window | **Breaking the Link to a Source File**

- Click the Office Button, point to Prepare, and then click Edit Links to Files.
- Click the link that you want to break, and then click Break Link.
- To break all the links in a document, press the Ctrl+Shift+F9 keys.

Because you used the Web Page, Filtered file type, the link to the worksheet containing Alison's chart was broken automatically. There's no need to break the link now. Instead, you can proceed with viewing the new Web page in a browser.

Viewing the Web Page in a Browser

You're now ready to view the finished Web pages in a Web browser and to test the hyperlinks. In a browser, you don't have to press the Ctrl key to use a hyperlink. Instead, you simply click the link.

To view the Web page in a Web browser and test the links:

▶ 1. Click the **Start** button 🏁 on the taskbar, and then click **Internet Explorer**. If you are asked if you want to connect to the Internet, click No. If your browser automatically attempts to connect to the Internet, wait until the connection is established before proceeding to Step 2.

▶ 2. If you see a menu bar in Internet Explorer, click **File** on the Internet Explorer menu bar, and then click **Open** to display the Open dialog box. If you do not see a menu bar, press the **Ctrl+O** keys to display the Open dialog box.

▶ 3. Click the **Browse** button, navigate to the Tutorial.07\Tutorial folder included with your Data Files, click **Green Fields Web Page**, click the **Open** button, and then click the **OK** button. If you see a warning dialog box indicating that Internet Explorer needs to open a new window, click the **OK** button. The Green Fields Web Page file opens in Internet Explorer. See Figure 7-36.

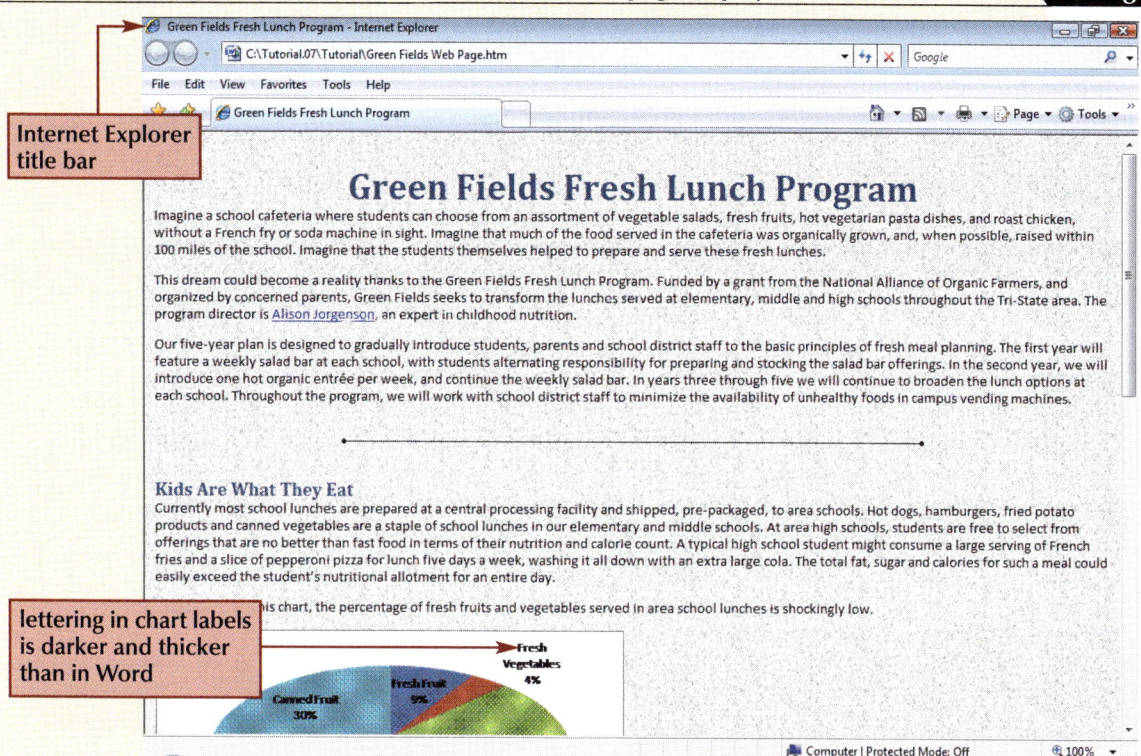

Internet Explorer title bar

lettering in chart labels is darker and thicker than in Word

▶ **4.** Scroll down and review the Web page. Notice that the labels in the pie chart are darker and less elegant-looking than they appeared in Word. Likewise, the embedded worksheet is a bit harder to read. This decrease in visual quality is a disadvantage of choosing the Web Page, Filtered file type. Keep in mind, however, that this file type has the all-important advantage of very small files, which makes transmitting the Web page faster and easier. If you preferred a better-looking Web page, you could choose one of the other Web page file types. Zoe is primarily concerned with making sure the Green Fields members can easily retrieve the Web page over the Internet, so she prefers to stick with the small-sized files provided by the Web Page, Filtered file type, at the expense of readability.

▶ **5.** Near the beginning of the Web page, click the **Alison Jorgenson** hyperlink. The Program Director section is displayed in the browser window.

▶ **6.** In the last paragraph of the document, click the **resume** hyperlink. The browser opens the Resume Web page.

▶ **7.** Scroll through the resume. Notice that when you view the resume in the browser, the table format disappears and Alison's address information is left-aligned. In this case, the format is still acceptable, so you don't have to make any additional changes in Word. But in another type of document, such a change might necessitate another round of editing in Word.

▶ **8.** At the bottom of the resume, click the **Return to Green Fields Web page** hyperlink. The browser displays the Green Fields Web page.

   Trouble? If any of the hyperlinks don't work properly, close the browser, return to Word, and then edit the hyperlinks so they link to the proper document.

▶ **9.** Close the browser window, start Word, open the **Green Fields Web Page** document from the Tutorial.07\Tutorial folder included with your Data Files, click the **Yes** button to update links, press the **Ctrl+End** keys to move the insertion point to the bottom of the Web page, press the **Enter** key twice, and insert the text **Prepared by** followed by your first and last name and a period.

▶ **10.** Save the Web page, print it, and close it. The printed Web page looks similar, but not identical, to the printed Word document.

Review | **Session 7.2 Quick Check**

1. True or False. A Web page is the same thing as an HTML document.
2. True or False. The Web Page file type results in the smallest possible total file size.
3. What's the difference between an intranet and the Internet?
4. What is the first step in creating a hyperlink to a location in the same document?
5. What term refers to the part of the Internet that transfers and displays Web pages?
6. Explain how to edit a hyperlink.
7. When saving a document as a Web page, which file type should you choose if you want to ensure that all OLE links to a source file are severed automatically?

Review | **Tutorial Summary**

In this tutorial, you turned on Track Changes in a document and inserted comments. Then you compared and combined documents, accepted and rejected changes, deleted comments, embedded an Excel file in a Word document, linked an Excel file with a Word document, edited an embedded Excel file, and edited a linked Excel file. You made a document suitable for online reading by adding hyperlinks, previewing the document in Web Layout view, and modifying the document's appearance to make it more interesting. Finally, you converted a Word document into a Web page, added additional hyperlinks, edited a hyperlink, and previewed the Web page in a browser.

Key Terms

bookmark	Internet	source file
balloons	intranet	source program
break a link	link	spreadsheet program
browser	linking	target
cell	merge	URL
combine	Microsoft Internet Explorer	Web
compare	Mozilla Firefox	Web address
destination file	object	Web Layout view
destination program	object linking and embed-	Web page
embedding	ding (OLE)	Web server
HTML document	online	Web site
home page	publish	worksheet
hyperlink	revision marks	World Wide Web
Hypertext Markup		
Language (HTML)		

Practice	**Review Assignments**

Apply the skills you learned in the tutorial using the same case scenario.

Data Files needed for the Review Assignments: Expenses.xlsx, Menu.docx, Progress.docx, Progress HD.docx, Rates.xlsx

The first year of the Green Fields Fresh Lunch program was a success. Now Zoe and the staff of Rios Communication need to create a progress report to summarize the program's effectiveness. Zoe has written a draft of the progress report and e-mailed it to Henry. While Henry reviews it, she plans to turn on Track Changes and continue work on the document. Then she can combine her edited version of the document with Henry's, accepting or rejecting changes. Next, she needs to insert an Excel worksheet as an embedded object and insert an Excel chart as a linked object. She then wants to create an online version of the document with hyperlinks, format the document for online viewing, save it as a Web page, and view it in a browser. (Note: Text you need to type is shown in bold for ease of reference only; do not bold the text unless otherwise instructed.)

1. Open the file named **Progress** from the Tutorial.07\Review folder included with your Data Files. Save the file as **Progress Report** in the same folder.
2. Turn on Track Changes, and then edit the document by formatting the first two headings with the Heading 1 style. Delete "concerned" in the first main paragraph.
3. In the last line of the first main paragraph, insert the word **generous** before the word "grant," so the sentence reads "...by a generous grant...." In the middle line of the third main paragraph, select the word "thirty" and insert a comment that reads **Remember to verify this number**.
4. In the Current Membership section at the end of the document, replace "Marti Sundra" with your name. Save your work.
5. Combine the Progress Report document with Henry's edited version, named **Progress HD**. This file is in the Tutorial.07\Review folder included with your Data Files.
6. Close the Progress Report document (saving changes if necessary) and save the new document as **Progress Report Rev** in the Tutorial.07\Review folder included with your Data Files.
7. Turn off Track Changes, and then accept all the changes in the document except Henry's deletion of "extremely." Review the comments and then delete all comments in the document. Save your work.
8. Replace the placeholder [Insert Excel worksheet] with the budget in the Expenses.xlsx file in the Tutorial.07\Review folder included with your Data Files. Insert the budget as an embedded object, and then close Excel.
9. Center the embedded object, and then edit it to change the Parent Education value from $2,500 to **$3,000**.
10. Delete the placeholder [Insert Excel chart], make sure the insertion point is located in a blank paragraph between the two paragraphs of text, start Excel, open the workbook named **Rates.xlsx** file in the Tutorial.07\Review folder included with your Data Files, and then save it as **Rates Copy.xlsx**. Copy the chart and insert it as a linked object in the **Progress Report Rev** document at the insertion point. Save your work.
11. Return to Excel and change the Last Month participation rate for middle schools from 40% to **90%**. Save and close the **Rates Copy.xlsx** file and close Excel. Update the linked object in Word.
12. Print the **Progress Report Rev** document.

13. In the list of board members at the end of the document, select the word "Chair" and insert a bookmark named **Board**. At the end of the first main paragraph, insert the sentence **The Board of Directors is responsible for overseeing the grant.** Format "Board of Directors" as a hyperlink that targets the Board bookmark. Test the hyperlink to make sure it works.

14. In the paragraph below the heading "Year One: What Went Right?," click after the first sentence and insert the following: **(Click here for a typical salad bar menu.)** Select the word **here** and insert a hyperlink that targets the Word document named **Menu** in the Tutorial.07\Review folder included with your Data Files. Test the hyperlink to make sure it works, and then close the Menu document.

15. Switch to Web Layout view, and then format the report's background with the Newsprint texture.

16. Before every heading except the first, insert a black horizontal line with circles on each end.

17. Increase the font size for the first heading, "Green Fields Progress Report," to 28-point, and then center the heading. Save the document.

18. Save the report as a Web page in the Tutorial.07\Review folder using the Web Page, Filtered file type. Use **Progress Report Web Page** for the filename and **Green Fields First Year Progress** as the page title.

19. Use the hyperlink to open the **Menu** document, and save then save the Menu document in the Tutorial.07\Review folder as a Web Page using the Web Page, Filtered file type. Use **Menu Web Page** as the filename, and **Green Fields Typical Menu** as the page title. Format the menu's background with the Newsprint texture, and then save the close the file.

20. Close Word, open your browser, open the **Progress Report Web Page** from the Tutorial.07\Review folder, review the Web page in the browser, test the hyperlinks, and then close the browser.

21. Use your e-mail program to send the **Progress Report Rev** document to a fellow student. In most e-mail programs, you need to create a new message, and then attach the file to the message. Ask the recipient of the file to open it and test the various links. Can he or she access the source file for the Excel file? Why or why not? Do the other links in the document work? Why or why not?

22. Submit the documents to your instructor, in printed or electronic form, as requested.

Apply | **Case Problem 1**

Apply the skills you learned to create an investment statement.

Data Files needed for this Case Problem: Cook.docx, Statement.xlsx

KingFish Financial Planning You have just started work as a certified financial planner at KingFish Financial Planning. At the end of every quarter, you need to send a letter to each client containing a statement that summarizes the client's investment portfolio. The letter is a Word document, and the investment data for each client is stored in an Excel file. You need to insert the Excel data in the Word document. Because your assistant updates this data every morning, you plan to insert the data as a linked object. That way, when you print and mail the statement at the end of the quarter, you can be sure that it will contain the most current data. In the following steps, you will create a statement for a client named Isabella Cook. You will also practice pasting copied worksheet data into a document as a Word table. (Note: Text you need to type is shown in bold for ease of reference only; do not bold the text unless otherwise instructed.)

1. Open the file named **Cook** from the Tutorial.07\Case1 folder included with your Data Files. Save the file as **Cook Letter** in the same folder. The letter is based on the Oriel Letter template.

2. Use the Date document control to select the current date. In the signature line, replace "Student Name" with your name.

3. Delete the placeholder "[Insert Excel worksheet.]."

4. Start Excel and open the file named **Statement** from the Tutorial.07\Case1 folder included with your Data Files. Save the file as **Cook Statement** in the same folder.

5. Copy the worksheet data to the Clipboard and insert it into the Word document in the blank paragraph that previously contained the placeholder text. Insert the data as a linked Microsoft Office Excel Worksheet Object.

6. Save and close the Word document.

7. Return to the **Cook Statement** worksheet and change the Year to Date value for the Roth IRA to **$28,000**. Save and close the Excel file.

8. Open the **Cook Letter** document in Word and verify that the Year to Date value for the Roth IRA has been updated to $28,000.

9. Save and print and the **Cook Letter** document.

10. Save the letter again as **Cook Letter** 2 in the same folder. Delete the worksheet object.

⊕ **EXPLORE** 11. Open the **Cook Statement** file in Excel again, and then copy the worksheet data to the Office Clipboard again. Return to the Word document, and this time simply paste the worksheet data into the document using the Paste button. Adjust column widths in the new table as necessary to make the statement easy to read.

12. Save and print the document.

13. Close Excel.

14. Submit the finished documents to your instructor, either in printed or electronic form, as requested.

| Apply | | **Case Problem 2** |

Apply the skills you learned to create a Web page for an upscale dog kennel.

Data Files needed for this Case Problem: Kreelie.docx, Sun.docx

Kreelie Kennels Web Page   Brianna Kreelie is the owner of Kreelie Kennels, an upscale dog boarding facility in Knoxville, Kentucky. She would like your help in creating a Web page for her business. She has created a first draft and saved it as a Word document. In the document, she included some comments explaining the edits she would like you to make. After you edit the document and remove the comments, she would like you to format it for online viewing and save it as a Web page. (Note: Text you need to type is shown in bold for ease of reference only; do not bold the text unless otherwise instructed.)

1. Open the file **Kreelie** from the Tutorial.07\Case2 folder included with your Data Files, and then save it as **Kreelie Edits** in the same folder.

2. Turn on Track Changes, review the comments, and make the changes requested in the comments. When you are finished, delete the comments. At the end of the document, insert a comment that reads **I made all the changes you requested**.

⊕ **EXPLORE** 3. Save and print the document using the default print settings. Notice that the margin balloons and revision marks are printed by default.

4. Save the document as **Kreelie Final** in the Tutorial.07\Case2 folder.

5. Turn off Track Changes, and then accept all your changes in the document except for the deletion of the word "fleece," which you should reject. Delete your comment at the end of the document, and then save your work.

6. Open the document named **Sun** from the Tutorial.07\Case2 folder, save it as **Sundeck** in the same folder, and then close it.

7. In the **Kreelie Final** document, at the end of the "Fun in the Sun" section, format the word "here" as a hyperlink that opens the **Sundeck** document. For now, don't be concerned if the link is formatted in a color that is hard to see. Test the link, and then return to the **Kreelie Final** document.

8. Open the Theme Colors menu and preview the various color sets, noticing the different color applied to the hyperlink in each theme. Select the Technic theme colors.

✦ EXPLORE

9. Format the page background for the **Kreelie Final** document and the **Sundeck** document using the yellow tile under Standard Colors in the Page Color menu.

10. Review the Kreelie Final document and the Sundeck document in Web Layout view. Save both documents in Web Layout view. Do not print the documents unless your instructor asks you to, because the yellow background could be problematic on some printers.

11. Save the Kreelie Final document as **Kreelie Web Page** in the Tutorial.07\Case2 folder, using the Web Page, Filtered file type. Use **Kreelie Kennels** as the page title. Save the Sundeck document as **Sundeck Web Page** in the same folder, using the same file type. Use **Kreelie Kennels Sundeck** as the page title.

12. Edit the hyperlink so it targets the correct file, and then save your work.

13. Close Word and open the **Kreelie Web Page** file in a browser. Test the hyperlink. Close the browser.

14. Submit the finished file to your instructor, either in printed or electronic form, as requested.

Create | **Case Problem 3**

Use your Web page skills to create the Web page shown in Figure 7-37.

Data Files needed for this Case Problem: Survey.xlsx

Seabird Optical Web Page You have been asked to create a Web page for Seabird Optical, a supplier of high-quality eyeglasses in Bellingham, Washington. Perform the following steps to create the Web page shown in Figure 7-37.

Figure 7-37

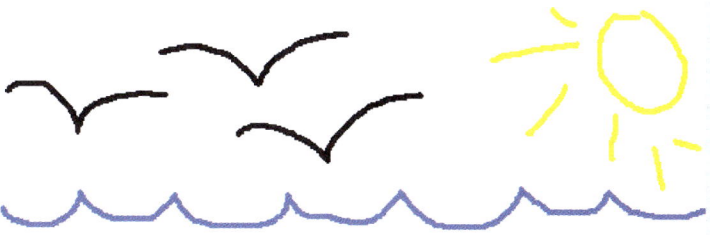

Seabird Optical

3421 Island Way, Bellingham, Washington 98225

Think you don't need glasses? Think again. Our customer surveys show a surprising number of people don't discover they need glasses until they have an eye exam. The following chart prepared by Student Name summarizes our findings:

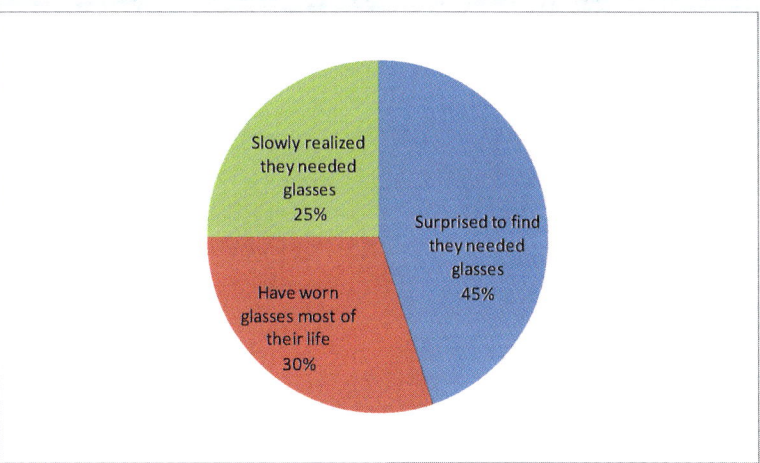

1. Open a new, blank document and save it as a document (not as a Web page) using the name **Sea** in the Tutorial.07\Case3 folder included with your Data Files. Insert two blank paragraphs.

⬡ EXPLORE 2. When creating Web pages and online documents, you might sometimes need to create simple graphics. To learn how, click the Start button on the taskbar, click All Programs, click Accessories, and then click Paint.

   a. Click Image on the menu bar, click Attributes, and then change the Width setting to 500 and the Height setting to 200.

    b. Click the Brush button on the toolbar, click a blue box in the color palette, and draw the waves shown in Figure 7-37. Continue using these tools to draw the yellow sun and the black birds. (If you don't like your first attempt, use the Erase button to erase your work.) Don't expect to produce a perfect work of art; your goal is just to get familiar with using Paint.

    c. Save the logo as a JPEG file named **Birds** in the Tutorial.07\Case3 folder, and then close Paint.

3. On the Insert tab, use the Insert Picture button to insert the **Birds** file into the first blank paragraph of the document. Center the picture at the top of the document.

4. In the second paragraph of the document, insert the company name as WordArt, as shown in Figure 7-37. Center the WordArt object.

5. Below the WordArt title, insert the text shown in Figure 7-37. Replace "Student Name" with your name. Format the text as shown in Figure 7-37.

6. Open the Excel file named **Survey** from the Tutorial.07\Case3 folder included with your Data Files, and then save it as **Survey Copy**.

7. Insert a linked copy of the chart from the Survey Copy file in the Word document. Close Excel.

8. From within Word, revise the linked chart to change the percentage for "Surprised to find they needed glasses" to 45%. Change the percentage for "Have worn glasses most of their life" to 30%. Update the link.

9. Format the page background with the Blue tissue paper texture. Insert a turquoise horizontal line as shown in Figure 7-37.

10. Break the link to the Excel file.

11. Review the document in Web Layout view, and then save it as a Web page using the Single File Web Page file type. Use **Seabird Web Page** as the filename and **Seabird Optical** as the page title.

12. In Web Layout view, resize the Excel chart to make it as wide as the last line of text in the paragraph above it, and then save your changes.

13. Close Word and open the Web page in a browser.

⊕ EXPLORE   14. Print the Web page from your browser, and then close your browser.

15. Submit the finished files to your instructor, either in printed or electronic form, as requested.

Challenge	**Case Problem 4**

Go beyond the skills you've learned to create a FAQ Web page.

Data File needed for this Case Problem: FAQ.docx

Great Falls Health Resource   Sebastian Morey is publications director at Great Falls Health Resource, a county agency in Great Falls, Montana, that helps county residents manage health and health insurance-related issues. Sebastian asks you to help create a FAQ (Frequently Asked Questions) page that answers some basic questions related to health insurance. So far, he has created the basic structure of the FAQ and inserted a few questions. He wants you to add the necessary hyperlinks.

1. Open the file named **FAQ** from the Tutorial.07\Case4 folder included with your Data Files, and then save it as a Word document using the name **Insurance FAQ** in the same folder.

2. At the bottom of the document, replace "Student Name" with your name. Replace "Date" with the current date.

EXPLORE   3. Create a system of hyperlinks that makes it possible for a user to click a topic in the Table of Contents and jump immediately to the relevant section in the Web page. Add hyperlinks to the "Back to top" text that jump to the "Table of Contents" heading at the beginning of the document. Use a heading as the target of each hyperlink rather than a bookmark.

    4. At the bottom of page 1, delete the placeholder "[Insert chart here.]," and then verify that the insertion point is located in a blank paragraph between two other blank paragraphs.

EXPLORE   5. In the Illustrations group on the Insert tab, use the Chart button to insert the default type of column chart. Drag the mouse to select the bottom row of data and then delete it. In the same way, delete the data in columns C and D. Drag the border between the column headers for Columns A and B to the right to make Column A about four times wider than its default width. Replace the first three rows of data with the following data:

      • No employee contribution: 5%

      • Required for family coverage: 60%

      • Required for employee coverage: 80%

    Replace "Series1" with **Employee Contributions**. Locate the bottom-right corner of the selection box around the data, and drag it up and to the left so that it encloses the data you just typed. Close the Chart in Microsoft Office Word window. There's no need to save the chart in this window because it will be saved with the Word document.

EXPLORE   6. Double-click the chart in the Word document, and then examine the various Chart Tools tabs. Use a button on the Chart Tools Layout tab to turn off the chart legend. Use a button on the Design tab to edit the data, changing the percentage for "Required for family coverage" from 60% to 93%.

EXPLORE   7. Near the end of page 2, in the section on finding health insurance statistics on the Web, format the word "here" as a hyperlink that targets the Web site for the U.S. Census Bureau. In the Address box of the Insert Hyperlink dialog box, enter the following URL: **www.census.gov**. (Do not include the period at the end.) If your computer is connected to the Internet, test the hyperlink, and then close the browser.

    8. Save the document and print it.

    9. Save the document as a Web page using the file type that results in the lowest total file size. Use **Insurance FAQ Web Page** as the filename and **Insurance FAQ** as the page title.

    10. Close Word and open the **Insurance FAQ Web Page** in a browser. Test all the table of contents and "Back to top" hyperlinks. If your computer is connected to the Internet, test the U.S. Census Bureau hyperlink.

    11. Submit the finished files to your instructor, either in printed or electronic form, as requested.

Research | Internet Assignments

Go to the Web to find information you can use to create documents.

The purpose of the Internet Assignments is to challenge you to find information on the Internet that you can use to work effectively with this software. The actual assignments are updated and maintained on the Course Technology Web site. Log on to the Internet and use your Web browser to go to the Student Online Companion for New Perspectives Office 2007 at **www.course.com/np/office2007**. Then navigate to the Internet Assignments for this tutorial.

Assess | SAM Assessment and Training

If you have a SAM user profile, you may have access to hands-on instruction, practice, and assessment of the skills covered in this tutorial. Log in to your SAM account (**http://sam2007.course.com**) to launch any assigned training activities or exams that relate to the skills covered in this tutorial.

Review | Quick Check Answers

Session 7.1

1. Verify that the document is displayed in Print Layout view, click the Review tab, and then click the Track Changes button in the Tracking group. Verify that Final Showing Markup is displayed in the Display for Review list box in the Tracking group. Edit the document as you ordinarily would.
2. New Comment button on the Review tab
3. Combine
4. An embedded object is a copy of the original object; edits to an embedded object do not affect the original. A linked object is shortcut to the original object in the source file; edits to a linked object also affect the original object.
5. Object
6. Paste button arrow on the Home tab
7. True

Session 7.2

1. True
2. True
3. An intranet is a self-contained Web-based network that is owned by a single organization. The Internet is a worldwide network incorporating many organizations.
4. Create a bookmark
5. World Wide Web
6. Right-click the hyperlink, click Edit Hyperlink in the shortcut menu, and then select a different target file.
7. Web Page, Filtered

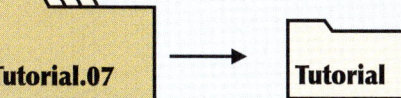

Tutorial.07 →

Tutorial

Green Fields Web Page_files (folder)
Resume Web Page_files (folder)
Chart Copy.xlsx
Green Fields.docx
Green Fields Rev.docx
Green Fields Web Page.htm
Resume.docx
Resume Web Page.htm

Review

Menu Web Page_files (folder)
Progress Report Web
    Page_files (folder)
Menu.docx
Menu Web Page.htm
Progress Report.docx
Progress Report Rev.docx
Progress Report Web Page.htm
Rates Copy.xlsx

Case1

Cook Letter.docx
Cook Letter 2.docx
Cook Statement.xlsx

Case2

Kreelie Web Page_files (folder)
Sundeck Web Page_files (folder)
Kreelie Edits.docx
Kreelie Final.docx
Kreelie Web Page.htm
Sundeck.docx
Sundeck Web Page.htm

Case3

Birds.jpg
Sea.docx
Seabird Web Page.mht
Survey Copy.xlsx

Case4

Insurance FAQ Web
    Page_files (folder)
Insurance FAQ.docx
Insurance FAQ
    Web Page.htm

Reality Check

At this point, you should feel confident that you have the word-processing skills to create, revise, and distribute polished, useful documents in the business world. But there's no need to wait to use your new word-processing skills. You can use them to create some practical documents right now. In the following exercise, you'll create documents using the Word skills and features presented in Tutorials 5 through 7.

Note: Please be sure *not* to include any personal information of a sensitive nature in the documents you create to be submitted to your instructor for this exercise. Later on, you can update the documents with such information for your own personal use.

1. Create a new report template to use for school reports or another type of report that you might have to create on a regular basis. Start with one of the templates installed with Word, delete or edit document controls as necessary, insert placeholder text as necessary, and customize the theme. Select an appropriate style set, and create at least one new style that will be useful in your report.

2. Use your template as the basis for a new report. Insert a file containing the text of a report you wrote for one of your classes, or insert appropriate text of your choosing, and then format the text using the template styles. Remember to include a table of contents in the report. At the end of the report, include a hyperlink that jumps to the beginning of the report.

3. If you are familiar with Excel, open a new workbook, enter some data that supports one of the points in your report, and then embed the worksheet data in your report. If you don't know how to enter data in Excel, you can embed the data from the Budget file in the Tutorial.07\Tutorial folder included with your Data Files, and then edit the data as necessary. Note that you can widen a column in Excel by dragging the right border of the column's header (the letter at the top of the column).

4. If possible, e-mail a copy of your report to a fellow student and have him or her edit the document with Track Changes turned on.

5. Turn on Track Changes in your copy of the report, and then edit it carefully for grammar, word choice, and punctuation. If you were able to ask a fellow student to edit another copy of the report, combine the two documents, and then accept or reject changes as necessary. Save the new, combined combined document with a new name.

6. Choose a type of information, such as e-mail addresses or birthdays, that you would like to organize in a single document. Create a Word table, and then enter fictitious versions of the information into the table. You can replace this with real information later for your personal use, after you've handed in your assignments. Sort the information based on one of the columns.

7. Create a main document for a directory that includes a dot leader. Use your Word table from Step 6 as the data source. Insert the necessary merge codes into the main document and complete the merge.

8. Format the merged document with a textured background and add a title. Format the title appropriately. Save the document as a Web page that consists of only one file.

9. Submit your documents to your instructor in electronic or printed form, as requested.

Customizing Word and Automating Your Work

Automating Documents for a Function Hall

Case | Forsythe Plaza

Geoff McLay manages the Forsythe Plaza, a building with four large function halls in Quechee, Vermont. The function halls are rented out for weddings and other large parties, and are usually booked more than year in advance. Geoff sends letters confirming bookings to customers who have sent in deposits. He wants to create letterhead for these letters. Also, prospective customers often visit or call to make preliminary choices about which of the rooms they want to rent and which caterer and band they want for their event. Geoff wants to create a template he can use to collect this information. Finally, Geoff is working to market the Plaza more aggressively for corporate and other functions. He wants to create a separate template for these corporate events. He also wants to create a brochure to mail out in a marketing campaign. He asks you to help him create these documents.

tarting Data Files

Tutorial.08 →

Tutorial
Brochure.docx
Flowers.jpg
Letter.docx
PicMacs.bas
Plaza Details.docx
Rings.jpg

Review
Bride.jpg
Brochure2.docx
Flowers2.jpg
Flyer.docx
Letter.docx

Case1
LCNLetter.docx
LCNReply.bas
frmLCNReply.frm
frmLCNReply.frx

Case2
List.docx
Logo.jpg
Water.jpg

Case3
Fax.docx

Case4
(none)

Session 8.1

Creating Templates

The templates you'll create for Geoff will ensure that all replies to queries about Forsythe Plaza include the same type of information, in the same order, and with the same format. The first document Geoff wants you to create is a letterhead template. The template will contain formatted text and graphics and a variety of helpful features designed to streamline the process of creating a document. The following list describes some common template elements:

- **Boilerplate** text and graphics, which is material that you want to appear in every document created using the template
- **Quick Parts**, which are stored words, blocks of text, or graphics that you can insert with the click of a button
- **Fields**, which are special codes that insert information automatically from various sources
- **Macros**, which automate a series of keystrokes or mouse operations

You'll include these features in the templates you prepare for Geoff.

As you saw in Tutorial 5, you can create templates for many kinds of frequently used documents: proposals, invoices, fax cover sheets, reports, contracts, or any document for which you want to automate your work and maintain a consistent look and feel. Using a template to create a document has the following advantages:

- **Consistency**. All documents based on the template will have the same format and some of the same text and graphics.
- **Accuracy**. The use of boilerplate text or graphics in a template helps prevent a user from introducing typos and other errors into the document.
- **Efficiency**. Customized styles, Quick Parts, and macros help simplify and automate the process of creating a document.

As you know, to create a document template, you save a new or existing document just as you would any other Word document, except that you change the file type to Word Template. After you save the template, you can copy or move it just as you would other files. You can then use it as the basis for any document which should have the same text, graphics, look, and feel as the template.

You'll begin helping Geoff by creating a letterhead template for Forsythe Plaza. You'll start with a new document and save it as a template. Then you'll copy information from existing documents into the template and add color, a photo, and a text box labeling the photo.

To create the letterhead template:

1. Open the file **Letter** from the **Tutorial.08\Tutorial** folder included with your Data Files, make sure you are in Print Layout view, and that nonprinting characters and the ruler are displayed. This is a letter that was written to a customer to confirm that a deposit has been received. The Opulent theme was used.

2. Click the **Office Button** , and then point to **Save As**. The list on the right side of the menu shows the Save As options.

3. In the list on the right side of the Office menu, click **Word Template**. The Save As dialog box opens with Word Template listed in the Save as type box.

4. Type **Letterhead** in the File name box, and then click **Save**. The file is saved as a document template.

▶ **5.** Select the date in the letter (be careful *not* to select the paragraph mark after the date), click the **Insert** tab, and then, in the Text group, click the **Date & Time** button. The Date and Time dialog box opens, as shown in Figure 8-1.

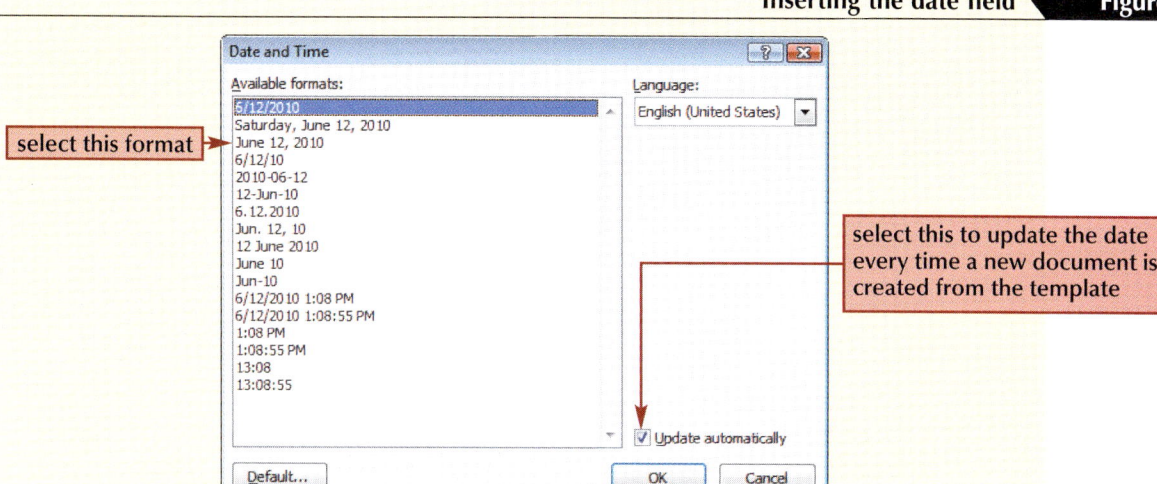

▶ **6.** In the Available formats list, click the third format in the list (in the format "June 12, 2010"), click the **Update automatically** check box to select it, if necessary, and then click the **OK** button. Now every time a new document is created using the Letterhead template, the current date will be inserted automatically.

Trouble? If the first line of the inside address jumps up to the same line as the date, you selected the paragraph mark along with the date in Step 5. On the Quick Access Toolbar, click the Undo button, and then repeat Steps 5 and 6, making sure you do not select the paragraph mark.

▶ **7.** In the inside address, replace "Ms. Pamela Lindeman" with **Name**, replace "145 South Main St." with **Address**, and then replace "Dover, NH 03820" with **City, State Zip**.

▶ **8.** In the salutation, delete **Ms. Lindeman,** (including the comma).

▶ **9.** Delete the rest of the text in the letter, and then save your changes.

Geoff wants the letters to be printed on a colored background. You'll add this color to the template next.

Adding Color to the Page Background

To make the Plaza letterhead template stand out, Geoff wants you to add color to the page. To do this, you use the Page Color button on the Page Layout tab. You can click a color on the color palette or create a custom color. If you click Fill Effects, you can add gradient shading, a textured background, a pattern, or a picture. You'll add a gradient shading of light lavender to the template.

To add a page background to the template:

▶ **1.** Click the **Page Layout** tab, in the Page Background group, click the **Page Color** button, and then click the **Lavender, Background 2** color tile (third tile in the top row). The background of the entire page changes to a pale lavender color. It's a little dark, so you'll add white to it.

▶ **2.** In the Page Background group, click the **Page Color** button again, and then click **Fill Effects**. The Fill Effects dialog box opens with the Gradient tab on top. The examples in the Variants section show shading from lavender to dark gray.

▶ **3.** In the Colors section, click the **Two colors** option button. Two boxes appear to the right of the option buttons, Color 1 and Color 2. The Color 1 box contains the lavender color.

▶ **4.** Click the **Color 2** arrow, and then click the **White, Background 1** color tile (first tile in the first row). The examples in the Variants section show shading from lavender to white.

▶ **5.** In the Shading styles section, click the **Vertical** option button, and then in the Variants section, click the bottom-left square. The Sample box changes to show gradient shading from the lavender color to white and back to lavender again. See Figure 8-2.

Figure 8-2 ▶ **Selecting gradient shading for the page**

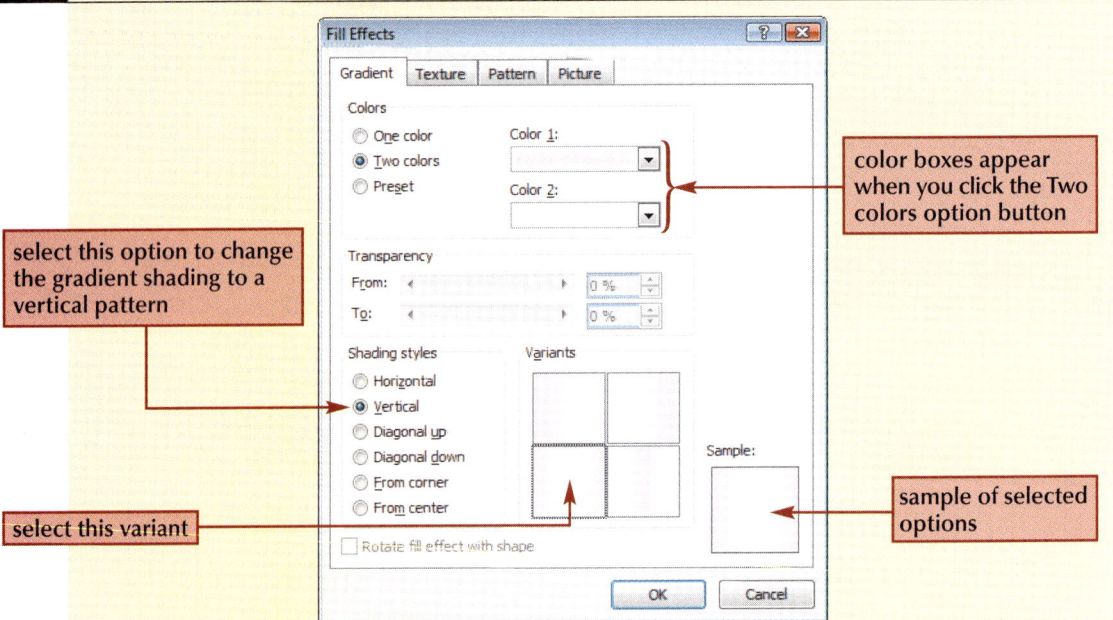

6. Click the **OK** button. The page background has the gradient shading you selected, as shown in Figure 8-3.

Gradient shading applied to page background ◀ **Figure 8-3**

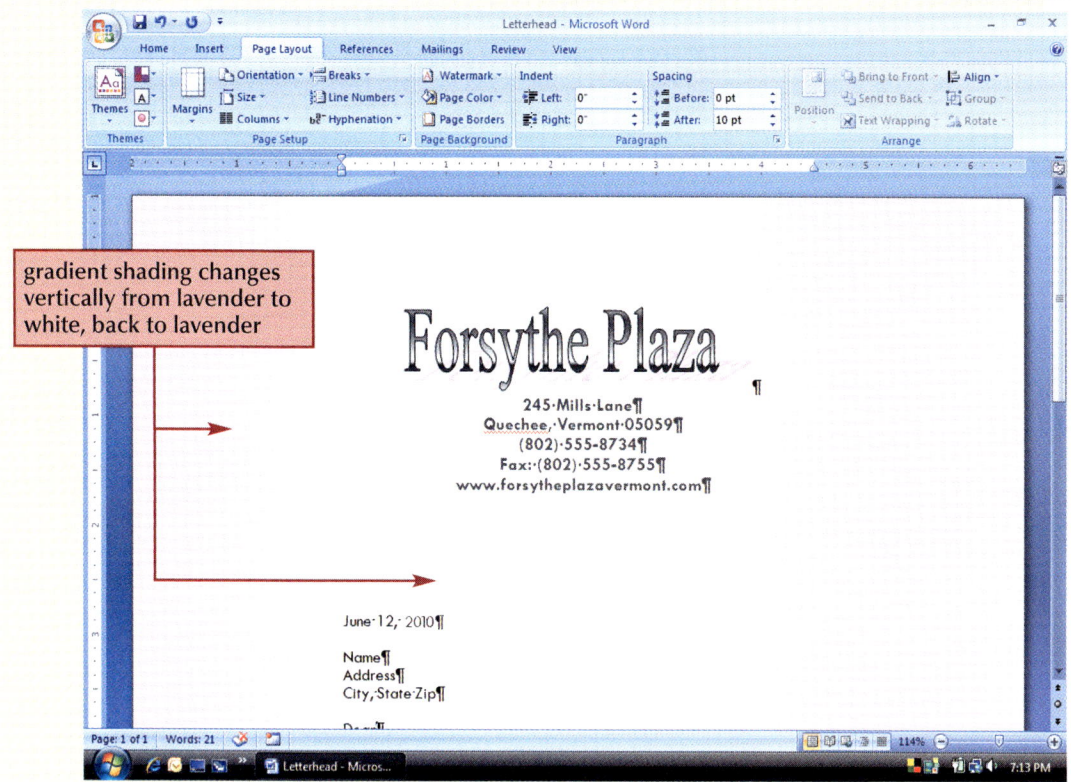

gradient shading changes
vertically from lavender to
white, back to lavender

▶ **7.** Save your changes to the template.

Next you'll add a picture of flowers in one of the gardens at Forsythe Plaza to the template. You'll position the flowers at the bottom of the document.

Adding a Picture to a Template

Geoff would like to add a picture of one of the gardens at the Plaza to the letter template. The photo is a JPEG file (with the file extension .jpg), which you can import into the template just as you would into a normal document.

To add a picture to the template, format it, and reposition it:

▶ **1.** With the insertion point anywhere in the document, click the **Insert** tab, in the Illustrations group, click the **Picture** button, navigate to the **Tutorial.08\Tutorial** folder included with your Data Files, click **Flowers**, and then click the **Insert** button. The picture is inserted in the template, and the Picture Tools Format tab becomes the active tab on the Ribbon.

▶ **2.** In the Size group, click the value in the Shape Height box, type **2**, and then press the **Enter** key. The picture is resized proportionately so that it is two inches high.

▶ **3.** In the Picture Styles group, click the **More** button (the bottom of the three arrows to the right of the five main picture styles), and then click the **Soft Edge Oval** style (the last style in the fourth row). The image changes to an oval shape with blurred edges.

Tip

You can recolor a selected image by clicking the Recolor button in the Adjust group on the Picture Tools Format tab. You can change the image to grayscale, sepia tones, or a washed-out effect, or you can change it to dark or light shades of one color in the theme color palette.

► **4.** In the Adjust group, click the **Brightness** button, click **+30%**, click the **Contrast** button, and then click **−10%**. The colors in the image are softened.

► **5.** In the Arrange group, click the **Position** button, click the bottom-left style on the menu, and then scroll to the bottom of the page. The image is changed from an inline graphic to a floating graphic, with the Square text wrapping style, and repositioned in the bottom-left corner of the page inside the margins. See Figure 8-4.

Figure 8-4 ▶ **Picture positioned in the lower-left corner of the document**

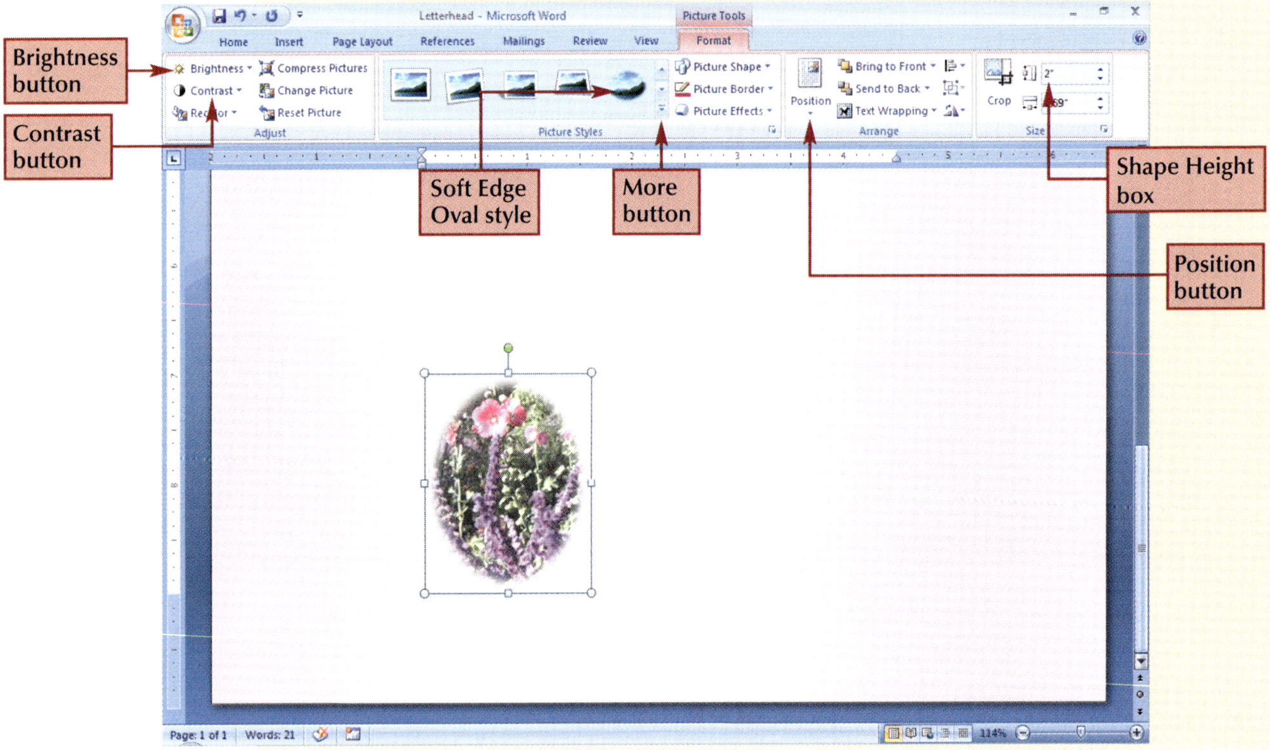

Now any document based on this template will contain the photo of the flowers in the gardens at Forsythe Plaza.

Compressing Pictures

When you add a picture to a file, the size of the file increases. Sometimes you need to keep the file size of a document small, for instance, if you need to send the document via e-mail. To make a file smaller, you can **compress** it, which means to remove certain unnecessary parts of the file. For example, when you crop a photo, you remove part of it from view, but you do not change the size of the file. However, if you compress the cropped picture, one of the ways the file is made smaller is that the cropped parts are actually removed from the file. You decide to compress the picture in the letterhead template.

To compress the picture in the letterhead template:

► **1.** On the Picture Tools Format tab, in the Adjust group, click the **Compress Pictures** button. The Compress Pictures dialog box opens.

► **2.** Click the **Options** button. The Compression Settings dialog box opens.

▶ **3.** Make sure the **Automatically perform basic compression on save** and **Delete cropped areas of pictures** check boxes are selected, and then click the **E-mail (96 ppi)** option button.

▶ **4.** Click the **OK** button. There is only one picture in the template. The default is for the compression settings to apply to all pictures in a document. If there were more than one picture in the document and you wanted to compress only the selected picture, you would click the Apply to selected pictures only check box.

▶ **5.** Click the **OK** button. The Compress Pictures dialog box closes. The picture is now compressed.

▶ **6.** Click anywhere in the document outside the picture to deselect it, and then save your changes.

You want to let people know that they can take photographs using the gardens as a backdrop. You decide to add text identifying the picture as one of the gardens and explaining this.

Adding a Shape with Text to a Template

You can add shapes to your documents to draw attention to something or to add interest. You can leave the shapes empty or you can add text to them. On the Insert tab, click the Shapes button in the Illustrations group to open a menu of shapes organized in categories, such as lines, rectangles, circles, and many types of arrows. In addition, callouts are a special category of shapes. **Callouts** are shapes that contain text and have a line attached to them so that you can point to something in the document.

You can add text to shapes in two ways. You can create a **text box**, an object that contains text, and place it over the shape. Or you can right-click a shape, and then click Add Text on the shortcut menu to add an integrated text box to the shape. Note that to add text to callouts, you don't have to do either of these steps; you can just click in the shape and start typing.

Adding a Shape with Text	Reference Window

- Click the Insert tab, and then in the Illustrations group, click the Shapes button.
- Click the desired shape.
- Drag the pointer to draw the shape in the document.
- Use the options on the Drawing Tools Format tab to format the size, placement, color, lines, and so on, of the shape.
- Right-click the shape, and then click Add Text on the shortcut menu.
- Type the text in the shape.
- Select the text and format it as necessary.

You'll add a rounded rectangle shape below the picture of the gardens, and then add text to the shape to label the picture.

To add a shape with text:

▶ **1.** Click the **Insert** tab, and then in the Illustrations group, click the **Shapes** button. The Shapes gallery opens, as shown in Figure 8-5.

Figure 8-5 ▶ Shapes gallery

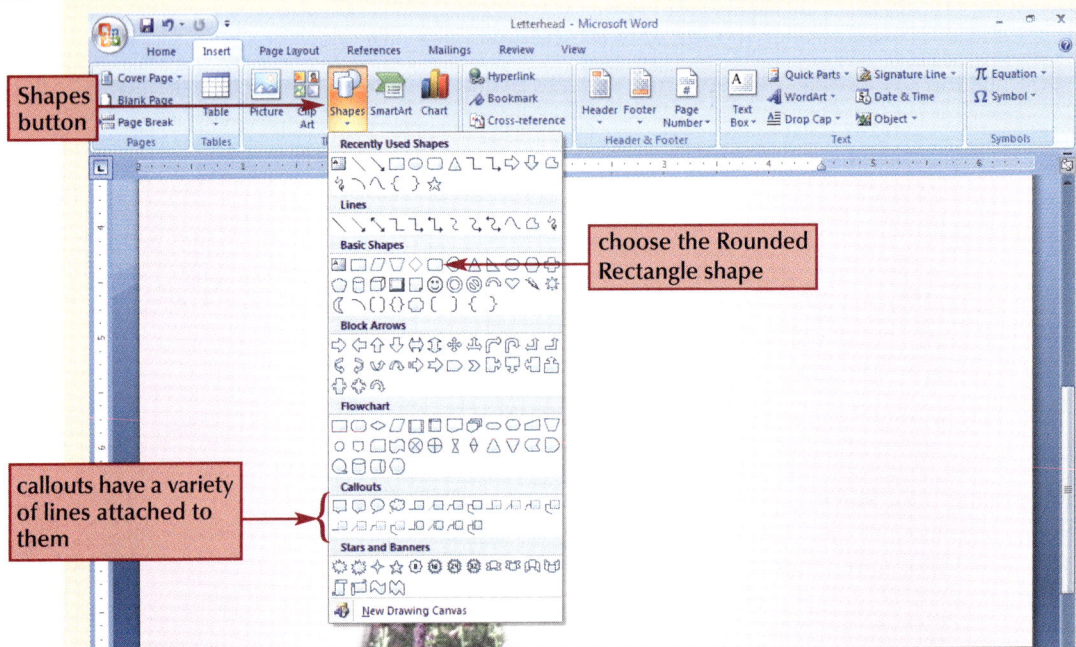

▶ **2.** Under Basic Shapes, click the **Rounded Rectangle** shape (first row, sixth shape). The menu closes and the pointer changes to $+$.

▶ **3.** Below the flowers picture, drag to draw a rectangle approximately two and one-half inches long and one-quarter-inch high. The rectangle appears in the document.

▶ **4.** Right-click the rectangle, and then click **Add Text** on the shortcut menu. A text box is added to the shape, and the insertion point is blinking in the text box.

▶ **5.** Type **Take photographs in any of our three beautiful gardens!**, click the edge of the text box to select it, change the font size to 8 points, and then italicize the text.

▶ **6.** If necessary, drag either of the **side sizing handles** to resize the rectangle so that it's large enough to fit the text all on one line.

▶ **7.** Click the **Text Box Tools Format** tab, if necessary, in the Text Box Styles group, click the **Shape Fill button arrow**, and then click **No Fill**. The white background is removed from the shape.

▶ **8.** In the Arrange group, click the **Position** button, click the bottom-left style on the menu, and then use the arrow keys to position the rectangle so it is centered just under the image, as shown in Figure 8-6.

Shape with text below image ◀ Figure 8-6

9. Deselect the text box, and then save your changes. Don't close the document.

Geoff is happy with the completed Letterhead template. You left it open so you can use elements from the Letterhead template to create the inquiry form that Geoff designed.

You'll start the template for Geoff's inquiry form by copying the logo and the address from the Letterhead template. Then you'll copy details about the plaza (choices of rooms, caterers, and bands) from another document that Geoff has.

Managing Multiple Documents to Create a Document

The next template you'll create for Geoff is a form that Forsythe Plaza employees can fill out when a prospective customer asks about reserving a function room for a wedding. The form will ensure that all replies to queries about Forsythe Plaza include the same type of information, in the same order, and with the same format.

When you create a new document, you can sometimes use content that already exists in other documents. When you need an entire file to be copied into your document, you use the Object button on the Insert tab to insert the whole file. However, if you need only selections from other documents, it makes more sense to copy and paste. You can do this one selection at a time, switching back and forth among the documents, but this gets cumbersome if you're working with several documents. Instead, you can open the Office Clipboard to copy all the items you need from one document, then the items you need from another document, and so on, and finally paste them (individually or all at once) into your new document.

To create the inquiry form template for Geoff, you will use text from the Letterhead template you just created and text from a document Geoff has that contains information about choices customers can make when they reserve a function room. You'll start by copying material from the Letterhead template and from Geoff's file. Then, you'll paste the selections into your new document.

To use the Office Clipboard to copy content to the template:

▶ 1. Create a new, blank document, and then save it as a Word template named **Inquiry Form** in the Tutorial.08\Tutorial folder included with your Data Files. First you need to copy the logo and address from the Letterhead template.

▶ 2. On the taskbar, click the **Letterhead – Microsoft Word** button. The Letterhead document is the active document again. Because you'll be copying information from another document as well, you'll open the Office Clipboard.

▶ 3. Click the **Home** tab, if necessary, and then in the Clipboard group, click the **Dialog Box Launcher**. The Clipboard task pane opens to the left of the document window.

▶ 4. Scroll up to the top of the document, position the pointer in the left margin until it changes to ⌐, drag to select the WordArt and the address information at the top of the letterhead, and then, on the Home tab in the Clipboard group, click the **Copy** button ⧉. A small version of the selected text appears in the Clipboard task pane.

▶ 5. Open the file **Plaza Details** from the **Tutorial.08\Tutorial** folder included with your Data Files, and then if it's not open already, open the Clipboard task pane in this document window.

▶ 6. Select all the text below the "Rooms and Vendors" heading, and then copy it to the Office Clipboard.

▶ 7. On the taskbar, click the **Inquiry Form – Microsoft Word** button, and then if it's not open already, open the Office Clipboard in this document. You want to paste all of the information on the Office Clipboard into the document.

▶ 8. In the Clipboard task pane, click the **Paste All** button. All of the contents of the Office Clipboard are pasted into the document, as shown in Figure 8-7.

All the contents of the Office Clipboard pasted into the document ◀ **Figure 8-7**

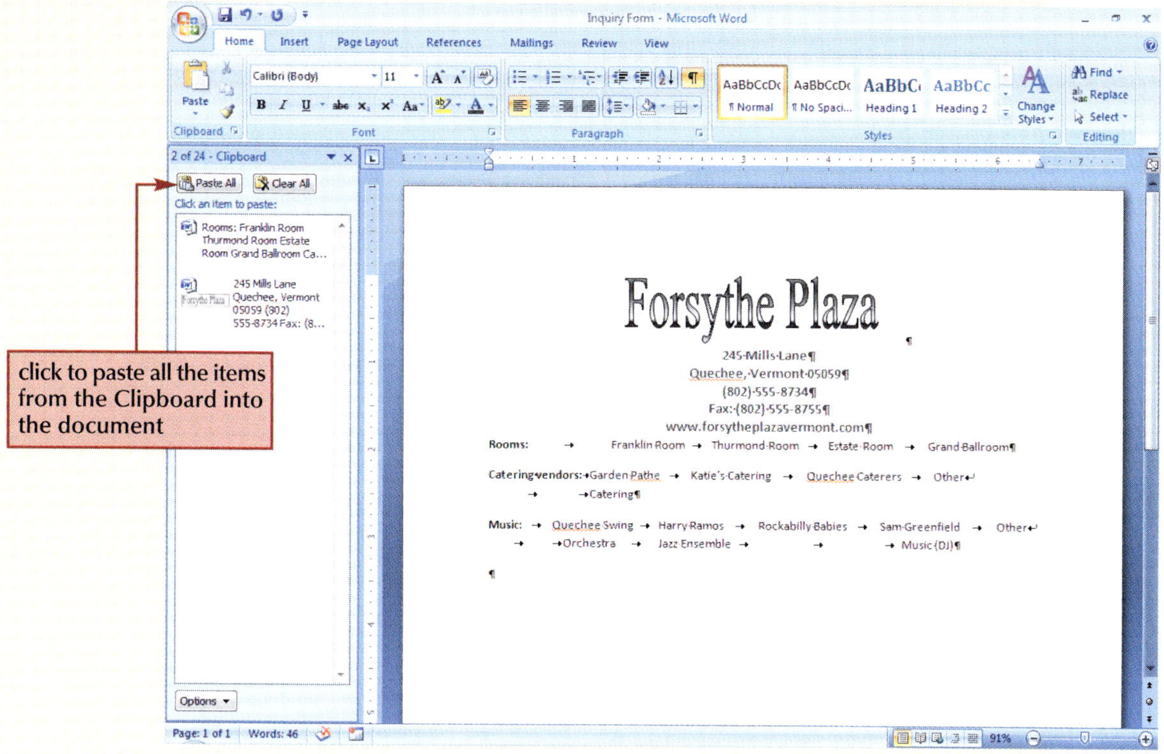

click to paste all the items
from the Clipboard into
the document

9. Save your changes to the template.

Now you can close the documents you are finished working with.

To close multiple open documents:

▶ **1.** In the Clipboard task pane, click the **Close** button ☒. The Clipboard task pane closes.

▶ **2.** Switch back to the **Plaza Details – Microsoft Word** document, close the Clipboard task pane, and then close the document.

▶ **3.** Switch to the **Letterhead** document, close the Clipboard task pane, click the **Close** button ☒ in the title bar, and then, if a dialog box opens asking if you want to save changes, click the **No** button. The Letterhead template closes, and then Inquiry Form is the current document again.

You've created part of the template. Now you need to add places to insert the name of the customer who wants to reserve the Plaza, as well as an introductory paragraph and a title. You'll do this next.

To create the rest of the template text:

▶ 1. Click at the end of the line containing the Web site address, press the **Enter** key, and then change the style to **Normal**. The AutoCorrect feature formats the Web site address as a hyperlink.

▶ 2. Right-click the Web site address, and then click **Remove Hyperlink** on the shortcut menu.

▶ 3. Click in the blank paragraph below the Web site address, type **Customer Inquiry Form--Wedding** (using two hyphens after "Form"), and then press the **Enter** key. The AutoCorrect feature changes the two hyphens to an em dash, a long dash used in typesetting.

▶ 4. Type the following paragraph:

   Thank you for your recent inquiry about renting our facility for your wedding. We will keep the following information on file for two months. If you decide you want to book one of our function rooms, please send a deposit of $1,500.

▶ 5. Press the **Enter** key, and then type the following list of terms, pressing the **Enter** key after each one (remember to insert a colon each time): **Customer name:**, **Address:**, and **Phone:**.

▶ 6. Type **Number of guests:**; do not press the Enter key this time.

▶ 7. Position the insertion point after "Phone:", click on the ruler at the **3½-inch** mark to insert a left tab stop, press the **Tab** key, and then type **E-mail:**.

▶ 8. Change the word "Rooms" to **Desired room**, and the word "vendors" to **vendor**.

▶ 9. Save your changes to the template.

Now you need to format the title and labels in each line so they stand out. You'll make these changes next.

Customizing Quick Styles

One way to make text more prominent in a document is to add a paragraph border. Geoff asks you to add a border to the document title so it stands out from the letterhead. He also wants the labels in each line (Customer name, Address, and so on) to be more prominent. To make these changes, you'll format the text and then customize a Quick Style and create new Quick Styles.

Changing a Quick Style Definition

Because Geoff wants all the documents sent out from Forsythe Plaza to have a consistent look, he wants you to change the theme to the Opulent theme and the fonts to the Median theme fonts; this is the theme and the font set used in the Letterhead template. Then you'll format the document title and update the Heading 1 Quick Style in the template so it matches the formatting of the title.

First, you'll change the theme and the set of fonts used in the theme.

To change the theme and the set of fonts used with the theme:

▶ 1. Click the **Page Layout** tab, in the Themes group, click the **Themes** button, and then click the **Opulent** theme.

▶ 2. In the Themes group, click the **Theme Fonts** button [A⁻]. The Theme Fonts gallery opens.

▶ 3. Scroll down the list until you see Median. The font used for both the body text and headings in the Median theme is Tw Cen MT.

▶ 4. Click **Median**. The gallery closes, and the fonts in the document are changed to Tw Cen MT.

▶ 5. Save your changes.

Tip

To restore the theme to the original template theme, on the Page Layout tab in the Themes group, click the Themes button, and then click Restore to Theme from Template.

Setting a New Default Theme and Style Set   InSight

When you create a new document, the default theme is the Office theme, and the default style set is the Word 2007 style set. You can change both of these so new documents open with the theme and style set of your choosing. To change the default theme, click the Page Layout tab on the Ribbon, and then click the Themes button to choose the built-in or custom theme you want to use. Then click the Home tab, in the Styles group, click the Change Styles button, point to Style Set, and then click the built-in or custom style set you want to use as the default. Finally, click the Change Styles button in the Styles group again, and then click Set as Default.

Next, you'll format the document title, and then you'll change the Heading 1 Quick Style to match your formatting. This way, Geoff can reuse the revised Heading 1 Quick Style in any document he creates based on the Inquiry Form template.

To change the Heading 1 Quick Style definition:

▶ 1. Select the text **Customer Inquiry Form—Wedding** (including the paragraph mark), click the **Home** tab, and then in the Styles group, click the **Heading 1** style. The text is formatted bold 14-point Tw Cen MT in a dark pink color, which is specified by the Opulent theme for Heading 1.

▶ 2. Change the font size to **24**, and then center the text. In the larger font size, the bold text now looks too dark.

▶ 3. With the text still selected, in the Font group, click the **Bold** button [B]. The bold formatting is removed from the text. Now you want to add a border around the text.

▶ 4. In the Paragraph group, click the **Borders button arrow** [⊞ ⁻], and then click **Borders and Shading**. The Borders and Shading dialog box opens with the Borders tab on top.

▶ 5. In the Setting list on the left, click the **Box** button to select it.

▶ 6. In the Style list, click the **down scroll** arrow once, click the bottom dashed line style, click the **Color** arrow, and then click the **Pink, Text 2, Darker 25%** color tile. The Preview changes to show a dark pink dashed line border around the paragraph, as shown in Figure 8-8.

Figure 8-8 ▶ Borders tab in Borders and Shading dialog box

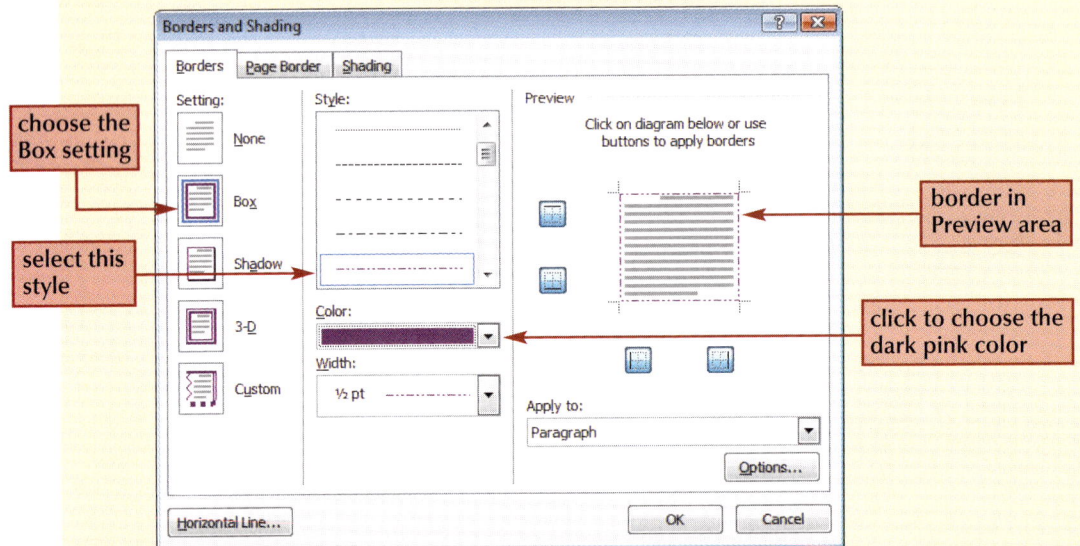

choose the Box setting

select this style

border in Preview area

click to choose the dark pink color

▶ 7. Click the **OK** button. The dashed line border appears around the document title text.

▶ 8. Click the **Page Layout** tab, and then in the Paragraph group, change the values in the Before and After boxes to **6 pt**. See Figure 8-9.

Figure 8-9 ▶ Title with border and adjusted spacing before and after

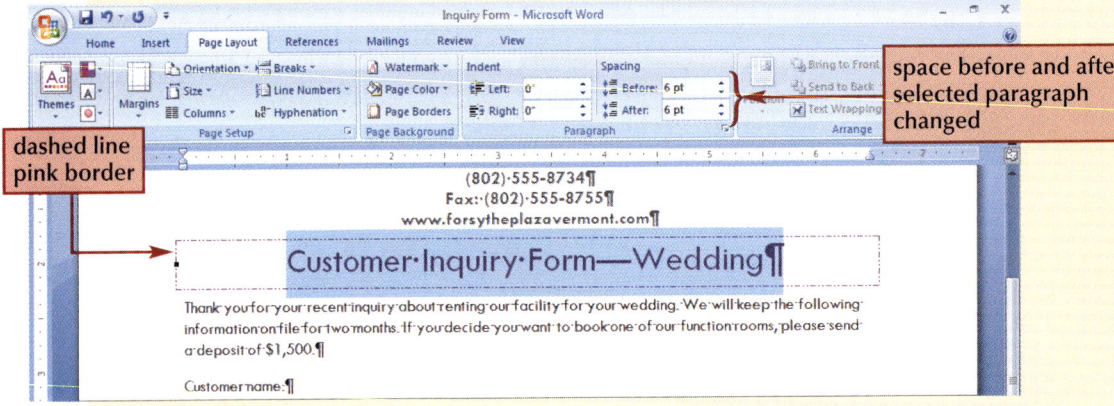

space before and after selected paragraph changed

dashed line pink border

Geoff likes this formatting, so now you'll change the Heading 1 Quick Style definition so he can easily reuse the style.

▶ 9. Click the **Home** tab, in the Styles group, right-click the **Heading 1** Quick Style, and then click **Update Heading 1 to Match Selection** on the shortcut menu. The shortcut menu closes, and the sample of text in the Heading 1 Quick Style button changes to match the formatting of the selected text. Note that this change affects only documents based on the Inquiry Form template; you have not changed the Heading 1 Quick Style that is part of the Normal template.

Now you'll test the new style.

▶ 10. Click anywhere in the "Customer name:" line, and then in the Styles group, click the **Heading 1** Quick Style. The text is formatted with the new Heading 1 style.

▶ **11.** On the Quick Access Toolbar, click the **Undo** button 🔄 , and then click the **Save** button 💾 to save your changes.

Next, you need to format the labels in the rest of the document. You decide to create quick styles for these as well.

Creating New Quick Styles

You want to make the labels in each line of text stand out. Because you'll be formatting more than one label, you'll create a new character style and save it as a new Quick Style. You also want to format each line that has a label with extra space before it so that if someone prints the template to fill it in by hand, there will be enough space to write in.

To create new styles and save them as new Quick Styles:

▶ **1.** Select the text **Customer name:** (but do not select the paragraph mark), and then apply bold formatting and change the font size to 12 points.

▶ **2.** On the Home tab, in the Styles group, click the **More** button, and then click **Save Selection as a New Quick Style**. The Create New Style from Formatting dialog box opens with the text in the Name box selected, as shown in Figure 8-10.

Creating a new style from existing formatting ◀ **Figure 8-10**

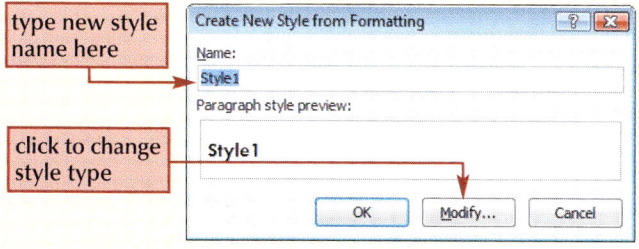

3. In the Name box, type **Template Labels**. The default is to create a paragraph style, and this is a character style, so you need to modify it.

▶ 4. Click the **Modify** button. A larger Create New Style from Formatting dialog box opens. Notice at the bottom of the dialog box that the Only in this document option button is selected. As when you updated the Heading 1 definition, the default for creating a new Quick Style based on a selection is to save the style in the current document only.

▶ 5. Click the **Style type** arrow, click **Character**, and then click the **OK** button. The new style appears as a Quick Style in the Styles group on the Home tab.

   Now you need to create a new paragraph Quick Style to format each of the lines with additional space after them.

▶ 6. Click the **Page Layout** tab, and then in the Paragraph group, click the **After** up arrow to change the value to 12 pt.

▶ 7. Click the **Home** tab, in the Styles group, click the **More** button, and then click **Save Selection as a New Quick Style**. Because this is a paragraph style, you don't need to modify the definition.

▶ 8. In the Name box, type **Template Entries**, and then click the **OK** button. The paragraph style Template Entries is added as a Quick Style.

Next, you'll apply the new Quick Styles to the other labels.

To apply the new Quick Styles to other text:

▶ 1. Select all the lines of text below "Customer name" through the end of the document, and then in the Quick Styles group, click the **Template Entries** style.

▶ 2. Select **Address:**, and then apply the **Template Labels** character style.

▶ 3. In each line, select the label and the colon, and then apply the **Template Labels** character style. When you applied the Template Entries style, the paragraph style overrode the left tab mark that you inserted in the Phone: line.

▶ 4. Position the insertion point in the Phone: line, and then click on the ruler at the 3½-inch mark to place a left tab stop there again. Now there is plenty of room to fill in the information by hand.

▶ 5. Save your changes to the template.

As you look over the form, you decide that the top part of the form, which contains the customer data, and the bottom of the form, which contains information about the event, should be visually separated. You decide to add a border between the two sections.

Adding Custom Paragraph Borders

Borders not only draw attention to text, they can separate parts of a document so the user doesn't get confused. You'll add a line between the top and bottom parts of the form to keep them visually separate and distinct.

To insert a horizontal border line in the template:

1. With the insertion point positioned in the Phone: line, in the Paragraph group on the Home tab, click the **Borders button arrow** , and then click **Borders and Shading**. The Borders and Shading dialog box opens with the Borders tab on top.

2. In the Setting list on the left, click the **Custom** button, in the Style list, click the **down arrow** three times, and then click the three lines style at the bottom of the list.

3. Click the **Color** arrow, and then click the **Pink, Text 2** color tile (fourth tile in the top row).

4. In the Preview section, click at the bottom of the paragraph. A triple purple line appears at the bottom of the paragraph in the Preview section.

5. Click the **OK** button. A dark pink triple line appears below the Phone: line, as shown in Figure 8-11.

Template with horizontal border added | **Figure 8-11**

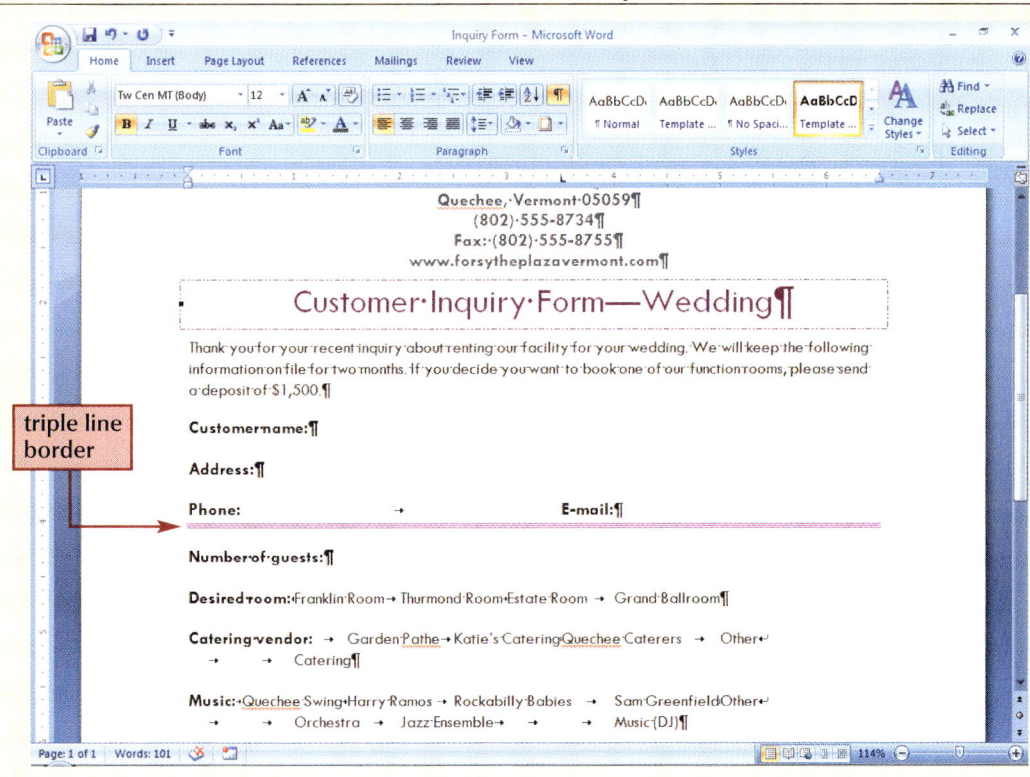

6. Save your changes to the template.

Geoff is pleased with the form so far, but he wants to add one final touch. Because this form will be used for weddings, he wants to add a picture of two hands with wedding rings as a watermark. You'll do this next.

Creating a Watermark

A **watermark** is a graphic that appears behind or in front of existing text on the printed pages of a document. Usually, the watermark appears in a light shade in the background of each printed page. When you add a watermark to a header or footer, it appears on every page in the document (or on every page on which the header or footer appears).

Geoff gave you the file containing the picture of the hands with wedding rings. You'll use this as the watermark.

To insert a photo as a watermark:

▶ 1. Click the **Page Layout** tab, in the Page Background group, click the **Watermark** button, and then click **Custom Watermark**. The Printed Watermark dialog box opens.

▶ 2. Click the **Picture watermark** option button, and then click the **Select Picture** button. The Insert Picture dialog box opens.

▶ 3. Navigate to the **Tutorial.08\Tutorial** folder included with your Data Files, click **Rings**, and then click the **Insert** button. The Printed Watermark dialog box should look like the one in Figure 8-12.

Figure 8-12	Printed Watermark dialog box with photo selected

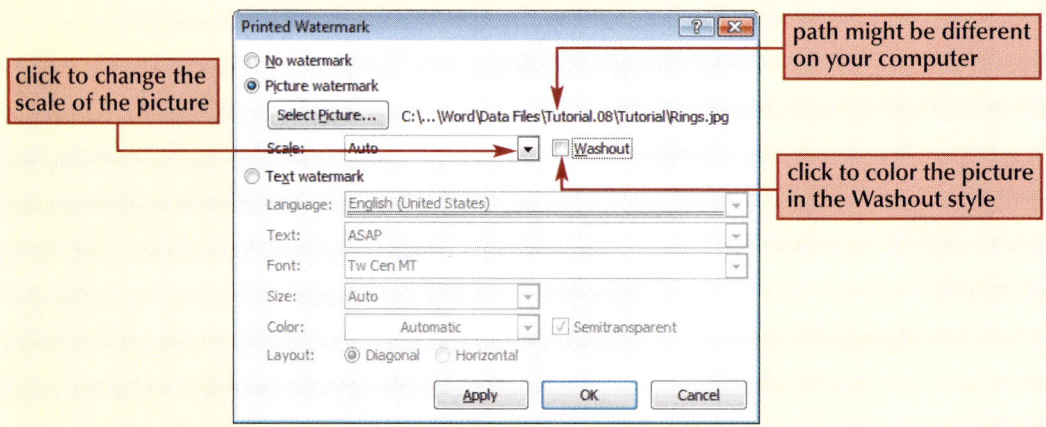

click to change the scale of the picture

path might be different on your computer

click to color the picture in the Washout style

Tip

Another way to add a picture as a watermark is to insert a picture using the Picture button on the Insert tab, change it to a floating graphic behind the text, and then on the Picture Tools Format tab, click the Recolor button and click the Washout style under Color Modes.

▶ 4. Click the **Scale** arrow, click **150%**, and then click the **Apply** button. The picture of hands with wedding rings appears as the background of the form behind the dialog box. It's too dark and makes the text difficult to read.

▶ 5. In the Printed Watermark dialog box, click the **Washout** check box to select it, if necessary, and then click the **OK** button. The dialog box closes and picture colors appear washed out, making the text much easier to read.

▶ 6. Save your changes.

Using Smart Tags

So far you have learned about several features that you can use to automate your work. Another useful automated option in Word is the smart tag feature. As you might have noticed when working with documents, Word marks certain words or phrases (names, dates, addresses, and so forth) as smart tags. A **smart tag** appears as a dotted purple underline in a document. When you place the mouse pointer over the smart tag (or when the insertion point is located within the smart-tagged text), a Smart Tag Actions button appears. This button displays a menu of commands that you can use to perform certain actions involving the smart-tagged word or phrase. The commands available on this menu depend on the type of information that has been marked with a smart tag. For example, you can use a smart-tagged name to send that person an e-mail message or add that person to the Microsoft Outlook address book (or another electronic address book). Or you can use a smart-tagged address to open your Web browser and display a map from the Internet showing you how to get to that address, or you can also choose to add that address to Outlook (or to another electronic address book).

You can choose which types of data Word recognizes as smart tags. To choose smart tag settings, open the Word Options dialog box. In the list on the left, click Proofing, click the AutoCorrect Options button to open the AutoCorrect dialog box, and then click the Smart Tags tab. See Figure 8-13.

Selecting options for smart tags   **Figure 8-13**

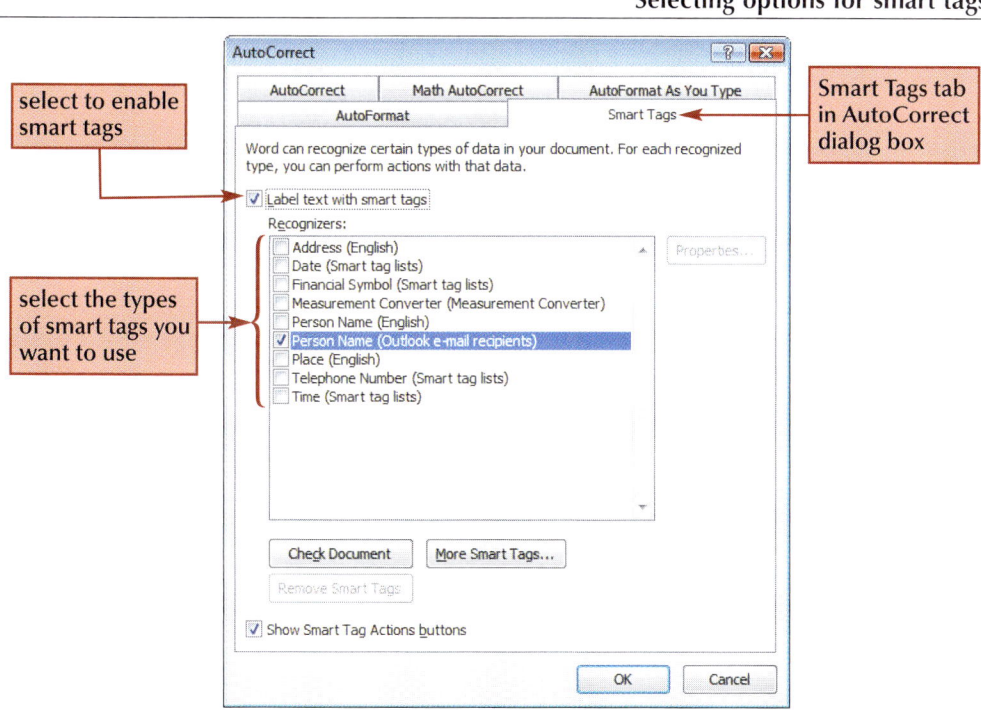

select to enable smart tags

Smart Tags tab in AutoCorrect dialog box

select the types of smart tags you want to use

To ensure that smart tags are used, first select the Label text with smart tags check box. Then, to specify what kinds of data you want marked as smart tags, in the Recognizers list select the smart tags you want labeled. For example, if you click the Person Name (English) check box, text in your documents that Word recognizes as names will be flagged with the dotted underline that indicates a smart tag.

Reference Window | **Working with Smart Tags**

- Click the Office Button, click Word Options, in the left pane click Advanced, and then in the Show document content section, click the Show Smart Tags check box if it is not already selected.
- In the left pane of the Word Options dialog box, click Proofing, click the AutoCorrect Options button, click the Smart Tags tab, and then click the Label text with smart tags check box.
- Under Recognizers, click the check boxes to select the type of content you want Word to mark with smart tags.
- At the bottom of the dialog box, make sure the "Show Smart Tags Actions buttons" check box is selected.
- To check the current document for smart tags, click the Check Document button in the AutoCorrect dialog box, and then click the OK button twice to close the AutoCorrect dialog box and the Word Options dialog box. To close the dialog box without checking the current document, click the OK button.
- In a document, position the pointer over text marked with a smart tag, or click anywhere within the tagged text to display the Smart Tag Actions button, and then click the Smart Tag Actions button to open the shortcut menu.
- Click the desired action item in the shortcut menu, and then complete the actions as directed.

You'll have a chance to use smart tags in the second case problem at the end of this tutorial. For now, you'll turn your attention back to the Inquiry Form template. At this point, the template contains boilerplate text and graphics and modified styles. In the next session, you'll add Quick Parts, columns, a pull quote, document properties, and fields.

Review | **Session 8.1 Quick Check**

1. What is a document template? List three types of documents for which you might create a template.
2. What is boilerplate? How are templates and boilerplates related?
3. List three advantages of using templates.
4. Briefly describe how to create and save a template.
5. How do you add text to a shape that you draw?
6. How do you change the definition of a Quick Style?
7. What is a watermark?

Session 8.2

Automating Tasks with Building Blocks

Building blocks are frequently used items such as text, graphics, and formatting that you can insert into your documents quickly and efficiently. Word comes with many built-in building blocks for a wide variety of items, including cover pages, calendars, numbering, text boxes, and more. You've already used some of these built-in building blocks, probably without realizing that they are building blocks. For example, on the Insert tab, when you click the Header or Footer button, the predesigned choices in the gallery are building blocks. Building blocks are stored in the global Building Blocks template, which is available to all documents.

Quick Parts are building blocks that you create. For example, you might make your signature block for a letter ("Sincerely," four blank lines, your name, and your title) a Quick Part so you can quickly insert that text without typing it as usual; or, you might create a Quick Part that is a company name and logo. Two advantages of Quick Parts are speed and accuracy. After you create an error-free Quick Part, you can easily insert it into documents, without worrying about creating spelling or typographical errors. This is especially valuable for difficult-to-type text such as phone numbers, serial numbers, e-mail addresses, or other words and numbers not in the Word dictionary.

To create a Quick Part, you select the text, graphic, or formatting that you want to reuse, click the Quick Parts button in the Text group in the Insert tab, and then click Save Selection to Quick Part Gallery. You can store Quick Parts in the global Building Blocks template so that they are available to anyone who uses Word on that computer, or you can store them in a document template so that they are available only in that template. The advantage of storing a Quick Part with a template is that you can send the template to someone else, and that person will have access to those Quick Parts.

Once you've created a Quick Part, you can insert it in your documents. To insert a Quick Part, use the Quick Parts button in the Text group on the Insert tab. You can use the same button to access the various built-in building blocks that come with Word.

Creating and Inserting Quick Parts

In Geoff's Inquiry Form template, you'll create Quick Parts to insert formatted contact information for Geoff and another employee.

Creating a Quick Part | Reference Window

- Select the text or graphics you want to be a Quick Part.
- Click the Insert tab, in the Text group, click the Quick Parts button, and then click Save Selection to Quick Part Gallery.
- In the Create New Building Block dialog box, replace the text in the Name box with a descriptive name for the Quick Part, if desired, to help you remember what the Quick Part is.
- If you don't want to save the Quick Part in the Quick Parts gallery, click the Gallery arrow, and then choose the gallery to which you want to save the Quick Part.
- If you don't want to save the Quick Part to the global Building Blocks template, click the Save in arrow, and then click the name of the template in which you want to save the Quick Parts.
- Click the OK button.

Now you're ready to create your first Quick Part: contact information that Geoff can insert at the end of the many letters he sends out. You'll create a similar Quick Part for Maria Chavez, one of Geoff's customer service representatives.

Most of the time, you'll want to store your Quick Parts in the Building Blocks template, so that they can be used in all documents created on your computer. In this case, however, you'll create the Quick Parts only for the Inquiry Form template so they'll be available any time an employee uses the template and on any computer to which the template is copied. In addition, by saving the Quick Part to the template, you'll leave the Normal template unchanged, which is important if you are using a computer in a lab.

To create the text for Geoff's contact information:

▶ **1.** If you took a break after the last session, make sure the Inquiry Form template is open and that the ruler and paragraph marks are displayed.

▶ **2.** Move to the bottom of the document, and then in a blank paragraph below the last line, type **If you have any questions, please call me.**

▶ **3.** Press the **Enter** key, and then type the following:

Geoff McLay, Event Manager

Forsythe Plaza

(802) 555-8734

Geoff.McLay@forsytheplazavermont.com

▶ **4.** Select all four lines of text, change the Quick Style to **No Spacing**, select **Geoff McLay, Event Manager**, and then change the font size to **12** points and apply bold formatting.

▶ **5.** Select the four lines of text again, in the Paragraph group, click the **Borders button arrow** 📋 ▾, click **Borders and Shading**, and then in the Setting list on the left of the Borders tab, click the **Box** button.

▶ **6.** In the Style group, click the **down arrow** 10 times, select the bottom style (a double line consisting of a thick line above a thin line), click the **Color** arrow, and then click the **Pink, Accent 1, Darker 25%** color tile (fifth row, fifth column).

▶ **7.** Click the **Shading** tab, click the **Fill** arrow, and then click the **Gold, Accent 4, Lighter 80%** color tile (eighth tile in the second row). The Preview box shows a pale yellow fill color.

▶ **8.** Click the **OK** button. The dialog box closes and the four lines of text have a border around them and are shaded with pale gold.

▶ **9.** With the four lines of text selected, drag the Right Indent marker on the ruler 🔺 to the 3½-inch mark. The right border of the paragraph is indented to the 3½-inch mark, as shown in Figure 8-14.

Figure 8-14 | **Formatted contact information**

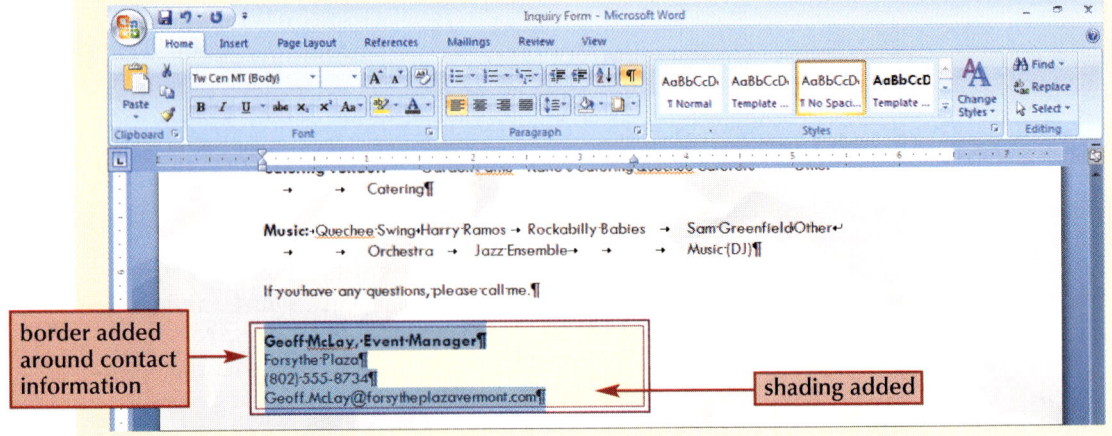

Now that you've inserted and formatted the text, you can save it as a Quick Part.

To create the Quick Part:

1. With the four lines of text selected, click the **Insert** tab, in the Text group, click the **Quick Parts** button, and then click **Save Selection to Quick Part Gallery**. The Create New Building Block dialog box opens.

2. In the **Name** box, delete "McLay," so that the contents of the Name box is "Geoff."

3. Click the **Save in** arrow, and then click **Inquiry Form**. See Figure 8-15. The Quick Part named "Geoff" will be saved as part of the template.

Creating a new Quick Part ◄ Figure 8-15

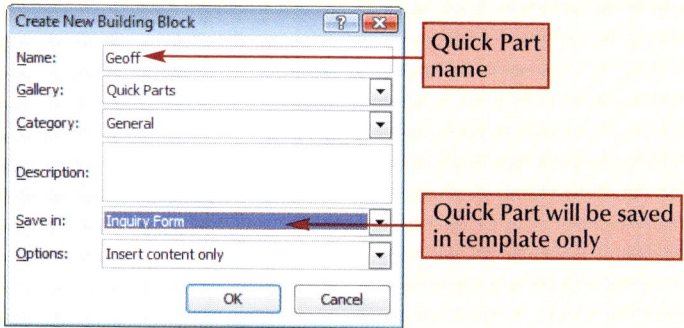

4. Click the **OK** button.

You'll also create a Quick Part for another employee, Maria Chavez, who is a Customer Service Representative.

5. In the document, replace "Geoff McLay, Event Manager" with **Maria Chavez, Customer Service Representative**, and then replace "Geoff.McLay" in the e-mail address with **Maria.Chavez**.

6. Select the four lines surrounded by the border, and then in the Text group, click the **Quick Parts** button. The Quick Part named Geoff appears at the top of the Quick Parts gallery. See Figure 8-16.

Quick Part on Quick Parts menu ◄ Figure 8-16

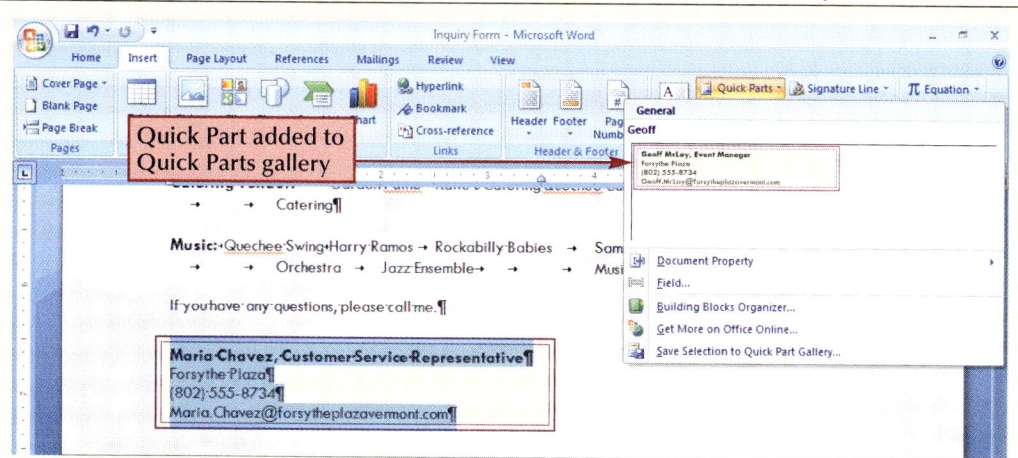

7. Click **Save Selection to Quick Part Gallery**, change the text in the Name box to **Maria**, change the Save in location to **Inquiry Form**, and then click the **OK** button. Now there are two Quick Parts saved in the template.

You should test one of the Quick Parts you created for this template to make sure it works properly.

To test Geoff's new signature Quick Part:

1. Delete the four lines of text surrounded by the border, and then create a blank paragraph below the last line of text in the document, if necessary.

2. In the Text group, click the **Quick Parts** button. The two Quick Parts you created appear at the top of the Quick Parts gallery in alphabetical order.

3. Click the **Geoff** Quick Part. Geoff's formatted information appears at the location of the insertion point.

4. Save your changes.

The Quick Part works as it should.

Managing Building Blocks

Geoff would like you to look at all the building blocks available in Word to see if there are some that he could be using to save time as he creates documents for Forsythe Plaza. You can see a list of all the building blocks in the global Building Blocks template by opening the Building Blocks Organizer dialog box. If you have a template open when you open the Building Blocks Organizer, any building blocks that are part of that template will also be listed. With the Building Blocks Organizer dialog box, you can sort the building blocks in various ways. You can also use the Building Blocks Organizer to insert a building block into the document, edit the properties of a building block, or delete a building block.

Building blocks are stored in galleries, which you've seen often. For example, when you inserted a header, you saw the building blocks in the Headers gallery. When you created the Quick Parts for Geoff and Maria, you stored them in the Quick Parts gallery, which is why they appeared on the menu when you clicked the Quick Parts button. You could have clicked the Gallery arrow in the Create New Building Block dialog box, however, and stored your Quick Part in any gallery.

Geoff would like you to explore the Building Blocks Organizer and then modify the two Quick Parts you created for him earlier.

To manage building blocks:

▶ 1. Make sure the Insert tab is the active tab, in the Text group, click the **Quick Parts** button, and then click **Building Blocks Organizer**. The Building Blocks Organizer dialog box opens. See Figure 8-17.

Building Blocks Organizer dialog box   Figure 8-17

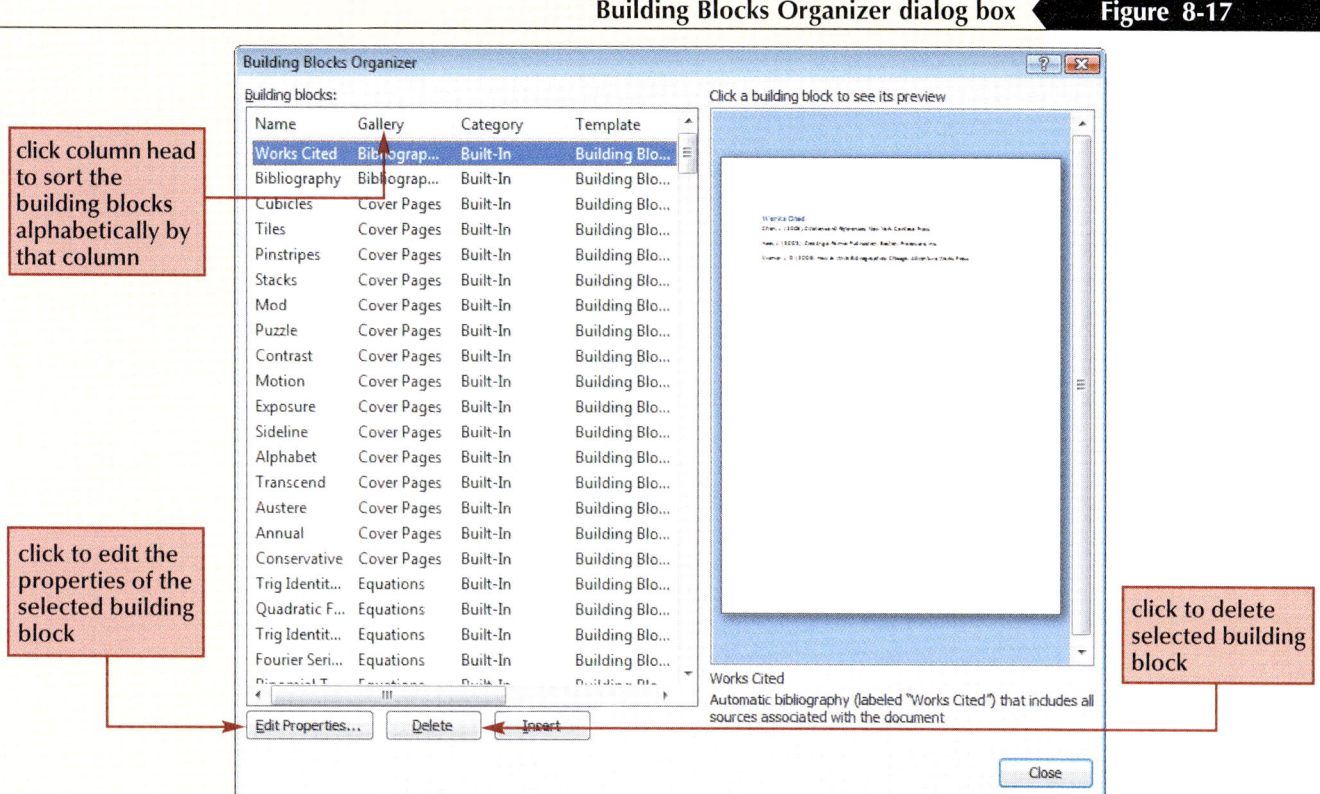

click column head to sort the building blocks alphabetically by that column

click to edit the properties of the selected building block

click to delete selected building block

▶ 2. Click the **Name** column head. The list is sorted in alphabetical order by name.

▶ 3. Click the **Gallery** column head. The list is sorted in alphabetical order by gallery.

▶ 4. Scroll down until you see the two entries in the Quick Parts gallery, click the **Geoff** building block, and then click the **Edit Properties** button. The Modify Building Block dialog box opens. It is identical to the Create New Building Block dialog box.

▶ 5. Click in the **Description** box, type **Contact info for Geoff McLay**, and then click the **OK** button. A dialog box opens asking if you want to redefine the building block entry.

▶ 6. Click the **Yes** button.

▶ 7. In the list of building blocks, click the **Maria** Quick Part, click the **Edit Properties** button, click in the Description box, type **Contact info for Maria Chavez**, click the **OK** button, and then click the **Yes** button. The properties for both Quick Parts that you created have been updated.

▶ 8. In the Building blocks Organizer dialog box, click the **Close** button.

▶ 9. Save your changes.

> **Tip**
>
> To delete a building block in the Building Blocks Organizer, select it, and then click the Delete button.

Another way to organize building blocks is to use categories. When you open the Create New Building Block dialog box, you can click the Category arrow, and then click Create New Category to open the Create New Category dialog box. Type a category name, and then click the OK button. You can sort the building blocks in the Building Blocks Organizer dialog box by category to help you keep track of Quick Parts you create.

You can use the Building Blocks Organizer dialog box to insert building blocks, even the ones that are available in a gallery that you open when you click a button. For example, to insert a formatted footer, you can click the Quick Parts button in the Text group on the Insert tab, click Building Blocks Organizer, click the footer in the Building blocks list in the Building Blocks Organizer dialog box, and then click the Insert button. This usually requires more steps than using the Footer button on the Insert tab. However, if you are using the Building Blocks Organizer to search for the building block you want, it's helpful to be able to insert it directly rather than switch to the Insert tab.

Now that you've learned how to use Quick Parts, you'll learn how to customize a related feature, AutoCorrect.

Customizing AutoCorrect

Recall that Word's AutoCorrect feature corrects certain spelling and typographical errors as you type, such as correcting letter transposition errors ("adn" to "and"), capitalizing a sentence that begins with a lowercase letter, and correcting two initial capital letters ("PHotography" to "Photography"). You can customize AutoCorrect by adding words to the AutoCorrect list that you frequently misspell or mistype. For example, Geoff frequently mistypes the word "Forsythe" as "Frosythe," so he wants this misspelling added to the AutoCorrect list.

Sometimes AutoCorrect makes unwanted corrections. For example, there is a default setting, "Capitalize first letter of sentences," which capitalizes any word that follows a period, exclamation point, or question mark. This is usually a good thing. But because Forsythe Plaza is owned by a larger corporation called Diamond Luxury Properties, Ltd., the next word following "Ltd." should not always be capitalized. Geoff would like you to create an exception to the "Capitalize the first letter of sentences" rule so that he can type "Ltd." without the next word being capitalized automatically. To set this exception, you need to add "Ltd." to the Exceptions list in the AutoCorrect dialog box.

Customizing AutoCorrect | Reference Window

- Click the Office Button, click Word Options, in the list on the left, click Proofing, click the AutoCorrect Options button, and then click the AutoCorrect tab in the AutoCorrect dialog box.
- Select or deselect the check boxes on the tab to set AutoCorrect options.
- To add an entry to the AutoCorrect list, click in the Replace box, type the misspelling you want to add, click in the With box, type the correct spelling, and then click the Add button.
- To remove an entry from the AutoCorrect list, click the entry, and then click the Delete button.
- To add an exception to the AutoCorrect rules, click the Exceptions button to open the AutoCorrect Exceptions dialog box, click the appropriate tab, type the exception, click the Add button, and then click the OK button.
- To delete an exception, click the exception in the list in the AutoCorrect Exceptions dialog box, click the Delete button, and then click the OK button.
- Click the OK button in the AutoCorrect dialog box, and then click the OK button in the Word Options dialog box.

You'll customize the AutoCorrect options next.

To create an AutoCorrect entry and add an Exception:

▶ 1. Click the **Office Button** , click **Word Options**, and then in the list on the left, click **Proofing**, if necessary. The dialog box shows proofing options.

▶ 2. Click the **AutoCorrect Options** button. The AutoCorrect dialog box opens.

▶ 3. If necessary, click the **AutoCorrect** tab. See Figure 8-18.

Customizing AutoCorrect settings | Figure 8-18

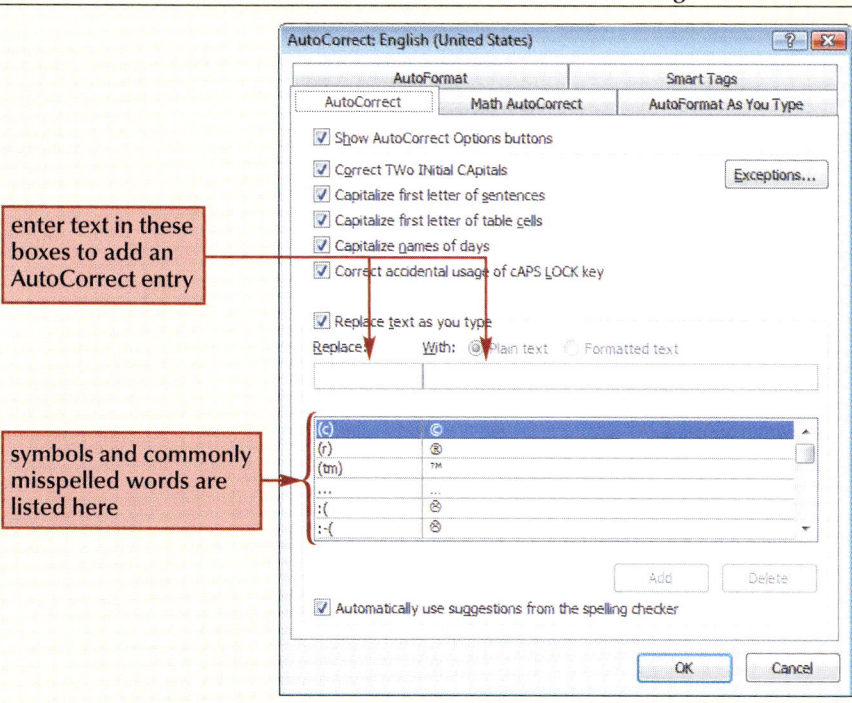

enter text in these boxes to add an AutoCorrect entry

symbols and commonly misspelled words are listed here

You use the check boxes on this tab to set the AutoCorrect options. Commonly misspelled or mistyped words are listed alphabetically in the box at the bottom of the tab. The correct spellings that AutoCorrect inserts in the document when you press the Enter key appear on the right side of the list. The first few items listed in the box are not misspellings but characters that represent a symbol. If you type the sequence of characters, AutoCorrect automatically inserts the symbol in place of the characters.

▶ **4.** Click in the **Replace** box, and then type **Frosythe**.

▶ **5.** Click in the **With** box, type **Forsythe**, and then click the **Add** button. The misspelling is added to the list.

The check boxes at the top of the tab control the AutoCorrect options. The third option is the one that controls the automatic capitalization of words after end-of-sentence punctuation marks.

▶ **6.** Click the **Exceptions** button in the AutoCorrect dialog box to open the AutoCorrect Exceptions dialog box, and then click the **First Letter** tab, if necessary. Here you'll type the text you want as an exception to the Capitalize first letter of sentences rule.

▶ **7.** Type **Ltd.** in the Don't capitalize after box, and then click the **Add** button. The word "Ltd." is added to the list of exceptions in the AutoCorrect Exceptions dialog box so that when Geoff types "Ltd.", AutoCorrect won't capitalize the following word. You won't actually change the default settings for now.

▶ **8.** Click the **OK** button in the AutoCorrect Exceptions dialog box, and then click the **OK** button in the AutoCorrect dialog box. The dialog boxes close and AutoCorrect is customized with your changes.

▶ **9.** Click the **OK** button in the Word Options dialog box. Now you'll insert text using the customized AutoCorrect entry and exception.

▶ **10.** In the first line in the paragraph under the heading "Customer Inquiry Form—Wedding," select **our facility**, type **Frosythe**, and then press the **spacebar**. The word you typed autocorrects to "Forsythe."

▶ **11.** Type **Plaza (a Diamond Luxury Properties, Ltd. company)**. The word "company" does not change to "Company" even though it is the first word after a period because "Ltd." was added to the exceptions list.

▶ **12.** Save your changes to the template.

Generally, AutoCorrect entries are short and are not formatted. Also, keep in mind that AutoCorrect corrections happen automatically once you add them to the AutoCorrect list. You need to undo them as you're working if you decide you don't want the correction to occur in a particular instance. Quick Parts need to be actively inserted into the document. Like Quick Parts added to the Building Blocks template, AutoCorrect entries are available only on the computer on which they were created; they don't become part of a template. Also, Quick Parts can be organized and sorted in several ways, which is useful if you plan to create a lot of them; AutoCorrect entries can be sorted only alphabetically and cannot be grouped into categories.

Now you'll remove the customizations you added to AutoCorrect.

To remove the AutoCorrect customizations:

1. Click the **Office Button**, click **Word Options**, in the list on the left click **Proofing**, click the **AutoCorrect Options** button, and then click the **AutoCorrect** tab, if necessary. The dialog box changes to show proofing options.

2. Scroll down the list of AutoCorrect entries until you see "Frosythe." (Note that the list is sorted in alphabetical order by the words in the Replace column.)

3. Click **Frosythe** to select that entry, and then click the **Delete** button. The entry you added is deleted.

4. Click the **Exceptions** button, scroll down the list until you see Ltd., click **Ltd.**, and then click the **Delete** button.

5. Click the **OK** button in each of the three open dialog boxes.

Next you want to reformat the body of the form so that you have space to insert a formatted quote from a satisfied customer.

Creating Columns of Different Widths

You want to insert a quote from a satisfied customer in the document. To create space for this, you will format the information in the body of the form in two columns. Instead of creating columns of equal width, you'll create a narrow left column and a wider right column. You want the categories to appear in the left column and the choices to appear in the right column.

To create columns of different widths:

1. Select all the text below the "Number of guests:" line and above the sentence "If you have any questions, please call me."

2. Click the **Page Layout** tab, if necessary, in the Page Setup group, click the **Columns** button, and then click **Left**. The selected text is formatted in two columns. The left column is narrower than the right column. However, the results are not exactly what you had expected. You wanted the boldface labels in the left column and the choices in the right column. You'll fix this now.

3. On the Quick Access Toolbar, click the **Undo** button. The text is formatted in a single column again.

4. Position the insertion point immediately after the colon after "Desired room," press the **Enter** key, position the insertion point immediately after the colon after "vendor," press the **Enter** key, position the insertion point immediately after the colon after "Music:," and then press the **Enter** key. Each label is now on its own line.

5. Select **Catering vendor:** and the paragraph mark, drag it up so it appears in the line below "Desired room," select **Music:** and the paragraph mark, and then drag it up so it appears in the line below "Catering vendor." See Figure 8-19.

Figure 8-19 Document after moving text

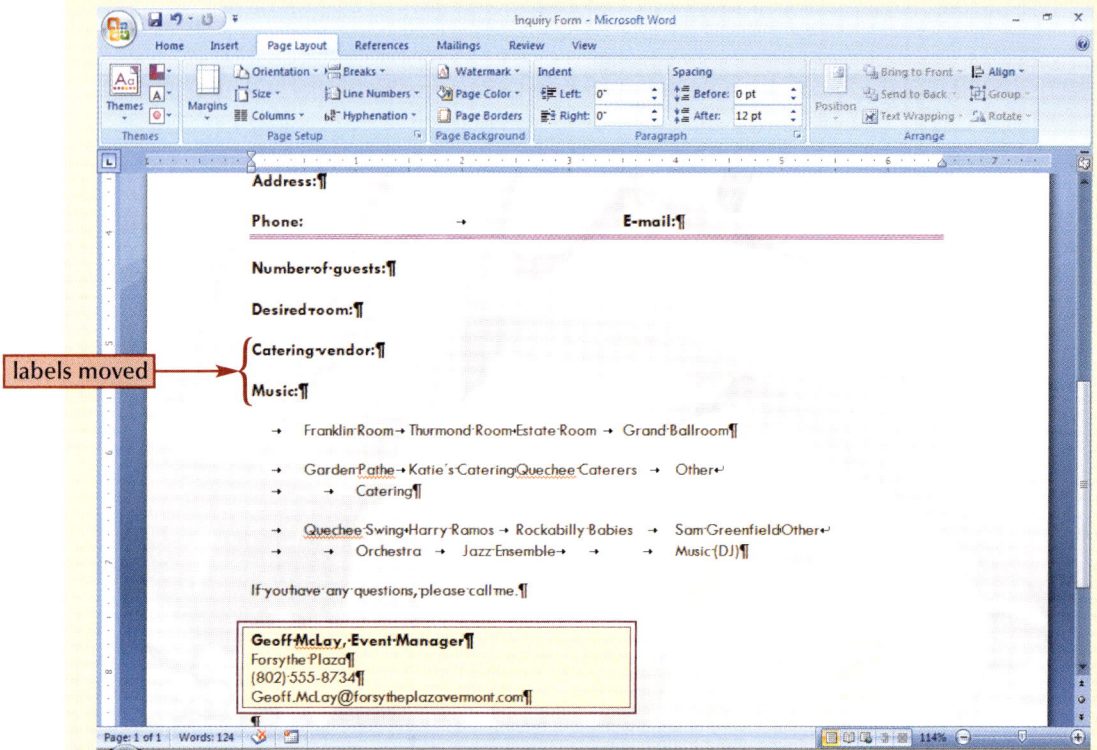

labels moved

Tip

To customize the width of the columns, on the Insert tab, in the Page Setup group, click the Columns button, and then click More Columns. In the Columns dialog box that opens, change the values in the Width and Spacing boxes as desired.

6. Select all the text below the "Number of guests:" line and above the sentence "If you have any questions, please call me.", in the Page Setup group, click the **Columns** button, and then click **Left**. The selected text is formatted in two columns and continuous section breaks are inserted before and after the columns. Now you need to force the second column to start with the list of rooms.

7. Position the insertion point before the tab mark in the line under "Music," in the Page Setup group, click the **Breaks** button, and then click **Column**. A column break is inserted, as shown in Figure 8-20.

Document after formatting text in two columns ◀ **Figure 8-20**

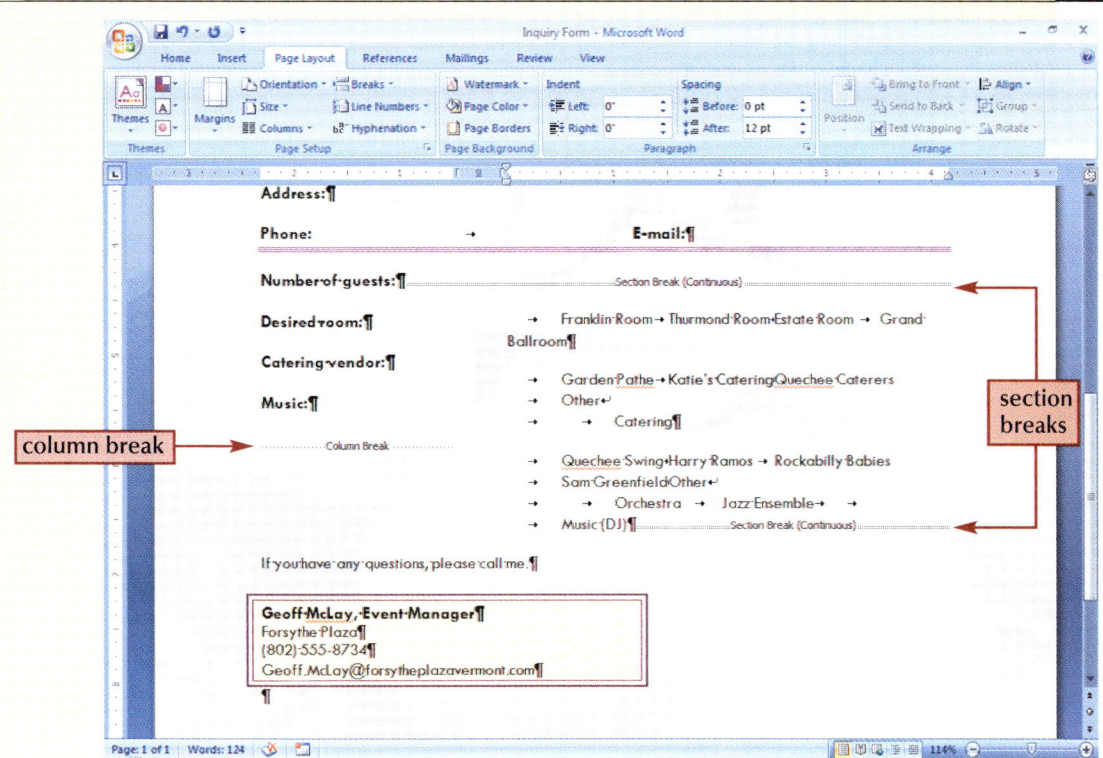

Now that you've formatted the text in columns, you need to move sections so that the labels in the left column align with the correct choices in the right column.

To restructure and format the columns:

▶ **1.** Position the insertion point before the tab mark at the top of the second column (the tab in front of the word "Franklin"), and then press the **Delete** key.

▶ **2.** Position the insert point after "Franklin Room", and then press the **Shift**+**Enter** keys. A manual line break is inserted, and the insertion point is blinking on the next line.

▶ **3.** Delete the tab marks in front of "Thurmond Room," "Estate Room," and "Grand Ballroom," and then insert manual line breaks after "Thurmond Room" and "Estate Room."

▶ **4.** In the second set of choices, delete the tab mark in front of "Garden," and then delete the tab marks and insert manual line breaks after "Pathe," "Katie's Catering," and "Quechee Caterers." Notice that the there is already a manual line break after "Other," and the word "Catering" is by itself below "Other."

▶ **5.** Cut **Catering** in the line below "Other" (do not cut the paragraph mark after the word), paste it after "Garden Pathe," position the insertion point between "Other" and the manual line break formatting mark, and then press the **Delete** key three times. The manual line break after "Other" and then two tab marks on the next line are deleted and the paragraph mark now appears after "Other."

▶ **6.** In the third set of choices, delete the tab mark before "Quechee," and then delete the tab marks and insert manual line breaks after "Swing," "Ramos," "Babies," and "Greenfield."

▶ **7.** Move **Orchestra** so it comes after "Swing," move **Jazz Ensemble** so it comes after "Ramos," move **Music (DJ)** so it comes after "Greenfield," and then delete the manual line break after "Other," the tab marks on the next line, and the blank paragraph, if necessary. Make sure you insert any spaces needed between words.

▶ **8.** Click anywhere in the phrase **Catering vendor:**, then in the Paragraph group, change the value in the Before box to **54 pt**, and then change the paragraph spacing before the paragraph containing "Music" to **54** points as well. Now the choices are aligned with each category label. See Figure 8-21.

Figure 8-21 ▶ **Text in columns repositioned and aligned**

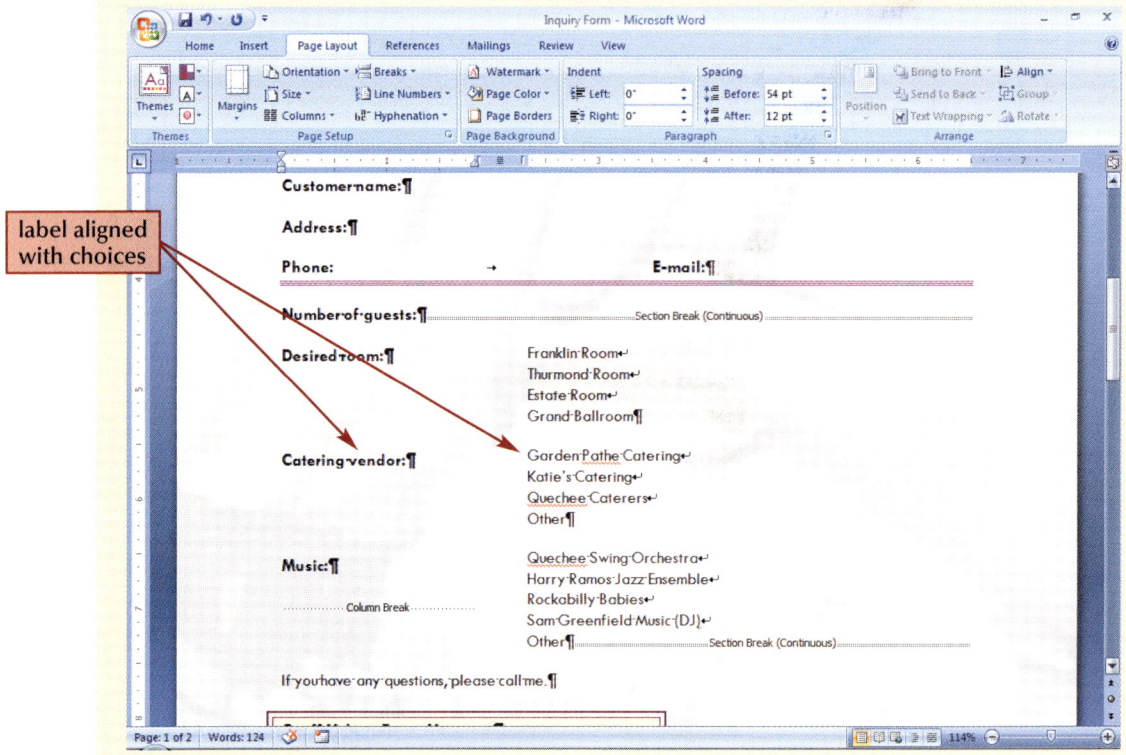

▶ **9.** Save your changes.

Now you can insert the text box with the quote from a satisfied customer.

Inserting Formatted Text Boxes

In Session 1, when you inserted text into the rounded rectangle below the picture of the flowers in the Letterhead template, you actually created a text box that became part of the shape. A text box is an object that contains text and that you can treat as an inline or a floating object in a document. Text boxes that contain text copied (not cut) from the document are called **pull quotes**, because they contain text "pulled" from the document. Pull quotes are eye-catching and provide relief from unbroken text, which is especially important in long documents. A variation on pull quotes is **sidebars**, which are text boxes that contain additional, related information that is not contained in the main document.

You can create plain text boxes that you leave plain or format yourself, or you can insert preformatted text boxes from the Text Box gallery. Either way, you start by clicking the Text Box button in the Text group on the Insert tab or by clicking the text box you want to insert in the Building Blocks Organizer dialog box. If you start with a plain text box, you can format it with fill color and border color, as well as change the font and font styles used in the text box. When you insert a preformatted text box, you can of course change the formatting if you choose.

Another aspect of text boxes you have to consider is whether they are inline with the text of the document or float over the document text. You also have to decide how you want the document text to wrap around the text box. You've made similar formatting decisions with the pictures, WordArt and clip art objects, and charts and graphs that you've worked with.

Geoff would like you to insert a formatted text box to contain a quote from one of his satisfied customers.

Tip

To create a plain text box from existing text, select the text, click the Insert tab, in the Text group, click the Text Box button, and then click Draw Text Box.

To insert a formatted text box:

1. With the insertion point anywhere in the document, click the **Insert** tab, and then, in the Text group, click the **Text Box** button. A gallery of text boxes opens. The colors used in the text boxes in the gallery change depending on the theme colors.

2. In the gallery, click the down scroll arrow once, and then click the **Braces Quote 2** text box. A purple text box is inserted in the right middle of the page. The placeholder text is selected in the content control.

3. Type **Thanks to the fantastic staff at Forsythe Plaza, all of our guests had a wonderful time at our wedding.**

4. Press the **Enter** key, and then type **Jack and Camille Perreira**.

5. Select the text in the text box, and then change it to **12 points**.

6. Click the **Text Box Tools Format** tab, if necessary, and then use the boxes in the Size group to change the size of the text box to **2" × 2"**.

7. Drag the text box to position it approximately centered in the area to the right of the list of choices. See Figure 8-22.

Tip

You can use the Quote or Intense Quote Quick Style to format text as a quote. Both styles italicize the text. The Quote style removes space before and after the paragraph, and the Intense Quote style adds bold formatting, indents the text from the left margin, and changes the space after the paragraph to 14 points.

Figure 8-22   **Formatted text box inserted in document**

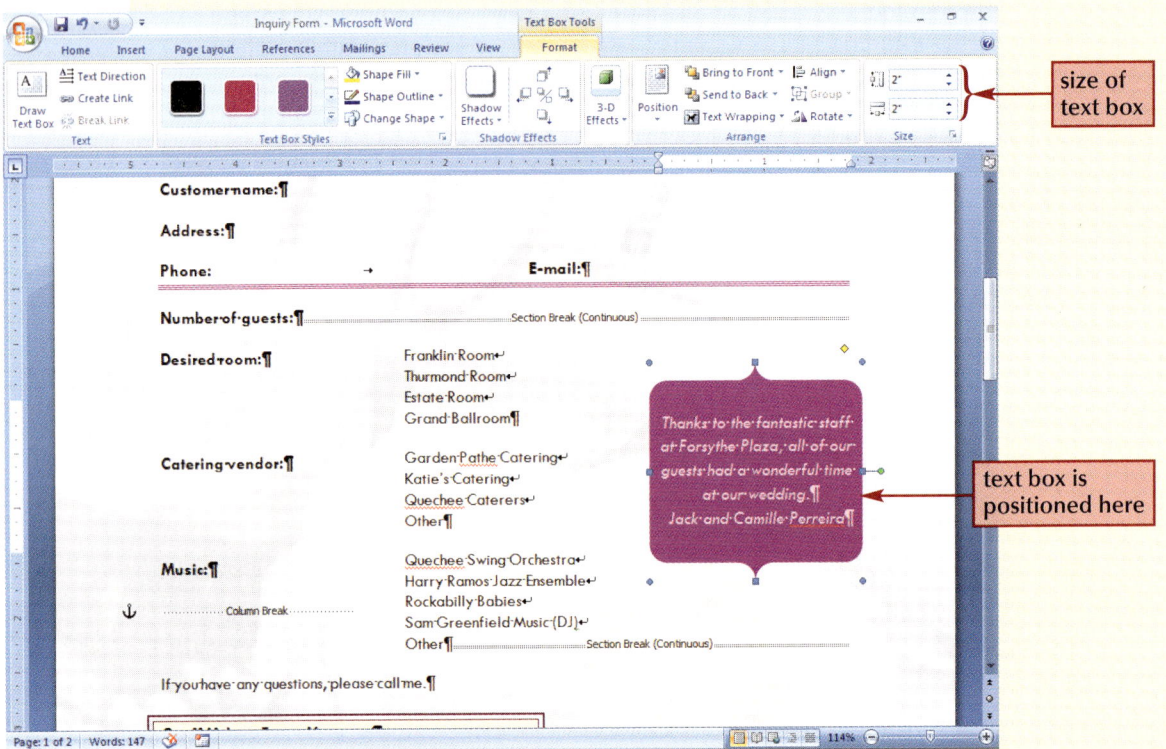

> **8.** In the Shadow Effects group, click the **Shadow Effects** button, and then under Drop Shadow in the gallery, click **Shadow Style 5** (the only style in the second row in the Drop Shadow section).

> **9.** In the Text Box Styles group, click the **More** button, and then click the **Horizontal Gradient – Accent 2** style (seventh row, third column).

> **10.** Deselect the text box, and then save your changes.

Geoff wants you to send the new form to his manager at Diamond Luxury Properties. Before you do this, you'll add information to the document to help identify it.

Understanding Document Properties

When you save a file, identifying information about the file is saved along with it, such as the author's name and the date the file was created. This information is known as the file **properties**. You can use properties to organize documents based on specific properties or to search for files that have specific properties.

Document controls can be linked to document properties so that the controls "pick up" and display the property information. For example, if you insert a header or a cover page that includes a Title document control, that content is automatically tied to the Title document property, and the Title property displays the information stored in the Title box in the Document Information Panel. The connection works both ways, so that if you change the title in the Title box in the Document Information Panel, the change will appear in every Title document control in the document.

Adding Document Properties

Geoff wants you to add properties to the Inquiry Form template. You'll do this now.

To add document properties:

▶ 1. Click the **Office Button** 🔘, point to **Prepare**, and then click **Properties**. The Document Information Panel opens at the top of the document window. When a document is created, the Author property is picked up from the User name box in the Word Options dialog box. See Figure 8-23.

Setting document properties in the Document Information Panel ◀ **Figure 8-23**

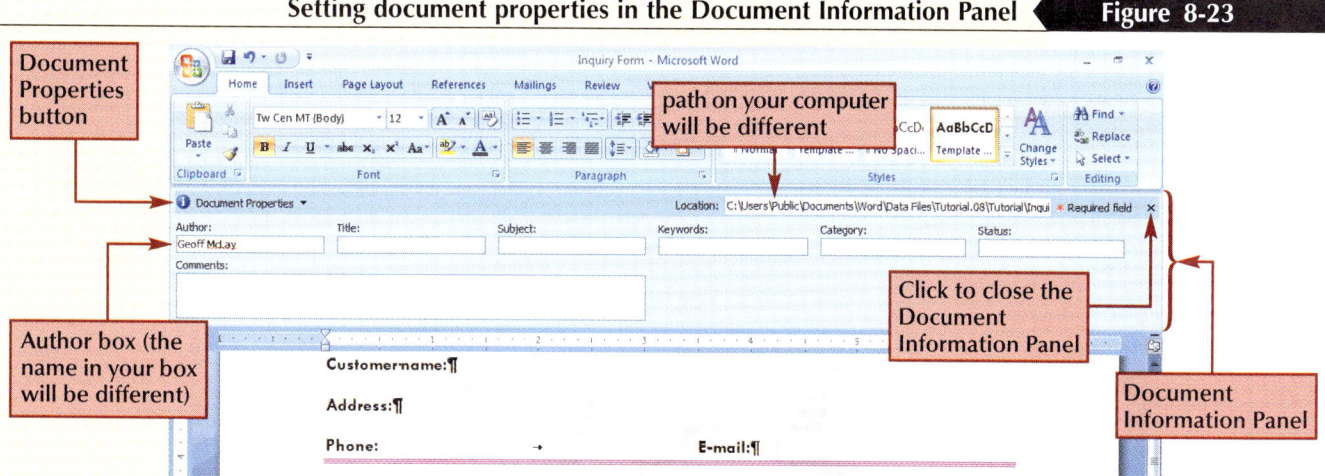

▶ 2. If your name doesn't appear in the Author box, select the name, and then type your name. If your name is already in the Author box, skip to Step 3.

▶ 3. Click in the **Title** box, and then type **Customer Inquiry Form**. The Title property is not the same as the filename. The title you insert here appears in any Title controls you insert in the template, and it would appear in the title bar of a browser if you saved the document as a Web page.

▶ 4. Click in the Keywords box, and then type **new customers, weddings, inquiry**.

▶ 5. Click in the **Status** box, and then type **Draft**.

▶ 6. In the upper-left corner of the Document Information Panel, click the **Document Properties** button, click **Advanced Properties**, and then, in the Inquiry Form Properties dialog box, click the **Summary** tab. The Title, Author, and Keywords boxes contain the text you entered in the Document Information Panel.

▶ 7. Click in the **Company** box, and then type **Forsythe Plaza**. Like the other properties, the Company property is used in document controls that appear on several cover pages, headers, and footers. Leave this dialog box open.

Geoff would also like you to indicate that this template was created by the Events department at Forsythe Plaza. You need to use the Custom tab to specify the department.

To add a custom document property:

▶ **1.** In the Inquiry Form Properties dialog box, click the **Custom** tab.

▶ **2.** In the list near the top of the dialog box, click **Department**. "Department" appears in the Name box above the list.

▶ **3.** Click in the **Value** box, type **Events**, and then click the **Add** button. "Department" and the value you gave it appear in the Properties list, as shown in Figure 8-24.

Figure 8-24 ▶ Adding a custom property to the Inquiry Form template

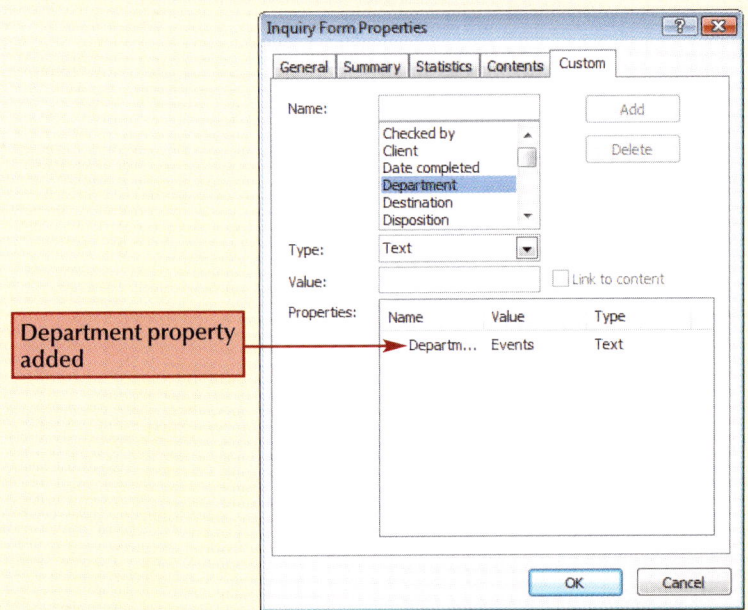

Department property added

▶ **4.** Click the **OK** button. The dialog box closes.

▶ **5.** In the upper-right corner of the Document Information Panel, click the **Close** button ☒.

▶ **6.** Save your changes.

The properties you inserted will make it easy for Geoff to organize and locate files based on these properties, and now he won't have to insert text into content controls that are linked to these properties.

Inserting a Document Property as a Quick Part

When you send the Inquiry Form template to Geoff's manager at Diamond Luxury Properties, Geoff wants you to indicate that the document is a draft. You could use the built-in Draft watermark, but that would remove the picture he inserted as a watermark. Instead you'll insert into the footer the document property that holds this information. You'll use the Quick Parts menu to do this. Geoff also wants to include the department name in the footer. You'll insert this using the Quick Parts menu also.

To insert a document property as a Quick Part:

▶ **1.** Click the **Insert** tab, in the Header & Footer group, click the **Footer** button, and then click **Edit Footer**. The footer area in the document becomes active, and the Header & Footer Tools Design tab is active on the Ribbon.

▶ **2.** Click the **Insert** tab, in the Text group, click the **Quick Parts** button, and then point to **Document Property**. A submenu of many of the document properties opens.

▶ **3.** Click **Status**. A document control labeled Status appears in the footer with "Draft" in it. Now, you want to insert the Department property, but that property does not appear on the Document Property submenu on the Quick Parts menu. You'll use the Field command to insert the Department property.

▶ **4.** Press the → key, press the **Tab** key twice, in the Text group, click the **Quick Parts** button, and then click **Field**. The Field dialog box opens.

▶ **5.** Click the **Categories** arrow, and then click **Document Information**. The Field names list is filtered to include only fields in the Document Information category.

▶ **6.** In the Field names list, click **DocProperty**. The right side of the dialog box changes to display options for the DocProperty field.

▶ **7.** In the Property list, click **Department**, and then click the **OK** button. "Events" appears in the footer.

▶ **8.** Save your changes.

Next, you'll insert the date using a field.

Automating Documents Using Fields

Another powerful method for automating a document is using fields. As you recall from Tutorial 5 on mail merge, a field is a special code that instructs Word to insert information that might change, such as the current date or page number, into a document. You've already used fields when you inserted these elements, although you were not aware of it. You also used fields when you created a mail merge. In Word 2007, you don't need to use fields very often, because there are simpler and faster ways of accomplishing the same tasks. For example, you can insert a date field, or you can use the Date & Time button in the Text group on the Insert tab. However, it's a good idea to understand how fields work, and then you can take advantage of them if you want.

Figure 8-25 lists common fields that you can include in documents.

Figure 8-25 Common fields

Field	Code (Example)	Action
Date	{DATE \@ "MMMM d, yyyy"}	Inserts the current date/time according to a date-time picture
Fill-in	{FILLIN "Your name?" * MERGEFORMAT}	Inserts information filled in by the user
NumPages	{NUMPAGES}	Inserts the total number of pages in the document
Page	{PAGE}	Inserts the current page number
Ref	{REF BookmarkName}	Inserts the contents of the specified bookmark

When you insert a field into a document, the corresponding field code includes the name of the field and optional instructions and switches, which are enclosed in braces { } (also called French brackets or curly brackets). An **instruction** is a word or phrase that specifies what the field should do, such as display a **prompt**, which is a phrase that tells the user how to proceed. A **switch** is a command that follows *, \#, \@, or \! and turns on or off certain features of the field. For example, a switch can specify how the result of the field is formatted. Figure 8-26 shows a field code that contains a field name, instructions, and a switch.

Figure 8-26 Components of a field code

The field name, FILLIN, specifies that this field asks the user to supply (fill in) some information. The instruction is a prompt (Product name:) that tells the user what to type. The switch (\@ MERGEFORMAT) specifies that the field's result (the user fill-in information) should retain any formatting applied to the field even if the user fills in new information.

All field codes must include braces and a field name, but not all field codes include instructions and switches. The Field dialog box, which you'll access later, shows which elements each field code must contain. To better understand fields, you'll examine an existing field in the document.

Viewing Fields in the Document

When you inserted the Status document property, a document control was inserted. When you inserted the custom Department property, however, a field was inserted. You'll examine the field code for this field now.

To examine field codes:

▶ 1. If necessary, double-click the footer to make the footer area active.

▶ 2. Right-click **Events**, and then click **Toggle Field Codes** on the shortcut menu. The field codes for the field you right-clicked appear instead of the content. The field code for the Department document property is { DOCPROPERTY Department * MERGEFORMAT }.

▶ 3. Right-click **Draft**. The Toggle Field Codes command is not on this shortcut menu because this is a document control, not a field, and although some document controls contain fields, this one does not.

▶ 4. Right-click the field code for "Events" at the right margin in the footer, and then click **Toggle Field Codes**. The field codes are hidden, and you again see only the content of the field.

▶ 5. Click the **Header & Footer Tools Design** tab, and then in the Close group, click the **Close Header and Footer** button. The footer area becomes inactive.

Next, you'll insert the current date, examine the field code, and then revise its format.

Inserting and Updating the Date Field

You're already familiar with the Date field, which inserts the current date and time or specifies parts of the date and time in the format you select, such as the full name for the current month (for example, February) without the day, year, or any part of the time.

Fields are updated when you open a document, but sometimes they must be updated while you are working on a document to ensure they contain the most recent information. For example, if you insert the NumPages field, which identifies the total number of pages in a document, and then create additional pages in the document, you need to update the field. This is important if you plan to print the document before closing it. The field is updated automatically when you open the document.

Inserting and Editing Fields | Reference Window

- Move the insertion point to where you want to insert the field.
- Click the Insert tab, in the Text group, click the Quick Parts button, and then click Field to open the Field dialog box.
- Click the Categories arrow, click a category, and then click a field in the Field names list.
- If necessary, set the field properties in the middle section of the dialog box.
- If necessary, set the field options in the right section of the dialog box.
- To view the codes in the Field dialog box, click the Field Codes button. To hide the codes in the Field dialog box, click the Hide Codes button.
- To edit the field's instructions or switches in the Field dialog box, click the Field Codes button, click the Options button, make changes in the Field Options dialog box, and then click the OK button.
- Click the OK button.
- To edit the field code from within the document, right-click the field, click Edit Field, edit the information in the Field dialog box, and then click the OK button.

You want the template to be updated with the current date whenever it is opened. You'll insert the date field using the command on the Ribbon, and then you'll examine the field codes for the date field.

To insert the date field and view the field codes:

▶ **1.** In the "Customer name:" line, position the insertion point to the right of the colon.

▶ **2.** To the left of the ruler, click the **tab marker** icon twice to switch to the right tab marker, on the ruler, click just to the left of the right margin marker, and then drag the new right tab marker on top of the Right Indent marker △ on the ruler.

▶ **3.** Press the **Tab** key. The insertion point is blinking at the right margin in the Customer name line.

▶ **4.** Click the **Insert** tab, in the Text group, click the **Date & Time** button, click the format fifth from the bottom in the Available formats list (the format in the style 6/12/2010 3:21:43 PM), click the **Update Automatically** check box to select it, if necessary, and then click the **OK** button. The current date and time to the second is inserted in the document.

▶ **5.** Click the date. Although this is a field, the borders of a document control appear around the date, and the title tab includes an Update button.

▶ **6.** On the title tab of the document control, click the **Update** button. The time is updated to be a few seconds later than when you inserted it. See Figure 8-27.

Figure 8-27 ▶ Updating the date field

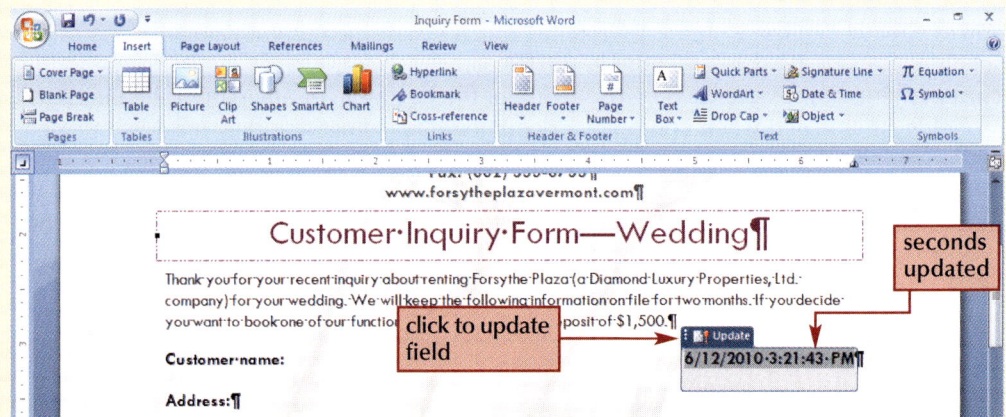

▶ **7.** Right-click the date, and then click **Toggle Field Codes** on the shortcut menu. The field codes for the field you right-clicked appear instead of the content. The field code for the format you chose is { DATE \@ "M/D/yyyy h:mm:ss am/pm" }.

The field code for the date specifies how the date is formatted. This notation is known as a **date-time picture**. You could designate the exact format of the date by editing the field code, but it is much easier to choose a format in the Date and Time dialog box when you insert the date (or choose a different format for a date field already inserted by using the Edit Field command on the field's shortcut menu). You'll change the format of the field you inserted for Geoff so it includes just the date, without the time.

To edit the Date field format:

▶ **1.** Right-click the field you inserted, and then click **Edit Field** on the shortcut menu. The Field dialog box opens. Date is selected in the Field names list in the Please choose a field section on the left, and the format you chose is selected in the Date formats list in the Field properties section in the middle. You can view the field code and the general syntax of the field code from this dialog box, as shown in Figure 8-28.

Editing the Date field ◀ **Figure 8-28**

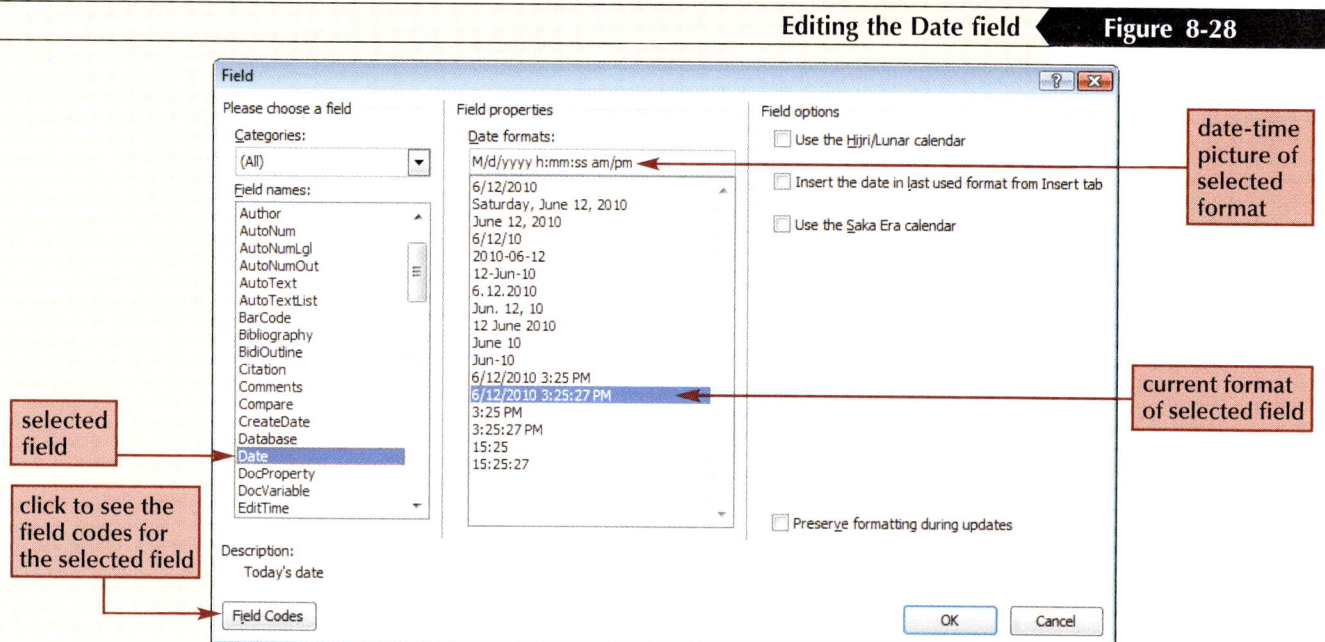

2. Click the **Field Codes** button. The right side of the dialog box changes to display the Advanced field properties section with the field code for the selected format listed in the Field codes box, and the general format for the syntax of the DATE field under the Field codes box.

▶ **3.** Click the **Options** button. The Field Options dialog box opens with a list of switches you can use with the Date field. At the bottom, under Description, the switches are identified as options that affect the Date-Time display options, which is the date-time picture. Each field has a different list of available switches.

▶ **4.** Click the **OK** button to close the Field Options dialog box, and then click the **Hide Codes** button. The Advanced field properties section disappears and the list of formats reappears.

▶ **5.** In the Date formats list, click the top format (in the format 6/12/2010), and then click the **OK** button. The Field dialog box closes and the date appears in the new format. Note that the field codes automatically toggled off.

▶ **6.** Right-click the date, and then click **Toggle Field Codes** on the shortcut menu. The field code is now { DATE \@ "M/d/yyyy" }; because this format doesn't include the time, the switches to display the time (h, s, m) are no longer part of the field code.

▶ **7.** Hide the field codes, and then save your changes.

Next, you'll use the Fill-in field to make it easy for Geoff to modify the template for events other than weddings.

Inserting and Editing the Fill-In Field

Although Forsythe Plaza is very popular for weddings, other types of functions (such as company dinners, lectures, and so on), can also be scheduled there. Geoff has been working on an extensive advertising program to market the Plaza to corporations for business functions. He decided that he wants to print customized inquiry forms for various functions. To customize the form, he needs to remove the picture watermark and delete the line with the music choices. He also wants to customize the title to suit each potential client. To customize the title for each client, you can insert the **Fill-in field** to prompt the user to insert the new title. When this field is updated, Word prompts you to fill in specific information.

Geoff would like you to insert a Fill-in field, and then you'll edit it to provide an appropriate prompt.

To insert a Fill-in field in the template:

▶ 1. Click the **Office Button** 🔘, point to **Save As**, click **Word Template**, and then save the template as **General Inquiry Template** to the **Tutorial.08\Tutorial** folder included with your Data Files.

▶ 2. In the title, delete the word **Wedding**, click the **Insert** tab, in the Text group, click the **Quick Parts** button, and then click **Field**. The Field dialog box opens.

▶ 3. Click the **Categories** arrow, click **Mail Merge**, and then in the Field names list, click **Fill-in**. You need to type the text that will appear when the document is opened in the Prompt box.

▶ 4. Click in the **Prompt** box in the Field properties section of the dialog box, and then type **Enter the type of function:** (with a colon at the end).

▶ 5. Make sure the two check boxes at the top of the Field options section are unchecked.

▶ 6. Click the **Preserve formatting during updates** check box to uncheck it. When this check box is checked, Word preserves any formatting that the user applies to the field; that is, if the user changes the format to, say, red italics, and the check box is checked, the red italics will appear when you update the field. If you clear this check box, Word will not only update the field information but also update the formatting to the original; that is, Word will clear the red italics. You cleared the check box, so now, if someone using the document changes the formatting of the text in the Fill-in field, the new formatting will not be preserved when the field is updated, and the Fill-in field will revert to the original formatting.

▶ 7. Click the **OK** button. A Microsoft Office Word dialog box appears with the prompt you typed, "Enter the type of function". You want the user to enter the type of form each time a new document is created from the template, so you will close this dialog box without entering any text.

▶ 8. Click the **OK** button without entering any text. The dialog box closes. It looks as if there is no change in the document.

▶ 9. Press the **Alt+F9** keys. All the field codes in the document are displayed. The Fill-in field code appears in the title. The Fill-in field code has no switch, but it does include the text you specified for the prompt. You can click anywhere in the field code to modify the prompt or to add a switch.

▶ 10. Press the **Alt+F9** keys to hide the field codes, and then save your changes.

When a Forsythe Plaza employee uses this template to create new queries, the template will provide a prompt to change the event title.

In addition to the fields you used, there are a few other fields, for which there are no content controls to insert the equivalent information, that are useful to know about. These fields are described in Figure 8-29. They are all available in the Field dialog box.

Useful fields | **Figure 8-29**

Field	Description of inserted text
FileName	Name of the saved file
FileSize	Size of the file on disk
NumPages	Total number of pages
SaveDate	Date the document was last saved
UserInitials	User initials on the Popular page in the Word Options dialog box
UserName	User name on the Popular page in the Word Options dialog box

In the next session, you'll explore how to customize various Word Options settings, and you'll record a macro to help create a brochure for Geoff.

Session 8.2 Quick Check | Review

1. What is a Quick Part?
2. How can you see all the available building blocks?
3. In the AutoCorrect feature, define *exception*.
4. What is a pull quote?
5. How do you access document properties?
6. How do you update a field?
7. What symbol surrounds field codes?

Session 8.3

Customizing Word Options

Before you create macros for his Forsythe Plaza template, Geoff asks you to explore some more of the customization features in Word. You know that you can customize many features of Word using the Word Options dialog box. You access the Word Options dialog box on the Office menu. When you open the dialog box, you click a category in a list on the left, and the right side of the dialog box changes to display options and commands in that category. The categories available in the Word Options dialog box are described in Figure 8-30.

Figure 8-30 ▷ **Word Options dialog box categories**

Category	Description
Popular	Options for selecting popular customizations in Word, including changing the user name and initials
Display	Options for changing how a document looks on the screen and when it is printed
Proofing	Options and commands for changing the way text is corrected when using the spelling and grammar checker and the AutoCorrect feature
Save	Options and commands for changing the default format in which documents are saved and the default locations to where files are saved
Advanced	Advanced options and commands for changing the display, proofing, and save defaults
Customize	A list of the commands available in Word and commands for adding them to the Quick Access Toolbar and modifying them
Add-Ins	Commands for working with add-ins, small programs that enhance Word's functionality
Trust Center	Links to Web sites that explain Microsoft privacy and security policies, and a command for opening the Trust Center, where you can set security settings
Resources	Links to use to contact Microsoft and to check for updates online

Recall that to open the Word Options dialog box, click the Office Button, and then click Word Options. The dialog box opens with Popular selected in the list on the left. See Figure 8-31. Several popular customization options are listed here, including the personalization section, where you can add your name and initials. As you learned when you used the Track Changes feature in Tutorial 7, you can change the user name and initials so that your name appears as the author of the tracked changes. The name in this box is also picked up as the Author control in new documents.

Word Options dialog box with Popular selected | **Figure 8-31**

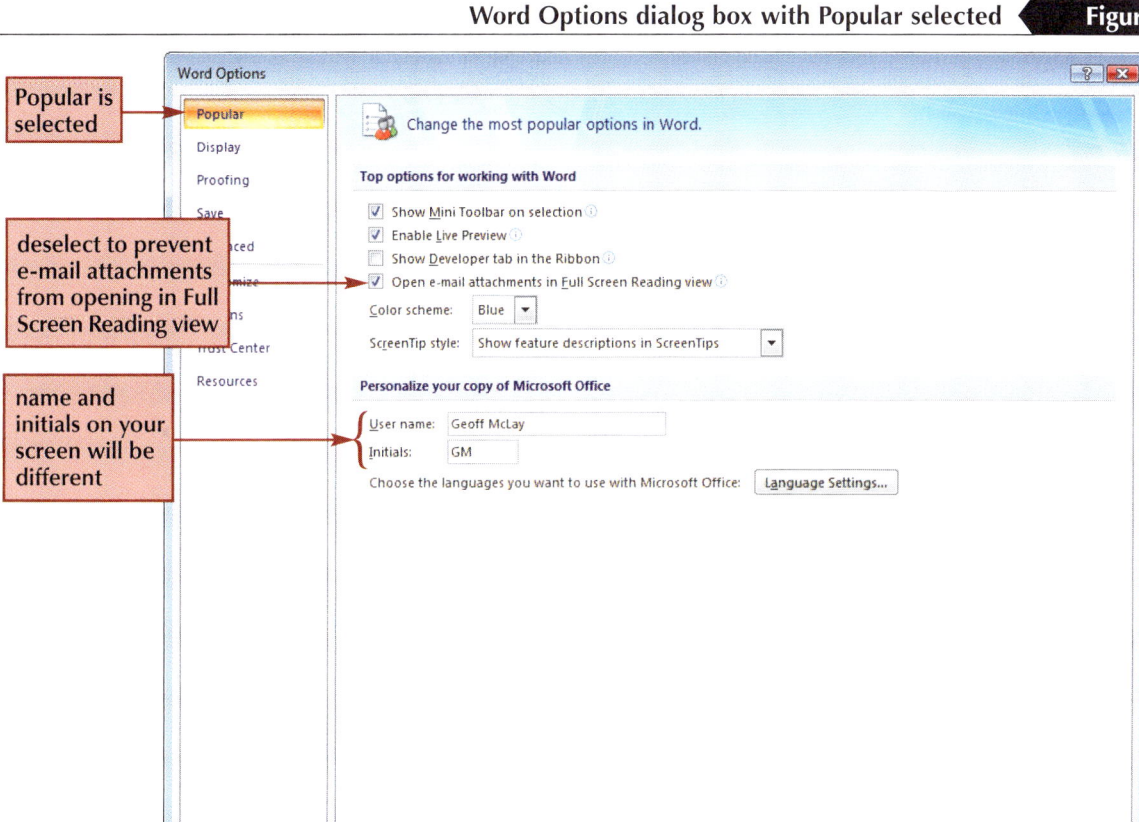

Popular is
selected

deselect to prevent
e-mail attachments
from opening in Full
Screen Reading view

name and
initials on your
screen will be
different

Another important customization in the Popular category of the Word Options dialog box is the ability to choose whether to have e-mail attachments open in Full Screen Reading view. With this option selected, if someone sends you a Word document as an e-mail attachment and you open it while it is still attached to the message (rather than saving it to a folder first), the document opens in Full Screen Reading view. It is easier to read the document onscreen in this view, but you cannot see what it will look like when printed in this view. To disable this feature, deselect the Open e-mail attachments in Full Screen Reading view check box.

Another helpful customization is to change the default Save location. When you use the Open or the Save As command, the Open or Save As dialog box lists the Documents folder as the default location for documents. If you store your documents in another location, it is a hassle to change the location every time you open or save a file. You can change the default location by clicking Save in the list on the left in the Word Options dialog box, and then changing the path and folder name in the Default file location box. See Figure 8-32. Note that you can also change the default file format here as well, by clicking the Save files in this format arrow, and then clicking the new default file format.

Figure 8-32 Save settings in Word Options dialog box

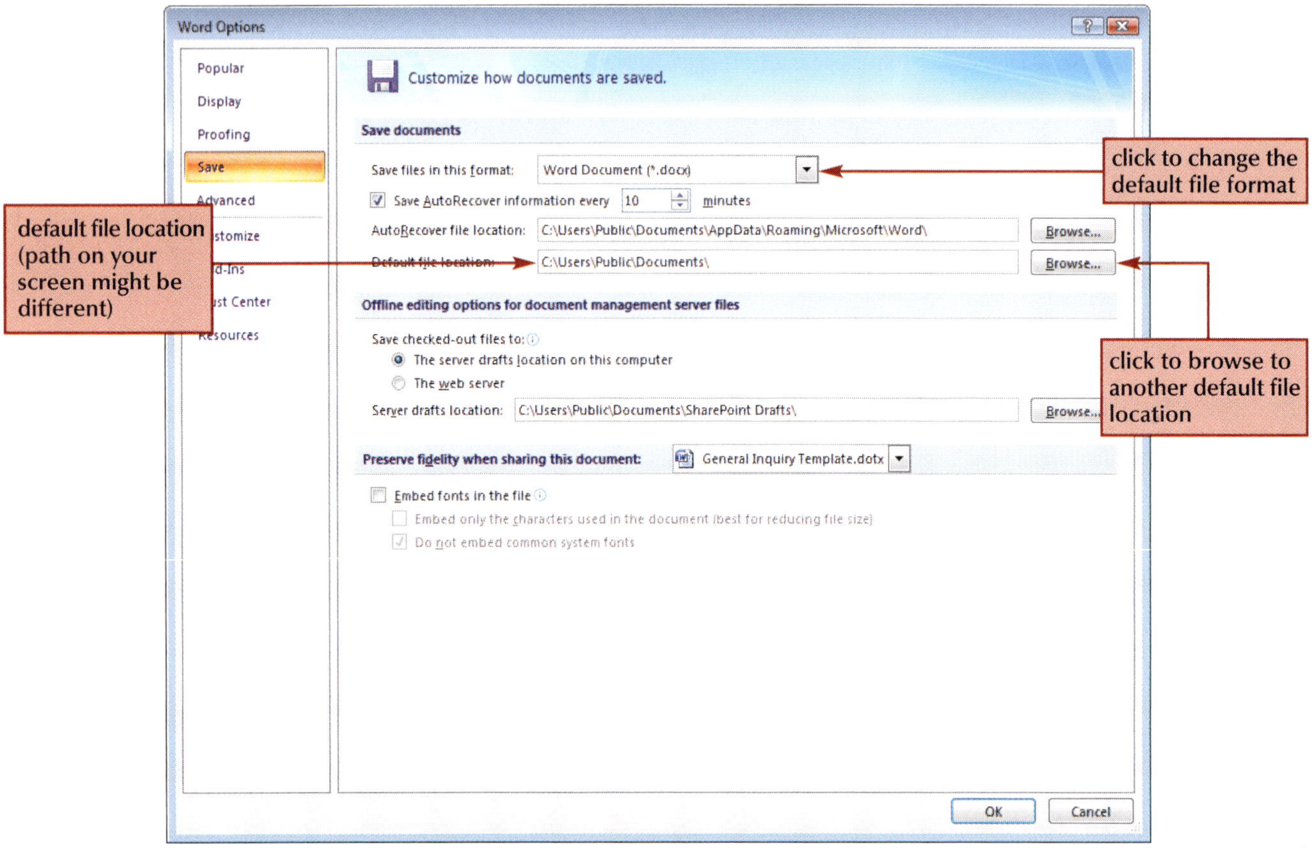

Reference Window | **Customizing Popular Features in Word**

- Click the Office Button, and then click Word Options to open the Word Options dialog box.
- To change the user name and initials, click Popular in the list on the left, and then change the name and initials in the User name and Initials boxes.
- To open e-mail attachments in Print Layout view, click Popular in the list on the left, and then click the Open e-mail attachments in Full Screen Reading view check box to deselect it.
- To change the default save location, click Save in the list on the left, and then edit the path name in the Default file location box or use the Browse button to locate the new default folder.
- To change the default file format for files you save, click the Save files in this format arrow, and then click the desired file format.
- When you are finished customizing Word, click the OK button.

The Customize category in the Word Options dialog box allows you to modify the Quick Access Toolbar by adding, modifying, and removing buttons from it. You'll do this next.

Customizing the Quick Access Toolbar

Although you cannot add buttons to or remove buttons from the Ribbon, you can customize the Quick Access Toolbar to suit your working style. Geoff asks you to add the View Field Codes button to the Quick Access Toolbar so that he can easily see the field codes in the template you created.

Customizing the Quick Access Toolbar | Reference Window

- To add a button, on the Quick Access Toolbar, click the Customize Quick Access Toolbar button, and then click a command in the list or click More Commands to open the Customize category in the Word Options dialog box; or click the Office Button, click Word Options, and then in the list on the left, click Customize.
- Click the Choose commands from arrow above the list of commands on the left, and then click a category of commands to filter the list of commands.
- In the Choose commands from list, click the command you want to add to the Quick Access Toolbar, and then click the Add button.
- Click the command in the Customize Quick Access Toolbar list, and then click the up or down arrow buttons to move the command up or down in the list.
- To reset the Quick Access Toolbar, click the Reset button.
- Click the OK button to close the dialog box.
- To remove a button from the Quick Access Toolbar, open the Customize section of the Word Options dialog box, click the command in the Customize Quick Access Toolbar list, and then click the Remove button; or right-click the button on the Quick Access Toolbar, and then click Remove from Quick Access Toolbar on the shortcut menu.

Geoff would like you to add the View Field Codes button to the Quick Access Toolbar.

To add a button to the Quick Access Toolbar:

▶ **1.** If you took a break after the last session, open the General Inquiry Template template, and then make sure the ruler and paragraph marks are displayed.

▶ **2.** Click the **Customize Quick Access Toolbar** button ⬇. A menu opens displaying common commands that you can add to the Quick Access Toolbar. Notice that the Save, Undo, and Redo commands have check marks next to them; these are the commands that already appear on the Quick Access Toolbar.

▶ **3.** Click **More Commands**. The Word Options dialog box opens with Customize selected in the list on the left. The list on the left contains commands available in Word; the list on the right contains commands that appear on the Quick Access Toolbar.

▶ **4.** Above the list on the left, click the **Choose commands from** arrow. A list of categories of commands opens.

▶ **5.** Click **Commands Not in the Ribbon**. The list changes to show only commands that are not available on the Ribbon.

▶ **6.** In the list on the left, drag the scroll box to the bottom of the scroll bar, and then click the up scroll arrow.

▶ **7.** At the top of the list, click **View Field Codes**, and then click the **Add** button. The View Field Codes command is added to the Customize Quick Access Toolbar list on the right, as shown in Figure 8-33.

| Figure 8-33 | Adding a button for the View Field Codes command to the Quick Access Toolbar |

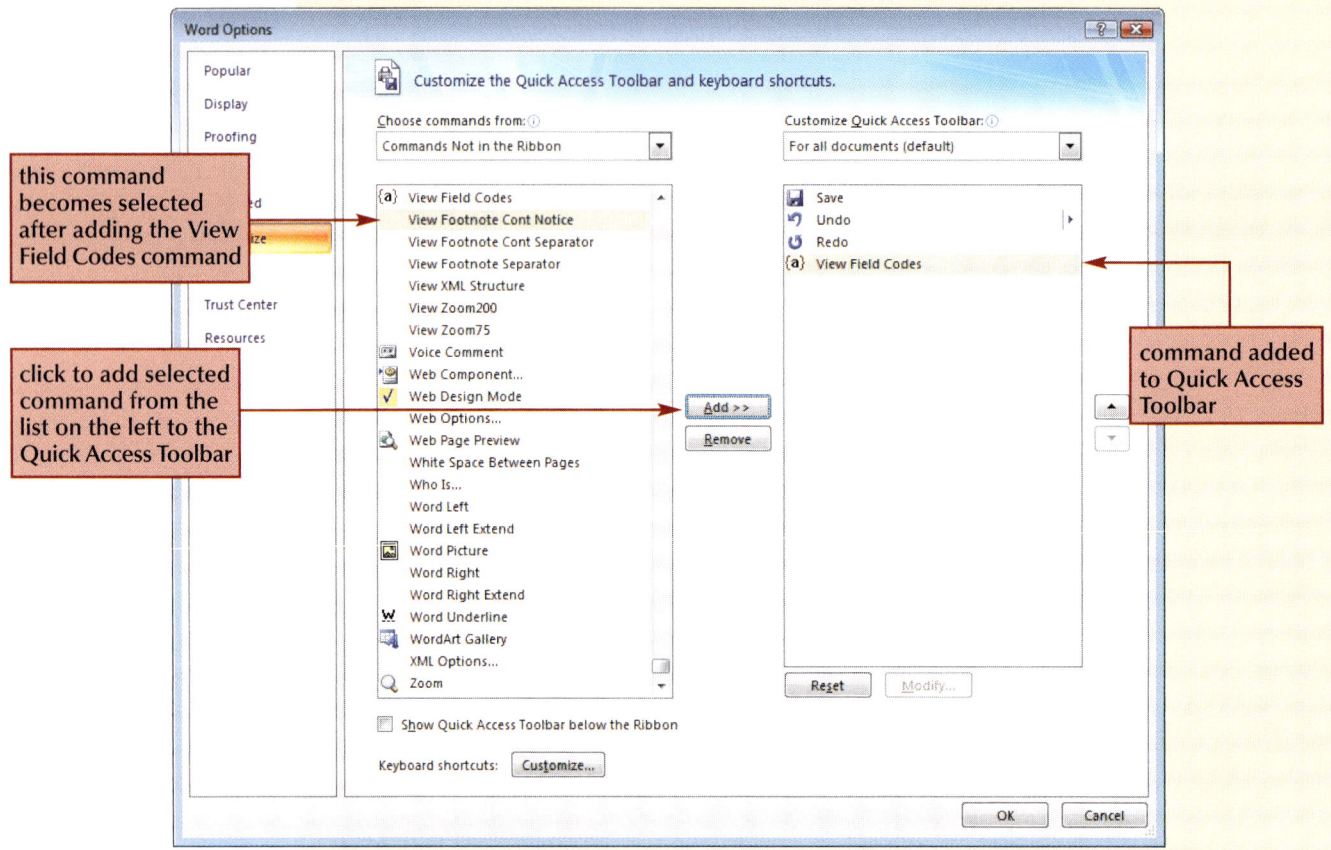

▶ 8. Click the **OK** button. The dialog box closes and the View Field Codes button appears on the Quick Access Toolbar.

Next, Geoff wants you to add a new keyboard shortcut so he can quickly execute the View Field Codes command without using his mouse.

To add a keyboard shortcut to a command:

▶ 1. Click the **Office Button** 🔘, click **Word Options**, and then in the list on the left, click **Customize**. This is the same dialog box that opened when you used the Customize Quick Access Toolbar button.

▶ 2. At the bottom of the dialog box, click the **Customize** button next to Keyboard shortcuts. The Customize Keyboard dialog box opens, as shown in Figure 8-34. Notice that the Save changes in box lists General Inquiry Template. By default, keyboard shortcuts are saved in the current template.

Customize Keyboard dialog box   **Figure 8-34**

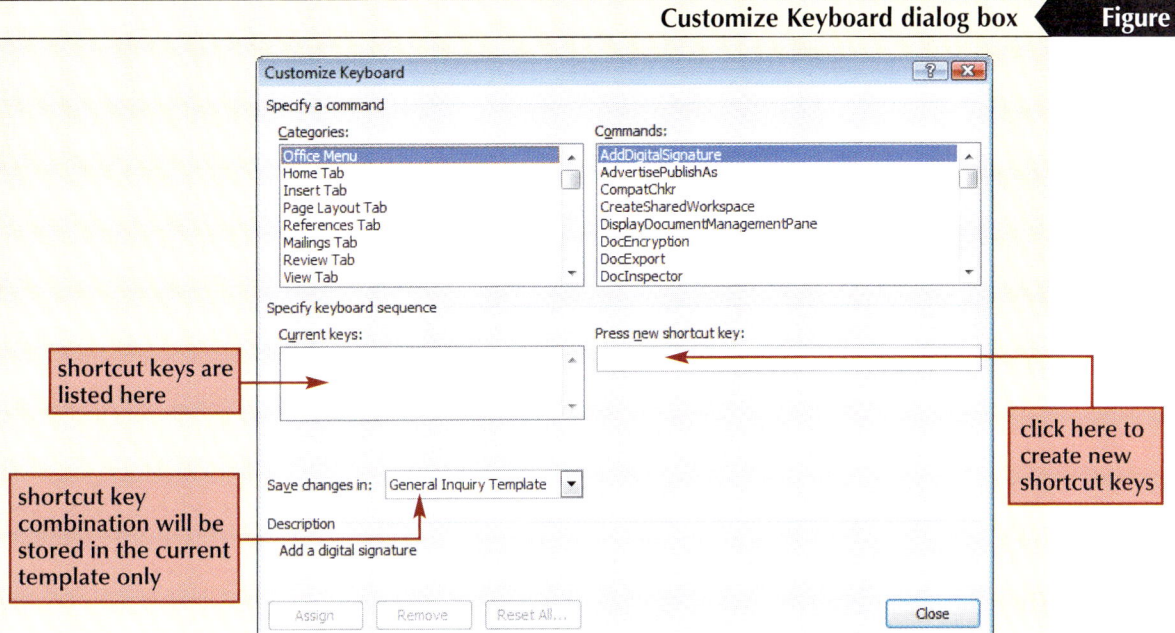

shortcut keys are listed here

shortcut key combination will be stored in the current template only

click here to create new shortcut keys

▶ **3.** In the Categories list on the left, drag the scroll box down to the bottom of the scroll bar, and then click **All Commands**. The Commands list on the right changes to list all the commands in Word.

▶ **4.** In the Commands list, scroll down the alphabetical list, and then click **ViewFieldCodes**. The Current keys box changes to show the current shortcut keys associated with the selected command. Currently, you can press the Alt+F9 keys to view field codes.

▶ **5.** Click in the **Press new shortcut key** box, and then press the **Alt+Ctrl+V** keys. Below the Current keys box, text appears telling you that the new shortcut keys you pressed are currently assigned to the EditPasteSpecial command.

▶ **6.** Press the **Backspace** key to delete all the text in the Press new shortcut key box, and then press the **Alt+V** keys. The text under the Current keys list indicates that this shortcut key combination is currently unassigned.

▶ **7.** Click the **Assign** button. The new shortcut key combination appears in the Current keys list.

▶ **8.** Click the **Close** button, and then click the **OK** button. The dialog boxes close.

Now Geoff can use the button or the new keyboard shortcut to use the View Field Codes command.

Removing Buttons from the Quick Access Toolbar

After adding buttons to the Quick Access Toolbar, you might decide that you don't want them there after all. If you're not working on your own computer, you should remove any customizations you make.

You'll test the button and the keyboard shortcut you created, and then you'll remove both of these customizations.

To test the customizations and then return Word to its default state:

▶ **1.** On the Quick Access Toolbar, click the **View Field Codes** button [a] . The button works as it should: the field codes appear in the document and the button on the Quick Access Toolbar is selected.

▶ **2.** Press the **Alt+V** keys. The shortcut keys also work as they should: the field codes disappear and the View Field Codes button on the Quick Access Toolbar is no longer selected. Now you'll return Word to its original state.

▶ **3.** On the Quick Access Toolbar, right-click the **View Field Codes** button, and then click **Remove from Quick Access Toolbar**. The shortcut menu closes, and the button is removed from the toolbar.

You don't need to remove the keyboard shortcut because that is saved only in the template. Remember that buttons you add to the Quick Access Toolbar are saved with the Word program, not with a template.

Automating Word with Macros

Geoff has heard a great deal about macros and how they can help automate repetitive tasks. A **macro**, in its simplest form, is a recording of keystrokes and mouse operations that you can play back at any time by pressing a key combination or by using the mouse. In its fullest form, a macro is a computer program that can perform complex functions based on document conditions or user input.

Using macros to run frequently executed commands has two main advantages. Combining a number of keystrokes and mouse operations into a macro saves time and helps you complete your work faster. Also, assuming you record a macro accurately—without typos or other mistakes—the keystrokes and mouse operations will always play back error-free. A macro that inserts text or performs formatting operations will consistently insert the same text and perform the same formatting operations.

Before you record the steps (keystrokes and mouse clicks) of a macro, you do the following:

• **Name the macro**. A macro name must begin with a letter and can contain a maximum of 80 letters and numbers; the name can't contain spaces, periods, or other punctuation. The macro name should summarize its function. For example, if you record a macro to resize a picture, you could name the macro "ResizePic."

• **Describe the macro (optional)**. You should provide a detailed description of a macro to help you recall its exact function. This is especially important if a macro performs a complex series of operations that can't be summarized in the macro name. For example, a simple macro name, such as PositionPicLeft, doesn't describe the picture features, such as borders and text wrapping. You could include that type of information in the description.

• **Attach the macro to a template or document**. Unless you specify otherwise, every macro you create is attached to the global template, Normal.dotx, and is available in every Word document, regardless of what template you used to create the macro. If you attach a macro only to the document or template you're editing, the macro is available only in that document or documents created from that template.

• **Assign the macro to a toolbar button, menu, or keyboard shortcut (optional)**. A macro is easier to run if you assign it to a button that you add to the Quick Access Toolbar or assign it a keyboard shortcut. Otherwise, it requires at least four mouse clicks to run.

Geoff wants to learn more about macros. He is working on a new brochure that he plans to send out in a direct mail campaign. A friend of his wrote two macros for resizing and repositioning a picture. He asks you to import the two macros into the brochure, and then run them to see how they work. To "run" a macro means to execute it—to have it perform the steps you programmed it to do.

Importing Macros

The two macros that Geoff's friend wrote are named ResizePictureLeft and ResizePictureRight. The two macros are similar: each opens a simple dialog box, asks the user to type a percentage, expands or reduces the picture size by the given percentage, and then positions the picture at the left or right margin. To create these macros, Geoff's friend did more than record keystrokes. He used **Microsoft Visual Basic**, a feature built into Word and other Office applications that provides a complete environment for writing new Visual Basic code and editing existing Visual Basic code and procedures. Writing complete Visual Basic programs and using most of the Visual Basic editor features are beyond the scope of this tutorial, but you'll learn how to record macros and use Visual Basic for simple editing.

Geoff's friend wrote the two macros in a Word document, and then exported them from Word into the file PicMacs.bas. The .bas file extension indicates that the file contains one or more Visual Basic macros. You will import the PicMacs.bas file into a document and then to test it to see how a macro works.

To access Visual Basic directly, you need to display the Developer tab, which contains commands for working with codes, controls, XML, and document protection in Word.

To open the Brochure document and display the Developer tab:

▶ **1.** Open the file **Brochure** from the **Tutorial.08\Tutorial** folder included with your Data Files, and then display nonprinting characters and the rulers, if necessary.

▶ **2.** Save the document as **Brochure Draft** to the same folder.

▶ **3.** Click the **Office Button**, and then click **Word Options**. The Word Options dialog box opens with Popular selected in the list on the left.

▶ **4.** Click the **Show Developer tab in the Ribbon** check box to select, it, if necessary.

▶ **5.** Click the **OK** button. The Word Options dialog box closes, and the Developer tab appears on the Ribbon to the right of the View tab.

▶ **6.** Click the **Developer** tab.

The Code group on the Developer tab contains commands for working with macros. Clicking the Visual Basic button opens the Visual Basic program window. Clicking the Macro Security button opens the Trust Center, where you can change your security settings for working with macros. You can also access some of these commands from the View tab.

Geoff is ready for you to import his friend's macros into the Brochure Draft document so you can test them.

To import macros:

▶ **1.** In the Code group, click the **Visual Basic** button. The Microsoft Visual Basic window opens. Instead of a Ribbon with tabs and buttons, the Visual Basic window contains a menu bar and toolbar. This window also contains various smaller windows (called panes) for creating and editing macros. One of the open panes is the Project – Project pane in the upper-left corner of the window.

   Trouble? If the Project – Project pane isn't open, click View on the Visual Basic menu bar, and then click Project Explorer.

▶ **2.** If necessary, maximize the Visual Basic window, and then click **Project (Brochure Draft)** in the Project – Project pane. See Figure 8-35.

Figure 8-35 ▶ **Preparing to import macros**

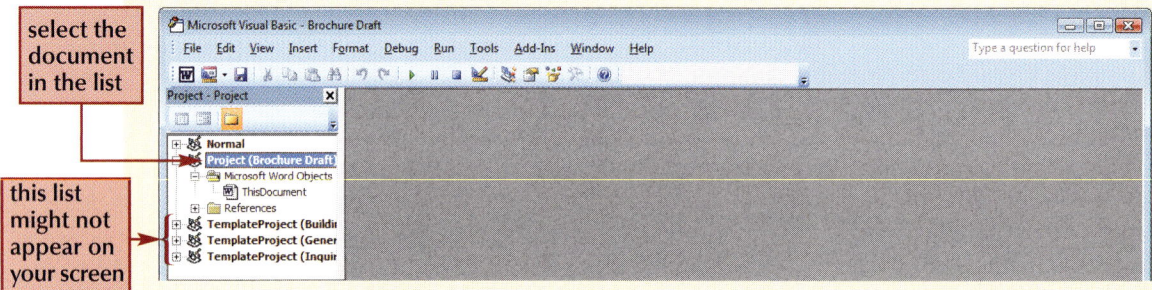

▶ **3.** On the menu bar in the Visual Basic window, click **File**, and then click **Import File**. The Import File dialog box opens.

▶ **4.** Click the **Look in** arrow, select the drive or folder in which your Data Files are stored, and then double-click folders as needed to navigate to the **Tutorial.08\Tutorial** folder included with your Data Files.

▶ **5.** Click **PicMacs.bas**, and then click **Open**. "Modules" appears in the Project (Brochure Draft) section in the Project – Project pane.

▶ **6.** In the Project (Brochure Draft) section in the Project – Project pane, click the **plus sign** next to the **Modules** folder. The folder opens, and the macros in the folder are listed below it. You see PicMacs, which is the name of the set of macros that you imported.

▶ **7.** Double-click **PicMacs** in the Project – Project pane. A window containing the macro code for PicMacs opens on the right.

▶ **8.** Maximize the window containing the PicMacs code. See Figure 8-36.

Visual Basic window with imported PicMacs code | Figure 8-36

Modules in Project (Brochure Draft)

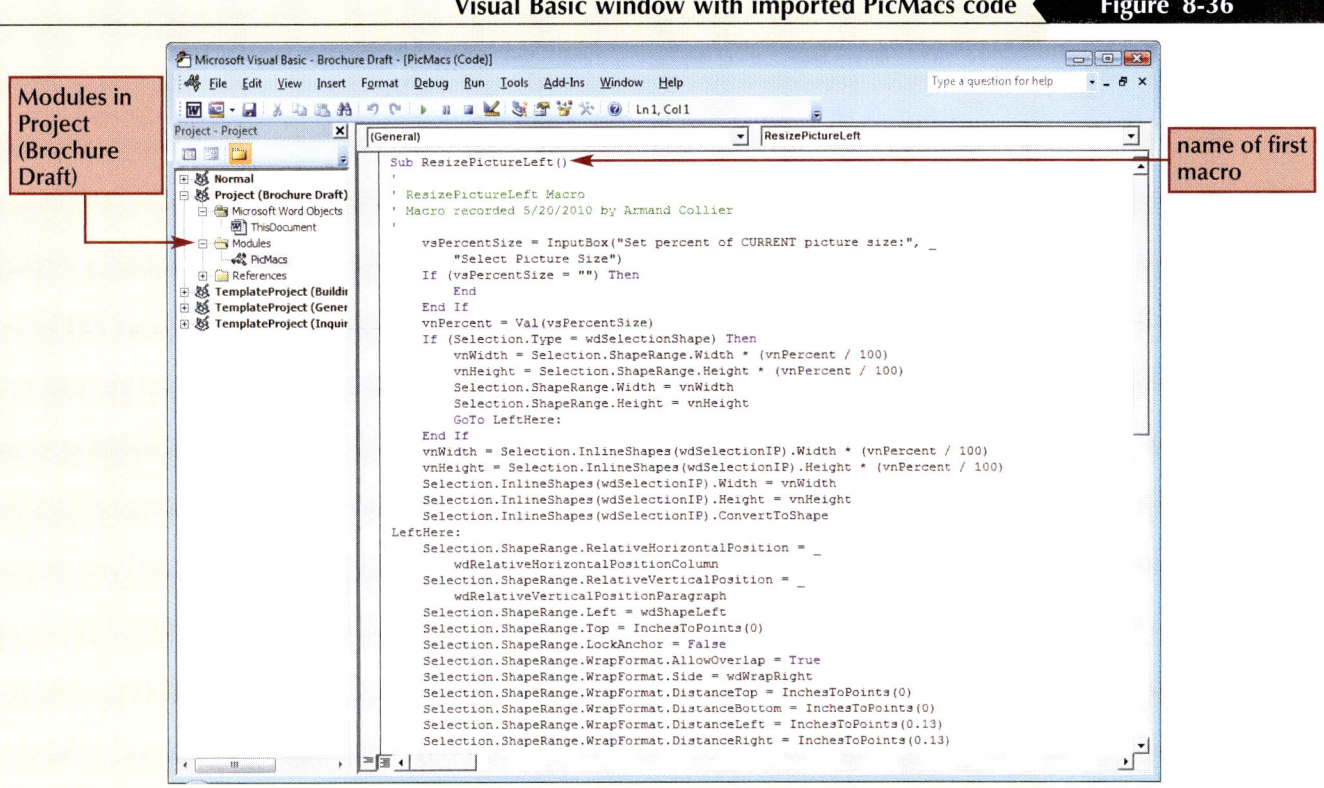

name of first macro

As you can see, the first macro is ResizePictureLeft, which resizes a photograph and positions it at the left margin of your Word document. If you scroll down the macro window, you can see the second macro, ResizePictureRight, which has the same function as ResizePictureLeft, except that it positions the picture at the right margin.

▶ 9. Click the **Close** button [X] on the Visual Basic window title bar to close it and return to the document.

Now that the two picture macros are imported, you're ready to run them.

Running Macros

To run a macro, you need to open the Macros dialog box. You do this by clicking the Macros button in the Code group on the Developer tab, or by clicking the Macros button in the Macros group on the View tab.

Because Geoff's macros are designed to format pictures, before you can run the macros you must have a picture inserted into your document, and the picture must be selected.

Tip

You can also open the Macros dialog box by clicking the Developer tab, and then in the Code group, clicking the Macros button.

To insert and select a picture and then run the PictureResize macros:

▶ 1. Click the **Insert** tab, in the Illustrations group, click the **Picture** button, navigate to the **Tutorial.08\Tutorial** folder included with your Data Files, and then double-click **Flowers**. The Flowers photo is inserted in the document. The picture is selected, as indicated by the sizing handles, and the picture is inserted as an inline graphic. Now you're ready to run one of the macros.

▶ 2. Click the **View** tab, in the Macros group, click the **Macros button arrow**, and then click **View Macros**. The Macros dialog box opens, as shown in Figure 8-37.

Figure 8-37 Choosing a macro to run

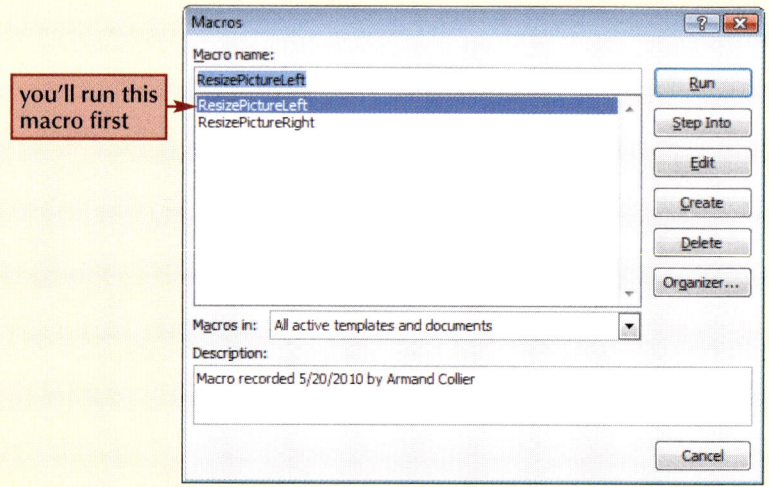

Trouble? If you see other macros listed in the Macros dialog box, they are probably from your Normal template. Just continue with the next step.

▶ 3. If necessary, click **ResizePictureLeft** (the first of the two macros) to select it, and then click the **Run** button. The macro displays a dialog box and waits for you to type a percentage of the current picture size. For example, if you wanted the height and width of the picture to be half their current values, you would type 50; if you wanted the height and width to be double their current values, you would type 200.

Trouble? If a dialog box appears with a message indicating that macros are disabled, you should change your security settings. Click the Cancel button in the Macros dialog box, click the Developer tab, and then in the Code group, click the Macro Security button to open the Trust Center dialog box with Macro Settings selected in the list on the left. Note which option button is selected in the Macro Settings section, and then click the Enable all macros option button. Click the OK button, and then repeat Steps 2 and 3. If they still won't run, exit Word without saving your changes, restart Word, repeat the steps in the Importing Macros section, and then repeat Steps 1–3 above. If the macros still won't run, read but do not execute the steps in this section.

▶ 4. Type **50**, and then click the **OK** button. The macro reduces the size of the picture by 50%, changes the picture to a floating graphic, sets the picture so that the document text wraps around it on the right side, and positions the picture at the left margin. See Figure 8-38.

Picture after running the ResizePictureLeft macro ◀ **Figure 8-38**

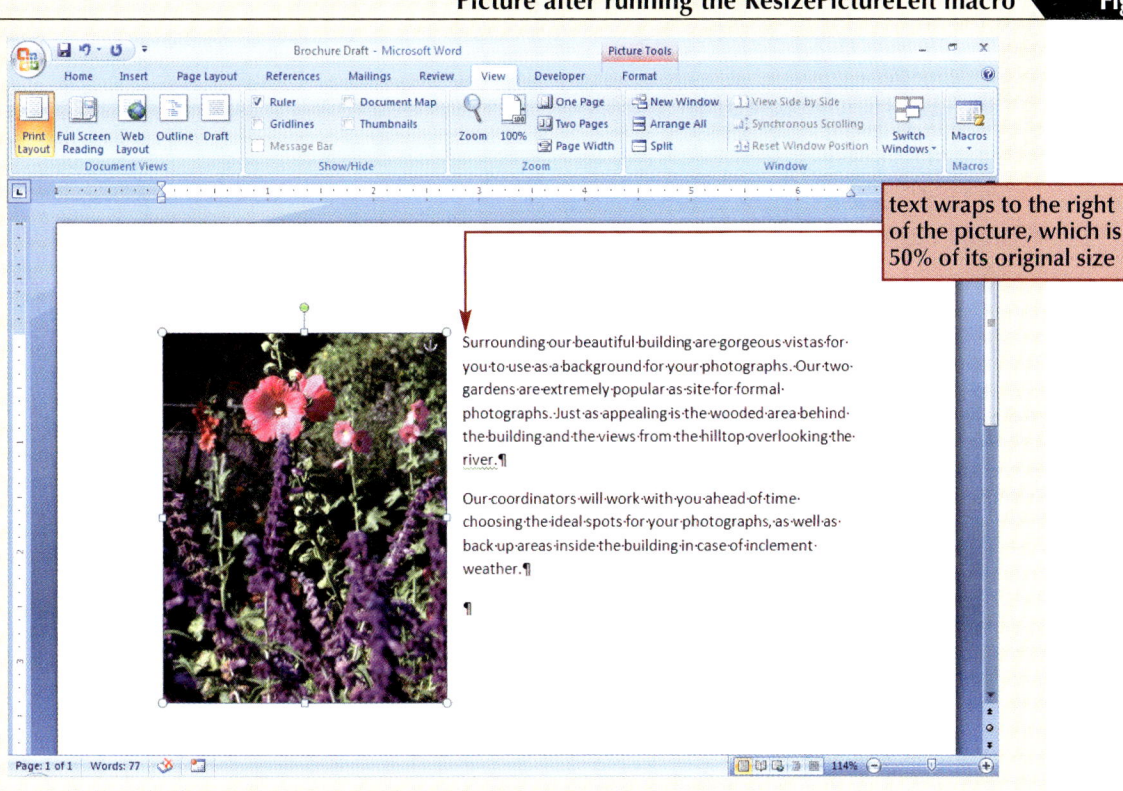

text wraps to the right of the picture, which is 50% of its original size

Next, you'll test the other macro, ResizePictureRight.

▶ **5.** With the picture of the flowers still selected, run the **ResizePictureRight** macro, type **40** as the percentage, and then click the **OK** button. The macro reduces the picture width and height to 40% of its current values and positions it at the right margin. Note that the picture dimensions are 40% of the current picture size, not 40% of the original size.

Now that you've seen how the macros work, you want to save the document with the macros.

Saving a Document with Macros

You want to save the work you've done on the brochure and be able to run the macros because you plan to insert more pictures. In order to run macros in a document, the document must be saved as a Macro-Enabled Document or a Macro-Enabled Template. If you try to save a document or a template that contains macros in the ordinary Word Document or Template file format, a warning dialog appears asking if you want to save the document as a "macro-free" document—in other words, without the macros—and you are given the opportunity to change the file type.

To save a document with macros:

▶ **1.** On the Quick Access Toolbar, click the **Save** button 🔲. A dialog box opens warning you that the macro cannot be saved in a macro-free document and asking if you want to continue saving as a macro-free document. This is not what you want.

▶ **2.** Click the **No** button. The dialog box closes, and the Save As dialog box appears.

▶ **3.** Click the **Save as type** arrow. Notice that there are two file types that are macro-enabled, a Word document and a Word template. You want to save this as a macro-enabled document.

▶ **4.** Click **Word Macro-Enabled Document**, and then click the **Save** button. The document is saved along with the macro.

| InSight | | **Understanding Filename Extensions** |

Recall that all files have filename extensions, which are several letters after a period at the end of a filename. The default setting in Windows is to hide filename extensions. Filename extensions identify the file type, such as .docx for normal Word documents, .jpeg or .bmp for pictures, .exe for program files, and so on. When you save a document as a Word Template, the filename extension is .dotx, which distinguishes these documents from ordinary Word documents. When you save a file as a Macro-Enabled Document, the filename extension is .docm, and when you save a file as a Macro-Enabled Template, the filename extension is .dotm. One other filename extension that you should be aware of is .doc, the extension for Word documents created in versions of Word prior to Word 2007.

Now that you've seen how to import and run macros and how to save a document with macros, you'll learn how to record your own macro.

Recording a Macro

Geoff would like you to record a macro that inserts the slogan for Forsythe Plaza as a footer. Once you've recorded the macro for him in the Brochure document, he can use the macro in other documents to save time.

Recording a macro is similar to recording your voice on a cassette tape: you turn on the tape recorder, speak into the microphone, and then turn off the tape recorder when you're finished. When you play back the cassette recording, you hear exactly what you recorded. Similarly, to record a macro, you turn on the macro recorder, perform keystrokes and mouse operations, and then turn off the macro recorder. When you play back the macro, Word performs the same sequence of keystrokes and mouse clicks. You can't use the mouse within the document window while you record a macro, but you can use the mouse to select buttons and options on the Ribbon.

Recording a Macro | Reference Window

- Click the View tab, in the Macros group, click the Macros button arrow, and then click Record Macro; *or* click the Developer tab, and then in the Code group, click the Record Macro button; *or* on the status bar, click the Start Recording button.
- In the Record Macro dialog box, type a name for the macro in the Macro name box.
- To save the macro in the current document or template, click the Store macro in arrow, and then select the desired active document or template.
- To assign the macro to a button on the Quick Access Toolbar, click the Button icon to open the Word Options dialog box, make sure the Customize category is selected, click the macro in the list on the left, and then click the Add button.
- To assign a shortcut key combination to the macro, in the Word Options dialog box, click the Customize button next to Keyboard shortcuts to open the Customize Keyboard dialog box, *or* in the Record Macro dialog box, click the Keyboard button; click a category in the Categories list on the left, click a command in the Commands list on the right, click in the Press new shortcut key box, press two or more keys to insert a shortcut key combination, click the Assign button, and then click the Close button.
- Click the OK button to start recording the macro.
- Perform the mouse movements and keystrokes you want to record the macro.
- On the View tab in the Macros group, click the Macros button arrow, and then click Stop Recording; *or* on the Developer tab in the Code group, click the Stop Recording button; *or* on the status bar, click the Stop Recording button.

Now you'll record a macro to insert the slogan for Forsythe Plaza in the brochure footer.

Before you record the tasks as a macro, you'll name the macro "InsertSlogan," attach the macro to the Brochure document, add a description of the macro, and assign the macro to a Quick Access Toolbar button and to a shortcut key combination.

To prepare to record the InsertSlogan macro:

▶ 1. Click the **View** tab, in the Macros group, click the **Macros button arrow**, and then click **Record Macro**. The Record Macros dialog box opens. Notice that Word suggests a macro name (Macro1). However, you should use a name that describes the function of the macro.

▶ 2. Type **InsertSlogan** in the Macro name box.

▶ 3. Click the **Store macro in** arrow, and then click **Brochure Draft (document)** to attach the macro only to the current document.

▶ 4. Click in the **Description** box, and then type **Inserts Forsythe Plaza slogan as a footer** (without any punctuation). The Record Macro dialog box now looks like Figure 8-39.

Tip

You can also click the Start Recording button 📧 in the status bar at the bottom of the document window to start recording a macro, or you can click the Developer tab, and then in the Code group, click the Record Macro button.

Figure 8-39 | Preparing to record a macro

Next, you'll assign the macro to a button that you'll add to the Quick Access Toolbar.

▶ **5.** Click the **Button** icon in the Record Macro dialog box. The Word Options dialog box opens with Customize selected in the list on the left.

▶ **6.** Click **Project.NewMacros.InsertSlogan** in the list on the left, and then click the **Add** button. The macro is added to the Customize Quick Access Toolbar list on the right.

▶ **7.** Click the **Modify** button. The Modify Button dialog box opens.

▶ **8.** In the last row in the dialog box, click the blue **A** (fourth from the right), and then click the **OK** button. The icon you selected replaces the macro icon in the Customize Quick Access Toolbar list on the right.

▶ **9.** Click the **Customize** button to open the Customize Keyboard dialog box, in the Categories list, scroll down, and then click **Macros**.

▶ **10.** Below the Current keys box, click the **Save changes in** arrow, and then click **Brochure Draft**. The three macros in the current document (two that you imported plus the one you're about to record) appear in the Macros list at the top of the dialog box on the right. (You might see additional macro as well.)

▶ **11.** In the Macros list, click **InsertSlogan**, if necessary, click in the **Press new shortcut key** box, and then press the **Alt+Ctrl+Shift+Z** keys. The message below the Current keys box tells you that this key combination is unassigned.

▶ **12.** Click the **Assign** button. The key combination you chose appears in the Current key list. Now when you press the Alt+Ctrl+Shift+Z keys, you will run the macro you are about to record.

▶ **13.** Click the **Close** button in the Customize Keyboard dialog box, and then click the **OK** button in the Word Options dialog box. The dialog boxes close, and the pointer changes to ⬚, indicating that you are recording a macro. On the status bar, the Stop Recording button ◼ appears (in place of the Start Recording button).

From this point, Word records every keystroke and mouse operation until you stop the recording, so perform these steps carefully, and complete them exactly as shown. If you make a mistake, you can stop recording and start over.

To record the InsertSlogan macro:

▶ **1.** Click the **Insert** tab, in the Header & Footer group, click the **Footer** button, and then click **Edit Footer**. The footer becomes active.

▶ **2.** Type **Forsythe Plaza--New England's Premier Wedding Facility**.

▶ **3.** Use the keyboard to select the text you just typed, and then format it so it is bold and italic.

▶ **4.** Click the **Home** tab, if necessary, and then in the Paragraph group, click the **Align Text Right** button ▤. The text is right-aligned.

▶ **5.** Click the **Header & Footer Tools Design** tab, and then in the Close group, click the **Close Header and Footer** button.

▶ **6.** Click the **View** tab, in the Macros group, click the **Macros button arrow**, and then click **Stop Recording**. The pointer changes back to the normal pointer, and the button on the status bar changes back to the Start Recording button 📄.

   Trouble? If you made a mistake while recording the macro, delete the button you added to the Quick Access Toolbar, return to the previous set of steps ("To prepare to record the InsertSlogan macro;"), and then repeat all the steps to this point. Click the Yes button when Word prompts you to replace the existing macro.

The InsertSlogan macro you just recorded will insert Geoff's slogan text into the footer of his documents. He'd like you to test the macro now. First, you need to remove the footer that was inserted when you recorded the macro.

To run the InsertSlogan macro:

▶ **1.** Click the **Insert** tab, in the Header & Footer group, click the **Footer** button, and then click **Remove Footer**.

▶ **2.** Click the **View** tab, and then in the Zoom group, click the **One Page** button. You can see that the footer no longer appears at the bottom of the page.

▶ **3.** Press the **Alt+Ctrl+Shift+Z** keys. The formatted footer is entered in the footer area, the document window becomes active, and the footer area becomes inactive. The macro works as it should. You can use the Undo button to see the list of tasks the macro performed.

▶ **4.** On the Quick Access Toolbar, click the **Undo button arrow** ↺ ▾. See Figure 8-40. Notice that the top several actions all begin with "VBA-." These are the recorded actions that the macro performed.

Tip

You can also stop the recording of a macro by clicking the Stop Recording button 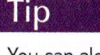 in the status bar.

Figure 8-40 **Undo list after running the macro**

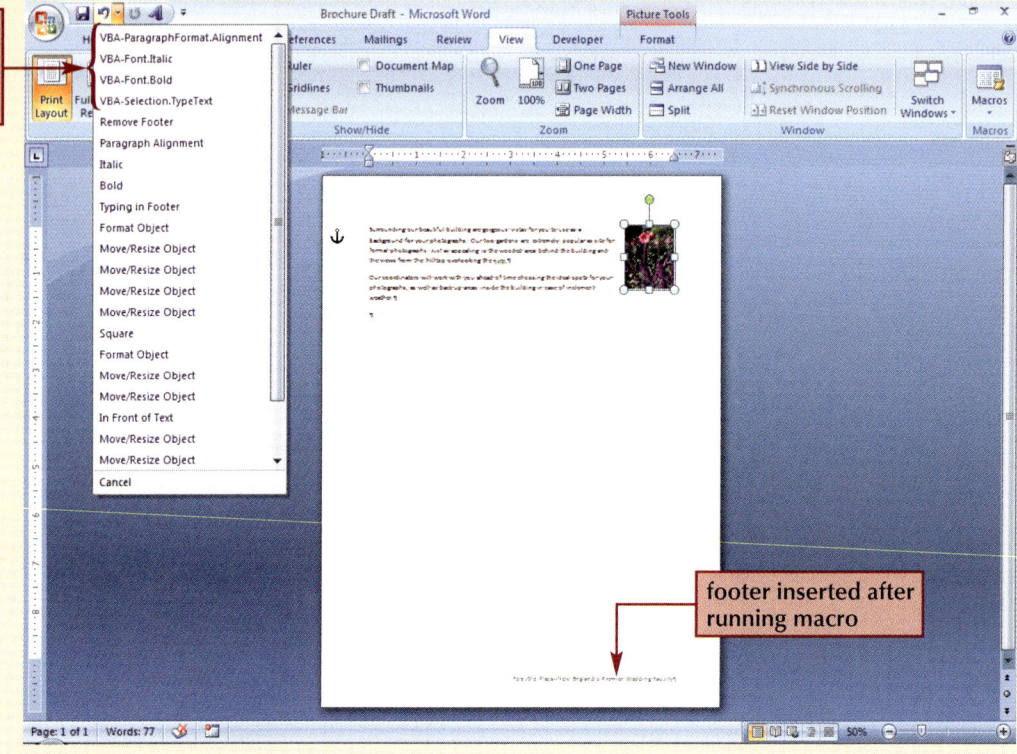

5. Press the **Esc** key to close the Undo menu.

Geoff decides he wants the slogan to be centered. You could record a new macro, but it's easier to edit the one you already recorded.

Editing a Macro Using the Visual Basic Window

To edit a macro, you open the macro in the Visual Basic window, where you can see a list of the commands that make up the macro. You can make simple changes to the commands themselves in this window without needing a thorough understanding of Visual Basic.

To edit a macro:

1. Click the **View** tab, if necessary, then in the Macros group, click the **Macros button arrow**, and then click **View Macros** to open the Macros dialog box.

2. In the list of macros, click **InsertSlogan**, and then click the **Edit** button. The Visual Basic window opens and displays the InsertSlogan macro commands in the right pane.

3. Maximize the code window, if necessary, and then adjust the panes as needed so that you can see most or all of the macro code, as shown in Figure 8-41.

Code for InsertSlogan macro in Visual Basic window ▸ **Figure 8-41**

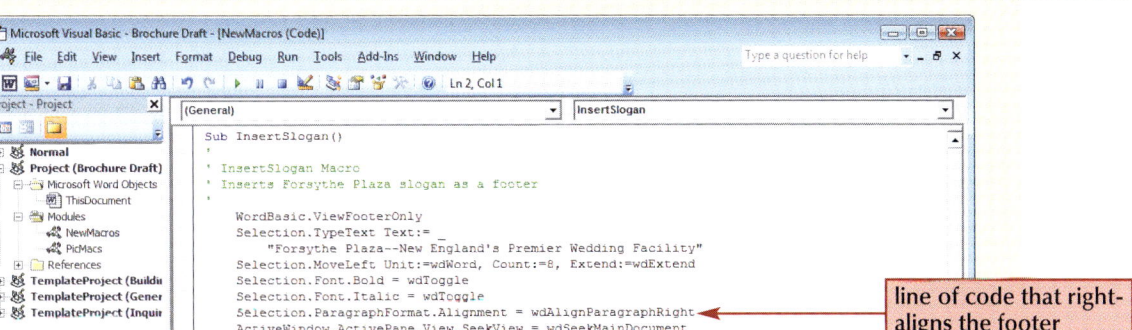

Notice that most lines of the code begin with "Selection." This is a Visual Basic command that performs an action on the selected text. The third line from the bottom is the line that was recorded when you clicked the Align Text Right button.

▸ **4.** In the third line of code from the bottom, select **Right,** and then type **Center**.

Trouble? If the second to last line beginning with "ActiveWindow" moves up to the end of the line that you just modified, position the insertion point after the word "Center," and then press the Enter key.

▸ **5.** Close the Visual Basic window. Changes you have made to the code are saved automatically with your Word document, and will be saved to the disk when you save the document. Now you'll test the macro.

▸ **6.** Remove the footer, and then on the Quick Access Toolbar, click the **Project. NewMacros.InsertSlogan** button 📧. The footer entered in the footer area is centered this time. Now you need to return to the default state on your computer, so you'll remove the button from the Quick Access Toolbar.

▸ **7.** On the Quick Access Toolbar, right-click the **Project.NewMacros.InsertSlogan** button 📧, and then click **Remove from Quick Access Toolbar**.

▸ **8.** Save your changes, and then close the Brochure Draft document. The General Inquiry Template is the current document.

Geoff is glad that he learned a little about how macros work. He realizes that macros are useful for complicated tasks and that for his slogan, saving it as a Quick Part would be easier. He'll do that later.

For now, you'll return to the General Inquiry Template, where you'll record a macro that finds the word "wedding" in the introductory paragraph so that the person filling in the form remembers to change it to suit the event being planned.

Recording an AutoMacro

To make the General Inquiry Template even more useful, you will add an AutoMacro. An **AutoMacro** is a macro that runs automatically when you perform certain basic operations, such as starting Word, creating a document, opening a document, closing a document, and exiting Word. Figure 8-42 lists the AutoMacros and their purposes. These AutoMacro names are reserved macro names in Word. Word reserves these special names so that when you create the macro using one of them, the macro runs automatically at the time determined by the reserved name.

Figure 8-42 Description of AutoMacros built into Word

AutoMacro Name	Purpose
AutoExec	Runs each time you start Word
AutoNew	Runs when you start a new document
AutoOpen	Runs each time you open an existing document
AutoClose	Runs each time you close a document
AutoExit	Runs each time you exit Word

Geoff asks you to record an AutoNew macro in the General Inquiry Template so that whenever a new document is created from the template, the macro will execute the Find command and select the word "wedding" in the introductory paragraph. This will remind the employee to change that word to match the event for which the customer is planning a party.

To create the AutoNew macro:

1. Make sure General Inquiry Template is the current document, and then press the **Ctrl+Home** keys to move the insertion point to the beginning of the document.

2. Click the **View** tab, in the Macros group, click the **Macros button arrow**, and then click **Record Macro**. The Record Macro dialog box opens.

3. Type **AutoNew** in the Macro name text box. This macro name tells Word to run the macro when you begin a new document.

4. Click the **Store macro in** arrow, and then click **Documents Based On General Inquiry Template** so the macro runs only if a new document is opened from the General Inquiry Template.

5. In the Description box, type **Find instance of "wedding."**. You won't assign this macro to a toolbar or the keyboard because it will run automatically when the new document is opened.

6. Click the **OK** button. You're now ready to record the commands of the AutoNew macro.

7. Click the **Home** tab, and then in the Editing group, click the **Find** button. The Find and Replace dialog box opens.

8. Type **wedding** in the Find what text box, and then click the **Find Next** button. Word finds the word "wedding" in the introductory paragraph.

9. Click the **Cancel** button in the Find dialog box. This completes the operations for the AutoNew macro.

10. Click the **View** tab, in the Macros group, click the **Macros button arrow**, and then click **Stop Recording**.

11. Save the file as a **Word Macro-Enabled Template**, changing the name to **General Inquiry Template with macros**.

The AutoNew macro will run whenever an employee starts a new document from the General Inquiry Template with macros template. Now you need to test your template. Before you can run an AutoMacro, you need to change your security settings to allow it.

To change the security settings to allow macros to run:

▶ **1.** Click the **Developer** tab, and then in the Code group, click the **Macro Security** button. The Trust Center dialog box opens.

   Trouble? If you are working on a computer in a lab, check with your instructor or technical support person before performing these steps.

▶ **2.** If necessary, click **Macro Settings** in the list on the left. The right side of the dialog box lists options for running macros. All of the options for Macro Settings disable macros except the last one. See Figure 8-43.

Tip

You can also open the Trust Center dialog box by opening the Word Options dialog box, clicking Trust Center in the list on the left, and then clicking the Trust Center Settings button.

Enabling macros in the Trust Center dialog box ◄ **Figure 8-43**

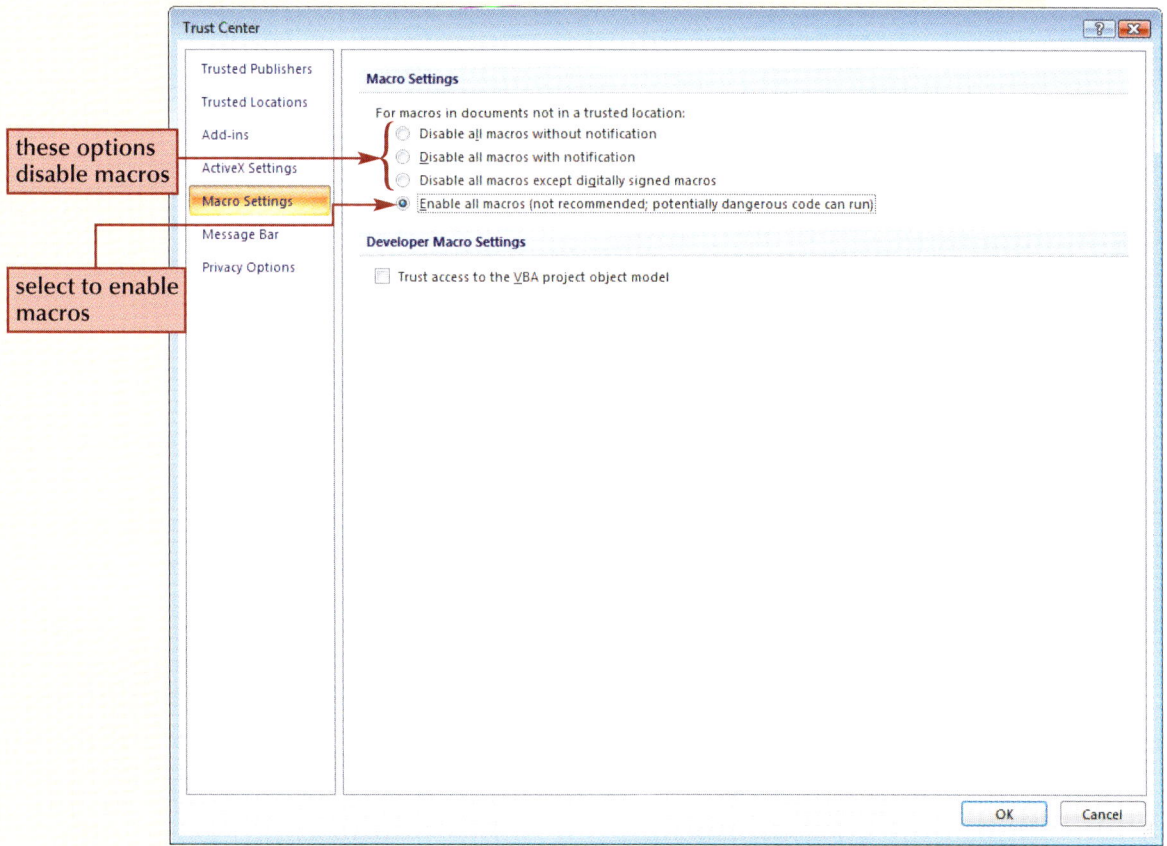

▶ **3.** Click the **Enable all macros** option button, and then click the **OK** button. The Trust Center dialog box closes.

Now that you have changed your security settings, you can use the macro in the General Inquiry Template with macros template.

To test the AutoNew macro in a new document based on the General Inquiry Template with macros template:

▶ **1.** Click the **Office Button** 🔘 , and then click **New**. The New Document dialog box opens.

▶ **2.** In the Templates list on the left, click **New from existing**. The New from Existing Document dialog box opens. Notice that the icon for General Inquiry Template with macros has an exclamation point on it. This indicates that the template or document is macro-enabled.

▶ **3.** Click **General Inquiry Template with macros**, and then click the **Create New** button. The New Document dialog box closes, and another dialog box opens as a result of the Fill-in field, asking you to enter the type of function. See Figure 8-44.

Figure 8-44 ▶ **Testing the AutoNew macro**

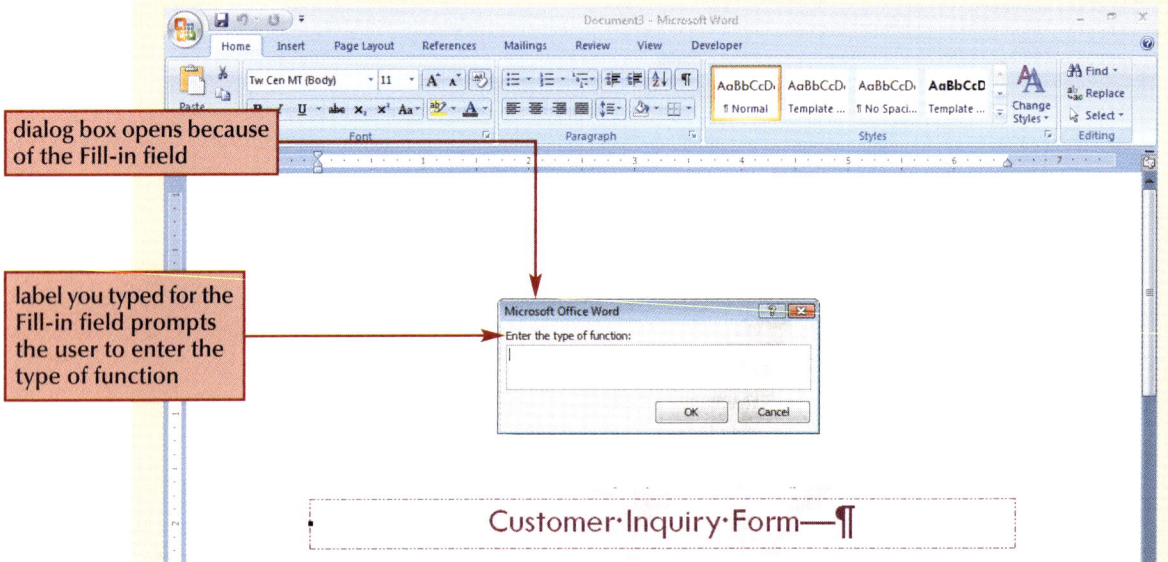

dialog box opens because of the Fill-in field

label you typed for the Fill-in field prompts the user to enter the type of function

▶ **4.** In the Enter the type of function box, type **Retirement Party**, and then click the **OK** button. The dialog box closes, and the document opens. "Retirement Party" appears in the title line to the right of "Customer Inquiry Form." This is where the Fill-in field is located in the document. The word "wedding" is highlighted in the introductory paragraph. This is a result of the AutoNew macro running.

▶ **5.** Type **retirement party** to replace "wedding" in the introductory paragraph.

▶ **6.** Save the document as a regular Word document in the **Tutorial.08\Tutorial** folder and name the file **Retirement Party Inquiry**.

Geoff wants to send his revised document to the corporate office for review. He knows that all the computers there have not been upgraded yet with Word 2007. He decides to check the document to see which features in the document are incompatible with Word 2003.

To check for features incompatible with previous versions of Word:

▶ **1.** Click the **Office Button** 🔵, point to **Prepare**, and then click **Run Compatibility Checker**. The Microsoft Office Word Compatibility Checker dialog box opens. Two items are listed as incompatible with previous versions of word: the content controls and the placement of the text box.

▶ **2.** If necessary, click the **Check compatibility when saving in Word 97-2003 formats** check box at the bottom of this dialog box to select it, and then click the **OK** button. To avoid any surprises, Geoff decides to save the document as a Word 97-2003 document.

▶ **3.** Click the **Office Button** 🔘 , point to **Save As**, and then click **Word 97-2003 Document**. The Save As dialog box opens with Word 97-2003 Document selected in the Save as type box.

▶ **4.** Type **Retirement Inquiry 97-2003** as the filename, and then click the **Save** button. Another Compatibility Checker dialog box opens, informing you that the same features you noted when you ran the compatibility checker are not supported in earlier versions of Word. This is because the Check compatibility when saving in Word 97-2003 formats check box is selected at the bottom of this dialog box.

▶ **5.** Click the **Continue** button. The document is saved in the Word 97-2003 format. Notice that "Compatibility Mode" appears in the title bar next to the filename.

Now Geoff wants to print the document on legal size paper so that he can easily take notes during a phone conference with his manager.

To print a document on different size paper:

▶ **1.** In the Editing group, click the **Select** button, and then click **Select All**. You need to select all the text in the document first. If you don't, the change to the paper size will affect only one section.

▶ **2.** Click the **Page Layout** tab.

▶ **3.** In the Page Setup group, click the **Size** button. A menu of paper sizes opens.

▶ **4.** Click **Legal**. The formatting of the document is changed to fit on legal size paper.

▶ **5.** Click the **View** tab, then in the Zoom group, click the **One Page** button. You can see the new page size.

▶ **6.** Save your changes.

Tip

If you don't see the size paper you want in the Size menu, click More Paper Sizes to open the Page Setup dialog box with the Paper tab on top, and then type the desired measurements in the Width and Height boxes.

The document is now ready to print on legal size paper. Now you should return Word to its original settings. You'll hide the Developer tab and return the security settings to the default state.

To restore Word to its default state:

▶ **1.** Click the **Office Button** 🔘 , and then click **Word Options**.

▶ **2.** Click the **Show Developer tab in the Ribbon** check box to deselect it.

▶ **3.** In the list on the left, click **Trust Center**, and then click the **Trust Center Settings** button.

▶ **4.** In the Macro Settings section, click the **Disable all macros with notification** option button or click the option button next to the option that was originally selected on your computer.

▶ **5.** Click the **OK** button in the Trust Center dialog box, and then click the **OK** button in the Word Options dialog box.

▶ **6.** Close all open documents.

Review | Session 8.3 Quick Check

1. What is the name of the dialog box in which you can customize many of the options in Word?
2. What is a macro?
3. What are three advantages to using a macro?
4. Briefly describe how to record a macro.
5. Why would you need to edit a macro? How would you do it?
6. What are AutoMacros?
7. Why might a template need an AutoNew macro?
8. How do you run a macro named MyMacro if it's not assigned to a button on the Quick Access Toolbar or to a shortcut key combination?

Review | Tutorial Summary

In this tutorial, you learned how to create, save, and use specialized document templates. You managed multiple documents and pasted information from other documents. You learned how to apply various advanced features to templates, including styles, borders and shading, Quick Parts, and watermarks. You added document properties and inserted them into a document using the Quick Parts button. You also learned how to customize Word to suit your working style, including customizing the AutoCorrect feature and automating parts of a document using field codes. Finally, you learned how to import, run, create, save, and edit macros.

Key Terms

AutoMacro	field	Quick Part
boilerplate	Fill-in field	sidebar
building block	instruction	smart tag
callout	macro	switch
compress	prompt	text box
date-time picture	property	Visual Basic
Document Information Panel	pull quote	watermark

Practice	**Review Assignments**

Apply the skills you earned in the tutorial using the same case scenario.

Data Files needed for the Review Assignments: Bride.jpg, Brochure2.docx, Flowers2.jpg, Flyer.docx, Letter.docx

Geoff McLay, Event Manager at Forsythe Plaza, wants you to create a brochure. He first wants you to create a brochure for customers who want to hold their wedding reception at the Plaza. Then he wants you to make suggestions for customizing the brochure for other functions. (Note: Text you need to type is shown in bold for ease of reference only; do not bold the text unless otherwise instructed.)

Complete the following:

1. Open the file **Brochure2** from the Tutorial.08\Review folder included with your Data Files, and then save it in the same folder as a document template with the file-name **Brochure Final**.
2. Open the file **Flyer** from the Tutorial.08\Review folder included with your Data Files, select all the text, and then copy it to the Office Clipboard.
3. Open the file **Letter** from the Tutorial.08\Review folder included with your Data Files, select the logo and address (through the URL), and then copy it to the Office Clipboard. Close the Flyer and Letter documents.
4. Go to the end of the Brochure Final document, and then use the Paste All command in the Office Clipboard to paste the contents of the Office Clipboard. Position the insertion point in front of the word "Gorgeous" in the second paragraph, and then press the Enter key.
5. Move the logo so it is positioned before the first word on the page, and then start a new paragraph after the logo. If there is not a blank line above the address at the end of the document, position the insertion point before the address, and then press the Enter key. Type **Forsythe Plaza** in the blank paragraph above the address.
6. Format the entire document in two columns, with the left column narrower than the right column. On the Page Layout tab, in the Page Setup group, click the Columns button, and then click More Columns. In the Col# 1 row, change the Width box to 2.8", and then click the OK button.
7. Insert a column break before the third paragraph, which starts with "Gorgeous."
8. Change the theme to Opulent.
9. Position the insertion point at the beginning of the second column, and then insert the picture **Flowers2** from the Tutorial.08\Review folder included with your Data Files. Format the photo with the Soft Edge Rectangle picture style. Use the Position button in the Arrange group on the Picture Tools Format tab to position the picture as a floating object in the upper-right corner of the document. If necessary, change the height of the picture to 1.44".
10. Position the insertion point at the end of the first column, and then insert the picture **Bride** from the Tutorial.08\Review folder included with your Data Files. Change the height of the photo to 2.5". Change the brightness of the photo to +20% and the con-trast to –20%. Format the photo with the Drop Shadow Rectangle picture style. Use the Position button to position the picture of the bride as a floating object in the lower-left corner of the document. Drag the photo and center it under the text in the first column.
11. Using the Rounded Rectangle shape, draw a rectangle below the picture of the flow-ers that is the same width as the flower picture and approximately ¼-inch high. Add the text **The rear garden** to the shape, change the font size to 10 points, and center the text. Fill the shape with Pink, Text 2, Lighter 80%, and change the outline to Lavender, Background 2, Darker 25%.

12. Change the color of the page background to a gradient fill using Lavender, Background 2 as the first color and White, Background 1, Darker 5% as the second color. Change the shading style to From corner and choose the variant in the lower-left.

13. Insert a watermark that identifies the document as a draft by opening the Watermark menu, and then clicking the Draft 1 style in the gallery.

14. In the first paragraph in the first column, select the text "Forsythe Plaza," and format it so that it is 12 points and bold, and change its color to White, Background 1, Darker 50%. Save this format as a new character style named FP Name.

15. Select all the text in the second paragraph in the first column, change it to 12 points and change the line spacing to 1.0. Redefine the Normal Quick Style to match this formatting.

16. At the bottom of the right column, select the text "Forsythe Plaza," and apply the FP Name style. Center this text if necessary and remove any space after the paragraph.

17. Insert a next page section break after the URL at the bottom of the right column. Change the format of page 2 to a single column, and change the orientation to Portrait.

18. On page 1, select the last six lines of text in the right column (the address information), open the Borders and Shading dialog box, and then choose a Box border. Drag the scroll box in the Style list to the bottom of the list, and then click the third style from the bottom. Change the color of the border to Purple, Accent 2, Lighter 40%. Add light purple shading using the Purple, Accent 2, Lighter 80% color.

19. Save the boxed lines as a Quick Part named FP Address stored in the Brochure Final template.

20. On page 2, insert the formatted text box called Sideline Sidebar. In the text box, type **Forsythe Plaza—New England's Premier Function Facility**, and then center the text in the text box. Drag the text box down to the bottom of page 2 and position it approximately two inches above the bottom of the page.

21. On page 2, insert the FP Address Quick Part at the top of the page.

22. Click the Insert tab, in the Header & Footer group, click the Footer button, and then click Edit Footer. In the footer, type **Updated**, and then press the spacebar. Insert the current date in the format 6/12/2010 so that it updates automatically.

23. Display the field code, and then edit the date field so the date will appear in the format 6/12/10. Toggle the field codes off.

24. Click after the date in the footer and then press the Tab key twice. Type **Prepared by**.

25. Open the document properties, and then type your name in the Author box. Open the advanced properties, and add the custom property Project with a value of **New Marketing Campaign**.

26. After "Prepared by" in the footer, insert the document property Author. Press the right arrow key, type a comma, press the spacebar, and then use the Field dialog box to insert the custom property Project. Close the footer.

27. On page 1, in the first paragraph in the left column, delete the word "weddings," and insert a second space. Position the insertion point between the spaces, and then insert the Fill-in field with the prompt **Enter type of event:**. Save the changes to the template.

28. Record a macro named **Slogan2** stored in the Brochure Final template. Assign the Alt+F keys as the shortcut key combination to run the macro. When the macro starts recording, click the Insert tab, in the Header & Footer group, click the Header button, click Edit Header, type **Forsythe Plaza makes it an event to remember!**, use the keyboard to select the text, format it as 16-point italic, and change the color to Purple, Accent 2, Lighter 40%, and then center the text. Close the Header area, and then stop recording.

29. Edit the macro so that the header is right-aligned instead of centered.

30. Remove the header and then run the macro.

31. Create an AutoNew macro stored in the Brochure Final template that opens the Document Information Panel and positions the insertion point in the Author box.

32. Save the template as a macro-enabled template named **Brochure Final with macro**, and then close the template.

33. Change your macro security settings to enable macros, and then create a new document based on the Brochure Final with macro template. Type **corporate function** in the Fill-in field dialog box that opens. When the Document Information Panel opens, edit the text in the Author box so **(student)** appears after your name. Close the Document Information Panel, and then save the document as a macro-enabled document named **Corporate Brochure Draft** to the Tutorial.08\Review folder.

34. Check for features incompatible with previous versions of Word.

35. If you changed the security settings for macros, reset the security to its original level, print the document on legal size paper if requested to do so, submit the documents to your instructor in electronic form, if requested, and then close all open documents.

| Apply | **Case Problem 1** |

Apply the skills you earned to create and se a new template nd import and use nacros in the emplate.

Data Files needed for this Case Problem: LCNLetter.docx, LCNReply.bas, frmLCNReply.frm, frmLCNReply.frx

Linnea's Crafts and Needles   Linnea Brown is the owner of Linnea's Crafts and Needles in Atlanta, Georgia. Linnea takes orders via telephone, mail, and the Internet from customers throughout Canada and the United States, and ships her crafts, sewing, and knitting products to her customers. One of her best sellers is her gift boxes of supplies for different types of crafts (scrapbooking, knitting, stamping, and so on). One of her responsibilities is to respond to customer complaints. Linnea asks you to help her prepare a document template to increase the efficiency with which her staff responds to complaints. Complete the following:

1. Open the file **LCNLetter** from the Tutorial.08\Case1 folder included with your Data Files, and then save it as a document template in the same folder with the filename **LCN Response**. Change your macro security settings, if necessary, so that you can run macros.

2. Change the theme to Civic and the theme colors to Paper.

3. Format the first line in the document so it is 16 points, bold, and Blue-Gray, Accent 6, Darker 25%. Redefine the Heading 2 Quick Style to match this formatting.

4. Change the format of any paragraph in the body of the letter so that the text is 10 points, the line spacing is 1.0, and the space after the paragraph is 12 points. Use this format to define a new Quick Style named LCN Body. Apply the new style to all the text in the letter except the company name and address, and then remove the space after the paragraphs containing the [NAME] and [STREET] placeholders in the inside address and "Carla Nieto" in the closing.

5. Set the page background color to Orange, Accent 2, Lighter 80%.

⊕ EXPLORE

6. Use clip art to create a watermark. Search for appropriate clip art (try using "knitting" as the keyword). Insert the clip, recolor it using the Washout style (on the Recolor button in the Color Modes section of the menu), and then change the text wrapping so it is behind the text.

7. Customize the Quick Access Toolbar by adding the Quick Parts button to it. Customize the Building Blocks Organizer command so that the shortcut key combination Alt+B executes the command. Save the shortcut key combination in the template only.

8. Select and replace [DATE] near the beginning of the letter with the current date set to update automatically.

🜨 EXPLORE

9. Edit the date field so the date appears in the format 12 June 2010. (*Hint*: Change the date-time picture to d MMMM yyyy.)

10. Select and replace the first occurrence of [NAME] (in the inside address) with a Fill-in field code to fill in the customer's name. Type an appropriate prompt.

11. Display field codes, copy the field code for the Fill-in field you just entered, and then paste it so that it replaces [NAME] after "Dear." Edit the prompt if necessary.

12. Select and replace [STREET] and then [CITY, STATE, ZIP] with an appropriate Fill-in field for each. Hide field codes.

13. Add a double-line border, colored Orange, Accent 2, below the URL.

14. Use the button you added to the toolbar to create a Quick Part from the company name and return address. (Be sure not to select the small empty paragraph at the top of the document.) Name it **LCN Address** and save it in this template. Delete the company name and address in the letter and then insert the Quick Part you created to test it. Create a second Quick Part consisting of just the company name, and name this **LCN**. Save this Quick Part in the template as well. Make sure you do not include the paragraph mark after the company name as part of the Quick Part. Save your changes to the template.

15. Position the insertion point at the beginning of the letter, and then create an AutoNew macro that moves the insertion point to the blank paragraph after the first sentence in the body of the letter. (Use the keyboard to move the insertion point.) Make sure the macro is saved in the template.

16. Open a Visual Basic window, and import the file **LCNReply.bas** (you might not see the file extension when you open the Import File dialog box), located in the Tutorial. 08\Case1 folder. This contains part of the code for a macro that Linnea wrote to help automate writing the response letter.

17. Import the file **frmLCNReply.frm**, located in the Tutorial.08\Case1 folder, in the Visual Basic window. This file contains a macro User Form, which is a customized dialog box. When you import this file, the file frmLCNReply.frx is imported automatically as well.

18. Close the Visual Basic window. Assign the key combination Alt+R to the macro LCNReply.

19. Move the insertion point to the end of the document, press the Enter key to insert a blank line, and then test the macro by pressing the Alt+R keys. The macro dialog box named "Response to Customer" appears and gives you the option of inserting one of four paragraphs, based on the type of customer complaint. The macro works as follows: Click "Nothing (Didn't receive order)" if the customer didn't receive an order; click "Wrong Order" if the customer received a product but not the correct order; click "Damaged Box" if the customer received the correct order but the gift box was damaged; or click "Poor Quality Product" if the customer complained about the quality of the crafts, sewing, or knitting products order; and then click the OK button. Test each option of the macro, and when finished, delete the inserted paragraphs and blank lines.

20. Save your changes as a macro-enabled template, and then close the document.

21. Open a new document based on the LCN Response macro-enabled template.

22. When prompted by the Fill-in fields, use your own name and address as the person to whom the letter is being written (the customer).

23. With the insertion point located in the blank paragraph below the first paragraph of the body of the letter, run the LCNReply macro, selecting the Damaged Box option. Move the insertion point to the left of the final period in the paragraph that you just inserted with the macro, press the spacebar, type "from," press the spacebar, and then use the LCN Quick Part to insert the company name.

24. Save the new letter as a macro-enabled document using the filename **Letter Final**, and then submit it to your instructor, either in electronic or printed form, as requested. If you changed the macro security settings, reset the security to its original level.

25. Remove the button you added from the Quick Access Toolbar, and then change the macro security settings back to the original setting, if necessary. Close all open documents.

Create | **Case Problem 2**

Explore more advanced features of Word by creating a shipping list template.

Data Files needed for this Case Problem: List.docx, Logo.jpg, Water.jpg

Seely Tech Books   Patric Melio is the manager of Seely Tech Books, a bookseller specializing in books about all forms of engineering. He has asked you to help him create a document template for a shipping list that he can include with each book shipment. Complete the following:

1. Open the file **List** in the Tutorial.08\Case2 folder included with your Data Files, and then save it as a macro-enabled template in the same folder with the filename **Shipping List**.

⊕EXPLORE   2. At the top line of the document, insert the Seely Logo, which is the graphic file **Logo** located in the Tutorial.08\Case2 folder included with your Data Files, and then format it using the Drop Shadow Rectangle picture style and the Round Diagonal Corner Rectangle picture shape.

3. Insert a watermark using the file named **Water** from the Tutorial.08\Case2 folder included with your Data Files.

4. To the right of the tab after "Shipment Method," type **Federal Express**, select that phrase, and then make it a Quick Part named **FedEx** in this template only. Delete the text "Federal Express" from the template. Repeat this action with **USPS**, saved as **USPS**, and **Fed Ex Ground**, saved as **Ground**.

5. To the right of the tab after "Payment Method," type **Credit Card**, and then save that phrase as a Quick Part named **CC** in this template only. Delete the text "Credit Card" from the template. Repeat this action with **Check**, saved as **Check**.

6. Define a new character Quick Style named "Packing Title" that is 14-point Book Antiqua (if Book Antiqua isn't available, use Times New Roman). Apply the Packing Title style to the following phrases, but do not include the colon that follows each phrase: Title, Author/Editor, Edition/Volume, and Copyright Year.

⊕EXPLORE   7. Insert Fill-in fields to the right of the tab after each phrase to which you just applied the Packing Title style. You should choose an appropriate prompt for each of the four items. (*Hint*: Create one Fill-in field, create its prompt, display field codes, select the Fill-in field, copy it to all the other locations where you want a Fill-in field, and then directly edit the prompt within the field code.)

8. With nonprinting characters displayed, insert the Date field to the right of the tab after "Date" below the section break. Format the date so that it appears in the style 4/8/2010.

⊕ EXPLORE   9. In the same section of the template, insert Fill-in fields to the right of the tab for Customer Number, Order Number, Date Ordered, Name, Company, and Street. You should choose an appropriate prompt for each of the items.

⊕ EXPLORE   10. Insert Fill-in fields to the right of the tab for City, State, and ZIP. Set the Default response for City to "Augusta", for State to "GA", and for ZIP to "30903", because most of the orders are from local customers. (*Hint:* Select the appropriate check box in the Field Options section of the Field dialog box, and type the default there.)

11. Insert a Fill-in field for the Price in cell B1 of the table. (*Note:* Cells B2 and B4 contain calculation fields, which you can see with the View Field Codes command. Inserting a calculation field in a table is covered in Tutorial 9.)

⊕ EXPLORE   12. Press the Ctrl+Home keys, and then create an AutoNew macro for this template only that moves the insertion point to the right of the tab after "Shipment Method" when a new document is opened based on this template. (Use the keyboard to position the insertion point.)

13. Hide formatting codes, save your changes, and then close the template.

14. Change the macro security settings to enable macros, if necessary. Open a new document based on the Shipping List template.

15. When prompted by the Fill-in fields, type the information as follows (the dialog boxes for the fields in your document might appear in a different order):
   - Customer Number: **23455**
   - Order Number: **087774**
   - Date Ordered: Use the current date.
   - Name: Use your name.
   - Company: Leave blank.
   - Street, City, State, and ZIP: Use your school or another address.
   - Title: **Ancient Bridges**
   - Author/Editor: **Martin Fasuli**
   - Edition/Volume: **2nd Edition**
   - Copyright Year: **2007**
   - Price: **82.75**

16. Verify that the insertion point is to the right of the tab after "Shipment Method," and then insert the FedEx Quick Part to insert "Federal Express." Move the insertion point to the right of the tab after "Payment Method," and then insert the CC Quick Part.

⊕ EXPLORE   17. In the table, update the Tax and Total fields (in the cells to the right of those labels), which are the calculation fields. (*Hint:* You update calculation fields the same way you update the results of other fields.)

18. Save the packing slip as a Word document in the Tutorial.08\Case2 folder included with your Data Files using the filename **Sample Shipping List**.

⊕ EXPLORE   19. Use the Advanced tab of the Word Options dialog box to turn on SmartTags, if necessary, and then use the Proofing tab of the Word Options dialog box to label names, addresses and phone numbers with smart tags.

⊕ EXPLORE   20. Save your changes, close the **Sample Shipping List** document, open it again, and then review the smart tags in the document.

⊕ **EXPLORE**

21. At the beginning of the document, where Word has marked the Seely Tech Books address with a smart tag, click the tagged text, click the Smart Tags Action button, click Add to Contacts (if that item appears in the menu), and then add the name and address of Seely Tech Books to your address book. In your address book, use the company name as both the name of the contact (full name) and the name of the company. Edit the address so it includes the full address, with ZIP code, on two lines. (*Note*: The Contacts window appears only if you have installed Outlook or some other compatible electronic address book. If the Contact window doesn't appear, skip this step.) When you are finished entering the contact information, print the contact information, save it, and close the Contact window.

22. Close the Sample Shipping List document. If you changed the security settings for macros, reset the security to its original level, and then submit the files to your instructor, in either printed or electronic form, as requested.

| Create | **Case Problem 3** |

Create a template and Word document for blacksmith company by using and expanding on the skills you learned in this tutorial.

Data File needed for this Case Problem: Fax.docx

Sierra Top Blacksmiths Petra Mincberg is the general manager of Sierra Top Black-smiths, a company that creates hand-forged iron products for solid-wood door manufacturers. Because shipping blacksmith products is so expensive, Petra wants to fax every customer an order acknowledgement that provides general information and lists the number of items in each style that the customer has ordered. Petra wrote the text for the acknowledgement fax, and asks you to create a document template, as shown in Figure 8-45, to generate the faxes. Then she asks you to use the document template to prepare a fax for a customer, as shown in Figure 8-46. (*Note:* Text you need to type is shown in bold for ease of reference only; do not bold the text unless otherwise instructed.)

1. Open the file named **Fax** from the Tutorial.08\Case3 folder included with your Data Files and save it as a macro-enabled template using the name **Fax Template**.

2. Insert a transparent hexagon shape that encloses the address at the top of the fax. Change the fill color of the shape to No Fill. Resize the shape as necessary so that the hexagon encloses the address without crowding it.

3. In the table below the company address, insert the fields shown in Figure 8-45.

Figure 8-45

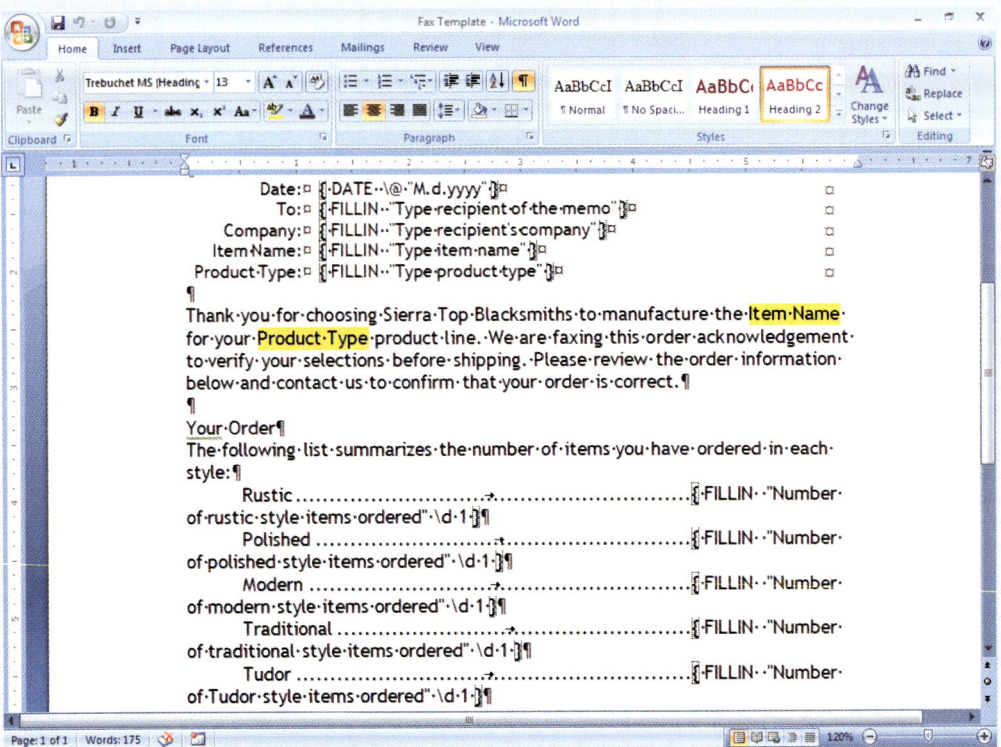

4. In the paragraph below the table, replace the highlighted placeholder text with the same fill-in fields that you used next to Item Name and Product Type in the table.

 **EXPLORE**

5. To the right of the dot-leaders in the "Your Order" section, insert Fill-in fields as shown in Figure 8-45. In each case, set the default number to **1**. (*Hint*: Select the Default response to prompt check box in the Field dialog box, and type **1** in the box next to that check box.)

6. Use Quick Parts to facilitate entering the names highlighted in the memo in the second to last paragraph. The completed template document should have six Quick Parts, three for the three account managers and three for three master blacksmiths. Use the person's initials as the Quick Part name. The completed template should have a space where a name should be located (rather than the highlighted list of names in brackets).

7. Include a macro in the template that moves the insertion point to the place where the first name should be inserted with a Quick Part in the paragraph below "Account Manager." The macro should run automatically when you start a new document using the template.

8. Save the completed **Fax Template** file to the Tutorial.08\Case3 folder and close it.

9. Use the **Fax Template** file to create the document shown in Figure 8-46. Use the current date. When you see the To: prompt, type your name.

Figure 8-46

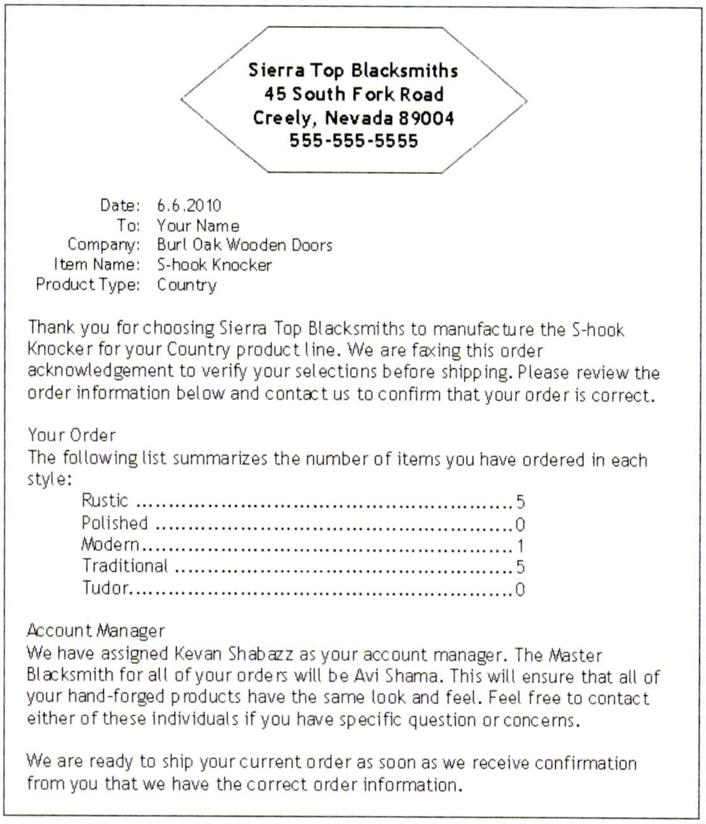

Sierra Top Blacksmiths
45 South Fork Road
Creely, Nevada 89004
555-555-5555

Date: 6.6.2010
To: Your Name
Company: Burl Oak Wooden Doors
Item Name: S-hook Knocker
Product Type: Country

Thank you for choosing Sierra Top Blacksmiths to manufacture the S-hook
Knocker for your Country product line. We are faxing this order
acknowledgement to verify your selections before shipping. Please review the
order information below and contact us to confirm that your order is correct.

Your Order
The following list summarizes the number of items you have ordered in each
style:

    Rustic 5
    Polished 0
    Modern...1
    Traditional 5
    Tudor..0

Account Manager
We have assigned Kevan Shabazz as your account manager. The Master
Blacksmith for all of your orders will be Avi Shama. This will ensure that all of
your hand-forged products have the same look and feel. Feel free to contact
either of these individuals if you have specific question or concerns.

We are ready to ship your current order as soon as we receive confirmation
from you that we have the correct order information.

10. In the second-to-last paragraph, insert **Kevan Shabazz** as the account manager, and **Avi Shama** as the Master Blacksmith.

11. Save the new letter as a document using the filename **Sample Fax**, and then print it.

12. Close the document.

13. Submit your documents to your instructor in electronic or printed form, as requested.

Research | **Case Problem 4**

Use the Internet and other sources to collect information about a play, and then create a newsletter introducing a theater company's production of that play.

There are no Data Files for this Case Problem.

Riverland Communications   You are a writer employed by Riverland Communications, a public relations firm located in Spring Green, Wisconsin. Riverland has been hired to create a series of newsletters for Red Barn Theater, a local community theater company, to publicize upcoming plays. Each newsletter should include the following three articles: a description of the play, information about the lead actor, and a biographical sketch of the playwright. It's your job to create a template that any writer at Riverland Communications can use to create these newsletters.

1. Create a sketch of the newsletter on paper. Plan to include a WordArt heading with the name of the theater company (Red Barn Theater). It should also include a sub-heading for the name of the current play. Plan to format the newsletter with multiple columns. Use varying widths if appropriate. Plan to include at least one shape with text. The Buildings folder in the Office Collections Clipart folder includes a clip art image of a barn and silo, which you could use as the logo for Red Barn Theater. Include any other newsletter features you want, such as drop caps, lines between columns, and a border.

2. Create a document and save it as a macro-enabled template named **Theater** in the Tutorial.08\Case4 folder.

3. Create the structure of the newsletter according to the plan you created in Step 1. Where appropriate, insert placeholder headings. Insert temporary text below the headings so you can see how the columns will look when filled with text. To insert temporary text (also known as random text), move the insertion point to a new paragraph, type **=rand()** and then press the Enter key.

4. Format the newsletter template and add any elements you planned in Step 1. Remember to include at least one shape with text as a decorative element and at least one piece of clip art.

5. Use fields to customize parts of the newsletter. For example, you might want to use Date and Fill-in fields. Keep in mind that the letter should have enough placeholder text and enough prompts so that you can use your document template to create a newsletter for any play staged by Red Barn Theater.

6. As part of the document template, create at least one macro. For example, create an AutoNew macro to move the insertion point to a certain location within the document when the document is first created, or record a macro that resizes a picture or clip art.

7. Create at least two Quick Parts that you save in the template. For example, one might be a Quick Part for the name of the company director, Milo Levetan, and for the name of the theater company, Red Barn Theater.

8. Close the **Theater** template, and then start a new document based on the **Theater** template. Save the document as a macro-enabled document named **Sample Newsletter** in the Tutorial.08\Case4 folder included with your Data Files.

9. Search the Internet for information on a play and then use the template to create a newsletter introducing Red Barn Theater's staging of that play. Based on your research, write the articles about the play and the playwright. Pick any famous actor as the lead actor, and then, doing more Internet research as necessary, write the article about the lead actor.

10. Save the completed newsletter, preview it, and print it.

11. Submit your documents to your instructor in electronic or printed form, as requested.

Research | **Internet Assignments**

Go to the Web to find information you can use to create documents.

The purpose of the Internet Assignments is to challenge you to find information on the Internet that you can use to work effectively with this software. The actual assignments are updated and maintained on the Course Technology Web site. Log on to the Internet and use your Web browser to go to the Student Online Companion for New Perspectives Office 2007 at **www.course.com/np/office2007**. Then navigate to the Internet Assignments for this tutorial.

Assess | **SAM Assessment and Training**

If you have a SAM user profile, you may have access to hands-on instruction, practice, and assessment of the skills covered in this tutorial. Log in to your SAM account (**http://sam2007.course.com**) to launch any assigned training activities or exams that relate to the skills covered in this tutorial.

Review | **Quick Check Answers**

Session 8.1

1. a file that you can use repeatedly to ensure all documents based on it contain the same text, graphics, and formatting, and therefore have a similar look and feel; examples are letters, reports, memos, invoices, contracts
2. text and graphics that are used repeatedly; templates can contain boilerplate text or graphics that should appear in every document based on the template
3. consistency, accuracy, efficiency
4. Create a normal Word document, customize or modify Quick Styles, themes, and shortcut keys, add fields, create macros, and then save as a Word Template.
5. Right-click the shape, click Add Text, and then start typing. (For callouts, simply click in the shape and start typing.)
6. Format text as desired, select the text, on the Home tab in the Styles group, right-click the Quick Style whose definition you want to change, and then click Update <style name> to Match Selection.
7. a graphic that appears behind or in front of existing text on the printed pages of a document

Session 8.2

1. frequently used text or graphics saved in a template that you can insert in a document with a few mouse clicks
2. open the Building Blocks Organizer dialog box by clicking the Insert tab, in the Text group, clicking the Quick Parts button, and then clicking Building Blocks Organizer
3. a word or phrase that the AutoCorrect feature does not automatically correct even if it fits one of the AutoCorrect rules
4. text copied from the document set off in a formatted text box
5. To access document properties, click the Office Button, point to Prepare, and then click Properties; to see advanced properties, click the Document Properties button, click Advanced Properties, and then click the Summary or Custom tab.

6. Select the field, and then press the F9 key, or right-click the field, and then click Update Field.

7. braces (also called French brackets or curly brackets)

Session 8.3

1. Word Options

2. a recording of keystroke or mouse operations that you can perform by pressing fewer key combinations or mouse operations

3. speed, accuracy, consistency

4. Start recording using the Macros button on the View tab, the Start Recording button on the Developer tab, or the Start Recording button on the status bar, give the macro a name and a description, optionally assign it to a keyboard or toolbar, record the keystrokes and mouse operations, and then click the Stop Recording button.

5. You would edit a macro if you've typed the wrong text or performed the wrong keyboard or mouse operations. Click the name of the macro in the Macro dialog box, click Edit, change the macro, and then return to the document.

6. macros that run automatically with certain Word events

7. An AutoNew macro might be used to perform some operation automatically when a new document is opened based on that template.

8. Open the Macros dialog box, click MyMacro, and then click the Run button.

Ending Data Files

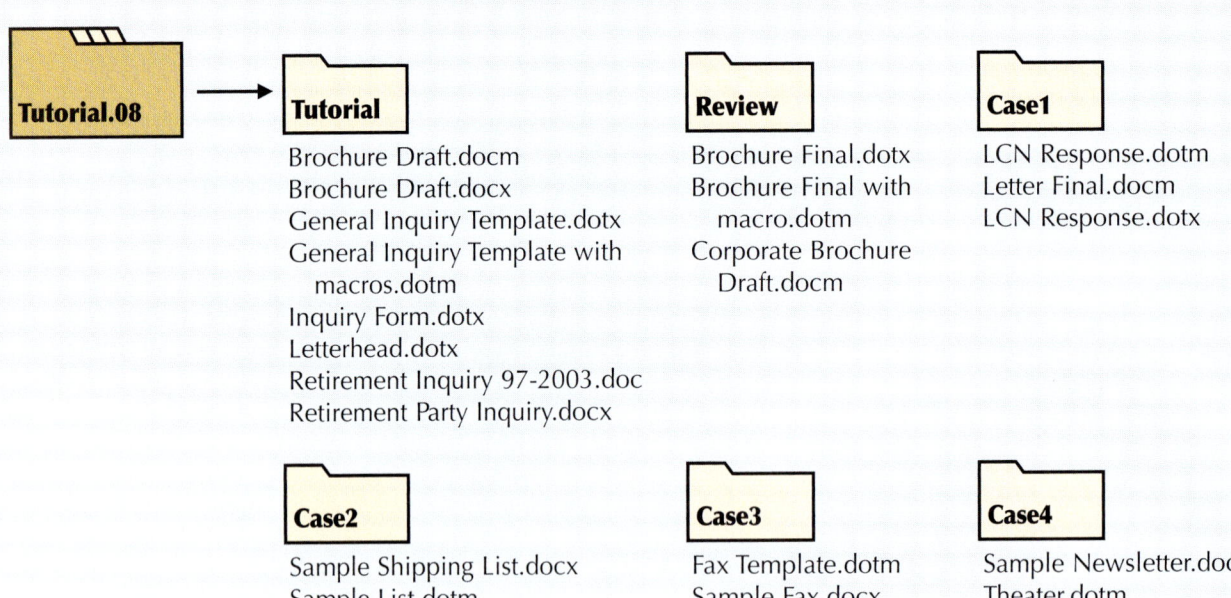

Tutorial.08 → **Tutorial**

Brochure Draft.docm
Brochure Draft.docx
General Inquiry Template.dotx
General Inquiry Template with
   macros.dotm
Inquiry Form.dotx
Letterhead.dotx
Retirement Inquiry 97-2003.doc
Retirement Party Inquiry.docx

Review

Brochure Final.dotx
Brochure Final with
   macro.dotm
Corporate Brochure
   Draft.docm

Case1

LCN Response.dotm
Letter Final.docm
LCN Response.dotx

Case2

Sample Shipping List.docx
Sample List.dotm

Case3

Fax Template.dotm
Sample Fax.docx

Case4

Sample Newsletter.docm
Theater.dotm

Creating On-Screen Forms Using Advanced Table Techniques

Developing an Order Form

Case | Scarborough Kung Fu Studios

Peter Dietz is the owner of Scarborough Kung Fu Studios in Scarborough, Maine. He teaches Kung Fu classes to children and teens. He opened his doors four years ago, and the business has grown from five classes a week to over 30 classes per week. He realized recently that his staff was spending quite a bit of time entering data for new students when they sign up for classes, so he decided to set up a computer on which new students or their parents could enter their own information in an online form.

Pete knows you are proficient in Word, so he asks you to create an on-screen registration form based on his design. Pete would like the customers to fill out the form, and then an employee can save a copy for the studio's records.

In this tutorial, you'll create and then test an on-screen registration form. You'll start with a partially completed form, which is a Word table that Pete created. First, you'll modify the structure and the format of the table. Next, you'll create different types of content controls and special fields to accept certain types of information, and you'll add placeholder text to help the user fill out the form. You'll add a formula to the table and use form fields to perform a calculation. When the form is complete, you'll add a password to protect the form from being changed accidentally, and then you'll test the form by completing a sample registration. Finally, you'll explore how Pete can fax or e-mail the form rather than printing it.

arting Data Files

Tutorial	Review	Case1	Case2	Case3	Case4
Child.jpg	AppForm.docx	NewStudent.docx	Dog.jpg	Landscaping.docx	Dance.dotx
RegForm.docx	Teen.jpg	Toddler.jpg			Dancer.jpg

torial.09

Session 9.1

Planning the Document

The on-screen registration form you'll create for Pete will consist of a Word table, formatted to be attractive and easy to read. The table will contain contact information for the family, the parent or guardian's credit card information, as well as other information required to register the child (such as the child's date of birth). The form will allow new students to enter the following information:

- **Photo:** A photo of the child taken during the registration process
- **Contact information for the child and the parent or guardian:** Name, address, phone numbers, and e-mail address
- **Child's date of birth:** Will be entered using a calendar the user can click
- **Credit card information:** Account type, card number, expiration date, and name on card
- **Note whether the child needs a uniform:** A simple yes or no question
- **Studio information:** The class the child will be placed in, the cost of the class, and the cost for an 8-week session

   As you work on the form, keep in mind that your goal is to make the form easy to use. The form should contain clear directions, and it should be easy to read and understand. The people who will be filling in the form are referred to as the users.

Creating and Using On-Screen Forms

An **on-screen form** is a Word template that contains places where the user enters information at a computer. You already have some experience working with Word templates, which are files that contain fixed text, graphics, and formatting and that make it easy to create a series of documents with a similar look and feel. When you create an on-screen form, you create a template file rather than a regular Word file so that users can't change the form itself when entering their information. In addition to the usual template elements (text, graphics, theme, styles, and placeholder text), an on-screen form template can contain content controls that you create. Recall that a content control is a space that stores a certain type of information, such as a name or a price. When a content control is linked to information in a document, that information is inserted by Word wherever that control appears in a document. Content controls in a form are areas that can contain only the type of information that you specify. You can also specify a format for the information stored in a control and create rules that govern what kind of information the control will accept. For example, Figure 9-1 shows a form with different types of information, including text, a date, and a value selected from a list.

| Figure 9-1 | Portion of an on-screen form |

Customer·Info¤		Credit·Card·Information¤	
Name:¤	John·Smith¤	**Account·Type:¤**	Visa¤
Address:¤	555·Main·St·¤	**Card·No.:¤**	555000011112222¤
City:¤	Chicago¤	**Expiration·Date:¤**	08/13¤
State:¤	IL¤	**Name·on·Card:¤**	John·T·Smith¤
Zip·Code:¤	60609¤	**Order·Date:¤**	May·25,·2010¤
Phone:¤	(xxx)·555-1234¤	☐·Ship¤	☒·Pick·Up¤

The fact that you can specify the type of information that can appear in a control and thereby allow only certain types of data helps prevent users from entering incorrect information. Placeholder text in each control tells the user what information is required for that particular part of the form.

Designing an On-Screen Form

Figure 9-2 shows Pete's design for the on-screen form.

Sketch of the structure of an on-screen form ◄ **Figure 9-2**

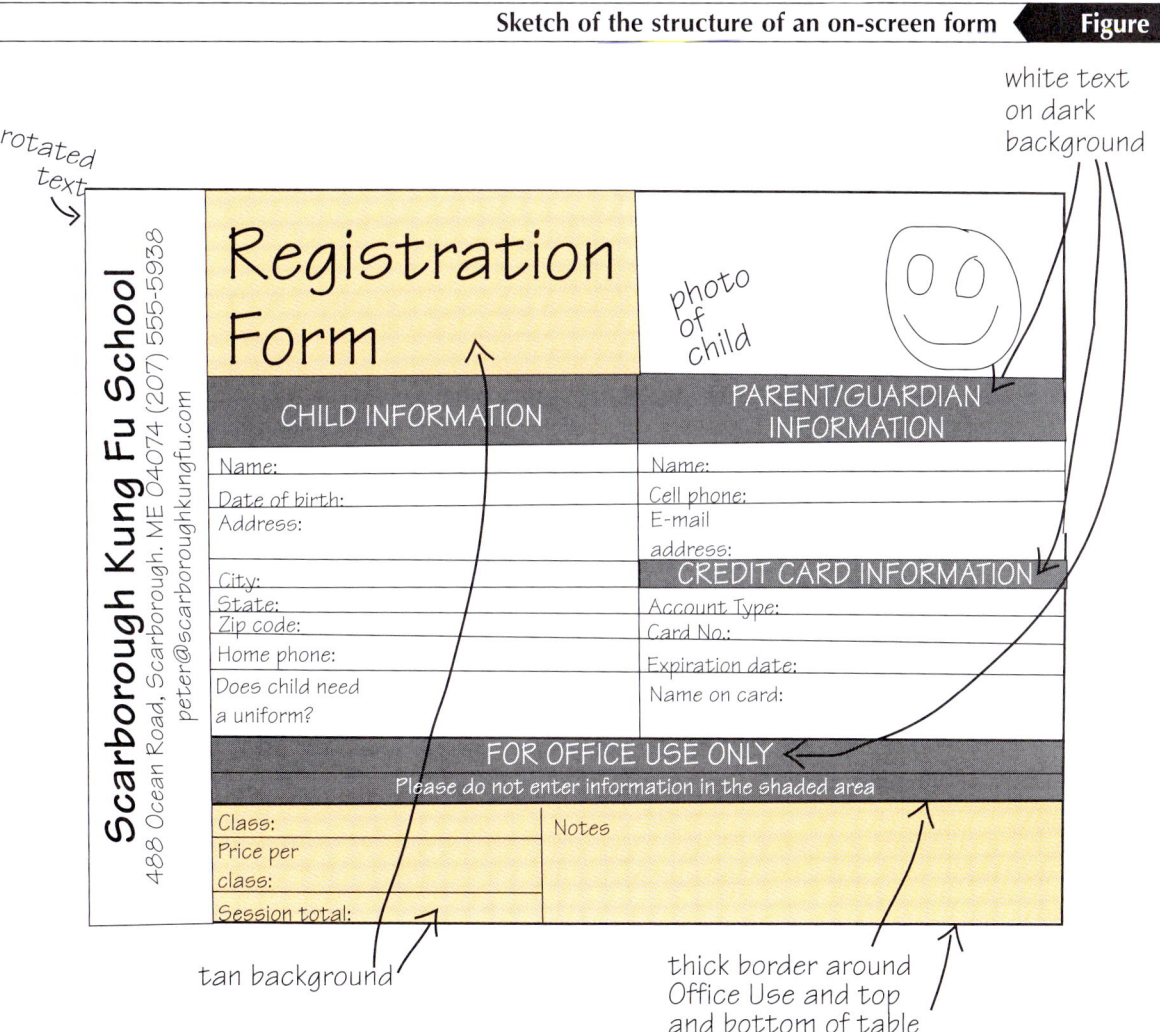

Pete designed the registration form as a table with the following features:

- The table uses two fonts (Verdana and Arial Rounded MT Bold), two font styles (normal and bold), two font colors (black and white), and rotated text.
- The table has border lines of different weights (½ point and 2¼ points), cells of different shading (none or white, tan, and dark gray), and cells with different types of contents (text, content controls, and fields).
- The table has cells of different heights and widths.

When designing an on-screen form, you don't need all of the features shown in Figure 9-2. In fact, you don't even need to use a table; you can insert controls into regular text. This flexibility means you can design nearly any type of on-screen form. For example, you might create a business contract with fields for entries such as payment terms and contract length. Using a table, however, helps you define the structure of the form, and it allows you to keep labels and the content controls next to each other.

Referencing Table Cells

When you work with a table, you need to be able to refer to specific cells in the table. Cells in a table are referenced by a letter that corresponds to the column and a number that corresponds to the row. The first column is column A, the second column B, and so on; likewise, the first row is row 1, the second is row 2, and so on. The cell in the first column and first row is cell A1, the cell in the first column second row is cell A2, and the cell in the second column, first row is cell B1. The importance of referencing cells in this manner will become clearer later in this tutorial when you learn how to insert a formula in a cell.

Modifying the Form Table

Pete already began creating the table for the on-screen form. You'll open his document, save it as a template, and then modify the table to include the features shown in Figure 9-2.

To open the document and save it as a template:

▶ **1.** Open the file **RegForm** located in the Tutorial.09\Tutorial folder included with your Data Files.

▶ **2.** Save the file as a Word template in the Tutorial.09\Tutorial folder, using the filename **Registration Form**. You will not be including any macros in this template.

   Trouble? Remember that to save a document as a template, you click the Office Button, point to Save As, and then click Word Template.

▶ **3.** Make sure the rulers and nonprinting characters are visible, that Word is in Print Layout view, and that your zoom is set to Page width.

Pete's table already has the necessary text for the registration form. Your first task is to format the table's font and font style in the first row in the table.

Changing Fonts, Font Sizes, and Font Effects

Pete wants to make the text in the top row of the table stand out. You'll do this by changing the font, font size, and styles.

To change the font of the headings in the table:

▶ **1.** Select **row 1** in the table. Recall that you can select a row by clicking ⚞ in the margin to the left of the row.

▶ **2.** In the Font group on the Home tab, click the **Font** arrow, and then click **Arial Rounded MT Bold**. The font of the selected text in the first row is changed. Next, you will change the style of text in cell A2.

▶ **3.** Select the text in cell **A2** ("Registration Form"), and then, in the Font group, click the **Dialog Box Launcher**. The Font dialog box opens.

4. In the Font style list, click **Bold**, scroll down the Size list and click **28**, and then, in the Effects section, click the **Engrave** check box. Notice that the preview at the bottom of the dialog box changes to reflect your choices.

5. Click the **OK** button, and then deselect the text. The Engrave effect sets the letters in white with a gray-shaded edge. Later you'll fill the cell with a gray background to make these letters stand out.

6. In cell A1, select the phrase **Scarborough Kung Fu School**, change the font size to **18** points, change the font size of the address, phone number, and e-mail address to **10** points, and then deselect the text. See Figure 9-3.

Tip

You can click the Underline style arrow in the Font dialog box to select from among 17 underline styles.

Form with modified fonts ◄ **Figure 9-3**

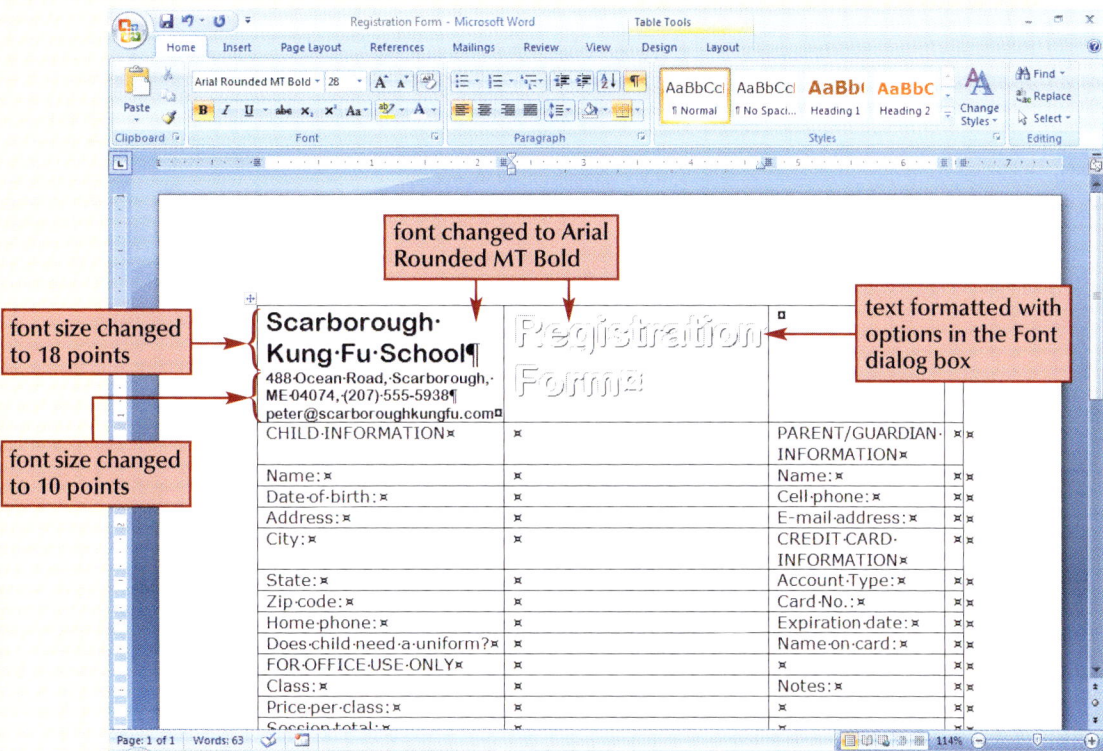

Later you'll make additional font and font style changes. For now, you need to insert a new column on the left side of the table for the company name. To do this the way Pete indicated in his sketch in Figure 9-2, you need to merge the cells of the new column.

Merging Cells

When you **merge** cells, you join two or more adjacent cells into one cell. You can merge cells in the same row, the same column, or the same rectangular block of rows and columns.

Merging Cells	**Reference Window**

- Select two or more adjacent cells in the same row, the same column, or in a rectangular block.
- Click the Table Tools Layout tab, and then, in the Merge group, click the Merge Cells button. *Or* click the Table Tools Design tab, then in the Draw Borders group, click the Eraser button, and then click or drag the Eraser pointer across the appropriate gridlines.

Pete wants you to insert a new column as the first column in the table, merge all the cells in it so it is one tall cell, and then move the studio name and address into that new cell. He also wants to merge cells that hold the headings of the form so they more clearly label the sections of the table. You'll do the first merge using the Merge Cells button, the second merge using the Table Eraser, and you'll choose the method for the rest of the merges.

To insert a new column and merge cells in the table:

▶ 1. Click anywhere in cell **A1**, click the **Table Tools Layout** tab, and then, in the Rows & Columns group, click the **Insert Left** button. A blank column is inserted to the left of the current cell, and all the cells of the new column are selected. The cell that contains the name and address of the company is now cell B1. Now you will merge all the cells in the new column A.

▶ 2. In the Merge group, click the **Merge Cells** button. The new column is now one cell—cell A1. See Figure 9-4.

| Figure 9-4 | Column merged into one cell |

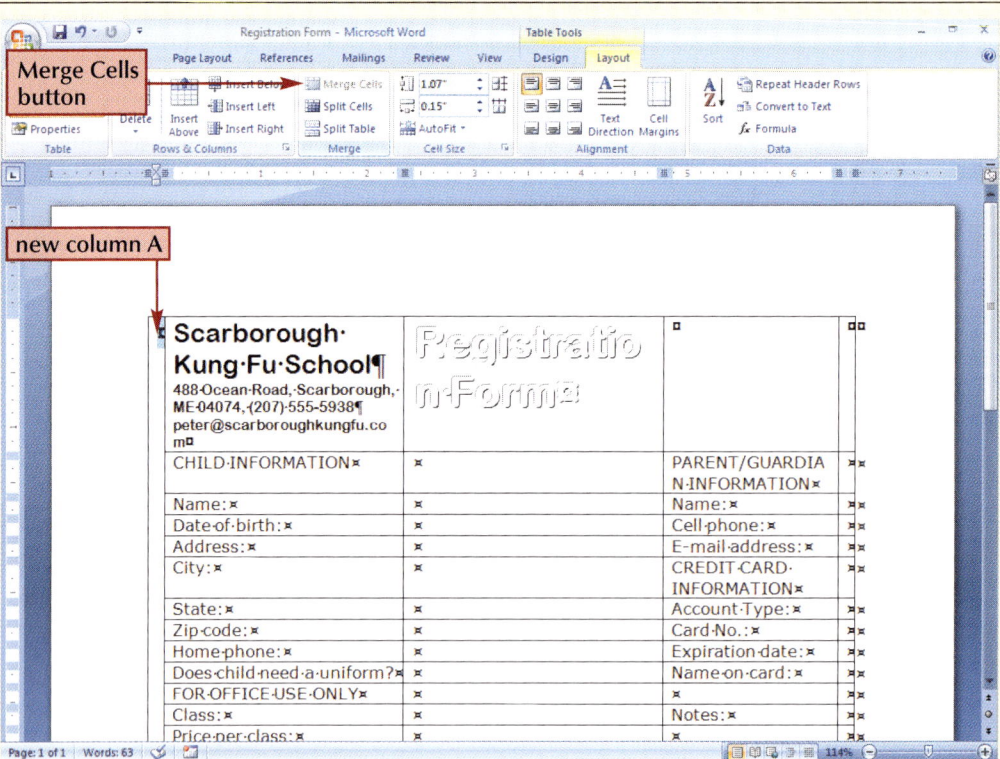

Next, you need to move the address information from cell B1 to the new cell A1.

▶ 3. Select all the text in cell B1, and then drag it to the new cell A1. Now you'll use the Eraser tool to merge cells.

▶ 4. Click the **Table Tools Design** tab. The commands on the Design tab appear on the Ribbon.

▶ 5. In the Draw Borders group, click the **Eraser** button, and then move the pointer on top of the document. When you move the pointer on top of the document, it changes to ✐. You can click a gridline or drag over several gridlines to merge cells.

6. Click the border between cells B1 and C1 (the first blank cell in the top row and the cell containing "Registration Form"). The cells merge into one cell. You also need to merge the last two cells in row 1 in preparation for inserting a photo of the child registering.

7. Click the border between cells **D1** and **E1**, and then, in the Draw Borders group, click the **Eraser** button to deselect it. Next, you'll merge cells to create section headings in the form.

8. Using either the Merge Cells button or the Eraser tool, merge cells **B2** and **C2** (the cell containing "CHILD INFORMATION" and the blank cell to its right), cells **D2** and **E2** (the cell containing "PARENT/GUARDIAN INFORMATION" and the blank cell to its right), cells **D6** and **E6** (the cell containing "CREDIT CARD INFORMATION" and the blank cell to its right), and cells **E12** through **E14** (the cell to the right of "Notes" and the cells beneath it), and then deselect the cells. See Figure 9-5.

Merged cells in table ◄ **Figure 9-5**

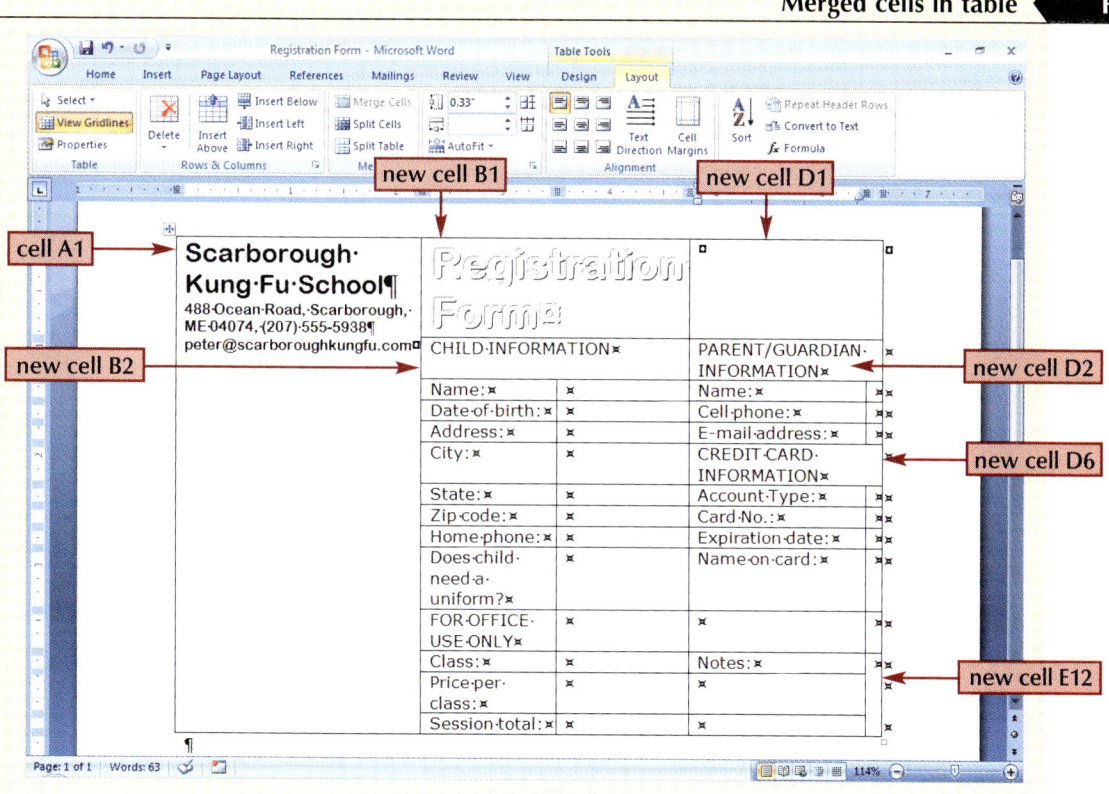

9. Save the template.

As you can see, by merging cells you can create cells that span more than one column and use them to enter headings. Merging cells is especially useful when you need to enter large amounts of information into a single cell. When you merge cells, the cell references change to reflect the removal of a cell or cells. A merged cell is referenced by the first column and the first row it is in. So the cell that contains "Registration Form" is cell B1, and the cell to the right of "Notes" is cell E12.

Splitting Cells

Just as you can merge cells, you can also split cells. When you **split** cells, you divide one cell into two or more cells. You can split cells vertically (to increase the number of columns in a row) or horizontally (to increase the number of rows in a column). You can also select multiple adjacent cells, and when you split them, you can specify whether you want them merged into one cell before the split, or whether you want each cell split.

Reference Window | **Splitting Cells**

- Select the cell or cells that you want to split.
- Click the Table Tools Layout tab, and then, in the Merge group, click the Split Cells button.
- In the Split Cells dialog box, set the number of columns and rows into which you want to split the current cell or cells.
- If you selected multiple cells, check the Merge cells before split check box if you want the cell contents to merge into one cell before they split into more columns or rows; or uncheck the Merge cells before split check box if you want the cell contents to split into columns and rows without merging first.
- Click the OK button.
or
- Click the Table Tools Design tab. In the Draw Borders group, click the Draw Table button, and then drag the Draw Table pointer to draw a new vertical or horizontal gridline.

In Pete's sketch, he indicated that he wants a row under the row containing "FOR OFFICE USE ONLY," but this row is not included in the table he created. You'll use the Split Cells button to merge the cells in row 11 into one cell and then split row 11 into two rows.

To split the "FOR OFFICE USE ONLY" cell into two rows:

▶ **1.** Select cells **B11** through **E11** (the cell containing "FOR OFFICE USE ONLY" and the three blank cells to the right of it), click the **Table Tools Layout** tab if necessary, and then, in the Merge group, click the **Split Cells** button. The Split Cells dialog box opens. See Figure 9-6.

Figure 9-6 ▶ **Split Cells dialog box**

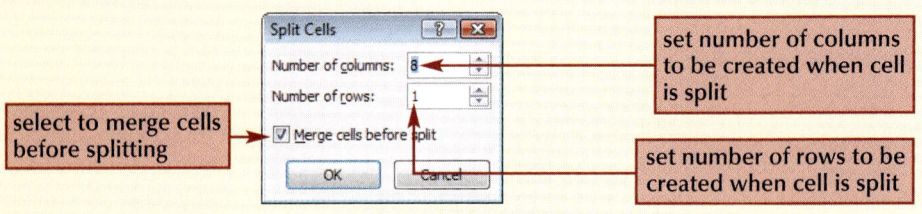

set number of columns to be created when cell is split

select to merge cells before splitting

set number of rows to be created when cell is split

2. Set the number of columns to **1** and the number of rows to **2**, and then make sure that the **Merge cells before split** check box is selected. Selecting this check box will merge these cells before splitting them into two rows.

3. Click the **OK** button. Cells B11 through E11 merge and then split into two rows to become cells B11 and B12. Now that you have split the cell, Word renumbers all the rows below the new one, so what was row 12 now becomes row 13; what was row 13 now becomes row 14; and so forth.

4. Click in cell **B12**, change the font size to **10**, and then type **Please do not enter information in the shaded area.** You'll add the shading later in the tutorial.

5. Save the template.

Tip

If you get unexpected results when you merge cells before splitting them, undo the split, and then try splitting the cells without merging them first.

Now you can turn your attention back to the text in cell A1. According to Pete's sketch, he wants it formatted so it reads from the bottom of the page up to the top. You'll do this next.

Rotating Text in a Table

Rotating text in tables allows you to fit long phrases or numbers into narrow columns. For example, if a table has many columns of 3- and 4-digit numbers, you could rotate the numbers in each cell to keep the columns narrow. Rotating the studio name and address will allow column A to be narrower and keep the text readable.

To rotate the studio name and address in cell A1:

1. Click in cell **A1**. You don't need to select any text because the command applies to all the text in the cell.

2. Click the **Table Tools Layout** tab if necessary, and then, in the Alignment group, click the **Text Direction** button. The text in cell A1 rotates so that it reads from top to bottom. Note that the icon on the Text Direction button changed to reflect this.

3. Click the **Text Direction** button again. The text in the cell and the arrows on the button change to show the text reading from bottom to top. If you clicked the button again, the text would read from left to right again. See Figure 9-7.

Figure 9-7 Table with rotated text

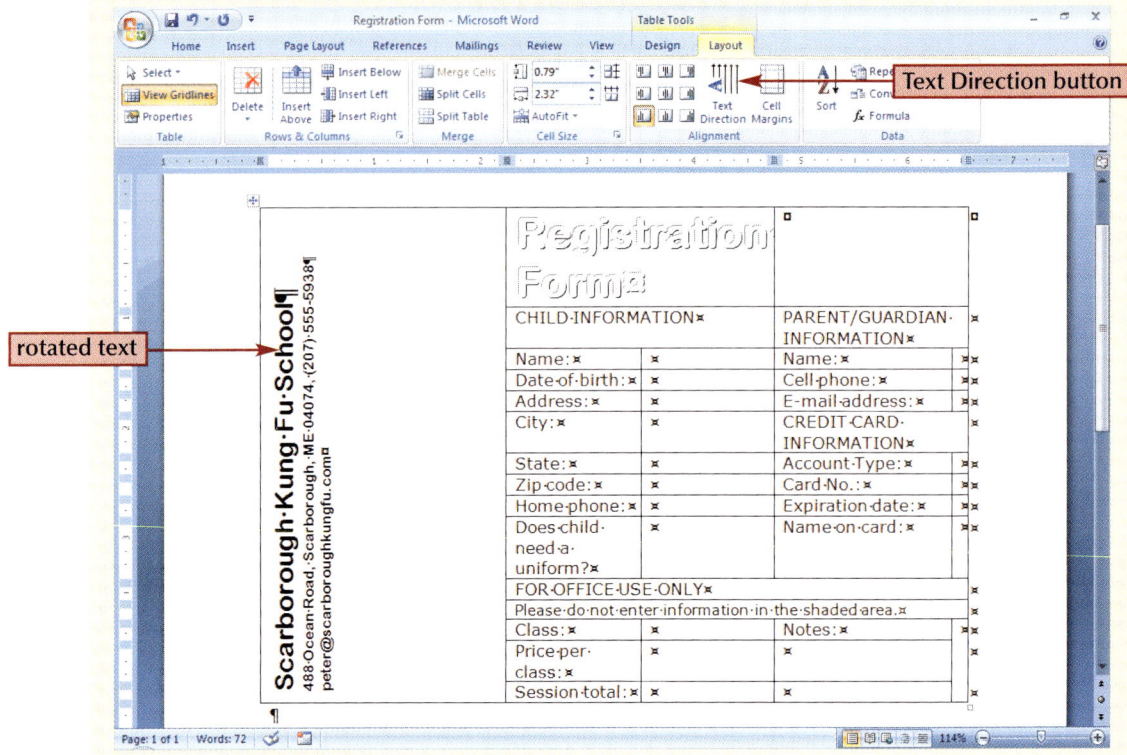

Now column A is much wider than it needs to be. You'll adjust the column widths and row heights next.

Moving Gridlines

Until now, the table columns have been automatically resizing to accommodate the widest entry in the column. For many tables, this is what you want. For this form, however, you want to control the column widths, because Word doesn't always format the columns as you would expect; for example, column A is still over two inches wide. You can specify exact column widths and row heights in the Table Properties dialog box, or you can drag the gridlines. Dragging the gridlines allows you to see the text or graphics you want to fit in your cell.

Before you can change the column widths and row heights in the table, you need to change the table property that causes the columns to automatically resize.

To turn off automatic resizing in the table's properties:

▶ 1. On the Table Tools Layout tab, in the Table group, click the **Properties** button to open the Table Properties dialog box, and then click the **Options** button. The Table Options dialog box opens. See Figure 9-8.

Table Options dialog box | Figure 9-8

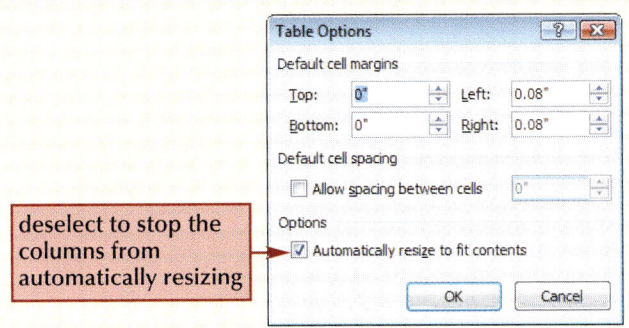

deselect to stop the columns from automatically resizing

2. Click the **Automatically resize to fit contents** check box to deselect it. This will stop the columns from automatically resizing.

3. Click the **OK** button, and then click the **OK** button in the Table Properties dialog box.

Understanding AutoFit Behavior in Tables | InSight

The default setting for tables in Word is for the columns to automatically resize as you enter text. If you want to create a table without the columns resizing, use the Insert Table dialog box to create the new table. (To open the Insert Table dialog box, click the Insert tab, then in the Tables group, click the Table button, and then click Insert Table.) After you set the number of columns and rows, you can click an option button to set the AutoFit behavior. The default is Fixed column width set to Auto. This means that the column widths will change as you enter text, but Word will allow the text to wrap in a cell so that one column does not get unreasonably wide. To set the column widths to a constant value, type the value (in inches) in the text box to the right of the Fixed column width option button. If you do not want the text to wrap in a cell and you want the columns to resize as you enter text, click the AutoFit to Contents option button. Each column will increase in width so that text does not wrap in a cell; this occurs until the table becomes wider than the page margins, and then the text in the cells will start to wrap, sometimes in unexpected ways. If you are creating a table for a Web page, select the AutoFit to Window option button. The table resizes to fit in the window in which it is being displayed.

Now you can move the table's gridlines. First you'll make column A and the cells that contain the labels narrower. It would also be helpful if the cells that will contain the user's data could be a little wider. The widths Pete wants are shown in Figure 9-9.

Figure 9-9 ▸ New column widths

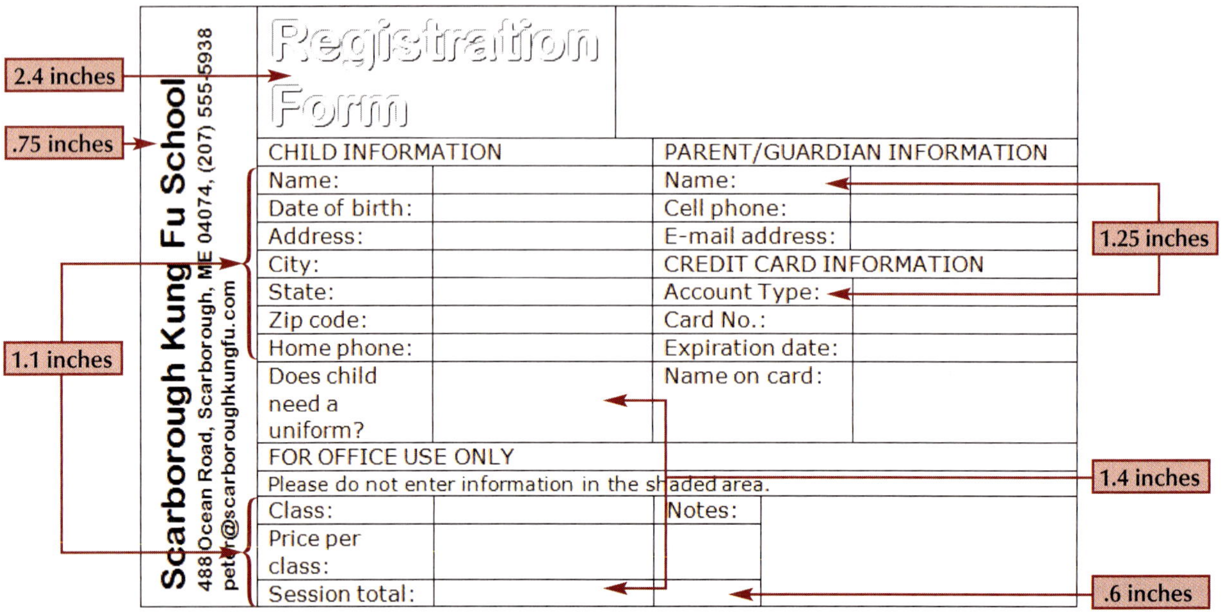

You can change the width of an individual cell or a group of cells without changing the entire column width. To do this, select the cell or cells, and then drag the gridlines to a new location.

To change the width of cells by moving gridlines:

▸ 1. Click in column **A**. On the ruler, notice that the Move Table Column marker ▦ between columns A and B is positioned approximately at the 2.25-inch mark.

▸ 2. Position the pointer over the gridline in the table between columns A and B (the right side of cell A1) so that the pointer changes to ◂‖▸ , press and hold the left mouse button, drag the gridline to the left until the Move Table Column marker ▦ is at the **.75-inch** mark on the ruler, and then release the mouse button. See Figure 9-10.

Resized column ◅ Figure 9-10

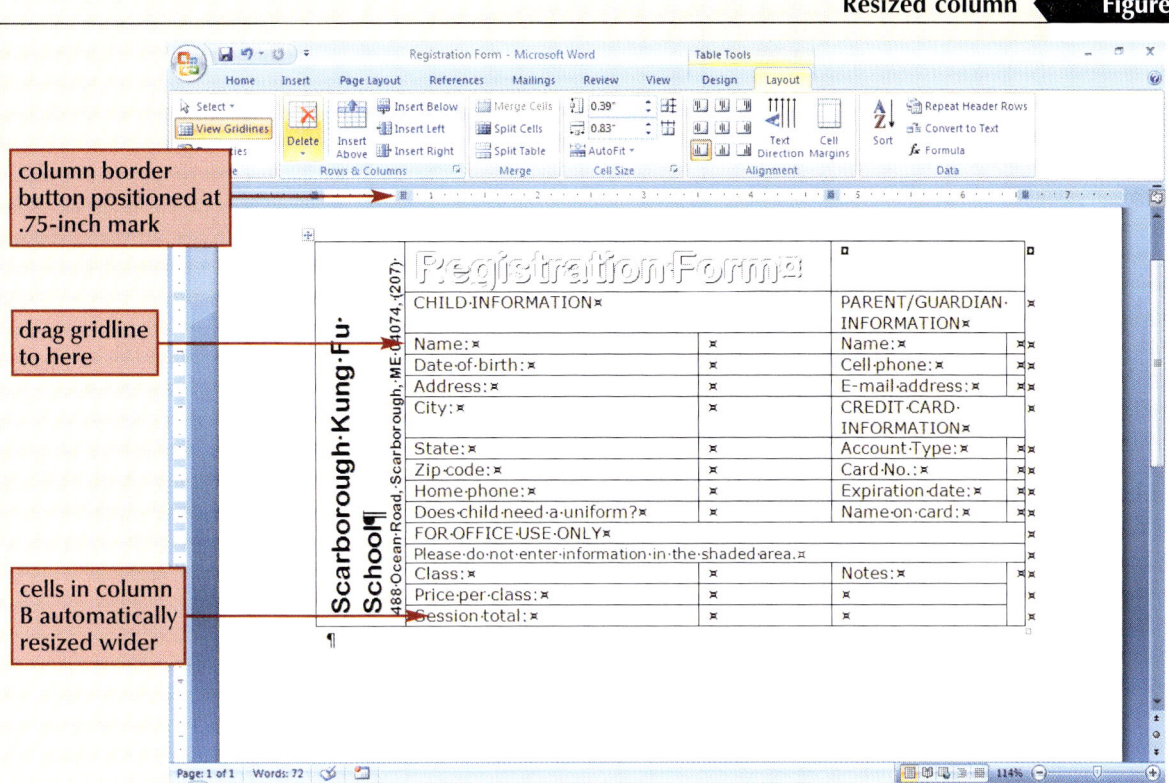

column border button positioned at .75-inch mark

drag gridline to here

cells in column B automatically resized wider

Trouble? If you dragged the Move Table Column marker on the ruler instead of dragging the gridline in the table, the whole table became narrower, not just column A. Click the Undo button ↶ , and then repeat Step 2, this time making sure that you drag the gridline in the table.

Some of the text in Column A is not visible. Don't worry about this for now. Notice that when you resized column A, the width of column B increased, but the width of the cells in column D decreased and the overall width of the table remained the same. You'll reduce the width of column B now.

▶ **3.** Select cells **B3** through **B10** (the cells below the "CHILD INFORMATION" heading), press and hold the **Alt** key, position the pointer over the gridline between columns B and C (the right side of the selected rectangle) so that it changes to ◂‖▸, and then press and hold the left mouse button. Notice that the ruler changed to indicate the exact widths of the columns. If you keep the Alt key pressed while dragging the gridlines, you can see the precise width of the selected column on the ruler.

Trouble? When you press the Alt key, the KeyTips appear on the Ribbon. You can ignore this while you are resizing the column.

▶ **4.** Using the ruler as a guide and keeping the Alt key pressed, drag the gridline left until the width of the selected cells in column B is approximately **1.1** inches, as shown in Figure 9-11.

Figure 9-11 | **Moving a gridline while pressing the Alt key**

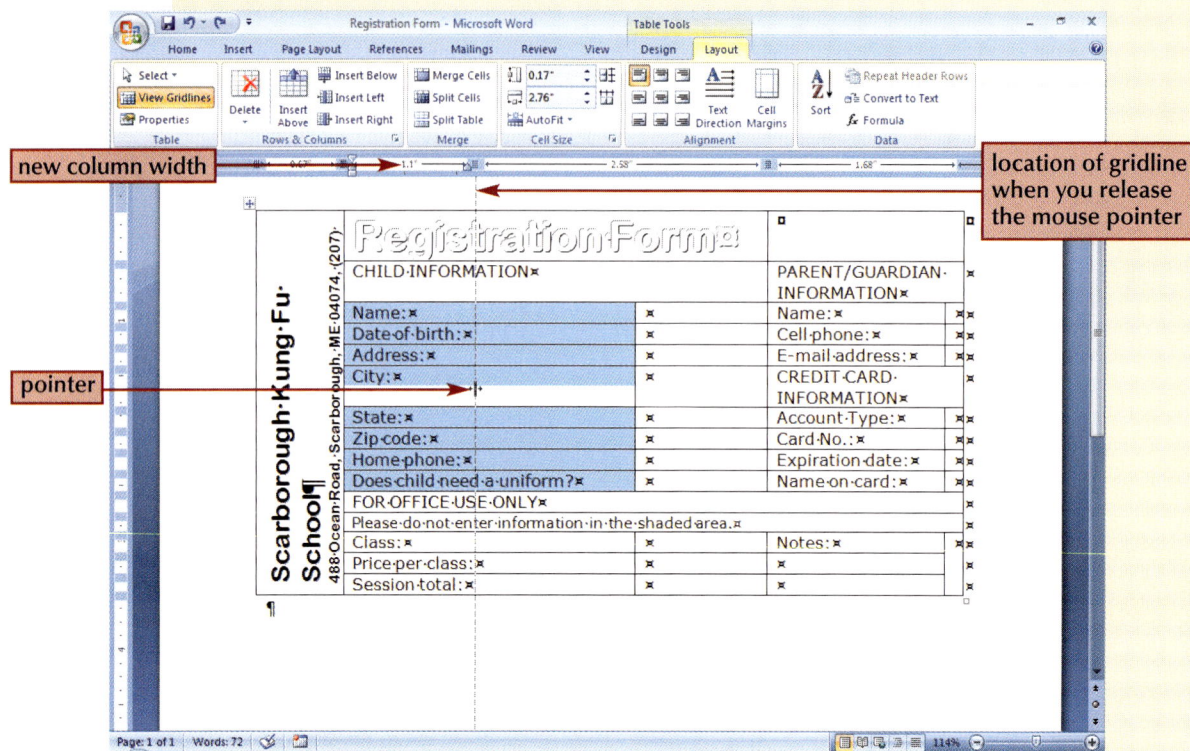

5. Release the **Alt** key and the mouse button.

6. Decrease the width of cells **B13** through **B15** (in the last three rows) to approximately **1.1** inches. Now you can resize column C. The section heading "CHILD INFORMATION" is in cell B2, but the right edge of this cell aligns with the right edge of column C. You want the section heading to remain above columns B and C, so you need to select this cell when you resize cells C3 through C10.

7. Select cell **B2** ("CHILD INFORMATION"), and then drag down in column C through **C10** (the cell to the right of "Does child need a uniform?"). Cell B2 and cells C3 through C10 are selected. See Figure 9-12.

Column C selected in table **Figure 9-12**

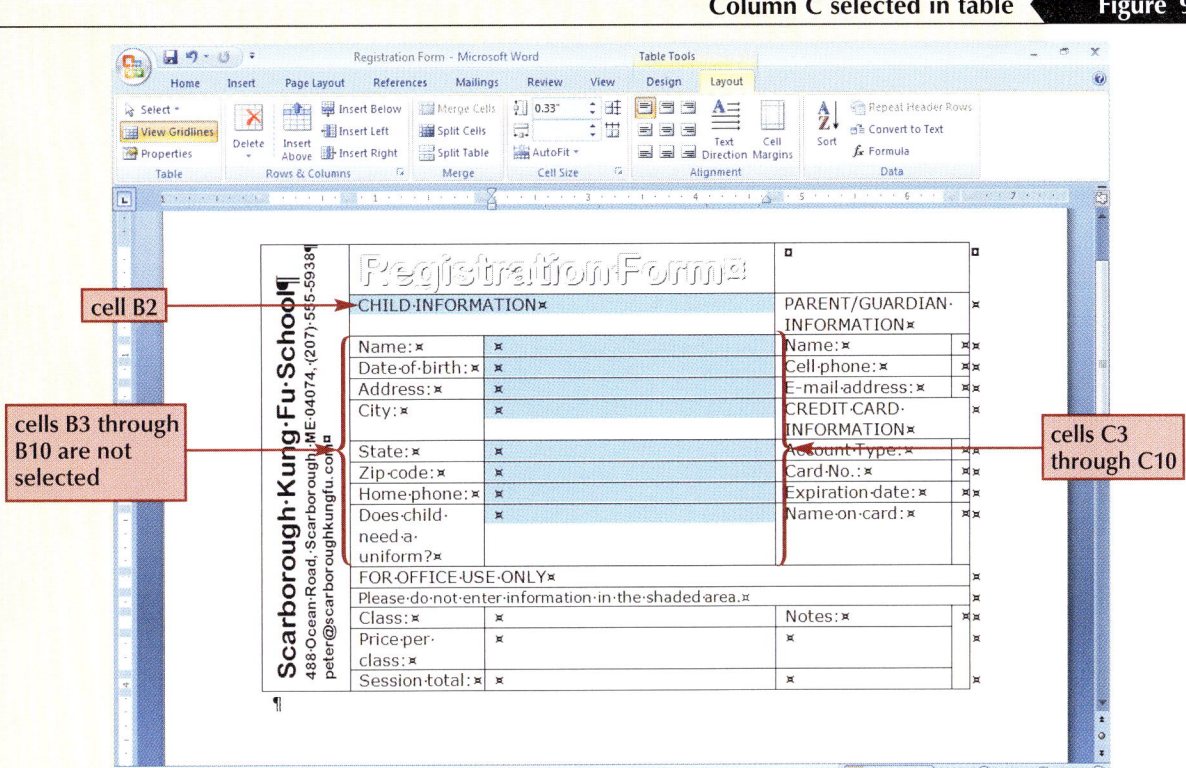

8. Press and hold the **Alt** key, and then drag the right border of the selected cells so that the selected cells in column C are approximately **1.4 inches** wide.

9. Resize cells **C13** (the cell to the right of "Class") through **C15** (the cell to the right of "Session total") to approximately **1.4 inches**.

10. Resize cells **D3** through **D5** (the cells below the "PARENT/GUARDIAN INFORMATION" heading) to approximately **1.25 inches**, and then do the same for cells **D7** through **D10** (the cells below "CREDIT CARD INFORMATION"). Now that you've resized the cells to the left of column E, the width of column E in the upper half of the table is fine. Next you need to resize the cell containing the label "Notes" and the cells below it.

11. Resize cells **D13** through **D15** (the cell containing "Notes" and the two cells beneath it) to approximately **.6** inches. Finally, you need to adjust cells B1 and D1.

12. Click in cell **B1** ("Registration Form"), then drag the gridline to the left until it is positioned to the right of the "n" in "Registration." The column should be approximately 2.4 inches wide. Compare your screen to Figure 9-13.

Figure 9-13   **Table with resized columns**

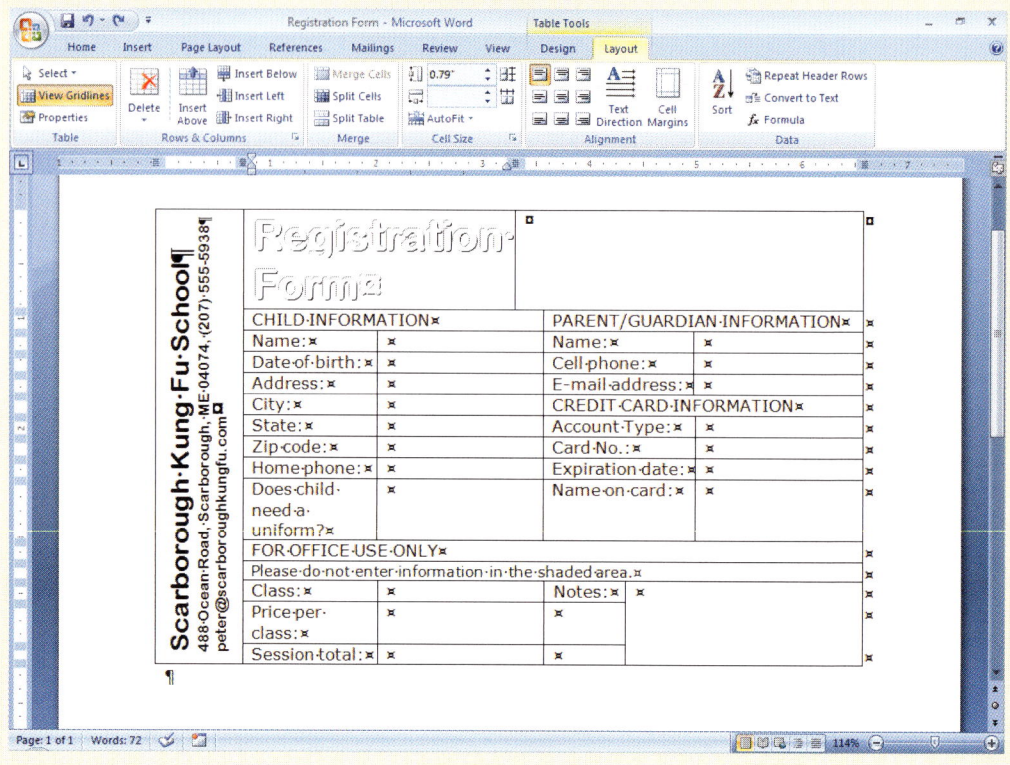

You can also adjust the height of rows. To visually separate the various sections of the form, you'll increase the height of the section headings rows (row 2 and 11).

To change the height of the section heading cells by moving the gridlines:

1. Click anywhere in the table, making sure that no text is selected, and then position the pointer over the bottom border of row **2** so that it changes to ⬍.

2. Drag the bottom border of row 2 down until the row is approximately double its original height.

3. Drag the bottom border of row 11 ("FOR OFFICE USE ONLY") down so that it is approximately double its original height. See Figure 9-14.

Rows resized in table   Figure 9-14

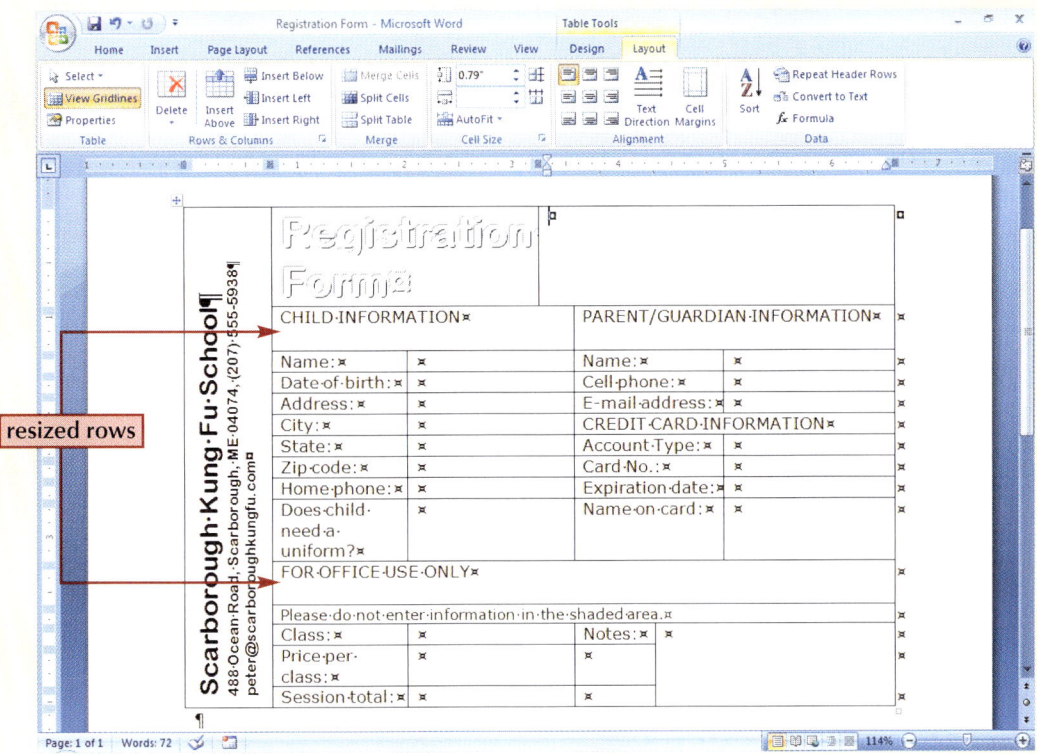

4. Save the template.

You don't want to change the row height of row 6 (containing the section heading "CREDIT CARD INFORMATION") because it is part of the Parent/Guardian Information section, and because the row also contains ordinary labels and content. Changing the height of row 6 would make the height of these cells too large.

Now that you've got the row heights and widths finalized, you can align the text within cells.

Aligning Text in Cells

The text in the cells of a table is, by default, left aligned and positioned at the top of the cell. To make the registration form more attractive and easier to read, you'll center the text for the section headings horizontally and vertically. On the Table Tools Layout tab, in the Alignment group, there are nine buttons you can use to align text in a cell. You can align text at the left and right edges of the cell, and you can center align it. You can also position the text at the top, middle, or bottom of the cell.

To center the section headings horizontally and vertically:

1. Select cells **B2** ("CHILD INFORMATION") and **D2** ("PARENT/GUARDIAN INFORMATION").

2. Click the **Table Tools Layout** tab if necessary, and then in the Alignment group, click the **Align Center** button ▤. The text is centered horizontally and vertically in the cell. See Figure 9-15.

Figure 9-15 **Text centered horizontally and vertically in cells**

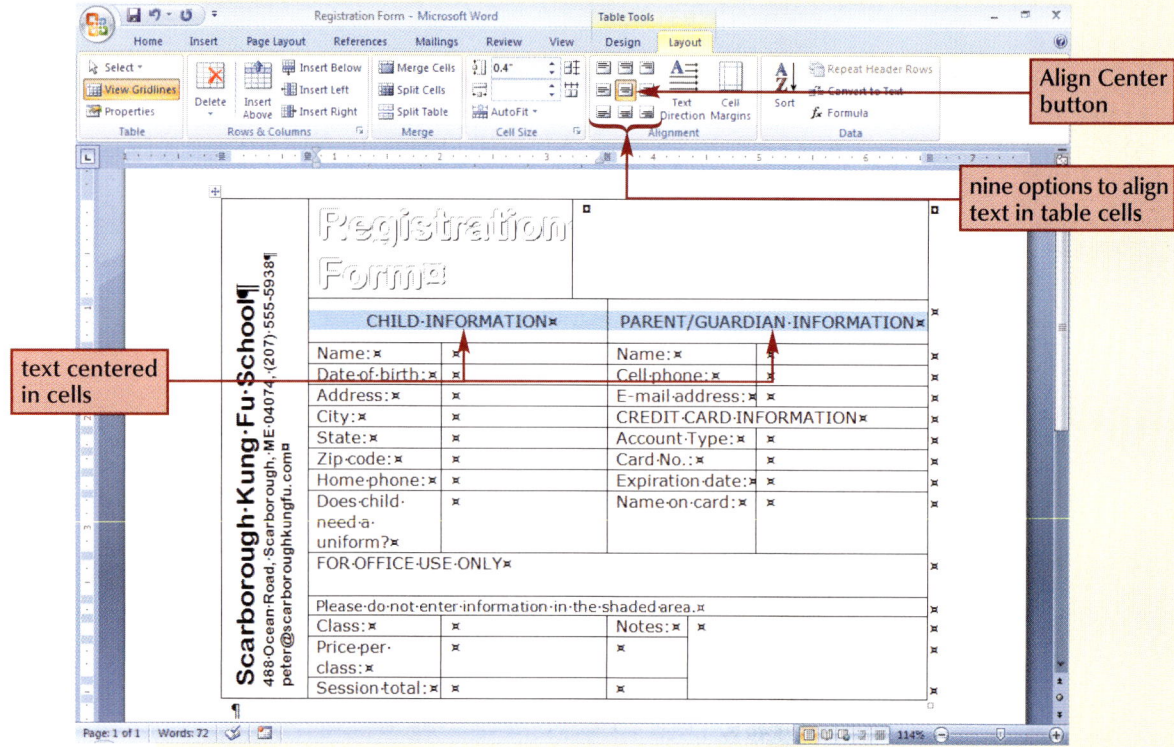

3. Format the text in cells **A1**, **B1**, **D6**, **B11**, and **B12** so the text is centered horizontally and vertically in the cells.

4. Save the template.

Next, you'll add shading to several cells to make the table more attractive and readable.

Shading Cells

Recall that the Engraved effect you applied earlier to the "Registration Form" heading in cell B1 made it a little hard to read, so you decide to add shading to it. Also, according to Pete's sketch, he wants you to add shading to the cells in the "FOR OFFICE USE ONLY" section.

To shade the "FOR OFFICE USE ONLY" cells:

1. Click cell **B1** ("Registration Form"), and then click the **Table Tools Design** tab.

2. In the Table Styles group, click the **Shading button arrow** to open the color palette, and then click the **Tan, Background 2** tile in the top row, third column from the left. Cell B1 becomes shaded with a light tan color.

3. Select cells **B11** through **D15** (the cell containing "FOR OFFICE USE ONLY" and all the cells below it except cell E13), and then, on the Quick Access Toolbar, click the **Repeat Shading Color** button. Your previous action is repeated, so the selected cells are shaded with the same light tan color.

4. Click in cell **E13** (the last cell in the table), then click 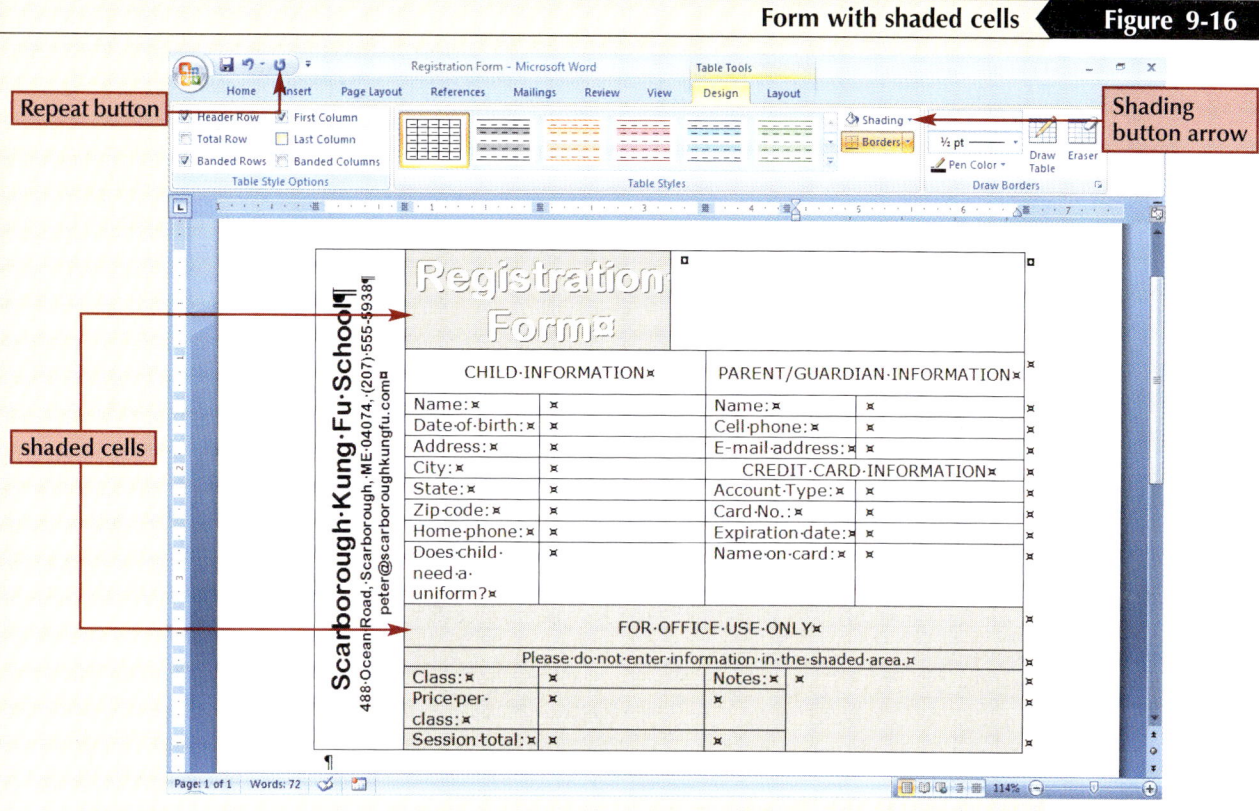 again. See Figure 9-16.

Form with shaded cells | Figure 9-16

Pete also wants the cells with the section headings to have a dark background. (Refer to Figure 9-2.) You'll shade those cells next.

Formatting Text as Reverse Type

To make the section headings stand out, Pete next wants you to shade those cells with a dark color. Shades of gray are usually measured by the amount of black mixed with white. Another way to make text stand out is to format it in reverse type. **Reverse type** (also called **dropout type** or **surprinted type**) is white text on a black background—the opposite of the usual black text on a white background. Reverse type is effective for making a line of text or a title attract the reader's eye; however, large amounts of reverse type can be difficult to read.

Creating Reverse (Light on Dark) Type in Table Cells | Reference Window

- Select the table cell or the text you want to set in reverse type.
- On the Home tab in the Paragraph group or on the Mini toolbar, click the Shading button arrow. *Or*, on the Table Tools Design tab, click the Shading button arrow.
- Click a dark-colored tile in the color palette.
- If the text is not automatically reformatted as white text, select it, and then, in the Font group on the Home tab or on the Mini toolbar, click the Font Color arrow, and then click the White (or any light color) tile.

You'll change the section headings to reverse type now.

To create reverse type for the table headings:

▶ 1. Select cells **B2** ("CHILD INFORMATION") and **D2** ("PARENT/GUARDIAN INFORMATION").

▶ 2. In the Table Styles group, click the **Shading button arrow**, and then point to—but do not click—the **Black, Text 1, Lighter 50%** tile (second row, second column under Theme Colors). The Live Preview shows the cells in the table shaded with a gray background.

▶ 3. Point to each of the next three tiles in that column, stopping at the **Black, Text 1, Lighter 15%** tile (second to last row under Theme Colors). See Figure 9-17. As you point to each tile, the live preview shows you the shading getting progressively darker. When you point to the Black, Text 1, Lighter 15% tile, the text color automatically changes from black to white. This is one way to create reverse type. But you can also format the text directly.

| Figure 9-17 | ▶ | **Using Live Preview to choose a shading color** |

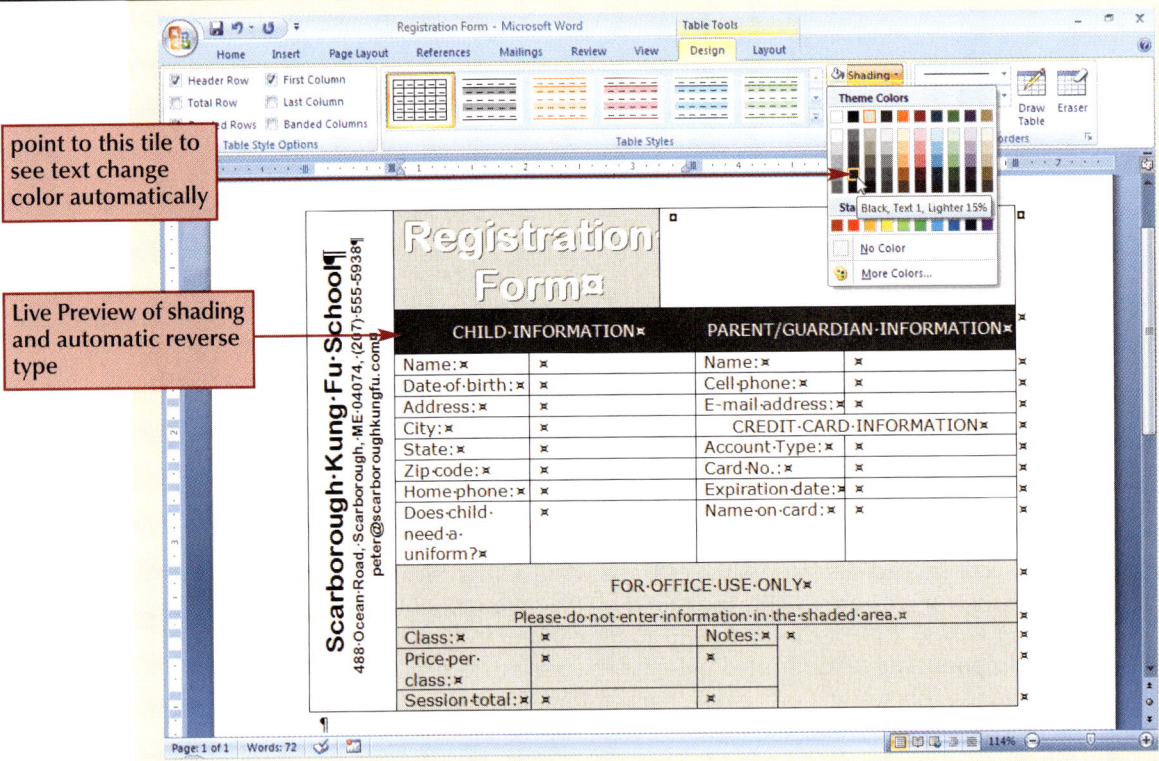

point to this tile to see text change color automatically

Live Preview of shading and automatic reverse type

▶ 4. Move back up one tile and click the **Black, Text 1, Lighter 25%** tile, and then deselect the cells. The cells are shaded with dark gray; the black text is barely visible.

▶ 5. Select the cells **B2** and **D2** again, click the **Home** tab, in the Font group click the **Font Color** arrow, click the **White, Background 1** tile (first column, first row under Theme Colors), click the **Bold** button **B**, and then deselect the cells.

▶ 6. Format cells **D6** ("CREDIT CARD INFORMATION") and cell **B11** ("FOR OFFICE USE ONLY") with **Black, Text 1, Lighter 25%** shading and **bold**, **white** text, and then format cell **B12** in the same manner but without the bold formatting.

▶ 7. Save the template.

Referring again to Pete's sketch (see Figure 9-2), you notice that there are no gridlines between the cells with labels and the cells where users enter information. You will remove the borders from between these cells next.

Drawing and Erasing Borders

As you know, gridlines are the lines that define the location and size of the rows, columns, and cells of a table. The gridlines, which define the structure of a table, do not print. You can display or hide gridlines while you are working; but even when hidden, the gridlines still define the table's structure. Table **borders**, on the other hand, are drawn lines that visually frame the table and cells. Borders do print. When you create a table, $1/2$-point borders appear along all the gridlines by default.

You'll modify Pete's table by removing the borders between the labels and empty cells next to them, to make it more attractive. You'll begin by removing the right border of cells that contain labels.

To remove borders from a group of cells using the Borders button:

▶ 1. Select cells **B3** through **B10** (the cell containing "Name" through the cell containing "Does child need a uniform?"), click the **Table Tools Design** tab if necessary, and then in the Table Styles group, click the **Borders button arrow**. The Borders menu opens. All of the border options in the Borders menu are selected except No Border and the Diagonal borders. You want to remove the right border.

   Trouble? If the Borders menu did not open, you clicked the Borders button instead of the arrow next to it. Undo the change, and then repeat Step 1.

▶ 2. Click **Right Border**. The menu closes and the right border is removed from the selected cells. Even though you removed the right border from these cells, the gridline that defines the structure of these cells is still there.

▶ 3. Verify that cells **B3** through **B10** are still selected, and then click the **Borders button arrow** again. Note that now, not only is the Right Border command deselected, but the All Borders and Outside Borders commands are deselected as well. The View Gridlines command is at the bottom of the menu.

▶ 4. If the View Gridlines command is *not* selected, click **View Gridlines**; if it *is* selected, click a blank area of the document to close the menu without making any changes.

▶ 5. Deselect the cells. The blue dotted line at the right edge of cells B3 through B10 indicates the gridline that creates the structure of these cells. See Figure 9-18.

Tip

You can also click the View Gridlines button in the Table group on the Table Tools Layout tab to display or hide gridlines.

Figure 9-18 **Form after border between columns B and C is removed**

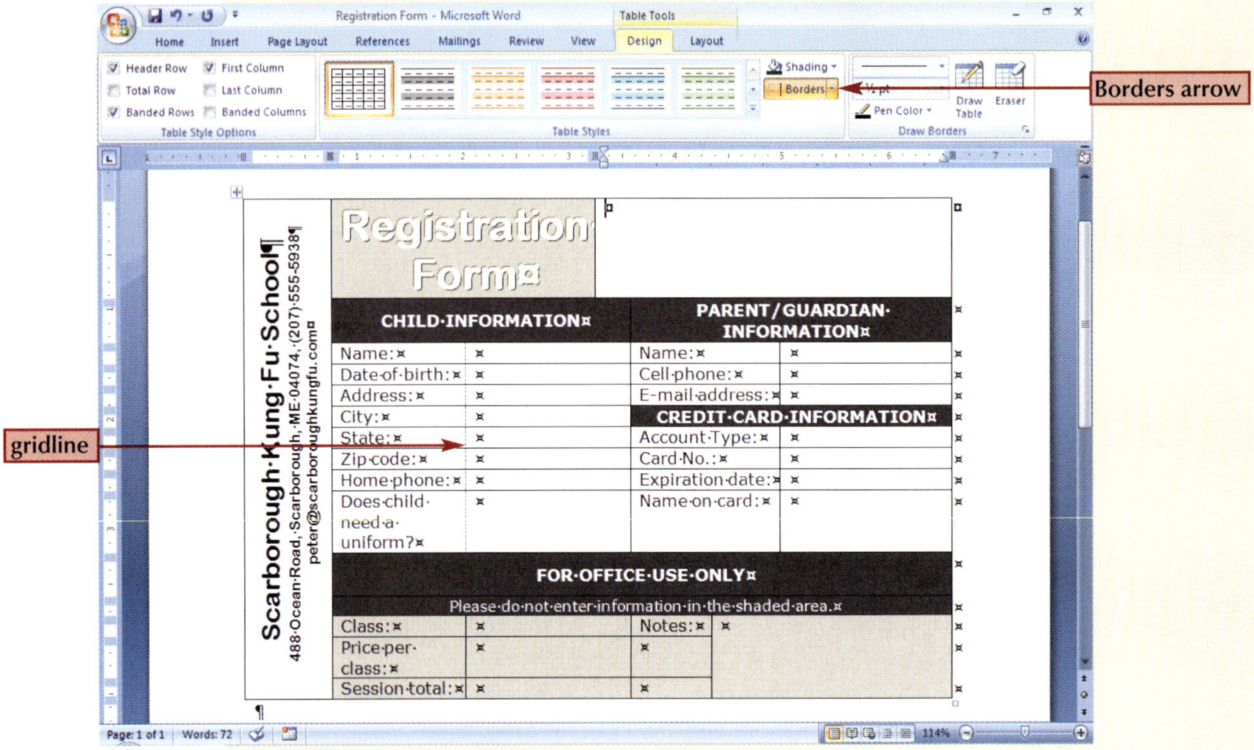

Sometimes it's hard to figure out exactly which commands on the Borders menu should be selected or deselected, so you might find it easier to use the Borders and Shading dialog box to modify or remove borders. You'll use this method for the other borders that Pete wants you to remove.

To remove borders using the Borders and Shading dialog box:

▸ 1. Select cells **D3** through **D5** (the cells under PARENT/GUARDIAN INFORMATION from "Name" through "E-mail address").

▸ 2. In the Table Styles group on the Table Tools Design tab, click the **Borders button arrow**, and then click **Borders and Shading**. The Borders and Shading dialog box opens with the Borders tab on top. See Figure 9-19. In the Apply to list box at the bottom of the Preview section, note that Cell is selected. The Preview section illustrates the borders on the selected cells.

Borders tab in the Borders and Shading dialog box ◄ Figure 9-19

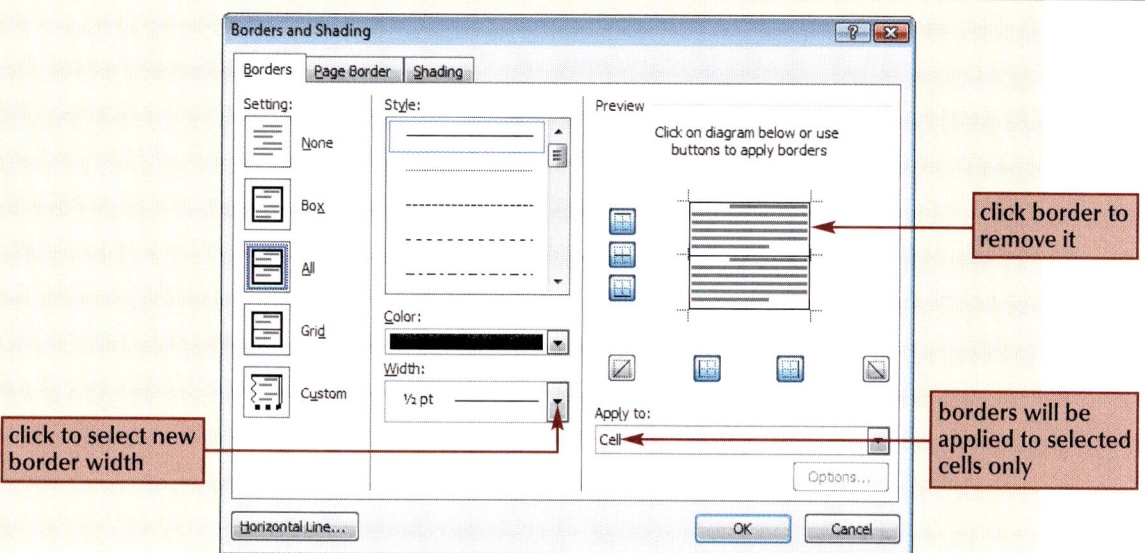

click border to remove it

click to select new border width

borders will be applied to selected cells only

3. In the Preview section, click the **right border**. The border disappears.

   Trouble? If one of the other borders disappeared instead, click that border to make it reappear, then repeat Step 3.

4. Click the **OK** button, and then click a blank area of the table to deselect the cells. The dialog box closes, and the right border of the cells you had selected is gone.

5. Remove the right border of cells **D7** through **D10** (the cells under "CREDIT CARD INFORMATION"), cells **B13** through **B15** ("Class" through "Session total"), and cells **D13** through **D15** (the last three cells in column D). Now you need to remove the bottom borders of cells D13 and D14.

6. With cells **D13** through **D15** still selected, click the **Borders button arrow**, and then click **Inside Horizontal Border**.

7. Save the template.

   Next, you'll use the Draw Table tool to draw thicker borders at the top and bottom of the table and around the Office Use area of the table.

To draw thicker borders at the top and bottom of the table and around the Office Use section:

1. On the Table Tools Design tab, in the Draw Borders group, click the **Draw Table** button to select it, and then position the pointer on the document. The pointer changes to ⬚.

2. In the Draw Borders group, click the **Line Weight button arrow** [½ pt ——— ▾], and then click **2¼ pt**. Now any borders you insert will be 2¼ points thick rather than the default ½ point.

3. Drag along the top line of the table, at the top of row 1. As you drag, make sure the line that you draw is a thick gray line, not a dotted rectangle, so that you don't insert a new row above row 1.

   Trouble? If you inserted a new row above row 1, undo the change and then try again.

> **Tip**
>
> The Borders button changes to reflect the most recent selection, so you can click it to apply the current settings to the new set of selected cells or to quickly open the Borders and Shading dialog box.

> **Tip**
>
> Remember that using the Eraser button on the Design tab merges cells because you erase the gridline. To remove a border, you can click the Line Style arrow in the Draw Borders group, click No Border, and then drag along a border to remove the border without removing the gridline.

▶ 4. In three separate operations, drag ✏ first along the bottom of cells **A15** through **E15** (at the very bottom of the table), then along the right borders of cells **E11** through **E15** (the right edge of the Office Use section), and finally along the top of cells **B11** through **E11** (the top of the Office Use section).

Trouble? If you make a mistake, undo your changes until the new border disappears, and then repeat the necessary steps to draw the borders correctly.

▶ 5. Drag along the left borders of cells **B11** through **B15**. The border all along the entire right edge of cell A1 is drawn thicker. This is because the left border of cells B11 through B15 is also the right border of the merged cell A1. You need to use the Borders and Shading dialog box to customize the left border of cells B11 through B15.

Tip

To use the Borders and Shading dialog box to place a border around cells, click Box in the Setting column on the left, click the Width arrow and select the desired width, and then click the Apply to arrow and select Cell.

▶ 6. On the Quick Access Toolbar, click the **Undo** button 🔄, click the **Draw Table** button to deselect it, and then select cells **B11** through **B15**.

Trouble? If you are having trouble selecting cells B11 through B15, make sure you drag down through column B, not column C.

▶ 7. In the Table Styles group, click the **Borders button arrow**, and then click **Borders and Shading**.

▶ 8. In the middle pane in the dialog box, click the **Width** arrow, and then click **2¼ pt**.

▶ 9. Verify that **Cell** is selected in the Apply to box below the Preview section; then, in the Preview section, click the **left border** of the box. A thick border is added.

▶ 10. Click the **OK** button, and then deselect the cells. The dialog box closes, and the thick border is added to the left of cells B11 through B15.

▶ 11. Compare your table to Figure 9-20, and then save the template.

Figure 9-20 | **Form after drawing thick borders**

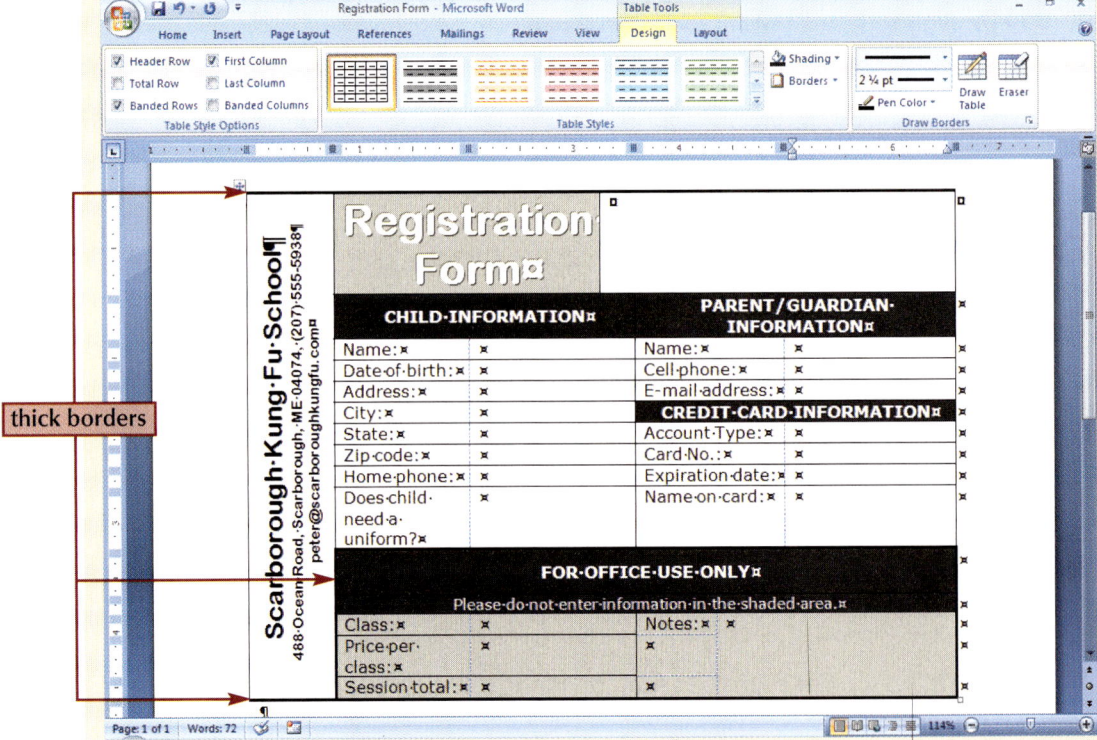

You have completed the table structure for the registration form. In the next session, you'll add content controls to the registration form.

1. What is an on-screen form?
2. What does it mean to merge cells in a table?
3. What does it mean to split cells in a table?
4. How do you rotate text in a table cell?
5. In a table, what is a border? How does it differ from a gridline?
6. How do you align text in a cell?
7. How do you add shading to a cell?
8. What is reverse type?

Session 9.2

Using Content Controls

You have formatted the Registration Form template to make it attractive and easy to read. Now you need to insert the most important elements of an on-screen form—content controls. The content controls will help users enter information into the registration form quickly and efficiently. You have used content controls when you worked with headers, footers, and cover pages. In this session, you will learn how to insert your own content controls, rather than just inserting information into content controls that are already there.

Word provides several types of content controls, as described in Figure 9-21.

Types of content controls | Figure 9-21

Type	Purpose
Rich Text	Holds text the user inserts; by default, the user can format the inserted text and enter multiple paragraphs
Text	Holds text the user inserts; the user cannot format the text, but the control can be set up to allow the user to enter multiple paragraphs
Picture	Holds a picture the user inserts
Combo Box	Holds a list of choices from which the user can pick, and allows the user to type alternate text if none of the choices is correct
Drop-Down List	Holds a list of choices from which the user must choose; the user is not allowed to type alternate text
Date Picker	Holds a calendar from which the user chooses a date
Building Block Gallery	Holds a list of Quick Parts from which the user must select; the user is not allowed to type alternate text

Each content control has properties associated with it that you specify when you insert it. For all of the content controls, you specify a title, which appears in a title tab at the top of the content control. You can also choose whether to allow the content control to be deleted and whether to allow the user to edit the contents of the control after they have entered information. Each type of content control has other properties that are specific to that control.

Inserting Text Content Controls

To allow a user to input any kind of text into a form, you insert Text or Rich Text content controls. The difference between Text and Rich Text content controls has to do with whether the user can format the text that is entered. **Rich Text content controls** allow the user to format the content he or she is entering. Usually you want the user to be able only to enter text—formatting is usually unnecessary. So for a form, you should usually use the **Text content control**.

Reference Window | **Inserting a Text or a Rich Text Content Control**

- Click the Developer tab, and then in the Controls group, click the Design Mode button.
- In the Controls group, click the Text button.
- In the Controls group, click the Properties button.
- In the Title text box, type the control title.
- If you want the text to be formatted differently than the default format, click the Use a style to format contents check box, and then click the Style arrow and select a style, or click New Style to define a new style.
- Click the Content control cannot be deleted check box to prevent users from deleting the content control.
- Click the Contents cannot be edited check box to prevent the user from changing the placeholder text.
- For a Text content control, click the Allow carriage returns (multiple paragraphs) check box to allow the user to insert more than one paragraph.
- Click the Remove content control when contents are edited check box to delete the content control and leave only the text the user inserts.
- Click the OK button.
- If desired, replace the default placeholder text with specific instructions to the user.

You need to add Text content controls to the form so the new students can enter their information. You'll insert Text content controls in the form now.

To insert a Text content control for the child's name and set the control's properties:

▶ 1. If you took a break after the previous session, open the **Registration Form** file, make sure the rulers and nonprinting characters are visible and table gridlines are displayed, that Word is in Print Layout view, and the zoom is set to Page width. The content controls are located on the Developer tab.

▶ 2. Click the **Office Button** 🔘, click the **Word Options** button, click the **Show Developer tab in the Ribbon** check box to select it, if necessary, and then click the **OK** button. The Developer tab appears on the Ribbon to the right of the View tab.

▶ 3. Move the insertion point to cell **C3** (to the right of the first "Name" cell), click the **Developer** tab, and then in the Controls group click the **Text** button [Aa]. A Text content control is inserted in cell C3. See Figure 9-22.

Text content control inserted in cell C3 | Figure 9-22

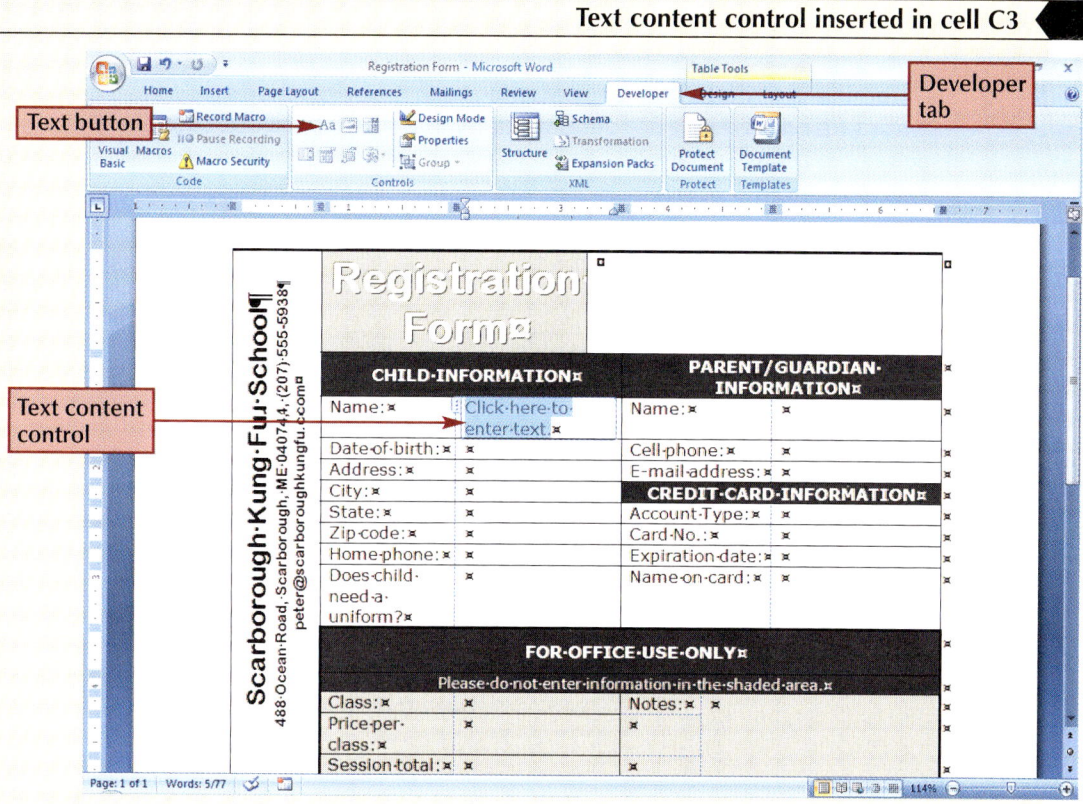

Now you can set the properties for the new Text content control.

4. In the Controls group, click the **Properties** button. The Content Control Properties dialog box opens. See Figure 9-23.

Content Control Properties dialog box | Figure 9-23

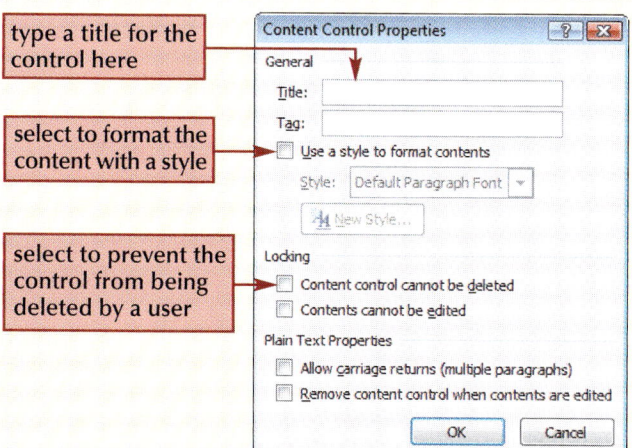

Tip

If the user will need to enter multiple paragraphs in a Text control, click the Allow carriage returns (multiple paragraphs) check box in the Content Control Properties dialog box.

5. Type **Child Name** in the Title text box. This is the text that will appear in the tab at the top of the control in the form. To make the child's name stand out, you will format it with the Strong style.

6. Click the **Use a style to format contents** check box, click the **Style** arrow, and then click **Strong**. Next, you'll set a property in the control so users won't be able to delete the content control.

7. Click the **Content control cannot be deleted** check box, and then click the **OK** button. The Content Control Properties dialog box closes and the control appears in the form. Notice that the title "Child Name" appears on the tab of the content control.

8. Click a blank area of the table to deselect the content control.

Usually, the user knows what information to enter into a control just by looking at the title. However, someone using the form for the first time might need instructions, and both new and experienced people sometimes need clarification regarding how to enter information into special controls, such as the Date Picker. To assist in answering user questions, you can customize the placeholder text to give the user specific instructions for each control.

Pete wants you to include instructions for the people who will be filling out the form. You decide to modify the placeholder text to include instructions. To change the placeholder text, you need to switch to Design mode, where you can edit content controls. If you are not in Design mode, you would enter information into the control instead of editing the control.

To change the placeholder text in the Child Name control:

1. In the Controls group, click the **Design Mode** button. The button is selected, and tags appear at the beginning and end of the control. Tags mark the location of the control in the document. Tags are useful when you plan to use your form in another program. Because you didn't type anything in the Tag text box in the Content Control Properties dialog box, the Tag is the same as the Title property. The Title property identifies the content control for the form developer.

2. In cell C3, drag to select the placeholder text, "Click here to enter text.", and then type **Child's first and last names.** You can remain in Design Mode to add additional content controls.

   Trouble? If any of the text you type is black instead of gray, undo your change, carefully select just the current placeholder text, and then type the new placeholder text in Step 2.

Tip

To delete a control, make sure the form is in Design mode, right-click the control, and then on the shortcut menu, click Remove Content Control.

3. In cell **E3**, insert a **Text** content control with the title property **Parent/Guardian Name** and do not allow the control to be deleted.

4. Change the placeholder text for the content control to **Parent/guardian name**.

5. Enter Text content controls as indicated in Figure 9-24. Do not allow any of the content controls to be deleted.

Text content control locations, properties, and placeholder text ◄ **Figure 9-24**

Cell	Title property	Placeholder text
C5	Address	Enter address.
C9	Home Phone	Enter home phone number.
C14	Class Price	Enter class price.
E4	Cell Phone	Cell phone number or type None.
E5	E-mail Address	E-mail address or type None.
E8	Credit Card No.	Credit card number exactly as shown on card.
E10	Name on Card	Name exactly as shown on credit card.
E13	Notes	Enter any notes.

Tip

If your replacement place-holder text appears as black text instead of gray text, format it the same as the original placeholder text by using the Format Painter to copy the format-ting from placeholder text in another content control.

You decide to format the word "None" in cells D10 and D11 in italics so the instruc-tion is clearer to the user.

To format the word "None" in the placeholder text in italics:

1. In cell **E4** (the cell to the right of "Cell phone"), select the word **None**.

2. Click the **Home** tab, and then, in the Font group, click the **Italic** button I.

3. In cell **E5**, format the word **None** with italics.

4. Save the template.

You have inserted all the Text content controls into the registration form template. Before you insert the rest of the content controls, Pete suggests you test the ones you already entered to verify that they work.

Protecting and Testing a Form

Protecting a form means that any changes to the text or structure of the form are prohibited. It is not mandatory that a form be protected in order for someone to enter text into a content control; however, it is a good idea if you don't want any of the other text or the table structure to change. An easy way to protect the content of a form is to use the Group command, available in the Controls group on the Developer tab.

To use the Group command for a form in a table, select the entire table, and then, in the Controls group on the Developer tab, click the Group button, and then click Group. When you apply the Group command to a table, you cannot type in any of the cells except to enter content in a content control.

You'll apply the Group command, and then test the form.

Tip

If you plan to group or pro-tect a form, do not set a Text content control so that the control is removed when contents are edited. If you do, as soon as you type one character, the control will be deleted and you will not be able to type anything else because only content con-trols can be modified in a protected form.

To protect the form with the Group command and test the form:

1. Move the pointer over the table so that the table move handle ⊞ appears above the upper-left corner of the table, and then click the **table move handle** ⊞.

▶ **2.** Click the **Developer** tab, in the Controls group click the **Group** button, and then click **Group**. Because you're working in Design mode, you see that the entire table is surrounded like it was a large content control, and you see the Group tags in the first and last cells of the tables. See Figure 9-25. To properly test the form, you need to turn Design mode off.

Figure 9-25 ▶ **Grouped table**

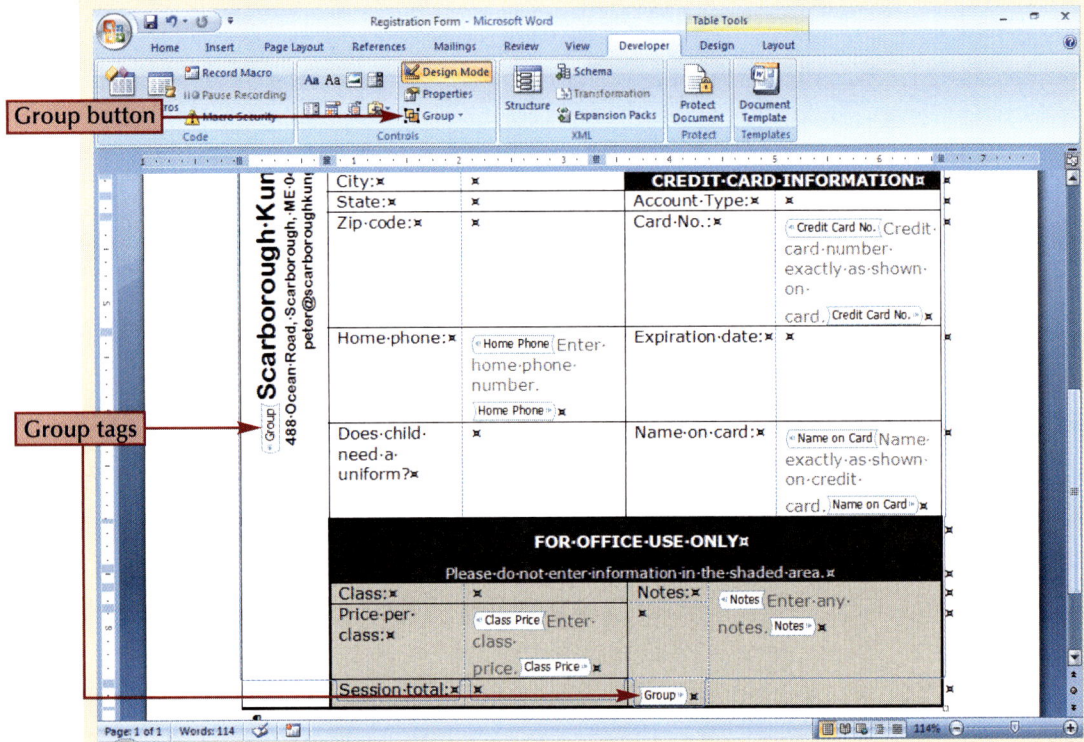

Tip

To lock all the content controls and prevent them from being deleted, select the grouped table, and then in the Controls group, click the Properties button to open the Group Properties dialog box. Select the Content control cannot be deleted check box.

▶ **3.** Make sure the whole table is still selected, scroll, if necessary, so you can see the word "Scarborough" in cell A1, and then, in the Controls group, click the **Design Mode** button to deselect it. Note that the insertion point is blinking in cell A1 in front of the word "Scarborough."

▶ **4.** Type your first name. Nothing appears on the screen at the insertion point. Because cell A1 does not contain a content control, you cannot insert text there.

▶ **5.** Click in cell **C3** ("Child's first and last names"). This cell contains a content control.

▶ **6.** Type **Jane Doe**. The text is entered into the content control.

▶ **7.** Click cell **E4** ("Cell phone number or type None"), and then press the **Delete** key. The placeholder text disappears temporarily from cell E3, but the content control is still there. When you move to another content control, the placeholder text will reappear, as it should if a user were to press the Delete key.

▶ **8.** Click anywhere in the table. The placeholder text in cell E4 reappears.

▶ **9.** Click in cell C3, select the text in the cell, press the **Delete** key to delete "Jane Doe," and then press the **Tab** key. The placeholder text reappears. When you test a form, you should reset Text content controls with the placeholder text you entered.

The form works as it should. Now that you have finished testing the controls, you need to ungroup them so you can continue to design the form. To ungroup the controls in the table, the insertion point must be in the table, but you cannot select the entire table.

▶ **10.** Click in the table to place the insertion point without selecting any text or cells, in the Controls group click the **Group** button, and then click **Ungroup**. The cells in the table are ungrouped.

▶ **11.** Save the template.

When you ungroup the controls in a table, the entire table cannot be selected. If you select the entire table, the only command on the Group button menu is Group; the Ungroup command will be gray (unavailable). If you click Group again, you will add a second set of Group tags to the table.

You're finished testing the Text content controls you've inserted so far. Next, you'll enter controls that allow the user to insert dates.

Inserting Date Picker Content Controls

Pete wants you to insert a content control that allows only a date to be entered for the cell containing the child's date of birth and the cell containing the credit card expiration date. To create a content control that contains a date, you use the **Date Picker content control**.

When you insert a Date Picker content control, you can specify what the date will look like in the final document. To do this, you can select a format from a list, or you can create your own **date-time picture**, which is a pattern of letters indicating a specific style for the date. For example, the date-time picture d-MMM-yy displays the date January 3, 2010, as 3-Jan-10, and the date-time picture dddd, MMMM dd, yyyy displays the date as Wednesday, January 03, 2010.

Inserting a Date Picker Content Control | Reference Window

- Switch to Design mode, then in the Controls group, click the Date Picker button, and then click the Properties button.
- In the Title text box, type the control title.
- If you want the text to be formatted differently than the default format, click the Use a style to format contents check box, and then click the Style arrow and select a style, or click New Style to define a new style.
- Click the Content control cannot be deleted check box to prevent the user from deleting the content control.
- Click the Contents cannot be edited check box to prevent the user from changing the placeholder text.
- In the Display the date like this list, click a format in the list for the date, *or* replace the text in the text box with a date-time picture.
- Click the OK button.
- If desired, replace the default placeholder text with specific instructions to the user.

To insert two Date Picker content controls in the registration form:

▶ 1. Click in cell **C4** (the blank cell to the right of "Date of birth"), and then, in the Controls group, click the **Date Picker** button . A Date Picker content control is entered in cell C4.

▶ 2. In the Controls group, click the **Properties** button. The Content Control Properties dialog box for a Date Picker control opens. The top of this dialog box is the same as the Content Control Properties dialog box for a Text control. See Figure 9-26.

Figure 9-26   **Content Control Properties dialog box for a Date Picker content control**

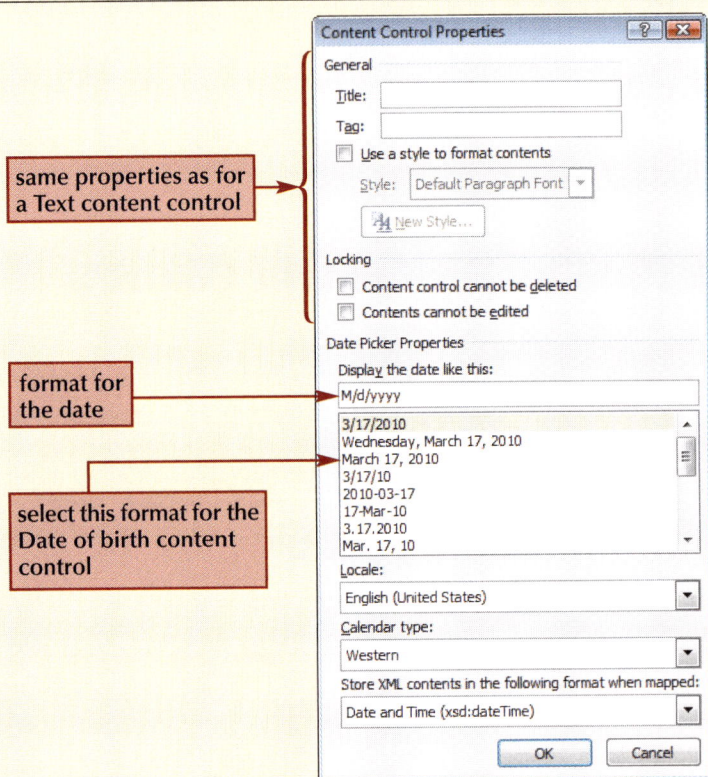

same properties as for a Text content control

format for the date

select this format for the Date of birth content control

▶ 3. Type **DOB** in the Title text box, and then click the **Content control cannot be deleted** check box. Now you need to select the format of the date.

▶ 4. In the list in the Date Picker Properties section of the dialog box, click the **third** date format. The Display the date like this box changes to MMMM d, yyyy.

▶ 5. Click the **OK** button. Now you need to change the placeholder text.

▶ 6. In the Controls group, click the **Design Mode** button to select it, and then replace the placeholder text in cell C4 with **Click arrow, then use calendar.**

You also need to add a Date Picker control to cell E9. You want this to show just the month and year. That format does not exist in the list in the Content Control Properties dialog box, so you will create a custom date-time picture.

To insert a Date Picker control with a custom date-time picture for the expiration date:

▶ 1. Click in cell **E9** (the blank cell to the right of "Expiration date"), insert a **Date Picker** control, and then, in the Controls group, click the **Properties** button.

2. Type **Exp. Date** as the Title, and then click the **Content control cannot be deleted** check box.

You want the month and the year to appear as two digits each; for example, if a card expires in March 2012, it would appear as 03/12.

3. Change the text in the Display the date like this box to **MM/yy**, and then click the **OK** button.

4. Replace the placeholder text with **Click arrow, then use calendar.**

5. Save the template.

Now you will test the Date Picker content control for the expiration date. You'll save time by testing it without using the Group command. First, you must turn off Design mode.

To test the Expiration date content control:

1. In the Controls group, click the **Design Mode** button to exit Design mode.

2. Click cell **E9** (the cell containing the Exp. Date content control). The content control is selected and an arrow appears at the right edge of the control.

3. Click the **arrow** in cell E9. A calendar appears showing the current month and with an orange box around the current date. See Figure 9-27. To change the date, you click the forward ▶ or backward arrows ◀ next to the month name. The Today button at the bottom inserts the current date and closes the calendar.

Using the Date Picker content control to select a date ◀ **Figure 9-27**

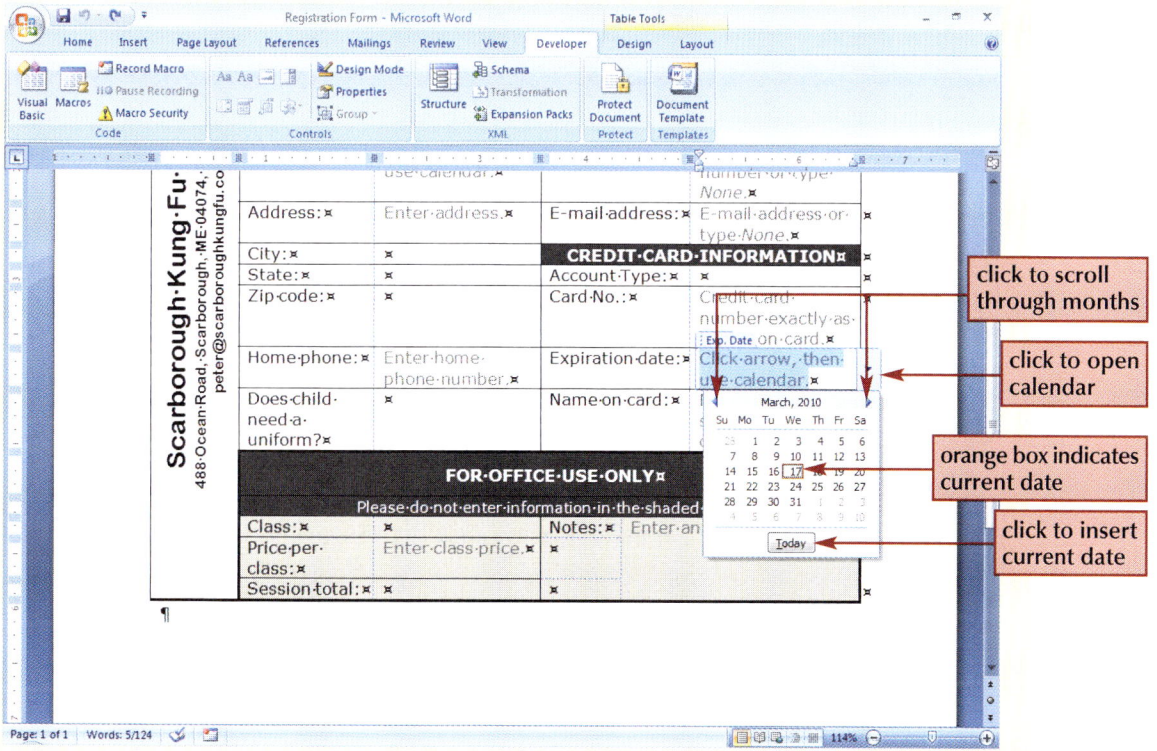

4. Click the **forward** arrow ▶ as many times as necessary to move to March 2013, and then click **1**. The calendar closes and the date you chose appears in the cell in the format you specified—in this case, 03/13. Because this format shows only the month and year, you could have clicked any date in March 2013.

5. Drag to select the date in the cell, if necessary, and then press the **Delete** key. The date you selected is removed from the document.

6. Click in any other cell in the table. The placeholder text reappears in cell E9.

Your Date Picker content control works as it should. You have now specified the content controls that will be used to store text or a date. Next, you need to enter the content controls that offer the user a list of choices.

Inserting List Content Controls

When the information required in a form is limited to a specific list of entries, you can use content controls that offer the user a list of choices from a list. You create a list of choices, and the user clicks one of the choices in the list. This type of content control makes it possible to complete a form faster and without making any spelling errors. There are three types of list content controls: Drop-Down List, Combo Box, and Building Block Gallery.

Inserting Drop-Down List Content Controls

Drop-Down List content controls restrict the user to clicking a choice from a list. When you insert the control, you add items to the list, and arrange them in an order that suits you. When users complete the form, they are allowed to choose only one item from the list. They cannot type anything else in the control.

Reference Window	**Inserting a Drop-Down List or Combo Box Content Control**

- Switch to Design mode, then in the Controls group, click the Drop-Down List button *or* the Combo Box button, and then click the Properties button.
- In the Title text box, type the control title.
- If you want the text to be formatted differently than the default format, click the Use a style to format contents check box, and then click the Style arrow and select a style, *or* click New Style to define a new style.
- Click the Content control cannot be deleted check box to prevent the user from deleting the content control.
- Click the Contents cannot be edited check box to prevent the user from changing the placeholder text.
- Click the Add button, then in the Display Name text box of the Add Choice dialog box, type an entry for the list, and then click the OK button. Repeat for each entry you want to include in the list.
- To change the wording of an entry, click the entry in the list, click the Modify button, replace the text in the Display Name text box in the Modify Choice dialog box with specific instructions to the user, and then click the OK button.
- To move an entry up or down in the list, click it, and then click the Move Up or Move Down buttons.
- To remove an entry from the list, click it, and then click the Remove button.
- Click the OK button.
- Replace the default placeholder text with specific instructions to the user.

Because Pete accepts only certain credit cards, he wants you to insert a Drop-Down List control that includes these cards in the list.

To insert a Drop-Down List control for the credit card type:

1. Click in cell **E7** (the blank cell to the right of "Account Type"), in the Controls group click the **Drop-Down List** button, and then click the **Properties** button. The Content Control Properties dialog box for Drop-Down Lists appears. See Figure 9-28.

Content Control Properties dialog box for a Drop-Down List control ◄ **Figure 9-28**

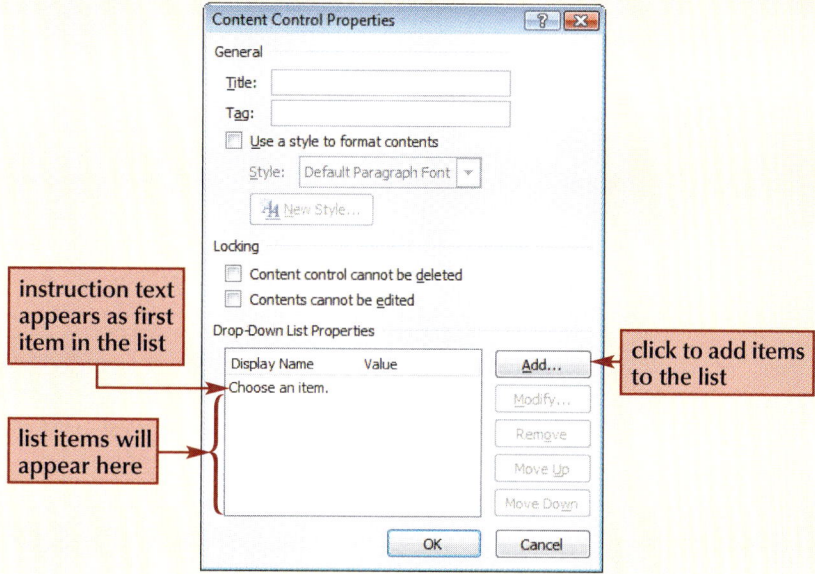

2. Type **Account Type** in the Title text box, and then click the **Content control cannot be deleted** check box. Now you need to add the items that will appear in the drop-down list below the instruction text.

3. Click the **Add** button to open the Add Choice dialog box, type **MasterCard** in the Display Name text box, and then click the **OK** button. As you typed in the Display Name text box, the same text appeared in the Value text box. You can connect a form to an Access database, and if you do, the contents of the Value field is entered into the database. You can ignore this for now. The Add Choice dialog box closes and "MasterCard" appears as the first item in the list.

4. Add **American Express**, **Discover**, and **Visa** to the list. Pete reminds you that he does not accept the Discover card.

5. In the list, click **Discover**, and then click the **Remove** button. Now you want to move "Visa" up so it is the first item in the list below the "Choose an item" instruction text.

6. In the list, click **Visa**, and then click the **Move Up** button two times. "Visa" is now the first item in the list below the instruction text. Now you want to modify the instruction text.

7. Click **Choose an item.**, and then click the **Modify** button. The Modify Choice dialog box opens. It's identical to the Add Choice dialog box.

8. Replace the text in the Display Name text box with **Click to select card type.**, and then click the **OK** button. See Figure 9-29.

Figure 9-29 — List items added to Drop-Down List control

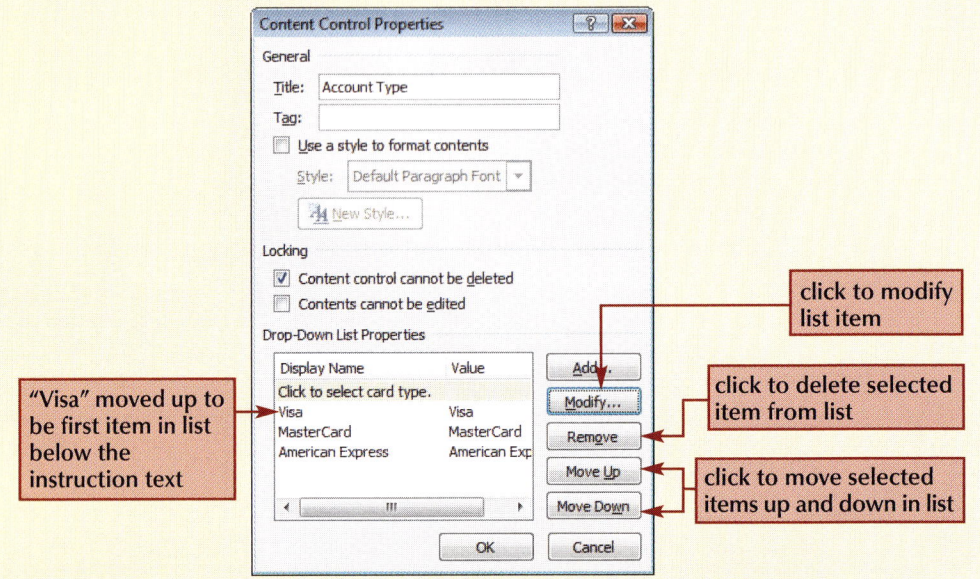

▶ **9.** Click the **OK** button to close the dialog box, turn on Design mode, select the placeholder text in cell E7, and then type **Click, then click arrow.**

▶ **10.** Save the template.

You still need to add one more Drop-Down List content control—the control for the class the student will be taking.

To insert a Drop-Down List control for the class:

▶ **1.** Click in cell **C13** (the blank cell to the right of "Class"), in the Controls group, click the **Drop-Down List** button 🔲, and then click the **Properties** button.

▶ **2.** Type **Class** in the Title text box, click the **Content control cannot be deleted** check box, and then add the following to the list: **Tiny Tots, Preschool/ Kindergarten, Youth, Teen,** and **Advanced Teen.**

▶ **3.** Modify the first item in the list to **Click to select class.**, and then click the **OK** button.

▶ **4.** Replace the placeholder text with **Click to select class.**

▶ **5.** Save the template.

Next, you will insert content controls that provide options in a list and allow users to type their own content.

Inserting a Combo Box Content Control

Because the school is located in Scarborough, Maine, most of Pete's students live there, but some live in other communities. Pete also gets a few children who visit only in the summer. Instead of using Drop-Down List controls for the child's city, state, and zip code, you can use **Combo Box controls**, which offer a list of the most likely choices but also allows users to type their own information if it's not in the list you provide.

To insert a Combo Box control for the child's city:

1. Click in cell **C6** (the blank cell to the right of "City"), in the Controls group, click the **Combo Box** button 🔳 , and then click the **Properties** button. The Content Control Properties dialog box for a Combo Box control appears. It looks identical to the Content Control Properties dialog box for a Drop-Down List control.

2. Type **City** as the Title, and do not allow the control to be deleted.

3. Add **Scarborough** as an item in the list.

4. Modify the first item in the list to **Click to select Scarborough or type your city/town.**

5. Click the **OK** button, and then replace the placeholder text with **Click, then click arrow.**

Now you need to enter Combo Box content controls in the cells to the right of State and Zip.

To insert Combo Box controls for the child's state and zip code:

1. In cell **C7**, insert a **Combo Box** control with **State** as the title, and do not allow the control to be deleted.

2. Replace the first item in the list with **Click to select ME or type your two-letter state abbreviation.**

3. Add **ME** as the second item in the list.

4. Click the **OK** button to close the dialog box, and then replace the placeholder text with **Click, then click arrow.**

5. In cell **C8**, insert a Combo Box content control with **Zip Code** as the title, and do not allow the control to be deleted.

6. Replace the first item in the list with **Click to select zip code or enter by typing.** Scarborough has two zip codes, so you will enter them both in the list.

7. Click the **Add** button, type **04074** in the Display Name text box, click the OK button, and then add **04070** to the list.

8. Click the **OK** button to close the dialog box, and then replace the placeholder text with **Click, then click arrow.**

9. Save the template.

Now you'll test the list content controls.

To test the Combo Box and Drop-Down List content controls:

1. Turn off Design mode, and then click the **City** Combo Box content control (cell C6). The placeholder text is highlighted and a drop-down arrow appears on the right edge of the control.

2. Click the **drop-down arrow** for the City control. See Figure 9-30.

Figure 9-30 Using a Combo Box content control

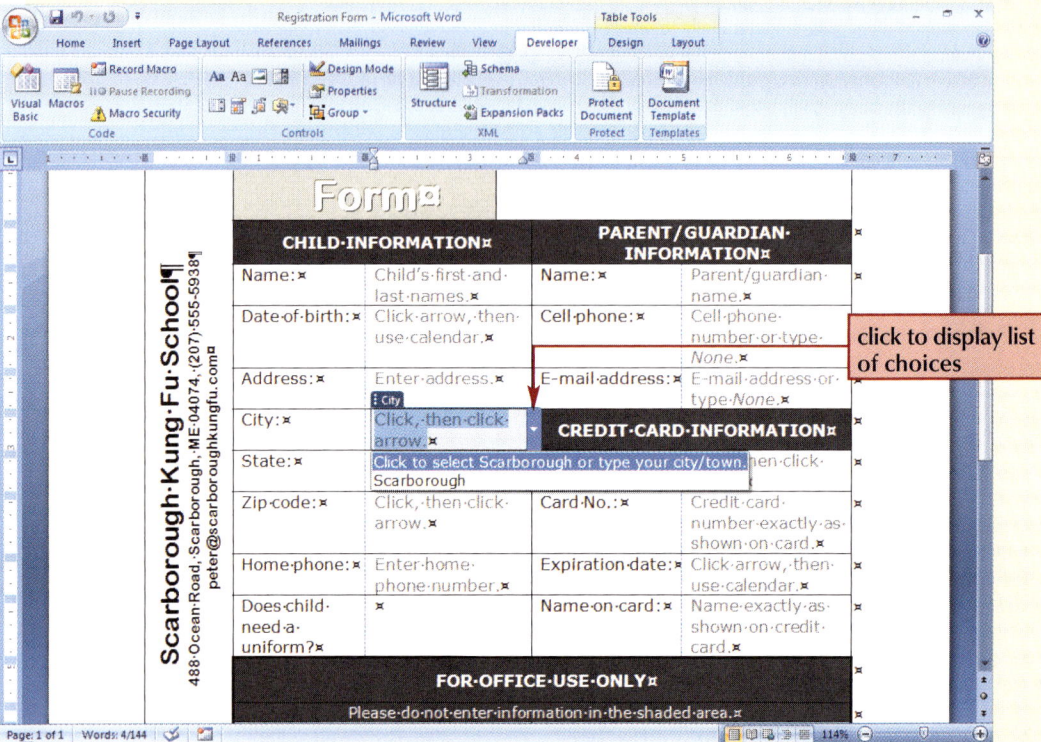

▶ **3.** In the list, click **Scarborough**. "Scarborough" appears in the cell.

▶ **4.** With "Scarborough" selected in the cell, type **Portsmouth**. "Portsmouth" replaces "Scarborough" in the control. This control works as it should.

▶ **5.** Click the **State** content control in cell C7, and then type **NH**. The text you typed replaces the placeholder text.

▶ **6.** Click the **Account Type** content control (cell E7), click the **drop-down arrow** that appears, and then click **Visa**. "Visa" appears in the control.

▶ **7.** Click the **drop-down arrow** again, and then click **American Express**. Your selection replaces "Visa" in the control.

▶ **8.** With "American Express" selected, type any character. Nothing changes because this is a Drop-Down List control and not a Combo Box control; you cannot type anything into the control.

▶ **9.** Click the **drop-down arrow** for the Account Type control again, click the first item in the list (the instruction text), and then do the same with the **City** and **State** content controls. The placeholder text reappears in the controls.

The list content controls you added to the form work as you expected. The third type of list content control, the Building Block Gallery content control, uses building blocks to populate the list from which the user can choose.

Inserting Building Block Gallery Content Controls

Sometimes the information required in a form is information that already exists in Quick Parts that you created. In this case, you can use a Building Block Gallery content control. **Building Block Gallery content controls** are similar to Drop-Down List content controls, but the choices in the list are connected to building blocks in the template or on the computer. You can also create building blocks that are saved with the template and restrict the user to selecting one of those. From the user's point of view, the Building Block Gallery content control is the same as the Drop-Down List control. The user must select an item in the list and cannot type to enter different text.

If you use Building Block Gallery content controls in a form, you can use the Group command to protect the form from inadvertent changes, but if you protect the entire form, the user will not be able to access the building blocks you assign to the list.

Inserting a Building Block Gallery Content Control | Reference Window

- Switch to Design mode, then in the Controls group, click the Building Block Gallery button, and then click the Properties button.
- In the Title text box, type the control title.
- If you want the text to be formatted differently than the default format, click the Use a style to format contents check box, and then click the Style arrow and select a style, *or* click New Style to define a new style.
- Click the Content control cannot be deleted check box to prevent the user from deleting the content control.
- Click the Contents cannot be edited check box to prevent the user from changing the placeholder text.
- Click the Gallery arrow, and then select the Building Block gallery from which you want the user to be able to select building blocks.
- Click the Category arrow, and then click the category from which you want the user to select building blocks, *or* leave the default choice (All Categories).
- Click the OK button.
- Replace the default placeholder text with specific instructions to the user.

Peter doesn't have any Quick Parts stored and doesn't want to use any other building blocks to populate a drop-down list in the form, so you don't need to use the Building Block Gallery control. Next you will insert a Picture content control at the top of the form.

Inserting Graphics into Cells

You can insert a **Picture content control** so that users can insert pictures into a form. Users can choose a picture from any accessible folder on the computer.

Reference Window | **Inserting a Picture Content Control**

- Switch to Design mode, then in the Controls group, click the Picture Content Control button, and then click the Properties button.
- In the Title text box, type the control title.
- Click the Content control cannot be deleted check box to prevent the user from deleting the content control.
- Click the Contents cannot be edited check box to prevent the user from changing the placeholder text.
- Click the OK button.
- If you want to include instruction text for the user, position the insertion point to the right or left of the content control, and then type the instruction text; use the Format Painter or format the instruction text directly to match the color and font of the placeholder text in other cells.

Pete wants to include a photo of each child with his or her registration form. His staff will photograph the child at the start of the registration process, and they will store the photo on the computer on which the parent or guardian will be completing the online registration form.

To insert a Picture content control in the form and test it:

▶ 1. Scroll up to the top of the document, click in cell **D1** (the blank cell to the right of "Registration Form"), in the Controls group click the **Picture Content Control** button 🖼, and then click the **Properties** button. The Content Control Properties dialog box for Picture content controls opens.

▶ 2. Type **Child Photo** in the Title text box, click the **Content control cannot be deleted** check box, and then click the **OK** button. You want the picture to be centered in the cell.

▶ 3. Click the **Child Photo** title tab on the content control to select the entire control. The control is highlighted.

▶ 4. Click the **Table Tools Layout** tab, and then, in the Alignment group, click the **Align Top Center** button 🖼. Notice that there is no placeholder text for this content control. You will include instructions below the content control.

▶ 5. Click in a blank area of cell **D1** to deselect the control, press the → key to move the insertion point to the right of the picture control, press the **Enter** key to insert a blank line below the picture control, and then type **Click the icon, and then double-click your child's name in the list.** Next, you'll format the instruction text in cell D1 to look the same as the placeholder text in the other cells.

▶ 6. Select all the text in cell D1, change the font to **Verdana (Body)**, change the font color to **White, Background 1, Darker 50%** (the last tile in the first column under Theme Colors), and then deselect the text.

▶ 7. Make sure Design mode is turned off, point to the button 🖼 in the middle of the Picture content control. A ScreenTip appears telling you to click the button to insert a picture. See Figure 9-31.

Using a Picture content control | **Figure 9-31**

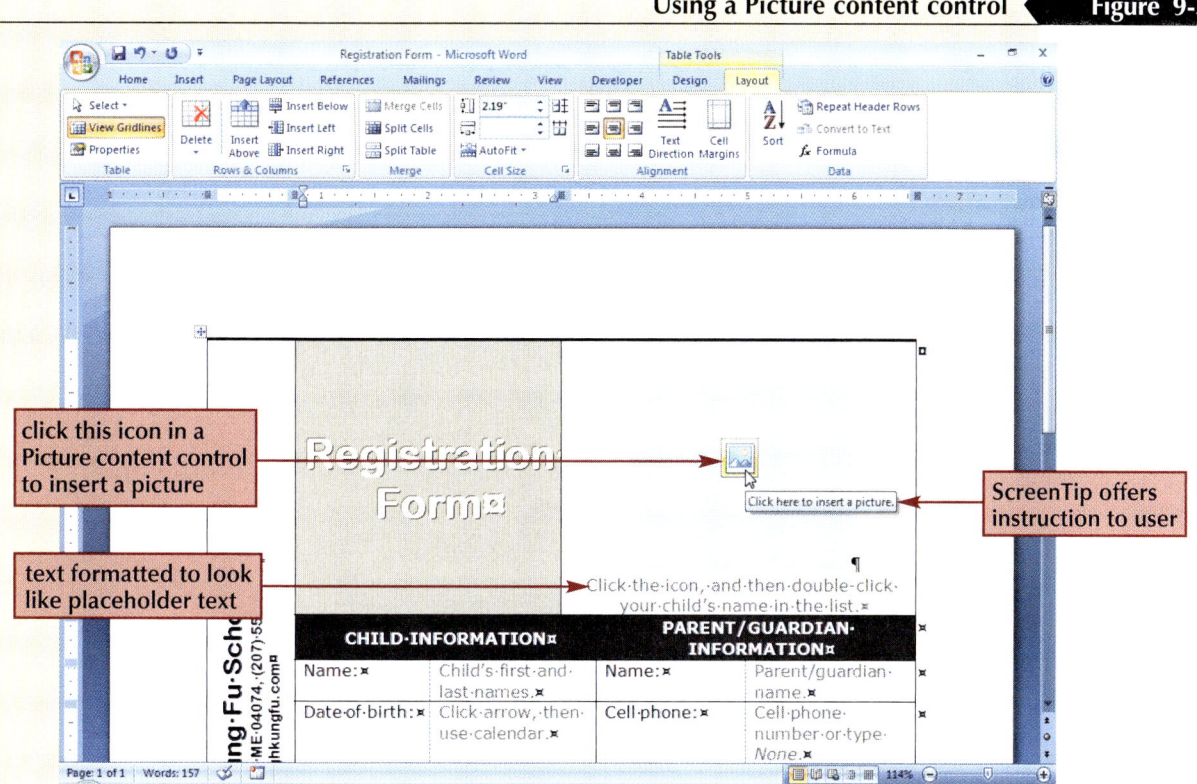

click this icon in a Picture content control to insert a picture

text formatted to look like placeholder text

ScreenTip offers instruction to user

8. Click [icon]. The Insert Picture dialog box opens. When the form is saved on the computer the new students will be using, Pete will make sure the photos are stored in the default folder, but for now, you need to locate the photo you will insert.

9. Navigate to the **Tutorial.09\Tutorial** folder, and then double-click **Child**. A photo appears in the Picture content control.

10. Press the **Delete** key to delete the photo you inserted, and then click a blank area of the document to return the Picture content control back to its original state. The picture control works as it should.

▶ 11. Click the **View** tab, and then in the Zoom group, click the **One Page** button. Compare your screen to Figure 9-32.

> **Tip**
>
> You can insert a graphic into a table cell in the same way you insert a graphic any place in a document—click the Insert tab, and then click one of the buttons in the Illustrations group.

Figure 9-32   **Form with all the content controls inserted**

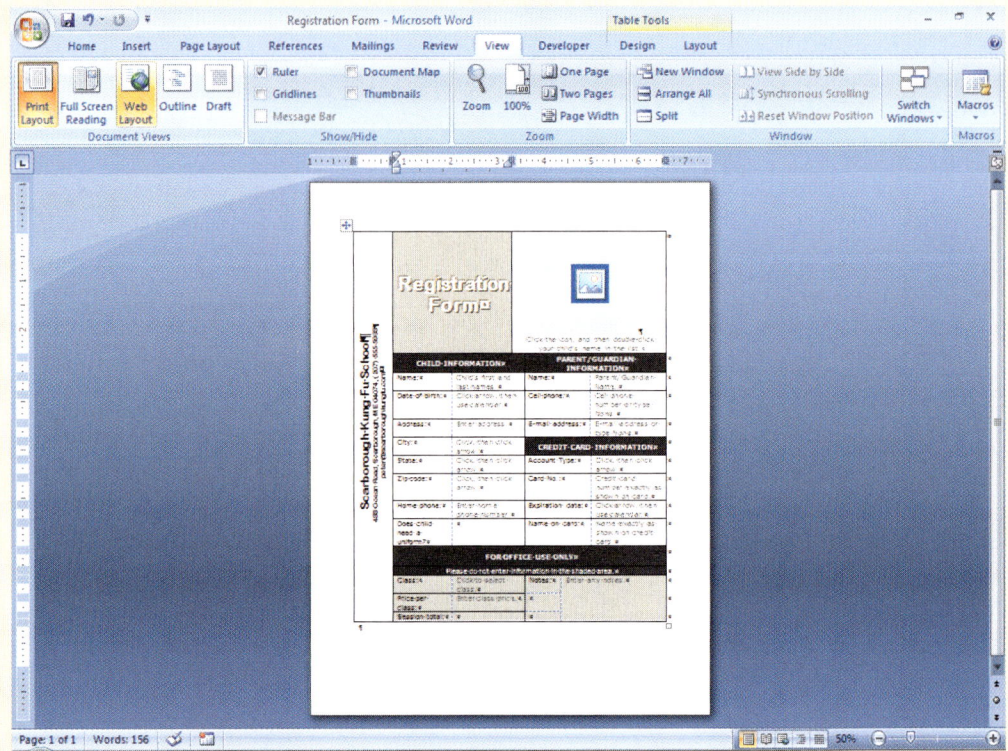

▶ **12.** In the Zoom group, click the **Page Width** button, and then save the template.

You've almost completed creating the form. In the next session, you will add a check box field and fields to calculate the cost of a session of classes.

Review | **Session 9.2 Quick Check**

1. What is the difference between a Text content control and a Rich Text content control?
2. How do you provide instructions for using a content control to a user?
3. Does a form that contains content controls need to be protected in order to test it?
4. True or False: The date-time picture MM/dd/YYYY displays the date in the form 03 February 2010.
5. Name a situation in which you would use a Combo Box content control instead of a Drop-Down List content control.
6. What type of content is included in the list for a Building Block Gallery content control?

Session 9.3

Using Legacy Form Fields

Pete would like a check box to appear in the cell to the right of the cell that asks if the child needs a uniform. To insert a check box, you need to use a form field. **Form fields** are similar to content controls; they are spaces in a document that contain a specific type of information and are able to be filled in by a user when a document is protected. Form fields are one of the legacy tools available to Word 2007 users. **Legacy tools** are tools that were available in previous versions of Word—thus the term *legacy*. **Legacy form fields** provide some capabilities that content controls do not have; for example, you can insert a check box form field that the user can click to check or uncheck, and you can insert a form field that will perform a calculation.

Inserting Check Box Form Fields

Many dialog boxes you have used in Word and in other programs include check boxes that you can click to display or remove a check mark to select and deselect items. Similarly, a **check box form field** is a box-shaped field that users can click to insert or remove an X. If you want to allow users to select any number of options in a list, you can list each option as text in the appropriate cell of the template, and then place a check box form field to the left of each item. You might include check box form fields in an on-screen survey form for questions such as, "Which of the following items do you plan to purchase in the next six months?"

Inserting a Check Box Form Field | Reference Window

- Switch to Design mode, and then, in the Controls group, click the Legacy Tools button.
- On the submenu, click the Check Box Form Field button.
- In the Controls group, click the Properties button.
- Specify whether the check box should be checked by default.
- Click the OK button.

According to Pete's sketch in Figure 9-2, the registration form needs to indicate whether the new student needs a uniform, so you'll add a check box form field to the form. Legacy form fields do not have placeholder text, so if you want to include instructions for the user, you need to type them directly in the cell.

To insert a check box legacy form field:

1. If you took a break after the previous session, open the **Registration Form** file as a template, make sure the rulers and nonprinting characters are visible, that table gridlines are displayed, that Word is in Print Layout view, that your zoom is set to Page width, and that the Developer tab is displayed.

2. Click in cell **C10** (the cell to the right of "Does child need a uniform?"), type **Click check box to remove the X if child doesn't need a uniform.**, and then press the **spacebar**.

3. Click the **Developer** tab, and then in the Controls group, click the **Legacy Tools** button 📷. A menu opens.

4. In the first row of buttons under Legacy Forms, click the **Check Box Form Field** button ☑. A check box form field is inserted in the cell. See Figure 9-33.

Trouble? If the check box is white instead of gray and if the words CheckBox1 appear next to it, you clicked the Check Box (ActiveX Control) button instead. Click the Undo button ↻, and then repeat Step 4, making sure you click the Check Box Form Field button in the first row on the menu.

Figure 9-33 | **Check Box form field inserted in form**

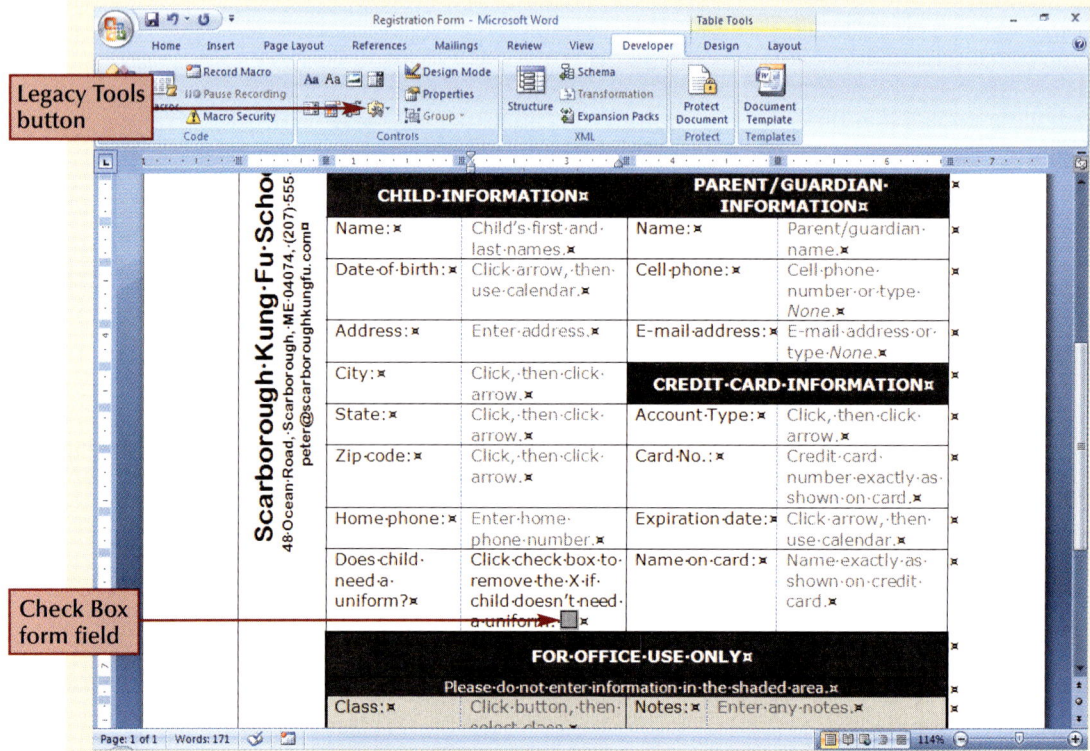

▶ **5.** In the Controls group, click the **Properties** button to open the Check Box Form Field Options dialog box. See Figure 9-34. Because most new registrants will need a uniform, you'll change the default value for this to checked.

Figure 9-34 | **Check Box Form Field Options dialog box**

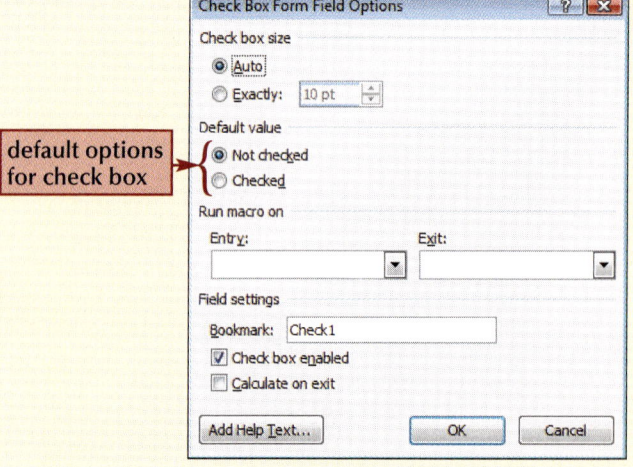

6. In the Default value section of the dialog box, click the **Checked** option button. Now the check box will have an X in it when a new form is opened.

Note the Add Help Text button. With legacy form fields, you can add help text, so that when the user's insertion point is in the form field, the text appears in the status bar or when the user presses the F1 key. This provides help that is similar to the placeholder text displayed for a content control. Because placeholder text in content controls is used in the rest of the form to display instructions to the user, you won't use the Add Help Text feature for the form field.

7. Click the **OK** button to return to the form. The check box is selected by default.

Protecting the Document and Testing a Check Box Form Field

Unlike content controls, to test form fields, the form must be protected. However, the Group command only allows you to edit content in content controls. If you use the Group command now, you would not be able to deselect or select the check box. Instead, to test form fields, you need to protect the entire document.

Protecting and Unprotecting a Form | Reference Window

- Click the Developer tab, and then in the Protect group, click the Protect Document button.
- In the Restrict Formatting and Editing task pane, click the Allow only this type of editing in the document check box to select it, click the arrow, and then click Filling in forms.
- Click the Yes, Start Enforcing Protection button. If the button is grayed out (not available), then in the Controls group on the Developer tab, click the Design Mode button to turn off Design mode.
- If you want to use a password, in the Start Enforcing Protection dialog box, type a password in the Enter new password (optional) text box, type the same password in the Reenter password to confirm text box, and then click the OK button; or, if you do not want to use a password, just click the OK button.
- To turn off protection, click the Stop Protection button at the bottom of the task pane.
- If you used a password, type the password in the Password text box in the Unprotect Document dialog box, and then click the OK button.

To protect the form, it must not be in Design mode. You'll turn off Design mode, protect the entire document, and test the check box form field.

Protect the document and test the check box form field:

1. Make sure the **Design Mode** button is deselected, and then in the Protect group, click the **Protect Document** button. The Restrict Formatting and Editing task pane opens to the right of the document window.

2. In section 2. Editing restrictions, click the **Allow only this type of editing in the document** check box to select it. The list box below that check box becomes active, and additional text appears below that.

When you protect the entire document, you need to specify that it is protected for filling in forms, which means that the user will be able to enter content in content controls and form fields.

▶ **3.** Click the **section 2** arrow, and then click **Filling in forms**. The button in section 3. Start enforcement becomes active. See Figure 9-35.

Figure 9-35 ▷ **Protecting a document for filling in forms**

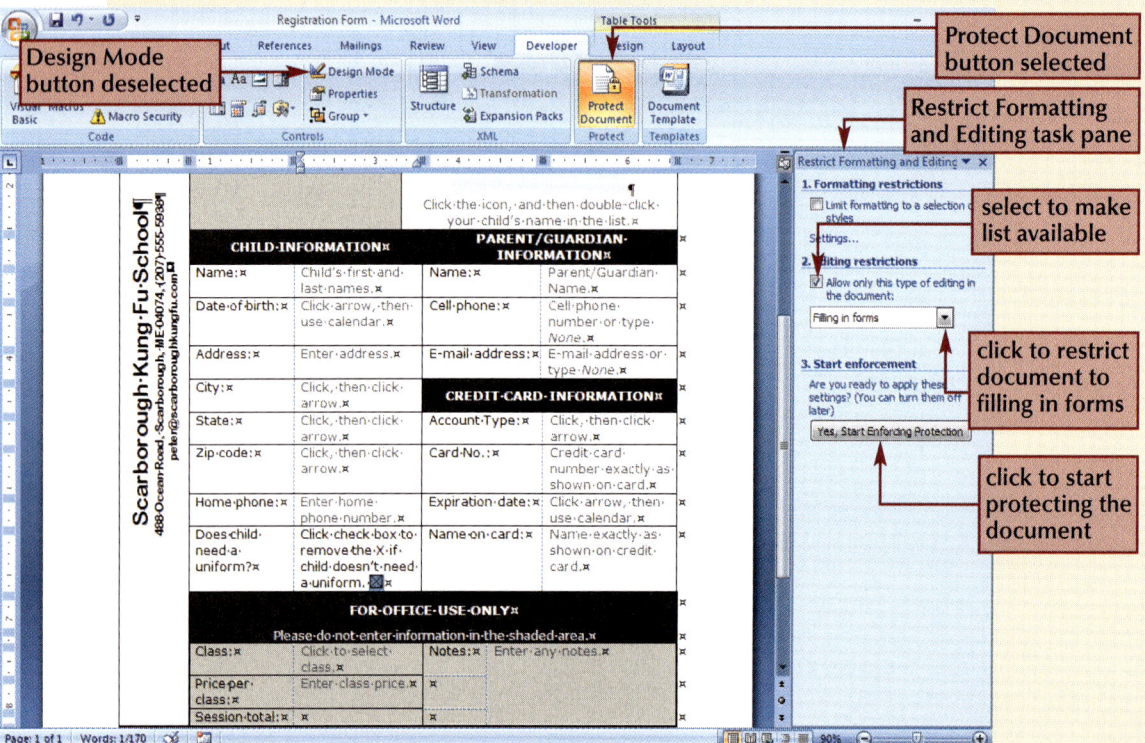

▶ **4.** Click the **Yes, Start Enforcing Protection** button. The Start Enforcing Protection dialog box opens, in which you can enter a password. You're just testing the form, so you won't enter a password now.

▶ **5.** In the dialog box, click the **OK** button. The dialog box closes, the task pane changes to inform you that the document is protected from unintentional editing, and a Stop Protection button appears at the bottom of the task pane. Because you can't edit the form now, most of the buttons on the Ribbon are unavailable (dimmed). See Figure 9-36.

Form with protection turned on   **Figure 9-36**

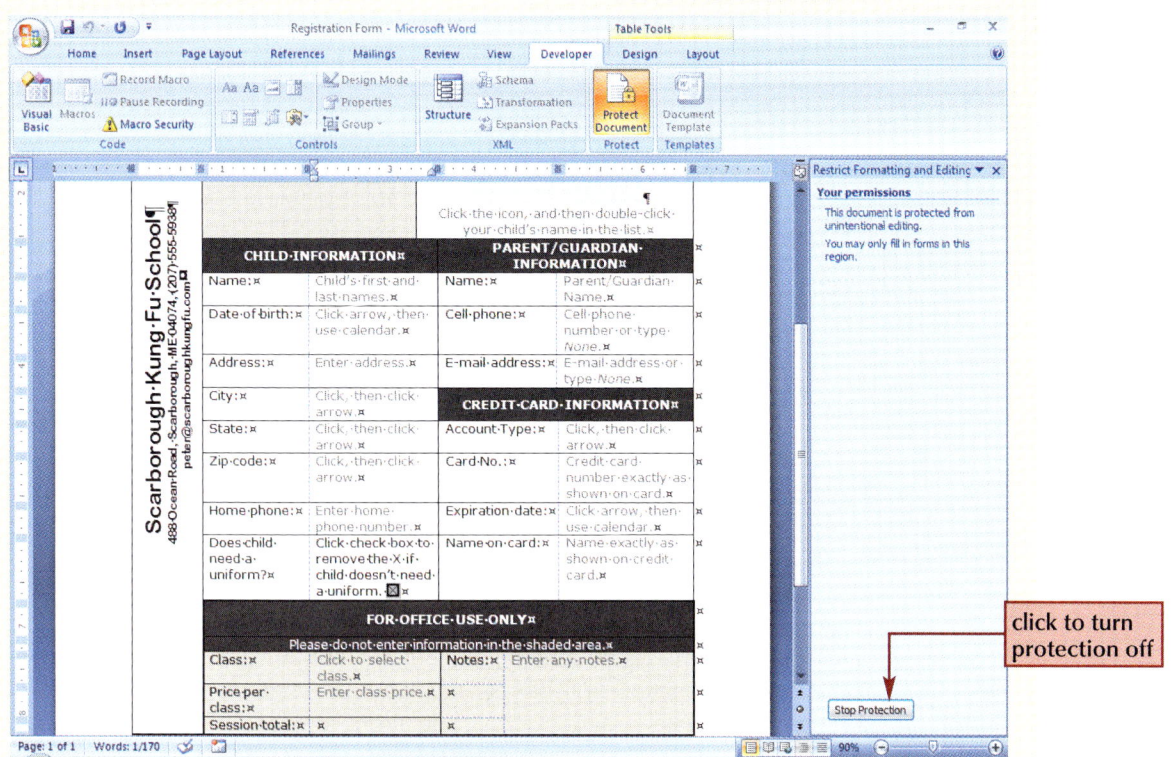

> click to turn
> protection off

6. In cell C10, click the **check box**. The "X" in the box disappears.

7. Click in cell **D10** ("Name on card"). The content control in cell E10 is selected instead of the insertion point being placed in cell D10. When the form is protected, if you click anywhere in the document window except within a content control or a form field, the insertion point moves to the next content control after the location where you clicked.

8. Click the **check box** in cell C10 to select it, in the Restrict Formatting and Editing task pane, click the **Stop Protection** button, and then, in the task pane title bar, click the **Close** button ☒. The task pane closes, and the buttons on the Ribbon are available again.

    Now you'll format the instruction text that you added to the cell so that it looks the same as the placeholder text in the other cells.

9. Select all the text in cell C10, change its color to **White, Background 1, Darker 50%**, and then deselect the text.

10. Save your changes to the template.

In computer terminology, *legacy* refers to hardware or software that existed in an older version and is still available in the new version, but is retained only for "backward compatibility"—to allow the new software or hardware to work with an older version of it, or for the software to create something the older version can use. For example, the term *legacy form fields* refers to tools such as the check box form field that are still available only because Microsoft knows that many people created forms using these older tools and they want to make sure the users can continue to work with those forms. To take full advantage of everything Word 2007 offers, you should try to avoid using the legacy tools; for example, if you are planning to take advantage of the XML capabilities of Word 2007 (a way of communicating with other programs), you should avoid using legacy form fields and stick with content controls. However, if you are creating a form that will be used by someone running Word 2003 or an earlier version, you should use only legacy tools because earlier versions of Word do not recognize content controls.

Using Formulas in a Table

The "For Office Use Only" section of the registration form contains the fields for entering the price of a class and the total for a session. There are eight weeks per session, so this total can be calculated by multiplying the number the employee enters in the cell to the right of the Class Price label by eight. When filling out the bottom part of the form, an employee could do this calculation in his or her head, but to avoid any mathematical errors, you can set up a formula to perform the calculation. You can format the result so it appears as a dollar amount.

Understanding Formulas

A **formula** is a mathematical statement that calculates a value. To insert a formula into a table cell, you click the Layout tab on the Ribbon, and then, in the Data group, click the Formula button to open the Formula dialog box. See Figure 9-37.

Figure 9-37	Formula dialog box

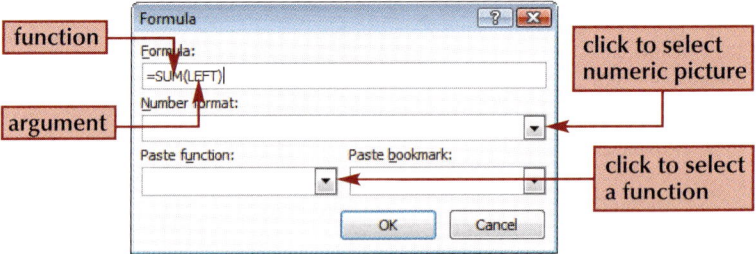

As shown in Figure 9-37, you enter a formula in the Formula text box. To indicate that the text in this box is a formula, it always starts with an equal sign. Numbers, variables, or a function can appear after the equal sign. If you type =1+2, the result 3 will appear in the cell.

Most formulas include at least one **variable**, which is a symbol for a number that can change. In formulas in Word, variables are named by the cell reference. So, for example, if the number 1 were in cell A2, and the number 2 in cell A1, you could type into cell A3 the formula =A1+A2. The formula "looks" in the referenced cells (A1 and A2) and uses the contents to calculate the result of the formula. It displays the answer in the cell where you inserted the formula (cell A3).

To make things easier, you can also use a function. A **function** is a relationship between variables; basically, it's a shorthand way of writing a formula. The most commonly used function is the SUM function, which adds numbers, usually stored in adjacent cells. All functions take arguments; an **argument** is a value that the function needs in order to calculate its result. Arguments appear between parentheses immediately after the name of the function. In our example—with 2 in cell A1, 1 in cell A2, and the formula in cell A3—you could use the SUM function to add the contents of cells A1 and A2. To do this, you would type =SUM(A1,A2) in cell A3. Finally, because tables are grids, and functions such as SUM are frequently used at the bottom of a column or the end of a row, you can use LEFT, RIGHT, ABOVE, and BELOW as the argument and SUM will add the contents of all the cells in that direction. So the formula in our cell A3 could be =SUM(ABOVE).

There are 18 functions you can use in Word tables. Of course, if you plan to do complex calculations, Word is not the best tool to use, but for simple calculations, the Formula dialog box is very handy.

Inserting a Formula in a Table Cell

When you insert a formula, you can specify how the result will be formatted in the document. The key to controlling the content and format of a number is selecting an appropriate numeric picture. Similar to a date-time picture, a **numeric picture** is a pattern of digits and symbols, such as $#,###,### or 00.00, that describes how the number will look. When you assign a numeric picture to a formula, Word takes the number entered by the user and formats it in a certain way. In some cases, Word also prevents the user from entering incorrect characters. For example, you could use a numeric picture that would take a single digit entered by the user and display it with a decimal point and a trailing zero. (That is, if the user entered "5," Word would display "5.0" in the cell.) The numeric picture doesn't change the number itself (provided you enter an appropriate number), but only how it is displayed.

To understand numeric pictures, you first need to understand the symbols used in them. Figure 9-38 shows the most commonly used numeric picture symbols.

Figure 9-38 Numeric picture symbols

Symbol	Purpose	Example
0 (zero)	Displays a digit in place of the zero in the field result. If the result doesn't include a digit in that place, the field displays a zero.	Numeric picture "00.0" displays "05.0" Numeric picture "0" displays an integer of any number of digits
#	Displays a digit in place of the # only if the result requires it. If the result doesn't include a digit in that place, the field displays a space.	Numeric picture "$##.00" displays "$ 5.00"
. (decimal point)	Determines the decimal point position.	See examples above
, (comma)	Separates a series of three digits.	Numeric picture "$#,###,###" displays "$3,450,000"
- (hyphen)	Includes a minus sign if the number is negative or a space if the number is positive.	Numeric picture "-0" displays an integer as " 5" or "-5"
; (semicolon)	Separates the positive and negative numeric picture.	Numeric picture "$##0.00;-$##0.00" displays "$ 55.50" if positive, "-$ 55.50" if negative
(parentheses around negative number)	Puts parentheses around a negative result.	Numeric picture ""$##0.00;($##0.00)" displays "$ 55.50" if positive, "($ 55.50)" if negative
$, %, etc.	Displays a special character in the result.	Numeric picture "0.0%" displays "5.0%"

You are ready to insert a formula in the table to calculate the session total.

To insert a formula for the session total:

1. Move the insertion point to cell **C15** (to the right of the label "Session total"), click the **Table Tools Layout** tab, and then in the Data group, click the **Formula** button. The Formula dialog box opens. Because there are cells to the left of the current cell, the default function =SUM(LEFT) appears in the Formula text box. You need to change this function to multiply the value in cell C14 by eight.

2. Delete all the text in the Formula text box except the equal sign, click the **Paste function** arrow, scroll down the alphabetical list, and then click **PRODUCT**. The function is inserted in the Formula text box, followed by parentheses, and the insertion point is blinking inside the parentheses so that you can enter the arguments.

3. Type **C14,8**. You want the result to be displayed with a $ whether or not the employee entering the data types $ before the value in cell C14.

4. Click the **Number format** arrow, and then click **$#,##0.00;($#,##0.00)** to set the number format as a dollar amount.

5. Click the **OK** button. The dialog box closes. The result of the calculation—"$ 0.00" —appears in the cell to the right of Session Total field. The result is $0 because there is no value in cell C14. Recall that fields update when the document is opened, when you click the Update Field command on the shortcut menu, or when you press the F9 key. Now test the formula.

6. Click in cell **C14** ("Enter class price"), type **15**, click the formula field in cell **C15**, and then press the **F9** key. The field updates to $ 120.00. See Figure 9-39.

Result of a formula displayed in a cell ⟩ **Figure 9-39**

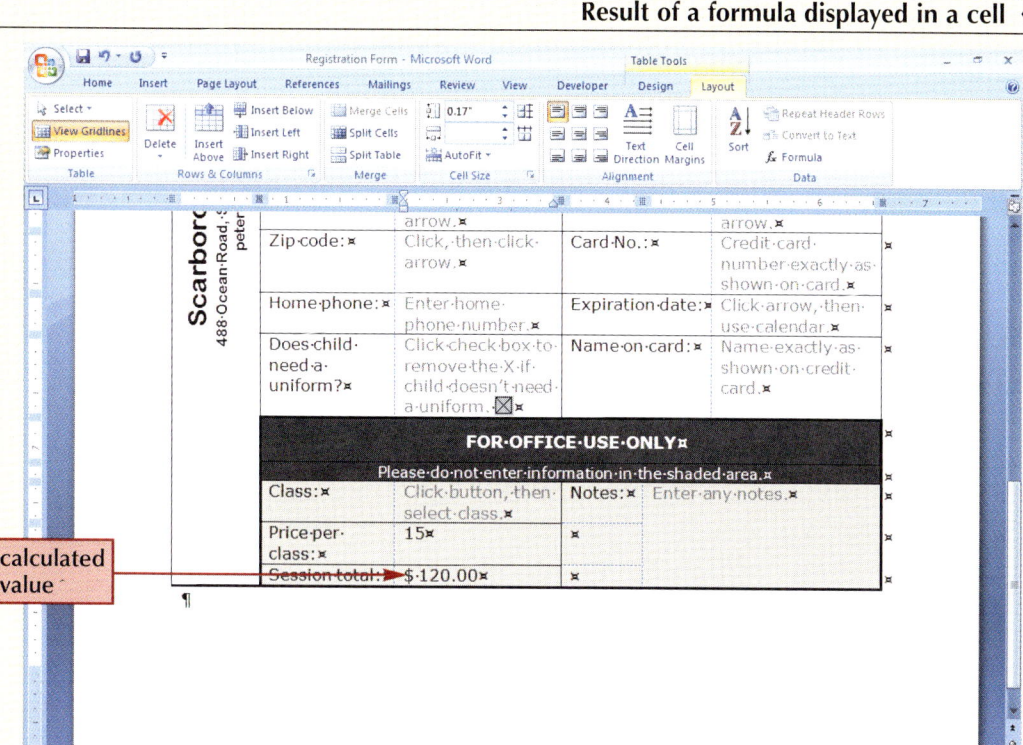

calculated value

7. On the Quick Access Toolbar, click the **Undo** button as many times as needed to remove the "15" from cell C14, and then save the template.

Next, you should make sure the field is calculated correctly when the form is protected.

To test the formula field in the protected registration form:

1. Protect the document for filling in forms.

2. Click in cell **C14** (the cell containing the Price per class content control), and then type **15**.

3. Click in cell **C15**, and then press the **F9** key. The field does not update. In fact, if you watch closely, you'll notice that when you click in cell C15, the check box in cell C10 becomes selected.

4. On the Quick Access Toolbar, click the **Undo** button, turn off protection, and then close the task pane.

The field did not update. What happened? When you protected the document and chose Filling in forms in the Editing Restrictions list, you specified that only content controls or legacy form fields can be modified while the form is protected; this means that ordinary fields will not be modified. There are no content controls that calculate a value, but you can use a legacy text form field and specify that it is the Calculation type to perform a calculation. For the Calculation type field to calculate while the form is protected, any values used in the formula must also be legacy form fields. This means you need to change cells C14 and C15 to legacy text form fields.

Using Legacy Text Form Fields to Perform Calculations

To calculate the session total in the registration form, you'll insert two legacy form fields—one to specify the class price and one to calculate the session total. Both fields are **text form fields**, but with a legacy text form field, you can specify the type of information the field will accept (that is, the input type). You can choose regular text (any string of alphanumeric characters), numbers, calculations, or dates only. For each type, you can set different properties; for example, for a text form field that you specify as regular text, you can set the maximum number of characters a user can enter.

Inserting Numeric Text Form Fields

You'll add a numeric text form field in cell C14, the cell to the right of "Price per class." When you insert this form field, you'll specify that the field can accept only a number, and you'll format the number as currency. When you choose the numeric picture that formats input as currency, Word displays it with a dollar sign and usually with a decimal and two digits to the right of the decimal. Because this is the number that will be used in the calculation, you need to select the Calculate on exit check box. Selecting this check box means that after you enter a value in this field, the value of the field will be updated in any calculations that depend on it.

Reference Window | **Inserting a Numeric Text Form Field**

- Switch to Design mode, and then, in the Controls group, click the Legacy Tools button.
- On the menu, click the Text Form Field button.
- In the Controls group, click the Properties button.
- Click the Type arrow, and then click Number.
- Click the Number format arrow, and then select the desired numeric picture.
- If desired, set the Maximum length of the input and the Default number.
- If the number will be used in a calculation, click the Calculate on exit check box to select it.
- Click the OK button.

You'll insert the two form fields Pete needs to calculate the cost of the session total now.

To insert a numeric Text form field in cell C14:

▶ 1. Turn on Design mode, right-click the content control in cell **C14** ("Enter class price"), and then on the shortcut menu, click **Remove Content Control**. You must be in Design mode to remove a content control.

▶ 2. Make sure the insertion point is in cell C14, in the Controls group, click the **Legacy Tools** button 🖼️▾ , and then click the **Text Form Field** button |ab| . A text form field appears in cell C14.

▶ 3. In the Controls group, click the **Properties** button. The Text Form Field Options dialog box opens. See Figure 9-40. You need to change the field type to a number.

Text Form Field Options dialog box | Figure 9-40

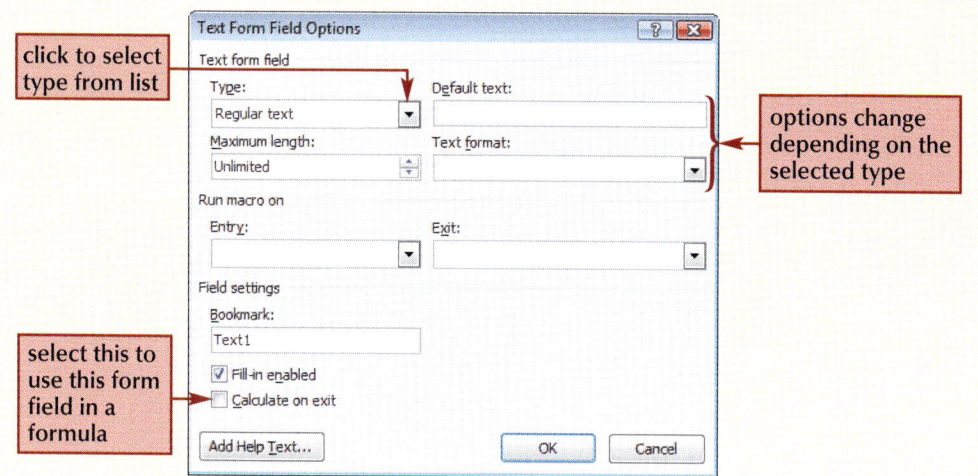

click to select type from list

options change depending on the selected type

select this to use this form field in a formula

4. Click the **Type** arrow, click **Number**, click the **Number format** arrow, and then click **$#,##0.00;($#,##0.00)**. Because this field will be used in the calculation, you need to set it to calculate automatically.

5. Click the **Calculate on exit** check box, and then click the **OK** button.

Inserting Calculation Text Form Fields

Now you need to replace the formula in cell C15 with a text form field that you set to the Calculation type. You will insert the same formula, but because you are using a form field instead of just an ordinary formula, the field will recalculate when you enter a value in the field the formula is dependent on (cell C14).

To insert a calculation text form field in cell C15:

1. Select all the text in cell C15, and then press the **Delete** key.

2. In the Controls group, click the **Legacy Tools** button ![icon], and then click the **Text Form Field** button ![ab icon].

3. In the Controls group, click the **Properties** button, click the **Type** arrow, and then click **Calculation**. The other text boxes in the dialog box change to reflect options related to a Calculation field. Notice that the text box to the right of the Type box changed to the Expression text box and an equal sign is in the text box. You will type the formula here.

4. Click in the **Expression** text box to position the insertion point after the equal sign, and then type **PRODUCT(C14,8)**. Note that you must type the function name in all uppercase letters, and the cell reference must also use an uppercase letter.

5. Click the **Number format** arrow, click **$#,##0.00;($#,##0.00)**, and then click the **OK** button. The dialog box closes and $0.00 appears in the cell.

Now you can test the form. Remember, you need to turn on protection in order to test legacy form fields.

▶ **6.** Turn Design mode off, turn protection on for filling in forms, click in cell **C14**, type **15**, and then press the **Tab** key. Because you checked Calculate on exit in the Text Form Field Options dialog box for the form field in cell C14, the result of the calculation that uses the value in cell C14 appears in cell C15. It was calculated when you pressed the Tab key and exited cell C14. Note that you must press the Tab key to exit the cell. If you click to place the insertion point somewhere else in the form, the value will not calculate.

▶ **7.** Delete the text in cell C14, press the **Tab** key, turn off protection, and then close the task pane.

▶ **8.** Save the template, click the **View** tab, and then, in the Zoom group, click the **One Page** button. Compare your screen to Figure 9-41.

Figure 9-41 ▶ Registration Form in One Page view

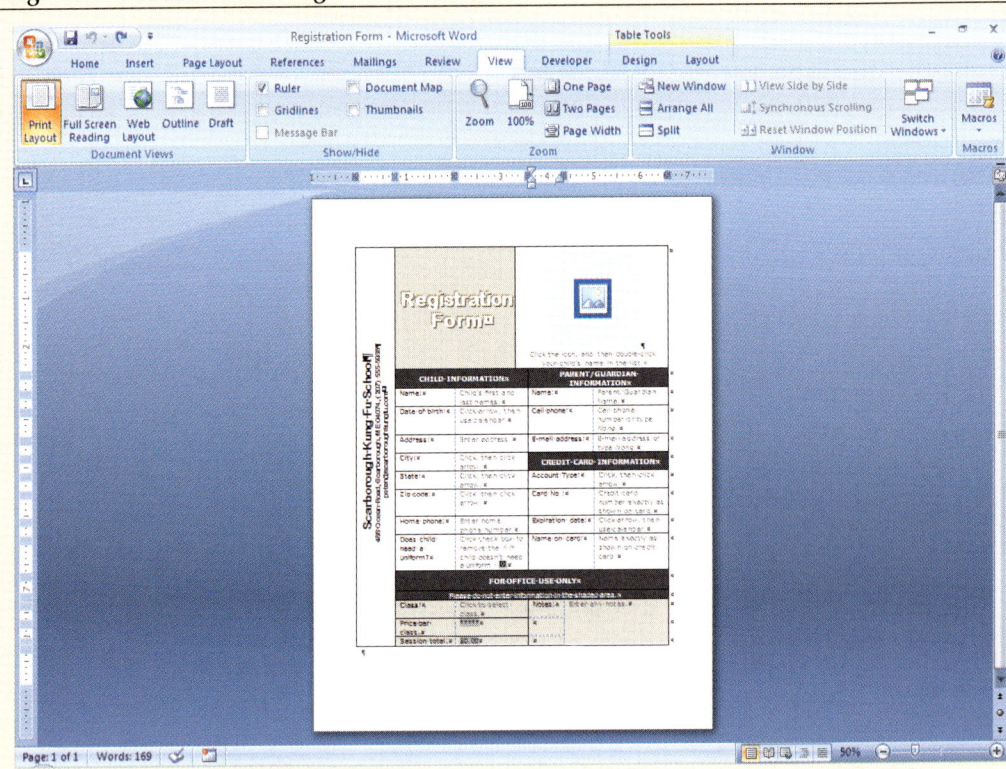

Trouble? If your order form doesn't match Figure 9-41, make any necessary changes.

It is important to note that if you want to include calculation form fields in a form, there cannot be any content controls horizontally or vertically between the fields referenced by the calculation and the calculation itself. For example, in the registration form, if the content control next to the Notes label were in row 14 instead of row 13, the calculation in C15 would not work properly.

The registration form is now complete. Keep in mind that a text form field that is set up to perform calculations displays the result of the calculation, not the formula used in the calculation. You should also be aware that, when the user fills in a protected form and presses the Tab key to move from one content control to the next, the insertion point doesn't stop at calculation fields, but skips past them to the next content control that requires input.

Protecting and Saving the On-Screen Form

The registration form for the school is now completed. Because this is the final version of the form, you'll add a password so that no one accidentally turns off protection. There's no way to add a password using the Group command, but you can use the Protect Document command and set a password so that no one can turn protection off.

To protect the form with a password:

1. Change the view back to Page width, click the **Developer** tab, make sure Design mode is turned off, and then in the Protect group, click the **Protect Document** button. The Restrict Formatting and Editing task pane opens.

2. If necessary, in section 2. Editing restrictions, click the **Allow only this type of editing in the document** check box to select it, click the **section 2** arrow, and then click **Filling in forms**.

3. Click the **Yes, Start Enforcing Protection** button. The Start Enforcing Protection dialog box opens.

4. In the Enter new password (optional) box, type **peterd**. The characters you typed appear as round bullets in the text box. See Figure 9-42. This is to prevent anyone from seeing your password over your shoulder.

Password showing as bullets in Start Enforcing Protection dialog box ◄ Figure 9-42

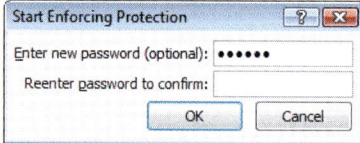

5. Press the **Tab** key, type **peterd** in the Reenter password to confirm text box, and then click the **OK** button. Passwords are case sensitive, so *PeterD* is not the same as *peterd*. The dialog box closes, and the Stop Protection button appears in the task pane.

6. Close the task pane, and then, on the Quick Access Toolbar, click the **Save** button 🖫 to save the final, password-protected template.

7. Click the **Office Button**, and then click **Close** to close the template but leave Word running.

   You have finished protecting the form and saving it in the Templates folder. Now you are ready to test the complete form as if you were registering a new student at Scarborough Kung Fu School.

Filling in the On-Screen Form

So far you have been acting as a form designer and creator. Now it's time to try out the form from the user's point of view to make sure there are no unexpected glitches. You can do this by filling in the form just as a user would.

To open a new registration form from the template:

▶ **1.** Click the **Office Button** 🔘 , and then click **New**. The New Document dialog box opens.

▶ **2.** In the Templates pane on the left, click **New from existing** to open the New from Existing Document dialog box, and then navigate to the **Tutorial.09\Tutorial** folder included with your Data Files.

▶ **3.** Click **Registration Form**, and then click the **Create New** button. The registration form opens in a new document window.

▶ **4.** If necessary, change the view to Page width and scroll up to the top of the document. The Picture content control in the top row is selected.

Now you will enter some information in the form.

To enter information into the form:

▶ **1.** In the Picture content control in the top row, click 🖼 , navigate to the **Tutorial.09\Tutorial** folder included with your Data Files, if necessary, and then double-click **Child**. The photo of a child is inserted into the document.

▶ **2.** Click cell **C3** (to the right of the first "Name" label), type **Greg Dunstan**, and then press the **Tab** key. The text you typed appears in the cell and is formatted in bold because of the Properties settings you entered earlier, and the next cell containing a content control, cell E3, is the current cell.

▶ **3.** Type **Patricia Dunstan**, and then press the **Tab** key. The content control in the cell to the right of "Date of birth" is selected.

▶ **4.** Click the **arrow** at the right of the cell, click the **backward** scroll arrow ◀ to the left of the month name in the calendar as many times as necessary to scroll to **December 2005**, and then click **12**. December 12, 2005 appears in the cell.

▶ **5.** Press the **Tab** key, type **207-555-3920**, press the **Tab** key, type **12 Birch Lane**, press the **Tab** key, type **patty@dunstanfamily.name**, and then press the **Tab** key. The content control to the right of "City" is selected. This is one of the Combo Box content controls. The next content control, the cell to the right of State, is also a Combo Box. You'll enter text in one and select from the list in the other.

▶ **6.** Type **South Portland**, and then press the **Tab** key. The State content control is selected.

▶ **7.** Click the arrow that appears in the content control to the right of the "State" label, click **ME**, and then press the **Tab** key. The content control to the right of "Account type" is a Drop-Down List control.

▶ **8.** Click the **arrow**, click **Visa**, press the **Tab** key, type **04106**, press the **Tab** key, type **1234 5678 9012 3456**, press the **Tab** key, type **207-555-3112**, and then press the **Tab** key. The Expiration Date content control is selected.

▶ **9.** Use the calendar to select any date in **February 2014** as the expiration date, and then press the **Tab** key. The expiration date for the credit card appears as 02/14, and the content control in the cell beneath the cell containing the expiration date is selected.

▶ **10.** Type **Patricia E Dunstan**, and then press the **Tab** key. The content control next to "Class" is selected. This is in the section of the form that only employees will be using. You realize that a customer filling out the form might not see the cell asking if the child needs a uniform. You'll format it to draw attention to it when you are finished testing the form.

▶ **11.** In the cell to the right of "Does child need a uniform?", click the **check box** to remove the X.

▶ **12.** Click in cell **C13** (the cell to the right of "Class"), click the **arrow**, click **Preschool/ Kindergarten**, press the **Tab** key, type **Call cell phone number first.**, and then press the **Tab** key. The insertion point does not move. Pressing the Tab key moves the insertion point to the next content control. Cell C14, the cell next to "Price per class," contains a form field.

▶ **13.** Click in cell C14, type **14**, and then press the **Tab** key. $112.00 appears in cell C15.

▶ **14.** Drag the **Zoom slider** to the left to change the zoom to 80%. Your completed form should look like the one shown in Figure 9-43.

Completed test form ◀ Figure 9-43

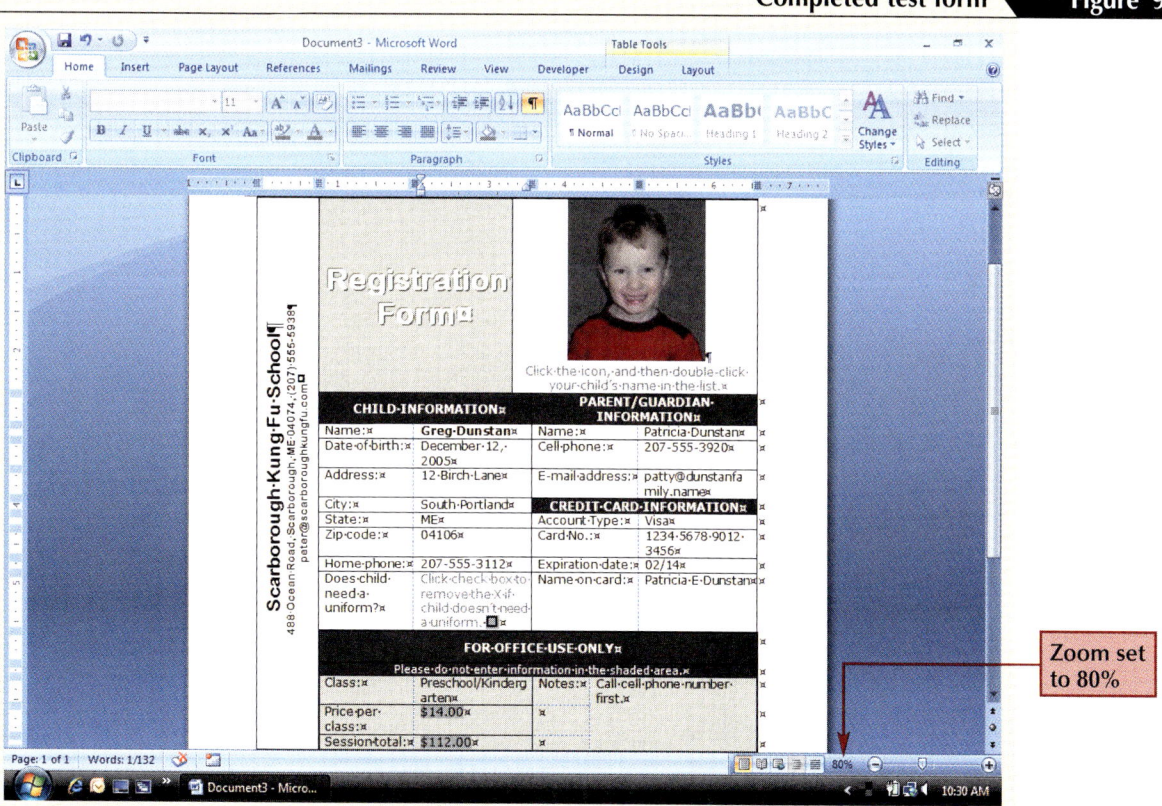

Zoom set to 80%

▶ **15.** On the Quick Access Toolbar, click the **Save** button 🖫 , navigate to the **Tutorial.09\Tutorial** folder included with your Data Files, replace the text in the File name text box with **Test Form**, and then click the **Save** button.

▶ **16.** Close the Test Form document, but leave Word running.

The form you created in this tutorial contains information organized in a logical way for the person who needs to create and store the form. However, as you might have noticed when you entered the information in the form, it is not set up in the most logical way for the user who is pressing the Tab key to move from one control or field to the next. When you design a form, keep the Tab key behavior in mind and try to come up with a design that works for both the person entering the data and the person who will be reading the form.

Now you will format the section containing the check box to draw the user's attention to it in case they press the Tab key to move from control to control. Before you can do this, you need to open the form template and turn off protection.

To open the template and change the formatting of the check box label and field:

▶ **1.** Click the **Office Button** 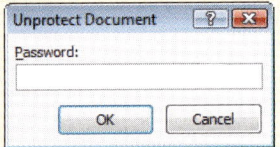, click **Open** to open the Open dialog box, navigate to the **Tutorial.09\Tutorial** folder included with your Data Files, and then double-click **Registration Form**. The form opens as a template, not a new document, so any changes you make will be saved in the template. Before you can make any changes to the password-protected template, you need to turn off protection.

▶ **2.** Click the **Developer** tab, in the Protect group click the **Protect Document** button, and then, in the Formatting and Editing Restrictions task pane, click the **Stop Protection** button. The Unprotect Document dialog box opens. See Figure 9-44.

Figure 9-44 ▶ **Unprotect Document dialog box**

▶ **3.** In the Password text box, type **peterd**, click the **OK** button, and then close the task pane. Now you can change the format of the cells.

▶ **4.** Select cells **B10** and **C10** (the cell containing "Does child need a uniform?" and the cell to its right). To make these cells jump out at the user so they won't inadvertently skip over this check box, you'll fill them with a bright color.

▶ **5.** Click the **Table Tools Design** tab, in the Table Styles group click the **Shading button arrow**, under Standard Colors in the last row of the color palette, click the **Yellow** tile, and then deselect the cells.

You've finished making the final touches to your form.

▶ **6.** On the Quick Access Toolbar, click the **Customize Quick Access Toolbar** button ⯆, click **Minimize the Ribbon**, change the zoom to **80%**, and then use the scroll bar to center the form in the document window. The final form should look like Figure 9-45.

Completed form template Figure 9-45

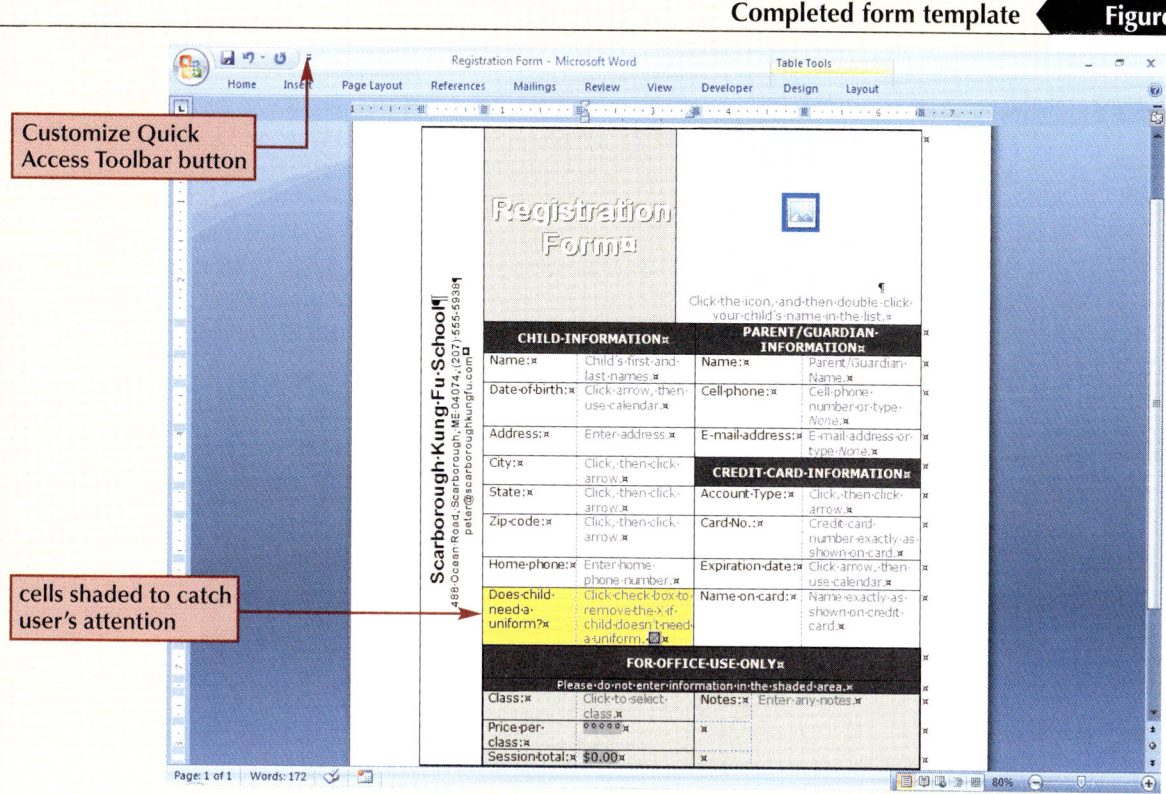

7. On the Quick Access Toolbar, click the **Customize Quick Access Toolbar** button , and then click **Minimize the Ribbon** to restore the Ribbon.

8. Turn on protection using the same password you did before (**peterd**), close the task pane, and then save the changes to the template.

9. Click the **Office Button**, click **Word Options**, click the **Show Developer tab in the Ribbon** check box to deselect it, and then click **OK**. The Developer tab no longer appears on the Ribbon.

10. Close the document and exit Word.

Now that you've finished filling in the form, you can be satisfied that it works as Pete planned. The last thing Pete wants you to do is to look into how he can get copies of the completed registration forms to the parents or guardians of the children they've enrolled.

Faxing or E-Mailing a Document

After completing a registration form, the employee at the Kung Fu school needs to give a copy of it to the student's parent or guardian. One way to do this is to use the Send command on the Office menu, which you can use with an Internet fax service to fax the document directly from the computer. You can also use the Send command to send a copy of the completed form as an attachment to an e-mail message.

Faxing a Document Directly from Word

To send a fax from your computer without having to print first and then send the paper through a fax machine, you need to have either a fax modem that you can set up as a printer, or you need to have subscribed to a fax Internet service. If you have a fax modem, you can open the Print dialog box, click the Name arrow, and then click Fax in the list. After you click OK, the Fax Setup Wizard starts. Click Connect to a fax modem, and then follow the steps in the wizard. You'll need to have administrative rights on your computer to complete the wizard. When you're finished, the New Fax message box opens ready for you to type a fax number in the To box. This message box looks similar to a new e-mail message box. Just like an e-mail message, you can type a Subject in the Subject box. The fax is a graphic attachment to New Fax message. See Figure 9-46. When you're ready, click the Send button on the toolbar.

Figure 9-46   New Fax message box

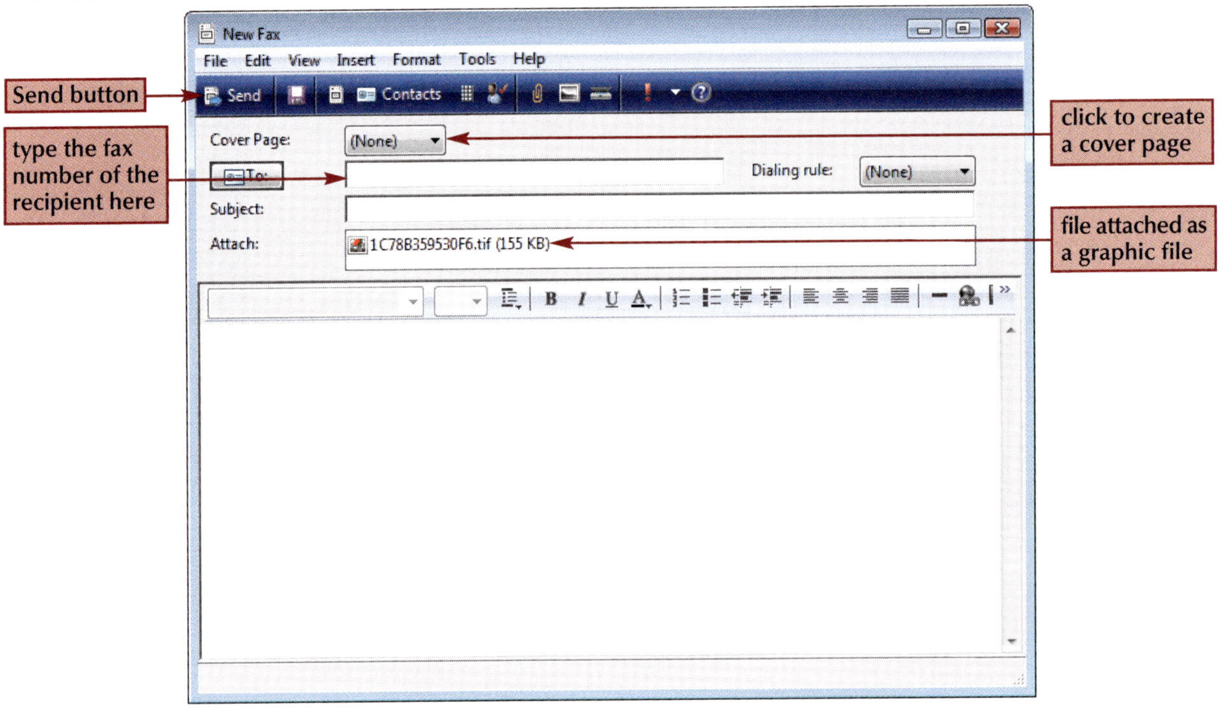

To subscribe to an Internet fax service from within Word, click the Office Button, point to Send, and then click Internet Fax. If you have not subscribed to an Internet fax service yet, a dialog box opens informing you that you need to sign up with a fax service provider. If you click the OK button in this dialog box, your browser starts and a Web page on Microsoft Office Online opens listing the available fax services that work with Word and links to sign up with the services. See Figure 9-47.

Available Fax Services Web page on Microsoft Office Online **Figure 9-47**

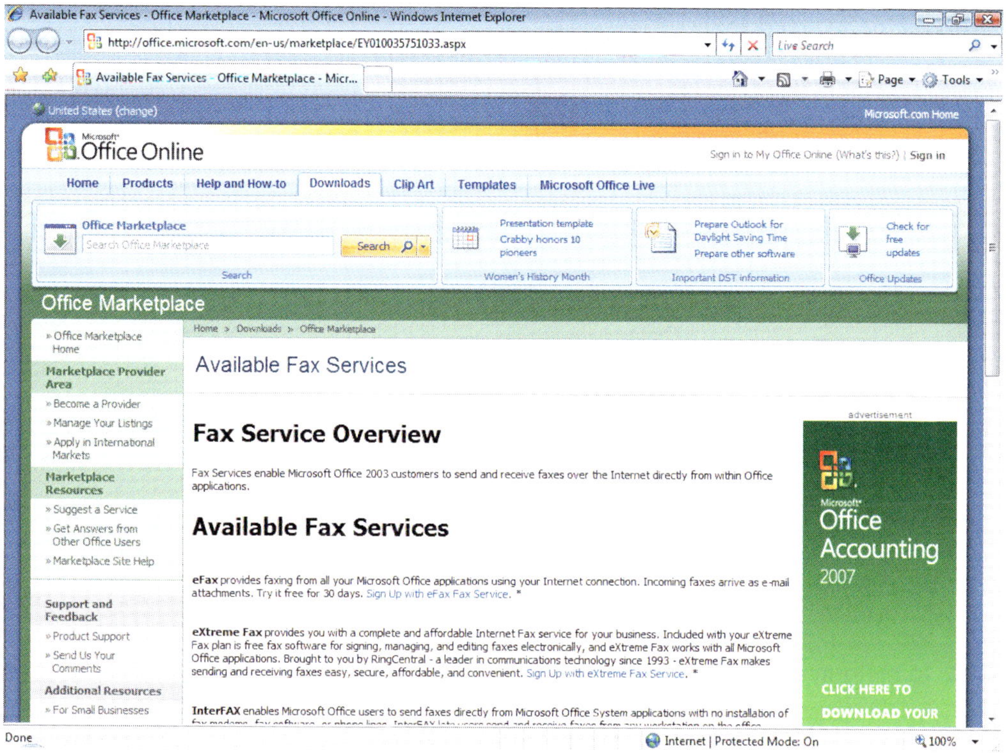

Once you've signed up with a fax service, clicking the Internet Fax command opens a new e-mail message window in Outlook or opens the fax service's interface. You can type the recipient's name and fax number as well as the subject of the fax, and then send the fax.

Sending a Document as an E-Mail Attachment Directly from Word

If you want to share a document with a group of people who have access to e-mail, and if you want to accumulate comments and corrections from members of the workgroup, then you might want to route the document instead of faxing it. When you **route** a document, you send it as an attachment to an e-mail message; the message (with the document attached) then travels to a group of people, one person at a time. The recipients of the e-mail are specified in a **routing slip**. After each person reads the document and makes comments and corrections, he or she sends it to the next recipient on the routing slip. Each recipient then has the benefit of seeing all the comments and corrections of previous reviewers. When the document returns to you, it will have accumulated comments and corrections from all the reviewers.

To understand another use of routing, suppose that Scarborough Kung Fu Studio is preparing to host a special series of classes for women on self-defense. Each time a person signs up for the class, an employee prepares a registration form that can include some information about the woman's fitness level. The employee can then route the order form to Pete so that he can track the number of women taking the courses and so that he can assign the woman to a class level, then to the course coordinator who arranges accommodations for the class participants, then to the class teacher, and so on. If any person in the routing doesn't approve the form, it doesn't go on to the subsequent members of the workgroup. Whether the form is approved or not, it returns to the originator of the routed document.

To e-mail a document as an attachment to an e-mail message, you click the Office Button, point to Send, and then click E-mail. A message window opens with the document attached. You can then address it and send it as usual.

Pete is pleased with the appearance of the form you created and with how well it works. He's sure it will make the process for enrolling new students more efficient as well as improve the accuracy of the records kept at the studio.

Review | Session 9.3 Quick Check

1. Why would you use a legacy form field? When should you *not* use a legacy form field?
2. How do you set the default value of a check box form field to checked?
3. What is a formula?
4. What is a variable?
5. What is an argument?
6. How does the number 34 appear if the numeric picture is $##0.00;($##0.00)?
7. What is always the first character in a formula in a Word table?
8. To perform a calculation using a legacy text form field, you need to check the Calculate on exit check box in the Text Form Field Options dialog box. Do you check this in the Form Field Options dialog box for the form field used in the formula, or in the Form Field Options dialog box for the form field that displays the result?

Tutorial Summary | Review

In this tutorial, you formatted a table using advanced table features, including merging and splitting cells, changing borders, rotating text in a cell, and formatting text and cells. Next, you added content controls and legacy form fields to create an on-screen form. You saved the form as a template so users could fill in the form online. Finally, you protected the form with a password, tested it, and explored options for sending it.

Key Terms

argument	form field	Rich Text content control
border	formula	route
Building Block Gallery content control	function	routing slip
check box form field	legacy form field	split (table cells)
Combo Box content control	legacy tools	surprinted type
Date Picker content control	merge (table cells)	tag
date-time picture	numeric picture	Text content control
Drop-Down List content control	on-screen form	text form field
dropout type	Picture content control	variable
	protect (an on-screen form)	weight
	reverse type	

| Practice | **Review Assignments** |

Data Files needed for the Review Assignments: AppForm.docx, Teen.jpg

Peter Dietz, owner of Scarborough Kung Fu Studios, wants to hire more staff. He asked you to develop an on-screen form that potential employees can fill out. He created a basic table. You need to format the table, insert content controls, and test the form. Complete the following:

1. Open the file **AppForm** from the Tutorial.09\Review folder included with your Data Files, and then save it in the same folder as a document template with the filename **Application Form**.

2. Select cells A1 through D1, and then split the selected cells into one column and two rows, merging the cells before you split them. Move the text "Application for Employment" into the new cell A2.

3. Format the text in cell A1 as bold 18-point Cambria with a shadow effect, and then format the text in cell A2 as bold 14-point Calibri.

4. Merge the following cells:
   - B3 through D3 (the cells to the right of "Photo")
   - C4 and C5 (the cell containing "Gender" and the cell beneath it)
   - A7 through D7 (the cell containing "Previous Work Experience" and the cells to its right)
   - A8 and B8 (the cell containing "Dates Employed" and the cell to its right)
   - C9 and C10 (the cell containing "Employer Address" and the cell beneath it)
   - D9 and D10 (the cells to the right of the merged "Employer Address" cell)
   - D11 through D14 (the last four cells in column D)

5. Select cells A6 through D6, and then split them into six columns and one row, merging the cells before you split them. Drag "Zip:" to cell E6, drag "ME" to cell D6, and then drag "State:" to cell C6.

6. Split cells D4 and D5 into two columns, deselecting the Merge cells before split check box (this will keep the same number of rows). Repeat this for cells A11 through A14. Drag the contents of cells A11 through A14 to the cells in the same row in column B. Merge cells A11 through A14, and then type **Office Use Only** in the new cell A11.

7. Rotate the text in cell A11 so that it reads from bottom to top.

8. Turn off automatic column resizing, and then resize the columns as shown in the table on the next page. Make sure you resize the columns in the order they are listed below. Note that after you resize cells C11 through C14 in the last step, the width of cells D11 through D14 changes to approximately .6 inches.

Cell	Width (in inches)
A3 ("Photo")	.35
A4 and A5, and then A6 ("Name" through "City")	.9
B4 and B5 (blank cells to the right of "Name" and "Address")	2.75
C4 ("Gender")	.8
D4 and D5 ("Male" and "Female")	.6
A9 and A10 ("From" and "To")	.6
A8 through B10 ("Dates Employed" through cell to the right of "To")	1.35
C8 through C9 ("Employer Name" through "Employer Address")	1.15
A11 ("Office Use Only")	.5
B11 through B14 ("Position Applied For" through "Overtime Rate")	1.2
D11 through D14 ("Notes" and cells beneath it)	1.25
C11 through C14 (to the right of "Position Applied For" through "Overtime Rate")	1.75

9. In row 6, drag the left borders of the cells after you select each of them to change the widths as follows: resize cell E6 ("Zip") to .3 inches, cell D6 (cell to the left of "Zip") to .8 inches, and cell C6 ("State") to .5 inches.

10. Resize row 7 ("Previous Work Experience") so it is approximately twice its original height.

11. Center the text in cells A1 ("Scarborough Kung Fu") and A2 ("Application for Employment") horizontally and vertically. Align the text in cell A7 ("Previous Work Experience") so it is left-aligned horizontally and centered vertically.

12. Shade cell A7 ("Previous Work Experience"), cell A11 ("Office Use Only"), and all the cells to the right of cell A11 with the light blue color in the second row, fifth column, under Theme Colors in the Shading button color palette (Blue, Accent 1, Lighter 80%). Fill cell A2 ("Application for Employment") with the dark blue color in the fifth row, fifth column, under Theme Colors in the Shading button color palette (Blue, Accent 1, Darker 25%), and format the text as reverse type.

13. Add a 2¼-point border above cell A1 ("Scarborough Kung Fu"), below cell A2 ("Application for Employment"), and above cell A7 ("Previous Work Experience"). Add a 2¼-point border around the shaded "Office Use Only" section at the bottom of the table.

14. Remove the borders (but do not erase the gridlines) from the right of the following cells:
    - A3 ("Photo")
    - A4 ("Name") through A6 ("City")
    - C4 ("Gender")
    - D4 ("Male") through D5 ("Female")
    - C6 ("State")
    - E6 ("Zip")
    - C8 ("Employer Name") through C9 ("Employer Address")
    - A9 ("From") through A10 ("To")
    - B11 ("Position Applied For") through B14 ("Overtime Rate")
    - D11 ("Notes") through D14

15. Remove the bottom border (but do not erase the gridlines) from the following cells: D4 through E4 ("Male" and the cell to its right), A8 ("Dates Employed"), A9 ("From") and B9, D11 ("Notes"), D12, and D13. (*Hint*: If a bottom border doesn't disappear, try selecting the cell below it and remove the top border from that cell.)

16. Show the Developer tab, and then insert Text content controls in the cells listed below. Do not allow the controls to be deleted. Use the contents of the cell to the left of the content control as the title of the control. Revise the placeholder text as indicated below.

Cell	Located to the right of	Placeholder text
B4	"Name"	Enter your name.
B5	"Address"	Enter your street address.
D8	"Employer Name"	Enter the name of your former employer.
D9	"Employer Address"	Enter the address of your former employer.
E11	"Notes"	Enter notes.

17. Change the properties of the Name content control (cell B4) so that it uses the Strong style. Change the properties of the Employer Address content control (cell D9) and the Notes content control (cell E11) to allow carriage returns (multiple paragraphs).

18. Insert Date Picker content controls in cell B9 (to the right of "From") and B10 (to the right of "To"). Use **Start Date** as the title of the control in cell B9 and **End Date** as the title of the control in cell B10. Do not allow the controls to be deleted, and use M/YYYY as the date format. Change the placeholder text in both cells to **Click arrow to select month and year.**

19. Insert a Drop-Down List content control in cell C11 (to the right of "Position Applied For"). Use **Position** as the title, do not allow the control to be deleted, and add **Assistant**, **Lead Assistant**, **Receptionist**, and **Teacher** as the choices in the list. Change the instruction text at the top of the list and the placeholder text to **Select position applied for**.

20. Insert a Drop-Down List content control in cell C12 (to the right of "Decision"). Use **Decision** as the title, and do not allow the control to be deleted. Add **Deferred**, **Hired**, and **Not hired** as the choices in the list. Move Deferred so it is the last choice in the list. Change the instruction text at the top of the list and the placeholder text in the control to **Choose hiring status**.

21. Insert a Combo Box content control in cell B6 (to the right of "City"). Use **City** as the title, do not allow the control to be deleted, add **Scarborough** as the only item in the list, and change the instruction text at the top of the list and the placeholder text in the control to **Click Scarborough or type your city/town.**

22. Insert a Combo Box content control in cell F6 (to the right of "Zip"). Use **Zip Code** as the title, do not allow the control to be deleted, add **04074** and **04070** as the items in the list, and change the instruction text at the top of the list and the placeholder text in the control to **Click zip code or type yours if different.**

23. Insert a Picture content control in cell B3 (to the right of "Photo"). Align the control at the top center of the cell. Insert **Click icon to insert your photo.** under the control in the cell, and format it as dark gray using the White, Background 1, Darker 50% tile in the Font Color palette. (You do not need to set any properties for this control.) Rotate the text in cell A3 so it reads from bottom to top and center the text horizontally and vertically in the cell.

24. Insert check box form fields in cells E4 and E5 (to the right of "Male" and "Female"). Insert **(click box to select)** under "Gender:" in cell D4, and format the text you inserted as dark gray using the White, Background 1, Darker 50% tile in the Font Color palette.

25. Insert Text form fields in cell C13 (to the right of "Hourly Wage") and cell C14 ("Overtime Rate"). Change the type in cell C13 to Number and in C14 to Calculation. Change the format in both cells to show currency. Set the field in cell C13 to calculate on exit. Type **=PRODUCT(C13,1.5)** as the Expression property in cell C14.

26. Protect the template for filling in a form with the password **peterd**, and then save the completed template form to the Tutorial.09\Review folder. Hide the Developer tab.

27. Open a new document based on this form. (*Hint*: Use the New command on the Office menu to open the New Document dialog box, and then click New from existing in the Templates pane.) Fill in the form using the name **Olivia Johnson** and fictitious (but reasonable) information for the rest of the controls. Insert your name in the cell to the right of "Notes." Use **Teen.jpg**, located in the Tutorial.09\Review folder, as the photo.

28. Save the completed form as **Test Application Form** to the Tutorial.09\Review folder included with your Data Files. Submit the final documents to your instructor in electronic or printed form, as requested. Close all open documents.

Apply | Case Problem 1

pply the skills you arned to create a ew template form.

Data File needed with this Case Problem: NewStudent.docx, Toddler.jpg

Sanborn Preschool Michelle Naughton owns Sanborn Preschool in Sanborn, Illinois. Every year, when new students register, she and her assistant spend hours retyping the information parents entered on paper forms into the computer. She wants to automate this process and have the parents enter information in an on-screen form. She asks you to help her by preparing the form. She does not want any of the content controls to be deleted as people use the form. Complete the following:

1. Open the file **NewStudent** from the Tutorial.09\Case1 folder included with your Data Files, and then save it in the same folder as a template with the filename **New Student Registration Form**.

2. Insert a new column A, and then merge the cells in column A so it becomes one cell. Fill the cell with Orange, Accent 3, Lighter 40%.

3. Merge cells C2 through D2 (the cells to the right of "Address").

4. Select cells B3 ("City") through E3 (to the right of "State"), and then split them into six columns and one row, merging them first. Drag "IL" to cell E3, and then drag "State" to cell D3. Type **Zip:** in cell F3.

5. Merge cells D5 and E5.

6. Resize column A to be approximately .4 inches wide, and then resize the rest of the cells containing labels so they just fit. (*Hint*: If you're having trouble resizing individual cells, select all the text and the end-of-cell mark in the cell you are trying to resize, and then drag the gridline.) Finally, resize cell C6 (to the right of "Photo Date") to be approximately 1 inch wide.

✦ **EXPLORE**

7. Use the Draw Table button to draw a new row with ½-point borders at the top of the table. After making the Draw Table pointer active, drag a rectangle above the top row of the table, starting approximately ¼-inch above the upper-left corner of the table and ending at the upper-right corner of the table. Type **Sanborn Preschool** in the new cell A1, format the text as 16-point Berlin Sans FB, and center align the text in the cell. Fill the cell with Orange, Accent 3, Lighter 80%.

8. Change the top border of the table and the border above cells B6 ("Photo Date") through D6 (the merged cell in the last row) so they are 2¼ points thick.

9. Insert a Text content control in cell A2 (the merged cell shaded orange to the left of the main part of the table) with a title of Last Name. Change the placeholder text to **Type child's last name.** Center the control in the cell.

✦ **EXPLORE**

10. Create a new style for the control in cell A2. In the Content Control Properties dialog box, click the New Style button to open the Create New Style from Formatting dialog box. In the Name text box, type LastName. At the bottom of the dialog box, click the New documents based on this template option button. Click the Format button, and then click Font to open the Font dialog box. In the Font style list, click Bold. In the Size list, click 16. In the Effects section, click the Small caps check box. Click the OK button twice.

11. Rotate the contents in cell A2 so they read from bottom to top.

12. Insert Text content controls in cells C2 (to the right of "Name") and C3 (to the right of "Address") with appropriate titles and placeholder text.

13. Insert a Date Picker content control in cell C6 (to the right of "Photo Date") with the title **Photo Date** and the placeholder text **Date photo was taken.** Use the format MMMM yyyy.

14. Insert a Picture content control in cell D6 with the title **Current Photo**. Center the content control in the cell.

15. Insert Combo Box content controls with appropriate titles in cells C4 (to the right of "City") and G4 (to the right of "Zip"). Add **Sanborn** as an item in the City Combo Box list, and **60222** and **60223** as items in the zip code list. Modify the instruction item in the list and the placeholder text to let the user know that he or she can select an item in the list or type different information.

16. Insert a Drop-Down List content control in cell E5 (to the right of "Program") with **Program** as the title and **Choose a program** as the instruction and placeholder text. Add **Preschool, Toddler, Nursery,** and **Kindergarten Prep** as the items in the list. Change the order of these items so that "Preschool" is the third item in the list.

17. Insert five check box form fields in cell C5 (to the right of "Allergies") to the left of each item. Set the check box next to "None" as checked by default. In cell C5, add the following above the list: **Deselect *None* if necessary and select all that apply.**

18. Protect the form, save your changes, and then close the form without exiting Word. Create a new document based on the New Student Registration Form and save it as **Preschool Test Form** to the Tutorial.09\Case1 folder.

19. In the Preschool Test Form document, test the form by inserting pretend data. Dese-lect the None check box and select at least one of the other check boxes. Use the file **Toddler.jpg**, located in the Tutorial.09\Case1 folder as the picture to insert. Save the final, filled-in form.

20. Submit the final documents to your instructor in electronic or printed form, as requested. Close all open documents.

| Create | | Case Problem 2 |

*eate a form for a
obile pet grooming
mpany using the
ills you learned in
is tutorial.*

Data File needed for this Case Problem: Dog.jpg

Minneapolis Mobile Pet Minneapolis Mobile Pet is a mobile pet-grooming service owned by Karl Fahlstrom. Karl has a fleet of eight vans that are kept busy with his full schedule. He recently equipped all the vans with laptop computers so his groomers can input information at their appointments. This way they won't have to spend time at the office transferring data from paper to the computer. He asked you to create a simple form for his groomers to use. To complete this case problem, you'll create and test the form shown in Figure 9-48.

Figure 9-48

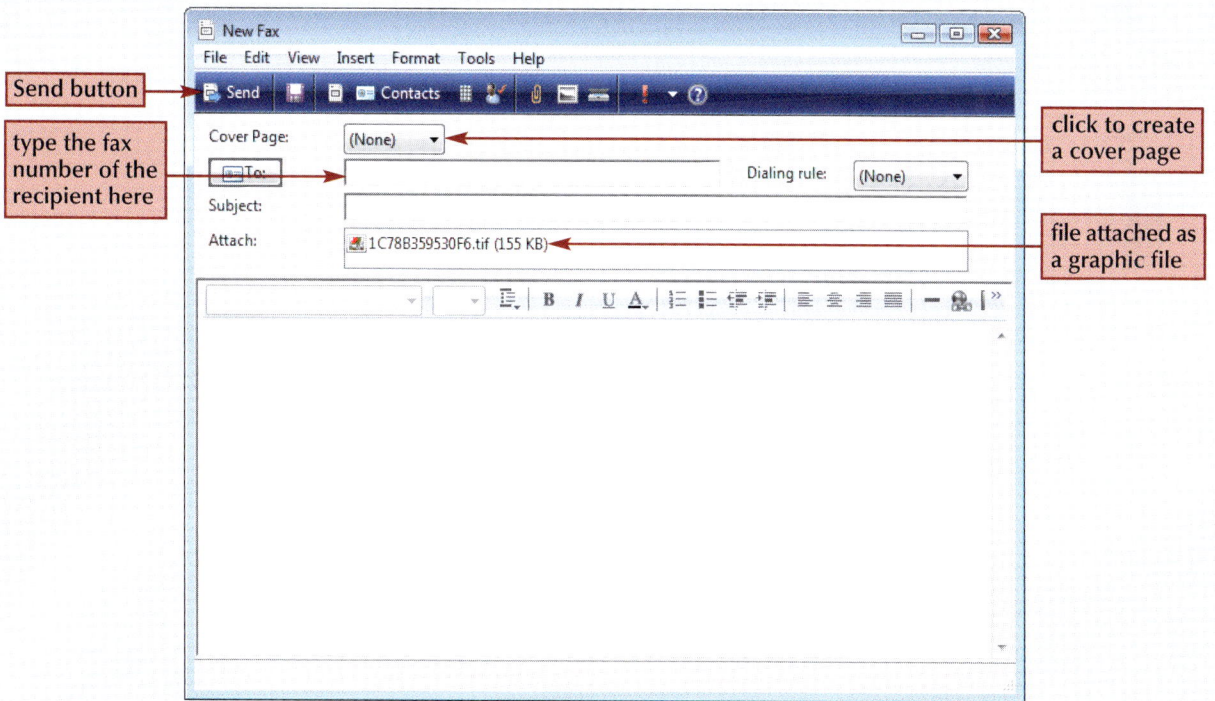

To help you create the form, use the following guidelines:

1. The theme used for the form is the Foundry theme, but the font used in the table is 12-point Corbel. The text in cell A1 is 16-point bold.

2. The thick border used around sections in the form is $2\frac{1}{4}$ points wide.

3. The shading in cell A1 is Olive Green, Text 2, the shading in cells D4 through E7 is Tan, Background 2, Darker 10%, and the shading in cells B4 through C6 is Rose, Accent 6.
4. The format of "Minneapolis Mobile Pet" above the table is 28-point Rockwell set in italics in Olive Green, Text 2, Darker 25% with the small caps effect.
5. Cells C1, C2, and C3 contain Text content controls. The control in cell C2 allows the user to press the Enter key to create multiple paragraphs.
6. Cell E1 contains a picture content control.
7. Cell E3 contains a Combo Box control with **Mark**, **Isaiah**, and **Corrine** as the values in the list.
8. Cells C4, C5, and C6 contain Drop-Down List controls with **Bath**, **Trim**, and **Nail clipping** as the values in the list in each control.
9. Cells E4, E5, E6, and E7 contain text form fields. The function used to calculate the result in E7 is =SUM(ABOVE).
10. The font for the placeholder text in all the cells with content controls is 11-point Rockwell, and it is colored White, Background 1, Darker 50%.

After you have created the form template, complete the following:

11. Protect the document for filling in forms using **PET** as the password, and then save it as a template named **Grooming Form** in the Tutorial.09\Case2 folder.
12. Create a new document based on this form. Use the file **Dog.jpg**, located in the Tutorial.09\Case2 folder, to insert a picture in the cell E1, and type **Retriever** as the breed. Type any name you want for the Pet Name and then type your last name. Type your name in the Combo Box in cell E3. Select a different service in each of the three service lists in cells C4, C5, and C6. The cost of a bath for a retriever is $45, the trim is $10, and nail clipping is $10.
13. Save the completed form as **Retriever Form** in the Tutorial.09\Case2 folder.
14. Submit the final documents to your instructor in electronic or printed form, as requested. Close all open documents.

Apply | **Case Problem 3**

Apply the skills you learned in the tutorial to create an order form for a landscaping company.

Data Files needed for this Case Problem: Landscaping.docx

Lakeville Landscaping You have recently been asked to design a customer form for Lakeville Landscaping. Mario Ramirez, the owner, has started selling plants directly to his customers. He wants his office staff to be able to input plant orders directly into the computer. He created a table with the information he wants included in the form. To complete this case problem, you'll design and create a form to allow employees to take plant orders. Complete the following:

1. Open the file **Landscaping** from the Tutorial.09\Case3 folder. Save it as a Word template named **Landscaping Order** to the same folder.
2. Create a new column consisting of only one cell to the left of the table. Move the name of the company to this cell and rotate it so it reads from bottom to top.
3. In the top row, merge the cells in columns B, C, and D.
4. Format the text in cell B1, the labels in column B, and the label in cell D2 with bold.
5. Format the name of the company in cell A1 so it is bold and with the font effects Engrave and Small caps.
6. Format the text in cells A1 and B1 so that it is 14 points.

7. Fill cell A1 with a dark green and reverse type. Fill cell B1 with a light green.

8. Change the width of column A to approximately .57 inches and column B to approximately 1.5 inches.

9. Right-align the text in cells B2 through B7, and then remove the vertical border between the cells in columns B and C and rows 2 through 6.

10. Remove the border below cells D2 and below D4, D5, and D6. Fill cells D4, D5, D6, and D7 with the same green that you used in cell B1.

11. Draw a 3-point border around the outside of the table.

12. Insert a Text content control in cell C2 with the title **Type of plant** and formatted with the Intense Emphasis style. Change the placeholder text to **Enter type of plant.**

13. Insert a Combo Box content control in cell C3 with the title **Employee**. Include **Sonia**, **Sun**, and **Leah** as the names in the list. Reorder them in alphabetical order. Change the first item in the list and the placeholder text to **Click an employee name or type your name**.

14. Insert a Date Picker content control in cell D3 with the title **Delivery Date** and the format Fri, June 4, 2010. (*Hint*: Choose a format in the list and then modify the date-time picture. Note that the day of the week is abbreviated, and only one number appears for a single-digit date.)

15. Insert text form fields in cells C4, C5, C6, and C7. Change the type of the form fields in cells C4 and C5 to Number, and the type of the form fields in cells C6 and C7 to Calculation. The formula in cell C6 should add the values in cells C4 and C5 and then multiply the result by 7%. The formula in cell C7 should add the values in the cells above it. Change the number format of all four form fields to show currency.

16. Protect the document using the password **PLANT**, and then save and close the document, but do not exit Word.

17. Create a new document based on the newly created form. Fill in the information for the form using real or fictitious (but reasonable) information. For the employee name, use your own name.

18. Save the completed form as **Completed Order** in the Tutorial.09\Case3 folder.

19. Submit the completed documents to your instructor in electronic or printed form, as requested. Close all open documents.

Challenge | Case Problem 4

pand the skills you arned in the tutorial create a form that ks permission to use photo in a Web site r a dance studio.

Data Files needed for this Case Problem: Dance.dotx, Dancer.jpg

Donna Vasquez Dance Donna Vasquez owns and operates a dance studio. Her students perform in competitions and recitals throughout the year. The studio has a Web site, and Donna posts photos of some of her students on it. She always gets permission from the students' parents or guardians first. She asked you to create an on-screen permission form that the parents or guardians can sign. An employee will fill out the form and then send the form via e-mail to the parent or guardian. Design an on-screen fill-in form by completing the following:

1. Read through each step for this entire Case Problem. Then, using paper and pencil, design an on-screen fill-in form with the features mentioned in the following steps. As you plan, make function and appearance your main concerns.

2. Open the template **Dance** located in the Tutorial.09\Case4 folder included with your Data Files. Save it as a template named **Photo Permission** in the same folder. This template appears blank but it contains Quick Parts. Choose the theme, color scheme, and fonts that you want to use.

3. Create a table at the top of the document. Start with one that is four columns and six rows. You can modify it if necessary.

4. Modify the table so that the first row includes the name of the form, and the first column has the name of the dance studio (Donna Vasquez Dance). The cell in the first row should span the width of the table, and the cell in the first column should span the table height (except for the first row). Shade these cells with different, complementary colors. Use an attractive, interesting font for the name of the dance studio.

5. The second row should include a place for the student's name and a place for the photo the studio wants to post on the Web site.

6. Include a label and content control that allows the employee to select the style of dance only from a list. The dance styles are ballet, tap, jazz, lyric, and hip-hop.

7. Include a content control that allows the employee to select the student's teacher from a list or type the name of teacher not included in the list (such as teachers who teach only one or two classes.) The full-time teachers at the studio are Miss Julie, Miss Tania, Miss Sophie, and Mr. Karl.

⊕ **EXPLORE** 8. Include a Building Block Gallery content control that allows the employee to select the dancer's level from a Quick Part stored with the template. (*Hint*: Click the Insert tab, and then in the Text group, click the Quick Parts button to see the Quick Parts stored with the template.)

9. Include a control for selecting the date of the photo and another control for the date the parent or guardian is contacted. Include a control for typing the parent or guardian's name.

10. Do not allow any of the content controls to be deleted.

11. Modify placeholder text to give helpful instructions, and add any shading and formatting you think will make your form attractive and easy to read. Use thicker border lines if appropriate, and remove any border lines that are distracting.

12. Below the table, type the following: **By signing this document, you give permission for Donna Vasquez Studios to publish the above photo on our Web site.** Below this text, type a line that is long enough to hold a signature.

13. Use the Group command to protect the content controls in the table.

14. Save and close the template, and then create a new document based on the template. Save the document as **Photo Signature Form** in the Tutorial.09\Case4 folder included with your Data Files.

15. Fill out the form using real or fictitious (but reasonable) information. Use your name as the teacher's name. Use the photo **Dancer.jpg**, located in the Tutorial.09\Case4 folder included with your Data Files. Save the completed form.

⊕ **EXPLORE** 16. Click the Office Button, point to Send, and then click E-mail. In the To box in the new e-mail message window that opens, type your e-mail address.

17. Start your e-mail program and retrieve your messages. Open the Photo Signature Form document attached to the message you sent to yourself. If you were filling out this form for a real dance studio, you would sign the form and mail it back to the dance studio.

18. Close your e-mail program.

19. Submit the final documents to your instructor in electronic or printed form, as requested. Close all open documents.

Research | **Internet Assignments**

to the Web to find
formation you can
e to create
cuments.

The purpose of the Internet Assignments is to challenge you to find information on the Internet that you can use to work effectively with this software. The actual assignments are updated and maintained on the Course Technology Web site. Log on to the Internet and use your Web browser to go to the Student Online Companion for New Perspectives Office 2007 at **www.course.com/np/office2007**. Then navigate to the Internet Assignments for this tutorial.

Assess | **SAM Assessment and Training**

If you have a SAM user profile, you may have access to hands-on instruction, practice, and assessment of the skills covered in this tutorial. Log in to your SAM account (**http://sam2007.course.com**) to launch any assigned training activities or exams that relate to the skills covered in this tutorial.

Review | **Quick Check Answers**

Session 9.1

1. a Word template used for entering information at the computer
2. join two or more adjacent cells into one cell
3. divide one cell into two adjacent cells, or divide one column or row of cells into two or more columns or rows of cells
4. Click in the cell containing the text you want to rotate, click the Table Tools Layout tab, and then in the Alignment group click the Text Direction button.
5. Borders are drawn lines that visually frame a cell or group of cells. Borders appear when you print the table. Gridlines define the structure of the table and appear only on the screen.
6. Click in the cell containing the text you want to align, click the Table Tools Layout tab, and then in the Alignment group click one of the nine alignment buttons.
7. Click the cell you want to shade, click the Table Tools Design tab, click the Shading button, and then click a color tile.
8. white text on a black background

Session 9.2

1. The user can format the content he or she enters in a Rich Text content control. Also, the user is allowed to enter multiple paragraphs by default in a Rich Text content control; in a Text content control, a property must be set in order for the user to be able to enter multiple paragraphs.
2. you modify the default placeholder text
3. no
4. False: MM/dd/YYYY displays the date in the form 02/03/2010; dd MMMM YYYY displays the date in the form 03 February 2010.
5. to enable users to select from certain options, but also allow them to enter their own information if needed
6. building blocks stored in the template or on the computer

Session 9.3

1. because legacy form fields provide some capabilities that content controls do not have
2. in the Default Value section of the Check Box Form Field Options dialog box, click the Checked option button
3. a mathematical statement that calculates a value
4. a symbol for a number that can change
5. a value that a function needs in order to calculate its result
6. ($34.00)
7. = (the equal sign)
8. in the Form Field Options dialog box for the form field used in the formula

Ending Data Files

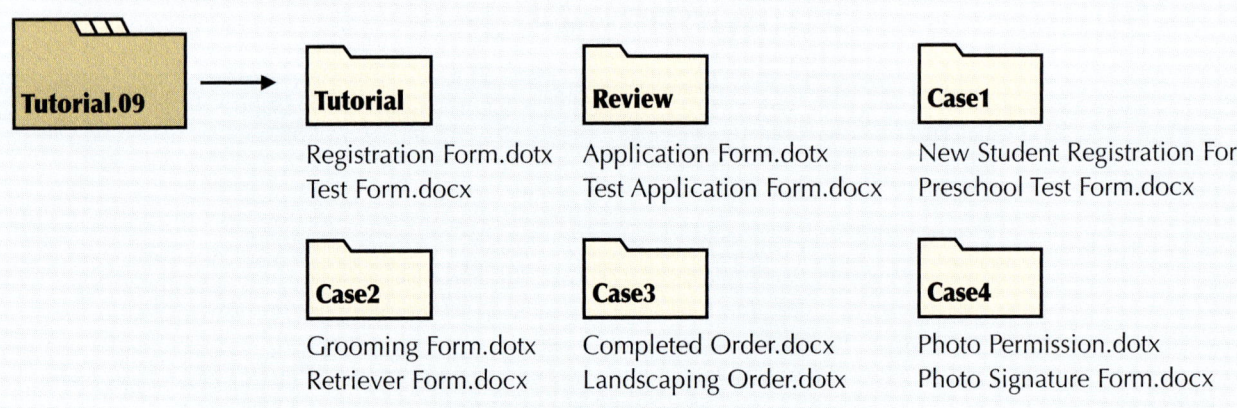

Tutorial.09 →

Tutorial
Registration Form.dotx
Test Form.docx

Review
Application Form.dotx
Test Application Form.docx

Case1
New Student Registration Form.◄
Preschool Test Form.docx

Case2
Grooming Form.dotx
Retriever Form.docx

Case3
Completed Order.docx
Landscaping Order.dotx

Case4
Photo Permission.dotx
Photo Signature Form.docx

Managing Long Documents

Creating a Broadband Subscriber Survey Report

Case | Continental Broadband Association

The Continental Broadband Association (CBA) is a consortium of broadband suppliers headquartered in Cambridge, Massachusetts. The companies belonging to CBA supply high-speed Internet access to residential customers, as well as to small and large businesses. Recently, CBA contracted with a market research company named Market Data Now, Inc. (MDNI) to obtain information about the attitudes of typical broadband subscribers. MDNI's research included an extensive subscriber survey. MDNI also conducted a series of focus groups.

Three of MDNI's market researchers, Michael Balczak, Katarina Thao, and Lori Tollefson, have been assigned to the research team for this project; Michael will oversee the entire project. In networking terminology, the team is considered a **workgroup**, a group of colleagues who have access to the same network server and work together on a common project. The group has finished conducting surveys and holding focus group meetings and is now working on a multipart report summarizing its findings. Each member of the workgroup has written at least one of the parts.

It's your job to help the workgroup combine the parts of the report into one master document, and then help edit the report to make it more attractive and easier to read. The report will include **front matter** (title page, table of contents, and list of figures), an index, and a bibliography. The team will set up the report to print on both sides of the paper, so the report will require different formats and footers for even and odd pages. When you are finished with the report, you will safeguard it against unauthorized edits by encrypting it. You will also verify its authenticity by adding a digital signature.

rting Data Files

torial.10	Tutorial	Review	Case1	Case2	Case3	Case4
	Kayla.jpg	Anls1.docx	Back.docx	Cyber.docx	Legal.docx	(none)
	Report.docx	Anls2.docx	Exec.docx			
	Report 2.docx	Intro.docx	Mar.docx			
	Res.docx	Table.jpg	Plan.docx			
	Small.docx	Wireless.docx				

Session 10.1

Working with Master Documents

Manipulating many pages in a long document can be cumbersome and time-consuming. On the other hand, splitting a long document into several shorter documents makes it hard to keep formatting consistent and to ensure that section and page numbering are always correct. To avoid these problems, you can use a master document, which combines the benefits of splitting documents into separate files with the advantages of working with a single document. A **master document** is a long document divided into several smaller, individual files, called **subdocuments**. Figure 10-1 illustrates the relationship between master documents and subdocuments.

Figure 10-1 ▶ **Master document and subdocument**

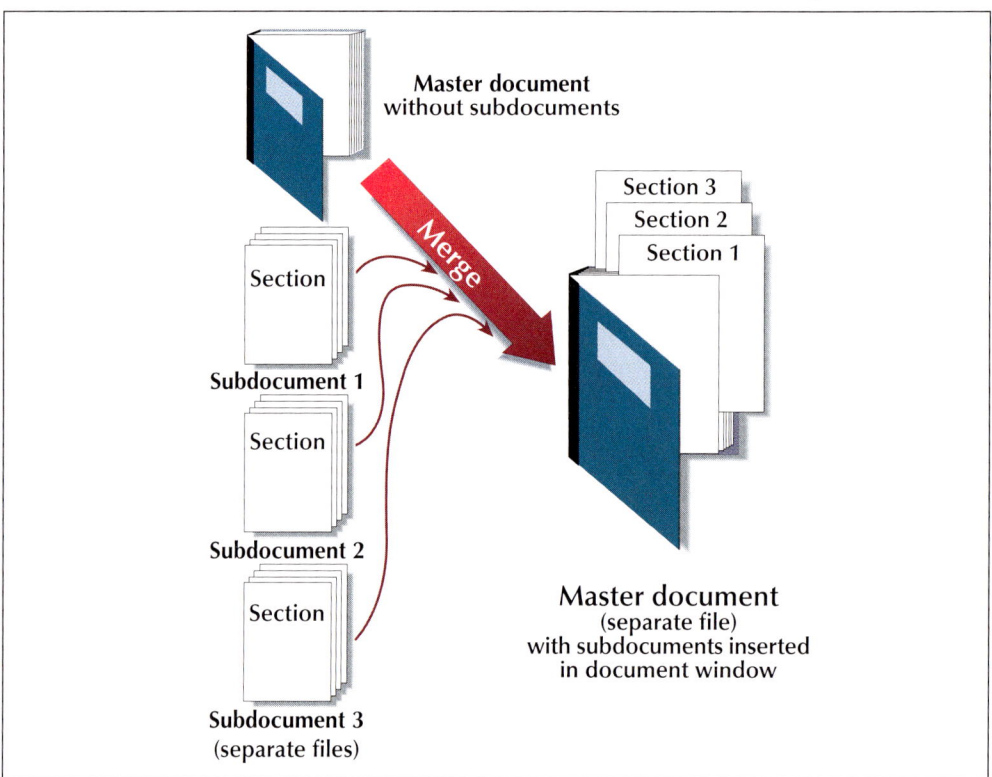

Using a master document is helpful when you are working with a document that consists of multiple parts. By working on each part individually, you avoid the extra time required to open, save, and edit a very large file. A master document is also helpful when several people are simultaneously working on different parts of the same document. Each member of the team can submit a separate document; you can then quickly organize these individual documents into a single, complete document by creating a master document. Finally, you might also want to use the master document feature when working with a document that contains many graphics, which require a large amount of computer memory and disk space.

Although you could work with and print smaller documents individually, combining them into a master document has several advantages:

- **Consistent formatting elements**. You set up styles, headers, footers, and other formatting elements in only the master document; the subdocuments get the same formatting.
- **Accurate numbering**. You can number the master document, including all subdocuments, with consecutive page numbers, heading numbers, and figure numbers. If you rearrange, delete, or add material, Word updates the numbers to reflect your changes.
- **Accurate cross-referencing**. You can refer to figures or tables in subdocuments and Word will keep the cross-references updated.
- **Complete table of contents, index, and bibliography**. You can easily compile a table of contents and create an index for a master document.
- **Faster editing**. You can edit the master document all at once, or you can edit each subdocument individually. Any changes in the master document automatically take effect and are saved into the subdocument files, and vice versa.

The various workgroups at MDNI often use master documents to combine multiple files into one long document. You'll learn how this feature works as you help Michael and his workgroup complete their report on broadband subscribers.

You can convert an existing document into a master document and convert its parts into subdocuments. You can also insert existing files as subdocuments into another document, which then becomes the master document.

In the first method, converting an existing document into a master document and subdocuments, you apply the Word built-in heading styles (Heading 1, Heading 2, and so forth) to the headings in the document, and then divide the document into subdocuments at the location of a heading level you select. For example, if you divide a master document into subdocuments at the Heading 1 style, each Heading 1 and its accompanying text are saved as a separate subdocument.

In the second method, creating a master document from existing documents, you insert existing files as subdocuments into an open Word document. Word converts the inserted files into subdocuments and the open document file into the master document. Unlike the first method, the subdocuments don't have to begin with a built-in heading style.

You probably will use both methods to create and manage a master document. For example, you might divide your original document into a master document and subdocuments, and then insert separate files as subdocuments into the master document.

You can convert any document into a master document. After you do create a master document, you can open, edit, and print its subdocuments individually; or you can open, edit, and print the entire master document as a single unit. When you save a master document, Word saves the file for each subdocument. The master document file contains only the filenames of its subdocuments, but not their text and objects (such as graphics).

Inserting subdocuments into a master document is different from inserting Word files into a document. Inserted Word files become part of the document in which they're inserted, whereas the files of subdocuments remain separate from the master document in which they're inserted.

Before you begin working with master documents, you must first switch to Master Document view. In **Master Document view**, you can insert, create, or remove subdocuments.

Converting a Document into a Master Document

Michael has written the title page and Rationale part of the report using the company's standard styles. You'll open the report document and make sure Word is set up so that it doesn't apply built-in styles as you type. Then, you'll convert the document into a master document.

To convert an existing file into a master document:

▶ 1. Open the file **Report** from the Tutorial.10\Tutorial folder included with your Data Files.

▶ 2. Save the file as **Broadband Report** in the same folder.

▶ 3. Display nonprinting characters.

▶ 4. Click the **Outline** button on the status bar. The document switches to Outline view, and the Outlining tab is displayed.

▶ 5. If necessary, click the **Show Level** arrow, and then click **All Levels** so you can see your entire document's text in Outline view, and, if necessary, change the Zoom setting to **100%**.

▶ 6. In the Master Document group on the Outlining tab, click the **Show Document** button to select it. When the Show Document button is selected, the Outlining tab displays a set of buttons for managing master documents. See Figure 10-2.

Figure 10-2   **Master Document view**

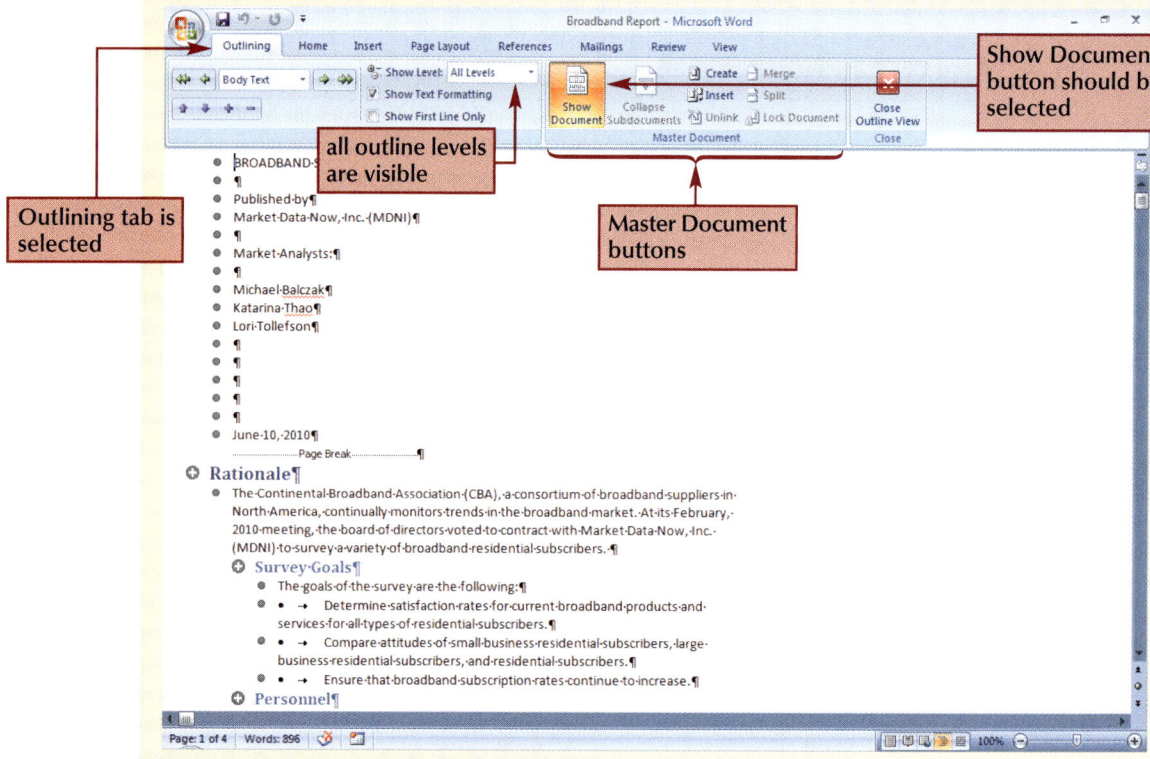

Even though the Show Document button is selected, the Broadband Report won't be a true master document until you insert a subdocument. Before you do this, however, Michael asks you to make backup copies of the files you'll use as subdocuments. Then, if a problem arises as you compile your master document and its subdocuments, you can start again with the original files. It's always important to make backup copies when working with any document, but backups are especially important when you are working with master documents and subdocuments. You'll first make a copy of the document written by Katarina (the analysis of residential subscribers) and then the one by Lori (the analysis of small business subscribers).

To make a backup copy of the subdocuments:

1. At the top left of the screen, click the **Office Button**, click **Open**, and then, if necessary, navigate to the **Tutorial.10\Tutorial** folder.

2. Right-click the file **Res**, and then click **Copy** on the shortcut menu.

3. Press the **Ctrl+V** keys to paste a copy of the Res file into the current folder. The file Res - Copy appears in the file list in the Open dialog box.

4. Right-click the file **Res - Copy**, click **Rename** on the shortcut menu, type **Residential**, and then press the **Enter** key to change the name of the file.

   Trouble? If an error message appears indicating that you're trying to change the file-name extension, click the No button, and use the filename "Residential.docx" (with the .docx filename extension). If you can't successfully rename files in the Open dialog box, open Windows Explorer, display the files in the Tutorial.10\Tutorial folder, and then repeat Step 4.

5. Repeat Steps 2 through 4 to create a copy of the **Small** file with the filename **Small Business**.

6. Click the **Cancel** button in the Open dialog box to return to the report without opening a document.

Now you can insert two subdocuments into the master document.

Inserting Subdocuments

When you insert a subdocument into a master document, the subdocument opens within the master document at the location of the insertion point. The subdocument appears in a box marked with a Subdocument icon 📇. Word inserts section breaks at the beginning and end of the subdocument. Sometimes a Lock icon 🔒 appears near the Subdocument icon to indicate that the subdocument is locked. You can't edit locked subdocuments, and all Ribbon options are unavailable when the insertion point is positioned in a locked subdocument. The Lock feature is important when more than one person is working on a master document, because it allows only one person at a time to edit a subdocument.

Inserting Subdocuments | Reference Window

- Move the insertion point to where you want to insert the subdocument.
- Click the Insert button on the Outlining tab.
- Select the document you want to insert as the subdocument.
- Click the Open button.

Michael asks you to insert the document named Residential (written by Katarina) into the master document, and then insert the document named Small Business (written by Lori). You'll start with Katarina's document.

To insert subdocuments into the master document:

▶ **1.** Scroll down and click to the left of the "L" in the level 1 heading "Large Business Subscribers." This is where you'll insert the first subdocument. To do this, you need to use the button labeled "Insert" in the Master Document group. Note that the labels on the buttons in the Master Document group don't necessarily match the name you see in the button's ScreenTip. For example, the button labeled "Insert" in the Master Document group has a ScreenTip that reads "Insert Subdocument." These steps refer to the buttons according to the label that appears on the button itself.

▶ **2.** Click the **Insert** button in the Master Document group on the Outlining tab. You see the Insert Subdocument dialog box, which is similar to the Open dialog box.

▶ **3.** Double-click the file **Residential**, located in the Tutorial.10\Tutorial folder. The file is inserted as a subdocument at the location of the insertion point (just above the heading "Large Business Subscribers").

▶ **4.** Scroll up so you can see the beginning of the subdocument at the heading "Residential Subscribers," if necessary. See Figure 10-3. Note that Word inserts a Next Page section break before the newly inserted subdocument and a Continuous section break after the newly inserted subdocument. The Subdocument icon is visible above and to the left of the heading "Residential Subscribers." A box appears around the subdocument, although the sides of the box are broken in places.

Figure 10-3 **Subdocument inserted into master document**

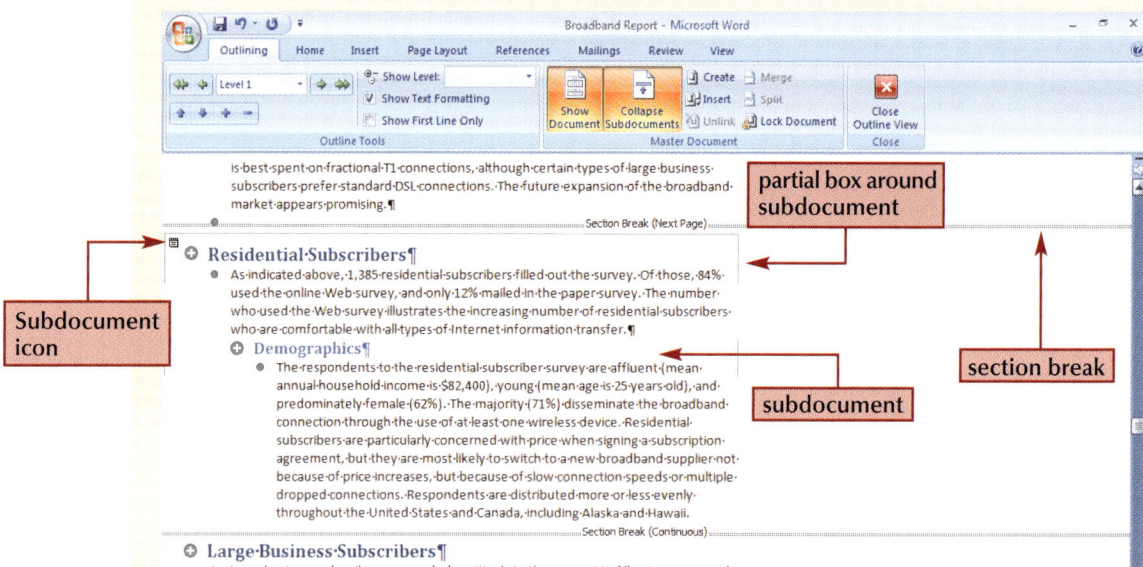

Now you'll insert the document written by Lori.

▶ **5.** If necessary, click to the left of the level-1 heading "Large Business Subscribers" again, and then repeat Steps 2 through 4 to insert the second subdocument, **Small Business**. The Small Business subdocument is inserted after the Residential document and before the heading "Large Business Subscribers." See Figure 10-4.

Second subdocument inserted and expanded ◄ **Figure 10-4**

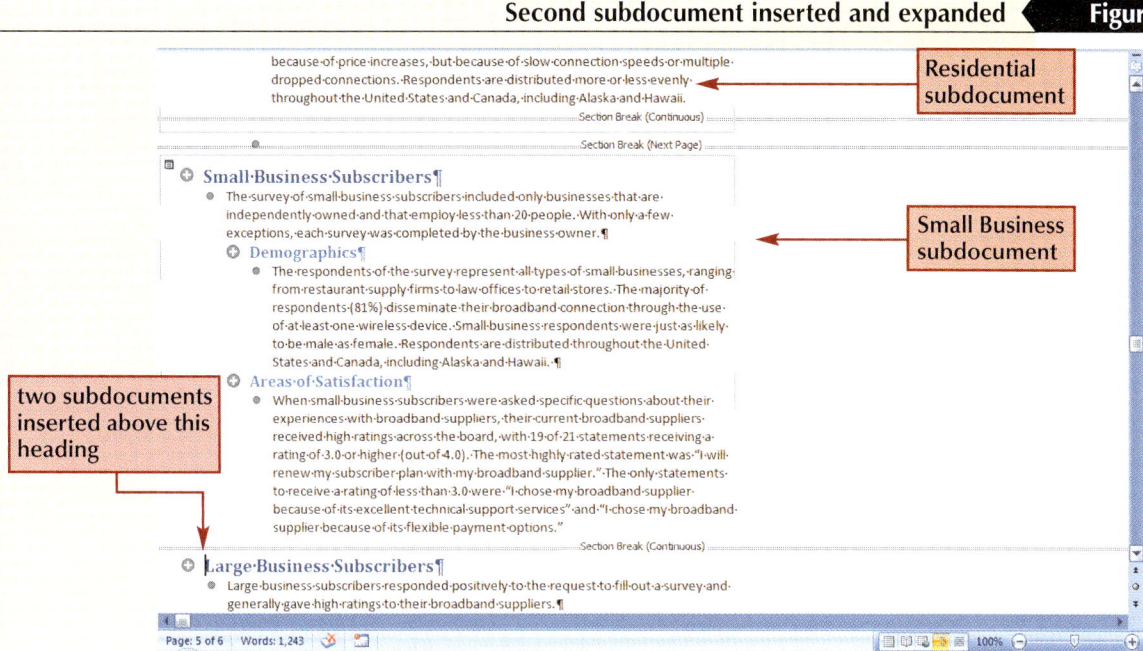

The master document Broadband Report now contains two subdocuments. Even though you can manipulate the subdocuments in the master document, the text of these subdocuments continues to be stored in the files Residential and Small Business, and not in the Broadband Report file. This is still the case even after you save the master document, which you'll do in the next section.

Saving the Master Document

After you insert subdocuments, you should save the master document. You save the master document the same way you save any other file.

To save the master document:

1. Click the **Save** button 🖫 on the Quick Access Toolbar. The Broadband Report file is now saved as a master document with two subdocuments.

The names and locations of the two subdocument files, Residential and Small Business, are recorded in the master document. The subdocuments will continue to appear in the master document as long as the files aren't renamed or moved.

Working with Subdocuments

One benefit of working with master documents is the ability to reorganize subdocuments. Another benefit is that you can create additional subdocuments from parts of the master document if the master document itself becomes too long and unwieldy.

Creating a Subdocument

When you create a subdocument by converting a part of the master document, Word creates a new subdocument file using the name of the subdocument's first heading (that is, the first paragraph that is formatted with a heading style). The new subdocument file is saved in the same folder as the master document, and the text of the new subdocument is no longer saved in the master document file.

| Reference Window | **Creating a Subdocument** |

- Make sure the document is in Master Document view.
- Locate the heading for the part of the document you want to transform into a subdocument.
- Click the Expand icon to the left of the heading to select the heading and its subordinate text.
- Click the Create button in the Master Document group on the Outlining tab.

Note that it's customary to refer to a part of a document that begins with a heading as a "section." Don't confuse this use of the word "section," with the more technical use of the term—as in a document that is divided into sections by section breaks.

Now Michael wants you to transform the "Large Business Subscribers" section into a subdocument.

To create a subdocument:

▶ **1.** Scroll down so you can see the heading "Large Business Subscribers," and then click the **white plus sign** ⊕ to the left of "Large Business Subscribers." The "Large Business Subscribers" heading and all the text and subheadings below it through the next heading formatted as Heading 1 are selected. Now you're ready to create the subdocument.

▶ **2.** Click the **Create** button in the Master Document group on the Outlining tab. Word puts a box around the Large Business Subscribers section, inserts section breaks before and after the Large Business Subscribers section, and displays the Subdocument icon at the beginning of the new subdocument.

▶ **3.** Save the Broadband Report file with the new subdocument. Word creates a new file named "Large Business Subscribers," using the subdocument's first heading for the filename. The subdocument is saved in the same folder as the master document.

You have successfully transformed a part of the master document into a subdocument. As you'll see in the next section, you can also split an existing subdocument into two separate subdocuments.

Splitting Subdocuments

If one subdocument becomes too long and unwieldy, or if you want two people to work on what is currently one subdocument, you can split the subdocument by dividing it into two subdocument files.

Michael wants to split the "Residential Subscribers" subdocument. After the split, the original "Residential Subscribers" subdocument will consist of the level-1 heading "Residential Subscribers." The new, second subdocument will have the filename "Demographics," and will consist of the level-2 heading "Demographics." The "Residential Subscribers" subdocument will retain its original filename, "Residential."

To split the subdocument:

1. Scroll up and click to the left of the "D" in the "Demographics" heading in the middle of the first subdocument (which starts with the heading "Residential Subscribers"). Note that there are two "Demographics" headings in the master document, and you want the first one. As you can see in the Outline Level list box on the Outlining tab, this "Demographics" heading is a level 2 heading, which means it is formatted with the Heading 2 style.

2. Click the **Split** button in the Master Document group on the Outlining tab. Word draws a box around the new subdocument and inserts a Continuous section break to separate it from the Residential subdocument above it.

3. Save the report with the new subdocument. Word creates a new file named "Demographics."

4. Click the **Office Button** 🏢 , click **Open**, navigate to the **Tutorial.10\Tutorial** folder, if necessary, and then verify that this folder contains the files named Demographics and Large Business Subscribers (the two subdocuments you created).

▶ 5. Click the **Cancel** button in the Open dialog box to return to the master document.

So far, you've learned how to insert a subdocument into a master document, to create a subdocument from master document text, and to split an existing subdocument into two subdocuments. Next, you'll learn how to combine, or merge, two subdocuments.

Merging Subdocuments

If your master document contains adjacent subdocuments that are fairly short and simple with few graphics or tables, it's sometimes helpful to merge the subdocuments. When you merge subdocuments, you combine the files and text of two adjacent subdocuments. Word inserts the text of the second subdocument into the first one, so that when you save the master document, the first subdocument file contains the text of both subdocuments. The second subdocument file remains on your disk, but is no longer used by the master document. You could delete this file without affecting your master document.

You should merge only subdocuments that will be edited by the same person. If two subdocuments will be edited by different people, it makes more sense to keep them separate, no matter how short they are.

Merging Subdocuments

- Make sure the document is in Master Document view.
- Click the Subdocument icon of the first subdocument.
- Press and hold the Shift key while you click the Subdocument icon of an adjacent subdocument.
- Release the Shift key, and then, in the Master Document group on the Outlining tab, click the Merge button.

Michael asks Lori to edit both the Small Business subdocument and the Large Business subdocument. These subdocuments are adjacent, so first Lori will merge them.

To merge two subdocuments into one:

1. Scroll down, move the insertion point anywhere in the "Small Business Subscribers" heading, and then click the **Collapse** button in the Outline Tools group to display only the headings within this subdocument and not the text below them.

2. Repeat Step 1 for the "Large Business Subscribers" heading. This allows you to see all the headings for both subdocuments at one time.

3. Click the **Subdocument** icon of the Small Business subdocument. Take care to click in the middle of the icon. The entire Small Business subdocument is selected.

   Trouble? If you click the Subdocument icon but the entire subdocument isn't selected, move the pointer to the center of the icon and try again. Keep trying until the entire subdocument, and not just the heading, is selected.

4. Press and hold the **Shift** key, click the Subdocument icon next to the "Large Business Subscribers" subdocument heading, and then release the **Shift** key. With both subdocuments selected, you can now merge them.

   Trouble? If you click the Subdocument icon but both of the subdocuments are not selected, click anywhere outside a subdocument, and then begin again with Step 3. Keep trying until both subdocuments are selected.

5. In the Master Document group on the Outlining tab, click the **Merge** button, and then click anywhere in the master document to deselect the text. The two subdocuments become one. See Figure 10-5. You can see that the Subdocument icon no longer appears next to the "Large Business Subscribers" heading.

Figure 10-5 ▶ **Two subdocuments merged into one**

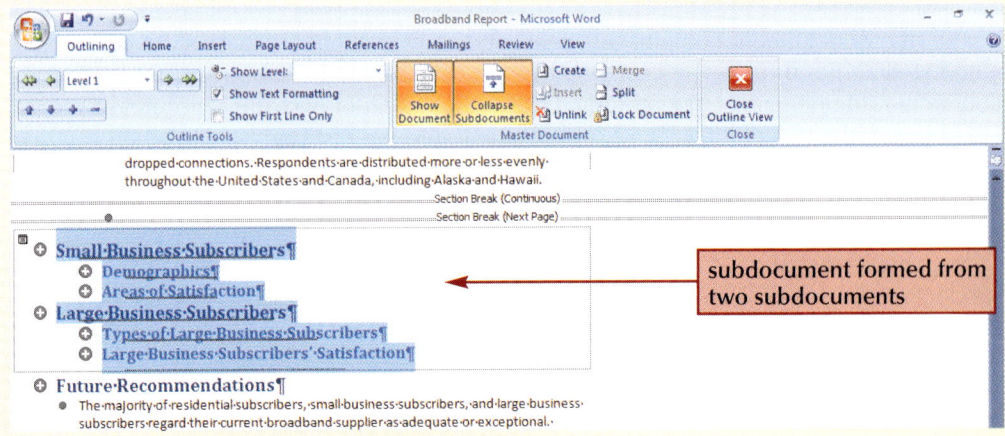

subdocument formed from two subdocuments

6. Save the master document. The text from the Large Business Subscribers file merges with the document named Small Business; the master document can no longer access the Large Business Subscribers file.

Tip

You can still open the Large Business Subscribers document from outside the Broadband Report master document.

The master document now has a title page and three subdocuments—Residential, Demographics, and Small Business.

Removing a Subdocument

It's also possible to remove a subdocument—that is, to incorporate the text of a subdocument into the master document. This decreases the number of subdocuments but increases the size of the master document. The removed subdocument file still exists, but the master document file can no longer access it. You can delete this unused subdocument file without affecting the master document.

Removing a Subdocument	Reference Window

- Make sure the document is in Master Document view.
- Click the Subdocument icon for the subdocument you want to move into the master document.
- In the Master Document group on the Outlining tab, click the Unlink button.

Michael decides that the short "Residential" subdocument (which includes only one heading followed by one paragraph) doesn't have to be a subdocument. He asks you to remove this subdocument and return it to the master document.

To remove the Subscribers subdocument:

1. Scroll up so you can see the heading "Residential Subscribers" in the Residential subdocument, and then click the **Subdocument** icon 🗐 for the "Residential" subdocument to select all the text in it.

2. In the Master Document group on the Outlining tab, click the **Unlink** button. The "Residential Subscribers" heading and its accompanying text become part of the master document. Your master document now consists of the title page, Rationale, Executive Summary, Residential Subscribers, and Future Recommendations sections. It also includes the subdocuments Demographics and Small Business.

3. Click anywhere in the document to deselect the Residential Subscribers section, and then save the master document. The folder that contains the master document still includes two extra files, Large Business Subscribers and Residential, which are no longer subdocuments of the master document.

You have learned how to manipulate subdocuments within a master document. Next, you'll deal with problems that arise from undesirable page and line breaks.

Controlling Page Breaks

As you know, in Print Layout view, page breaks are marked by blue space between the bottom of one page and the top of the next page. If the page break is also a section break, the double-line section break appears below the last line of text on the page, with the text "Section Break (Next Page)." You'll now look at the location of page breaks in the Broadband Report document to make sure the breaks are in reasonable places. As you have seen, when you insert a new subdocument in a master document, Word inserts a Next Page section break (that is, a section break that also starts a new page) before the new subdocument and a Continuous section break after the subdocument. In the following steps, you will switch to Print Layout view and examine the report's page and section breaks.

To view the page and section breaks in the report:

1. Switch to Print Layout view, change the Zoom to Page Width, and then scroll through the document, noting the page break after the text on page 1 and the Next Page section break on page 3. When you inserted the Residential subdocument, Word inserted a Next Page section break just before the new subdocument. Word also inserted a Continuous section break on page 4, at the end of the original Residential subdocument. Even though you merged the Residential subdocument with the rest of the document, the Continuous section break remains. Note also, the Continuous section break before and after the Demographics subdocument, and the Next Page section break after thet text on page 4, which Word inserted just before the Small Business subdocument. Finally, note the section break in the middle of page 5, at the end of the Small Business subdocument.

> **Tip**
>
> Click the View tab and then click the Two Pages button in the Zoom group to see two pages at once.

2. Zoom out until can see two pages side by side, and scroll through the document, noting the short page of text on pages 3 and 4. See Figure 10-6.

Figure 10-6 ▶ **Pages 3 and 4**

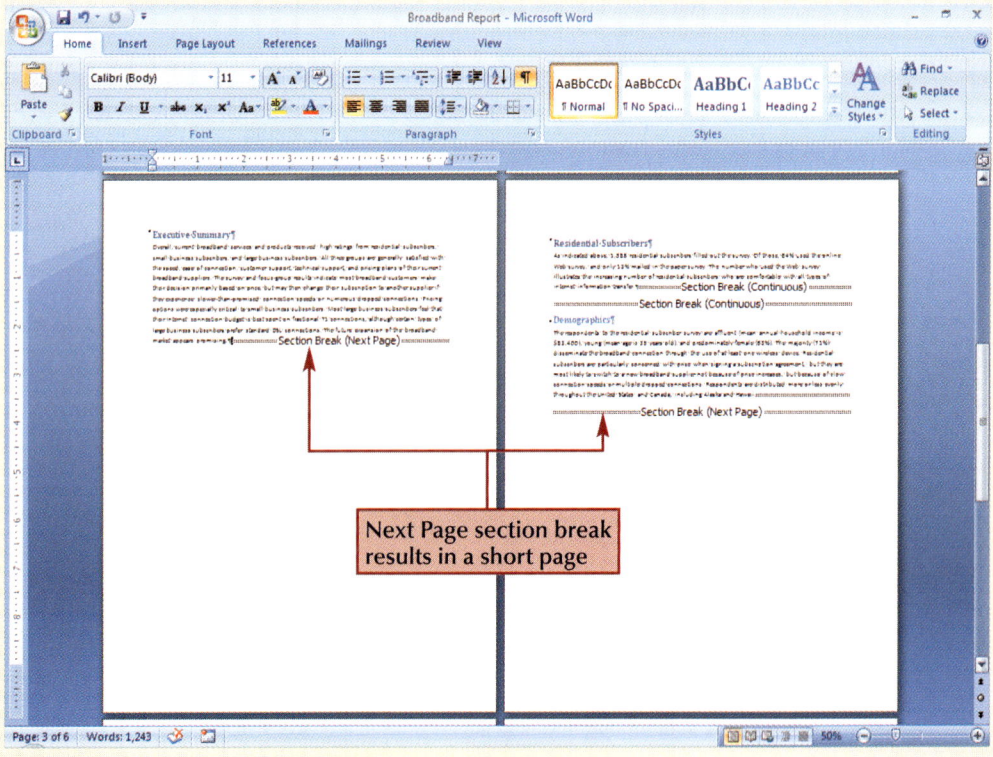

Next Page section break results in a short page

The shortness of page 4 is a result of the Next Page section break before the Small Business subdocument, which begins on page 5. You can't delete this Next Page section break without merging the Small Business subdocument with the rest of the document. Lori plans to add more text to the Small Business subdocument later, so for now you'll leave the subdocument and its accompanying Next Page section break as is. Later, after Lori is finished revising the subdocument, Michael can merge it with the rest of the document if he wants and delete the Next Page section break on page 4. At this point, however, you can delete the Next Page section break on page 3, which became unnecessary after you merged the Residential subdocument with the rest of the document.

3. Change the Zoom to Page Width, scroll so you can see page 3, click to the left of the section break line so that the insertion point is positioned just to the right of the paragraph mark. See Figure 10-7. When deleting section breaks or page breaks, it's important to position the insertion point correctly, so that you don't accidentally delete a paragraph mark, which might in turn affect the formatting of subsequent paragraphs.

Deleting a Next Page section break   **Figure 10-7**

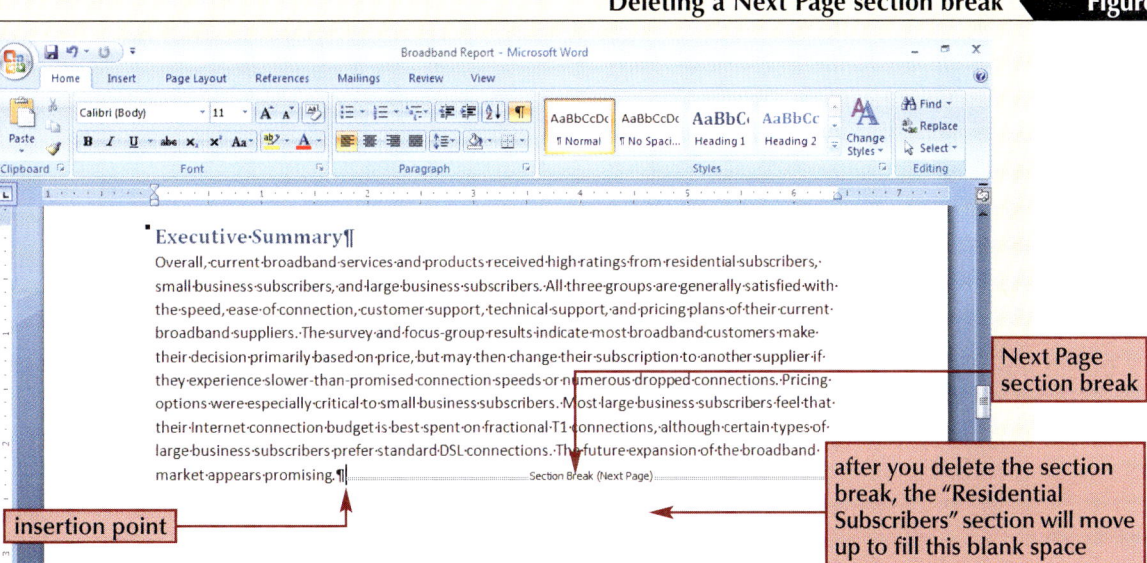

4. Press the **Delete** key. The Next Page section break is deleted, and the "Residential Subscribers" heading moves from page 4 to the current page.

When working on a long document with multiple writers, you need to check the page and section breaks in the document to make sure text flows properly from one page to another. In particular, scan the pages for widows and orphans, as explained in the next section.

Tip

You can also delete page breaks and Continuous section breaks by clicking to the left of the break and pressing the Delete key.

In publishing terminology, a **widow** is the last line of a paragraph that appears alone at the top of a page. A widow looks out of place and can be hard to read. An **orphan** is the first line of a paragraph isolated at the bottom of a page. A reader can easily miss an orphan, jumping instead to the next page. Isolated headings that are stranded at the bottom of a page, with the paragraph following it on the next page, are similar to orphans.

By default, Word documents are set up to prevent widows and orphans. Also, Word's default heading styles prevent headings from being stranded on the bottom of a page. However, when you are working with a group of writers, or if you are working with a document that does not include Word's default heading styles, you might inadvertently incorporate some material into your document that includes these problematic elements. To get rid of a widow or orphan in a document, you could insert a page break. However, this usually creates more problems than it solves. For example, you could insert a page break just before an orphan—that is, just before the first line of a paragraph that is stranded on the bottom of a page—so that the line moves to the next page, joining the rest of its paragraph. But if you then added more text above the page break, and that text spilled over to another page, the page break you added would shift, possibly resulting in a nearly blank page. As you can see, you would have to continually insert and delete hard page breaks to fix widows and orphans as you edit a document.

A better option, as you saw in Tutorial 2, is to use the Keep with next option in the Line and Page Breaks tab of the Paragraph dialog box to tell Word you want to keep a paragraph on the same page as the following paragraph. These check boxes in the Line and Page Breaks tab of the Paragraph dialog box give you even more control over text flow and page breaks:

- Widow/Orphan control—This check box is selected by default in a new Word document. If you notice problems with widows and orphans in a document created by someone else, verify that this check box is selected.
- Keep lines together—This check box tells Word to keep all the lines of a paragraph together on the same page.
- Page break before—This check box tells Word that the paragraph should always begin a new page.

Note that you can also assign page break settings to specific document styles, as follows:

1. Open the Styles window, point to the heading you want to modify in the Styles window, and then click its list arrow.
2. Click Modify to open the Modify Style dialog box, click the Format button, and then click Paragraph to open the Paragraph dialog box.
3. If necessary, click the Line and Page Breaks tab, select the Pagination options you want, and then click the OK button in both dialog boxes to return to the document.

In addition to page breaks, you should also look through your document for awkward line breaks. For example, in the last paragraph of the document (on page 5), "e-businesses" is split between two lines. Although this isn't a serious problem, readers might be confused to see "e-" at the end of a line. To prevent Word from breaking a hyphenated word, you need to use a hard **nonbreaking hyphen**, which is a hyphen that won't allow the word or phrase containing it to break between two lines. By contrast, a **soft hyphen** is a hyphen that allows the word containing it to appear on different lines. To insert a soft hyphen, you simply press the hyphen key on your keyboard.

Next, you'll replace the soft hyphen in the word "e-business" with a nonbreaking hyphen. You'll use the Go To feature to move quickly to the correct page.

To insert a nonbreaking hyphen:

1. At the bottom of the vertical scroll bar, click the **Select Browse Object** button to open the Browse Object menu, and then click the **Go To** icon → to display the Go To tab in the Find and Replace dialog box. In the Go to what list box, you can select the item in the document you want to go to. In this case, the default option, Page, is correct, because you want to go to a specific page.

▶ 2. Type **5** and then click the **Go To** button. The insertion point moves to the top of page 5, to the left of the "Future Recommendations" heading.

▶ 3. Click the **Close** button to close the Find and Replace dialog box, and then move the insertion point immediately to the left of the hyphen in "e-businesses" at the end of the third-to-the-last line.

▶ 4. Press the **Delete** key to delete the soft hyphen. The "e" becomes joined to "businesses," and, as a result, "ebusinesses" appears on the next line. Now you'll insert the nonbreaking hyphen.

▶ 5. Click the **Insert** tab, in the Symbols group click the **Symbol** button, and then click **More Symbols** to open the Symbol dialog box.

▶ 6. Click the **Special Characters** tab. As you can see, Word offers a wide variety of special symbols, including the nonbreaking hyphen.

▶ 7. Click **Nonbreaking Hyphen**, and then click the **Insert** button to insert the hyphen into the document at the location of the insertion point.

▶ 8. Click the **Close** button in the Symbol dialog box. The Symbol dialog box closes, and the word "e-businesses" (which now contains a nonbreaking hyphen) no longer breaks at the end of the line.

▶ 9. In the last sentence of the paragraph, replace the soft hyphen in "high-speed" with a nonbreaking hyphen.

▶ 10. Click the **Office Button** and then click **Close** to close the master document without closing Word, saving changes when prompted.

Tip
You can also press the Ctrl+Shift keys to insert a nonbreaking hyphen.

Another important special character is the nonbreaking space. A **nonbreaking space** is a space that won't allow the words on either side to break between two lines. For example, the phrase "10 KB" (where KB stands for kilobytes, as in a 10 KB file) might be hard to read or distracting if the "10" appears at the end of one line and "KB" appears at the beginning of the next line. To avoid this problem, you can insert a nonbreaking space between the "10" and the "KB." You can insert the nonbreaking space by using the Special Characters tab in the Symbol dialog box or by pressing the Ctrl+Shift+Spacebar keys. The Broadband Report doesn't contain any words that require a nonbreaking space.

You have completed setting up MDNI's Broadband Report using Word's master document feature. In the next session, you'll use Word features to number sections and figures, and then you'll edit the report.

Session 10.1 Quick Check | Review

1. Define the following terms:
   a. master document
   b. subdocument
   c. widow
   d. orphan

2. Describe how to split a subdocument, how to merge subdocuments, and how to remove a subdocument from a master document.
3. What are three advantages of using a master document to manage long documents, rather than working with separate, smaller documents?
4. True or False. After you create a subdocument from text in a master document, Word creates a new file that contains the subdocument.
5. What are the two methods for creating a master document?
6. What is a nonbreaking hyphen? A nonbreaking space? Why would you use them?

Session 10.2

Reopening a Master Document

When you open a master document that has one or more subdocuments, Word doesn't open the subdocuments, but rather displays their filenames as hyperlinks in underlined blue text and enclosed in a rectangular outline. The Subdocument icon 📖 and the Lock icon 🔒 are also enclosed in the outline. When you click a subdocument hyperlink, Word opens the subdocument in another document window, not into the master document.

However, in this case, you don't want to open the subdocuments into other document windows. You want to open them into the master document, a process known as expanding the subdocuments. To expand subdocuments means to open the subdocuments, currently displayed only as hyperlinks, into the master document so that you can read and edit the text of the subdocuments. When you expand the subdocuments, the Lock icon disappears, indicating that the text is now available to be modified. Conversely, to collapse subdocuments means to close the subdocuments so that the subdocuments appear only as hyperlinks in the master document. You'll open the master document and expand subdocuments now.

To expand subdocuments:

▶ 1. Open the master document **Broadband Report**, switch to Outline view, and then click the **Show Document** button in the Master Document group on the Outlining tab to select it.

   Trouble? If you didn't close the master document at the end of the previous session, close it now and then perform Step 1.

▶ 2. Display nonprinting characters, if necessary, and then scroll so you can see page 3, which at this point contains hyperlinks to the subdocuments and not the subdocuments themselves. See Figure 10-8.

Figure 10-8 ▶ **Master Document with hyperlinks to the subdocuments**

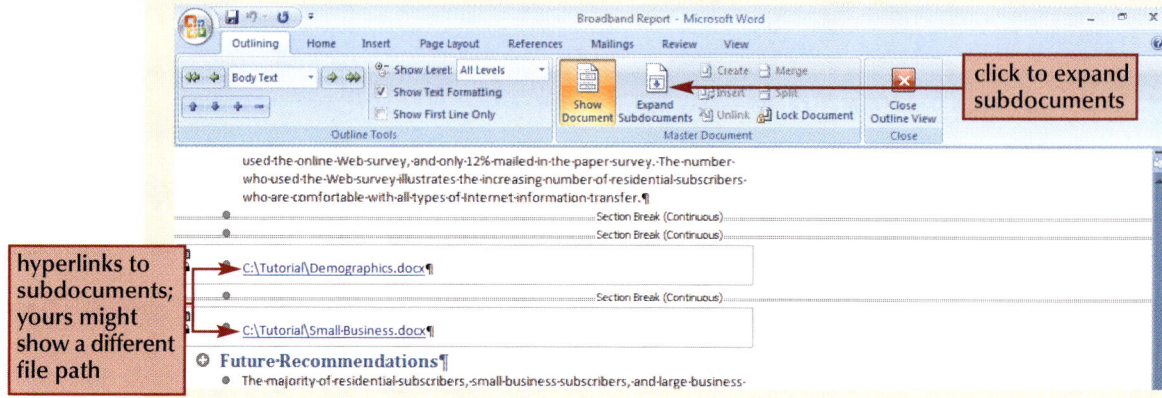

Trouble? If, instead of blue underlined hyperlinks, you see code that begins with "{HYPERLINK . . .," press the Alt+F9 keys to hide the field codes and display the actual hyperlinks.

3. In the Master Document group on the Outlining tab, click the **Expand Subdocuments** button. Word replaces the hyperlinks with the text of the subdocuments.

You've successfully expanded the subdocuments into the master document. You can now read and modify the subdocument text.

Adding Section Numbers to Headings

To help readers find the information they need, Michael asks you to give each major heading a number—for example, "1. Rationale" and "2. Executive Summary." You could manually insert text such as "Section 1" before each heading, but what would happen if you had to add, reorder, or delete a heading? You would need to review every heading and change the numbers—a time-consuming process, especially in a long document. Instead, you can number the parts of a document by automatically numbering the headings. This feature has several advantages:

- **Automatic sequential numbering**. Word keeps the heading numbers consecutive even if you add, delete, or move a section.
- **Numbering across subdocuments**. Word numbers the same-level headings of all the subdocuments in the master document consecutively. Then the members of a writing team don't need to know the number of each heading as they write their own subdocuments.
- **Consistent style**. Subdocuments have the number style specified in the master document.

Numbering Headings Automatically | Reference Window

- Click the Home tab, and then in the Paragraph group, click the Multilevel List button arrow.
- Click the heading numbering style you want to use.
- As you edit a document that contains numbered headings, you may occasionally find that the heading number disappears from some headings. If that happens, apply the correct heading style (which, after you numbered the headings in the document, contains the heading numbering) to the affected headings.

In the next set of steps, you'll modify the document headings to include automatic numbering.

To number headings automatically:

1. Click anywhere in the level-1 heading "Rationale" at the beginning of page 2. In the Outline Tools group on the Outlining tab, click the **Show Level** arrow, and then click **Level 2**. Only the level-1 and level-2 headings are displayed. This will make it easier to see the numbers applied to the headings.

2. Click the **Home** tab, and then, in the Paragraph group, click the **Multilevel List** button. The Multilevel List menu opens. The List Library contains four list styles that can be used with headings. Michael wants to use the numbering style that shows a number followed by "Heading 1". This style is sometimes called the legal paragraph numbering style. See Figure 10-9.

Tip

When you add numbers to the headings in a document, Word actually modifies the document's heading styles to include the numbers. You can see a sample of the numbering style you select in the heading options in the Quick Styles gallery.

Figure 10-9 **Multilevel list styles**

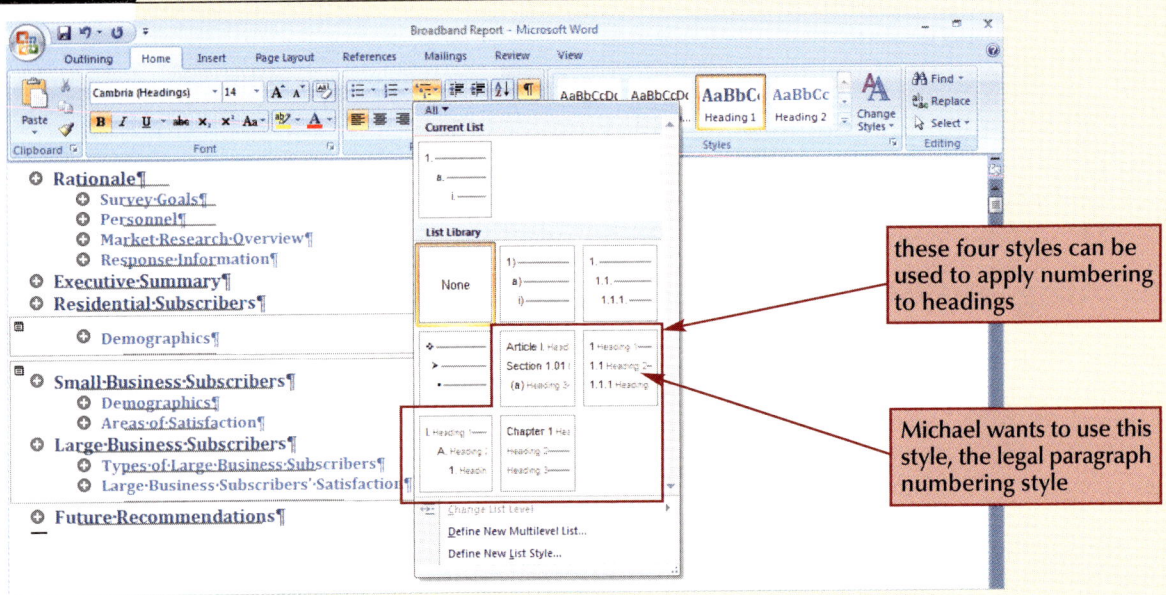

these four styles can be used to apply numbering to headings

Michael wants to use this style, the legal paragraph numbering style

3. Click the legal paragraph numbering format (the style in the second row of the List Library, in the right column). The numbers are applied to the document headings. A sample of the numbering style is now included as part of the heading styles in the Quick Styles gallery. Each level-1 heading (that is, each heading formatted in the Heading 1 style) has a single number. The numbers assigned to the level-2 headings consist of the number of the level 1 heading just above it, followed by a period, and then a sequential number. See Figure 10-10.

Figure 10-10 **Collapsed document with numbered headings**

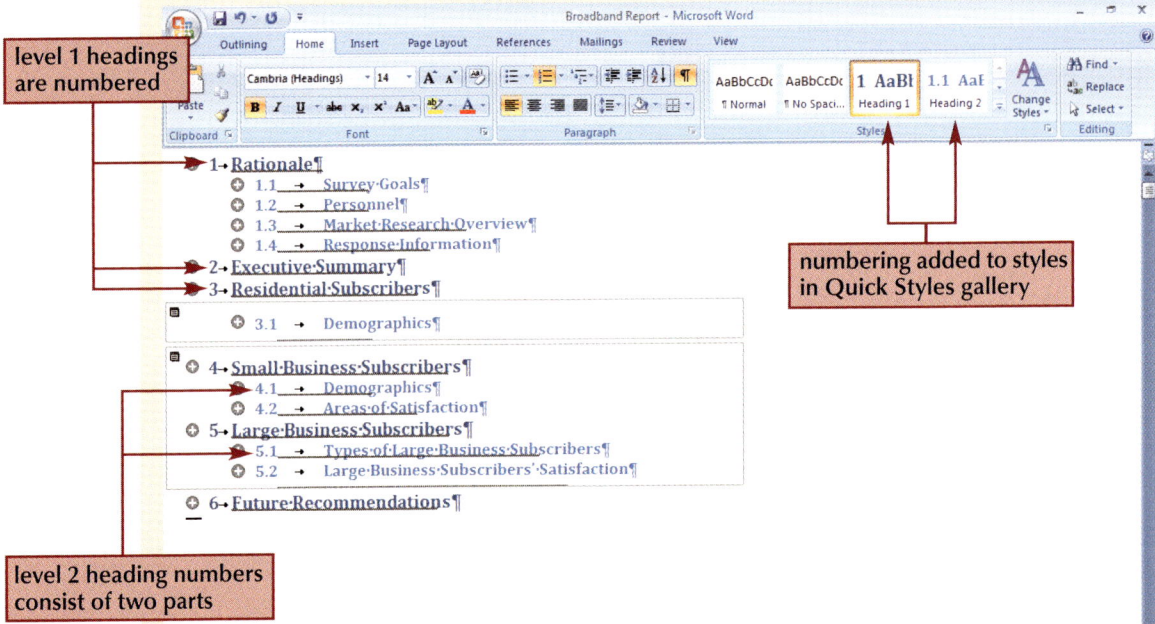

level 1 headings are numbered

numbering added to styles in Quick Styles gallery

level 2 heading numbers consist of two parts

Next, you want to customize the numbering format so that each number is followed by a period.

4. Click the **Multilevel List** button  and then click **Define new Multilevel list**. The Define new Multilevel list dialog box opens. You want to change the default setting "1" for Heading 1 styles to "1." (with a period following the number) and Heading 2 styles to "1.1." (with a period following the second number).

5. Make sure **1** is selected in the Click level to modify list, click to the right of the number in the Enter formatting for number box, and then type a period.

6. Click **2** in the Click level to modify list, click to the right of the number in the Enter formatting for number text box, and then type a period after "1.1". Make sure your settings match those in Figure 10-11.

Define new Multilevel list dialog box ◄ **Figure 10-11**

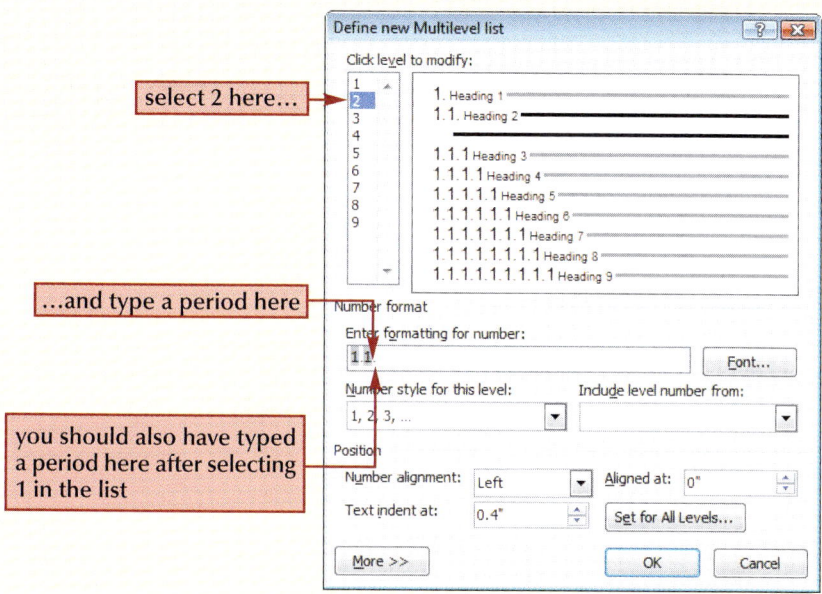

7. Click the **OK** button, and then save the master document. Now all text formatted with a heading style has automatic section numbering.

All the headings now have numbers, making it easy to refer to a specific heading or subheading by its number. Furthermore, from now on, if Michael adds, removes, or rearranges the headings, Word will renumber the numbers consecutively. Note that as you edit a document that contains numbered headings, heading numbers might sometimes disappear from some headings. If that happens, select the affected heading, and then apply the correct heading style from the Quick Style gallery (which, after you numbered the headings in the document, applies the heading number). In this tutorial, if you notice missing heading numbers as you are editing Michael's report, correct the problem by re-applying the correct heading style from the Quick Style gallery.

Inserting Numbered Captions

Michael suggests that you include figures to illustrate key points in the report. A **figure** is any kind of illustration, such as a photograph, clip art, chart, map, or graph. Specifically, in section "1.2. Personnel," he wants you to add a picture of Kayla West, the liaison between Market Research Now, Inc. and the Continental Broadband Association. Also, in section "1.4. Response Information," you need to add a pie chart showing the age range of the residential respondent. Finally, in section "6. Future Recommendations," you need to add a SmartArt graphic illustrating one possible future trend. Because graphics are not visible in Outline view, you'll switch to Print Layout view.

To insert figures into the report:

▶ 1. Switch to Print Layout view, if necessary, change the zoom to Page Width, and then move the insertion point immediately to the left of "Kayla West" below "1.2. Personnel," on page 2.

▶ 2. Click the **Insert** tab, in the Illustrations group click the **Picture** button to open the Insert Picture dialog box, navigate to the **Tutorial.10\Tutorial** folder included with your Data Files, and then double-click the image file **Kayla**. Word inserts the picture of Kayla into the document. You'll now change the text wrapping to resize the picture.

▶ 3. Verify that the picture is selected, in the Arrange group on the Picture Tools Format tab click the **Text Wrapping** button, and then click **Square**. The text, including the heading, wraps to the right of the picture.

Tip

To see a ScreenTip with the name of a style in the Picture Styles group on the Picture Tools Format tab, move the mouse pointer over a style.

▶ 4. In the Size group, click the **Shape Height** box, type **1.5**, and then press the **Enter** key. The photo increases in size, with the width changing to match the new height. Next, you will format the picture with a Quick Style from the Picture Styles group on the Picture Tools Format tab.

▶ 5. In the Picture Styles group, click the style on the far left (the "Simple Frame, White" style), and then drag the picture down a little so that it is below (and not to the left of) the heading "1.2. Personnel," and the text wraps as shown in Figure 10-12.

Figure 10-12 ▶ **Document with inserted picture**

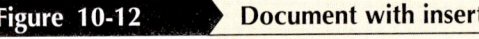

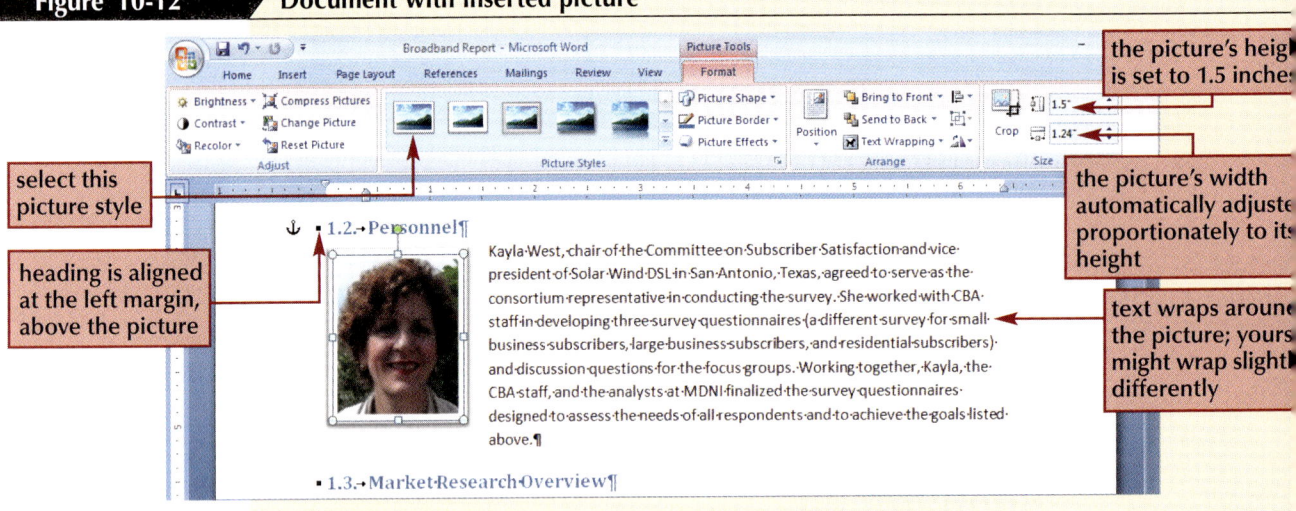

▶ 6. Save the master document.

Michael wants to include captions for each figure so the text can refer to them. He asks you to insert captions with automatic figure numbering. With automatic figure numbering, Word updates the figure numbers if you insert a figure before an existing figure, move a figure, or reorder the parts of the document. When creating a caption, you can choose to number the captions sequentially as they appear in the document (1, 2, 3, etc.) or you can include the number of the first heading above the caption that is formatted with the Heading 1 style. For example, you could use 1-1 for the first caption under the heading "1. Rationale," 1-2 for the second caption under the heading "1.Rationale," etc. The captions in the "2. Executive Summary" section would then be numbered 2-1, 2-2, and so on. This type of numbering is sometimes called double-numbering.

Creating Captions | Reference Window

- Select the table or figure to which you want to apply a caption.
- Click the References tab, and then, in the Captions group, click the Insert Caption button.
- Click the Label arrow, and then click the type of object to which you're applying the caption (for example, figure or table).
- Use the Position arrow to specify whether you want the caption to appear above or below the figure.
- To use double-numbering that includes the number of the preceding Heading 1 heading (for example, 1-1 for the first caption under the heading "1. Rationale," 1-2 for the second caption under that heading, etc.), click the Numbering button, select the Include chapter number check box, and then click the OK button.
- Click the OK button in the Caption dialog box.

Now you are ready to create a numbered caption for the figure you just inserted.

To create a numbered caption:

1. With the picture of Kayla still selected, click the **References** tab, and then, in the Captions group, click the **Insert Caption** button. The Caption dialog box opens.

2. Make sure the Caption text box at the top of the dialog box displays **Figure 1** and that the Label list box displays **Figure**. Also, make sure **Below selected item** is selected in the Position list box.

   Trouble? If the Caption text box displays "Figure 1-1," click the Numbering button to open the Caption Numbering dialog box, click the Include chapter number check box to uncheck it, and then click the OK button.

3. With the insertion point to the right of "Figure 1" in the Caption text box, type : (a colon), press the **Spacebar**, and then type **Kayla West**. See Figure 10-13.

Tip

To change the format of the caption number, such as to Figure 1-1, click the Numbering button in the Caption dialog box.

Creating a numbered caption   **Figure 10-13**

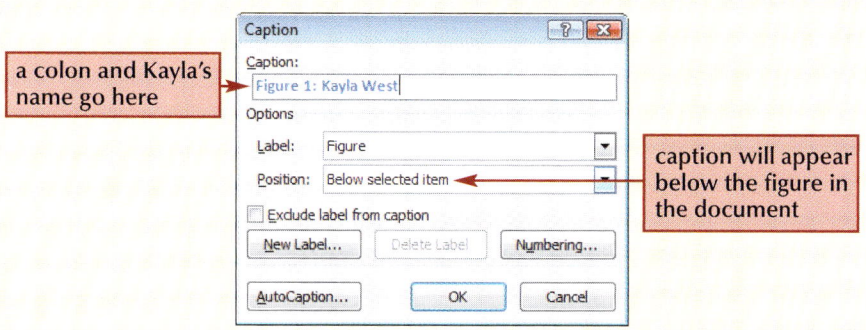

a colon and Kayla's name go here

caption will appear below the figure in the document

4. Click the **OK** button. The numbered caption is inserted below the figure as a floating text box with a border.

Trouble? If the caption number is anything except 1, select the number by dragging the pointer over the caption, and press the F9 key to update the field code.

▶ **5.** Drag the **bottom-center sizing handle** up so that the caption box just accommodates the caption.

▶ **6.** Verify that the heading "1.3.Market Research Overview" is positioned below the caption and aligned at the left margin. If it is not, adjust the position of the picture and the caption box until the heading is aligned at the left margin, below the caption. When you are finished adjusting the caption and the picture, click anywhere in the document to deselect them, and verify that the report text wraps as shown in Figure 10-14.

| Figure 10-14 | Figure with numbered caption |

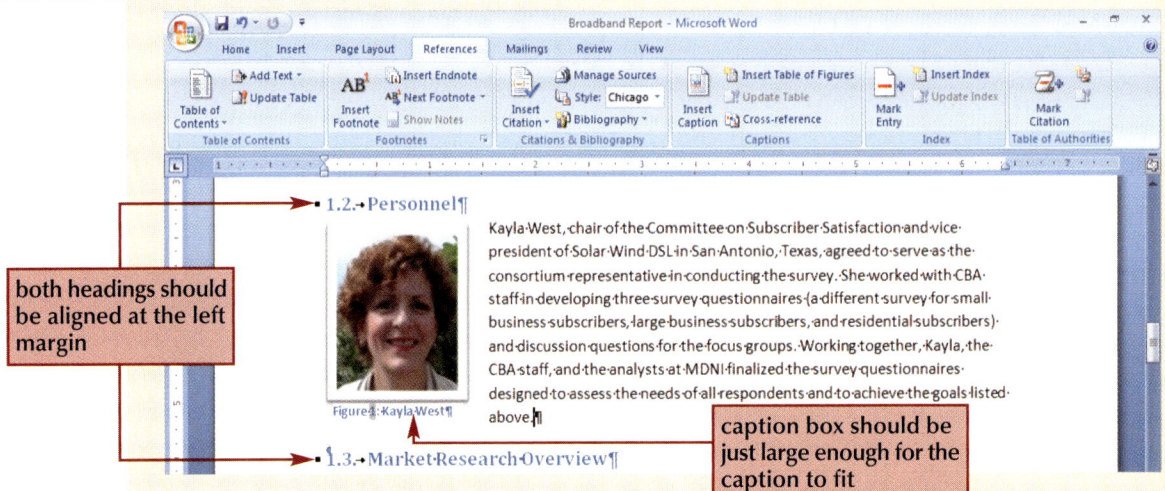

Trouble? If the caption box has a border around it, right-click the edge of the caption text box, click Format Text Box on the shortcut menu, click the Colors and Lines tab, and then, in the Line section, click the Color arrow and click No Color. This removes the border lines from around the caption.

Now, using the same procedure, you'll insert another figure with a numbered caption. This figure will be a SmartArt graphic illustrating one possible future trend in the broadband industry.

To insert a SmartArt graphic with a numbered caption:

▶ **1.** Use the Go To feature to go to page 5, click at the beginning of the last paragraph in the document, click the **Insert** tab, and then, in the Illustrations group, click the **SmartArt** button. The Choose a SmartArt Graphic dialog box opens.

▶ **2.** In the left pane, click **Process**, and then, in the middle pane, click the **Basic Process** format (in the top row, first column on the left). The right pane of the Choose a SmartArt Graphic dialog box shows a sample of the Basic Process graphic, which consists of three rectangles separated by two arrows.

▶ **3.** Click the **OK** button to close the Choose a SmartArt Graphic dialog box. The SmartArt graphic is displayed inside a border.

4. If the Text Pane is open next to the SmartArt graphic, click the **Text Pane** button in the Create Graphic group on the SmartArt Tools tab to close it.

5. In the SmartArt graphic, click the far-left rectangle, type **Static Connection Speeds**, click the middle rectangle, type **Increased Prices**, click the far-right rectangle, and type **Consumer Dissatisfaction**.

6. Display the ruler, if necessary, and then drag the lower-right corner of the SmartArt border up and to the left so the border is 3 inches wide.

7. Position the mouse pointer over the middle of the bottom border so the mouse pointer changes to a white double arrow ⬍ and drag the border up so it is positioned just below the three rectangles. In the same way, drag the top border down so it is positioned just above the three rectangles. Continue dragging the top and bottom borders by small amounts until the SmartArt graphic is about 1 inch high.

8. Click the **Page Layout** tab, in the Arrange group click the **Text Wrapping** button, and then click **Square**. If necessary, adjust the position of the graphic until it matches the one shown in Figure 10-15.

> **Tip**
>
> To reset the SmartArt graphic to its original size and shape, click the Reset Graphic button in the Reset group on the SmartArt Tools Design tab.

Text wrapped around SmartArt graphic ◄ **Figure 10-15**

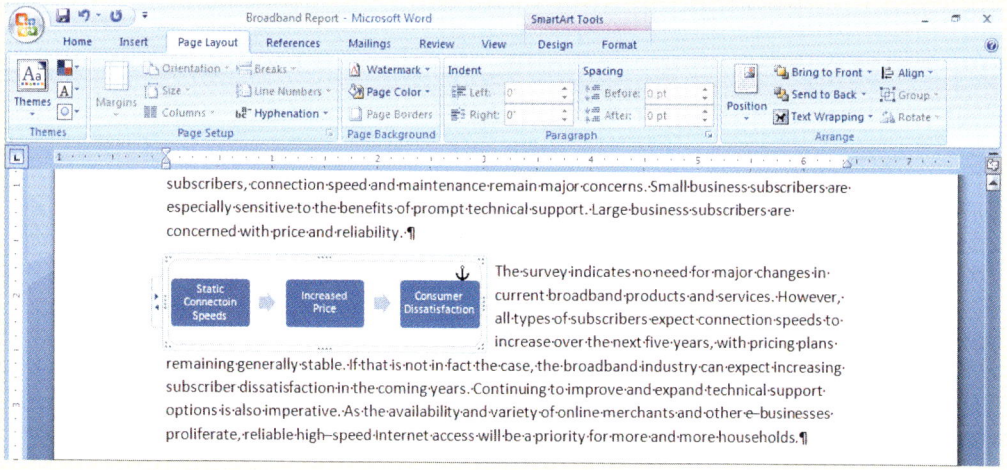

You are finished creating the new figure. Now you can add a numbered caption to the figure.

To create a caption for the SmartArt graphic:

1. With the graphic still selected (that is, with the border still displayed), click the **References** tab, and then, in the Captions group, click the **Insert Caption** button. The Caption dialog box opens. Notice that the Caption text box automatically displays "Figure 2," because this will be the second caption in the document.

2. Edit the caption in the Caption text box to read **Figure 2: Possible Future Trend**, click the **OK** button, and then drag the bottom border of the caption box up so that it just accommodates the caption. Adjust the position of the caption box or the SmartArt graphic as necessary to make the text wrap similar to the text shown in Figure 10-16. Don't be concerned if your text doesn't wrap in exactly the same way as in the figure.

Figure 10-16 | Figure with new caption

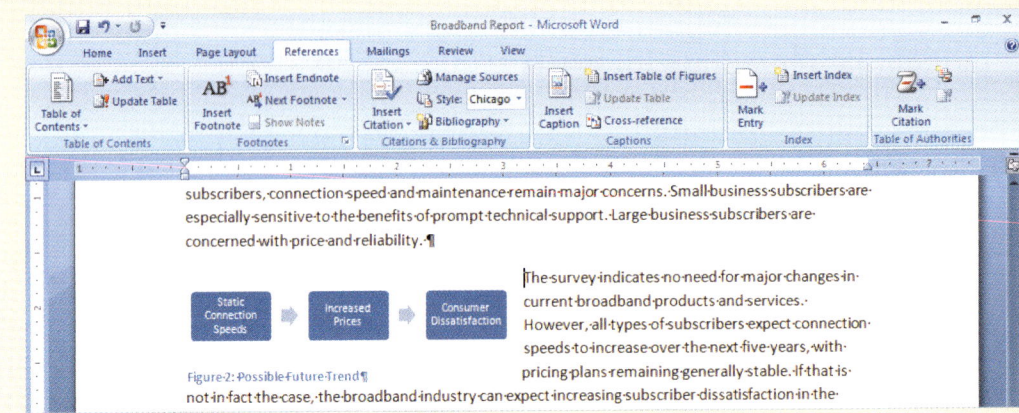

▶ **3.** Save the master document.

Now you're ready to add another graphic element to the report—the pie chart that Michael requested.

Inserting a Graph or Chart

Michael would like you to add a pie chart in section "3.1. Demographics" to show the range of annual household income among residential subscribers. You'll create this pie chart using Microsoft Graph. **Microsoft Graph** is a program you can use with Word to create simple charts and graphs. To use Microsoft Graph, you start Microsoft Graph via the Object button in the Text group on the Insert tab, select the type of chart or graph you want, and then modify the information in the datasheet. The **datasheet** is a grid of cells, similar to an Excel worksheet, to which you can add data and labels. The columns in the datasheet are labeled A, B, C, and so on, and the rows are labeled 1, 2, 3, and so on. As you add the data and labels, Microsoft Graph automatically creates the chart or graph.

Note that you can also create a chart in Word by clicking the Chart button in the Illustrations group on the Insert tab. This opens the Insert Chart dialog box, where you can select a type of chart and then click OK to open a Microsoft Excel window where you can enter the data for your chart. This method is useful if you are already familiar with Excel. However, if you are not familiar with Excel and you want to create a simple graph or chart, Microsoft Graph is the better option.

Because Lori is not familiar with Excel, she asks you to use Microsoft Graph to create the pie chart.

To create a pie chart in Microsoft Graph:

▶ **1.** Move the insertion point to the beginning of the paragraph just below the heading "3.1. Demographics" on page 3 (just to the left of the sentence that begins "The respondents to the residential...").

2. Click the **Insert** tab, in the Text group click the **Object** button (not the Object button arrow), click the **Create New** tab, if necessary, click **Microsoft Graph Chart**, and then click the **OK** button. Microsoft Graph opens within the Word window, displaying a sample bar chart and a datasheet. The sample bar chart is inserted at the location of the insertion point. The datasheet is floating over the document, possibly obscuring the sample chart. In the next step, you will make some adjustments to ensure that your Microsoft Graph window matches the figures in this book.

3. Drag the datasheet by its title bar, if necessary, so that it doesn't cover the sample chart. See Figure 10-17.

Microsoft Graph open in Word ◀ **Figure 10-17**

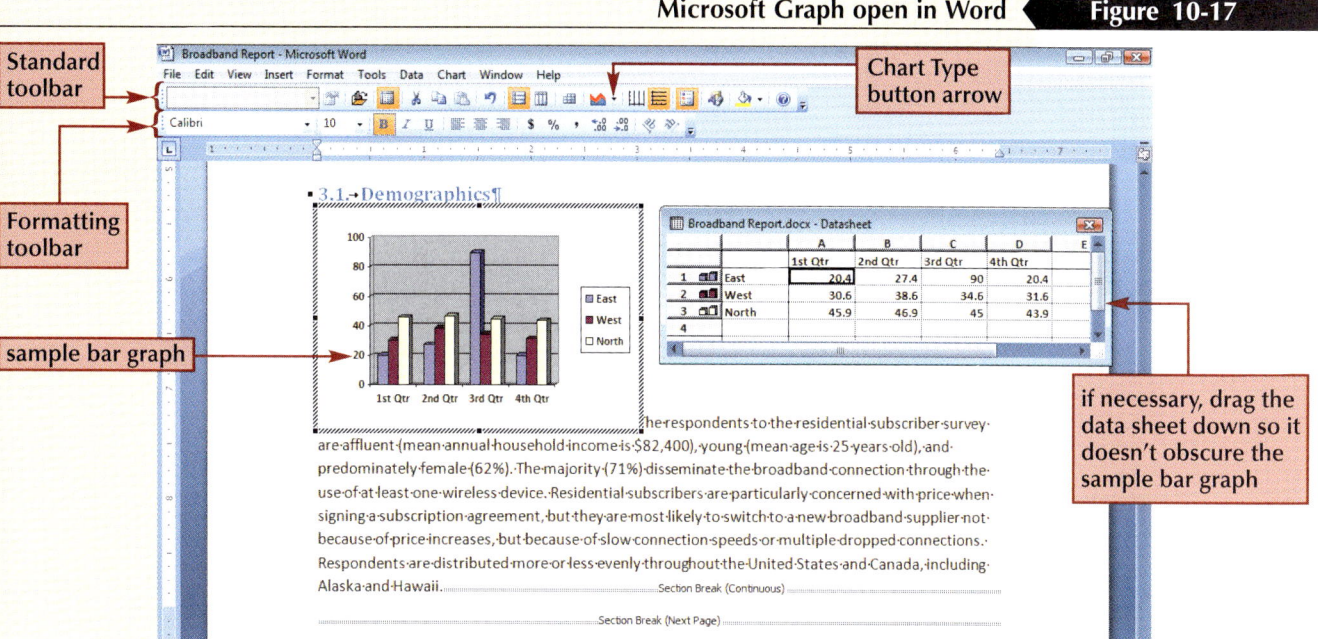

Standard toolbar

Formatting toolbar

Chart Type button arrow

sample bar graph

if necessary, drag the data sheet down so it doesn't obscure the sample bar graph

Instead of a Ribbon with multiple tabs, which you are used to seeing in Word, the Microsoft Graph window includes two toolbars, each of which contains buttons that you can use to perform various tasks. Your toolbars might appear in a single row or they might be stacked on top of each other. In the next step, you will stack your toolbars on top of each other, if they aren't already.

4. If your toolbars currently appear in a single row, click the **Toolbar Options** button on the right edge of the toolbar row, and then click **Show Buttons on Two Rows**. The toolbars are displayed in two separate rows. The top toolbar is called the Standard toolbar, and the bottom one is called the Formatting toolbar.

5. Click the **Chart Type button arrow** on the Standard toolbar (the top toolbar) to display a menu of chart types, and then click the **Pie Chart** button . The chart changes to a pie chart.

Trouble? If the sample chart changes to a different type of chart, you clicked the Chart Type button rather than the Chart Type button arrow. Undo the change, and then repeat Step 5, taking care to click the Chart Type button arrow.

6. Click the datasheet's title bar to make sure the datasheet window is selected, click the blank, gray button in the upper-left corner of the datasheet (two rows above row 1 and two columns to the left of column A) to select the data in the datasheet, and then press the **Delete** key to erase the current data. Because the datasheet is now blank, the chart window is also blank. See Figure 10-18.

Figure 10-18 | **Data deleted from datasheet**

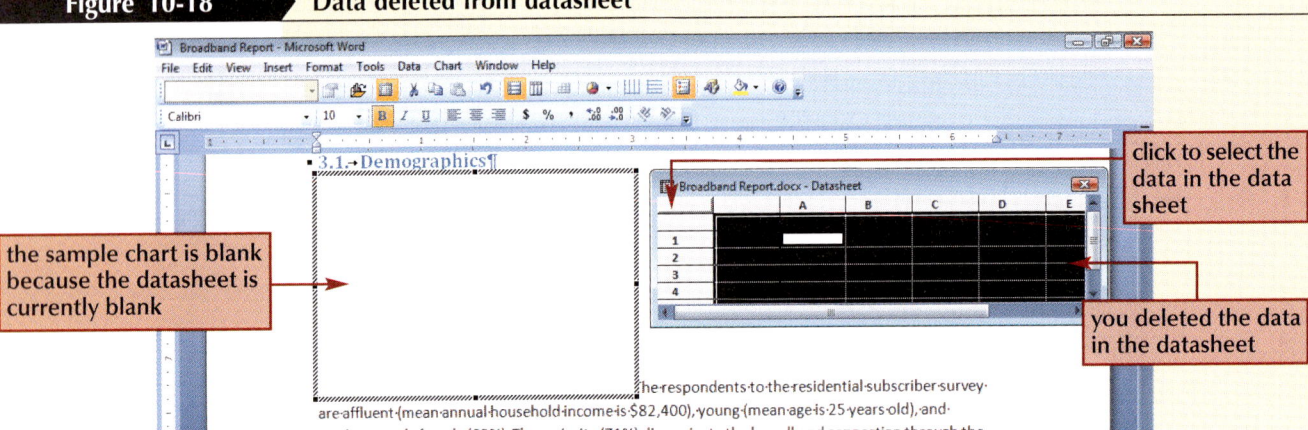

the sample chart is blank because the datasheet is currently blank

click to select the data in the data sheet

you deleted the data in the datasheet

▶ **7.** Click the top cell in column A. This is now the active cell, the cell that is ready to accept age data for residential respondents.

▶ **8.** Type **18 to 29**, and then press the **Tab** key. The active cell moves to cell B1.

▶ **9.** Type **30 to 49**, press the **Tab** key, type **over 50**, and then press the **Tab** key.

▶ **10.** Click **cell A1** (the cell at the intersection of column A and row 1, directly below the label "18 to 29"), and then, using the Tab key to move from cell to cell, type the following data in row 1: **60%**, **25%**, and **15%**. Press the **Enter** key after typing the last percentage to enter data in the datasheet. The pie chart is re-drawn to reflect the new data. See Figure 10-19.

Figure 10-19 | **Pie chart created with Microsoft Graph**

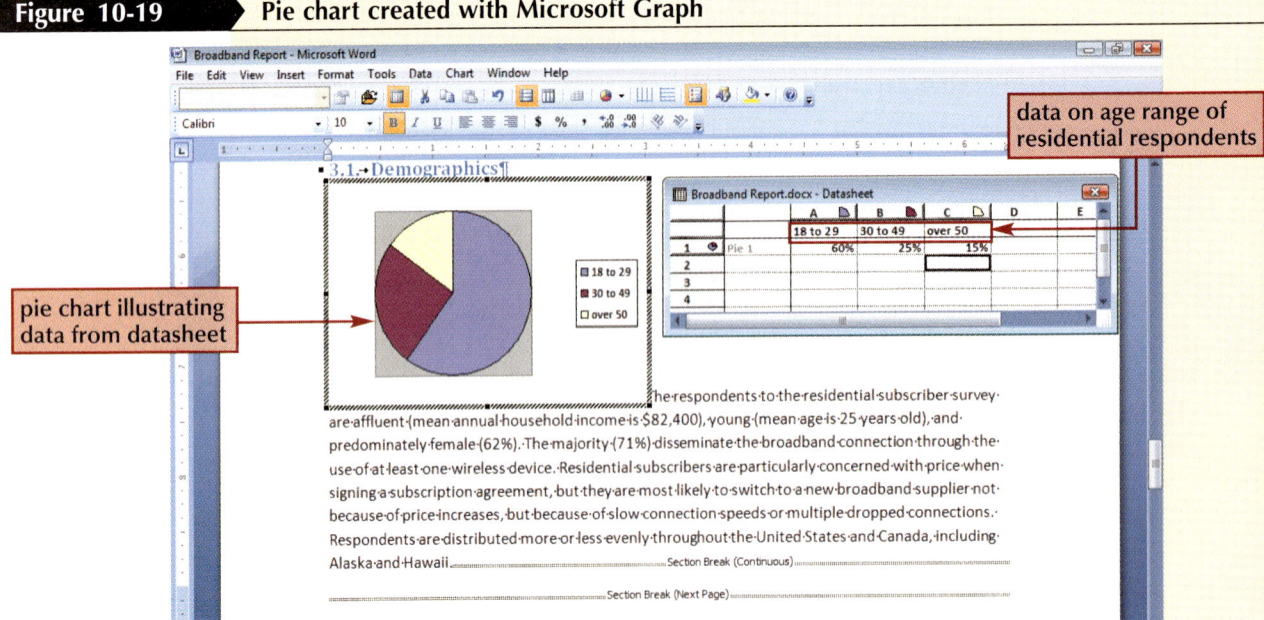

data on age range of residential respondents

pie chart illustrating data from datasheet

11. Click anywhere outside the chart or datasheet to return to the Word document. The datasheet window closes, and the border around the pie chart disappears.

Next, you'll wrap the text around the left side of the chart, position the chart on the right side of the page, and then create a caption for the pie chart figure. You'll start by using a different method for wrapping text around a graphic.

To position the chart, wrap the text, and create a caption:

1. Right-click the **chart**, click **Format Object** on the shortcut menu, click the **Layout** tab, click the **Square** icon in the Wrapping style section, click the **Right** option button in the Horizontal alignment section, and then click the **OK** button. The pie chart moves to the right, with the document text wrapped to its left. See Figure 10-20.

Pie chart with text wrapped to its left — **Figure 10-20**

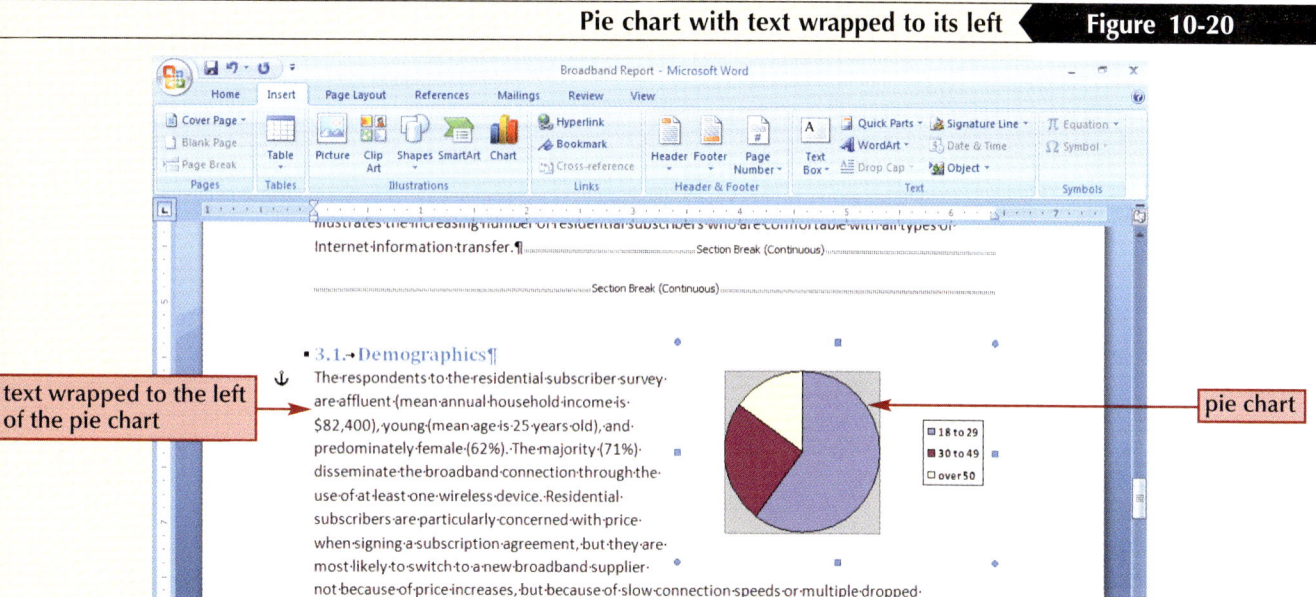

text wrapped to the left of the pie chart

pie chart

2. Verify that the pie chart is selected, and then open the Caption dialog box. Note that the Caption text box displays "Figure 2." Word automatically numbers this Figure 2 because you are inserting it before the previously numbered Figure 2. The old Figure 2 is renumbered Figure 3.

3. Change the figure caption to **Figure 2: Age Range of Residential Respondents**, click the **OK** button, drag the bottom border of the caption box up until it just accommodates the caption, click anywhere in the paragraph to deselect the caption box, click the caption box again to display its dotted selection border, drag the caption box up slightly so that two full lines of text wrap below it, and then click anywhere in the paragraph to deselect the caption box.

4. Scroll down and note that the SmartArt graphic has been renumbered as Figure 3.

5. Save the document.

Now that you have inserted three figures with captions, you need to refer to each of them in the text. For that, you'll use cross-references.

Creating Cross-References

A **cross-reference** is a notation within a document that points the reader to a figure, table, or section. If you refer to figures within the text—for example, "See Figure 2"—you need to make sure the cross-references change if the figure numbers change. This might be necessary if you add or delete figures or reorganize a document. Word updates cross-references automatically, just as it updates the heading numbering and figure captions.

Reference Window | **Creating Cross-References**

- Move the insertion point to the location where you want to insert the cross-reference.
- Type the text preceding the cross-reference, such as "See" and a space.
- Click the References tab, and then, in the Captions group, click the Cross-reference button.
- Select the Reference type—for example, figure, table, equation, or heading.
- In the "Insert reference to" list box, select the information you want to appear in the cross-reference—for example, entire caption, only label and number, or page number.
- Indicate whether you want the cross-reference formatted as a hyperlink. (When the user clicks a hyperlink cross-reference, the insertion point moves to the item being cross-referenced.)
- Click the Insert button, and then click the Close button.

Michael wants the figures in the report referenced within the text, so you'll insert cross-references to the three figures.

To insert a cross-reference to a figure:

► 1. Scroll up to the heading "1.2. Personnel," click to the right of "Kayla West" in the paragraph of text (not in the figure caption), press the **Spacebar**, type (**see** and then press the **Spacebar** again. When you are finished, the sentence should read "Kayla West (see ". Now you're ready to insert the automatically numbered cross-reference.

► 2. Click the **References** tab, if necessary, and then in the Captions group, click the **Cross-reference** button. The Cross-reference dialog box opens.

► 3. Click the **Reference type** arrow, scroll down if necessary, and then click **Figure**.

► 4. Click the **Insert reference to** arrow, and then click **Only label and number**.

► 5. Make sure **Figure 1: Kayla West** is selected in the For which caption list box. See Figure 10-21.

Figure 10-21

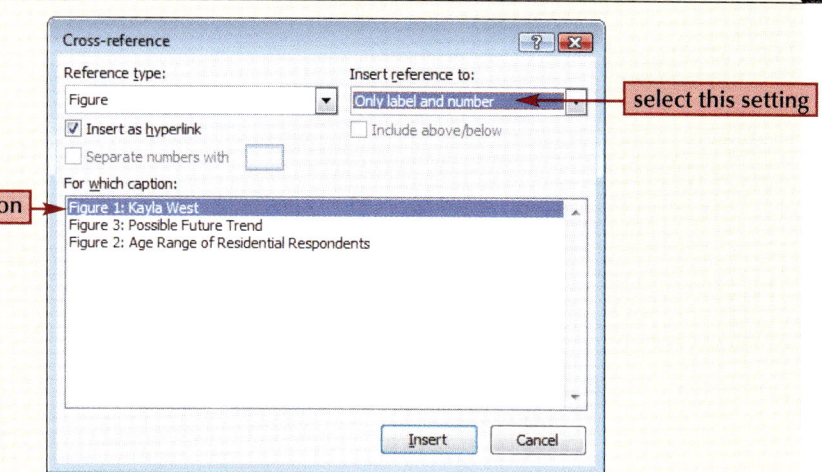

select this setting →

select this figure caption →

6. Click the **Insert** button to insert this cross-reference, click the **Close** button to close the dialog box, and then type **)** after the cross-reference to close the parentheses. The phrase "(see Figure 1)" appears in the report, so that the sentence reads "Kayla West (see Figure 1), chair of the...." Notice that the cross-reference you created is automatically numbered to match the figure caption number.

Trouble? If the figure number changes to 2 (or another number) as you edit the document, select the figure caption, press the F9 key to update the caption field codes, click anywhere in the document, press the Ctrl+A keys to select all the text in the document, and then press the F9 key again to update the cross-references.

The power of all automatic numbering features in Word—heading numbering, caption numbering, and cross-references—becomes evident when you edit a long document with many figures. Now you'll add cross-references to the other two figures.

To insert additional cross-references:

1. Scroll down to the section that begins with the heading "3.1. Demographics," click at the end of the first sentence below the heading, and then, using a cross-reference, insert the sentence **See Figure 2.** Do not include parentheses. Also make sure you include a space after the newly inserted sentence.

2. Find the sentence that begins "If that is not in fact the case...", and then click at the end of that sentence. Insert the following as a cross-reference: **(See Figure 3.)** This time, take care to include the parentheses and appropriate spacing. Depending on how the text is wrapped around the graphic and the caption box, you may find that the nonbreaking hyphen you inserted earlier in the word "high-speed" (in the last sentence of the paragraph) now prevents the word from breaking over two lines. See Figure 10-22.

Figure 10-22 ▶ **Cross-reference to figure**

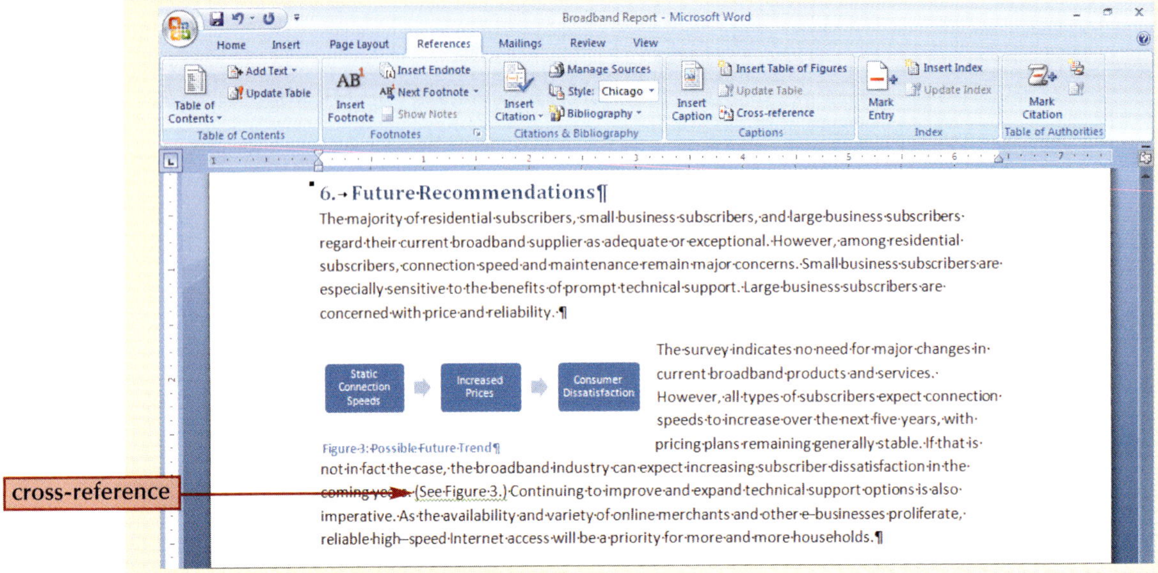

cross-reference

▶ **3.** Save the master document.

Next, you'll help Michael control the kinds of changes the other writers at Market Data Now can make to the Broadband Report.

Protecting a Document

Because Michael has already done a fair amount of work on the master document, he'd like to retain some control over the kinds of changes the other writers make to it, so he decides to protect the document. When you **protect** a document, you restrict the kinds of formatting changes and edits that Word will allow in the document. When specifying formatting restrictions, you can limit formatting in the document to a specific list of styles. You can also block certain formatting changes, such as selecting a new theme.

When specifying editing restrictions, you can choose from the following options:

- **Tracked changes.** Allows users to make any editing changes and the formatting changes allowed by the formatting restrictions, but all changes are marked with revision marks.
- **Comments**. Allows users to insert comments, but not to make any other changes.
- **Filling in forms**. Allows users to fill in forms only; you used this option in Tutorial 9 to protect a form.
- **No changes (Read only)**. Allows users to read the document but not to make changes.

It's also possible to specify user exceptions—that is, you can allow some users to remove the protection and edit the document freely, no matter what formatting and editing restrictions you have specified for other users. The users to whom you apply exceptions must be part of your workgroup (so that Microsoft Word has access to their user names) or must be specified in the Microsoft Office 2007 Information Rights Management (IRM) program, which you can download from the Microsoft Office Web site.

As you learned in Tutorial 9, when you protect a document you can choose to require a password in order to turn off protection. If you are protecting a document because you are concerned that someone might make unauthorized changes to the document, then you should definitely use a password. However, if you are protecting a document that will be shared among a small group of colleagues, and you are using the protect feature simply to ensure that all changes are tracked with revision marks, then a password typically isn't necessary.

Protecting a Document | Reference Window

- Open the document you want to protect.
- Click the Review tab, and then, in the Protect group, click the Protect Document button to open the Restrict Formatting and Editing task pane.
- To specify formatting restrictions, under "1. Formatting restrictions", select the "Limit formatting to a selection of styles" check box, click Settings to open the Formatting Restrictions dialog box, select the restrictions you want, and then click the OK button.
- To specify editing restrictions, under "2. Editing restrictions", select the "Allow only this type of editing in the document" check box, click the list arrow, and then click the editing restriction you want. For example, to protect a document for tracked changes, you would click Tracked changes.
- To specify user exceptions, verify that you have set up IRM, under "Exceptions (optional)" select a group of users in the list box, or click More users and select additional users.
- Under "3. Start enforcement", click the Yes, Start Enforcing Protection button.
- If desired, type a password in the "Enter new password (optional)" text box and in the "Reenter password to confirm" text box.
- Click the OK button.

Because Michael wants to be able to see exactly what changes the other writers make to the text, he decides to protect the master document by applying the Tracked changes editing restriction. This is sometimes referred to as "protecting a document for tracked changes." You already have some experience working with the Track Changes feature, which marks additions, deletions, moved text, and formatting changes with revision marks. Once you protect a document for tracked changes, you should keep in mind the following:

- Revision marks don't necessarily show up even when tracking is on. You can choose to display or hide the revision marks. Even if you can't see them, they are stored in your document for you or others to view when necessary.
- You can use the tracking feature without protecting the document. The difference between tracking changes with protection on or off is this: if the document is unprotected, you can turn on and off revision tracking at will. If the document is protected, you can't turn off revision tracking, unless you remove the restrictions first.
- When you protect a master document for tracked changes, Word creates revision marks for any change made in the master document text or in the subdocuments that are expanded in the master document. However, even if the master document is protected, you can still open the subdocuments in separate document windows and edit them, without tracking the revisions. In other words, protecting a master document doesn't protect the separate subdocument files.

In addition to protecting the document for tracked changes, Michael wants to apply one formatting restriction—in particular, he wants to block any user from changing the document theme. You're ready to begin protecting the Broadband Report document.

To apply formatting and editing restrictions to the document and then protect it:

1. Click the **Review** tab, and then, in the Protect group, click the **Protect Document** button. The Restrict Formatting and Editing task pane opens. First, you'll take care of the formatting restrictions. Michael doesn't care whether the other writers apply new styles to the document, so you'll start by making sure the first check box does not contain a check mark.

▶ **2.** In the "1. Formatting restrictions" section, deselect the **Limit formatting to a selection of styles** check box if necessary. Next, you will block users from changing the document theme.

▶ **3.** Click **Settings** to open the Formatting Restrictions dialog box, and then near the bottom of the dialog box select the **Block Theme or Scheme switching** check box. See Figure 10-23.

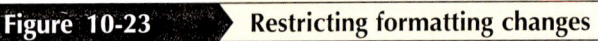

Figure 10-23 ▶ **Restricting formatting changes**

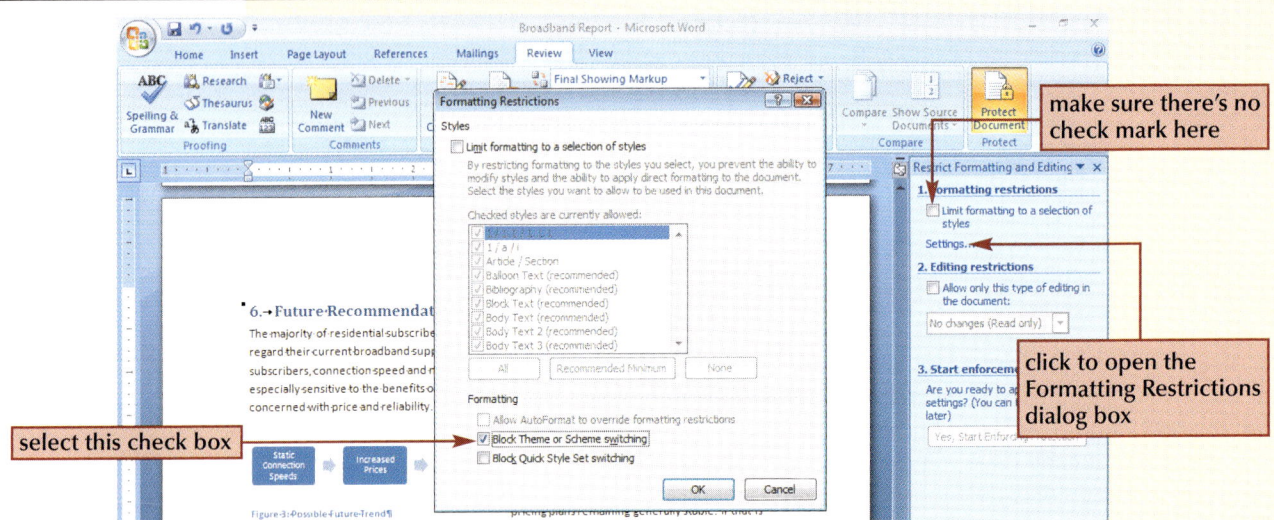

▶ **4.** Click the **OK** button to close the Formatting Restrictions dialog box. Next, you will apply an editing restriction.

▶ **5.** In the "2. Editing restrictions" section of the task pane, click the **Allow only this type of editing in the document** check box. A new section of the task pane, labeled "Exceptions (optional)," opens. You can use this section of the task pane to select users who will be allowed to edit the document freely, no matter what formatting or editing restrictions you specify. Michael does not want to specify any user restrictions, so you can ignore this section of the task pane.

▶ **6.** Click the arrow button in the Editing restrictions section—which by default is set to No changes (Read only)—and then click **Tracked changes**. The user exceptions section of the task pane closes; when Tracked changes is selected, all users are free to make any changes they want, so there's no need to exempt some users.

▶ **7.** In the "3. Start enforcement" section of the task pane, click the **Yes, Start Enforcing Protection** button. The Start Enforcing Protection dialog box opens, where you have the opportunity to specify a password.

▶ **8.** Click the **OK** button to close the dialog box without entering a password.

▶ **9.** Close the task pane, and then save the document.

Choosing When to Protect a Document | InSight

It's not convenient or useful to protect every document you create. But most people don't use this feature as much as they should. If you plan to send a document around to colleagues for their comments, you should definitely take the time to protect the document first, so that your colleagues' changes are tracked with revision marks. Otherwise, you might encounter some surprises in documents after they are published, mailed, or e-mailed. For example, a colleague might introduce an error by changing an important sales figure using outdated sales information, and then forget to tell you later. You can prevent this kind of problem by protecting your shared documents for tracked changes. Unless you are concerned about someone trying to sabotage your work, it's probably not necessary to use a password. Simply protecting a document for tracked changes informs your colleagues that you need to be aware of all changes. Of course, as always when using revision marks, it's extremely important that you accept or reject all changes and turn off Track Changes before finalizing the document.

Now that the document is protected for revisions, neither you nor anyone else can make changes without having the changes tracked with revision marks.

Editing a Protected Document

Now Lori asks you to revise the Executive Summary section.

To edit a document with revision marks:

1. Make sure the Broadband Report document is in Print Layout view, and scroll until you see the heading "2. Executive Summary." Lori realizes that the word "generally" in the second sentence is unnecessary, so she asks you to delete it.

2. Double-click the word **generally** located in the second sentence below the heading "2. Executive Summary," and then press the **Delete** key. Normally, "generally" would simply be removed, but because the document is protected for tracked changes, Word draws a strikeout line through it, displays the deleted word in red, and adds a revision line in the margin.

   Trouble? The deletion on your screen might be marked with a balloon in the right margin.

3. Click the **Page Layout** tab, and notice that the options in the Themes group are unavailable. You blocked all users from changing the document theme, so Word prevents you from using these options. See Figure 10-24.

Editing a protected document | Figure 10-24

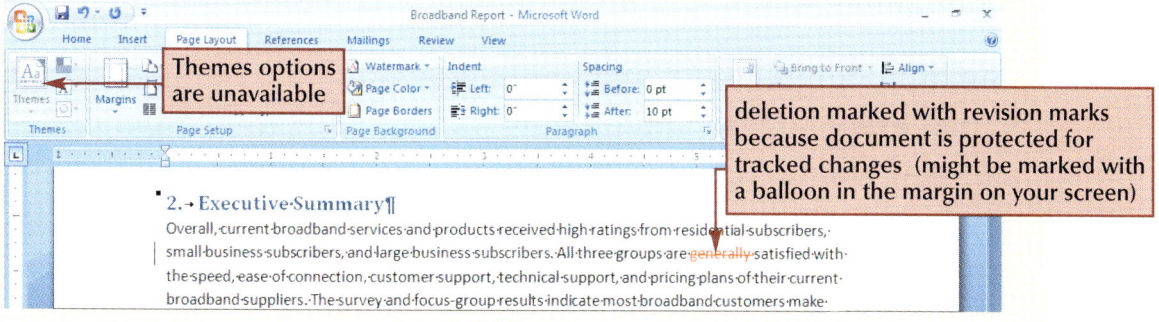

> **Trouble?** Your revision marks might be a different color than the ones shown in Figure 10-24.

Now you'll turn off the document protection and remove the formatting restriction.

To unprotect the document and turn off the formatting restriction:

▶ 1. Click the **Review** tab, and then, in the Protect group, click the **Protect Document** button. The Restrict Formatting and Editing task pane opens.

▶ 2. Click the **Stop Protection** button at the bottom of the task pane. From this point on, Word will no longer automatically mark changes with revision marks.

▶ 3. In the "1. Formatting restrictions" section of the task pane, click **Settings** to open the Formatting Restrictions dialog box, deselect the **Block Theme or Scheme switching** check box, click the **OK** button to close the dialog box, in the "2. Editing restrictions" section of the task pane, click the **Allow only this type of editing in the document** check box to remove the check mark, and then close the task pane.

You'll now see what the document would look like if you accepted Lori's revision—that is, if no revision marks appeared in the document.

To review the document with changes accepted:

▶ 1. In the Tracking group, click the **Display for Review** arrow (which is currently set to Final Showing Markup), and then click **Final**. The document now appears as it would if you accepted Lori's revision. Using the Display for Review arrow, you can also show how the document looked before the revisions and show the original version with markup.

▶ 2. Save the document. At this point, the document still contains Lori's deletion of the word "generally" marked with revision marks, although you can't see the revision marks.

As you have seen, the Display for Review list in the Tracking group on the Review tab provides a lot of flexibility when working with revision marks. It's often helpful to use the Final setting to display the document as if all the revision marks have been accepted or rejected, without actually accepting or rejecting the revision marks. However, after you review the document using the Final setting, it's easy to forget to go back and accept or reject the revision marks. If you do forget, you might then accidentally send out a document that contains revision marks to a client or to your superior. Such a mistake could make you look unprofessional, or, even worse, depending on the nature of your revisions, inadvertently reveal sensitive information. To make sure a document doesn't contain any revision marks, or any other types of information that you don't want to reveal to readers of your document, you can use the Document Inspector.

Checking a Document with the Document Inspector

The **Document Inspector** automatically checks a document for comments and revision marks. If it finds any, it gives you the opportunity to remove them with a click of a button. When you remove revision marks with the Document Inspector, all changes are accepted, as if you had used the Accept button in the Changes group on the Review tab.

You can also use the Document Inspector to check a document for personal information stored in the document properties, headers, or footers. In addition, it can search for hidden text (text that is hidden from display using the Hidden check box on the Font tab of the Font dialog box) and for special types of data that can be stored along with the document. You'll use the Document Inspector now to check for revision marks. Before using the Document Inspector, you should save the document.

To check the document using the Document Inspector:

1. Click the **Office Button** 🔘 , point to **Prepare**, and then click **Inspect Document**. The Document Inspector dialog box opens.

   Trouble? If you see a dialog box indicating that the file has not been saved, click the Yes button.

2. Deselect all the check boxes except the first one, so that Word will only check for items related to tracked changes and comments. See Figure 10-25.

Document Inspector

To check the document for the selected content, click Inspect.

leave a check mark here →
- ☑ **Comments, Revisions, Versions, and Annotations**
  Inspects the document for comments, versions, revision marks, and ink annotations.

deselect these check boxes →
- ☐ **Document Properties and Personal Information**
  Inspects for hidden metadata or personal information saved with the document.

- ☐ **Custom XML Data**
  Inspects for custom XML data stored with this document.

- ☐ **Headers, Footers, and Watermarks**
  Inspects the document for information in headers, footers, and watermarks.

- ☐ **Hidden Text**
  Inspects the document for text that has been formatted as hidden.

[Inspect] [Close]

3. Click the **Inspect** button. You see a message in the Document Inspector dialog box indicating that revision marks were found in the document.

4. Click the **Remove All** button. You see a message in the Document Inspector dialog box indicating that all the items were removed.

5. Click the **Close** button. The Document Inspector dialog box closes.

6. Verify that the Executive Summary section is visible, click the **Review** tab if necessary, in the Tracking group click the **Display for Review** arrow (which currently displays "Final"), and then click **Final Showing Markup**. If the document did contain revision marks, you would see them now. Because you used the Document Inspector to remove all revision marks, Lori's edit has been accepted and the word "generally" has been deleted.

The Document Inspector is especially useful when you are working on a long document and you are collaborating with other writers who might have made changes to a document without your knowledge. Another useful tool for long documents is synchronous scrolling, as explained in the next section.

Managing Multiple Documents Simultaneously with Synchronous Scrolling

One of the hardest parts about collaborating on a document with other people is keeping track of which copy of the file is the correct one, and making sure that all the intended edits are entered into the correct file. Using the Master Document feature can go a long way toward ensuring that all edits are made in the correct file. But if confusion does arise, you can open up both documents, display them side-by-side, and then scroll through both documents at the same time. Scrolling two documents at once—a process known as **synchronous scrolling**—allows you to quickly assess the overall structure of two documents. If this side-by-side comparison suggests numerous differences between the document, you can then use the Compare feature (as explained in Tutorial 7) to examine, in detail, the differences between the two documents.

While Michael was out of the office, Katarina made a copy of the Broadband Report document, and then edited the chart in the "3.1. Demographics" section. Michael decides to use synchronous scrolling to compare Katarina's new copy of the document, which is named Report 2, with his Broadband Report document. Note that in the Report 2 document that you will be using in the following steps, the subdocuments have been merged with the master document. That way you won't have to take the time to expand the subdocuments before proceeding with the synchronous scrolling steps. You'll start by scrolling to the top of the Broadband Report document and examining some options in the View tab. Then you will open the Report 2 document and use synchronous scrolling to pinpoint the differences in the two documents.

To examine some options in the View menu and display two documents side-by-side:

▶ 1. Press the **Ctrl+Home** keys to move the insertion point to the beginning of the Broadband Report document.

▶ 2. Click the **View** tab. The Window group on the View tab contains several buttons that you can use to manipulate the document window for one or more documents. The Split button allows you to divide the current document window in two, so you can display two different parts of the same document at once.

▶ 3. In the Window group, click the **Split** button. The mouse pointer changes to ≑ and a gray horizontal line appears in the document window, moving up and down as you move the mouse.

▶ 4. Move the mouse pointer to the middle of the document window and click. The window is split into two, with two separate vertical scroll bars that you can use to scroll to different parts of the document.

▶ 5. In the bottom window, scroll down to display the chart in the "3.1. Demographics" section. See Figure 10-26. Note that what you see in the bottom window is part of the same document that you see in the top window.

Trouble? If the heading number has disappeared from the "Demographics" heading next to the chart, click anywhere in the heading and format it with the Heading 2 style.

Splitting the document window | **Figure 10-26**

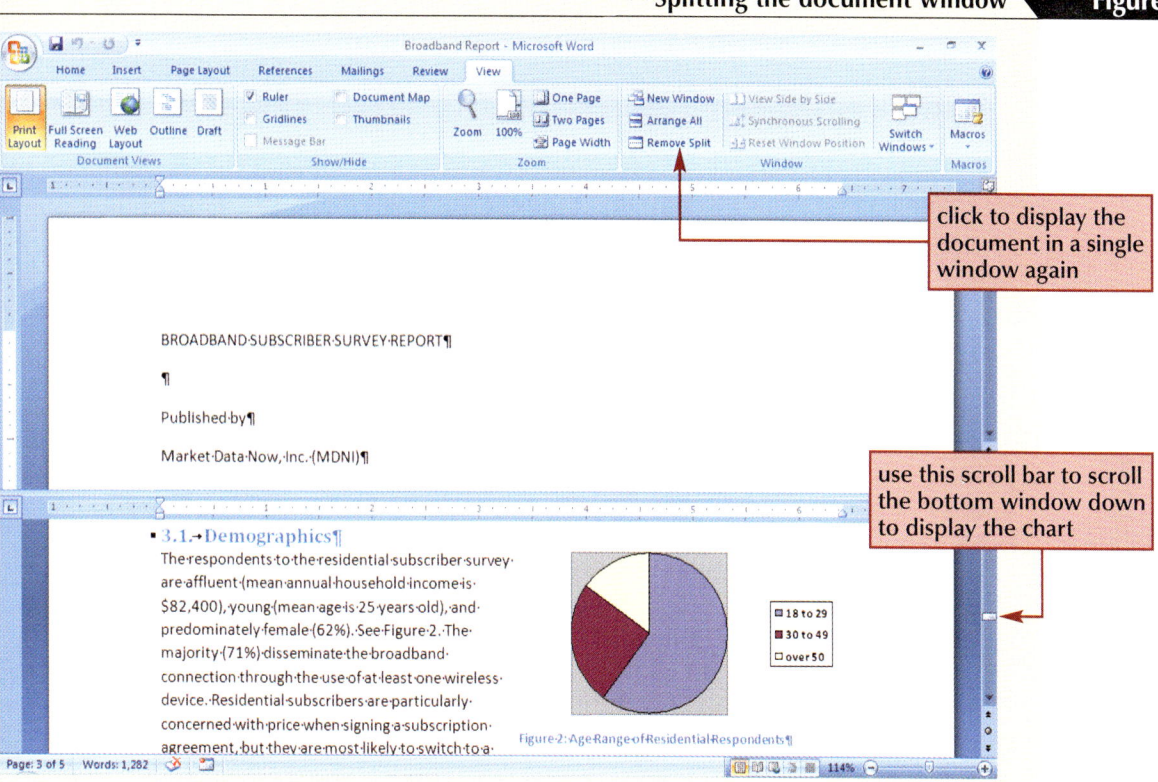

click to display the document in a single window again

use this scroll bar to scroll the bottom window down to display the chart

6. In the Window group on the View tab, click the **Remove Split** button to display the document in a single window again, scroll up if necessary to display the beginning of the Broadband Report document, and then open the document named **Report 2** from the Tutorial.10\Tutorial folder included with your Data Files.

7. In the Report 2 document window, click the **View** tab, and then in the Window group, click the **View Side by Side** button. The documents are probably displayed side by side, but they might be stacked one on top of the other. In the next step, you will display your documents side by side if necessary.

8. If necessary, click the **Reset Window Position** button in the Window group in the Report 2 document window, and then verify that your document windows are displayed side by side, as in Figure 10-27. In the figure, the Broadband Report document is on the right, but on your computer it might be on the left.

Tip

If more than two documents are open when you click the View Side by Side button, the Compare Side by Side dialog box opens so you can select the document you want to compare.

Figure 10-27 ▶ **Two documents displayed side by side**

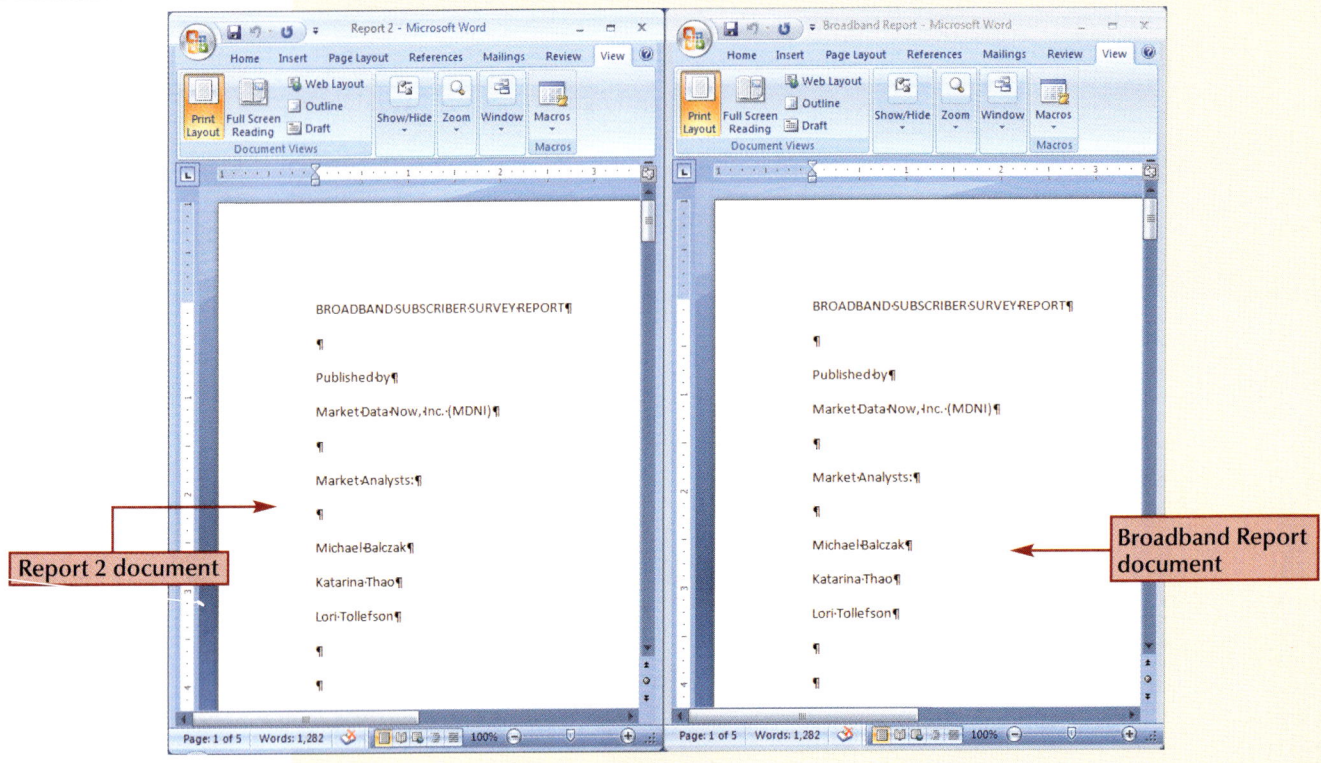

Report 2 document

Broadband Report document

Synchronous scrolling is turned on by default when you display documents side by side. In the next step, you will verify that it is turned on.

▶ 9. In the Report 2 window, click the **Window** button to open the Window menu, verify that **Synchronous Scrolling** is selected, press the **Escape** key to close the Window menu, and then use the vertical scroll bar in the Report 2 document to scroll down to the "3.1. Demographics" section. Note that the vertical scroll bar in one document controls both documents, so that they scroll simultaneously.

▶ 10. When you see the "3.1. Demographics" section in both documents, use the horizontal scroll bar in the Report 2 window to scroll slightly right, so you can see the chart in both windows. In the Report 2 document, the chart is a bar graph; in the Broadband Report document, you see Michael's pie chart. In order to see the chart and the text next to it at the same time, you can stack, or tile, the document windows on top of each other.

Trouble? If you don't see horizontal scroll bars in the document windows, your screen is too small to display them. Skip Step 10 and proceed to Step 11.

Trouble? If the heading number has disappeared from the "Demographics" heading, use the Heading 2 Quick Style button on the Home tab to reapply the heading style.

▶ 11. In the Report 2 window, click the **Window** button, and then click the **Arrange All** button. The documents are stacked, or tiled, on top of each other, with the Report 2 document on top. Note that Synchronous Scrolling is still turned on in both windows. If you wanted to scroll through the documents separately, you could deselect Synchronous Scrolling in either window.

Tip

When the document windows are displayed side by side, you see one larger button for each group on the Ribbon, except for the Document Views group. Click one of these buttons to access the buttons in that group.

Next, Michael wants to add some color to the "3.1. Demographics" section so he'll remember to look at the chart again later. He'll start by adding **highlighting**—that is, a bar of color that looks as if you drew a line over the text with a highlighting pen. Then he'll experiment with **paragraph shading**, which applies a background color to an entire paragraph.

To add highlighting and paragraph shading to a paragraph:

1. In the Report 2 document window, scroll down, if necessary, so you can see the figure reference, "See Figure 2," click the **Home** tab, in the Font group click the **Text Highlight Color** button 📇 , and then move the mouse pointer over the Report 2 document text. The pointer changes to a highlighting pointer ⟋ .

2. In the second line of the paragraph below the heading "3.1. Demographics," drag the ⟋ pointer over the sentence **See Figure 2.** The sentence is highlighted in yellow in the Report 2 document window. The same sentence in the Broadband Report document remains unchanged. In the next step you'll remove the highlighting.

3. In the Font group in the Report 2 document window, click the **Text Highlight Color button arrow** 📇 ▾ to open a palette of highlight colors, click **No Color,** drag the ⟋ pointer over the highlighted sentence, and then press the **Escape** key to turn off the highlighting pointer. The highlighting is removed. Next, you will practice applying shading to the entire paragraph. Because paragraph shading is a type of paragraph-level formatting, you start by verifying that the insertion point is located in the paragraph you want to format.

4. In the Report 2 document window, verify that the insertion point is located in the paragraph below the "3.1. Demographics" heading, in the Paragraph group in the Report 2 document window click the **Shading button arrow** 🖌 ▾ to open a palette of shading colors, and then, under "Standard Colors," click the **orange box**. The entire paragraph in the Report 2 document, including the blank space between lines, is highlighted in orange. See Figure 10-28.

Figure 10-28 **Two documents tiled on top of each other**

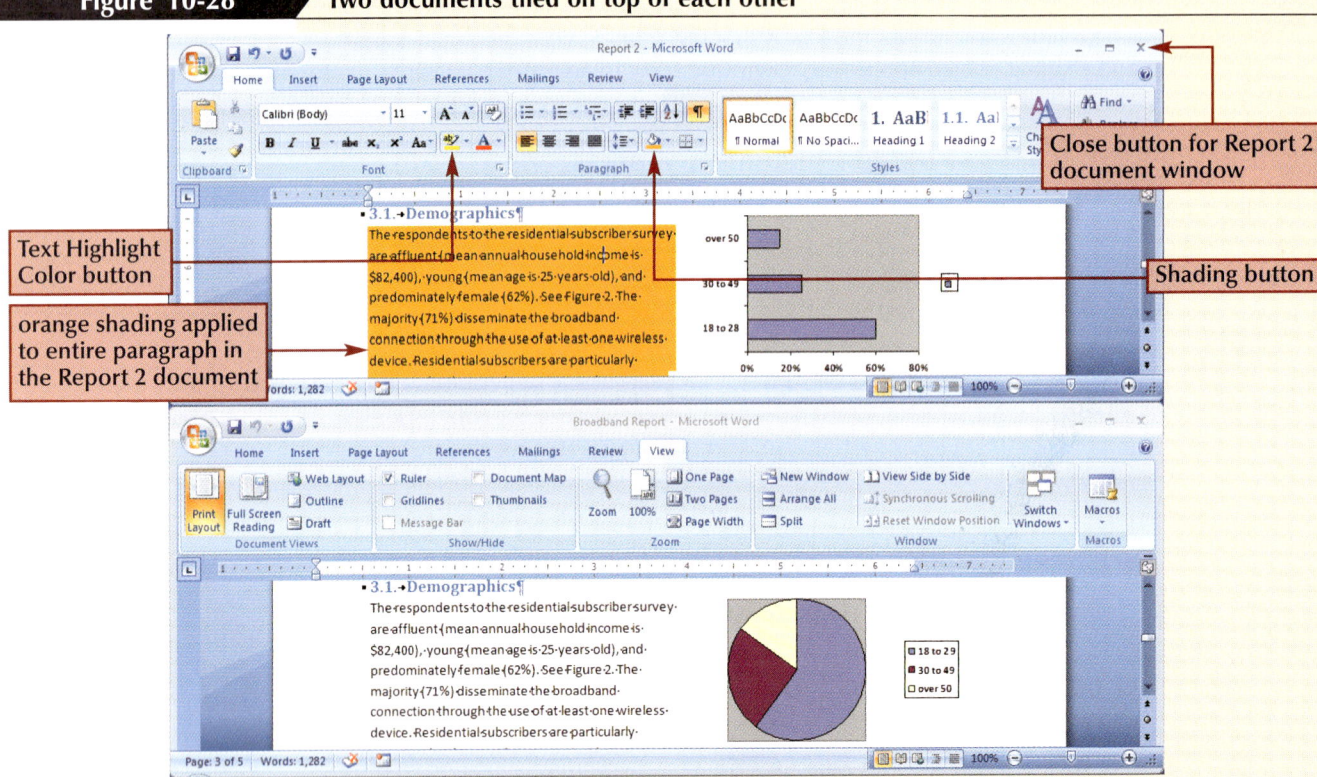

As a rule, you should use the Shading button when you want to apply color to create a dramatic effect. The Text Highlight Color button is more of an editing tool that you can use to quickly draw attention to material that needs more attention.

5. In the Report 2 document window, click the **Office** button and then save the document as **Report 2 Shaded**, and then close the Report 2 Shaded document window. The Report 2 Shaded document closes, and the Broadband Report window is maximized.

Be sure to use the options on the View menu when you are working with multiple documents. If you need to move quickly around a single, long document, consider using thumbnails instead, as explained in the following section.

Using Thumbnails to Navigate a Document

Thumbnails are another way of navigating in a document; they show miniature views of the document pages in a pane on the left side of the Word window. Clicking the thumbnail for a particular page displays that page in the document window. You'll use thumbnails now to navigate through the Broadband Report document.

To navigate using thumbnails:

1. Verify that the View tab is displayed, and then, in the Show/Hide group, click the **Thumbnails** check box to select it. The Thumbnails pane opens. See Figure 10-29.

Displaying document thumbnails | Figure 10-29

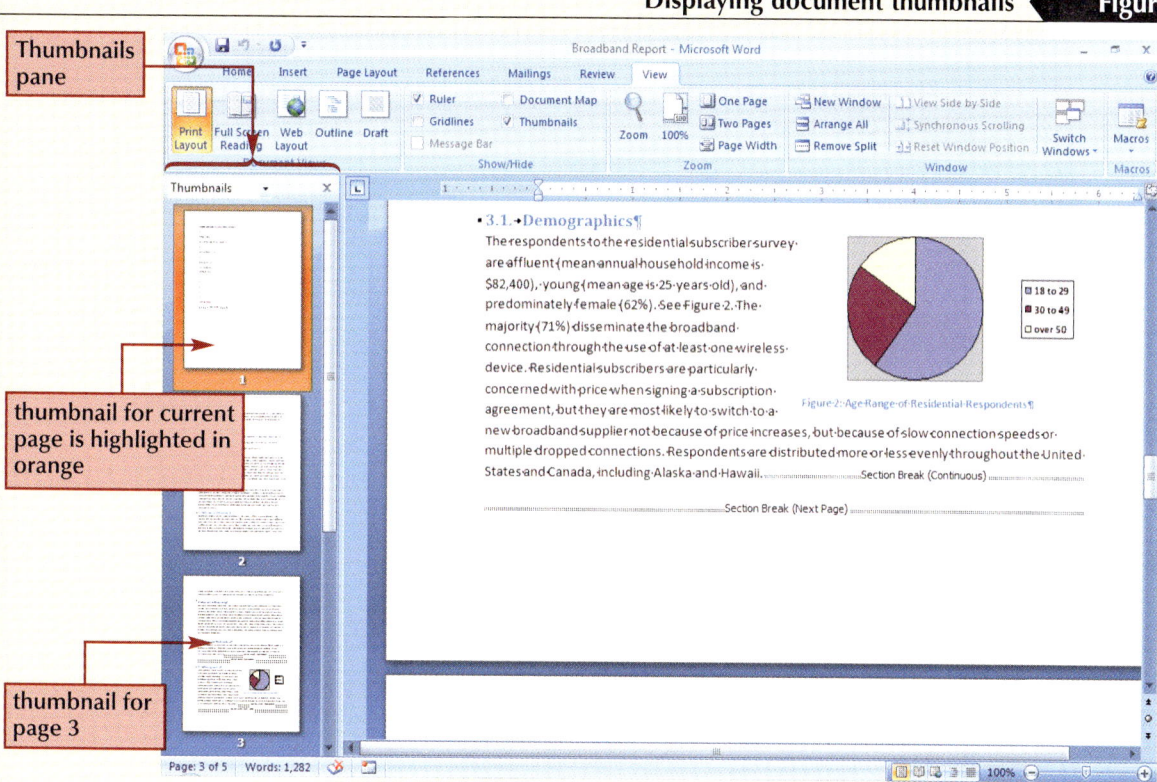

- Thumbnails pane
- thumbnail for current page is highlighted in orange
- thumbnail for page 3

2. Click **thumbnail 2** in the Thumbnails pane. The document window jumps to the second page in the document.

3. Click **thumbnail 1** in the Thumbnails pane. The document jumps back to the title page. Now you'll close the Thumbnails pane.

4. In the Show/Hide group, click the **Thumbnails** check box to deselect it. The Thumbnails pane closes.

5. Close the Broadband Report document, saving your changes.

In the next session, you'll format the document for printing and add a table of contents, list of figures, index, bibliography, and footers.

Session 10.2 Quick Check | Review

1. True or False. When you open a master document that has one or more subdocuments, Word also displays the subdocuments within the master document.

2. Explain how to add automatic numbering to section titles in a master document.

3. What button do you use to insert a figure caption?

4. True or False. Microsoft Graph can only be used to create pie charts.

5. Suppose you want to include the text "(see Figure 3") in a report and you want to make sure the figure number is automatically renumbered, if necessary, to reflect additions or deletions of figures in the document. What should you do?

6. What kind of editing restrictions can you specify when protecting a document?

7. Explain how to start the Document Inspector.

Session 10.3

Numbering Pages with Number Formats

Michael wants to add footers to the Broadband Report that include the name of the section and page numbers. Like most books, reports, and other long documents, the report will use a different page-numbering scheme for the front matter—the pages preceding the report itself, and which includes material such as the title page and table of contents. Front matter is usually numbered with lowercase Roman numerals (i, ii, iii, iv), whereas the main sections of a report are numbered with Arabic numerals (1, 2, 3, and so on). The first page of the report itself typically begins with page number 1.

You'll begin by formatting the title page and creating several other front matter pages, and then you'll set up the page numbers for the front matter.

To insert new front matter pages and format the title page:

1. Open the master document **Broadband Report**, expand the subdocuments, display nonprinting characters, switch to Print Layout view, and set the zoom to Page Width.

2. Move the insertion point to the end of page 1, immediately to the right of the date "June 10, 2010." Here you will insert a section break, so that you can format the title page with a format that is different from the other pages in the front matter.

3. Click the **Page Layout** tab, in the Page Setup group click the **Breaks** button to open the Breaks menu, and then, under "Section Breaks," click **Next Page**. Word inserts a new page following a section break. The insertion point moves to the new page, along with the Page Break line that was originally on page 1. Next, you will insert a heading for the table of contents and a new page and heading for the list of figures. Note that in the publishing industry, it's traditional for the table of contents heading to be the single word "Contents," not "Table of Contents."

4. Type **Contents,** press the **Enter** key three times to add some space below the heading, press the **Ctrl+Enter** keys to insert a page break, and then type **List of Figures**.

5. Press the **Delete** key to delete the paragraph mark after "List of Figures," and then press the **Delete** key again to delete the page break; insert three blank paragraphs below the text "List of Figures," click at the beginning of the heading "1. Rationale," which moved up onto the current page when you deleted the page break, and then insert a Next Page section break. You've created two new pages, each with a heading and each in a new section. You'll create the table of contents and the list of figures for these pages later. For now, you'll just format the headings.

6. Scroll up and select the paragraph containing the **Contents** heading, click the **Home** tab, and apply the **Heading 1** style. The "Contents" heading is formatted to match the other headings, including a heading number. Typically, the headings in a document's front matter are not numbered consecutively with the rest of the headings in the document. You will clear the Heading 1 style from the heading and re-format it using the options in the Font group on the Home tab.

7. In the Font group, click the **Clear Formatting** button 🔳 to format the "Contents" heading in the Normal style, and then use the options in the Font group to format the selected paragraph in 14-point, Cambria, with boldface. Next, you need to add the same font color as the other headings in the document.

8. In the Font group, click the **Font Color button arrow** 🔳 to open a color palette, and then, under "Theme Colors," point to the square for the color whose ScreenTip reads "Blue, Accent 1, Darker 25%." You'll find this square in the fifth column from the left, second box up from the bottom. This is the same color that is applied by the Heading 1 and Heading 2 Quick Styles, which are used elsewhere in the document. See Figure 10-30.

Selecting a font color ◄ **Figure 10-30**

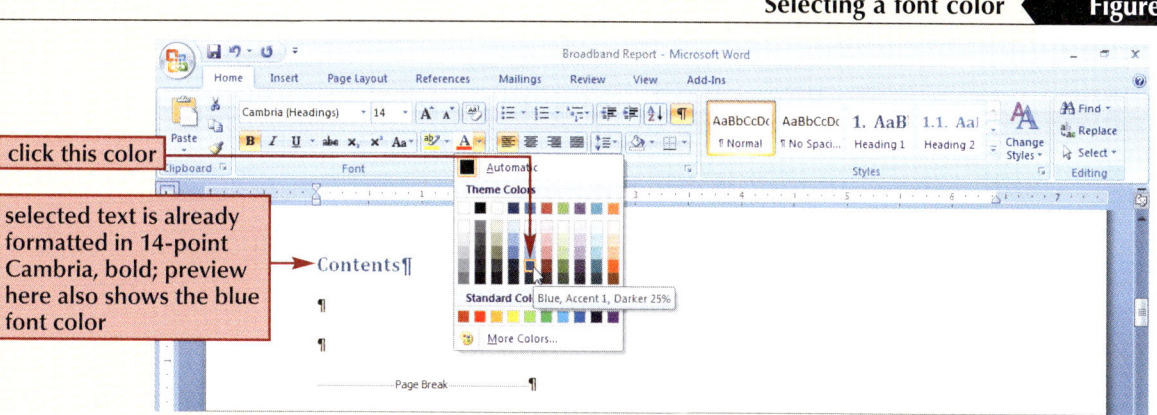

9. Click the **Blue, Accent 1, Darker 25%** color box, and then use the Format Painter to format the "List of Figures" heading to match the "Contents" heading.

Next, you'll format the title page. You already know how to insert a preformatted cover page, using the Cover Page button in the Pages group on the Insert tab. It's also helpful to know how to take existing text and format it as a cover page.

To format the cover page:

1. Move the insertion point anywhere on page 1 (the title page), click the **Page Layout** tab, in the Page Setup group click the **Dialog Box Launcher** to open the Page Setup dialog box, and then click the **Layout** tab (if necessary).

2. Click the **Vertical alignment** arrow, click **Center**, and then make sure **This section** appears in the **Apply to** list box (in the Preview section of the dialog box). This tells Word that you want the text in this section (which consists only of the title page) to be centered between the top and bottom margins.

3. Under "Headers and footers," select the **Different first page** check box. This ensures that the first page in this section (that is, the only page in this section, the title page) will not include a page number later, when you add page numbers to the rest of the document. See Figure 10-31.

Figure 10-31 ▶ **Aligning text vertically on the page**

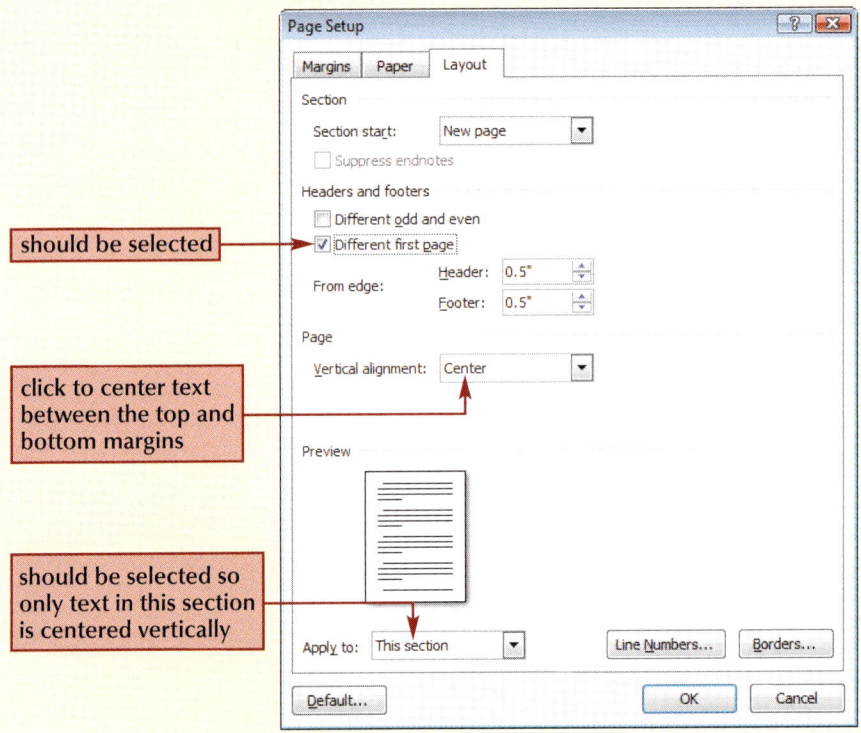

- should be selected
- click to center text between the top and bottom margins
- should be selected so only text in this section is centered vertically

▶ **4.** Click the **OK** button, zoom out so you can see the whole page, and verify that the text is centered vertically and horizontally on the page.

▶ **5.** Select the title page text, click the **Home** tab, and then, in the Paragraph group, click the **Center** button 三. The text is now centered horizontally (between the left and right margins) and vertically (between the top and bottom margins).

▶ **6.** Format the title page text in 16-point Cambria bold. Apply the same font color you used for the "Contents" heading, and then save the document.

Now you're ready to set up the page numbering for the front matter (that is, the title page, table of contents, and list of figures). You'll start by inserting a page number using one of the default page number styles. Then you will format the page numbers as lower-case Roman numerals (i, ii, iii, etc.).

To set up page numbers for the front matter:

▶ **1.** Change the zoom to Page Width, and then move the insertion point to the left of the "Contents" heading on page 2.

▶ **2.** Click the **Insert** tab, in the Header & Footer group click the **Page Number** button to open the Page Number menu, point to **Bottom of Page** to open the Bottom of Page menu, and then click **Plain Number 3**. The document switches to Header and Footer view, the Header & Footer Tools Design tab is displayed, and a page number field is inserted on the right side of the footer.

▶ **3.** In the Header & Footer group, click the **Page Number** button, and then click **Format Page Numbers**. The Page Number Format dialog box opens.

4. Click the **Number format** arrow, click **i, ii, iii, ...** so the page numbers will be low-ercase Roman numerals, and then make sure that the **Include chapter number** check box does not contain a check mark.

5. In the Page numbering section, click the **Start at** option button, and then make sure **i** (Roman numeral one) is displayed in the Start at text box. See Figure 10-32. (In your dialog box, the "i" will be selected and possibly hard to read.)

Page Number Format dialog box   **Figure 10-32**

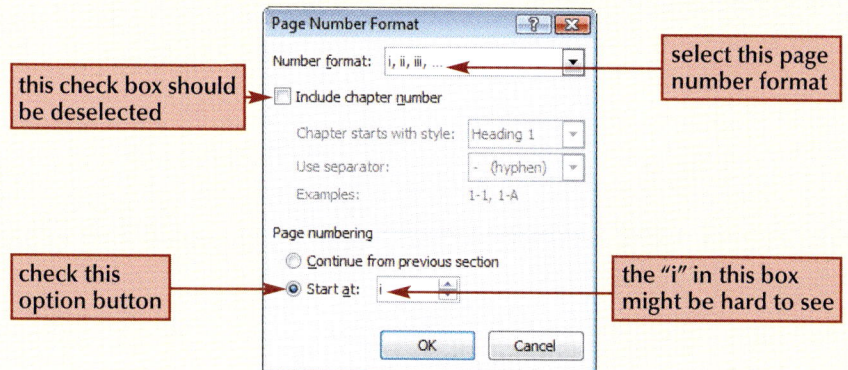

this check box should be deselected

select this page number format

check this option button

the "i" in this box might be hard to see

6. Click the **OK** button to close the Page Number Format dialog box. The page num-ber field in the footer on the Contents page displays the page number "i."

The page numbers you just inserted appear in the footer of every page in the docu-ment except the title page. However, the Roman numeral format was only applied to the current section. The page numbers in the report itself are formatted to use Arabic numer-als (1, 2, 3). The first page of the report (which contains the heading "1. Rationale") is currently numbered as page 3. In the next steps, you will set up the page number so the page is numbered page 1.

> **Tip**
>
> In Header and Footer view, the Different First Page check box serves the same function for the current section as the Different First Page check box in the Page Setup dialog box.

To set up the page numbers for the page that begins with the "1. Rationale heading":

1. While still in Header and Footer view, scroll down until you can see the page num-bered 3, in the footer for Section 3. This is the first page of the report itself.

2. Click the **3** page number to select the page number field, and then, in the Naviga-tion group, click the **Link to Previous** button to deselect it.

3. In the Header & Footer group, click the **Page Number** button, and then click **Format Page Numbers** to open the Page Number Format dialog box.

4. In the **Number format** list box, make sure **1, 2, 3, ...** is selected, and then make sure the **Include chapter number** check box is not selected. Next, you need to indicate that you want this section to begin with page number 1.

5. Click the **Start at** option button in the Page numbering section to select it, and then make sure **1** (Arabic numeral one) appears in the Start at text box.

▶ **6.** Click the **OK** button to return to the document, and then scroll down to view the footers in the rest of the document. Note that the section numbers in the footers on the last few pages of the document are not sequential. This reflects the many section breaks in the document that were inserted when you inserted and merged subdocuments. All that matters is that the page numbers in these sections are consecutive. The numbering starts with page 1 on the page containing the heading "1. Rationale" and proceeds consecutively through the document.

▶ **7.** Close Header and Footer view.

You have set up the page numbering for the master document. All the sections after the title page are numbered with consecutive Arabic numerals, and the front matter is numbered with consecutive lowercase Roman numerals. When you create the table of contents and the list of figures later, they'll appear on pages i and ii of the front matter.

Changing the Footer and Page Layout for Odd and Even Pages

Most professionally produced books and reports are printed on both sides of the paper and then bound. The blank space on the inside of each page, where the pages are bound together, is called the **gutter**. When you open a bound book or report, odd-numbered pages appear on the right, and even-numbered pages appear on the left. Often, the headers and footers for odd-numbered pages have text that is different from the headers or footers for the even-numbered pages.

Michael wants to follow these standards in the Broadband Report. Specifically, he wants you to use the page layouts shown in Figure 10-33.

Figure 10-33 ▶ Page setup for odd and even pages

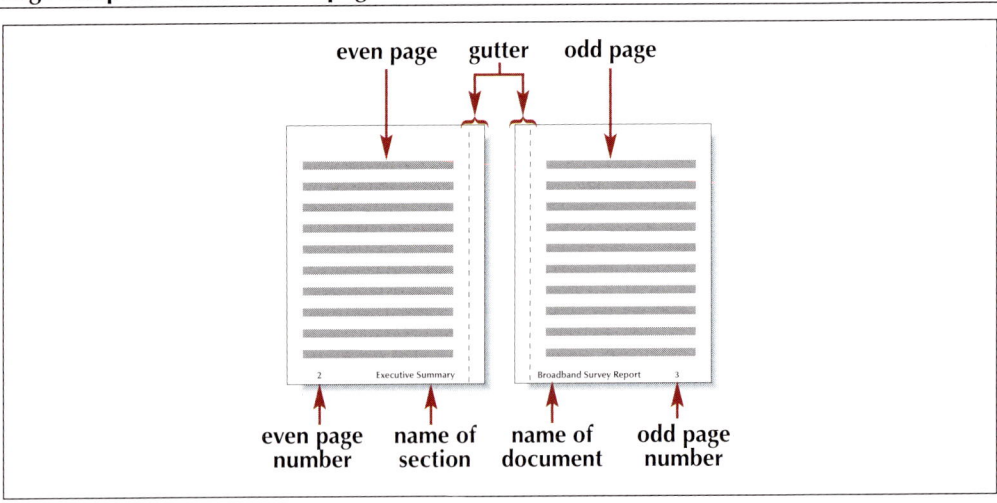

Use the following guidelines:

- Set the gutter to one-half inch. This will cause Word to shift the text on odd pages to the right ($\frac{1}{2}$ inch in this case), leaving a wider margin on the left, and to shift the text on even pages to the left (again, $\frac{1}{2}$ inch), leaving a wider margin on the right. When the even and odd pages are printed back-to-back (in a printing format called **two-sided printing**), the gutters line up on the same edge of the paper, thus leaving room for the binding.
- Change the location for page numbers so it's different on odd and even pages. In a page layout that distinguishes between odd and even pages, the page numbers are usually printed near the outside edge of the page rather than near the gutter to make them easier to see in a bound copy. On odd pages, the page numbers appear on the right; on even pages, page numbers appear on the left.
- Type different text for the footers on odd and even pages. In many books, the section title is included in the header or footer of odd pages; at the same time, the book or chapter title is included in the header or footer of even pages. Sometimes this text is shifted toward the gutter (just as page numbers are shifted toward the outer edge). MDNI's standard style is for the odd-page footers to include the document title (for example, "Broadband Report") and the even-page footers to include the section title (for example, "Residential") closer to the gutter.

First, you'll change the page setup in the master document to distinguish between odd and even page footers, and then you'll increase the size of the gutter to allow enough room to bind the report without obscuring any text. To make these changes, you'll use the Page Setup dialog box.

To change the page setup for printing odd and even pages:

1. Move the insertion point to the second page of the document (numbered page i, with the heading "Contents"), click the **Page Layout** tab, and then, in the Page Setup group, click the **Dialog Box Launcher** to open the Page Setup dialog box.

2. Click the **Margins** tab, and then change the setting in the Gutter text box to **0.5"**.

3. Click the **Layout** tab, and then click the **Different odd and even** check box in the Headers and footers section. This allows you to enter page numbers and text differently in odd and even pages.

4. Click the **Apply to** arrow, and then click **This point forward** so these options apply to the remainder of the report.

5. Click the **OK** button. The Page Setup dialog box closes. Now the footers in the odd pages of the document will differ from those on the even pages. This change doesn't affect the title page because you selected "This point forward" in Step 4.

   Because you set the gutter to .5 inch with odd and even pages different, the body text on each page has shifted.

6. Make sure the Zoom is set to Page Width, and scroll through the document to see that the body text on odd pages (for example, the Contents page) is shifted to the right; in other words, the left margin has increased in width, and the right margin has decreased. Conversely, on the even pages (for example, the List of Figures page) the body is shifted to the left; in other words, the left margin has decreased in width, and the right margin has increased. You no longer see the page number on the even page. You will fix this problem next, when you edit the footers.

Tip

The page number in the status bar reflects the total number of consecutive pages in the document, not the page number schemes created for document sections.

You have specified that odd and even pages should be set up differently. Now you'll type the footer text and format page numbering differently in the odd and even footers. Then you will view the pages side by side, so you can clearly see the differences between the two types of footers.

To format different footers for odd and even pages:

1. Scroll to display the footer area of the Contents page, and then double-click the footer area to open Header and Footer view. The label "Odd Page Footer –Section 2–" appears on the left side of the footer area. This is the odd page footer in the second section of the document. In the right margin, the footer contains the page number "i." Because this is an odd page, you'll leave the page number at the right and insert the document name at the left.

2. If necessary, click to the left of the page number to insert the insertion point there, and then press the **Backspace** key twice to move the insertion point to the left margin. The page number field moves with the insertion point. You'll move it back to the right margin after you enter the document name.

   Trouble? If the insertion point did not move when you pressed the Backspace key, the paragraph is right-aligned. With the insertion point to the left of the page number, follow Step 3. When you press the Tab key in Step 3, the text you type in that step will move to the left margin.

3. With the insertion point at the left edge of the footer text box, type **Broadband Report**, and then press the **Tab** key twice to move the page number field back to the right margin, where it is aligned at a right tab stop.

4. Scroll down to the next page until you can see the footer text box labeled "Even Page Footer – Section 2." When you set up the document for even and odd pages, the page numbers on the even pages were removed. You'll re-insert the page number in this footer now.

5. Click the blank paragraph on the left side of the footer, in the Header & Footer group click the **Page Number** button, point to **Bottom of Page**, and then click **Plain Number 1**. A page number field appears above the blank paragraph, displaying the page number "ii."

6. In the Navigation group, click the **Next Section** button to move the insertion point to the footer labeled "Odd Page Footer – Section 3," verify that the insertion point is located to the left of the page number field, press the **Backspace** key twice to move the insertion point to the left margin, type **Broadband Report**, press the **Tab** key twice to move the page number field back to the right margin, and then scroll down until you can see the even page footer at the bottom of the page containing the chart.

   Trouble? If the section numbers in your document footers don't match those in this tutorial, don't be concerned. Results can vary when inserting page numbers in a master document.

So far you've set up the odd page footers with the report title on the left margin and the page number on the right margin. In even page footers, you've included a page number on the left margin. The footers for the front matter and the report itself are the same, except that the page numbers in the front matter are lowercase Roman numerals, and the page numbers in the report itself are Arabic numbers. Next, you'll add heading text to the even page footers.

Inserting a Style Reference into a Footer

In long reports, it's customary to have the even page footers display the heading for the main section on that page. For example, in an even page that includes the heading "2. Executive Summary," you would insert the heading "Executive Summary" in the footer. Rather than manually entering a heading in each footer, it's easier to have Word insert the proper text automatically using a style reference.

A **style reference** is a field code that inserts text formatted with a particular style. Like many of the Word features you've used in this tutorial, style references are useful because they allow Word to update information automatically in one part of a document to reflect changes made in another part of a document. For example, in the footer for each even page, Michael wants you to insert a style reference to the Heading 1 style. As a result of this style reference, the footer on each page will include the text of the first heading on that page that is formatted with the Heading 1 style. As the heading text for the various parts of the document changes only from one page to another, the heading text in the footer will change accordingly. Furthermore, if Michael changes a section heading, the text in the footer will change accordingly.

To insert a style reference to the section title into the footer:

1. In the Even Page Footer box at the bottom of the page containing the chart, click to the right of the page number field, if necessary, and then press the **Tab** key twice. The insertion point jumps to the right margin.

2. Click the **Insert** tab, in the Text group click the **Quick Parts** button, click **Field** to open the Field dialog box, click the **Categories** arrow, and then click **Links and References**.

3. In the Field names list box, click **StyleRef** (an abbreviation of "style reference"). Next, you'll indicate which style you want the StyleRef field code to refer to.

4. In the Style name list box, click **Heading 1** (the style applied to the main headings in the document). See Figure 10-34.

Inserting a style reference to the Heading 1 style | **Figure 10-34**

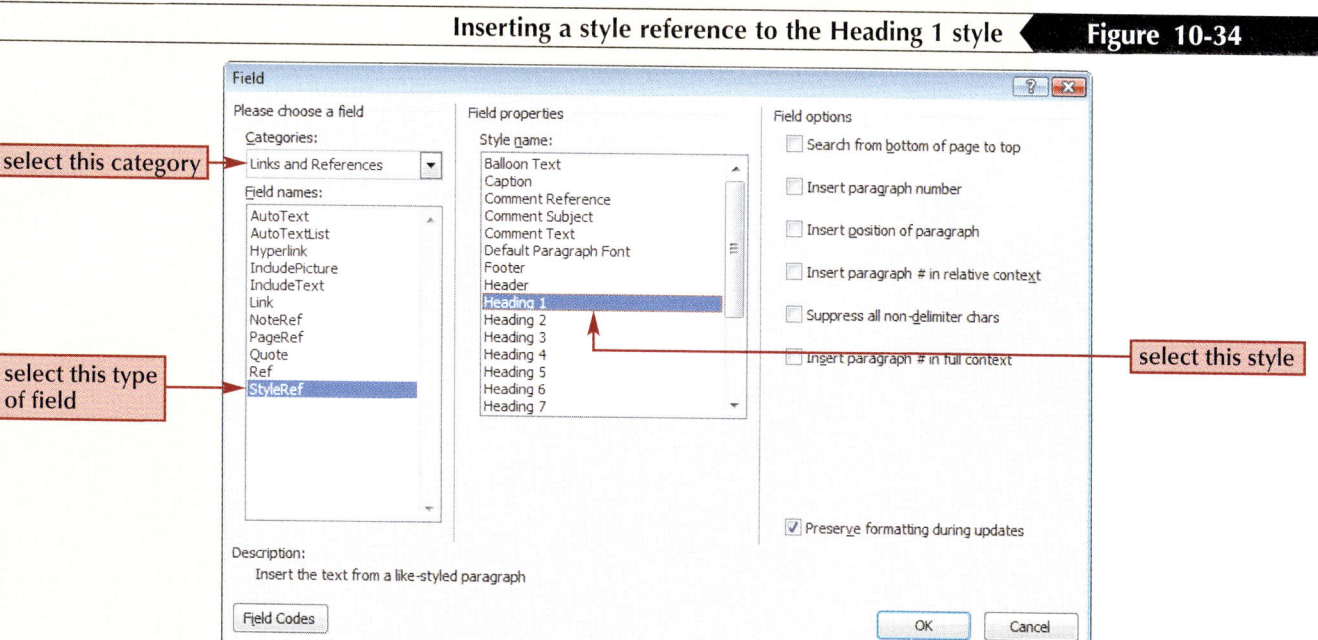

▶ **5.** Click the **OK** button. The Field dialog box closes. The text "Executive Summary" appears in the footer, because that is the first heading on the page that is formatted with the Heading 1 style.

▶ **6.** Click the **Heater & Footer Tools Design** tab, and then in the Close group click the **Close Header and Footer** button to return to Print Layout view.

▶ **7.** Preview the document in the Print Preview window, scroll so you can see the title page, and then in the Zoom group on the Print Preview tab, click the **Two Pages** button. The title page appears on the right side of the window. You see only one page because the title page is an odd-numbered page, belonging on the right.

▶ **8.** Scroll down to see the next two pages. A blank page appears on the left side of the window. See Figure 10-35. This is because you set up the document for different odd and even pages, and then you set up the Contents page to be numbered with the odd number i. The title page, which isn't numbered, is still the first page in the document, and so is considered by Word to be an odd page. However, you can't have two odd-numbered pages in a row (the margins, gutter spacing, and footer text would be off), so Word inserted a blank, even-numbered page between the title page and the Contents page. Note that you can't see this blank page in Print Layout view, but the total page count in the status bar includes this blank page.

Figure 10-35	▶	Blank page added after title page

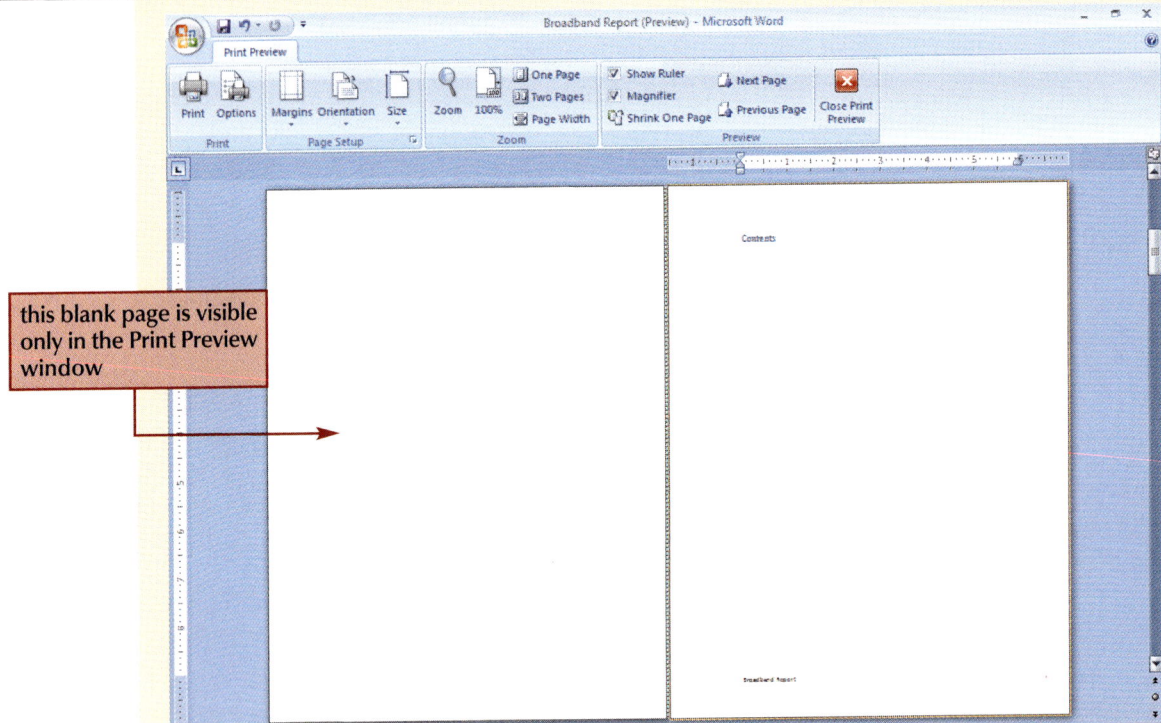

this blank page is visible only in the Print Preview window

▶ **9.** Close the Print Preview window, move the insertion point to the "Contents" heading, note that the page count in the lower-left corner of the document window tells you that this is page 3 of the document, scroll up to the title page and notice that the blank page between the title page and the "Contents" page is not visible.

▶ **10.** Save the document.

Reviewing Your Document in Print Preview | InSight

The blank page after the title page, which you saw in Print Preview, is not visible in Print Layout view. Nevertheless, it is part of the document, and when you print the document your printer will include a blank page after the title page. This is exactly what you want in a document that will be printed on both sides of each page. When the document is printed on both sides of each page, the blank page ensures that the back of the title page remains blank. If the document did not include this blank page, then the Contents page would be printed on the back of the title page, turning the Contents page (which is set up to be an odd page) into an even page. The remaining odd and even pages would also be reversed.

This significant difference between the appearance of the document in Print Layout view and Print Preview underscores the importance of reviewing your documents occasionally in Print Preview to make sure it will look the way you want when printed.

The report is set up so Michael can print the document on both sides of the page. Next, you will create an index.

Creating an Index

Michael wants you to create an index to help readers locate specific information in the report. As you probably know, an **index** is a list of words and phrases (called entries) accompanied by the page numbers on which they appear in a printed document. For example, if customers want information on "competition," they should be able to look in the index and find a list of all the pages on which the entry "competition" appears in the report.

Compiling an index by hand is tedious, time-consuming, and error-prone. It's also inefficient because if you insert, delete, or move text from one part of the document after you create the index, the page numbers might change. You would then have to go through the entire index again, making any necessary page number changes. On the other hand, once you set up an index using the Word Index feature, the page numbering is automatic, no matter how much you reorganize the document.

When you create an index with Word, you generate entries in one of four ways:

- Select a word or phrase and have Word search the document for every occurrence of that entry. This is fast, efficient, and accurate. It isn't, however, foolproof. For example, sometimes a portion of the document contains a particular topic which doesn't use the exact phrase you selected for that topic.
- Move the insertion point to the location where you want an entry, and insert an index entry.
- Select a range of pages, assign it a bookmark, and then mark the bookmarked pages as an index entry. This would result in an entry such as "business subscribers, 4–6" (where the 4–6 refers to the bookmarked range of pages).

You'll use all these methods as you create the index for the Broadband Report.

Marking Index Entries

When you mark an index entry, you select the word or phrase you want to appear in the index, and then use the Mark Index Entry dialog box to refine the text. For example, you can specify that the text appears as the main entry, and then provide subentries related to it. That way, the index includes a main topic, such as "Broadband connections," with an indented list of associated subtopics, such as "cable modem" and "DSL." When you mark an index entry in your document, Word inserts a field code that appears if you display nonprinting characters. You can hide these codes if necessary after you finish marking the index.

Michael asks you to create an index for the Broadband Report. You'll start by marking the main entries for the index.

Reference Window | **Marking Index Entries and Subentries**

- Select the word or phrase you want to mark as an index entry.
- Press the Alt+Shift+X keys to open the Mark Index Entry dialog box. Alternately, click the References tab, and then, in the Index group, click the Mark Entry button to open the Mark Index Entry dialog box.
- If necessary, type an index entry in the Main entry text box, and then, if desired, type an entry in the Subentry text box.
- Make sure the Current page option button in the Options section is selected.
- Click the Mark button to mark this occurrence, or click the Mark All button to mark every occurrence in the document.
- Click the Close button.

You'll start creating the index by selecting the first occurrence of a word or phrase that you want as an index entry, and then telling Word to mark every occurrence of it throughout the document. The first entry you'll mark is "Canada."

To mark every occurrence of a main index entry:

▶ 1. Press the **Ctrl+Home** keys to move the insertion point to the beginning of the document, use the Find feature to find the first occurrence of the word "Canada" and then close the Find and Replace dialog box. Now you can add this word to the index.

▶ 2. Click the **References** tab, and then, in the Index group click the **Mark Entry** button. The word you selected, "Canada," appears in the Main entry text box of the Mark Index Entry dialog box.

▶ 3. Make sure the **Current page** option button in the Options section of the dialog box is selected. This ensures that the current page of this entry will appear in the index.

Tip

The "XE" in the field code stands for "index entry."

▶ 4. Click the **Mark All** button. Word searches your document for every occurrence of "Canada" and marks each as an index entry. In the document, you can see that Word has inserted the field code {XE "Canada"} next to the word "Canada." See Figure 10-36.

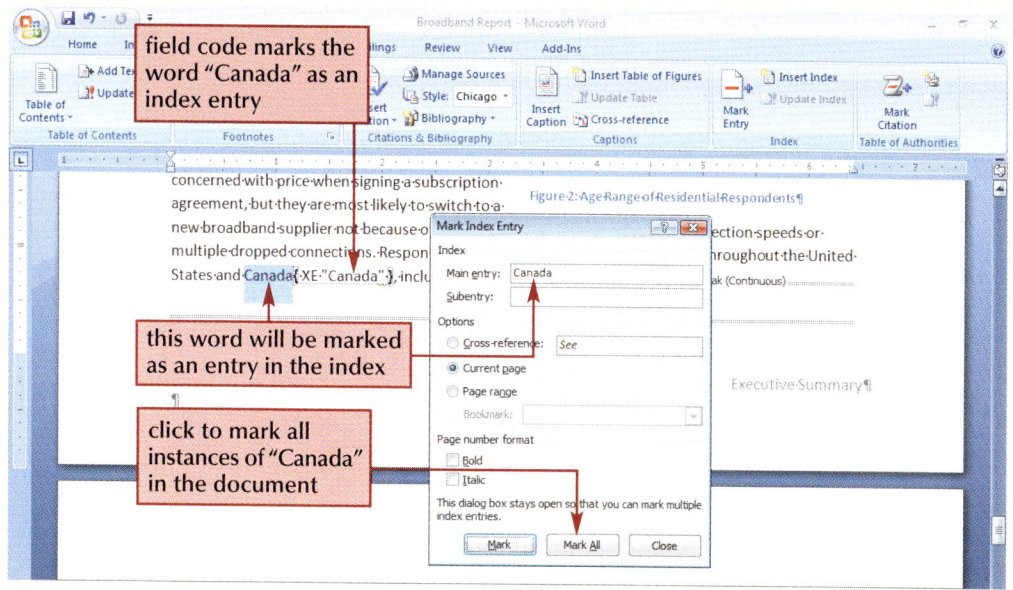

5. Close the Mark Index Entry dialog box to return to the document window.

6. Scroll to the paragraph below the heading "3.1. Demographics." Note that the word "Canada" in this paragraph is also marked as an index entry.

Throughout the report, Word has marked "Canada" as an index entry, as indicated by the {XE "Canada"} field code to the right of each instance of the word. You'll mark a few more index entries now.

To mark additional index entries:

1. Scroll to display the first paragraph below the heading "1. Rationale."

2. Select the phrase **Continental Broadband Association** in the first sentence of the paragraph.

3. Press the **Alt+Shift+X** keys to open the Mark Index Entry dialog box, and then click the **Mark All** button. Word marks every occurrence of Continental Broadband Association with the XE field code.

4. Without closing the Mark Index Entry dialog box, click in the document window, and then select the phrase **Market Data Now, Inc.** in the same paragraph. If necessary, drag the dialog box out of the way to see the phrase, but don't close the dialog box. The Mark Index Entry dialog box is one of the few dialog boxes that you can leave open while you scroll through a document and select text.

5. Click the **Mark All** button in the Mark Index Entry dialog box. Even though the button was dimmed (because the document window is active, rather than the dialog box), Word immediately activates the dialog box and the button when you click the button, and marks the highlighted phrase throughout the report. The highlighted phrase now appears in the Main entry text box.

6. Select the word **products** in the first bulleted item below the heading "1.1. Survey Goals," and then click the **Mark All** button in the Mark Index Entry dialog box.

▶ **7.** Repeat this procedure for the words **services** in the first bulleted item and **attitudes** in the second bulleted item. Leave the Mark Index Entry dialog box open.

Your index contains six entries so far, which is sufficient to demonstrate the power of this feature. If you were creating a full index for a complete document, you would continue to mark words and phrases as index entries. Instead, you'll add some subentries to the index.

Marking Subentries

A high-quality index contains subentries as well as main entries. A **subentry** is an index item that is a division or subcategory of a main entry. For example, in the Broadband Report, you want to create a main entry for "respondents," and three subentries for "Residential Subscribers," "Small Business Subscribers," and "Large Business Subscribers."

To create subentries in an index:

▶ **1.** Scroll down until you see the heading "1.3. Market Research Overview," and then select the phrase **small business subscribers** in the first sentence.

▶ **2.** Click the **title bar** of the Mark Index Entry dialog box to make it active without marking an index entry.

▶ **3.** Select the text in the **Main entry** text box, type **respondents**, press the **Tab** key to move the insertion point to the Subentry text box, and then type **small business subscribers**. This creates a main entry for "respondents" with the subentry "small business subscribers."

▶ **4.** Click the **Mark All** button. Word marks all occurrences of "small business subscribers" with the entry "respondents" and the subentry "small business subscribers."

▶ **5.** Repeat Steps 1 through 4, except select the words **large business subscribers** and **residential subscribers** and create the index entries with "respondents" as the main entry and "large business subscribers" or "residential subscribers" as the subentries.

▶ **6.** In the middle of the paragraph, select the word **respondents** in the phrase "to the three types of respondents," and mark it as a main entry, without a subentry, for all occurrences of the word throughout the text. Don't close the Mark Index Entry dialog box.

You have marked several subentries for a main index entry. Next, you'll create a cross-reference index entry.

Creating Cross-Reference Index Entries

A cross-reference index entry is a phrase that tells readers to look at a different index entry to find the information they seek. For example, you've already marked "Continental Broadband Association" as an index entry, but what if someone looks up CBA? You'd want the index to say: "*CBA. See* Continental Broadband Association." You'll create the necessary cross-reference now.

To create a cross-reference index entry:

1. Scroll up to display the paragraph below the heading "1. Rationale" and then select the abbreviation **CBA**, located in parentheses in the first line of the paragraph.

2. Click the **title bar** in the Mark Index Entry dialog box.

3. With "CBA" as the main entry, click the **Cross-reference** option button in the Options section of the dialog box, click to the right of the word *See* in the text box, and then type **Continental Broadband Association**.

4. Click the **Mark** button. You can't click the Mark All button, because a cross-reference entry appears only once in the index and doesn't carry a page number. Now you'll create the "MDNI" cross-reference that tells readers to look up "Market Data Now, Inc." in the index.

5. In the paragraph below the heading "1. Rationale," select **MDNI** (which is in parentheses in the second-to-last line of the paragraph), and mark it with a cross-reference to **Market Data Now, Inc.** Don't close the Mark Index Entry dialog box.

The index you're creating for the Broadband Report includes two cross-references. Next, you'll add an index entry that refers to a range of pages.

Creating an Index Entry for a Page Range

In addition to main entries and subentries that list individual pages, sometimes you'll want to include an index entry that refers to a range of pages, such as the range of pages for the Small Business section. This requires a more complicated procedure: you must select the pages of the section you want to mark as an index entry, create a bookmark for the selected pages, and then mark that bookmark name as the page-range entry.

Creating a Page Range Index Entry | Reference Window

- Select a range of pages—for example, a section.
- Click Insert tab, and then in the Links group, click the Bookmark button.
- Type the name of the bookmark, and then click the Add button. The Bookmark dialog box closes.
- Make sure the Mark Index Entry dialog box is open, click the Page range option button, click the Bookmark arrow, and then click the bookmark name.
- Click the Mark button.

Next, you need to create an entry for "Residential Subscribers." This entry will span a range of pages.

To create an index entry with a reference to a range of pages:

1. Scroll until you see the heading "3. Residential Subscribers."

2. Switch to Outline view and select the entire "Residential Subscribers" section, including the "3.1 Demographics" subsection.

3. Click the **Insert** tab, and then, in the Links group, click **Bookmark** to open the Bookmark dialog box.

4. Type **Residential** as the bookmark name, and then click the **Add** button to create a bookmark for the selected range of pages.

▶ **5.** With the text still selected, click the **Page range** option button in the Mark Index Entry dialog box, click the **Bookmark** list arrow, and then click **Residential**.

▶ **6.** Verify that **Residential Subscribers** appears in the Main entry text box. See Figure 10-37.

Figure 10-37 ▶ **Creating a page range index entry**

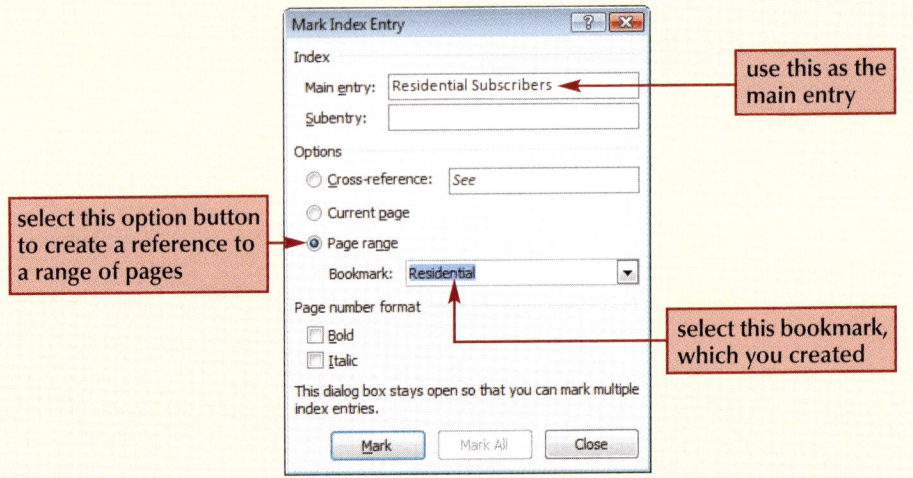

▶ **7.** Click the **Mark** button to mark this index entry.

▶ **8.** Select the entire section titled "4. Small Business Subscribers," including its subsections; assign it the bookmark **SmallBusiness** (all one word, no spaces), and then create a page range index entry, with the main entry **Small Business Subscribers**. Do the same for the section titled "Large Business Subscribers," naming the bookmark **LargeBusiness**. These sections don't span multiple pages now, but they will eventually, after Lori and Katarina add more text to them.

Trouble? If paragraph numbering disappears from some paragraphs, don't worry; you'll fix it later.

▶ **9.** Close the Mark Index Entry dialog box, and then save the document.

Although you have marked only a few words and phrases in the document, you have learned how to create all the different types of entries.

Compiling and Updating an Index

After you mark all the desired index entries, subentries, cross-references, and page-range references, you're ready to **compile** the index—that is, you're ready to tell Word to generate the index using the marked entries. Most often, indexes appear at the end of books, reports, or long documents.

Compiling an Index | Reference Window

- Move the insertion point to the location where you want to insert the index.
- Hide nonprinting characters. This is necessary because the hidden text of the field codes takes up extra space and changes the pagination of the document.
- Click the References tab, and then, in the Index group, click the Insert Index button. Click the Index tab, if necessary.
- Select the desired options controlling the appearance of the index.
- Click the OK button.

You'll compile the index on a new page at the end of the Broadband Report.

To compile the index:

1. Switch to Print Layout view, press the **Ctrl+End** keys to move the insertion point to the end of the document, press the **Ctrl+Enter** keys to insert a page break below the last paragraph, type **Index**, and then press the **Enter** key to insert a blank line below the heading. You will insert the index at the insertion point.

2. Double-click **Index** to select it, and then format it in 14-point, Cambria bold. Apply the same "Blue, Accent 1, Darker 25%" font color you used for the "Contents" heading.

3. Turn off nonprinting characters so the XE codes are no longer visible, move the insertion point to the blank line below the heading, and then make sure the blank line is formatted in the Normal style. You're ready to compile the index.

4. Click the **References** tab, and then, in the Index group, click the **Insert Index** button to open the Index dialog box. Click the **Index** tab, if necessary.

5. Make sure **From template** appears in the Formats list box to ensure that the index is formatted using the document's template styles.

6. Make sure **2** appears in the Columns text box and that the Right align page numbers check box is not selected.

7. Click the **OK** button to compile the index, make sure the document is in Print Layout view, and then scroll to view the completed index. See Figure 10-38.

Index for the Broadband Report document | **Figure 10-38**

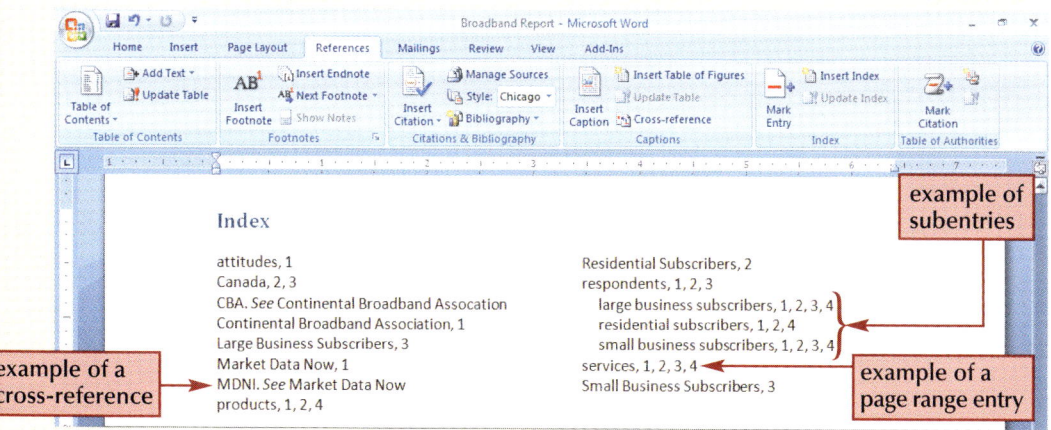

Trouble? If your page numbers aren't the same as those shown in Figure 10-38, make sure the nonprinting characters are hidden, and then go on to the next set of steps, where you'll regenerate the index. If the pages are still not the same, don't worry—differences in printers can cause page numbering differences. Also, if you accidentally deleted a page or section break when working with subdocuments, your page numbers might differ from the figure.

Your index is short but representative of the entries that would appear in a full index. Michael asks you to add one more entry to the index. You'll mark the entry, and then update the index to include the new entry.

To update an index:

▶ 1. Scroll up to see the last paragraph of the document, just above the index, and then select the term **e-businesses** in the second-to-last line of the paragraph.

▶ 2. Mark all occurrences of "e-businesses" as main index entries.

▶ 3. Close the Mark Index Entry dialog box, and then hide nonprinting characters.

▶ 4. Scroll down to display the index, click anywhere in the index, click the **References** tab, and then in the Index group, click the **Update Index** button.

▶ 5. Scroll down and verify that the term "e-businesses" appears in the index.

The index is complete. Next, you turn your attention to creating a bibliography.

Creating a Bibliography

When preparing long documents, you often research information in books, articles, or on the Web to support your claims or you report based on the conclusions of experts. To summarize the works you research, you can prepare a **bibliography**, a list of sources you refer to in the document or consulted as you wrote. The sources listed in a bibliography usually include information such as the name of the author, the title of the work, its publication date, and its publisher.

Reference Window | **Creating a Bibliography**

- To select a bibliography style, click the References tab, click the Style button arrow in the Citations & Bibliography group, and then click a style for the bibliography.
- Click at the end of the sentence or phrase you want to cite.
- To add a citation for a new source, in the Citations & Bibliography group on the References tab click the Insert Citation button, click Add New Source, enter information in the Create Source dialog box, and then click the OK button.
- To add a citation for an existing source, in the Citations & Bibliography group on the References tab click the Insert Citation button, and then click the source.
- Click where you want to insert a bibliography.
- In the Citations & Bibliography group on the References tab, click the Bibliography button.
- Click a bibliography format to insert the bibliography into the document.

To create a bibliography with Word, you first insert citations within the document. A **citation** is a reference to a book, article, Web page, or other source that includes enough details to identify the item. For example, a citation often includes the author, book title, and publication date. As you enter citations, you also enter or select sources, which are works such as books and articles that you are referencing. For example, if you are writing a report claiming that 60 percent of computer users in your area want expanded DSL service, you need to cite a source such as a survey or report to support your claims.

After entering citations and sources in a Word document, you select a place in the document—usually at the end—where you want the bibliography to appear. Word can then generate a bibliography based on the source information you provided for the document.

As you enter citations, Word keeps track of sources so that the bibliography lists each source only once and to save you time when inserting citations. For example, suppose you are writing a report and summarize demographic information from a marketing survey written by a researcher named Jeanne Riley. You can enter a citation to indicate the source of that demographic information. The first time you do, you enter information about the new source, including its author, title, and publication year. Word inserts the author's last name and publication date in parentheses as the citation, as in (Riley 2007). If you insert another citation to the marketing survey, you can select the survey from a list of sources. Word inserts the same (Riley 2007) citation in the document, but lists the survey information only once in the bibliography.

Michael wants to develop a bibliography for the Broadband Report document. You'll start by selecting a style for the bibliography.

Selecting a Bibliography Style

Recall that when you enter a new citation in a document, you enter information about the new source, such as the author, title, and publisher. The source information you provide is determined by the type of source, which can be one of dozens of kinds of publications, including books, articles, reports, Web sites, recordings, and interviews. The source information is also determined by the style you choose for the bibliography. For example, a bibliography using the Modern Language Association (MLA) style is designed for academic articles in the humanities. Before you enter a citation in a document, you should choose a bibliography style that your audience expects or that your instructor or publisher requires.

Choosing the Best Bibliography Style for Your Document | InSight

The style you select for a bibliography sets the format of its citations and sources. Organizations in professional and academic fields publish style guides for bibliographies that are appropriate for their fields. Be sure to choose a bibliography style that suits the purpose and audience of your document or that is required by your instructor or publisher. Besides the MLA style, which is appropriate for research papers, you can select the APA style, developed by the American Psychological Association for publications in the social sciences, or the Chicago style, based on *The Chicago Manual of Style*, which is appropriate for the social sciences and humanities. Word offers other styles, including Turabian (similar to Chicago), GB7714 (from the Standardization Administration of China), GOST (from the Federal Agency of the Russian Federation on Technical Regulating and Metrology), SIST02 (from the Standards for Information of Science and Technology by Japan Science and Technology Agency), and ISO 690 (from the International Organization for Standardization).

The document you and Michael are creating is a business report, so it can use the APA, MLA, or Chicago bibliography styles, which are standard styles for academic and business publications in the United States. Michael is familiar with the Chicago style, so you'll choose that style for his report.

To select a bibliography style:

▶ 1. Click the **References** tab, if necessary, and then, in the Citations & Bibliography group click the **Style button arrow** to display the list of bibliography styles, as shown in Figure 10-39. "Chicago" is selected in Figure 10-39, but it might not be on your computer.

Figure 10-39 ▶ Selecting a bibliography style

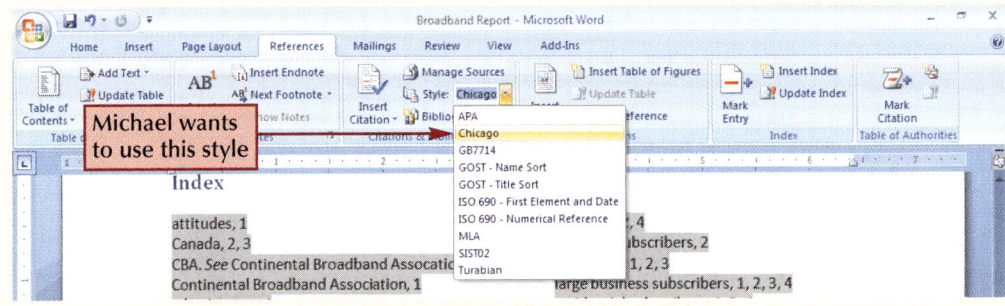

▶ 2. Click **Chicago**, if necessary.

Word will use the Chicago bibliography style when creating citations, sources, and the bibliography itself. Now you're ready to add a new citation and source to the document.

Inserting a Citation and a Source

When you add a new citation to a document, you start by creating a source. The source will appear as a single item in the bibliography even if more than one citation uses the same source. If you don't know the source information, you can insert a placeholder instead. That way, you can still create a citation and then provide the source information later. You can also use the Research task pane to find sources or research additional information about sources you are citing. For example, you can search a reference Web site or library database for books and articles related to your topic, and then insert the citation information from the Research task pane.

You want to insert two citations in the Broadband Report document. Both of the citations use the same source: a report written by Liam Welper, a marketing analyst at Market Data Now, Inc. You'll start by adding a sentence to the report and then entering a citation and source for this new information.

To insert a sentence and add a citation and source:

▶ 1. Scroll until you can see the heading "5.2. Large Business Subscribers' Satisfaction," click at the end of the paragraph below the heading, and then insert a space.

▶ 2. Type **This response is in marked contrast to the survey conducted in 2006.** The new sentence is now the last one in the paragraph.

▶ 3. Click the **Insert Citation** button in the Citations & Bibliography group on the References tab, and then click **Add New Source**. The Create Source dialog box opens.

4. Click the **Type of Source** arrow, and then click **Report**. The bibliography fields change so that they are appropriate for a Report source.

5. Click in the Author box. An example of an author entry appears near the bottom of the Create Source dialog box. You can also refer to the examples as you enter the rest of the source information.

6. Type **Welper, Liam** in the Author box.

7. Click in the Title box, and then type **Internet Subscriber Report**.

8. Press the **Tab** key, and then type **2006** in the Year box.

9. Press the **Tab** key three times, and then type **Market Survey** in the Report Type box. See Figure 10-40.

Creating a source for a bibliography | Figure 10-40

10. Click the **OK** button. The citation "(Welper 2006)" appears at the end of the "5.2. Large Business Subscribers' Satisfaction" paragraph.

You want to add another citation to the same source in the Broadband Report document, but before you do, Michael notices that the title of Liam's 2006 report is "Internet User Report," not "Internet Subscriber Report." You'll edit the source to correct that error.

Modifying an Existing Source

After you insert a citation, you can edit the citation itself to display only the author's name and not the year of publication, for example, or to include a page reference in the citation, as in "(Welper, Internet Subscriber Report 2006, 3-4)." You can also modify the source information you provided so the entry appears correctly in the bibliography. If you have already generated a bibliography, you can update it so it reflects the source corrections you entered. You can make all of these changes using the Citation Options menu, which you can access from the citation itself. (Click a citation and then click the Citation Options arrow button to open this menu.)

When you create a source, Word adds it to a master list of sources, which is stored in the Source Manager dialog box. (Click the Manage Sources button in the Citations & Bibliography group on the References tab to open this dialog box.) The master list includes sources you can use in any Word document. To change source information in the master list, you can select a source in the Source Manager dialog box, and then edit the author, title, or other source information. If you use the Citation Options menu to change the source information, Word displays a dialog box asking if you want to update the master list and the source information in the current document. If you click the Yes button, Word updates the source information in both locations. If you click the No button, Word updates only the source information in the current document.

You are ready to modify the source you entered for the new citation in the Broadband Report.

To edit a source:

▶ 1. Click the **(Welper 2006)** citation you entered, and then click its arrow button. The Citation Options menu opens. See Figure 10-41.

Figure 10-41 | **Citation Options menu open for a citation**

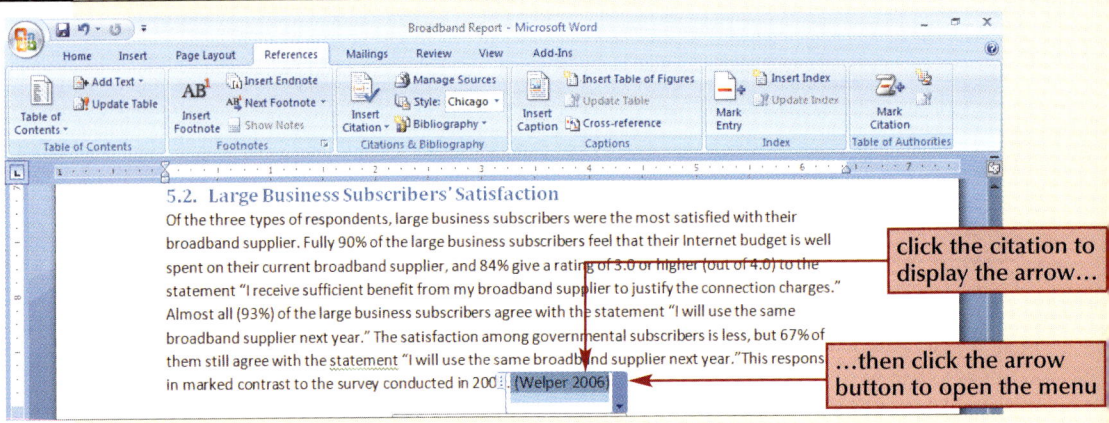

▶ 2. Click **Edit Source**. The Edit Source dialog box opens, displaying the information you entered for this source.

▶ 3. Double-click **Subscriber** in the Title box, and then type **User** so the title now appears as "Internet User Report."

▶ 4. Click the **OK** button. A message dialog box opens asking if you want to update the master source list and the current document.

▶ 5. Click the **Yes** button.

Now you will add another citation to the Internet User Report. Then you'll be ready to generate the bibliography.

To add a citation to an existing source:

▶ 1. Scroll down to the "6. Future Recommendations" section and click at the end of the first paragraph after the heading, after the sentence that ends "...concerned with price and reliability."

2. Click the **Insert Citation** button in the Citations & Bibliography group on the References tab, and then click **Welper, Liam** in the list of available sources. Word inserts a second (Welper 2006) citation.

Although you've inserted only two citations using one source in the document, you can generate the bibliography to review its format. Later, after Michael adds other sources, he can update the bibliography so it's more complete.

Generating a Bibliography

After inserting at least one source in a document, you can generate a bibliography for that document. When you do, Word scans all the citations in the document, gathers the source information for each citation, and then assembles each unique source in a list. You can insert a built-in list that uses "Bibliography" or "Works Cited" as the title. You can also insert a generic bibliography with no title. Both the built-in and generic bibliographies format entries according to the style you chose for the bibliography, such as Chicago or MLA. For example, the Chicago style inserts the full name of each author, as in "Welper, Liam," whereas the APA style uses only an initial for the first name, as in "Welper, L."

You want to insert a bibliography near the end of the document, just before the Index, and use "Bibliography" as its title, so you'll choose a built-in bibliography for your document.

To insert a bibliography:

1. Scroll down to the Index page, and click at the beginning of the "Index" heading.

2. Turn on nonprinting characters, press the **Ctrl+Enter** keys to insert a page break, and then press the up arrow key ↑ to move the insertion point up to the new blank page, just before the page break. This page retains the formatting from the "Index" heading on the preceding page, so you need to clear the formatting.

3. On the Home tab in the Font group click the **Clear Formatting** button 🅰️, press the **Enter** key to insert a blank paragraph before the page break, click in the new, blank paragraph, and then verify that the new paragraph is formatted in the Normal style.

4. Click the **References** tab, and then in the Citations & Bibliography group, click the **Bibliography** button to display the built-in types of bibliographies.

5. Click **Bibliography**. Word inserts the "Bibliography" title and lists the sources cited in the document. There is only one source now; but later, after Michael revises the document, there will be more. The "Bibliography" heading is formatted in the Heading 1 style, so it includes a section number. See Figure 10-42.

Figure 10-42 ▷ **Bibliography inserted in the document**

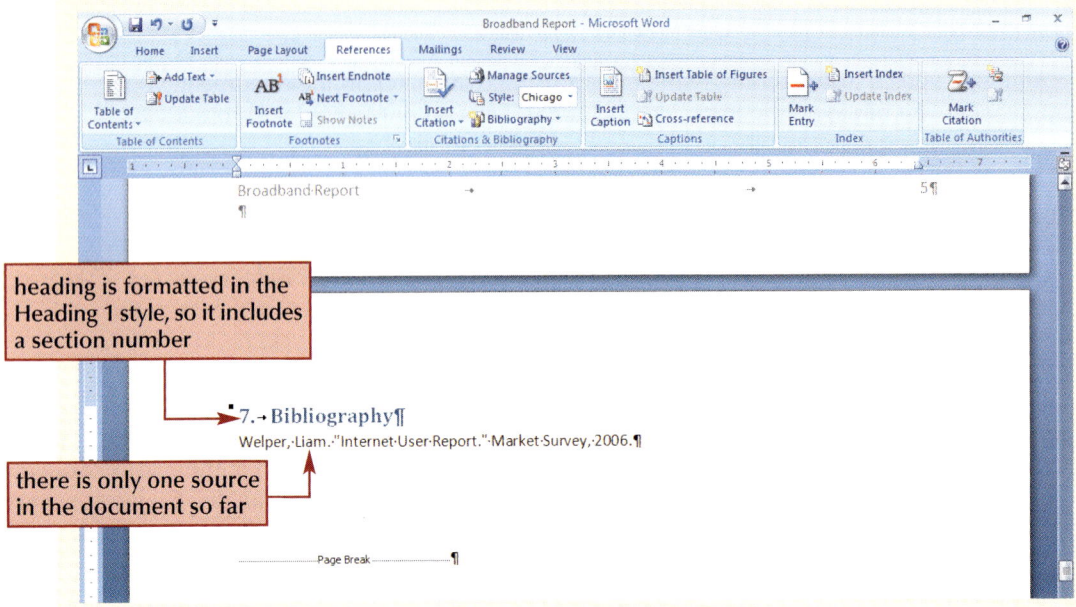

heading is formatted in the Heading 1 style, so it includes a section number

7.→Bibliography¶
Welper, Liam. "Internet User Report." Market Survey, 2006.¶

there is only one source in the document so far

Page Break ¶

Michael asks you to add another citation to the document to support the demographic statistics described for the small business subscribers. After you do, you can update the bibliography to reflect the changes.

Updating a Bibliography

If you add or change citations or source information after generating a bibliography, you can update the bibliography to include the new information. You'll insert a citation to the Small Business Subscribers section and add a new source that refers to the MDNI Web site. Then you'll modify the bibliography to include this change.

To add another citation and source:

▶ 1. Scroll up to the heading "3.1. Demographics" and then click at the end of the paragraph below the heading.

▶ 2. Click the **Insert Citation** button in the Citations & Bibliography group on the References tab, and then click **Add New Source**. The Create Source dialog box opens.

▶ 3. Click the **Type of Source** arrow, scroll the list, and then click **Web site**.

▶ 4. Click in the **Name of Web Page** text box, and then type **Market Data Now**.

▶ 5. Press the **Tab** key, and then type **2010** in the Year text box.

▶ 6. Click in the URL text box, and then type **www.mdni.course.com**.

▶ 7. Click the **OK** button. Word inserts a citation for the Market Data Now Web site.

Because you've added another citation and source to the document, you need to update the bibliography.

To update a bibliography:

1. Scroll down to display the bibliography.

2. Click the **Bibliography** heading. A toolbar appears above the title. See Figure 10-43.

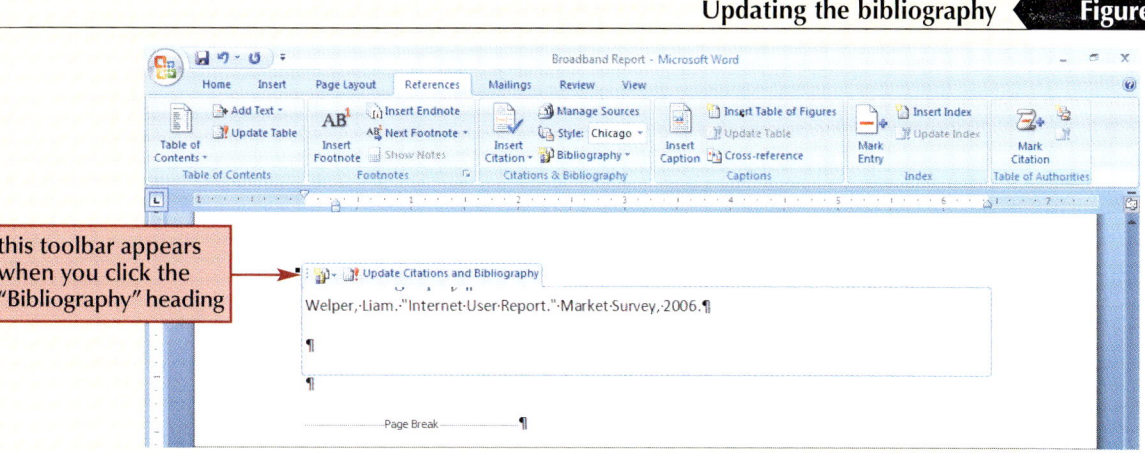

this toolbar appears when you click the "Bibliography" heading

3. On the toolbar, click **Update Citations and Bibliography**. Word adds the Market Data Now Web site source to the bibliography.

4. Click anywhere on the page outside the bibliography to deselect it.

You've completed work on the bibliography for now, so you can turn to your next task, which is to create a table of contents and a table of figures.

Creating a Table of Contents and a Table of Figures

As you learned in Tutorial 5, the Table of Contents feature automatically compiles a table of contents made up of text formatted with Word's heading styles. You'll create a table of contents for the Broadband Report document now, following the steps you learned in Tutorial 5. Then you'll use a similar procedure to compile a list of all the figures in the document.

To create a table of contents:

1. Move the insertion point to the first blank paragraph below the heading "Contents" on page i in the front matter. This is where you'll insert the table of contents. Recall that the predefined table of contents formats available on the Table of Contents menu include a heading. Because you've already typed and formatted the "Contents" heading, you will use the Table of Contents dialog box to create the table of contents.

2. Click the **References** tab if necessary, then in the Table of Contents group click the **Table of Contents** button, click **Insert Table of Contents**, and then make sure the Show page numbers and Right align page numbers check boxes are selected, that the Tab leader list box is set to a dotted line, that the Formats list box is set to From template, and that Show levels is set to 3.

▶ **3.** Click the **OK** button. Word generates the table of contents based on its predefined heading styles. The only problem with the table of contents is that it does not include the "Index" heading. You could scroll down to the "Index" heading, select it, and then add it to the table of contents using the Add Text button and the Update Table button in the Table of Contents group on the References tab, as explained in Tutorial 5. However, that method would result in the "Index" heading being formatted with the Heading 1 style, which would in turn add a heading number to it, so that the heading would read "8. Index." Michael would like the Index heading to remain unnumbered, so he decides to add a line below the table of contents that looks like it is part of the table of contents, but is really made up of the text "Index," a dot leader, and a page number field that displays the page number on which the "Index" heading is currently located.

▶ **4.** Scroll down to the "Index" heading on the last page of the document, and create a bookmark to the "Index" heading. Name the bookmark **Index**.

▶ **5.** Scroll back up to the table of contents, move the insertion point to the blank paragraph below the table of contents, and then type **Index**. Now you will insert a right tab stop with a dot leader that will align the page number for the Index section below the other page numbers in the table of contents.

▶ **6.** Click the **Home** tab, open the Paragraph dialog box, click the **Tabs** button, type **5.9** in the Tab stop position text box, in the Alignment section click the **Right** option button, in the Leader section click the **2...** option button, click the **OK** button to return to the document, and then press the **Tab** key.

▶ **7.** The insertion point moves to the right margin, and a row of dots appears to the right of the word "Index." Next, you can insert a page number field that will display the page number of the Index bookmark.

▶ **8.** Click the **Insert** tab, in the Text group click the **Quick Parts** button, click **Field** to open the Field dialog box, in the Field names list click **PageRef**, in the Bookmark name list click **Index**, and then click the **OK** button. The "Index" heading now appears to be included in the table of contents. See Figure 10-44.

Figure 10-44 ▶ **Line with page field below the table of contents**

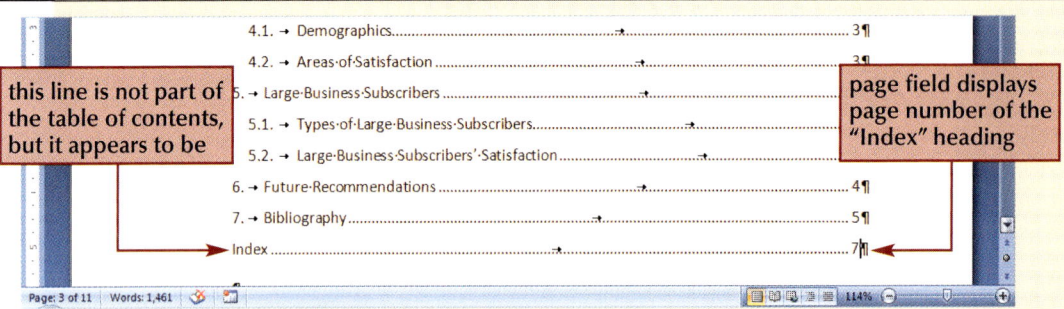

Keep in mind that, if the page flow in the report changes as a result of editing and revisions, and Michael has to update the table of contents later using the Update Table button in the Table of Contents group on the References tab, the page field in the "Index" line would not be updated. Instead, Michael would have to update the page number field by right-clicking it, and then clicking Update Field in the shortcut menu.

▶ **9.** Save the master document.

You have completed the index, the bibliography and the table of contents. Your next task is to create a **table of figures**, which is a list of the captions for all the pictures, charts, graphs, slides, or other illustrations in a document, along with the page number for each. As with a table of contents, the entries in a table of figures are links to the captions to which they refer. You can click an entry in a table of figures to jump to that caption in the document. Although a table of figures in a short report such as the Broadband Report is unusual, it is not unusual in manuals, dissertations, technical documents, textbooks, and other long documents. Creating one for the Broadband Report will give you the practice you need to create a table of figures for longer documents.

To create a table of figures:

1. Move the insertion point to the first blank paragraph below the heading "List of Figures" on page ii in the front matter. This is where you'll insert the list of figures.

2. Click the **References** tab, and then, in the Captions group, click the **Insert Table of Figures** button. Make sure the Show page numbers and the Right align page numbers check boxes are selected, that the Tab leader list box is set to a dotted line, that the Formats list box is set to From template, and that the Caption label list box is set to Figure.

3. Click the **OK** button. The table of figures is inserted in the document, as shown in Figure 10-45.

Table of figures inserted in document ◄ **Figure 10-45**

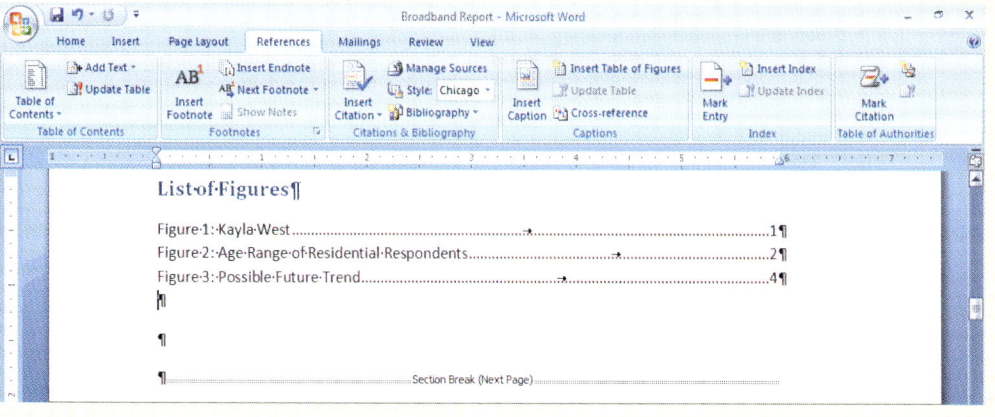

4. Scroll up to the title page and add your name on the blank line after "Lori Tollefson."

5. Save the master document.

Besides tables of contents and lists of figures, Word can also generate other lists. When creating legal documents, you may have to create a list called a **table of authorities**, which is a list of references to cases, statutes, or rules. Similar to other Word-generated lists, a table of authorities includes the page numbers on which the references appear. To create a table of authorities:

1. Mark all the citations (references). To mark a citation, select it, click the References tab, in the Table of Authorities group click the Mark Citation button to display the Mark Citation dialog box, select the category (Cases, Statutes, Rules, Treatises, and so forth), and then click Mark or Mark All.

2. Generate the table of authorities. In the Table of Authorities group on the References tab, click the Insert Table of Authorities button.

3. To update a table of authorities after adding more citations to a document, click the Update Table of Authorities button in the Table of Authorities group on the References tab.

You're now ready to print the Broadband Report document.

Updating Fields Before Printing

Many of the elements you have added to the Broadband Report, such as the cross-references, the bibliography, and the table of contents, include fields. Before printing a document containing fields, you should make sure that Word is set up to update fields before printing. By default, updating fields before printing is turned off.

To set up Word to update fields before printing:

▶ 1. Click the **Office Button** 🔘, click the **Word Options** button to open the Word Options dialog box, click **Display,** and then, under "Printing options," click the **Update fields before printing** check box to select it, if necessary, and then click the **OK** button. This ensures that fields (those in a table of contents, table of figures, index, etc.) are always updated when you print a document.

▶ 2. Click the **OK** button to close the Word Options dialog box.

▶ 3. Scroll through the report, and if any heading lacks a heading number, open the Styles window, click anywhere in the heading (in the document), and click that heading's style in the task pane.

▶ 4. Print the Broadband Report document. A dialog box opens prompting you to update the table of contents.

▶ 5. Click the **OK** button. If you see the same dialog box again, click the OK button again. Next, you should turn off Update fields before printing so you leave Word in the same state you found it when you started this tutorial. If the Update fields before printing check box was selected by default when you performed Step 1, then skip the following step.

▶ 6. Click the **Office Button** 🔘, click the **Word Options** button to open the Word Options dialog box, click **Display**, and then, under "Printing Options," click the **Update fields before printing** check box to deselect it, and then click the **OK** button.

Michael plans to post the final version of the survey report file on his company's network. When he does, he wants to make sure anyone who reads the report knows that it really was created by writers at Market Data Now, Inc.. He also wants to prevent any unauthorized readers from opening the report. In the next section, you will learn about two Word features that allow you to protect a final document from unauthorized access or from unauthorized modification: encryption and digital signatures.

Creating Digital Signatures and Encrypting and Finalizing a Document

To **encrypt** a file is to modify the data structure to make the information unreadable to unauthorized people. When you encrypt a Word document, you assign a password to the file. The only way to open the file is by entering the password.

Encrypting a Document | Reference Window

- Click the Office Button, point to Prepare, and then click Encrypt Document to open the Encrypt Document dialog box.
- Type a password in the Password text box, and then click the OK button to open the Confirm Password dialog box.
- Retype the password in the Reenter password text box, and then click the OK button.
- To open an encrypted document, open the file as usual, type the password in the Password dialog box, and then click the OK button.
- To remove a password, click the Office Button, click Save As to open the Save As dialog box, click Tools, click General Options, select the password, press the Delete key, click the OK button, click Save, and then click Yes if necessary.

A **digital signature** is an electronic attachment, not visible within the contents of the document, which verifies the authenticity of the author or the version of the document by comparing the digital signature to a digital certificate. Once a signature is added, the document is marked as final and can't be modified. If you remove the Mark as Final status so that you can make changes to the document, the signature is marked as invalid (because it is no longer the same document the signatory signed).

You should understand the following additional information about digital signatures:

- You can obtain a digital certificate from a certification authority, or you can create one yourself on your computer that can only be used to validate a document on the same computer.
- Only digital certificates obtained from an official certification authority are verified (i.e., officially valid and reliable). Only a certification authority can provide legitimate, certifiable digital signatures.
- When you open a digitally signed document, an icon appears in the status bar. You can click this icon to view the digital signature.
- If you modify a digitally signed document in any way and then save the modified version, Word will strip the digital signature from the document. (You'll be warned of this when you try to save the document.) Thus, if a document has a certified digital signature, you can be fairly certain that no one has modified the document.
- You can't add a digital signature to a master document, but you can add one to each of its subdocuments.
- You can maintain the security of a document in other ways than using digital signatures—for example, by protecting the document with a password, encrypting the file with a password, and sending the file only through secure networks.

You can insert a signature line with information about the signer, such as his or her title, and you can include instructions to the signer. When the signer double-clicks the signature line, he or she can type a name to sign the document, and that signer's digital signature is attached to the document. You'll save the Broadband Report document as a new document. Then, because you can't add a digital signature to a master document, you will merge the subdocuments with the rest of the document. Then you will encrypt the new document and add a digital signature.

To encrypt a copy of the current document:

▶ **1.** Save the Broadband Report master document one more time, so you are sure you have saved all your work.

▶ **2.** Save the document again using the name **Final Report** in the Tutorial.10\Tutorial folder included with your Data Files.

▶ **3.** Switch to Outline view, in the Master Document group click the **Show Document** button, scroll down to the "3.1 Demographics" section, click its **Subdocument** icon 🔲 , click the **Unlink** button in the Master Document group, scroll down to the "4. Small Business Subscribers" section, click its **Subdocument** icon 🔲 , and then click the click the **Unlink** button again. The Final Report document no longer contains any subdocuments. You are ready to encrypt it.

▶ **4.** Click the **Office Button** (🔵) , point to **Prepare**, and then click **Encrypt Document**. The Encrypt Document dialog box opens. Here you'll type a password.

▶ **5.** Type **survey** in the Password text box (using all lowercase letters), notice that instead of the password you typed you see a series of six black dots, and then click the **OK** button. The dialog box changes to the Confirm Password dialog box.

▶ **6.** Type **survey** again to verify the password (using all lowercase letters), and then click the **OK** button again. Now, when you save the file, it will be in an encrypted format, so that it can't be opened except by a person knowing the password. (Normally, you would use a stronger password—one that included numbers or some uppercase letters, but for the sake of simplicity here, you are using a password that is easy to remember.)

Next, you'll add the digital signature to this file.

To insert a signature line in the document:

▶ **1.** Press the **Ctrl+Home** keys, position the insertion point after "2010" and before the section break (at the bottom of the first page), press the **Enter** key three times, and then press the ↑ key to move the insertion point up one line.

▶ **2.** Click the **Insert** tab, and then in the Text group, click the **Signature Line** button.

▶ **3.** If a dialog box opens containing an explanation of the purpose and limitations of a digital signature, read the information in the dialog box, and then click the **OK** button. The Signature Setup dialog box opens, as shown in Figure 10-46.

Figure 10-46 ▶ Signature Setup dialog box

4. In the Suggested signer box, type **Michael Balczak**. You could also type a title and an e-mail address in the appropriate boxes, or select the check box to allow the signer to add comments in the Sign dialog box. Note that the default is for the current date to appear in the signature.

5. Click the **OK** button. The dialog box closes and a signature line appears with Michael's name underneath it. See Figure 10-47.

Signature line in document ◄ **Figure 10-47**

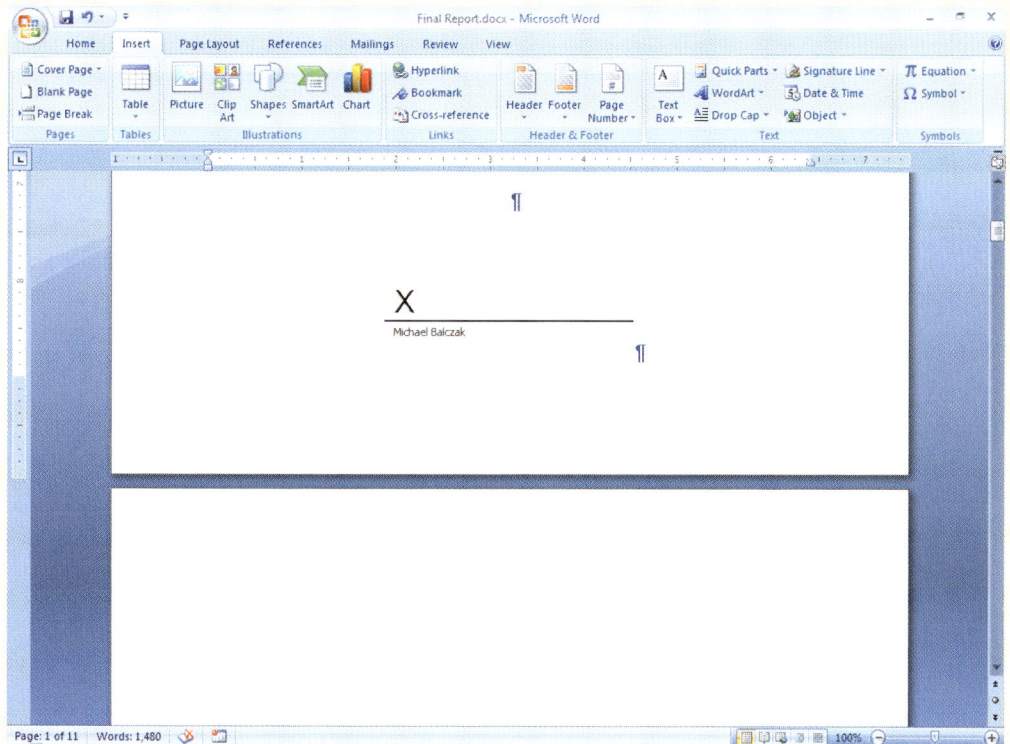

Now Michael can digitally sign the document.

6. Double-click the area just above the signature line, and then if the dialog box containing an explanation of digital signatures opens again, click the **OK** button.

If the Get a Digital ID dialog box opens, that means that there is no digital certificate stored on the computer you are using. You could click the Create your own digital ID option button and create your own digital certificate, but then others can't verify your digital signature, and you can verify it only on the current computer. Click the Cancel button, and then read but do not execute Steps 7 through 9 in this section. After reading these steps, you should perform the last step, Step 10.

If the Sign dialog box opens, the insertion point is blinking in the Purpose for signing this document box. The name at the bottom is the name on the certificate issued to or created on this computer.

7. If you see the Sign dialog box, type **Michael Balczak**, and then click the **Sign** button.

▶ **8.** If the Signature Confirmation dialog box opens, click the **OK** button. Word saves the document using the default filename and location. Michael's name appears on the signature line, the current date appears in the upper-right corner of the signature line box, and the Signatures task pane opens listing the name on the certificate. The document is marked as being digitally signed, as indicated by the icon 🧑 in the status bar.

▶ **9.** Close the Signatures task pane.

▶ **10.** Whether or not you created the digital signature as described in these steps, close the Final Report document.

With the document now encrypted and signed, you can no longer edit it or add comments.

To open the encrypted document and view its digital signature:

▶ **1.** Open the **Final Report** document located in the Tutorial.10\Tutorial folder included with your Data Files. The Password dialog box appears.

▶ **2.** Type **survey** in the text box (using all lowercase letters), and then click the **OK** button. The document opens as usual. If you did create a digital signature in the preceding set of steps, you can now view the document's signature to verify that it is indeed authentic. If you did not create a digital signature, read Steps 3 and 4 but do not perform them.

▶ **3.** Scroll down so that you can see the bottom of page 1, click the **Office Button** 🔘, point to **Prepare**, and then click **View Signatures**. The Signatures task pane opens. The signature you added is listed as a valid signature.

▶ **4.** Close the Signatures task pane, and then close Final Report document.

Encryption and digital signatures are designed to help make your documents secure against unauthorized changes. If security isn't a vital concern—perhaps because you will only be sharing a document among a few colleagues—consider using the Mark as Final feature instead. When you mark a document as final, all editing features are turned off and the document file becomes a read-only file. Also, the Final icon is visible in the status bar. Note that anyone can turn off the Mark as Final feature, so it does not provide actual security. However, in an informal setting, it offers a convenient way to alert readers that you are not expecting any changes to a document.

To mark a document as final, you would follow these steps:

1. Save the document.
2. Click the Office Button, point to Prepare, click Mark as Final, and then click the OK button.
3. If you see a message indicating that the document has been marked as final, click the OK button.
4. To turn off the Mark as Final Feature, click the Office Button, point to Prepare, and then click Mark as Final.

Congratulations on finishing a very long and complicated document. The skills you learned in this tutorial will be extremely useful to you as you create long documents for school and in the workplace.

Session 10.3 Quick Check | Review

1. What type of page numbers are typically used in front matter?
2. How do you format a document's page numbers?
3. Define "gutter" and explain how to change the size of a document's gutter.
4. Define "style reference."
5. What are the basic steps in creating an index?
6. True or False. When a document is digitally signed, you can no longer edit it or add comments to it.
7. What do you need to do before you can compile a bibliography?

Tutorial Summary | Review

In this tutorial, you learned how to create master documents and subdocuments. You learned how to split, merge, and remove subdocuments, and how to control page and text flow in long documents. You learned how to organize a document using section numbers, numbered captions, and cross-references. You learned how to create and insert a chart using Microsoft Graph. Then you learned how to use protect a document with formatting and editing restrictions and how to check a document with the Document Inspector. Next, you learned how to manage and navigate documents using synchronous scrolling and thumbnails. You learned how to format pages with different page setups for odd and even pages and how to insert field codes in a footer. You also learned how to create, compile, and update an index, a bibliography, a table of contents, a table of figures, and a table of authorities. Finally, you learned how to set up Word to update Fields before printing, how to create and add a digital signature, and how to encrypt a document.

Key Terms

bibliography	gutter	soft hyphen
citation	highlighting	style reference
compile	index	subdocument
cross-reference	master document	subentry
datasheet	Master Document view	synchronous scrolling
digital signature	Microsoft Graph	table of authorities
Document Inspector	nonbreaking hyphen	table of figures
encrypt	nonbreaking space	thumbnails
figure	orphan	two-sided printing
front matter	paragraph shading	widow
	protect	workgroup

Practice	**Review Assignments**

Get practice in the skills you learned in the tutorial using the same case scenario.

Data Files needed for the Review Assignments: Anls2.docx, Anls2.docx, Intro.docx, Table.jpg, Wireless.docx

The Market Data Now, Inc. (MDNI) team of Michael Balczak, Katarina Thao, and Lori Tollefson asks for your help with another project. The team has to prepare another report for the new Wireless Services Committee (WSC). The WSC was formed to study attitudes about citywide wireless networks and the Internet access they provide. The MDNI team developed, administered, and analyzed print and Web surveys of wireless users to determine their attitudes about wireless technology and what they want from it. Each member of the team wrote a section of the report. It's your job to compile the report as a master document and to perform the necessary revisions such as creating an index and a bibliography. (*Note*: Text you need to type is shown in bold for ease of reference only; do not bold the text unless otherwise instructed.)

1. Open the file **Wireless** from the Tutorial.10\Review folder included with your Data Files, and save it in the same folder using the filename **Wireless Report**.

2. On the title page (page 1), below "Lori Tollefson" in the list of market analysts, insert a new paragraph and type **Assisted by** followed by a space and your name.

3. In the Tutorial.10\Review folder, make copies of the three files **Anls1**, **Anls2**, and **Intro** and rename the copies **Analysis 1**, **Analysis 2**, and **Introduction**, respectively.

4. Display nonprinting characters, switch to Master Document view, move the insertion point to page 4 (which is blank), and then insert the **Introduction** file as a subdocument in the Wireless Report.

5. Immediately after the first subdocument, insert the files **Analysis 1** and **Analysis 2** as additional subdocuments. Review the master document, and note that it includes headings formatted with the Heading 3 style, in addition to headings formatted with the Heading 1 and Heading 2 styles. Note the highlighted placeholder text, which you will replace later with various items.

6. Merge the Analysis 1 subdocument (which begins with the heading "Survey Results and Analysis") with the Analysis 2 subdocument (which begins with "Subscription Rates").

7. Split the first subdocument (which begins with the heading "Background") into two subdocuments. The second subdocument should begin with the level-1 heading "Demographics of Respondents" and include the "Executive Summary" section.

8. Unlink the first subdocument (which begins with the heading "Background") so it becomes part of the master document.

9. Use the Show Level button to display the first two levels of headings, and then, using the legal paragraph numbering format, double-number all the section headings. Add a period after each heading number. In the Define new Multilevel list dialog box, keep in mind that the document contains level 3 headings in addition to level 2 and level 1 headings.

10. Now Michael wants to insert a table that Lori created in another program and saved as a JPEG file. Go to page 5, delete the placeholder that reads "[INSERT TABLE AS JPEG FILE]" and insert the picture file named **Table** from the Tutorial.10\Review folder included with your data files. Resize the table so it is about 3.25 inches wide, wrap text around it using the Square option, insert a caption below the figure that reads "Figure 1," and then adjust the size of the caption box and placement of the table so that the heading "3. Executive Summary" wraps below it.

11. On page 9, delete the placeholder text "[INSERT SMARTART GRAPHIC]," and then insert a SmartArt graphic using the Multidimensional Cycle format from the Cycle category, which shows three rectangles arranged in a triangle. In the top rectangle type **Training**, in the bottom-right rectangle type **Promotion and Advertising**, and in the bottom-left rectangle type **Communication**. Resize the graphic so it is about 3 inches wide, wrap text around it using the Square option, and then drag it up to position it so the three bulleted items wrap to its right. Insert a caption below the graphic that reads "Figure 2." Adjust the size of the caption box so it is just high enough to accommodate the caption.

12. On page 10, delete the placeholder "[INSERT PIE CHART]," and in its place insert a pie chart that illustrates the data shown in Figure 10-48. Resize the pie chart so it's about 3 inches wide. Wrap text around the chart using the Square option. Next, drag it up to position it on the left side of the paragraph below the heading "4.4.1 Project Managers," with the paragraph text wrapping to the right. Insert a figure caption below the pie chart that reads "Figure 3." Adjust the position and size of the chart and the caption box so that the heading and the first two lines of the paragraph wrap above the chart, with the rest of the paragraph text wrapping to the right of the chart.

Figure 10-48

High	Average	Low
70%	19%	11%

13. Create a cross-reference to each figure, replacing the highlighted cross-reference placeholder text in the document.

14. Save the Wireless Report document, save it again in the same folder as **Protected Report**, combine the two subdocuments with the rest of the master document, and then protect the document by blocking changes to the theme and allowing only changes marked with tracked changes. Do not require a password. Save and close the Protected Report document.

15. Reopen the **Wireless Report** document and expand its subdocuments. Center the title page between its top and bottom margins and select the Different first page check box in the Layout tab of the Page Setup dialog box. Format the title page text to match the Heading 1 style, without actually using the Heading 1 style, except use 16-point font and no numbering.

16. Open the **Wireless** document from the Tutorial.10\Review folder, display it side-by-side with the Wireless Report document, and use synchronous scrolling to see how much you have added to the Wireless Report document. Close the **Wireless** document.

17. In the front matter of the **Wireless Report** document, insert lowercase Roman numeral page numbers on the right side of the footer, with page i starting on the Contents page, and then set the remainder of the report to Arabic numerals, with page 1 starting on the page containing the heading "Background."

18. Set up the pages for two-sided printing, with a 0.5-inch gutter.

19. Set up footers so that the odd-page footers include the document title "Wireless Report" at the left margin, and the page number at the right margin; and the even-page footers have the page number at the left margin, and the Heading 1 text at the right margin.

20. Create an index with index entries for every occurrence of "Market Data Now, Inc.," and "WiFi." Create a cross-reference for the abbreviation "MDNI" to "Market Data Now, Inc."

21. Select the entire section "4. Survey Results and Analysis," mark it with the bookmark "ResultsAndAnalysis" (all one word), and then mark that section with the index entry "Survey Results and Analysis."

22. Hide nonprinting characters, move the insertion point to the end of the document, below the heading "Index," and generate the index. Then, below the "Contents" heading in the front matter, insert a table of contents.

23. Below the "List of Figures" heading in the front matter, insert a list of all the figures.

24. If necessary, select Chicago as the bibliography style. At the end of the second paragraph on page 6 (just after the Figure 1 cross-reference), insert a citation to a report by Eli Zimmerer, entitled "CBA Demographics Report," from the year 2006. The report is a Market Survey report.

25. At the end of the second paragraph after the heading "4.5 Potential for Growth", insert another reference to the same report. Then insert a new, blank page before the Index page and insert the bibliography.

26. Update the table of contents to include the new "Bibliography" heading and add the "Index" heading to the table of contents using a combination of text, a dot leader, and a page reference.

27. Review the document in Print Preview. Ignore the extra space and pages; assume Michael will remove this extra space after he has added more text to the report and combined the subdocuments with the master document. Review the headings and re-apply heading styles as necessary to ensure that all heading numbers are used consistently. Save the document.

28. Unlink all the subdocuments, and then save the document as **Wireless Report Final**. Encrypt the document using the password **MDNI**. Add a signature line to the cover page with Michael Balczak as the signer. If you have a certificate installed, sign the document. Submit the completed report to your instructor in printed or electronic form, as requested.

| Apply | **| Case Problem 1** |

Apply what you've learned in this tutorial to help create a business plan for a promotional products company.

Data Files needed with this Case Problem: Plan.docx, Back.docx, Exec.docx, Mar.docx

Big Picture Products   Loren Stravusky of Eugene, Oregon, has recently started a business named Big Picture Products. The company will produce and market mugs printed with color photographs, which can be used by businesses as promotional items. She and her three partners have written the various parts of a business plan. She asks you to help her put the document together, format it, and add the remaining sections. (Note: Text you need to type is shown in bold for ease of reference only; do not bold the text unless otherwise instructed.)

1. Open the file **Plan** from the Tutorial.10\Case1 folder included with your Data Files, and save it in the same folder using the filename **Business Plan**.

2. On the title page (page 1), below Loren Stravusky's name, type **Assisted by** followed by a space and your name.

3. In the Tutorial.10\Case1 folder, make copies of the three files **Back**, **Exec**, and **Mar**, and rename the copies **Background**, **Executive**, and **Market**, respectively.

4. Move the insertion point to the blank paragraph below "List of Tables," insert a section break that begins a new page, and then on the new page insert the document named **Executive** as a subdocument in the Business Plan. If you see a dialog box indicating that a Heading 1 style exists in the Executive document and the Master Document, click Yes. When incorporating documents from multiple writers, it's common to encounter some style inconsistencies. In that case, it's best to click Yes in this dialog box to use the styles of the master document. Immediately after the first subdocument, insert **Background**, and then **Market** as additional subdocuments.

5. Merge the two subdocuments named **Executive** and **Background**, and then delete both section breaks above the heading "Background." (After you delete the section breaks, you might have to reapply the Heading 1 style to "Background" and make other formatting adjustments.)

6. Split the new, larger subdocument named **Executive** at the heading "The Company" to create a new subdocument.

7. Make sure that the Normal style has widow and orphan control turned on. (It should be active in your documents already, but it's a good idea to double-check.)

8. Double-number all the section headings and then edit the heading numbers to add a period after each heading number.

9. In the second paragraph below the "1. Executive Summary" heading, replace the hyphens in "high-quality" and "low-priced" with nonbreaking hyphens.

⊕EXPLORE 10. Add captions to the two tables where indicated in the master document by the highlighted placeholder text. You add table captions the same way you add figure captions except that, in the Caption dialog box, you select Table in the Table list box. For the caption text, use the word "Table" and a number. Don't be concerned if a page break separates the Table 2 caption from its table. You'll adjust the page break settings later in these steps.

11. Insert cross-references to the two tables where indicated in the master document by the highlighted placeholder text. In the Cross-reference dialog box, be sure to select Table in the Reference type list box.

⊕EXPLORE 12. Below the "List of Tables" heading in the front matter, insert a list of all the tables. Use the same procedure as when inserting a list of figures, but select Tables as the caption label if necessary.

13. Just before the "Index" heading, insert a vertical bar chart where indicated by the highlighted placeholder text. Use the data in Table 2 as the data for the chart. Do not wrap text around the chart.

14. Add a figure caption for the chart. Also add a cross-reference to the new figure where indicated by the highlighted placeholder text.

15. Center the title page between its left and right margins, and between its top and bottom margins.

16. Set the page numbering of the front matter to lowercase Roman numerals, with page i starting on the "Contents" page, and then start Arabic numeral numbering with page 1 on the "Executive Summary" page.

17. Set up the pages for two-sided printing, with a 0.5-inch gutter.

18. Set up the footers so that the odd-page footers (starting on page 1, which is Section 3) include the text "BPP Business Plan" at the left margin and the page number at the right margin; the even-page footers should have the page number at the left margin and the Heading 1 text at the right margin.

19. Create an index with entries for every occurrence of "mugs." Mark the abbreviation "BPP" as a cross-reference in the index to "Big Picture Products." Select the "6. Sales Forecast" section, mark it with the bookmark "SalesForecast" (all one word), and then mark that section with the index entry "Sales Forecast."

20. Move the insertion point to the end of the document, below the heading "Index," insert a page break if necessary before the "Index" heading, and then generate the index using the default settings.

21. Below the "Contents" heading in the front matter, insert a table of contents using the default settings.

22. Save the **Business Plan** document, and then save it again in the same location as **Business Plan Final**. Combine the subdocuments with the master document, review the headings and reapply heading styles as necessary to ensure that all heading numbers are used consistently. Delete any unnecessary page or section breaks, and then review the document in Print Preview to make sure it is set up correctly.

23. Save the **Business Plan Final** document again, and then mark it as final.

24. Save the document, and then submit the completed report to your instructor in printed or electronic form, as requested. Close any open files.

Challenge		**Case Problem 2**

Challenge yourself by exploring Word features to help create an informational cyber security report for a consulting firm.

Data File needed with this Case Problem: Cyber.docx

Cronkite Security Consulting Terrell Prassad is a computer security consultant at Cronkite Security Consulting (CSC). He is working on an informational report for CSC's clients. The report summarizes the essential elements of an effective cyber security policy for large and small organizations. He asks you to prepare front and back matter for the report and to create two subdocuments within the master document so his staff can review each section individually. You'll help Terrell manage the various sections of the report, format the document, and prepare it for printing. (Note: Text you need to type is shown in bold for ease of reference only; do not bold the text unless otherwise instructed.)

1. Open the file **Cyber** from the Tutorial.10\Case2 folder included with your Data Files, and save it in the same folder using the filename **Cyber Security**. Review the document, reading the comments and noting that it contains three levels of headings.

2. Check the document with the Document Inspector and remove any comments, revisions, versions, or annotations.

3. Change the document theme to Aspect.

4. Insert a preformatted cover page using the Mod format. For the document title use **Cyber Security,** for the subtitle use **An Informational Report**, delete the abstract document control, insert your name as the author, and select the current date.

5. At the end of the document, insert a page break, and then insert the heading "Index", applying the Heading 1 style.

6. Transform the "Modern Threats" section and the "Modern Solution" section into subdocuments. Return to Print Layout view.

7. Open the **Cyber** document from the Tutorial.10\Case2 folder, display the two documents side-by-side, and scroll through them using synchronous scrolling. Close the **Cyber** document.

8. Save the **Cyber Security** document, and then save it again as **Cyber Protected**.

9. In the **Cyber Protected** document, combine the two subdocuments with the master document.

10. Protect the **Cyber Protected** document against changes to its theme; also protect it for tracked changes. Assign the document the password **Crk4Scrty** (which you can remember because it stands for "Cronkite for Security"). Be extremely careful as you type the password (you have to type it twice) so that you can open the document later on. Remember to use uppercase letters for the "C" and the "S."

11. In the first paragraph under "Rationale," delete the words "the following" so the phrase reads "...of this report are:" and then, in the first line below the bulleted list, delete the word "specifically."

12. Save the **Cyber Protected** document and close it.

13. Re-open the **Cyber Security** document and expand its subdocuments.

14. In the "Location Security" section, insert a SmartArt graphic where indicated by the highlighted placeholder text. Use the Segmented Pyramid style from the Relationship group. For the SmartArt text, use the following: **IT Doors Locked** (for the bottom-left triangle)**, Outer Doors Locked** (for the bottom-right triangle), **Server Doors Locked** (for the middle triangle), and **Backups Off Site** (for the top triangle). Resize the graphic so it is two inches tall and two inches wide, wrap text around it using the Square option, and then position it so the four bullets in the "Location Security" section wrap to its right.

15. Insert a figure caption below the new figure, and then insert cross-references to the figure at both locations indicated by highlighted placeholder text. Make sure you have deleted the blank paragraph where the [INSERT SMARTART GRAPHIC] used to be located.

16. Set up the document so the title page will not have a header or page number when you add one to the rest of the document, and then insert a page number on the bottom of every page (except the title page) using the Brackets page number style.

EXPLORE 17. In Header and Footer view, move the insertion point to the header on the first page after the title page, and then use the appropriate check box in the Options group on the Header & Footer Tools Design tab to set up the document for different even and odd pages. Check the footers on odd and even pages, and re-insert the page number if necessary. Use the Page Setup dialog box to change the gutter to 0.5 inches.

EXPLORE 18. In the first even header, insert a header using the Mod Even Page header style. In the first odd header, insert a header using the Mod Odd Page header style. Make sure the current date and the title appear in the header. Verify that the header does not appear in the title page.

EXPLORE 19. Replace all occurrences of "e-mail" (with a hyphen) with "e-mail" (with a nonbreaking hyphen). This prevents the word from being split between two lines. (*Hint*: In the Find and Replace dialog box, click the More button, and then click Special.)

20. Mark index entries for all occurrences of "password." Mark "IT" as a cross-reference to "See Information Technology." Generate an index at the end of the document.

21. Select the APA style and then, on the second page of the document, replace the highlighted placeholder text with a citation to a Web site. Enter **Calliam, Lucy** for the author, **Modern Security**, as the name of the Web page, **2010** for the year, and **www.modernsecurity.course.com** as the URL. Below the Index, on the same page as the index, insert a bibliography.

22. Review the document in Print Preview and make any necessary adjustments. Save your changes.

23. Save the document as **Cyber Security Unlinked**, and then unlink all the subdocuments. Add a signature line to the cover page with Terrell Prassad as the signer, and then, if you have a digital certificate installed, sign it with your name, and then print and close the document. Submit your documents to your instructor in electronic or printed form, as requested.

| Create | **Case Problem 3** |

Compile a table of authorities for a legal brief and create a document with the headings shown in Figure 10-49.

Data Files needed with this Case Problem: Legal.docx

Kekoanui and Lee LLP   Naomi Kamei is paralegal at the law offices of Kekoanui and Lee, in Honolulu, Hawaii. The firm is handling a lawsuit filed by Peli Promotions, an advertising company, against a competitor. It's your job to help generate a table of authorities for a legal brief. Naomi also needs your help in preparing the structure of a report she is preparing for the law firm's partners. The report summarizes the firm's pro bono activities (that is, legal work donated for free) on behalf of nonprofit agencies, government agencies, and individuals over the past five years. The report will be presented to the firm's board of directors. Leah has not written the report yet, but she would like you to set up the document with the appropriate title page, headers, footers, page numbers, and so on. (Note: Text you need to type is shown in bold for ease of reference only; do not bold the text unless otherwise instructed.)

1. Open the file named **Legal** from the Tutorial.10\Case3 folder included with your Data Files and save it as **Legal Brief**. This document includes the beginning of a 30-page legal brief.

⊕ EXPLORE

2. Go to page 3, and in the third paragraph, select the phrase **Sydney v. Rogan Publishing, Corp., 81 F.2d 49, 56 (2d Cir. 1935)**. Don't include the space before the phrase or the semicolon after this phrase. Mark this citation for a table of authorities, using the category "Cases."

3. Similarly, mark the other seven citations in this paragraph.

⊕ EXPLORE

4. Move the insertion point to the blank paragraph below the heading "Table of Authorities" on page 2, and then generate a table of authorities, using the default settings. You should see eight items in the table of authorities. If you see fewer, mark the citations you missed and update the table of authorities.

5. Save the **Legal Brief** document, print it, and then close it.

6. Open a new, blank document and save it as **Pro Bono Report** in the Tutorial.10\Case3 folder included with your data files.

7. Insert a title page of your choice. Use **Law Offices of Kekoanui and Lee** as the company name, **Pro Bono Report** as the title, **2006–2010 Activities** as the subtitle, and your name as the author. Include the current date.

8. Add the headings shown in Figure 10-49, using the Heading 1 and Heading 2 style. Be sure to include one blank paragraph formatted in the Normal style after each heading.

Figure 10-49

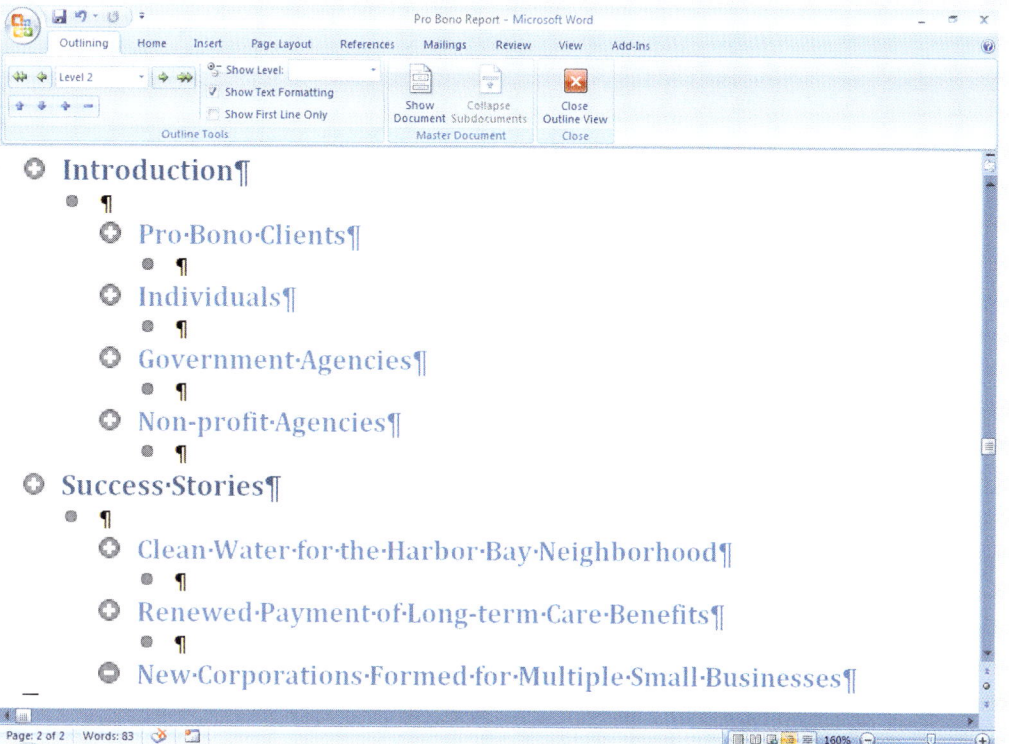

9. Add heading numbers and then format the level 1 numbers as uppercase letters (A, B, C, etc.). Add a period after the level 2 numbers.

10. Select a theme of your choice.

11. Before the "Introduction" heading, insert a Next Page section break. Add a "Contents" heading to the blank page and format the heading to match the other headings in the document, without using the Heading 1 style. Insert a blank paragraph formatted in the Normal style after the "Contents" heading.

12. Transform the "Introduction" section (including its three subsections) into a subdocument. Do the same for the "Success Stories" section (including its three subsections). Make sure there is one blank paragraph between the last heading in the document and the last section break; insert one if necessary. Check to make sure the blank paragraph after each heading is formatted in the Normal style.

⊕ EXPLORE 13. Click in the blank paragraph after the "A. Introduction" heading, type **=rand()** and press the Enter key to insert three paragraphs of random text in the document. Inserting this placeholder text makes it easier to see what the finished document will look like. Insert random text after each heading.

14. Insert the table of contents.

15. Set up the document for two-sided printing, with a 0.5-inch gutter. In a document containing a preformatted cover page, it is difficult to number the page after the cover page as page 1, so insert a Next Page section break before the "Contents" heading to create a blank page.

16. Insert the Alphabet header on each page of the report except the blank page and the cover page. Insert a plain page number in the middle of the document footer on each page of the report except the cover page, the blank page and the Contents page. On the page containing the "A. Introduction" heading, start the page numbering at 1. (Note that this will insert a blank left page after the Contents page.)

17. Save the **Pro Bono Report** document and review it in Print Preview. Note that Word did insert a blank page after the Contents page, because the page containing the "A. Introduction" heading is numbered as page 1.

18. Make any changes you think are required, including reformatting headings if necessary.

19. Encrypt the document using the password **ProBono**, save your changes, print the **Pro Bono Report** document, and then close it.

20. Open the two subdocument files, note that they are still formatted in the Office theme, print the subdocuments, and then close them.

21. Submit your documents to your instructor in electronic or printed form, as requested.

| Research | **Case Problem 4** |

Use the Internet and other sources to collect information about preparing a guided tour.

No data file is associated with this Case Problem.

Preparing a Guided-Tour Brochure   Your instructor will divide your class into workgroups of three to six students and appoint a workgroup leader or have each workgroup select one. Each workgroup will collaborate to prepare a document that provides a guided tour of a real or imaginary place. Your goal is to create a brochure like you might receive from a chamber of commerce that introduces you to a city or county. You might want to select a place in which most of your workgroup has some interest and at least one member of the group has expertise, such as your school campus or your city. Alternatively, you could select an unfamiliar place and then conduct the necessary research to learn about your chosen location. Another approach is to create a guided tour of the landscape in your favorite online role-playing game or of the geographical area discussed in a favorite novel.

Working together, your group should do the following:

1. Discuss in a planning meeting how the workgroup will accomplish its goals and how it can make all the chapters consistent in style and format.

2. Create a detailed outline for the guided tour brochure. Plan to divide the brochure into chapters and to include numerous figures, so the brochure is well-illustrated. You can include digital photographs, drawings, or other types of illustrations. If you are writing about an online role-playing game, include screenshots of selected locations. (Remember to include complete citations that explain your sources, including the source of any screenshots.)

3. Plan the brochure's overall formatting. Pick an appropriate theme, as well as theme fonts, theme colors, and theme effects. Decide if you want to use the default heading styles or modify the heading styles. Also, decide how you want to format figures and tables, including how you want text to wrap around these elements. You will use two-sided printing, so plan the headers and footers accordingly.

4. Write the chapters, dividing them up so each workgroup member writes at least one. Each workgroup member should base his or her chapter on research or personal knowledge. Include illustrations, but do not include captions or cross-references at this point. Format the chapter according to the formatting plan created in Step 3, and then protect the chapter for tracked changes (without a password).

5. Each group member should review each of the chapters written by the other members of your workgroup. Review the chapters electronically. Make at least one edit per document (the changes should be marked with revision marks) and include at least one comment, and then pass each document file along to the next group member, so that all of the group's changes are made in a single copy of each document file. When you are finished, each workgroup member should have a copy of his or her document file that contains edits and comments from all the members of the workgroup.

6. Retrieve the file for your chapter or chapters, unprotect the document, and accept or reject the edits made by the other workgroup members. Delete any comments. Discuss the chapter with the other group members as necessary until you all agree on the final status of all the chapters.

   For the remaining steps, you have two options: 1) Perform the remaining steps as a group; or 2) Perform the remaining these steps individually, so that each member of the workgroup creates his or her own copy of the guided tour brochure. Ask your instructor if you should work alone or as a group.

7. Create a new document to be used as the master document for the brochure, save it as **Guided Tour** in the Tutorial.10\Case4 folder included with your data files, insert a title page, write a brief preface or introduction, and set up headings for the table of contents, for the list of figures and/or list of tables, the bibliography, and for the index.

8. Insert the various chapter files as subdocuments, and then format the document consistently according to the formatting plan you agreed on in Step 2. Add figure captions and cross-references.

9. Set up the brochure for two-sided printing. Create appropriate headers or footers for the odd and even pages. Make sure you include page numbers, the brochure title, and chapter names in the headers or footers.

10. Add all the necessary citations and then insert the bibliography.

11. Insert the table of contents.

12. Mark appropriate index entries and then insert the index.

13. Review the document in Print Preview, and make any necessary changes to ensure that your brochure looks polished and professional.

14. Update fields and print the document. Print on both sides of the document pages if possible.

15. Submit your documents to your instructor in electronic or printed form, as requested.

Research | Internet Assignments

The purpose of the Internet Assignments is to challenge you to find information on the Internet that you can use to work effectively with this software. The actual assignments are updated and maintained on the Course Technology Web site. Log on to the Internet and use your Web browser to go to the Student Online Companion for New Perspectives Office 2007 at **www.course.com/np/office2007**. Then navigate to the Internet Assignments for this tutorial.

| Review | Quick Check Answers |

Session 10.1

1. a. Word document divided into several smaller, individual files, to help you organize and maintain a lengthy document
   b. one of several small, separate files that are part of a master document
   c. the last line of a paragraph appearing alone at the top of a page
   d. the first line of a paragraph appearing alone at the bottom of a page
2. To split a subdocument, select the heading to be the start of the new subdocument, and then click the Split button in the Master Document group on the Outlining tab. To merge subdocuments, Shift-click the subdocument icons of the subdocuments you want to combine, and then click the Merge button in the Master Document group on the Outlining tab. To remove a subdocument from a master document, click the subdocument icon for the subdocument you want to remove, and then click the Unlink button in the Master Document group on the Outlining tab.
3. consistent formatting elements; accurate numbering; accurate cross-referencing; complete table of contents and index; faster editing
4. True
5. Convert an existing document into a master document, and then divide it into subdocuments using built-in heading styles; insert existing disk files into a Word document.
6. a hyphen that won't allow the word or phrase it connects to break between two lines; a space that won't allow the words on either side to break between two lines; when you want to keep two words on the same line of text

Session 10.2

1. False
2. Click the Home tab, in the Paragraph group, click the Multilevel List button arrow, click a heading numbering style.
3. Insert Caption button in the Captions group on the References tab
4. False
5. Insert the text "Figure 3" as a cross-reference.
6. Tracked changes, Comments, Filling in forms, No changes (Read only)
7. Click the Office Button, point to Prepare, click Inspect Document

Session 10.3

1. Lowercase Roman numerals
2. Insert page numbers using the Page Number button in the Header & Footer group on the Insert tab. Click the Page Number button in the Header & Footer group on the Insert tab, click Format Page Numbers, click the Number format list arrow and select a format, and then click the OK button.
3. A gutter is the blank space on the inside of each page in a bound book. Open the Page Setup dialog box, click the Margins tab, enter a value in the Gutter text box, click the Layout tab, select the Different odd and even check box, and then click the OK button.
4. A field code that inserts text that is formatted with a particular style.
5. Mark index entries and subentries, and then compile the index.
6. True
7. Create citations for sources in the document.

ling Data Files

rial.10 →

Tutorial

Broadband Report.docx
Demographics.docx
Final Report.docx
Large Business Subscribers.docx
Report 2 Shaded.docx
Residential.docx
Small Business.docx

Review

Analysis 1.docx
Analysis 2.docx
Demographics of Respondents.docx
Introduction.docx
Protected Report.docx
Wireless Report.docx
Wireless Report Final.docx

Case1

Background.docx
Business Plan.docx
Business Plan Final.docx
Executive.docx
Market.docx
The Company.docx

Case2

Cyber Protected.docx
Cyber Security.docx
Cyber Security Unlinked.docx
Modern Solution.docx
Modern Threats.docx

Case3

Introducion.docx
Legal Brief.docx
Pro Bono Report.docx
Success Stories.docx

Case4

Guided Tour.docx
Various subdocument files

Reality Check

After finishing this book, you have many advanced word-processing skills at your disposal. Using these skills, you can add more complexity to documents you may have already created for work, school, or home, and you can create new, complicated documents from scratch. In the following exercise, you'll create or revise a number of documents by using the Word skills and features presented in Tutorials 8 through 10.

Note: Please be sure *not* to include any personal information of a sensitive nature in the documents you create to be submitted to your instructor for this exercise. Later on, you can update the documents with such information for your own personal use.

1. Collect the Word documents you use regularly, and add document properties to help you keep your files organized.
2. If you are working on your own computer, customize the Quick Access Toolbar by adding buttons that you frequently use.
3. Open a new document. If you are working on your own computer, create Quick Parts that you save to the Building Blocks template that you can use for a future report for school or work. If you are not working on your own computer, save the document as a template, and then save the Quick Parts in the template.
4. Take a long report that you have already created for school or work, and pick out text in the document that you want to draw attention to with special, character-level formatting. For example, you might choose to format a company name that is used repeatedly in a different font and font color. Record a macro that applies the formatting you want, and then use the macro throughout the document to apply the formatting.
5. Add a text or picture watermark to the report.
6. Create a form that collects information that you can include in your report from colleagues or friends. Format the form attractively. Use the Picture content control if appropriate.
7. Include a pull quote or sidebar somewhere in the report. Change its format so it looks attractive in the document.
8. Expand the report by adding figures with captions. Include cross-references to the figures within the report text. Format the pictures with picture styles.
9. If possible, insert additional material in the report as one or more subdocuments.
10. Add a preformatted title page, and format the document headings with heading styles, using a theme, theme colors, and theme font of your choice.
11. Add a table of contents and a table of figures.
12. Set the document up for two-sided printing, with appropriate headers and footers. Don't forget to include page numbers, with a different style of page number for the front matter.
13. Add citations for any material from other sources. If your report does not include material from other sources, add an opening quotation from another source and include a citation for it. Add a bibliography at the end of the document.
14. Create a useful index that includes all the important terms and concepts in your document.
15. Update the document fields.
16. Check the document for hidden or personal data and remove that data.
17. Save the document, mark it as final or digitally sign it, and then print it.
18. Submit your documents to your instructor in electronic or printed form, as requested.

Creating a Form Letter and a Program

Case | Washington Engineers Society

Angela Notraga is an engineer and is active in the Washington Engineers Society, which annually awards scholarships to students. Angela needs to send a letter to this year's winning students inviting them to the Society's annual banquet. She also needs to prepare a program for the banquet.

1. Open the file **Engineer** from the AddCases folder included with your Data Files, and save the file as **Engineer Form Letter** in the same folder.

2. At the top of main document, insert the picture file **Logo** in the AddCases folder.

3. Change the scale of the height of the picture from 34% to 42%, leaving the width of the picture at 34%. (*Hint*: Open the Size dialog box, deselect the Lock aspect ratio check box, and then change the Height percentage.)

4. Replace the [Date] placeholder with a date field in the "11 Feb 2010" format so that the date appears directly below the logo.

5. Begin a mail merge using Engineer Form Letter as the main document. Use the file **Engineer Data** from the AddCases folder as the data source.

6. In the letter, replace the bracketed text with merge field codes from the Engineer Data data source. Use the format "Joshua Randall, Jr." in the Address Block merge field and format the Greeting Line merge field as "Dear Joshua,". Replace the [Your name] placeholder with your name, and then save the document.

7. Preview the merge, correct any errors, and then merge the Engineer Letter main document with all records of the data source to a new document. Save the merged document as **Engineer Award Letters** in the AddCases folder. (If the logo does not appear in the first merged letter, close the document and then open it again.)

8. Print the last letter of the merged document, and then close all the documents. Do not save changes to the Engineer Form Letter document.

9. Open a new document, save it as **Program Main** to the AddCases folder, and then begin a Directory mail merge using the **Engineer Data** from the AddCases folder as the data source.

ting Data Files

dCases

jineer.docx
jineer Data.mdb
jo.jpg

10. Insert the following merge fields: First_Name and Last_Name separated by a space. Press the Tab key, and then insert the City, Award_Name, and Award_Amount fields separated by tabs. Press the Enter key. Save your changes.

11. Merge all the records to a new document. Save the document as **Dinner Program** to the AddCases folder.

12. Create the document shown in Figure 1-1. The theme is Foundry. All the text is formatted with Quick Styles, and some of the formatting is then modified. Make sure the tab stops include a dot leader, and that you include the Draft watermark. Save your changes.

Figure 1-1

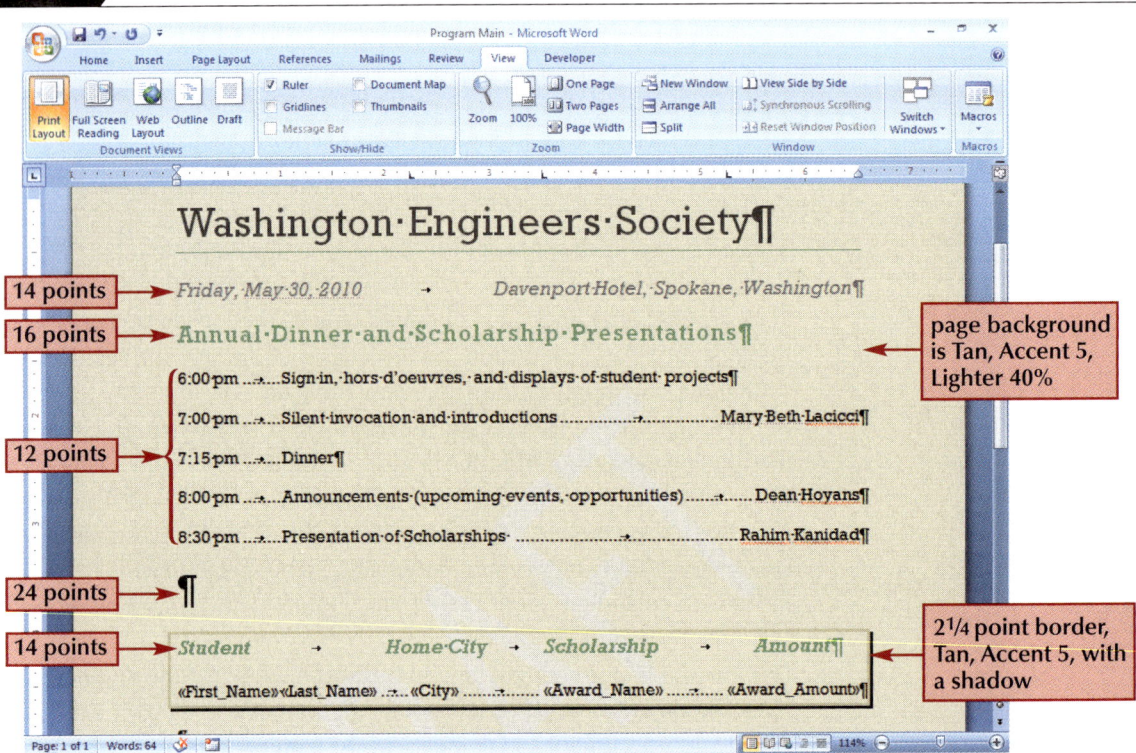

13. Close all open documents without saving changes. Submit the completed documents in electronic or printed form, as requested.

Ending Data Files

Dinner Program.docx
Engineer Award Letters.docx
Engineer Form Letter.docx
Program Main.docx

Creating a Promotional Flyer

Case | PersonalRec

Bruno Lambert owns and operates a small business in Portland, Maine, called PersonalRec, which coordinates and sponsors active recreational trips to destinations in the United States and Europe. Bruno rents or ships equipment so that travelers can sail, ski, surf, and enjoy other forms of recreation as soon as they arrive. His signature service is to provide clients with a hot-air balloon ride at the end of their trip. Bruno asks you to help him create an appealing and informational flyer that he can distribute at athletic meets and recreational events to advertise his business. Complete the following:

1. Open the file **RecFlyer** from the AddCases folder included with your Data Files, and then save the document in the same folder using the filename **PersonalRec Flyer**.
2. Change the page setup so that the top and bottom margins are 0.5 inch and the left and right margins are 1 inch.
3. In the table, adjust the width of the Description column so that the table spans the width of the page. (The page itself should be 6.5 inches wide.)
4. Sort the rows of the table so that the categories in column 2 appear in alphabetical order.
5. In cell A2, delete the text "RecGolf" and then insert the graphics file **RecGolf**—that is, the file whose name you just deleted. Repeat this procedure in cells A3 through A7—that is, delete the name of the graphics file and then insert the graphics file (digital image) into the cell. All the image files are located in the AddCases folder included with your Data Files. Adjust the height (with the aspect ratio fixed) of each of the pictures to 1.0 inch.
6. Apply the Table Colorful 1 table style to the table.
7. Change the font of the text in cells B1 and C1 to white, 14-point Trebuchet MS italic. If your computer doesn't have the Trebuchet MS font, use Arial.

ectives

ust the margins of a
cument
ange the text font,
, color, and effect
ort and modify
ital pictures
ize graphics
text wrapping
ions
ate and modify a
artArt graphic
dify the style set of
document
the rows of a table
ly a table style and
dify elements of
style

ting Data Files

dCases

Bal.jpg
Flyer.docx
Golf.jpg
Logo.jpg
Sail.jpg
Ski.jpg
Snow.jpg
Surf.jpg

8. At the top of the flyer, insert the PersonalRec logo, **RecLogo.jpg**, located in the AddCases folder.
9. Set the size of the logo to 1.0 inch in height (keeping the aspect ratio locked), and then position the logo in the top left with the text wrapping set to Square.
10. Change the font of the company name ("PersonalRec") to 28-point Trebuchet MS. (If your computer doesn't have Trebuchet MS, use Arial bold.)
11. Change the font color of the company name to Blue, Accent 1, and change the font effects to Shadow.
12. Apply the Modern style set. Delete any extra blank paragraphs.
13. Adjust the widths of the table columns so they match those in Figure 2-1.

Figure 2-1

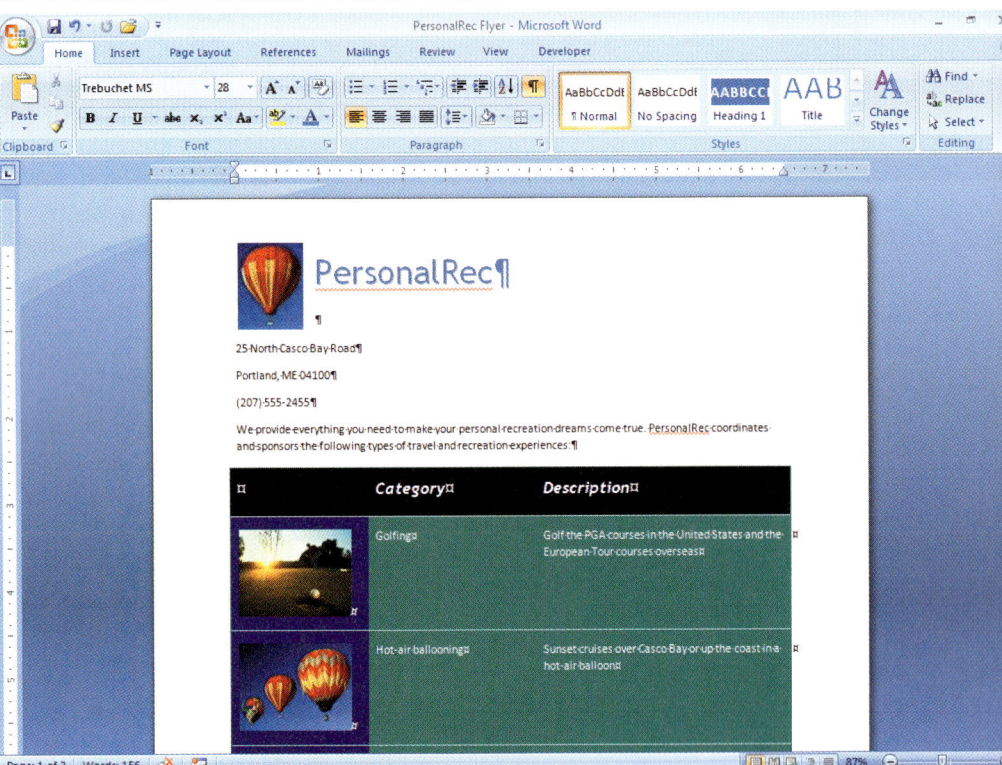

14. At the end of the document, insert the Converging Arrows SmartArt graphic from the Relationship category. In the shape on the left, insert the text **Achieve your personal best!** and in the shape on the right, insert the text **Adventure recreation travel!**
15. Change the colors of the SmartArt graphic to Gradient Range – Accent 1.
16. Make sure the entire flyer fits on two pages.
17. Save the file, and then submit the completed document to your instructor in printed or electronic form, as requested.
18. Close all open windows.

Ending Data Files

AddCases

PersonalRec Flyer.docx

Creating a Confirmation Order Form

Case | Pictures!

Miranda Lajoie is the owner of Pictures! in Lafayette, Kentucky. Pictures! puts customers' photos and messages on mugs, plates, and t-shirts. Miranda asks you to create an order form for the customers to fill out by hand that an employee can then enter into the computer. The employee will scan or store the customer's photo at the same time and include the photo in the onscreen form. This completed form can be confirmed as correct by the customer and will follow the item through the whole process so that the employees who put the photos on the items can double-check that they are putting the correct photo on the correct item. You will prepare these forms.

1. Open the document **Order** from the AddCases folder included with your Data Files, and then save it as **Order Request** in the same folder.
2. Insert WordArt using the text **Pictures!** at the top of the document using WordArt style 13. Center the WordArt in the line.
3. Format the label "Name:" as Strong, and then change the font size to 12 points and the color to Orange, Accent 5, Darker 25%. Redefine the Strong Quick Style to match this format, and then apply the redefined format to the other labels in the customer contact section.
4. Format the label "Photo description:" with the redefined Strong Quick Style, change the color of the text to black and the size to 14 points.
5. Format the table with any table style that looks attractive in the document.
6. Add your name as the author property. Save your changes.
7. Open a new, blank Word document. Save it as a Word template named **Order Confirmation** in the AddCases folder. Change the theme and theme colors so they match the Order Request document.
8. Copy the WordArt logo, the address, customer contact information, and the date field from the Order Request document to this document. Change the space after the "Name," "Address," and "City" lines to 10 points.
9. Use the Modify Style dialog box to redefine the Normal style so it is 12 points.
10. In the paragraph below the date field, type: **Please confirm that the photo and the items ordered are correct. If you have any corrections, please let your sales representative know. Your items will be ready in approximately one hour.**

11. Remove the line leaders in the customer information section, and then insert a Text content control after each label in that section. Adjust the tab stops as needed.

12. Position the insertion point after the date field, press the Tab key twice, and then insert the time in the format 1:36 PM to be updated automatically. Format the time as 14 points and bold.

13. Create a 6×7 table below the last paragraph. Type **Item**, **Quantity**, **Price**, and **Total** as column labels, skip the fifth column, and then type **Personalization** as the last column label.

14. Copy the items and their prices from the Order Request document to the second through fourth rows in the table in the form. Match the destination formatting.

15. Insert Text form fields of the type Number in the first three rows under Quantity. Set these fields to calculate on exit, and set the default value to be zero. (*Hint:* Type **0** in the Default number box in the Text Form Fields Options dialog box.)

16. Insert Calculation Text form fields in the first three rows under "Total" to calculate the total price for each item. (*Hint:* Use the Product formula and the argument Left.) Format the numbers with two decimal places (but no dollar sign). Set these fields to calculate on exit because the results will be used in another calculation.

17. Merge the six cells in the last two rows and the first two columns. In this cell, type: **Items left for more than 30 days will be discarded or resold.** Format this in bold.

18. In the last three cells in the "Price" column, type **Subtotal**, **Tax**, and **Total**.

19. In the cell to the right of "Subtotal," insert a Calculation Text form field to add the numbers above it and set it to calculate on exit. In the cell to the right of "Tax," insert a Calculation Text form field that multiplies the amount in the cell to the right of Subtotal by .06—sales tax in Kentucky is 6%—and set it to calculate on exit. (*Hint:* The Subtotal value is in cell C5.) Format both of these numbers with two decimal places (but no dollar sign).

20. In the cell to right of Total, insert a Calculation Text form field that adds the amounts in the two cells above it. Format this number as currency.

21. Merge all the cells in the last column. Insert a Photo content control in the merged cell. Merge the six cells below the "Personalization" head in the last column, and then insert a Text content control.

22. Format the table attractively. Format at least one cell so it is filled with black and uses reverse type.

23. Protect the template for filling in forms, save your changes, and then close the document.

24. Create a new document based on the Order Confirmation template. Insert your own information in the Text content controls in the customer contact section.

25. Enter **5** as the number of mugs sold, **3** as the number of plates, and **2** as the number of t-shirts. Type **Happy Birthday Grandma!** in the last cell.

26. Insert the photo **Boys**, located in the AddCases folder, in the Photo content control.

27. Save the completed table as **Order Test** to the AddCases folder.

28. Submit the completed documents in electronic or printed form, as requested.

Ending Data Files

AddCases

Order Confirmation.dotx
Order Request.docx
Order Test.docx

Creating an On-Screen Order Form

Case | Cardenas Transcription, LLC

Shiana Cardenas is the owner of Cardenas Transcription, LLC, located in Phoenix, Arizona. She and her employees type transcriptions of legal and medical notes. Shiana asks you to help her design an online order form so that as her employees receive requests for services, they can fill out a standard form.

1. Open the template file **Cardenas** from the AddCases folder included with your Data Files, and then save it as a document template in the same folder using the filename **Cardenas Form**.
2. Change the page orientation from portrait to landscape, and set the top and bottom margins to 0.7 inch.
3. Increase the width of column B until the right edge of the table is at 9 inches on the ruler, and decrease the width of column A to 2.25 inches.
4. Change the theme to Verve, but select the Urban theme colors.
5. Format the company name (in cell B1) to 20-point, bold, and then format the company address, telephone number, and e-mail address in the Heading 2 style. Center all the text in cell B1 horizontally and vertically, and then apply the Purple, Accent 3, Lighter 80% shading to cell B1.
6. In cell A1, insert the clip art image of a woman in a purple shirt sitting in front of a computer. The image is in the Business subfolder of the Office collections folder. Resize the image so it is 1.5 inches high. Center the image between the cell's left and right borders.
7. Merge the cells containing the text "Order Information," "Legal Services," and "Medical Services" with the cells to their right. In the new cells, change the font size to 14-point bold, and center the text between the left and right borders. Apply Indigo, Accent 1, Lighter 40% as shading to the cell.
8. Split cell B14 (the blank cell next to "Dictation Method" in the "Legal Services" section) into two columns. In the new cell B14 (the middle cell), insert a check box form field, with the default set to checked. To the right of the check box, insert a space and then the text **Telephone.** In the new cell C14, insert a check box form field, with the default set to unchecked. To the right of the check box, insert space and then the text **Digital Recorder.**
9. Split cell B20 (the blank cell next to "Dictation Method" in the "Medical Services" section) and insert identical text and check boxes.
10. Insert a date/time field in cell B3 (the cell to the right of "Date"), so that the date and time automatically appear in the form Aug 06 2010 4:42 PM.

ting Data Files

dCases

rdenas.dotx

11. Insert Combo Box controls for the city, state, and ZIP code with the following list values: for the city and state, use Phoenix, AZ, and for the zip code, use 85003.

12. In cell B13 (to the right of "Type of document"), add a Drop-Down List control with the values **None**, **Letter**, **Contract**, **Brief**, **Report**, **Speech**, and **Other**.

13. In cell B18 (to the right of "Specialty"), insert a Drop-Down List control with the values **General Practitioner**, **Dermatology**, **Oncology**, **Pediatric Medicine**, **Surgery**, and **Other**.

14. In cell B24 (to the right of "Approx cost (in dollars)"), add a Calculation form field to calculate the number of hours (cell B23) multiplied by $65, and format it as currency. Insert a Number type Text form field in cell B23 and set it to calculate on exit.

15. Insert Date content controls in cells B16 (to the right of "Due date"), B19 (to the right of "Date of patient appointment"), and B22 (to the right of "Due date").

16. Insert Text content controls in the rest of the cells in column B.

17. Protect the completed document template form for filling in forms, and then save and close it.

18. Create a new document based on **Cardenas Form** in the AddCases folder. Fill in the report using the information shown in Figure 4-1. (*Hint:* Deselect and select the appropriate check boxes last. If the form will not accept input in a content control, unprotect the form, and then protect it again.)

Figure 4-1

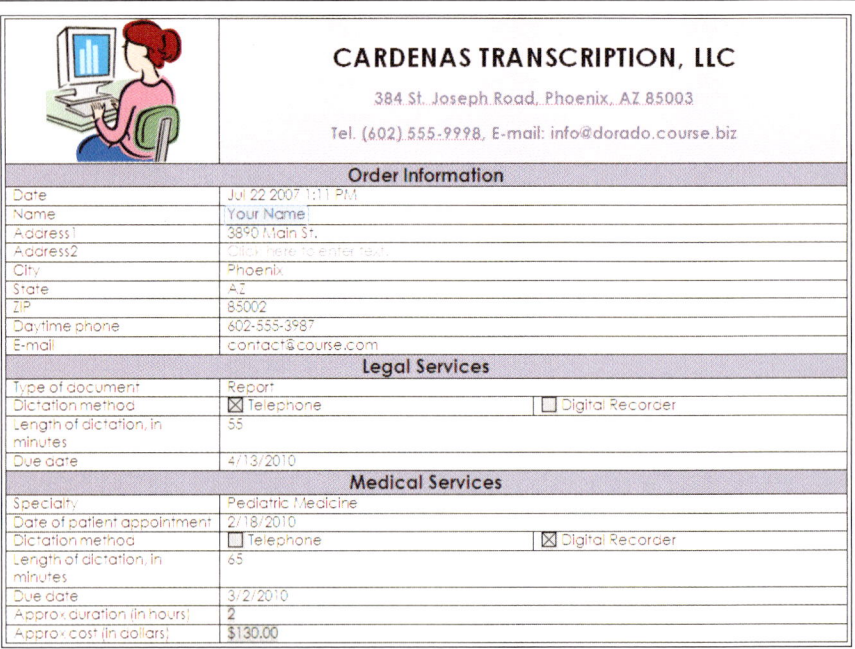

19. Save the filled-in form as a Word document named **Cardenas Order**.

20. Submit the completed documents in printed or electronic form, as requested.

Ending Data Files

Cardenas Form.dotx
Cardenas Order.docx

Structuring Documents Using XML

Using XML to Identify Data

Case | Decision Data, Inc.

Albert Kjar works as a market researcher at Decision Data, Inc. (DDI), a market research company in Lowell, Massachusetts. As part of a workgroup, he recently completed a report for the American Association of Recreation Homebuilders (AARH) about its magazine, *Cabin and Condo Living*. The AARH is indeed pleased with the report from DDI, but the AARH would like DDI to send the information in a format that allows people to use software to search for, extract, and process the data quickly and efficiently.

To do this, Albert will use XML, a programming language. Albert has asked you to help him prepare the XML-formatted document so that he can send it to the AARH along with the Word report.

rting Data Files

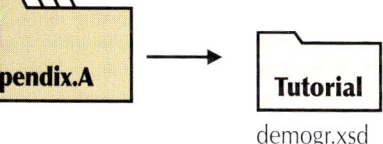

pendix.A   **Tutorial**

demogr.xsd

Understanding XML

XML, which stands for **Extensible Markup Language**, is language analogous to, but much more powerful than, HTML; it allows data to be formatted in such a way that software can search for, extract, and process the data quickly and efficiently.

To understand the power of XML, let's compare a regular Word document, namely the Market Survey Report prepared by Albert, with a Word document structured using XML. The Market Survey Report is "human-friendly" in the sense that, as you read the document, you can easily differentiate between a person's name (like Gladys Kocherhans) and a magazine name (like *Cabin and Condo Living*). Furthermore, you can read and understand the demographic data: the mean average age of subscribers is 47 years old, 72% of subscribers are female, and 58% of subscribers own a cabin (see paragraph "3.1. Demographics").

But computer programs don't think as humans do, so Market Survey Report is not software-friendly; that is, a computer program would have a difficult time differentiating between a person's name and a magazine title or extracting and processing the demographic data. A computer program could search for a phrase like "cabin owners," but it would have no way of extracting information about the cabin owners.

An XML-structured Word document, on the other hand, uses tags to mark data in such a way that computer programs can find, extract, and analyze the data; this is sometimes referred to as **data mining**. When you create an XML-structured document, you use a **schema**, which is a file that defines the structure and type of data that an XML document can contain. A schema specifies **elements** (a tagged item), **attributes** (a feature that modifies or amplifies the information in an element), and **data types** (dates, financial numbers, alphanumeric words and phrases, etc.). Each element can have **child elements**, which are subelements (analogous to a directory folder within another folder). For example, a schema might define how information about subscribers to *Cabin and Condo Living* is stored in the document. When you want to structure a Word document using a particular schema, you attach the schema file to the document, and then the elements of the schema appear in the XML Structure task pane ready for you to apply. To apply a schema element, you can select the applicable text in your Word document, choose the desired schema element, and thus apply an XML tag to the text. For example, you could select the name of the magazine (*Cabin and Condo Living*) and apply an XML tag called "MagazineName." In that way, a computer program that is trying to extract information from your XML document will be able to identify the name of the magazine for which the XML document is being prepared.

Once a document is structured using XML, you can apply an **Extensible Stylesheet Language Transformation (XSLT)** file to the XML document. An XSLT file can transform XML documents into other types of documents, such as HTML, for posting to the Web.

Understanding the Office Open XML Format

Word 2007 files use the .docx filename extension, indicating that the file is saved in the Office Open XML format. **Office Open XML** is a compressed file format, which means that it compresses the XML file automatically. You can see this in action by using a program that can open compressed files, including Windows Vista. Start the compression program and open a Word 2007 document in it. The .docx file will appear as several smaller XML files. Figure A-1 shows the contents of a Word file named Sample Word Document. The contents are displayed in a Windows Vista folder named Inside Sample Word Document.

XML components in a Word 2007 file   Figure A-1

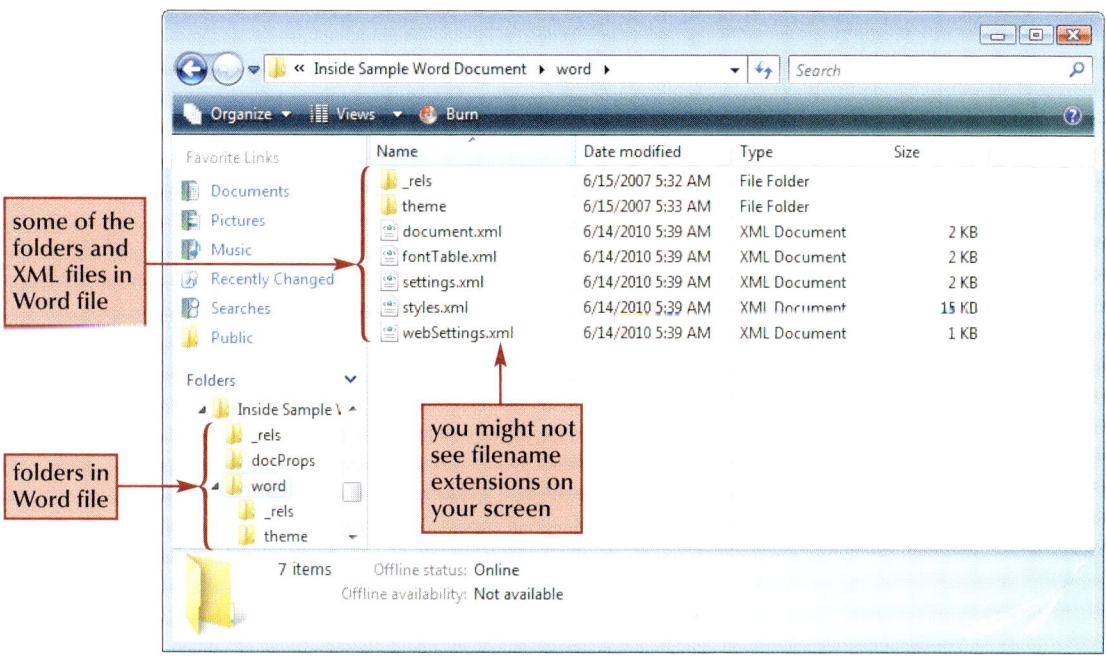

some of the folders and XML files in Word file

folders in Word file

you might not see filename extensions on your screen

Each XML file contains different information about the file; for example, one XML file contains information about the theme, another contains the document properties, and another contains the actual file contents. If you double-click one of the XML files, your browser starts and you can see all of the elements that make up the XML file. Figure A-2 shows the file named document.xml from the Sample Word Document open in Internet Explorer. When you are creating ordinary Word documents, this underlying XML format has no effect on your work and you don't need to think about it.

XML file displayed in an Internet Explorer window   Figure A-2

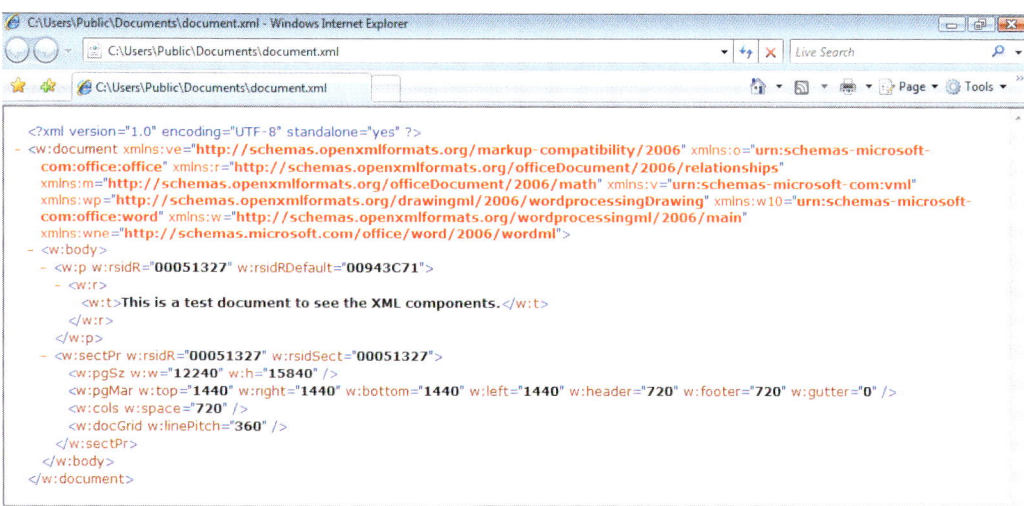

Applying an XML Schema

Albert Kjar asks one of the DDI programmers to prepare a sample XML schema that can be applied to a Word document and structure the document for information about a DDI report. The programmer saved the schema in a file named demogr. You'll begin by creating an XML document and adding a schema to the **Schema Library**, which is the location in a Word document where one or more schema are stored. For the schema to function, your computer must be connected to the Internet so that Word can access validation files from the Microsoft Web site.

To create an XML document and add a schema to the Schema Library:

▶ **1.** Create a new, blank document.

▶ **2.** Hide formatting marks, if necessary, and then switch to Page width view.

▶ **3.** Show the Developer tab on the Ribbon, and then click the **Developer** tab to make it active.

▶ **4.** In the XML group, click the **Schema** button. The Templates and Add-ins dialog box opens with the XML Schema tab on top.

▶ **5.** Click the **Add Schema** button, navigate to the **Appendix.A\Tutorial** folder included with your Data Files, click **demogr.xsd**, and then click the **Open** button. The Schema Settings dialog box opens. You need to give an alias to the schema. An **alias** is a user-friendly nickname for the schema. You can choose any name you want, but usually you'll want a name that describes the function of the schema. In this case, the function is to provide demographics data for a DDI report.

▶ **6.** Type **ddi-demographics** in the Alias text box, and then click the **OK** button. The schema now appears in the Templates and Add-ins dialog box. See Figure A-3.

Figure A-3 ▶ XML Schema tab in Templates and Add-ins dialog box with schema added

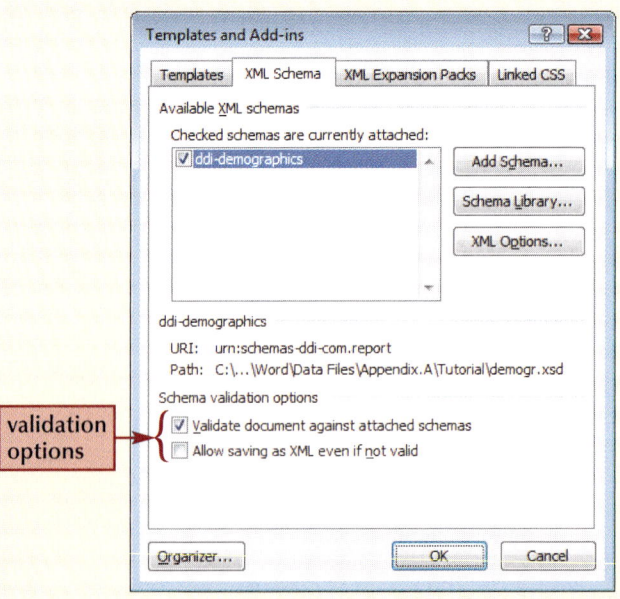

validation options

▶ **7.** In the XML Schema tab of the Templates and Add-ins dialog box, make sure that the **ddi-demographics** check box is checked, the **Validate document against attached schemas** check box is checked, and the **Allow saving as XML even if not valid** check box is unchecked. These two validation check boxes ensure that you save the XML information in the proper format and that the information is complete. (Of course, the XML validation only checks for proper format and data type but has no way of knowing that the information is accurate. For example, someone could type a dollar amount, like "$72,400" in complete, proper format, completely acceptable by the XML document, but this number might be a typographical error and actually should be "$82,400.")

8. Click the **OK** button. The dialog box closes and the XML Structure task pane appears to the right of the Word document window. Notice also that the Structure button in the XML group on the Ribbon is selected. The XML Structure task pane provides information about the XML schema.

You have opened a new XML document, added a schema to the Schema Library, and attached the schema to the current document. Your next task is to apply the schema elements to the document. You'll first apply the element "report" and then apply elements of the report to your document.

To apply schema elements:

1. In the XML Structure task pane, in the Choose an element to apply to your current selection box, click **report**. Word inserts the "report" element into the document, displays the begin and end tags of the element, and displays the child elements of "report" in the task pane, as shown in Figure A-4.

Tip

When you create a content control, the text you type in the Tag field in the Properties dialog box for the content control is an XML tag.

XML document with "report" element inserted | **Figure A-4**

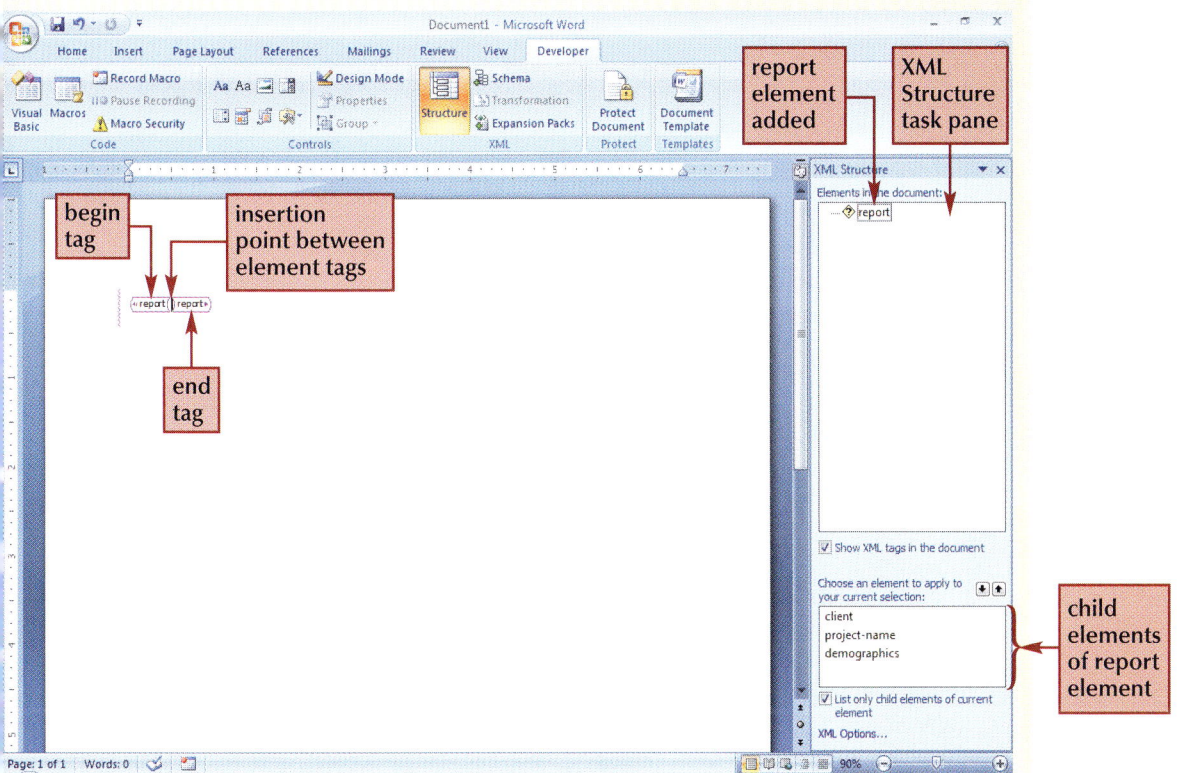

You'll now insert hard returns between the "report" begin and end tags so the elements and information you type between the tags are more readable. Be aware, however, that adding hard returns is not necessary for valid information.

2. Press the **Enter** key twice, and then press the ↑ key to move the insertion point to the blank line between the begin and end tags.

▶ **3.** In the XML Structure task pane, in the Choose an element to apply to your current selection box, click **client**. The begin and end tags of the "client" child element are inserted in the document. Notice that "client" has no child elements, so the Choose an element to apply to your current selection box that lists elements in the task pane is empty. You'll now type the name of DDI's client.

▶ **4.** Type **American Association of Recreation Homebuilders**, press the → key to move the insertion point past the "client" end tag, and then press the **Enter** key. The insertion point is now on a blank line, and the three child elements of "report" again appear on the task pane.

▶ **5.** In the XML Structure task pane, in the Choose an element to apply to your current selection box, click **project-name**, and then type **Analysis of Cabin and Condo Living**. As you can see, "project-name" also has no child elements. You'll now apply the element demographics, which has four child elements.

▶ **6.** Press the → key, press the **Enter** key, click **demographics** in the task pane, press the **Enter** key twice, and then move the insertion point up to the blank line, as shown in Figure A-5.

Figure A-5 ▶ **Insertion point positioned to insert child elements**

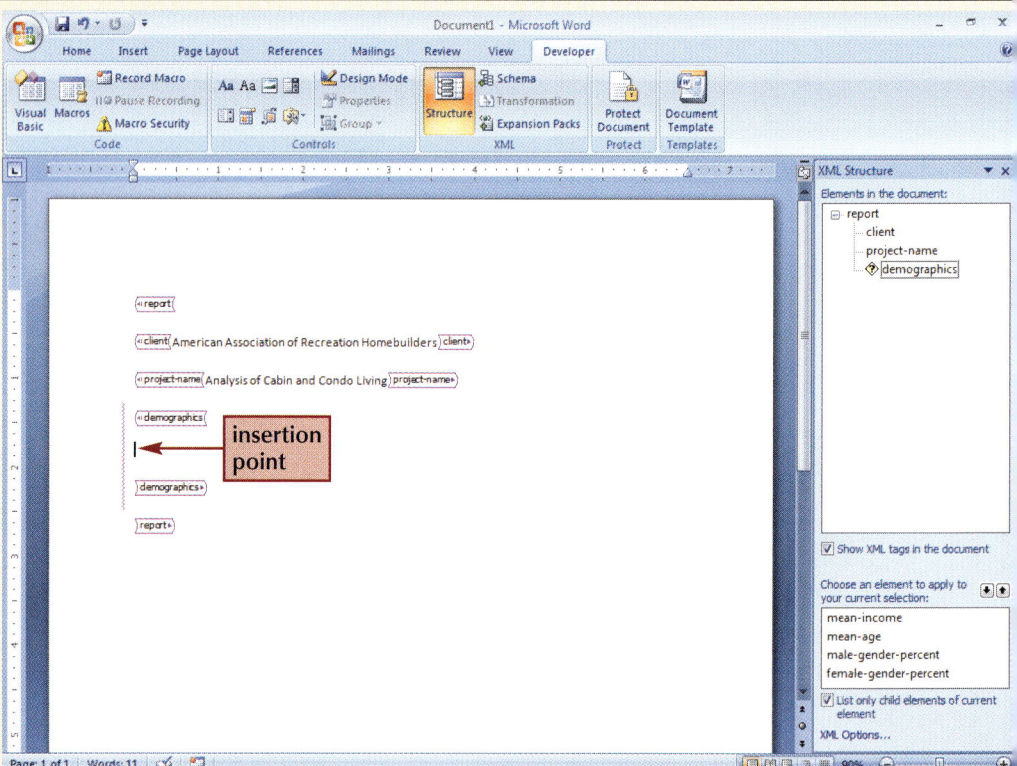

The "demographics" element allows you to insert demographic information into your XML document, including the mean income of subscribers to *Cabin and Condo Living*, the mean age of subscribers, and the percent of male and female subscribers.

▶ **7.** Insert the first three child elements of "demographics," and then type the information for each of these child elements, as shown in Figure A-6. Insert the tags and information exactly as shown, even though, as you'll see later, the information is incomplete and, in one case, incorrectly formatted.

Incomplete XML document ◀ **Figure A-6**

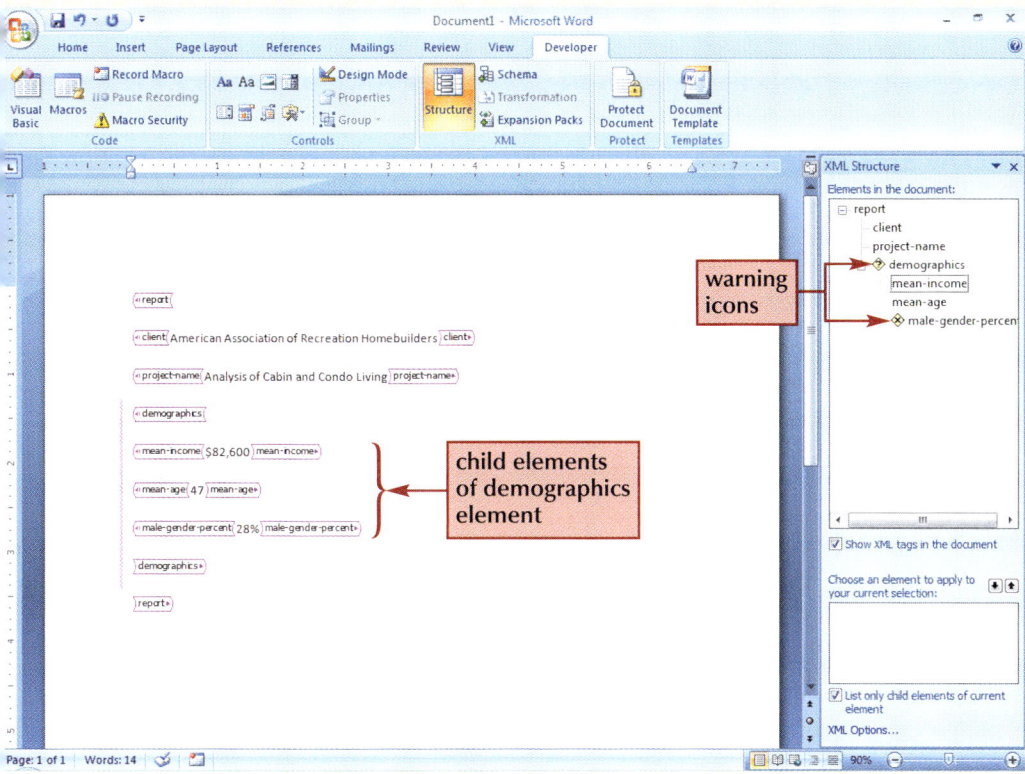

Trouble? If you make a mistake, click the Undo button on the Quick Access Toolbar and reenter the element or retype the information.

You have applied the schema you created to the XML document. Next, you'll evaluate the document and correct any validation errors.

Fixing Validation Errors in XML Documents

If you tried to save the XML document in its current form, Word would give you an error that its "structure violates the rules set by the schema," unless someone had changed the XML Options to allow saving the document with invalid information. How do you know if an element is invalid? How do you know how to fix it? The answer lies in the yellow warning icons in the XML Structure task pane, as shown in Figure A-6. You'll now check the warnings and fix the problems.

To fix validation errors in an XML document:

1. In the task pane, right-click the yellow warning icon to the left of **demographics** in the **Elements in the document** box in the task pane. Word displays the message, "Some required content is missing." The problem is that "demographics" has four child elements, but you have inserted only three elements. To be complete, the document needs the "female-gender-percent" child element.

2. Click anywhere in the window to close the shortcut menu, and then right-click the yellow warning icon to the left of **male-gender-percent** in the upper box of the task pane. Word displays the message "This must be a number." The problem is that with the percent sign, the value for male-gender-percent is not a pure number. You'll fix these validation problems.

▶ **3.** In the document window, click between the percent sign and the end male-gender-percent tab, and then press the Backspace key. The warning icon next to male-gender-percent in the task pane disappears.

▶ **4.** Press the → key, press the **Enter** key, in the task pane, click **female-gender-percent**, and then type **72**. Figure A-7 shows the completed XML document.

Figure A-7 ▷ **Completed XML document**

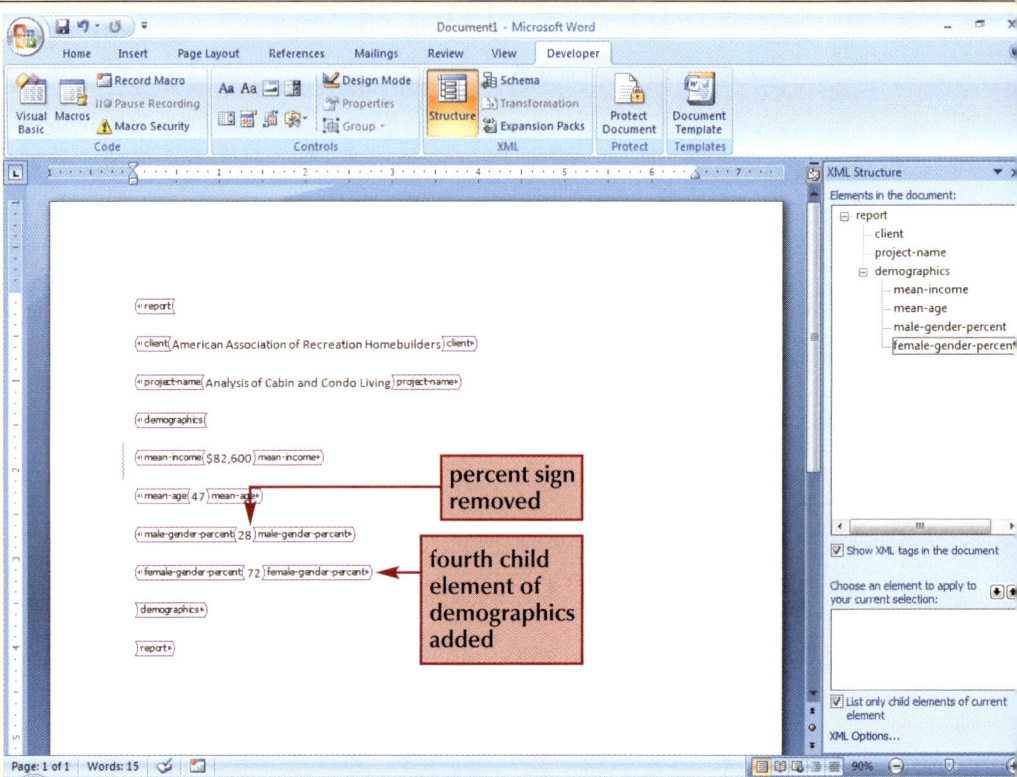

Now that you have fixed the invalid data and completed all the required information, you're ready to save the document. Because Word uses the Office Open XML format, you can save it as a Word document and preserve the XML formatting. You can also save it as a pure XML document; when you save the document in this file format, none of the formatting information included with a Word document, such as the theme and styles, is included. You'll save it as a pure XML document.

To save an XML document:

▶ **1.** On the Quick Access Toolbar, click the **Save** button 🖫, just as you would if you were saving a normal Word document.

▶ **2.** Make sure the Save in location is set to **Appendix.A\Tutorial**.

▶ **3.** Click the Save as type arrow, and then click **Word XML Document**.

▶ **4.** Change the filename to **DDI-Report**, and then click the **Save** button. The file is saved as an XML document.

You can now edit the data that you typed in the XML document in many ways similar to a normal Word document. For example, you can edit the information, cut and paste elements and data, and insert and delete elements. You can also change XML options by clicking XML Options at the bottom of the XML Structure task pane. This displays the XML Options dialog box, as shown in Figure A-8.

XML Options dialog box   **Figure A-8**

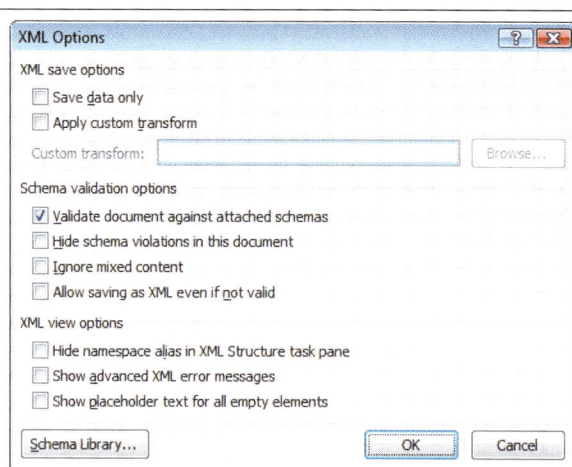

As you can see, you can set the options to save the data only (without the XML tags), to change the schema validation options, and to change the XML view options.

Deleting a Schema from the Schema Library

Once you've applied a schema to a document, you can delete a schema from the Schema Library without affecting the document. You'll now delete the demographics schema from the Schema Library.

To delete a schema from the library:

1. On the Developer tab, in the XML group, click the **Schema** button, and then in the dialog box, click the **Schema Library** button. The Schema Library dialog box opens.

2. Click **ddi-demographics** in the Select a schema list, click the **Delete Schema** button, click the **Yes** button to verify that you want to delete the schema, and click the **OK** button in both open dialog boxes.

3. Close the **DDI-Report** document.

Even though you have deleted the schema from the library, the schema is still attached and functional in the XML document that you saved.

Albert sends a copy of the saved XML document to the American Association of Recreation Homebuilders. That company's programmers can then write software to extract the information, combine the information extracted from other XML documents, post information to the Web (by transforming the XML elements into HTML elements), and analyze the information—all automatically.

Review | Appendix A Quick Check

1. What does XML stand for?
2. True or False. Open Office XML is a compressed file format.
3. Explain the term "data mining."
4. What is the difference between an element and a child element?
5. True or False. You can delete a schema from the Schema Library once it has been applied to a document.
6. True or False. Once you have added data to an XML document, you cannot edit it.

Review | Appendix Summary

In this appendix, you learned about XML and how it can be used to extract data from a document. You also learned how to create an XML schema, add it to the Schema Library, and apply it to a document. You then learned how to fix errors in an XML document. Finally, you learned how to delete a schema form the Schema Library.

Key Terms

attribute
child element
data mining
data type
element

Extensible Stylesheet
  Language
  Transformation (XSLT)
Open Office XML
schema

Schema Library
XML (Extensible Markup
  Language)

Review | Quick Check Answers

1. Extensible Markup Language
2. true
3. using XML tags in such a way that computer programs can find, extract, and analyze the data in a document
4. An element is a tagged item in an XML document. A child element is a sub-element and is only accessible after an element has been applied.
5. true
6. false

Ending Data Files

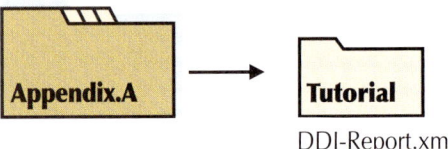

DDI-Report.xml

Glossary/Index

Task Reference

TASK	PAGE #	RECOMMENDED METHOD
Action, redo	WD 20	Click ↻
Action, undo	WD 20	Click ↺
AutoCorrect, customize	WD 403	See Reference Window: Customizing AutoCorrect
AutoCorrect, set options	WD 21	Click 🔴, click Word Options, click Proofing, click AutoCorrect Options
AutoMacro, record	WD 437–438	Click View tab, in Macros group, click Macros button arrow, click Record Macro, type one of the AutoMacro names (AutoExec, AutoNew, AutoOpen, AutoClose, or AutoExit), click Store macro in arrow, click desired template, click OK, record macro, click View tab, in Macros group, click Macros button arrow, click Stop Recording
Background, add textured	WD 357	Click Page Layout tab, click Page Color button in Page Background group, click Fill Effects, click Texture tab, click a texture, click OK
Bibliography, create	WD 586	See Reference Window: Creating a Bibliography
Bibliography, update	WD 592–593	Click bibliography in document, click Update Citations and Bibliography
Boldface, add to text	WD 78	Select text, in Font group on Home tab click **B**
Bookmark, create	WD 349–350	Move insertion point to desired location, click Insert tab, click Bookmark button in Links group, type bookmark name, click Add
Border, insert around page	WD 174	Click Page Layout tab, click Page Borders button in Page Background group, click Page Border tab, click Box
Building blocks, create category	WD 402	Select text, click Insert tab, click Quick Parts, click Save Selection to Quick Part Gallery, click Category arrow, click Create New Category, type category name, click OK, click OK
Building blocks, delete	WD 401	Click Insert tab, click Quick Parts, click Building Blocks Organizer, select Quick Part, click Delete, click Yes, click Close
Building blocks, edit properties	WD 401	Click Insert tab, click Quick Parts, click Building Blocks Organizer, select Quick Part Gallery, click Edit Properties, click Yes, click OK, click Close
Bullets, add to paragraph	WD 74	Select paragraph, in Paragraph group on Home tab click ☷
Captions, create	WD 549	See Reference Window: Creating Captions
Character spacing, adjust	WD 219	See Reference Window: Adjusting Character Spacing
Citation, insert	WD 588–589	Click References tab, in the Citations & Bibliography group, click Insert Citation, click desired citation
Clip art, crop	WD 166	Click clip art, click Format tab, click Crop button in Size group, drag picture border to crop
Clip art, find	WD 161	Click Insert tab, click Clip Art button in Illustrations group, type search criteria, click Go
Clip art, insert in document	WD 161–164	Click Insert tab, click Clip Art button in Illustrations group, click Organize clips, click picture, click Copy, click in document, press Ctrl+V
Clip art, resize	WD 165	Click clip art, drag sizing handle

TASK	PAGE #	RECOMMENDED METHOD
Clipboard, use to cut, copy and paste	WD 57	*See* Reference Window: Cutting (or Copying) and Pasting Text
Clipboard task pane, open	WD 57	In Clipboard group on Home tab, click Clipboard
Column, insert in table	WD 110	Click in column, click Table Tools Layout tab, click Insert Right or Insert Left button in Rows & Columns group
Column width, change in table	WD 112	Double-click or drag border between columns
Columns, balance	WD 173	Click end of rightmost column, click Page Layout tab, click Breaks button in Page Setup group, click Continuous
Columns, create different widths	WD 405	Click Page Layout tab, in Page Setup group, click Columns, click Left or Right
Columns, customize widths	WD 406	Click Page Layout tab, in Page Setup group, click Columns, click More Columns, deselect Equal column width check box, set widths in Width boxes, click OK
Columns, format text in	WD 158	Click where you want to insert columns, or select text to divide into columns, click Page Layout tab, click Columns button in Page Setup group, select options, click OK
Comments, delete	WD 329	*See* Reference Window: Accepting and Rejecting Changes and Deleting Comments
Comments, insert	WD 317	*See* Reference Window: Inserting Comments
Compressed files, extract	FM 18	Right-click compressed folder, click Extract All, select location, click Extract
Compressed folder, create	FM 17	Right-click a blank area of a folder window, point to New, click Compressed (zipped) Folder
Content control, Building Block insert	WD 493	*See* Reference Window: Inserting a Building Block Gallery, Content Control
Content control, Date Picker, insert	WD 485	*See* Reference Window: Inserting a Date Picker Content Control
Content control, Drop-Down List or Combo Box, insert	WD 488	*See* Reference Window: Inserting a Drop-Down List or Combo Box Content Control
Content control, insert	WD 479	Click Developer tab, in Controls group, click desired control, in Control group, click Properties, edit properties as desired, click OK
Content control, Picture, insert	WD 494	*See* Reference Window: Inserting a Picture Content Control
Content control, Text or Rich Text, insert	WD 480	*See* Reference Window: Inserting a Text or a Rich Text Content Control
Cross-references, create	WD 556	*See* Reference Window: Creating Cross-References
Data source, create for mail merge	WD 269	*See* Reference Window: Creating A Data Source for a Mail Merge
Data source, edit in Word	WD 285	*See* Reference Window: Editing a Data Source in Word
Data source, sort	WD 288	*See* Reference Window: Sorting a Data Source
Date field, insert	WD 276	Click Insert tab, click Date & Time button in Text group, click a date format, select Update automatically checkbox if desired, click OK
Date, insert with AutoComplete	WD 25	Start typing date, press Enter

TASK	PAGE #	RECOMMENDED METHOD
Developer tab, show	WD 427	Click , click Word Options, select Show Developer tab on Ribbon check box, click OK
Digital signatures, create	WD 598–600	Click , point to Prepare, click Add a Digital Signature, type purpose for signing, click Sign
Document, e-mail, send via	WD 515	Click , point to Send, click E-mail, address e-mail message, send message as usual
Document, encrypt	WD 597	*See* Reference Window: Encrypting a Document
Document, fax from Word	WD 514	Click , click Print, click Name arrow, click Fax, click OK, click Connect to a fax modem, follow steps in Fax Setup Wizard, type fax number in To box, type Subject, click Send
Document, open	WD 46	Click , click Open, select drive and folder, click filename, click Open
Document, open new	WD 5–6	Click , click New
Document, preview	WD 34	Click , point to Print, click Print Preview
Document, protect	WD 559	*See* Reference Window: Protecting a Document
Document, save with same name	WD 17	On Quick Access Toolbar, click
Documents, compare or combine	WD 325	*See* Reference Window: Comparing and Combining Documents
Drop cap, insert	WD 170	Click in paragraph, click Insert tab, click Drop Cap button in Text group, select options
Embedded object, modify	WD 340	Double-click object, use commands and tools of source program to modify object, click outside embedded object
Endnotes, create	WD 119	*See* Reference Window: Working with Footnotes and Endnotes
Envelope, create	WD 36	*See* Reference Window: Creating an Envelope
Field codes, view	WD 414–415	Right-click field, click Toggle Field Codes
Field, edit	WD 415	Right-click field, click Edit Field, make changes, click OK
Field, insert	WD 415	Click Insert tab, click Quick Parts, click Field, click field you want to insert, click OK
Field, update	WD 416	Right-click field, click Update Field
Fields, insert and edit	WD 415	*See* Reference Window: Inserting and Editing Fields
File, close	OFF 21	Click , click Close
File, copy	FM 14	*See* Reference Window: Copying a File or Folder
File, delete	FM 16	Right-click the file, click Delete
File, move	FM 12	*See* Reference Window: Moving a File or Folder
File, open	OFF 22	*See* Reference Window: Opening an Existing File or Creating a New File
File, print	OFF 27	*See* Reference Window: Printing a File
File, rename	FM 16	Right-click the file, click Rename, type the new name, press Enter
File, save	OFF 18	*See* Reference Window: Saving a File
Files, compress	FM 17	Drag files into a compressed folder

TASK	PAGE #	RECOMMENDED METHOD
Folder, copy	FM 14	*See* Reference Window: Copying a File or Folder
Folder, create	FM 11	*See* Reference Window: Creating a Folder
Folder, move	FM 12	*See* Reference Window: Moving a File or Folder
Folder, rename	FM 16	Right-click the folder, click Rename, type the new name, press Enter
Folder or drive contents, view in Windows Explorer	FM 7–8	Click ▷
Font, change typeface	WD 81	In Font group on Home tab, click Font arrow, click font
Font size, change	WD 82	In Font group on Home tab, click Font Size arrow, click point size
Footer, add	WD 129	Double-click in bottom margin, type footer text, select options on Head & Footer Tools Design tab
Footnotes, create	WD 119	*See* Reference Window: Working with Footnotes and Endnotes
Form field, check box, insert	WD 497	*See* Reference Window: Inserting a Check Box Form Field
Form field, numeric text, insert	WD 506	*See* Reference Window: Inserting a Numeric Text Form Field
Form, protect and unprotect	WD 499	*See* Reference Window: Protecting and Unprotecting a Form
Format, copy	WD 73	*See* Reference Window: Using the Format Painter
Graphic, crop	WD 166	Click graphic, click Format tab, click Crop button in Size group, drag to c
Graphic, find	WD 161	Click Insert tab, click Clip Art button in Illustrations group, type search criteria, click Go
Graphic, resize	WD 165	Click graphic, drag sizing handle
Graphic, wrap text around	WD 168	Click graphic, click Format tab, click Text Wrapping button in Arrange group, click text wrapping option
Header, add	WD 129	Double-click top margin, type header text, select options on Header & Footer Tools Design tab
Help task pane, use	OFF 24	*See* Reference Window: Getting Help
Horizontal line, insert	WD 360	On Home tab in Paragraph group, click Borders and Shading list arrow click Borders and Shading, click Horizontal Line, click a line style, click
Hyperlink, add type in document	WD 120	Type e-mail address or URL, press spacebar
Hyperlink, remove	WD 120	Right-click hyperlink, click Remove Hyperlink
Hyperlink, use	WD 120	Press Ctrl and click hyperlink
Hyperlink to a location in the current document, format text as	WD 149	*See* Reference Window: Linking to a Location in the Same Document
Hyperlink to an existing file or Web page, format text as	WD 353	*See* Reference Window: Creating a Hyperlink to Another Document
Index entries and subentries, mark	WD 580	*See* Reference Window: Marking Index Entries and Subentries
Index entry, page range, create	WD 583	*See* Reference Window: Creating a Page Range Index Entry
Index, compile	WD 585	*See* Reference Window: Compiling an Index
Italics, add to text	WD 79	Select text, in Font group on Home tab click *I*

TASK	PAGE #	RECOMMENDED METHOD
Keyboard shortcut, add	WD 424	Click 🔘, click Word Options, click Customize, click Customize, click Categories arrow, click desired category, click command in Commands list, click in Press new shortcut key box, press desired keys, click Assign, click Close, click OK
Line spacing, change	WD 32	Select text to change, in Paragraph group on Home tab click Line spacing button, click spacing option
Link, break	WD 364	*See* Reference Window: Breaking the Link to a Source File
Link, update	WD 344	In destination file, right-click linked object and then click Update Link
Macro security settings, change	WD 430	Click Developer tab, in Code group, click Macro Security, in Trust Center dialog box, click Macro Settings, click desired option, click OK
Macro, edit	WD 436–437	Click Developer tab, in Code group, click Macros, select macro, click Edit, make changes, close Visual Basic window
Macro, import	WD 427–428	Click Developer tab, in Code group, click Visual Basic, click project name, click File, click Import File, navigate to location of file, click desired file, click Open, close Visual Basic window
Macro, record	WD 433	*See* Reference Window: Recording a Macro
Macro, save a document or template with	WD 431–432	Click 🔘, click Save As, click Save as type arrow, click Word Macro-Enabled Document or Word Macro-Enabled Template, click Save
Mail Merge, perform	WD 264	Click Mailings tab, click Start Mail Merge in Start Mail Merge group, click Step by Step Mail Merge Wizard, follow steps in Mail Merge task pane
Mailing labels, create	WD 291	Click Mailings tab, click Start Mail Merge in Start Mail Merge group, click Step by Step Mail Merge Wizard, click Labels, click Next: Starting document, click Label options, select label type, click OK, click Next: Select Recipients, select or create data source, click Next: Arrange your labels, insert merge fields, click Update all labels, click Next: Preview your labels, click Next: Complete the merge
Margins, change	WD 65	*See* Reference Window: Changing Margins for a Document
Merge fields, insert in main document	WD 277	Click Mailings tab, click Insert Merge Field in Write & Insert Fields group, click a merge field
Nonprinting characters, show	WD 8	In Paragraph group on Home tab, click ¶
Numbered headings, create	WD 545	*See* Reference Window: Numbering Headings Automatically
Numbering, add to paragraphs	WD 76	Select paragraphs, in Paragraph group on Home tab click ▤
Object, embed	WD 337	Select and copy object in source program, return to Word, click destination location, on Home tab in Clipboard group click the Paste button arrow, click Paste Special, select Paste option button if necessary, in As list box select option that will paste object as an Object, click OK

TASK	PAGE #	RECOMMENDED METHOD
Object, link	WD 342	Select and copy object in source program, return to Word, click destination location, on Home tab in Clipboard group click Paste button arrow, click Paste Special, select Paste link option, in As list box select option that will paste object as an Object, click OK
Office program, start	OFF 3	*See* Reference Window: Starting Office Programs
Outline, create and edit	WD 238	*See* Reference Window: Creating and Editing Outlines
Options, popular, customize	WD 422	*See* Reference Window: Customizing Popular Features in Word
Page, view width	WD 10	Click Zoom level, click Page width, click OK
Page background, add color	WD 379–380	Click Page Layout tab, in Page Background group, click Page Color, select color from palette
Page break, insert	WD 103	Click where you want to break page, click Insert tab, click Page Break button in Pages group
Page number, insert	WD 130	Open header or footer, on Header & Footer Tools Design tab, click Page Number button in Header & Footer group
Page orientation, change	WD 123	Click Page Layout tab, click Orientation button in Page Setup group, choose orientation type
Paragraph, decrease indent	WD 72	In Paragraph group on Home tab, click
Paragraph, increase indent	WD 72	In Paragraph group on Home tab, click
Paragraph spacing, adjust	WD 221	*See* Reference Window: Adjusting Spacing Between Paragraphs
Picture, compress	WD 382	Select a picture, click Picture Tools Format tab, in Adjust group, click Compress Pictures, in Compress Pictures dialog box, click Options, set desired options, click OK, click Apply to selected pictures only check box if desired, click OK
Print Layout view, change to	WD 7	Click on status bar
Program, Office, exit	OFF 28	Click on title bar
Programs, Office, open	OFF 3	*See* Reference Window: Starting Office Programs
Properties, add to document	WD 410–411	Click , point to Prepare, click Properties, type properties in Document Information Panel, click Document Properties, click Advanced Properties to add additional properties, click OK, click Close button
Property, insert as Quick Part	WD 412–413	Click Insert tab, click Quick Parts, point to Document Property, click desired property
Quick Access Toolbar, customize	WD 423	*See* Reference Window: Customizing the Quick Access Toolbar
Quick Part, create	WD 397	*See* Reference Window: Creating a Quick Part
Quick Style, create new	WD 391	*See* Reference Window: Creating a New Quick Style
Quick Style, redefine	WD 388–389	Format text as desired, right-click a Quick Style, click Update Style to Match Selection
Research task pane, open	WD 249	Click Review tab, in Proofing group click Research button, Thesaurus button, or Translate button

TASK	PAGE #	RECOMMENDED METHOD
Research task pane, use	WD 248–249	Connect to the Internet if possible, open Research task pane, type term you want to research in Search for text box, click the list arrow and select a reference work, click ➡
Row, delete from table	WD 111	Click row, (or select multiple rows) click Delete button in Rows & Columns group on Table Tools Layout tab, click Delete Rows
Row height, change in table	WD 112	Drag divider between rows; to see measurements, press and hold Alt while dragging
Rulers, display	WD 7	*See* Reference Window: Displaying the Rulers
Schema, add to the Schema Library	WD A4	Click Developer tab, in XML group, click Schema button, click Add Schema, navigate to schema file, click Open, type an alias, click OK
Schema, apply	WD A5	Click Developer tab, in XML group, click Schema button, click alias of desired schema, click validation check boxes as desired, click OK
Section, insert in document	WD 122	Click where you want to insert a section break, click Page Layout tab, click Breaks button in Page Setup group, click a section break type
Shading, apply to table	WD 113	Click table, click Design tab, click More button in Table Styles group, click shading style
Shape with text, add	WD 383	*See* Reference Window: Adding a Shape with Text
SmartTags, use	WD 396	*See* Reference Window: Working with Smart Tags
Source, create	WD 588–589	Click References tab, in the Citations & Bibliography group, click Insert Citation, click Add New Source, in Create Source dialog box click Type of Source arrow, click desired type, add information to fields, click OK
Special character, insert	WD 172	*See* Reference Window: Inserting Symbols and Special Characters
Spelling, correct individual word	WD 23	Right-click misspelled word (as indicated by a wavy red line), click correctly spelled word
Spelling and grammar, check	WD 50	*See* Reference Window: Checking a Document for Spelling and Grammar Errors
Style, apply from Quick Styles gallery	WD 100	Select text you want to format, in Styles group on Home tab click a style in Quick Styles gallery; if style you want is not visible in Quick Styles gallery, click the More button in Styles group, click style you want
Style, apply from Styles window	WD 224–225	Select text you want to format, click style in Styles window
Style, create a new	WD 227	*See* Reference Window: Creating a New Style
Style, modify	WD 223	*See* Reference Window: Modifying Styles
Styles window, open	WD 223	In Styles group on Home tab, click Styles Dialog Box Launcher
Subdocument, create	WD 536	*See* Reference Window: Creating a Subdocument
Subdocument, insert	WD 533	*See* Reference Window: Inserting a Subdocument
Subdocument, merge	WD 538	*See* Reference Window: Merging Subdocuments
Subdocument, remove	WD 539	*See* Reference Window: Removing a Subdocument
Subdocument, split	WD 537	*See* Reference Window: Splitting a Subdocument

TASK	PAGE #	RECOMMENDED METHOD
Symbol, insert	WD 172	*See* Reference Window: Inserting Symbols and Special Characters
Tab stop, set	WD 116	*See* Reference Window: Aligning Text with Tab Stops
Table, create in Word	WD 104	Click Insert tab, click Table button in Tables group, drag pointer to select columns and rows
Table, format	WD 113	*See* Reference Window: Formatting a Table with a Built-in Table Style
Table, sort	WD 108	*See* Reference Window: Sorting the Rows of a Table
Table borders, draw	WD 477	Select table, click Table Tools Design tab, in Draw Borders group, click Draw Table, Click Line Style button arrow and select desired line style, click Line Weight button arrow and select desired weight, click Pen Color button arrow and select desired color, drag on table to draw border
Table borders, erase	WD 475	Select table, click Table Tools Design tab, in Draw Borders group, click Eraser, drag over border
Table cells, create reverse type	WD 473	*See* Reference Window: Creating Reverse (Light on Dark) Type in Table Cells
Table cells, merge	WD 459–460	*See* Reference Window: Merging Cells
Table cells, split	WD 462	*See* Reference Window: Splitting Cells
Table of Contents, add text to	WD 233	*See* Reference Window: Working with a Table of Contents
Table of Contents, create	WD 593–594	Click References tab, in Table of Contents group click Table of Contents, click Insert Table of Contents, select desired options, click OK
Table of Contents, update	WD 233	*See* Reference Window: Working with a Table of Contents
Table of figures, create	WD 595	Click References tab, in Captions group click Insert Table of Figures, click Insert Table of Figures, select desired options, click OK
Template, saving a document as	WD 233	*See* Reference Window: Saving a Document as a Template
Text, align	WD 69–71	Select text, click ≡, ≡, ≡, or ≡ on Mini toolbar
Text, copy and paste	WD 57	*See* Reference Window: Cutting (or Copying) and Pasting Text
Text, find and replace	WD 62	*See* Reference Window: Finding and Replacing Text
Text, move by drag and drop	WD 54	*See* Reference Window: Dragging and Dropping Text
Text, select entire document	WD 30	Press Ctrl and click in selection bar
Text, select multiple adjacent lines	WD 30	Click and drag in selection bar
Text, select multiple nonadjacent lines	WD 30	Select text, press and hold Ctrl, select additional lines of text
Text, select multiple paragraphs	WD 30	Click and drag in selection bar
Text, wrap around WordArt	WD 154	Click WordArt, click Format tab, click Text Wrapping button in Arrange group, click text wrap option
Text box, insert	WD 383–384	Click Insert tab, click Text Box, click Draw Text Box, type text

TASK	PAGE #	RECOMMENDED METHOD
Text box, insert formatted	WD 408–409	Click Insert tab, click Text Box, click desired style, type text
Text boxes, link	WD 385	Select text you want to link, click Insert tab, in Text group, click Text Box button, click Draw Text Box, drag to draw text box, click outside the text box, in Text group click Text Box button, click Draw Text Box, drag to draw second text box, click in text box containing the content, click Text Box Tools Format tab, in Text group, click Create Link, and then click 🖱 in the empty text box
Theme, create a custom	WD 210	See Reference Window: Customizing the Document Theme
Theme, save as default	WD 389	Customize theme, click Home tab, in the Styles group, click Change Styles, click Set as Default
Theme colors, customize	WD 215	See Reference Window: Creating Custom Theme Colors and Theme Fonts
Theme fonts, customize	WD 215	See Reference Window: Creating Custom Theme Colors and Theme Fonts
Track Changes, use	WD 316	See Reference Window: Tracking Changes in a Document
Track Changes, accept and reject	WD 329	See Reference Window: Accepting and Rejecting Changes and Deleting Comments
Watermark, create	WD 394	Click Page Layout, in Page Background group click Watermark button, click desired text watermark or click Custom Watermark, in the Printed Watermark dialog box, click Picture watermark option button and then select picture, or click Text watermark and type text in Text box, click OK
Web page, save document as	WD 359	See Reference Window: Saving a Word Document as a Web Page
Web page, view in Web Layout view	WD 355	Click 🖳
Window, close	OFF 6	Click ❎ or click ✕
Window, maximize	OFF 7	Click ⬜ or click ⬜
Window, minimize	OFF 7	Click ➖ or click ➖
Window, restore	OFF 7	Click ❐ or click ❐
Windows Explorer, start	FM 7	Click 🟢, click All Programs, click Accessories, click Windows Explorer
Word, start	WD 3	Click 🟢, click All Programs, click Microsoft Office, click Microsoft Office Word 2007
WordArt, change shape	WD 153	Click WordArt, click 🅰 in WordArt Styles group, click shape
WordArt, edit text	WD 152	Click WordArt, click Format tab, click Edit Text button in Text group, edit text, click OK
WordArt, insert	WD 149	See Reference Window: Creating WordArt
WordArt, wrap text	WD 154	Click WordArt, click Format tab, click Text Wrapping button in Arrange group, click text wrap option
Workspace, zoom	OFF 8	See Reference Window: Zooming the Workspace
Zoom setting, change	WD 10	Drag Zoom slider